D0850814

Companion to
Women's Historical Writing

Companion to Women's Historical Writing

Edited by

Mary Spongberg,
Ann Curthoys and
Barbara Caine

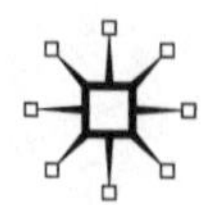

First published 2005 by
PALGRAVE MACMILLAN
Houndmills, Basingstoke, Hampshire RG21 6XS and
175 Fifth Avenue, New York, N.Y. 10010
Companies and representatives throughout the world

PALGRAVE MACMILLAN is the global academic imprint of the Palgrave Macmillan division of St. Martin's Press, LLC and of Palgrave Macmillan Ltd. Macmillan® is a registered trademark in the United States, United Kingdom and other countries. Palgrave is a registered trademark in the European Union and other countries.

ISBN-13: 978–1–4039–1508–5 hardback
ISBN-10: 1–4039–1508–3 hardback

This book is printed on paper suitable for recycling and made from fully managed and sustained forest sources.

A catalogue record for this book is available from the British Library.

Library of Congress Cataloging-in-Publication Data
Companion to women's historical writing / edited by Mary Spongberg, Ann Curthoys, Barbara Caine.
p. cm.
Includes bibliographical references and index.
ISBN-13: 978–1–4039–1508–5 (hardback)
ISBN-10: 1–4039–1508–3 (hardback)
1. English prose literature—Women authors—History and criticism—Handbooks, manuals, etc. 2. Literature and history—English-speaking countries—Handbooks, manuals, etc. 3. Women and literature—English-speaking countries—Handbooks, manuals, etc. 4. Historiography—English-speaking countries—Handbooks, manuals, etc. 5. English-speaking countries—Historiography—Handbooks, manuals, etc. 6. American prose literature—Women authors—History and criticism—Handbooks, manuals, etc. 7. Commonwealth prose literature—Women authors—History and criticism—Handbooks, manuals, etc. 8. Women—English-speaking countries—Intellectual life—Handbooks, manuals, etc. 9. Historical fiction, American—History and criticism—Handbooks, manuals, etc. 10. Historical fiction, English—History and criticism—Handbooks, manuals, etc. 11. Women historians—English-speaking countries—Handbooks, manuals, etc. I. Spongberg, Mary, 1965– II. Curthoys, Ann. III. Caine, Barbara.
PR756.H57C66 2005
828′.08—dc22 2005043034

10 9 8 7 6 5 4 3 2 1
14 13 12 11 10 09 08 07 06 05

Printed and bound in Great Britain by
Antony Rowe Ltd, Chippenham and Eastbourne

Contents

List of contributors
vi

Acknowledgements
xiii

Introduction
xiv

The Companion to Women's Historical Writing
1

Bibliography
618

Index
667

List of contributors

Steven Angelides is Senior Research Fellow in the Australian Centre at the University of Melbourne. He is the author of *A History of Bisexuality* (2004) and has written widely on the areas of queer theory and the history and theory of sexuality.

Michelle Arrow is Lecturer in the Department of Modern History at Macquarie University. Her monograph *Upstaged: Australian Women Dramatists in the Limelight at Last* was published in 2002 and was shortlisted for five national prizes.

Paula Bartley has written a number of history texts for schools and universities and co-edited the Women's History series for Cambridge University Press. Her more recent books include *The Changing Role of Women* (London, 1996); *Votes for Women* (London, 1998, second edition 2002); *Prostitution: Reform and Prevention in England, 1860–1914* (London, 1999) and *Emmeline Pankhurst* (London, 2002). She currently lives in Hungary.

Faith E Beasley is Associate Professor of French at Dartmouth College in the United States. She is the author of *Revising Memory: Women's Fiction and Memoirs in Seventeenth-Century France* (1991) and *Salons, History, and the Creation of Seventeenth-Century France: Mastering Memory* (forthcoming, Ashgate 2006). She has also edited, with Katharine Ann Jenson, *Approaches to Teaching Lafayette's The Princess of Clèves* (1998). She has written numerous articles on women writers of the French classical period, the literary public and the salons. She is currently editing *Options for Teaching Seventeenth- and Eighteenth-Century French Women Writers*, to be published by the Modern Language Association.

J Lea Beness teaches at Macquarie University. Her research interests are in ancient world gender studies, Roman republican history and underwater archaeology.

Kelly Boyd is Senior Lecturer in History at Middlesex University, London. She is the author of *Manliness and the Boys' Story Paper in Britain, 1855–1940: A Cultural History* (2003) and the editor of the *Encyclopedia of Historians and Historical Writing* (1999). Her current research focuses on the cultural impact of television on post-war Britain.

Susan Broomhall is ARC Research Fellow in the School of Humanities at the University of Western Australia. Her research principally concerns women and gender in early modern Europe.

Miriam Elizabeth Burstein is Assistant Professor of English at the State University of New York, College at Brockport. She is the author of *Narrating Women's History in Britain, 1770–1902* (2004).

Barbara Caine is Professor of History at Monash University. She has published extensively on the history of feminism. Her most recent work is *Bombay to Bloomsbury: A Biography of the Stracheys* (2005).

Amanda L Capern is Lecturer in Early Modern Women's History at the University of Hull. She is the author of *The Historical Study of Women 1500–1700* (Palgrave, 2006) and has written articles on women's landed property and power in the family.

Jane Chance, Professor of English, has taught at Rice University since 1973. Editor of the series Library of Medieval Women, she has published 20 books which include *Woman as Hero in Old English Literature* (1986), a translation of *Christine de Pizan's 'Letter of Othea to Hector'* (1990), and two edited collections, *Gender and Text in the Later Middle Ages* (1996) and *Women Medievalists and the Academy* (2005).

Ann Curthoys is Manning Clark Professor of History at the Australian National University. She writes on many aspects of Australian history and about historical practice. Her most recent book is *Freedom Ride: A Freedomrider Remembers* (2002), and her next book, with John Docker, is entitled *Is History Fiction?*

Desley Deacon is Professor of Gender History in the Research School of Social Sciences at the Australian National University. She is the author of *Elsie Clews Parsons: Inventing Modern Life* (1997). Her forthcoming book is *Mary McCarthy; Four Husbands and a Friend*. She is now working on a biography of the Australian-American actor Judith Anderson.

Judith A Dorn teaches Eighteenth-Century English Literature as Associate Professor at St Cloud State University in Minnesota. Her book project on English and French 'secret histories', which has yielded articles on Ann Yearsley's historical novel *The Royal Captives* and Charlotte Lennox's women's periodical, explores relations between history and literature and the emergence of distinctions among humanities disciplines in the early modern period.

Lisa Featherstone is Associate Lecturer in the Department of Modern History at Macquarie University, where she has taught in Australian history and women's history. Her research interests include reproduction, sexuality and medical history.

Hilary Fraser holds the Geoffrey Tillotson Chair in Nineteenth-Century Studies at Birkbeck, University of London. Her books include *The Victorians and Renaissance Italy* (1992), *English Prose of the Nineteenth Century* (with Daniel Brown 1997) and *Gender and the Victorian Periodical* (with Stephanie Green and Judith Johnston 2003).

Patricia Grimshaw is Max Crawford Professor of History at the University of Melbourne, where she teaches United States and Australian history, and in the Gender Studies Programme. Recent publications include the co-edited *Women's Rights and Human Rights: International Perspectives* (2001) and *Letters from Aboriginal Women of Victoria, 1867–1926* (2002) and the co-authored *Equal Subjects, Unequal Rights: Indigenous Peoples in British Settler Colonies 1830 to 1910* (2003).

T W Hillard is Senior Lecturer in Ancient History at Macquarie University. His previous publications have been in the fields of Roman social history (with a focus on Women's History), Republican political history and maritime archaeology.

Claire Hooker began her intellectual journey at the University of Sydney where she studied the history of women in science, now available to all readers in her book, *Irresistible Forces* (2004). She is co-editor of *Contagion: Epidemics History and Culture from Smallpox to Anthrax* (2002) with Alison Bashford and is currently Sidney Sax Postdoctoral Research Fellow in Public Health at the Universities of Sydney and Toronto, researching the occurrence and resolution of health scares.

Sarah Howard is Project Officer at the Australian Academy of the Humanities. Her current research interests include higher education policy. She has worked previously as a freelance research assistant in the fields of Australian, American and British history, the history of science and medicine, and gender and feminist history.

Marnie Hughes-Warrington is Senior Lecturer in World History and Historiography in the Department of Modern History at Macquarie University, Sydney. She is the author of *Fifty Key Thinkers on History* (2000), *'How Good an Historian Shall I Be?': R. G. Collingwood, the Historical Imagination and Education* (2003) and the editor of *Palgrave Advances in World Histories* (2004).

Sarah Irving is a Commonwealth scholar and doctoral candidate at King's College, Cambridge. Her PhD explores the influence of natural science on the intellectual origins of the British Empire.

Cecily Jones is a lecturer in Gender and Sociology in the Department of Sociology at the University of Warwick. Her teaching and research concern the intersections of race, gender, class and sexuality in the colonial slave plantation societies of the Americas. She is also Director of the Centre for Caribbean Studies at Warwick University, an interdisciplinary research centre.

Amanda Laugesen is Lecturer in History at the University of Southern Queensland. She completed her PhD, 'Making Western Pasts: Historical Societies of Kansas, Wisconsin and Oregon, 1870–1920', at the Australian National University. She has published in both American and Australian history.

Philippa Levine teaches at the University of Southern California in Los Angeles. Her recent publications include *Prostitution, Race and Politics: Policing Venereal Disease in the British Empire* (2003) and an edited volume in the Companion Series of the Oxford History of the British Empire, entitled *Gender and Empire* (2004).

Devoney Looser is Associate Professor of English at the University of Missouri, Columbia and is the author of *British Women Writers and the Writing of History, 1670–1820* (2000), the editor of *Jane Austen and Discourses of Feminism* (1995) and the co-editor of *Generations: Feminist Academics in Dialogue* (1997).

Vera Mackie is Australian Research Council Professorial Research Fellow in History at the University of Melbourne. Major publications include *Creating Socialist Women in Japan: Gender, Labour and Activism, 1900–1935* (1997) and *Feminism in Modern Japan: Citizenship, Embodiment and Sexuality* (2003).

Alison Mackinnon is Professor of History and Gender Studies at the University of South Australia and the author of several books including *Love and Freedom: Professional Women and the Reshaping of*

Personal Life, which won a NSW Premier's literary award in 1997. She has an honorary doctorate from Umea University in Sweden (2000) and is a former president of the Australian and New Zealand History of Education Society.

Susan Magarey is Adjunct Professor in History at Adelaide University, where she was also Foundation Director of the Research Centre for Women's Studies and Foundation Editor of *Australian Feminist Studies*. She has written two monographs (one a prize-winner), some 50 articles, edited five books and co-edited two more.

Roger D Markwick lectures in History in the School of Liberal Arts, the University of Newcastle, Australia. He is author of *Rewriting History in the Soviet Union: The Politics of Revisionist Historiography 1956–74* (Palgrave, 2001) which was awarded the Alexander Novel Prize in Russian, Soviet and Post-Soviet Studies in 2003.

Susan Marsden is a consultant historian who has also worked as National Conservation Manager for the Australian Council of National Trusts and as South Australia's State Historian. Recent publications include: *Urban Heritage: The Rise and Postwar Development of Australia's Capital City Centres* (2000), *Our House: Histories of Australian Homes* (www.heritage.gov.au/ourhouse) and *Newcastle – a Brief History* (2004).

Louella McCarthy holds a PhD in history and an MA in women's studies from the University of New South Wales, Sydney. She has taught Australian history at UNSW and public history at the University of Technology, Sydney. As a specialist in the history of women and medicine, she has published on the impact of gender ideologies on modern medical practice. Recent articles have appeared in journals such as *Social History of Medicine* and *Women's History Review*. Her current projects include women and cancer research and treatment, and the place of hospital heritage in the Australian landscape. She is vice-president of the NSW Society for the History of Medicine and its newsletter editor. With Dr Amanda Capern (University of Hull), she is series editor for Gender and History (Palgrave Macmillan).

Rosemary Ann Mitchell is Senior Lecturer in History at Trinity and All Saints College, University of Leeds, and previously worked as a research editor on *The Oxford Dictionary of National Biography* (2004). She has published on Victorian women's history-writing in *The Journal of Victorian Culture* and *Women's History Review* and is the author of *Picturing the Past: English History in Text and Image, 1830–1870* (2000).

Pauline Nestor is Associate Professor in English Literature at Monash University. She has published extensively on nineteenth-century women writers.

Lucy Noakes is Senior Lecturer in Social and Cultural Theory at the University of Portsmouth. Her research interests include war and society, theories of gender and national identity, popular memory, and the role of women in the armed forces. She is currently researching a history of women and the British Army.

Melanie Nolan is Associate Professor in the School of History, Philosophy, Political Science and International Relations at Victoria University of Wellington in New Zealand. She is the author of *Breadwinning: New Zealand Women and the State* (2000).

Maria Nugent is Postdoctoral Research Fellow based in the School of Historical Studies at Monash University. She specialises in Australian Aboriginal History, with particular interests in post-colonialism, public history, memory and oral history.

Patty O'Brien teaches Australian and Pacific History in the Center for Australian and New Zealand Studies at Georgetown University. She writes on gender and empire in Australia and the Pacific. Her book is *The Pacific Muse: Exotic Femininity and the Colonial Pacific,* forthcoming, University of Washington Press, 2006.

Alison Oram is Reader in Women's Studies at University College, Northampton, UK. She is co-author of *The Lesbian History Sourcebook: Love and Sex between Women from 1780 to 1970* (2001). Her current research is on stories of women's gender-crossing in the twentieth-century British popular press and their relationship to emerging ideas about lesbianism and transsexuality.

Ros Pesman is Emeritus Professor of History at the University of Sydney. She is author of *Duty Free: Australian Women Abroad* (1996). She co-edited the *Oxford Book of Australian Travel writing* (1996) with David Walker and Richard White. She is currently working on the involvement of British women in Italian politics and culture in the nineteenth century.

I M Plant is Lecturer in Ancient History at Macquarie University, New South Wales. He has recently published a comprehensive anthology of the extant literary texts of women writers from the Graeco-Roman world: *Women Writers of Ancient Greece and Rome* (2004).

Ilaria Porciani is Professor of Contemporary History and History of the Historiography at the University of Bologna. She is presently the editor of *Il mestiere di storico,* Yearbook of SISSCO. She published *L'Archivio Storico Italiano* (Firenze Olschki, 1979) and *La festa della nazione* (Bologna, Il Mulino, 1997: Acqui storia Prize for history in 1998) and edited several books on the history of the university and publishing. In 2004 she has edited together with Maura Palazzi *Storiche di ieri e di oggi* (Roma, Viella, 2004) and is presently editing together with Mary O'Dowd 'History Women' the special issue of the international journal *Storia della Storiografia* devoted to women historians in Europe. Within the European Science Foundation Project 'Representing the past', she is editing a European atlas of the historical institutions (1800–2005). See www.esf.org.publication/171/NHIST and www.uni-leipzig.de/zhs/esf.nhist.

Alison Prentice taught at Ontario Institute for Studies in Education, University of Toronto, focusing her research and writing on the origins of public schooling and the history of women teachers and professors. Now an adjunct at the University of Victoria, British Columbia, her current work deals with the history of women in the Professions, especially physics and history.

June Purvis is Professor of Women's and Gender History at the University of Portsmouth. She has published extensively on the British women's suffrage movement, her latest book being *Emmeline Pankhurst: A Biography* (2002). She is also the Founding and Managing Editor of the journal *Women's History Review* and the editor for the Routledge Series on Women's and Gender History.

Jennifer Ridden lectures in Modern British and Irish History at the Australian National University. Her particular research interest is national identity in nineteenth-century Ireland, Britain and the Empire.

Donna Robson has completed a doctorate in Romantic women's writing at the University of Sydney.

Jill Roe is Emeritus Professor in Modern History at Macquarie University, Sydney, where she recently taught a course on war and peace in world history. She is currently completing a biography of Australian writer and feminist Miles Franklin.

Penny Russell teaches History at the University of Sydney. Her research interests include gender and imperialism; subjectivity and history; identity, status and manners in colonial Australia; and a biographical study of Jane, Lady Franklin. She is the author of *A Wish of Distinction* (1994) and *This Errant Lady* (2002).

Clair Scrine completed her doctoral dissertation in 2003 on 'Conceptions of Nymphomania in British Medicine 1790–1900', which involved extensive research at The Wellcome Institute for the History of Medicine in London. Her research interests include the history of medical thinking about sexual desire, the history of women's relationship to sexual knowledge and notions of normalcy with regard to sexual practice.

Susan Sheridan is Professor of Women's Studies at Flinders University in Adelaide, South Australia. She has published widely on women writers, Australian literature and journalism, women's studies and feminist theory. Her books include *Christina Stead* (1988), *Along the Faultlines: Sex, Race and Nation in Australian Women's Writing, 1880s–1930s* (1995) and *Who Was That Woman? The Australian Women's Weekly in the Postwar Years* (2002). She is the editor of *Grafts: Feminist Cultural Criticism* (1988) and *Debutante Nation: Feminism Contests the 1890s* (with Susan Magarey and Sue Rowley, 1993). She was Reviews Editor of *Australian Feminist Studies* and also a member of the editorial boards of *Australian Humanities Review, Australian Literary Studies, Southern Review, Southerly* and *Hecate*.

Glenda Sluga is Associate Professor of History at the University of Sydney. Her most recent works include *Gendering European History* (co-authored with Barbara Caine) and *An International History of the Idea of the Nation between 1870 and 1920* (forthcoming).

Mary Spongberg is Associate Professor of History at Macquarie University. She is author of *Feminising Venereal Disease: The Body of the Prostitute in Nineteenth-Century Medical Discourse* (1997) and *Writing Women's History Since the Renaissance* (2002). She is also the new editor of *Australian Feminist Studies*.

Shurlee Swain is Reader in History at the Australian Catholic University and Senior Research Fellow in the Department of History at the University of Melbourne. She has researched widely in the areas of Women's History, Children's History and Comparative History and has most recently collaborated with Julie Evans, Patricia Grimshaw and David Phillips to produce *Equal Subjects, Unequal Rights: Indigenous Peoples in British Settler Colonies 1830s–1910* (2003).

Hsu-Ming Teo teaches European history and the history of travel in the Department of Modern History at Macquarie University. She co-edited *Cultural History in Australia* (2003) and has published articles on travel, gender, imperialism and popular culture. She is finishing a book on the culture of romantic love in Australia.

Joan Thirsk CBE is Reader Emeritus in Economic History and Honorary Fellow of St Hilda's College, Oxford. She is a veteran chronicler of the economic history of agriculture in England and former president of the British Agricultural History Society. Her published works include *The Rural Economy of England* (Hambledon and London, 1984), *Alternative Agriculture: A History from the Black Death to the Present Day* (1977) and *Rural England* (2000).

Clara Tuite is Senior Lecturer in the Department of English at the University of Melbourne. She is the author of *Romantic Austen: Sexual Politics and the Literary Canon* (2002), co-editor with Gillian Russell of *Romantic Sociability: Social Networks and Literary Culture in Britain, 1770–1840* (2002), and an associate editor of *An Oxford Companion to the Romantic Age: British Culture 1776–1832* (edited by Iain McCalman, 1999).

Charlotte Woodford is Fellow in German and Director of Studies in Modern Languages at Selwyn College, Cambridge, England. Her book, *Nuns as Historians in Early Modern Germany*, was published in 2002.

Angela Woollacott is Professor of Modern History at Macquarie University. She is the author of *On Her Their Lives Depend: Munitions Workers in the Great War* (1994) and *To Try Her Fortune in London: Australian Women, Colonialism, and Modernity* (2001). She is the co-editor, with Miriam Cooke, of *Gendering War Talk* (1993) and, with Mrinalini Sinha and Donna J Guy, of *Feminisms and Internationalism* (1999).

Acknowledgements

The editors of this project gratefully acknowledge the support of the Australian Research Council for the award of the grant that made this project possible.

Special thanks go to all those people who worked as researchers on the Companion. Michelle Arrow, Megan Edwards, Lisa Featherstone, Sarah Howard, Michelle Lyons and Jamie Agland all contributed generously and enthusiastically to the production of the Companion, showing much grace under pressure. Laina Hall, Margaret Sampson and Lorna Barrow also provided able teaching relief.

We would also like to thank our colleagues at Macquarie, Monash and the Australian National University for their assistance and encouragement with this project, with special thanks going to all those who contributed entries. Marnie Hughes-Warrington, who organised the Sydney workshop at Macquarie, requires special thanks. Josephine Spongberg saved us from many attachment dramas and much else, we are very grateful to her. Barbara Caine would particularly like to thank Barbara Russell. Ann Curthoys thanks Susan Magarey, John Docker, Desley Deacon, Jill Matthews and the History Programme RSSS for having her as a visitor while working on this project, and the School of Social Sciences, Faculty of Arts, for supporting her involvement in the project throughout.

Inter-library loans at Macquarie University also served the project with skill, enthusiasm and interest, often going beyond the call of duty to track down obscure texts from distant libraries.

It was not possible for individual contributors to thank colleagues and research assistants in the body of the essays. So we have included a list of acknowledgements here. Lucy Noakes would like to thank the trustees of the Mass-Observation Archive for allowing her to quote from the Archive. Joan Thirsk would like to thank Dr Kate Tiller for valuable help and criticism in preparing her essay Local History. Maria Nugent would like to acknowledge the importance for her essay on Oral Traditions of the doctoral work of Barbara Russell, whose forthcoming PhD thesis, 'History and the Maiden: Representations of Women through South Africa's Truth and Reconciliation Commission' (Monash University), deals with a number of the issues raised here.

Finally special thanks need to go to Margaret Alma Jones who provided the project with much-needed space in its final stages and most graciously read and commented upon various sections of the manuscript. We dedicate this book to you with thanks.

Introduction

In one of the final scenes in Jane Austen's last completed novel *Persuasion* (1817), a crucial exchange occurs between Anne Eliot, the novel's heroine, and Captain Harville on the subject of women's constancy in love. Captain Harville jokingly defends his position on women's inconstancy by telling Anne: 'But let me observe that all histories are against you, all stories, prose and verse . . . I do not think that I ever opened a book in my life which had not something to say upon a woman's inconstancy. Songs and proverbs, all talk of woman's fickleness. But perhaps you will say, these were all written by men.' Anne's reply does indeed point to the way in which control of the pen has determined the history:

> Perhaps I shall. Yes, yes, if you please, no reference to examples in books. Men have had every advantage of us in telling their own story. Education has been theirs in a much higher degree; the pen has been in their hands. I will not allow a book to prove anything.

While less cited than Austen's young heroine Catharine Morland, who regarded history as wearisome and tedious with 'the quarrels of popes and kings, with war and pestilences, in every page, the men all so good for nothing and hardly any women at all', Anne Eliot's statement, written in Austen's last year, reflects a more mature understanding of the ways in which accepted historical and literary traditions have shaped ideas about women. It serves also to reveal the limitations women felt in relation to their engagement with History and indeed all other forms of literary production. There is, however, much that is ironic in this exchange. Austen, a female author, is narrating the life of a women whose constancy, fidelity, adherence to domestic virtues, quiet patriotism and fate serve to contrast here strongly with the picture of women that is presented to her as an accurate reflection of her sex. Austen herself was well educated for a woman of her time, having spent much time in the only academy readily open to early modern women, her father's library. Like many women discussed in the Companion, Austen's 'education' allowed her to engage critically with dominant historical paradigms, and to offer alternative histories. Indeed, the novel *Persuasion* itself can be read as a domestic history of the Napoleonic Wars, dealing with social and economic changes that were significant in English county life at the time and contrasting as it does women's experiences of fear, sacrifice and loss with the adventure and bravery of war-scarred men. But the importance of the history that is contained in Austen's novels has only come to be recognized recently. Prior to this recent feminist re-evaluation, critics commented rather on her lack of interest in what was seen as the dominant historical issues of the time – most particularly the Napoleonic Wars, without recognizing either the extent to which she was offering an alternative history, focusing on the women who remained at home, and noting the relatively small impact of these wars on domestic society.

Although perhaps the best-known discussion of women's exclusion from history in literature, Austen's was certainly not the first – and nor was hers the first attempt to offer an alternative history that focused on women's lives. For centuries, women have resented their exclusion from the dominant historical narratives and have responded by generating a history of their own. The nun Baudonivia's *Life of Radegund* (seventh century), one of the first historical texts known to be written by a woman, was produced expressly to 'supplement' the male-authored vitae of Radegund's life. This has been variously interpreted as a challenge to the authority of the representation of Radegund in male-authored vitae and a desire on the part of the nuns of her abbey to present a woman-centered version of her life. Several centuries later **Christine de Pizan**, 'the first feminist', exclaimed in her epic poem *The God of Love's Letter* (1399): 'If women had written books, I know for sure they would have been written differently' (Blumenfeld-Kosinski 1997: 23). She then set about undermining the representation of women found in what she saw very much as the masculine historical tradition and to write books that established a tradition of woman-centred historical writing and inaugurated the *querelle des femmes*. For these women the authority of history served a higher moral purpose and allowed them a space to tell their own stories or the stories of other women that have been traduced in the historical tradition that was passed down from one generation of men to the next.

This Companion is devoted to exploring the many different ways in which women have researched and written history. In many cases, even if these writings were known, they were not considered to be 'history' because they lacked either the accepted formal qualities or the appropriate subject matter. Women, whether or not they were self-consciously feminist or interested in the position and the problems of their sex, often wrote about women's lives and the immediate and local societies in which they lived. The frequently wrote their own histories, versions of events or analyses of what women had done in reaction to work by men that distorted, obscured or vilified women's historical role. Women historians, like feminists and women practitioners in other fields, have often termed the canonical works and the great literary and disciplinary traditions as 'masculinist' in their unquestioned assumptions of male rationality and dominance and their disregard of women. Much of their own writing has been shown here to form part of a distinctly feminine (if not feminist) tradition that sought to insert women into the historical narrative and to generate a gendered understanding of the past.

The purpose of the Companion is not to establish an essentialist reading of women's historical production, but rather to show how the prescriptions of gender functioned to shape women's understanding of the past and their engagement in developing a history of their own. Few women depicted in this volume wrote 'women's history' and it is not the purpose of the Companion to focus on the history of women. Rather the Companion sets out to create a history of women's historical production in all its myriad forms. It is the purpose of the Companion to both expand our knowledge of women's historical production as well as to extend our definitions of 'History'. Thus while women's historical writings will include biographical writing, stories of women worthies, historical fictions, diaries and letter-writing, travelogue and chronicles as well as a range of more conventional kinds of history, the Companion will also explore how women writers negotiated the ostensibly masculinist genre of history, as well as the interconnectedness of women's historical production and other forms of women's writing. Women's historiography, once an obscure area of interest is now a highly contested field, engaging the interest of literary and cultural critics as well as historians.

This Companion is not a guide to feminist historiography, but it does demonstrate the relationship between women's historical production and the development of feminist consciousness. It is inevitably the case that a Companion of this kind will be partial in its coverage. The field of women's historical writing, both in the past and more particularly in the last four or five decades, is vast. The editors have had to be extremely selective in deciding on the topics for the long interpretive essays – and there are many others that could have been chosen. We have sought here to include the issues and areas that we saw as showing particularly interesting interventions by women and particularly significant developments in women's history. We have included a number of essays on particular national histories and a wide range of essays dealing in a cross-national way with themes and topics that have been extensively written about by women, including the body and sexuality, marriage and family life, nursing and medicine. In addition there are essays on particular kinds of history, for example local histories, or on particular kinds of approach, for example through biography. Thus while the Companion is not comprehensive, we hope that it includes at least some discussion of all the myriad different ways in which women have written history.

Critical to this endeavour has been the work of eminent scholars such as Natalie Zemon Davis, Bonnie G Smith, Gerda Lerner, Joan Thirsk and Joan Wallach Scott. Not only have these historians greatly enhanced our knowledge of the number of women engaged in historical production and the range of their work, they have also offered significant insights into continuities between women's writing in the past and the writing of women's historians in the present. The history of women's historical writing is now a vibrant and contested field, engaging interest from historians, literary critics, art historians and cultural theorists. Recent works by Billie Melman, Rohan Amanda Maitzen, Alison Booth, Rosemary Mitchell, Miriam Elisabeth Burstein, Greg Kucich, Devoney Looser and Daniel R Woolf have drawn much attention to women's historical production in the past, providing detailed and nuanced readings of women's historical writings and we have been fortunate to have some of these authors work with us on the Companion.

Entry categories

The Companion is made up of over a 150 separate entries ranging from 250 words to 7500 words, laid out in alphabetical order. The entries are divided into several categories as mentioned below.

Genre

The Companion is devoted to depicting the multiple ways in which women have chosen to write about the past, so a number of entries in this volume focus on women's historical production in fields such as auto/biography, fiction and memoir. We hope to show women as innovative in their co-option of new and various media to express their 'particular' view of the past.

Nation

A range of entries examines women's contributions to the history of the nation state. Expanding our understanding of both history and nationalism, these essays challenge the assumption that women have failed to engage in the making of national histories, while also confirming the marginalisation of women from writing the history of High Politics and Diplomacy and their absence in these most nation-bound sub-disciplines. The nation states examined in the Companion represent the Anglophone world, Australia, Canada, Great Britain, Ireland and the United States with Italy, France and Japan as counter-points.

Biographical

These entries examine the lives of women who have engaged in the writing of history within the Western tradition – from Baudonivia in the seventh century to the late Joan Kelly, one of the founders of the 'new Women's history'. The purpose of these entries is to demonstrate the range and extent of women's historical production within the context of their lives and to draw out continuities and connections, to establish a sense of women's historical production as part of a tradition. They should also be valuable for future workers in the field of women's historiography. Where possible we have included references to recent editions of their work.

Period

While some feminist historians have sought entirely new forms of periodisation thought more suitable for women, most historians have followed Joan Kelly's advice in 1976 to follow the usual periodisation but with a new focus on women's experiences. Many women historians have contributed to the study of particular historical periods, and here we examine some of the major ones from the ancient world until the Enlightenment.

Thematic

Women historians have written on many themes, both those once thought to be the particular province of 'women's history', such as the family, and those once considered the domain of men, such as war and revolution. Our entries cover those themes that have most engaged women historians, including industrialization, peace, colonialism and postcolonialism, empire and much else.

A

Abolition

Women's involvement in the movement to abolish **slavery** in the United States of America in the central decades of the nineteenth century has long attracted the interest of female historians and historians of women. Abolitionism has been widely viewed (not uncontroversially) as a precursor to the feminist movement in the US, particularly because the abolitionist movement split over the contentious issue of women's rights and participation.

Abolitionists used historical writing to advance their cause: historian and novelist **Lydia Maria Child**'s *An Appeal in Favour of that Class of Americans Called Africans* (1833) provided the first full-scale analysis of slavery for abolitionists. Child was also one of several activists to sponsor slave life histories. Elizabeth Cady Stanton, Susan B Anthony and Matilda Joslyn Gage's *History of Woman Suffrage* (1881) was the first history to situate the work of abolitionist women within the history of feminism, claiming that women were made aware of gender oppression through their agitation against racial oppression. This interpretation set the template for much of the subsequent historiography of women's abolitionism.

Women's contribution to the abolitionist struggle was marginalised in the general histories of the movement in the early to mid-twentieth century and women's histories of the movement were rare. There were some popular histories and biographical works, but until the mid-1960s, much of the historiography focused on male leaders and downplayed or ignored the role of women.

The beginnings of women's history in the 1960s saw women historians turn their attention to abolitionism. **Alma Lutz** produced the first contemporary study to feature women abolitionists, *Crusade for Freedom: Women in the Antislavery Movement* (1968), while Gerda Lerner published her *Grimké Sisters from South Carolina: Rebels against Slavery* in 1969 and Aileen S Kraditor published *Means and Ends in American Abolitionism*, her study of Garrison and his critics in 1969. Lerner and Kraditor were the first contemporary historians to study the intersections between abolitionism and feminism, exploring the ways that abolitionist rhetoric raised the consciousness of many women, and they also asked questions about the power relationships between white and black women in the movement, which were taken up by subsequent historians.

Much of the history of women in abolitionism has focused on the abolitionist feminists. For example, the first full-length study of women abolitionists, Blanche Glassman Hersh's *The Slavery of Sex: Feminist-Abolitionists in America* (1978), maintained that there was a strong connection between abolitionism and feminism. However, this was not an uncontested position: Ellen DuBois argued in 1979 that it was a common error of historians to attribute women's emerging consciousness about their oppression to their involvement in abolitionism, and that there was evidence of women's incipient feminism in other early nineteenth-century female activities.

In the 1970s and 1980s, the flourishing of women's history produced numerous histories of women's anti-slavery societies, famous women abolitionists and studies of the rhetoric and artefacts of abolitionism. However, as Nancy Hewitt noted, two aspects of anti-slavery historiography remained unchanged, despite the incursions made by women's history. The first was that general histories continued to minimise or ignore the activities of women abolitionists documented by women historians. Some male historians did include gender in their analyses, but most marginalised women's role in the cause (Hewitt 1994). The second issue Hewitt identified was the tendency of feminist historians to selectively document abolitionism, treating it as a prelude to the women's rights movement rather than analysing it on its own terms. Amy Swerdlow (1994) noted that there were women within the movement that opposed their own rights, and the place of these women in the history of abolitionism had been neglected.

As women's history continued to flourish, many historians revisited famous female abolitionists in **biographies** such as Deborah Pickman Clifford's *Crusader for Freedom: A Life of Lydia Maria Child* (1992) and Dorothy Sterling's *Ahead of Her Time: Abby Kelley and the Politics of Antislavery* (1991). Literary scholars and historians have examined the lives and writings of contemporary women writers who were sympathetic to abolitionism such as Carolyn L Karcher's *The First Woman of the Republic: A Cultural Biography of Lydia Maria Child* (1994) and Lyde Cullin Sizer's *The Political Work of Northern Women Writers and the Civil War 1850–1872* (2000). Other historians focused on the political culture of women's abolitionism, its place within the wider political culture and the gendered nature of abolitionist rhetoric, particularly in the various works of Jean Fagin Yellin such as *An Untrodden Path: Antislavery and Women's Political Culture* (1993) and *The Abolitionist Sisterhood: Women's Political Culture in Antebellum America* (1994) and Karen Sanchez-Eppler's *Touching Liberty: Abolition, Feminism and the Politics of the Body* (1993).

Just as much of the historiography of the 1960s onwards was inspired by the rise of second-wave feminism, the Civil Rights movement also influenced the writing of the history of abolitionism. Shirley Yee's *Black Women Abolitionists* (1992) was a key study of the collective role played by black women in the movement. Other historians focused on the ways that African-American women were positioned within the writing and iconography of abolitionism. Most recently, women historians of abolitionism have moved away from 'great women' to focus on what Julie Roy Jeffrey calls 'the Great Silent Army of Abolitionism' in her book of the same name (1998). Jeffrey argued that most abolitionism history has focused on the significance of the movement, the motives and achievements of its (male) leaders. Women's history has remedied the neglect of abolitionist women, but has mostly focused on the small number of radical women who became feminists. However, most abolitionists shied away from feminism but maintained the momentum of the movement through their tireless activism. Her work placed abolitionist activism in the context of daily life to offer a more representative and thus more complicated picture of the movement, and to further problematise the notion of separate spheres. Closely related to Jeffrey's work are the recent explorations of the ways that objects created by women with anti-slavery emblems illustrated the interconnections made by abolitionist women between public and private spheres.

This issue of the permeable nature of the boundaries between public and private spheres is one which recurs in the most recent historical work on abolitionism by and about women. Jeffrey (2001) has explored the ways in which abolitionist women conceptualised themselves and their activism within the ideology of separate spheres, and the ways the women exploited, contested and subverted conservative ideas about appropriate female behaviour through their activism. Carol Lasser argues that Jeffrey's work forces historians of women to call for new ways to understand the contest over gender relations and gender definitions. Perhaps the work of women abolitionist historians will provide new ways of dealing with the vexed question of separate spheres in women's history (Lasser 2001). The issue of separate spheres and of women speaking 'out of their place' was the cause of much consternation to observers of abolitionist women, and historians are still debating in and around it in relation to abolitionism more than 150 years later.

Michelle Arrow

References

DuBois 1979; Hewitt 1994; Jeffrey 1998, 2001; Lasser 2001; Swerdlow 1994.

Related essays

Civil Rights; Slavery; USA.

Adams, Hannah 1755–1831

Historian of religion, America's first professional woman writer. Born Medfield, Massachusetts. Daughter of Elizabeth (Clark) and Thomas Adams. Largely self-educated, she was introduced to the study of religion when given a copy of Broughton's *Dictionary of Religions*. Acquaintance with male-authored histories of religion left Adams 'full of mental indecision' as she perused the 'various and contradictory arguments adduced by men of piety and learning in defence of their respective religious systems'. She began to research this area herself. Forced by poverty to publish these researches, her first work, *An Alphabetical Compendium of the Various Sects*, appeared in 1784 and went through several editions (1791, 1801, 1817). She also published a *History of the Jews* (1812) and *Letters on the Gospels* (1824), an exposition on primitive Christian sects. Addressed to her 'Dear Nieces', it sought to advance the 'moral Christian edification of women'. Adams sought to present an impartial and sympathetic analysis of the religions she studied, quietly critical of the sectarian masculinist histories she drew upon. Adams also wrote several **local histories** including *A Summary History of New England* (1799). The abridgement of this text led her into a protracted legal dispute with the Reverend Jebidiah Morse. She produced an account of this dispute in 1814, in which she described the negative treatment of women authors by the publishing industry. Although she was one of the most popular writers of her time she was plagued by illness and poverty. She struggled to publish her work and again lamented the difficulties she faced as a female author in her **memoirs** published posthumously in 1832.

Sarah Howard

References

Tweed 1992; Vella 1993.

Ady, Cecilia Mary 1881–1958

English historian of the Italian Renaissance. Daughter of the art historian **Julia Cartwright** and the Reverend Henry Ady. Educated at St Hugh's College, Oxford, where she attained her MA and D.Lit. Ady was one of the first women to be awarded her degree in history from Oxford University. She was appointed tutor in modern history at St Hugh's in 1909. Her sacking from St Hugh's College in 1924 was the cause of much scandal. She did not return to the college until 1929, when she joined as a research fellow. She retired from St Hugh's in 1951 and was elected an honorary fellow.

Like her mother, Ady was interested in the cultural world of Renaissance Italy, particularly the role of the signorial families. She published *A History of Milan under the Sforza* in 1907, *Pius II: The Humanist Pope* in 1913, the *Bentivolgio of Bologna* in 1937 and *Lorenzo di Medici and Renaissance Italy* in 1955. She also wrote sections for general books such as *Italy, Medieval and Modern* (1917) and contributed a chapter on the 'Invasions of Italy' to the *Cambridge Modern History* in 1930. Although her work is sometimes characterised in scholarly opposition to her mother's more 'romantic' approach to history, it is possible to see continuity in themes and sources. Like her mother, Ady's histories showed evidence of women as shapers of culture and were drawn from similar source materials.

Interested in suffrage, Ady wrote a chapter on women's history in Zoe Fairfield's *Some Aspects of the Women's Movement* (1915), published by the Student Christian Movement. She drew on her mother's work citing 'the great ladies of the houses of Este and Gonzaga' as examples of women 'who achieved a name and fame by their own exertions' (1915: 49–50). Like **Lina Eckenstein**, Ady stressed the importance of monasticism to women's history. A committed churchwoman, she also wrote a booklet *The Role of Women in the Church* in 1948. Recognition of her role in the creation of the field of Renaissance studies came with the publication of E F Jacob's *Italian Renaissance Studies* (1960), a tribute to her, following her death.

Mary Spongberg

References

Emanuel 1989.

Aikin, Lucy 1781–1864

English poet, novelist, memoirist and historian. Daughter of Martha (Jennings) and John Aikin, Unitarian minister. Educated largely at home by her father. Aikin began her career, writing and collecting poetry for children. Her anthology *Original Poems for Infant Minds* was published in 1801. She published a sentimental novel *Lorimer* in 1814.

Aikin turned to history in 1810 with the publication of her epic poem *Epistles on Women, exemplifying their character and condition in various ages and nations.* The poem demonstrates an understanding of women's position in society, derived from Philosophical or conjectural history. Aikin's work reflects a post-revolutionary caution regarding feminism. Stressing the historical importance of women's role in the private sphere, Aikin simultaneously criticised women seeking to be 'inferior men' by usurping their role. There is a certain irony, however, to her suggestion that 'sex' not 'be carried into everything' and that the 'impartial voice of History' should testify that 'when permitted women have been worthy associates of the best efforts of men', as she goes on to rewrite the history of the world from a woman-centred perspective.

In her *Memoirs of the Court of Queen Elizabeth* (1818), a 'domestic history of her reign', Aikin presented a feminised version of history, focusing on the interior world of the court. Historicising the private sphere, emphasising the emotion and intrigue behind politics and diplomacy, Aikin recalls earlier traditions of *Memoirs* and *Secret Histories*, while also anticipating later feminist critiques of masculinist historical writing. She also produced *Memoirs of the Court of James I* (1822) and *Charles I* (1833). Aikin claimed to have 'more or less of personal acquaintance with almost every literary woman of celebrity who adorned English society' during her life. She was certainly known to **Elizabeth Hamilton** and **Sarah Taylor Austin** and wrote memoirs of her aunt Anna Laetitia Barbauld (1825) and friends **Elizabeth Ogilvy Benger** (1827) and Joanna Baillie. She also published biographies of her father, John Aikin (1823), and Joseph Addison (1843).

Mary Spongberg

References

Kucich 1993; Le Breton 1864; Smith 1984.

Ancient history, archaeology and classical studies

When Veronica Seton-Williams, who would in later life become famous for her Swan Hellenic Nile cruises and her (co-authored) *Blue Guide to Egypt* (1983), entered the University of Melbourne in 1931, she was disappointed that it was impossible to study Egyptology anywhere in Australia. She 'settled for the next best thing, History and Political Science' (Seton-Williams 1988: 17). There she was much influenced by Jessie Webb, the celebrated lecturer who handled Ancient History single-handedly. Webb had studied *inter alia* Greek, Latin, History, Philosophy, Constitutional History and Law at Melbourne graduating with Double Firsts in History and Political Economy in 1901. When Seton-Williams published her memoirs 57 years on from her matriculation, she dedicated them to Webb, the Egyptologist Margaret Murray and Tessa Wheeler, under whom she was first introduced to archaeological fieldwork.

The remembrance of Webb marks the presence of women's scholarship in Ancient History in the early twentieth century. Sometimes, this work was prompted by an interest in the women of antiquity; as, for example, Helen McClees' *Study of Women in Attic Inscriptions* (1920) and Grace Macurdy's *Hellenistic Queens* (1932). Sometimes it was not; Gertrude Smith's *The Administration of Justice from Hesiod to Solon* (1924) heralded her influential studies of Greek law, whilst Kathleen Freeman's *The Work and Life of Solon* (1926) was but the first of a number of works devoted to Greek philosophy, politics and law (all with an eye to contemporary politics and morality). But it is difficult to imagine that the present essay would have been commissioned had women traditionally made the same mark on History as had men. In Briggs and Calder's *Classical Scholarship* (1990), a repertory of 50 important 'classicists', only two women appear. Only one of those, **Lily Ross Taylor** would have regarded herself as an Ancient Historian. Her major works – *The Divinity of the Roman Emperor* (1931), *Party Politics in the Age of Caesar* (1949), *The Voting Districts of the Roman Republic* (1960) and *Roman Voting Assemblies* (1966) – established her as one of the giants in the field, and the last three in particular are still cited as reference points today. It will be appreciated that this advent of an outstanding female scholar in Ancient History is relatively late. The delay in women's appearance is significant, but not difficult to explain. If History generally excluded women, Ancient History positively celebrated this exclusion. Ancient Historians proved especially amenable to the re-establishment of a Thucydidean model, setting the parameters of their discipline in ways that replicated the domestic seclusion of women in classical Athens and their consequent placement outside the realms of History. In 1893 the eminent classicist Ulrich von Wilamowitz-Moellendorff recommended the reading of Thucydides precisely *because* of the absence of women (or rather the perfume of the boudoir) (Briggs and Calder 1990: xv). To give women a place in History was, as Bernadette Brooten in her analysis of early Christian women has so well observed, 'to contradict the presuppositions of male-centered historiography' (1985: 66).

Clearly not all women were deterred. **Lily Ross Taylor** is a case in point. Although her range of interests was extraordinarily broad, her focus would have been regarded at the time as 'mainstream'. When hospitalised with a broken ankle, she whiled away the time with Theodor Mommsen's monumental *Römisches Staatsrecht*. That was the intellectual company she sought.

Philology and archaeology

To assume, however, that women's historical interest in antiquity was restricted to those who practised within the confines of Ancient History would be a mistake and herein lies one of the themes of this essay. **Jane Ellen Harrison**, the only other woman registered in the abovementioned repertory of 50 outstanding 'classicists' and of whom it has been legitimately claimed that she changed the way we think about the ancient Greeks (Beard 2000: xi), is a reminder of the mark which women of earlier generations had *already* made. One avenue to the past had been through philology (used in its older sense of the study of a culture through its literature). Between 1674 and 1682, Anne Le Fèvre Dacier produced five volumes for the famous Delphin series of classical texts, editions with Latin notes of Callimachus and Florus (both in 1674), Dictys Cretensis with Dares (1680), Aurelius Victor (1681) and Eutropius (1682). As Fern Farnham observes: 'She was the only woman among the numerous editors to whom the work was assigned, and the only single editor to undertake and complete so many volumes and such a varied assortment of authors. Her work is unique, also, in that it includes the only Greek author in the whole series' (1976: 49). She also translated classical authors into the French vernacular. Her translation of Anacreon and Sappho was published in 1681, her Plautus in 1683, her Aristophanes in 1684 and her Terence in 1688. Dacier's crowning achievement was the translation of Homer, the *Iliad* appearing in 1711 and the *Odyssey* in 1716, produced whilst involved in the great literary debate of the time, the Quarrel between Ancients and Moderns, the latter seeking the removal of ancient authors from their pedestal in favour of new creative visions. She published her 'Concerning the Cause of Taste's Corruption', a passionate defence of the Ancients, in 1714. Her achievement was singular: '[H]er contribution to the *Grand Siècle* of France . . . would have been noteworthy for a man. For a woman of her time it was unique' (Malcovati 1953; Farnham 1976: 16).

Others would follow. Elizabeth Carter translated into English the works of Epictetus (1758). Henrica Malcovati's work on the fragments of Roman orators, *Oratorum Romanorum Fragmenta Liberae Rei Publicae* (first published in 1930), underpins studies of the life and politics of the Roman Republic; Ada Adler's five-volume edition of the tenth-century CE lexicon, the *Suda* (1929–1938), has seen her hailed as 'incontestably the greatest woman philologist who ever lived' (Calder and Hallett 1996–1997: 83); and the study of ancient Persian religion would be greatly the poorer without the prolific philological work of Mary Boyce (Bivar and Hinnells 1985: xi–xx).

But it was Archaeology that particularly excited the interest and accommodated the talents of women interested in the ancient world (Beard 1994; Díaz-Andreu and Sørensen 1998). In the absence of an academic discipline, the field also provided an entrée for those without qualifications in higher education, thus skirting a problem for a number of women at the end of the nineteenth century (Champion 1998: 176). Amelia Edwards, the celebrated English novelist, travel-writer and journalist, raised money to support the work of the famous Flinders Petrie and founded the Egypt Exploration Fund (1882) and, by bequest, the first chair of Egyptian Archaeology and Philology at University College, London. Her most famous work, *A Thousand Miles up the Nile* (1877), while providing an introduction to the spirit of Egyptian civilisation, was essentially a guide-book. She also wrote an immense number of popular articles on Egyptological subjects and *Pharaohs, Fellahs, and Explorers* (1891), based on the Egyptian lectures delivered during her tour of the United States in 1889–1890.

Reference to Edwards irresistibly draws the survey to Gertrude Bell: the quintessential 'bold Victorian woman'. Bell was in one sense an exception to the rule. From an early age she was interested in History, and did well at it. In 1888 she graduated from Oxford with a First in Modern History. Chaperoned to lectures, Bell had revelled in the conspicuous isolation of her small company in a room full of men. There was no suggestion, however, that she would pursue a career in Academe. Travel and adventure in part satisfied her restlessness. At the age of 31, she was entranced by the current excavations in Athens, watching as, to her mind, antiquity was brought to life: it made her 'brain reel' (Wallach 1996: 43). She took private instruction, and when she travelled east again she did so with purpose. The result was *The Desert and the Sown* (1907), an account of her peregrinations in Syria, with a particular focus on the archaeology and ethnography of the area. Her archaeological orientation was further underlined when she published the continuation of that enterprise, namely her journey through Cilicia and Lycaonia, in *Revue archéologique* 1906–1907. Bell's other major archaeological publications include *The Thousand and One Churches* (1909) with Sir William Ramsay and *The Palace and Mosque at Ukhaidír* (1914). One of her important contributions was the photographic record of archaeological sites in the Middle East. Throughout her crowded life, as she became a participant in history, described as the 'mother of modern Iraq', archaeology remained an interest. This interest provided her with a certain solace when she was eventually shut out of the world of affairs; and the fruit of that passion was the Baghdad Museum which she created.

By the time Bell's *The Desert and the Sown* had appeared, some outstanding women had already established themselves in a professional capacity in the field. The excavations of Harriet Boyd (Hawes) at Kavousi in Crete (1900) were published in the *American Journal of Archaeology* in 1901. In that year Boyd discovered the site of Gournia in Crete and her excavations there between 1901 and 1904 made her the first archaeologist to discover and excavate a Minoan town site of the Early Bronze Age. She married in 1906 and the final excavation report *Gournia, Vasiliki and Other Prehistoric Sites on the Isthmus of Hierapetra, Crete* (1908) was largely written during her son's first year. Surprise at this female achievement was denied but scarcely concealed in a review for the *Times Weekly Edition* of London:

> In these days of women's emancipation there should be nothing surprising in the successful conduct of a scientific

> excavation in the Near East by a lady, and least of all an American lady; but, as a matter of fact, Mrs. Hawes comes before us as actually the first of her sex who has both directed in person a scientific excavation in classic soil and edited in chief the scientific statement of its results . . . It is very much to Mrs. Hawes's credit that she lighted on the site at all, and, more, that she could explore it, when found, as thoroughly and intelligently as she did. (Allesbrook 1992: 134)

Her daughter was to write that Boyd Hawes was not so much antagonistic to convention 'as blissfully unaware of it'. That indifference to convention had limits. Whilst she found the dilemma posed by a marriage proposal a 'painful choice', she believed that a woman's work must 'be more or less interruptible [lest] family and society . . . suffer'. With regard to her professional insights, Boyd Hawes subscribed to the theory of women's particular psychology: 'We are deficient in logic', she wrote in 1912, 'but we have as an offset the gift of inference. And the faculty for correct inference . . . is beginning to be recognized as a legitimate power.' She thought women's academic work should parallel, or dovetail, with men's – not duplicate it. At the same time, she envisioned that research such as hers might occasion the modification of History (a conviction that grew with time): a proper reading of history – or a reading of proper history – would prove that the life of women had not been 'tame and without influence until recently' (Allesbrook 1992: 130, 228–9).

Boyd Hawes was a mentor to others (for whom Archaeology was being seen as an appropriate pursuit). Edith Hall (Dohan), having received a Fellowship for study at the American School at Athens in 1903 and an additional stipend from a fellowship founded to 'lift the restrictions on women in the study of archaeology', was invited to join the excavations of Harriet Boyd. From this flowed her doctoral dissertation submitted in 1907: *The Decorative Art of Crete in the Bronze Age*. Immediately thereupon, Hall became an instructor in classical archaeology at Mount Holyoke College, during which time she continued fieldwork in Crete for the Museum of the University of Pennsylvania. After a five-year interruption, occasioned by her marriage in 1915, she returned to academic life with a curatorship at the Museum and teaching stints at the prestigious women's college Bryn Mawr in the 1920s, becoming in 1932 the review editor of the *American Journal of Archaeology*, a position she held until her death. Hall's curatorial work at the University of Pennsylvania led her into Etruscan studies and her most important publication *Italic Tomb-Groups in the University Museum* (1942) was hailed as 'the first attempt ever made to establish a synchronology of seventh-century Etruscan graves'. In addition, she published some 50 articles in archaeological and museum journals.

Boyd had not been the first to direct excavations. In Egypt, Margaret Benson did so at the temple of Mut at Thebes in 1895–1898, despite having received no archaeological training. In Egypt also, the camps of the famous Flinders Petrie offered opportunities to a number of women. One of his students, Janet Gourlay, brought her training to Benson's dig at Thebes. Petrie's wife Hilda was an active collaborator from the time of their marriage in 1897 (Drower 1996: 231–48). Another was the suffragette Margaret Murray who specialised in both inscriptions and human remains. A student under Petrie from 1894, Murray was the first woman to devote herself fully to Egyptology, taking up fieldwork with the Petries at Abydos in 1902, at the same time as **Lina Eckenstein.** During that season, it was decided that Hilda Petrie would direct the excavation of the 'Osireion' with the assistance of Murray and Miss Hansard who came as an artist; an all-woman excavation and one not without danger (Drower 1996: 267–9). In the end the investigation had to be abandoned, because of the conditions, though the results were published by Murray in 1904 in *The Osireion at Abydos*. The next year saw the publication of the first volume of Murray's *Saqqara Mastabas*, Murray describing this in her memoirs as the work of a small team: herself, Miss Hansard and Jessie Mothersole (Murray 1963: 125–6). Murray went on to a long academic career. She produced over 80 books and articles on Egypt. Although much of her work has been overtaken, she left vivid memories, especially of her deep interest in witchcraft. In 1921 she published *The Witch-Cult in Western Europe* which established her reputation in that field, and in 1933 as a sequel intended for the popular market, *The God of the Witches*, both books attempting to base medieval and early modern witchcraft upon ancient pagan religion. Although her work in this area has received some serious academic criticism, *The God of the Witches* in particular became a best-seller (Hutton 1999: 194–201, 272). Her entry in the *Dictionary of National Biography* suggests that 'she possessed firm common sense and was quite unsuperstitious, although if she had lived in an earlier age she might have been thought of as a lady fit for burning'.

In 1921 the formidable Gertrude Caton-Thompson began her career with the Petries. At the age of 33 and after success in the civil service, she joined them at Abydos, encouraged by Murray and the paleozoologist Dorothea Bate. Caton-Thompson was invited the next year by Murray to join her women's team excavating on Malta. In 1924 she was back in Egypt, joining the Petrie camp at Qau, accommodated in a rock-cut tomb, 'roomy and cool and jointly owned by a family of three cobras' (Caton-Thompson 1983: 90–1). In the same year, having determined the potential importance of settlement sites rather than cemeteries (in this observation she was ahead of her time), she began her own excavations at the site of Hemamieh, which led to her co-authored work *The Badarian Civilisation* (1928). In 1925, she worked on the desert margins of the Fayum (north-western Egypt) with the Oxford geologist Elinor Gardner. Together they published *The Desert Fayum* (1934). Caton-Thompson's most famous work was conducted in 1929 at Zimbabwe, published with her usual speed in 1931. Subsequently, after work in the western desert with Gardner, the first such excavations in a Saharan oasis site, she produced *Kharga Oasis in Prehistory* (1952). In 1935, Veronica Seton-Williams was accepted onto the Petrie team in the Sinai, having learnt the elements of hieroglyphs from Margaret Murray. Amongst her publications were *Ptolemaic Temples* (1977), *El-Amarna* (1984) and *A Short History of Egypt* (1989).

This is not to suggest that the path was smooth in Archaeology. Women like Murray felt tested in ways their male counterparts were not (Murray 1963: 96–8; Caton-Thompson 1983: 83). The Schools of Archaeology at Athens and Rome were closed to French women until the 1960s (Coudart 1998: 73–4). Work with male relatives provided an avenue; but whilst connubial collaboration need not lead to the eclipse of the wife – the early example of the both liberated and supportive Jane Dieulafoy is a case in point (in that the excavation reports of the work undertaken with her husband in Persia were published in her own name), the contribution of others, like

Hilda Petrie and Tessa Wheeler, was not as widely known. Still others, despite fieldwork expertise, found their way forward in the 'housework' part of the profession, that is to say, museum management (Gero 1985). Some flourished. Semni Papaspyridi-Karouzou, one of the first women employed by the Greek Archaeological Service, was appointed as a curator at the National Archaeological Museum in Athens in 1921. Her subsequent career was outstanding, her commitment to the national heritage unwavering, despite political vicissitudes. Her professional containment, that is, her museum commitments, actually led to extensive publications (some 20 monographs and more than 120 articles) and international recognition (Nikolaidou and Kokkinidou 1998: 244–51). Also well known for her role in museum work was Winifred Lamb, honorary keeper of the Greek and Roman Department in the Fitzwilliam Museum, Cambridge, between 1920 and 1958. The classical collections in the Fitzwilliam grew significantly under Lamb and she was heavily involved in the display and publication of the collection. She wrote the standard text *Greek and Roman Bronzes* (1929), reviewed in *The Journal of Hellenic Studies* (1929) as 'at once a history of the subject and a book of reference . . . written with an appreciation of the beauty and humour of Greek art which is not the less attractive for sometimes being feminine'.

By the early decades of the twentieth century, then, women had established themselves in Archaeology. Esther Van Deman, who took her PhD from Chicago in 1898, was the first woman Roman archaeologist. Her studies of building materials and methods of construction such as *The Atrium Vestae* (1909), *The Building of Roman Aqueducts* (1934) and *Ancient Roman Construction in Italy from the Prehistoric Era to Augustus* (1947) laid the foundation for the serious study of Roman architecture. Hetty Goldman who took her PhD from Radcliffe in 1916 was known for her work at Halae, Colophon, Eutresis and Tarsus. The excavation reports from two of these sites, *Excavations at Eutresis in Boeotia* (1931) and the three collaborative double volumes of *Excavations at Gözlü Kule, Tarsus* (1950, 1956, 1963), are viewed as models of their kind. In 1936 she became the first woman professor at Princeton's Institute for Advanced Studies. Dorothy Garrod, whose work was principally in prehistoric archaeology (see, for example, *The Upper Palaeolithic Age in Britain* [1926] and *Environment, Tools and Man* [1946]), became in 1939, as the Disney Chair of Archaeology at Cambridge, the first woman to hold a chair in any subject at that university. Winifred Lamb was also active in the field. She conducted campaigns in Greece and Turkey, producing the important Bronze Age study *Excavations at Thermi in Lesbos* (1936). Her work at Kusura in Turkey (published in *Archaeologia* [1936]) saw pioneering progress towards cross-dating between the prehistoric Aegean and Anatolia (Gill 1999). Kathleen Kenyon, having first experienced the field as a photographer and assistant to Caton-Thompson, left an indelible mark on the discipline through her theories of excavation technique (the 'Wheeler-Kenyon method'); as one of the founders (in 1937) of the University of London's Institute of Archaeology; and through her excavation from 1952 of Jericho, as a result of which in texts such as *Digging Up Jericho* (1957) and *Archaeology in the Holy Land* (1960) she significantly rewrote the history of this are (Champion 1998: 189–90).

Crossing discipline borders: Jane Ellen Harrison

It was not only in Archaeology that women found interest and opportunity. In the first two decades of the twentieth century, **Jane Ellen Harrison**'s *Prolegomena to the Study of Greek Religion* (1903) and *Themis: A Study in the Social Origins of Greek Religion* (1912) had a profound impact on the way in which the modern world regards ancient Greek culture (Ackerman 1991: xiii). Harrison entered the recently founded Newnham College, Cambridge, as a student in Classics in 1874 but did not thrive in that field. It is generally recognised that as a rule women were ill-prepared, given the training that they had previously received, for the heavy concentration in Cambridge's Classical Tripos on language and philology (as it was there defined), particularly the emphasis on verse translation and textual criticism (Breay 1999). As Harrison remembered:

> Looking back over my own life, I see with what halting and stumbling steps I made my way to my own special subject. Greek literature as a specialism I early felt was barred to me. The only field of research that the Cambridge of my day knew of was textual criticism, and for fruitful work in that my scholarship was never adequate. (1926: 82)

Archaeology provided an initial escape. It was in London, at the British Museum, that Harrison found her place. Her interest in the Greek cultural landscape, however, was broader than the strictly archaeological. Harrison's chief contribution arose from her belief that myth had its origin in ritual and that from a study of the latter, using the broadest range of evidence and inference, it was possible to retrieve nothing less than the evolution of Greek culture. She embraced the new currents of anthropology, sociology and psychology: 'New ways in thinking were everywhere in the air and she inhaled them all. She often confessed that her head was seething with ideas. She cleared it by writing, and the result each time was the statement of a coherent position that was nevertheless riddled with paradox' (Robinson 2002: 8). Harrison acknowledged many debts – in particular to James Frazer, Gilbert Murray, Henri Bergson and Émile Durkheim – but in some ways she saw her contribution as gender specific. In 1915 she was to recall a thought which had lodged in her mind, though she could no longer remember where she had first read it: 'Woman is more *resonant* than man, more *subject to induction from the social current* . . . ' In the context, she was speaking to her belief that the 'present age is an age of [intellectual] co-operation, marked not so much by individual emergence as by interdependent, collective advance . . .', particularly where 'the imaginative reconstruction of the past' was concerned (Harrison 1915: 122–3, 126).

The history of art

Another refugee from Classics and one-time pupil of Harrison was Eugénie Sellers Strong. Obtaining a Third Class in the Classical Tripos, she decided to make archaeology her career, pursuing her interests at the British Museum. In the 1880s and 1890s she studied with a number of German archaeologists. Her first major work, *Roman Sculpture from Augustus to Constantine* (1907), established Roman art as a subject worthy of study in its own right. The second, *Apotheosis and After Life* (1915), explored the relationship between the visual arts and Roman ideologies of the afterlife. The approaches of

Harrison and Strong were quite distinct – but, as has been usefully observed by others, Strong did for Rome what Harrison did for Greece (Beard 2000: 28). They were cultural anthropologists drawing upon the visual arts and archaeology. In 1909, Strong was appointed Assistant Director of the British School at Rome, of which, from that time until her 'retirement' in 1925, she became the social and administrative hub. The milieu she created was likened to 'the salon of a great lady' (Thomson 1949: 72–4; see also Wiseman 1990: 15). At her retirement dinner in London, attended by almost 200 guests, Lord Asquith asserted 'that there is no more distinguished woman scholar to be found anywhere today' (Beard 2000: 15).

At that dinner was Gisela Richter who had that year begun her long reign over classical antiquities at the Metropolitan Museum in New York; Richter was the first woman in the United States to hold such a position. She also had been a student at Girton, where she had entered in 1901 and where she had been taught by Katharine Jex-Blake (resident classical lecturer 1885–1901, and then Director of Studies in Classics), a teacher who had been particularly alert to the disadvantages faced by women undertaking the Classical Tripos (Breay 1999: 59, 67) and who had collaborated as a translator with her close friend Eugénie Sellers Strong on *The Elder Pliny's Chapters on the History of Art* (1896). Richter's entrée to the Metropolitan Museum had been provided by Harriet Boyd who had taken up Richter as a protégé when the latter, in 1904, had been the only woman 'at' the British School at Athens, although not allowed to reside there. Staying instead at a pension, she had become friends with several women from the American School of Classical Studies. Boyd had invited Richter to Gournia and introduced her to the science of Minoan chronology whilst nursing the young woman through a bout of gastric fever. In 1905, Boyd invited Richter to come with her to the United States. Richter became an authority in Greek, Etruscan and Roman art, with Archaic Greek art her speciality; her books such as *Sculpture and Sculptors of the Greeks* (1929) and the *Handbook of Greek Art* (1959) have become standard sources for students.

Again, we have women with 'historical' instincts operating outside the discipline of History. A contemporary of Richter was Margarete Bieber, the first woman to be awarded a travelling fellowship for classical archaeology by the German Archaeological Institute and only the second woman professor in that country. In 1933, when Nazi race laws forced her to abandon her homeland, she briefly held a visiting post at Oxford, 'where she was treated as an honoured guest but never felt at home' (Harrison 1978: 574). She then transferred to the United States where she carved out an outstanding career (Bonfante 1979). Three of her works in particular have become classics: *The History of the Greek and Roman Theater* (1939), the first treatment of that subject which went beyond the literary aspect of theatre; *The Sculpture of the Hellenistic Age* (1955) and *Ancient Copies* (1977).

Her success underlines the seemingly more hospitable environment for women academics in the field of ancient world studies on the western side of the Atlantic. A longer tradition prevailed there. Helen Magill (White), the first American woman to receive a PhD, had taken it in Greek with a dissertation on Greek drama at Boston University in 1877. The Vassar departments of Latin and Greek before 1920 were staffed by 'a uniquely distinguished female faculty: *inter alias* Abby Leach,

Grace H. Macurdy, Lily Ross Taylor and Elizabeth Haight – four large presences in American classical studies . . .' (Lateiner 1996/1997: 154). The quietly influential Mary Swindler, who took her PhD in 1912 from Bryn Mawr where she became Professor of Classical Archaeology in 1931, was, from 1932 to 1946, the first woman editor-in-chief of the *American Journal of Archaeology*. Her field of expertise was art history, her chief work being *Ancient Painting* (1929) which ranged from Palaeolithic cave paintings to late antique mosaics and early Christian art. By the time, then, of Bieber's installation at Columbia in the 1930s, women had left their mark on the study of antiquity – but rarely had they done so as Historians.

Ancient History today

Lily Ross Taylor, the first woman to be spoken of in the same terms as the male 'Greats' who were her contemporaries in Ancient History, cut a very different figure to those of the scholars covered above; she would have seen her work based solely upon traditional *Wissenschaft*. In the preface to her *Divinity of the Roman Emperor* (1931) where she acknowledges her debts to previous scholarship (principally German), there is no mention of Strong's *Apotheosis and After Life*. The omission is striking, given the overlap of their residences in Rome. As much as Taylor's students and colleagues would remember that her interest had been in how people functioned *within* institutions and as much as Taylor's own professed aim was to make her students feel that they were 'walking the streets of Rome, and seeing and thinking what Romans saw and thought' (Broughton 1970: 735), she must have felt uncomfortable with Art History (even if she herself mobilised the evidence of the visual media) – or was she uncomfortable with the ways in which Strong sought to probe the psyche of imperial messages?

Taylor served as a model to future female scholars who might take an interest in both the more traditional and the developing fields within Ancient History. Of the 13 (perhaps 14) doctoral candidates whom she is known to have supervised a number went on to publish important works on Roman religion, politics and society. There is an Australian connection here (in which the authors may be indulged): Taylor's last graduate student, Beryl Wilkinson, went on as Beryl Rawson to become the first female Chair of Classics and Ancient History in Australia whilst Rawson's student, Suzanne Dixon, went on to become Australia's foremost scholar in Roman Women's History. The developing interests of these three women, and the matrilineage here invoked, might form an interesting social history in its own right; but the great wave of women's scholarship on the ancient world in the second half of the twentieth century must unfortunately be reduced to something of an epilogue here.

Much of that scholarship has been devoted to women's studies, with Sarah B Pomeroy's *Goddesses, Whores, Wives and Slaves: Women in Classical Antiquity* (1975) rightly being seen as a watershed (Culham 1987). One of the most notable achievements of so much women's scholarship in the final quarter of the twentieth century has been the challenge to traditional historiography and approaches to the past. Skinner (1985, 1987, 1989) argues that feminist approaches to the study of Graeco-Roman civilisation have critiqued the very nature of classical studies which she characterises as one of the most conservative, hierarchical and patriarchal of academic fields (see also Richlin 1991, 1992; Rabinowitz and Richlin 1993). Brooten finds that the *absence* of evidence regarding women in the ancient world highlights the tunnel vision of traditional historiography: 'Woman represents a crack in the system; her existence as central and not marginal demonstrates that both the ancient literary sources and contemporary historiography are not the mirrors or windows they claim to be' (Brooten 1985: 66, 68). Blok (1987: 38) points to the feminist reconsideration of the function of the ancient source material and to the interrogation of the limits of literary sources. This has led, Blok suggests, to a diversity of perceptions of antiquity. Archaeology has been subject to parallel influences. In 1984 Margaret Conkey and Janet Spector complained of the lack of a gendered perspective in that discipline. The campaign continued with Conkey and Joan Gero lamenting that the transformation of the social and historical sciences 'because of feminist-inspired critiques' had not yet impacted on archaeology (1991: 3–5). The results came quickly as Rita Worth was to observe: in just a little over a decade 'gender research [had] profoundly changed the way we think about people in the past' (1996: 1).

The impact of second-wave feminism on the study of the ancient world has not been confined to women's studies. Women's scholarship now treats every aspect of antiquity. To proffer one British example only, reference might be made to *some* of the works of Averil Cameron: *Agathias* (1970), *Continuity and Change in Sixth-Century Byzantium* (1981), *Procopius and the Sixth Century* (1985), *History as Text* (edited 1989) and *Christianity and the Rhetoric of Empire: The Development of Christian Discourse* (1991), together with her texts intended for the wider market, *The Later Roman Empire* (1993) and *The Mediterranean World in Late Antiquity AD 395–600* (1993). The high degree of consciousness that accompanied women's impact on the academy since the 1970s and the simultaneous search for the voice of women in antiquity might have created the illusion of Women's voice in scholarship. If ever such existed, the present spread of women's scholarship in the field of antiquity would seem to defy any quest for uniformity or gendered definition. Even Ancient Historians influenced by second-wave feminism had been divided on source interpretation, a division now characterised as between 'Optimist' and 'Pessimist' readings (Richlin 1993). By the end of the twentieth century the internal critique of identity politics has led to a perceived splintering within Women's Studies (Scott 1997). Other allegiances cut across gender. Debates centering on the issue of race provide an obvious example. Shelley Haley (1993) criticises the presuppositions of white female scholars whilst Mary Lefkowitz (1996) deplores 'Afrocentric ancient history' as espoused by both male and female champions alike. Third-wave feminism makes manifest the fragmentation of voices, with some third-wave feminists, such as Lynn Meskell, ridiculing the concentration on women in antiquity: 'Ancient Egypt is once again being Orientalized and feminized – not as a result of androcentric colonialist discourses, but through the new spate of studies devoted to the women in ancient Egypt' (Meskell 1998: 173). The study of antiquity, Meskell argues, has gone beyond the *add women and stir* phase. Moreover, debate between female scholars, on some fundamental issues, has been vigorous; the hypotheses of Marija Gimbutas reviving interest in the theory of early matristic societies (1974, 1989, 1999) have received some of their strongest criticism from other women scholars.

Polyphony prevails. Studies which are essentially gendered (and/or focus upon gender) flourish, while other scholars are alternatively attracted to the studies which *assume* gender or ignore it. Of the former, Rabinowitz's attempt to retrieve evidence of female homoeroticism from antiquity is an example; in particular, her emphasis on 'the effect of the lenses we use to view antiquity' (2002: 148). Those 'lenses' are not necessarily gendered; but in all probability are – in the first instance. A related phenomenon is the **Lesbian** Perspective; its proponents speak *as* women, but would not profess to speak for all women. The movement is of special interest here because at least one classicist spokeswoman asserts direct inspiration from Jane Ellen Harrison (Passman 1993: 180). But this discussion has drifted back, not inevitably, to the area of Women's Studies. Harrison's research was by no means confined to the latter – and those with a very different approach might also make a claim to inspiration in Harrison who once wrote: 'Rather, by a swing of the pendulum we are back in an inverse form of the old initial error, the over-emphasis of sex . . . and in this hubbub of man and woman the still small voice of humanity is apt to be unheard' (Harrison 1915: 85–6).

J Lea Beness
T W Hillard

References

Ackerman 1991; Allesbrook 1992; Beard 1994, 2000; Bivar & Hinnells 1985; Blok 1987; Bonfante 1979; Breay 1999; Briggs & Calder 1990; Brooten 1985; Broughton 1970; Calder & Hallett 1996–1997; Caton-Thompson 1983; Champion 1998; Conkey & Gero 1991; Conkey & Spector 1984; Coudart 1998; Culham 1987; Diaz-Andreu & Sørensen 1998; Drower 1996; Farnham 1976; Gero 1985; Gill 1999; Gimbutas 1974, 1989, 1999; Haley 1993; EB Harrison, 1978; JE Harrison, 1915, 1926; Hutton 1999; Lateiner 1996/97; Lefkowitz 1996; Malcovati 1953; Meskell 1998; Murray 1963; Nikolaidou & Kokkinidou 1998; Passman 1993; Rabinowitz & Richlin 1993; Rabinowitz 2002; Richlin 1991, 1992, 1993; Ridgway 1996; Robinson 2002; Scott 1997; Seton-Williams 1988; Skinner 1985, 1987, 1989; Thomson 1949; Thompson *et al.* 1974; Wallach 1996; Wiseman 1990; Worth 1996.

Related essays

Ancient world; Empire; Lesbian history; Local history; Orientalism; Travel.

Ancient world

While there is little extant evidence of the writing of women in the ancient world, recent research has discovered women as authors of works of philosophy, musical theory, grammar, literary criticism, astronomy, travel, magic, medicine, alchemy, mathematics, drama, prophecy and sex manuals (Plant 2004). However, few women in the ancient world were recognised as historians as the genre of history and its subject matter were considered almost exclusively the prerogatives of men (Snyder 1989). As early as the fifth century BC, Thucydides defined History in his *History of the Peloponnesian War* as being essentially about war and politics, and excluded women from it. In the second century AD Lucian, in his epistolary lecture *How to Write History*, cites Heraclitus' famous dictum, 'War is the father of all things', to conclude that war is the father of all historians. He argues that a historian needs first and foremost to understand war and to have been in camp himself. Such personal observation ('autopsy'), along with personal acquaintance with other eyewitnesses, was seen as crucial for the historian. Women were thus further precluded from the field of political/ military history as they could not claim specialist knowledge nor autopsy, nor would it have been proper for a woman to solicit witnesses as a man could.

The domestic seclusion of women in ancient Athens appears to have inhibited their literary production as only one female historian is attested from Classical Greece. Marcellinus (fifth–sixth century AD) noted that some readers had claimed that Book Eight of Thucydides' *History of the Peloponnesian War* was not written by Thucydides himself, but by his daughter. Marcellinus dismisses such claims and they seem unlikely to have been more than supposition. Why then was part of this history attributed to a woman? Thucydides died before he completed his *History* and Book Eight in particular is unfinished: the style is not polished, nor in this book are there the set speeches found in the rest of the history. The much simpler narrative style suggested a less highly accomplished writer, though Marcellinus argues that the quality of the work is still too good to have been written by a woman.

This prejudice exemplifies a popular perception in the Græco-Roman world that women were not capable of prose of high quality. This was not true, as a discerning reader like Cicero could attest: he states in *The Nature of the Gods* that the philosopher Leontion wrote in very good Attic Greek. Hortensia was remembered for her good rhetorical style too by Appian in his *Civil Wars* (mid-second century AD), and Valerius Maximus in *Memorable Deeds and Sayings* and Quintilian in his *Institutes of Oratory* (both first century AD). Women in the Græco-Roman elite were well educated and well read as references to the literary abilities of Sempronia, Perilla, Cornifica and Cynthia attest. Evidence for the education of women in Archaic and Classical Greece is less secure, though extant poetry by women from these periods shows that the elite were literate (Beck 1978: 1–8). However, even literate women were not expected to offer a critical voice in public as there was a taboo against a virtuous woman 'exposing' herself to men outside her family. A woman was expected to keep her speech, her feelings, character and temperament hidden, as well as her body.

The prejudice against women as writers of history is exemplified in Athenaeus' reservations about the history of Alexander the Great by Nicobule. Nicobule is dated to about 300 BC, and so lived a good 500 years or so before Athenaeus. We only know of Nicobule and her work through Athenaeus, but he expressed some doubt that the work attributed to her was really by her, speculating that it may have been written by a man. Similarly, some ancient writers thought that Pamphila's *Historical Commentaries* had really been written by her husband or her father. Pamphila lived in the reign of Nero (first century AD) in Egypt, a centre for scholarship in the Hellenistic world. Eleven fragments of the original 33 books of the *Historical Commentaries* remain, including the prologue in which Pamphila explains that her husband was a famous teacher and his lectures were an important source for her work, as were lectures by his visitors, as well as books. The fame of her husband, a misreading of this prologue, as well as prejudice against women writers, combined to lead some later readers to discredit her claim to authorship. Pamphila was a polymath, specialising in epitomes. She is credited with an epitome of Ctesias, a historian of Persia and India who lived in the fourth century BC. The extant fragments of her *Historical Commentaries* are biographical anecdotes about famous Greek philosophers, historians and politicians. In this respect it appears to have been similar to Nicobule's work, of which only anecdotes about Alexander remain. The works by Pamphila and Nicobule were derivative, historical summaries and biographical works. For these writers, as women, could not have personal access to oral informants, let alone demonstrate the autopsy demanded of a Historian. Even so, Pamphila felt the need to claim a form of autopsy. She asserted that she listened to lectures by her husband and his visitors. While the library was an important source for her too, it was the personal contact with informants that she stressed.

A contemporary of Pamphila, Julia Agrippina wrote historical commentaries (*commentarii*) which were also biographical. Agrippina was an important member of the Roman elite, the daughter of Germanicus, the wife of the emperor Claudius, sister of the emperor Gaius and the mother of the emperor Nero, and according to Tacitus, a major political figure herself. We have two references to her work: Pliny the Elder, a contemporary of Agrippina, tells us in his *Natural Histories* that she wrote about the birth of her son, Nero, and Tacitus cites her as the source for a story in his *Annals* about her mother, Agrippina the Elder. Family histories were very important to the Roman elite, and it is interesting to see a woman publish 'the story of her life and the misfortunes of her own family'. Her work is often labelled ***Memoirs***, a gendered interpretation of the Latin term *Commentarii*, implying to the modern reader a more personal, feminine and perhaps less important form of history. Calling her work memoirs distinguishes and distances it, for example, from Julius Caesar's histories of the Gallic and Civil wars, which were also called *Commentarii* and so to the Latin reader were works in the same genre as Agrippina's. Tacitus's brief citation suggests Agrippina's work was a revisionist history, an attempt to set the record straight about her mother, who had been persecuted by the emperor Tiberius. That Agrippina would write biography, even autobiography, seems to contradict the taboo against women revealing themselves, for what underpinned her work was her personal testimony. In autobiography, the writer's personal experience is what defines and legitimises the work.

Histiaea wrote a historical commentary rather than History in about 200 BC. The *Iliad* had been accepted by the Greeks as a poetic account of a real Bronze-Age war. In the fragment of her work which survives, Histiaea discussed the topography of Troy, making an astute observation that the plain in front of Ilium in her day was the result of later alluvial deposit. According to Strabo writing in the first century BC, Demetrius of Scepsis, who visited Ilium himself, cites Histiaea as an authority. Histiaea was probably a contemporary of Demetrius but nothing more is known about her.

The demand for autopsy in history, perversely, led to the generation of pseudonymous texts, such as the letters of Cornelia who lived in the second century BC and was later remembered as the 'mother of the Gracchi' and idealised as a model for Roman woman. Letters attributed to her were read by Cicero, Quintilian and Cornelius Nepos, and known to Plutarch. Pseudonymous philosophical texts were attributed to Theano, the wife of Pythagoras, and to his daughters. Where a woman was an eyewitness to events and confidante of key players she could add credibility to an account through her testimony. One famous woman who was later said to have been a historical writer was Septimia Zenobia, Queen of Palmyra in the third century AD. We should treat with caution the claim that she wrote an epitome history of Alexandria and the East. For the claim only appears in a semi-fictional work, the *Augustan History* (dated to the end of the fourth century AD), and is made by an author who freely invented many of the sources cited there. The context of the claim is nevertheless interesting. For the author of the *Augustan History* chose to extol Zenobia's intelligence, knowledge and command of languages by claiming she was a writer and a historian: this was to be seen as an outstanding achievement for her as a woman.

Perpetua may provide us with a second example of an autobiographical work. Few stories of Christian martyrs may be taken as historical, but the martyrdom of Perpetua, is generally taken to be an exception to this rule. Part of the story of the imprisonment, trial and execution of this young Christian woman in Carthage in AD 202 is given in the first person, purporting to be the words of Perpetua herself. Scholars hesitate to accept this, though the text is unusual in its focus on her experiences, rather than those of her four male companions (who were also executed and died as martyrs). Acceptance of female authorship makes this text particularly significant as it would stand as the earliest extant Christian literature written by a woman.

Egeria's *Itinerarium*, a journal of her pilgrimage and an account of the liturgy of Jerusalem, provides us with another type of historical work. Egeria, whom we only know through her text, described her visit to the Holy Land in the fifth century AD. She was evidently a wealthy woman and describes in detail the biblical sites, churches and monasteries she visited, the hospices she stayed in and bishops, laymen and monks whom she met. Her *Journal* takes the form of a letter, addressed to readers named 'sisters', which is best interpreted to mean fellow religious and so define Egeria herself as a member of a religious order. The text was probably not intended for general publication, and this may explain its rough and repetitive style.

In a community that saw a woman as, ideally, a hidden admirer of her husband's works, rather than as an active participant in a literary circle herself, opportunities for publication of texts were limited to the wealthy who had the leisure time to write and the resources necessary. The mode of publication also served to restrict women to literary genres deemed appropriate to their sex. For publication was not normally just a literary act. Publication was by performance, the reading of a text by its author. The text could then be circulated at the discretion and the expense of the author. While male writers might be sponsored by a rich patron, women were not.

There were, however, opportunities for aristocratic women to present a personal history. Select gatherings gave women the opportunity to tell historical stories. Cornelia was remembered as a model Roman woman, as a chaste wife and mother of famous sons. She was also remembered for the stories she told of her father, the famous Scipio Africanus, and her sons, Tiberius and Gaius Gracchus. In his *Letters* Pliny the Younger records anecdotes which Fannia told about her grandmother, the famous Arria. Non-aristocratic women also told stories. Plutarch records in his *Life of Pompey* (early second century BC) that the prostitute Flora used to repeat stories about her relationships with Pompey, Geminius and Caecilius Metellus, consequently forming an important source of oral history. Another prostitute, 'Hispana', who in her youth spent some time in a cave in Spain with Crassus also used to enjoy repeating her story in her old age. Writing in the early first century AD the historian Fenestella said that he himself often heard her tell this story. The subject of these women's stories was the lives of famous Romans, usually but not always men, with whom they had had relationships, as mother, daughter, granddaughter or companion. The choice of such biographical topics allowed women to contribute from their own experience.

In Rome then, the recitation not just the writing of history was important and women played a part in maintaining **oral traditions**. As written historical texts were read out loud, in delivery the personal accounts of these women would not have been so different from the performances of other historians. Cornelia's audience was select and the venue her beautiful home near Misenum: this was socially appropriate for a Roman aristocrat. Flora and 'Hispana' were mixing with wealthy Roman aristocrats in their youth, and again in their old age: perhaps they continued to make a living from their intimate knowledge of Roman aristocrats in their old age through their stories.

Women did write about great wars too, but not in a genre that we would recognise immediately as history. Proba, a Roman aristocrat, wrote an epic poem on Constantius's war against Magnentius (AD 350–352), a war fought in her own lifetime. While this work has not survived, she also wrote a Virgilian cento of nearly 700 lines which is extant. This can be read as a historical work too, as her subject is the creation of the world and other episodes from Genesis, Old Testament stories and the story of Christ. Another Christian writer Eudocia, an Athenian born about AD 400 who married the Emperor Theodosius II, wrote epic poetry including a historical poem on the Roman victories of her husband over the Persians in AD 421 and 422. Eudocia composed Christian works which could be considered historical too: a verse paraphrase of the *Octateuch* (the first eight books of the Old Testament), a paraphrase of the books of the prophets Zacharia and Daniel, an epic poem on the martyrdom of St Cyprian, of which nearly 800 lines survive, as well as a paraphrase by Photius; and an Homeric cento of about 2400 lines on the life of Christ, which has survived complete, along with other works.

History was a gendered genre, with a clear focus on war and politics. There was also a social barrier to participation by women in the way in which History was published. However, poetry was an acceptable genre for women, and, importantly, in poetry women did not have to satisfy the requirements of autopsy, but could call upon the Muses and divine inspiration as the ultimate sources of their knowledge as Proba did in her *Cento* 9–21. While women such as Proba and Eudocia could tackle the subject of war in epic poetry, this genre encouraged exaggeration, was designed to entertain rather than inform, and had evolved into a form of panegyric, with the heroising of historical figures.

I M Plant

References

Beck 1978; Plant 2004; Snyder 1989.

Related essays

Archaeology and ancient historians; Memoir; Oral traditions; War.

Anthony, Susan B 1820–1906

United States woman suffrage leader, historian. Born Adams, Massachusetts, daughter of Lucy (Read) and Daniel Anthony, farmer and cotton miller. Raised in Battenville, New York. Educated at a district school, at home and briefly at a Friends' Seminary near Philadelphia. From 1839 taught in district schools, private academies and families, ending as head of the female department in the academy at Canajoharie, New York, in 1846. Her parents and sisters had attended the 1848 woman's rights convention at Seneca Falls. When she quit teaching to run the family farm outside

Rochester in 1849 she became involved with them in the Western New York Anti-Slavery Society and the Daughters of Temperance. In 1850 she met Elizabeth Cady Stanton, with whom she formed a lifelong partnership.

Anthony began the peripatetic life of a reformer in 1852 as an agent for the Woman's New York State Temperance Society which she and Stanton founded to lobby for woman suffrage, married-women's property rights, mothers' custody rights, liberal divorce laws and rights for women in 'female' occupations. She combined this with her work as principal agent for the New York State American Anti-Slavery Society from 1856 until the Civil War. She and Stanton turned their focus onto the federal government when they founded the Women's Loyal National League in 1863 which urged Congress to abolish slavery by constitutional amendment. In 1869 they formed the National Woman Suffrage Association (NWSA) in order to test women's right to vote by virtue of their citizenship rights. Anthony was arrested and fined when she voted in 1872 as part of NWSA's campaign. From 1875 the NWSA's efforts focused on what came to be called the 'Susan B Anthony amendment' (the 19th Amendment) which was finally ratified in 1920. Anthony worked strenuously to link suffragists with other powerful women's groups. In 1890 she succeeded in merging the rival suffrage associations as the National American Woman Suffrage Association (NAWSA), presiding over it from 1892 to 1900 and cultivating younger talent.

Anthony and Stanton were both aware of their historic role from early in their careers. In the aftermath of the Centennial in 1876, they began, with their colleague **Matilda Joslyn Gage**, 'working for dear life – trying to gather up the threads of our Woman's Rights History'. They envisaged one volume of 600–800 pages, a general history interwoven with brief sketches of the leaders with their pictures. Stanton and Gage would write, collect, select and arrange material while Anthony would secure publication. Anthony, the more meticulous record-keeper, had kept clippings of their campaigns from 1855; trunks and boxes of old papers were shipped from her Rochester home to Stanton's home in Tenafly, New York. The three spent six months at Tenafly from 1880 to 1881, assembling the first volume of *The History of Woman Suffrage*, which appeared in May 1881, its 878 pages bringing them only to 1860. They began work again in July 1881 on Volume Two, covering 1861–1876, which was published in May 1882.

Anthony found the work 'appalling'. But the first two volumes were a labour of love for the friends as they laughed and squabbled over the 'swamp of letters and papers almost hopeless'. By the time they published Volume Three, covering 1877–1885 and published in 1886, they were ready to consign the work to younger hands, suggesting the publication at the end of each congressional term of a report on legislation that could be readily bound into similar volumes, 'thus keeping a full record of the prolonged battle until the final victory shall be achieved'.

The last three volumes essentially comprise that record. Volume Four, covering 1883–1900, begun half-heartedly by Anthony and Stanton in 1891, was finally completed by Anthony's young housemate Ida Husted Harper and published in 1902. After Anthony's death in 1906 Harper completed the *History* up to ratification with Volumes Five and Six, published in 1922, the final volume in association with the NAWSA. Harper also helped Anthony prepare her own two-volume

Life and Work of Susan B. Anthony, published in 1898. Anthony donated her books and scrapbooks to the Library of Congress and shipped thousands of volumes of the *History* and *Life and Work* to libraries.

Desley Deacon

Reference

NAW 1971.

Major works

Elizabeth Cady Stanton, Susan B Anthony & Matilda Joselyn Gage's *History of Woman Suffrage* (Salem: Ayer Co., 1985) and Anthony's papers are microfilmed and indexed as the *Papers of Elizabeth Cady Stanton and Susan B Anthony* (eds) Patricia G Holland and Ann D Gordon (1991).

Archives

Women writers of history have gained access to and made use of archival material in their published and unpublished work since at least the seventeenth century. One of the difficulties involved in constructing a history of women writers' use of archives involves determining what constitutes an archive. As Antoinette Burton reminds us, the word 'archive' derives from the Greek word *arkeion* – 'the house, residence, domicile of the archon (superior magistrate)' (2003: 6). From its beginning, 'archive' has implied a crossroads of public and private space. In her book *Dwelling in the Archive*, Burton asks, 'What counts as an archive? Can private memories of home serve as evidence of political history . . . [W]hat does it mean to say that home can and should be seen not simply as a dwelling-place for women's memory but as one of the foundations of history . . . conceived . . . as a narrative, a practice, and a site of desire?' (2003: 4). For contemporary historians, Burton argues, an archive is much more than a collection of documents found in a musty museum space, funded by government or private endowment and peopled with cataloguers and scholars.

We might carry Burton's conclusions into the past as well, in which case we would find women writers working in archives, broadly conceived, very early indeed. Early women's life-writing (diaries, biographies and autobiographies) could be said to draw on archival material. When we widen our sense of what constitutes an archive, and, at the same time, of what constitutes history, the possibilities for finding fruitful new subjects for study expands greatly. Recent books such as Charlotte Woodford's *Nuns as Historians in Early Modern Germany* (2002) illustrate the possibilities for locating previously unrealised material. To broaden our scholarly scope is exciting, but it also creates new problems. Do expanded definitions dictate that studying women in the archives requires the consideration of nearly everything that they recorded? If that is the case, all women writers might be said to have worked with archival sources.

For the purposes of this essay, a more conventional understanding of what constitutes an archive will be employed. Musty museum spaces of collected documents – and before those existed, private collections of statesmen's papers – have also been important sites for early women historians' labours. Very little work exists to document how women gained access even to these narrowly defined repositories of historical information, although studies of British, American, French and German women historians of earlier eras have appeared. Pre-twentieth-century women historiographers' use of archival material has yet to be explored in a thoroughgoing manner. As we will see, however, there is a great deal that might be described in such an account.

Prior to the mid-eighteenth century, few historians of either sex would have felt it necessary to consult documentary material in constructing a history, though exceptions may be found. English Civil War historians drew on documents in their own possession, and antiquarians sought documents for their scholarly pursuits. **Lucy Hutchinson** wrote *Memoirs of the Life of Colonel Hutchinson* (c.1671, published 1806) to document her own and her husband's participation in the war alongside larger historical events. It is her own archive' of her statesman husband's letters and her reconstructions of events in which he and she have participated that build the narrative. She couples this material with information she acknowledges adapting from Thomas May's *History of the Long Parliament of England* (1647).

Hutchinson's contemporary, **Margaret Cavendish**, the Duchess of Newcastle, also builds on her own memories of the war in her historical account of her era, her life and her husband. She argues that to do otherwise is to construct weak history. She calls her approach 'particular history' and deems it the most superior type, because of its narration by prime actors and spectators. In her view, inferior types of history include those written by travellers, navigators and statesmen. Cavendish does not include in her classification system a form of history-writing that consults original documents, except for those papers in one's own possession.

Prior to the eighteenth century, history practised as a scholarly pursuit fell to the antiquarians. Today these amateurs are most often understood as men whose activities involved gross misinterpretations of the past, as well as stultifying prose. Some women, too, were involved in antiquary endeavours. The most notable among them was Elizabeth Elstob. She was interested in the history of language and also published translated editions of Old English sermons. Although her work was scholarly and arguably drew from archival materials, it is unlikely to be categorised as history-writing by today's standards.

As we have seen, until the eighteenth century, historical writing did not necessarily entail the use of what we would call 'primary documents'. The famous contrast of British historians David Hume and William Robertson – the former of whom did not draw on archival material and the latter of whom did – has long served as a watershed moment in describing the development of British history-writing. Eighteenth-century women historians, too, might be crudely classified along this divide. The celebrated French writer **Germaine de Staël** did not consult documents, but her equally celebrated British predecessor, **Catharine Macaulay**, did.

De Staël, as a self-styled historical 'genius', drew on 'a set of emotions, psychic states, and bodily feelings' in creating her works (Smith 1998: 20). Her histories 'eschewed the realistic, linear chronicling of war, preferring the world of monuments and tombs, song and poetry' (Smith 1998: 25). She used materials from conversations, as well as descriptions of travel and of great historical actors with whom she had come in contact, in writing such books as *Considerations on the Principal Events of the French Revolution* (1818) and *On Germany* (1810). These procedures have been denigrated as 'amateur' and came to be associated with 'scribbling women' (Smith 1998: 37). Though 'as the nineteenth century opened, archival research was by no means the accepted road to historical truth' (Smith 1998: 19), some women writers were availing themselves of materials found in public and private archives.

Catharine Macaulay may well be the first woman historian publishing in English to incorporate materials housed in public archives. The British Museum's library, which opened in 1759, began to rival Oxford University's Bodleian Library as 'a place of pilgrimage and resort for the small but important world of historical and literary research' (Esdaile 1948: 53). Macaulay became the British Museum Library's first female regular reader in 1763. She had special permission to read the royal letters and used the resources of the library to construct her eight-volume *History of England from the Accession of James I, to That of the Brunswick Line* (later re-titled *to the Revolution*) (1763–1783). She also drew on archival material in private hands and is said to have unsuccessfully lobbied Lucy Hutchinson's descendants to publish her *Memoirs of the Life of Colonel Hutchinson* in the late eighteenth century (Looser 2000: 47).

Though acclaimed as a historian, Macaulay's personal life was frequently subject to harsh scrutiny, especially after her second marriage to a much younger man. This act, along with her Republican political sympathies, made her a target for criticism. It is therefore difficult to credit the posthumous accusation that she destroyed archival material. Isaac D'Israeli claimed that Macaulay was a 'dilapidator of manuscripts' who defaced seventeenth-century state letters while working in the British Museum Library. Although D'Israeli acknowledged that the rumour was 'impossible to authenticate', he maintained that Macaulay regularly destroyed any manuscript material unfavourable to her political leanings. He offered the so-called 'proof' of just one incident. Macaulay's widower William Graham and others came to her defence, and a flurry of letters was published in the periodical press. In the *Gentleman's Magazine* (1794), Graham responded publicly to D'Israeli asking, 'What your motive could be in making so wanton and malicious an attack on the memory of a most worthy and amiable woman, three years after her death, I am at a loss to conceive.' It is a sad fact that the first British female historian who drew extensively from archival sources was accused of misusing them.

Macaulay was not the first woman to be admitted to the British Museum Library. On 1 January, 1762, Lady Mary Carr and Lady Ann Munson were admitted together to the Reading Room. After Carr, Munson and Macaulay, it is believed that 'No other ladies appear to have been admitted during the first ten years' of the Library's existence (Barwick 1929: 34). Carr and Munson's admission together was no anomaly either. The tradition of women using the British Library in pairs was apparently long-standing, as the practice continued well into the nineteenth century. It is said that museum authorities waived their objections to music-and-education historian Maria Hackett's use of the library in 1827 'upon the condition of her finding a lady to study with her' (Bumpus 1891: 108). Her study partner was Mary Somerville, renowned author of books on physical geography and physical science (Bumpus 1891: 109). Though one historian of the British Museum indicates that he has found no official confirmation of the practice, he locates several instances of two ladies being admitted together (Barwick 1929: 65).

The British Museum Library emerged as the premier research centre for English-language materials, in that it was free and open to the public, and contained 435,000 volumes in 1850. By contrast, the United States's Library of Congress, founded in

1801, had just 80,000 volumes in the early 1860s. Although women had used that library for study since its earliest years, by the middle of the nineteenth century women were welcomed into or simply made themselves welcome in the British Museum Library's Reading Room. In the late nineteenth century, two long tables in the Reading Room were designated 'for the exclusive use of lady-readers'. Though women had the 'privilege . . . of taking a seat wherever they please,' the ladies's tables were ostensibly so designated because they provided hassocks (Nichols 1866: 9). When the room was redecorated in the early twentieth century, the 'ladies's area' was removed. After 1907, 'ladies who objected to the proximity of the other sex' were 'accommodated with a seat in the North Library' (Barwick 1929: 137). Such traditions quickly became antiquated. As Barwick notes, 'In 1906 it was found that the lady readers were about one-fifth of the daily average; in 1913 they had increased to about a third and are at present [1929] rapidly approaching the half' (1929: 144).

The uncelebrated women who were among the earliest users of the British Museum's Library illustrate the unacknowledged work of nineteenth-century women in libraries and archives. The aforementioned Maria Hackett – devoted to a cause (the welfare of choristers at St Paul's Cathedral School) as well as to writing – was a scholar and an activist. She published books on the history of St Paul's. She was also interested in the history and antiquities of London, though most of that work appeared in 'many letters from her graceful pen on archaeological and historical subjects' in the *Gentleman's Magazine* and other periodicals (Bumpus 1891: 114). Instead of using her name in full, she signed herself 'M. H.'

Hackett's historical contributions might be seen as more typical of women in the period, but one nineteenth-century female historian stands out as exceptional: **Agnes Strickland.** Strickland's histories led to great celebrity, and she drew heavily on archival material. Strickland (working with her sister Eliza) published nearly 50 works of history, poetry, fiction or letters during the years 1817–1871, a number that does not include anonymous work for periodicals. The most famous of the Stricklands' works are *Lives of the Queens of England* (1840–1848) and *Lives of the Queens of Scotland* (1850–1859). *The Queens of England* involved more than a dozen years of research and writing and employed materials from England's public record offices, among other places. Strickland excoriates the gossipy nature of the historical essay. She argues, ' "Facts, not opinions," should be the historian's motto' (*Lives*, I 1840: ix). She also describes the difficulties faced in using papers that 'have suffered much from accidents, and from the injuries of time. Water, and even fire, have partially passed over some; in others, the mildew has swept whole sentences from the page, leaving historical mysteries in provoking obscurity' (*Lives*, I 1840: xi).

If the documents themselves sometimes proved inscrutable, gaining access to public records was also a tricky business in the nineteenth century. British Home Secretary Lord John Russell initially blocked the Stricklands' request to use the State Paper Office by refusing to give them any facility for consulting documents. They got around him by using contacts who cleared the way for their use of the State Paper Office at any time they pleased. Later, the Stricklands were also given permission to use the Rolls Office. Because of the lack of organisation of the papers (the Calendar of State Papers was not printed until 1857 and 1865), their work was very slow going.

British historians had been lobbying the Commission of Public Records in the early 1830s, asking that the materials be better organised, protected and accessible. Accusations were made that important records were then being stored in stables or were being eaten by rats; that they were haphazardly indexed or entirely unindexed; and that large fees were assessed by keepers in order to see even these chaotic holdings. In 1838, the Public Record Office was called into being by Act of Parliament. It created at long last a central repository for these materials. Archival material in France endured a similar fate. It was claimed that the French archives in the Soubise Palace were in chaos, with cartons of documents lining halls and stairways, damaged by debris from falling ceilings, and subject to frequent thefts; the situation improved when the palace was refurbished in the 1840s (Smith 1998: 119).

When the public was finally admitted by ticket to the British Public Record Office, it was 'considered unsuitable that women should try and force their way in' (Pope-Hennessy 1940: 67). But the Stricklands and others, including **Lucy Aikin** and **Mary Anne Everett Green** found access. They became involved in activism to further extend reading privileges. Aikin, Green and Strickland signed an 1851 petition along with 80 men, asking the Master of Rolls to waive fees 'for people engaged in serious literary or historical scholarship, arguing that the fees were set for lawyers who consulted only a few documents, while literary and historical researchers often needed to consult many' (Laurence 2000: 125). In 1852, the fees for such researchers were abolished.

Even with better access to public records, research remained a challenge because many vital historical documents were in private hands. Sometimes information came directly to Strickland. As her sister-biographer Jane writes, 'Many learned and illustrious persons sent [Agnes] valuable extracts from their family archives, or directed her attention to scarce books' (1887: 24). Agnes Strickland, like others before her, found herself in correspondence with descendants of important historical personages, making requests to see their family papers. Through these means, she was able to use archives at Chatsworth and Hardwick, thanks to the assistance of the Duke of Devonshire. There she examined paintings, carvings and other objects, as well as papers. Despite this relatively easy access, she expressed the wish that all documents that were 'at present locked up in private collections, will in time be thrown open to the public' (*Letters*, I: xxii).

Gaining entry to archives sometimes required letters of introduction. The Stricklands used their contacts to gain access to materials. To complete research on Henrietta Maria, Catharine of Braganza and Mary of Modena, the Stricklands travelled to France in the mid-1840s and found assistance from statesman-historian François Guizot and historian Jules Michelet (*Lives*, I: xii–xiii). With such help, the sisters were admitted to the Archives du Royaume, Archives Etrangères and Bibliothéque des Rois, where they used State Papers and other documents. Though the Stricklands began diligently studying the papers themselves, it was suggested that they hire a copyist. Doing so freed them up to visit additional repositories and to sightsee (Pope-Hennessy 1940: 140).

Eliza Strickland most easily took to detail work and checking references. Research and composition were 'a serious labour' to Agnes, and she was admittedly less skilled in paleography than was Eliza (Laurence 2000: 129). But when Eliza refused to assist Agnes with a late project, *Lives of the Last Four Princesses of the House of Stuart* (1870),

Agnes undertook this work alone. It required new introductions and travel to sites and archives in Holland, Germany and Belgium. At age 73, she went abroad alone to research, instructing her family that if she should die abroad, she wished her remains to stay abroad (Pope-Hennessy 1940: 294). She received 'great kindness' from the royal librarian at The Hague, pleased that she was able to use 'works not to be obtained in the [British Museum], nor I believe in any library in England' (Pope-Hennessy 1940: 295). The Strickland sisters proved themselves diligent researchers, capable writers and popular authors of historical works. As Miriam Elizabeth Burstein argues, 'Strickland stands out from other women's historians in elevating a research agenda over moralization and commercial short-cutting' (1998: 220).

During the nineteenth century, across the West, profound changes in the availability and organisation of public records occurred. Anne Laurence has argued that 'the demand for free and open access to public records was both evidence of and contributed to the changes which took place, changes which affected women in rather different ways from men' (2000: 127). With the rise of 'scientific' history in the nineteenth century (generally said to derive from German methods and practices, led by such figures as Leopold Von Ranke) professional historians emerged. Scientific history, usually about men and nation states, was seen as factual and non-partisan; the history of women was discredited as partisan (Smith 1998: 147).

More full-time work for historians became available in the latter half of the nineteenth century, but it often required a university degree, membership in an historical association or affiliation with a record-keeping body. While this created a profession for men, it 'largely excluded women except as assistants to men and confirmed their restriction to writing in particular historical genres', such as popular history or children's books (Laurence 2000: 128). For late nineteenth- and early twentieth-century women who were not affiliated with a male researcher, menial and detail-oriented work for hire in archives was another possibility, as it was seen as their forte.

The late nineteenth century saw many wives and daughters contributing to their professional historian husbands' and fathers' work, sometimes with credit but more often without. Louise Creighton was introduced to the study of history by her husband, the Oxford and Cambridge University don Mandell Creighton, who was an historian of Renaissance popes. In 1873, while at Oxford, Mandell asked his wife to translate Leopold von Ranke's *Englische Geschichte*. Louise began 'spending her mornings reading [in the Bodleian Library] under her husband's direction' (Covert 2000: 92). He gave her assignments that required her to write as well as read history. Ultimately, she wrote and published many historical works of her own. But it was her husband who founded and edited the *English Historical Review* and who was in demand as a lecturer. Later, Louise became an activist – against women's suffrage, although she ultimately changed her mind (Covert 2000: 196).

Another pair of historians might be compared and contrasted to the Creightons. Americans **Mary Ritter Beard** and Charles Austin Beard were historians who wrote separately and together. Shortly after their marriage in 1900, Charles went to study at Oxford, and Mary accompanied him. While there, she became active in the women's suffrage movement. In 1915, she turned to writing and lecturing and became an expert on the labour movement and the history of women. She and her husband together wrote textbooks and monographs on American history. Rather than one having a byline and the other being a silent contributor, Mary and Charles Beard became acknowledged collaborators. She did not complete graduate work and faced hostility from male academics; her husband, on the other hand, was a professor at Columbia and founder of the New School for Social Research. In the 1930s, Mary attempted to establish a World Centre for Women's Archives to preserve the records of women's lives, believing that such a collection would 'encourage the recognition of women as co-makers of history' (Anke Voss-Hubbard 1995: 21). Although the Centre failed because of lack of funds many of the papers Beard gathered were preserved, forming significant sections of the Sophia Smith Collection at Smith College and the Schlesinger Library at Radcliffe (Cott 1991: 47).

Until recently, materials relating to non-aristocratic women were often not among those housed in public and private archives. Mary Beard was a trailblazer in bringing feminist attention to this problem and to women's history generally. Still, it is important to recognise that many of her predecessors wrote histories of women. As the nineteenth century progressed, there was a growing belief that women were the most appropriate authors of histories about women. Notable exceptions exist, but the path of least resistance for women historians was to specialise in topics dealing with notable women. By 'restricting themselves' to writing about women, women historians 'might use the authority conferred by their femininity' (Laurence 2000: 138). Unlike Macaulay before them, they could avoid public scepticism or accusations of masculine propensities by writing about feminine subjects. This did not preclude men from producing 'at least half, if not more, of the women's histories flooding the market' during Strickland's lifetime (Burstein 1998: 220).

In the United States, women were actively involved in historical and archival endeavours, though they seem to have gotten off to a later start than their British counterparts. Nina Baym's *American Women Writers and the Work of History* (1995) identifies 150 American women who produced historical writing in 350 works published between 1790 and 1860. Baym admits that she has not consulted archives in the American West and Southwest that 'must contain historical writings by non-Anglo women' (1995: 10). It is unclear how many of the texts Baym identifies employ archival research. She does indicate that few Anglo-women historians during this period 'had access to great libraries and fewer still could hope to devote their lives to scholarly inquiry' (1995: 32). This limited them to 'synthesizing or summarizing the relatively accessible published sources' so that 'their authority was in the strictest sense derivative, as they readily conceded' (1995: 32). A substantial number of women published textbooks for school or home use.

A notable exception to this pattern is **Mercy Otis Warren**. Her career as a historian and her correspondence with Catharine Macaulay demonstrate that there was also early movement from Great Britain to America (and from America to Great Britain) of archival information. Macaulay had contemplated and then abandoned (due to ill health) plans to write a history of the American Revolution. She had amassed letters and documents from John Adams, George Washington and others. Ultimately, Warren undertook the project, publishing it as her three-volume magnum opus, *History* *of the Rise, Progress, and Termination of the American Revolution* (1805), when she was 77 years old. In the introduction to that work, Warren notes that she was advantageously positioned to write such a work because she was in the habit of 'confidential and epistolary intercourse with several gentlemen employed abroad in the most distinguished stations, and with others since elevated to the highest grades of rank and distinction.' Because of this, she writes, 'I had the best means of information.'

As Warren's case shows, one could amass one's own archive, in the form of letters, primary documents in print or manuscript form or, more often, secondary sources. The Sotheby auction *Catalogue of the Library of Miss Agnes Strickland* (1876) is especially illustrative on this matter. It includes 212 lots of books in octavo size, 81 in quarto and 65 in folio. Among these lots were complete runs of periodicals and some manuscript materials. Included in the sale were a 1594 black-letter collection of Magna Charta statutes and a 1533 black-letter edition of Fabyan's *Chronycle*, as well as other sixteenth- and seventeenth-century works, though most of the volumes were histories published in the eighteenth and nineteenth centuries. The Strickland sisters were financially successful, and Agnes used some of her wealth to collect hundreds and hundreds of sources – her own 'archive' as it were.

There were many possibilities for engaging in archival research and historiography outside of an academic setting; they were just less valued and have subsequently become less visible. In her study of late nineteenth- and early twentieth-century America, Julie Des Jardins documents how a small group of black, middle-class clubwomen discovered historical writing 'as an effective means for promoting their race' (2003: 7). As Des Jardins argues, 'One need not have access to official documents, government repositories, or tenure in a university history department, they proved, to render original and empowered history of African American women, but simply the wherewithal to search for this hidden past in the most inauspicious of places' (2003: 8). The women used oral traditions and grassroots mobilisation, among other tactics, to complete historical work. There is a great deal of history to be told on these and other like matters relating to women and archives, and it is only beginning to be documented.

Over the past 100 years, information available to women scholars and even information *about* women in archival sources has become much more extensive. Special collections in libraries and indeed separate libraries related to the study of women or women's history have appeared. London's Fawcett Library (now The Women's Library) was established in 1926 as the Library of the London Society for Women's Service. Its collections first centred on the suffrage campaign. North American library collections related to women are also well established. Unfortunately, the growing number of collections related to women does not mean that the information has gone from obscure to transparent. As Carole Gerson reminds us, archives are not a 'neutral zone' (2001: 7). Such collections are 'developed from specific social assumptions that dictate what documents are available [and] social assumptions that construct priorities that often exclude women's documents' (Buss 2001: 2). Nevertheless, both bibliographical and theoretical resources specifically related to women in the archives have become more widely obtainable in manuscript, print, microfilm and electronic forms. This growth, if sustainable and continued, has the potential to change radically the ways that women appear in the archives – as well as the ways historians of women use archives – in centuries to come.

Devoney Looser

Related essays in the volume
Female biography; Great Britain; Private writings; Royal lives; United States of America.

Further reading
Barwick 1929; Baym 1995; Bumpus 1891; Burstein 1998; Burton 2003; Buss 2001; Cott 1991; Covert 2000; Des Jardins 2003; D'Israeli 1793; Esdaile 1948; Gerson 2001; Laurence 2000; Looser 2000; Nichols 1866; Pope-Hennessy 1940; Smith 1998; Strickland 1887; Voss-Hubbard 1995.

Art history

'The First Professional English Art Historian' was, according to Adele Holcomb, a woman: **Anna Brownell Jameson** (1983: 171–87). Three decades after her death, 'Aliquis', a writer on 'Art-Critics of To-Day' for the *Art Journal* in 1892, declared, 'We have not yet forgotten Mrs. Jameson', but by this point she does not stand alone. Indeed, as the pseudonymous author notes, 'Several of the most admirable writers on Art during recent years have been, and are, highly cultivated women. . . . among our contemporaries the names of Mrs. Oliphant, Miss Julia Cartwright, Miss Helen Zimmern, and others occur readily.' These writers are specifically distinguished as art historians as opposed to 'the regular critics of well-known weekly and daily journals', among whom 'a good many ladies are to be found'. The world invoked by this writer is one in which women play an active and seemingly integrated role. They are to be seen in the illustrations accompanying the article, both as single figures contemplating art works, and among the crowds of journalists on press day at the Royal Academy. Other names, such as Emilia Dilke and Vernon Lee, could be added to this roll-call of female art historians who produced substantial scholarly studies in the latter part of the nineteenth century.

Yet some prominent modern feminist art historians, whilst acknowledging the extensive participation of female art historians and critics of the intellectual stature of Dilke in late nineteenth-century artistic networks, have argued that they were complicit in the formation of a professional discipline that is deeply and fatally gendered. 'Their writings', Deborah Cherry contends, 'participated in the discipline of art history at a crucial stage in its development, and their silence contributed to the structural exclusions of women artists in the history of art and the public collections of the early twentieth century.' She concludes, '[I]n refuting sexual difference and refusing women artists, these writers assisted in the framing of those discourses of art which became hegemonic in the later nineteenth century, in which masculinity was inscribed as the central area of study and the pivotal term of reference' (1993: 72). Paradoxically, then, it seems, the pioneering women art historians of the nineteenth century played a significant part in creating the ideological construct of art history that it is the project of modern feminist scholars to undo. On the eve of the twenty-first century, in her book *Differencing the Canon: Feminist Desire and the Writing of Art's Histories*, Griselda Pollock posed a challenging question:

> Given that we can define art history as a hegemonic discourse, we are forced then to ask: can feminists be 'art historians' – that is, professionals

> within its extended remit of curation, history and criticism? Or does that not of itself imply self-identification with the hegemonic tradition embodied in institutionalised art history, with the canonical as a systematic pattern of inclusions and exclusions which are generated from and sustain deep structures of social and economic power? (1999: 11–12)

Pollock's feminist refusal of the title 'art historian' constitutes an ironic riposte to Jameson's first-wave claim to a professional identity. And yet such disavowals of their first-wave feminist legacy ignore some of the more radical contributions by women to the development of the discipline in the nineteenth century. Focusing first on this period which saw the invention and formulation of art history, and which also, I argue, saw the beginnings of its critique by feminism, this essay will reassess the historiographical work of women writers on art and their interventions in academic discourses, not only in the context of canon formation but also in light of *how* they write about art and its histories, and how they shape, disrupt and negotiate – theoretically, methodologically, strategically and politically – a discipline that, in truth, they are constantly remaking.

The canon

It is perhaps not surprising to find modern feminist art historians criticising their predecessors for promoting canonicity, since twentieth-century feminism's first task was to disrupt the very notion of the canon in the history of art and the gendered ways in which it produces meaning. For centuries, of course, women have been drawing attention to the work of women in the arts. **Christine de Pizan**, for example, converses with the allegorical figure of Reason about the famous women artists of antiquity in her early fifteenth-century *Cité des Dames*, and among her contemporaries praises a female illuminator, Anastaise, who she claims to be the equal of the finest craftsmen in Paris. In the nineteenth century itself, as well as writing on contemporary female artists, women devoted whole monographs to the history of women's art: **Elizabeth Ellet**'s *Women Artists in All Ages and Countries* appeared in 1859; Ellen Clayton's book on *English Female Artists* in 1876 and Clara Clement's encyclopedic *Women in the Fine Arts from the 7th Century BC to the 20th Century* in 1904. But, as Rozsika Parker and Griselda Pollock point out in *Old Mistresses: Women, Art and Ideology*, such accounts, whilst acknowledging women artists and sexual difference, because of their general tenor and because of the historical moment at which they were published were oddly counter-productive; for 'at the very moment of a numerical increase in the numbers of women artists working professionally, women artists were represented as different, distinct and separate on account of their sex alone' (1981: 44). Subsequent generations of artists and critics have had to struggle against 'Victorian ideologies of femininity and notions of women's art as categorically distinct from men's' that, they argue, have only been perpetuated and consolidated by the modern discipline of art history (Parker and Pollock 1981: 44–5).

Some of the most distinguished women writing about art in the nineteenth century did without doubt contribute to this legacy. Studies of male artists by women in this period include Emilia Dilke's work on *Claude Lorrain: Sa Vie et Ses Oeuvres* (1884), Maud Cruttwell's books on Signorelli (1899), Verrocchio (1904) and Pollaiuolo (1907), Julia Cartwright's on Mantegna and Francia (1881), Raphael (1895, 1905), Sandro Botticelli (1903) and on the nineteenth-century painters Jean-Francois Millet (1896), G F Watts (1896) and Edward Burne-Jones (1894). Anna Jameson herself wrote about the great male tradition in books such as her *Memoirs of the Early Italian Painters, and the Progress of Painting in Italy* (1845) and although she showed an awareness of female artists and emphasised feminine, even feminist, themes, her work is informed by the kinds of essentialist notions of sexual difference that Parker and Pollock find so pernicious. Jameson was notwithstanding deeply interested in women as producers of art, at a time when the work of the 'old mistresses' was very little known. On 21 April, 1840 she wrote in a letter to her friend Ottilie von Goethe that she had begun work on a 'Biography of female Artists, and their social position philosophically and morally considered', 'a work of a far more important nature', she claimed, than any other on which she was engaged (Needler 1939: 124). Regrettably, this cherished project was never realised. Nevertheless, discussion of women artists in her published work, tantalisingly brief though it is, gives some indication of the direction her projected book on female artists might have taken. Her *Visits and Sketches at Home and Abroad* (1835), for example, refers to a number of women artists: the three Anguisciola sisters, especially Sofonisba, whose 'most lovely works' are described by Jameson as 'glowing with life like those of Titian', Lavinia Fontana, who, according to Jameson, 'threw a look of sensibility into her most masculine heads' and the short-lived Baroque painter Elisabetta Sirani, of whom Jameson notes 'Madonnas and Magdalenes were her favourite subjects'. All of these artists were, Jameson maintains, 'women of undoubted genius; for they each have a style apart, peculiar, and tinted by their individual character' (1835: Vol. 2, 175–7). But, she claims, they were '*feminine* painters', and thus unable to paint history: 'They succeeded best in feminine portraits, and when they painted history, they were only admirable in that class of subjects which came within the province of their sex; beyond that boundary they became *fade*, insipid, or exaggerated' (1835: Vol. 2, 178).

Although Jameson displays an interest in women artists that was well ahead of her time, her subscription to the ideological formulation that men and women occupy 'separate spheres' and her application of such gender codification to art do of course identify her as an early Victorian and seem conservative to modern readers. Claire Richter Sherman suggests in her 1981 study of *Women as Interpreters of the Visual Arts, 1820–1979* that the lack of institutional employment for women in prestigious universities and their 'marginal position' in the new centres of academic art history may have 'discouraged women from taking new or controversial positions' (Sherman 1981: 40). But equally one might argue (with the benefit of postcolonial hindsight) that writing from the margins confers a kind of freedom that those who inhabit centres do not have. Women did not have to take the institutions that would not have them as seriously as those who were held in their ideological embrace. Writing from the sidelines, from the verge, their work is, we should not be astonished to discover, more often on the edge, more likely to refuse conventional categories. And so while many of them observed the canon, their approach to mainstream art was sometimes very differently inflected from those who were more centrally positioned.

Historiography and difference

Jameson herself is best known for her three-volume study *Sacred and Legendary Art*, which includes a book on Marian iconography, *Legends of the Madonna* (1852), the first major study of imagery of the Virgin. In her discussions of the representation in **Renaissance** art of both the Madonna and the Magdalen, here and elsewhere, Jameson draws attention to the iconic resonances of such heroic female figures for contemporary women. In works by female art historians writing towards the end of the century we find a still more determined focus on the role of women in the arts, more nuanced discussions of gender difference. This is evidenced in a greater consciousness of their own intellectual capital, their professionalism and their power both to shape and disrupt the discipline of art history. **Julia Cartwright**, for example, having established her reputation as a Renaissance scholar through her work on Raphael, Mantegna and Francia, turned her attention to female patronage, recognising the contribution of women as patrons and mentors, and thickening our understanding of the networks and politics and economies of cultural production.

Cartwright draws attention not only to the fact that our perspective on the past depends on which archival sources the historian uses, but also to the silences in the historical record, noting '[t]his is especially the case with the women of the Renaissance' (1926: v–vi). Her own work on the correspondence of Isabella d'Este, in the Gonzaga archives at Mantua, throws, she says, '[a] flood of light . . . on the history of Italy in the fifteenth and sixteenth centuries; public events and personages have been placed in a new aspect; the judgments of posterity have been modified and, in some instances, reversed' (1926: v). It is a new aspect that takes us from the masculine history of the public arena into the feminine private sphere: 'We see now, more clearly than ever before,' she writes, 'what manner of men and women these Estes and Gonzagas, these Sforzas and Viscontis, were . . . We follow them from the battlefield and council chamber, from the chase and tournament, to the privacy of domestic life and the intimate scenes of the family circle' (1926: v). Julia Cartwright's concern is most certainly with the 'exceptional' historical women who are typically the focus of early feminist studies (Kelly 1984). But Cartwright's work is nevertheless of great value in defamiliarising, by feminising, the Renaissance.

Cartwright makes it clear to her readers that she brings together for the first time 'the vast number of letters which passed between [Isabella d'Este] and the chief artists of the day', that have 'hitherto lain buried in foreign archives or hidden in pamphlets and periodicals, many of them already out of print' (1903: Vol. 1, ix). Cartwright had carefully acknowledged the work of the Gonzago archivists Alessandro Luzio and Rudolpho Renier; however, envious of her success, they accused her of stealing their work and violating international laws of copyright. Cartwright was publicly vilified, but completely exonerated (Emanuel 1989: 266). Interestingly other female art historians, such as Anna Jameson and Vernon Lee (1998), also had to contend with the criticism that their ideas were not their own.

One of the things that distinguishes later nineteenth-century women art historians from earlier writers such as Jameson is their insistence on the rigorous original scholarship that underpins their books, and their pursuit of new methodological approaches to the understanding of the art and culture of the past. Deborah Cherry argues that their work 'participated in the discipline of art history at a crucial stage in its development'

(1993: 72) and we do indeed see them engaging critically, even sometimes combatively, with the scholarly field, and asserting their authority. Emilia Dilke, for example, takes an uncompromisingly academic approach to her subject. In the four volumes of her *French Painters of the Eighteenth Century* (1899) she acknowledges but also quibbles with other scholars, such as the Goncourt brothers, and draws attention to the meticulousness of her research and how long it has taken her. Dilke was concerned that her work be understood for what it is, an original study rather than a 'mere compilation' of second-hand ideas. She proudly asserted 'I have described nothing, I have criticised nothing that I have not seen for myself.' She also accused others of cutting corners and depending on unverified secondary sources (Dilke 1899: vi, 115–16).

First-wave feminist historiography is sometimes taxed by modern historians for being insensitive to socio-economic factors. However, Dilke was clearly alert to such issues, and her interest in the socio-economic framework within which artists and craftsmen worked is everywhere apparent. In her study of eighteenth-century French art she draws on the 'Livre-Journal' or 'day ledger' of the powerful dealer, agent and patron Lazare Duvaux, and analyses his complex role in the creation of mid-eighteenth-century *décors* (Dilke 1901: 163). Dilke, who had been involved with the Women's Trade Union League from its foundation in 1874, and was its President from 1886 until her death, investigates the economics of production from the perspective of the artists and craftsmen engaged in making luxury items for the rich. And so she writes of the suffering and distress of the tapestry workers at the Gobelins and the Savonnerie and those engaged in the historic industries of Aubusson and Felletin. 'The wages of the tapestry workers were not only always in arrears but it was impossible to establish satisfactory rates of payment, as the piece-work system continued to prevail' (Dilke 1901: 110, 115). Dilke was as conscious of the economics of the modern market for eighteenth-century art as she was of the contemporary economics of production (Dilke 1901: vi, 203). She was particularly alert to the social and economic pressures that told against women.

The invisible ideological pressures and their power to exclude women from professional artistic life are explored more specifically in Dilke's *French Painters of the Eighteenth Century* (1899). Only three pages into the first volume, on painters, Dilke, who had herself studied art at South Kensington, launches into a discussion of the position of female artists in the French Academy. A vigorous campaigner for the rights of women to have access to life-drawing classes, she notes wryly 'the fulfilment by the administration of its often deferred promise to enable the Academy to open their Life School without charge, and the vigorous decision, taken in the same year [1706], not to receive women, in future, as "*académiciennes*" ' (1899: 3). Dilke goes on to explain how a few women did manage to gain admittance 'in spite of this fixed determination'. Indeed, Anne Vallayer and Mlle Roslin became Fellows in the same year. But, as Dilke acerbically observes,

> these two incursions of women, rapidly following on one another, were evidently regarded as dangerous, and the Academy took occasion to record that, though they liked to encourage women by admitting a few, yet such admissions, being in some sort foreign to their constitution, ought not to be multiplied, and thenceforth it was resolved never to admit more than four. (1899: 3)

The idea of the foreign has a special resonance for Dilke. The use of the word 'foreign' metaphorically signifies in her discussion of the French Academy's designation of women. Like a number of other women writing about art and its histories at this time, such as Vernon Lee, her appreciation of the difficulties facing women artists would have been enhanced by her sense of her own outsider status as an art historian. Dilke and Lee, formidably learned though they were, and well versed in current scholarship in their fields, write from a sense of difference, and attempt to articulate a different way of viewing art and of writing its history. Lee, for example, in her major studies of Renaissance art and culture, *Euphorion* (1884) and *Renaissance Fancies and Studies* (1895), abjures the grand narratives of conventional historiography, contrasting her work with the kind of comprehensive universal 'encyclopaedic atlas' of the Renaissance offered by male contemporaries such as John Addington Symonds. Rather, she explains,

> the Renaissance has been to me . . . not so much a series of studies as a series of impressions. I have not mastered the history and literature of the Renaissance . . . , abstract and exact, and then sought out the places and things which would make the abstraction somewhat more concrete in my mind; I have seen the concrete things, and what I might call the concrete realities of thought and feeling left behind by the Renaissance, and then tried to obtain from books some notion of the original shape and manner of wearing these relics, rags and tatters of a past civilisation. (Lee 1884: Vol. 1, 8–9, 16)

Lee aims at neither 'mastery' nor 'penetration' in her impressionistic art history. In an intriguing analysis of how, in Italy, 'we are subjected to receiving impressions of the past so startlingly life-like as to get quite interwoven with our impressions of the present', she interrogates her own attempts to reach out and touch the past:

> It seems as if all were astoundingly real, as if, by some magic, we were actually going to mix in the life of the past. But it is in reality but a mere delusion, a deceit like those dioramas which we have all been into as children . . . So also with these seeming realities of Renaissance life . . . we can see, or think we see, most plainly the streets and paths, the faces and movements of that Renaissance world; but when we try to penetrate into it, we shall find that there is but a slip of solid ground beneath us, that all around us is but canvas and painted walls, perspectived and lit up by our fancy; and that when we try to approach to touch one of those seemingly so real men and women, our eyes find only daubs of paint, our hands meet only flat and chilly stucco. (Lee 1884: Vol. 1, 21)

Such writing strikes a very different note from the confident empiricist histories that we associate with the nineteenth century, suggesting, and indeed enacting, alternative ways of engaging with the past, given the impossibility of a masculinist 'penetrating into' it. Vernon Lee enters the interstitial ficto-historical spaces between the 'real' Renaissance and its simulacra, the 'daubs of paint' on the 'flat and chilly stucco', in ways that, I suggest, trouble the notion implied by Pollock's account of the impermeability of art history's borders, of a kind of professional and disciplinary hegemony that has the power to resist such incursions.

Such a construction of the discipline anyway sits rather oddly with the fact that some of the most influential art historians in nineteenth-century Britain (at least) maintained a kind of independent amateur status (like Ruskin) or their status as art historians was contested (as Pater the Oxford don's was, ironically, by Emilia Dilke). Certainly art history was not a discourse from which women who were not specialists felt prohibited from speaking. A volume of ekphrastic poetry published collaboratively under the signature 'Michael Field' by Katherine Bradley and Edith Cooper, aunt and niece, lesbian lovers, entitled *Sight and Song* (1892) offers an intriguing example of the kind of experimental art historical work that women outside the profession were producing towards the end of the nineteenth century. Like Vernon Lee, lesbians writing under a man's name, doubly different, Bradley and Cooper as Michael Field further negotiate with conventional ways of writing about art in this collection of poems written in response to paintings they had studied together in British and Continental galleries. It is an extraordinary volume that articulates a dynamic stereoscopic gaze intersected by lesbian desire, a gay gaze, a way of looking at art that enables a decentring of the observing subject and a radical destabilisation of the gender binary.

Women's art histories today

Although writers such as Michael Field and Vernon Lee were doing genuinely innovative work in aesthetics and poetics, and developing alternative and, I suggest, gendered historiographical methodologies, their interest was in the relationship between the viewing subject and the historical art object rather than in the forgotten woman painter. It was not really until second-wave feminism asked the question, as Linda Nochlin bluntly puts it in her foundational essay, 'Why have there been no great women artists?' (1971), that the kinds of issues raised by Jameson, Cartwright and Dilke in relation to women in the art world were reverted to and analysed. For Germaine Greer, in *The Obstacle Race*, it is not only the institutional barriers identified by Dilke that have handicapped women practitioners, but the fact that they have been culturally conditioned and psychologically disabled from becoming great artists, for as Greer states: '[Y]ou cannot make great artists out of egos that have been damaged, with wills that are defective, with libidos that have been driven out of reach and energy diverted into neurotic channels' (1979: 327). Furthermore, according to Greer, female artists have been betrayed by the very women who might have bought and promoted their work, including female art historians:

> Women are consumers of art; they are also art historians, but they have not so passionately espoused their own cause that they have become a market which will impose its own values. They did not as a result of the 1906 exhibition [Une Exposition retrospective d'Art feminine] begin to haunt the salerooms on the qui vive for any scent of an Artimesia Gentileschi; they did not force the prices of women's work up by bidding at auctions. (1979: 1)

Since that time, works such as Mary Garrard's *Artimesia Gentileschi* (1989) and *Artimesia Gentileschi Around 1622* (2001),

Caroline Murphy's *Lavinia Fontana* (2003), Fredrika Jacob's *Defining the Renaissance Virtuosa* (1997), Deborah Cherry's *Painting Women* (1993), Pamela Gerrish Nunn's *Victorian Women Artists* (1987) and Susan Casteras' *A Struggle for Fame* (1994) have brought the work of neglected female painters into the public eye. Jan Marsh, particularly, has radically transformed our understanding of Pre-Raphaelitism, through her important books on the *Pre-Raphaelite Sisterhood* (1985) and on individual women in the Pre-Raphaelite circle such as Christina Rossetti and Elizabeth Siddal and by curating an exhibition on Jane Morris in 1988, the first exhibition of Elizabeth Siddal's work in 1991, and (with Pamela Gerrish Nunn) a major exhibition of Pre-Raphaelite Women Artists in 1997.

Work such as this has provided a much-needed corrective to the idea (that one might have garnered from the major exhibition of Pre-Raphaelite art at the Tate in 1982 for example) that there *were* no women artists producing work in this genre. But of course, as Deborah Cherry points out in *Painting Women*, 'feminist interventions into the history of art have not been satisfied with the simple addition of women artists into existing accounts'. Rather, '[R]ecognising that the production of knowledge is intimately related to the workings of power, feminist studies have concentrated on documenting the lives and works of women artists and analysing the meanings of representations of femininity in the broader fields of social relations' (1993: 2). The important recuperative work on forgotten women artists carries on, but it has been clear ever since second-wave feminism revolutionised the field, that the problems surrounding women and their place in art history will not be solved simply by revising the canon to include a few more women and artists of colour. The discipline of art history itself, the terms of discussion that constitute its discourse, its values and its methodologies, requires interrogation and reformation.

In the last three decades art historians within the academy, men as well as women, have been opening up to scrutiny, more explicitly than ever before, the ideological structures of the fields of art history. Their concerted critique takes a number of forms. It might, as we have seen, involve the recuperation and re-evaluation of neglected female practitioners. It might interrogate the representation of women in art as works such as Lynda Nead's *Myths of Sexuality* (1988) and *The Female Nude* (1992) or Lisa Tickner's book on the imagery of the suffrage campaign *The Spectacle of Women* (1987) have done. Linda Nochlin's *Women, Art, and Power* (1991), Griselda Pollock's *Avant-Garde Gambits* (1992), Reina Lewis' *Gendering Orientalism* (1996) and Julie Codell's *Orientalism Transposed* (1998) negotiate between the different trajectories of feminist work in art history and other fields to explore the relationship between visuality, subjectivity and difference. Anthea Callen's work is likewise interdisciplinary in its approach. Her 1995 study of Degas, *The Spectacular Body*, explores the visualisation of the human body, especially the female body, in late-nineteenth-century Paris, and shows how patriarchal representations of femininity and masculinity 'contain women and empower men' (1995: ix). Both here and in her work on the teaching of Anatomy in nineteenth-century Paris and London (Callen 1997) she is interested in the relationship between art and medicine in the formation of images of the human body.

Callen's earlier work on women's contributions to the British Arts and Crafts movement, *Angel in the Studio* (1979), was part of an important feminist challenge to the conventional division and ranking of 'art' and 'craft' within art history. Scholars such as Rozsika Parker, in her major study of embroidery *The Subversive Stitch* (1984), have given serious critical treatment to genres that have typically been thought of as both feminine and minor domestic art forms. Such critics are alert to the gendering of artistic movements within so-called high art itself, and of particular formal qualities and practices. Callen has recently explored the contemporaneous perception of Impressionist painting within the established artistic hierarchy of the day as 'feminised'. Focusing on Monet's series paintings of grainstacks and poplars, she considers Monet's strategy for a revised definition of the 'artist' in terms of his interest in and deployment of drawing and form (masculine), colour and light (feminine) (Callen 2000). Feminists have argued that these gendered hierarchies extend to the very materials with which artists work. Isabelle Bernier, for example, writing on the social connotations of art forms in 'In the Shadow of Contemporary Art' in 1986, comments on how oil paint connotes masculinity and therefore 'art', while ceramics connote femininity and 'craft' (Robinson 2001: 41–3).

Bernier is not an academic art historian but a practising artist whose own work engages with, interprets and extends the critical work of feminist art historians such as Parker and Pollock. Other contemporary feminist artists, such as Cindy Sherman, explore visually questions of history, identity and representation that exercise their colleagues in art history, and of course in the period since Anna Jameson made her mark as the 'first professional English art historian' there have been many women – artists in different media, writers and theorists in different fields – who have changed the way we think about women, art and its histories. Indeed it is notable that, whilst the number and profile of women in the academic discipline of art history has risen exponentially, some of the most important and influential work for art history has been produced outside the established institution of Art History identified by Pollock and others. Laura Mulvey's essay 'Visual Pleasure and Narrative Cinema' (1975), for example, and Jacqueline Rose's *Sexuality in the Field of Vision* (1986) demonstrate the radically transformative impact of film theory, psychoanalysis and semiotics on modern work in visual culture, while filmmakers and artists from Maya Deren to Sally Potter and Louise Bourgeois to Tracy Emin have contributed to the reshaping of the field.

Back in the mid-1980s, when feminists were defining their place in the 'new art history', Lynda Nead warned of the dangers of regarding feminism as an 'approach' to art history, and of thereby marginalising it as 'a term of difference for the traditional discipline', instead urging that 'Its importance lies in its project to demonstrate the work of visual representation and the social function of culture and cultural values' (Nead 1986: 120, 124). This she has gone on admirably to demonstrate in her own subsequent work, such as her richly suggestive book on nineteenth-century London, *Victorian Babylon* (2000). Lisa Tickner, writing at the same cultural moment of the late 1980s about the relationship of feminism to art history, argued similarly that a more radical strategy was required than tinkering at the edges of the dominant tradition as it was institutionally defined. Instead she proposed that the way forward is for feminism to dismantle the idea of the autonomy of the art object upon which conventional art history and connoisseurship are founded; for 'it is the object *as text* – a more porous entity – which is the concern of all approaches centred on the social production of meaning'. Feminist methodologies should enable the image to be understood as a 'site . . . for the production of meanings constantly circulated and exchanged among other texts and between other sites of social formation' (Tickner 1988: 92–128). The discipline, I suggest, like the text itself, must have this quality of 'porousness', must encourage this kind of circulatory creativity, as the women of the nineteenth century who participated in its birthing well knew, if feminists are to inhabit a position of greater integrity than that of 'art historians', in Hilary Robinson's phrase, 'masquerading in the discipline while working to undo it' (2001: 165).

Hilary Fraser

References

Callen 1995, 1997, 2000; Cartwright 1903, 1926; Cherry 1993; Dilke 1899, 1901: Emanuel 1989; Greer 1979; Holcomb 1983; Jameson 1835; Kelly 1984; Lee 1884; Mulvey 1975; Nead 1986; Needler 1939; Nochlin 1971; Parker & Pollock 1981; Pollock 1999; Robinson 2001; Sherman 1981; Tickner 1988.

Related essays

Great Britain; Modernity; Orientalism; Renaissance; Travel.

Ashurst Women: Emilie Ashurst Venturi 1826–1893; Eliza Ashurst Bardounau-Narcy 1820–1850 and Caroline Ashurst Biggs 1840–1889

Editor, translator, biographer, novelist, artist. Emilie Ashurst was the youngest of the four daughters of London barrister William Ashurst and Elizabeth Brown. Her sisters were Eliza Ashurst Bardounau-Narcy, Caroline Ashurst Stansfeld and Matilda Ashurst Biggs. The Ashurst daughters grew up in a household which was at the centre of mid-nineteenth-century radical and reform movements and strongly committed to the liberation of all subject groups including women. They were brought up to be independent and politically aware and active; in the words of the eldest sister, Eliza, allowed and accustomed 'to more freedom of intercourse than many other parents allow their children'.

Emilie Ashurst received some legal education in her father's chambers and then when she showed an interest in and aptitude for drawing was apprenticed to the artist Frank Stone. She worked mainly as a portraitist and her subjects included European revolutionary leaders Giuseppe Mazzini, Alexandre Ledru-Rollin and Lajos Kossuth. In 1844 Ashurst married Sydney Hawkes who was part of the family circle, the Muswell Hill 'brigade'. The marriage ended in divorce in 1861 and in the same year, she married Carlo Venturi, an Italian revolutionary who, after deserting the Austrian army in 1848, had fought with Garibaldi in South America.

All the Ashurst sisters were active in mid-nineteenth-century reform campaigns but from the late 1840s after they met Mazzini, the cause of Italian liberation became their focus. The sisters established very strong personal bonds with Mazzini, becoming his 'sisters', close confidantes and friends. Mazzini's relations with the Ashurst women can be traced through the more than 1500 letters that he wrote to members of the family which were collected by Ashurst Venturi and later published in a three-volume edition by her friend Elinor Richards. The collection, an incomparable source for the personal life of Mazzini, has been described by Denis Mack Smith as one of the most attractive literary products of the Risorgimento.

While all the sisters became deeply involved with Mazzini and the cause of Italian liberation, it was Emilie, 'the chief vestal of Mazzinianism', whose discipleship was most fervent and whose dedication was most productive. Felice Orsini, a former follower of Mazzini and failed assassin of Napoleon III, was very critical of what he represented as Mazzini's confiding too much in her; he claimed that at times the fortunes of Italy were in the hands of Ashurst and her brother-in-law James Stansfeld. Active in fundraising, in supporting refugees, as one of the 75 women members of *The Friends of Italy* and as a courier to the Continent and a clandestine Mazzinian agent in Italy, Ashurst's most substantial contribution to the Mazzinian cause was as a publicist, editor, translator, biographer and commentator. Her writing was influential in the creation of Mazzini's image in Britain and on nineteenth-century British readings of the Risorgimento.

Apart from translations and articles for the daily and periodical press in Britain, Emilie Ashurst was the translator of the first English edition of Mazzini's *The Duties of Man* (1862), a translator and editor for the six-volume *The Life and Writings of Joseph Mazzini* (1864–1870), the author of a brief biography, *Joseph Mazzini: A Memoir by E.A.V* (1875), and of *Mazzini's Foreshadowings of the Coming Faith* (1916). In collecting Mazzini's letters, including those written to his mother, she formed the nucleus of the vast Italian national edition of his correspondence.

In Ashurst Venturi's portrayal of Mazzini, he was first and foremost a religious thinker, a unique example among modern revolutionists in founding a political theory upon, and governed, during his whole career, 'by a religious idea'. Like other British women devotees of Mazzini, Ashurst Venturi highlighted his emphasis on duties rather than rights, an emphasis consonant with the Victorian bourgeois ethic. Mazzini himself was cast in the mode of the betrayed saviour who had given up everything – family, country and private life – for the holy cause of Italian liberation. There was little reference in Ashurst Venturi's representation to Mazzini the conspirator. From the late 1860s, Mazzini's closest followers in both Britain and Italy took a leading role in the movements to repeal state regulation of prostitution. The Ashurst network was particularly prominent in campaigns in both countries. From 1871 to 1886, Emilie Ashurst edited *The Shield*, the journal of Josephine Butler's Ladies National Association for the Repeal of the Contagious Diseases Act, if not always to the satisfaction of Butler.

Like her sisters, Caroline Ashurst Stansfeld and Matilda Ashurst Biggs, Emilie Ashurst was also active from the 1860s in campaigns for women's suffrage and to reform the married women's property law. She was also a supporter of Home Rule and an admirer of Parnell. Apart from her works on Mazzini, Ashurst Venturi published a novel, *The Owl's Nest in the City* under the pseudonym, Edward Lovel, and wrote another novel, *A Dull Day*, which was privately circulated.

Ashurst Venturi was not the only Ashurst woman engaged in writing, translating and editing. Her eldest sister, Eliza, before her death at the age of 30, translated a number of the novels of George Sand. Caroline Ashurst Biggs, the feminist daughter of Matilda Ashurst and Leicester manufacturer, Joseph Biggs, was very active in the mid-nineteenth-century suffrage campaign and in promoting the participation of women in local government. She was the editor of *The Englishwoman's Review* from 1871 until her death in 1889 and the author of political pamphlets and of the chapter on Britain in the *History of Woman Suffrage* edited by **Elizabeth Cady**

Stanton. She also published two novels, the three-volume *White and Black: A Story of the Southern States* (1862) and *Waiting for Tidings* (1874). Imbued with the family's passion for Mazzini, she sent him a copy of her first novel. In response, he wrote that it was amazingly good for a first novel, advising that her next attempt might be more 'autobiographical' and suggesting that the 'national struggles' might provide a subject.

Ros Pesman

References

Gleadle 2000; *ODNB* 2004.

Austen, Jane 1775–1817

English novelist, born in Steventon, Hampshire, the seventh of eight children of the clergyman Cassandra (Leigh) and George Austen, who had landed and aristocratic connections. She had two brief periods of formal education in Oxford and then at the Abbey school in Reading but was educated mainly at home, reading widely in her father's library and discussing books with members of her close-knit family, who were later to actively support her literary career. Living always within the family circle, after her father retired in 1801 Austen moved (albeit reluctantly) to Bath with her parents and her beloved sister Cassandra. In 1809 she settled in Chawton, Hampshire, with her mother and sister in a cottage owned by her brother Edward Knight, who lived in the nearby Great House. She died, most probably of a lymphoma, at the height of her creative powers. In 2003 Edward Knight's Elizabethan manor house opened after restoration as the Chawton House Library and Centre for the Study of Early English Women's Writing.

The relationship between the work of Jane Austen and historical writing and representation has long been a contentious topic. For many years, a dominant formalist criticism identified Austen's writing with an ahistorical realism. As a canonical form of the British domestic realist novel, Austen's *oeuvre* was traditionally seen to be generically opposed to historical representation. Austen's major novels were written in the wake of the French Revolution, during the Napoleonic Wars and its aftermath. Arguably, however, Austen's work has had a problematic relation to historical representation because it registers such contemporary historical events for the most part in highly oblique, allusive and indeed eloquently silent ways. With the emergence from the 1970s of critical languages of Marxism, feminism, new historicism and postcolonialism, Austen's work became a touchstone for changing conceptions of history and historical representation in literature. More recently, the so-called new formalism, together with more culturally rooted forms of historicism which associate history with cultural memory, has refocused interest in Austen's sense of memory as a form of history, in her innovative renderings of the affective practices of nostalgia, memory, recollection and cultural quotation.

It is in Jane Austen's juvenile writings that we find her most straightforward form of historical writing. Although a parody of conventional historiography, 'The History of England from the reign of Henry the 4th to the death of Charles the 1st, by a partial, prejudiced, & ignorant Historian' (c.1790) displays nonetheless an extraordinarily sophisticated historiographical understanding. It parodies the political histories of David Hume and Oliver Goldsmith, the stock genre of the lives of kings and queens, and schoolroom history's preoccupation with dates ('NB: There will be very few Dates in this History'). As a counter to the anti-Stuart bias of most Whig history, the young Austen, whose maternal ancestors had provided shelter for Charles I, offers fulsomely sympathetic accounts of the Stuarts, particularly Mary: '[M]y principal reason for undertaking the History of England being to prove [Mary's] innocence . . . and to abuse Elizabeth.'

References in later works also demonstrate that Austen read history widely. *Pride and Prejudice* (1813) is thought to evidence a reading of Gibbon's *Decline and Fall* (1776–1788); *Mansfield Park* (1814) demonstrates a reading of *History of the African Slave-Trade* (1808) by the anti-slavery campaigner Thomas Clarkson; and Austen's *Letters* declare herself 'in love' with Charles Pasley, author of *The Military Policy and Institution of the British Empire* (1810). However, the interpretation of these references in Austen's mature novels has been a fraught critical affair. For as Austen's work evolves, it practises an intriguing form of realist discretion, sparing in explicit references to contemporary historical events. This has meant that critics have often built a case about Austen's historical engagement upon sparse yet telling details. The late Edward Said's justly influential account of Austen and empire, built from a snatch of conversation and an eloquent silence in *Mansfield Park*, is a case in point. Some critics have argued that such a method is strained and overdetermining. However, it might also be argued that Austen's work demands precisely this kind of attention – offering as it does an almost allegorical form of realism within a narrative economy of legible absences and seemingly insignificant, inessential details nonetheless replete with revelatory significance.

The classical historical novel genre emerges in Austen's period (see **Historical Fiction**). Austen demonstrates her awareness of such a competing fictional genre in her admiration of Maria Edgeworth and in a famous letter to the Prince Regent's librarian: 'I am fully sensible that an Historical Romance, founded on the House of Saxe Cobourg might be much more to the purpose of Profit or Popularity, than such pictures of domestic Life in Country Villages as I deal in.' Despite the simplicity of this notoriously homespun aesthetic manifesto, Austen's novels offer an acutely ironic form of observation that belies the seeming naivete of the trope of 'pictures' with its suggestion of transparent reflection. Her 'pictures' are in this sense both symptomatic and critical social documents that chart what the Marxist critic Raymond Williams refers to as 'the making and remaking' of rural gentry families in a period of intense social upheaval, mapping complex interrelations between class, gender and social mobility. What these detailed 'pictures of domestic Life' offer then is a sense of the historicity and historical specificity of the present.

Even Sir Walter Scott, credited with initiating the modern historical novel (see Historical Fiction), acknowledged the historical significance of Austen's particular form of domestic realism. One of Austen's more perceptive early critics, Scott referred in a review of *Emma* (1816) to the 'Big Bow-wow strain I can do myself' of large-scale epic and public history, comparing it self-deprecatingly with Austen's 'correct and striking representation of that which is daily taking place'. Scott's sense of the importance of finding a suitable narrative form for documenting what is 'daily taking place' attests to the deeply significant function and innovative value of Austen's work in registering the historical specificity of the present. The term 'history' itself refers less often in Austen's writing to public or political history than to a narrative of local details or what we might now call the backstory of an individual's life. It is this sense of history that Austen's novelistic practice sought – successfully – to vindicate as a vital cultural form.

Austen's most eloquent presentation of memory as a form of history appears in her final complete novel *Persuasion* (posthumously published in 1818). Integrating local and national historical meanings and practices, *Persuasion* tells the history of a love affair as recollected by its heroine, Anne Elliot, upon the return from war of her former (and still) beloved Captain Wentworth. Austen's narrative deftly modulates from a detailed representation of Anne's elegiac interior retrospection to her spirited dialogue about the stories different genders tell, challenging proverbial 'talk of woman's fickleness', and making claims for what we would now call women's history: 'I will not allow it to be more man's nature than woman's to be inconstant and forget those they do love or have loved. . . . Men have had every advantage of us in telling their own story. Education has been theirs in so much higher a degree; the pen has been in their hands' Anne Elliott says in response to her male interlocutor's claim that 'all histories are against you, all stories, prose and verse'.

Such feminist declarations and self-reflexive claims on Austen's part for the power of the female pen occur within a subtle romance of the British navy that is undeniably warm with the patriotic afterglow of Napoleonic defeat (two of Austen's six brothers were naval officers). Broader claims for women's history are both enabled and limited by the nationalistic feminism which produces Anne's apotheosis as 'a sailor's wife' and the wry narrative observation that accompanies it that this is 'a profession more distinguished in its domestic virtues than in its national importance'.

Neither a radical Enlightenment feminist like **Mary Wollstonecraft**, nor a didactic Tory feminist like Hannah More, Jane Austen's vital place in the history of women's writing lies in her profoundly self-reflexive sense of the cultural agency of women's writing and reading – specifically of the novel – and her transformative novelistic practice which brought the genre a new cultural capital through the heightened aesthetic complexity it used to tell women's stories. Austen's achievement is to have brought a technical sophistication and subtlety to the representation of the social and affective lives of young women at a poignant moment of social and cultural transformation, registering the claims both of a new form of intelligent feminial subjectivity and its preferred cultural technology of the novel, and asserting the power of this gender and genre to tell the stories of domestic and national history.

Clara Tuite

References

Butler 1989; Looser 2000; Tuite 2002; Williams 1973.

Major work

The History of England (London: The British Library, 1993).

Austin, Sarah Taylor 1793–1867

English translator, historian. Born in Norwich, youngest child of Susanna (Cook) and John Taylor. Influenced by **Mary Wollstonecraft**, her mother saw that she received a liberal education at home and encouraged her facility for languages. The family home was a centre of Whig and Unitarian literary culture, and Sarah's circle included Laetitia Barbauld, **Eliza** and **Agnes Strickland** and various

Martineau relations. In 1820 she married the jurist John Austin. One child, Lucie, born in 1821. Moving to London, Austin created an extensive literary circle and formed close friendships with Harriet Grote and Jane Carlyle. Following John's retirement from the Chair of Jurisprudence at the University of London in 1832, Sarah became the family's main breadwinner, translating works from French and German, including Ranke's *History of Popes* (1840) and Guizot's *Causes of the Success of the English Revolution* (1850), and becoming the favoured translator and correspondent of these men. Her only work of history *Germany from 1760–1814 or Sketches of German Life* was published in 1854. In this work Austin attempted to sketch 'the influence of the social and domestic life of a nation on the great collective life called its History' (*Germany* 1854: vi). Much of the text was drawn from the writings of Johanna Schopenhauer and Madame Pichler. Austin avoided the scientific discussion of politics that defined the work of masculinist historians such as Ranke. Claiming a distinctly gendered perspective on social history, Austin argued 'Society is so much the province of women' that women should be considered 'the natural and proper historians of its changes'. Following the death of her husband, Austin edited and published his writings on jurisprudence. Her portrait was hung on the walls of Harvard Law School, in 1900, in recognition of these labours. Her granddaughter Janet Ross published several histories of her maternal family, detailing the life of Austin in *Three Generations of Englishwomen.*

Mary Spongberg

References

Smith 1984, 1998; Waterfield 1937.

Australia

Before the expansion of tertiary education after the Second World War, women who wrote Australian history were as likely to be novelists as historians, and most historical writing ignored the gendered character of its assumptions, subjects and pronouncements. The second half of the twentieth century however saw the development of feminist critiques of Australian history and with this emerged new accounts of aspects of Australia's history which located women and gender at their centre. Towards the end of the twentieth century, debates around difference prompted women to write histories which also took account of other sources of commonalities among Australians showing gender, like class, to be fissured by race, ethnicity and sexuality. In the globalising culture of the twenty-first century those fault lines were extended to the concept of nation, now seen in a transnational context.

Pioneers

The earliest authors of Australian women's history were novelists. Catherine Spence's first novel, *Clara Morison. A Tale of South Australia during the Gold Fever* (1854) is, as she wrote, 'a faithful transcript of life in the Colony' when all the men had left to join the gold rush in Victoria in the early 1850s. Brisbane's leaders are so realistically portrayed in Rosa Praed's *Policy and Passion* (1881) that it is possible to identify individual politicians amid the sexual politics of her fiction. Indeed, those engaged in the sexual politics, too, prompted speculation among readers in Queensland, where Praed's father was known for his sexual liaisons as well as for being a prominent parliamentarian (Clarke 1999: 61–2). Rosa Praed also depicted some of the horrors, and complexities, of relationships between the invading settlers and the local Aboriginal people in *Lady Bridget in the Never*

Never Land (1915), a novel drawing on her own childhood memories of living at Naraigin, a property in central Queensland, the Yiman people's country (Clarke 1999: 12–14). Ada Cambridge, in *The Three Miss Kings* (1883), offers a richly detailed picture of the Melbourne of the 1880 International Exhibition as backdrop to her story of three sisters, and in *An Australian Girl* (1890) Catherine Martin invokes the same society, 80 years later, during Melbourne's Centennial International Exhibition of 1888. Miles Franklin, in *Some Everyday Folk and Dawn* (1909), dramatises the arrival of votes for women in Penrith, where she spent part of 1904. In the justly renowned novel, *The Getting of Wisdom* (1910), Henry Handel Richardson provides a savage depiction of the Presbyterian Ladies College in Melbourne, an institution to be the subject of an academic historical study in the mid-1970s. Catherine Martin depicts an Aboriginal woman's efforts to pursue and rescue her son from settler kidnappers in *The Incredible Journey* (1923), a true story, she said (Martin 1987: x). Katherine Susannah Prichard's *Coonardoo* (1929) and the novel written jointly by Marjorie Barnard and Flora Eldershaw as M Barnard Eldershaw, *A House is Built* (1929), both present passionate critiques of the position of women – in *Coonardoo*, Aboriginal women, in the north-west of Western Australia – amid a wealth of historical detail. Eleanor Dark wrote *The Timeless Land* (1944), a thoroughly researched and vividly imagined novel about the arrival of British settlers in a land that was already thoroughly inhabited.

One pioneer who was not a writer, nor yet an academic or professional historian, was Myra Willard. An outstanding student at Sydney University during the second decade of the twentieth century, she won several prizes and graduated with first-class honours. One prize was for her postgraduate study of migration to Australia, *History of the White Australia Policy to 1920*, which became, in 1923, the first book published by Melbourne University Press. It remained the standard reference work on its subject for much of the century, with Willard adding minor corrections to a reprint in 1967. But she did not write any more history.

An early form of women's history in Australia was the anthology compiled to mark anniversaries of white colonisation and to demonstrate that women, too, were part of those events (see **Dominion women writers**). Important contributions to historical knowledge were made in these collections, for example, journalist Alice Henry's 'Marching Towards Suffrage' in the Victorian *Centenary Gift Book* (1934) and Miles Franklin's essay on Catherine Spence in *A Book of South Australia* (1936). The New South Wales sesquicentenary, *The Peaceful Army*, edited by Flora Eldershaw (1938), included another essay by Franklin, this time on Rose Scott, Dymphna Cusack's essay on ex-convict Mary Reibey, Winifred Birkett's useful account of 'Some Pioneer Australian Women Writers', artist Margaret Preston's inspiring story of pioneering women artists and novelist Eleanor Dark's 'Caroline Chisholm and Her Times'. Dark considered that '[h]istory as it has been mainly written is, very literally, the story of man'. But there have been, through time, she argued, women 'whose mental vitality was strong enough to survive the pressures of sex and custom' (Clarke 1998: 346). One of them was philanthropist Caroline Chisholm. Dark linked Chisholm's philanthropy to forces for reform in Britain in the early nineteenth century, and located Chisholm in a tradition that Chisholm herself would have rejected by linking her courage, commitment and independence to the political movement for rights for women (Eldershaw 1938: 57).

Caroline Chisholm was the subject of another work, a full-length biography (1950), by distinguished historian Margaret Kiddle, a tutor in the History Department at Melbourne University. Kiddle's congenital kidney disease precluded her from seeking academic security. But it did not prevent her travelling widely in England, Scotland and Ireland pursuing her research, nor did it prevent her extensive researches among the letters, diaries and station records of early settlers in the western district of Victoria, where her own forebears had established substantial pastoral properties. Kiddle wrought her researches into the monumental *Men of Yesterday: A Social History of the Western District of Victoria* (1961) a work completed, when she was 43, only with the continual support of a dialysis machine: 'Her bed covered by a welter of research notes, papers and books, she wrote the last words of the manuscript, said to [the doctor, her brother-in-law], "Now turn that thing off," turned her face to the wall and died' (Grimshaw and Carey 2001: 366). This book was a ground-breaker in many respects, among them Kiddle's including women as active participants in the creation of a frontier society and stressing the economic importance of the work that they undertook.

Kiddle was one of a very small number of women to have gained posts at a university before 1960. The environments in which these women worked evinced a clearly gendered division of labour with expectations that women would continue to be what Sir Keith Hancock called the 'charwomen' of the academic department. Even so, these pioneering academic women historians managed to produce important academic works, works in which women appeared as central figures. **Kathleen Fitzpatrick**'s *Sir John Franklin in Tasmania, 1837–1843* (1949), was equally a study of his wife, Jane Franklin, and the reasons for which the British Colonial Office cited Lady Franklin's 'inappropriate influence' as its ground for dismissing him from his post, a judgement that Fitzpatrick comprehensively contextualised. In her centenary history of Henry Handel Richardson's school, the Presbyterian Ladies College, Melbourne (1975), Fitzpatrick located her narrative in a broader account of women's struggle for education, emancipation and wider opportunities for employment throughout the western world. Both Fitzpatrick and Kiddle were bound by assumptions of class and race and their times: anxious to show their subjects to be properly feminine, that is, 'normal' wives and mothers, putting the care of husband and children above all others (Grimshaw and Carey 2001: 367–8). Their class assumptions separated them even further from the radical nationalists among their male colleagues in a period that saw the foundation of the Association for the Study of Labour History at the Australian National University. But they shared their assumptions about Indigenous Australians with other historians, beyond the universities as well as within.

Outside universities, women historians produced popular works of Australian history such as Marnie Bassett's pioneering study of Anna, wife of Philip Gidley King, *The Governor's Wife* (1940/1954), Alexandra Hasluck's engrossing biography, woven largely from the diaries and letters of botanical pioneer, Georgiana Molloy, *Portrait with Background* (1955), and Eve Pownall's *Mary of Maranoa*, (1959). All were unselfconsciously in and of a white settler tradition of writing about Australia. It was not that they ignored Aboriginal

Australians. On the contrary, Georgiana Molloy's letters included graphic descriptions of encounters with 'natives' intent, it seemed, on theft or menace to her own or her daughter's life. Pownall devoted her first chapter to 'Stone Age Women', 'Australia's First Housekeeper', drawing extensively on the research of writer Kathleen Langloh Parker, and early anthropologists R and C Berndt and Phyllis Kaberry. Writer Mary Durack's *Keep Him My Country* (1955) depicted a relationship between a European station-owner and an Aboriginal woman, setting questions of race and sexual relationships at the centre of her narrative, as had Prichard in *Coonardoo*, 25 years earlier. But the love story in Durack's novel can, nevertheless, be read as a defence of white colonisation, and however sympathetic Pownall's exposition, it still betrays a mighty condescension.

Histories of women

In a collection of articles on Australian women compiled by journalist Julie Rigg *In Her Own Right* (1969) the article on women's history was written by Left labour historian, Ian Turner. His piece impelled Ann Curthoys, a young postgraduate student, to write her landmark article 'Historiography and Women's Liberation' (1970). Turner's article failed, in Curthoys' view, to see connections between the social roles expected of women, the nature of the economy being established in Australia and the development of liberal-democratic political traditions. It also failed to identify the heavily male orientation of Australian ideologies, both around mateship and around the liberal and Christian ideal of the family. His trouble was that he considered the position of women as entirely separate from the mainstream of historical inquiry, as though women were a static condition of nature, quite distinct from the world of men and events. Instead, wrote Curthoys,

> A 'history of women' . . . should do more than restore women to the pages of history books. It must analyse why public life has been considered to be the focus of history, and why public life has been so thoroughly occupied by men. We must find out how the assumptions of female inferiority in public life and subordination in the home have operated in history, and ask why some societies differentiate more than others. We must especially find out the effect of industrialisation and Christianity on the position of women. The concepts usually operating in historiography, defining what is important, must be questioned. (1970: 4)

It was a clarion call, impelled by a new upsurge of activist feminism, a clear recognition that many of its burning questions could only be answered historically and a sense of profound disappointment in existing histories and their inability to offer answers to those questions. 'We had no past – or so, at first we thought,' Curthoys would write, five years later (Curthoys 1975: 89).

International Women's Year, 1975, brought an historiographical explosion in response: four major works endeavouring to rewrite the history of the nation, but differently, so that they would account historically for the position of women in the present. There was also a special issue of the journal, *Labour History*, devoted to *Women at Work*, edited by Ann Curthoys, Susan Eade [Magarey] and Peter Spearritt. Edna Ryan's and Anne Conlon's *Gentle Invaders: Australian Women at Work 1788–1974* was the most narrowly conceived and clearly executed of the four books. A work showing similarities to old Left labour histories, it was a study of the dual labour market, women's wages and the fight for equal pay to which Edna Ryan, an established labour activist, contributed importantly all her life. She would write another book, too, on the establishment of the distinctively Australian system for arbitrating industrial disputes: *Two-thirds of a Man: Women & Arbitration in New South Wales 1902–08* (1984). The most remarkable article in *Women at Work*, and the most innovative, was Merle Thornton's 'Women's Labour', a consideration of the economic, social and psychological functions of everything encompassed by the term 'housework', a first step in a field of analysis that had to wait for the 1980s to establish itself.

Beverley Kingston was already an historian at the University of NSW. Her book, *My Wife, My Daughter and Poor Mary Ann* (1975), focused on domestic work as an experience in which the great majority of women share, however differently, and proposed, provocatively, 'a symbiotic relationship between the great Australian male dream and the Australian woman's suburban nightmare'. The prize-winning journalist Anne Summers was a postgraduate student in Politics at the University of Sydney when her book, *Damned Whores and God's Police*, was published. *Damned Whores* was a work that she described as 'neither history nor sociology'. Summers explored the subject of 'women and the ideology of sexism which has governed so much of our lives – an ideology which has determined and limited the extent to which women have been able to participate in Australian society'. That ideology mobilised the concept of colonisation: all women are 'colonised' by men thereby creating the most important divisions between them which are not economic, ethnic or racial but rather, the attitudinal division embodied in the stereotypes of good and bad women, 'damned whores' and 'God's police', the latter term a quotation from Caroline Chisholm. Miriam Dixson was an historian at the University of New England. Her book, *The Real Matilda: Women and Identity in Australia 1788–1975*, argued that the formative years of a nation, like those of a child, mark its subsequent history in escapable ways forever. The degradation of convict women, she maintained, and their consequent low self-esteem had ensured the continuing misogyny of Australian society.

Writing in 1982, Kay Daniels, the first person to teach a course on women in history in an Australian university, at the University of Tasmania, developed a searching critique of Dixson's and Summers' perspectives on Australian history. Noting that Summers' and Dixson's focus on ideology allowed them merely to rework familiar material rather than looking for new sources, Daniels contended that such material trapped them into an old debate about cultural identity, a debate saturated with the sexist moralising of previous male historians; derivative, they were, of the works of the fathers of Australian history. Could this explain why these works have been so remarkably enduring? *The Real Matilda* has been republished once and *Damned Whores and God's Police* has never been out of print. Indeed, it has been republished twice, each time in a revised and expanded edition.

To create a woman-centred Australian history, Daniels maintained, women's historians needed not only conceptual debate but also sources. Information about the lives of women in the past seemed, at first, to be very thin on the ground. The new generation of women historians rejected the work of the Fitzpatricks and Kiddles for their class-boundedness, their focus on what could be considered exceptional women, rather than ordinary women – the women of the working class. The belief that there were no sources about working-class women, together with the analysis encapsulated in one of the early Women's Liberation slogans – 'the personal is political' – generated a slowly accumulating number of **memoirs** and memorials, autobiographical sketches and biographical studies, books of documents and tapes of interviews.

Many, like Mavis Robertson's sketch of Sally Bowen, Joyce Stevens' of Lucy Barnes, Nance Kingston's recollections of her time with the Australian Women's Army during the Second World War and Thelma Prior's autobiographical sketch, 'My forty-five years in industry' – papers presented to the first and second Women and Labour Conferences in 1978 and 1980 – were compiled for reasons which had more to do with intrinsic importance and personal validation than the needs of historians. So were a number of other works. Zelda D'Aprano's autobiography, *Zelda* (1977), was a life story of a trade union activist and pioneer of the Women's Liberation Movement. Joyce Stevens' *Taking the Revolution Home* (1987) included interviews with ten women, as the second part of her account of the personal, domestic and political lives of more of the women active in the Communist Party of Australia. Justina Williams' story of her life of struggle and commitment in the west, *Anger & Love*, published in 1993, was also about her days in the Communist Party.

Some autobiographical works coupled personal recollection with political reflection in a way that made them illuminating historical analysis. Audrey Blake's account of her joining the Young Communist League in 1932, in *A Proletarian Life* (1984), shows a fine irony: three young men interrogated this 15 year-old about her 'social origin', a question that she did not understand. She was relieved to learn that her father's job as a metal worker rendered her sufficiently proletarian (Blake 1984: 91–2). Daphne Gollan's article about her life with the Communist Party, Trotskyism and the Women's Movement combines an understated but searing account of growing up during the Depression and a hard-hitting critique of Leninist elitism and patriarchal attitudes with moments of hilarity. The article is titled 'The Memoirs of "Cleopatra Sweatfigure"' (1980), a pseudonym that Comrade Gollan tried to adopt while the Party was underground in the 1950s.

Some works, by contrast, were collected specifically for historians. The International Women's Year research project that Kay Daniels headed produced a two-volume annotated guide to historical sources, *Women in Australia*, finally published in 1977. Collections of documents followed: Kingston's *The World Moves Slowly* (1977), Daniels and Mary Murnane's *Uphill All the Way* (1980), Margaret Allen *et al.*, *Fresh Evidence, New Witnesses* (1989), Charles Fox and Marilyn Lake's *Australians at Work* (1990), Marian Aveling [Quartly] and Joy Damousi's *Stepping out of History* (1991), Patricia Grimshaw, Susan Janson and Marian Quartly's *Freedom Bound I* (1995), and Marilyn Lake and Katie Holmes's *Freedom Bound II* (1995).

Feminist history

The new social history as it emerged in the 1970s contributed to the development of feminist critiques within Australian history by broadening the range of concerns that could now be considered historical and by integrating the history of women into the history of society as a whole. Jill Matthews' *Good and Mad Women* (1984), Kerreen Reiger's *The Disenchantment of the Home*

(1985), Marilyn Lake's *The Limits of Hope* (1987) and Desley Deacon's *Managing Gender* (1989) showed influences of the new social history in their explicit discussion of the theories that they mobilised in their work, and in their analyses of specific sets of relationships in ways which endeavoured to illuminate the whole social structure. Lake gave an early statement of a contention that was central in several of her later works, too: that men as well as women are gendered, so that consideration of gender must examine masculinity as well as femininity. Reiger examined changes in the advice provided on housekeeping, mothering and child-rearing, identifying a new class of technocrats who sought to replace nineteenth-century bourgeois conceptions of the household and family as a haven in a heartless world with a rationally managed, efficient organisation of twentieth-century domestic life. Deacon argued for a detailed understanding of the history, interests, resources and effects of public servants as essential to comprehension of 'the processes of state formation and policy formulation and implementation'. Matthews, using the case notes on 60 women admitted to Glenside psychiatric hospital in Adelaide between 1945 and 1970, sought an understanding of the norms for femininity by considering the lives of those deemed to be deviant from or marginal to those norms.

Integrating a history of women into a history of the whole society was the explicit goal of a major work by four feminist historians published in 1994. *Creating a Nation* by Patricia Grimshaw, Marilyn Lake, Ann McGrath and Marian Quartly won a Human Rights award a year after it appeared. They announced their goals at the beginning of the book. 'The creation of nations has traditionally been seen as men's business. . . . We wish to challenge this view of history, by asserting the agency and creativity of women in the process of national generation. . . . Recognition of the interdependence of femininity and masculinity and of the way in which they shape and are shaped by all social relationships and processes', they continued, echoing north American feminist historian Joan Scott, 'has led to the identification of gender as a central category of historical analysis'. Their introduction also invoked 'post-colonial scholarship', rejected 'more radical post-structuralist conclusions', acknowledged 'the complexity of discussing the category "women" ', and commented: 'Women's history is now seen to be a more complex and contradictory saga than was evident in the heady days of the early 1970s.'

Of course, neither these women historians nor those of the 1970s to whom they gestured had the aspiration to write a new national history all to themselves. In the decade prefacing the bicentenary of white settlement in Australia in 1988, several of a growing number of women in History Departments in Australian universities were involved in the Bicentennial History project, two were even among the 26 volume-editors: Marian Aveling [Quartly] and Ann Curthoys. This project produced ten volumes titled *Australians: A Historical Library*. A politically alternative venture was the four-volume work, sub-titled *A People's History of Australia since 1788*, edited by Verity Burgmann and Jenny Lee. Women historians were certainly represented in its pages, but not especially prominently. A third effort to mark the bicentenary was the new *Oxford History of Australia*, under the general editorship of Geoffrey Bolton. This divided Australia's history into four segments of time and allocated each to an author, and this time women gained equal representation. The author of the first volume was Jan Kociumbas, and of the third, Beverley Kingston.

Agency and difference

By the 1980s there were two important developments in Australian women's historical writing. One derived from a political insistence among feminists upon the importance of 'agency', of recognising women as not merely victims of men's power, but, rather as self-determining actors in their own lives and the shape of their societies and polities. Such insistence is to be seen in what has become a steady stream of feminist biographies, among them my own study of Catherine Spence, *Unbridling the Tongues of Women* (1985), the 'Pioneering Profiles' in Barbara James' *No Man's Land: Women of the Northern Territory* (1989), Diane Kirkby's *Alice Henry, The Power of Pen and Voice* (1991), Judith Allen's *Rose Scott* (1994), Rita Huggins and Jackie Huggins's, *Auntie Rita* (1994), Carole Ferrier's *Jean Devanny: Romantic Revolutionary* (1999) and Marilyn Lake's biography of Faith Bandler, *Faith* (2002). There are other biographies on the way, too: Jill Roe's of Miles Franklin, the study of Edna Ryan by her daughter Lyndall Ryan, Margaret Allen's biography of Catherine Martin and Penny Russell's of Jane Franklin. Agency is a crucial element in the feminist biography that has been the subject of two special issues of the interdisciplinary journal, *Australian Feminist Studies* (1992, 2004) in which several of these biographers appear.

The other was the growing importance attached to questions of difference, especially in relation to race and sexuality. Early feminist considerations of race included the comprehensive study, *Race Relations in Colonial Queensland: A History of Exclusion, Exploitation and Extermination*, co-edited by Raymond Evans, Kay Saunders and Kathryn Cronin (1975), Elizabeth Windschuttle's collection, *Women, Class and History* (1980), which included Ann McGrath's discussion of pastoral and other work carried out by Aboriginal women in the Northern Territory in the early twentieth century, and Lyndall Ryan's *The Aboriginal Tasmanians* (1981), its title a neat reversal of colonial conventions. But it was not until the late 1980s that such analyses were being conducted by women who were also, themselves, Aboriginal, as in Jackie Huggins' discussion of the work of Aboriginal domestic servants between the two world wars, published in the interdisciplinary feminist journal, *Hecate*, in 1987–1988. Questions of difference of ethnicity surfaced, as well, notably in a paper that Stania Pieri, Mirna Risk and Anne Sgrò presented to the second Women and Labour conference in 1980. Questions of difference in sexuality appeared in Kay Daniels' wonderful article 'The Flash Mob: Rebellion, Rough Culture and Sexuality in the Female Factories of Van Diemen's Land' (1993) and in her collection of articles on prostitution, *So Much Hard Work* (1984).

Difference moved to the top of the agenda, among feminist historians and among many women historians who had no connection with the Women's Movement as well. Much Aboriginal women's life-writing was undertaken primarily for personal validation and political assertion. Margaret Tucker's autobiography, for instance, was titled *If Anyone Cared* (1977). Lilian Holt insisted that in writing about her identity, she was writing for herself and not on behalf of all Aboriginal women (Holt 1993: 175). Sally Morgan's prize-winning *My Place* (1987) combined autobiographical writing with the searing life stories of her mother and grandmother. Jan Critchett collected autobiographies: *Untold Stories: Memories and Lives of Victorian Kooris* (1998).

In 2001, Margaret Allen edited a special issue of *Australian Feminist Studies*, a selection of papers from the Fourth Biennial Conference of the Network for Research in Women's History, their general title 'Gender in the "Contact Zone" '. None of the seven contributors was Aboriginal, although the articles all contributed to reconceptualisations of Australian history in the light of Aboriginal history. A number of them, noted Allen, made whiteness problematic, a reversal of the colonising direction of concern, demonstrated most innovatively and comprehensively in the work of Aboriginal scholar Aileen Moreton-Robinson, in *Talkin' up to the White Woman* (2000). This work showed how the continuing privilege of 'subject position middle class white woman' extends from past to present, so that non-Indigenous women historians can be as complicit in colonising relationships as their colonising forebears.

Using autobiographical narratives among a range of other sources, Barbara Cummings' *Take this Child* (1990) and Christine Choo's *Mission Girls* (2001) pursued the lives of Aboriginal children taken away from their parents and kept in missions or children's homes. Inga Clendinnen, in the wake of an illness that prevented her continuing work on the history of Latin American cultures, turned her attention to the encounters that had been the subject of Eleanor Dark's *The Timeless Land*. *Dancing with Strangers* (2003) is a prize-winning work that insists, as had Dark's novel, that it tells two histories, not one. Others, too, aligned themselves with a politics increasingly referred to as postcolonial. Rebe Taylor pursued and found stories of the lives of Aboriginal women thought to be lost forever: *Unearthed: The Aboriginal Tasmanians of Kangaroo Island* (2002). Some postcolonial women historians essayed histories of non-Anglo-Celtic settlers. Susan Jane Hunt's *Spinifex and Hessian* (1986) was an exploration of the lives of women, 'Asians, poor Europeans, single working women and Aborigines' – as well as the wives of settler European men that focused on the differing hardships of their work in the north-west of Western Australia in the late nineteenth century. Regina Ganter traced the economics of another female occupation in *The Pearl-shellers of Torres Strait* (1994). Jan Ryan considered the lives of Chinese people in colonial Australia in *Ancestors* (1995), and Diana Giese charted 'changing perspectives on the Top End Chinese experience' in *Beyond Chinatown* (1995). Diana Giese's particular talent was with oral history, demonstrated in *Astronauts, Lost Souls & Dragons: Voices of Today's Chinese Australians* (1997).

Diversity

It might have been expected that there would also be a great deal of historiographical work that bore little relation to the politics of the Women's Movement. For, of course, as the long economic boom brought increasing numbers of women into universities, and the abolition of university fees in the 1970s enhanced that number even more, the number of academic and professional women historians grew. But it would be difficult to sustain such a claim; feminism seems to have had some effect on all women's history – whether the historians were feminist or not. Portia Robinson's *The Hatch and Brood of Time* (1985), for instance, and later Deborah Oxley's *Convict Maids* (1996) presented new histories about convict women, but their accounts were shaped at least partly by their desire to contradict Summers and Dixson, as Kay Daniels pointed out in her magisterial *Convict Women* (1998).

Women have also written many **local histories** dealing with both urban and regional Australia, and at least some have been concerned with women and gender.

Barbara James' consideration of the history of the northern territory was, appropriately, titled *No Man's Land* (1989). Raymond Evans and Carole Ferrier's *Radical Brisbane* (2004) included the story of the life of Emma Miller, socialist and feminist in the early twentieth century. Shirley Fitzgerald's brilliant study of Sydney in the late nineteenth century, *Rising Damp* (1987) made women's working environment – household and street – equal in importance to men's – factory and wharf – an analytical move that called into question all previous male historians depicting Australia as a 'working man's paradise'. Works of history written for occasions and celebrations included the collection of mini-biographies of '**women worthies**' in the history of Victoria, edited by Marilyn Lake and Farley Kelly, titled *Double Time* (1985), Heather Radi's extremely useful *200 Australian Women*, collected and published to mark the bicentenary of white settlement in Australia (1988) and Helen Jones' *In Her Own Name* (1994). Libby Robin's *Defending the Little Desert* (1998), an history of the rise of ecological consciousness in Australia was a subject which was also an important element in Verity Burgmann's *Power and Protest* (1993), an historical study of socio-political movements for change in the late twentieth century. Marilyn Lake's *Getting Equal* (2002) is a history of Australian feminism, a political history focused on campaigns for rights for women.

Memoirs continue to appear, notably by those who had been feminist activists in the 1970s. The first volume of Anne Summers' memoirs, *Ducks on the Pond* (1999), traced her life to the age of 31, the year after she published *Damned Whores and God's Police*. Susan Ryan's *Catching the Waves* (1999) offered insight into her years as Labour's Minister for Education and Minister for Women and her carriage of the Sex Discrimination Act of 1984, a landmark legislation. Wendy McCarthy's, *Don't Fence Me In* (2000), a story which included her early years with Women's Electoral Lobby in the 1970s, appeared a year later. The co-founder of the eminent and adventurous publishing house McPhee-Gribble, Hilary McPhee, too wrote her memoirs *Other People's Words* (2001). Another autobiographical work, Ann Curthoys' *Freedom Ride: A Freedom Rider Remembers* (2002), was far from being a conventional memoir; rather, it partook of both political and social history of a symptomatic political protest against the position of Aboriginal Australians in the mid-1960s. But it was, as well, personal recollection written by a feminist.

Cultural history

In the language of some feminist theorists – influenced by poststructuralism and postmodernism – questions of difference could concern difference within. The resulting historiographical moment came to be known by some as 'the linguistic turn'; for others it was broader, a turn to cultural history, a young cousin of the new social history. Sylvia Lawson's brilliant, prize-winning study of the *Bulletin*, the journal that became an icon of Australia's masculinist nationalism – *The Archibald Paradox: A Strange Case of Authorship* (1983) – anticipated many of the new emphases in cultural history by some years. *Labour History* published a special issue in 1991 on 'Women, Work and the Labour Movement in Australia and Aotearoa/New Zealand' which included an oral autobiography by Agnes Williams told to Jackie Huggins, presented as 'Experiences of a Queensland Aboriginal Domestic Servant', Diane Kirkby on photographs of barmaids, Gail Reekie's illuminating account of the working woman's wardrobe, 'Sexualised

Consumerism' and artist Ann Stephen's wonderful and innovative examination of advertising, 'Selling Soap: Domestic Work and Consumerism', as well as the similarly rich but more conventional labour history. The collection that I edited, together with Sue Rowley and Susan Sheridan, *Debutante Nation* (1993), linked literary and artistic with historical analysis. Penny Russell's *A Wish of Distinction* (1994) was a discussion of 'an endlessly reworked notion of "gentility" ' in nineteenth-century Melbourne. She pointed out the difference effected by her focus on a concept and its meanings, rather than a specific category of people:

> Attempts to deal with the gentry as a finite social category tend to privilege the experience of men, who possessed the wealth, titles, honours and professions which can most readily be used to define and select the group. Investigating the concept of gentility itself focuses attention on the experience of women. (1994: 3)

Katie Holmes explored the meanings that women gave to their lives in their diaries, in the 1920s and 1930s in *Spaces in Her Day* (1995). In 1996 *Australian Historical Studies* included Raelene Frances' examination of the Australian discourse on prostitution 'as part of a wider, international concern with "the white slave traffic" and venereal disease', and my own combination of conventionally political material from parliamentary debates and the records of activist groups in the campaign for women's suffrage, with a reading of an array of novels. I used a similar strategy in *Passions of the First Wave Feminists* (2001), though this was a book which owed as much to the new social history and Michel Foucault as it did to cultural history and consideration of meanings. That issue of *Australian Historical Studies* also included Ruth Ford's consideration of the challenges offered to identity politics by queer, post-structuralist and feminist theorists in her reading of lesbian Monty Punshon's scrap-books from the 1920s to the 1950s. Ford's contribution to cultural history appeared as well in a national touring exhibition titled 'Forbidden Love, Bold Passion: Lesbian Stories 1900–1990s', produced with Lyned Isaac and Rebecca Jones for the Australian Lesbian and Gay Archives. Joy Damousi turned from her consideration of convict women, *Depraved and Disorderly* (1997), to cultural history explorations of grief, *The Labour of Loss* (1999) and *Living With the Aftermath* (2001), and then to a history of the very internality, with its exploration of meaning and the shifting and evanescent, that had been an impulse in the development of cultural history, in her history of psychoanalysis in Australia, *Freud in the Antipodes* (2005).

Going global

A major development towards the end of the twentieth century was a growing interest in comparative and transnational approaches to history. In 1997 a collection compiled from the Third Biennial Conference of the Network for Research in Women's History appeared, it was edited by Patricia Grimshaw and Diane Kirkby and tellingly titled *Dealing With Difference*. It included articles which extended the work's focus on 'Gender, Culture and History' to an international array of Anglophone cultures. In 2001, another collection appeared, this one a selection of papers from the 1998 International Federation for Research in Women's History conference that Patricia Grimshaw convened at the University of Melbourne. Titled *Women's Rights and Human Rights: International Historical Perspectives* and edited by Grimshaw (2001), Holmes and Lake, it brought together articles from an even wider array of national cultures. Both texts were instances of what Fiona Paisley in 2001 called 'the comparative turn' in feminist history writing. Ann Curthoys later argued that 'Transnational history' captures better than 'comparative history' does the idea of historians looking at historical processes, at networks of influence and power that transcend the nation. The point of the exercise becomes not comparison, but a shift of focus, to the study of influence and interconnection (Curthoys 2003: 29).

Some feminist historians based in Australia were engaged in developing what north American feminist historian Antoinette Burton described as 'a more transnational approach to writing women's and feminist history . . . one that conceives of nations as permeable boundaries, subject to a variety of migrations, diasporic contests and refigurations not just after colonialism but throughout its history' (Burton 1998: 562; Paisley 2001: 275). Angela Woollacott, in *To Try Her Fortune in London* (2001), traced white women from Australia on their journeys to London, discovering themselves to be not only colonials but also colonisers. Fiona Paisley edited a special issue of *Australian Feminist Studies* (2001) in which contributors applied 'the comparative' to 'feminist cultural and social history projects'. They acknowledged the importance in their projects of earlier reworkings of imperial history, of the kind carried out by Catherine Hall, Burton and Mrinalini Sinha, which de-centred Britain as the heart of empire, making 'Englishness' as much a subject of investigation as might be identity in colonial societies, just as Moreton-Robinson had made whiteness. They also showed how a comparative framework applied to 'an anti-essentialising "new cultural history" allows women's historians to examine gender cross-culturally and historically, to analyse colonial encounters, and to rethink relationships between gender and other systems of power' (Paisley 2001: 272).

Susan Magarey

References
Burton 1998; Blake 1984; Clarke 1999; Curthoys 1970; Curthoys 1975; Daniels 1993; Eldershaw 1938; Grimshaw & Carey 2001; Martin 1987; Paisley 2001.

Related essays
Dominions; Empire; Historical Fiction; Feminist Bio/Autobiography; Local History; Memoir; Postcolonial; Travel.

B

Balfour, Clara Lucas 1808–1878

English Temperance advocate, biographer, historian of women. Born in New Forest, Hampshire, daughter of a mother 'of much intellectual power' and John Lydell Lucas, cattle dealer. Educated briefly at a girl's school. Following the death of her father, moved to London, where she engaged in needlework to survive. Married James Balfour in 1827. The marriage was troubled by James' sporadic employment and drinking. The couple became involved in the Temperance movement in 1837, when both signed a pledge of total abstinence. Balfour earned money to support their four children by proofreading for the prestigious *London and Westminster Review*. In 1841 she published a volume of Temperance poems entitled 'The Garland of Flowers'. Encouraged by friends in the movement, Balfour began to speak and write on a range of subjects, especially on the influence of women on society. The idea of women's moral influence as an historical force was developed more fully in her numerous books on women's history such as *Women of Scripture* (1847) where she compared the representation of women in 'general history' with 'Scriptural history'. The Bible she claimed was remarkable in its recognition of 'woman's moral responsibility' when read against other ancient texts. In *Woman and the Temperance Reformation* (1849) Balfour wrote that women were the 'most influential moral teachers of society' with a particular responsibility to 'promote virtue, and a mission to reform husbands, children, even vulnerable women themselves'.

In *Sketches of English Literature* (1852) Balfour began the restoration of Mary Wollstonecraft within Victorian feminist consciousness, suggesting that she should be considered alongside women such as Hannah More, whose life she also wrote on. Balfour drew on a tradition of self-help, stressing the importance of 'woman's mission' to the progress of history, continuing this theme in *Working Women of the Last Half-Century* (1854) and many later texts. As well as historical texts Balfour produced over 70 Temperance novels, stories and collections. She devoted much time to lecturing to Worker's Institutes and was a pioneer of adult education. She was elected president of the newly formed British Women's Temperance Association in 1877, a year before she died.

Mary Spongberg

References

Cunliffe-Jones 1992; Doern 1997.

Bateson, Mary 1865–1906

English Medievalist. Born near Whitby, daughter of Anna (Aikin) and William Henry Bateson, Master of St John's College, Cambridge. Educated at Miss Thorton's School, Cambridge, the Institut Friedländer in Baden, the Perse School for Girls, Cambridge. She began studies in Newnham College, which her parents helped found, in 1884. Won a first class in Cambridge's historical tripos in 1887, being placed second in 'an exceptionally good year'. Began teaching at Newnham in 1888. Keenly involved in suffrage activities, her mentor Mandell Creighton persuaded her to disengage from political activism and 'write true history'. Her early works demonstrate an interest in women's history. In 1899 she published an edition of the *Register of Crabhouse Nunnery* and an article in the *English Historical Review* on the 'Origin and Early History of Double Monasteries' (1899), drawing upon the work of **Lina Eckenstein**, recovering the lives of women such as **Hrotsvitha** and demonstrating that women sometimes had authority over men in such institutions.

Working extensively with Downing Professor of Legal History F W Maitland, Bateson turned to municipal history, publishing volumes such as the *Records of the Borough of Leicester* (1899–1905), *Charters of the Boroughs of Cambridge* (1901), the *Cambridge Guild Records* (1903) and *Borough Customs* (1904–1906). She was involved in the reform of the teaching of history at Newnham and helped establish research fellowships at the college. She wrote 108 entries for the *Dictionary of National Biography*, although none of her subjects were women. She also published *Medieval England*, a popular text – the first social history of the English middle ages. She was appointed editor of the *Cambridge Medieval History* shortly before her sudden death.

Mary Spongberg

References

DNB; Fenwick 1994.

Major works
Medieval England 1066–1350 (New York: Freeport Books, 1971).

Baudonivia seventh century

Frankish biographer, historian. Nun of the Holy Cross, Baudonivia wrote the first biography known to be written by a woman, the *Life of Queen Radegund* of Poitiers (sometime between 609–614). Little is known of Baudonivia's early life, although she boasted in her *Life of Radegund* that she has been 'nourished from the cradle' by the saintly queen. This relationship allowed her to claim a particular authority and audience, as two male-authored lives of Radegund already existed.

Baudonivia wrote her *Life of Radegund* to supplement one of these works by Venantius Fortunatus. Wishing to 'not repeat what the apostolic Bishop Fortunatus recorded of her blessed life' (McNamara *et al.* 1992: 86), Baudonivia claims that she will only speak of what he considered unworthy to mention. Commissioned by her Abbess Dedimia to write for the nuns at Saint-Croix, Baudonivia concentrated on those details of Radegund's life most pertinent to her community, her founding of the Holy Cross convent and her life among the sisters. Thus she established a woman-centred tradition of biographical writing, emphasising female traits in her depiction of Radegund's saintliness. She also depicted how the mediatory nurturing roles played by Merovingian noblewomen came to be assimilated into religious life. Baudonivia's account of Radegund's life acknowledges the role played by the Queen in the history of her people, merging her noble and saintly roles, stressing her active religious ministry, her destruction of pagan shrines and relic hunting, as well as her engagement in diplomacy and politics.

Mary Spongberg

References
Coon 1997; McNamara *et al.* 1992; Wemple 1981.

Major work
Baudonivia's *Life of Radegund* has recently been translated in McNamara *et al., Sainted Women of the Dark Ages* (Durham: University of North Carolina Press, 1992).

Beard, Mary Ritter 1876–1958

American suffrage activist, historian of women. Born in Indianapolis, one of seven children of Narcissa (Lockwood) teacher, and Eli Foster Ritter, lawyer. Class valedictorian of her high school in Indianapolis, Beard studied at de Pauw University, graduating with a Bachelor's degree in 1897. Taught German in the Greencastle public school system before marrying Charles Austin Beard, historian, in 1900. Following her marriage Beard moved to England where Charles was studying at Oxford. Both were involved in the establishment of Ruskin Hall. Settling in Manchester where Charles directed an extension division of Ruskin Hall, Beard became acquainted with the **Pankhursts** while they were associated with the Independent Labour Party. The searing poverty of Manchester caused Beard to develop a feminist consciousness and her later concern for labouring women can be traced through these Manchester connections.

Beard's first publications 'The Twentieth-Century Woman Looking Around and Backward' (1900) and the 'The Nineteenth-Century Woman Looking Forward' (1901) were published in *Young Oxford*, the journal of Ruskin Hall. In these essays, Beard questioned the 'completeness' of 'the history of the human race', as she had found women 'as makers of civilization' strangely absent from the historical record. The quest to discover women's historical role would characterise Beard's historical writing for the next half century.

Beard returned to the United States in 1901 following the birth of her daughter. She entered Columbia University as a graduate student in sociology in 1902, leaving in 1904 without completing her degree. Following the birth of her son in 1907 she worked for several women's voluntary organisations such as the National Women's Trade Union League and the Equality League for Self-Supporting Women. Beard supported women workers during the 1909 shirtwaist maker's strike and in 1911 she lobbied for protective legislation and stricter fire regulations following the Triangle factory fire.

Beard became a leading figure in the New York City Suffrage Party, and between 1910 and 1912 she served as an editor on *The Woman Voter*, the Party journal. In 1912 she published an article entitled 'Mothercraft' in that journal which anticipated her later work on women's agency in history. In 1913 Beard became involved in the most radical wing of the American suffrage movement, joining the Congressional Union for Women Suffrage (CU), who employed similar tactics to the militant suffragettes in England led by Emmeline Pankhurst. Beard became an executive member of the CU board and in 1917 she spoke before the Senate Committee on Women's Suffrage. Drawing on her knowledge of history she turned the Committee's attention to women's 'vital services' and 'equal and active participation' in the making of the American nation. Beard's primary concern, however, remained labouring women and she broke with the CU over their support of the Equal Rights Amendment, which would have seen protective legislation for women and children overturned. Beard's disillusionment with suffrage politics marked a shift in her historical understanding also, as she came to believe that equal rights feminism depended upon the myth of women's subjugation for its ideological basis. Beard's attempts to undermine this myth framed her later works of women's history.

Still Beard maintained a desire to educate women to citizenship and this led to her first collaboration with her husband in 1914 when they co-authored a high-school civics text, *American Citizenship*. Written at her instigation *American Citizenship* was designed to make girls as well as boys aware of their duties as citizens. This theme was continued in her next book, *Women's Work in the Municipalities* (1915), a text that combined her interest in civic reform with her growing understanding of women's historical agency. Their experience of worker's education in England saw the Beards committed to an ethos of education in the service of social progress. Both worked to initiate the Worker's Education Bureau of the United States and in 1920 Beard published *A Short History of the American Labour Movement* under its auspices. In 1920 they published *A History of the United States* and in 1927 *The Rise of American Civilisation*, the first part of a multi-volumed history of the United States appeared, followed by *America in Midpassage* (1939) and *The American Spirit* (1942). Beard also wrote a life of her husband *The Making of Charles A Beard* (1955) published several years after his death. Although Beard preserved her independence as a writer by never signing herself Mrs Charles Beard, her contributions to their co-authored texts were frequently rendered invisible by male critics, a fact that no doubt influenced her historical understanding of women's contribution to society.

In 1931 Beard published her first major historical study of women, *On Understanding Women*. Recognising that previous masculinist representations of women in history were fragmentary and flawed,

Beard called for a more cultural approach to women's history. Drawing influence from **Charlotte Gilman Perkins**, Beard maintained that anthropologists had a 'better memory' of women's contribution to the development of civilisation and suggested that historians interested in women would benefit from an interdisciplinary approach. Beard's critique of the masculinist nature of historical writing anticipated her husband's depiction of the partial and political nature of historical writing in his famous Presidential address to the American Historical Association in 1933.

In 1933 Beard published *America through Women's Eyes*, an anthology on women's historical writing in the USA, that included sections from feminist histories such as Elizabeth Cady Stanton's *History of Woman's Suffrage*, biographies of feminist activists, as well as more general works by women historians such as **Hannah Adams, Alice Morse Earle** and **Elizabeth Ellet**. In 1934 Beard published 'A Challenging Political Economy as It Affects Women', under the auspices of the American Association of University Women, a 56-page document constituting perhaps the first women's studies syllabus. Critical of the masculinist nature of education, Beard's syllabus sought not only to demonstrate the role women played in making civilisation, but to assert that men's and women's 'destinies are bound together'. She was unable to persuade any college to adopt her syllabus.

In 1936 Beard began the project that was most influential to the writing of women's history in America, her campaign to create the World Centre for Women's **Archives** (WCWA). The object of the WCWA was to assemble and preserve source material; the guiding principle of 'the projection of woman's personality out of the shadows of time and into the living force which is woman in fact, into written history' was clearly shaped by Beard's perspective on women's historical role. Beard became Director of the Archives and worked tirelessly to acquire the papers of prominent women and records of women's organisations. She envisaged that the Archives would lead to the creation of an Academy of Women that would provide an institutional base for research on women. Financial problems and lack of public support crippled the project and it was abandoned, with many of the papers being donated to Smith and Radcliffe College.

In 1946 Beard published the text for which she is best remembered, *Woman as Force in History*. As with her earlier work, Beard stressed women's contribution to civilisation, demonstrating women's agency, their 'force' in generating historical change. Also a 'study' of the idea that women 'were members of a subject sex', in this work Beard rejected earlier feminist interpretations of women's historical role that had focused on their oppression. Beard was also critical of the celebratory histories of first-wave feminism that had begun to appear during the interwar period. She consciously set out to challenge what she considered was women's history that privileged the activities of a few elite women who measured their progress in terms of the gaining of suffrage. Written in the wake of the Second World War, *Woman as Force in History* is also a pacificist text, written to stress women's active role in the promotion of **peace** throughout history.

In 1978 the Berkshire Conference of Women Historians at Mount Holyoke held a special session on the 'Legacy of Mary Beard', a belated recognition of her influence. No biography of Beard exists, perhaps in part due to the fact that she destroyed many of her papers and asked those women who corresponded with her to do likewise. In 1991 Nancy F Cott published the existing letters and provided the most detailed biographical and historiographical study of Beard to date, *A Woman Making History*.

Mary Spongberg

References

Cott 1991; Des Jardins 2003; Lane 1977; Turroff 1979.

Major works

Woman as Force in History (New York: Persea Press, 1987) and *Making Women's History: The Essential Mary Ritter Beard* (ed.) Ann J Lane (New York: Feminist Press, 2000).

Beauvoir, Simone de 1908–1986

French writer and philosopher, is best known for her major work, *The Second Sex* (1949). Here she provided a sweeping interdisciplinary analysis of women's status as secondary, the Other, the inessential, the less than human. Women, she urged, needed to reclaim their subjectivity, to fight against their biology for their individuality. Though primarily a work of philosophy this book also considered the history of women's subordination. After chapters on biology and psychology, the third chapter is entitled 'The Point of View of Historical Materialism'. Here, she outlines Frederick Engels' theory that the subjection of women arose with the emergence of private property, and questions why and indeed whether there was any necessary connection between the two. 'Historical materialism', she writes, 'takes for granted facts that call for explanation'. There are, she suggests, prior issues to consider, such as men's recognition of themselves as individual and autonomous, and the constitution of women as something lesser, or 'other'. Private property would involve women's subordination, she suggests, only if these basic habits of thought prevailed.

De Beauvoir was also a novelist and an autobiographer of great significance, writing several novels and four major autobiographical volumes plus some shorter works. Her novels, especially *She Came to Stay* (1943) and *The Mandarins* (1954), were based very much on her own life and circle, and prefigure the **autobiographies** in interesting ways. Most notable among the autobiographical works were *Memoirs of a Dutiful Daughter* (1958), *The Prime of Life* (1960), *Force of Circumstance* (1963) and *All Said and Done* (1972). De Beauvoir tells us that she conceived of the autobiographies first, and that *The Second Sex* was written in preparation for them, stating in *The Prime of Life*: 'Wanting to talk about myself, I became aware that to do so I should first have to describe the condition of woman in general.' The autobiographies are notable for their attention to detail and their evocation of the life of a female intellectual in the French intellectual milieux of the middle decades of the twentieth century.

All these works – novels, autobiographies and works of philosophy – were important for the **women's liberation** movement of the 1970s. *The Second Sex* was a major influence on key American feminist texts of this era; two of them, Shulamith Firestone's *The Dialectic of Sex* and Betty Friedan's *The Feminine Mystique*, were dedicated to de Beauvoir, and Kate Millett, the author of a third, *Sexual Politics*, later wrote: 'I owe a great debt to *The Second Sex*. I couldn't have written *Sexual Politics* without it.' Her work has since been subjected to intensive examination and critique by feminist scholars, and her life has been similarly scrutinised, some seeing her as an example of a woman who lived in the shadow of a man and others as a symbol of unparalleled independence. Despite these critiques, de Beauvoir was loved and respected by women around the world, especially for *The Second Sex*. After her death, one of her American biographers, Margaret Simon, spoke for many when she wrote: 'It makes me cry to think of her again; I wish she could have lived forever.'

Ann Curthoys

References

Bair 1990; Brosman 1991; Faillaze 1998; Forster 1989; Moi 1994; Pilardi 1999; Simons 1986; Vintges 1996.

Major works

All Said and Done (New York: G.P. Putnam's 1974); *Memoirs of a Dutiful Daughter* (Harmondsworth: Penguin, 1963); Force of Circumstance (London: Andre Deutsch & Weidenfeld and Nicolson, 1965); *She Came to Stay* (New York: World Publishing Company, 1954); *The Mandarins* (London: Fontana, 1986); *The Prime of Life* (London: Andre Deutsch & Weidenfeld and Nicolson, 1965) and *The Second Sex* (New York: Vintage Books, 1989).

Belgiojoso, Cristina di 1808–1871

Italian political journalist, theologian, historian. Born in Milan, daughter of Gerolamo and Vittoria Trivulzio. Following the death of her father in 1812, her mother remarried the Marchese Alessandro Visconti d'Aragona, an Italian nationalist. Educated at home by progressive governess, Ernesta Bisi. Married Prince Emilio Barbiano di Belgiojoso d'Este against the wishes of her family in 1824. They separated by mutual consent in 1828. One daughter.

Cristina found consolation in nationalist politics. Her anti-Austrian activities forced her into exile in France in 1830. She befriended Augustin Thierry, François Mignet and General La Fayette, who introduced her to Parisian society. She formed an influential salon in 1833, using it to promote Italian nationalism. Her fortune confiscated, she worked as a political journalist. Returning to Italy in the 1840s, she engaged in social and political reforms on her estates. This isolation allowed her to write. In 1842 she published a four-volume history of the development of Catholic dogma, questioning Augustinian authority. In 1844 she translated Vico's *Scienza Nova*. In the Italian revolutionary wars in 1848 Belgiojoso became a participant-observer, organising the first military nurse' corps and leading a battalion of volunteers from Naples to Milan. She wrote contemporary accounts of these revolutionary wars, including *L'Italie et la révolution italienne de 1848* (1848). Melchior de Vogüé of the *Académie Française* wrote of her that 'No other Italian of her sex has contributed more to the resurrection of Italy.' Exiled again from Italy she travelled to Turkey, where she wrote an **Orientalist** novella *Emina* (1856) and travel-writing demonstrating the domestic side of 'Mussulman [*sic*] society'.

Mary Spongberg

References

Brombert 1977; Gattey 1971; Marrone 2000.

Benger (or Benjays), Elizabeth Ogilvy 1778–1827

English poet, novelist, biographer, historian. Only child of Mary (Long) and John Benger. Benger showed a passion for reading from an early age. Her formal education began at 12 when her father allowed her to attend a boy's school to learn Latin. His death in 1796 left her in straitened circumstances. Arriving in London in 1800, she joined literary circles frequented by **Elizabeth Hamilton** and **Lucy Aikin**.

Benger showed a precocious interest in women's history. At the age of 13 she published *The Female Geniad* (1791), an epic poem celebrating female genius, depicting classical figures such as Aspasia and Sappho, as well as contemporaries such as **Catharine Sawbridge Macaulay** and **Helen Maria Williams**. She produced two novels *Marian* (1812) and *Valsimore, or The Heart & The Fancy* (1813) before returning to women's history publishing **Memoirs** of ***Elizabeth Hamilton*** (1818), *Anne Boleyn* (1821), *Mary Queen of Scots* (1823) and *Elizabeth of Bohemia* (1825). Like earlier **memoirs** Benger's work merged romance with history creating a 'tragical history of the passions'. Her focus on private life allowed her to criticise men's power over women, demonstrating women's suffering at their hands. **Lucy Aikin**, her biographer, wrote that Madame de Stäel considered her 'the most interesting woman she had seen during her visit to England'. In spite of such celebrity, Benger died in poverty.

Mary Spongberg

References
Aikin 1864; Kucich 1993.

Berry, Mary 1763–1852

English editor, diarist, social historian. Born Yorkshire, eldest daughter of Robert Berry. Berry and her younger sister Agnes led a nomadic existence, moving among relatives until their teens. Largely self-educated, Berry travelled to Europe in 1783 with Agnes. Acquaintance with Horace Walpole allowed the sisters to enter fashionable society upon their return in 1788. Walpole called Mary and Agnes his 'twin wives' and moved them onto his Strawberry Hill estate. Berry became engaged to General Charles O'Hara, but called off the engagement in 1795. The most significant relationship in her life was with Walpole's niece, the sculptor Anne Seymour Damer. Her first literary work, *The Fashionable Friends*, performed privately at Strawberry Hill in 1802 by Berry and Damer appears to have been a self-protective parody of their relationship.

Walpole's death saw Berry financially secure, as he left her property and the duty of literary executrix. She published a five-volume edition of his works within a year of his death. The death of her father and the loss of income that entailed propelled Berry to write. In 1819 she edited the *Letters of Rachel, Lady Russell*, providing an introductory biography. Her major work of history, *A Comparative View of Social Life in England and France*, was published in two volumes in 1828 and 1831. Drawing largely upon the biographical writings of **Lucy Hutchinson** and Margaret Cavendish, and the **memoirs** of the Duchesse de Longueville, Madame de Motteville and the Duchess de Nemours, Berry's history reveals much about the role of women at court and in the salon, the education of women and the impact of women's engagement in politics.

Berry's own salon was frequented by French and English literary figures such as **Madame de Staël** who considered her 'the cleverest woman in England' and **Harriet Martineau** who reported that her parties 'were rather *blue* . . .'. Entries on Miss Berry appear in Martineau's *Biographical Sketches* (1868) and Townshend Gertrude Mayer's *Women of Letters* (1894).

Mary Spongberg

References
Elfenbein 2001; Oldfield 1999; Sage 1999.

Blackburn, Helen 1842–1904

Anglo-Irish historian of suffrage. Only surviving daughter of Isabella (Lamb) and Bewicke Blackburn of County Kerry in Ireland. Nothing is known of her schooling. Blackburn became involved in the English suffrage movement in the 1870s.

Was appointed Secretary to the Central Committee of the National Society for Women's Suffrage in 1874 and served in that position until 1895. She was also sole editor of *Englishwoman's Review* between 1881 and 1890 and published numerous articles on the working conditions of women. Blackburn published the first book-length history of the English suffrage movement, *Women's Suffrage* (1902). She claimed that the 'effort to bring political liberty to the daily lives of women' formed 'part of the continuity of history' and like **Charlotte Carmichael Stopes** presented the struggle for the vote as the result of women's declining civil status since the Norman conquest. Her retrospective analysis drew on the example of **Anne Clifford** whose motto was 'Maintain your loyalty and preserve your rights'. The book, however, focuses on the struggle of women to gain suffrage since the Reform Act of 1832, with much space devoted to the life of suffrage agitator Lydia Becker and other moderate suffragists. Blackburn obscured the role of radical suffragists and ignored other campaigns of first-wave feminism such as the struggle to repeal the Contagious Diseases Acts. Blackburn retired from political activism to care for her aging father. Upon her death she bequeathed her library to Girton College, Cambridge.

Mary Spongberg

Reference

Holton 2000.

Body and sexuality

The past two decades have seen increased historical interest in the body and sexuality amongst women historians. A plethora of articles, books, dissertations, conferences and journals have been devoted to exploring the place of the body and sexuality in historical change, discourses about the body and sexuality, and conceptions of embodiment and sexual identities in varying historical periods. Women historians have been drawn to the body and sexuality for different reasons, and approached these concepts in varying ways. Some have considered the body and sexuality as fundamental to the historical exploration of people's identity formation and sense of self, others as central to examining people's oppression as well as resistance to those things that seek to control them, other women historians have seen these aspects of human experience as key concepts to examining a society's social order. While today the body and sexuality tend to be approached as integrated concepts basic to examining changing conceptions of sexual difference, this is a more recent phenomenon that, as this work will show, has largely come from changes within the historiography of each of these concepts and within the canon of women's history.

The unavoidable detour?

In the key areas of inquiry women historians have traditionally been drawn to, such as childbirth, motherhood, sexuality and labour, the body's life cycle lies at the heart of the historical investigation. Some historians have suggested that such is the centrality of the body in women's lives it cannot be avoided in their history. In 1984 French historian Catherine Fouquet questioned whether a history of women's bodies was inevitable in women's history given the extent to which the biological has shaped and determined women's lives. Fouquet also queried whether such biological determinism was in fact the cause of women's absence from the historical record given the enduring perception among many historians of women's lives as essentially ahistorical. 'For the majority of men who wrote history,' Fouquet argued, 'the feminine condition sprang out of that part of history they liked to consider unchanging: just as the earth is round, women work for the continuance of the species' (1984: 53). A fundamental gendered dichotomy between Nature and culture in which woman was conflated with her physiological processes was crucial to women's ahistorical identity.

Women historians examined the longevity of beliefs about woman's antithesis to culture and the way the female body was used to explain this alignment to a more inferior, primeval position. In *The Death of Nature: Women, Ecology and the Scientific Revolution* (1980), Carolyn Merchant initiated a concern with the links between changing conceptions of nature and assertions about woman's social role and position. She illustrated how changing perceptions of nature during the scientific revolution supported claims of woman's passive role in reproduction and the implications of this on conceptions of woman's capacities. Through such analysis, women historians exposed the culturally and historically specific and constructed nature of ideas about the female body. This process of unmasking the contrived nature of beliefs about the body was significant to the canon of women's history because of the challenge it posed to the myth of women's unchanging experiences and the ways in which it exposed the ideologies such a falsehood served.

In *Am I that Name? Feminism and the Category of Women in History* (1988), Denise Riley examined the shifting historical constructions of the category of 'women', in which differing conceptions of the body were central. Riley explored how the discourse of medieval theology constructed women as bodies only whose souls remain ungendered and therefore capable of divine grace. Riley argued that this medieval conception established a very different meaning of womanhood to that in the eighteenth century for instance, when discourses about the female body situated woman as part of the natural world and therefore distinct from the rational, political sphere. Riley demonstrated the culturally and historically specific nature of discourses and disciplinary practices about the female body and the impact this had on conceptions of women's position in the social order. In a slightly different way, in *The Woman beneath the Skin* (1991), Barbara Duden explored how the historical nature of discourses about the body established culturally and historically distinct bodily self-perceptions. Through her examination of the records of an eighteenth-century German physician who documented the medical histories of 1800 women (often recorded in their own words), Duden's work illustrated the crucial role historical and cultural factors play in women's bodily experiences and sense of self. While acknowledging that biology itself was a constant, unchanging phenomenon, Duden argued that historians should attend to the specific history of women's corporeality, and dismissed the idea that the female body offers women a sense of historical continuity because of some collective or essential bodily experience.

Other work by women historians has challenged even the idea of the biological body as a non-historical entity suggesting that it is not only women's experiences of their body that are culturally and historically contingent, but even the anatomical 'facts' about the female body. Women historians, like philosophers and sociologists, have been attracted to such anti-essentialism, seeking to expose the constructed nature of scientific 'truths' about the biological body and the natural laws that govern human life. Women historians have been particularly interested in analysing the social, cultural and historical nature of scientific statements about the female body and their relationship to the workings of the dominant social order of various historical epochs. In *Sexual Visions, Images of Gender in Science and Medicine between the Eighteenth and Twentieth Centuries* (1989), Ludmilla Jordanova examined the ways in which science reinforced particular cultural beliefs about racial and sexual biological differences which were then both legitimised by and entrenched within discourses of science and biomedicine. In both *The Mind Has No Sex? Women in the Origins of Modern Science* (1989) and *Nature's Body: Gender in the Making of Modern Science* (1993), Londa Schbeinger presented many examples of the ways in which eighteenth-century ideologies about relations between the sexes shaped specific developments within natural history and categories of scientific classification which then underpinned scientific claims of women's inherent inferiority. In *Beyond the Natural Body* (1994), Nelly Oudshoorn sought to debunk the myth of scientific narratives of 'discovery' by illustrating the selective process through which scientists decided which truths they would discover in relation to the development of theories about sex hormones. Oudshoorn argued that sex hormones, which comprise a large portion of the 'biological truth' about sex, were far from passive records of bodily functions and characteristics but culturally motivated and ideologically driven scientific discoveries (1994: 20).

The complex work of Caroline Bynum has taken the idea of the history of the body in rather different directions by exploring amongst other things, the historical nature of bodily behaviour. In *Resurrection of the Body in Western Christianity 200–1336* (1996) Bynum explored radical bodily behaviours that emerged in the thirteenth century such as somatic miracles, trances and levitations. Bynum suggested that these events must be seen as evidence of genuinely new and historically specific behaviour. Throughout her work, Bynum has argued that the historian should approach the body not simply as an appendage of the mind, nor a separate thing to which mind or soul is attached, but rather part of a complicated and unitary self which is itself historically and culturally contingent. In this text, Bynum also looked at the ways in which men and women in the Middle Ages viewed the relationship between themselves and their bodies – even after their deaths. This aspect of her work has been groundbreaking not only in furthering understanding of the way bodily self-perceptions and behaviours have a history, but also in showing the role of the body in ideas of the self in the medieval period and their connection to modern Western attitudes towards the body.

Body politics

Many women historians have examined the political implications of the construction of and the changing meanings accorded to the biological body. In *Women and the Public Sphere in the Age of the French Revolution* (1988) Joan Landes explored how the symbolic representation of the female body determined women's place (or lack of place) in definitions of citizenship, politics and the public sphere. Landes concluded that rhetorical claims of universality and the female embodiment of the nation disguised the extent to which the Republic was 'constructed against women' (1988: 171). In *The Body and the French Revolution: Sex, Class and Political Culture* (1989), Dorinda Outram examined the political upheaval and change wrought by the French Revolution through the prevailing class-based perceptions of the body. Characterising the Revolution as a struggle of the middle class's ideal of the (male) stoic and restrained body over the excessive and depraved bodies of women, the aristocracy and the lower orders, Outram too stressed the importance of the body in the political culture and the transformation of public space that accompanied the French Revolution. Developing this line of argument even further, in *The Family Romance of the French Revolution* (1992), Lynn Hunt provided a complex reading of the imagery and controversies surrounding the body of Marie-Antoinette. Hunt illustrated that the anxiety over the supposedly depraved sexual body of the Queen mirrored deeper concerns about women's political power and the feminisation of the new Republic.

Women historians have also been interested in studying the demarcation, regulation and manipulation of bodies within different historical periods and particular events, for example, in the Imperialist project. In *Imperial Leather: Race, Gender and Sexuality in the Colonial Contest* (1995) Anne McClintock illustrated the complex yet central role the body of the colonised woman played in colonial and Imperialist discourses of power and race. McClintock explored how social relationships between coloniser and colonised were infused with sexuality, and the way sexual codes and corporeal norms were largely governed by this power relationship. More recently, Ann Laura Stoler's *Carnal Knowledge and Imperial Power: Race and the Intimate in Colonial Rule* (2002) has explored the role of the sexual body in the making of colonial categories, and in notions of European supremacy and its colonised antithesis. Other women historians have been drawn to examining the role the body plays in effecting different forms of social control, social formation and in the development and definition of nation states. Isabell Hull's *Sexuality, State and Civil Society in Germany 1700–1815* (1996) and Kathleen Wilson's *The Island Race: Englishness, Empire and Gender in the Eighteenth Century* (2002) are notable for their complex study of the various ways cultural, political and economic change brought new (re)interpretations of bodies in the definition and demarcation of national identity, citizenship and civil society. A similar line of argument has been pursued in studies of fascism. Claudia Koonz's *Mothers in the Fatherland: Women, the Family and Nazi Politics* (1987) explored the ways women's reproductive function situated them within the Nazi regime, and how it was both a source of power and a means by which their control was effected. Victoria de Grazia's *How Fascism Ruled Women, Italy 1922–1945* (1992) analysed the regime's conflicting public discourses about femininity and uses of the female body, specifically the competing images of women in propaganda and commercial culture.

The relationship between feminism and women's history has been especially important to women historians' analysis and approach to the body. In the late 1960s, second-wave feminists across the western world rallied against biologically determinist perceptions of the female body that supposedly legitimated women's limited opportunities and social roles. In contesting the notion that a woman's biology determined her destiny, feminists sought to expose the various ways the female body was deployed to ensure the capitalist and patriarchal organisation of society. In *Sexual Politics* (1970), Kate Millet argued that by virtue of her body, woman was relegated to a limited role that tended to 'arrest her at the level of biological experience' (1970: 26). Millet concluded that 'all that can be described as distinctly human rather than animal activity (in their own way animals also give birth and care for their young) is largely reserved for the male' (1970: 26). Identifying patriarchy as a socially conditioned belief system masquerading as nature, Millett demonstrated the ways that patriarchal attitudes about the female body penetrated literature, philosophy, psychology and politics, and the role such cultural discourse played in reinforcing the systematised subjugation and exploitation of women.

The arguments articulated in *Sexual Politics* provided the inspiration for a great deal of feminist scholarship. Women historians began identifying the historical legacy of biologically determinist arguments and their role in the legitimation of the patriarchal organisation of western society. The fundamental goal of much of this early historical work was exploring the social construction of femininity to which the body was crucial. Such analysis tended to focus on the role medicine and male practitioners played in women's status as the 'lesser sex', seen particularly in Barbara Ehrenreich and Deirdre English's *Complaints and Disorders: The Sexual Politics of Sickness* (1973) and their collection *For Her Own Good: 150 Years of the Experts Advice to Women* (1979) as well as contributions to Mary Hartman and Lois Banner's collection *Clio's Consciousness Raised* (1974), and Elizabeth Fee's 'Science and the Woman Problem: Historical Perspectives' (1976).

Women historians have continued to be interested in examining medical discourse about the female body and its role in reinforcing particularly limited views of women including their fragility and incapacity for public life. Contributions to the edited collection *Body/Politics* (1990) explored the effects of scientific discourse on the feminine body and women's experience of their body, emphasising the control such thinking exerts over women's lives. Anne Digby's 'Women's biological straightjacket' (1989), Deborah Kuhn's *From Midwives to Medicine* (1998) and Ornella Moscucci's analysis of the female body within English gynaecology and obstetrics over the late eighteenth, nineteenth and early twentieth centuries in *The Science of Woman* (1990) illustrated the way the female body offered a source of power to men claiming authority over its functions and how such knowledge directly impacted on women's lives. Monica Green's work on gynaecology in the later Middle Ages, Lesley Dean Jones' *Women's Bodies in Classical Greek Science* (1994) and Helen King's *Hippocrates' Woman: Reading the Female Body in Ancient Greece* (1998) have also offered important new insights into the origins of the pathologisation of the female body at the hands of male medical elites, illustrating the longevity of certain ideas and assumptions within medical discourse.

While women historians' analysis of the body has tended to be dominated by an interest with the way medical conceptions of the female body reinforced particular patriarchal assumptions about women's lives, there have been some notable changes in the approach taken and the conclusions arrived at. The historical work of Mary Poovey in *Uneven Developments* (1988) was instrumental in convincingly problematising the idea of a straightforward connection between the construction of knowledge about women and cultural expectations of femininity. Poovey's work especially influenced historical analysis on the Victorian era with Jill Matus' *Unstable Bodies: Victorian Representations of Sexuality and Maternity* (1995), Kelly Hurley's *The Gothic Body: Sexuality, Materialism, and Degeneration at the fin-de-siecle* (1996), Mary Spongberg's *Feminising Venereal Disease: The Body of the Prostitute in Nineteenth-century Medical Discourse* (1997) and Regina Morantz–Sanchez's *Conduct Unbecoming a Woman: Medicine on Trial in Turn-of-the-century Brooklyn* (1999), all of which are concerned with emphasising the 'uneven' or discontinuous and contradictory nature of beliefs about the female body and their relationship to the gendered social order.

Disciplining the body

Many would argue that the writings of French theorist Michel Foucault have greatly influenced the historiography of the body. Foucault is generally credited with establishing the concern with the relationship between power relations and discourses about the body that has come to dominate the historiography of the body. Yet the earlier historical analysis by women historians on the disciplining of the female body and the concomitant regulation of women's lives such as Ann Douglas Wood's 'The Fashionable Diseases: Women's Complaints and Their Treatment in Nineteenth-century America' (1973) and Carroll Smith-Rosenberg's 'The Female Animal: Medical and Biological Views of Woman and Her Role in Nineteenth-century America' (1973) actually pioneered ideas about the power of discourse.

Certainly, Foucault's work has provided the impetus for some extremely productive and innovative historical work by women historians, although not all of this has been because women historians embrace Foucault. Many have been extremely critical of Foucault's failure to attend to the specifics of the female body and experiences of women. In addressing omissions within Foucault's approach, women historians have greatly enhanced and extended many of his initial ideas, particularly the role of the body as a site of both oppression and agency for women. American literary historian Elaine Showalter convinced many of the potential of this approach to the body in *The Female Malady* (1985). Showalter argued that the female body was a means by which women were controlled and suppressed, yet also that the body offered women an expression of resistance to the claustrophobic and conflicting demands of the feminine role in the nineteenth century. For Showalter, the body offered women access to passive anti-patriarchal protest spoken through a language of physical symptoms. Such ideas influenced a great deal of subsequent historical analysis by women historians keen to explore the role of the body in both women's oppression and their struggles against various regimes and techniques of domination.

Various debates and shifts within women's historiography have also contributed to the historiography of the body within women's historical analysis. The shift to gender within feminist scholarship that occurred over the course of the late 1980s and early 1990s was especially important to recognition of the body as the most pervasive system by which sexual difference is defined and naturalised. At this time, many feminists increasingly recognised the meanings accorded to biological sex as the most oppressive social division. In historical circles, many women saw exploring sexual difference in history as an ontological and analytical tool that could liberate them from the methodological constraints and divisions increasingly polarising women's history. Those who embraced this conceptual approach sought to explore the role the body played in determining the relations and positions of the sexes. As Julia Epstein and Kristina Straub pointed out in their introduction to *Body Guards*:

> Sex/gender systems as we understand them are historically and culturally specific arrogations of the human body for ideological purposes. In sex/gender systems, physiology, anatomy, and body codes (clothing, cosmetics, behaviours, miens, affective and sexual object choices) are taken over by institutions that use bodily difference to coerce gender identity. (1991: 3)

Within historical analysis, the concept of gender lends itself to an examination of the interdependency between perceptions of the female and male body, concerned as it is with the discursive construction of man and woman. By exploring the role of the female body in defining relations between the sexes, women historians exposed how the association of woman with the body reinforced men's disassociation with the corporeal and served to perpetuate the sense of women's alterity. Much of this work focused on the changes in anatomical thinking about sexual difference and developments in reproductive physiology that took place over the long eighteenth century. Contributions by Catherine Gallagher, Londa Schbienger, Laura Engelstein, Mary Poovey and Christine Buci-Glucksmann to *The Making of the Modern Body* (1987) were especially important to the analysis of these shifts in thinking about sexual difference. These historians illustrated, in various ways, how the shift from a one-sex conception of sexual difference saw long-held assumptions about the female body as simply an inferior version of the male body change to a conception of incommensurability and opposition between the sexes in which they were understood as constituted by completely different parts. It was these changes that were said to mark the modern era, modern bodies, and establish woman's absolute otherness in relation to the normative male body.

While many women historians have accepted the importance of the eighteenth century to the historical analysis of sexual difference, others have suggested that this has distorted the picture of previous centuries. Patricia Crawford and Sara Mendelson's *Women in Early Modern England 1550–1720* (1998) offered important new insights into ideas about sexual difference through their reconstruction of women's physical, emotional and cultural changes and experiences associated with work, marriage, maternity and menopause. Similarly, Joan Cadden's *Meanings of Sex Differences in the Middle Ages* (1993) and Mary Fissell's exploration of the representation of reproduction in early modern England all raise questions about the emphasis accorded to the 1700s with regard to the historical analysis of sexual difference. Fissel's work provides enough examples to directly challenge beliefs about the hegemony of the one sex model in medical thinking in the 1700s while Cadden illustrates how medieval natural philosophical theories and medical notions about reproduction, sexual impulses and experiences contributed to a specific delineation of what was 'feminine' and what was 'masculine'. All these texts have demonstrated the significance of the medieval and early modern periods to modern conceptions of the self and, in so doing, suggest there has been a degree of over-emphasis accorded to the 1700s.

Much of the historical work on sexual difference has shown the way dominant beliefs about womanhood and the female body tend to be defined and represented by sexuality – either through its overt presence or absence. Indeed, it is the fundamental importance of and interconnection between the body and sexuality in the historical analysis of sexual difference that has led to many women historians' incorporating both concepts within their historical examinations. This, however, was not always the case with regard to sexuality. While popular today among women historians, the history of sexuality and the concern with sexuality was, like attitudes to the body, generally seen as outside the scope of history. Although sex featured in all societies in the past it was not considered a product of history. While women historians initially dedicated themselves to restoring women to the historical record and portraying women as active agents of change, this did not immediately extend to the issue of women's sexuality.

Gradually women historians saw that just as history had denied women a place as historical actors, so too it had negated their place as sexual subjects. Influenced by contemporary feminist debates concerning women's sexuality, many women historians began to look to the past to find evidence to support their own feminist concerns. Some historians were influenced by arguments of the Women's Liberation Movement where women's rights to sexual pleasure – on their own terms – was regarded as symbolising their freedom and autonomy. In *Woman's Body, Woman's Right* (1976), Linda Gordon provided a detailed history of American women's access to birth control in terms of the progress and freedom such changes represented for many women's lives. In contrast, other women historians approached sexuality as the source of women's subordination and oppression, seeing in women's experiences of the past a legacy that continued in their own societies. Anna Clark's contribution to the London Feminist History Group's *Sexual Dynamics of History: Men's Power, Women's Resistance* (1983) explored women's vulnerability and powerlessness with regard to their sexuality and the way 'patriarchal assumptions shaped any organised protests against sexual victimization' (1983: 26). In the same collection Sheila Jeffreys examined the stance of pre-First World War feminists' against sex, arguing that such a unifying and transforming force was subject to attack by the attitudes of the sex-reform movement of the 1920s. Jeffreys concluded that such historical analysis was evidence that 'it cannot be assumed that the pursuit of sexual pleasure for women in relationships with men is automatically in women's interests' (1983: 202).

Pleasure and danger

Women historians' approach to women's sexual experiences in the past as either the source of their liberation or oppression was in many ways too polemic and tended to approach all sex for women as either wanted or unwanted heterosexual intercourse. In 1982, the 9th Scholar and Feminist conference held at Barnard College, New York, the papers from which appeared in Carol Vance's *Pleasure and Danger: Exploring Women's Sexuality* (1989), was dedicated to the theme of 'a politics of sexuality'. The conference explored the many tensions and contradictions in women's sexual experiences and in the construction of female sexuality. One contribution – Ellen DuBois and Linda Gordon's 'Seeking Ecstasy on the Battlefield' – criticised the trend amongst women historians pursuing women's sexual powerlessness. Like many papers in this collection, the authors argued for the need to accept sexuality as simultaneously a source of pleasure and danger for women, and address the complexities this posed.

The sense of polarity gave way to a recognition of the need for more nuanced assessments that accounted for complexities. Approaching the history of women's sexuality as a complicated and contradictory experience gradually opened out the historical record and saw some especially innovative analysis by women historians on the diverse range of women's experiences of their sexuality. The pioneering work of Leonore Davidoff (1983) on the complex sexual relationship between Englishman Arthur Munby and his servant Hannah Cullwick launched a series of similar investigations by women historians exploring the way wider social forces and cultural preoccupations of the Victorian era impacted on people's erotic behaviour. An important aspect of this work was attention to issues of class, race and gender and the way these played out in people's sexual practices, producing, in the case of Munby and Cullwick, disordered and contradictory hierarchies of social and erotic power. Similar attention to issues of race and class were made by contributions to Ann Snitow and Christine Stansell's collection *Powers of Desire: The Politics of Sexuality* (1983) which sought to explore not only the way sexuality was a form of control but also how people engage, resist and challenge the meanings accorded to sexual practices.

Women historians have continued to be interested in breaking down the operation of rigid and competing dichotomies such as liberated/oppressed, healthy/pathological, disciplined/undisciplined, purity/adulteration in their analysis of the historical representation of sexuality and people's sexual activities. Such an approach has found particular resonance for women historians interested in the examination of those whose sexual identity was constructed around notions of their 'deviancy'. Judith Walkowitz's *Prostitution and Victorian Society: Women, Class and the State* (1982) was especially groundbreaking in this regard. Walkowitz explored the ways in which the identity of the prostitute was formed from particular dominant class-based ideals embedded in the governing institutions and laws of Victorian society. She demonstrated how the deviant identity of the prostitute was a specific class construction formed from a relationship to an equally class-specific construction – the chaste and sexually passive middle-class woman. Walkowitz argued that amongst their own social class prostitutes occupied a different identity not as sexual deviants but as active independent women and, in so doing, demonstrated the absolute necessity for historians to attend to the specifics of class when examining the representation of women's sexuality. In 1990 Judith Allen broke new ground in Australian women's history with *Sex and Secrets: Crimes Involving Australian Women Since 1880*, offering unique insights gained from a feminist analysis of crimes involving women and their complex relationship to gender and sexuality. Allen's provocative survey of an array of evidence demonstrated how particular social changes and class shaped dominant sexual and political positions, which in turn informed responses to the representation and portrayal of those women whose behaviour was regarded as deviating from the norm.

While a great deal of work by women historians has countered limited stereotypical images of women's experience of and relationship to sexuality, there has also been an interest with exploring how women have engaged with and shaped the discourse and the role sexuality has assumed in women's social struggles and politics. Late nineteenth- and early twentieth-century feminist debates have offered women historians a great deal of material, especially as a source of contestation and debate between women. Research by Sheila Jeffreys in *The Spinster and Her Enemies* (1986), Susan Kingsley Kent's *Sex and Suffrage in Britain 1860–1914* (1987) and Margaret Jackson's *The Real Facts of Life* (1994) all demonstrate the extent to which sexuality permeated the suffrage campaigns, the post-war sex-reform movements and the work of radical-feminist birth controllers such as Marie Stopes and Stella Browne. More recent historical work such as Lucy Bland's *Banishing the Beast* (1995) and Lesley Hall's *Sex, Gender and Social Change* (2000) have contested some of the conclusions arrived at by these historians. Bland and Hall have led the way in opposing the assumption of a clear-cut opposition between those who advanced arguments for women's suffrage based on woman's moral purity and those advocating for sex reform. Both historians have convincingly illustrated that first-wave feminist's views on sexual morality were far from monolithic, and suggest previous studies have been misleading in their failure to address the racial and class agendas underlying claims of women's 'purity' and in regard to the complexity of women's views and experiences about sexuality. The extensive and somewhat prolific contribution of Lesley Hall to the history of sexuality has shown, among many things, how important the agitations of feminist radicals were to changes that took place over the course of the twentieth century, including women's access to birth control and the increasing acknowledgment of women's sexual satisfaction.

There have been many divisions and criticisms among women historians raised by their historical work on sexuality, yet it is these which have contributed to the development and changes within both the historiography of sexuality and women's history. One of the more influential criticisms was made by Adrienne Rich in the 1980s in her essay 'Compulsory Heterosexuality and Lesbian Existence' which highlighted the heterocentric assumptions within many women's scholarship. Rich argued that much historical work not only denied or ignored lesbian existence, but failed to acknowledge it as a source of knowledge and power available to all women. Contesting the falsity of the heterosexual–homosexual binary within the examinations of women's lives, Rich argued for the need to explore and acknowledge a 'lesbian continuum' whereby feminist scholars engaged with 'forms of primary intensity between and among women, including the sharing of a rich inner life' (1983: 192). Rich's essay articulated the significance of lesbian sexuality and its cultural invisibility and had a profound impact on the approach of many women historians. Interestingly, the trend now is generally to reject or negate the idea of an essentialist sexual experience or identity that can be identified through time. Rather, many women historians have become interested in historicising sexual categories and identities and exploring how theories about the sexual body have shaped cultural perceptions of people's sexual identity and practices. Central to much of this work is the medicalisation of sex and the role of scientific theories in the construction of the 'abnormal' sexual body.

The work of Valerie Traub, Theresa Braunschneider and Katherine Park has highlighted how ideas about lesbians (tribades) from the early modern period were explained by recourse to certain 'facts' about their particular genital morphology. In 'Clitoral Corruption: Body Metaphors and American Doctors' Construction of Female Homosexuality, 1870–1900' (1997), Margaret Gibson extended the analysis by exploring the medical construction of the female homosexual in America between 1870 and 1900, a period that witnessed a series of medical theories about 'female inversion'. Gibson argued that by the late nineteenth century the idea of a constitutional deviancy was not limited to the body of the homosexual but corresponded to assumptions about the bodies of lower-class, deviant and non-white women. Gibson concluded that the overlapping nexus between ideas about the female homosexual and other categories of 'deviant' women were literally embedded in ideas about the size of the clitoris (1997: 111). Women historians' interest with constitutional deviancy has also seen some important examinations of the connections between theories of race and the construction of sexual bodies. Anne Fausto-Sterling's contribution to Jennifer Terry and Jaqueline Urla's edited collection *Deviant Bodies: Critical Perspectives on*

Difference in Science and Popular Culture (1995), on Sarah Bartman the 'Hottentot Venus', examined the significance and meanings nineteenth-century comparative anatomists accorded to the appearance of Bartman's clitoris, pelvis and breasts. Fausto-Sterling illustrated how the presentation of Bartman's sexual body was used and taken as proof of the inherent uncontrollable sexuality of the primitive female and epitomised scientific attempts to find distinct morphological characteristics that proved the existence of racial boundaries between black and white women's sexual bodies.

Many historians accept that understanding and negotiating the relationship between an individual subject and their social context is not easy. The focus on people's experience of their body and sexuality, as opposed to discourse, requires a great deal of conjecture by the historian, and for this reason has been criticised for projecting contemporary values and desires into the historical narrative. The challenge for many women historians remains finding ways in which history can account for the experience and construction of subjectivity in a manner not deterministic or voluntaristic, yet without dismissing the power of discourse within people's lives. Current trends towards pursuing the uneven, discontinuous and contradictory in historical discussions and representations of sexuality and the body reflect the desire of many women historians to challenge the idea of a seamless continuity between discourse and practice. Rather than seeking consensus, many historians are concerned with a sense of plurality and rupture as a way of attempting to reflect a more realistic sense of people's experiences and engagement with discourse. There is also an increasing concern with moving away from isolating changes to the history of discourses about the body and sexuality to particular periods and events and, instead, emphasising the persistence and co-existence of conceptions and beliefs across historical periods.

One glaring omission from women historians' work on the body and sexuality has been the lack of analysis on the way that men experienced their bodies and sexual difference. In some ways this is inevitable given the legacy of the conflation of 'the body' with the feminine and woman as 'the sex'. Yet what women historians are starting to appreciate is that much of what was written about the female body and women's sexuality can actually be read as about masculinity. This realisation appears to be gaining increasing attention among more recent women graduates who are looking at the evidence anew, seeing not simply a history of women, but a story of men's precarious relationship to their body and their sexual subjectivity, especially a pervasive sense of anxiety. Such scholarship suggests that despite the wealth of history on the body and sexuality produced over the last 30 years by women historians, much of the history of sexuality and the body remains yet to be explored.

Clair Scrine

References

Bland 1995; Braunschneider 1999; Davidoff 1983; Digby 1989; DuBois & Gordon 1984; Epstein & Straub 1991; Fausto-Sterling 1995; Fee 1976; Gallagher & Laqueur 1987; Gibson 1997; Jacobus *et al.*, 1990; Jordanova 1989; Jeffreys 1983; Millet 1970; Park 1997; Rich 1983; Roper 1994; Showalter 1985; Smith-Rosenberg 1973; Traub 1995; Wood 1973.

Related essays

Feminism; Revolution; Science.

Brittain, Vera Mary 1893–1970

English journalist, novelist, autobiographer, historian of women. Daughter of Arthur Brittain, a paper manufacturer, and

Edith Mary (Bervon). She had one brother, Edward, to whom she was very close. Hers was an affluent and conservative middle-class family, whose conventional life, first in Staffordshire and then in Buxton, she found suffocating. She attended the Grange School in Buxton before becoming a boarder at St Monica's, a new school in Kingswood, Surrey, that offered a solid, well-rounded education rather than stressing purely social 'feminine' attainments. She still required coaching to pass the Oxford University entrance examinations, but was awarded a Somerville College exhibition to study English literature in 1914. Before going to Oxford, she had met Roland Leighton, a close friend of her brother, who introduced her to the writings of Olive Schreiner and to whom she became engaged. Brittain's university life was interrupted by the outbreak of war: as Roland Leighton and her brother and his friends began to volunteer for military service, she felt that she too must relinquish her studies to assist in the war effort. In 1915 she became a nursing assistant and then applied to join the voluntary aid detachment through which she was sent to France – until her parents decided that she was needed back home in 1918. The War brought her great personal loss as both Leighton and her brother Edward were killed. In 1919, Brittain returned to Somerville to read History – feeling a need to understand how the war had happened, and how and why her generation had agreed to be used and slaughtered. She met Winifred Holtby, with whom she set up house in London in 1921, and who became a central and integral part of her life. She married a political scientist, George Catlin, with whom she had an unconventional relationship as he taught at Cornell University in New York State for many years, while she remained based in London, continuing often to share her home with Holtby. She had two children: John Edward Brittain-Catlin and, in 1930, Shirley Vivian (who became the MP Shirley Williams).

The story of Brittain's life is important, because it provided the focus and subject matter for her most significant historical work, the autobiography *Testament of Youth: An Autobiographical Study of the Years 1900–1925* (1933), which was and remains one of the most graphic and moving accounts of a woman's experience of the First World War. It provides both a personal account and a history of Brittain and her generation, including an analysis of the ways in which the war divided men and women, the impact of the War on morals and mores, and of the ways in which it brought greater freedoms for women in terms of both sexual knowledge and the ending of Victorian customs. This was followed by a number of other autobiographical volumes: *Testament of Friendship: The Story of Winifred Holtby* (1940), in which she dealt extensively with Holtby's War experience and the ways in which her life had been played out against the wider changes in British society. This in turn was followed by *Testament of Experience: An Autobiographical Story of the Years 1925–1950* (1957). She also published an early work of women's history, *Lady into Woman: A History of Women from Victoria to Elizabeth II* (1960), which traced what she saw as 'the revolutionary changes brought by this century to the position of women' in terms of their recognition as equal citizens with men, a view that was easily sustained in a text that dealt only with the lives of middle-class white women. Brittain felt that there was still a long way to go before 'women's values in social and political thinking' were adequately incorporated into the social and political order. Brittain attempted also to explore recent historical developments in her novels, most notably, *Honourable Estate: A Novel of Transition* (1936), a family saga based on the recent history of the Brittain and Catlin families and in which she dealt with questions of feminism, pacifism and contemporary history (see **Peace** essay). In addition, she published *Women at Oxford: A Fragment of History* (1960), *Pethick-Lawrence: A Portrait* (1963) and *The Rebel Passion: A Short History of Some Pioneer Peacemakers* (1964). But nothing else that she wrote approached the importance or popularity of *Testament of Youth*.

Barbara Caine

References

Berry & Bostridge 1995; Gorham 1996.

Major work

Testament of Youth (London: Fontana, 1979) with Preface by Shirley Williams.

Butler, Josephine Elizabeth 1828–1906

English social reformer and women's activist. Born at Milfield Hill, Glendale, Northumberland, Josephine was the fourth daughter and seventh child of Hannah Eliza (Annett), and John Grey. Except for two years at a school in Newcastle, Josephine was educated at home. In late adolescence, she suffered an intense religious crisis, apparently because while she felt called to some great mission, she could not yet envisage exactly what it was. In 1852 Josephine Grey married George Butler, a university teacher and Anglican clergyman.

During the late 1860s Butler became increasingly involved in the campaign for women's rights. She signed the petition for women's suffrage presented to parliament by John Stuart Mill in 1866, served as president of the North of England Council for Promoting the Higher Education of Women (1867–1873), petitioned Cambridge in 1868 to provide special examinations for women and joined the Married Women's Property Committee, remaining on it until the passage of the Married Women's Property Act of 1882. In 1869 she became involved in her major cause by becoming honorary secretary of the Ladies National Association for the Repeal of the Contagious Diseases Acts.

Butler wrote extensively on education and employment, often making clear her sense that the current situation of women reflected a decline in their status that followed from the ways in which industrialisation and the separation of home and work place had reduced the range of activities in which women were involved. In *Women's Work and Women's Culture* (1869) she suggested that women were victims of a 'transitional' period of industrialisation, 'stranded' by the elimination of many of their traditional employments while being prohibited from pursuing new opportunities.

In addition to this, Butler wrote a great deal on the recent history of her own family, all of which serves both to explain the background and context of her feminist involvement and to link it to an historical liberal tradition. The first of these, *Memoir of John Grey of Dilston* (1869), dealt with her father. This was followed by a book about her husband, *Recollections of George Butler* (1892) and finally one about her favourite sister, *In Memoriam Harriet Meuricoffre* (1901). She also wrote her own version of the history of the movement against the Contagious Diseases Acts, *Personal Reminiscences of a Great Crusade* (1896).

Alongside this contemporary history, Butler wrote a biography of the fourteenth-century saint, *Catherine of Sienna* (1878). Her desire to establish historical roots and traditions for herself is evident in this work too, with its celebration of Catherine as a pioneering example of a female activist and Christian mystic. She identified herself with Catherine's struggle to carve out a public role for herself, and sought also to draw a connection between the problems Catherine saw in Medieval Sienna and those of Victorian Britain.

Long seen as the most sympathetic and interesting of Victorian feminists, Butler has recently been subjected to extensive critical analysis because of her imperialist leanings. In regard to India, for example, while condemning the cantonment regulations which imposed even more severe conditions on Indian women deemed to be prostitutes than had obtained in Britain under the Contagious Diseases Acts, she continued to defend Britain's imperial destiny and to argue that British feminists had a special imperial mission of representing female colonial subjects that paralleled their special role in representing the interests and sufferings of poor women within the nation. Taking this argument even further in the case of South Africa, Butler strongly defended the British part in the Anglo-Boer War against all critics. In *Native Races and the War* (1900), while acknowledging the ruthlessness and ambition of Rhodes and Jameson, and the ill-treatment of some 'natives' by individual settlers, she stated her firm belief that England remained the best of nations – and the one most committed to the care of and regard for those without rights.

Butler wrote *An Autobiographical Memoir* (1909), which was published posthumously. She has been the subject of several biographies, including Jane Jordan's recent study *Josephine Butler* (2001).

Barbara Caine

References

Burton 1998; Caine 1992; Walkowitz 1980.

C

Cam, Helen Maud 1885–1968

English medievalist. One of nine children of Kate (Scott) and the Reverend William Herbert Cam, headmaster of Roysse's School. Educated at home. Awarded an open scholarship to Royal Holloway in 1904, Cam took out a first class honours degree in History in 1907. Won a research fellowship at Bryn Mawr in 1908, where she took advanced classes in Anglo-Saxon and became immersed in American history. Unable to find employment in the academy upon her return to England in 1909, Cam taught at the Cheltenham Ladies College until 1912, when she was offered a lectureship at Royal Holloway. Moved to Girton College as a Pfeiffer Research Fellow in 1921. Elected to a Staff Fellowship in 1927, Cam was also appointed to a university lecturership in that year. Keenly committed to the cause of adult education, Cam also lectured at the Hillcroft College for Working Women. Became Director of Studies in History at Girton in 1940. Elected Fellow of the British Academy in 1948, the same year she became the first woman professor in the faculty of Arts and Sciences at Harvard when she was appointed Zemurray Radcliffe Professor in history, a position she held until her retirement in 1954. She was elected a Fellow of the British Academy in 1945 and was the first woman to deliver the Raleigh lecture to that body. She was also the first woman to become a member of the Selden Society. Became President of the International Commission for the History of Representative and Parliamentary Institutions and in 1957 was awarded a Commander of the British Empire. In 1962 she received an honorary

LittD from Oxford University and was made an honorary fellow of Somerville College in 1964.

The suffrage agitation caused Cam to examine the basis of political rights and she became an ardent supporter of womanhood suffrage and lectured on this subject. A lifelong member of the Labour Party and committed socialist, Cam stood for election to County Council in 1928. The workings of local government were her primary historical focus and much of her writing is devoted to the subject of medieval local government. Her first major work *Local Government in Francia and England* (1912) was published from her MA thesis. *Studies in the Hundred Rolls* (1921) was published as part of Paul Vinogradoff's *Oxford Studies in Social and Legal History*. She became Britain's foremost expert on the Hundred Rolls, publishing *The Hundred and the Hundred Rolls* (1930). In 1944 she published *Liberties and Communities in Medieval England*, a collection of her articles. She also wrote popular history such as *England Before Elizabeth* (1950) and a study of historical fiction, *Historical Novels* (1961), for the Historical Association. Her contribution to the field of medieval history was honoured with a festschrift prepared by scholars from 13 countries, which was published as *Album Helen Cam* in 1960.

Mary Spongberg

Reference

Sondheimer 1996.

Canada

In late August of 1940, a flurry of phone calls and telegrams passed between Chester New, of McMaster University in Hamilton, Ontario, and Margaret Anchoretta Ormsby, then living with her family in rural British Columbia. Professor New was hoping that Dr Ormsby could hang in for a few more days, while he sought permission from the elusive chancellor of his university to hire her as an instructor in the Department of History. In an interview much later, Ormsby explained New's problem. McMaster was a Baptist institution and Ormsby was an Anglican. McMaster expected its staff to be dry; Dr Ormsby enjoyed a glass of sherry. Eventually, both parties came to an understanding. Ormsby would not drink in public and she would attend Baptist religious observances on campus. Later, she recalled regaling McMaster faculty and students with one or two 'good Anglican sermons.' But she stuck to her agreement regarding alcohol while in Hamilton, although one might imagine her being driven to drink; her office during the years she worked for McMaster was a table in the ladies' washroom (Boutilier and Prentice 1997; Prentice 1997).

The hiring of Margaret Ormsby by McMaster marked a shift in the history of women historians in Canada. Although women taught in English-Canadian university history departments during the early decades of the twentieth century, their positions were never sufficiently secure to support them as writers of history; few, if any, held their jobs for more than a decade. Just after the First World War, for example, New Brunswick-born Latin-Americanist Vera Brown [Holmes] taught at McGill, the major Anglophone university in the province of Quebec, while she completed her Bryn Mawr doctorate. But for permanent employment Brown had to look south. It was at an American college for women that she made her career and composed her innovative volumes on the history of the Americas. More than a decade after Brown's departure from McGill, its chairman of history told Sylvia Thrupp that the men in his department would never hire another woman. They had once had one 'whom they didn't like' and planned never to take the risk again. A medievalist trained at the University of London, Thrupp taught for ten years at her alma mater, the University of British Columbia, but by 1945 she too had decamped to the US where a brilliant future as a social and economic historian awaited her (Prentice 1997). In the meantime, UBC had invited Margaret Ormsby back to her home province and university, giving her a job that would become permanent and support her studies in federal–provincial relations and the tensions between hinterland and metropolis in the social, political and economic history of British Columbia (Norris 1976–1977). At about the same time, the University of Saskatchewan made space for a contemporary, hiring former student, Hilda Neatby, to pursue her interests in the history of post-conquest French Canada. Although not uninterested in national history, grand narratives or big questions, for a variety of reasons – and like many Canadian women historians who preceded or would follow them – both Neatby and Ormsby made their historical reputations as regionalists (Norris 1976–1977; Hayden 1983).

These stories of early academic women suggest some patterns. Clearly, the interwar years saw a growing number of women pursuing graduate degrees in history and seeking employment in universities. Because western Canadian institutions had greater difficulty getting staff than older, eastern ones, they were more open to the idea of hiring women. It was their undergraduate universities that eventually engaged Ormsby and Neatby on a permanent basis. When, in the mid-1960s, both women had been elected to the presidency of the Canadian Historical Association – the first to be so honoured – we might say that women historians had made their mark in the academy. But therein lies a question: Has academic belonging been the most useful or stimulating route to the writing of history for Canadian women?

Learning our mysteries

It certainly has not been the only route. Canada had a significant recorded history long before Anglophone populations spread across the continent. British imperialism eventually put a particular cultural stamp on the territories that would become Canada, but would never entirely engulf either its indigenous or the earlier arriving Francophone peoples, let alone the many other cultures that eventually created the nation. Women contributed to the historical enterprise long before their employment by university history departments. If we include under the heading 'historical writing' the recording of contemporary events, women were involved from the seventeenth century. In New France, the founder of the Quebec Ursulines, Mother Marie Guyart de l'Incarnation, was the most famous of many female recorders of history. The writer of countless letters to France, she documented and sometimes analysed the extraordinary daily history of herself, her sisters in religion, her aboriginal and non-aboriginal students and the life of the settlement in which they all lived (Marshall 1967). Part of a tradition in which women religious had long written, sometimes for relatives, but more often for the members of their congregations or their ecclesiastical superiors, Marie de l'Incarnation observed that 'writing teaches us our mysteries'. As Elizabeth Smyth has pointed out, most religious women wrote 'under obedience', to preserve their own histories in convent annals and countless other documents that their superiors required them to create, not only in New France but in French and English convent communities that would continue to flourish in British North America and then Canada (Smyth 1997). But Marie de l'Incarnation's truth held, for in writing for any public the writer teaches herself as much as she teaches others.

Women religious wrote history within a structure. Their convents educated them and supported, as well as ordering, their historical writing. Married or single laywomen who wrote history had different sources of support but, of necessity, they too were embedded in structures that sustained their work. Catharine Parr Traill and Susanna Moodie (see **Strickland**), who emigrated to Upper Canada from England early in the nineteenth century and achieved considerable renown for their reports on life in British North America, came from a family of writers that included their older sister historians Agnes and Elizabeth. Educated at home by their father, in British North America they were supported by a settler community that included a well-established brother and husbands who offered moral if not always steady financial support. Their works, which supplemented family income, were very different from the letters and annals of convent women, but significant contemporary histories nonetheless, written chiefly for a British audience. Just as convent writings became rich sources for later historians, so the writings of these sisters would long be mined for their insights into life in British North America (Gray 1999).

Women diarists, letter writers and essayists had been writing in the Atlantic colonies of British North America since the late eighteenth century and for similar reasons: the need to explore and sometimes tell others about their lives in a new country. Like Traill and Moodie, such women were educated and wrote from a domestic base. Rebecca Byles, who came to Nova Scotia from Boston in 1776 with her loyalist clergyman father, mother and siblings, was taught at home in Halifax, as well as in small private schools, before attending a ladies' academy. For over 50 years, she wrote to two aunts who remained in Boston, describing life in a colony that, unlike their own, had remained part of the British Empire. These letters reveal Rebecca questioning, among other things, the annoyances caused by the Revolutionary War or, later, the growing number of British women authors in print. Perhaps she had a literary bent herself. Was it wise for women to write for public consumption? She reported on her extensive reading, the marriage market in Halifax and her own marriage. Her writings did not see print during her lifetime, but they left much for future historians to ponder (Conrad *et al.* 1988).

Marie de l'Incarnation, Catharine Parr Traill, Susanna Moodie and Rebecca Byles had no sense of vocation as historians; if they saw themselves as 'writers', it was as storytellers, recorders or commentators on their times. Although their letters may have circulated widely, two of the four were not published in the formal sense. But all reported and occasionally critiqued the daily domestic round, the doings of their friends and families, and the larger social, religious, political, economic and intellectual worlds in which they lived. These historians of contemporary life were also politically motivated. They wrote about power, about how things worked in their new environments, and they took a stance on the issues of the day.

For convent women, the power in history was divine providence. If struggles were sent to them, they were tested; if their congregations survived and prospered, this was God's work. It was important to tell this story to themselves and to others (Smyth 1997). The laywomen who wrote of lives lived in the colonies of British North America had different motives. They wrote, in some cases to maintain networks with friends and relatives, in others to inform a larger public. However, they too wrote of their struggles: with themselves, with strange neighbours, with children who chose paths they had not sanctioned, or the power of the wilderness. Byles' stance, in the end, was a defence of loyalism and tradition, while Traill and Moodie wrote partly to warn other British women of the perils that awaited emigrants. If lay writers referred less to divine providence than did their sisters in religion, they nevertheless documented their ultimately successful settlement and the continuation of the generations. Despite many challenges, these women had survived in what, to them, was a challenging new country.

The past as another country

The shift to writing about *the past* as another country occurred for Canadian women in the second half of the nineteenth century. In 1867 the British North American colonies of Nova Scotia, New Brunswick, Lower Canada (now renamed Quebec) and Upper Canada (newly named Ontario) had joined in Confederation; later the annexation of more provinces and territories would extend Canada from coast to coast. The birth of the new nation prompted explorations of its imperial origins and 'national' heritage or heritages. Early exemplars of this wave of historical writing are two almost contemporary Ontario women: Agnes Maule Machar and Sarah Curzon. Machar, the daughter of a Presbyterian clergyman, grew up and lived most of her long life in the town of Kingston, where her father was for a time principal of Queen's University. Turning as a young, single woman to writing as her vocation, she eventually won considerable acclaim as an essayist, journalist, poet and author of historical fiction for children. Curzon, a married British immigrant who probably settled in Toronto in the middle 1860s, was the mother of a grown daughter when she took up historical writing in the 1880s. Machar undoubtedly earned money for her work, but depended chiefly on her parental family for financial security; in contrast, Curzon may have turned to writing to help restore family fortunes (Boutilier 1997; Hallman 1997).

Political motivation is clear in the work of both. Machar began with family and neighbourhood stories, but soon shifted to the larger community of the emergent Canadian nation. Her writings promoted British patriotism, friendly attitudes towards the Francophone peoples of Canada, the higher education of women and civic virtue. Curzon too saw history as a vehicle for inspiring love of both Canada and the Empire. But she also wrote for the community of women. An activist involved not only in the struggle for women's admission to universities, but also in the more controversial struggle for women's suffrage, in 1895 Curzon was the co-founder and first president of the Canadian Women's Historical Society of Toronto, through which she hoped more women would become involved in the creation of historical memory. Her play *Laura Secord, the Heroine of 1812* (1887) proclaimed the importance of women's labours to the development of empire and nation. The imperialist and nationalist educational concerns of Machar and Curzon would be echoed across the country, particularly among early twentieth-century women teachers who wrote history texts for Canadian schools (Boutilier 1997). An entirely different tack was taken by the extraordinary teacher-historian from Toronto, Florence Deeks, who dreamed of writing **world history** as an *antidote* to nationalism. Penned just before the First World War, Deeks' history of the western world would have showcased women's roles in a variety of settings. It never saw publication, however, and may have been plagiarised by H G Wells (McKillop 2000).

Of the generation of women writing imperial and national history who laboured in the first half of the twentieth century, **Isabel Skelton** stands out as a follower of Curzon in emphasising the work accomplished by pioneer women and other heroic female figures from Canada's past. Skelton's classic *Backwoodswoman* was published in 1924. Foreshadowing cultural history, this volume linked the exceptional women of New France with less famous female pioneers of later settlements. Few women were to be found in Canadian history books, she noted. 'Yet in all save the earliest years they have formed nearly half the population and have done almost half the work' (Skelton 1924: 7). If she criticised male historians for neglecting the history of women and the family, she also scrutinised Susanna Moodie's and Catharine Parr Traill's complaints about pioneer life. Their class position, she argued, had blinded them to the far greater difficulties and tragedies endured by Canada's backwoods poor. *Backwoodswoman* would now be seen as unduly celebratory, but it reflected the historical writing of her period. On its publication, Skelton turned to biography, again focusing on the ordinary as well as the exceptional, and writing in the midst of a family life that became increasingly complicated and demanding (Crowley 1997, 2003).

Skelton and Deeks aspired to national and international themes, but most Canadian women writing history in the first half of the twentieth century focused on their own regions. In Quebec, women religious began to publish multi-volume histories of their congregations. Hagiographic in that they emphasised the sterling qualities of founders and leading figures, some were nevertheless grounded in meticulous research and met the scholarly standards of their day. Sister Henriette (Darie Lemyre-Marsolais) published the first of 11 volumes that became known as Histoire de la Congrégation de Notre-Dame de Montréal (1910–1974). In this and subsequent volumes she explored her community's economic concerns and occasional battles with male ecclesiastics as well as its religious odyssey. In frequently vibrant prose, she demonstrated the strength of women who not only dealt with serious financial matters, but also stood up to bishops. In two volumes published in the 1920s, Mère Marie-Antoinette (previous name unknown) examined the lay charities in nineteenth-century Montreal that were the basis of her community. In her four-volume *L'Institut de la Providence: Histoire des Filles de la Charitè, servantes des pauvres, des Soeurs de la Providence* (1925–1928) power struggles involving women and ecclesiastical authorities can be read between the lines; once again the religious who engaged in these struggles emerge as heroines of the story (Jammal 1999).

Laywomen exploring Quebec's history were similarly productive and provocative. Librarian Marie-Claire Daveluy's *L'Orphelinat catholique de Montréal*, the history of a Montreal orphanage founded in 1832, is dated 1919, while journalist Eve Circé-Côté's *Papineau: son influence sur la penseé Canadienne*, her first historical work and a psychological study of the patriot, was published in 1924. From 1919 until her death, Daveluy produced a steady stream of lyrical histories and romantic novels set in Quebec's recent and distant past. Both of these historians were Francophone as well as Canadian nationalists. Although Circé-Côté's work had the more critical edge, she rejected clericalism only to embrace the liberal secularism that opposed it (Jammal 1999).

Perhaps the most committed of the regional historians was Constance Lindsay Skinner. Raised in the interior of British Columbia, Skinner eventually made a living from writing although, to do so, she had to move to New York City and take up American subjects. The wildly successful *Chronicles of Canada* (which employed only one woman – the Ontario writer Agnes Laut, author of *The Cariboo Trail,* (1916) inspired its publisher to create the similar *Chronicles of America.* Its editor reached out to several women writers, one of whom was Skinner, by then a well-known journalist. Drawing on her childhood experience of pioneer life in Canada, she produced two stunning volumes pioneers of the Old Southwest (1919) and, *Adventures of Oregon: A Chronicle of the Fur Trade* (1920). Skinner not only knew how to write but also had a strong aversion to dullness or prejudice in historical writing. 'American written history . . . has no vitality in it because it is not literature', she complained. 'It is dead stuff because the drama of human souls has been left out of it.' Constance Skinner eventually made enough money from her *Chronicles* to pay the rent, continuing to publish essays, reviews, poetry, short stories, historical fiction for juveniles and works of popular history, much of the latter two categories set in the Canadian Northwest. Continuing her regional focus, she also planned the Rivers of America series, which was an enormous success, although she lived to see only one of its volumes in print (Barman 1997, 2002).

Amateurs to professionals

Skinner died in 1939. It was early in the same decade that Margaret Ormsby and Sylvia Thrupp had written the University of British Columbia's first MA theses dealing with the history of Canada's most western province. Surrounded by other women students with similar interests and much encouraged by the provincial archivist, D C Harvey, they were participating in an important national trend. Harvey's move to the Nova Scotia Archives in 1931 coincided with – or perhaps initiated – similar developments in Eastern Canada. Margaret Ells was one of his earliest protégées, but the best known was Phyllis Blakeley who eventually rose to the position of provincial archivist herself. Blakeley's published studies began to appear in the 1940s and ranged widely over the social, economic and cultural history of her region. Her history encompassed Black loyalists, as well as early Nova Scotian music and musicians, women literary figures and the Mi'kmaq First Nation (Duff 1987). By the 1950s, she and Margaret Ormsby were corresponding in connection with the local history committee of the Canadian Historical Association.

The most renowned of the Maritimes regionalists was New Brunswick historian Esther Clark Wright. Educated during the First World War at Acadia University, Wright took some time to find her métier. Liberated from responsibilities at home in Fredericton by her marriage to a British scholar, Wright at first dedicated herself to the support of her husband's academic career. But when this failed, she determined to pursue her own scholarly interests. With a Harvard doctorate in economic history and family wealth ensuring her financial independence, Wright was able to devote the second half of a long life to writing widely acclaimed books and essays on the economic and social history of her region. Her studies were grounded in archival and statistical research that was often innovative. She also contributed *The St John River* (1949) to the Rivers of America series initiated by Constance Skinner. Commenting on her life's work in 1968, Esther Clark Wright declared that her histories dealt not only with place, but with people: where they came from, what they did and how they lived (Townsend 1990; Moody 1997).

A little younger than Wright, Irene Biss Spry travelled an even more circuitous route to a career in Canadian regional history. Born in Africa and educated at the University of London when women historians like **Eileen Power** were making their mark, she pursued further economic studies at Cambridge and an MA in social research and social work at Bryn Mawr, before moving to a doctoral programme at the University of Toronto under the economic historian Harold Innis. Marriage and the Second World War ended the doctorate, but not Spry's studies, to which she eventually returned. *The Palliser Expedition* (1963) among other innovative works significantly altered how historians viewed the fur trade and influenced a whole generation of younger historians. Although, like Esther Clark Wright, Spry did some university teaching, for most of her career she was an independent scholar, dedicating time and energy to conservation and international rural women's movements, as well as to history (Friesen 1985).

In 1969 J M S Careless noted that 'limited' rather than national identities were becoming a significant feature of Canadian historiography (Careless 1969). Men like Careless and D C Harvey joined the women scholars who framed Canadian history more broadly and regionally than most male historians of their time. These women and men sympathised with the many equally passionately engaged but 'amateur' local historians writing during the same period. Many of the latter were women who concerned themselves with the histories of their own villages, towns and counties. Such women looked self-consciously at the past, gathering up fast-disappearing evidence, with agendas less ambitious but otherwise similar to those of Esther Clark Wright: to find out who they and their neighbours were, where they had come from, what they had built and perhaps why. Some worked under the auspices of Canadian-born, rural organisations known as the Women's Institutes. They explored the methods of modern historical scholarship, but most chafed at the criticisms of their work that university-based historians offered. Community, not professional scholarship, was their basic concern (Ambrose 1997).

By the late 1940s and 1950s, women historians were also working thematically. In the Atlantic provinces, for example, mature-aged student Katherine MacNaughton turned her University of New Brunswick master's thesis in educational history into the first sophisticated history of a provincial school system, *The Development of the Theory and Practice of Education in New Brunswick* (1947). In Ontario, Mary Quayle Innis snatched time from a busy life supporting the career of her husband and raising their four children to launch her scholarly career. Almost all her edited works dealt with the history of Canadian women's paid and voluntary work. Her own research and writing resulted in the first history of the Canadian Young Women's Christian Association, *Unfold the Years* (1949).

Innis' focus on women's employment, and on subjects that were national in scope, foreshadowed much that was to come. The first major study of the history of the suffrage movement in Canada grew out of an American PhD thesis, but the third quarter of the twentieth century finally saw enough women taking doctoral degrees to initiate a new era in Canadian historical writing. Ontario-born Margaret Prang was among the first of this new generation of women who moved into the academy to do their work. Launching her career in the late 1940s in political and social history, she would become chair of the UBC History Department and be elected as the third woman president of the Canadian Historical Association for 1976–1977. In her later years, Prang published important work in the history of Canadian women and religion. In Québec Louise Dechêne was beginning her penetrating historical explorations, drawing on the approach of the *Annales* school and, at the same time, transforming it. Her pioneering volume on the social history of Montreal *Habitants et marchands de Montréal au XVIIe siecle* (1974) was acknowledged from the outset as a classic. The erudition of her later *Le partage des subsistances* (1994) which explored the imperial and institutional history of that colony in the eighteenth century ensured her reputation as the pre-eminent historian of New France in her generation. Equally at home in demographic, economic, legal and institutional history, she was an inspiration to many younger historians both in and outside of Quebec.

Women historians and women's history

By the late 1960s and the 1970s the number of women starting academic careers in history had expanded so significantly that listing individual women and their areas of interest becomes problematic. It seems important, however, to name women whose work reflected the emergence of second-wave feminism in Canada and who wrote the first doctoral theses in the history of women. Veronica Strong-Boag and Wendy Mitchinson tackled the history of late nineteenth- and early twentieth-century Canadian women's organisations. Their work was echoed in that of contemporaries specialising in British history. Kathleen McCrone was encouraged by Hilda Neatby to explore the history of British women and sport; later Deborah Gorham's PhD examined the history of women and education in Britain. Ruth Pierson, another contemporary, came to Canada with a doctorate in German history, but by the late 1970s had shifted her focus publishing innovative studies in Canadian history such as *'They're Still Women After All': The Second World War and Canadian Womanhood* (1986). Although many of them would turn to other topics, at this time national themes and institutions attracted these historians. However, during the same period other academically oriented women continued to work regionally – and many of the new regional historians were also historians of women. Reflecting the labour history movement, which emerged at about the same time as the women's history movement, and frequently Marxist in outlook, they often dedicated themselves to the history of women's work, activists sometimes joining them in this endeavour. In Ontario, for example, an activist collective put together a volume of essays entitled *Women at Work, Ontario 1850–1950* (1974). Another early thesis writer in women's history, Sylvia Van Kirk, analysed the labours and family systems of women in the western British North American fur trade, opening up not just a new field in the history of women's work but also the history of Aboriginal and Metis women. Her *'Many Tender Ties': Women in Fur-Trade Society* (1980) would become a classic. In Québec, Marie Lavigne and Jennifer Stoddart co-authored a master's thesis and articles exploring the history of women's work in that province, while Suzanne Cross focused on women's employment in industrialising Montréal (See Pedersen 1996). Micheline Dumont and Nadia Fahmy-Eid were soon to begin their pioneering studies in the history of women's work in education and religion (*Maîtresses de maison, maitresses d'école* 1983), eventually attracting a large following of students to these fields.

In the meantime, women Canadianists were exploring many other themes. Some, like Susan Houston and myself wrote on the history of education, *Schooling and Scholars in Nineteenth-Century Ontario* (1988). Susan Mann Trofimenkoff's *The Dream of A Nation* (1982) explored the intellectual history of Quebec; Barbara Roberts' *Whence They Came* (1988) examined the history of immigration and ethnicity; and Joy Parr's

The Gender of Breadwinners (1990) presented an innovative perspective on Canadian labour history. Nova Scotia historian Margaret Conrad worked on political subjects publishing *George Nowlan: Maritime Conservative in National Politics* in 1986. But as we have seen, women historians were also by no means wedded only to the history of Canada, although some who were initially or chiefly historians of other countries were sometimes attracted to it, just as historians working in other fields were often drawn to women's history. From a general history of women in the European and western tradition (1982) Mary Kinnear moved to Canadian subjects, penning among other works an important study of the gendering of the professions in Manitoba (1995) (see **Education**). Margaret Macmillan's early research focused on women of the British Raj; her study of international peace-making, *Paris 1919* (2003), encompassed the world.

There were significant efforts in the 1970s and early 1980s to publish documentary studies in Canadian women's history and there were also efforts at synthesis. In the mid-1970s Naomi Griffiths took time from her studies in the history of the Acadians to pen an influential volume of reflections on the history of women in Europe and Canada entitled *Penelope's Web* (1976). There were also collectively authored or edited works. One of the most innovative and influential was *L'Histoire des femmes au Québec depuis quatre siècles* (1982) whose four authors identified themselves as the *Collectif Clio*. With these exceptions, Canadian women scholars have perhaps not been involved in synthesis as much as historians of other nations have been. Just as it took four women to produce the first history of women in Québec, it took a collective of six (Alison Prentice, Paula Bourne, Gail Cuthbert Brandt, Beth Light, Wendy Mitchinson and Naomi Black) to create the first general history of women in Canada as a whole, *Canadian Women: A History* (1988). Who can define a '**nation**' of women, when that nation has been characterised by linguistic, cultural, racial and regional diversity from the beginning – let alone try to synthesise it? Much Canadian women's historical work has explored relatively finite subjects and appeared in article form in journals or collections of essays, rather than as monographs possibly for the same reason. Regionalist approaches, in particular, may dominate because women historians juggle the financial and family costs of travelling to distant archives.

First and other nations

Perhaps Olive Patricia Dickason's story best illustrates women's passion for history overcoming such obstacles. The daughter of a First Nations woman, Dickason worked as a highly successful journalist and raised three daughters before she could pursue her scholarly dreams. Her education during the interwar years included correspondence school, the run of a neighbour's library in the northern Manitoba bush and, eventually, a Roman Catholic seminary in Saskatchewan that granted degrees from the University of Ottawa. But it was decades before she could attend that university in person to earn her doctorate. Her advanced age when she completed her PhD did not stop her from obtaining a post at the University of Alberta, however, and becoming the much-loved author of the classic *Canada's First Nations* (1992). Nor did compulsory retirement, which she fought all the way to the Supreme Court of Canada, stop Dickason. Her contributions continued to pour out long after she reached the magic age of 65.

As Dickason's story suggests, in the late 1980s, 1990s and early years of the twenty-first century, many of the historians mentioned above, along with their colleagues and younger women, explored topics that previous generations had all but ignored. Many took to gender studies and investigated post-modernist approaches to history. They introduced sexuality, the body, peace and war, race and religion, to historical studies that for too long had ignored or marginalised these topics. As a result we have studies by women historians in the history of medicine, psychiatry and pacifism, as well as in the history of First Nations and Blacks in Canada. Works of note in the last two fields include Veronica Strong-Boag and Carole Gerson's brilliant reappraisal of Mohawk writer E Pauline Johnson's historical and literary oeuvre, *Paddling Her Own Canoe* (2000) and the innovative and multi-authored (Peggy Bristow, Dionne Brand, Linda Carty, Afua P Cooper, Sylvia Hamilton and Adrienne Shadd) *'We're Rooted Here and They Can't Pull Us Up'* (1994) exploring the history of African-Canadian women.

Sojourning Sisters (2003), a recent study by Jean Barman of two school-teaching sisters who migrated from Nova Scotia to British Columbia in the 1880s, recalls Isabel Skelton's work but with many new – and sometimes painful – understandings. Barman reveals the imperialist/colonial ethos, the exclusions of First Nations and mixed blood neighbours and other prejudices that Jessie and Annie McQueen embodied, as well as the more positive work they did towards the domestication of western Canada. The building of the Canadian nation, she argues, involved the labour of such ordinary women, in their case, women who brought the gendered understandings of an eastern Canadian farm community and a particular brand of Protestantism to the creation of settler society in the west. As Barman's focus on women teachers and this essay suggest, we have become increasingly involved in histories of women's work in the professions and recently 'historian' has been added to the list.

Which leads us back to Margaret Ormsby and her contemporaries and followers. With their entry into the academy, women historians adopted practices laid down for the men of the profession. What have women gained – or lost – in the professionalisation of their historical work? One thing that has been gained is institutional support, although we are still by no means as well supported in the academy as men. Women like Margaret Ormsby, Hilda Neatby, Louise Dechêne and Margaret Prang began a struggle that continues. Nor are the struggles initiated by the women religious or by Sarah Anne Curzon, Isabel Skelton and Mary Quayle Innis resolved, as married and single women continue to snatch time from community or family work for their work in history. Perhaps this accounts for the remarkable number of books that are co-authored, co-edited or collectively produced by Canadian women historians.

Moreover, as bodies of literature expand, the work grows more complex and demanding. Economic history informed the work of Spry and Dechêne and academics participating in the early women's history movement were much influenced by Marxist economic thought – to a degree far greater, for example, than comparable Americans seem to have been. Quantitative approaches added to both the expense and complexity of our studies. But the earlier feminist historians were not unduly burdened by theory and most followed the maxim about clear prose taught to Irene Spry by Eileen Power: namely that one should write for generally literate audiences as well as for other scholars. Have women academics, in addressing theory and complexity, cut themselves off from the larger public, particularly the public of women? Certainly, they are not the only female interpreters of the past, as women who remain outside the academy continue to write vibrant biography, autobiography, family and community history. And what about First Nations women, among others, who speak or sing their history, in preference to writing it? (Cruikshank *et al.* 1991; Ahenakew and Wolfart 1992).

Aboriginal women are among those who call into question the very existence of the Canadian nation, let alone a coherent body of literature by Canadian female historians that might in any way represent them. Yet, they too have increasingly taken to the writing of history, emphasising oral sources, story telling, pictures and their own unique approaches to what constitutes historical truth (Louis 2002; Brown 2003). First Nations and other women have criticised malestream historical practice, just as each generation of historians has critiqued the one before. There is no doubt that we have much to learn from modes other than scholarly writing. There is also no doubt that we are just beginning to understand how Canadian women have explored and conveyed our mysteries through the writing of history.

Alison Prentice

References

Ahenakew & Wolfart 1992; Ambrose 1997; Barman 1997, 2002; Boutilier 1997; Boutilier & Prentice 1997; Brown 2003; Careless 1969; Conrad 1988; Crowley 1997, 2003; Cruikshank 1991; Duff 1987; Friesen 1985; Gray 1999; Hallman 1997; Hayden 1983; Jammal 1990; Louis 2002; Marshall 1967; McKillop 2000; Moody 1997; Norris 1976–1977; Pedersen 1996; Prentice 1997; Smyth 1997; Townsend 1990.

Related essays

Archives; Australia; Convents; Dominions; Great Britain; Local history; Nation United States of America.

Cartwright, Julia 1851–1924

English art critic and historian, biographer and novelist. Born in England, into the Northamptonshire gentry, Cartwright was the third child of Mary Freemantle and Richard Cartwright. Educated largely at home. Married Reverend Henry Ady in 1880. One daughter Cecilia Mary.

A life-long diarist, Cartwright also wrote poetry, art criticism, novels and song lyrics before turning to art history in the 1880s. Her works of art criticism were published in both popular and scholarly journals, and like **Anna Jameson**, whom she admired, her popular writings made Cartwright an influential figure within the Victorian Arts and Crafts movement. In 1881 she published *Mantegna and Francia*, the first of a number of studies of **Renaissance** artists. Around the same time she began to write novels, moral tales for young people, for the Society for Promoting Christian Knowledge (SPCK).

Her first efforts at **female biography** appeared as essays in *Macmillan's Magazine* in the early 1890s. Books from these essays, *Sacharissa*, on Lady Dorothy Sidney and *Madame* on Henrietta Stuart were published in 1893 and 1894. Considered historical 'Romances' by Cartwright, these works were idealised portraits of their subjects, reflecting their image in **art** and literature. Cartwright believed that Sidney and Stuart represented all that was 'fair and excellent in womanhood', and she stressed their virtue and moral influence. Like many courtly **memoirs** produced by women, these works focused on the interior world and were drawn largely from women's private correspondence. The domestic realm would be particularly important to Cartwright's biographical writing, and she familiarised herself with the homes and personal possessions of her subjects.

Her later works *Beatrice d'Este* (1899) and *Isabelle d'Este* (1903) can be read as part of a broader trend to rewrite the Renaissance, led by her friend Vernon Lee and J A Symonds. Cartwright, however, presented a particularly feminised or maternalist view of history, stressing the historical importance of women in the private sphere while simultaneously recovering evidence of women's skills in diplomacy and politics. Cartwright also anticipated later feminist critiques of the **Renaissance**, attributing to women, qualities and powers usually reserved for the men of the period. The quality Cartwright most idealised in her subjects was the desire to educate their children. This was of importance in her own life as well, as she spent much of the money she earned from her writings on educating her daughter **Cecilia Mary Ady**. Ady studied at St Hugh's in Oxford, becoming a major scholar of the Renaissance. Although conservative in her political interests, Cartwright was a strong supporter of the campaigns to allow women full membership to Oxford and Cambridge.

As well as historical works Cartwright also produced a number of studies of contemporary artists such as Edward Burnes-Jones, G F Watts and Jean Francois Millet. In her later years she continued to produce art history and criticism. Following the First World War, she campaigned to restore Italian studies to British universities until her death in 1924.

Mary Spongberg

References

Emanuel 1989; Fraser 1998.

Cary, Elizabeth Lady Falkland 1585–1639

English playwright, translator, poet, historian. Born in Oxfordshire, only child of Elizabeth (Symondes) and Lawrence Tanfield. Taught herself to read 'and loved it much' and was fluent in French, Spanish, Italian, Latin, Hebrew and 'Transylvanian' by 'four or five'. Began her literary career translating Seneca's *Epistles* and Abraham Ortelius's *Le Miroir du Monde*. Displayed precocious interest in religion, disputing Calvin's *Institutes of Christian Religion* while still a child, anticipating her later conversion to Catholicism. Married Sir Henry Cary, Viscount of Falkland, in 1602. Bore eleven children, nine of whom survived to adulthood.

Following their marriage, Henry Cary went to fight in the Low Countries, was captured and imprisoned in Spain. During this time Cary produced several literary works including a verse-biography of Tamburlaine, now lost. Her play *The Tragedy of Mariam* (c. 1609), a Senecan closet drama was drawn from Josephus, whose *Antiquities* had been translated into English by Catholic scholar Thomas Lodge in 1602. The play is unusual for its focus on Mariam, the subject of domestic and political tyranny and for its insistence on a wife's right to speech, public and private. The play alluded to the divorce of Henry VIII from Catherine of Aragon and the split of the Church of England from the Church of Rome.

Throughout her marriage Cary maintained a process of self-education, reading 'History very universally'. She continued to question Protestant theology and disputed with noted clerics. At court she associated with women known for their Catholic sympathies. Cary broke with her husband when her conversion to Catholicism became public in 1626. Abandoned by him and disinherited by her father, she was left destitute until the Privy council intervened. During this period of persecution she wrote verse-biographies of Mary Magdalene, Agnes the Martyr and Elizabeth of Portugal, now lost. She also translated Cardinal Perron's reply to

King James. This work was publicly burned by the Archbishop of Canterbury.

One of her four surviving daughters wrote *The Lady Falkland: Her Life*, one of the first biographies written in English. While hagiographic in intent, it reveals the Lady Falkland as resistant to social mores and patriarchal control. Lady Georgina Fullerton published a biography of Lady Falkland in 1872. More recently she has been the subject of extensive feminist scholarship identifying her as the author of *The History of the Life, Reign and Death of Edward II*, previously attributed to her husband. Written around 1627, the period marking the height of Cary's persecution, the author identified only as 'EF' claims to have written the text 'to out-run those weary hours of a deep and sad passion'. Merging biography and political history, *Edward II* presents a sympathetic portrait of Edward's maligned wife Isabel, giving her great agency in the power struggles around the King and blaming her infidelity on his debauchery.

Mary Spongberg

References

Beilin 1987; Kronitiris 1990; Travisky 1987; Weller & Ferguson 1994.

Major works

The Tragedy of Mariam edited by Barry Weller & Margaret W Ferguson (Berkeley: University of California Press, 1994) includes the biography *The Lady Falkland*.

Catalogs of women

Catalogs originated from catalog verse, a metered or rhymed list organised around a common theme. Catalogs can be found in every genre of literature either appearing alone or as part of another text. Early examples of catalogs are found in the works of Hesiod or in the form of genealogical tables in the Bible. Catalog lists are didactic, presenting moral instruction or rudimentary history lessons (McLeod 1991: 11). As the catalog tradition developed, it purported to transmit conventional wisdom and cultural consensus, drawing on evidence gleaned from a variety of historical and literary sources (McLeod 1991: 12). During the **Middle Ages**, catalogs were produced for the edification of the reader, providing a moral example to imitate and were supposed to transmit the wisdom of written authority. Catalogs of women were formed within the masculinist literary tradition to reflect on the status of women and to define femininity through historical *exempla*. The examples of womanhood presented in catalogs came to stand as argument within other texts. The question of women's innate virtue or essential vice and its role in shaping history was a constant feature of this literature; thus catalogs of women usually took one of two forms, either celebrating illustrious women or reviling infamous women, although these were not mutually exclusive categories. The catalog was frequently chosen by male writers entering into debates about women as it allowed them to act as a 'judge who gazes at womankind and then selects individual women for his purposes and pleasure' (Teague and De Haas 1998: 251).

While catalogs of famous or notorious women are by far the most common genre in which men represented female historical figures such as queens and saints, their historicity is questionable. Male-authored catalogs usually presented women in ways that denied them historical subjectivity or represented them in ways that are external and antithetical to history. The earliest examples of catalogs of women appear in Hesiod's epic the *Eoiae* and Homer's *Odyssey*. These texts feature catalogs of women as a genealogical list, depicting the mothers of Greek heroes. In these catalogs women's status was defined in relation to their biological function, consequently they embody no historical subjectivity in themselves, serving only as referents to history, as the 'incubators of heroes' (McLeod 1991: 14). This reduction of women to their biological function aligned women with nature and identified them with the private sphere, consequently positioning them outside history. While later male-authored catalogs allowed that women could have a role beyond their biological function and a place beyond the domestic sphere they too contained women's historical subjectivity. Such catalogs depict women's activities outside the domestic sphere as extraordinary, or argue that women who engaged in such activities were essentially acting 'above their sex'. This is the case in Roman catalogs such as Plutarch's *The Virtues of Women*, where women are called into history-making action only in exigent circumstances. In catalogs produced during the Christian era such as St Jerome's defence of chastity *Adversus Jovianum*, women can only attain historical subjectivity by denying their sexuality, effectively acting above and beyond their sex.

Christine de Pizan is the first female writer known to have used catalogs in defence of women. A short catalog of women appears in Christine's poem *The God of Love's Letter* (1399) featuring Dido and Penelope, figures emblematic of female fidelity, as well as Medea, a woman reviled in the misogynist tradition. Christine's rehabilitation of Medea anticipates her more expansive revisionism in the *Book of the City of Women* (1405). In this text Christine uses a catalog to form a moral defence of women against institutionalised misogyny. Although it is uncertain whether Christine was familiar with Plutarch, she followed him in making women's and men's virtue essentially comparable. She followed Boccaccio too, claiming that men and women who are outstanding should receive equal praise, while no doubt questioning his assumption that women's frailty made them more praiseworthy. While both male authors avoided directly comparing examples of male and female excellence, Christine organises her catalog around this very issue. Thus she states in her opening sketch of Nicaula, Queen of Ethiopia: 'Please tell me where there was ever a king endowed with greater skill in politics, government and sovereign justice, and even with such lofty and magnificent style as one can read about the most noble Empress, Nicaula' (Richards 1982: 32). In making such comparisons Christine undercut the idea that such women's behaviour was 'exceptional', while also generating a positive history of women's contribution to civilisation.

Christine's use of catalog was innovative in that she did not merely use the catalog to bolster argument, rather she allowed it to function as a form of self-definition. The women featured in the catalog serve as role models for her and her women readers (McLeod 1991: 114). She recorded the deeds of women worthies from the past, substantially revising their histories to form a counter-narrative to the masculinist tradition. While her choice of subject matter resembles earlier catalogs of women, Christine presents them in ways that are unique. Following Christine, a number of women created catalogs as acts of self-definition, particularly when defending themselves as learned women. Isotta Nogarola, her younger compatriot, drew upon catalogs of learned women to defend herself against the slanders that greeted a female scholar and to ask for assistance to further her education. In her letters and in her orations the figure of the learned woman instructing great men featured prominently, reflecting her own desire to fulfil this role (King and Robin 2004). Whereas Christine built a city of women to protect women from the slander of men, Laura Cereta used the imagery of a family tree of brilliant women in an epistolary essay, creating for herself a line of matrilineal descent. This imagery reinforced the theme of maternal authority that looms large in her writings (Robin 1997). Writing biography in the voice of the subject in her collection *Les femmes illustres* (1642) **Madeleine de Scudéry** allowed women such as Sappho and Cleopatra to demonstrate the superiority of women in the study of art and literature while also defending her own participation in this field (Newman 2003).

Women writing during the early modern period also drew upon the catalog tradition to defend womanhood against the scurrilous claims of men made in specific misogynist tracts. Usually appearing in defence of women, these catalogs served as historical evidence to counter men's slander and to prove women's excellence. Responding to Guiseppe Passi's satirical diatribe *The Defects of Women* (1599), Lucrezia Marinella in *The Nobility and Excellences of Women* (1600) drew upon this tradition, while also providing a lengthy catalog of men who condemn women by their 'flippant and vain reasoning' and an extensive list of male 'defects and vices' (Dunhill 1999). Marinella's text represents one of the earliest examples of women explicitly deconstructing the masculinist historical tradition, while also attacking patriarchal privileges. In England the female respondents to Joseph Swetnam's *Arraignment of Lewd Women* (1617) reacted to his catalog of infamous women playfully. Rachel Speght, author of *A Mouzell for Melastomus* (1617), claimed that it would be just as easy (if not easier) to produce a list of infamous men, while the pseudonymous Ester Sowernam, in her *Ester hath hang'd Haman* (1617), countered Swetnam by providing a list of good women to undercut his list of bad.

By the eighteenth century, texts featuring catalogs of women gave way as a tradition of female prosopography developed. Like catalogs these collective biographies of women functioned to both generate female role models from history and narrate the progress of civilisation through the achievements of women.

Mary Spongberg

References

Dunhill 1999; King & Robin 2004; McLeod 1991; Newman 2003; Richards 1982; Robin 1997; Teague & De Haas 1998.

Related essays

Defences of Women, Female Biography, Women Worthies, World History.

Caulkins, Frances Manwaring 1795–1869

American local historian. Born in Connecticut, the second and youngest child of Fanny (Manwaring) and Joshua Caulkins. Trading in Haiti, her father died of yellow fever before she was born. Educated at various girls' schools in Norwichtown, Caulkins was at one time taught by Lydia Hunter (later Sigourney). After leaving school she lived with an uncle, Christopher Manwaring, in New London. Gaining access to his library, she contributed **local history** articles to the provincial newspapers. She became a school teacher in 1819 and ran various girls' schools in Norwichtown and New England until 1834. Following her conversion to the Congregationalist church in 1831, Caulkins began writing religious inspirational tracts for the American Tract Society and contributing to the Society's publication, *American Messenger*. She also produced inspirational poetry, six volumes of Bible studies for children and *Eve and Her Daughters or Women of the Bible*.

In 1845 she published her *History of Norwich, Connecticut*. This endeavour saw her honoured in 1849 when she became the first (and for over a century, the only) woman elected to membership in the oldest historical society in the United States, the Massachusetts Historical Society. Active in various local associations, Caulkins became an authority on the structures of community life and in 1852 she published her last work *History of New London*, a study of her hometown.

Sarah Howard

References

NAW 1971; Scanlon & Cosner 1996; Sklar 1976.

Cavendish, Margaret, Duchess of Newcastle 1623–1673

English Philosopher of science, author and playwright. Margaret Lucas was born into an aristocratic family, as her father was the Earl of Colchester. Upon the outbreak of the English Civil Wars in 1642, Margaret became maid of honour to Queen Henrietta Maria, wife of Charles I. Staunchly royalist, she joined the exodus to Paris, where in 1645 she married the widower William Cavendish, Marquis (later Duke) of Newcastle (1593–1676). The Cavendish family was prominent in intellectual circles and had close connections to Francis Bacon and Thomas Hobbes.

Margaret Cavendish was one of the most prolific Anglophone female authors of the seventeenth century. Notable for its copious adventurousness, her work spans a variety of genres including poetry, utopia, drama, oratory, letters, fiction, biography and, most importantly, natural philosophy. Her most famous works include *Poems and Fancies* (1653) which saw three editions during her lifetime, *The World's Olio* (1655, 1671), *Philosophical and Physical Opinions* (1655) which was republished as *The Grounds of Natural Philosophy* (1668), *Observations Upon Experimental Philosophy, to Which is Added, The Description of a New World, Called the Blazing World* (1666) and the biography of her husband.

Cavendish's chief intellectual project was a critique of experimental and mechanical philosophy, the Baconian scientific doctrine of the Royal Society. In *Observations Upon Experimental Philosophy* (1666), she directly criticised Robert Hooke's *Micrographia* (1665), a treatise of mechanist philosophy, which described objects seen through the microscope. Cavendish developed an organicist materialism which challenged the epistemological assumption that nature was a structured machine and that the men as knowing subjects of knowledge were in a privileged position to discover scientific principles.

Her scientific work, however, was largely sidelined as a novelty by her contemporaries, largely because of the disarming persona she created for herself. The most characteristic aesthetic feature of Cavendish's writing is her lucid experimentation with genre and form, through which she constructs a spectacle of her own identity. In much of her work, Cavendish appears as a character in a variety of masques. She is an eccentric, hermaphroditic individual. In her utopia *The Description of a New World, Called the Blazing World* (1666), for example, Cavendish metamorphoses into the Empress Margaret I, who is the absolute ruler of her kingdom. This fascination with constructing a variety of hybrid personas took place in a social setting in which women were formally excluded from public debate. But while this was true per se, Cavendish's status enabled her to negotiate points of entry into masculine arenas. In 1667, for example, she managed to arrange a visit to the Royal Society in London. She also had exchanges with Marin Mersenne, Thomas Hobbes and Rene Descartes. Cavendish's continuous assertion of her own identity, particularly her insistence upon publishing under her own name, enhanced her status as a social and intellectual maverick.

Although claiming to be 'ignorant of the rules of writing histories', Cavendish produced a biography of her husband William Cavendish, the Duke of Newcastle, *Life of the Thrice Noble . . . Duke* (1667) to which she appended an autobiographical piece written a decade earlier entitled *A True Relation of My Birth, Breeding and Life* (1656) (see **Renaissance** essay). She has been the subject of several recent biographies including Kathleen Jones' *A Glorious Fame: The Life of Margaret Cavendish, Duchess of Newcastle* (1988) and Kate Whitaker's *Mad Madge: Margaret Cavendish, Duchess of Newcastle: Royalist, Writer and Romantic* (2003).

Sarah Irving

References

Major works

Cavendish's autobiographical fragment can be found in Elspeth Graham *et al.* (eds) *Her Own Life: Autobiographical Writings by Seventeenth Century English Women* (London: Routledge, 1989) Other selections of her writings can be found in Sylvia Bowerbank & Sara Mendelson (eds) *Paper Bodies: A Margaret Cavendish Reader* (Peterborough: Broadview, 2000).

Child, Lydia Maria Francis 1802–1880

Historical novelist, poet, political journalist, historian of women. Born in Medford, Massachusetts. Youngest child of Susannah (Rand) and Convers Francis. Child's father actively discouraged her education, allowing her to attend Miss Swan's Academy for a year in 1814, then sending her to her sister Mary Francis Preston in Norridgewock, Maine. In Norridgewock Child was exposed to Native American culture, visiting the camps of the Abenaki and Penobscot families. Child developed the cross-cultural perspective that shaped her work as a reformer and historian as a result of this exposure. Child left Maine in 1821 to live with her brother Convers, Unitarian minister in Watertown Massachusetts. A Harvard graduate, Convers shared the benefits of his education with his sister. Child's awareness that her sex had been the cause of the disparity in their educations informed her social activism.

Child's first novel, *Hobomok* (1824), was an historical romance set in colonial America. *Hobomok* represents a revision of the masculinist history of Puritan settlement and a rejection of the masculinist literary canon, bringing together themes that inflected Child's work for the rest of her life. Centred around a romance between Puritan heroine Mary Conant and the 'Indian' warrior Hobomok, the novel rejected the prescribed 'manifest destiny' of women and 'Indians', signalling Child's advocacy of inter-racial marriage as a means of overcoming white supremacy, a theme continued in her writings on abolition. In this and later writings on the 'Indians' such as 'The Adventures of the Bell' (1827) and 'The Church in the Wilderness' (1828), published in her influential children's journal the *Juvenile Miscellany*, Child explored the history of conquest from varying cultural perspectives. Founded in 1826, *Juvenile Miscellany* was critical to the development of children's literature and radical in its sympathetic depiction of Native Americans and slaves. Contributors to the journal included **Margaret Fuller** and **Sarah Josepha Hale**. The journal was forced to close in 1834 because of Child's radical abolitionist views. In 1825 Child published *The Rebels or Boston before the Revolution*, a political novel that won the attention of David Lee Child, editor of the *Massachusetts Journal*, who she married in 1828 after a protracted courtship. From the start the Childs viewed their marriage as a political partnership. Together they campaigned against the removal of the Cherokee from their land. Child published anonymously *The First Settlers of New England* (1829), decrying their dispossession. Her marriage was marred by her husband's financial mismanagement and both pragmatism and expediency can be seen in her publication of *The Frugal Housewife* (1829) and *The Mother's Book* (1831), texts that combined domestic advice and recipes with commentary on the state of the Republic and the role of women within it. *The Mother's Book* particularly encouraged women to read history as a republican duty (see **Female Biography** essay).

Following the success of these works, Child began a five-volume history project for the Ladies Family Library, that included *Biographies of Madame de Staël and Madame Roland* (1832), *Biographies of Lady Russell and Madame Guyon* (1832) and a collective biography Good Wives (1833). Moving beyond the **women worthies** mode, Child created hybrid texts that merged historical documents with historical romance, insisting, like **Madame de Staël**, that such details 'supply the deficiencies of history'. **De Staël** had been a heroine of Child's since she had first read *De l'Allemagne* (1813) with **Margaret Fuller**. Child also produced a compendium world history, the *Condition of Women in Various Ages and Nations* (1835). This three-volume text combined ethnological discussion of women throughout the world with a general history of women living under patriarchy. Although the text drew on historical sources such as Herodotus and Josephus, much of it is devoted to quasi-anthropological observations about women's distinctive culture, their productive labour and the customs and ceremonies pertaining to marriage, childbirth and divorce. Child revised masculinist myths about women and drew attention to inconsistencies in the male historical record around figures such as Artemesia and Aspasia. **Elizabeth Cady Stanton** cited this text as an invaluable resource for women in their struggle against patriarchy.

This text reflected Child's growing abhorrence for slavery and her interest in racial intermarriage. Meeting radical abolitionist David Lloyd Garrison in 1830, Child became fervently involved in this cause, publishing her *Appeal in Favor of That Class of Americans Called Africans* in 1833. A compendium history of slavery, Child's Appeal used history to refute racist myths and called for emancipation and an end to miscegenation laws (see **Slavery** essay). The publication of the *Appeal* embroiled Child in scandal with many publishers refusing to take her work. This created strain in her marriage and she separated from her husband in 1841, moving to New York as editor of the *National Anti-Slavery Standard*. Her column *Letters from New York* inaugurated the journalistic sketch and revitalised Child's career.

An emotional crisis in 1847 launched Child on a religious quest that culminated in her *Progress of Religious Ideas* (1855). Prompted by a desire to counteract religious bigotry, Child's three-volume text analysed various world **religions**, challenging the Judeo-Christian dominance of religious history and contesting Christianity's claim to divine inspiration and rejecting its sexual asceticism. Around 1848 she reconciled with her husband and returned to Massachusetts. She wrote a number of children's stories, numerous anti-slavery tales and anti-slavery tracts, including the widely circulated *Correspondence between Lydia Maria Child and Governor Wise and Mrs Mason of Virginia* (1860). The Civil War was agony to Child who sought the emancipation of the slaves, but was also a pacifist. In 1865 she compiled *The Freedman's Book,* a school reader for ex-slaves and in 1867 she published her last novel *A Romance of the Republic,* holding up racial intermarriage as America's destiny. In old age she campaigned for suffrage for African-Americans while also supporting womanhood suffrage. Child was one of the women to whom **Elizabeth Cady Stanton, Susan B Anthony** and **Matilda Joselyn Gage** dedicated their *History of Woman Suffrage.*

Mary Spongberg

Reference
Karcher 1994.

Major works
Hobomok and Other Writings on Indians (ed.) Carolyn L Karcher (New Brunswick: Rutgers University Press, 1986); *An Appeal in Favor of that Class of Americans called Africans* (ed.) Carolyn L Karcher (Amherst: University of Massachusetts Press, 1996) and *A Romance of the Republic* (ed.) Dana D Nelson (Lexington: University of Kentucky Press, 1997).

Civil rights movement

Women historians have made many significant contributions to the historiography of the African-American Civil Rights movement of the 1950s and 1960s, just as women activists were vital to the success of the movement's campaigns to tackle segregation and discrimination. The movement was both intensely documented and self-documenting (Nasstrom 1999a), generating an enormous body of literature. A good deal of civil rights scholarship has been written by former participants in the movement, and it has a strong sense of engagement, stressing positive interpretations and shying away from asking critical questions (Eagles 2000). Women's role in the movement was long minimalised in the historiography by a focus on male leaders and, as Ann Standley notes, 'the omission of women from many of the histories of the movement is also apparent in the widespread use of the metaphor of reaching manhood to describe the self-confidence that blacks gained from the movement' (1993: 183). Much of the growing body of scholarship that deals with female participation in the movement has not been incorporated into larger civil rights histories, and historiographical surveys tend to obscure the contributions of female historians.

Early histories presented the civil rights movement as a political force that garnered legislative and judicial triumphs, producing a nationally oriented political history with a chronology centred on key events in the life of Martin Luther King, Jr (Lawson 1991; Nasstrom 1999a). This focus, many argued, obscured local struggles, the place where the civil rights movement obtained its dynamism (Lawson and Payne 1998). Women were also obscured in these accounts, which Joan C Browning attributed to the male journalists who covered the civil rights story. In her essay 'Invisible Revolutionaries: White Women in Civil Rights Historiography', Browing has argued that they identified only male leaders and described the movement with masculine metaphors, noting 'the feminine roles of building consensus . . . [and] sustaining community . . . cannot be described in win/loss records' (1996: 201).

By the late 1970s the rise of the new social history saw the unified story of a national movement give way to a myriad of local studies (Lawson 1991). The variety and scope of these community studies has forced reconsideration of basic questions in the historiography, including the periodisation of the movement, the scope of actions that constituted it, and the nature of its activism and leadership (Nasstrom 1999a). Many women historians have written local studies, such as Darlene Clarke Hine's *Black Victory: The Rise and Fall of the White Primary in Texas* (1979), Joan T Beifuss' *At the River I Stand: Memphis, the 1968 Strike, and Martin Luther King Jr* (1985), Kim Roger's *Righteous Lives: Narratives of the New Orleans Civil Rights Movement* (1993), Glenda Alice Rabby's *The Pain and the Promise: The Struggle for Civil Rights in Tallahassee, Florida* (1999) and Elizabeth Jacoway's *Understanding the Little Rock Crisis: An Exercise in Remembrance and Reconciliation* (1999). Other works have examined specific themes within local contexts, such as Catherine A Barnes' *Journey from Jim Crow* (1983) on desegregation and Mary Aickin Rothschild's *A Case of Black and White* (1982) on the role of Northern volunteers. More recently, local studies on areas outside the South have appeared such as Gretchen Cassel Eick's *Dissent in Wichita* (2001), Martha Biondi's *To Stand and Fight: The Struggle for Civil Rights in Postwar New York City* (2003) and Jeanne Theoharis and Komozi Woodard's edited collection *Freedom North* (2003). Local studies such as Vicki Crawford *et al.*'s *Women in the Civil Rights Movement* (1993) and Bettye Collier-Thomas and V P Franklin's *Sisters in the Struggle: African-American Women in the Civil Rights – Black Power Movement* (2001) have revealed thousands of female activists, showing that women were much more active in the movement than a national focus revealed. Running parallel to this emphasis on the local, other women historians have expanded the parameters of civil rights scholarship, not just by looking at the pre-civil rights era (such as Patricia Sullivan's *Days of Hope* 1996), but by placing the civil rights movement in an international context in works such as Brenda Gayle Plummer's *Window on Freedom: Race, Civil Rights and Foreign Affairs 1945–1988* (2003), Mary L Dudziak's *Cold War Civil Rights* (2000) and Carol Anderson's *Eyes Off the Prize: The United Nations and the African-American Struggle for Human Rights, 1944–1955* (2003).

Much of the scholarship on women in the civil rights movement has attempted to explain the apparently anomalous (to political scientists) nature of women's high levels of participation in the movement. Historians like Darlene Clark Hine (1986) have argued that women were able to tap into the infrastructure of secular clubs and sacred associations to mobilise protest. Rhonda Lois Blumberg in her essay 'White Mothers as Civil Rights Activists' (1990b) argued that the civil rights movement was a revolutionary movement that was violently opposed, and that this had special implications for women in the movement, as well as women's social position, thus volunteers were more likely to be found amongst lower paid workers and women fell into this category. Blumberg also contended that in the South, black women tended to take leadership roles because of the presumed greater danger that men would face (1991: 136).

An extension of this analysis of women's participation was the analysis of women's organisational roles – why were women such effective organisers for the civil rights movement? And why were they not as well represented in its leadership? How did gender impact on conceptions and experiences of leadership in the civil rights movement?

Ann Standley says that 'the role of black women in the civil rights movement . . . was complicated by their ambivalence about what it ought to be', noting that women were reluctant to criticise their black male leaders (1993: 201). Paula Giddings argued in *When and Where I Enter* (1984) that sexist and authoritarian views of leadership held by church leaders prevented women from assuming command of organisations. However, Kathryn L Nasstrom claimed that the problem was a historiographical one: 'In recent scholarship, organisation is being recognised as a critical movement activity in its own right and as an under-appreciated form of leadership' (1999b: 114). Yet as she noted, organising was a multi-skilled task, so 'why hasn't organising been valued as much as leadership or seen as a form of leadership, and was it always this way? How did leadership in the civil rights movement become so thoroughly associated with men, and what are the consequences of that connection?' (1999b: 115).

The recovery and analysis of women's leadership by female scholars has attempted to address this. In *How Long? How Long? African-American Women in the Struggle for Civil Rights* (1997) Belinda Robnett coined the term 'bridge leadership' to describe the intermediate level of leadership that women took on in the movement. She claimed that bridge leadership between larger organisations and potential constituents is vital to the sustenance of a social movement, and that in the civil rights movement, this role was largely played by women. Her framework explains how black women were able to play leadership roles even though their gender almost always barred them from formal leadership positions.

The connection between the women's movement and the civil rights movement is a widely accepted, but not uncontroversial, one. Sara Evans, author of *Personal Politics: The Roots of Women's Liberation in the Civil Rights Movement and the New Left* (1979), and historians like Rhoda Lois Blumberg (1991) claimed that women's experiences of sexism and leadership in the civil rights movement led them away from this struggle into the women's liberation movement. The question of the sexism of the civil rights movement is a contentious one: Paula Giddings argued that women were not excluded from leadership positions, but that their influence decreased from the mid-1960s, relegated to minor responsibilities 'in part because of indiscriminate sexual behaviour' (1984: 302). She claims that black women did not rise up against sexism in the movement because they saw race as a more pressing issue than gender. While some black female activists were offering feminist criticisms of the movement in the 1960s, others denied that sexism was a problem – Joyce Ladner recalled that black women played key roles and drew on a black female cultural tradition where women assumed a great deal of responsibility (Breines 1996). Blumberg noted that the emergence of the feminist movement has prompted participants to reexamine the movement from the perspective of gender. For example, Septima Clark was involved in the feminist movement after the civil rights movement and, Blumberg argued, 'learned to comprehend her own story . . . in a framework very different from that through which she experienced it' (1991: 20).

The surge in civil rights history in the 1970s and 1980s coincided with the growing popularity of oral history which has been used to document local activists who leave few documents and might otherwise remain obscure. Oral history projects such as Ruth Edmond Hills' *Black Women Oral History Project: From the Arhut and Elizabeth Schlesinger Library on the History of*

Women in America (2001), have collected interviews with leaders and participants, or conducted interviews with female activists. Civil rights historians have embraced oral history because it can give clues about why people joined and stayed in the movement (Rogers 1988), as well as raise questions on the periodisation of the movement in histories (Nasstrom 1999a). Oral history has been used in numerous local studies and to document the lives of women activists such as in Cheryl Lynn Greenburg's *A Circle of Trust: Remembering SNCC* (1998) and Judith Rollins's *All is Never Said: The Narrative of Odette Harper Hines* (1995).

There was a major surge in civil rights literature on women after 1980 and much of this was biographical (Eagles 2000). Like oral histories, autobiographies and biographies have served to document individual lives within a larger movement, emphasising women's contributions and also showing the ways that many people were active in the movement, but also either side of it. Life-writing has added immediacy and emotion to movement historiography, and many activists such as Mary King (1987), Virginia Foster Durr (1985), Pauli Murray (1987) and Sara Murphy (1997) have written memoirs and autobiographies. Some life histories became a force in the movement itself, as women such as Daisy T Bates (1962) and Anne Moody (1968) told of their lives under segregation. Many historians have written biographies of activists including Cynthia Stokes Brown on Septima P Clark (1986), Judith Rollins on Odette Harper Hines (1995), Cynthia Griggs Fleming on Ruby Doris Smith Robinson (1998), Kathryn L Nasstrom on Frances Freeborn Pauley (2000) and Barbara Ransby on Ella Baker (2003).

One of most contentious issues in the historiography of women in the civil rights movement is the role of white women. White women were variously characterised as marking time before they defected into the women's movement or blamed for causing tensions between black men and women and the resentment of Southern whites, for engaging in taboo interracial sex (Blumberg 1990a). This has coloured the depiction of white women in civil rights historiography and indeed, the controversial issue of interracial sex has not yet featured in civil rights historiography (Eagles 2000). Browning argued that the relative scarcity of white women in civil rights historiography proves that they are casualties of their race and gender.

> White women were always part of the civil rights movement from the very beginning. And yet, historians's treatment of the movement renders them almost invisible. When included in Civil Rights movement history, their contributions are unclear, marginalised, disregarded or defined by identification with men. (Browning 1996: 198)

Women's historians have made some steps towards recovering white activists, in works such as Debra Schultz's *Going South* (2001) on Jewish women, Catherine Fosl's *Subversive Southerner* (2002), a study of Anne Braden, Patricia Sullivan's collection of Virginia Foster Durr's letters *Freedom Writer* (2003) and Florence Mars' *Witness in Philadelphia*, (1977), an account of a white woman who testified against the Ku Klux Klan in the trial of the murderers of three civil rights workers. Former activist Constance Curry recently published *Deep in Our Hearts: Nine White Women in the Freedom Movement* (2000), the reminiscences of nine white women activists.

Most civil rights historians have examined either white actions or black actions, rarely considering the two together (Fairclough 1990: 398). The only whites to appear in most civil rights histories are usually racist whites, but neither side was monolithic. Barbara Ransby (2000) argued that civil rights historians needed to understand the roles of white women and that it should be considered in the context of emerging work on whiteness. Lynne Olsen (2001), for example, has tried to deal with both black and white women in her account of the movement, yet as Eagles pointed out, most historians have told the stories of supportive whites, telling only one side of the story, from within the movement. Very little has been written about those who opposed it, although Beth Roy (1999), for example, undertook an oral history study of the whites of Little Rock Central High, in an attempt to understand, rather than demonise segregationists.

Adam Fairclough has also argued that historians have neglected the distinctive culture of the civil rights movement 'and its subjective political, emotional, religious and psychological dimensions' (1990: 398). Some women historians have done work on the role of song in the civil rights movement, such as Kerran L Sanger's *"When the spirit says sing!": The Role of Freedom Songs in the Civil Rights Movement* (1995) and Berenice Johnson's essays on 'The Lined Hymn as a Song of Freedom' (1990). Reagon has also written about the role of black women as transmitters of culture (1993). Others have written about the portrayal of the movement in culture produced by women, in texts such as Melissa Walker's *Down from the Mountaintop: Black Women's Novels in the Wake of the Civil Rights Movement* (1991) and some of the essays in Ling and Montieth's collection *Gender and the Civil Rights Movement* (1991). Graham has written on the impact of the movement on popular culture, especially film and television, with emphasis on the depiction of white Southerners.

Historical films about the civil rights movement have tended to downplay the role of women in the struggle, although African-American filmmaker Julie Dash made *The Rosa Parks Story* for television (2002). African-American musicians the Neville Brothers have paid tribute to Rosa Parks in their song 'Rosa Parks': 'Thank You Miss Rosa / you were the spark / that started our freedom movement / thank you sister Rosa Parks.' This kind of popular history-making has kept certain women civil rights activists at the forefront of American national memory.

Michelle Arrow

References

Bates 1962; Blumberg 1990b, 1991; Breines 1996; Brown 1986; Navarro, Wild Trees Press. Browning 1996; Durr 1985; Eagles 2000; Evans 1979; Fairclough 1990: Fleming 1998; Giddings 1984; Hine 1986; King 1987; Lawson 1991; Lawson & Payne 1998; Moody 1968; Murphy 1997; Murray 1987; Nasstrom 1999a,b, 2000; Olsen 2001; Ransby 2003; Reagon 1990, 1993; Rollins 1995; Rogers 1993; Roy 1999; Standley 1993.

Clark, Alice 1874–1934

English historian of women. Born in Somerset, fourth child of Helen Bright, feminist and dress reform advocate, and William Clark, an original partner of C & J Clark Shoemakers. Attended the Brighthelmston School, Southport. Passed Cambridge entrance examination with honours, hoping to study at Newhnam. She did not, however, initially pursue higher education, choosing instead to work in the family company.

When the business became a private limited company in 1903, Clark was made a director for life.

Clark was the great-niece of Anna Maria, Mary Priestman and Priscilla Bright McLaren, part of the 'Quaker sisterhood' active in the English women's suffrage movement. Through these women, links were established with American suffragists Harriot Stanton Blatch and her mother **Elizabeth Cady Stanton**. Her mother's political activism, campaigning against the Contagious Diseases Acts, also brought Clark into contact with **Josephine Butler**. Clark herself was active in the suffrage movement, forming the Women's Liberal Association in Somerset in 1890 and working on the Executive Committee of the National Union of Women's Suffrage Societies until she became ill with tuberculosis.

Recovering her health, Clark took up the Charlotte Shaw Fellowship in 1914 to study economic history at the London School of Economics (LSE) under the supervision of **Lilian Knowles** and **Eileen Power**. Interested in the working lives of women, Clark analysed their economic status in seventeenth-century Britain. The war interrupted Clark's research, and she threw herself into Quaker humanitarian aid. In 1919 Clark's research was published as the *Working Life of Women in the Seventeenth Century*. Challenging the idea that women's lives were 'a static feature in social developments', Clark argued that the rise of industrialisation caused the decline of women's economic and social status. Based on archival research from guild-company and borough records, household books and memoirs, letters and household accounts, Clark presented a detailed analysis of how the decline of home-based industry impacted upon women. Following **Olive Schreiner**, Clark maintained that industrialisation had robbed women of their 'ancient domain of productive and social labour' and compromised their ability to devote themselves to their families. Like historians such as **Beatrice Webb** and **Barbara Hammond**, Clark presented an essentially pessimistic view of the impact of industrialisation, claiming that the 'triumph of capitalistic organisation' was the decline of women's status. Although she does not appear to have been a member of the Fabian Women's Group, its influence on the *Working Life of Women in the Seventeenth Century* is evident, and similarities between her text and Mabel Atkinson's *The Economic Foundations of the Women's Movement* have been noted.

Clark's conclusions were at odds with those of her supervisor Lilian Knowles, who maintained that the Industrial Revolution brought positive changes to production and that the factory system was an improvement on home-based production. In the next decade Clark's ideas were challenged by **Ivy Pinchbeck** and M Dorothy George. Clark did not engage in further historical research, choosing to work in the family business until her death.

Mary Spongberg

References

Berg 1992; Chaytor & Lewis 1982; Holton 1996.

Major work

Amy Louise Erickson (ed.) Alice Clarke, *Working Life of Women in the Seventeenth Century* (London: Routledge, 1992).

Clifford, Anne Countess of Dorset, Pembroke and Montgomery 1589–1676

Diarist, family historian. Only child of Margaret Russell and George Clifford, third Earl of Cumberland. Educated in 'true religion and moral virtues' by her mother, Clifford was also tutored by the historian Samuel Daniel, whose memory she celebrated in the Appleby triptych, a pictorial record of her familial and intellectual connections. Married first to Richard Sackville, Earl of Dorset in 1609 and after his death to Philip Herbert, Earl of Pembroke in 1630. Clifford bore seven children, five sons who died in infancy and two daughters. Following the death of her father, Clifford and her mother became involved in a protracted legal battle over control of the estates of Westmoreland and Craven. This placed her in conflict with both her husband and James I. These lands reverted to Clifford upon the death of her father's male heirs in 1643. She did much to rebuild her estates, defying the authority of Cromwell's occupying forces and creating various monuments to her female ancestors.

Clifford wrote history as an appellant, using the historical record to validate her identity as heir and producing detailed records of her struggles in two major works – the *Knole Diary*, a journal recording the years in which she contested her father's will (1616–1619) and the three-volume *Great Books of the Records of Skipton Castle*, a genealogical history of her ancestors, that included memoirs of her mother and father written in the tradition of Plutarch's *Lives*. Clifford also appended an autobiographical study, the 'Life of Me', to these memoirs. Through these works she buttressed her claim to her lands, celebrating her matrilineal heritage and reversing the patriarchal concepts of inheritance by claiming her ancestor Isabella de Viteripont as founder of the Clifford line. Clifford looked to her female ancestors as examples of resistance to male authority, thus justifying her own actions and defending the rights of women to take up positions of power. Clifford drew on her knowledge of history referring to texts such as *Holingshed's Chronicle & Stow's Chronicles & all Other Chronicles of England*, correcting mistakes or omissions she found and sympathetically representing women traduced in the masculinist record.

Biographical accounts of her life appear in Louisa S Costello's *Memoirs of Eminent English Women* (1848), and **Helen Blackburn** cites her as an example of female resistance to patriarchy in *Women's Suffrage* (1902). She also served as a model of feminine agency in history for her female descendants, such as Vita Sackville-West who edited the *Knole Diary* (1923) and was dispossessed of this estate to a male heir. Recent work on **Virginia Woolf** has identified Anne Clifford as the young Orlando in her novel of the same name (1928). It has also been suggested that Woolf drew on Clifford in 'The Journal of Mistress Joan Martyn' (1906), an unpublished account of a female historian who discovers the journal of a fifteenth-century woman, while researching the English land tenure system.

Mary Spongberg

References

Hallet 1995; Suzuki 2001.

Major works

Vita Sackville-West (ed.) *The Diary of the Lady Anne Clifford* (London: Heinnemann, 1923); Katherine Acheson, *The Diary of Anne Clifford 1616–1619: A Critical Edition* (New York: Garland, 1995).

Collective and collaborative writing

Since the early Middle Ages women have engaged in collaborative historical writing, sometimes involving only two authors, sometimes writing as a collective or group. The first known collaborative historical writing by women emerged within **convent** communities and may have started as early as the eighth century when groups of nuns from the Abbey at Chelles are believed to have written the *Annals Mettenses Priores* for their Abbess, Gisla, sister of Charlemagne (Ferrante 1997: 69). By the fourteenth century, German nuns are known to have written collective biographies of the inhabitants of their convents, known as 'sister books', reflecting the sense of familial history such texts were meant to evoke. Sometimes these efforts at collective historical writing would last for several generations, as was the case with nuns from Saint Monica's Convent in Louvain (Grundy 1992: 128).

With the rise of first- and second-wave feminism another form of sisterhood created the desire among women to write history collectively. Like earlier forms, such endeavours involved groups of authors or editors, who may not even be named individually, and usually evolved as a communal enterprise, particularly if produced by feminist historians. The distinction between collaborative and collective writing is not clear-cut, even in feminist works. This is illustrated in a feminist history of **Australia**, *Creating a Nation* (1994). The book was written collaboratively by four historians: Patricia Grimshaw, Marilyn Lake, Ann McGrath and Marian Quartly, who each wrote individual chapters. 'Our writing was also a collective enterprise, however, the product of continual discussion, comment and rewriting' (1994: 5).

Early suffragists collaborated to produce their own histories, such as the multivolume *History of Woman Suffrage* produced in the USA in 1881 by **Elizabeth Cady Stanton, Susan B Anthony** and **Matilda Joslyn Gage**. For histories produced in the nineteenth and early twentieth centuries collective writing must be assumed where no individual author is named. Many women's organizations used history on occasion as a vehicle for promoting their aims, for example the Young Women's Christian Association and the Woman's Christian Temperance Union. Some organisations had overtly historical aims, notably, the national society, Daughters of the American Revolution (DAR), founded in Washington DC in 1890. 'Women felt the desire to express their patriotic feelings and were frustrated by their exclusion from men's organizations formed to perpetuate the memory of ancestors who fought to make this county free and independent' (see **USA** essay). The early history-writing of the DAR appears to have been collective, in that individual authors are not named in material prepared for the Daughters of the American Revolution Museum, also established in 1890, which focused on historic decorative arts, nor in its book, *Early History, Daughters of the American Revolution* (1908).

A philosophy of collectivism characterized the Women's Liberation Movement of the 1960s and 1970s. Most of the collective histories produced by women during this period had common aims in writing women back into history and in documenting women's experiences. A model for self-consciously collective writing was provided early in the period of second-wave feminism in the United States, when the Boston Women's Health Book Collective published *Our Bodies, Ourselves* about women's health and sexuality in 1970. The book was not historical but the methodology was influential: '[W]e would research our questions, share what we learned in our group, and then present the information' (Norsigian *et al.* 1999). Collective historical writing also emerged from the first women's studies programmes offered at universities. Guided by feminist historian **Joan Kelly**, the Sarah Lawrence women's studies programme produced the collectively written text *Workbook on*

Sterilization and Sterilization Abuse (1978). Kelly also worked collectively with Renate Bridenthal, Amy Swerdlow and Phyllis Vine to produce a feminist family history, *Household Kith and Kin* (1980). Like other feminists Kelly's commitment to collective writing was political and she wrote that she felt 'energized' by 'the incredible women's network that connected me to myself and my sisters'. Following Kelly's death in 1982 a collective of women edited and published her papers as the immensely significant text, *Women History and Theory* (1984).

Among feminist women there were deliberate efforts to depict continuities between early and later women's movements. Feminist practices such as Consciousness Raising (CR) particularly encouraged collective story-telling. CR allowed women to create a collective identity as feminists and consequently influenced historians of women to seek out examples of collective feminist activity in the past. The feminist publishing company Virago reissued in 1977 *Life as We Have Known It* by Co-operative Working Women, first published with an introduction by Virginia Woolf in 1931. These were **memoirs** of British working women who were members of the Women's Co-operative Guild, founded in 1882. The proliferation of women's organisations from the 1970s and collective female activism produced a substantial number of histories. The types of history that lent themselves to such writing tended to be anthologies and reference works. Several of the major feminist texts of the 1970s and 1980s were written collectively, such as the London Feminist History Group, *The Sexual Dynamics of History* (1983) and the London-based Lesbian History Group, *Not a Passing Phase: Reclaiming Lesbians in History, 1840–1985* (1984). Much women's history-writing combined individual authorship of chapters or essays in an anthology which was collectively planned, edited and published. Feminists also recognised the necessity of controlling the means of production and distribution as well as preparing the works, establishing feminist printing presses and publishers.

The importance of these collective works extended beyond their content or their methodologies. *Not a Passing Phase*, for example, contributed to a public discourse that established lesbians as a group, probably for the first time in history (Cottingham 1996: 2). In 1983 the Manchester Women's History Group gave advice in *Spare Rib* on starting a feminist history group by suggesting that women think about the kind of group they wanted. For example, this could be 'a support group for women actively engaged in historical research . . . to share their work and the common problems of isolation' and their struggle with the questions thrown up by women's history and in particular, 'discuss what constitutes feminist history'. Another kind of group could be set up 'to study local women's history as a collective enterprise, arising out of a common interest in your community' (London Feminist History Group 1983: 205). Both forms of collective history writing have persisted but the former has, as the Manchester group's advice implied, focused on feminist history and the 'support group' has been mainly a function of academic historians and is evidenced in feminist anthologies such as *Australian Feminism: A Companion* (1998) and this volume.

Most collective history writing by women has focused on women's history although there is a tradition, also dating from the nineteenth century, of women collectively writing local history. Within Australia, this form of history writing was promoted by the largest women's organisation, the Country Women's Association (CWA), first formed in New South Wales in 1922 and by the end of the century numbering more than 1800 branches. The CWA's concern with education, recreation and crafts also found expression in compiling local and regional histories. Women's groups also promoted women's role as citizens especially on commemorative occasions (see **Local history, Dominion women writers**).

Much feminist history writing, even when single-authored, was essentially collaborative, reflecting the fact that many historians work within their communities to ensure they are not robbed of their historical subjectivity. The African-American historian Darlene Clark Hine states that her work aims to give voice to people who otherwise would be ignored and forgotten, or rendered invisible and dismissed as unimportant (Hine 1994). The author of many works on the experience of African-American women, including a multi-authored 16-volume historical encyclopedia documenting *Black Women in America* (1993), Hine has also been involved in establishing the black women's history **archive**. The creation of such archives is always a collective activity involving collaboration between historians, archivists and the community. Such collaborations allow many voices to be heard and as a result sometimes challenge long-held historical 'truths.' This was the case with the Buffalo Oral History Project established by lesbian historians Elizabeth Lapovsky Kennedy and Madelaine D Davis in collaboration with the Buffalo lesbian community. The collection of oral histories as part of this project enabled women of this community to speak for themselves, allowing Kennedy and Davis to draw a more nuanced and complex history in their *Boots of Leather, Slippers of Gold* (1993), and enabling their subjects a degree of collaboration in writing their own history.

Since the nineteenth century, women's history-writing has had a persistent aim: education, both of women themselves and their wider communities. For this reason, many histories have been both collectively prepared and presented in forms other than the monograph such as oral histories, newsletters, exhibitions, artworks, films and, since the 1990s, the Internet. Increasingly collective history writing finds expression in material published on the Internet. An early example was the work of the National Women's History Project, an American organization founded in 1980 to 'promote multicultural women's history awareness' by providing information and educational materials and programs. The Project originated with the Educational Task Force in California that instigated Women's History Week in 1978. This has been continued by the National Women's History Project that also maintains an Internet site (www.nwhp.org) that offers a wide range of historical information and resources.

Susan Marsden

References

Cottingham 1996; Ferrante 1997; Grimshaw *et al.* 1994; Grundy 1992; Hine 1994; London Feminist History Group 1983; Norsigian *et al.* 1999.

Coman, Katharine 1857–1915

American economic historian and social reformer. Born in Newark, Ohio, the fourth of seven children of Martha Seymour and Levi Parsons Coman. Coman attended Steubenville Female Seminary and when the Principal of that institution refused to give her more advanced work her father transferred her to the high school of the University of Michigan. An outstanding student, Coman graduated from Michigan University with a PhD in 1880. Finding work as instructor in rhetoric at Wellesley College, by 1883 Coman was made professor of political economy and history. In 1900 she organised a separate department of economics and became professor of economics and sociology, a position she held until her retirement. Coman was not married, but for much of her adult life lived with Katharine Bates and both of their mothers. Following her death, Wellesley established a chair named after her.

Coman was a founder of the College Settlements Association and chaired the Boston Settlement Committee. From 1900 to 1907 she was president of the electoral board and chairman of the standing committee of the National College Settlements Association, and helped develop a fellowship programme enabling young college graduates to spend a year or more at one of the association's settlement houses. Coman was an early supporter of the Consumers' League which sought to improve factory conditions by bringing consumer pressure to bear on manufacturers. She was a member of the executive branch from its inception in 1899 until 1905. In 1910 she went to Chicago to assist a strike of seamstresses seeking union recognition. As chair of the committee on grievances of the Women's Trade Union League of Chicago she helped publicise the reasons for the strike, which ended successfully in 1911. In 1913, after retiring from Wellesley because of ill health, she volunteered to serve with the National Progressive Service division of the Progressive Party. Despite serious illness she spent much of 1914 in Europe, studying the operation of social insurance programme in Europe. Her findings and observations were published in a series of articles in *Survey* magazine and posthumously as *Unemployment Insurance: A Summary of European Systems* (1915).

Coman was a pioneer in the field of economic history. She used quantitative analysis and practised a scientific method of history. She went directly into the field, travelling the routes of fur traders and railroad men and interviewing survivors of these earlier times. She established a national reputation for rigorous research as well as writings on classroom technique. She published three main texts in this area: 'Contract Labor in Hawaii' (1903), a long monograph published by the American Economic Association; *Industrial History of the United States* (1905), a textbook widely used and published in several editions; and *Economic Beginnings of the Far West* (1912), published in two volumes. In 1894, with Elizabeth Kendall, she published *The Growth of the English Nation* for the Chautauqua Reading Circle series. In 1899, again with Elizabeth Kendall, she published *A History of England for High Schools and Academies*. In 1902 she and Katharine Lee Bates edited *English History Told by the Poets*.

Coman revealed her commitment to women workers through her historical research and extracurricular activities with settlements and workers' collectives, and her articles 'A Sweated Industry' and 'The Supreme Court Decision on the Oregon 10 Hour Law' are examples of this. She was one of only three women members of the American Historical Association in its early years.

Sarah Howard

References

Des Jardins 2003; Palmieri 1983.

Convents and writings by nuns

History forms an important part of the life of a convent. Nuns have always been reminded of it through the convent buildings themselves, the tombs, portraits and memorials celebrating former members of the convent, and other physical reminders of historical figures and events (Wunder 1999). Nuns' daily prayers, for example, call to mind their religious duty to remember the souls of the convent's founders and benefactors. Even in the early days of female monasticism, careful records were usually kept of former nuns, and the anniversaries of their deaths were commemorated throughout the year. Nuns have also been conscious throughout history of a responsibility to preserve the convent's knowledge and traditions, power, wealth and land for future generations who thanked and remembered them in turn.

The early modern period, however, stands out as a time when nuns were particularly concerned with writing history. This period stretches from the monastic reforms of the late fifteenth to the secularisation of the eighteenth century. At this time, history writing generally was seen as an unusual genre for a woman. Nuns, however, were set apart from most women because they were educated to a high standard, and often had a more receptive audience for their work. They wrote histories of and for their own communities as part of a widespread tradition throughout the older, contemplative orders, for a number of different reasons, which this essay will explore. Despite the attacks on monastic life by the different Protestant churches during and after the **Reformation**, female monasticism still received strong support across Europe during the early modern period, and was beginning to spread to South America.

Nevertheless, in the 'scientific' age of the eighteenth century, the rationalist philosophy of the Enlightenment began to undermine seriously this social support for contemplative orders (McNamara 1998: 544–62). A movement to suppress monastic houses swept through Europe in the last quarter of the eighteenth century. Although nuns' defence of their contemplative lifestyle was as strong as it had been during the Reformation, relatively few convents survived the secularisation intact. Some of the most powerful older convents had their rights restored in the course of the nineteenth century, but many nuns from contemplative orders joined newer, active orders, such as the Ursulines, whom society valued for their work in female education. The face of female monasticism in Europe was greatly changed. This essay will focus on the period before this great change, examining the writing of history in communities that in many cases had been dissolved by the end of the period.

The convent

Natalie Zemon Davis's early essay on female historians in the early modern period indicates the problems women usually had accessing material about their subject matter, or gaining the experience of life and politics that men took for granted (1984: 154). By contrast, nuns were easily able to find materials to research their subject, provided they were allowed access to the convent's archive. They had that 'sense of connection' about which Davis writes, for not only was the history of the convent also their own history, but the history of the convent was often closely linked to the political or civic history of their immediate surroundings (Lowe 2000). Nuns sometimes had access to models, such as those found in the library of a monastery with which their house had close ties. The Abbess Elisabeth Herold used a chronicle of the Cistercian monastery of Kaisheim, written by Johannes Knebel, for her history of the Cistercian convent of Oberschönenfeld in Bavaria (Woodford 2002). Knebel was a Humanist, who, drawing on Cicero, conceived of history as a stock of educative role models, a view which undoubtedly influenced Herold. Histories written by nuns had both an immediate function within their community and a ready-made audience. Juliana Ernst, the prioress of a Poor Clares' house in Villingen, Germany, wrote a hagiographical account of her convent's founding abbess, Ursula Haider (Woodford 2002: 144–84). She was partly motivated by 'the constant imploring of some of my fellow nuns who bear a particular love and respect for our late mother' (Ernst 1881: 141).

It is possible to demonstrate from the textual evidence that large numbers of histories of convents were certainly written by women, rather than by confessors or other clerics. Nuns often gave their name to accounts, since they felt no shame in writing for their communities, indeed they hoped that future generations would remember and pray for them. Where accounts are anonymous, the authors are often identified by a convent office; authors tend often to have held important offices within a convent, such as abbess or prioress. They had to manage their work around their devotions and other duties. Elisabeth Herold from Oberschönenfeld worked late into the night on her long history of the convent since its foundation in 1211. It is structured according to the period of rule of each abbess, and is a great intellectual achievement, for which she used hundreds of documents and letters from the archive, which she read through many times. She was also responsible for the re-organisation of the convent's archive. The Italian Franciscan historian Orsola Formicini from SS. Cosma e Damiano in Rome undertook a similar work of re-organisation when she became abbess (Lowe 2000: 109). Recent studies have focused on further works of history by Italian nuns of the same period (Evangelisti 1992; Lowe 2003). In the community of Port-Royal in France, the author Angélique de Saint-Jean had to neglect her history of the convent's foundation for many years because of her other duties as sub-prioress and novice mistress (Weaver 1978: 126, 136). So in some convents, abbesses delegated to others. From the chronicle of the Bridgettine convent of Maihingen, Bavaria, we learn that it was the prioress' work to write, because the abbess would not have time (Woodford 2002: 57). Caritas Pirckheimer, abbess of the Poor Clares' convent in Nuremberg, Germany, probably had a scribe copy up rough versions made on a wax tablet. In the important Benedictine abbey of Frauenchiemsee in Bavaria, chronicles were kept during the period of rule of each abbess. These were most likely written by another nun or nuns, and one at least, belonging to Magdalene Auer, was written by a confessor (Woodford 2002: 66–77).

Reformation and dissent

Nuns not only researched histories of their convent's past but also wrote eyewitness accounts of important events. They wrote in the vernacular, for that was the language most commonly understood and used by their sisters. The texts were usually transmitted as manuscripts, and sometimes re-copied by later generations. Authorisation from the abbess was needed to access the documents necessary to do research, and for an account to be preserved in the archive or library, the history usually needed to conform to the convent's ideals and outlook. Authors usually acted with the superior's blessing or under her instruction. It is thus very difficult for a subversive account to survive. One interesting example of a dissenting text, however, is an eyewitness account of the Counter-Reformation enclosure of the Puttrich house of Franciscan tertiary nuns in Munich (Strasser 2002). The Puttrich nuns had an active ministry in Munich, caring for the sick and dying in the city until the Council of Trent decreed the strict enclosure of all female religious (Strasser 2002: 221). The King of Bavaria, Maximilian I, invited the reformers to the convent, and in 1621 a male clerical and political hierarchy enforced reform on the reluctant women. The account is written by the gatekeeper – one of the nuns – and suggests that enclosure was opposed, and bitterly resented. However, as Ulrike Strasser demonstrates, by the end of the century the convent's official history, printed in two versions for public consumption in 1695 and 1721 denied any resistance to reform in a celebration of its enclosed and contemplative lifestyle (2002: 221–2). Strasser points out how a comparison of the different versions of the events of 1621 alerts us to the problem that 'male-oriented conventions of remembrance' may be at work even in sources which we consider to be female voices (2002: 239). The gatekeeper's history, written for consumption within the convent, represents the women's grief at the loss of their active ministry, and demonstrates their collective dissent against the male hierarchy. By contrast, the later public histories have internalised the values of the male reforming clerics and 'sequestered . . . part of the female past' (2002: 239).

Although far more research is needed on the similarities and contrasts between histories written by nuns in different language areas, the tradition crosses political borders and seems to be found in all the pre-Tridentine monastic orders. There was a very strong tradition of writing historical chronicles in Birgittine houses. Important examples exist from Maihingen and Altomünster in Bavaria, Germany. In Maria Troon in Dendermonde in the Netherlands, Marie van Oss wrote a chronicle spanning 50 years and noting the convent's connections to 23 other Birgittine houses (Olsen 1999: 241). Her contemporary, the Abbess Margareta Nicolai or Clausdaughter of Vadstena in Sweden, wrote a chronicle in Swedish about the life of St Birgitta and the saint's family (Olsen 1999: 242). Nicolai herself was a relative of the saint. There were close links between the different convents and the impetus to write history was probably passed on through such connections. Birgittine houses were founded mostly in the late fourteenth and early fifteenth centuries, and their histories seem often to have been written in an attempt to preserve the memories of nuns who had witnessed the convent's foundation, at a time when the oral history transmitted by the oldest generation was about to be lost. Angélique de Saint-Jean Arnauld of Port-Royal des Champs in France made a similar effort to write her community's history just as the founding generation was disappearing (Weaver 1981; Kostroun 2003). She did so initially without consulting her aunts, *Mère* Angélique Arnauld and *Mère* Agnes Arnauld, who were the founding mothers. However, upon the death of *Mère* Angélique in 1661, *Mère* Agnes herself ordered all the nuns to write down everything they could remember about the reverend mother (Weaver 1978: 126). The convent was under threat from the clerical and political hierarchy for its adherence to Jansenist practices, and so the writing of its history played an important part in its self-justification beyond the cloister.

In England, monastic houses were suppressed during the English Reformation. However, many nuns moved to the Low Countries or France to join communities of the same order, and gradually founded English communities there. Histories from such convents often commemorate the bravery and religious commitment of the earliest members of the community who risked their lives for their faith (Foster 1986; Grundy 1992). One important example is the convent of Augustinian Canonesses of St Monica's in Louvain, settled in 1609 by English nuns from the convent of St Ursula there (Grundy 1992: 35–7). They were proud to recall illustrious connections with important martyrs and saints who were persecuted during the Reformation, such as Thomas More and Margaret Clitheroe. The English nuns after the Reformation came largely from the minor gentry, and Claire Walker suggests that these connections provided a substitution for the aristocratic connections, on which convents would previously have drawn to validate their position (Walker 2003).

In Germany too, nuns' histories recall the religious upheaval of the early modern period. In 1525, the Imperial Free City of Nuremberg in Germany decided to adopt Lutheranism and close down its religious houses. Out of four monasteries and two convents, only one house, that of the Poor Clares, led by the Abbess Caritas Pirckheimer, resisted (Barker 1995; Woodford 2002). Throughout that year, Pirckheimer negotiated extensively with the City Council over her convent's rights and refused to release her nuns from their solemn vows. The nuns were verbally abused from outside the cloister. Three young nuns, whose families had willingly placed them in the convent only six or seven years previously, were forcibly removed from the convent by their mothers, as a public spectacle. Eventually, the reformer Philipp Melanchthon achieved a compromise: the convent would remain, but no new nuns could be admitted and it was denied Catholic sacraments, with the result that it died out in 1596. To demonstrate for posterity that the community had used every means possible to protect itself, Pirckheimer had the nuns create a written record, usually called the *Denkwürdigkeiten* (Pfanner 1962; Woodford 2002: 78–105). It comprises important letters written to the convent's adversaries, interspersed with narratives by Pirckheimer depicting the most important conversations and events.

The *Denkwürdigkeiten* is a very striking account, using vivid, emotive language, such as describing the mothers of the young nuns as 'she-wolves', and saying of the daughters' resistance: 'all three fell to the floor and screamed, wept and bawled, and their demeanour indicated such grief that the Lord above must surely have pitied them' (Pfanner 1962: 79). While it would be easy to read the account simply as a true and vivid record of events, it is important to bear in mind the ideological standpoint of the author, and the effect this had on the language used and events selected. Pirckheimer was the sister of the humanist Willibald Pirckheimer, and received a humanist's classical education. Her style and rhetoric are very carefully selected; this can be seen in her polemical descriptions of her adversaries and repeated assertions of the nuns's unanimous obedience. Hers was a reformed convent and it may be that discipline was so strict that the nuns could be relied upon to follow her lead. However, early in 1528, one of the nuns, Anna Schwarz, left the convent voluntarily, after a long struggle to do so, during which she kept herself apart from the other nuns and refused to accept Pirckheimer's authority. This incident is not mentioned by Pirckheimer, but added by a later chronicler. In fact, Schwarz may well have been stirring up trouble in the convent as early as 1525, for the account is both defensive and didactic. It justifies Pirckheimer's course of action, defending her inability to maintain the convent's right to the Catholic sacraments and to accept new members. It presents a picture of exemplary resistance and obedience, not only as a model for future generations, but as a reminder to her 80 nuns of the right way to behave.

Monastic writing

History writing in convents probably developed as a tradition in the early Middle Ages alongside the writing of history by male religious (Woodford 2002). It was used to justify the rights of a monastic house and lay claim to its lands. However, histories of monasteries, which were all written by male religious and hence were often in Latin, have been the subject of far more research; histories of convents are often overlooked by studies. In the fifteenth century, the monastic reform movement led to an increase in the writing of history in convents and monasteries and a shift in its function. The reform movement, which grew out of the Church councils of the early fifteenth century, attempted to counter what it perceived as a weakening of discipline in monastic life in the late Middle Ages. The reformers were largely men, and women were in many ways disproportionately affected by the reforms, through which male control over female monastic life was strengthened. Strict enclosure – the *clausura* or cloister – was advocated for all women who had taken solemn vows. It prevented abbesses from travelling to imperial diets and all nuns from caring for the sick and dying within their local community, looking after their families, or earning a living in the town, which had been important for communities which were not well endowed financially, such as many of the Franciscan tertiary nuns. This restriction on women's freedoms was often bitterly resisted, especially by women who had become nuns less out of religious conviction than as part of a family strategy deliberately to limit the number of daughters who had to make costly marriages (McNamara 1998: 385–418). History writing formed an important tool in persuading nuns (and, in monasteries, monks) to accept the reforms of the Church. Through histories of a convent's earliest days, a golden age was depicted, when religious discipline was as strict as the Church advocated and the nuns were holy women whose example the community should seek to emulate. History became a didactic tool, and depictions of female monasticism in the past were carefully calculated to reflect the ideals of the present.

With her biography of the Abbess Ursula Haider, written during the Counter-Reformation, Juliana Ernst presents her nuns with a model for their behaviour in both spiritual life [*vita contemplative*] and other duties [*vita activa*]. She begins with Haider's youth, emphasising her commitment to virginity, and her desire only to enter a reformed, that is enclosed, convent with strict religious discipline. Ernst's readers all live in such a convent, but by reminding the nuns of the founder's commitment to such a strict lifestyle, she intends to strengthen the readers' acceptance of it, perhaps with the intention of increasing the severity of adherence to the rule. The young Haider is depicted as having model obedience towards her superiors in the convent, and tirelessly engages in the washing, cleaning and care for the sick and elderly, which many nuns probably found onerous.

Ursula Haider began her religious life in the reformed Poor Clares' convent of Valduna, and she was 67 before she was called to go to Villingen and reform the small open convent there. Ernst provides a very rich narrative of the hardships undergone by the small group of nuns, after Haider had enclosed the new convent in 1480: 'the blessed little cloister was built just like a secular house: it was in ill state of repair, small and dark . . . It would have been no surprise if the women had not fallen ill from their strict lifestyle and airless house, for they only had one narrow, dark room and a chamber' (Ernst 1881: 37). Important for Ernst is the perseverance of the nuns, driven by their commitment to the ideals of reformed monasticism: '[T]he nuns suffered frost and cold, even hunger and thirst . . . with great forbearance. When they tried to go to sleep at night they had no rest because there was so much vermin; mice and rats ran over their faces and bit them in the forehead and the hand' (Ernst 1881: 37). This description is similar to the account of life in St Ursula's in Louvain (Grundy 1992: 137). The nuns were 'gentlewomen' but they 'did willingly accommodate themselves to the hard fare and simple diet of the cloister . . . which indeed was so very mean as to deserve to be recorded to posterity, that we might know with what fervour our sisters began to serve God in holy religion' (Hamilton 1904/6: 34–5). They lived on rye bread, small beer, porridge made with water, and only very small amounts of poor meat and broth. The rule was observed very strictly, and the women had to carry out work which they would usually have had done by servants. They washed linen and wool clothes, made bread, weeded, swept and wove linen, 'which was indeed a man's work, and very hard for tender, weak women' (Hamilton 1904/6: 36).

In both cases, the nuns surely did suffer in their dedication to the monastic rule, and the account fulfils the important religious function of *memoria*, ensuring that the readers remember to pray for the souls of those who suffered such hardship to provide them with a secure convent environment. However, the detailed depiction of the suffering also suggests a desire by a later generation to create narratives of the past which could assist the convent in its aims; justifying the convent's existence through the virtue of its founding generation and exhorting the present readership to emulate that generation in its own devotion to the rule.

The depiction of hardships in the chronicles from Villingen and St Monica's is mirrored in Elisabeth Herold's chronicle of Oberschönenfeld too, although here she is drawing on her own memories of the community's fate in the Thirty Years' War. Her community fled to the Austrian Alps during the Swedish advance of 1631. It need not necessarily have fled; many communities remained in their buildings. However, it should have made preparations to send its numerous treasures and archives to safety. These preparations were not taken, for which Herold (who became abbess in exile) levies bitter criticism at her predecessor:

> Perhaps one simply thought that the storm would not reach us here, or that God would miraculously conceal our convent, against the natural order of things, from the eyes of the enemy (that would certainly have been desirable), but one has never heard or read of such a thing happening before, and still less could or should one have reasonably imagined it would happen here. (1995)

Herold was drawing on her own experience for the depiction of these hardships. But they are still described in a way deliberately calculated to elicit admiration and sympathy. She wrote that for four weeks the community of 35 people lived in a cramped farm with a single room: 'the professed nuns had their resting place in the main room on the earth and on the benches; the others [the lay sisters and maids] were in the barn on the hard floor. There was not a wisp of straw or a handful of hay to rest our heads on. Rather we lay fully clothed like poor beggars' (Herold 1995). When her community returned to Oberschönenfeld, it had been looted, and Herold had lost control over some of its estates. She had to search through the archives to find documentation justifying the abbey's control over its lands. She wrote the chronicle as part of her quest to have its full legal rights restored, and as a demonstration of its power and status (Woodford 2002).

Spiritual autobiographies

Convent history also provided women with an opportunity to write their own history. Catherine Burton, a Carmelite, and Catherine Holland, an English Augustinian Canoness from Bruges, both wrote spiritual autobiographies in the second half of the seventeenth century, which they present as a part of their community's history (Grundy 1992: 128). Catherine Holland depicts her life and spiritual turmoil up to the point when she made her profession as a nun in 1664 (Grundy 1992: 131). The worldly pleasures of youth, such as dancing, cards and music characterised her formative years (Durrant 1925: 276). Monastic life had no attractions for her: 'I thought it a miserable Life always to be locked up as in a Prison . . . I little thought, I was to be one of those, I thought them so unhappy' (Durrant 1925: 277–8). However, Divine Providence led her to her true vocation, and her story is clearly edificatory for any young pupil or novice, for it demonstrates how the most worldly girl might become a contented religious. Maria Anna Junius, a Dominican nun from Bamberg, and Clara Staiger, prioress of the Augustinian nuns of Eichstätt, both give much briefer narratives of their lives at the start of their accounts of the Thirty Years' War in Germany (Woodford 2002). Junius wrote a very detailed history of the Swedish War, which contains large sections that have nothing to do with her convent at all, but rather depict in a broader sense the progress of the Swedish army's campaigns in South Germany. This perhaps demonstrates how closely she felt her convent's history to be connected to that of the region as a whole and her own history with both. Staiger's is a personal diary. She took office just as the War began to affect Eichstätt; the nuns had to flee after the convent was attacked. Later it was burned down, and the community impoverished. Staiger's occasional outbursts demonstrate the pressure she suffered. After managing to buy a horse to replace one which was stolen, she writes: 'It is impossible to believe how much trouble this cost me, and I have not had any sleep, nor any rest day and night for worrying about the misery that is before my eyes, as well as how we will find food in the future. Rather, I have been constantly worrying and weeping' (Staiger 1981: 166). The start of Junius's account tells briefly of the persecution of witches in Bamberg, in which her father and mother both perished. Maria Anna enters into a form of self-censorship, however. She suppresses the connection with her parents, and does not mention them, merely allowing herself to question whether the persecution had not claimed many innocent victims.

Research into history writing by nuns is an area in which much work still needs to be done. Many histories by nuns have not yet been the subject of detailed analysis, and many more probably remain to be discovered in the archives. Further extensive bibliographical work as well as studies of individual writings are essential if any broad picture is to emerge. Some of this work has been undertaken within the convents themselves, which continue to display a strong interest in researching their own past. The chronicle of Elisabeth Herold from Oberschönenfeld was continued until the convent's secularisation in 1802, and again since its restoration in 1836 until the present day (Woodford 2002: 182–3). Currently, the abbey is in the process of publishing the chronicle in excerpts in its biannual newsletter (Herold 1995). Similarly, the abbey of Frauenchiemsee, the oldest female house in Germany, has published one of its seventeenth-century chronicles, while other convents, such as St Marienstern or Altomünster, have organised exhibitions and produced volumes examining their long history. Nevertheless, many writings exist from convents that were suppressed and hence have no successors to research them. Every monastic house has its own unique history and situation. However, convents across Europe were subject to many similar influences. Further research may demonstrate that there are far more similarities in the writing and function of history, both across monastic orders and between different language areas, than has previously been acknowledged.

Charlotte Woodford

References

Barker 1995; Davis 1984; Durrant 1925; Ernst 1881; Evangelisti 1992; Foster 1986; Grundy 1992; Hamilton; 1904, 1906; Herold 1995; Kostroun 2003; Lowe 2000, 2003; McNamara 1998; Olsen 1999; Pfanner 1962; Proksch 1994; Staiger 1981; Strasser 2002; Walker 2003; Weaver 1978, 1981; Woodford 2002; Wunder 1999.

Related essays

Middle Ages; Reformation; Religion; Travel.

Cooper, Anna Julia Haywood 1858–1964

African-American feminist, pan-Africanist, educator, historian. Born in Raleigh, North Carolina, daughter of Hannah Stanley, slave. Educated at Saint Augustine's Normal School and Collegiate Institution, where she became a teacher following graduation. Married George A C Cooper, a theology student in 1877. He died prematurely several months after his ordination. Following his death Cooper entered Oberlin College, where she studied classics, languages and mathematics, earning her AB degree in 1884 and her MA degree in 1887. As one of the few African-Americans with a graduate degree she was recruited to teach in Washington DC at the Preparatory High School for Coloured Youth (known popularly as the M Street School) where she spent much of her career.

In 1892 she published her first major work *A Voice from the South: By a Black Woman from the South*, one of the first works of African-American feminism. A collection of essays and addresses which merged autobiography, oratory and literary criticism, this work forcefully challenged the muting of the voices of African-American women and offered an historical analysis of their oppression. Cooper was critical of the racism of the white women's movement, anticipating arguments made by historians such as Paula Giddings and bell hooks almost a century later. Cooper herself was heavily involved in the black women's club movement. A founding member of the Colored Women's League of Washington, she attended and spoke at events such as the American Conference of Educators, the Congress of Representative Women, the National Conference of Colored Women and the National Federation of African-American Women. She attended the first Pan-African Conference in London in 1900 and presented a paper on 'The Negro Problem in America'. Became Principal of the M Street School between 1902 and 1906 when she was removed from this position for refusing to concede to the Board of Education's demand that her students be given 'a course of study commensurate with their alleged inferior abilities'. Served as chair of languages at Lincoln University in Jefferson City, Missouri, between 1906 and 1910, when she returned to the M Street School.

Travelled to France to study at the Guilde Internationale in the summers of 1911, 1912 and 1913 to study French history, literature and phonetics. In 1914 at Columbia University, she began her course work requirements for the PhD. She transferred her studies to the Sorbonne, completing her thesis *Le Pèlerinage de pendant la Révolution*, a study of the relations between revolutionaries in France and the inhabitants of her richest colony, Santo Domingo. Cooper's thesis inserted the dimension of race into the history of the revolution, shifting the focus of revolutionary causes away from the feudalism of the *ancien regime* and onto the institution of chattel slavery. In 1925 Cooper became one of the first women in France to obtain a doctorate from the Sorbonne.

Appointed the second President of Frelinghuysen University in Washington DC in 1930. Frelinghuysen was a group of schools devoted to providing 'social services, religious training and educational programs for people who most needed them'. Following the financial demise of this institution, Cooper retired from teaching, although she remained active in education reform until the 1940s.

Mary Spongberg

References

Alexander 1995; Keller 1975; NBAW 1996; Washington 1988.

Major work

A Voice from the South (ed.) Mary Helen Washington (New York: Oxford University Press, 1988).

D

Dall, Caroline Wells Healey 1822–1912

American biographer, social scientist, historian of women. Born Boston, eldest daughter of Caroline Foster and Mark Healey, a banker. Educated by governesses and at a private school in Boston. Engaged in 'relief work' through the Unitarian Church, Dall operated a nursery for working mothers between 1837 and 1842. From 1842 until 1844 she taught in a school in Georgetown, DC. Married Reverend Charles Henry Appleton Dall, Unitarian minister in 1844. Two children. Following her marriage she engaged in abolition work and assisted slaves to escape to Canada.

Dall became interested in **feminism** after reading **Harriet Martineau**'s 'Political Non-existence of Women' in 1837. It was not, however, until 1855, when she was effectively abandoned by her husband, that she became involved in campaigns for women's rights. Working with **Paulina Wright Davis** on *The Una*, Dall organised the Boston Women's Rights Conventions in 1855, where she delivered an exhaustive report on the legal status of women. She also organised the New England Women's Rights Convention in 1859, delivering one of its principal addresses, later published as *Women's Right to Labor or Low Wages and Hard Work* (1860), a text she dedicated to **Anna Jameson**. Dall criticised women's restricted opportunities for employment, claiming this made for their unequal status. Her edited work *A Letter from Marie E Zakrzewska MD* (1860) illustrated the possibilities of women training in medicine, a theme she revisited in *The Life of Dr Anadabai Joshee* (1888). Dall's economic analysis of women's oppression foreshadowed that of **Charlotte Perkins Gilman**.

Historical Pictures Retouched drew together articles Dall had written for *The Una*, including biographical studies of Aspasia, Hypatia, **Madame de Staël** and **Margaret Fuller** and essays on the contribution of women to medical science and on the duties and influence of women. Dall believed the writing of **Female Biography** served a feminist purpose by rewriting the masculinist historical record. With *Women's Rights under the Law* (1861) she produced a comparative study of women's 'civil disabilities'. Parts of this text were republished in the *Englishwoman's Journal*. In 1865 she co-founded the American Social Science Association and served as its director until 1880. Dall believed the link between feminism, social science and history was self-evident. She had written in *The Una*, 'Without reading the past clearly, it is impossible to go on to the root of present evils.' In 1867 Dall brought together her research on the history of women's work and legal status into her most acclaimed book *The College, the Market and the Court* (1867). She was awarded an LLD from Alfred University in 1877.

In 1895 Dall drew on her own history in *Margaret and Friends* based on notes taken during her attendance at Margaret Fuller's weekly 'conversations' in 1841. *Lecture on Transcendentalism in New England* (1897) presented a feminine history of the evolution of this movement claiming its origins in Anne Hutchinson and placing **Margaret Fuller** on equal footing with Ralph Waldo Emerson. Dall was one of the women to whom **Elizabeth Cady Stanton, Susan B Anthony** and **Matilda Joselyn Gage** dedicated their *History of Women's Suffrage*.

Mary Spongberg

Reference

Conrad 1976.

Davis, Paulina Wright 1813–1876

Suffrage activist, editor, publisher, historian of women. Born in New York, one of the five children of Polly (Saxton) and Captain Ebenezer Kellogg. Orphaned when aged seven, she was brought up by her aunt. Married Francis Wright, a merchant, in 1833. Wright became involved in Abolition and Temperance activities. In the late 1830s she petitioned the New York legislature for a married women's property law. She became involved in health reform, studying anatomy and physiology. After her husband's death left her independently wealthy, she lectured women on physiology and established the Providence Physiological Society. In 1849 she married Thomas Davis, an anti-slavery Democrat elected to Congress in 1852.

Following this marriage Wright Davis focused her energies on the woman's rights movement. Co-ordinating the meetings for the National Woman Suffrage Movement in New York City, she gave the keynote address at the first US Woman's Rights Convention in 1850. In 1853 she began to publish, at her own expense, a monthly periodical called the *Una*, one of the first publications dedicated to the woman's rights movement. The *Una* promoted women's historical writing by recording the history of the present, documenting the progress of the Woman's Rights Movement for posterity and by drawing on the past to highlight women's present situation. Davis hoped to provide stenographers to the conventions and wrote that she would 'endeavour to preserve a correct history, not only of this specific movement, but of the lives of those engaged in it'. She wrote for the *Una* detailed accounts of the woman's rights conventions, editorials and informative articles, outlining the achievements of women. After two years the magazine floundered and Davis felt that her attempts to bring about united action among women had failed. **Caroline Dall** worked on the *Una* keeping it afloat until it ceased publication in 1855. Davis wrote for a number of woman's rights periodicals, including **Susan B Anthony** and **Elizabeth Cady Stanton**'s *Revolution*, and in 1870 she established another reform paper, the *New World*. Much of her writing drew on history, as well as mythology and the Bible. Davis believed that cultural perceptions of women were based on the past, and often reinterpreted history, mythology and religion in order to define or redefine the role of women.

Davis' principal work was *A History of the National Woman's Rights Movement* (1871). Davis described herself as a compiler and much of the *History of the National Woman's Rights Movement* is made up of documents she has collected, interspersed with the barest of details or commentary, usually in the form of an introduction for each successive document. Many of the introductions were rhetorical in nature and personal, as if the book was written as a convention speech. It might also be described as part **memoir** of an activist part documentary history. Davis is one of the women to whom **Elizabeth Cady Stanton**, **Susan B Anthony** and **Matilda Joselyn Gage** dedicated their *History of Woman Suffrage*.

Sarah Howard

References
Derbyshire 1993; *NAW* 1971.

Defences of women

Stemming from the tradition of **catalog** literature defences of women were the most common form of women's history produced during the early modern period. Defences of women were formulated to question the proposition that women were inferior physically, mentally and morally to men. While not primarily written as 'women's history', defences of women functioned partly to restore women to history, by establishing the excellence of women through historical examples and to make humanist arguments, particularly for the education of women. The Italian humanist Giovanni Boccaccio between 1361 and 1375 is often said to have written the first 'defence of women' *Concerning Famous Women* (c.1360–1375). This text draws on various catalogs from the classical and early Christian era, as well as the lives of the saints, to create the first collection of biographies devoted exclusively to women. While frequently cited as a 'defence of women' Boccaccio wrote to 'praise' rather than to defend 'the sex' and feminist scholars have commented upon an overpowering ambivalence towards women in the text (McLeod 1991: 59–80). Boccaccio singled out for inclusion in his text, only women who transcended their 'soft frail bodies and sluggish minds' to attain a 'manly spirit' (Brown 2003: 4). Thus while *Concerning Famous Women* presents the history of women whose 'deeds are worthy of remembrance' it simultaneously limits the potential of women attaining historical subjectivity as women, recording the actions of virile women, while praising only those who are chaste, silent and obedient.

What is truly unique in Boccaccio's text, however, is its inclusion of learned and cultured women such as painters, writers, sculptors and scholars (McLeod 1991: 61). This innovation heralded a new interest in women's potential for learning, indeed a new interest in defining womanhood, inspiring the *querelle des femmes*. Following Boccaccio numerous male-authored 'defences of women' appeared. Like *Concerning Famous Women*, these texts contained catalogs of Biblical, Classical and Christian heroines demonstrating the possibility of female excellence. Male-authored defences of women written following Boccaccio were concerned to rhetorically determine the question 'Quid est mulier?' [What is woman?]. Historical information about 'illustrious women' formed a rhetorical strategy in these texts. Such lives were not presented as models for imitation, but rather as 'objects of demonstration'; consequently it was irrelevant whether the women presented were mythical or had historically existed (Rang 1998: 51–2). Like *Concerning Famous Women* many of these defences of womanhood were deeply ambivalent and by the middle of the sixteenth century one observer complained that such texts were 'cold, tedious and monotonous re-workings of old themes written . . . to demonstrate wit and cleverness, or to satisfy . . . the greed of the popular press' (Benson 1992: 65). The printing press made such texts available to a wider audience, but it also encouraged the development of a virulent pamphlet literature that defamed women and reviled marriage. Texts such as Jacques Olivier's *Alphabet of Women's Imperfections and Malice* (1617) and Joseph Swetnam's *Arraignment of Lewd Women* (1617) were less scholarly and more polemical than male-authored defences, but also more popular, often running through numerous editions.

While male authors produced defences as exercises in rhetoric and chivalry, female-authored defences of women were frequently written in response to specific misogynistic texts. In their defences women drew upon the authority of history to counter misogynistic claims and used historical figures to demonstrate women's capacity for both civic and domestic virtue. The first female defender of women, **Christine de Pizan**, wrote specifically to counter the writings of Jean de Meun and Mathéolus. In a series of works in different genres Christine drew upon myth as well as sacred and secular history to defend women from the misogynous slurs. *The Book of the City of Women* written in response to 'the wicked insults about women and their behaviour' promulgated by 'learned men' (3) offers her most extensive defence. *City of Women* can also be read as response to Boccaccio's *Concerning Famous Women*. It is known that Christine drew upon this text for examples; however, the *City of Women* offers a substantial reworking of *Concerning Famous Women* both structurally and in terms of its argument. Whereas Boccaccio's text offered faint praise for women, Christine's work was structured as a rhetorical defence of womanhood, consequently it is both defensive in its aim to promote a better understanding of women's capabilities and aggressive in its desire to protect women from slander. While Boccaccio stressed the exceptionality of his subjects, Christine drew upon the same subjects as evidence for the excellence of all women. Christine essentially rewrites Boccaccio's text as a woman-centred history of women, making the female experience universal, and thus decentring the masculine as author and subject of history.

A number of Christine's compatriots followed her example producing defences of women that rewrote history from a feminine perspective. While most female-authored defences of women included catalogs of **women worthies**, they also adopted other generic forms and like Christine sought to revise or reform them. The Brescian prodigy Laura Cereta wrote epistolary essays that drew upon Boccaccio's *Concerning Famous Women* while also challenging and revising the material he used in this text (Robin 1997: 63). While Boccaccio had focused on virile women, women who had achieved fame by overcoming their sex, Cereta created a maternalist history of women, presenting women's unique biological function as an engine of history, calling women to action. The Venetian writer Moderate Fonte's (Modesta Pozzo) *The Worth of Women* (1592) usurped the masculinist tradition by creating a symposium of women engaged in a dialogue on marriage.

In questioning women's subservient status Fonte rewrote scriptural history suggesting the story of the Fall had been misinterpreted and vindicating Eve of blame. In this text she draws on an extensive knowledge of ancient history to depict the 'magnanimity and patriotism of women'.

Other women followed Christine in writing defences of women to answer specific misogynistic texts. The prolific Venetian writer Lucrezia Marinella hastily composed her *Nobility and Excellence of Women* (1600) in response to Giuseppe Passi's diatribe *On the Defects of Women* (1599). Written as a formal debating treatise Marinella's text not only defends women against scurrilous accusations, it also features a blistering attack on masculine imperfections. In the Preface to this text Marinella personally upbraids Passi, while also claiming that Aristotle 'was led by scorn, hate and envy in many of his books' and this caused him to 'to vituperate and slander the female sex'. The publication of Joseph Swetnam's *Arraignment of Lewd Women in England* produced no less than three responses claiming to be written by women, although only one author Rachel Speght used her real name. Speght, the daughter of a Puritan minister, drew upon an impressive knowledge of Scripture and the historical writings of the Church fathers such as Eusebius to challenge Swetnam's conclusions in *A Mouzell for Melastomus* (1617). When the Reverend Sprint published his famously patriarchal wedding sermon *The Bride-Woman's Counsellor* (1700), two English women responded in verse: the pseudonymous 'Eugenia' (Sarah Fyge Egerton) who drew upon Scriptural history to question each of his premises in *The Female Advocate* (1770) and Lady Mary Chudleigh who wrote *The Ladies' Defence* (1701).

As women came to write in defence of womanhood, they were sometimes subject to vicious personal attacks and thus wrote to defend themselves. As early as 1439 Isotta Nogarola was the subject of a vituperative anonymous attack that merged scorn at her 'eloquence' and 'erudition' with a scurrilous charge of incest (King 1980: 77). Such charges not only connected Nogarola with the crime most damaging to the social order, it also linked her in the public imagination to the women most reviled in the masculinist catalog tradition, Messalina and Agrippina. Following this attack she would write elegantly in a letter to a male patron that 'many women surpass not only other women but also men in every kind of virtue and excellence' appending a catalog of women worthies such as Cornelia, mother of the Gracchi and Sappho as evidence of her claim (King and Robin 2004: 98–9). Laura Cereta was also frequently attacked by hostile critics and she defended herself so valiantly that her championship of female learning forms a major theme in her work (King 1980: 90).

The defence of female learning also formed a theme in the writings of women beyond Italy. In various texts the French writer Marie de Gournay complained about men's devaluing of women, especially their intellectual ability. In her *The Equality of Men and Women* (1622) she drew upon 'glorious witnesses' such as Plato and Socrates to derive a catalog of learned women such as Hypatia, Themistoclea, the sister of Pythagoras and the legendary Nicostrata who Boccaccio claimed to have invented the Latin alphabet, thus turning the masculinist tradition upon itself. De Gournay also mentions contemporary women of learning such as Anna Maria van Schurman from Holland, who was known as 'the most learned woman of the age'. England's Bathusua Reginald Makin also mentions van Schurman in her *An Essay to Revive the Antient Education of Gentlewomen* (1673). Van Schurman herself wrote a treatise entitled *Whether the Study of Letters is Fitting for a Christian Woman* (1638). In this text she carefully distinguished herself from earlier women writers who had sought to reverse traditional gender relations, claiming only that religious and moral virtue in women would be enhanced by study (Irwin 1998: 10). Unlike other defences of women written by women Van Schurman did not draw upon historical examples to bolster her argument, perhaps because the example of extraordinary women undermined her modest claims. Other writers were more innovative. **Madeleine de Scudéry**, one of France's most prolific novelists, created first-person 'autobiographical' accounts of women such as Cleopatra and Sappho in her *Les femmes illustres, ou Les harangues héroïque* (1642). For each of the women worthies represented in the text, de Scudéry presents an 'Argument', a prefatory and concluding poem, the oration or harangue itself, and a brief statement of its effect, essentially giving the moral of the story (Newman 2003: 9).

By the end of the seventeenth century women felt confident enough in making their defences to urge for the rejection of the masculine world and the values that shaped it. Mary Astell's *A Serious Proposal to the Ladies* (1694) defended women, arguing that girls should be taught to use their intellect and radically proposed a separatist educational community for women, in order that they might prepare themselves to be teachers for the next generation. This text focused on logical argument rather than celebratory lists and said little about history. In her later text, *The Christian Religion Profess'd by a Daughter of the Church of England*, Astell thoroughly discounted history, claiming that 'Men, being the historians seldom condescend to record the great and good actions of women' (1705). While it appears she was unfamiliar with her predecessors who revised masculinist history to reclaim the 'great and good actions of women' in the past, she too critiques the exceptionality of male-authored texts, indeed coining the phrase that women featured in them 'acted above their sex'.

By the middle of the eighteenth century defences of women drawing on the catalog tradition gave way to more encyclopedic studies of women's excellence. In line with the Enlightenment impulse to catalog and categorise, brief biographical sketches gave way to dictionaries and encyclopedias of celebrated women. In England George Ballard's *Memoirs of Several Ladies of Great Britain* (1752) marked the new direction in male-authored texts. Ballard's *Memoirs* drew largely upon the unpublished work of Elizabeth Elstob. As a young woman Elstob had been one of the foremost scholars of Saxon in Britain, but had retired from society following the death of her brother. Struggling in genteel poverty, Elstob had to abandon a volume on learned women she had hoped to write (Perry 1985: 24). The success of Ballard's text may have encouraged women to work on similar projects. Some 20 years later Ann Thickness produced *Sketches of the Lives and Writings of the Ladies of France*, the first work of collective biography by a named woman author (Oldfield 1999: 30). In France **Louise de Keralio [Robert]** began publication of a similar work, the 12-volume *Collection des meilleurs ouvrages français composés par des femmes* in 1786. This work constructed a female literary tradition in France beginning with Héloïse (Hesse 1993: 240–1). Although these works were not defences they functioned in a similar way, promoting the education of women through biographical studies of learned women.

Defences of women have remained of interest to historians of women as evidence of the widespread and virulent nature of early modern misogyny, but also as evidence of female agency during this period. Pioneering works of women's history such as **Emily Putnam**'s *The Lady* (1910), Myra Reynolds' *The Learned Lady in England* (1920), Lula McDowell Richardson's *The Forerunners of Feminism in French Literature of the Renaissance* (1929), Ruth Kelso's *Doctrine for the Lady of the Renaissance* (1955) and **Doris Mary Stenton**'s *The English Woman in History* (1957) drew on these defences as evidence of women's engagement in the world of politics and letters in the past. More recently **Joan Kelly** has suggested that such texts can be read as early examples of feminist philosophy, arguing that defenders of women from Christine de Pizan to **Mary Wollstonecraft** were women who felt themselves and all women maligned by misogynist ideology. In defending women as a 'social group', Kelly suggests these women created 'an intellectual tradition' that 'kept alive the memory of the feudal rule of women' (1984: 69). This memory had informed the work of first-wave feminist historians, such as **Helen Blackburn**, Caroline **Ashurst** Biggs and Charlotte Carmichael Stopes, who argued that womanhood suffrage was a demand for the restitution of women's feudal rights (Holton 1999: 150).

Mary Spongberg

References

Brown 2003; Hesse 1993; Holton 1999; Irwin 1998; Kelly 1984; King & Robin 2004; Newman 2003; Oldfield 1999; Perry 1985; Rang 1998; Robin 1997.

Related essays

Catalogs; Female Biography; Renaissance; Women Worthies; World History.

Dominion women writers

Ambivalent identities

In 1913 an American woman, Miss Jessie Ackermann, inaugural President of the Woman's Christian Temperance Union of Australasia and a notable reformer for women's rights, published a book entitled *Australia from a Woman's Point of View*. Ackermann had witnessed the swift movement of Australian women in the 1890s and early 1900s to full political citizenship, and puzzled that women rarely rated in written accounts of the new nation. The existing literature, she declared, presented 'the man's point of view'. The position of women in the country that pioneered women's citizenship had scarcely been described, much less 'properly set forth in its vital bearing on national life' (1913: vii). This situation she set about to rectify vigorously, if idiosyncratically, in her text.

In her first book, *The World through a Woman's Eye*, published in 1896, Ackermann had expressed surprise that the women in the British colonies she had visited as an organiser for the World Woman's Christian Temperance Union, 'the recipients of more courtesy and greater civility than those of any other race or tongue', were rarely content. Rather, the air was 'electric' with 'a great unrest among womankind', a striving for more than family and domestic life had to offer. One outcome, perhaps, of the unrest that Ackermann observed, was women's engagement with the writing of the national history, initially seeking to be included but increasingly differentiating their place in the dominant pioneer/progress narratives (1896: 18).

In the British Dominions of Canada, South Africa, Australia and New Zealand during the first decades of the twentieth century white women gained political rights, and a modest number of educated middle-class women entered the professions. A select few became academic historians, but commonly their writing left unchallenged the dominant narratives that their male counterparts had constructed as objective accounts of these new white societies; there was little space here for women's experiences or issues of gender. National celebrations of significant moments in white settlements provided the first opportunity for women to define a distinctive female past. Women writers, mostly outside the universities, wrote primarily for non-academic readers. This is not to suggest that their writing was insignificant. The educated housewives and single working women who bought, read and gave these books as presents to female relatives and friends were arguably as important as any academic readership to the construction of a national identity-in this case, one inclusive of women.

Such writers offered an imagined heroic past for their women citizens. Yet their gender-inclusivity was contained within a white project. The claims of these white women served in varying degrees to further exclude, marginalise or patronise the indigenous women and men who shared their past, the peoples whose dispossession had provided the basis for the white nationhood of whose development the writers claimed women's share. The Dominions were the sites of Empire where colonists had displaced indigenous peoples, to set their own stamp on these lands, their politics and their histories. In Canada and South Africa, formed into national entities in 1867 and 1910 respectively, the colonising process had been shared with the French in the former and the Dutch 'Afrikaaners' in the latter. In the seven Australasian colonies, British rule was unchallenged though the French and Germans claimed smaller Pacific islands. The six Australian colonies federated to form the Commonwealth of Australia in 1901, while the seventh colony, New Zealand, stood alone as a separate nation. The new white Dominions were unashamedly stamped with white supremacy but by mid-century some writers, women among them, began to recognise the pre-emption of an indigenous past and made some hesitant steps to rectification. This essay examines the ways in which these writers situated women of indigenous origin in their attempts to develop a gender-inclusive national history.

Canada

Canada, the oldest of the Dominions, provided a considerable space for women writers in the first decades of the twentieth century. Their emphasis, however, was on reclaiming the women's role within what were seen as the two founding peoples. The anonymous author of the Historical Sketch in the National Council of Women's *Women of Canada: Their Life and Work* (1901) argued: 'No woman's name appears among the discoverers and early explorers of Canada', yet 'it is the woman who assaults fortune for the sake of home and a fair future assured to her children. It is the woman, too, who perhaps has ever most cared for social advancement.' However, women exerted influence through their husbands rather than exercising political power in their own right. Although the early explorers had observed the power of the Mohawk Women's Council, the writer noted, 'the men of this nation . . . were the fiercest savages of the New World . . . and the liberty granted by them to their women commended itself no more highly to civilised Europeans than did their other heathen practises [*sic*]'.

The first historians to take up the challenge of including women within the pioneer story focused on French Canada. In her *Maids and Matrons of New France*, Mary Sifton Pepper compared the pioneer women of New France to the women who had accompanied the Pilgrim Fathers to America (1901: 1–2). The first three sections of her book tell the stories of individual women in the French settlements of Acadia, Québec and Montréal, struggling 'to establish a Christian commonwealth in the midst of a savage infected forest' (1901: 152–3). The last focuses on the 'sprightly, coquettish maids', whose later migration served 'to prevent the young men from allying themselves with Indian women', avoiding the birth of 'half-breeds . . . of doubtful value as future citizens' (1901: 242). Pioneer women were surrounded by indigenous women but the latter had no place in the future nation. An exception was made for the small number of Christian converts who 'provided with a dowry by benevolent French women . . . in time married Frenchmen and from them many Canadians of today claim their origin' (1901: 107–8).

Corinne Rocheleau's 1924 dramatic tableaux focused on several of Pepper's 'heroines', depicting them as 'courageous women who confronted the dangers of this savage and unknown country' (1924: 11–12). Her story opens with *La Huronne*, an indigenous woman encountering *les blancs*, who will take away all that she held precious (1924: 19–22). The indigenous women that follow are shown either as threats to or objects of charity for the 11 wives, daughters and religious whose contribution to the new settlement is being celebrated. However in the epilogue the women of New France, conquered by the English, are depicted as sharing the fate of *La Huronne*, their culture in danger of being lost (1924: 119).

Commemorative histories of English-speaking Canada culminated in triumph rather than defeat. Founded in 1896, the Women's Canadian Historical Society of Toronto met regularly to hear papers locating women in the stories of the Empire Loyalists who had laid the foundations of British Canada (FitzGibbon 1896). These papers established a pattern that was to mark the writing of women's history in the new century, which can be seen in works such as Emma Currie's *The Story of Laura Secord* (1900) Margaret Hart's *Janet Fisher Archibald* (1934) L Montgomery's *Courageous Women* (1934) and Isabel Skelton's *The Backwoodswoman* (1924). Nellie de Bertrand Lugrin's *The Pioneer Women of Vancouver Island* (1928) takes the reader to a cabin in the forest where 'the sweep of tides on lonely shores, rush of wind through the forest, dip of Indian paddles, [and the] chant of returning braves' was disrupted by 'the sharp cry of a woman in travail and the wail of the babe new-born'. While her husband envisioned 'days to come and the cities to be', the pioneer woman focused on 'the love for her mate and the guarding and rearing of her young' and as such was 'responsible for the birth of a nation' (1928: 1–2). Lugrin then documents the stories of the various groups of women who came to the Island. 'Pioneer women' are celebrated for their whiteness and purity, providing a striking contrast to the 'Indian wives' they were displacing (1928: 17). The fact that Amelia Douglas, the wife of the colony's first effective Governor, was herself of indigenous descent is disguised. Depicted as distressed at having become so 'tanned' during the journey to join her husband, there is relief when the sunburn quickly faded leaving the

'Little Snowbird's . . . cheeks . . . as lily and rose as before' (1928: 16; Perry 1999: 85–6). Douglas is presented as a benefactor rather than a sister to British Columbia's increasingly marginalised indigenous women (Lugin 1928: 18–19). The 'Indian nurse [who] was in attendance when the first babies came' is transformed into the increasingly unreliable servant and finally dismissed as the 'primitive' who when 'the smoky lodge fires beckoned, the easy, lazy ways lured, . . . returned to the old gods' (1928: 96).

This marginalisation of indigenous women reflected their place in a nation that saw 'Indian status' as incompatible with citizenship. Proponents of women's rights wrote within this understanding. Author and campaigner Nellie McClung saw herself as responsible for all the world's children. 'I wanted to do something about the inequalities of the world, I wanted to make other women feel their responsibility; organise their instinctive mother love to do away with evils that prey on childhood, like slums, undernourishment, child labour, and drunkenness' (Savage 1979: 46). McClung's writings evoked history to argue for the need for change. 'History, romance, legend and tradition' had always been written by men. The views of 'the more spiritual half' of the population had yet to be heard (McClung 1972: 15–19). Her wartime treatise *In Times Like These* (1915) set out to demolish the myths which buttressed male superiority, arguing that women needed to articulate their own concerns rather than shelter within flawed assumptions that their interests were represented by their husbands. The women of McClung Canada, asserted, no longer endured the struggles of their pioneer mothers and grandmothers, but could use similar qualities to improve their communities.

The racism implicit in McClung's writing has been the subject of lively debate, but less attention has been paid to her explicit attitudes towards Canada's indigenous population (Fiamengo 1999/2000). A child of the first prairie 'settler' generation, McClung was not silent on issues of dispossession. In her first autobiographical work, *Clearing in the West*, she presented her mother as uncomfortable about living amongst indigenous peoples, persuading her husband to move away from Winnipeg because 'there are too many jet black eyes and high cheekbones here. I like them very well when they belong to the neighbours' children, but I would not like to see them in my grandchildren' (1935: 52). Later the mother explained the serious illness of one of her children as an Indian curse on those who have unjustly taken their land (1935: 79). McClung depicted her child self as more enlightened, defending the 'half-breeds' during the 1885 rebellion and joining in acts of benevolence to Indian children (1935: 88–9, 168–9). But as an adult she saw indigenous women as impediments to rather than co-beneficiaries of women's advancement (1935: 306). In her later autobiography, *The Stream Runs Fast*, indigenous women disappeared entirely, as McClung reflected gloomily on the failure of Canadian women to rewrite history and grasp the responsibilities that came with full citizenship (1965; Buss 1990: 160–2).

The marginalisation/elimination of indigenous women is one of several features of McClung's writing that show a greater congruence with the celebratory narrative of the pioneer woman than the feminist stance of *In Times Like These* would suggest. McClung's view of women located them 'as angels on the hearth if not mats on the doorsill' (Wood 1980: 354). While she campaigned tirelessly for women's rights, she did so in order that they could use these rights as 'agents of civilisation'. The Canadian woman was to use her feminine qualities to improve rather than challenge the settler project, ignoring the dispossession on which it was based.

South Africa

The much newer Union of South Africa offered less space for women to position themselves within the national story. In the early years of the twentieth century, Olive Schreiner, author of *The Story of an African Farm* (1883), a novel famous for its radical views on marriage, stands almost alone. While she was to receive further international acclaim with the publication of her theoretical analysis *Woman and Labour* in 1911, Schreiner was increasingly preoccupied with issues of race, and particularly with developing a history which would contribute towards a healing of the rifts opened up during the Boer War. This involved the construction of a South African identity which acknowledged the shared, if often antagonistic, history of European settlement, and looked to a time when 'there will be no Dutchman . . . no Englishmen . . . but only the great blended South African people' (Schreiner 1899: 30). In this analysis, settler women are positioned as shared stakeholders with men in a land threatened with destabilisation by the inflow of immigrants interested only in exploiting its mineral wealth (1899: 66). Co-existing with but standing outside this concept of nation were the many indigenous peoples whose incorporation Schreiner could not contemplate (Krebs 1997: 427).

Schreiner's experiences during the Boer War intensified her admiration for the Afrikaaner woman, 'the true citadel of her people' (Krige 1968: 116). The treatment of non-combatants during the war, she argued, had created a generation of women who died for their country (Brink 1990: 278). This corresponded closely with and acted to confirm the Afrikaaner notion of the *volksmoeder*, the mother of the nation. Introduced in the nineteenth century and consolidated in the twentieth, this image, Elsabe Brink has argued, provided a place for women in the national history. Primarily the construct of the male writers Willen Postma and Eric Stockenström who produced the first histories of women in South Africa (*The Boer Woman, the Mother of her Nation*, 1918; *Die Vrou in die Geskiedenis van die Hollands-Afrikaanse Volk*, 1921), it was incorporated without critique in a 1938 series of female-authored magazine articles on South African women's history. The *volksmoeder* extended to the *volk* the care a good mother offered to her children (Brink 1990: 284–5). English-speaking South Africans produced their own, somewhat paler, model of the *volksmoeder* in the pioneer wife, 'the women who trekked hundreds of miles and left their colonial homes to live in a dirty tent, strangers in a strange land, sharing all the hardships and the thousand indignities of life that were worse than the hardships . . . [but] carried . . . all through their travels an atmosphere of home' (Williams 1992: 1).

Although Schreiner did, on occasions, counterpose the independence of the Boer women to the apparent meaninglessness of English women's lives, the focus of her writing was to expose the gendered limitations that white women shared (Krige 1968: 136–8; Berkman 1989: 142). No woman in South Africa, she argued, was the equal of white men in the eyes of the law (Clayton 1997: 88). She worked with South African suffragists in staking a claim to separate representation by demonstrating that a woman's interest was not identical to that of her husband. The 'women's cause', the 'right to be regarded as an intelligent human being, freed from the shackles of laws ... that relegate women married in community of property to practically the same grading as children and lunatics', leading suffragist Bertha Solomon recalls, was one of the few instances in which English and Afrikaans women spoke as one (1968: 239–40).

Non-white women, however, were excluded from this consensus. Solomon justified this exclusion by arguing that 'the half loaf is better than no loaf, if only because it provides a springboard to press for the other half', even though she provides no evidence of that springboard being used (1968: 71). Schreiner was less pragmatic, breaking ranks with the suffrage movement because of what she saw as its betrayal of non-white women (Buchanan-Gould 1948: 198). Her response encoded a sense of responsibility rather than sisterhood. Her sympathy was great, she declared, 'with all women fighting to do away with any sex disabilities'. She felt strongly, however, 'it is just the poorest & most helpless women we have to fight for: not only for *ourselves* ... native & coloured women suffer much more from the mere fact they are women than we do. We who are well educated, or are rich, can do much better without the legal recognition of our state' (Stanley 2002: 259).

Few suffragists, however, were in disagreement with white supremacy. Rather, Walker argues, they were 'women who were wanting to expand the existing political structure ... to incorporate themselves. They were not wishing to overthrow the structure on which, ultimately, their privileges rested' (1982: 23). The few histories of women that appeared in South Africa before the Second World War reflected this racially compromised view, charting the achievements of white women while leaving the story of the majority population to anthropologists and missionaries (Ballinger 1938: 326–38; Maud 1933: 379–85).

Australia

Unlike South Africa historians of women in Australia were writing from a position of demographical dominance. Aborigines, who had confronted European intruders from the disadvantage of small hunter-gatherer bands, were by the early twentieth century reduced to a small proportion of the population. From the earliest days of the Commonwealth of Australia, historians stressed the whiteness of the country. A handful of women embarked on the task of defining Australian history, taking recognised watersheds as their starting point and following accepted male paradigms of relevance and selection to make a bid for mainstream attention. Marjorie Barnard and Flora Eldershaw, in *My Australia* in 1939, saw themselves as presenting 'a shape of history, a review of the raw material from which we shall mould our future'. They reported that Australia had been 'a man's world ... The life of the road was the norm. Within its limits it demanded a high standard of courage and endurance, of resourcefulness and, above all, mateship, the solidarity of men against the bush' (1939: 30). Kylie Tennant's 1953 *Australia: Her Story* described a history centred on male actors from convicts and diggers onwards, as did Helen G Palmer and Jessie MacLeod in *The First Hundred Years* (1954).

Earlier attempts to record women in Australian history used memoir and autobiography. In 1911 Elinor Mary Mordaunt, using the pseudonym E M Clowes, published *On the Wallaby: Through Victoria*, a work that showed greater aspirations for breadth. Clowes relied on her own observations and oral sources for insight into women's past, recording the efforts of poor pioneer women keeping house in one-room log huts plastered with mud and roofed with bark; and squatters' wives left alone in isolation and fear in the wilderness. 'For the good of Australia and the Australians, the history of such people ought to be written,' she declared (1911: 6). Two years later Jessie Ackermann's *Australia from a Woman's Point of View* developed a new conceptual approach with chapters organised around such topics as 'Mothers, Children, and the Birth-rate', 'Men in Australia as Husbands and Fathers', 'Women and Wages' and 'Women of Australia as Citizens'.

As with Canada, state or national commemorations of white history brought women together to produce collaborative histories. *The Peaceful Army: A Memorial to the Pioneer Women of Australia 1788 to 1938* organised by Flora Eldershaw, President of the Sydney branch of the Fellowship of Australian Writers, to mark the sesquicentenary of white settlement was the most prominent. Contributors included well-known published authors such as Eldershaw's collaborator, Marjorie Barnard, Dymphna Cusack, Miles Franklin, Eleanor Dark, Kylie Tennant, and artist, Margaret Preston. State centenary volumes in Victoria and South Australia interspersed poetry, memoir and illustrations amongst chapters by notable intellectuals, all of which unashamedly celebrated women's achievements. As feminists they were convinced that women were likely to be ignored in the commemorations, they set out to argue for their status as pioneers. The educated writers positioned themselves as the beneficiaries of the pioneer women who, in spite of the harshness of their lives, left a positive legacy to their children and grandchildren.

Editing the 1934 Victorian centennial volume, Nettie Palmer and Frances Fraser honoured those women who made the great venture to come with their men-folk 'to this unknown land, enduring the great privations with a spirit that inspired husbands and sons to persevere in spite of all'. Women, they argued, did far more than cook and sweep. 'They milked cows, dug for gold, sowed the corn, and even literally put their hand to the plough. They tended the sick and dying, they comforted the homesick, and in every way passed down to the women of today their splendid heritage of courage and initiative.' *A Book of South Australia: Women in the First Hundred Years* (1936), edited by Louise Brown, similarly emphasised the 'noble' part played by early women settlers, filled with 'fortitude in the face of privation and danger'. In the foreword Lady Duggan reminded readers, 'Today we are reaping the benefit of their great endeavour, of their determination to win through and of their faith.' *The Peaceful Army*, again, celebrated 'the heroism and devotion of the women who have shared, and are still sharing, the hardships of this struggle . . . [they] deserve all the recognition we can give them' (1938: 61).

These volumes included biographies of notable women excluded from mainstream history. From the colonial period through to the present, the writers agreed, women were always pioneering, making a place for themselves in almost all walks of life and forging new spaces for their sisters. 'A pioneer', Kylie Tennant's *Peaceful Army* contribution argued, was 'a person who surveys his environment, decides it isn't good enough, sees what is needed, and gets to work to supply the need'. In hundreds of organisations in the cities, and the bush women were doing their best 'to improve, not only their own environment, but everyone else's . . .' (1938: 142). The battlers keep on battling. Women, Palmer and Fraser asserted in the foreword to their *Centenary Giftbook* (1934), showed themselves the mates rather than rivals of men. 'Their courage and perseverance have been shown in making better conditions for women and children.' They told the story of women who 'blazed the trail' as 'firsts' – the first woman telegraphist, the first woman elected to a municipal council, as well as early women artists and writers. They discussed improvements in girls' and women's education, entry to citizenship, women in trade unions, clubs, welfare work and nursing. The South Australian volume similarly recorded the victories of women in science, medicine, law, drama and social welfare.

Written by and for women who lived in the southeastern seaboard cities where few indigenous people resided, these volumes paid little attention to Aborigines. Primarily they were mentioned, as one of the trials of pioneering. The (white) women well knew the dangers of the new country: 'Hostile blacks, escaped convicts, bushrangers, snakes, floods, fires, droughts . . .', Mary Grant Bruce wrote. She invited her readers to picture what it would be like to bear children and rear them in solitude that held such danger (Fraser and Palmer 1934: 17). An amateur poet tried her hand at more graphic description, inviting her readers to imagine the frightening situations of bush women, fearing always the 'creeping black shadows, half man and half spear', which made 'shivering night of the sunniest days' (1934: 66). Not all were so negative. If Daisy Bates was scarcely credible when she proclaimed the prodigious good will of settler women towards indigenous women (Brown 1936), a few other writers more reliably recorded some amiable encounters. Mary Grant Bruce told of a woman who gave birth to 11 children – 'the blacks were her friends, and she learned from them as well as taught them' (Brown 1936: 16). A landowner's wife, we hear, taught her own and station children in the day and the 'native' children at night (Brown 1936: 91). E Marie Irvine in her *Certain Worthy Women* told of two indigenous women, 'Narraben' and 'Old Nan', who loyally helped white people who had shown their people kindness (1939: 91). The South Australian ethnologist K Langloh Parker recorded and published Aboriginal myths (Brown *et al.* 1936).

If the poet Mary Gilmore's 'Ode to the Pioneer Women', the 'Women upon whose long endurings rest / The might and majesty acclaimed by us today . . . / Of such as these was born the ANZAC and his pride', represents the dominant evasions of the colonial past, Eleanor Dark's discussion of white treatment of Aborigines is noteworthy for its indication that some progressive white women were beginning to question this interpretation. A nomad race, she said, found 'its country invaded, its streams polluted, its hunting grounds commandeered, cleared, fenced, sown with crops'. White men killed the kangaroos as a matter of course, but 'if the hungry Aborigines kill a sheep for a meal there is the devil to pay' (Eldershaw 1938: 65). It was understandable that whites should have defended themselves when attacked but murder and poisoning were different matters; 'these, with disease, alcohol and "civilisation" have come near to exterminating a race to which, too late, we are beginning to give the respect which is deserved' (Eldershaw 1938: 66).

New Zealand

In New Zealand the centenary of the signing in 1840 of the Treaty of Waitangi between Maori chiefs and representatives of Queen Victoria that marked the formal

British annexation of the islands as a colony provided a trigger for the writing of women's history. Keen amateur historians in the Women's Division of the New Zealand Farmers' Union, advocates for improved living conditions for isolated farmers' wives, compiled *Brave Days: Pioneer Women of New Zealand* (1939), a collection of life stories of elderly women many of whom grew up as daughters in the homes of the original pioneers. The book was seen as a treasure trove for those who cared about history and a storehouse for future researchers. ' "Not marble, nor gilded monuments of princes" shall keep a memory honoured more than theirs', the women writers declared of their subjects.

There were initially to be three official commemorative volumes: a general history; a history of women; and a history of the Maori people. The latter was never completed, but the second, *Women of New Zealand*, written by Masters graduate and *Brave Days* contributor Helen Simpson appeared on time in 1940. Essentially a white chronological narrative, the book moved from the lives of the earliest arrivals, the wives of the Anglican and Methodist missionaries, through women's lives in colonial communities, the coming of urban development and waged work for women, and the growth of women's organisations and political citizenship in the twentieth century.

For white New Zealanders the Treaty symbolised the country's essentially cordial biracial character which, they believed, compared favourably with 'race relations' in Australia. While British soldiers and settler militias fought wars against hostile Maori in the mid- to late nineteenth century, the country's history overall was characterised by racial harmony. Unable to hide racial conflict the commemorative publications recorded white women's fears of Maori but they also recorded and praised the assistance Maori gave to settlers. Unlike the self-conscious inclusions into Australian histories, in New Zealand Maori were integral to the national story. The stance of all the writers, however, remained unambiguously white, aligned with the female figures who, while subordinate to white men, nevertheless dominate these narratives of female prowess, and reduce Maori women to the role of actors on the white women's stage.

Where issues of race were believed 'settled,' Dominion women felt increasingly confident in embarking on the writing of women's history, yet they still faced a dilemma. When women wrote mainstream history they were forced into a dominant narrative that excluded women's past; if they wrote separately, as women for women, male historians could cite their work to justify this exclusion. In excluding women from his *National Portraits*, Australian critic and writer Vance Palmer argued that *The Peaceful Army* had already told their story (1940: v–vi). This was a dilemma that Dominion writers, making a bid to assert women's significance in the past, were unable to resolve (Grimshaw 1985, 1991). It was left to feminist writers in the post-war decades to forge fresh narratives grounded solidly in the bases that their predecessors had laid.

Patricia Grimshaw and Shurlee Swain

References

Ackermann 1896, 1913; Ballinger 1938; Barnard & Eldershaw 1939; Berkman 1989; Brink 1990; Brown *et al.* 1936; Buchanan-Gould 1948; Buss 1990; Clayton 1997; Clowes 1911; Eldershaw 1938/1988; Fiamengo 1999/2000; Fitzgibbon 1896; Fraser & Palmer 1934; Grimshaw 1985, 1991; Irvine 1939; Krebs 1997; Krige 1968; Lugrin 1928; McClung 1935, 1972; Maud

1933; Palmer 1940; Palmer & MacLeod 1936; Pepper 1901; Perry 1999; Rocheleau 1924; Savage 1979; Schreiner 1899; Soloman 1968; Walker 1982; Williams 1992; Wood 1980.

Related essays
Australia; Canada; Empire; Local History; Postcolonial.

Dowriche, Anne 1560–1613

English Puritan poet, historian. Daughter of Elizabeth (Tregian) and Sir Richard Edgcumbe. Married Hugh Dowriche, Puritan minister in 1580. Four children. In 1589 Dowriche wrote *The French History* (1589), a lengthy narrative poem describing the persecution of Huguenots that culminated in the St Bartholomew's day massacre in 1572. Dowriche took as her source Thomas Tymmes' *The Three Parts of Commentaries Containing the Whole and Perfect Discourse of the Civil Wars of France* (1574), a translation of Jean de Serres' *Commentariorum de statu religionis & republicae in regno Galliae libri* (1572–1575) and echos also John Fox's *Actes and Monuments* (1563) and Francois Hotman, *De Furoribus Gallicis* (1573). Although Dowriche chose to disguise her role as historian by driving her narrative in the masculine voice of 'a godlie French exile', the poem can be read as a distinctly feminine account of these events. Dedicating the poem to her brother Pearse, Dowriche wrote 'If you finde anie thing that fits not your liking, remember I pray, that it is a woman's doing.' While such a statement is typical of the rhetorical authorial modesty claimed by early modern women writers, it also explicitly identifies the poem 'as a feminist interpretation of history'. Unlike the male-authored martyrologies she drew upon that served a retributive purpose, Dowriche's *History* presents execution as sacrifice and worship, empowering Protestant martyrs with the gift of mercy to their enemies. Dowriche's narrative is also remarkable for its depiction of Catherine de Medici as a charismatic politician exhorting her male co-conspirators to action. This depiction reinscribes female agency to European politics and presents Catherine as the first Machiavellian figure in English literature. Dowriche also wrote *The Gaoler's Conversion* (1596) commendatory verse attached to one of her husband's sermons.

Mary Spongberg

References
Beilin 1987; Martin 1999; Sondergard 2002.

Major work
'The French historie' is reprinted in Susan Woods *et al.*, *The Poets I: Isabella Whitney, Anne Dowriche Elizabeth Melville, Aemilia Lanyer, Rachel Speght, Diana Primrose Anne, Mary and Penelope Grey* (Aldershot: Ashgate, 2001).

E

Earle, Alice Morse 1851–1911

US historian of women. Born in Worcester, Massachusetts to Abby (Mason Clary) and Edwin Morse. Educated at Worcester High School and Gamet's Boarding School in Boston. Married Henry Earle, a stockbroker, in 1874, moved to Brooklyn, where the couple raised four children. Began writing to support her family following the death of her husband. A collector of antiques, Earle drew on her interest in the material conditions of early colonial life for her first book *The Sabbath in Puritan New England*

(1891), an account of an ancestor's church. The history of the material and cultural life of early colonial America formed a dominant theme in her works such as *China Collecting in America* (1892), *Customs and Fashions of Old New England* (1893), *Costumes of Colonial Times* (1894) and *Two Centuries of Costume in America 1620–1820* (1903). She also published on the history of American gardens, *Old Time Gardens* (1901) and *Sun Dials and Roses of Yesterday* (1902).

A member of the Daughters of the American Revolution and the Society of Colonial Dames, Earle wrote a major history of 'ordinary women' in Colonial America, *Colonial Dames and Good Wives* (1895). Drawn largely from court records of the early colonies, *Colonial Dames and Good Wives* demonstrated the role of women as a civilising influence in the new colony and the socio-economic importance of marriage. Like **Elizabeth Ellet**, Morse stressed women's bravery in the face of adversity. She mentions Margaret Brent, 'the first woman in America to demand suffrage' in 1647 (*Good Wives* 1895: 44) and recovers women reviled in the masculinist historical records such as Anne Hutchinson. She was a pioneer in the history of childhood, publishing *Child Life in Colonial Days* in 1899. She also edited the diary of Boston schoolgirl Anna Green Winslow in 1894 and published a biography of Margaret Winthrop in 1895.

Mary Spongberg

Reference

NAM 1971.

Major works

Colonial Dames and Good Wives (New York: Ungar, 1962); *The Sabbath in Puritan New England* (Detroit: Omnigraphics, 1998); *Child Life in Colonial Days* (Bowie: Heritage Classics, 1997); *Customs and Fashions of Old New England* (Bowie: Heritage Books, 1992); *Costumes of Colonial Times* (Detroit: Omnigraphics, 1999); *Diary of Anna Green Winslow* (Bedford: Applewood Press, 1996) and *Old Time Gardens* (Hanover: University Press of New England, 2005).

Eckenstein, Lina 1857–1931

English medievalist, translator, archaeologist, historian of women. Born in London, daughter of Julie (Helmke) and Frederick Eckenstein. Privately educated. Fluent in German, French, Latin, Middle High German and Middle English. Began working-life in the British Museum, translating Albrecht Dürer's notes for William Martin Conway's *Literary Remains of Albrecht Dürer*. She later published her own work on Dürer in the Popular Library of Art series. Her first publication was a collection of four children's stories, *The Little Princess and the Great Plot* (1892). She maintained an interest in children's literature throughout her life publishing *Comparative Studies of Nursery Rhymes* in 1906. Politically progressive, Eckenstein was a member of the Fabian Women's Group, where she read historical papers on subjects such as prostitution and the impact of the Reformation on women. She was also a member of the Men and Women's Club.

Eckenstein never married and her most important relationships were with women. She had a **Romantic Friendship** with Maria Sharpe, who married Karl Pearson, founder of the Men and Women's Club. Eckenstein dedicated her major work *Woman under Monasticism* (1896) to the Pearsons. Drawn largely from hagiographical and biographical sources, *Woman under Monasticism* presents a history of female saints and religious women from 500 to 1500 AD. Reflecting her interest in feminism and Fabianism, Eckenstein suggested that many of the rights women were demanding in the late nineteenth century were 'analogous to the rights which the convent secured' prior to the Reformation. Eckenstein represented medieval nuns as the precursors of modern feminists and she hoped that her study would influence contemporary debate on women's education and work. Perhaps mindful of a growing morbidification of romantic friendships, Eckenstein was keen to show that women who were neither married nor mothers led lives 'which still have living value'. *Woman under Monasticism* anticipates much recent feminist revisionist history of the Reformation by suggesting that the closure of convents had a negative impact upon women.

Eckenstein was also a keen Egyptologist. She accompanied friends Sir W M Flinders Petrie and his wife Hilda on several expeditions to Egypt. She wrote an article on moon cults in Sinai that discussed aspects of female divinity for Petrie's journal *Ancient Egypt*. She also produced a *History of Sinai* (1921) and a fictional recreation of a pharaoh's wife *Tutankh-aten* (1924). Her two final works *A Spell of Words* (1932) and *The Women of Early Christianity* (1935) were published posthumously.

Mary Spongberg

References

Alexander 2001; Bland 2001; Johnson 1997.

Major work

Woman under Monasticism: Chapters on Saint-Lore and Convent Life between A.D. 500 and A.D. 1500 (New York : Russell & Russell, 1963).

Education

In 1866, Emily Davies asked the question: 'As to authority what constitutes it?' This essay is concerned with questions of authority. How are women to gain authority, to find positions from which to speak? Women have considered the education of their sex the key to remedying their disabilities in public and private life throughout history. Thus they have written widely in the history of education. In this essay I look at three time frames to consider if any notion of a tradition, of a dominant theme over time, can be upheld. The first period might be termed the pre-institutional period when women wrote from a range of perspectives and in many genres about the education of women and girls. It could be described, to use Bonnie Smith's term, as the age of the amateur (Smith 1998: 6–7). The second time frame is the early phase of the discipline from its beginnings in the late nineteenth century. This period paralleled the growth of teachers' colleges and university departments of education and there is a discernible stream of writing in the area. Much of that writing is in the 'heroic' mode. The third period is the current period from the last quarter of the twentieth century to today – the period categorised as 'revisionist' in the history of education as it challenged the frameworks of the 'heroic' period, and is seen by some as containing the seeds of its own destruction. I shall devote scant space to the first as it pre-dates the history of education as a discipline, considerably more to the second period and even more to the third. It is in the last 30 years that women have come into their own in the history of education, defining it in their own ways and challenging their omission from earlier work and indeed the very frameworks of analysis.

The pre-institutional period

While legions of women wrote on women's education before the late eighteenth century we might start with **Mary Wollstonecraft**; her strong, wide-ranging work is often seen as providing a turning point in women's analysis of their place in the world. Her major work, *A Vindication of the Rights of Woman* (1792), warrants a place here. For she recommended a system of national, equal, co-educational state schools (Spender 1982: 112), arguing as many did before and after that an educated woman would be both a full citizen and a better wife and mother. Describing women's minds as forced like flowers planted in too rich a soil, 'strength and usefulness sacrificed to beauty', Wollstonecraft lamented their early maturation and rapid fading. This 'barren blooming' Wollstonecraft attributed to 'a false system of education, gathered from the books written on this subject by men, who, considering females rather as women than human creatures, have been more likely to make them alluring mistresses than affectionate wives and rational mothers' (Wollstonecraft 1792/1985: 317). A child's first educator, the mother, must herself 'have sense', she argued, that is, she must be educated rationally.

Half a century later Emily Davies in *The Higher Education of Women* (1866/1988) also made a case for the equal education of women, drawing from history to make her points. Like Wollstonecraft she wrote a sustained argument, embodying the notion of women's rational self, seeking to influence those who opposed her reasonable views. She openly sought authority for women, seeing it for her 'young ladies' as best vested in 'examination by men of high repute' and through examination by 'official bodies such as universities' (Davies 1866/1988: 103). Thus she fought for the admission of women to universities. These books might well be characterised as forerunners of the field of women-writing in the history of education although they were written for very different audiences and at very different periods. Both were writing to convince a sceptical public, both men and women, that men and women shared a common humanity and thus women should be educated in the same fashion as men.

Until the more secular twentieth century, religion provided the source of inspiration for most writers on education. Within religious thought two major discernible traditions can be traced. The dissenters (radical dissenters, Unitarians, Quakers and others) later allied with more humanist thinkers, wrote of progressive education and stressed that the power of reason resided in both men and women (Hilton and Hirsch 2000). They often supported co-education. The established church, on the other hand, particularly in its nineteenth-century evangelical form, privileged woman's separate place and her role as moral guide (Hole 1996). Such writers tended to support separate schools and university colleges for women. Yet some writers confounded such easy distinctions, drawing inspiration for their pens from religion, politics and the issues of the day. Emily Davies, for instance, can well be called conservative, but her determination that women should have the same education as men belied that terminology (Caine 1992). She drew great strength from her Anglican beliefs. However, from the Enlightenment onwards humanism vied with religion, often intertwined with it, as a wellspring of educational writing.

One inspirational amateur was **Anna Jameson**, self-educated, a governess until her marriage and an independent author and illustrator after separating from her husband, who wrote books for women on a wide range of cultural issues and art history at a time when young men were sent on grand tours of Europe but young women were not. She urged the importance of training and education for women with 'an almost desperate passion', in Ray Strachey's words (Clarke 2000: 70). She claimed a rare form of authority as Clarke argues: the ability to claim a voice in lectures to the public. Jameson wrote through the words of a fictionalised female author:

> I do not choose presumptuously to fling these opinions in the face of the world in the form of essays on morality and treatises on education. I have rather chosen to illustrate certain positions by examples and leave my readers to deduce the moral themselves, and draw their own inferences.

Resisting systems and methods, she champions 'the pursuit of an authentic, independent self fed freely by the multiple and unpredictable richness of the world' (Clarke 2000: 77).

The history of education in the heroic era: The birth of a discipline

The discipline of history of education as we know it arose from the growth of the modern teachers college and the department, school or faculty of education in universities, a development that began in the late nineteenth and early twentieth centuries in the English-speaking world (Campbell and Sherington 2002: 46ff.). This development paralleled the rise of modern state school systems, often seen by historians as a triumph of social 'reform'. As Craig Campbell and Geoffrey Sherington put it, 'the job of history of education was to celebrate, justify and explain the present' (2002: 51). For the trainee teacher it provided a 'civic function' and contributed to the building of 'newly professional and increasingly confident teachers, and educators in general' (2002: 51). Roy Lowe in the UK and Craig Campbell in Australia have both commented on the 'uncritical tradition' in the history of education which lasted virtually from the 1880s to the 1950s and 1960s, a tradition that was 'narrow, profession-focussed, and believed that its approach would ensure progress upon the Whig tradition' (Campbell and Sherington 2002: 51). Within this tradition differentiation between girls and boys as students, or men and women teachers, rarely appeared. Within the grand narratives of parliamentary reform, 'great' or 'pioneering' headmasters [*sic*], administrators and schools, and sectarian struggles, any notion of 'the authentic, independent self' championed by Jameson faded from view.

The professionalisation of the discipline of history of education resulted in the marginalisation of amateur women's writing until well into the last quarter of the twentieth century. The dominant triumphal view of the history of education was mainly the preserve of male historians. At the time women rarely filled the university posts or the senior positions in teachers' training colleges which would enable them to write the heroic works that characterised the period. And, as Bonnie G Smith reminds us, where the topic of the nation state was central, female amateurs tend to disappear (Smith 1998: 70). Yet women were present in large numbers as teachers in the schools provided by that consolidating nation state; creating the nation, as it were, through their work. As Campbell and Sherington (2002: 52) usefully point out Australia, 'a superior guide' to the realities of modern state schools might be found in the works of novelists such as Dymphna Cusack and Christina Stead, who wrote scathingly of the lives of the women teachers who flocked to the profession (Theobald 1996).

Yet throughout the English-speaking world there were many women who wrote about the history of education, specifically about the history of the education of women and girls. They were a parallel stream to that of the dominant discipline. In some instances their work can be viewed as part of the heroic tradition, particularly where they wrote histories of pioneering women educationalists and of exemplary schools. How much their works appeared in mainstream reading lists is debatable, although several survey texts had an obligatory chapter on women's education (see, for instance, Hughes and Klemm 1907, cited in Campbell and Sherington 2002: 51). Some were curious about other countries. In the United Kingdom Sarah Burstall wrote *The Education of Girls in the United States* (1894/1971) and *English High Schools for Girls* (1907), both describing the systems in place and documenting the battles to obtain good secondary and university education for British and American girls. (*The Education of Girls in the United States* was reprinted in 1971 in the series American Education: Its Men, Ideas and Institutions.) Burstall was a highly respected mistress of the pioneering North London Collegiate School for Girls, a scholar of Girton College, Cambridge and the recipient of a prized Gilchrist Trusteeship to study secondary schools and training colleges for women in the United States. Some years after those earlier works, she published a biography of Frances Mary Buss: an educational pioneer who established the North London Collegiate School (Burstall 1938). Barbara Stephen's *Emily Davies and Girton College* (1927) put on the record the pioneering work of Emily Davies. Years later Josephine Kamm wrote the well-known *How Different from Us: A Biography of Miss Buss and Miss Beale* (1958), the title playing on the famous ditty amongst supporters of schools for girls:

> How different from us, Miss Beale
> and Miss Buss,
> Cupid's dart they ne'er feel, Miss Buss
> and Miss Beale.

This reference to the assumed spinsterish nature of the famous pioneering headmistresses does not detract from their importance and that of their schools, which remained a magnet for women writing about an academic education for girls. The verse demonstrated that authority came at a price: women who led the new girls' schools were 'different from us'. Kamm's book was followed by the significantly titled *Hope Deferred* in 1965 and *Indicative Past: A Hundred Years of the Girls Public Day's Trust School* in 1971.

In the United States over the first half of the twentieth century a literature too vast to detail here mapped women's admission to college and universities, celebrated great institutions for women (such as Troy, Oberlin, Cornell, Bryn Mawr) and the women who led them (Mary Lyon, Catherine Beecher, Mrs Emma Willard, M Carey Thomas and many others). These works can be seen as both amateur works and as part of the heroic tradition, blurring the boundaries between such categories as they celebrated the struggles and far-sightedness of early leaders in women's education. They provide rich sources for those who followed such as Barbara Miller Solomon whose scholarly work *In the Company of Educated Women* (1985) mapped three generations of women's higher education in the US. In 1959, however, Mabel Newcomer's landmark work *A Century of Higher Education for American Women* departed from that quasi-celebratory stance. She documented a period of advance and then decline in women's higher education and demonstrated that women's relative position in the academic world was falling. Patricia Graham (1978) also feared that with the rise of the research university in the US and a downplaying of the role of teaching, women's role began to decline. There had been a sea change from the early part of the twentieth century when women wrote of the triumphs of women's entry to academic secondary schooling and university study through the proud records of the pioneering women. By mid-century Kamm and Newcomer both were lamenting the fact that 'progress' seemed to have stalled, hope to have been 'deferred'. This would provide a rallying point for the next generation who emerged through the new social history of the 1960s and the women's movement of the 1970s.

In the 1950s and early 1960s women were not entirely absent from the mainstream of history of education but they rarely wrote about women's issues. For that generation, stories of feminist pioneers were out of fashion: a focus on women (particularly unmarried women headmistresses) was decidedly not modern. In the journal *Melbourne Studies in Education* (MSE), for example, Olive Wykes, lecturer in education at the University of Melbourne, wrote several articles in the late 1950s and early 1960s on France, her area of specialty, providing historical reviews of French secondary education. Ailsa Zainu'ddin (1964) made an early appearance in the discipline with a comparison of national education in two pluralist societies, England and Australia, and on Indonesian education. In the 1972 edition of MSE Barbara Falk wrote about protest in contemporary society. In the United States Geraldine Joncich Clifford wrote a key work on Edward L Thorndike (1968, 1984). Women were present within the history of education and were happy to have their voices heard, their scholarship acknowledged. Some voices presaged change. In 1967 Clifford's compatriot Maxine Greene, editor of the *Teachers College Record*, wrote an important piece questioning the 'difficult question of the discipline's [history of education] significance in teacher education' (Greene 1967). Criticising current practitioners, Greene lamented their lack of explanation, their tendency to write for 'strategic reasons or political ones'. She argued for the historian of education as an interpreter, one who could pursue meanings, and offer the student teachers possibilities for the shaping of large perspectives. The historian of education could 'make it possible for him [*sic*] to confront the human condition and to take his stance as a teacher who is a human being with respect to the indifference of the sky' (Greene 1967: 190). This larger agenda, this meaning, was to resonate with the next generation writing the history of education.

History of education in the contemporary era: Revival and revision

History of education as a contemporary discipline developed out of the old discipline but turned against its approaches, espousing the new trends that swept across history in general in the late 1960s and 1970s. This renewal was underpinned by an increasing post-war need for trained teachers and the growth of Bachelor of Education degrees and Diplomas of Education taught at universities and at colleges of education. Larger numbers of trainee teachers filled the universities in the 1960s as primary and secondary schools expanded. New faculty frequently included historians who had been trained in history departments, rather than through the history of education itself. Furthermore, historians of education frequently felt marginalised by historians in history departments, who saw the type of history they taught as narrow and institutional. And indeed it was, as we have seen, often focusing on administrations, legislatures and heroic principles.

By the 1970s new entrants into history of education were expressing interest in larger issues such as the reproduction of social class through schooling. This was the new social history, informed by anthropology and sociological approaches. It was not just concerned with the great and famous but with wider social processes. Informed by the theories of Marx and Gramsci, on the one hand, and of psychohistory on the other the new history took as its canvas childhood, studies of youth and work, and of families and social reproduction. It drew from such diverse fields as anthropology and the quantitative approaches of demography. The 1970s also brought the new insights of the women's movement, although they were slow to make their way into the field. Before women presented their challenges, a new wave of historians interested in education, rather than educational historians, swept into the field bringing issues of social class, nation-building and 'history from below' to the fore. This resulted in the new 'revisionist' history of education which was to provide a vehicle for women historians of education to enter the debate. In 1983 the English scholar Joan Simon wrote a key piece in the Australian *History of Education Review* titled 'The History of Education and the "New" Social History' (1983), laying out the new approaches and new opportunities within the field. From this time on the parallel stream of women-writing about the history of education began to merge with the mainstream to provide some turbulent challenges.

A brief look at the English and Australian scene in the latter part of the twentieth century typifies these challenges and the connections between them. In other English-speaking countries such as the United States, New Zealand and Canada similar trends can be observed.

England: 'It's all in the melting pot'

In England in December 1967 the History of Education Society was formed at a conference attended by 150 people, 'mainly teachers of the subject in colleges and departments of education'. The aims of the new society were to further the study of the history of education, to provide opportunities for discussion amongst those engaged in the study and teaching of the history of education, to organise conferences and meetings and to publish a bulletin. Among the eight founding committee members was one woman, Nanette Whitbread, from the City of Leicester College of Education. The new society's members aimed to publish two bulletins a year with hopes of eventually launching a journal.

According to the first *History of Education Society Bulletin* (1968), several major themes engaged the founding members – themes that contemporary historians of education recognise all too well. What part should the history of education play in general education courses? Speakers were concerned that history was often subordinated to sociological, psychological and comparative subjects in training teachers. A second theme dealt with approaches to teaching the history of education: How far should one try to escape from the traditional, chronological treatment? Ought topics to be preferred . . .? And, finally, who would teach the history of education? What degree of separation should exist between historians in the education department and those in the history departments of the university? The society aimed to reflect 'all shades of interest and opinion among members of the Society, with special emphasis on teaching and research in the subject'.

One of the first articles in this edition of the *Bulletin* was Nanette Whitbread's report on a survey on current teaching in the history of education in the three-year certificate course in colleges of education in England and Wales. The report detailed a sorry tale of dull and unimaginative teaching, of 'Grinding out of "Acts and facts" ' by non-historians and of a desire for more enlightened approaches (1968: 4–5). Whitbread noted that the comment 'it's all in the melting pot' was typical of respondents more generally. It was time for change.

The humble *Bulletin* of 1968 became *History of Education: Journal of the History of Education Society* in 1972 with the hope of promoting a 'much wider conception of the history of education than has been usual in the past' (History of Education Society 1972: 3). It was not until 1977, however, that the journal *History of Education* contained the first article by a woman historian on women, Joan Burstyn's article 'Women's Education in England during the Nineteenth Century: A Review of the Literature, 1970–1976'. This was to become a vital addition to the reading list of every woman historian of education, this author included, from then on. 'The women's movement of the 1970s has led scholars to redefine women's relationships to events and movements traditionally studied by historians', she began (Burstyn 1977: 11). Not only did Burstyn plan to review recent writings and work presented since 1970 but she wanted to 'place them within the framework of reconceptualisation that women's scholars of women's history are constructing'. This was an exciting and ambitious project. Burstyn, then at Douglass College, Rutgers, outlined the key work that scholars such as **Joan Kelly** and Gerder Lerner were propounding – the notion that women's position in society has always to be measured in relation to men's, that women were a separate social category, that women's absence from historical studies has been due to historians' blindness to them, not to a 'natural lack of significance in women's lives' (Burstyn 1977: 11). Drawing on Hilda Smith, she suggested that women must define for themselves the significant source material. Burstyn drew from this exciting new work several questions for historians of education, some redolent of Emily Davies' cry: Where were the sources of power and authority in nineteenth-century educational institutions? How did they change during the century? Did women have access to them? Shortly after this important piece Margaret Bryant wrote one of the defining British texts of the period: *The Unexpected Revolution: A Study in the History of Education of Women and Girls in the Nineteenth Century* (1979) (see also Fletcher 1980). The education of women and girls was back on the agenda and attracted the energies of most women writing in the field.

Australia: 'signs of an interdisciplinary awakening'

The history of education as a renewed discipline in Australia also has its roots in the mid-1960s, when academics teaching the history of education began to consider forming an association (McMahon 1996). Ailsa Zainu'ddin was the only woman present at the first annual general meeting of ANZHES in 1971 but she made her presence felt. As McMahon notes, '[f]ollowing some stimulus the Executive of the Society decided to invite members to read papers about the history of women in education at the 1974 Sydney conference' (1996: 6). The following story is typical of the early efforts of many women in their professional societies. Zainu'ddin was unable to attend but protested to the organising committee about the lack of women participants. John Lawry, on behalf of the Executive, claimed that considerable effort had been spent on locating any woman prepared to read a paper on the history of women in education (McMahon 1996: 6). The conference went ahead: four of the seven papers presented were about the history of women in education or the subjection of women, no doubt a useful consciousness-raising issue for the men who delivered them. From 1975 on more women joined the society and began to publish in the *ANZHES Journal*.

The first journal article by a woman on a topic about women was Helen Jones' 1975 piece, '"Pinnacle of the State-School System": The Advanced School for Girls, Adelaide', followed later by her book on educational change in South Australia (1985). This work represented a vital step forward in the inclusion of both women writing history of education and writing about women and girls. Ailsa Zainu'ddin was the first woman historian of education to present a paper in 1976 to the ANZHES society. That paper was titled 'Women and the Teaching Profession, 1906–1914'. Earlier she had written a key piece for *Melbourne Studies in Education* titled 'The Admission of Women to the University of Melbourne, 1869–1903' (1973). This article connected strongly with the earlier tradition by locating women's admission to Melbourne University within the debates canvassed by English reformers such as Emily Davies and Josephine Kamm. From the mid-1970s in Australia, England, the United States and Canada, the women's movement propelled a legion of women, often those trained in the teachers' colleges and university departments of education, into the history of education where they sought to reclaim a place in the field. Conversely, historians from the wider field turned to educational history to understand women's continuing secondary status. Jill Ker Conway, trained as an historian in Sydney and at Harvard, entered women's educational history in the United States, writing *inter alia* a key article on the history of women's education (Conway 1976). She was particularly critical of the then dominant notion that coeducation was necessarily liberating for women. She wrote of the need to invoke 'the skepticism [*sic*] which feminists normally extend to male interpretations of women's experience' (1976: 1). Invoking that scepticism Alison Mackinnon edited an issue of the Australian *History of Education Review* in 1984 on the theme of women and education. Her lead article, titled 'Women's Education: Linking History and Theory', pointed to a new development for many women: the challenge of incorporating the new feminist theory into their historical writing.

For many of this feminist generation the old school of Josephine Kamm *et al.* represented a narrow, indeed slavish, following of male models of educational provision and a misunderstanding, indeed denigration, of women's culture. The foremothers of the heroic era had, like the novelists Thackeray and Elliot, scorned the narrow accomplishments-based schooling for women of the nineteenth century. Australian historian of education Marjorie Theobald radically overturned that perception in her groundbreaking piece 'Mere Accomplishments?' (1991), a re-evaluation of the importance of that form of female education. The engagement of historians of education with the earlier generation of women writers and teachers helped forge women's new voice, one that proclaimed the importance of women's culture and the embodied nature of men and women.

The flourishing: Women writing the history of education

In the last two decades of the twentieth century, women not only wrote about the history of women and girls in education, but many also re-entered the wider field re-examining state building and institutions from the newer revisionist perspectives. In Canada, for instance, Susan Houston and Alison Prentice wrote the magisterial work *Schooling and Scholars in Nineteenth-Century Ontario*, 'a comprehensive account not simply of the early evolution of the public school *system* in Ontario but of schooling itself', thus combining the older form of concern about school systems ('the shared mania for school promotion') with the new focus on schooling and the broad experience it entailed (Houston and Prentice 1988: viii, original emphasis). Some built on educational history to range far and wide across social history, viewing education as part of broader transformations. Pavla Miller, for example, wrote two major scholarly works which brought together issues of gender with class formation, families and age relations in general (Miller 1986, 1998). In the United States Geraldine Clifford questioned American education, and its institutional setting in the academy (1976, 1988). In 1996 American Julie Reuben wrote *The Making of the Modern University: Intellectual Transformation and the Marginalization of Morality*, a major work of intellectual history within the history of education.

Revisionism did not attract the support of all women writing in the field. Yet it has been around the question of authority for women that many women writing in the field have converged. Women scholars in all parts of the English-speaking world and beyond have mapped a wide range of areas concerning women and girls. Works focusing on the provision of schools for girls and women both by the state and through private ventures include Majorie Theobald's *Knowing Women: Origins of Women's Education in Nineteenth Century Australia* (1996), Noeline Kyle's *Her Natural Destiny: The Education of Women in New South Wales* (1986), Carole Dyhouse's *Girls Growing up in Late Victorian and Edwardian England* (1981), Linda Eisenmann's *Historical Dictionary of Women's Education in the United States*, and June Purvis' *Hard Lessons: The Lives and Education of Working-Class Women in nineteenth Century England* (1989) and *History of Women's Education in England* (1991). The key role of teachers and teachers' work has been explored in texts such as Alison Prentice and Majorie Theobald's *Women Who Taught: Perspectives on the History of Women Teaching* (1991), Kathleen Weiler's *Women Teaching for Change* (1988), Kathleen Weiler and Sue Middleton's *Telling Women's Lives* (1999) and Kay Whitehead's *The New Women Teachers Come Along* (2003). The admission of women to universities and women's colleges has been the subject of works such as Carole Dyhouse's *No Distinction of Sex? Women in British Universities 1870–1939* (1995), Patricia Ann Palmieri's *In Adamless Eden: The Community of Women Faculty at Wellesley* (1995), Geraldine Clifford's *Lone Voyages: Academic Women in Coeducational Institutions, 1870–1937* (1989), Alison Mackinnon's *The New Women: Adelaide's Early Women Graduates* (1986) and Jana Nidiffer's *Pioneering Deans of Women: More than Wise and Pious Matrons* (2000). Other works have sought to map the impact of that education on women's professional and personal lives such as Barbara Miller Solomon's *In the Company of Educated*

Women (1985), Joyce Antler's *The Educated Woman and Professionalization* (1987), Mary Kinnear's *In Subordination: Professional Women 1870–1970* (1995) and Alison Mackinnon's *Love and Freedom: Professional Women and the Reshaping of Personal Life* (1997), to mention but a few. In some ways they might be seen to be revisiting the areas that amateur historians of the late nineteenth century had so successfully mapped. Bonnie G Smith reminds us of their work, their 'thickly painted historical surface of everyday life, material culture, working women's lives, and, to a lesser extent, women's activism' (Smith 1998: 183) – all grist to the mill of women writing in the history of education today. Beyond the mapping of the territory, however, others seek to create new frameworks for interpretation (Eisenmann 2001). As politics and state building have faded from historical agendas and the new social history and women's history and theory have redefined the field, women writing in the history of education have come into their own, plundering forgotten archives and revelling in new areas such as the Foucauldian-inspired subjectivity and governmentality (Theobald 1996). Foucault's notions of discipline and regulation – as well as 'moral discourses' – lend themselves admirably to historians of education as *Discipline, Moral Regulation and Schooling: A Social History*, a Canadian-based collection, attests (Rousmaniere, Delhi and de Coninck-Smith 1997).

A tradition?

Can we then use the lens of retrospect to construct a tradition as Joan Scott (1997: 37) suggests? There are discernible threads that run through the work of women writing within the history of education. An ongoing concern is to map the ways in which women benefit from a rigorous non-gender-specific education, to recount women's accomplishments in establishing institutions for women and to acknowledge their leaders. The fear that women will be omitted from mainstream historical accounts is constant, ensuring that restoring women to history has a long past and will probably have a healthy future. Issues of power and authority, as Burstyn noted and Davies pondered, still remain central (Eveline 2002). It is still unusual, for example, to find women in the major histories of universities written by men.

Within revisionist and 'post-revisionist' history of education women, like their male colleagues, have imaginatively explored a wider set of issues which include state building, gender relations, the creation of categories of youth and adolescence and issues of colonialism and race. The issue raised by Campbell and Sherington needs to be confronted here. In drawing such a wide bow have women writing within and beyond the history of education contributed unwittingly to its demise – its transformation in Australia and the UK at least into broader historical fields, into gender studies, cultural studies and women's history? Is it possible to conceive of a history of education per se in an era in which the state school is no longer celebrated as the centrepiece of the strong nation state, but seen as a residual category, besieged by market forces? Was the history of education a discipline that paralleled, indeed met the needs of an era, one that has now almost certainly ended? This is too harsh a conclusion: women's writing can also be seen as part of a broader process of renewal of the discipline. In a recent *History of Education* editorial two British women editors wrote hopefully of 'a continually developing field', one that can adapt to new sources, new questions, new theories and methods and new disciplines (Goodman and Martin 2004: 10). Emily Davies, wondering what might constitute authority, could take comfort there. As editors of an academic journal with a long pedigree, as full members of university communities, Goodman and Martin show that women writing within the history of education have claimed a voice, can indeed speak with authority.

Alison Mackinnon

References

Burstall 1938; Burstyn 1977; Caine 1992; Campbell & Sherington 2002; Clarke 2002; Clifford 1976, 1988; Conway 1976; Eisenmann 2001; Eveline 2002; Fletcher 1980; Graham 1978; Greene 1967; Hilton & Hirsch 2000; Hole 1996; Houston and Prentice 1988; Jones 1975, 1985; Mackinnon 1984; McMahon 1996; Miller 1986, 1998; Scott 1997; Smith 1998; Spender 1982; Theobald 1986, 1991, 1996; Whitbread 1968; Wollstonecraft 1792/ 1985; Zainu'ddin 1964, 1973.

Eldershaw, M. Barnard

Marjorie Barnard (1897–1987) and Flora Eldershaw (1897–1956) were two Australian women who wrote together under the joint pseudonym M Barnard Eldershaw in the middle decades of the twentieth century. Both born in Sydney, the two women met while both were History students at the University of Sydney. Marjorie graduated with first class honours in History in 1920, and was awarded a graduate place at Oxford which paternal intervention meant she was unable to accept; instead she worked as a librarian at Sydney Technical College. Flora became a teacher, rising to senior English mistress and head of the boarding school at the prestigious Presbyterian Ladies' College, Croydon. She also was active in Sydney literary circles, becoming the first woman president of the Fellowship of Australian Writers in 1935.

The two women began writing together with an historical novel set in nineteenth-century Sydney, *A House Is Built* (1929), which as the joint winner of a prestigious literary award made them instantly famous within the Australian literary scene. It was followed two years later by a second historical novel, *Green Memory* (1931), also set in nineteenth-century eastern Australia. In 1935 Marjorie resigned from her library position to write full-time, and the writing duo became extremely productive. After two more novels, *The Glasshouse* (1936) and *Plaque with Laurel* (1937), the two women jointly wrote three histories, *Phillip of Australia: An Account of the Settlement at Sydney Cove 1788–1792* (1938), *The Life and Times of Captain John Piper* (1939) and *My Australia* (1939). The first two histories explore early Australian colonial history on the basis of extensive primary research, using the life of their subjects, one a governor and the other a leading figure in Sydney society, to illuminate the history of British rule in New South Wales. The third, *My Australia* (1939), was a general history, based largely on secondary sources; it was divided into two sections – 'New World', a history of white people in Australia, and 'Old World', about the land, its ecology and its indigenous people. In 'The Dispossessed', a chapter near the end of the book, the authors mourn the lack of interest the settlers took in Aboriginal knowledge and culture, but see both their ignorance and the disappearance of the Aboriginal people as inevitable and final: 'He (the Aboriginal) has gone back into the earth like one of his mia-mias, and his secret with him.'

Flora left teaching and became a public servant in Canberra in 1941; the following year Marjorie returned to librarianship at the CSIRO (which lasted until 1950, after which she returned to full-time writing).

Despite the fact these were busy years for both women, they wrote another collaborative work, which was to prove their last, the historical and science fiction novel, *Tomorrow and Tomorrow* (1947). Here their love of Australian history was again evident but this time in a much more experimental context. The novel opens in an ordered and technologically advanced twenty-fourth century; the leading character reads to a friend a novel he has written about working-class life in Sydney between the wars. Partly because of its vision of an invasion of Australia by a right-wing international police force followed by a revolutionary uprising and finally the destruction and abandonment of Sydney, the novel was censored in 1944 and published only after 393 lines were cut. It was poorly received and attracts diverse responses today. With the apparent failure of this novel, Eldershaw and Barnard stopped writing together and Eldershaw died in 1956.

Now working alone, Barnard turned back to her first love, history. She wrote *Sydney* (1956), a short popular book, without notes or bibliography, on the history of her home city. Then she turned to something more ambitious, a general history of Australia. The earlier jointly written *My Australia* had been modest in approach, more a sketch for a general history than anything else; as the authors wrote: 'This is not a history of Australia, it is no more than a shape of history, a review of the raw material from which we shall mould our future.' Now, Barnard wrote something much more ambitious, *A History of Australia* (1962). Based on printed primary and secondary sources, it was reasonably comprehensive, though like the other more academic texts of its era, confined the history of Aboriginal people to a separate chapter, 'The Dark People', near the end of the book. Given the scarcity of such texts and the growing popularity of Australian history in an expanding education system, this book became very well known. Part of the reason for its popularity was Barnard's easy and engaging writing style, also evident in her later book, *Macquarie's World*, both a biography of an early colonial governor of New South Wales and a history of his time. Despite Barnard's radical politics, this book shared with all the others a very brief treatment of colonial dispossession, allocating only four-and-half pages out of 233 for a discussion of Aboriginal–European relations. Indeed, she wrote, Aboriginal people had been 'already driven off the map', a statement that cannot help but jar the modern reader.

Ann Curthoys

Reference

Modjeska 1981.

Eliot, George (Mary Anne, Mary Ann, Marian Evans, Marian Evans Lewes, Mary Ann Cross) (1819–1880)

English novelist, essayist, translator, poet, editor of The *Westminster Review*. Born in Warwickshire to Robert Evans, estate manager, and his second wife, Christiana Pearson, Mary Anne was the youngest of five surviving children. Eliot was educated conventionally at local schools, but the modesty of her formal education was entirely eclipsed by her prodigious appetite for self-education. She grew up to become one of the great polymaths of the century, fluent in seven languages, proficient in all branches of contemporary scientific theory and a cultural commentator on matters as various as the history of religion and the future of German philosophy. Under the influence of free-thinking Coventry friends Eliot abandoned the zealous evangelical Christianity of her adolescence and subsequently translated two texts which were decisive in the period's great shift from religious to secular ethics – Strauss's *The Life of Jesus* (1846) and Feuerbach's *The Essence of Christianity* (1854).

Following the death of her widowed father in 1849, Eliot was freed to move to London, where she supported herself as a reviewer and became editor of The *Westminster Review* in 1851. In 1854 her elopement with George Lewes began a profoundly supportive relationship which was to last until his death in 1878. With his encouragement, she published *Scenes of Clerical Life* in 1858, the first of eight works of fiction, as well as two volumes of poetry and a collection of essays. Eliot's novels were characteristically studies of English provincial life set in the recent past, a device which enabled the creation of a world at once familiar, comprehensive and completed. The one exception to this is *Romola*, a historical romance set in fifteenth-century Florence. While offering a brilliant study of personal and public politics, the novel is burdened by the excessive erudition with which Eliot sought to 'animate the past'. Yet in that very endeavour it is typical, for Eliot always aspired to render history 'incarnate' through a scrupulous realism, founded at once on fidelity to detail and psychological veracity. Like the dazzling metaphor of the coachman's journey which opens *Felix Holt*, offering a panorama of continuity and change, Eliot saw the present as only comprehensible in the context of the accumulated past.

Pauline Nestor

References

Beer 1986, 2000; Hardy 1970; Nestor 2002; Shuttleworth 1984.

Major works

Scenes from a Clerical Life (ed.) Thomas A Noble (Oxford: Oxford University Press, 1985); *Romola* (ed.) Andrew Sanders (New York: Penguin, 1980) and *Felix Holt, the Radical* (ed.) William Baker & Kenneth Womack (Peterborough: Broadview, 2000).

Ellet, Elizabeth Fries Lummis 1812–1877

Born in New York. Daughter of Sarah (Maxwell) and William Nixon Lummis, physician. Educated at the Quaker Female Seminary in Aurora, where she showed an early facility for languages and an interest in Romanticism. Began writing career by publishing poetry for the *American Ladies Magazine*. Her first published work *Euphemio of Messina* (1834), a translation of the tragedy by Silvio Pellico, was published anonymously. Her own historical tragedy *Teresa Contarini* and a small volume of poetry were published in 1835, the year she married William Henry Ellet, Professor of Chemistry, Columbia University.

In 1836 the couple moved to Columbia, where her husband took up a position at South Carolina College. While in Carolina, Ellet produced three books: *The Characters of Schiller* (1839), *Scenes in the Life of Joanna of Sicily* (1840) and *Rambles about the Country* (1840) and wrote for various periodicals. Returning to New York in 1848 she published a long essay on the subject of women's role in the Revolutionary Wars in Godey's *Lady's Book*. Like **Sarah Josepha Hale** Ellet believed in an old style of Republicanism that privileged civic virtue over personal desire. The figure of the Republican mother looms large in Ellet's major study *Women of the American Revolution* (1848–1850), a three-volume study of women who lived through the Revolution. Descended from veteran Captain John Maxwell on her mother's side, Ellet used this connection to correspond with and interview elderly survivors of the revolutionary wars. In this work Ellet celebrated the ideal of Republican motherhood. Ellet's analysis of women's role in the Revolution reflects a romantic sense that women shaped history by personal influence and force of sentiment. While Ellet recorded instances of women moving into the masculine realm of soldiering and politics, she created a domestic history of the revolution, stressing the importance of women's heroism within their own sphere, suggesting that there were two separate but equal narratives of the war. This theme was continued in *A Domestic History of the Revolution* (1850) which limited the details of major battles in order to focus on the experience of war 'derived from domestic pictures drawn from real life'. *Pioneer Women of the West* (1852) presented biographies of 'pioneer matrons' documenting through domestic life their role in the 'progressive settlement of the whole country'.

Ellet became editor of *The Practical Houskeeper: A Cyclopedia of Domestic Economy* in 1857. Later works such as *Queens of American Society* (1867) and *Court Circles of the Republic; or, Beauties and Celebrities of the Nation* (1870) focused upon America's socially dominant families, stressing the way in which prominent women influenced politics through their social role. She involved herself in philanthropy, especially the rescue of homeless women, and converted to Catholicism shortly before her death.

Mary Spongberg

References

Baym 1995; Caspar 1995; Kerber 1997.

Major work

Revolutionary Women in the War for American Independence (A one-volume revised edition of Ellet's *Women of the American Revolution* 1848) (ed.) Lincoln Diamant (Westport: Praeger, 1998).

Empire

Writing in 1992 on women in the Middle East, Billie Melman wrote in *Women's Orients* that few historians had looked 'at the relations between imperialism and gender' (1992: 6). Melman, without question, was in the vanguard of an extraordinary sea change, for in the dozen or so years since she wrote this, the field of imperial history has changed radically as a result of feminist interventions. The 1990s saw a veritable explosion of interest not only in topics related specifically to women's history but to the application of feminist theories to questions of imperialism and colonialism. And while this essay will focus on the contributions to the field of the British Empire, this rich vein of scholarship is by no means limited to scholars of that particular empire. The Dutch, French and German colonial worlds (Stoler 1991; Clancy-Smith and Gouda 1998; Locher-Scholten 2000; Wildenthal 2001), the colonies of the earlier Roman empire (Richlin 1992; Golden and Toohey 2003) and those of the early modern Spanish empire (Chambers 1999; Socolow 2000) have all come within the purview of feminist scholars and each has been transformed by a belief in the mutual constitution of empire and gender. Feminist scholars, reading the phenomenon of colonial power through the lens of gender, have reshaped a field once dominated by a deeply traditional and just as deeply masculine attention to diplomacy, high politics, military warfare and a top-down flow of ideas and policies from 'centre' to 'periphery'.

The sheer breadth of Britain's huge empire, the largest of the modern period, has produced a diverse range of work. Scholars as varied in their strategies and methodologies as Kathleen Wilson, Tanika Sarkar, Catherine Hall, Vron Ware, Antoinette Burton, Clare Midgley and Adele Perry (to name but a handful in a very talented and now quite crowded field) have all insisted that colonialism in its modern guise cannot be properly understood apart from the hierarchies of gender, as of race and class. Some of these scholars have made empire as an entity the focus of their interests; others have concentrated on one particular colonial location. They have sought to question how and whether domestic categories of gender differentiation operated in colonial situations as Mrinalini Sinha does in *Colonial Masculinity* (1995). They have asked what effect gendered thinking about, for example, family and sexuality has had on the related categories of race and class; in works such as Luise White's *The Comforts of Home: Prostitution in Colonial Nairobi* (1990) and Anne McClintock's *Imperial Leather* (1995), as well as Philippa Levine's *Prostitution, Race and Politics: Policing Venereal Disease in the British Empire* (2003). Antoinette Burton in her essay 'Who Needs the Nation? Interrogating "British" History' (1997) and Catherine Hall in *Civilizing Subjects* (2002) have asked tough questions about the relationship between metropole and colony. Burton in *Burdens of History* (1994) has also investigated how far western feminism has meaning in subaltern contexts, while Vron Ware in *Beyond the Pale: White Women, Racism and History* (1992) asks whether 'sisterhood' is a term that can survive the violence and the strife of the modern colonial enterprise.

But thinking historically about the British Empire is not the exclusive domain of today's feminist historians. Women's writings have long engaged with this theme. Though afforded little official role in the business and management of empire, women nonetheless visited the empire, travelled in it, lived and worked in it and frequently made it central in their writings, whether as a foil for comparing the rights of women in various societies, as a setting for fictional tales or in that fashionable nineteenth-century genre, the travel memoir. Feminist journals, which began to appear in Britain in the mid-nineteenth century, frequently discussed imperial questions, mostly but by no means exclusively in relation to questions of women's rights and the fight to win and expand those. In all of these instances, we commonly find writings imbued with an historical sense of Britain as a major and exceptional power at home and abroad, boasting an empire qualitatively different from its predecessors and its competitors, an empire whose historical trajectory would be different and, most thought, better. This striking avowal of an imperial exceptionalism for Britain was moulded, of course, by a perception of British history as itself exceptional.

Non-British women writers also engaged with questions of empire, and not surprisingly an exceptionalist stance was less frequent among them. One might find elements of British exceptionalism among white colonial women, but among colonised women, writing was largely an arena in which to discuss the phenomenon of imperialism critically. There were often fewer outlets for publishing their opinions and voices even than there were for British women, but colonised women nonetheless actively engaged with the imperial experiences that in so many ways governed their lives. This essay will look briefly at some examples of all of these different historically shaped writings about empire by women.

Travel and travel writing

Women's writing on empire pre-dates the era of nationalism, as the work of Lady

Mary Wortley Montagu illustrates. Wife of the British consul to the Ottoman Emperor and resident in the eastern Mediterranean for some 15 months in 1717 and 1718, Montagu became interested in Ottoman culture and practice, and particularly in the lives of women. En route to Turkey, and whilst living in Adrianople and then Constantinople, Montagu wrote copiously, richly descriptive letters to her friends and family in England. Subsequently collected and published as *Letters from the Levant during the Embassy to Constantinople, 1716–18* (1838), these letters represent what Melman calls 'the very first example of a secular work by a woman about the Muslim Orient' (1992: 2).

Montagu's interest in the position and life of women in Ottoman Turkey made her seek out the company of local women, many of whom lived in the seclusion dictated by local custom and religion. Her letters constantly played with the kind of 'equality-difference' antagonism that twentieth-century feminists have treated so frequently. Over and over, Montagu reminded her correspondents that eastern manners and customs were not so different from those of west. Writing to her sister about urban upper-class marital infidelity, Montagu remarks, 'the manners of mankind do not differ so widely as our voyage writers would make us believe' (1838/1971: Letter xxxi). Montagu resists the typical and orientalist reading of the eastern woman as peculiarly and grossly oppressed. Women, she told the Countess of Bristol, 'are bought and sold as publicly and as infamously in all our Christian great cities' (1838/1971: Letter xlvi). Unlike many Western writers for whom *purdah* and veiling epitomised barbarism and the rejection of modernity, Montagu delighted in its potential. The total robing required of women when they went abroad in public offered them, she thought, 'entire liberty of following their inclinations without danger of discovery' (1838/1971: Letter xxxii).

Sceptical as she was regarding an east–west binary, Montagu was nonetheless critical of what she saw as Ottoman despotism, writing to one of her correspondents disapprovingly of witnessing 'arbitrary government in its clearest and strongest light' (1838/1971: Letter xxxi). She was apt to hold British constitutionalism up as the model of perfect governance even while she counselled her correspondents not to dismiss the east as a savage and primitive world. It is perhaps this satisfaction with the English polity that made Montagu, despite her more radical statements, a key figure in the nineteenth century, widely read by travellers and others. Montagu's influence reached far and offered a wide range of readers an alternative view of the eighteenth-century Ottoman empire: woman-centred, unusually lacking in Eurocentrism and open to new ideas.

As we move into the nineteenth century, there is a far greater body of published work by women about empire, mirroring the proliferation of print materials, of cheaper books and of growing literacy. Moreover, as travel became more widespread, greater numbers of women were able to move about the empire, and many wrote prodigiously about their experiences. Their **travel** was not monodirectional: women moved from Britain to the colonies, between colonies, and from the colonies to Britain. In the twentieth century, in particular, young men and women from the white settler colonies spent time living and working in London, even while successive immigration laws restricted such opportunities for their non-white counterparts. For those travelling from places such as South Africa and Australia, the long sea journey offered the opportunity to 'see the world' en route. A trip to the 'Mother Country,' as Ros Pesman in *Duty Free: Australian Women Abroad* (1996) and Angela Woollacott in

To Try Her Fortune in London (2001) illustrate, was often a must-do prior to the traditional path of marriage and motherhood, which awaited those who made the return journey, as most did. The writings of those who undertook such journeys offer us more than merely a glimpse into the typical voyaging of young middle-class colonial society. The writings of these women constitute a form of historical writing for the insights they offer us as to the fractured nature of colonialism, the particular ways in which gender shaped the journeying and the opinions of white colonial women, and how women reared in **Dominion** arenas reacted to what was constantly represented as the centre of their imperial world, London. White colonial women's opinions and behaviours were historically shaped by the particular versions of empire to which white settler colonialism had given rise since the eighteenth century. Products of their particular environment, they brought to bear both on Britain and its empire – their own countries included – the weight of that historical specificity.

In the empire

Although in far smaller numbers than the relatively affluent white women from Dominion countries, other colonised women came to the 'heart of the empire' too. Freed (and frequently literate) African-American slaves were brought across the Atlantic by abolitionists to plead their cause. Their experience of slavery was historically rooted in the empire, for the eighteenth-century British Empire was built in large part on the success of the slave trade. Their writings reveal much about empire, most particularly in their reading of British anti-slavery activism as typifying a characteristically British support for personal liberty. Ellen Craft, former Georgian slave, famously declared in the *Anti-Slavery Advocate* in December 1852 that she would 'much rather starve in England, a free woman, than be a slave for the best man that ever breathed upon the American continent'. Declarations such as that of Craft, largely concerned with pressing contemporary issues, self-consciously invoked a British past of liberty and reason, revealing a highly edited version of both the British past (and present) which ignored the centrality of Britain in the imperial slave trade and overlooked the almost total excising of women from political representation at the imperial centre.

There were also many for whom empire was the explicit focus of their writings. When the women who accompanied their husbands to colonial postings in crown colonies and protectorates or to isolated farmsteads where they hoped to make their fortunes through cheap property wrote of their lives in such places, they did so through a gendered imperial lens. For some, comparison was uppermost, as they wearily described the harsh climate or gruelling conditions which pioneer living forced upon them and which contrasted so radically with the gendered gentility which so many hoped to achieve by moving to the colonies. For such women, it was the isolation of life in unfamiliar surroundings that was key, but in other cases – tellingly, among the wealthier classes – we see women expertly re-creating familiar social hierarchies and expectations in their new environs. We see such women most often through their diaries and correspondence rather than through 'professional' writings, and while such textual forms themselves perform certain functions vis-à-vis audience and author, theirs are markedly different productions than among those consciously seeking a wider audience through the medium of formal publishing. Both often abided by certain writerly conventions, and in both instances the kinds of domestic assumptions that defined women's lives would further have modified the nature of these writings, yet a difference between formal and informal writing is often discernible. In each case, however, the assumptions and trajectories of their lives and work, their feelings about empire, all bear the mark of an historical background against which they measured and shaped their own imperial lives. Trained in a particular and historical mode of womanhood and frequently conscious of their Britishness, these women often struggled to make sense of life in unfamiliar environments.

The same might be said of non-white women faced with the racial as well as the gendered hierarchies of empire. Pandita Ramabai was a high-caste Indian woman who, in the 1880s, spent three years in Britain. Ramabai was a prolific author and correspondent whose publications allowed her an unusual self-sufficiency among women in her day. She came to Britain to study medicine, and shortly after arriving converted to Christianity, rapidly proving a tenacious critic of the Anglican Church. She wrote abundantly about her considerable doctrinal differences with her mentors in the Church of England. These differences more often than not turned on the question of authority, and to the frustration of the Anglican women who tutored Ramabai, on what they regarded as her wilful flouting of church authority. Ramabai moved quickly from being seen by her English supporters as an object of pity and interest to becoming a thorn in their side. While the press and her 'handlers' before she espoused such independent thought had sought to cast her as heroic victim – orphaned, widowed and tragically determined – she herself worked to fashion a very different self. Meera Kosambi in *At the Intersection of Gender Reform and Religious Belief* (1995) and Antoinette Burton in *At the Heart of the Empire* (1997) have read Ramabai's writings and her life to make broader claims about Indian nationalism and British feminism, and how each relied upon a backdrop of empire for their force. Ramabai's own writings may not have spoken directly to concerns of empire, but if we adopt a more generous and inclusive view of what constitutes women's historical writings about empire, we might read Ramabai – through her writings as well as her actions – as a woman whose life was shaped by the kinds of gendered considerations that contemporary feminist historians have insisted upon revealing as central to understanding empire.

Feminism and empire

Feminists writing about empire in the nineteenth century seldom saw a contradiction, as Ramabai might have done, between support for imperialism and their own demands. Indeed, the position of the 'native' woman was often used as a foil for the demands of British women, well into the twentieth century. The work of scholars such as Antoinette Burton, Laura Mayhall and Julia Bush has shown how white women in Britain made a critique of women's position in imperial locations a powerful tool in their own fight for political representation. Nineteenth-century women writers were by no means uncritical of empire but their critiques often rested on practice rather than principle. When Florence Nightingale called for sanitary reform in India, in a paper she read at the Social Science Congress in 1873, she did so not only because of the benefits she thought would accrue to those living there but also because such reforms would render it 'an easy matter to hold the great Indian Empire by a British force' (Tuson 1995). These are hardly the sentiments of a woman critical of the principles of colonialism.

It was also in the area of sanitary reform that one of the biggest controversies around empire in the late nineteenth century erupted, the furore over the continued regulation of prostitution in the empire after its repeal in Britain in 1886. The House of Commons had in June 1888 passed a resolution extending the condemnation of compulsory genital examination of registered prostitute women to India. Despite that victory anti-regulationists were sceptical that the parliamentary voice was being heeded. What ensued was an elaborate and lengthy fight, by no means limited to India, for the genuine abolition of registered prostitution – and the Contagious Diseases (CD) Acts and Ordinances that enunciated it – throughout the British Empire. While the campaign was not limited to feminists, they were prominent among the abolitionists, and through their prolific writings on the topic we glimpse a woman's world structured profoundly and substantially by both imperialism and Christianity. The basis of abolitionist opposition rested, obviously, on the double moral standard enshrined in both colonial and domestic versions of the CD laws, but in the imperial phase of the campaign the movement also revealed an interesting and largely pro-imperial stance in which Britain featured as a power which should – but was failing to – uphold the historical principles of liberty on which British power rested. Alongside a distaste for partial laws which blamed women and not men for spreading sexually transmissible diseases, many activist women saw in the empire a place where Christian moral principles were urgently needed. The empire, for many women involved in this fight, was itself a Christian duty of the highest order, and the government's inability to impose moral restraint therein destabilised both religion and the historical justifications for a British Empire. **Josephine Butler**, doyenne of the repeal movement, wanted imperialism to take up more profoundly what she saw as its inexorable moral obligations. 'What an opportunity lies before her [England], of laying her strong imperial hand on a wrong which is crying to heaven for vengeance' (Butler 1899: 144). J Ellice Hopkins, writing at the same time in *The Power of Womanhood* (1899), called the 'great British Empire, the greatest civilising, order-spreading, christianising world power ever known' (Hopkins 1900:297)

In the early twentieth century, a new phenomenon emerged in women's writing about empire. While white women in the earlier British empire had been predominantly wealthy women seeking adventure, poor women seeking employment and sometimes a marriage partner, or women accompanying husbands, fathers and brothers posted abroad, the twentieth century gave rise to the academic woman, interested in questions of imperialism and travelling in the empire, seeking answers to her questions. Well known amongst this group of women was Margery Perham, frequently dubbed Britain's 'conscience on Africa.' Well educated and upper-middle class, Perham moved throughout her adult life in typically masculine environments: the academy, the Colonial Service and the empire itself. Enamoured of travel and with an impressively staunch constitution, Perham embarked on what would be a lifelong interest in Africa when in the early 1920s, she undertook a lengthy visit to the Sudan ostensibly to visit her sister Ethel, who in 1911 had married New Zealander Harry Rayne, now a district commissioner in British Somaliland. Feminine visiting styles were not, however, to dictate Perham's extraordinary adventures on that first of many trips. As she would with many subsequent travels, Perham wrote lovingly and engagingly of her far from sedate experiences.

On that trip she rode horseback over mountains and rough terrain, camped extensively and visited isolated settlements, a far cry from the gentility of tea and tennis that was many a woman visitor's experience of empire. Perham was a prolific author, penning a slew of policy works on colonialism, a biography of her friend and mentor, Frederick Lugard, and a couple of novels alongside her extensive travel memoirs. Her writings about empire are thus unusually varied, comprising a lively mix of fiction, travel writing, private correspondence and diary entries, biography and policy papers. In Perham's work, we see again that historically inflected understanding of the contemporary empire and we can use her writings, too, to reveal much about the continued obstacles which women faced in the masculine environment of the colonial world.

Perham's work was distinctive in a number of respects. Not only was she, as a woman in a distinctively male universe, sensitive about her own role and power as she moved through the empire, but she was always concerned deeply with questions of racial inequality. She understood acutely the obstacles as well as the advantages her femaleness offered her, and she also recognised the difference that race made in terms of privilege and access. Both feature repeatedly in her writings, and most especially in her more personal writings, the diaries that were later published as travel memoirs as Perham's stature grew. Over and over, she commented on the operation of gender in her own situation, although she was always hesitant to broaden the analysis to the social structures of the colonies of which she writes. For Perham, gender was largely a terrain she navigated personally rather than an issue she regarded as relevant across national lines. As a result there is very little in her work on gender as a colonial issue, or on the colonial world as other than accidentally all male. This seeming inability to translate her own standing in the world with a broader critique is echoed, as well, in her writings on race. Although endlessly critical of and concerned about the corroding effects of racism, Perham sometimes wrote with surprising naiveté about racial prejudice. In *The Colonial Reckoning* (1961), written at the moment of her retirement, and in the unusually public spotlight of the Reith Lectures, she comfortably argued that it was merely an accident, albeit a 'very unfortunate' one, that 'most of the people whom the Western colonial nations conquered were coloured'.

Perham's writings about gender were only slightly more sophisticated than her reading of the racial-imperial axis as merely a bad coincidence. She was deeply sensitive to her own subject position as a woman. 'How much easier all this is for men!' she remarked of travelling in general, in *Pacific Prelude: A Journey to Samoa and Australasia, 1929* (1988: 35). On her way by boat across the Pacific she noted of her fellow passenger, the new Governor of American Samoa: 'I envied him his job – and his sex' (1988: 77). Such comments are common, sprinkled across the pages of all her travel memoirs, yet she seldom drew broader or deeper conclusions from such observations. Women such as Perham were simultaneously insiders and outsiders, their gender separating them from the privileges that accrued to men of their class and race, but their class and race assuring their safety as they travelled. In a similar vein Ellen Jacobs, writing about **Eileen Power** and her travels in China and in India, notes that while discrimination kept Power out of important institutional fraternities, her winning of a prestigious travel scholarship 'reinscribed her privileges of race, class and professional status as a "translator" of colonial cultures and civilisations' (Jacobs 1998: 299). Perham's travels, too, were funded by a scholarship more commonly awarded to men than to women; Power travelled on a Kahn Fellowship, Perham on a Rhodes scholarship.

At the opposite end of the political spectrum to Perham and travelling within the empire only a handful of years earlier was **Beatrice Webb.** She and her husband Sidney spent some four months touring British India and the princely states in 1912 and kept a diary of their doings. Though the diary entries are written largely using the plural pronoun, Beatrice was the principal diarist of the couple. Like Perham, the Webbs visited colonial officials, sought out intellectuals among Indians and were interested in questions of social reform and political representation. They approached their imperial travels, in this respect, in very similar ways to Perham.

And like Perham, Sidney and Beatrice Webb, too, found it hard not to conceive of India as a place where the British might educate and modernise. It was 'enlightened' Muslims, they wrote in *Indian Diary*, whose womenfolk were out of *purdah*. Of native rulers, they lamented 'it is a terrible problem how to bring up these native Rulers', assuming the necessity and desirability of British influence on ostensibly independent Indian lands (1990: 76). Yet missionaries, in particular, the Webbs despised for an attitude of superiority remarkably akin to their own unrecognised position. 'The theological representatives of England in India seem to be as cocksure as our military or civilian or commercial representatives that we are in all respects the superior people, kindly vouchsafing to stoop to administer at liberal salaries the affairs of an inferior "subject race" ' (1990: 126).

The ambivalence of both Perham and Webb – wanting to see colonised peoples as equal but still caught up in a strong belief that modernity was a benevolent product that colonialism could deliver for the good of humanity – is perhaps a characteristically twentieth-century contradiction. Perham and Webb both wrote at a time when struggles over suffrage and over the meaning of democracy were critical, and especially for women. Both were educated women who rejected the domestic existence that would routinely have been the future for women of their background in favour of political involvement. Markedly different in their political beliefs they were both, however, the recipients of changes in women's freedoms that were yoked, at least rhetorically, to broad questions of modernity and progress in much the same ways that the 'civilising mission' was represented as ultimately liberating for colonial peoples. Yet open and degrading racism repulsed them, given their belief in (and perhaps their fledgling albeit spotty experience of) equality. As colonial nationalism in the twentieth century began to demand many of the same freedoms women had fought for – and only sometimes won – theirs was a perhaps necessarily ambivalent position. It was a position, moreover, that has significant repercussions for understanding the historical nature of these women's views of empire, for in their assumption that modernity would be beneficial and had to be taken *to* the colonies, both women had a particular and western historical reading premised on a belief in western progress and in the frozen historical development of backward colonies requiring to be brought into the modern world. As Perham insisted in her autobiographical *African Apprenticeship* (1974), 'by any balanced historical judgment . . . our colonial rule . . . was . . . an immense and essential service to Africa'.

Mary Louise Pratt, in her influential book *Imperial Eyes: Travel Writing and Transculturation*, sees a difference in eighteenth- and nineteenth-century accounts of travel by men and women. While the men focus often on achievement and dominance, women writers, she finds, 'emplot quests for self-realization, and fantasies of social harmony' (1992: 168). The writings considered here suggest some adherence to that general principle, for these were women often focused on social reform issues and how a resolution of these matters would better people's lives. This was not a vision that in any way presupposed or dictated anti-imperialist views; for many women, social reform was precisely why imperialism was necessary. Katherine Dixon went so far as to argue, in *An Appeal to the Women of the Empire Concerning Present Moral Conditions in Our Cantonments in India,* that 'the uplift of Indian men and women is our only justification for being in their country at all' (1916: 7).

Gender and empire

Women from the colonies (and more especially from the non-white colonies) were far likelier to criticise the principles of colonialism, though even in such instances we neither can nor should categorise all colonised women as anti-imperialists. Instead we should perhaps pay close attention to what Adrienne Rich, more than 20 years ago, dubbed the 'politics of location', a term that signifies class and racial location as much as geographical. Women's writings about empire can no more be essentialised than those of men. Their social status, their personal beliefs and politics, their geography and their interactions with others all affected how they regarded empire. We might be more confident in asserting the concrete effects of empire on women's lives; their writings about the phenomenon certainly suggest its centrality in their lives. Despite the common exclusion of women from imperial decision-making and office, the plethora of writings – fictional and non-fictional, published and unpublished – evidence that women wrote about, thought about and experienced empire in many ways.

Chandra Mohanty has observed in her much-cited essay, 'Under Western Eyes: Feminist Scholarship and Colonial Discourses', that 'feminist scholarly practices . . . are inscribed in relations of power – relations which they counter, resist or even perhaps implicitly support. There can, of course, be no apolitical scholarship' (1991: 53). When women wrote about empire, they wrote within and of politics but they wrote frequently of a politics far broader, far more encompassing, than that in which the history of colonialism was written when the field was dominated by men who were policymakers as much as they were historians, men whose lives and careers were bound to the maintenance of empire (Midgley 1998). Whether we look at the writings of contemporary feminist historians or the women for whom empire was both an immediate reality *and* an historical construct and wherever those women stood on the political spectrum, women have engaged historically with the theme of empire throughout the chequered history of that powerful and always gendered phenomenon.

Philippa Levine

References

Burton 1997; Butler 1899; Chambers 1999; Clancy-Smith & Gouda 1998; Dixon 1916; Golden & Toohey 2003; Hopkins 1899; Jacobs 1998; Levine 2003; Locher-Scholten 2000; McClintock 1995; Melman 1992; Midgley 1998; Mohanty 1991; Montagu 1838/1971; Perham 1974; Perham 1988; Perham; Perry 2001; Pratt 1992; Richlin 1992; Sinha 1995; Socolow 2000; Stoler 1991, 2002; Tuson 1995; Webb 1990; Ware 1992; Wilson 2003; Wildenthal 2001; White 1990.

Related essays

Dominion; Orientalism; Postcolonialism; Travel.

Enlightenment

'Enlightenment' refers both to an intellectual and a political movement and an age of enlightened political and social philosophy associated with 'reason'. Its chronological boundaries coincide approximately with 'the long eighteenth century' viz. c.1680–1800. The Enlightenment was a self-conscious movement: contemporaries spoke of 'enlightenment' (Britain), 'l'age de lumiere' (France), 'Aufklarung' (Germany) and 'Illuminismo' (Italy); they also spoke of the imperative 'to enlighten'. Crucial to understanding what separates 'Enlightenment' from 'Renaissance' is rejection by the 'moderns' of the late seventeenth century of the sole intellectual authority of classical texts. The 'moderns' eschewed the 'ancients', or those scholars they accused of being intellectually trapped by 'custom'.

Enlightenment philosophers rejected the political authority of the Church, historical authentication through scriptural texts and intellectual authority through faith. Enlightenment thinkers genuinely displaced God as the central actor in the historical narrative, and providential visions of God's intervention in the affairs of 'men' were replaced by an interest in the human condition, free will and historical agency. The deism of Enlightenment thinkers subjected religion to 'reason' and replaced the idea that God's will was revealed in nature with empirical observation of the natural world. Thus, 'The Enlightenment' was secularising and its impact was felt throughout Europe. It spawned a secondary political movement associated with monarchs like Catherine II of Russia who claimed a modernity of thinking that drove political policies aimed at social equality. It also encouraged a radical politics exemplified at the end of the period by **Mary Wollstonecraft**'s *A Vindication of the Rights of Woman* (1792).

Enlightenment historiography developed symbiotically with the idea of human progress. Crucial to historical methodology were two works – Pierre Bayle's *Dictionnaire Historique et Critique* (1697) and Giambattista Vico's *Scienza Nuova* (1725). Bayle's work was an attempt to discredit Catholic historical interpretation. It also pre-figured 'scientific' historical method, with his extensive explanatory footnotes, bibliographical citations and explanatory notes. Vico's dictum of *verum ipsum factum* (the theory that the true and the made are the same) underlay his vision of historical narrative that revealed laws governing the nature of states whose historical progress was discoverable and explicable. These works indicated that historical knowledge was no longer bound by the finite resource of God's laws and was replaced by the belief in the infinite acquisition of fact. As Peter Gay argued in his influential two-volume essay on the Enlightenment (1969), the 'science of man' that was Enlightenment history was a 'strategic science' that acted as a template for all other disciplines. History as a combination of archival research (empirical method) and social criticism (particularly about 'superstition'), exemplified by works such as Pietro Giannone's *Storia Civile del Regno di Napoli* (1723), provided a methodology that was co-opted by other disciplines such as 'mechanical science'.

The iconic Enlightenment project was the *Encyclopédie* (1751) of Denis Diderot and Jean le Rond d'Alembert. This was a collective effort at systematised knowledge in 17 volumes of text with 11 volumes of plates. In 72,000 articles 140 Encyclopedists demonstrated their belief that humanity could quantify its knowledge and insisted upon the division between human and natural sciences. The *Encyclopédie* first appeared in a decade that saw also the reworking of the

Renaissance biographical form in works like *Age of Louis XIV* (1751) by François Marie Arouet (Voltaire). This work was more than just a celebration of a monarch; it linked Voltaire's philosophy with his criticism of the *ancien regime* and his mission to bring history to bear on social and political reforms. In Voltaire it is possible to see that the Enlightenment world that believed history was made by humans, also believed that humans were currently making history. **World** and 'universal' histories abounded alongside national histories as historians classified themselves, in the phrase of Ernst Breisach, as 'interpreters of progress and nation'. The most ambitious historical project of the Enlightenment was Edward Gibbon's *Decline and Fall of the Roman Empire* which emerged in six volumes between 1776 and 1788. It was published when Enlightenment historiography reached its apogee just as the German Enlightenment had witnessed the establishment of the Historical Library at the University of Göttingen and Emmanuel Kant published his *Critique of Pure Reason* (1781), arguing that history as a series of evolutionary laws.

Women's 'exclusion' from the historical record was diminished by the way in which they were *included* in historical accounts such as the *Encyclopédie*. 'Man' as a generic term for 'man and woman' in history was a concept that depended for its very existence on making women the *object* of study especially through explorations of sexuality. Several articles written by Diderot for the *Encyclopédie* examined sexual desire and pleasure, lingering on female fidelity and romanticising the sexuality of Polynesian women. Women's 'exclusion' also resulted from identification of female subordination with Montesquieu's concept of 'civil slavery'. Montesquieu argued that 'all men are born equal' but that women were subject to 'personal' and 'real' slavery brought about in 'nations remarkable for their simplicity of life'. Carole Pateman (1988) has argued that '[c]ivil slavery' was thus turned into a legitimate human contractual relationship; the whole burden of Rousseau's works like *Discourse on Inequality* (1754) and *The Social Contract* (1762) was to argue that the enslaved *agreed* to their slavery when society moved from a state of nature to civil society. Women were, thus, made the *object* of historical study as one measurement of 'civilisation'.

The Encyclopedists also separated human and natural science and underpinned the separation with the gendered association of women with one object of study – the world of nature. Hilda Smith (2000) has argued that these ideas were in place at the beginning of the Enlightenment and led to what she has called 'the false [discursive] universal' of 'man' as hegemonic and representative of humankind. One newspaper in 1755 was simply entitled *Man: A Paper for Enobling [sic] the Species*. Men were trained into their role as 'humankind' while women were constructed as the supporting cast. John Dunton's *The Athenian Mercury* addressed 'all men and both sexes' in 1690 and Hume's *Treatise of Human Nature* (1739–1740) made a clear distinction between 'man' and female 'nature'. This is a work in which 'mankind' is 'inventive' and in which 'man' was discussed in terms of property, origins of government, political allegiance and so on while women were discussed obliquely in relation to men's need for 'chastity'.

Enlightenment relegation of women as a 'species' for study may be seen in William Alexander's *The History of Women, from the Earliest Antiquity, to the Present Time* (1779). In this verbose and taxonomic work, Alexander admitted to the historical oppression of women which he concluded was the consequence of men's love and desire to protect the female sex. 'Female society' was discussed in relation to its value for shaping the nature of 'man': '[o]f all the various causes which tend to influence our conduct and form of our manners, none operate so powerfully as the society of the *other* sex'. Theoretically, enlightenment philosophy as espoused in the *Encyclopédie* and in essays on human morality by David Hume promoted sexual equality. However, in sociological and historical practice the search for the condition of 'man' universalised the male subject.

'The mind has no sex'

The impact of 'Enlightenment' thought and politics on the role of women was both profound and contradictory. It depended upon the changing concept of 'woman' embodied in medical treatises, works of natural philosophy, works of the *querelle des femmes* and of early feminist tracts. The Enlightenment rejected the intellectual foundations from Genesis and the Aristotelian/Galenic nexus that had led to a negative gender construction of 'woman' as 'daughter of Eve' and the 'weaker vessel'. Eighteenth-century ideas about human progress were potentially liberating for women; as Sylvana Tomaselli has observed women became 'the barometer on which every aspect of society, its morals, its laws, its customs, its government' was measured (Tomaselli 1985). The concept of civil society was formed around an ideology of separate spheres, which defined women as 'woman' as different from, but equal to, man. Underpinning such enlightened ideas was a belief in the educability of women articulated in texts such as François Poullain de la Barre's two Cartesian works – *On the Equality of the Two Sexes* and its sequel, *On the Education of Ladies* – that argued that because 'the mind has no sex' society should reject the 'custom' of leaving women in ignorance. Present too was a growing discourse of sensibility that conflated an ideal of progress with the feminisation of society. The idea that women were morally superior to men became prominent in conduct books written by men such as Richard Allestree's *The Ladies Calling* (1673). Allestree's motivation was to instruct women in life based on the idea that God's Creation could be improved upon. '[I]n the sublimest part of humanity [i.e. the soul]' he told his readers women were capable of 'infinite beatitude' and, after chapters on such desirable feminine traits as 'meekness', 'compassion' and 'affability', he told women that if God found his own image in them 'they then become like the King's daughter, all glorious within too'. This left the way open for personal introspection, reform and a proselytising role in society that would end with women being raised to the 'heavenly crown'.

While men dominated the discussion of women's conduct, women too began to articulate their own ideas about their role in society. In England, Mary Astell's *A Serious Proposal to the Ladies* (1694) argued that if the daughters of gentlemen were educated it would be 'no inconsiderable advantage to the Nation' because educated women made better wives. Astell called for a 'seminary to stock the kingdom with pious and prudent ladies'. She wrote within the context of a Europe-wide debate about the need for girls' schools. 'Incapacity, if there be any, is acquired not natural', Astell told her readers and she argued that 'custom' alone rendered women under-educated. Her attack drew upon the enlightened discourse of François Fénelon whose *De L'Education des Filles* (1687) inspired Madame de Maintenon to establish a school for 250 girls at Saint-Cyr. Bathsua Makin's *An Essay to Revive the Antient Education of Gentlewomen* (1673) argued for a *revival* of female education so that women could 'answer the end of [your] Creation, to be meet helps to [your] Husbands'. The message appealed to the merchant men of London who sent their daughters to her new school in Tottenham where they could learn dancing, music, singing, writing, needlework and account-keeping (Gardiner 1929: 209–17).

Enlightened ideas about women's education in Europe led to a small number of prominent female scholars in the academy. In 1678 Elena Cornaro received a doctorate of philosophy from the University of Padua and in 1732 Laura Maria Caterina Bassi followed her example in Bologna before holding a teaching post there until 1778. The percentage of girls who received some level of education in many European countries rose. In 1768 Catherine the Great founded the Smolny Institute for Girls and in 1786 she extended primary and secondary education to Russian children in some of the large provincial towns. Gradually the percentage of Russia's school population that was female rose to 10 per cent and the number of highly educated and creative women rose fairly dramatically in number through the eighteenth century. In France, the Abbé de Saint-Pierre's projected curriculum of 1730 resulted in a programme of development for free day schools and boarding schools. As the debate about female education gathered pace in France it came to cohere around Jean-Jacques Rousseau's influential work *Émile* (1762) which advocated the role of mother as perfect educator. The rise of female literacy rates are suggestive of this impact: from just 1 per cent of the female population in the sixteenth century to 25 per cent by the mid-eighteenth century and, according to some estimates, 75 per cent in urban areas.

With increased female literacy came concern about what women were reading. Conduct manuals and other prescriptive literature recommended the reading of history for women interested in furthering their education. As a rule when women were offered serious-minded digests of historical accounts, they showed a clear preference for 'frivolous' histories which spoke to their domestic concerns. Hester Chapone in her conduct book of 1773 advised women to read history for 'improvement of the mind', but most read history for that Enlightenment staple – 'imagination'.

Salons and salonnières

While schooling and even university education became a possibility for women during the Enlightenment, women also used institutions such as the salon to expand their education and to engage in the creation of knowledge. The salon had emerged in seventeenth-century France as an alternative space to the court, serving firstly as school of *civilité*, encouraging social mobility and extending the reaches of polite society beyond the court system. Politeness was established through 'the commerce of discourse' in the salon. Indeed, the origins of 'polite society' may be found in the feminine space of the *chambre bleue* of the Marquise de Rambouillet in the 1620s and there is a sense in which the salon was the space that created the 'public sphere' of political discourse as conceptualised by Jürgen Habermas. Indeed the French referred to the salon as '*le monde*', the world.

The rise of salon culture was accompanied by a discursive construction of sexual 'inclusion' that included a 'feminocentric' debate about the role of female speech. Lawrence Klein (1993) has argued that 'in a world that was being constructed around the touchstone of refined sociability or politeness women had an assured place'. Women benefited from the culture of 'politeness' (though also, more obliquely, of 'libertinism' and, therefore, 'un-politeness') that came to define masculinity and femininity and generate rules of social behaviour. 'Libertinism', with all of its sexual talk, 'vernacularised' Enlightenment and allowed a freedom of sexual action that could be at once liberating and oppressing for women (Cryle and O'Connell 2004). The print market was flooded with advice on correct speech and deportment and assumed 'conversation' shared *between* the sexes. According to Klein 'gendered notions of conversation and discourse played a positive role in defining the character of the public sphere in the eighteenth century and also of endorsing the female voice' (Klein 1993: 104, 111). The female 'voice' gained legitimacy in public discourse through the idea that it had a 'civilising influence' on 'conversation'.

Madeleine de Scudéry, author of a number of voluminous historical fictions satirising contemporary French society, was perhaps most famous for her conversation. As well as being mistress of her own salon, Scudéry was author of numerous tracts advising women on conversation, rhetoric and other elements of polite and learned speech. These works, so-named *Conversations* (*Conversations sur divers sujets* 1680; *Conversations nouvelles sur divers sujets* 1684) were so popular they were used as textbooks in Mme de Maintenon's school for girls from 1686 to 1691 (Donaworth and Strongson 2004: 25). Scudery's *Les femmes illustres; ou Les harangues héroïques* adapted the **catalog** of **women worthies** to a new form of speech or oration (DeJean 1989: 101–2). Comtesse de la Fayette, author of historical fiction such as *La Princesse de Clèves* (1678), was also famed in the salon. Drawing on the heated sexual politics of the salon, Lafayette 'proposed a new model for the historical novel in which affairs of state are dominated by marital politics' (DeJean 1991: 96).

In the eighteenth century these women were followed by Julie de Lespinasse and Marie de Vichy-Chamrond, Marquise de Deffand whose salons were visited by leading Enlightenment figures from all over Europe including Montesquieu, Voltaire and Hume. As the attendance of such men suggests, the eighteenth-century salon had become a centre of enlightenment rather than *civilité*. During this period conversation itself became reified as an indispensable component of 'enlightened' and 'polite' society. The reach of salon culture was extended during this period to Britain and America, where 'bluestockings' and 'frenchified dames' mixed polite conversation with literary and politic debate (Kelly 1999; Branson 2001). The 1696 tract *Defence of the Female Sex* is evidence of the beginnings of this process; the work of a Tory (either Judith Drake or Mary Astell), it ridiculed the 'coffee house politician' who 'is never without some notable discovery of . . . a dangerous plot to be found in a Meal Tub [a reference to the Elizabeth Cellier case in England in 1680]' and asked the question 'whether the time an ingenious Gentleman spends in the Company of Women, may justly be said to be misemploy'd' before arguing the case that 'conversation' 'profit[ted] . . . the Improvement of the Understanding' and could be attained 'by the Society of Women'. Perhaps the greatest Salonnière of the late eighteenth century was **Madame de Staël** whose salon was at the heart of Parisian political and literary culture. Through her salon, de Staël wielded immense political power. It was said that the first republican constitution was debated in her drawing room.

The rights of woman

Print culture was, as Jürgen Habermas' *The Structural Transformation of the Public Sphere* (1962) pointed out, democratic (and gender-neutral) in its inclusiveness and it was the emergence of print culture in Europe, more than anything else, that allowed women to participate in the creation of Enlightenment thought and to engage in what has been recently called 'oral activism'. Print culture and oral culture embraced one another and the idea that female speech was 'civilising' (and female company morally cleansing) became encapsulated in works like Richard Steele's *The Ladies Library* of 1714. Women too embraced the culture of print, a number becoming engaged in the profession itself. Elinor James ran a printing press in London for 40 years from about 1665 and said 'I have a great love for it'. She used her press to write works like *Advice to the King and Parliament* (1715). In Italy Elisabetta Caminer Turra, the *donne illustre*, ran one of Venice's most successful publishing houses between 1780 and 1794 and was a celebrated and powerful woman member of the Italian 'Republic of Letters'. **Louise de Kéralio**, France's first '*historienne*', ignored the laws prohibiting women from becoming publishers to launch a publishing business in 1785. During the Revolution she published the radical *Journal de l'etat et du Citoyen* only to be vilified by male journalists as a '*phenomène politique*' and an '*amazone*' (Hesse 1993: 245).

The Enlightenment explosion of print culture also expanded the range of literary pursuits with which women could engage. Public lectures, lending libraries and debating societies all potentially included women in the Enlightenment project. In the 1780s *La Belle Assemblee* allowed unescorted women to subscribe and deliver lectures. The emergence of periodical literature aimed directly at women allowed them to participate in a discourse that explicitly celebrated the rise of sensibility and the consequent feminisation of society. Following a successful career as both a novelist and the author of several scandalous **secret histories, Eliza Haywood** became editor of *The Female Spectator* (1744–1746), the first journal to confine itself to a female readership. Haywood's earlier works such as *Memoirs of A Certain Island* (1724) and *Adventures of Eovaai* (1736) satirised contemporary politics and connected the rise of Republicanism to the declining political instrumentality of women (Ballaster 2000). Haywood used this periodical to reinvent herself as a model of propriety. *The Female Spectator* offered 'True Histories', moral tales drawn from life, that spoke of 'improvement' in emulation of the 'French Ladies'. While women's periodicals were written for a distinctly feminine audience, the genre of the secret history commanded an extensive male readership in the eighteenth century and by the early nineteenth century had a popular readership of both sexes. *Lady Hamilton's Secret History of the Court of England* (1832) was a highly desirable text because of its details about the English regency court.

The emergence of a woman-centred print culture initiated debate about women's qualifications for and rights to 'citizenship'. 'Sophia's *Woman not Inferior to Man* (1739) was a popular treatise which argued that 'custom' led to the oppression of women and that women had a 'natural right . . . to a perfect equality of Power . . . with . . . Men'. What was new about the argument was the suggestion that men had not historically proved that they were better able to govern than women and that women had not been 'improved' by male rule. A fine piece of rhetoric, the tract appealed to the female imperative of 'improvement', the author attacking male speech, and paying tribute to women's intellect and capacity for University employment and public office. The author declared '[o]ur souls are as perfect as theirs'; thus, 'Sophia's case about women's right to full citizenship was based on the premise of the equal 'perfection' (and perfectibility) of their souls.

Historical production

Despite women's participation in Enlightenment knowledge culture, their role in the production of historical knowledge was largely limited to what Daniel Woolf (1997) has called 'the social circulation of [historical] knowledge'. There was a close connection between gender construction and genre and women tended to populate areas of historical writing that were romantic, confessional and fictionalised such as romantic historical novels and **auto/biography**, antiquarianism/ **local history** and **family** history/geneaology. What might be termed *feminine histoire* flourished, the generic foundations of which were to be found in the social construction of femininity. Women's **memoirs** were one gendered component of European historical memory, particularly in France where the 'particular history' of women was differentiated from the *ars historica* from the beginning of the Enlightenment period. Sometimes the first person account was co-opted for biography as seen in Madeleine de Scudéry's *Story of Sapho* (1653).

Women were also amongst a generation of antiquarians and genealogical researchers who combined empirical research with an interest in local culture. They included **Cassandra Willoughby** and Elizabeth Elstob. Willoughby used estate records to produce a two-volume history of her family and Elstob produced a collection of the Saxon homilies of Alfric, archbishop of Canterbury. Elstob was a philologist whose *Rudiments of Grammar* (1715) made an impression on George Ballard, author of *Memoirs of British Ladies Who Have Been Celebrated for Their Writings or Skill in the Learned Languages, Arts or Sciences* (1752). Irish antiquarian research was carried out by Charlotte Brooke, whose studies of folklore came to underpin the burgeoning cultural nationalism demonstrated in works by later Irish writers such as Maria Edgeworth and **Sydney Owenson, Lady Morgan.**

Travel was another area that allowed women to engage in the production of historical knowledge. For many women travel represented the beginnings (rather than the end) of an education that remained deficient. If the *esprit* of the age was located for men in the parlour or salon where they gained 'enlightenment' surrounded by women's conversation, for women it was to be gained more readily by their escape to foreign shores. When Celia Fiennes recorded her travels in Britain she also described the human landscape that she encountered, often mentioning in her journal when she visited 'historic sites' (Woolf 1997: 653). Mary Wortley Montagu wrote a series of letters when she accompanied her husband on an ambassadorial visit to Constantinople in 1716. Published as *Turkish Embassy Letters* in 1718, the letters represent a woman-centred account of contemporary politics and history lessons on architecture, literature, manners and government (Looser 2000: 78). Mary Astell's preface to the 1718 edition commented:

> I confess I am malicious enough to desire that the World shou'd see to how much better purpose the LADYS travel than their LORDS, and that whilst it is surfeited with Male Travels, all in the same Tone and stuft with the same Trifles, a *Lady* has the skill to strike out a New Path and to embellish a worn-out Subject with variety of fresh and elegant Entertainment.

A handful of European women worked in the same historical idiom as men. In France women's historical concerns were shaped by the same desire to construct systematised knowledge as Diderot's *Encylopédie*. Marie Charlotte Pauline Robert de Lézardière's *Théorie des loix politiques de la monarchie française* (1792), a four-volume study of French political, institutional and legal history, was clearly influenced by more philosophical approaches to history and was underpinned by detailed archival research. Marie-Geneviève-Charlotte Darlus Thiroux d'Arconville's *Vie de Marie de Médici* (1774) was also based on detailed analysis of manuscripts and documents in the royal library (Davis 1980: 167). A scientist as well as an historian, d'Arconville adopted the rigours of science into her analysis of history in ways similar to her male counterparts. **Catharine Sawbridge Macaulay**, dubbed by Edmund Burke 'the republican virago', represented the first woman in Britain to write political history. 'Patriot historian' republican and radical Macaulay loved her country ahead of monarchy and defended the American rebellion. Like many of her contemporaries in France she held her own salon and was a central figure in English political and literary circles. Macaulay's *History of England* published between 1763 and 1783 was a narrative of Stuart England from the civil war to the 'glorious revolution' and was imbued with the neoclassical political views that characterised the radical politics of the Enlightenment. Macaulay was probably the first woman historian to use the records of the British Museum, reflecting a more 'scientific' approach to history. Her epistolary *History of England from the Revolution to the Present Time* was her only nod at *feminine histoire* and she abandoned the work after only one volume. Like other Enlightenment figures Macaulay was committed to the improvement of women's education and in her last work *Letters on Education* (1791) she articulated the common argument of Enlightenment feminists that women would gladly 'give up indirect influence for rational privileges'.

Macaulay's arguments in *Letters on Education* anticipated many of those made by **Mary Wollstonecraft** in her *Vindication of the Rights of Woman* (1792). The standard text of Enlightenment feminism, written quickly and for profit, the *Vindication* expressed commonplaces about 'the perfection of our nature . . . [being] estimated by the degree of reason, virtue and knowledge' alongside the more controversial claim that men used reason 'to justify prejudices'. Barbara Taylor's (2003) intellectual biography of Wollstonecraft points out that she was a 'jacobin philosophe' of the 1790s and not a modern feminist. This seems obvious, but needs restatement here. Wollstonecraft was *the* quintessential feminine product of the European Enlightenment. Like Macaulay she had written a tract on female education, *Thoughts on the Education of Daughters* (1786). In her one work of history, the *Historical and Moral View of the Origins and Progress of the French Revolution*, she argued that 'man' could achieve 'new-modelling . . . at each epoch of civilization'. However, in *Vindication* she demonstrated her belief in a *feminine* version of this Enlightenment project by arguing (against Voltaire) that women were taught 'a puerile kind of propriety' by their mothers to gain the protection of men who then kept them in ignorance and falsely extended childhood. In 1792, for Wollstonecraft, the *feminine* Enlightenment remained distinctly a Christian one – she equated God and nature and argued that women should turn to God to seek perfection, an argument that exactly echoed Richard Allestree in 1673 at the beginning of the Enlightenment.

The 'enlightened' female voices of Macaulay and Wollstonecraft were echoed throughout Europe. In 1794 Rosa Califronia in Italy complained that the French Revolution had been nothing more than a bellicose demand for the 'rights of MAN' and in 1795 'P.B.v.B' condemned the exclusion of women from participation in government (Offen 2000: 68–9). Feminist Enlightenment thinkers were 'moderns' who rejected the 'custom' of leaving women undereducated. However, their **modernity** often looked back to Christian traditional values and the classical construction of female 'virtue' to rescue women from 'frivolity' and 'excess' with the result that 'history' was devalued as a discipline for women's training. The Enlightenment 'politics of facts' defined 'fact' as political, 'masculine' and part of the new 'public sphere'. Historical writing targeted at women became devalued as peddling 'insignificant' facts and fictionalising the historical record. It was the very kind of historical writing that 'feminist' women, like Mary Wollstonecraft, rejected as corrupting. Thus, the 'long eighteenth century' was a cultural moment that produced the feminist critique necessary to allow women to write history, while it simultaneously devalued the work of women historical writers.

The French **Revolution** and the Napoelonic wars that followed produced a distinct decline in women's engagement with political history. Women retreated into genres of history more acceptably feminine. **Mary Hays**, biographer of Macaulay and friend of Wollstonecraft, wrote *Female Biography* (1803) in six volumes. This work fitted into the long *querelle des femmes* tradition of creating **catalogs** of **women worthies** while also looking forward to the more ambitious female biography of historians like the **Strickland** sisters. A distinct genre of **historical fiction** emerged at the end of the Enlightenment concomitant with the rise of Romantic nationalism. Works such as Maria Edgeworth's *Castle Rackrent* (1800), **Sydney Owenson**'s *The Wild Irish Girl* (1806) and **Germaine de Staël**'s *Corinne* (1807) inaugurated a new historical genre, the national tale. Disguising political history as patriotic fiction, national tales reinscribed the sexual status quo by reaffirming the domestic virtues over the emancipation of women. In this new historical world, Madame de Staël moved seamlessly from writing romantic novels to cultural history in *De l'Allemagne* (1810).

Amanda L Capern

References

Ballaster 2000; Branson 2001; Cryle & O'Connell 2004; Davis 1980; DeJean 1989, 1991; Donaworth & Strongson 2004; Hesse 1993; Kelly 1999; Klein 1993; Looser 2000; Offen 2000; Pateman 1988; Smith 2000; Taylor 2003; Tomaselli 1985; Woolf 1997.

Related essays

Catalogs; Defences; Family; Historical Fiction; Local history; Memoir; Modernity; Nation; Orientalism; Renaissance; Revolution; Romantic Women Writers; Secret History; Travel; Women Worthies; World History.

F

Family

From antiquity until well into the modern world, the family has been a major focus of women's historical writing. Their own immediate or extended families offered women a subject that allowed them to express their piety and devotion to parents and ancestors in writing in ways that seemed to accord with their appropriate domestic and familial role. At the same time, it could offer them scope to comment on wider social, political and historical questions. Indeed, for at least the last century, focusing on the family has enabled women historians to offer new interpretations of major religious, social and political developments including the Renaissance, the Reformation and the modern industrial world. In the process, women historians have offered innovative and important ways of understanding the family as a social, political and religious institution, as a set of interlinked networks and relationships, and as a kind of imaginary bond that articulates particular kinds of identity.

The importance of the family in women's historical writing derives from its centrality in their lives. Thus the earliest writings by women from the time of late antiquity involved the recording of the lives of family members and the history of their own families. Initially such family histories were the prerogative of women from the imperial or royal household. Texts such as the *Commentarii* (first century CE) of the Roman empress Julia Agrippina, the epic verse of Frankish Queen Radegund (sixth century CE) and the *Alexiad* (1143–1148) of the Byzantine Princess **Anna Komnena** told the history of eminent relatives while also inserting the author's life into the historical record. Sometimes this form of writing mirrored their domestic role, as women produced self-effacing accounts of the lives and significant deeds of husbands and fathers for the benefit of their brothers, sons and grandsons. In periods of social and political and upheaval, however, a focus on the family could allow scope for wider concerns. In the sixteenth and seventeenth centuries, the religious upheavals associated with the **Reformation** and more particularly the English Civil War offered women new opportunities, even while writing ostensibly about the valiant deeds or the sufferings of their own menfolk, to comment on wider political, religious and military events. **Lucy Hutchinson**'s *Memoirs of the Life of Colonel Hutchinson,* for example, while ostensibly following this earlier form included stringent criticism of the British monarchy.

Women continued to write or to edit histories, correspondence and **memoirs** of their own or of their husband's families across the eighteenth, nineteenth and into the early twentieth centuries. Sometimes they focused on contemporaries, but many women offered a broader view of their extended families over several generations or centuries. In the course of the nineteenth century, other approaches to the history of the family also emerged, sometimes in different literary forms. The novel in particular provided an opportunity for women to discuss critically the nature of marital and familial relationships and their changes over time. Jane Austen is perhaps the best known novelist to explore the changing nature of marriage and of family life from the mid-eighteenth to the early nineteenth century, but several of her contemporaries did so too – most notably, perhaps, Suzanne Ferrier in her novel called simply *Marriage*. These issues continued to be of interest to women novelists across the nineteenth century and indeed, one can track quite closely nineteenth-century British feminists' critiques of marriage and of family life within women's novels (Dyhouse 1989). In the 1840s and early 1850s, for example, the novels of Elizabeth Gaskell explore marital incompatibility and questions of parental responsibility for the rearing of daughters, in terms not very far removed from Austen. A decade later, however, **George Eliot** dealt in far more complex ways with the terrible contrast women faced between their expectations of marriage, encouraged by courting behaviours, and the often harsh realities of married life. Eliot explored also the ways that family life and expectations affected those girls and young women who sought a life that was more extensive than that of their own mothers. Finally, at the end of the nineteenth century, the novels of Sarah Grand and Mona Caird pointed first to the devastating impact of the sexual double standard with its privileging of male sexual freedom on the life and health of married women and their children, and secondly to the ways in which familial demands destroyed women's own lives (Ledger 1997).

The origin of the family

At the turn of the nineteenth and twentieth centuries, women engaged in research and discussion about the history of the family in a number of different ways. Some of these reflected their close involvement in the anthropological debates concerning the origin of the family associated initially with Bachofen in Germany and subsequently taken up by Friedrich Engels in his *Origin of the Family, Private Property and the State*, and by Lewis Morgan in the United States. These anthropological theories of matriarchy both challenged and reinforced positivist and essentialist ideas about the naturalness of patriarchy. These questions about the origin of the family were of particular interest to those women who were beginning to collect materials for and to write histories of feminism. Understanding the origins of women's oppression has always been an important issue for feminist activists and in the nineteenth century both **Elizabeth Cady Stanton** and **Matilda Joslyn Gage** sought to contribute to this debate, taking up Bachoffen's suggestion of an early matriarchal society that was brutally overthrown by the establishment of patriarchal families and patriarchal power. Stanton developed this theme in a number of speeches and articles like 'The Matriarchate or mother-age', first delivered to the National Council of Women in 1891, in which she argued that patriarchal power was violently created and centred on the oppression of women. Matilda Joslyn Gage developed this argument further in her *Woman, Church and State: A Historical Account of the Status of Women through the Christian Ages; With Reminiscences of the Matriarchate* (1893). As Ann Taylor Allen (1999) has argued recently, both women turned Bachofen on his head, depicting the period of matriarchal rule not as one based on promiscuity which gave way to an orderly patriarchal family life, but rather 'in its mature period as a model of female humanitarianism, justice, and equality'.

Interest in the history of the family over many centuries was shown by other feminists as well. In 1903, the small French Group for Feminist Studies (the *Groupe Française d'études Feministes*) produced a series of essays on the history of the family which they used as the basis of their demand for reform of the marriage laws. In England, at the same time, the distinguished classicist **Jane Ellen Harrison** took up Bachoffen and other matrilineal theorists to argue that the ancient matrilineal society in Greece had revered the forces of life, nature, change and sexuality through its worship of male and female deities such as Dionysus – and that these deities had been replaced in later Greek civilization by the male-dominated Olympic pantheon (headed by a domestic tyrant, Zeus) in order to impose the patriarchal conservatism that still dominated western society.

This insistence on recognition of the existence of a matriarchal stage prior to the continuing patriarchal one, and hence of the central importance of the history of the family in explaining the origin and the nature of women's oppression was taken up by a number of feminist writers at the turn of the eighteenth and twentieth centuries, including Mona Caird, Frances Swiney, Olive Schreiner and **Charlotte Perkins Gilman.** All of these writers based their critique of women's current domestic subordination and isolation on their sense that this situation was neither necessary nor natural, but was the result of a particular history of the family which had seen the original power of women within the family taken from them with the establishment of patriarchal control. This had resulted also in their loss of the capacity to contribute to production and their confinement to reproduction. Not all feminists accepted this analysis. Indeed, as Carol Dyhouse has shown, the question of how best to interpret the place of women within the family or of how to resolve the problems that family life imposed on women remained a very complex one (Dyhouse 1989).

Social and economic histories of the family

As professional women historians came to write about the history of the family in the course of the 1920s, discussions about earlier matriarchal societies and family formations gave way to a new interest in the ways in which the family had changed in historical time – particularly in relation to other economic, social and political developments. The importance of marriage and families in the lives of women meant that even those women historians concerned more with the question of women's work than with their private and domestic lives inevitably addressed the issue of family life. The changing nature of the sexual division of labour within families, and the related question of the power and influence of wives and mothers was brought to the fore by a group of pioneering women historians in Britain located primarily at the London School of Economics. In the 1920s and early 1930s, both **Eileen Power** and **Alice Clark** explored the nature of marital relationships and the place of women within family life and through it in the wider society in their discussions respectively of medieval and early modern life.

The first major historiographical debate amongst women historians focused on this question, and more particularly on the question of the impact of industrialisation on the status of women and their familial and social role. In *The Working Life of Women in the 17th Century* (1919), her path-breaking book on women's domestic and familial life, Alice Clark argued that both economic necessity and the political exigencies of the English Civil War made seventeenth-century marriages into partnerships in which women were often required to function as heads of households and to take considerable responsibility for the economic well-being of their families and indeed for the running of family farms and businesses. In her view, this expansive role for women led to a greater equality in marriage than was evident after the industrial revolution with its ever-increasing emphasis on separate spheres between women and men. Writing shortly after Clark, Ivy Pinchbeck, in *Women Workers and the Industrial Revolution* (1930), queried this view, insisting rather that women's role was always a subordinate one in family farms and businesses. In her view, industrialisation benefited women and family life in two different ways. On the one hand, the trend towards the separation of home and workplace made homes and familial life considerably more pleasant than had been the case before. On the other, the growing possibilities that industrialisation offered women for financial independence without marriage contributed far more to the higher status of women than could any enhanced view of wifedom.

This debate continued to be important, even central in women's history, until well into the 1970s and 1980s. In those later decades, the emergence of historical demography, with its focus on population size on the one hand, and the new social history on the other, led to an unprecedented interest in the family. For social historians, the family was both an important site for the exploration of ordinary and everyday life, and the institution at the intersection of private and public life – an institution that was seen as a crucial indicator and mediator of social change. There was much criticism amongst feminist historians at the time of the approach and the assumptions of historical demographers, most of whom assumed that the sexual division of labour and the hierarchical relationship between male heads of household and the rest of the family were natural and unproblematic. Nonetheless, women historians made some notable contributions to this work. Perhaps the most important was Tamara Hareven for whom the family was the one institution that would enable historians to understand the experience and the meaning of everyday life for ordinary people. But she sought also to use the insights of historical demography in slightly new ways in order to explore more closely the ways in which family life could both illuminate and mediate a range of other forms of social change. One of her central interests lay in mapping the different ways in which individuals interacted with and experienced family relationships across the life course. In sole-authored and in a series of collaborative and edited works, she researched and encouraged others to explore the life course in relation to the family in many different societies: in American urban societies, in European peasant and urban societies and in her later works also in urban Japanese societies (see particularly her *Family Time and Industrial Time: The Relationship between Family and Work in a New England Industrial Community* [1982] and her edited volume, *Transitions: The Family and the Life Course in Historical Perspective* [1978]).

Feminism and the family

Although recognising the importance of this earlier work, many feminist historians commented on how gender blind much of it was and how little recognition it showed of the hierarchical nature or the internal divisions within the family. They rejected the idea that the views of the male head of household could be taken as representing those of the whole family and demanded a more critical investigation of how families actually operated and functioned. The many works critiquing the sexual politics of family life in the present produced by feminist theorists suggested new questions that might be addressed to the question of family life in the past. These included questions about the precise ways in which sexual hierarchies had functioned, their implications for the distribution of resources and work within families and about the strategies which women and children often had to devise to negotiate the power of male heads of households – or to survive when they were absent or unable to provide the leadership assumed to accompany their role.

In the mid-1970s, at a time when feminist theory was seeking to address the question of women's agency both in the present and in the past, there was considerable interest amongst some women historians in establishing the significance and the nature of women's contribution to family survival or well-being in the past. In an important article entitled 'Women and the Family Economy in Eighteenth-Century France', published in 1975, Olwen Hufton argued that while men might formally be the heads of families, it was women amongst the poor in eighteenth-century France who held the family together. The presence of a mother, not a father, she argued was what determined whether a family unit could survive. If a man left his wife and children, the wife would usually ensure the survival of the unit by organising either the casual labour or the resort to charity that would enable herself and her children to manage. By contrast, the death or other form of departure of a wife and mother would signal the end of the family as a unit, as male heads of household proved unable or unwilling to hold the unit together. These insights were expanded in a broader discussion of women's different place in the family economy in Britain and France across the late eighteenth and nineteenth centuries in Louise A Tilly and Joan W Scott, *Women, Work, and Family* (1978). A different approach to the question of women's contribution to family life was taken in Patricia Branca, *Silent Sisterhood: Middle Class Women in the Victorian Home* (1975). Focusing on married women who did not engage in paid labour, Branca argued that in their roles as wives and mothers, these women introduced their families to modern ways of living through their approach to motherhood (and their demand for fewer children) and to domestic management.

While some women historians sought to expand the ways in which women's role in family life was seen, others undertook a more radical critique of the whole concept of family life in the past as in the present. The interdisciplinarity evident in a wide range of feminist scholarship was very important here. Thus, for example, the first major examination of the history of the family to be published in *Feminist Studies* in 1979 included two historians, Ellen Ross and Renate Bridenthal, and an anthropologist, Rayna Rapp. It was Rapp who articulated the general case that was accepted by a number of women historians in her insistence that 'the family', seen as a natural and biological entity with necessary, even inevitable structure and functions in western society and history, was an ideological concept rather than an actual entity. If one looked at different societies, she argued, it was possible to discern many very different arrangements for managing sexuality, domestic life and reproduction. Emphasis on 'the family' tended to obscure these differences – and to provide an ideological framework that focused more on the question of how people should live within households and who should be included within them, than on describing what actually happened. It was thus a prescriptive and normative concept rather than a neutral label.

This emphasis on the need to recognise the ideological underpinnings of much discussion of the family, on the one hand, and to analyse exactly how the different component parts of sexual reproduction and domestic life had functioned or changed historically was significant in much work by women historians. One can see it first and most clearly in the emphasis on the connection between the family and other social and political institutions and the rejection of the idea that the family belonged entirely in the private sphere. This insistence on the importance of the family as a social institution was closely connected to the critique levelled by both feminists and by many women historians at the idea that private and public spheres actually existed in the social realm, and their insistence that the very notion of 'public' or 'private' was an ideological one, with a strong gender component, and something that changed markedly over time.

It is scarcely surprising that one period in which women historians were particularly interested was precisely that of the late eighteenth and nineteenth centuries, the period usually seen as one in which the division between public and private became more and more pronounced, particularly for the middle class. The 1970s and 1980s saw the publication of a number of works by women exploring middle-class family life, and the place of women within it. Few of these works challenged the idea that middle-class women were increasingly drawn into the home in the period from the late eighteenth through to the mid-nineteenth century, or that they were increasingly limited and confined to their marital and familial roles. What they argued rather was that this process had to be seen not as something that was important only in terms of changing ideas about marriage and family life, but rather that it was the key strategy by which a middle class established its distinctive sense of itself and hence provided the basis of its demand for the political and social recognition that was the concomitant of its economic power. Mary Ryan made this case in relation to the United States in her influential *Cradle of the Middle Class: The Families of Oneida County New York 1790–1865* (1981). A similar case was made a few years later by Leonore Davidoff and Catherine Hall in their possibly even more influential work *Family Fortunes* (1987).

Historical interest in marriage and family life was certainly not confined to the later modern period. The 1980s and early 1990s also saw important works by women exploring the nature of marriage and family life in the Renaissance, the Reformation, the Enlightenment and the French Revolution as well. There were a range of different themes and issues raised in these works, many of which were echoed later in relation to other periods. The problematic nature of marriage for women during the Renaissance, for example, when they were forced to leave their own families and were taken into the families of their husbands, but continued to be seen as outsiders was explored in detail by Kristiane Klapische-Zuber in her *Women, Family and Ritual in Renaissance Italy* (1985). Most poignant were her discussions of the fate of widows, who became complete outsiders in the families of their husbands and were often separated from their children either if they remarried or if they returned to their own birth families. The patriarchal nature of marriage, its importance in integrating the family into a hierarchical and authoritarian society, on the one hand, and its oppression and subordination of women on the other was strongly emphasised by Klapische-Zuber. This question was dealt with in a slightly different way by Lyndal Roper in *The Holy Household – Women and Morals in Reformation Augsburg* (1991) a few years later. Roper sought to stress the importance of a particular kind of male-dominated household in establishing and maintaining the beliefs and values of the German Reformation and in setting up the kind of society that served to re-enforce them.

While these historians stressed the importance of particular family and household forms and values in the maintenance of social harmony, Lynn Hunt, in *The Family Romance of the French Revolution* (1992), looked at the other side of this question in her discussion of the ways in which images of the family and of family values, or rather the transgression of those values, was invoked in popular hostility to Louis XVI and Marie Antoinette in the course of the French Revolution. Drawing on Carole Pateman's reading of the importance of patricide in the establishment of a fraternal social contract, Hunt argued that the execution of Louis XVI was both regicide and, in light of the family model often invoked by the French monarchy, also patricide – and it raised questions about the nature of the fraternal bonds and power that would follow. The family was invoked equally directly in the depiction of Marie Antoinette as an evil mother who engaged in many deviant sexual behaviours, including incest and lesbianism. Hunt's reading of the family and of its place both in opposition to the French monarchy and in determining the framework of a new society stresses the extent to which the French Revolution was imagined as both private and public, involving intimate questions about sexuality and identity alongside political ones about a new society and government.

The emphasis in Hunt's work on the ways in which concepts and relationships like that of fatherhood and motherhood were both imagined and constructed in the lead up to and in the course of the French Revolution pointed to a new interest both in exploring more fully some of the particular relationships which could be found within the broad category of family and also the importance of the imaginary and the unconscious, on one hand, and of broad social and political developments, on the other, in the construction of all these relationships and indeed of the concepts on which any notion of family depended. The question of motherhood was perhaps the one on which feminist historians focused most extensively as they sought to explore the ideological pressures that went into the creation of particular ideas and ideals of motherhood and the ways in which women sought to negotiate the social and economic pressures that they faced in attempting to deal with the changing expectations of their role in relation to their husbands, on the one hand, and their care for children, on the other.

While some women historians researched questions about white and European family life in the 1980s and 1990s, many others sought to explore the impact and importance of these developments within an imperial framework. The extensive recent interest in the ways in which imperialism drew on, re-enforced or undermined existing gender relations has pointed constantly to the impact of imperialism on family life. The opportunity that empire offered to men seeking an escape from marriage and parenthood and for women seeking alternative lives has been a subject of historical interest for at least four decades. More recently, women historians have focused specifically on the question of how imperial groups and individuals managed their marital and familial lives and on the impact of imperial relationships, including not only concubinage and mixed race sexual relations, but also the employment of indigenous domestic staff, on family life. Ann Laura Stoler's *Carnal Knowledge and Imperial Power: Race and the Intimate in Colonial Rule* (2002) offers the most extensive recent analysis of this issue.

The question of imperial relations raises many of the same questions as does that concerning race in relation to family history. This question was extensively debated in the context of American History where it drew on the earlier debates that had followed the publication of the Moynihan Report in 1965. Under the rubric of President Lyndon Johnson's 'War on Poverty', Daniel Moynihan had sought to explain and find a solution to black urban poverty and social disorder. At the heart of the deterioration of the fabric of Negro society, he concluded, was the deterioration of the Negro family. It is the fundamental cause of weakness in the Negro community. This weakness in turn derived from the lack of status and authority of black men in both familial and social life – and the resulting black matriarchal family. The report caused an immediate outcry from black political and community groups as well as from sociologists and historians. Some questioned the reality of Moynihan's idea of a black matriarchy, while others stressed the need to question the assumption that there was only one acceptable family pattern – that exhibited in contemporary white-American society. Others, like Paula Giddings, pointed to the extreme sexism evident in the Moynihan suggestion that, in order to increase employment levels amongst black men, more jobs needed to be available. Black women's jobs, he suggested, might need to be redesigned to make them suitable for men! (Giddings 1984). This new questioning of the particular nature of the black family, combined with the expansion in social and family history, led to a range of new work on the impact of **slavery** on black families. In *Labor of Love, Labor of Sorrow: Black Women, Work and the Family from Slavery to the present* (1985), the most comprehensive study of this issue, Jacqueline Jones explored the many different ways in which black women sought to support their families and the constant and complex interplay between their labour and their family lives.

The question of race and family life has been the subject of considerable interest in Australian women's historical writing too, in recent years, although both its focus and its impetus were a little different from those evident in the United States. The question of family life and its importance for women became an issue of debate and contention amongst Australian feminists in the course of the 1970s when Aboriginal women took exception to the broad critique of family life as one of the sources of women's oppression. Like some black women in the United Kingdom, they argued that far from feeling any need to free themselves from family ties, they found within their families refuge and support against a hostile and racist society. What they demanded was the right to undertake the family roles and duties that they chose. Their demands contrasted with those of white feminists on every point. Thus where white feminists sought 'abortion on demand', black women sought rather the right to bear and to maintain children without state intervention – and most particularly without the threat of having their children forcibly removed. It is this last question: the policy of removing Aboriginal children, especially those deemed 'half caste' according to contemporary racial classifications, and incarcerating them in religious or state run institutions, a policy that was the subject of a Royal Commission of Inquiry in the 1990s and has been deemed 'genocidal' by the Australian Human Rights Commission. Australia was not the only country in which children were removed from parents deemed unfit or unsuitable and recently Margaret Jacobs has explored the differences and similarities evident in the policies regarding child removal amongst Australian Aborigines and American Indians. In the Australian case Katherine Ellinghaus (2003) has argued recently, both this policy and the attempts to control Aboriginal marriage reflected the view that was widely held by government officials and others in the early twentieth century, that as primitive and inferior peoples, Aborigines would inevitably die out – either through becoming assimilated with the dominant and superior white population or by simply ceasing to exist. In accordance with this view, government policies concerning inter-racial marriage in most Australian states contrasted strongly with their American counterparts. Where marriages between blacks and whites were deemed completely unacceptable in the United States, for the most part in Australia this was not the case – as it seemed to many that it would involve the absorption of Aborigines into white society and thus was part of the inevitable flow of history. Other forms of miscegenation, most specifically the inter-marriage of Aborigines with Asians or

Pacific Islanders, were deemed absolutely unacceptable.

All of this work has, of course, contributed to a broader feminist argument concerning the need to see every aspect of marriage and family life as part of the broad public and political, subject to regulation and control in ways similar to other social institutions. Many women historians have argued that marriage, motherhood and childhood have been subject to ever-increasing public and state regulation from the late eighteenth century to the present. Motherhood, and the question of state involvement in it, either directly through legislation, or through powerful voluntary organisations has been of particular concern to feminist historians over the past two to three decades. The medicalisation of childbirth and the growing power of doctors within it have been explored in a number of countries, as has the way in which women have been expected and even directed to 'modernise' their family and home (Lewis 1980; Reiger 1985). State regulation has not only set a framework for how motherhood should be undertaken, but has also determined which women are deemed fit to be mothers and which are not. In the Australian case, as Marilyn Lake and others have argued, for much of the twentieth century, maternal rights and benefits were exclusively the preserve of white women and were denied both to Aboriginal women and to many migrants (Lake 2000). While state regulation could be and often was both discriminatory and punitive, it was sometimes possible for women to negotiate it and to use it for their own benefit. In the case of American history, in a series of very innovative studies Linda Gordon has explored the ways in which women sought to use often punitive and intrusive welfare services to deal with the domestic problems, including poverty and violence, which sometimes enabled them to maintain some measure of control of their own family life in her, *Heroes of Their Own Lives: The Politics and History of Family Violence Boston, 1880–1960* (1988). She has extended this work on the ways in which the state and its welfare services approach single mothers, in *Pitied but not Entitled: Single Mothers and the History of Welfare, 1890–1935* (1994).

In Britain too, the late nineteenth and early twentieth centuries have been the focus of much interest, as this was the period in which, as Ellen Ross has argued, a particular concept of modern motherhood came into being in which 'mothers are responsible to the state and are, under its scrutiny, expected to turn out a child schooled in specific ways and cared for as prescribed by medical and associated professionals' (Ross 1994). While Ross offers an extensive and indeed definitive account of this development, aspects of this new concern with motherhood have been explored for the last two decades. The new emphasis on motherhood and the connection between maternal conduct and duty and national efficiency that was associated with the rise of eugenics and the aggressive imperial expansion of the late nineteenth century was analysed in an influential article by Anna Davin 'Imperialism and Motherhood (1978). The emphasis on maternal responsibility for both infant health and infant mortality in this period – even in situations where individuals were powerless in the face of poverty, lack of appropriate and nutritious food and appalling sanitation, was explored by Carol Dyhouse too in 'Working-class Mothers and Infant Mortality in England, 1895–1914' (1978). The broad question of how motherhood was constructed in all its various forms, from the question of where and how birth should occur through the many questions associated with infant care and welfare and the ways in which ideas about these questions changed was explored also by Jane Lewis (1980).

While some women focused on questions about motherhood, others sought instead to explore the changing nature of childhood and the changing ways in which children were seen and treated within both the familial and the wider social and political context. In Britain, Ivy Pinchbeck was a pioneer in this area, as she had been earlier in relation to women and work and her two-volume *Children in English Society* (jointly authored with Margaret Hewitt [1969–1973]) set the framework for a range of subsequent debates. Here, as in her work on industrialisation, Pinchbeck espoused a view of almost continuous progress in the treatment of children. The Elizabethan world, her starting point, was depicted as one in which marital and familial relationships were instrumental and often brutal. Children were required to treat parents with the utmost respect and deference. Obedience was demanded and brutally enforced in familial relationships marked by distance and hierarchy. Familial relationships became less distant and more affectionate over the subsequent centuries, while the growing concern about children and the higher value placed on their lives was evident also in the expanding role of the state. While many subsequent historians viewed the nineteenth-century legislation that brought children under state control as often brutal and as enforcing middle-class norms on all families, Pinchbeck saw it clearly as evidence of growing concern within the wider community for the health and well-being of children and hence with the necessary regulation of certain aspects of family life.

A strongly contrasting view of English childhood amongst the poor was provided by Anna Davin in *Growing Up Poor: Home, School and Street in London 1870–1914* (1996). Where Pinchbeck assumed the benevolence of state and welfare agencies, Davin insisted rather on their imposition of a rigid ideological framework based on middle-class values. In accordance with this framework, they distrusted the poor and regarded them as unfit parents who lacked the capacity to develop the character of their children adequately, nor could they accept that working-class practices allowed for what they deemed to be a proper childhood. The education offered to the poor served further to inculcate the class and gender values of the middle class, with its ready acceptance of absenteeism amongst girls who were required to look after younger siblings and for whom domestic and child-rearing skills were deemed more important than other forms of learning, and its assumption that a 'sense of shame' amongst the poor indicated a higher level of civilisation.

In recent years, there has been a growing sense of unease about and criticism of the history of the family amongst feminist historians, many of whom argue that the very naming of a singular 'family' in historical research serves to reify a particular normative and prescriptive idea of the family and that scholarly endeavour ought rather to be directed towards critically examining this idea and the many different kinds of relationships that have been and are established amongst kin. This case is put very forcefully in Leonore Davidoff *et al.* (eds) *The Family Story: Blood, Contract, and Intimacy, 1830–1960* (1999). In the introductory chapter, Davidoff points to the constructed and often imaginary nature of families in which all markers, including surnames, are complex, often designating a desire for a sense of belonging rather than any coherent unit or institution. The stress here is on the need to explore the many different kinds of relationship that can develop and have developed around sexuality, reproduction and the establishment of kinship. Mothering is particularly important – including of course the many different kinds of single motherhood that produce units often not designated 'family'. Special attention is also given to sibling ties and relationships as a particularly important tie that has long been neglected amongst historians. Women historians have long accepted many of these views and indeed a number have also been very active in exploring sibling relationships, particularly those amongst sisters. Since the 1970s, the relationships of sisters, in both large and small families from the eighteenth century to the present has been of particular interest to a number of women historians who have seen in these relationships both a new way of exploring the daily lives of women and also a way of showing how family connections could provide women with assistance and support as well as helping to maintain a prevailing gender order. The next step in this pathway, as foreshadowed by Davidoff and evident in the work of others, is to explore the relationships between brothers and sisters as well, and then to move into wider networks in exploring the kinship bonds and ties that have long been neglected by a focus on nuclear families.

Barbara Caine

References

Allen 1999; Dyhouse 1978, 1989; Ellinghaus 2003; Giddings 1984; Grimshaw 1999; Hufton 1975; Lake 2000; Ledger 1997.

Related essays

Ancient History; Australia; Female Biography; Feminism; Great Britain; Memoir; Reformation; Religion; Revolution; Slavery; USA.

Fanshawe, Ann 1625–1680

English memoirist, historian. Born in London, daughter of John Harrison, MP of Balls Park in Hertfordshire, and Margaret (Fanshawe) of Fanshawe Gate, Derbyshire. Her family was wealthy and she received a good education until the death of her mother in 1640 when her fortunes changed. The family was royalist, pledging the king large sums of money and losing their estates to sequestration after the arrest of her father in 1642. In 1643 she moved to royalist Oxford, and in 1644 she married her cousin, Richard Fanshawe (b. 1608), who was the newly appointed Secretary of War to Charles, Prince of Wales. Her marriage resulted in a life of travel and exile, first going with her husband to Bristol, then the West Country, the Scilly Isles and Jersey during war campaigns. In 1647 they went to Paris carrying a packet of letters for Henrietta Maria. In 1649 they travelled to Ireland and survived the Cork Rebellion, in 1650 she was in Spain and in 1651 her husband was captured at the Battle of Worcester after which she successfully petitioned for his release. After the Restoration, Richard Fanshawe negotiated the marriage of Charles II to Catherine of Braganza before being appointed Ambassador to Portugal in 1662 and Spain in 1664.

Fanshawe's **memoirs** were completed around 1676 and circulated privately in manuscript until publication as *The Memoirs of Ann, Lady Fanshawe* in 1829. They begin with an account of her immediate family that reveals much about the social devastation caused to the gentry by the English Civil Wars. This is followed by a detailed account of the couple's movements and travails during the second Civil War and interregnum. Her narrative juxtaposes political events with the hardships suffered by royalists whose loyalty 'cost them dear'. Fanshawe, unusually, wrote in a secular rather than providential style. She described the closeness of her marriage and juxtaposed her tale of devotion with the story of 'nearly thirty years suffering by land and sea'. The writing style is highly pictorial. Of the Alhambra she said 'the entry into this great palace is of stone for a porter's lodge, but very magnificent (though the gate be low), which is adorned with figures of forest work, in which the Moors did transcend'. This contrasts with the minimalist style in which she recorded the deaths of her infants: in the court of Madrid she 'was delivered of my first daughter that was called Elizabeth . . . upon the 13 of July . . . [s]he lived but 15 days and lies buried in the chapel of the French Hospital'. Such contrasts reveal her primary motivation as a narrator of public events. She had 14 live children (and 6 miscarriages), only 5 of whom survived at the time of Richard Fanshawe's death in 1666. One of these was their only surviving son, Richard Fanshawe, for whom Fanshawe wrote her 'memoirs' which were republished again in modern editions by Beatrice Marshall in 1905 and H C Fanshawe in 1907.

Amanda L Capern

References

Hudson 1993; *NDNB 2004*; Sage 1999; Todd 1989.

Major work

John Loftis (ed.) *The Memoirs of Anne, Lady Halkett and Ann, Lady Fanshawe* (Oxford: Clarendon Press, 1979).

Female biography

Female biography has been the most persistent and popular genre of women's historical writing. In its various guises – the lives of saints, **catalogs, defences of women,** individual and collective biographical studies – female biography has been the dominant form of female historical production since antiquity. Although initially only a handful of women engaged in such writing, by the nineteenth century female biographies written by women were so common as to constitute a minor literary phenomenon (Maitzen 1998: 371). Until recently such works have received but scant historical attention. Like much historical writing by women, female biography has been all but ignored within the masculinist tradition. Histories of biography such as John A Garraty's *The Nature of Biography* (1958) or Donald Stauffer's *English Biography before 1700* (1964) treat men as the universal subject of biography and always gender the biographer male. While feminist scholars have recognised that women engaged in biographical writing, they have often ignored or discounted such work, referring to it unkindly as the history of **women worthies.** This was particularly true in the 1970s as women historians sought to distance the new 'women's history' from older forms of women's writing they considered of dubious historicity. Modern women engaging in biographical writing themselves have also been slow to recognise their foremothers. They have depicted earlier efforts at female biography as conservative and anti-feminist. Carolyn Heilbrun, biographer of the feminist Gloria Steinem, has written '[F]emale Biographers, that is, if they wrote about women, chose comfortable subjects whose fame was thrust upon them. Such subjects posed no threatening questions; their atypical lives provided no disturbing model for the possible destinies of other women' (1988: 21–2).

The publication of Bonnie G Smith's ground-breaking essay 'The Contribution of Women to Modern Historiography in Great Britain, France and the United States' (1984) challenged many previously held assumptions about women's historical writing, and has allowed for more complex readings of genres such as female biography. According to Smith, women's production of individual and collective biographies 'inspired massive historical research into the character of women's existence, produced an important tradition of women's historiography, and set the initial terms for assessing women's historical significance' (1984: 715). Since then female biography as a form of women's history has received more scholarly interest. Literary critics such as Miriam Elizabeth Burstein and Rohan Maitzen have offered complex and nuanced ways of reading 'Female Biography' as women's history, yet there remains an overarching assumption that 'the most obvious characteristics of these biographies . . . is the emptiness of the exemplary lives they present' (Burstein 1999: 51).

Such ideas echo the concerns of certain women on the subject of female biography in the past. For the most part such concerns reflected the ways in which men had written women's lives. The English feminist Mary Astell in *The Christian Religion as Profess'd by a Daughter of the Church of England* (1705) was critical of the representation of women in history, claiming that the only women history recognised were those who had 'acted above their Sex', those who were effectively 'men in petticoats'. **Mary Wollstonecraft** in her *Vindication of the Rights of Woman* (1791) was also critical of a focus on great women, because such women were always regarded as 'exceptional to the general rule'. By the nineteenth century female biographers themselves were questioning the potential for women's lives to sustain the interest of the reader. Elizabeth Sandford, author of *The Lives of English Female Worthies*, stated in this text that she feared that female biography was necessarily deficient in interest. 'Women', she wrote, 'even of high excellence, do not possess that individuality which characterises the illustrious amongst men . . .' (1833: x). It would be wrong, however, to take the concerns of Mrs Sandford seriously. Not only had she already published extensively on the subject of women, writing works on *Female Improvement* (1831) as well as a history of Woman, in 'her social and domestic character'. Her writings formed part of the most commercially successful segments of the publishing market during this period.

Criticism of Female Biography has tended to conflate the subject matter with the genre. Because women worthies and women's worthiness have formed the basis of much female biographical writing it has tended to be viewed only as a prescriptive and reactionary genre, designed to educate women into unachievable ideals of femininity. The desire to define the female ideal through biography derives from biography's relationship to **hagiography**, a discourse that centred the *exemplarity* of saintly lives. In earlier forms of female biography such as the lives of saints, catalogs and defences of women, *exemplarity* formed the rationale for such works. While vitae sought to present examples of holy women for emulation, catalogs and defences of women used biographical sketches of famous and infamous women to define femininity and to 'understand' women through historical example. By the nineteenth century female biographies had come to function like conduct manuals and domestic fiction, as a 'textual means for engendering bourgeois subjectivity'. The lives of 'great women' were marketed to serve as role models for middle-class 'ladies' (Booth 2004).

This essay will focus not on the notion of women worthies, but rather on the ways in which women sought to generate alternative historical narratives through the writing of women's lives. Tracing women's biographical writing since the seventh century, it will argue that various forms of female biography can be read as counter-narrative to the masculinist historical tradition, a narrative that questioned the authority and historicity of male-authored texts and masculine understandings of the nature of history itself. Indeed as shall be shown, the fact of female authorship, an unfeminine act in itself, has always meant subtle subversions of the genre, even **hagiography**. This essay will examine the development of the genre since antiquity, focusing on certain key texts, texts that have served as correctives, as ways of recovering women lost to history and as a means of asserting women's historical subjectivity. Such texts have formed important sites where ideas about the construction of gender have been contested, misogynistic assumptions about women's role in history have been refuted and relations between the sexes have been questioned. While few female biographers claimed to be feminist, their works celebrated women's transcendence of the private sphere and demonstrated the importance of women to the nation state.

The vitae of saints

The first known examples of woman-authored biographical texts, indeed the first extant evidence of women's historical production, are a small corpus of saints' lives written by cloistered women living in Europe between the seventh and eleventh centuries. The first and best-known text, the *Life of Radegund* (609–14), written by **Baudonivia** serves as an important example of how woman-authored biographical texts not only alter our historical perspective by centring upon the life of a woman, but offer counter-narratives questioning the authority of male-authored texts and the masculine historical tradition. The saintly queen Radegund had been the subject of two male-authored vitae before Baudonivia attempted to write of her life. Gregory of Tours (538–94) wrote of the life of Radegund in his *History of the Franks* and detailed the events of her funeral, over which he had presided, in the *Glory of the Confessors* (McNamara *et al.* 1992: 61). Radegund's friend, the poet-bishop Venantius Fortunatus (530–609), also produced a *Life of Radegund* shortly after her death. According to Baudonivia, her *Life of Radegund* was written to supplement this text, at the request of her abbess Dedimia. Baudonivia's text was written specifically for the edification of the nuns at Sainte-Croix and consequently it focused upon Radegund's life while she was living at the monastery. In her preface Baudonivia wrote:

> I am the smallest of small ones she nourished familiarly from the cradle as her own child at her feet! So that I may offer a public celebration of her glorious life to the ears of her flock, in devout, though unworthy language I pray that you will aid me in prayers for I am more devoted than learned. In this book, we will not repeat what the apostolic bishop Fortunatus recorded of her blessed life but speak of what he omitted in his fear of prolixity. (McNamara *et al.* 1992: 86)

Later critics of this text have read this statement as typical of the rhetorical humility expected of authors of vitae. Her claim to be writing a supplementary text in 'rustic rather than refined language' has been generally accepted without question, because it presented a conventionally gendered complementarity. The male-authored text represented the learned and public version of Radegund's life, while Baudonivia's text represented the homely and private Radegund, fit only for the consumption of her community. Yet this rhetorical strategy can also be seen to be used to authorise Baudoni via's unique spiritual and political narrative of Radegund's life. The fact that both Dedimia and Baudonivia believed that a supplementary life of Radegund was necessary has been taken by feminist historians to mean that these women felt Fortunatus' *Life* was somehow deficient and that it did not present an effective role model for her nuns to follow. Although Fortunatus claimed friendship with Radegund, Baudonivia claimed a daughterly relationship, thus assuming a particular authority through this relationship.

As other historians have shown, the lives of Radegund evince distinct differences that might be attributed to the gender of the biographer. The primary focus of Baudonivia's text falls on Radegund's life cloistered at Sainte-Croix, but it would be wrong to think that she ignores Radegund's public and political role. Baudonivia emphasises Radegund's contribution to public life, acknowledging her influence in Merovingian politics and the power of the institution that she founded (Coon 1997: 127). The characterisation of Radegund as a mother figure, a peacemaker and a promoter of a dynastic cult centre was unique to Baudonivia's vita (Wemple 1981: 184). Fortunatus mentions nothing of this, nor does he discuss Radegund's successful diplomacy in acquiring ornate editions of gospels, relics of important martyrs and a piece of the holy cross from the patriarchs in Jerusalem and the Byzantine emperors (Coon 1997: 127). Baudonivia's life places much emphasis on Radegund's acquisition of the relic of the holy cross, showing how it formed an important part in her plans to develop the monastery into an agency of intercession on behalf of kings. Baudonivia stresses that Radegund regarded the relic 'as an instrument whereby the salvation of the kingdom would be secured and the welfare of the country assured' (Wemple 1981: 185).

The absence of a public or political role for Radegund in Fortunatus' text is typical of male-authored vitae that represented women in ways that 'rendered them innocuous in the context of secular power' (McNamara *et al.* 1992: 4). Both Gregory of Tours and Fortunatus formed their lives of Radegund to fit the *topoi* of heroic martyrdom which shaped the literary representation of male saints (Coon 1997: 123). In these texts Radegund is represented as an asexual female saint, a virago whose imitation of masculine forms of self-mortification allowed her to attain sanctity. Although Baudonivia claims that she will not discuss aspects of Radegund's life already narrated by the 'apostolic bishop' she does draw upon his description of the queen's self-mortification, subtly rewriting and revising his version of these events. Fortunatus, like other male authors of vitae, presents Radegund's saintliness as deriving from graphic scenes of self-mutilation, while Baudonivia emphasises Radegund's prayers and vigils, suggesting these were more powerful displays of sanctity (Kitchen 1998: 142–3). While Fortunatus' Radegund attained saintliness through self-abnegation and at the expense of her historical subjectivity, Baudonivia's *Life* breaks with this *topoi* of heroic martyrdom, allowing Radegund a degree of individuality and hence historical subjectivity.

Baudonivia's *Life of Radegund* created an influential model of female piety for noble and holy women to follow and there is evidence that later female-authored vitae of saints, such as the *Life of Bathild* produced by an anonymous nun of Chelles, were written following Baudonivia. Writing the history of female saints, Baudonivia and the women writers who followed her introduced feminine values and ideals into hagiography. They focused on the lives of women in relational ways, depicting their importance within kinship and dynastic networks. Given that the female-authored vitae of saints were written specifically to provide models for emulation for women, it is significant that they can be characterised as demonstrating women's active public roles or as Joan Ferrante has observed, 'the roles they can, do and perhaps should play in history' (1997: 69).

The defence of womanhood

During the Renaissance defences of women, biographical catalogs of women to which were attached rhetorical discussion regarding the educability of women, were the principal vehicle through which a history of women was articulated. While the Italian humanist Giovanni Boccaccio is frequently attributed with creating the first defence of women, it was in fact **Christine de Pizan** who initiated this genre. Boccaccio's claim to have written the first defence of women stems from his authorship of *Concerning Famous Women* (c.1360–1375). Written in 'praise of women' this text contained 104 chapters each shaped around the 'biography' of a famous woman. While innovative in its discussion of learned women, Boccaccio's text drew on a tradition of Roman and Christian catalogs, known for their invective towards women. Thus while Boccaccio claimed 'to praise women' this intention is largely peripheral to his biographical writing. As a number of feminist scholars have suggested, Boccaccio's depiction of women is ambivalent. He was drawing upon two contradictory historical traditions: one that represents feminine virtue in the seclusion of the domestic sphere and thus outside the realms of history and another that claims femininity and civic virtue are incompatible. As a consequence Boccaccio represents women who engage in civic life as viragos, manly women acting 'above their sex' (Jordan 1987; Mc Leod 1991: 66–7).

Christine de Pizan was the first feminist scholar to recognise the impossibility of depicting praiseworthy women within the masculinist tradition. Challenging the depiction of women found in Ovid and other misogynist texts in her first playful critique of the tradition, *The God of Love's Letter* (1399), Christine not only questioned the authority of such writers, she also consciously began to rewrite the history of women. Thus while Boccaccio represents Medea as 'the cruelest example of ancient treachery' (Brown-Grant 2003: 37), Christine depicts her as a woman 'treated falsely, treacherously, deceitfully and mendaciously' (Blumenfeld-Kosinski 1997: 23). Underpinning Christine's revision of the masculinist historical tradition was her sense that her own experience showed the error of these misogynist representations. This sentiment found its fullest expression in her *Book of the City of Ladies* (1405), a text in which she created a woman-centred universal history to counter the masculinist historical tradition. Christine's innovation in this text lies in her adoption of a rhetorical strategy that allowed her to reshape the dominant ideology by manipulating authoritative allegories of speech and genre in the figures of Reason, Rectitude and Justice. These 'daughters' of God appear to Christine and command her to create a new tradition of women by building the City of Ladies to protect 'ladies and all valiant women . . . against the various assailants' (Richards 1982: 10). The intervention of these ladies allows Christine to draw upon the evidence of her own experience to authorise her version of the lives she presents. They remind her that most women are honourable, intelligent and virtuous. While Christine had initially questioned her judgement when faced with the enormity and virulence of the masculine tradition, she is reprimanded by this heavenly authority who command her to trust her own intellect rather than the spurious inventions of men. These figures ask Christine why do you shun 'what you know for a certainty and believe what you do not know or see or recognise except by virtue of many strange opinions?' (Richards 1982: 6). They highlight the inconsistencies and contradictions in the works of male authorities and question the motives of these authors. They describe Mathéolus, who prompted in Christine such misgivings about her own sex, as 'an impotent old man filled with desire' (Richards 1982: 19).

Until recently the various forms of female biography Christine de Pizan produced have tended to be read as imitations of Boccaccio as she drew on the biographies of famous women presented in *De mulieribus claris* and other works such as the *Decameron*. Christine, however, used female biography in ways that differed from Boccaccio in style and content as well as in intention. While Boccaccio had drawn on classical authority, Christine drew upon a higher authority. This allowed her to subvert the authority usually invested in the masculinist historical tradition and rewrite it, while also claiming her own authority through experience and observation. While the biographical catalog she presents resembles Boccaccio's in certain superficial ways, it actually has been constructed and ordered in ways that manipulate Boccaccio's authority. Thus Christine does not hesitate to highlight when Boccaccio praises women and uses his authority to validate hers. Nor is she above overstating Boccaccio's praise as is evident when their lives of Sappho are compared. But she also consciously rewrites Boccaccio's biographies in ways that demonstrate a distinctive feminine perspective. This is clearly evidenced in her representation of women reviled in the masculinist tradition. The example of Semiramis is perhaps the most telling. Boccaccio describes Semiramis as 'constantly burning with carnal desire', taking her own son Ninyas for her lover (Brown-Grant 2003: 11). Christine reports that Semiramis married her son, as 'she wanted no other crowned woman in the empire besides herself' and that no other man was worthy of her (Richards 1982: 40). Moreover she insists that Semiramis cannot be judged in terms of contemporary morality, as she lived at a time when there was 'no written law' and people acted according to Nature. Had she known of moral injunctions against such actions Christine reports 'she would never have done this, since she had such a great and noble heart and so deeply loved honour' (Richards 1982: 40). While Christine does not discount the incest, she desexualises the story of Semiramis, focusing upon her skills of governance and her military prowess. As a woman creating a new historical tradition, Christine acknowledged the possibility that women could engage in the public realm while still remaining virtuous. This was impossible for Boccaccio as he was writing within a tradition that conflated women's actions in the public sphere with sexual and social disorder.

Female biography as it is presented in the *Book of the City of Ladies* functioned not only to defend women against the slanders of men, but also to create models for women to imitate; consequently, Christine stifles the suggestion omnipresent in Boccaccio's work that the lives of the women he records are extraordinary. Boccaccio used the exceptionality of a few women to demonstrate the moral and intellectual inferiority of 'the Sex' more generally. Christine made the experience of women an allegory for all humanity, suggesting that meritorious acts these women had performed presented a moral and spiritual lesson for all humanity (Richards 1996: 126). Christine also defined her task in producing female biography in terms of achieving self-knowledge consequently marking a textual shift in her own self-perception, as she no longer views her writerly self in manly terms, as she had in earlier works. Women such as Isotta Nogorola, Laura Cereta, Lucrezia Marinella, **Madeleine de Scudéry**, who produced biographical catalogs and defences of women following Christine, used female biography to define themselves within a tradition of virtuous and learned women (see **Renaissance** essay). Although it is uncertain whether such writers had access to Christine's text, they were inspired by the same spirit and used the example of history to demonstrate women's scholarship and cultural production, as well as to defend their own participation in these fields.

Feminine biography

By the eighteenth century, texts featuring catalogues of women gave way as a tradition of female prosopography developed. Early models of this genre such as **Louise de Kéralio**[**Robert**]'s *Collection des meilleurs ouvrages français composés par des femmes* (1786–1789) attempted to create an alternative literary history of France, not only by including women within history, but also by challenging the masculinist assumptions that had framed earlier models (De Jean 1991: 186). More prosaic examples such as Ann Thickness' *Sketches of the Lives and Writings of the Ladies of France* (1760) and Mary Pilkington's *A Mirror for the Female Sex* (1798) were written to defend the right of women to education, a theme that would define the genre in the nineteenth century. It was not until the nineteenth century that female biography became a literary phenomenon. The kinds of biographical sequences composed in an era provide a clue to the mind of an age, so it is not perhaps surprising that a century marked by the 'Woman Question' produced an outpouring of female biography.

This outpouring of female biography is attributable to the crises of gender and genre occasioned by the revolutionary upheavals that had ended the eighteenth century. On both sides of the Atlantic, **revolution** had heightened paradoxes in the already equivocal cultural codes that determined feminine propriety. Revolution had posed a direct threat to the principle of subordination which governed feminine behaviour, bringing the issue of women's rights to attention, while simultaneously generating a conservative backlash that threatened to eliminate the question of women's rights altogether. In writing works of female biography, women were seeking not only to re-evaluate their political status, but also their role as writers and historians.

At the height of the French Revolution, British historian **Catharine Sawbridge Macaulay** had written a poignant plea for women's advancement, *Letters on Education* (1791). In this work Macaulay presented women as a civilising force in history. Usurping notions of historical progress popularised by philosophical historians such as Condorcet, Adam Ferguson, William Robertson and John Millar, Macaulay suggested that 'the first springs of the vast machine of society were set a going by women' (Macaulay 1791/1974: 214–15). Macaulay looked to the example of the past to assert women's rights, claiming: 'To do the Sex justice, it must be confessed that history does not set forth more instances of positive power abused by women, than by men; and when the sex have been taught wisdom by education, they will be glad to give up indirect influence for rational privileges' (1791/1974: 215). Macaulay's framework and argument shaped women's historical writing for the next century. The conflation of women and civilisation underpins many collections of female biography written by women during this period and would frame the feminisation of history that such collective works proposed (Burstein 1999).

Indeed the first major collective biography of women produced in the nineteenth century, **Mary Hays**' six-volume *Female Biography, or Memoirs of Illustrious and Celebrated Women, of all Ages and Countries* (1803), responded directly to Macaulay's challenge to look to history. Written as a memorial to 'those women whose endowments, or whose conduct have reflected lustre upon the sex', *Female Biography* presented detailed portraits of eminent women, moving beyond hagiographic depictions that characterised earlier studies of women worthies. Hays, friend and eulogist of Wollstonecraft, had been extremely active in Jacobin literary circles during the 1790s and was already the author of two romantic novels, *The Memoirs of Emma Courtney* (1796) and *The Victim of Prejudice* (1799). Her shift from romance to biography had been prefigured in her novel *Emma Courtney*, when Emma's father discouraged her reading of Rousseau's *La Nouvelle Héloise*, but encouraged her reading of Plutarch's *Lives*. An afternoon with Plutarch leaves Emma's mind 'pervaded with republican ardour, [her] sentiments elevated by high-toned philosophy and [her] bosom glowing with the virtues of patriotism' (1796/1996: 27). While this novel saw its heroine remain in the thrall of Rousseau, her later works bear the influence of Plutarch.

Women's education was the central theme of Hays' text and she was concerned to create a new type of female biography, a history that would speak to women and teach them of their rights and duties. She claimed to 'have at heart the happiness of [her] sex' and aimed at 'their advancement on the grand scale of rational and social existence' (1803: Vol. 1, iv). Echoing Macaulay and Wollstonecraft, Hays presented a new version of rational womanhood: 'A woman who, to the graces and gentleness of her own sex, adds the knowledge and fortitude of the other, exhibits the most perfect combination of human excellence' (1803: Vol. 1, iv). The education that Hays had in mind was distinctly feminist. Hays' revision of the masculinist historical record was shaped by a desire to dispel the myths of chivalry and benevolent patriarchy articulated by conservative men during the Revolution and to demonstrate that women were frequently the victim of social injustices at the hands of such men. For Hays the Revolution had drawn women 'together in a common cause against the despotism and tyranny of men', a sentiment no doubt heightened by the vilification she had experienced during the 1790s (Hays 1821: 127).

While Christine blamed the misogynist literary tradition for the demeaning historical representation of women, Hays went further demonstrating how patriarchy subordinated women through 'disadvantages civil and moral', while simultaneously presenting women who violated those structures as mad or bad (Kucich 1993: 6). Thus Joan of Arc was executed as a witch, Hays declared, because of her 'violati[on] . . . of the decorums of her sex' (Kucich 1993: 6). Women such as Agrippina the younger, especially reviled in the masculinist tradition, were offered redemption in this text. Agrippina is described as being 'corrupted' by her brother Caligula and her worst excesses are blamed on the 'feebleness' of her husband, Claudius. It is even possible to perceive a grudging admiration for Agrippina in Hays' portrait, as she writes 'Checked by no impediment in her career of ambition, absolute in power, and magnanimous in defeat, we are compelled to mingle admiration with our abhorrence of her guilt . . . ' (1803: Vol. 1, 14). *Female Biography* was not well reviewed, perhaps because it moved so boldly beyond the women worthies model. In 1821 she published *Memoirs of Queens, Illustrious and Celebrated*, an abridgement of *Female Biography*, aimed at the growing market in courtly memoirs and **royal lives**. Even in this sanitised text Hays could not resist depicting the hapless Queen Caroline as a victim of male perfidy.

While few other nineteenth-century female biographers were as strident in their articulation of women's 'civil and moral disadvantages', most followed Macaulay and Hays in using the genre for the advancement of women. The notion of women as civilisers or as bearers of culture was ubiquitous in the genre and frequently these two ideas became conflated, so the fate of civilisation was linked to the advancement of women. Avoiding the Enlightenment notion of the 'rights' of women, women writers nonetheless sought to define a significant place for women within post-revolutionary European and American society. Shaped by an ideology of separate spheres female biography generated a history of patriotic heroines to complement the political histories of great men. As **Sydney Owenson, Lady Morgan**, Irish nationalist and author of the biographical *Woman and her Master*, wrote, 'politics can never be a woman's science; but patriotism must naturally be a woman's sentiment' (1809: xiii).

The gendering of patriotism is particularly apparent in the work of American women such as **Lydia Maria Child**, **Elizabeth Ellet** and **Sarah Josepha Hale**, who were dedicated to defining a patriotic role for women within the new Republic. Child produced a series of biographies in the 1830s including *Biographies of Madame de Staël and Madame Roland* (1832) of *Lady Russell and Madame Guyon* (1832) and a collective biography *Good Wives* (1833) from Panthea to Madame Layfette. Perhaps the most conservative and least original of all Child's work, *Good Wives* nonetheless clearly expressed the ideology of Republican motherhood that shaped American women's political engagement in the antebellum period. The figure of the Republican mother enabled women to transcend the boundaries of the private sphere, in that it deemed them responsible for the inculcation of the virtues necessary to sustain the infant Republic. Elizabeth Ellet's collective biography, *The Women of the American Revolution*, literarily suggested that women gave birth to the new Republic as she wrote: 'Patriotic mothers nursed the infancy of freedom' (1848: Vol. 1, 24). This imagery of women nurturing the state into existence was not an uncommon feature of the genre. On the other side of the Atlantic, **Agnes Strickland** described her regal subjects in *Lives of the Queens of England from the Norman Conquest* as 'nursing mothers to the Christian faith of this Island' (1857 I: xxi) and in other works as 'nursing mothers of the Reformation'.

Such imagery did not merely insert women into histories of state formation and nation-building which had previously ignored them, it functioned to domesticate and feminise history, presenting women's maternal and domestic duties as critical to historical progress. This feminisation of history meant that the genre itself was configured in ways that stressed its appropriateness as a form of women's writing, that is, private, domestic and morally influential. Thus while History was characterised as manly, biography was increasingly characterised in terms that stressed its essentially feminine qualities. As the anonymous female author of *Select Female Biography* opined:

> History and Biography are the two great mirrors in which we contemplate the human character. The first too

> often presents a frightful tissue of crimes and horrors, whilst the second frequently reflects from its calm and polished surface, everything that is excellent, lovely and of good report.

While certain observers claimed that '[T]he humbler walk of Biography' was 'less unfitted to feminine power' (Stodart 1842: 128), because it did not require the same level of masculine restraint, rationality and pedagogical authority that history demanded, female biographers tended to suggest that the masculinist nature of History made it unfit for the new age of women. As the Irish historian **Julia Kavanagh** asserted in her *Women of Christianity*:

> What share have women in this history of men? We hear of empresses and queens, of heroines and geniuses, and even of women who have won perilous fame through the power of loveliness or surpassing grace; but woman in the peace and beauty of domestic life, in the gentleness of her love, in the courage of her charity, in the holiness of her piety, we must not hope to find. History has been written in the old pagan spirit of recording great events and dazzling actions: not in the lowliness of the Christian heart, which affecting to despise the great, still loves and venerates the good. (1852: vii)

No text articulated these sentiments more clearly than Sarah Josepha Hale's *Woman's Record* (1853). A monumental collective biography of 1650 'distinguished women' from Eve to Hale herself, the *Woman's Record* presented a history of women drawing upon diverse figures such as Medea, Joan of Arc and Mary Wollstonecraft (albeit under her married name of Godwin). The *Woman's Record* was also a **world history**, in which Hale presented her unique perspective on historical progress, naming the nineteenth century as 'the Destiny of Women' (1853: vii). Hale structured her text in order to demonstrate her theory that the rise of civilisation was dependent upon women's moral influence and that the United States represented the pinnacle of civilisation as a Protestant republic. The biographies themselves functioned as evidence that women in each age had performed the duties of teacher and inspirer of 'virtue'. Linking the progress of society ('the permanent improvement of our race') with the progress of virtue, Hale maintained each was dependent upon 'the manner in which [woman's] mission is treated by man' (1853: xxxv).

While Hale was vigorously opposed to womanhood suffrage, she nonetheless maintained that if women were to perform their civilising duties, they needed to receive an education similar to men's. Like earlier biographers of women she believed that the genre of biography itself both educated women and made an argument for the education of women, as she wrote: '[I]f examples of women are to be found in every age and nation, who without any special preparation, have won their way to eminence in all pursuits tending to advance moral goodness and religious faith, then the policy, as well as justice of providing liberally for female education, must be apparent to Christian men' (1853: viii). This desire to reform women's condition was a striking characteristic of most women engaged in the writing of collective biographies. While few female biographers were overtly involved in feminist campaigns, most were involved in proto-feminist or 'womanist' activities such as abolition and temperance. Child's conservative *Good Wives* appeared shortly before her most radical and 'unwomanly' piece of writing, the scandalous *Appeal in Favour of that Class of Americans Called Africans* (1833) was published. **Clara Balfour Lucas,** author of some forty biographical collections, produced much of her oeuvre to educate society on the importance of Temperance. Sarah Bolton, author of *Successful Women* (1888), *Famous Types of Womanhood* (1892), *Leaders among Women* (1895) and almost as prolific as Lucas, was also an ardent supporter of Temperance. Both women asserted that female biography demonstrated women's role as influential moral teachers in society.

Anticipating the feminism of radical suffragists such as the **Pankhursts,** female biographers came to assert the need for women to domesticate the public sphere and to use their moral influence beyond the confines of the domestic realm. Women's biographical writing may appear to have supported a more conservative feminism as it emerged out of the eighteenth century, but by the mid-nineteenth century it had laid the foundation for something more radical. Indeed feminists such as **Caroline Wells Healy Dall, editor** of the first major American suffrage journal *The Una*, produced numerous biographical sketches of women (later compiled in her *Historical Pictures Retouched*, 1860) to depict intellectual excellence in women, to recover women reviled in the masculinist historical tradition and to plead for women's rights. With the rise of first-wave **feminism** the theme of women's moral influence gave way to a more overt discussion of heroines who insisted upon the rights of women, particularly to education, moral reform and suffrage. These works clearly anticipated the histories of feminism that emerged out of the suffrage movement and **feminist auto/biography** that evolved in the twentieth century.

Mary Spongberg

References

Blumenfeld-Kosinski 1997; Booth 2004; Brown-Grant 2003; Burstein 1999; Coon 1997; De Jean 1991; Hays 1796/1996, 1803; Heilbrun 1988; Jordan 1987; Kitchen 1998; Kucich 1993; Macaulay 1791/1974; Maitzen 1998; McNamara *et al.* 1992; McLeod 1991; Morgan 1809; Richards 1982; Sandford 1833; Smith 1984; Stodart 1842; Wemple 1981.

Related essays

Catalogs; Defences of women; Feminism; Feminist auto/biography; Hagiography; Royal Lives; Women Worthies; World History.

Feminism

The involvement of women in writing the history of feminism began at almost the very moment that organised campaigns for women's rights emerged in Britain and the United States in the mid-nineteenth century. Early women's rights activists recognised that the absence of women from the historical record paralleled their absence from the political stage and took care to record and chronicle their own campaigns. As Ellen DuBois has argued recently, they 'thought the preservation of history would contribute to "the cause"' (DuBois 1991: 61). This pattern by which feminist activists were also amateur historians of feminism continued well into the 1920s and 1930s, producing a number of stirring narratives of feminist struggle. For the most part, these works were emphatically histories of feminist campaigns, paying very little attention to the question of feminist ideas. **Ray Strachey**, for example, devoted just one sentence of her book, *The Cause: A Short History of the Women's Movement in Great Britain* (1928) to **Mary Wollstonecraft**'s *A Vindication of the Rights of Woman* (1792): '[I]n this book,' she noted, 'the whole extent of the feminist ideal is set out, and the whole claim for equal human rights is made. . . . It has remained the text of the movement ever since' (Strachey 1928/1978: 12). Like other early activists, she seems here to assume that the case of Wollstonecraft is almost self-evident.

Defining feminism

In the past few decades, this assumption has been completely rejected as feminist historians, alongside philosophers and literary, intellectual and cultural theorists, have addressed themselves extensively to researching the changing nature of feminist ideas and theories. The ways in which earlier feminists understood and negotiated prevailing ideas about sexual difference and femininity has become a subject of considerable interest, as have questions about the importance of religious belief to many forms of feminism and the relationship of feminist ideas to other forms of political and social theory. The ways in which feminist analyses were sustained, reworked or popularised in literary works have also been extensively discussed.

This is not to suggest that earlier feminist campaigns have lost their appeal to historians. However, approaches to writing the history of feminist activism have changed markedly. Contemporary professional historians have come to focus attention not so much on whether or not particular campaigns gained their ostensible objectives, but rather on the strategies they employed, the networks of relationships on which they were based, and the ideas and beliefs that underpinned them (Levine 1990). At the same time, the objectives of feminist campaigns have come under new scrutiny, as critical historians have pointed to the ways in which many feminists themselves endorsed class privilege and racial and imperial assumptions, which led them to demand rights only for some women, often at the expense of others (DuBois 1978; Burton 1994).

It is worth noting here that while the term 'feminism' is commonly used to designate the ideas or the activities of those who criticised or opposed the oppression of women from the ancient world to the present, it did not come into use until the very end of the nineteenth century (Caine 1997: 8–9). First used in France in the course of the 1890s, it was slowly taken up thereafter in Britain and the United States, becoming reasonably common in the Anglophone world just before the First World War. Prior to that, there was no single label or term to designate those women who criticised prevailing assumptions about sexual difference or who sought to extend women's rights or to ameliorate their condition. Some of those involved in the British nineteenth-century campaigns to extend women's access to education and employment as well as to gain their enfranchisement used the clumsy phrase 'women's rights women', or if they were concerned primarily with the suffrage, 'suffragists'. This late advent of the term 'feminism' has led to some discussion concerning whether or not it should be applied to earlier periods. Nancy Cott, for example, in *The Grounding of Modern Feminism* (1987) argued that the advent of the term in itself pointed to new feminist developments. Its introduction in the United States, she insisted, marked the end of an older 'woman movement' that had been preoccupied with suffrage and other legal and political rights and has assumed the underlying unity of all women, and the start of a new phase in which questions about the meaning of women's freedoms and questions about the connection between private life and political action became more central (Cott 1987: 11–13). While accepting that the language of feminism, the willingness to use the term and the meanings it is given are important facets of any kind of historical study, other historians have accepted the need to use the term as the only existing one that makes questions about sexual difference or about the position of women central to their analysis (Offen 2000).

First-wave feminism

From the mid-nineteenth century onwards, many of those concerned about women's rights sought not only to record their own activities and to note the progress and development of feminist campaigns, but also to ensure that due recognition was given to outstanding women in the past, some of whom they regarded as their forerunners. Initially, this was done primarily through periodicals. In Britain, the *English Woman's Journal* (1858–1864) was the first of these, followed in Britain by the short-lived *Victoria Magazine* and the longer lasting *Women's Suffrage Journal*, and the *Women's Review of Social and Industrial Questions*. In the United States, Lucy Stone established the *American Women's Journal* in 1870. Soon there were books to accompany these ephemeral publications, most notably the monumental *History of Woman Suffrage*, begun by **Elizabeth Cady Stanton, Susan B Anthony** and **Matilda Joslyn Gage** in the late 1870s. The six volumes in this work continued to appear over four decades. As its founding editors aged and died, their task was taken over by Ida Husted Harper, who produced the final volume in 1922.

As Cady Stanton and her colleagues indicated in the preface to their *History of Woman Suffrage*, they believed that their work would provide both an historical record and a compendium of useful information for those who would subsequently become involved in the struggle. They sought, they explained, to put into 'permanent shape the few scattered reports of the Woman Suffrage Movement still to be found and to make an arsenal of facts for those who are beginning to inquire into the demands and arguments of the leaders of this reform' before all the pioneers are dead. They intended to include and interweave personal reminiscences with the threads of history, secure in the belief that their readers wanted to know 'the impelling motives to action; the struggle in the face of opposition; the vexation under ridicule; and the despair in success too long deferred', and that they would be especially interested in a history written from a subjective point of view (Stanton *et al.* 1889/1969: Vol. 1 6–10). This work, perhaps the most ambitious attempt to record the history of a feminist campaign ever undertaken, was very broad in scope. It was a compilation of writings by many different authors and encompassed not only the suffrage campaign in the United States, but also international developments particularly in the British Empire and in Europe.

While there was no work in Britain as expansive as this *History of Woman Suffrage*, several British activists shared the underlying concerns reflected in the volume and wrote their own histories of the particular campaigns that had been most important to them. **Josephine Butler**, leader of the campaign against the Contagious Diseases Acts, published her *Personal Reminiscences of a Great Crusade* in 1896, and this was followed by **Helen Blackburn**'s *Women's Suffrage: A Record of the Suffrage Movement in the British Isles* (1902), and Millicent Fawcett's *Women's Suffrage* (1912) a decade later. The 1890s also saw a new historical consciousness evident particularly in a growing interest in Mary Wollstonecraft. The scandalous life of Wollstonecraft had made her a figure of some embarrassment to many Victorian feminists, but the advent of the 'new woman' of the 1890s cast her in a new light and led to the publication of at least two new biographies and several editions of her *Vindication of the Rights of Woman* (Taylor 2003: 246–53). Other early feminists, especially Mary Astell, were the subject of renewed interest, as were William Thompson and Anna Wheeler.

From the start, it was the suffrage campaign that had tended to dominate historical work on feminism. Inevitably, the political outlook and the divisions between different suffrage organisations tended to be reflected in the way that history was written. This was particularly the case in Britain where, as Sandra Holton (1998) has argued, early twentieth-century histories of suffrage campaigns were written from either a moderate constitutional position, or from a militant one. Thus Millicent Garrett Fawcett, the leader of the moderate National Union of Women's Suffrage Societies, in her book on *Women's Suffrage* and her later **memoirs** clearly endorsed the strategy and approach of the moderates. By contrast, the memoirs of Christabel and Emmeline **Pankhurst** suggested rather how little had been achieved in the nineteenth century and emphasised the dramatic new energy brought to the suffrage campaign with the advent of militancy in 1905. This battle over which approach to suffrage had been most important and which strategy most significant in the ultimate enfranchisement of women continued to emerge from the inter-war years in the two most significant histories of the suffrage movement, Ray Strachey's *The Cause* and Sylvia Pankhurst's *The Suffragette Movement* (1931).

The Cause was regarded for many decades as 'the classic' account and the best introduction to the history of British feminism in the nineteenth and early twentieth centuries. Its easy style and its celebratory tone served to make it an inspiring and engaging book. It was notable for many other things as well: its endorsement of a particular kind of liberal feminism, its emphasis on the central importance of Strachey's revered leader, Millicent Garrett Fawcett and its cursory treatment of her adversaries and opponents. But it is significant here too as the first work that extended beyond a single campaign and sought to delineate the British women's movement in an extensive and comprehensive way and to provide a framework for it that connected it to major eighteenth-century economic and intellectual developments. The 'Women's Revolt,' Strachey insisted, was a product of both the Industrial and the French Revolutions and its effective starting date was that of the publication of Mary Wollstonecraft's *Vindication of the Rights of Woman* in 1792. While ceding pride of place to Wollstonecraft in this respect, Strachey also insisted on including the work of women philanthropists and educators including Hannah More and Mrs Trimmer, Caroline Norton and Florence Nightingale in her account of the ways in which women sought to break out of 'the prison house of home.' She then proceeded to delineate the development and emergence of an organised women's movement that encompassed demands for improved education and entry to universities, greater employment opportunities, the campaign against the CD Acts and finally the suffrage campaign. Strachey's endorsement of liberal feminism and of the moderate approach of the constitutionalist National Union of Women's Suffrage Societies (NUWSS) is evident throughout this work, and particularly through its emphasis on the importance of Mill's ideas and its stress on the importance of using reason and careful strategies to obtain the suffrage. It is evident equally in her discussion of the militant campaign of the WSPU. From the start of the militant campaign, in her view, 'patience and trust were abandoned and indignation and bitterness took their place' (Strachey 1928/1978: 292). The complete contrast she insists on between the militants and the moderates emphasises constantly the 'moral violence', the lack of procedure, the unscrupulousness of the WSPU – and also its lack of effectiveness. It was the constant growth and expansion of the moderate campaign that mattered in her view – far more than the short-lived flash of the militants who, she insists, ceased to be important after 1912 (Strachey 1928/1978: 327).

A very different history, and indeed one that seems almost designed as a response to this work, was offered in Sylvia Pankhurst's *The Suffragette Movement*. Pankhurst's socialist convictions, her concerns about working-class women and her sympathy with radical causes led to a very different sense of how the movement developed and what was important about it. As her title makes clear, it was the militant suffrage movement with which Pankhurst was concerned, and the earlier suffrage campaign is seen largely as its forerunner. Moreover, her discussion of the rise of the women's suffrage movement focuses very much on radical activities in Manchester. The organisation which she saw as the one anticipating the WSPU was the Women's Franchise League, which was considerably more radical than were any of the London-based suffrage committees. Sylvia Pankhurst's work gives pride of place to the Pankhurst family – and makes very clear her adulation of her father and her difficult and conflictual relationships with her mother and older sister Christabel. At the same time, it pays almost no attention to the moderate NUWSS, commenting only on its reactions to the militant campaign and to the government attempts to suppress it.

These contrasting and even competing versions of the history of the women's movement in Britain had a counterpart in the United States. There, as Ellen DuBois argues, the two wings into which the suffrage movement split in the final stages of the battle for the nineteenth amendment to the Constitution which enfranchised women battled as intensely over the history of the women's rights movement as they did over immediate questions of strategy. The moderate National American Women's Suffrage Association and the more militant National Women's Party disagreed over which wing had been the more important in the ultimate gaining of suffrage – and each produced histories which wrote the other group out of the story (DuBois 1991: 65–6).

Works by participants in the suffrage movement inevitably came to an end in the late 1920s and 1930s. That period, however, also saw a number of pioneering biographies of feminist leaders and alongside this a marked concern to ensure that the records and papers of earlier feminists were collected, archived and protected for later historical research. In some cases it was family members, especially feminist daughters, who archived the papers of their mothers. Harriet Stanton Blatch, for example, arranged for the papers of her mother, Elizabeth Cady Stanton, to be deposited at the Library of Congress. But there was also a wider concern to collect feminist documents and records internationally which was spearheaded and organised by **Mary Beard** (DuBois 1991: 75–6). Beard herself worked to collect and to ensure the proper preservation of documents about American suffrage, but she corresponded with women in many other countries in an effort to ensure an international approach to this question.

The work of activist historians was followed in the late 1950s and 1960s by a number of important books offering a very different approach to the whole question of suffrage. The first of these was **Eleanor Flexner**'s *Century of Struggle: The Woman's Rights Movement in the United States* (1959), which sought to offer a comprehensive analysis of the position of women and of their struggle for access to education, for political rights and for better working conditions from the early colonial period until the final granting of women's suffrage in 1920. Flexner was not a professional historian, gaining both her knowledge of and her interest in history rather from her political involvements in the Communist Party and in the trade union movement. She sought and received support from professional historians, however, and her work reflects her very extensive archival research. It also reflects her strong political interests and her commitment to the union movement with its extensive discussion of women's work and their struggle for acceptance in the Labour Movement. Of all the early histories of women's struggle for rights, Flexner's is the most enduring and the one still considered most significant – not least because of its insistence on the importance of seeing the struggles of black women and of white working-class women as central parts of the story.

Second-wave feminism

In Britain, new studies of the women's movement did not appear until the following decade with the publication of both Miriam Ramelson's *The Petticoat Rebellion* and Constance Rover's *Women's Suffrage and Party Politics in Britain, 1866–1914* in 1967. Ramelson, like Flexner, was motivated to write this history by her own left-wing political involvement, and her work draws particular attention to the political activities of working-class women and the relationship between the labour movement and the militant suffrage campaign. While Ramelson sought to ensure the inclusion of working-class women in histories of the women's movement, Constance Rover took a slightly different tack in emphasising the political dimensions of the suffrage movement. She sought in her analysis of the suffrage movement, above all, to avoid 'the heroics and the personalities' that filled earlier narrative accounts, and to provide a political analysis that focused on the arguments on which the suffrage claim was based, the policies and tactics adopted and the relationship between the suffrage movement and the major political parties. Hers was the first critical and analytical study of the suffrage movement and it set a direction that was followed by many other works in subsequent years.

The history of feminism was transformed in the course of the 1970s with the advent of the women's liberation movement and the new approaches to women's history that accompanied it. The socialist commitment that had inspired Flexner and Ramelson was very significant in the early stages of the women's liberation movement and brought increasing attention to bear on socialist traditions and on their importance in the development of feminism. In Britain in the late 1960s and early 1970s, Juliet Mitchell and Sheila Rowbotham both extended the work of Ramelson and sought to show the ways in which feminist traditions influenced by socialism had developed. In place of a history that regarded feminism as essentially an outgrowth of the liberal theories of John Stuart Mill, they stressed the importance of the European socialist and feminist traditions stemming from Engels, Bebel and Klara Zetkin or Alexandra Kollontai. They were concerned, not with middle-class suffrage committees, but rather with the emergence of women's organisations connected within the German and Russian socialist movements and with the ways in which women had been involved in trade union organisation, and campaigns for legislative protection in Britain. Groups that had previously been given relatively little attention were given new prominence in their work, including the Fabian Women's Group, the Women's Cooperative Guild and the many women trade union activists.

In the course of the 1970s and 1980s, this revised and expanded idea of the history of feminism incorporating socialist views and organisations was written not only in relation to Britain, but also to Germany, France and Russia. The place of women within European socialist movements, the complicated relationships between bourgeois and socialist women, and the difficulties that many socialist women had in gaining acceptance of their feminist views were all questions discussed in a number of different works. Jean Quataert's *Reluctant Feminists in German Social Democracy, 1885–1917* (1979) made the difficulties evident in its very title and she, along with Marilyn Boxer, expanded on this discussion in their edited volume *Socialist Women: European Socialist Feminism in the Nineteenth and Early Twentieth Centuries* (1978). The importance of feminism and the difficulties faced by feminists like Alexandra Kollontai within the Bolshevik movement was the subject of much interest at the time. Kollontai was the subject of two biographies and of a number of major historical studies in the course of the 1980s (Farnsworth 1980).

The question of feminist claims and struggles in earlier socialist movements was also explored in the course of the 1980s, most notably in Barbara Taylor's *Eve and the New Jerusalem* (1983), an outstanding study of women in the Owenite movement in Britain, and one which pointed to the continuing importance of Mary Wollstonecraft amongst radicals and socialists who were attracted to, rather than being deterred by, her desire for new forms of sexual relationships and of marital and domestic life. The importance of utopian socialism in the articulation of feminist ideas was also explored in France in Claire Moses' *French Feminism in the Nineteenth Century* (1984).

This focus on working women and on the relationship between feminism and the labour movement brought a renewal of interest in nineteenth-century women's movements too. In *One Hand Tied behind Us: The Rise of the Women's Suffrage Movement* (1978), Jill Liddington and Jill Norris offered a quite new account of the suffrage movement, in which they stressed the role of radical suffragists, the working women in the north of England, who came into the suffrage movement via trade unions and combined their demand for suffrage with a very strong sense of the particular needs of working women. Several of these women became paid full-time organisers, employed by the National Union of Women's Suffrage Societies to expand their support base in the north of England. Extending this discussion of the links between the suffrage and labour movements, Sandra Holton's *Feminism and Democracy: Women's Suffrage and Reform Politics in Britain, 1900–1918* (1986) explored the ways in which, at the beginning of the twentieth century, an older generation of suffragists were forced reluctantly to accept the interest in social democracy and in the labour movement evident amongst many of their younger colleagues. The relationship between women's suffrage and other forms of political radicalism was discussed at the same time in the United States, most extensively by Ellen Carol DuBois' *Feminism and Suffrage* (1978) which focuses on the radicalism of the suffrage leader, Elizabeth Cady Stanton.

While this work served to show how much more complex and extensive feminist debates had been than was suggested by those earlier heroic works focusing only on an organised middle-class women's, that movement was subjected to a range of new critiques. In the very process of exploring links between suffragists and the labour movement, Liddington and Norris, for example, stressed the narrow class-base and the limited and often conservative political vision evident amongst organised campaigners for women's rights who sought to allow middle- and upper middle-class women to enjoy the rights and privileges of their men folk without questioning the implications of this position for working women. In the United States, the connection between early feminist campaigns and demands, and the abolitionist movement was the subject of much discussion. But so too was the racism and hostility to black rights evident in some branches of the woman suffrage movement after the American Civil War. Ellen DuBois explored in some detail the ways in which even ostensibly radical women, like Elizabeth Cady Stanton, came to oppose the enfranchisement of Afro-American men after the Civil War, fearing that the needs of women would cease to be important – but revealing also levels of racism not previously recognised in her thought.

But while some women commented on the limitations of earlier feminist analyses, others insisted rather on the need to examine the differences between feminism and other forms of political and social thought and the distinctive ideas of feminists, especially the importance to them of questions about sexual difference and sexual oppression, and at the importance for feminists of attacking the many different forms of discrimination and exploitation that arose from the sexual double standard. This framework produced a number of new works, especially on nineteenth-century feminism. Here too, Constance Rover was a pioneer, and her book *Love, Morals and the Feminists* (1970) was one of the very first to look at the connection between feminism and 'the great moral problems of Victorian and modern times.' This approach was taken up and extended by Susan Kingsley Kent's *Sex and Suffrage* (1987), and Sheila Jeffrey's *The Spinster and Her Enemies* (1985) and by Judith Allen's *Sex and Secrets* (1990). All these works argued that it was necessary to explore in more detail the extent to which feminism encompassed a critique of the sexual double standard and demands for reform in sexual and marital conduct. The latter two pointed also to the more fundamental critique evident amongst some nineteenth-century feminists of male sexuality and of the ways that heterosexual relationships were understood. Jeffries went furthest along this line of analysis, seeking also to argue that the feminist canon should include some of the women once regarded as excessive in their concern with sexual morality and social purity, and who had evinced little interest in women's suffrage, because of their concern with the sexual exploitation of women. The need to provide a new framework for analysing feminist theories and ideas, and to recognise the limitations of the notions of 'radical', 'liberal' or 'conservative' derived from other forms of politics in describing feminists, was also urged by a number of women historians who stressed the combination of ostensibly radical and conservative elements in the thought, for example, of Josephine Butler or Emmeline Pankhurst.

Cultural feminism

While the political dimensions and the outlook of earlier feminists were being scrutinised by some, other women historians became increasingly interested in the distinctive ways in which feminist groups and campaigns had come into being and in the ways in which they reflected particular women's cultures and values. Following the lead of Carroll Smith-Rosenberg (1975), a number of women historians began exploring the private, familial and social worlds of feminists. Where previous histories had stressed the ways in which women met and organised and sought access to the public sphere for themselves in order to campaign for greater public recognition, some of the newer histories of feminism focused rather on the extent to which feminist organisations were composed of and fostered networks of close family and friends who offered each other the emotional support that made sustained and difficult activity possible. Nancy Cott's *The Bonds of Womanhood* (1977) pointed to the ways in which, in the United States, the female groups and circles acceptable within the broad framework of domestic ideology allowed women to work together and to begin to articulate their dissatisfaction with their lot, while Judith Walkowitz's *Prostitution and Victorian Society* (1980) and Philippa Levine's *Feminist Lives* (1990) examined the kinds of female relationships that underlay British feminist campaigns.

Another major shift in writing the history of feminism that became very significant in the late 1980s centred on the increasing attention that was paid to feminist ideas. This is clearly evident in the publication of a number of major studies on the ideas of Mary Wollstonecraft. Some historians and literary critics were made uneasy by her anxiety about women's sexuality, but others insisted rather on her concern with natural rights, and importance as an innovative political theorist, who sought to combine reason and emotion in new and significant ways (Landes 1988; Sapiro 1992). This discussion of Wollstonecraft's ideas was accompanied in Britain by a broader interest in assessing the ideas of other important feminists and their relationship with the political, social and cultural context from which they emerged. Dale Spender's edited collection *Feminist Theorists: Three Centuries of Women's Intellectual Traditions* (1983) provided a widely read and accessible statement of this new approach, introducing a spate of other works that focused on the ideas, rather than the activities and campaigns of prominent feminists including Josephine Butler, Millicent Fawcett, Emily Davies in the UK, Elizabeth Cady Stanton, Susan B Anthony and **Charlotte Perkins Gilman** in the US, Rose Scott in Australia and **Olive Schreiner** in South Africa.

One of the key concerns here, the questions of the relationship between feminism and Enlightenment thought, was being discussed extensively also in France and the United States, as some women historians questioned the once widely accepted assumption that Enlightenment rationalism and individualism provided a basis for feminism. The hostility to women's rights expressed by Rousseau and evident in the denial of rights to women and the suppressing of women's clubs and political activities in the early years of the French Revolution led historians like Joan Landes to argue in *Women and the Public Sphere in the Age of the French Revolution* (1988) that it was not the Enlightenment but the denial of rights to women in bourgeois liberalism that inspired the articulation of feminist demands. The precise nature of this nexus and ways in which sexual difference came to be understood and aggressively asserted in the early stages of the French and American revolutions was explored in a number of works by women historians in France (Fraisse 1995; Ozouf 1997; Offen 2000), Britain (Rendall 1985) and the United States (Kerber 1980; Norton 1980). The breaking of this nexus between Enlightenment ideas and feminism led to new analyses of the importance to feminism of religious ideas and beliefs, and of theoretical and practical developments in the sciences (Behnke 1982). The broad parameters of feminist thought at any particular time was also a subject of new interest, as was the changing nature of feminist critiques over time and the question of whether there were significant national differences in feminist ideas – or, as Karen Offen suggested, fundamental differences between the basically individualist framework of Anglo-American feminism, on the one hand, and the relational approach of European feminists, on the other (Offen 2000).

The last two decades have seen further developments in all of these areas, alongside some new ones. Feminist campaigns, organisations and ideas have continued to be explored, and often in new ways. In Britain in particular, discussion about the objectives and the effectiveness of the suffrage campaign has given way rather to an interest in its extraordinary range and variety. Lisa Tickner's path-breaking *The Spectacle of Women* (1987) was perhaps the most significant work here, with its wonderful analysis of suffrage art and craft, and its insistence on the ways in which suffrage pageantry and use of art and symbols in monster demonstrations served to transform British political campaigns in the early twentieth century. This new approach has led to extensive discussion and analyses of suffrage costumes, music, drama and fiction, all of which serve to show both how important suffrage was in the daily lives of its supporters and how central it became in the national imagination in the early twentieth century. The impact of feminist beliefs and activities on individual lives, and the need to research the lives of women who, while never becoming national leaders, had devoted themselves to the feminist cause was a new line of research undertaken by Sandra Holton, June Hannam and many others. In the course of undertaking this kind of research, women historians came to re-evaluate earlier beliefs about the division between militant and moderate suffragists in England, as many women managed to belong to and support both campaigns.

Global perspectives

While much work continues to be done on national feminisms, particularly in Britain and the United States, there has also been a growing interest in looking at feminism from an international and global perspective. One strand of this has centred on the need to encompass within the history of feminism the insights that have come from new imperial histories, and to recognise the many ways in which imperial assumptions alongside imperial power pervaded European and American feminism. This has been explored most extensively in regard to nineteenth- and early twentieth-century British feminism, especially in terms of how many British feminists endorsed the dominant imperial outlook of their time, which often served to empower them by giving them a sense of the global importance of their claims for political rights on the one hand, while sometimes giving them a sense of a mission to assist and support their 'little' sisters in the territories over which Britain ruled on the other. The special mission that many British women felt in regard to Indian women has been particularly thoroughly explored (Burton 1994). The complex imperial framework of Australian feminism has also been explored, in terms of the ways that Australian feminists were, as Marilyn Lake has argued, both colonised, in relation to Britain, and colonisers, in relation to the Australian Aborigines whose inferior status they often took for granted – even as they sometimes protested against the abuses that Aboriginal women suffered (Lake 1999).

While some women historians have pointed to the imperial assumptions underlying specific national feminisms, others have focused rather on the ways in which feminists from the late nineteenth century onwards sought international links and collaboration. The international organisations that were established at the turn of the twentieth century, the International Women's Suffrage Alliance and the Women's Christian Temperance Union, have been the subject of extensive research, as have rather more radical groups, like the Women's International League for Peace and Freedom that opposed the national policies of their governments and sought to assert their pacifism and internationalism even in the face of war. International links amongst feminists were evident even before this, as Bonnie Anderson has argued in her study of the first international women's movement, *Joyous Greetings* (2000). This work traces some of the links between women in Britain, Germany, France and the United States, arguing that they constitute 'an early, loosely knit, international woman's movement', all the participants of which saw themselves as working together for an international cause. The internationalism of feminists in the interwar period has also been the subject of new research, alongside work on the ways in which women concerned about women's rights sought to further their objectives, first through the League of Nations and then through the United Nations.

In the past couple of decades, the history of feminism has continued to be a subject of much interest to women in many different disciplines and many different countries. In Britain, the United States and Europe attention has come to be focused on many different aspects of the culture of feminism, in its literary, visual and popular manifestations, and on analysing different kinds of feminist lives. At the same time, women historians in a number of African, Asian and South American countries have sought to explore not only the impact of imperialism on women, but the specific forms that feminism took within different ethnic and cultural frameworks. The importance of recognising the multifold natures of different feminisms has been stressed constantly – and has immeasurably enriched research within this field.

Barbara Caine

References

Behnke 1982; Burton 1994; Caine 1997; Cott 1987; DuBois 1978, 1991; Farnsworth 1980; Fraisse, 1995; Holton 1998; Kerber 1980; Lake 1999; Landes 1989; Levine 1990; Norton 1980; Ozouf, 1997; Rendall, 1985; Sapiro 1992; Smith-Rosenberg 1975; Strachey 1928/1978; Stanton *et al.* 1889/1969; Taylor 2003.

Feminist autobiography

Like the writing of feminist history, the writing of feminist autobiography began almost at the start of organised campaigns for women's rights in the mid-nineteenth century. Although most of those involved in the early campaigns for women's rights did not write their own memoirs until late in the nineteenth or even early in the twentieth centuries, a number of them were concerned to write and record the lives of other women they regarded as pioneers in the cause, either in the periodicals they produced or in the histories they wrote. Indeed, the need to record and acknowledge the lives of those pioneering women who had made significant contributions to the emancipation of their sex, and thus to ensure their place within the historical record, was regarded as something of the utmost importance to many feminists across the nineteenth and twentieth centuries.

Feminist autobiographies and biographies have, moreover, played an important part in the development and dissemination of both feminist theory and feminist history. The preoccupation with the self, with its making and its differentiation from others which has been so central to the western preoccupation with the individual over several centuries has made autobiography into a particularly important literary, philosophical and historical genre in western culture. But this self has always been explicitly a masculine one – as has the subject of traditional autobiography. Thus, as Sidonie Smith argues, any form of women's autobiography challenges 'the narrative itinerary of traditional autobiography'. Woman, mother and the feminine, in her view, function in a traditional autobiography as part of the 'mess and clutter' that the autobiographer has to clear out in the struggle for self-identity and a coherent past which is the core concern of the genre (Smith 1993: 19). As a consequence, women, like other excluded groups, have used autobiography as a way of 'talking back', or insisting that there is a story within the 'mess and clutter' that deserves to be told, and as a way of resisting official memories and narratives that exclude them. It is in their autobiographies, she argues that feminists like **Elizabeth Cady Stanton** can be seen most effectively to subvert ideals of femininity and the gendered division of public and private by writing about their lives in ways that simultaneously claim masculine territory, explore the author's subjectivity, allow them to create a coherent narrative of the past – and demand recognition of their own private and emotional worlds.

For Cady Stanton herself, and for a number of other late nineteenth-century feminists who sought to criticise prevailing ideas of marriage and prevailing sexual mores even more critically than she had done, it was the life of **Mary Wollstonecraft** that offered an important example. Wollstonecraft's 'irregular life', her sexual relationship with a man to whom she was not married and with whom she had a child, and her later unusual relationship and marriage to Godwin had made her a pariah for much of the nineteenth century. But what Barbara Taylor calls her 'sexual heterodoxy' was of great importance in the 1890s, when 'new women' and advanced feminists in Britain and elsewhere were challenging dominant sexual norms. To women like Elizabeth Wolstenholme Elmy and Olive Schreiner, seeking to live new and sexually radical lives, she provided a model – and the number of biographies and biographical studies of her that appeared in the 1890s suggest that they were not alone in this interest (Caine 1997; Taylor 2002).

The importance of the autobiographies or biographies of earlier feminists to a later generation has also been made clear recently in regard to **Simone de Beauvoir**. Although the *Second Sex* is usually taken as her most significant theoretical contribution to feminism, it was through her autobiographies and novels that her ideas were most thoroughly absorbed by feminists in the 1960s and 1970s. The autobiographies, Ann Curthoys argues, 'became nothing less than a guide for fashioning a new feminine self' (2000). De Beauvoir herself recognised the close connection between *The Second Sex* and her autobiographical work, as she explored the condition of becoming and of being a women in general before examining the ways in which femininity had impacted upon or had to be resisted in her own life. Her work was of particular importance to the next generation because of her combination of concern to find a new form of personal life and her intense involvement with the contemporary intellectual, political and social world – hence the autobiographies provided a history of that world and an analysis of de Beauvoir's often difficult engagement with it.

In this essay I will seek to explore the changing patterns evident in the ways that feminists over the past century and a half have written about themselves, or been written about by others, looking at the ways in which they represent the emergence of a female self and at the question of which aspects of their lives they deemed important to write about. I want also to look at the ways in which they consciously sought to write history and to address, interrogate or extend the historical record.

Feminist autobiography before the era of women's rights

As in other areas of feminist thought and writing it is not always easy to establish precisely which works to include in an essay on feminist autobiography and biography. The relatively late introduction of the term 'feminism' into discussions about women's rights (its use became widespread in Britain and the United States, for example, in the years just preceding the First World War) means that many of those nineteenth-century women, now commonly referred to as 'feminist leaders', would not have described themselves in those terms. This is not a matter of particular concern when it comes to the autobiographies and biographies of those who led or who dedicated much of their time to the various nineteenth-century campaigns for women's rights, like Elizabeth Cady Stanton, or Millicent Garrett Fawcett, or Frances Power Cobbe, all of whom wrote some form of autobiography. But it does raise questions about others, such as Harriet Martineau or Florence Nightingale, for example, both of whom were regarded as important pioneers by many of those who devoted themselves to campaigns for women's rights, but whose own feminist commitments remain a little ambiguous.

Martineau's interesting and important *Autobiography* (1877) is particularly interesting text here. Born in 1802, Martineau lived much of her life in the decades before the advent of organized movements for women's rights in either Britain or America. She addressed many questions of importance to women in her writings, advocating improvements in their education, exploring the nature and the problems women faced in finding employment, and indicating some support for women's suffrage. She was an early opponent of the Contagious Diseases Acts in Britain and a signatory to the first Ladies' Appeal against them, and wrote also on the problem of domestic violence and the sexual double standard (Pichanick 1980). Nonetheless, Martineau remained equivocal about campaigns for women's rights – and especially about who should be involved in demanding them. While vocal and eloquent in anatomizing women's oppression, she would not always have seen herself as participating in a broader movement for women's rights. She refused to speak publicly on the subject of women's rights, giving as a response when asked a firm statement about the need for women not to appear as victims, but to improve their lot themselves. 'Whatever a woman proves herself able to do, society will be thankful to see her do', was her response to those who appealed to her to speak on this cause (Martineau 1877: Vol. I, 400–1). Her autobiography is, moreover, very different in content and form from those of most other prominent nineteenth-century feminist activists or sympathisers. Drawing on an earlier tradition of introspective biography, she sought rather to explore her own early life and feelings, and to analyse the point at which she emerged as moral and fully conscious being. She regarded it as her duty to write about her life, she insists in her *Preface*, because she had derived so much profit from the autobiographies and reminiscences of others – a sense of duty that was increased when her life 'became evidently a somewhat remarkable one'.

There is no question that Martineau, in Smith's terms, worked to subvert the dominant forms of autobiography. The 'mess and clutter' of her life is palpable, as is her deep misery and pain – and the story of her intellectual development and emergence as a prominent writer is never really separated from it. Although the story is very clearly particularized, Martineau's anguish-ridden account of her painful childhood and early life does also illustrate the misery and discomfort of those women who failed to fit into the approved feminine framework. Her frequent physical discomfort, exacerbated by her deafness, was the constant accompaniment to her sense of being an unloved and unvalued daughter. Her desire to be educated, noticed and to excel only underlined further her lack of the more acceptable feminine qualities. Finding no source of human comfort, she turned instead to religion. Begun in the 1850s, at a time when her recurrent ill health made her feel that her life was nearly over, Martineau's autobiography bears a marked similarity to George Eliot's autobiographical novel, *The Mill on the Floss*, which serves also to recount the deep misery experienced by a little girl whose exceptional intelligence, and passionate and impetuous nature are as much a source of dislike and discomfort to her and her family as are her unusual looks.

Autobiography and the nineteenth-century movements for women's rights

Martineau's work is markedly different in approach and in tone from the spate of autobiographies of the first generation of women's rights activists that began to appear in the 1890s. In place of her intense individual unhappiness, many of these later works stress the integration of the woman in her own community – and her sense that her own sufferings were a function of her sex and of the place of women in society. Elizabeth Cady Stanton's *Eighty Years And More Reminiscences 1815–1897* (1897) is a particular case in point. Although written at a time when Stanton's religious and political radicalism had made her somewhat isolated in the increasingly conservative American woman suffrage movement, and when her once very close friendship with suffrage leader, **Susan B Anthony**, was subject to considerable strain, Stanton presents the autobiography as one written by a woman closely integrated into both family and community. Dedicated to 'my steadfast friend for half a century', Susan B Anthony, it refers in the preface also to the desire expressed by her family and friends to have the story told, and hence locates itself immediately as a work that has an audience and comes from a life shared with many others. Stanton used this work also to emphasise both the range and richness of her personal experience and the breadth of her intellectual, social and feminist interests. Thus her marriage, her experiences of motherhood and her deep concerns about the need for a radical reform of approaches to child care and early education feature prominently in the book, alongside her sense of the connection between her interest in women's political rights with abolitionism on the one hand, and with the need for the new and radical critique of Christianity that she sought in her project for a 'Woman's Bible' on the other. The feminist content of the work is thus expansive and every aspect of Cady Stanton's life is connected with it. Her feminism is also grounded in her early personal and emotional life, and the unhappiness she experienced as a child and a young woman, particularly in the face of her father's dismissive comments and his constantly reiterated wish that she had been a boy rather than a girl. But all of this is presented in ways that emphasise the relationship between her personal distress and the broader question of the status of women – rather than suggesting that she was personally wretched and unloved.

For Cady Stanton, as for many of her contemporaries both in Britain and the United States, the writing of an autobiography was thus closely connected to the feminist cause. It provided a history of that cause and the networks of women that sustained it on the one hand, while implicitly criticising marriage and many of the assumptions that underlay family life on the other. This same combination of the promotion of a feminist cause and the detailing of alternative ways of life for women is evident in the autobiography of the British feminist, Frances Power Cobbe. Shortly before writing her *Life* (1902), Cobbe wrote to her old friend, the suffrage leader Lydia Becker, to tell her that she was 'planning to write, for a last book, a sketch of my life in which I shall make a point of showing how I came to be concerned with Women's Rights and why I support them' (Caine 1992: 111). As Nina Auerbach has argued, Cobbe's autobiography also celebrated her rich and full life as a single woman, albeit an exceptionally able and active one – whose feminism was based 'on the refreshing assumption that legislation on behalf of women must measure up to the high standard her life had already set' (Auerbach 1982: 123). Where Cady Stanton wrote at length of motherhood, Cobbe insisted rather on the kind of domestic companionship and friendship that women could offer each other – and on their ability to live well and happily without any connection with men. Like Cady Stanton, much of her autobiography serves to explain her complex sense of the nature of women's oppression and her growing realisation of the need for legal, political and social reform. Thus her appalling schooling, with its emphasis on useless accomplishments and its disregard of anything intellectually demanding and substantial, like her difficult home life, especially after the death of her mother, when she was the housekeeper and domestic companion of an autocratic father with whom she had nothing in common, all serve to stress the need for reform in the situation of women and the reasons for her supporting women's rights. Cobbe stressed too the importance of her discovery in Italy of the possibilities of a very full life for single women who determined to be independent and to engage in artistic or philanthropic activity – and she placed a heavy stress on the essentially philanthropic nature of her feminism and its fundamental concern with the sufferings of women who were less well treated than her.

One of the interesting features of the autobiographies of nineteenth- and early twentieth-century feminists is the careful balance that many of them attempted to maintain in their writing between public and private lives. As women seeking legislative change and a wider political and social role, they were of course demanding a much more expansive public life than was normally available to women. From their own point of view, moreover, and in accordance with the dominant historical framework of their time, it was their public life and activities that made them historically significant. At the same time, as autobiographies, their work necessarily dealt in some ways with their private lives – and they used them to detail the changing nature and the history of the female and domestic sphere and of middle-class women's education. Moreover, one of the ways in which they could ensure that the autobiographies contributed to their feminist cause was precisely in demonstrating the extent to which they shared the common feelings and experiences of women and performed their feminine duties. Thus

Cady Stanton's emphasis on motherhood, like Millicent Garrett Fawcett's description of the marital devotion between herself and her husband, or Frances Cobbe's insistence on how much she enjoyed the role of housekeeper and that of undertaking the philanthropic work that was expected of the womenfolk of substantial landowners, all served to further the insistence of the women's movements at the time that feminism did not remove women from the domestic sphere, but rather made them occupy it in a more intelligent, dutiful and effective way. The treatment of their familial and domestic lives rarely involved intimate revelations, of course. Like other Victorian and Edwardian writers of autobiography, they maintained a strong sense of decorum. Affection for parents, spouses, female partners and children was almost taken for granted and described only in very general terms. There was little space for any domestic incompatibility. It is her silence, for example, that points to Cady Stanton's matrimonial difficulties. Frances Cobbe was unusual here in making clear her relief when his death finally freed her form the burden of caring for her father.

The question of how to maintain this balance between public and private life, and how to represent one's public activity, was a complex one – and the tensions evident in some autobiographies stress the difficulties women had with the form. Josephine Butler, leader of the campaign against the Contagious Diseases Acts in England, chose a different form in which to do this than either Stanton or Cobbe. Butlers wrote several volumes of reminiscences and memoirs, but all of them focused ostensibly either on other people or on her great campaign. It was in the form of memoirs or recollections that she chose to pay tribute to the most important figures in her life: her father (*Memoir of John Grey of Dilston*, 1869), her husband (*Recollection of George Butler*, 1892) and her sister (*In Memoriam: Harriet Meuricoffre*, 1901). She is the dominating presence in all of these works, however, and they provide her with a platform for elucidating her own life without ostensibly claiming the main ground. As a result of this earlier writing, her *Personal Reminiscences of a Great Crusade* (1896) is very much her story of the campaign against the Contagious Diseases Acts, dealing with her growing awareness of the issue, and of her feelings and concerns throughout; this volume begins with the passage of the Acts themselves and of responses to them – rather than dealing with any of her personal life in the preceding years. All of this had been covered in the works in which she ostensibly paid tribute to others – while detailing her own early life and experiences. In this process, she too questions the normal autobiographical form and offers new ways of writing and thinking about it.

The suffrage struggle

While the autobiographies of Butler, or of Millicent Fawcett, stress familial closeness, this is not the only model. The several autobiographical and biographical writings produced by the **Pankhurst** family taken together, as June Purvis has argued, serve rather to illustrate deep underlying tensions and hostilities, especially those between Sylvia and Christabel. One can see also, in the Pankhurst autobiographies, a shift in the balance between public and private life. Private life had almost no place in the Pankhurst's autobiographical and biographical writing; the campaign was all and in the case of both Emmeline and Christabel, it overwhelmed everything else. Christabel Pankhurst's autobiography, *Unshakled* (published in 1959, a year after her death), is the most extreme example of this, suggesting that she had no private or emotional life outside the suffrage struggle and that she was entirely consumed by it. Hers is literally a story without a self – and her first chapter on 'Family History' takes as its central character not herself, but the early life, marriage and development of political interest of her mother. Her concern in the next chapter, 'The Years of Preparation', is to emphasise that she was her mother's 'right hand'. One might well want to question some of the ways in which Christabel Pankhurst painted her subordination to her mother. But the devotion and the lack of any sense of other life remain striking.

The drama of the militant phase of the suffrage struggle was so great as to overpower almost any other aspect of the lives of suffragettes. Emmeline Pethick-Lawrence's *My Part in a Changing World* (1938), for example, offers somewhat more insight into her private life than do the Pankhurst stories, dealing as it does with her early life and interests, and her marriages as well as suffrage work. But it is the latter that dominates completely and her autobiography, like those of Emmeline and Christabel Pankhurst, provides not only a way of telling her own story, but also of offering her version of some of the conflicts that occurred within the militant suffrage movement.

Important as it was, the suffrage movement is less dominating in one of the very few autobiographies written by working-class women in this period, Hannah Mitchell's posthumously published *The Hard Way Up* (1956). In part this reflected Mitchell's desire to describe a working life with its attendant hardships and difficulties to a largely middle-class readership – and possibly also to show why, as a worker and a socialist, she had come to see women's rights as so important. Mitchell's life was incomparably harder than that of any of the other women described to date, both materially and emotionally. Her autobiography is clear and uncompromising in its description of her impoverished childhood, her difficult relationship with an unloving and violent mother, and the keen sense of gender inequalities she acquired in watching her brother's leisure while she was required constantly to do domestic chores. Mitchell left home at the age of 14, after seizing the stick with which her mother was beating her and attempting to strike back. Her working life as a seamstress, her marriage and her very early (and unsuccessful) attempt to establish in it a relationship in which domestic chores were shared, her desire to limit the size of her family, her entry into labour politics and feminism (and her resentment at being rendered invisible by middle-class women) are dealt with in a very direct way – and with an unusual frankness.

All of these women emphasised the close connection between their own individual life and the broader public developments of their time, thus emphasising the extent to which their autobiographies were also works of contemporary history. Some did so by locating their lives within the framework of significant national events. Millicent Garrett Fawcett, for example, explains on the first page of *What I Remember* that 'the year of my birth was the year of the Irish Famine and the repeal of the Corn Laws, and the following year saw the downfall of half the old autocratic Governments of Europe' – thus immediately connecting herself with some of the great liberal issues of the nineteenth century. She stresses too, the importance of local history: of her family and their community ties. Stanton and Butler focus on different questions, connecting themselves rather with important reforming traditions, particularly abolitionism. Mitchell in turn did so by connecting her life with trade union and socialist developments in Lancashire and with the broader sweep of labour history.

Feminist autobiography in the interwar period

Just as feminist activists can be seen in generational terms, not only in age, but in interest and preoccupation, so too one can see generational shifts in feminist autobiography. Those that appeared in the interwar years are clearly demarcated from their late nineteenth and early twentieth - century forerunners in their greater degree of discussion of private life and sometimes also in their approach to feminism. Economic independence and the question of work became much more important in the interwar period than had been the case earlier when suffrage was the dominant issue – and some interwar autobiographies reflect this.

The First World War itself and its impact on individuals and on society was an issue too in some feminist autobiographies – most especially in **Vera Brittain**'s *Testament of Youth* (1933), probably the most widely read of any feminist autobiography. Although the central focus of Brittain's story is the terrible losses suffered during the war, and her own particular loss of fiancé, brother and close friends, the work also explores the development of her feminism, and the ways in which she suffered as a woman from the conflict between parental expectations and her own wishes, and desires, on the one hand – and from her exclusion from the world of her fiancé and brother, on the other. The book also allows Brittain to explore the changes in social and sexual behaviour that came with the war, as young women like herself who, before 1914 were not even allowed to have tea with a male friend unchaperoned, travelled to war fronts or were involved in the intimate care of male bodies in hospitals. The strongly marked hostility to the war, and the sense of terrible and pointless waste that it involved is far more pronounced in this work written in the late 1920s than was the case in Brittain's war-time diaries. While Brittain discussed aspects of her relationship with her fiancé, Roland Leighton, far more openly than was the case in most earlier autobiographies, she was considerably more reticent when it came to talking about relationships between women. *Testament to Friendship* (1940), the book she wrote about her close friend Winifred Holtby, is a case in point. Brittain deals in some measure with Holtby's women friends, and includes a discussion of some of their life together as two young women graduates, setting up home and attempting to establish independent lives as writers against the background of the post-war world. This work has raised far more questions than Brittain's earlier testament, however, because of its combination of apparent openness, and its reticence and evasion about the nature of Holtby's sexuality in general and about the emotional relationship between her and Brittain. There is a fierce insistence on Holtby's heterosexuality – and no hint at all of the possible complexity that later writers have seen in Holtby's immersion in the life of Brittain – or of Brittain's dependence on her friend.

The need simultaneously to talk about private life and to negotiate carefully their discussion of private, and especially sexual, life was an issue for almost all feminists until the 1960s. One can see this clearly in the case of the suffragette and composer Ethel Smyth, for example, whose passionate friendships with women, including Emmeline Pankhurst and **Virginia Woolf**, were well known to many friends and colleagues, but were dealt with in a somewhat restrained fashion in the several volumes of autobiography that she produced: *Impression that Remained*, 2 vols (1919), *Streaks of Life* (1921), *Female Pipings in Eden* (1933), *As Time Went on . . .* (1936), *What Happened Next* (1940). She certainly made it clear that all her intense and important relationships were with women, and that her women friends were the 'shining threads in my life', but she did not provide any detail about them. Her autobiographical volumes offer extensive discussion of her musical and suffrage career and often contain acute observations on individuals and on episodes in her life, but little detail of her own emotional life. 'I should like an analysis of your sex life as Rousseau did his,' Virginia Woolf wrote to her, advising her to provide '[M]ore introspection. [M]ore intimacy'. But Smyth kept the details of her emotional and sexual life firmly out of her books. At the same time, Smyth's work did challenge accepted autobiographical models, by drawing on the musical patterns of which she was so knowledgeable as a composer. Indeed, one recent commentator has argued that the pattern of her writing and her revelations follows the complex one of the fugue (Wood 1994).

Smyth's refusal to deal openly with her emotional or sexual relationships with women was a common feature of interwar feminist autobiography and biography. Cicely Hamilton, for example, was equally cautious in her autobiography, *Life Errant* (1935), as Mary Stocks was in *Eleanor Rathbone: A Biography* (1950). Stocks, who was a friend of Rathbone's, was careful to avoid any reference to Elizabeth Macadam, Rathbone's close female companion for more than 40 years. Macadam herself insisted that she be kept out of the story and kept a close eye on Stocks to ensure that this was done. Indeed, the first work on Rathbone to discuss this relationship is Susan Pedersen, *Eleanor Rathbone and the Politics of Conscience* (2003).

It was not only in Britain that feminists sought to avoid too much emotional introspection. The American feminist, **Charlotte Perkins Gilman**, for example, followed much the same pattern. Although her autobiography dealt with her early life and painful childhood including her difficult relationships with her mother, her first marriage and its breakdown, its tone is determinedly stoical. Exhibiting what one recent commentator sees as a 'fear of feeling'. Gilman refused absolutely to delve into her own emotions. Indeed, she sought rather to deny their importance, distinguishing in her posthumously published *The Living of Charlotte Perkins Gilman*, between 'life' and 'living'.

> The difference is great between one's outside 'life', the things which happen to one, incidents, pains and pleasures, and one's 'living'. Outside there was a woman undergoing many hardships and losses, and particularly handicapped by the mental weakness which shut down on her again, utter prostration and misery but inside her was a conscious humanity, immensely beyond self; a realization of the practical immortality of that ceaseless human life of ours, of its prodigious power, its endless growth. (1935; 181)

As Gilman's biographer, Ann J Lane comments, it is extraordinary to regard 'mental weakness' and 'utter prostration and misery, as *not* being part of an inner life – and it points to her refusal to allow any analysis of or delving into the dark places in her life' (Lane 1997).

Autobiography and women's liberation

There is both continuity and change in approach in the most recent feminist autobiographies, those written by the women who were actively involved in the Women's Liberation Movement of the 1960s and 1970s. Some of them reflect very clearly the impact of the sexual revolution of the 1960s, and the growing interest in psychology and psychoanalysis not only in the openness with which they discuss intimate sexual and emotional questions, but also in the ways in which they treat their complex relationships and ambivalence about the whole women's liberation movement. But others resemble their turn-of-the-century forerunners in their emphasis on the women's movement, and their disinclination to delve into personal aspects of their life.

Kate Millitt's *Flying* (1974) illustrates most clearly a new approach both to feminism and to autobiography in its detailed and intimate discussion of her emotional and sexual life. Beginning with her strict Irish-Catholic upbringing in St Paul, Minnesota, it explores the guilt and anxieties associated with her first sexual relationship with another woman, her many close female friendships and the 'problem' of her bisexuality. Millett deals in some detail with her relationship with her husband, the Japanese sculptor Fumio Yoshimur – and with the difficulties of reconciling this with her feminist persona. She also offers a frank account of the impact on her of the success of *Sexual Politics*, her major feminist text, and of the difficulties she faced when she found herself suddenly a leading figure in the women's movement – and facing new pressures around her sexuality.

In many ways, Millett stands out as the most significant autobiographer of the women's liberation movement. She is certainly the most prolific and the most revealing, not only in terms of her sexual relationships as in *Elegy for Sita* (1979), but also in relationship to her family of origin and her battles with manic depressinon and psychiatric institutions. *The Loony-Bin Trip* (1990) deals with her struggle to regain control of her life after being forcibly committed to mental hospitals as a manic depressive, both in the United States and subsequently in Ireland. Most recently, *Mother Millett* (2001) deals with her recollections of and relationship with her mother, combining stories of her childhood memories with discussions of her mother's final years. As she notes in the Introduction, much of the book is more about her than her mother – as 'I rarely write about any subject except myself'.

The publication of *Sexual Politics* (1970) catapulted Millett, then in her twenties, into international prominence. But hers was not the only kind of story associated with women's liberation. In Australia, the first significant autobiography to deal with the women's movement, Zelda D'Aprano's *Zelda the Becoming of a Woman* (1977) offered a very different kind of book and a very different life. Born in 1928 to a working-class Jewish family that had only recently migrated to Australia from Poland, D'Aprano was already in her fifties when she became involved in a Women's Action Committee that articulated the standard demands of women's liberation. But this was a crucial point for her – and much of the story of her life is told in terms of the illumination and understanding that feminism and the women's movement offered her about much of her earlier suffering both at home and at work. Hers too is a very frank account, dealing with early episodes of sexual abuse and rape – and the question of why she, and other women, remained silent about these things, to avoid embarrassment to or disruption of social, familial or working relationships. Her marriage and its ultimate breakdown and her other sexual relationships, her close ties with her mother and her daughter are all described as the constant battles she faced as a woman needing to support herself and her child in labouring jobs. D'Aprano's working life, much of it spent sorting mail in the post office, was also one in which there was constant discrimination and victimization as skilled work, like positions of union leadership, was regarded as a male prerogative. Her own emergence as an activist and a public figure is described too, but so is the cost, not only in emotional terms, but also in terms of the harassment she suffered from unions, from male opponents – and from a conservative government that placed her under constant surveillance.

While writing in detail of her own life, D'Aprano follows in some ways an earlier pattern of British working-class autobiography in seeking through the details of her life to acquaint a readership with issues and problems that they might not otherwise notice or acknowledge. The importance of the goals of women's liberation, and the 1970s feminist critique of male dominance in every aspect of women's lives is thus made evident in her discussions of her experience of sexual abuse, of discrimination at work and also in relation to questions of her health and maltreatment by a male-dominated medical profession. She cites several episodes when, suffering from pain and illness, she sees male doctors who are negligent and dismissive. She is told the cystitis she contracts after marriage, for example, is likely to be a venereal disease, for example. The final episode in *Zelda* deals with her having a hysterectomy, after some years of considerable pain. However neither she nor any of the women that she meets in hospital are adequately prepared for what is involved, or give information about after care, or told of the consequences.

The slogan, 'the personal is political' that was so important within the women's liberation movement was dealt with in a number of different ways in feminist autobiographies. Millett and D'Aprano illustrate its significance very clearly by exploring the ways in which sexual politics was evident or played out in their own lives. But others approached it in rather different ways. Betty Friedan's *Life So Far* (2000), for example, deals at some length with the difficulties she had in accepting the implications of her feminist critique in terms of her own life, pointing to the conflict between her public and private life at a time when she was gaining both national and international reputation as a feminist activist and organiser, demanding more access to employment and better pay, while being locked into an abusive and violent marriage – that her fear of divorce made it hard for her to leave.

A more common pattern in recent feminist autobiography is that of linking personal and political stories in works which point to the ways in which student life and involvement in radical politics in the course of the 1960s and 1970s was connected to sexual experience – and often to a growing sense of the inadequacy of marriage, or the incapacity of men with impeccable left credentials to acknowledge the entitlement of women to equality in either personal or public life. In some cases, there is an underlay that comes from an earlier sense of injustice or discrimination within a familial framework: Anne Summers' account of the violent hostility she suffered at the hands of her alcoholic father, in *Ducks on the Pond: An Autobiography 1945–1976* (1999), for example, provides an important and framing background to her later involvement in women's liberation. For her, as for a number of autobiographical works by significant British or American feminists, it is important also to detail the nature of the broader political and social climate of the 1960s, and especially of the high level of active opposition and resistance amongst students and young people to the Vietnam War, to a range of economic, social and political institutions – and to conservative governments and law enforcement agencies. The extent to which the decade of the 1960s is seen as a central aspect of people's lives is evident even in the titles of some autobiographies – for example, Sheila Rowbotham, *Remembering the Sixties* (2004) or Susan Brownmiller's *In Our Time: Memoir of a Revolution* (1999).

The emphasis on the 1960s, and the very particular nature of the politics of that decade, which included a strong emphasis both on direct protest and on a connection between political protests and personal life, does serve in some ways to differentiate the most recent feminist autobiographies from their nineteenth-century predecessors. At the same time, the dominance of public and political events, and the telling of life stories that privilege the campaigns and the politics of the women's liberation over any discussion of personal life, as Brownmiller does in the United States, or as Wendy McCarthy does in Australia in her autobiography *Don't Fence Me In* (2000), are very reminiscent of the work of an earlier period. There is certainly a difference in the kinds of lives that women can lead, and in the ways in which it has become accepted that the telling of a life story requires some discussion at least of personal difficulties with families and of sexual relationships, but while dealing often quite extensively with the particular historical context in which they become feminists, many recent feminist autobiographies follow an earlier pattern in their disinclination to reveal to much about themselves. While accepting the idea that 'the personal is political', it remains hard to work this into a life story – and for many contemporary feminists, as for their nineteenth-century forerunners, the sense of the importance of their feminist political activity seems to outweigh any inclination for personal revelation.

Barbara Caine

References

Auerbach 1982; Caine 1992; Lane 1997; Pichanick 1980; Smith 1993; Stanley 1992; Taylor 2002; Wood 1993.

Related essays

Female Biography; Feminism; Family; Women's Liberation.

Fitzpatrick, Kathleen 1905–1990

Australian historian. A major force in the History Department at the University of Melbourne for many decades, at a time when women academic historians were rare. She was educated at the University of Melbourne and then Somerville College Oxford. Hired by the History Department in 1938, she gradually rose through the ranks to associate professor in 1948, retiring in 1963. She was known as an inspiring teacher, especially for her lucidity, scholarship and wit.

Fitzpatrick wrote some well-esteemed history books, starting with *Sir John Franklin in Tasmania, 1837–1843* (1949). Unusually well-researched for its day, this book made extensive use of colonial archives. Fitzpatrick's emphasis was on the nature of the penal society Franklin governed for six years: 'I have tried', she says, 'to reconstruct the framework of circumstances within which Sir John Franklin worked in Van Diemen's Land, and to exhibit how it was that with so much goodwill he found himself unable to be the liberal, reforming governor he wished to be.' She paid considerable attention to Franklin's wife, Lady Jane Franklin, and their relationship, yet it is hard to distinguish her work from that of male historians of the period. This was followed by *Australian Explorers: A Selection from Their Writings with an Introduction* (1958), a compilation of explorer journals with a brief introduction. Always interested in literature, her work took a rather different turn with *Martin Boyd* (1963), a short biography and critical assessment of an Australian expatriate writer whom she defined as 'a delightful minor novelist' and also as a 'regional novelist' of Melbourne and its environs.

In contrast with her academic histories, her later work, written after her retirement, shows a growing interest in the history of women and especially of women's **education**. Her history of the Presbyterian Ladies College, Melbourne, called *PLC, Melbourne: The First Century, 1875–1975* (1975), placed the particular history of the school within a broader account of women's struggle for education, emancipation and wider opportunities for employment. Today her best-known book is possibly her autobiography, *Solid Bluestone Foundations and Other Memories of a Melbourne Girlhood, 1908–1928*, published in 1983 when she was 78. Ending with some chilling accounts of her experiences as both a 'colonial' and a woman at Oxford in the 1920s, this book provided an excellent insight into the childhood and education of a female academic historian in the mid-twentieth century.

Ann Curthoys

References

Carey & Grimshaw 2001; Grimshaw & Strahan 1982.

Major works

PLC, Melbourne: The First Century, 1875–1975 (Burwood: Presbyterian Ladies College, 1975) & *Solid Bluestone Foundations and Other Memories of a Melbourne Girlhood, 1908–1928* (Ringwood: Penguin, 1986)

Flexner, Eleanor 1908–1995

American historian of women. Daughter of Anne Crawford, playwright, and Abraham Flexner, educational reformer. Studied at Swarthmore College, majoring in history and English. Her honours thesis on Mary Tudor won her a fellowship to study for a year at Somerville College, Oxford. Like her mother, Flexner was drawn to the theatre. Becoming involved in the progressive theatre movement of the 1930s, she wrote several plays dealing with social and economic unrest and the rise of fascism. For a time she edited *New Theatre* magazine and in 1937 she published her first work *American Playwrights 1918–1938: The Theatre Retreats from Reality*, a critique of the impact of commercialism on American theatre. Around this time she joined the American Communist party and it was this connection that shaped her interest in women's political organisation. During the Second World War Flexner joined the Congress of Industrial Organisations' campaign to unionise workers across industries. Following the war she served as secretary to the Congress of American Women, then worked for the Speakers Bureau of the Foreign Policy Association (FPA), where she became familiar with the names of many women associated with the suffrage movement. While working for the FPA she met Helen Terry who became her companion. Terry lived with Flexner until her death in the mid-1980s.

While teaching courses on American women's history at the Jefferson School of Social Science, Flexner's ideas about the historical development of the struggle for women's rights began to crystallise. The death of her mother allowed her the income to devote herself to writing and she began detailed archival research in the Sophia Smith collection, the Schlesinger collection at Radcliffe as well as collections at Howard University and Schomburg branch of the New York Public Library in Harlem. In 1959 Flexner published *Century of Struggle: The Women's Rights Movement in the United States*, a work that traced the progress of campaigns for women's rights from the colonial period until the granting of suffrage. Flexner's work was unusual in that her connection with radical politics made her aware of the importance of the political contribution of African-American, working class and immigrant women. With this emphasis *Century of Struggle* provided the 'sex/class/race' framework that now characterises much feminist history of the United States. By examining the history of women's rights Flexner provided a new way of conceiving the history of feminism in America that moved beyond the hagiographic and highly contested histories of suffrage that proliferated during the interwar years. Flexner's text can be seen as an important precursor to women's liberation as it inspired Betty Friedan, author of *The Feminine Mystique*, who claimed that *Century of Struggle* provided many clues to the 'truth behind the feminine mystique and its monstrous imagery of the feminists'.

Following the publication of *Century of Struggle*, Flexner worked with the editors of the biographical dictionary *Notable American Women* to identify significant radical women and wrote entries on suffrage leaders, trade unionists and women of colour such as Carrie Chapman Catt, Ida B Wells-Barnett and Maud Younger. In 1972 Flexner published her biography of **Mary Wollstonecraft**. Naming Wollstonecraft as the first woman to 'effectively challenge[d] the age-old image of her sex as lesser and subservient human beings'. Flexner recognised her as a foremother of women's liberation. Flexner's biography is the first overtly feminist analysis of Wollstonecraft's life. *Century of Struggle* was republished in International Women's Year (1975) with Flexner including a discussion of the improved state of women's rights during this decade.

Mary Spongberg

References

DuBois 1991; Fitzpatrick 1996.

Major work

Century of Struggle (ed.) Ellen Fitzpatrick (Cambridge, MA: Belknap Press, 1996).

France

Women's works have been crucial to establishing what constitutes a valid record of the French past, whether it be their own memories as women of differing social, cultural or racial groups, emotional and social realms, or developing a speculative history of the motivations of individuals and groups. Female historians have produced narratives in varied genres such as essays, biographies and novels that have enabled them to pursue histories depending on their access, interest and valuation of particular source materials and research techniques. Whether in direct and conscious opposition to the prevailing views of male writers and academia, or simply by pursuing their own agendas of what constitutes subjects of historical interest, women's historical works have continually pushed the boundaries of what constitutes the history of France.

The Reformation

Prior to the Reformation, autobiographical writing was the primary medium through which women could contribute to an understanding of the French past. In letters written to her former lover and tutor Peter Abelard around 1135, the abbess Héloïse produced an alternative perspective, of their tragic relationship and of her emotional trauma since their separation, to that circulated in Abelard's *Historica calamitatum*. Héloïse's deeply interiorised history of her experiences mirrored the personal and particular histories to which later women writers were drawn. Likewise in **Christine de Pizan**'s *L' Avision Christine* (1405) Christine outlined her personal and public achievements in the world since childhood, but also drew on a wide knowledge of French political history. In so doing she paralleled her own story with that of France – which she described as an unhappy widow fallen on hard times. Other autobiographical accounts surfaced in different forums. Later Francophone author Eleanor de Poitiers in her *Les Etats de France* combined memoirs and instruction in her manual of the elaborate etiquette rituals at the fifteenth-century court of Burgundy, intended for the edification of younger noblewomen. Eleanor's description of ceremonial conduct offered a unique female account that differed from those of contemporary male chroniclers and revealed how gender caused even the most rigid court rituals of France and Burgundy to fluctuate.

The turbulent politics of the Reformation allowed women to produce texts that were less inward-looking and more concerned with present-focused historical events. Religious and civil warfare between Catholics and Protestants over the course of the later sixteenth century in France led to destruction, struggles and changes to everyday life in both urban and rural areas. Those who had first-hand experience of these events found a ready audience for their historical memoirs and commentaries which were widely disseminated by printers and publishers, eager for profit. Women who held power, such as Jeanne d'Albret, Queen of Navarre, produced *Ample déclaration sur la jonction de ses armes des Reformés en 1568*, a memoir of the turbulent decade of the 1560s in which she justified her actions as queen and leader of the Huguenot forces in France. Marguerite de Valois, sister of three French monarchs and queen herself, compiled her *Mémoires de la roine Marguerite* towards the end of the sixteenth century (published 1628) in which she reviewed her role in the world of political intrigue at court.

The events of the later sixteenth century, however, affected more than just monarchs. Abbess of the Poor Clares of Geneva, Jeanne de Jussie, composed *Le Commencement de l'hérésie de Geneve* (c.1611), a retrospective history of her convent's struggle to maintain a Catholic monastic institution in the Protestant city of Geneva. Although the sisters were eventually forced to relocate to Annecy in France, Jussie's account presented a triumphant vision of Catholic solidarity against the heretical message of the Genevan reformers. Françoise Guyart, a nun in the Annonciades convent at Bourges, began in the 1560s a history of that order's foundations under Jeanne de France, the very decade in which Jeanne's tomb was desecrated in Protestant attacks. Both Jussie and Guyart's texts presented different ways in which the spiritual focus of Catholic institutions could be galvanised through historical writing during the religious troubles. At a time when nuns were encouraged to retreat from public discussion and view, religious women's narratives often emphasised the effects of religious turmoil on the interior 'domestic' life of the community, but their works simultaneously indicated a desire to recognise women's experiences in the historical narrative of their era.

Both Catholic and Protestant laywomen were inspired by religious fervour to produce other kinds of histories, which were circumscribed by domestic duties and limited access to historical records. Protestant women used family history to commemorate relatives lost or to demonstrate God's mercy in protecting the family members, particularly after the St Bartholomew's Day Massacre of 1572. The massacre, an event that shocked Catholics and Protestants alike beyond the borders of France, had repercussions in England where

Anne Dowriche recounted the recent history of persecution of Huguenots in her poem 'The French History' (1589). Family histories by Catholic women, in which they documented births, marriages and deaths using easily accessible family records and their own memories, recounted tales of triumph for future generations of the family to emulate. Jeanne du Laurens composed her *La Généalogie des Messieurs du Laurens* (1631), a tale of hard work and persistence against life challenges, in what was ostensibly the history of her father and brothers, one of whom became physician to the king, Henri IV. Du Laurens' depiction of her widowed mother's exemplary work in keeping the family together and allowing her sons to pursue medical studies also embedded the significance of women's familial duties into the national narrative.

Memory and fiction in the seventeenth century

The definitions of official 'state history' became increasingly regulated under the patronage of powerful Bourbon monarchs over the seventeenth and eighteenth centuries. Louis XIV in particular commissioned court historians to produce history that was defined by his own presence and focused on royal acts, achievements and official documentation (Beasley 1990: 11–20). Women who wished to contribute to the historical record of their own time, as well as shaping the predominant historical narrative, were not able to procure such commissions, although many found other ways to offer an alternative to the scope of official history.

Eyewitness accounts by women, particularly in the form of memoirs, continued to be a dominant method by which women participated in creating the historical record of their century. Louise Bourgeois' *Récit véritable de la naissance de Messeigneurs et Dames les Enfants de France* (1617), **memoirs** of her work as midwife to Queen Marie de Medici, highlighted the intrigues of court life. Her domain of expertise and commentary largely concerned the court medical and household community with whom she worked. Françoise Bertaut, dame de Motteville, was a lady-in-waiting to Queen Anne of Austria. After the death of her mistress, Motteville composed her *Mémoires pour servir à l'histoire d'Anne d'Autriche* (1723), an historical account of the queen from notes she had maintained during Anne's lifetime. Motteville, like Bourgeois before her, claimed that her distinctive working relationship with the monarch gave her memoirs a particular validity and uniqueness. As male historians increasingly sought out archival administrative evidence to document the nation's past, women drew upon their personal experiences and memories of the particular to offer a different perspective on court life.

Other memoir writers were noblewomen who wrote about the political and social history of particular movements such as the Fronde. This was a rebellion driven by the elite protesting the power and influence of the regent Anne of Austria's favoured minister, Jules Mazarin. Because male-authored accounts of such political events obscured or ignored women's roles, women sought to insert themselves in these narratives through memoirs recording their political involvement. 'La Grande Mademoiselle', Anne-Marie-Louise-Henriette d'Orléans, cousin of Louis XIV, produced *Mémoires* (1718) spread over four volumes, emphasising her own central significance to the official history of France, and creating a subversive counter-history to that of the monarch (Beasley 1990: 123–4). Marguerite-Jeanne Cordier, Baronne de Staal-Delaunay, who served the powerful Duchesse du Maine, wrote of her first-hand knowledge of the political intrigues at court in *The Mémoires de Madame de Staal-Delaunay* (1775). Other elite women wrote memoirs both inside and outside the court, which were less concerned with the political intrigues but rather commented upon the social mores of their time. Some women used memoirs to highlight the sexual politics of the court, as did Marthe-Marguerite de Villette de Murcay, Marquise de Caylus, in her *Souvenirs* (1770) of Louis XIV's court. The *Mémoiris* written by Madame du Hausset provide an important corrective on the relationship between Louis XV and his influential mistress, the Marquise de Pompadour. Hausset was able to observe Pompadour's fragile grasp on power in the corrupt and decadent surroundings of Louis XV's Court.

Women's memoirs also explored the realm of emotional relationships of the individuals and events they recounted. In doing so they, like sixteenth-century women's personal religious history of salvation and trauma, contributed to the more self-reflexive focus of later autobiographical works. Women's emphasis on the significance of sentiment as a means to understand motivations in history also was pursued through historical fiction. **Madeleine de Scudéry**'s epic historical novels such as *Clélie, histoire romaine* (1654–1660) and *Artamène ou Le Grand Cyrus* (1649–1653) may have been set in ancient times, but the social world they evoked was that of seventeenth-century France. Over the course of the century, the favoured chronological and geographical location of such historical fictions shifted from the exotic and classical to the more recent and local. Increasingly, female historians chose to examine the immediate past of their own nation, focusing particularly on the French courts of the sixteenth century. In doing so, authors' claims to a new kind of historical focus were drawn closer to the history of the nation. The tales of monarchs and court life of the sixteenth century produced by Charlotte-Rose Caumont de La Force such as her *Histoire secrète de Henry IV* (1695), *Histoire de Marguerite de Valois, reine de Navarre, soeur de Francois 1er* (1696) earned her a pension from the reigning monarch, Louis XIV. The best-known exponent of this genre was Marie-Madeleine Pioche de la Vergne, Comtesse de Lafayette, whose influential novel *La Princesse de Clèves* (1678) explored the psychological and social world of her own century providing unique insight into women's historical role. Fiction allowed women to produce a more imaginative and speculative form of history than that composed by contemporary male historians. Memoirs, historical fiction and secret histories could explore motivations of individuals and groups without reference to official records. By focusing on court intrigue and matters of sentiment, women fashioned a different perspective on the historical narrative proposed by royal history, one in which psychological and social analyses dominated acts and achievements in the public world.

Science, rationality and Enlightenment history

In the eighteenth century, the Enlightenment would impact on women's historical writings as they engaged with its ideals of independent truth. Best expressed through the contemporary Encyclopedia project, this philosophy, which espoused that all knowledge was to be questioned and verified by scientific methods of empirical observation, appeared to offer new possibilities for female historians to insert women (both as historians and agents) into the national narrative. A kind of scientific rational history developed whereby truth could be uncovered through methodical assessment of **archives.** Some women applied these methodologies to participate as equals in the production of the national historical discourse. Marie Charlotte Pauline Robert de Lézardière pursued exacting requirements for documentary evidence in her *Théorie des loix politiques de la monarchie française* (1792), her four-volume study of French political, institutional and legal history. Other female historians conducted rigorous archival research to reconstruct the experiences of women in the French past. Marie-Geneviève-Charlotte Darlus Thiroux d'Arconville produced her *Vie de Marie de Médici* (1774) based on study of manuscripts and documents in the royal library (Davis 1980: 167). As a scientific scholar, as well as through her work translating male-authored historical texts, d'Arconville was exposed to the conventions of impartial proof developing in the sciences and in the professionalised 'science of history'. However, for many female authors, access to archival sources would still prove a bar to their ability to produce this kind of history.

The era also produced new narratives of human progress suggesting that all civilisations could be charted by a constant, atemporal series of levels, ending with the pinnacle of achievement, the Enlightenment in Europe. One measure of human progress was the status of women. Widespread public debate deliberated about what constituted appropriate education and civil rights for women, since an enlightened nation required educated but obedient women to raise the civilised citizenry of the future. This sparked a renewed interest among male historians for charting a separate, and usually emancipatory, history of women. In such histories women were rarely represented as agents of historical change in their own right, but as passive recipients of the increasing social and political advantages bestowed upon them by men (Spongberg 2002: 54). In response, women historians frequently aimed to show the influence of women themselves as social and political agents who could shape, as well as be shaped by, historical events. In her *Eloges des illustres savantes anciennes et modernes* (1668) Marguerite Buffet produced a history of eminent women known for their eloquence and conversational abilities in which she argued that women's linguistic abilities could be a source of equality with men. Madame de Coicy continued to emphasise the influence of women throughout history, from antiquity to the pre-revolutionary era, in her work *Les Femmes comme il convient de les voir* (1787). As an 18-year-old, **Louise-Felicité Guynement de Kéralio [Robert]** produced the *Collection des meilleurs ouvrages français composés par des femmes* (1786–1789), a 12-volume history of literary texts composed by women in which she pursued the notion that women had a separate but equally important history in need of public recognition. Kéralio's works won her wide fame as an historian, and she was elected to the Academy of Arts in 1787. In such texts, women gave recognition to a long tradition of female contributions to history, particularly a sophisticated literary history, and participated in contemporary debate on female education by demonstrating via historical examples the manifold advantages to the French nation of civilised and educated women.

Revolution and liberty in France

Elite female historians of the late eighteenth century often reflected the broad education and free speech that they experienced in the mixed-sex salon culture of the era. The period of the Revolution produced an array of historical texts by women. Some women continued to use memoirs to voice a particular perspective on the national narrative, and were concerned to rehabilitate the reputation of the *ancien régime* court and particularly its leading individuals. Jeanne-Louise-Henriette Genest Campan produced *Mémoires sur la vie privée de la Reine Marie Antoinette* (1823), a sympathetic portrait of her mistress, the queen Marie-Antoinette. Béatrix-Etiennette Renart de Fuchsamberg d'Omblimont de Lage de Volude, a noblewoman attached as a companion to the Princesse de Lamballe in the last decade of the *ancien régime* wrote *Souvenirs d'émigration de Madame la marquise de Lage de Volude, dame de S.A.S. Madame la Princesse de Lamballe, 1792–1794* (1869), memoirs that spoke of the experiences of elite families who were forced into exile as the Revolution took hold. As national history was made in the court environments to which elite women had access, their memoirs and those of their retainers treated these themes as a matter of course.

Other women celebrated the fall of the monarchy and embraced the possibilities the Revolution seemed to offer women for liberty and equality in its first few years. Kéralio pursued her interest in women's history, writing unsympathetically of the crimes of French queens in her *Les Crimes des reines de la France* (1791). English women were instrumental in the early historicisation of the Revolution. Both **Helen Maria Williams** and **Mary Wollstonecraft** lived in Paris as the bloody events unfolded, and their reportage and documentation of the Revolution's social and intellectual origins were vital to its perception abroad. While foreigners looked on in horror at the barbarity of some revolutionary acts, Williams, a supporter of the moderate Girondin party, pleaded the Republican cause, crafting a carefully balanced history of the Revolution's intellectual thought and cultural developments in her *Letters from France* (1790, 1792, 1796). After witnessing the cruelty and continued poverty firsthand, Wollstonecraft argued in *Moral and Historical View of the Origin of the Revolution* (1794) with measured optimism that the human potential for good and the attempt to create a more equitable form of government would be the Revolution's enduring legacy. Responsible for producing some of the first British accounts of the Revolution, both women were crucial in providing recognition of its intellectual and social merits to a sceptical foreign readership.

The historical analyses of Helvetian **Anne-Louise-Germaine de Staël** straddled both historical themes of rehabilitative history and revolutionary celebration of the possibilities for liberty. In her work on the French Revolution, de Staël examined the role of her father, Jacques Necker, who had been a key finance minister in the government of Louis XVI and served in the first years of the Revolution. De Staël had both direct knowledge of contemporary economic, political and social transitions, and a personal interest in understanding and shaping the historical construction of events in which her own family were involved. Moreover, the work celebrated how women could participate in revolutionary ideals of liberty through intellectual pursuits and dialogue. At first de Staël embraced what seemed like new possibilities for liberty and learning. Increasingly, however, she became disillusioned with the growing tyranny of the Napoleonic regime. Her Romantic vision of the possibility of a history and identity for Germany, *De L'Allemagne* (1810) posited a radical alternative to the hegemony of the aggrandising Napoleonic empire and a critique of Napoleon's personal imperial aspirations. De Staël's identification of politically and culturally distinct nation states was feared as so influential that Napoleon ordered the text to be pulped in 1810.

Eight years later, de Staël wrote her *Considerations sur les principaux événements de la Révolution* (1818) which celebrated both her father's and her own role in the early stages of the Revolution. The nineteenth century saw female historians beginning to offer a critical view of the Revolution's success, dissecting the reasons why it had not delivered its promised liberty and equality for their sex. Marie d'Agoult, Comtesse de Flavigny, held an elite salon where republican ideals and radical politics were debated amongst its members, some of whom were leading historians of her day. She believed that women, like the working class, could be involved in the processes of democracy if given appropriate education, and identified this as one of the failures of the French Revolution, which contributed to the later events of the 1848 Revolution. Although she offered a critical perspective on the Revolution's claims to equality in texts such as *Essai de la Liberté* (1847) and *Histoire de la Révolution de 1848* (1850–1853), she still held out hope for a republic in which both male and female educated citizenry could participate.

Nineteenth-century amateurs and educators

Biographical works, particularly of women, abounded from the pens of female historians in nineteenth-century France. Fanny de Mongellaz, in her study of the influence of women on the manners and destiny of nations, *De l'influence des femmes sur les moeurs et les destinées des nations* (1828), and Henriette Guizot de Witt in her study of 'women in history', *Les Femmes dans l'histoire* (1888), emphasised women's impact on recognised historical events. Women also pursued a separatist agenda claiming that women had a history of their own. Fortunée Briquet's *Dictionnaire historique, littéraire et bibliographique des françaises et étrangères naturalisées en France* (1804), an historical dictionary of women, supported an important separatist claim to women's history. In such works, female historians demonstrated the influence of women in French history, but they were also laying claim to a different narrative of history – one that emphasised the importance of other events in the lives of French women.

Female historians also chose exemplary women in history whose lives could be used for the edification of female, juvenile and religious readers. Adélaïde-Gillette Billet Dufrenoy composed collections of short stories about the lives of French women in history as well as her biographies of famous young women of history, designed as a pedagogical text of exemplary models for her adolescent readers to emulate such as *Biographies des jeunes demoiselles ou vie des femmes célèbres* (1816) and *Françaises* (1818). Mathilde Bourdon's historical subjects were frequently female saintly religious leaders in France's history such as St Genevieve, St Radegund and St Jeanne de Valois. Adélaïde Celliez also produced *Les Saintes de France* (1853) as well as a series of royal lives such as *Les Reines de France* (1846), *Les Reines d'Angleterre* (1852), *Les Reines d'Espagne* (1856) and *Les Impératrices. France, Russie, Autriche, Brésil* (1860). In such historical literature, nineteenth-century women adopted a different agenda to their Revolutionary and Romantic predecessors. Female biographers used historical protagonists to define a quintessential and ahistorical feminine virtue that could then be used prescriptively. It was through these specifically feminine virtues that women could impact upon French history, as did Joan of Arc, the humble peasant girl whose purity, innocence and chastity enabled her to alter the course of the entire French nation. Since the virtues their works extolled for female readers were recognised by contemporaries as appropriate and desirable characteristics in women, female biographers wrote from a moral, rather than intellectual, truth and authority. This was a different kind of contribution that was proposed by male professional historians.

Access to local sources, rather than national archives, gave 'amateur' women historians opportunities to create regional and local histories. Albertine Clément-Hémery argued, in her detailed histories of local customs of France such as *Histoire des fêtes civiles et religieuses, des usages anciens et modernes du département du Nord* (1834) and *Histoire des fêtes civiles et religieuses, usages anciens et modernes de la Flandre* (1845), that local, social and cultural dynamics could impact on a national scale. Increasingly over the nineteenth century and into the twentieth century, a number of women began to produce local, autobiographical and observational works that documented lives of those beyond the elite. Marguerite Donquichotte, who wrote as Marguerite Audoux, described her childhood as an orphan and servant in the rural Sologne region in works such as *Marie-Claire* (1910) and *L'Atelier de Marie-Claire* (1920). Women's belief that their life stories were of value to the historical record marked an important change, as French history was democratised to include the experiences of a wider sector of the population. Female historians provided detailed local and personal studies that framed French history with new perspectives and narratives.

Women and the academy

Towards the end of the nineteenth century, education for women was being increasingly promoted as achieving similar moral and domestic aims for the French nation as female biographers argued in the texts of their female protagonists. With the promotion of a new intellectual women's syllabus from the 1880s, women could begin to make inroads into the academic institutions where professionalised history was being produced, although paid employment within the discipline remained elusive (Davis 1992: 121–37). Women were often heavily involved as researchers, editors and writers in the production of male historians' works. The successive wives of university lecturer and politician François Guizot researched and prepared lectures for him, and the family's daughters, Pauline and Henriette Guizot de Witt, both became published historical writers. Athénaïs Michelet, second wife of the historian Jules Michelet, researched for his historical texts and supervised publications after his death (Smith 1998: 83–101). This 'handmaiden status' was replicated in the twentieth century, where women were crucial to the historical work produced by the *Annales* school. The contributions of women such as Lucie Varga, Suzanne Febvre, Thérèse Sclafert, Yvonne Bézard, Eugénie Droz, Germaine Rouillard and Paule Pradel, sometimes as wives, lovers, friends and students of academic historians, were often not recognised in the historical works produced by such men as Marc Bloch, Lucien Febvre and Fernand Braudel; yet their influence on such works has helped to shape modern French academic historical writing and practice (Davis 1992: 121–37).

Feminism was embedded in the intellectual institutions of France rather earlier than many other Western nations. **Simone de Beauvoir**'s highly influential ideas exposed in *Le Deuxième Sexe* (1949), a radical feminist philosophical work in which she argued that women were constructed as the 'other' by men and that their oppression was linked to their bodies, were later absorbed into the feminist movement's organised campaigns in the late 1960s for abortion and contraceptive rights. Political and social concerns of both popular and intellectual feminist groups, such as *Mouvement pour la libération des femmes* (MLF), were one of many causes championed during the dramatic May 1968 student and workers' protests in France. Female historians sought answers to these contemporary interests by examining Frenchwomen's sexual and reproductive history. However, the ahistoricity of Beauvoir's arguments that the locus of oppression is universally to be found in women's bodies and the relationships between men and women has been problematic. In works such as *La raison des femmes* (1992) and *Muse de la raison* (1994) historian and philosopher Geneviève Fraisse has explored the historicity of sexual difference itself and seeks to establish a new starting point for the history of French women than difference between the sexes.

The status of feminism as an intellectual tradition in the academy has enabled many historians to pursue an explicitly feminist agenda within the professionalised history discourse. Academics such as Michelle Perrot have taught the history of women in French universities since 1973. Women's history adopted, then adapted, many of the techniques of conventional academic history, increasingly pursuing new avenues of research, re-evaluating types of source materials, and contributing alternative scope and visions. From her foundations in nineteenth-century French social history and class struggles, Perrot now draws upon anthropological and ethnological standpoints to explore how women, largely excluded from the public sphere, created a material history and record of their individuality and subjectivity through objects such as clothes. In these ways, women such as Perrot have complicated the philosophical underpinnings of French history inside and outside the academy.

The history of women in France has been characterised by a highly interdisciplinary approach, as French historians have absorbed sociological, anthropological and *Annalistes* insights into their interpretative frameworks. Trained as an archivist, Edith Thomas has produced a diverse range of historical studies, from short stories and novels, to more academic texts such as *Jeanne d'Arc* (1947) and *Les Femmes de 1848* (1948). Her work focused on female protagonists as diverse as the Bible heroines, George Sand, Louise Michel and the female arsonists of the 1848 Revolution. Academic sociologist Evelyne Sullerot, perhaps best known for her texts on the history of women's working lives and conditions such as *Histoire et sociologie du travail féminin* (1968), has more recently turned to novels and autobiography as forms of historical expression.

The **Revolution** – perhaps more than any other single moment in French history – has undergone major revision as a result of the work of feminist historians internationally, who have questioned its role in women's social, economic and political emancipation. Olwen Hufton in *Women and the Limits of Citizenship* (1992) and Christine Faure in *Démocratie sans les femmes* (1991) have highlighted the limitations of revolutionary claims to democracy for women, while Joan B Landes has analysed theoretical and practical challenges to restrictive republican ideas brought about by radical female activism during the Revolution in *Women and the Public Sphere* (1988). Mona Ozouf has examined the interplay of gender in revolutionary politics and discourse in *La fête* *révolutionnaire, 1789–1799* (1976), while Sarah Maza has foregrounded the politicisation of a gendered domestic morality in *Private Lives and Public Affairs* (1993). Their views add to the debate about the novelty of the revolutionaries' ideas – particularly in regard to the political and social status of women, as well as other marginalised groups.

History and memory

In understanding more recent events of French history, women have challenged the status of memory and oral histories as valid historical sources, particularly for the recognition of marginalised voices. Women, whether professional historians or not, have broken down strictly conceived boundaries of conventional academic history. Many female authors in the twentieth century have found in the novel a freedom to record loosely autobiographical works. Here they explore psychological and emotional relationships with no emphasis on documentary evidence to support their positions. The *nouveau roman* innovations that exploit the interplay between truth and fiction have also had impact in the domain of historical writing. Marguerite Donnadieu, writing as Marguerite Duras, examines the significance of the act and context of writing on meanings and use of historical memories by re-visioning her own life experiences in different textual spaces in works such as *L'Amant* (1984) and *L'Amant de la Chine du nord* (1991). In so doing women writers have problematised the boundaries of conventional historical writing as well as the underlying conception of history itself.

Debates over the subjective value of memory and of the notion of truth have highlighted and challenged autobiography specifically as a form of historical writing, but also raised questions about the objectivity of an historical truth more generally. France's occupation during the Second World War and the experiences of its Jewish citizens have been highly influential on France's collective post-war identity. Female writers and historians have contributed to France's national memories of trauma, persecution and resistance, by experimenting with the borderlands between autobiography, history and fiction. Novelist Elisabeth Gille has explored the possibilities for speculative historical work in her fictional autobiography of her mother who died in Auschwitz, *Le Mirador* (1992).

Women's historical works examining postcolonial narratives have also helped to shape the changing identity of the French colonial empire, particularly since conflicts in French Indochina and Algeria in the 1950s and 1960s. Fatima-Zohra Imalayène, who writes as Assia Djebar, proposes a new vision of Algerian history, interweaving this with her own personal narrative in texts such as *L'amour, la fantasia* (1985), *Ombre sultane* (1987) and *Loin de Medine* (1991). Djebar contributes historical insight into the exploitation and role of Algerian women over the past two centuries. She merges the experiences of individuals' lived experiences with the broader national history created by study of its archives. Through the work of female historians, the experiences of the displaced marginal and the female are beginning to be recognised and included in the national narrative of migration and postcolonialism in the later twentieth century.

Susan Broomhall

References

Beasley 1990; Davis 1980, 1992; Smith 1998; Spongberg 2002.

Related essays

Convents; Memoir; Nation; Revolution; Secret History.

Fuller [Sarah] Margaret 1810–1850 American journalist, social critic, translator, historian of women. Born Cambridge, Massachusetts, the oldest of eight children of Margarett Crane, teacher, and Timothy Fuller, lawyer. Tutored at home by her father who had read **Mary Wollstonecraft**, Fuller learned Greek, Latin, French, logic and rhetoric at an early age. She attended various private schools in Cambridgeport and Boston, completing her schooling at Miss Prescott's Young Ladies Seminary at Groton in 1824. Unable to attend university, Fuller maintained a process of self-education, throwing herself into the social and cultural life of Cambridge. In 1825 she met **Lydia Maria Child** at the salon of Harvard professor George Ticknor. Together they read the works of **Madame de Staël**. Throughout her life Fuller was influenced by and emulated de Staël, earning herself the title the 'Yankee Corinne'.

Interested in **Romanticism** Fuller began to study German in 1832 and within a year had read the major works of Goethe, Tieck, Schiller and Novalis. In 1834 her first publication, a reply to the historian George Bancroft, appeared in the *North American Review*. In this essay she questioned Bancroft's depiction of Brutus in an essay he had published on slavery in ancient Rome. Her methods in this essay, particularly her revision of classical sources, foreshadowed her style in later historical writing. Around this time Fuller began a translation of Goethe's *Torquato Tasso* and planned to travel to Europe to gather materials to write a biography of Goethe. Her father's sudden death in 1835 left the family in straitened circumstances. To support the family Fuller taught at private schools in Boston and Providence, a task she found onerous. To supplement her income Fuller held her series of 'Conversations' (between 1838 and 1844), a series of classes designed to supply 'a point of union to the well-educated and thinking women' of Boston, so that they might acquire 'the precision in which our sex are so deficient'. It was attended by **Lydia Maria Child** who encouraged Fuller to become involved in abolitionism and **Caroline Dall** who wrote an historical account of her experience, *Margaret and Friends* (1895). **Elizabeth Cady Stanton** said of Fuller's 'Conversations' that they had been 'a vindication of a woman's right to think'.

In 1839 Fuller published a translation of Eckermann's *Conversations with Goethe*. She also began to translate the correspondence of Karoline Gunderode and Bettine von Arnim, two German aristocratic women intellectuals. Although she never completed this task, a slim volume of her translation appeared in 1842. (Fuller also wrote on these women in 'Bettina Brentano and her friend Gunderode' [1842], an essay idealising female friendship for the *Dial*.) Friendship with Ralph Waldo Emerson led to engagement with Transcendental philosophy. In 1840 she began her career as editor, working with Emerson and George Ripley on the *Dial*, journal of the Transcendental club. In a number of essays Fuller wrote for the *Dial*, women were the subject. Her most famous essay, 'The Great Lawsuit: Man versus Men. Woman versus Women', was published after her resignation as editor. The arguments made in this essay underpinned her most famous work, *Woman in the Nineteenth Century* (1845). In 1843 Fuller travelled through Illinois, Michigan and Wisconsin, writing of her experience in *Summer on the Lakes* (1843), a hybrid text that merged travelogue with poetry and social commentary.

Like 'The Great Law Suit', *Summer on the Lakes* demonstrated Fuller's growing concern with women's position in American society. These texts won Fuller the attention of New York publisher Horace Greeley and he offered her a place on his staff at the *New York Tribune*. Greeley also encouraged Fuller to expand 'The Great Law Suit' into a book. Moving to New York in 1844 Fuller became the *Tribune's* literary editor and the first woman critic to earn a living from her journalism. In this capacity she also wrote often on women in essays of social criticism on subjects such as 'benevolent' institutions and prostitution. She also favourably reviewed the work of other women such as Child, **Anna Jameson** and George Sand. *Woman in the Nineteenth Century* appeared in 1845. While not a systematic history of women, *Woman in the Nineteenth Century* represents a major feminist revision of history anticipating many of the themes that occupied historians of women for the next century. Trained in Classics, Fuller criticised masculinist interpretations of history, re-reading ancient sources to present women's role in the public sphere more favourably and to undercut male arguments about women's inferiority. Fuller also presented a diverse group of historical women (Semiramis, Sappho, **Mary Wollstonecraft**) to demonstrate women's power and influence. She pointedly depicted the invidiousness of women's unequal social status, likening it to slavery. *Woman in the Nineteenth Century* helped 'set the tone, if not the precise agenda for the Seneca Falls convention in 1848', making it a landmark text in American feminism.

Visiting Europe in 1846 as a correspondent for the *Tribune*, Fuller expanded her network of like-minded women. In England she met with **Harriet Martineau** and Jane Carlyle, and in France with socialist-feminists, such as Clarisse Vigoureux, Pauline Roland and George Sand. She also met a number of revolutionary exiles such as the Italian patriot Guiseppe Mazzini and Polish poet Adam Mickiewicz, who told her that her 'mission' was 'to contribute to the deliverance of the Polish, French and American woman'. In 1847 Fuller travelled to Italy becoming an eyewitness to the revolution unfolding there. Reporting her excitement at these events in dispatches to *The Tribune*, she noted that she 'would gladly be its historian'. While in Italy Fuller married Giovanni Ossoli, an Italian aristocrat and nationalist, although the date of the wedding has never been established. A son was born in September 1848. In 1849 she joined her husband in Rome, where he was engaged in republican service as Captain of the Civic Guard. During the siege of Rome Fuller worked with the **Princess Belgiojoso**, nursing those who fell defending the city. Her last work, a history of the Italian revolution, appears to have been influenced by Mary Wollstonecraft and **Madame de Staël**, as it was to have included 'extended observations upon the Social, Political, Religious and Aesthetical condition' of Italy. The manuscript was lost when Fuller died at sea returning from Europe.

After her death 'Margaret Fuller Clubs' sprang up all over the United States. Elizabeth Cady Stanton and **Susan B Anthony** wrote that Fuller 'possessed more influence upon the thought of American woman than any woman previous to her time'. Ralph Waldo Emerson, James Freeman Clarke and William Henry Channing pieced together fragments from an autobiographical sketch (1840), letters and journal entries to produce the unreliable *Memoirs of Margaret Fuller Ossoli* (1852). Emerson sold more copies of these **memoirs** than any of his other works. Fuller was also the subject of several biographies in the late nineteenth century, including T W Higginson's sympathetic biography *Margaret Fuller Ossoli* (1884) which went through nine editions and Julia Ward Howe's *Margaret Fuller, Marchesa Ossoli* (1884).

Second-wave **feminism** saw renewed interest in Fuller, with Bell Gale Chevigny publishing her study of Fuller, *The Woman and the Myth*, in 1976. More recently Donna Dickenson produced the first full-length critical study of Fuller's writing, *Margaret Fuller: Writing a Woman's Life* (1993).

Mary Spongberg

References

Capper 1992; Dickenson 1993; Kelley 1994; Reynolds & Smith 1991.

Major works

Woman in the Nineteenth Century (ed.) Larry J Reynolds (New York: W W Norton, 1997) and Margaret Fuller's European dispatches for the *New York Tribune* have been published as *These Sad but Glorious Days: Dispatches from Europe 1846–1850* (eds) Larry J Reynolds & Susan Belasco Smith (New Haven: Yale University Press, 1991).

G

Gage, Matilda Joslyn 1826–1898

US women's rights leader, lecturer, writer and historian. Born in Cicero, New York, only child of Helen Leslie and physician Hezekiah (Joslyn), a supporter of woman suffrage, abolition, temperance and free thought. Educated by her father and at the Clinton Liberal Institute, New York, she made unsuccessful attempts to gain a medical education in 1843–1844. Married Cicero merchant Henry H Gage in 1845 and had five children. Lived in Syracuse and Manlius before settling in Fayetteville, New York. A close friend of **Elizabeth Cady Stanton** since she spoke on women's intellectual abilities at the National Woman's Rights Convention in Syracuse in 1852. She was an original member of the National Woman Suffrage Association (NWSA) in 1869 and vice president and secretary of the New York State Woman Suffrage Association. She became president of both associations in 1875. She contributed to the NWSA's newspaper *The Revolution* and testified before House and Senate committees.

Gage was a writer and intellectual with a strong historical sensibility. In 1870 she published a pamphlet on *Woman as Inventor*. In 1876 she wrote, with Stanton and **Susan B Anthony**, the *Woman's Declaration of Rights* read at the 1876 Independence Day celebration in Philadelphia. She edited and published the NWSA's opinionated monthly newspaper, *National Citizen and Ballot Box*, from 1878 to 1881. From 1876 to 1884 she worked with Stanton and Anthony on the first three volumes of the six-volume *History of Woman Suffrage* (1881–1922). Gage's 1881 essay 'Preceding Causes' provided the first chapter of the *History*, placing the woman's rights movement within a historical context in which church and state were twin barriers to human rights. She contributed two other chapters: the final chapter of the first volume on 'Woman, Church, and State' and 'Women's Patriotism in the War', the opening chapter of Volume II. Gage shared Stanton's opposition to misogynist religious teachings and like her, she concentrated her intellectual energies on this issue in the 1890s. In 1890 she left the NWSA to found the Woman's National Liberal Union whose objectives combined woman suffrage, exposure of the religious denigration of women and the fight for a constitutional amendment guaranteeing the separation of church and state. In 1893 she published the scholarly and widely read *Woman, Church and State*.

Her gravestone read: 'There is a word sweeter than Mother, Home, or Heaven; that word is Liberty.' Her life and work were dedicated to elucidating the history of the repression of women's liberty in order to gain legal, economic, political and intellectual freedom for women. Her Woman Suffrage Scrapbooks are housed in the Library of Congress.

Desley Deacon

References

Leach 1980; *NAW* 1971; Willard & Livermore 1893.

Major works

Elizabeth Cady Stanton, Susan B Anthony & Matilda Joselyn Gage's *History of Woman Suffrage* (Salem: Ayer Co., 1985).

Gender

Gender operates as an analytic concept in a wider field of study denoted by related concepts such as 'women' and 'men', 'male' and 'female', 'masculinity' and 'femininity', 'sex' and 'sexuality'. It usually denotes the social, cultural and historical distinctions between men and women, and is sometimes described as the study of masculinity and femininity.

Modern usage of the term 'gender' emerged first in sexology and psychoanalysis in the 1960s, in the work of Alex Comfort (*Sex in Society*, 1963) and Robert Stoller (*Sex and Gender*, 1968). Following Stoller in particular, sex came to be regarded as the biological foundation of male–female differences, while gender was a social and cultural construction. This separating of biology and culture provided the Women's Liberation movement with an intellectual basis for repudiating biological determinism and asserting the possibility of sexual equality. Gender was what made it possible to think of a future different from the past and the present.

Feminists saw all societies, past and present, as having valued and treated the two sexes differently, creating, in Gayle Rubin's term, a 'sex/gender system'. For feminist historians, specifically, their task was to explain the origins, development and universality of this system. Yet it took some time for historians to truly adopt the 'gender' part of 'sex/gender system'. In the early years of the new women's history, historians usually spoke more freely of 'women's oppression', 'sex role differentiation', 'male domination' and 'patriarchy'. An early but fleeting use of 'gender' by an historian is evident in Natalie Zemon Davis' '"Women's History" in Transition: The European Case' which stressed that women's history provided new understandings of power and social structure. It was important, she wrote, to 'understand the significance of the sexes, of gender groups in the historical past' (1976: 90). 'Gender' was still on the margins in **Joan Kelly**'s influential 'The Social Relation of the Sexes: Methodological Implications of Women's History' (1976) published that same year. Rather than gender, she wrote of the 'social relation of the sexes', and 'the roles and positions women hold in society by comparison with those of men'. After criticising attempts to categorise women as a class, caste or minority group, she writes 'we are a sex', refers to 'categorization by gender' and 'the sexual order'. She also writes of the social order as patriarchal.

By the 1980s, these somewhat clumsy formulations were being replaced by 'gender'. Elizabeth Fox-Genovese, in 'Placing Women's History in History' (1982), said historians would need henceforth to 'adopt gender system as a fundamental category of historical analysis'. She emphasised 'the mutability of gender systems', warning that it is 'fruitless to look for a uniform oppression of women, or a universal form of male dominance' (1982: 15). Fox-Genovese's approach was strongly Marxist with its stress on structures and systems; when Joan Scott made some somewhat similar points a year later, she was influenced by poststructuralist approaches derived from French theorists such as Foucault, Derrida, Kristeva, Lacan, and Irigaray rather than Marxism. This meant a new emphasis on discourses and identity, and a turning away from a notion of social structure as something underlying the surface of society. In 'Gender: A Useful Category of Historical Analysis' (1986), Scott opposed feminism's common binary opposition between men and women as two distinct social groups and argued that gender history could be anywhere, including political history. Her essay was enormously influential, and during the second half of the 1980s 'gender' increasingly replaced all the earlier formulations. Also important for historians' changing and increasing use of 'gender' was the work of political theorist Judith Butler in *Gender Trouble* (1990), which emphasised 'gender' as a *process*, a doing, as something that is performed in daily life. Gendered subjectivity, Butler suggested, is produced in a series of competing discourses, rather than by a single patriarchal ideology, and gender relations are a process involving strategies and counter-strategies of power. Butler's work led to a growing fashion for speaking of 'gendering' and 'engendering', and of 'engendered' social processes.

With growing attention to the effects of race, and a continuing interest in class, historians were finding it increasingly difficult to manage the separate dimensions of gender, race and class. By the 1990s there was a turn away from adding these to one another, or trying to decide which was more important or determinative of the others. Instead, historians tried rather to grasp their intersection and mutual construction. This new emphasis on gender in a way which avoided both binary and additive modes of analysis made it a much more flexible (though some might argue, less powerful) concept. One consequence was a new attention to **masculinity**. Another was a broadening of focus to almost any human activity.

Many feminist historians had noted the male-centredness of the discipline, in its concerns, membership and self-representation. Bonnie G Smith took this to a new level in *The Gender of History: Men, Women, and Historical Practice* (1998). Here, the gendered assumptions of the men who built the discipline, and the definitions of history that excluded much of women's historical writing, were analysed in detail.

Ann Curthoys

References

Butler 1990; Carroll 1976; Davis 1976; Fox-Genovese 1982; Kelly 1976; Rubin 1975; Scott 1986.

Gilman, Charlotte Perkins Stetson 1860–1935

American feminist, social reformer, historian of women. Born in Hartford, Connecticut. The third of four children of Mary (Westcott) and Frederick Beecher Perkins. She was the grand-niece of Catharine Beecher. Largely self-educated, she supplemented a few years of formal schooling by extensive reading, particularly in the fields of anthropology, sociology and economics. She also completed one year at the Rhode Island School of Design, paid for by her estranged father and justified as vocational education.

She married Charles Walter Stetson in 1884. One child, Katherine Beecher. She separated from her husband in 1890 and moved with her daughter to California. She was divorced in 1894. She married her cousin George Houghton Gilman of New York City in 1900. Gilman worked primarily as a lecturer. She traveled all over the Mid-West, sometimes speaking twice a day for a few dollars on a range of subjects including, 'Nationalism and Religion', 'Love', 'The Goodness of Common Men' and 'Womanhood Suffrage'. **Susan B Anthony** called her an extraordinary speaker.

Gilman was a member of the executive board of the Woman's Congress Association of the Pacific Coast which had been formed to interest women 'in matters which tend to improve moral and social conditions'. She participated actively in its first convention, held in 1894, on the theme 'Woman and the Affairs of the World as They Affect and Are Affected by Her'. The theme of the second conference was 'The Home'. She spoke on 'Organization in Home Industry', a subject she would later revisit in various published works. Through her involvement in the Woman's Congresses Gilman came to consider some of the most influential women of the movement. In 1912 with 25 other women she formed a club called Heterodoxy – a club for unorthodox women. It was a luncheon club located in Greenwich Village and its members embraced a wide range of political opinions and included married, heterosexual women, lesbians, free-love advocates, radicals and reformers of all kinds. Gilman wrote in her autobiography of her leaving the club that, 'when the heresies seemed to center on sex psychology and pacifism, I wearied of it'. She served on the National Advisory Council of the Woman's Party, a breakaway group of the National American Woman Suffrage Association (NAWSA) between 1916 and 1920.

Gilman wrote in a number of genres. Her best-known piece of fiction, *The Yellow Wallpaper*, a short story about insanity was published in January 1892 in the *New England Magazine*. In 1893 she published a slim volume of poetry, *In This Our World*. Other works of fiction include *What Diantha Did* (1910), *The Crux* (1911), *Moving the Mountain* (1911) and *Herland* (originally published in *Forerunner* in 1915). *Herland* was a **utopian** piece about a mythical country called 'Herland' populated only by women descended by parthenogenesis from an aboriginal virgin mother.

Gilman engaged history in a very broad and general sense, adopting a meta-narrative to underpin her theorizing about social, sexual and economic relationships between men, women and children in works such as *Women and Economics* (1898), *Human Work* (1904), *The Man-Made World; or Our Androcentric Culture* (1911) and *The Home* (1910). Gilman's main thesis which underpinned much of her work was interdisciplinary in its explanation of women's condition. Drawing on classical economics she argued first that the major influence in our lives is the way we earn a living, and second that all imbalance in society and the historical model and precedent for all subsequent inequities, including those based on class, is underpinned by what she termed the 'sexuo-economic relationship', a relationship between males and females (and peculiar to the human species alone) in which the female is dependent on the male for food. This formulation, presented in her book *Women and Economics* (1998), informed all of Gilman's subsequent work. In this work she traced women's economic autonomy from primitive cultures and argued that ultimately the distinctive attributes of men and women together created civilized culture. Her sense of history, as it is engaged in these arguments, however, is very general, and she was not concerned with the classic historical question of origins as such.

Gilman was the first to attempt to forge a new social philosophy by analyzing society through the prism of gender. She located the oppression of women and children in the home and in their economic subservience to men, arguing that women and children alike would benefit from wider participation in the public sphere and from greater autonomy. She sought to elevate the normally feminine responsibility of child rearing to a position of social importance equal to that of the public work of men. She saw beyond the sentimentality of marriage and motherhood and revealed the power dynamic that imprisoned women and children in the home. She argued for the complete and genuine equality and autonomy of both sexes, and she repudiated gender difference.

Historians Charles and **Mary Ritter Beard** suggested that she was the major intellectual leader of the struggle for women's rights almost exclusively championing women's suffrage. Her powerfully insightful critique of the material conditions of women's lives was particularly novel during the period in which she wrote and she anticipated a number of modern writers on the subject like **Simone de Beauvior** and Margaret Mead.

Gilman's autobiography *The Living of Charlotte Perkins Gilman* was published posthumously in 1935. Since then a number of biographical studies have been produced including Mary A Hill's *Charlotte Perkins Gilman: The Makings of a Radical Feminist* (1980) and Ann J Lane's *To Herland and Beyond: The Life and Work of Charlotte Perkins Gilman* (1990).

Sarah Howard

References

Degler 1956; Des Jardins 2003; Hill 1980; Kessler 1995; Lane 1990.

Great Britain

Despite the difficulties they have encountered both in the earlier periods and as history developed into a professionalised discipline, women have played a significant role in the development of British historiography and in the development of new historical fields, often in a variety of genres other than the conventional history book. They have also contributed to the development of new methodologies, being pioneers of archival research, scholarly editing of texts and social scientific approaches, and they have offered challenges to dominant historical orthodoxies, such as the 'Whig interpretation of history'. John Kenyon's 'History Men' have never been without their female counterparts.

The early modern period

British women were writers of history in a variety of genres between 1600 and 1800. Their focus was on person and place, the particular rather than the general, and the cultural and social rather than the political. They helped to develop a new dimension to humanist and Enlightenment historiographies, in which history was frequently quarried for lessons in princely and civic conduct during the turmoil of the Civil War and the subsequent political realignments of the eighteenth century. Many women played a role as family archivists and historians, as historians of convents, as folklorists and local historians. Women also contributed to the development of history writing in Great Britain through editing and translating texts: Elizabeth Elstob was the translator of an Anglo-Saxon homily (1709) and an Anglo-Saxon grammar (1715). She also provided George Ballard with many of the sources from which he drew his monumental *Memoirs of Several Ladies of Great Britain* (1756). Other writers explored cultural issues with an historical angle to them – Elizabeth Montagu, for instance, published an *Essay on the Writings and Genius of Shakespeare* (1769). Meanwhile, drawing on the French novelistic tradition of the **'secret history'**, **Delariviere Manley** wrote subversive contemporary history in the form of the satirical *roman a clef*: *The Secret History of Queen Zarah, and the Zarazians* (1705) that targeted Queen Anne's favourite, Sarah Churchill.

One emerging literary genre in which women pursued the past most energetically was the novel, in particular the Gothic novel. Clara Reeve's *The Champion of Virtue* (1777), better known as *The Old English Baron*, was one of the earliest examples of a Gothic novel by a woman writer, but of more interest is *The Recess; or, a Tale of Other Times* (1783–1785) by Sophia Lee. This recounted the tale of the (fictional) twin daughters of Mary Queen of Scots by her marriage to the Duke of Norfolk, apparently derived from an 'obsolete manuscript'. Their romantic passions for Lord Leicester and the Earl of Essex are doomed by their lovers' and Queen Elizabeth's thirst for power. In this text the harsh world of politics is opposed to and becomes the destroyer of the private sphere of love, familial and romantic, which is represented by their retreat, 'the recess' (Spencer 1986: 195–201). The novel thus presents an alternative fictional version of the past which creates a space for women who – as Catherine Morland famously points out in *Northanger Abbey* (1818) – received little attention in history books. The Gothic novel allowed other eighteenth-century women writers such as Ann Radcliffe – and, indeed, male writers – to focus on women's feelings and experiences within an historical setting.

Such novels often explored the issue of patriarchal domination through the persecution of the heroine by powerful male relatives, aristocratic seducers or sinister monks. This empathetic engagement with the persecuted heroine informed, and continues to inform, the biographies of historical 'victims' such as Mary Queen of Scots and (more recently) Diana, Princess of Wales. **Jane Austen**'s semi-serious partisanship in favour of Mary and her corresponding denigration of Elizabeth I in her *History of England* thus proved prophetic of much Romantic history writing by women. But women Romantic novelists championed the cause of persecuted nations as well as individuals. A transitional romance, *The Scottish Chiefs* (1810) by Jane Porter, which drew on Scottish legends to narrate the life of William Wallace, was an important precursor of the **historical fiction** of Walter Scott. But it can also be seen as an example of the regional or 'national tale', a genre in which Maria Edgeworth, author of *Castle Rackrent* (1800), and **Sydney Owenson, Lady Morgan**, author of *The Wild Irish Girl* (1806), both published. Porter's sympathies for suppressed and especially Celtic nationalism was further evidenced in *Thaddeus of Warsaw* (1803) and her play *Owen: Prince of Powys* (1822), and it can be no surprise that Napoleon banned the translation of such an anti-imperialist work as *The Scottish Chiefs*.

The outstanding figure among British women writers of the **Enlightenment** was **Catharine Sawbridge Macaulay**, the only woman to produce a multi-volumed political history. While many **Romantic women writers** tended to support the victims and lost causes of history and to disrupt Enlightenment narratives of improvement, Macaulay appeared to endorse them. Her *History of England* (1763–1783) offered a Whig revision of the English Revolution to counter Hume's reputedly Tory *History of England* (1754–1762). It was also more carefully researched in the primary sources than Hume's *History*. Macaulay showed little interest in the historical involvement or experience of women, but – when women figured positively in her text – they were shown adopting the role of the Republican matron, sternly sacrificing personal feelings for the greater good. So, rather than celebrating the alternative private sphere of family and feeling and attempting to regender the past, Macaulay called upon women to deserve their (limited) role in the public sphere and the political history book by the enactment of public and manly virtues (Hicks 2002). She also drew liberal intellectuals into a discussion of 'ancient rights' held under the Anglo-Saxon constitution, but lost following the Norman invasion. The notion of lost ancient rights would inform later constitutional histories written in support of womanhood suffrage.

Personal pasts: female biography and court history

The nineteenth century was in many ways the heyday of women's history writing in Great Britain, and many of the fields and genres which women historians and writers helped to pioneer remain popular with them in the twenty-first century. Women made a substantial contribution to the writing of amateur or 'picturesque' history, which had a continuity with their earlier approaches to the past: practitioners of picturesque history emphasised the 'feel' and experience of the past, drawing on a wide range of primary sources to attempt reconstructions in text and image in a variety of genres other than the conventional history book (Mitchell 2000). Their enthusiasm for biography, art, culture, travel and social history laid the foundations for many of the historical disciplines which developed in the late nineteenth and twentieth centuries. They also demonstrated a commitment to popularising history, even as the professionalisation of the discipline was underway in the universities. Although there were of course many male practitioners of picturesque history and the role of such male historians as T B Macaulay and J R Green in the development of social history is undeniable, by the end of the nineteenth century picturesque history was seen as feminine, while academic or 'scientific' history became a masculine preserve (Smith 1998).

One area in which women writers were particularly dominant was female biography, especially of **women worthies** and **royal lives** (Maitzen 1995). Here they challenged the assumption of many Victorians that the history of Britain was essentially the biographies of great men. In a few cases, women managed to move from the writing of women's biography to other fields of endeavour. **Mary Anne Everett Green** who produced *The Lives of the Princesses of England from the Norman Conquest* (1849–1855) secured a post with the Public Record Office, in 1855, for editing domestic state papers (Krueger 2003). This transition from popular biographer to archive editor reflected a trend for women historians towards the end of the century: the job of archivist or editor gave women historians the chance to practise professional history, but often only as handmaidens to the male historian. While some biographies, such as those of the Stricklands and Everett Green, involved methodological innovation in the form of considerable archival research, many biographies did not and some showed very little critical awareness: Mrs Matthew Hall's *The Lives of the Queens before the Conquest* (1854) received (and deserved) very poor reviews. Many mid- and later nineteenth-century **female biographies**, such as Ellen Clayton's *Notable Women* (1859) and *Women of the Reformation* (1861), were essentially hackwork.

Many nineteenth-century female biographies perpetuated the ideal of the Victorian domestic woman, as is apparent in Elizabeth Sandford's *Female Worthies* (1833) which functioned as an historical companion volume to her 1831 advice manual, *Woman in Her Social and Domestic Character*. Nevertheless, they often advanced a womanist, if not a feminist, perspective on historical events. In Agnes Strickland's prolonged defence of Mary, Queen of Scots, in the *Lives of the Queens of Scotland*, it is possible to see the Romantic heroine resurface, representing the embodiment of feminine virtues, victimised by the men about her, whose martyrdom offered a critique of power politics. The Stricklands presented a Tory reinterpretation of the dominant Whig historiography of the English Revolution. Unlike Catharine Macaulay, who had achieved the opposite effect by writing a rival political text, the Stricklands's reinterpretation of seventeenth-century history focused on the domestic virtues of Stuart kings and queens, allowing a more sympathetic reappraisal of Jacobite politics as 'wrong but Romantic'. Sympathies were enlisted on the side of the Stuarts – not because divine right was justified, but because they were good wives and husbands, mothers and fathers (Mitchell 2000). Such biographies represented typical examples of the Victorian revisionist tradition, generally Tory, Catholic and Romantic in its emphases, which involved the championing of 'lost causes' and controversial figures who had fallen foul of the dominant Whig narrative of Protestantism, progress and prosperity. Women were keen contributors to this revisionism. Like the Strickland sisters, Caroline Halsted's *Life of Richard III* (1844), based on key primary sources such as Harleian MS 433, also presented a controversial account of a much-maligned monarch. Catholic women historians such as Mary Helen Allies, Anne Hope and Jean Mary Stone also played a key role in the revision of the British historiographical tradition, helping to open up new areas of research such as Recusant studies and producing reinterpretations of the events and personalities of the English Reformation. Based on the queen's privy purse accounts, Stone's *The History of Mary I, Queen of England* (1901) offered a sympathetic reappraisal of 'Bloody Mary', building on Elizabeth Strickland's earlier, controversial attempt to critique the popular perception of the queen.

In the twentieth and twenty-first centuries, women have continued to make an important contribution to British history through writing female biographies and court histories. Many have produced popular, well-researched biographies that offer a challenge to historical orthodoxies. Cecil Woodham-Smith's *Florence Nightingale* (1950) rescued the Victorian celebrity from her debunking by Lytton Strachey. Lady Antonia Fraser, the author of biographies of Mary Queen of Scots (1969), Cromwell (1973) and Charles II (1979) is, perhaps, the modern doyenne of the popular historical biography, following in the footsteps of her mother, Elizabeth Longford, biographer of queens Elizabeth and Victoria. Alison Weir's recent biographies of Tudor queens and princesses and Amanda Foreman's *Georgina, Duchess of Devonshire* (1998) also belong to this tradition. The popular history retains the potential to innovate and revise traditional historiography. Fraser's biography of Mary of Scotland offered a sympathetic revision of its subject, while *The Weaker Vessel* (1984) took her into the field of women's history and contributed considerably to understanding of the lives of ordinary women in seventeenth-century Britain. Elizabeth Mavor's joint biography *The Ladies of Llangollen* (1973) is an early work in the field of **lesbian history**.

Particular pasts: Places, folklore, family, texts

Although the world of the gentlemanly antiquary had always been a difficult sphere for the woman writer, women antiquaries and **local** historians began to proliferate in the eighteenth and nineteenth century (Thirsk 1995, 1996). Antiquarianism contributed greatly to the development of picturesque history in the Victorian period and increasingly became identified with it. One of the earliest women antiquaries was Elizabeth Ogbourne who published the first volume of *A History of Essex* in 1817. As folklore studies developed in the later nineteenth century, women such as Charlotte Sophia Burne, author of *Shropshire Folklore: A Sheaf of Gleanings* (1883), and Jessie M E Saxby, writer of *Foys and Fanteens: Shetland Feasts and Fasts* (1915), played a key role. A classical example of the Victorian woman local historian is Mary Stapleton, lady of the manor at Souldern manor in Oxfordshire, a member of the North Oxfordshire Archaeological Society and the author of *Three Oxfordshire Parishes: A History of Kidlington, Yarnton, and Begbroke* (1893). Charlotte Fell Smith pursued the career of the woman local historian more fully: she edited the letters of Essex's seventeenth-century Quaker Steven Crisp (1892) and contributed to the antiquarian journal, the *Essex Review*. Her pursuit of the history of the marginal and marginalised, through her interest in local Non-conformity, was characteristic of the Victorian woman historian. Her career also reflected the increasing involvement of turn-of-the-century women historians in collaborative projects: she contributed 231 articles to the *Dictionary of National Biography* and accounts of Essex industries to the *Victoria County History*. This latter enterprise was a major employer of women writers with local history interests. A professional academic historian who took up the local history tradition was **Mary Bateson**, her first published work was *The Register of Crabhouse Convent* (1889) which she produced for the Norfolk and Norwich Archaeological Society. She then turned to municipal history, editing archives in Leicester and Cambridge.

Local studies were also linked to travel writing, which proved both a route into history writing for many women, and also an alternative way of exploring the past. Like many Romantic writers, they were profoundly conscious of the *genius loci* and they also shared the antiquarian interest in the physical remains of the past. Louisa Costello was the author of conventional history works such as *Memoirs of Eminent Englishwomen* (1844), but much of her history writing also appears in her tours of Britain and the Continent, such as *Falls, Lakes, and Mountains of North Wales* (1845). Janet Ross wrote *The Story of Pisa* (1909) and Mary Dormer Harris wrote *The Story of Coventry* (1911), both in Dent's Medieval Towns series. The family history work of Maria Margaret, Lady Verney – who edited the important papers of the Verney family – shed new light on domestic and social life during the English Civil War, exploring the impact of the political on the personal, a key theme for the woman historian. Editing of documents was an important activity for the later Victorian woman historian and a path into a professional historical career: Lucy Smith Toulmin, who edited texts including the *York Plays* (1885) for societies such as the Early English Text Society and the Camden Society, followed the career trajectory of Everett Green, becoming librarian of Manchester College, Oxford, in 1894.

Women have continued to practise 'particular history'. A twentieth-century example of the continuity of this tradition is Joan Wake who was at once a local and a family historian and an editor of texts, playing a key role in the editing of local, legal and clerical records for the Northamptonshire Records Society and producing a family history of *The Brudenells of Deene* (1953). Her guide to *How to Compile a History and Present Day Record of Village Life*, produced for the Federation of Women's Institutes, hints at the continuing role of countless women as local and family historians in the twentieth and twenty-first century.

Popularising the past: Textbook history and the historical novel

As amateur historians, many Victorian women writers were committed to popularising historical knowledge and understanding. Their involvement was reflected in their role in producing textbook histories, in which women writers often featured as promoters of more domestic and social interpretations of the past, as well as educational innovators. The best-known early nineteenth-century history textbooks were all produced by women: Richmal Mangnall's *Historical and Miscellaneous Questions* (1800); Elizabeth Penrose's *History of England* (1823), which she produced under the pseudonym of Mrs Markham; and Maria, Lady Callcott's *Little Arthur's History of England* (1835). Although it now appears a sure route to rote learning, Mangnall's question-and-answer technique was innovative in its time. Penrose's 'Conversations', which appeared at the end of each chapter of her work, allowed her to introduce information about customs and dress, which was supplemented by illustrations drawn from the antiquarian works of Joseph Strutt. Writers such as Julia Corner who published a series of histories of England and European countries in 1840–1848 continued Penrose's tradition of including 'manners and morals' in history. Maria Hack, author of *Grecian Stories* (1819) and *English Stories* (1820–1825), also rejected lengthy political narrative, emphasising the importance of story-telling and the development of comprehension rather than memory skills. Although educational reform and the increasing importance of history as an education for the citizen led to the rise of the professionally qualified male textbook writer in the later Victorian period, women writers such as Charlotte Yonge still continued to produce history textbooks, although often for the younger age group. An early twentieth-century textbook writer such as Henrietta Marshall, author of *Our Island Story* (1905), *Our Empire Story* (1908) and *Scotland's Story* (1906), the last of which was still appearing in a revised edition in the 1960s, demonstrates the longevity of this female story-telling tradition in the textbook.

Problems of exclusion from academe in the twentieth century may well help to explain the continuing vitality of the woman writer of popular history. In the twentieth century, historical fiction has continued to be a popular genre for women, with Georgette Heyer's Regency romances and Jean Plaidy's fictional biographies of historical women remaining perennially popular. Many of these historical novels make a genuine contribution to historical understanding of unexplored areas of the past: Heyer's portrait of elite customs and values is fully detailed and realised, as too is the depiction of life in fifth-century Romano-Britain in Mary Stewart's Arthurian trilogy (1970–1979). While Heyer and Stewart excel in establishing historical atmosphere and setting, Josephine Tey's *The Daughter of Time* (1951), a detective novel exploring the case of the princes in the tower which exonerates Richard III, has been used as a textbook for raising questions on historical method. Rosemary Sutcliffe's long series of historical novels for children *The Armourer's House* (1951), *The Eagle of the Ninth* (1954) and *Knight's Fee* (1960) have ably supplemented textbook histories for several generations of children. They continue the tradition, so popular with women historians, of exploring major historical events and eras from the perspective, and through the experience, of the ordinary individual.

New agendas: Social and economic history

In the nineteenth century women played a significant role in the transformation of the history of 'manners and morals'. In the twentieth century they have been integral to the transformation of the disciplines of social and economic history. The contributions of women writers to the development of social and economic history sometimes reflected conventional ideas about women's role in the domestic sphere. This can be evidenced in texts such as Jessie Bedford's *Home Life under the Stuarts 1603–49* (1903) and *Social Life under the Stuarts* (1904), and in her pioneering study of the history of infancy (1907). But others, such as Georgiana Hill's *Women in English Life* (1896), took a feminist perspective, arguing that medieval women had enjoyed greater social, cultural and political freedom than their descendants. This thesis of a lost Golden Age for women, followed by a period of oppressive patriarchy, became a key theme in women's history writing by the late Victorian and Edwardian period. **Lina Eckenstein** argued in *Women under Monasticism* (1896) that it was the Reformation in England and Germany that restricted women's opportunities to the domestic sphere.

Indeed, as both socialism and feminism began to impact on the writing of history, women writers increasingly explored the history of the common people, and in particular the common woman rather than the lives of women worthies. The use of techniques and ideology from the social sciences was also increasingly apparent. Several of these women worked within husband and wife teams and were influenced by the Fabian socialist tradition which encouraged feminism. **Beatrice Webb** worked with her husband Sidney on British social, labour and administrative history. **Barbara Hammond** explored with her husband J L Hammond the impact of industrialisation on the working classes. Such egalitarian partnerships make a heartening contrast with the family lives of Victorian male historians such as E A Freeman, whose work owes an unacknowledged debt to his daughters. Many women historians of this period were associated with the London School of Economics (Berg 1992). These included **Lilian Knowles,** author of *The Industrial Revolutions in Great Britain during the Nineteenth Century* (1921), **Alice Clark,** whose *Working Life of Women in the Seventeenth Century* (1919) argued that the Industrial Revolution had limited women's working and social lives, and **Ivy Pinchbeck,** author of *Women Workers and the Industrial Revolution, 1750–1850* (1930). But the doyenne of the group was **Eileen Power** who played a leading role both in the development of women's history and economic history at the London School of Economics. In the 1920s and 1930s Power studied the medieval wool trade, incorporating anthropological, sociological and comparative approaches in a manner reminiscent of the *Annalistes*. In so doing she avoided the narrowly economic and statistical approaches of many male contemporaries. Her more picturesque social histories, *Medieval People* (1924) and *Medieval Women* (1975), are still popular with the general reading public (Berg 1996).

The development of social and economic history from the 1930s illustrated the process by which a new historical discipline pioneered by women became professionalised and gradually less accessible to the female historian. Many women scholars such as Eleanor Lodge, Eleanora Carus, Mabel C Buer, M Dorothy George and Caroline Skeel continued to work in the field of social and economic history. But in the 1940s and 1950s, women historians did not continue to enjoy the access to academe and the participation in the expansion of new subject areas that Eileen Power and her colleagues had experienced. When the *Oxford History of England* was published in the 1950s and 1960s, only one volume was written by a woman: *The Fourteenth Century 1307–1399* (1959) by May McKisack, professor of history at Westfield College, London. **Helen Mary Cam**, an expert on medieval local government, was awarded a professorial chair by Cambridge, Massachusetts, not Cambridge, England (Sondheimer 1996). Possibly as a result of this development, many women academics retained an interest in and a concern for popular history.

New agendas: Women's history

The rise of first-wave feminism saw a number of women engage in the revision of British political history. Recalling Macaulay a feminist version of lost ancient rights evolved. In **Charlotte Carmichael Stopes**'s *British Freewomen: Their Historical Privilege* (1894), she suggested that the Norman Conquest had destroyed the ancient freedoms of British women, reprising a line of argument which Hannah Lawrance had explored earlier in her *History of Woman* (Holton 1998). Feminism not only transformed the traditional male-orientated Whig historiographies of the Victorians; increasingly, it generated a new area of historical study. As the suffrage movement developed, women writers began to record its history and its heroines: **Helen Blackburn**'s Women's Suffrage: *A Record of the Suffrage Movement* appeared in 1902 and **Ray Strachey**'s *The Cause: A Short History of the Women's Movements in Great Britain* followed in 1927. The interest of women writers and scholars in women's history never really died after the suffrage period. **Doris Mary Stenton** reiterated the Golden Age theory as late as 1957 in her *English Woman in History* – but the emergence of second-wave feminism in the 1960s significantly boosted enthusiasm for research into British women's history. Ruskin College and the History Workshop Group, led by radical and socialist historians such as Raphael Samuel and E P Thompson, focused on 'the people's history'. But this new socialist version of the past tended to exclude working-class women. In 1970 women arranged a Women's Liberation Movement Conference at Ruskin College to draw attention to women's rights and women's history. Women scholars involved in the Workshop – Sheila Rowbotham, Anna Davin, Sally Alexander and Barbara Taylor – played a key role in re-invigorating women's history. They explored women's roles in radical and revolutionary movements in the past in works such as Rowbotham's *Women, Resistance, and Revolution* (1972) and Taylor's *Eve and the New Jerusalem* (1983). Rowbotham also explored the impact of **industrialisation** and **modernity** on women's lives in *Women's Consciousness, Man's World* (1973). Women involved in History Workshop pioneered new methodologies in women's history, making use of **oral** sources and discovering new **archives**. Elizabeth Roberts, in her *A Woman's Place. An Oral History of Working-Class Women 1890–1940* (1984), illustrated the benefits of oral history for retrieving the experience of women.

Women's history became a major field of historical study in late twentieth-century universities, affecting every period and subject area of British history. Lindsay Allason-Jones has explored the history of Roman Britain in works such as *Roman Women: Everyday Life in Hadrian's Britain* (2000) and in numerous archaeological studies. Christina Fell has studied the experience of Anglo-Saxon women (*Women in Anglo-Saxon England* 1984) as well as producing various studies of Britain during this period. Henrietta Leyser has written biographical studies of medieval women (*Christina of Markyate* 2004) as well as writing a social history of women in Britain between 400 and 1500, *Medieval Women* (1995). The social and cultural world of early modern British women has been explored by Anne Laurence in her general survey, *Women in England 1500–1760* (1994). Pauline Stafford's *Queens, Concubines and Dowagers* (1983) and *Queen Emma and Queen Edith* (1997) and Jennifer Ward's *Women of the English Nobility and Gentry* (1995) have explored the lives of elite women in the early and later medieval period. The impact of the English Revolution on women has been examined in works such as Patricia Crawford and Sara Mendelson's *Women in early modern England* (1998) and Stevie Davies *Unbridled Spirits* (1998) and *A Century of Troubles* (2001). Women's experience of work in the eighteenth century has been explored by Bridget Hill in texts such as *Servants* (1996), *Women Alone* (2001) and *Women, Work and Sexual Politics in Eighteenth-Century England* (1989). Works by Amanda Vickery such as *The Gentleman's Daughter* (1998) and *Women, Privilege and Power* (2001) have presented the leisured world of aristocratic and gentry women during the same period. Areas such as the nineteenth-century woman and first-wave **feminism** are the foci of intense research. The establishment of both the Fawcett Library and the Virago Press proved crucial in encouraging the development of British women's history, as too do academic journals such as *Women's History Review*. Increasingly, women historians are moving away from the rediscovery of the lives of women (important though this still is) towards integrating the history of women with that of men, and towards the exploration of the nature and impact of gender as a category.

New agendas: National, British, and imperial history

Women historians have always played a particularly significant role in the redefinition of national and British history through the exploration of regional identities. Their contribution to the development of regional and Celtic historiographies in the early modern period has continued into the twentieth century. **Alice Stopford Green** explored the history of her native Ireland, publishing *The Making of Ireland and its Undoing, 1200–1600* (1908), an account that suggested Tudor imperialism had destroyed a previously flourishing economy and culture: her pro-Gaelic stance may be linked to her growing sympathy for the feminist movement (Melman 1993; Holton 2002). More recently, this link between the history of the marginalised Celtic countries and the history of women has been confirmed in works of historians such as Rosalind Mitchison and Leah Leneman who have explored Scottish women's history in the early and modern period, while Angela V John and Deirdre Beddoe have led research into modern Welsh women's history. Meanwhile, Linda Colley has examined the eighteenth-century creation of the British identity in *Britons: Forging the*

Nation 1707–1837 (1992), revealing both how the Whig narrative of Protestantism, progress and prosperity was constructed and the role played by women in this process. Women historians have also colonised the formerly male-dominated domain of British imperial history, playing a key role in its postmodern transformation from the history of high politics at the metropolis to an exploration of the experience and representation of life in the peripheries. The imperial experience has been investigated in Antoinette Burton's *The Burdens of History* (1994), Vron Ware's *Beyond the Pale* (1992) and Catherine Hall's extensive body of work. Such texts have analysed the roles played by women as well as men in the construction of the British imperial identity and the interplay within it of ethnicity and gender. Like many of their predecessors, such women historians continue to challenge hegemonic grand narratives, producing a more inclusive, complicated and multifaceted picture of the British past.

Rosemary Ann Mitchell

References

Berg 1992, 1996; Burstein 1998, 1999; Davis 1983; Fenwick 1994; Grundy 1992; Gunn 1964; Hicks 2002; Hill 1992; Holton 1998, 2002; Johnson 1997; Krueger 2003; Looser 2000; Maitzen 1995; Melman 1993; Mitchell 1998, 2000; Sherman & Holcomb 1981; Smith 1998; Spencer 1986; Thirsk 1995, 1996; Weaver 1997; Woolf 1997.

Related essays

Archives; Enlightenment; Empire; Education; Female Biography; Feminism and Suffrage; Feminist Biography and Autobiography; Historical Fiction; Industrialisation; Local History; Modernity; Oral traditions; Renaissance; Romantic Women Writers; Royal Lives; Women worthies.

Green, Mary Anne Everett 1818–1895

English historian and archivist. Born in Sheffield, daughter of Robert Wood, Wesleyan minister. Childhood spent in Lancashire and Yorkshire. Educated at home. Moved to London in 1841 when her father took up a post at the Methodist Chapel in Islington. There she pursued her own course of study in the British Museum, Lambeth Palace Library and the Towers Records Office. She also became acquainted with the collections of antiquarians such as Sir Thomas Phillips and Dawson Turner. In 1843 she had completed a draft of *Lives of the Princesses of England*; however, her publisher Henry Coburn withheld it until he had completed the publication of **Agnes Strickland**'s *Lives of the Queens of England* (1842–1848). Three volumes of her *Letters of the Royal Ladies of Great Britain* appeared in 1846, the year she married George Pycock Green, an artist. Four children.

Upon marriage Green moved to Europe where her husband studied art and she visited archives and private collections with a view to revising her *Lives*. Green attached the same importance to consultation of original documents as Agnes Strickland. In the preface to her *Letters* Green stated that she had paid 'the strictest attention to fidelity in the transcripts and to correctness in the translations'. In the preface to *Lives* she claimed that she investigated the available documents 'in almost every civilized country in Europe'. The *Lives* were published in six volumes between 1850 and 1856 and were favourably compared to Strickland's. When Strickland declined to write the lives of the Brunswick queens on the grounds that it was disrespectful to Queen Victoria, Green took on the task but the proposed *Lives of the Queens of England of the House of Brunswick* never appeared.

Green returned to Britain in 1848, settling in Gower Street, close to British Museum. Her meticulous researches drew her to the attention of Sir John Romilly who appointed her as the first external editor of the *Calenders of State Papers* in 1855. She worked in this capacity in the Public Records Office for 40 years, producing 41 of the 800-page volumes of the domestic Calenders of State Papers covering the reigns of Edward VI, Mary Tudor, Elizabeth Tudor, James I the Interregnum and Charles II. As well as editing these Green produced prefaces to many of these volumes, which taken together constitute a political history of seventeenth-century England.

Green also edited *The Diary of John Rous* (1856) and the *Life of William Whittingham* (1871) for the Camden Society. She also contributed articles to the *Athenaeum, the London Review* and the *Gentleman's Magazine*.

Mary Spongberg

References

Krueger 2003; Laurance 2000; Thirsk 1985.

H

Hagiography

Sacred discourse representing the lives of the saints in the form of short lives or *vitae*. Drawing on the classical and Hebrew tradition, early Christian writers have produced lives of holy men and women since the third century AD. Hagiography aims at edification and such lives were intended for public reading at events such as the anniversary of the saint's death, and were frequently recited within monastic communities for the instruction of the clergy (McNamara 1992: 2–3). While hagiography maybe historical, the lives of saints were not necessarily written as objective reports or analyses of events, rather hagiographical accounts were often written to establish legal, dynastic or miraculous claims and to offer models of behaviour to be followed or avoided (Ferrante 1997: 69). Unlike modern biography, sacred biography stressed the exemplarity of their subject rather than their individuality. Although lives of the saints continue to be written, the bulk of these texts were produced before the **Renaissance** (see **Religion**, **Reformation**).

It was not until the seventh century that women are known to have produced vitae of saints. **Baudonivia**, a nun of the Holy Cross in Poitiers, produced the first *vita* known to be written by a woman, the life of the saintly Queen Radegund, between 609 and 614 AD. Written to supplement the male-authored vitae of Radegund, Baudonivia's *Life of Radegund* created an influential model of female piety for noble and holy women to follow. There is evidence that later female-authored vitae of saints were written following Baudonivia (Wemple 1981: 184). Women writing *vitae* were likely to be acquainted or related to their subject. Baudonivia claimed a quasi-maternal relationship with Radegund who had 'nourished' her 'from the cradle'. This proximity allowed women writers to claim a certain authority and allowed them access to sources unavailable to men. Being of the same convent was also advantageous and hagiographers such as Berta, a nun of the Abbey of Willich, wrote the life of Saint Adelheide, first abbess of Willich, drawing on the testimony of older nuns from this convent known to the saint.

Gender shaped both the writing of hagiography and the representation of saintly lives. Male-authored *vitae* represented women saints in ways that 'rendered them innocuous in the context of secular power' (McNamara 1992: 4). Hence women were represented as passive vessels of God's will. In the small number of extant female-authored vitae it is possible to see women introducing feminine values and ideals into hagiography (Wemple 1981: 183). As models of behaviour for women the lives of saints written by women 'were invariably slanted' towards demonstrating to women 'the active roles they can do and perhaps should play in history' (Ferrante 1997: 69). This feminine perspective permitted a degree of individuation contrary to the hagiographic tradition. Consequently although women such as Baudonivia were sometimes criticised for their 'barbarous' style' they have been considered better historians than their male counterparts (Kitchen 1998: 127–8).

Mary Spongberg

References

Ferrante 1997; Kitchen 1998; McNamara *et al.* 1992; Wemple 1981.

Hale, Sarah Josepha 1788–1879

Poet, novelist, editor, biographer, historian of women. Born in New Hampshire, daughter of Martha (Whittlesey) and Captain Gordon Buell, a revolutionary soldier. Educated at home by her mother and brother Horatio. At eighteen Hale established a school where contrary to convention she taught girls Latin. Schooled in the ideology of Republican motherhood, Hale advocated women's rational education throughout her life. Closing the school upon her marriage to lawyer David Hale in 1813, she began to write, encouraged by her husband who disciplined her 'predilection for pompous words'. Pregnant with her fifth child when her husband died in 1822, Hale looked to writing to support her family. A book of poetry *The Genius of Oblivion* appeared in 1823. A novel *Northwood: A Tale of New England* was published in 1826. *Northwood* advocated colonisation not abolition, a theme she returned to in her later historical novel *Liberia* (1853). In both these novels, Hale historicised slavery as God's way of introducing Christianity into Africa. *Northwood* drew the attention of the Rev John Lauris Blake, who offered Hale the editorship of his publication, *The Ladies' Magazine*, which she took up in Boston in 1828. Under her editorship the *Ladies' Magazine* focused on issues such as women's education and women's employment and was novel in its promotion of American culture. While working as editor, Hale published two books *Sketches of American Character* (1829) and *Traits of American Life* (1835) both demonstrating Hale's desire to promote the virtue in the citizens of the new Republic. Hale also published a number of children's books at this time. Hale worked as editor of the *Ladies' Magazine* until it was bought by Louis A Godey, who made Hale editor of his periodical the *Lady's Book* in 1837.

Although opposed to women's suffrage Hale used her platform as editor of the *Lady's Book* to promote various women's causes such as the right of women to teach in public schools, day nurseries for working mothers and increased wages for women. She encouraged Matthew Vassar to create a college for women along the same lines as Harvard and to hire female faculty members. Her feminism has been described as maternalist as she regarded motherhood 'the most important vocation on earth'. In the *Lady's Book* Hale consciously promoted the reading of history over other genres and drew on women's historical writing in her editorials. She believed women to be 'God's appointed agent of morality', and in her major historical study, *Woman's Record* (1853), maintained that woman's moral agency was the engine of historical progress. Hale used the genre of **Female Biography** to present a woman-centred universal history and drew upon sources that included **Mary Hays, Anna Jameson, Sydney Owenson, Lady Morgan, Agnes Strickland** and **Julia Kavanagh**. *Woman's Record* contains over 2000 biographical sketches of 'women of eminence' including an autobiographical note on Hale. She issued revised and expanded editions of *Woman's Record* in 1855 and 1870. She published her last editorial at the age of 89.

Mary Spongberg

References

Baym 1990, 1995; NAW 1971; Okker 1995; Oldfield 1999.

Halkett, Anne 1623–1699

English memoirist, historian. Born in London, daughter of Thomas Murray, Provost of Eton College, and Jane (Drummond). Her father died three months after her birth and her mother became governess to the younger children of Charles I. Halkett received a good education in music, French and some medical science. Her early life featured loss – Thomas Howard with whom she fell in love, secretly married someone else in 1646 and her mother died in 1647. In the same year she became involved with the married royalist Colonel Joseph Bampfield. Between 1647 and 1648 she was involved in Bampfield's espionage work, helping the Duke of York to escape in April 1648 in women's clothes. In 1649 she was forced to leave London because of Bampfield's imprisonment and the social scandal about their affair. She steadfastly refused to believe he was married and only in 1653 accepted the truth after moving to the Castle of Fyvie at the invitation of the Earl of Dunfermline. In 1656 she finally turned her back on Bampfield and married Sir James Halkett, a widower with four children, and lived at Pitfirrane in Fife.

Halkett was a deeply pious woman who wrote 21 volumes of devotional manuscripts and a godly treatise – *The Mother's Will to Her Unborn Child*. Extracts were published by Simon Couper in 1701. Her only historical writing was her **memoirs**, written between 1677 and 1678. The memoirs were first published in 1875, edited by John Gough Nichols and then reprinted in modern editions in 1965 and 1979. Halkett's autobiography is a remarkable testament to her royalist support during the civil wars. Her account of the escape of the Duke of York disguised as a woman is vivid and generous in details: 'His highness called "Quickly, quickly, dress me" and putting off his clothes I dressed him in the women's habit that was prepared, which fitted his Highness very well . . . he was very pretty in it.' Equally compelling is her narrative of nursing wounded royalist soldiers in Scotland after the regicide. Her recollections of events during the civil war are in an intimate first-person style and convey the sense of anxiety shared by many women. Halkett wrote without apology for making herself the subject of historical narrative: 'The earnest desire I had to serve the king made me omit no opportunity wherein I could be useful, and the zeal I have for his Majesty made me not see what inconveniencies I exposed myself to.' She felt empowered to write her history out of partisan loyalty and the text features her fears for royalist friends and factual information not found in other civil war memoirs about the military activities of the Duke of York and royalists in Dumfermline in the 1650s. The text ends abruptly and sections of the manuscript have also been torn away suggesting self-censorship.

James Halkett died in 1670 and Anne Halkett went on to live a quiet life on a pension supplied by James II when he came to the throne in 1685.

Amanda L Capern

References

Hudson 1993; *NDNB* 2004; Sage 1999; Todd 1989.

Major work

John Loftis (ed.) *The Memoirs of Anne, Lady Halkett and Ann, Lady Fanshawe* (Oxford: Clarendon Press, 1979).

Hamilton, Elizabeth 1758–1816

Irish novelist, satirist, biographer, historian. Born in Belfast, third child of Katherine (MacKay) and Charles Hamilton. Death of both parents during her childhood left Hamilton in the care of her paternal aunt in Scotland. Attended boarding school briefly, but largely self-educated. Her aunt advised her to 'avoid any display of superior knowledge' and Hamilton was compelled to hide 'Lord Kaims' [*sic*] *Elements of Criticism*' under a cushion 'lest she be detected in a study which prejudice and ignorance might pronounce unfeminine'. This tension between expected gender roles and her desire for a literary life shaped her writing. Her first attempt to write an historical novel based on the life of Arabella Stuart remained incomplete. Her first essays and poetry were published in *The Lounger* in 1785. The return of her brother Charles from India in 1786 marked a turning point. Hamilton moved to London and immersed herself in literary and diplomatic circles. In England to translate the Persian Code of Islamic Law for the Colonial administration, Charles also wrote a history of the Rohilla Wars. He fostered his sister's literary talent and she worked with him on his translations. His death in 1792 left Hamilton devastated as he had 'taught her to explore her own latent and hitherto unappropriated treasures'. It proved the occasion that spurred her on to a serious literary career. Writing *Letters of a Hindoo Rajah* (1796) assuaged her grief as she fondly recalled his conversations on such subjects. Combining various generic forms this work presented a feminised historical perspective on Anglo-Indian relations. *Letters* has also been read as a veiled commentary on the impact of the French Revolution on Europe. Hamilton's anti-Jacobin sentiments received fuller treatment in *Memoirs of Modern Philosophers* (1801). She particularly savaged **Mary Wollstonecraft**'s companion **Mary Hays** who appears in the text as Bridgetina Botherim. Hamilton's works on women's education, however, are in keeping with Wollstonecraft's assertions on women's rationality. In *Letters on Elementary Principles of Education* (1801) she claimed that women's education encouraged 'beautiful imbecility'.

Interested in the rival claims of history and fiction, Hamilton published *Memoirs of Agrippina* in 1804. Written to illustrate the psychological principles expounded in her work on education, the text provided a detailed biographical account of Agrippina, the Elder, drawn from Tacitus and a philosophical history of women. The *Memoirs* represent an early attempt to feminise history as she critiqued the interest history excites 'in the fate of heroes and conquerors', claiming that it 'may mislead an ardent mind' with images of false glory. Awarded a pension by George III 'in consideration that her talents had ever been exerted in the cause of religion and virtue', she spent her last years in Edinburgh. Her influence can be seen in the works of **Lucy Aikin** and **Elizabeth Benger** who produced her biography in 1818.

Mary Spongberg

References
Benger 1818; Jones 1986; Rendall 1996.

Major works
Translation of the Letters of a Hindo Rajah (ed.) Pamela Perkins & Shannon Russell (Peterborough: Broadway Literary Texts, 1999) and *Memoirs of Modern Philosophers* (ed.) Claire Grogan (Peterborough: Broadway Literary Texts, 2000).

Hammond, [Lucy] Barbara 1873–1961

English historian. Youngest child of Ellen Johnson and Edward Henry Bradby. Headmaster of Haileybury College. The family moved to Toynbee House, the Oxford Settlement in East London, during her teens. Educated at St Andrews and St Margaret Hall, Hammond had the distinction of being the first woman to take Firsts in Classical Moderations and Greats. Began employment as a Fellow at St Margaret's but left after a year to work for the Women's Industrial Council with **Beatrice Webb** and Clementina Black. In 1901 she addressed the Berlin Congress of Women on the issue of equal pay. Married liberal journalist John Lawrence Hammond in 1901. Both campaigned against the Boer War and for a free Ireland. Developed tuberculosis in 1905, rendering her unable to have children and forcing her to give up politics. Around this time wrote a semi-autobiograpical novel that went unpublished. In 1906 she took up historical research in intellectual collaboration with her husband. The Hammonds wrote a series of ground-breaking works of labour history, including the trilogy *The Village Labourer* (1911), *The Town Labourer* (1917) and *The Skilled Labourer* (1919). Barbara Hammond's research was critical to the conception of the Industrial Revolution, as the discovered extensive evidence of civil disturbances in the British Home Office records. The Hammonds sought to present a vivid and picturesque view of the past, emphasizing the emotional life of their subjects, anticipating the work of E P Thompson and E J Hobsbawm. Their books became subject of great debate following the publication of J H Clapham's *Economic History of Modern Britain* (1926). Both were awarded an honorary Dlit from Oxford in 1933. They also wrote *Lord Shaftesbury* (1923), *The Rise of Modern History* (1925), *The Age of Chartists* (1930) and *The Bleak Age* (1934).

Mary Spongberg

References
Applegate 2002; Weaver 1999.

Major works
The Village Labourer 1760–1832: A Study in the Government of England before the Reform Bill (Gloucester: Sutton, 1987), *The Town Labourer* (London: Longman, 1978) and *The Skilled Labourer* (London: Longman, 1979).

Harrison, Jane Ellen 1850–1928

English scholar with broad interests who acquired an international reputation for her work on ancient Greece. The third daughter of Elizabeth (Hawksley) and Charles Harrison, a wealthy and successful timber merchant. Her mother died a month after her birth. Her early education was directed by a series of governesses, one of whom encouraged Harrison's love for languages. She received further education at Cheltenham Ladies' College where she excelled. At Newnham College, Cambridge, from 1874 to 1879, she read classics and was placed in the second class of the classical tripos. She went on to study archaeology at the British Museum and between 1880 and

1898 lectured there on Greek art. In this period she twice applied unsuccessfully for the Yates Chair of Classical Archaeology at University College, London. In 1898 Harrison returned to Cambridge as Lecturer in Classical Archaeology at Newnham where she remained until 1922. She was the first woman to lecture in University buildings at Cambridge, her lectures characterised by her enthusiasm and theatricality. Between 1900 and 1903 she became the first holder of a Research Fellowship at Newnham, her work in time establishing the college as a base of classical research.

Her early works include the art-historical essays *Myths of the Odyssey in Art and Literature* (1882) and *Introductory Studies in Greek Art* (1885). Three visits to Greece and study of the topography of Athens inspired *The Mythology and Monuments of Ancient Athens* (1890). It contained a translation by her friend Margaret Merrifield Verrall of the section on Attica in Pausanius' ancient guidebook to Greece and a detailed commentary on current archaeological excavations supplied by Harrison. In her preface to the book Harrison drew out the interrelationship between religious ritual and Greek myth, a consistent theme of her work:

> I have tried everywhere to get at, where possible, the cult as the explanation of the legend. My belief is that in many, even in the large majority of cases, *ritual practice misunderstood* explains the elaboration of myth. Some of the loveliest stories the Greeks have left us will be seen to have taken their rise, not in poetic imagination, but in primitive, often savage, and I think, always practical ritual.

Harrison's two most important books were *Prolegomena to the Study of Greek Religion* (1903) and *Themis: A Study of the Social Origins of Greek Religion* (1912). The *Prolegomena* had a profound impact on the intellectual landscape. Using classical archaeology and comparative evolutionary anthropology Harrison fundamentally challenged scholarly consensus on Greek thought and religion. The work also heralded the appearance of the 'Cambridge Ritualists', the group centred on Harrison which continued to champion evolutionary anthropology and had a major impact on classical studies. In *Prolegomena* Harrison supported the theory of matriarchy, arguing that the frequency of cults dedicated to goddesses was an indication of the elevated social status of women. By the time *Themis* was published, Harrison had changed her views on matriarchy, firmly distinguishing between it and matrilineality. Although drawing principally upon the Greek sphere, Harrison proposed in *Themis* a general theory for the evolution of religion as a human institution, drawing on the irrationalist sociology of Durkheim and the vitalistic philosophy of Bergson. She argued that the Greeks conceived of the goddess Themis as 'social ordinance, the collective conscience projected, the Law or Custom that is Right', reflecting as did annual ritual a tendency towards 'emotion, union, indivisibility'. Harrison would later describe *Themis* as her 'central work'.

Deeply disturbed by the First World War which according to Harrison in her Preface to the second edition of *Themis* (1927) 'shattered much of academic tradition, scattered my fellow-workers all over Europe to be killed or drilled, and drove me, for I am no Archimedes, to fly from Greece and seek sanctuary in other languages and civilisations', she took up other interests, one of which was Russian which she studied in Paris. Returning to Newnham, she lectured on Russian until her 'retirement' which she spent in Paris and London. Her latter years were spent with a young writer Hope Mirrlees, with whom she published translations of the Russian religious autobiography

Life of the Arch-Priest Avvakum (1924) and Russian bear stories in the form of *The Book of the Bear* (1926).

Harrison also published a collection of lectures and pamphlets entitled *Alpha and Omega* (1915) which contains autobiographical elements. Within the volume is her 'Homo Sum' in which she advocates the granting of female suffrage, albeit that it is a gift which she says she must steel herself to receive. She also wrote a short memoir, *Reminiscences of a Student's Life* (1925). She exercised influence on her friend **Virginia Woolf**, especially on the essay *A Room of One's Own* (1929). In Harrison's paper 'Scientiae Sacra Fames' she had dealt with the topic of women's hunger for knowledge, asserting that '[o]ne of the most ominous signs of the times is that woman is beginning to demand a study'. *A Room of One's Own*, a memorial to Harrison, was imbued with Harrison's presence and the imagery and themes of her work.

In recent decades there has been a renewed interest in Harrison's work, not only because of the milestone which that work represents and the abiding vitality of her prose style, but because of the inspiration claimed by the Goddess movement and the advocates of the **Lesbian** Perspective. This has provoked a reaction from other admirers who claim her legacy has been abused. It has been said that Harrison did much to foster the aura of legend that surrounded her. That being the case, she may not have been surprised by the revisionism a legend enjoys (or suffers).

J Lea Beness
T W Hillard

References

Ackerman 1991; Beard 2000; Robinson 1994, 2002; Schlesier 1990, 1991.

Major works

Prolegomena to the Study of Greek Religion (Princeton: Princeton University Press, 1991) and *Themis. A Study of the Social Origins of Greek Religion* (New York: The World Publishing Company, 1962).

Hays, Mary 1760–1843

English novelist, biographer, historian of women. Daughter of Rational Dissenters. Largely unschooled. Developed a love of learning while engaged in secret correspondence with fellow Dissenter John Eccles. Following family disapproval an engagement was formed in 1780, but Eccles died before they could wed. Hays spent much of the next decade in mourning and 'solitary self-education'. Her first work, *Cursory Remarks* (1791), a defence of nonconformist practices, was published under the pseudonym Eusebia, perhaps anticipating her feminisation of history. This work brought her into contact with Radical circles, where she became acquainted with **Mary Wollstonecraft**, who encouraged her literary ambitions and edited her *Letters and Essays, Moral and Miscellaneous* (1793).

Hays (re)introduced Wollstonecraft to her husband William Godwin and attended her deathbed. She published two obituaries of Wollstonecraft, one in the *Monthly Magazine* (1797) and another in the *Annual Necrology 1797–8* (1800). Both women's lives were marred by unfortunate romantic attachments. Encouraged by Godwin, Hays turned to writing to deal with romantic disappointment, producing the *Memoirs of Emma Courtney* (1796), a complex and hybrid text that merged romance and philosophy, autobiography and fiction and dealt with issues of women's lack of sexual, political and economic autonomy. *Emma Courtney* also served as an oblique attack on the paternalist and patriarchal ideals espoused by Edmund Burke and other British anti-Jacobins, a theme she revisited in *Appeal to the Men of Great Britain* (1798) and in her novel *The Victim of Prejudice* (1799).

The publication of *Emma Courtney* saw Hays parodied as a 'philosophess' and Godwinian, whose novel 'undermine[d] religion.' She was the subject of an unflattering caricature in **Elizabeth Hamilton**'s *Memoirs of Modern Philosophers*. Hays' shift from romance to biography was prefigured in *Emma Courtney*, when Emma's father discouraged her reading of Rousseau's *La Nouvelle Heloise*, but encouraged her reading of Plutarch's *Lives*. In 1803 Hays published *Female Biography, or Memoirs of Illustrious and Celebrated Women*. Written as a memorial to 'those women whose endowments, or whose conduct have reflected lustre upon the sex', *Female Biography* presented detailed portraits of eminent women, moving beyond the hagiographic depictions that characterised earlier works of **Female Biography**, pre-empting the modernisation of the genre of biography by almost a century. Women's education was the central theme and she was concerned to create woman-centred history that would speak to women and teach them of their rights and duties. She also astutely demonstrated how women's lives were moulded by patriarchy and the suffering women experienced being subject to laws they had no hand in creating.

Female Biography was tepidly reviewed and Hays retired from public life. She continued to write history to support herself, publishing works for children such as the third volume of Charlotte Smith's *History of England* (1806). In 1821 she published *Memoirs of Queens Illustrious and Celebrated*, a sanitised abridgement of *Female Biography*. A brief biography of her appears in **Sarah Josepha Hale**'s *Woman's Record*.

Mary Spongberg

References

Kelly 1993; Kucich 1993.

Major works

Memoirs of Emma Courtney (Oxford: Oxford University Press, 2000) and *The Victim of Prejudice* (Peterborough: Broadview Press, 1998).

Haywood, Eliza c.1693–1756

English actress, journalist, novelist, historian of women. Much that has been reported of Haywood's early life cannot be substantiated. In her own writings Haywood presented contradictory statements about her education, claiming in *The Fatal Secret* (1724) that she had been 'depriv'd of those Advantages of Education' only to write later in the *Female Spectator* that she had 'an education more liberal than is ordinarily allowed my Sex'. The first authentic public record of her life shows that she appeared on the stage in Dublin, playing as Chloe in Thomas Shadwell's adaptation of *Timon of Athens* in 1715. Haywood published her first novel *Love in Excess* (3 volumes) between 1719 and 1720. With this came immense literary success. *Love in Excess* was the most popular work of fiction in Britain before the publication of Richardson's *Pamela* (1740). Encouraged by this success Haywood published an amatory novel on average every three months during the 1720s, earning herself the title 'the Great Arbitress of Passion'.

Haywood also published a series of **Secret Histories**, scandal chronicles presenting thinly disguised attacks on contemporary political and literary figures. *Memoirs of a Certain Island*, a Tory satire of courtly society modelled on **Delarivier Manley**'s *The New Atalantis* appeared in 1724. *Memoirs of . . . Utopia* (1726) and *The Secret History of Present Intrigues of the Court of Caramania* (1727) satirised members of the court of George II and a later text the *Adventures* *of Eovaai* (1736) formed a vituperative assault on Robert Walpole, the Prime Minister. *Bath Intrigues in Four Letters to a Friend in London* (1725) modelled on Manley's *Court Intrigues and Letters from the Palace of Fame* (1711) is sometimes ascribed to Haywood. Through these 'secret histories' Haywood commented on current political events, linking Republicanism with misogyny and the declining political instrumentality of women. Haywood also published *The Secret History of Mary, Queen of Scots* (1725), her only secret history referring explicitly to an historical figure. Sometimes referred to as a 'fictional' biography, Haywood called this a 'True History' distinguishing it from Romance and drew on an extensive range of French sources. Anticipating later Romantic revisions of Mary's life, Haywood presented the fate of Mary Stuart in terms critical of male-authored histories and their appropriation of women's private lives and suggested that the role of the woman writer/historian should be to serve as a corrective to the errors of men. Her secret histories saw her publicly traduced by Alexander Pope in his poem the *Dunciad* (1728). She responded, writing part of *The Female Dunciad* (1729).

Haywood was active in the London theatre scene, writing and appearing in several plays such as *The Fair Captive* (1721), *A Wife to be Lett* (1723), an historical tragedy *Frederick, The Duke of Brunswick* (1729) and an opera *The Opera of Opera's* (1733). She was among the players Henry Fielding assembled in 1736 at the New Theatre and appeared in a number of his plays. Haywood also produced a compendium of theatrical criticism and history, *The Companion to Theatre, or the Key to the Play* (1735). Her stage career ended in 1737 when the Licensing Act was passed.

In 1744 Haywood appeared as editor and publisher of *The Female Spectator*, the first magazine by and for women. A collection of 'True Histories', moral tales drawn from life, *The Spectator* was designed to acquaint her reader 'with other People's Affairs' so they might learn 'to regulate their own'. Following the demise of the *Spectator* Haywood published the short-lived political journal *The Parrot*, 'A Compendium of the Times' explicitly committed to Tory causes. Like **Manley**, Haywood was arrested for seditious libel, when in 1749 she published a pamphlet entitled 'A Letter from H——G——esq . . . To a Particular Friend'. Turning to domestic fiction and conduct manuals in later life, Haywood published the *Anti-Pamela of Feign'd Innocence Detected* (1741), *Life's Progress through Passions, or the Adventures of Natura* (1748), *The History of Miss Betsy Thoughtless* (1751) and *The History of Leonora Meadowson* (1788).

Although Haywood frequently drew upon personal histories to morally instruct her readers, she left little evidence of her own, resisting early biographers' attempts to chronicle her life for she feared 'improper liberties' would be taken with her 'History' following her death. George Frisbie Whicher published the first twentieth-century biography of Haywood, *The Life and Romances of Mrs Eliza Haywood* in 1915. Some 70 years later Mary Anne Schofield published *Eliza Haywood* (1985) and more recently a critical study of her works *The Passionate Fictions of Eliza Haywood* (2000) was edited by Kirsten P Saxton and Rebecca P Bocchicchio.

Mary Spongberg

References

Ballaster 1992; Hollis 1997; Saxton & Bocchicchio 2000.

Major works

Adventures of Eovaai: Princess of Ijaveo: A Pre-Adamatical History (ed.) Earla Wilputte

(Peterborough: Broadview Press, 1997); *Memoirs of a Certain Island Adjacent to the Kingdom of Utopia* (ed.) Josephine Grieder (New York: Garland Publishing, 1972); *The Secret History of the Present Intrigues of the Court of Caramania* (ed.) Josephine Grieder (New York: Garland Publishing, 1972) and *The Female Spectator* (ed.) Gabrielle M Firmager (Bristol: Bristol Classical Press, 1993).

Historical fiction

Early contexts

The long history of debate about the relationship between the discourses of history and fiction emerges in the sixteenth century, when attempts were made by religious writers and pedagogues to enforce a hierarchical distinction between history and fiction. However, these boundaries were often contested, as in the work of the seventeenth-century French author **Madeleine de Scudéry** who wrote in her historical romance *Artamène, ou le Grand Cyrus* (1648–1652), 'the intrigues of war and peace are better, many times, laid open and satyriz'd in a Romance, than in a downright History, which being oblig'd to name the persons, is often forc'd for several reasons to be too partial and sparing'. Scudéry's historical romances, originally published under the name of her brother, initiated the genre of the historical novel known as the *roman héroïque* and laid the ground for the development of the modern novel. This genre also became widely influential in England, its anatomy of 'intrigues' influencing genres such as the court memoir, the so-called **secret history** or scandalous memoir, the most famous being Delarivier Manley's *Secret Memoirs of the New Atalantis* (1709), a Tory *roman à clef* which publicised alleged sexual indiscretions of members of the Whig cabinet during Queen Anne's reign. While such genres are not historical fiction in the sense to which we have become accustomed, this emphasis on the private life behind the public stage became critically important to the practice and theory of historical fiction for women authors, who enunciate their prerogative both for fiction and for history through the rich interpenetration of public and private history which became their specialty.

Another significant context for the development of historical fiction is the eighteenth-century debate over the relation between romance – associated with invention, courtly ideals and older aristocratic forms of narrative such as pastoral – and realism, associated with social and psychological observation, the rendering of detail and individualised particularities, and a supposed likeness to life. Both these competing modes are to varying degrees nevertheless constitutive of the novel genre, but as the novel gained more cultural capital during the early nineteenth century it did so under the aegis of formal realism while romance became a largely devalued term. This debate was conducted in fiction, prefaces and in works of critical history such as English writer Clara Reeve's *The Progress of Romance* (1785), a polemical dialogue which offered the first systematic distinction between the romance and the realist novel. As Reeve's history suggests, the lowly status of the novel within the generic hierarchy derives from its identification with a female romance readership associated with low culture, passion, sentiment and naivete.

In the wake of the French Revolution of 1789 historical fiction started to take on the features we now associate with the genre of the classical historical novel – its particular formal strategies, thematic concerns and larger social and cultural functions. These features include an integrated social, cultural and psychological realism; an interest in periodisation; an engagement with spatio-temporality, including a sense of the historicity of place, which is part of a new conception of the historicity of entire social cultures in a given place and time; and an ethnographic focus on the culture of everyday life of the common people. In particular, the genre focuses on individuals not as heroic models to emulate but as complex subjects whose experiences are contingent upon and symptomatic of a given time and place. As the Marxist critic Georg Lukács puts it in his groundbreaking critical study *The Historical Novel,* this genre involves a new representational practice of 'defining the individuality of characters from the historical peculiarity of their age' (1983: 19).

The nineteenth century: Nationalism and the national tale

The emergence of nationalism at the end of the eighteenth century is another critical development. In the British context, the historical novel grows out of emergent nationalist movements engaged in the collection, documentation, celebration and memorialisation of local, regional cultures which were threatened with extinction as an effect of industrialisation and the creation of the political entity of the United Kingdom. The emergence of the historical novel is therefore part of a larger culture of Romantic antiquarianism but also a lyricising alternative to it as a form of remembering the past. The genre is also to some extent a genre of ethnography. With its ethnographic focus on the common people rather than great events and its documentary impulse to represent all the intricacy and minutiae of what we would now call everyday life, the historical novel engages in the textualisation of local culture and oral tradition.

The early nineteenth century sees the consolidation of the genre of the historical novel in the context of the emergence of a vast diversity of genres of historical fiction. The period was an extraordinarily rich one for a whole range of genres which integrated fiction and the historical imagination: the Jacobin and anti-Jacobin novel that engaged the French Revolution, the Gothic novel, the national tale, the regional novel, tales of village life, the futuristic romance, the historical romance, together with the historical novel, are all powerful forms which emerge in this period. Women writers were at the forefront at experimentation in these forms and in consolidating the genre of the modern historical novel.

The genre of the historical novel played a critical role in the broader upward mobility of the novel genre. A decisive event in this regard was the publication of Sir Walter Scott's *Waverley* in 1814. An examination of the intertextual relations between Scott and women contemporaries demonstrates both the vitality of women is writing in this form, and the emergence of the assumption that historical fiction is a male genre, paradoxically, in the very period in which women represented the highest number of practitioners. As Peter Garside has argued, '[t]he 1810s show [a clear] pattern of female dominance of novel writing . . . Scott's earliest historical novels were launched when male authorship of fiction was at a lower than usual ebb' (2000: 74–5). In Lukács' study, Scott's work apotheosises the new genre of the historical novel. However, as Katie Trumpener argues, 'most of the conceptual innovations attributed to Scott were in 1814 already established commonplaces of the British novel' (1997: 130); and, as Ina Ferris argues in *The Romantic National Tale* (2002), they were established mainly in the work of women writers. The genre of the national tale was a natural form for women writers who were traditionally excluded from the roles of public office that provided masculine subjects with routes into mainstream forms of historical writing. Given this exclusion, women writers worked in para-historical or liminal historical genres such as genealogy, family history, natural history, antiquarian topography, manners, testimony, legend, anecdote, rumour and myth, as well as other genres of oral history. These genres can be seen to inform the national tale and the historical novel, with their ethnographic focus on particularities of lifestyle, daily life and regional custom. Lukács refers to Scott's female contemporaries dismissively: '[W]ith Scott, in particular, it was the fashion to quote a long list of second- and third-rate writers (Radcliffe, etc.), who were supposed to be important literary forerunners of his' (1965: 30). In fact, women writers like Maria Edgeworth, Elizabeth Hamilton and Mrs Grant were Scott's important forerunners, as Scott himself acknowledged in print on a number of occasions, not the least of which was the Postscript to *Waverley* and the 1829 'General Preface' to his Collected Novels.

A particularly critical figure whose work was overlooked as an effect of the gendered distinction between the domestic novel and the historical novel that emerged in the wake of Scott was the Anglo-Irish writer Maria Edgeworth (1767/1768–1849). Edgeworth pioneered the Irish regional novel and was the most financially successful and critically acclaimed novelist in Britain during the 1800s and early 1810s – before the publication of *Waverley* in 1814. As Marilyn Butler writes, '[f]rom 1800, when she published *Castle Rackrent*, to 1814, when Scott published *Waverley*, Maria Edgeworth was easily the most celebrated and successful of practising English novelists' (1972: 1). The example of Maria Edgeworth offers a particularly interesting case study of genre and gender. The fact that she practised the genre of the domestic and the historical novel, often in the same novel, meant that her work fell between the genres of domestic novel and historical novel, as they were being associated with Austen and Scott, respectively. Given the new ethnographic focus on history as everyday life and culture in a specific time and place, the regional novel is a critical genre to consider in the story of the development of historical fiction. Edgeworth's reputation as the initiator of the Irish novel rests on four Irish novels, *Castle Rackrent* (1800), *Ennui* (1809), *The Absentee* (1812) and *Ormond* (1817). The first and most famous of these, *Castle Rackrent*, published in the same year as the Act of Union, the parliamentary act by which Ireland was incorporated politically within England (Scotland had already been incorporated earlier in 1707, and Wales before that in 1536), was set during the 1782 Irish Parliamentary Independence. And while *Castle Rackrent* is not usually regarded as an historical novel, its framing device of the subtitle 'An Hibernian Tale taken from the Facts, and from the Manners of the Irish Squires, before the year 1782' clearly sets out to foreground a particular period.

Generally regarded as the first regional novel, *Castle Rackrent* presents a social world, the individuals who comprise it and a way of life that was vanishing. It is presented in the form of the 'memoirs' of Thady Quirk – 'an illiterate old steward', as Edgeworth's 'editor' refers to him in the Preface – who 'tells the history of the Rackrent family in his vernacular idiom'. *Castle Rackrent* was the first novel to feature a narrator who speaks dialect. It also suggested that the ideal historian might be an uneducated or indeed unreliable narrator or native informant. Such an emphasis suggests that historical fiction does not necessarily see its function as the production of truth but as representing different ways of remembering the past. *Castle Rackrent* adds the framing and distancing devices of a preface, coda and glossary to translate Irish words, drawing attention to the ethnographic function of historical fiction in translating culture, and in recasting living history into a textual (and ultimately commodifiable) form. However, Edgeworth's editor also claims that 'Thady's idiom is incapable of translation', arguably making a bid to preserve the distinct identity of this particular cultural form and to resist its translation.

Edgeworth's Preface to *Castle Rackrent* offers an implicit defence of historical fiction. Edgeworth attacks history as its own kind of romance, citing the excesses by which 'The heroes of history are so decked out by the fine fancy of the professed historian'. She also makes claims for the category of anecdote, usually 'censured and ridiculed by critics, who aspire to the character of superior wisdom' but stemming, she argues, from 'that love of truth [that] leads to a love of secret memoirs and private anecdotes'. She claims too that '[w]e are surely justified in this eager desire to collect the most minute facts relative to the domestic lives, not only of the great and good, but even of the worthless and insignificant'. Invoking a pervasive trope of historical fiction, Edgeworth claims that the genre enables the reader to go 'behind the scenes, that we may take a nearer view of the actors and actresses' of history.

Another of Edgeworth's Irish novels, *The Absentee*, traces the social and cultural effects of the Union upon the lives of absentee Anglo-Irish landlords in fashionable London. It explores the difficulties of the Anglo-Irish Union through the Romantic union between Colambre, an Anglo-Irish landlord, and Grace Nugent, his orphan cousin, a character named after a heroine of Irish nationalism and something of a cipher of wild Ireland. The central drama turns on the misrepresentations of a family genealogy, which have a 'blot' on Grace's maternal name passed on through oral legend. In this way, the novel represents the possibilities of misrepresentation that attend both oral and supposedly official documents of historical record. The interplay between the oral and the textual transmission of culture is a critical theme for Edgeworth. The novel arguably rescripts yet eventually ratifies the Anglo-Irish Union by presenting the domestication of Grace Nugent through marriage and the discovery of her true identity as an heiress. This deeply allusive and extraordinarily wide-ranging novel works into the courtship romance allegories of Classical culture, Jewish exile, Jacobite conflict, the relation of Catholic emancipation to French, English and Irish Jacobinism, and British imperialism in the Caribbean.

Whether Edgeworth's Irish novels present a nostalgic or critical view of the pre-Union world and to what extent their vision is complicit with English imperialism, are ongoing subjects of critical debate. What is indisputable, however, is the complexity of these fictional representations – often neglected in critical accounts that highlight Edgeworth's Ascendancy social position. For in *The Absentee* there are arguably two competing impulses. One is fragmenting, localising, ironising and palimpsesting, and the other is harmonising, unifying and working to smooth over difference, vindicating the political union by making it over into a cultural romance. The intricacy- and ultimate radical irreconcilability – of these distinct modes of representation in this profoundly self-divided, multi-layered and deeply poignant novel draws attention to how histories are constructed, and renders Edgeworth's work one of the most sophisticated and complex forms of the genre of historical fiction.

Many critics attribute Edgeworth's popularity in the period before Scott to her appeal for a middle-class English audience as a member of the Protestant Anglo-Irish Ascendancy. And this explanation carries some weight if we consider another important Irish historical novelist, the Irish nationalist, **Sydney Owenson, Lady Morgan.** Owenson was also enormously successful in commercial terms, and something of a Regency celebrity, but never received the same critical celebration as Edgeworth, even though her most famous work *The Wild Irish Girl: A National Tale* (1806) is widely regarded as the first national tale. This relative critical neglect of Owenson until very recently can be attributed to effects of class, gender and nationalist politics, in that Owenson's work and celebrity persona embodied a quite excessive mode of traditional femininity and an outspoken Catholic Irish nationalism. *The Wild Irish Girl* has strong elements of romance, sensibility and 'boudoirising' – a world away from the rational, realist emphasis on ethnographic representation which is such a keenly organising feature of Edgeworth's fictions, and which was perhaps just as suited to second-wave liberal-feminist canons of taste as to those of early nineteenth-century middle-class England.

As the fictions of Maria Edgeworth and Sydney Owenson demonstrate, these early female historical fictioneers celebrated the personal, the domestic and the prerogatives of romance to varying degrees. However, women writers were not by any means limited to the private and domestic sphere. They were often intensely engaged with national struggles at the larger public and political levels. What marks women's historical fiction of the nineteenth and twentieth centuries is not so much this focus on the domestic, private and local as opposed to the public, military and national, but the ways in which these two modes are interimplicated. For many of these fictions are inflected by national, gender or religious politics, using the historical setting as an allegory for contemporary politics, and therefore using the form of the historical novel politically and transformatively in order to mediate between past and present. **Elizabeth Hamilton**, for example, in *Memoirs of Agrippina* (1804), offers a Christianised reading of the decline of Rome as an allegory for the decline of England since 1688 and of the French Revolution.

The fiction of Jane Porter integrates private and public in its focus on military history and national heroism. Porter wrote tales of national heroism, or what she herself called 'biographical romances', such as *Thaddeus of Warsaw* (1803), based on the life of the polish soldier and patriot Tadeusz Kosciusko, which saw ten editions by 1819, and *The Scottish Chiefs* (1810), a tale of William Wallace. In the original Preface to *Thaddeus of Warsaw*, Porter engages existing preconceptions about gender and genre directly in an address to her female readers: 'But if the reader be one of my own sex, I would especially solicit her patience while going through the first portion of the tale, its author being aware that war and politics are not the most promising themes for an agreeable amusement; but the battles are not frequent, nor do the cabinet councils last long.' Despite this somewhat cocky identification with the masculine trappings of historical fiction, Porter is in fact true to her word. Her fiction does not dwell long on war and politics and clearly prefers the business of romance, so much so that Scott was said to have thought her version of Wallace to be too genteel (read: too feminine). Not that this stopped Porter from claiming to have influenced Scott. In the 1831 Preface to her 'simply-told biographical legend of Poland', Porter claims that Scott 'the once Great Unknown – now the not less great avowed author of the *Waverley* Novels . . . did me the honour to adopt the style or class of novel of which

"*Thaddeus of Warsaw*" was the first'. Porter's fiction embodies the kind of uneasy hybrid of historical realism with historical romance that later becomes the hallmark of popular feminine historical romance. It does this nevertheless very interestingly, in its selective use of historical realism, its heady, chivalric form of courtship romance, its somewhat showy speechifying and a generalised pastness that marks the historical romance paradoxically – with a certain kind of ahistoricity, as in *The Scottish Chiefs*, ' "Why, brave knight, will you ever sully the fair field of your fame, with an ensanguined tide? It is the fashion of the times;" replied Kirkpatrick, roughly.'

Porter also makes claims for the accuracy of her fiction as a mode of reportage of contemporary events. A General Gardiner, who had been at the Polish court, is invoked to testify in the Preface to *Thaddeus*: 'On his reading the book, he was so sure that the facts it represented could only be learnt on the spot, that he expressed his surprise to several persons that the author of the work, an English lady, could have been at Warsaw during all the troubles there and he not know it.' But, of course, Porter, a young English woman, had never been to Poland. 'The author has never been to Poland.' 'Impossible!' replied the General. This claim suggests a proximity to the genre of the eyewitness history, which also develops in this period, as in **Helen Maria Williams'** *Letters Written in France* (1790), an eyewitness account of the French Revolution. The emergence of the eyewitness history concurrently with these new genres of historical fiction testifies to a new sense of history as something in process, a new sense of the historicity of the present. It shows too how the French Revolution challenged existing understandings of history. Porter's Preface to the first edition of *Thaddeus* bears out Hayden White's account of the epoch-making significance of the French Revolution as an event which defied existing models of historical explanation and involved 'social processes and structures [which] seemed "demonic" ' (White 1978: 124). Explaining her choice of theme, Porter writes, 'There certainly were matters enough for the exhibition of all that human nature could suffer and endure, and, alas! perish under, in the nearly simultaneous but terrible regicidal revolution of France; but I shrunk from that as a tale of horror, the work of demons in the shape of men [. . .] and human monsters.'

While it would be inaccurate and reductive to claim a uniform agenda for such a varied body of writing, it is reasonable to suggest that most of these texts self-consciously mark themselves out as feminine and female-authored, and as writing from a marginal position in relation to mainstream historiography. Most are also concerned with struggles of class and nationalism.

Historical fiction is not simply fiction set in the past. It is marked too by an engagement with the present and the future. Mary Shelley's futuristic historical romance, *The Last Man* (1826), is an apocalyptic history of the future set in the twenty-first century. One of the first works to take the entire earth as its stage, set in Europe but with its radar attuned to events as far afield as America and Australia, it narrates the destruction of the world as an effect of the plague visited by imperial expansion. Offering on one level a searching critique of British imperialism, it also functions at another as a nostalgic grand tour, retracing the author's steps around Europe with her husband, Percy Bysshe Shelley, and Lord Byron. *The Last Man* fantasises an English Republic, and presents a romance of ruins of an empire in answer to the work of the French historiographer Constantin Volney, *The Ruins, or a Survey of the Revolutions of Empires* (1791).

A new confidence in historical sources which emerged after Thomas Macaulay's *History of England* (1848–1855) had an enormous impact on historical novelists from the 1850s. An examination of the changing status of the 'detail', that central category of realist narrative, helps us to understand what is at stake in the changing debate about generic distinctions between history and fiction. As science and empiricism gained status in the nineteenth century, and as novelistic realism came to be associated with the emergence of scientific models of historical explanation, so too did the novel come to be seen as a source of real knowledge. But this had mixed effects on the fortunes of the genre. For later in the nineteenth century, the categories of the material artefact and the detail became more fraught in the practice of the historical novel, particularly for the woman writer, who was often seen to be encroaching upon the male territory mapped out by Scott. In a cultural context where, as a recent critic has suggested, 'the Victorian preference in matters of memory [was] for the inexplicit, the vague, the generaliseable, the nostalgic' (Dames 2001: 211), the practice of assembling historical detail was particularly fraught for the woman writer. George Eliot's *Romola* (1863), for example, set in fifteenth-century Florence, came under critical attack for what was perceived to be its attention to detail at the expense of imaginative engagement with a generalised sense of the life of the past. It was seen to be too erudite, too weighted with detail, too antiquarian, too masculine.

Modernism and postmodernism

In the twentieth century, historical fiction remained a critical genre for women writers and theorists in a variety of forms, crossing popular romance, modernist experimentation, feminist political fiction and postmodernism. Modernism's rediscovery of Classical culture marked much historical fiction by women writers in the first half of the twentieth century, as in the work of Mary Renault, celebrated for its meticulous historical research in the depiction of ancient Greece, which engages male homoerotic themes, as does the French writer Marguerite Yourcenar in her epistolary novel *Memoirs of Hadrian* (1951).

Georgette Heyer can be credited with establishing historical romance as a women's genre in the twentieth century. She starts her career writing 'swashbucklers', or tales of masculine adventure, with *The Black Moth* (1921), heavy on gambling and sword fighting, which she wrote originally for a sick brother. With *These Old Shades* (1925), Heyer created the modern feminial historical romance which features romantic plots involving the stock types of the aristocratic rake, the Regency beau and the virtuous but passionate heroine, like Serena, from *Bath Tangle* (1955): 'a vital, passionate creature . . . headstrong and obstinate, sometimes quite dreadfully mannish . . . but with all these faults . . . she had a wealth of kindness and of generosity, and a chivalry which made her beloved amongst her father's dependants.' Chivalry is a byword of historical romance, referring to archaic social and affective forms from an earlier yet not clearly defined age – it names in fact those very same forms of aristocratic culture which were beginning to be commodified and romanced in the Regency period itself. Hand in hand with this romance of chivalry, we see a proto-feminist ironising of the august social institution that Heyer refers to as 'the Marriage Mart'. Set in the country houses, Bath spas and London parties of the Regency, Heyer's romances feature a wealth of period detail, lovingly 'recreated', and create a frisson of authenticity with the introduction of historical figures such as the Prince Regent and the original dandy Beau Brummell. Heyer's work, and the genre of Regency romance which it initiated, was for many years derided as escapist fantasy. However, more recent feminist critical reception appreciates the period detail and the cultural literacy of the genre, which relies on a knowledge of Jane Austen. *Regency Buck* (1935), for example, refers to *Pride and Prejudice* (1813) and works to refunction the iconic cultural milieu of the Regency.

Another development of the historical romance is the genre of the family saga, and the epic costume romance of Margaret Mitchell's *Gone with the Wind* (1936), set during the Civil War, which won the 1937 Pulitzer Prize. Also set in the Civil War is Toni Morrison's *Beloved* (1987), which won the 1987 Pulitzer Prize and is widely regarded as the most significant historical fiction by a contemporary woman author. Based on the story of a fugitive slave, Margaret Garner, who murdered her child to free it from **slavery**, *Beloved* reworks the genre of the slave narrative and rewrites the history of Black Reconstruction, using the ghost of the murdered child to metaphorise history as a process of trauma and haunting. *Beloved* has been read as magic realist on account of its use of the supernatural to present historical events that are horrific but nonetheless real. Pioneered in Latin American literature, where it is associated mainly with Gabriel García Márquez and Isabel Allende, the magic-realist genre is often engaged in postcolonial contexts. Magic realism also informs the historical fictions of writers such as Jeanette Winterson, who, for example, in *Sexing the Cherry* (1989), invents the grotesque figure of the Dog-woman to elaborate an historical allegory between Thatcher's England in the 1980s and the Puritan Commonwealth of the 1640s, focusing on the interrelations of sexual hypocrisy and aesthetic iconoclasm.

A particularly rich and significant form of women's historical fiction is the feminist **utopianism** and dystopianism which involve science fiction as a speculative form of future-oriented historical romance and critique, and can be seen to continue the feminist science-fiction tradition of Mary Shelley's *Frankenstein* (1818). The 1970s produced important feminist speculative fictions, such as Ursula Le Guin's *The Dispossessed: An Ambiguous Utopia* (1974) and Marge Piercy's *Woman on the Edge of Time* (1976), which engage the history of the present by imagining the future. More recently, Margaret Atwood's *Oryx and Crake* (2002) presents a futuristic dystopia that centres on the violence of genetic engineering and Western cultural and sexual imperialism.

The late Susan Sontag's *The Volcano Lover: A Romance* (1992), which recounts the canonical romance story of Emma Hamilton, the wife of William Hamilton and lover of war-hero Nelson, and dramatises the Neapolitan Revolution of 1799, offers a postmodern reworking of the romance genre. Some feminist readers regard this as a conservative work which derides popular culture and slums it with decadent royalty, doing far too little (and far too late in the novel) with the feminist and revolutionary figures of **Mary Wollstonecraft** and Eleanora Pimentel. Others see it as a compelling feminist version of Linda Hutcheon's highly influential coinage 'historiographical metafiction', which refers to postmodern fiction which is highly self-reflexive but also lays claim to history, and engages historiography as a subject of representation. Formulated in *A Poetics of Postmodernism: History, Theory, Fiction* (1988), Hutcheon's is the most influential account of the genre of historical fiction after Lukács's. While Hutcheon has come under criticism for promoting a largely masculine postmodern canon, her work has proved enormously useful as a model for what might be called 'feminist historiographical metafiction'.

Recent critical accounts of historical fiction such as Amy J Elias' *Sublime Desire: History and Post-1960s Fiction* (2001) suggest the wider (if not explicitly acknowledged) influence of feminism upon literary studies in the reconsideration of the romance genre as an important transformative mode of fiction.

In 1810, the Enlightenment feminist and Dissenter Anna Laetitia Barbauld quipped that '[W]here history says little, fiction may say much' (1810: Vol. 1, 25). Prefacing her 50-volume collection of novels – the first major and comprehensive collection of novels in English – Barbauld's quip anticipates the so-called linguistic turn of new cultural historians of the 1970s for whom the rhetorical functions of narrative performed a vital yet neglected role in remembering the past. In contemporary culture, the legacy of the new cultural history has entailed a far-reaching reconsideration of the importance of affective and imaginative modes of historical engagement and given new value to those 'subjective' modes of historical experience and practice that were once excluded from mainstream history. Key questions for the practice of history today, such as what is the role of memory in shaping the need for historical understanding, foreground the claims of the personal, the anecdotal and the imaginative, thereby opening up the claims of fiction to history. Indeed, so influential has this linguistic turn been that academic and popular debate is now marked by a tendency to privilege the fictional side of the equation, and by the almost ritualistic invocation of the questionable assertion that 'Historical fiction is more truthful than history itself' (Lowenthal 1983: 227). Arguably, however, fiction and history are not engaged in finding the truth but in meaningful ways of remembering the past. Such a privileging of fiction above history, predicated on a simplistic assertion of the authenticity of the subjective, ignores the fact that all writing functions according to generic, social and institutional conventions. Within these conventions fiction's brief has always been – for better or worse – the production of the private and the subjective. As Michel Foucault writes, literature operates by a 'kind of injunction to flush out the most nocturnal and the most everyday aspect of existence' (Foucault 1979: 90). From this perspective, the mystification of this fictional prerogative in the name of a critique of the discourse of history has limited strategic value. Similarly, with regard to the relationship between genre and gender, while many women writers make claims for greater freedom within the genre of fiction, a consideration of the institutional and historical entailments of the genres of history and fiction should serve to caution against naturalising the terms of opposition that associate history with masculinity and fiction with femininity. The most searching historical fictions do not simply assert the priority of fiction over history but work to complicate the relations between them, and to stress the mutually interrogative relations between the narratives of fiction and those of history. They ask how can fiction be used to contest received versions of the past, what kinds of historical claims can these fictionalisations make, what political effects can aestheticised representations of history lay claim to and what is their specific kind of value? In asking these questions, the most powerful historical fictions dramatise the ways in which genealogies of genre are themselves battlegrounds of the constitution of historical knowledge and cultural value. In this they say much.

Clara Tuite

References

Barbauld 1810; Butler 1972; Chandler 1998; Dames 2000; Ferris 2002; Foucault 1979; Garside 2000; Lowenthal 1983; Lukács 1937/1983; White 1978; Woolf 1997.

Related essays
Enlightenment; Great Britain; Ireland; Memoir; Romantic Women Writers; Secret History; Slavery; USA.

Historical organisations

Since the professionalisation of history in the nineteenth century many Western countries have established a tradition of historical associations and societies. These organisations have played an important role in buttressing and shaping the nature of the historical profession and in participating in the making of historical culture within the broader community. The story of women within these organisations touches on many broader issues about women both within the profession and within the making of public historical culture.

Definitions
This brief essay will explore several aspects of women and historical organisations. But first, an attempt to define the nature of historical associations and societies needs to be made. Historical associations in this essay will refer to professional historical organisations, usually made up of historians practising history within the academy, and representing in some way a forum for professional historical research, teaching and employment concerns. The Australian Historical Association, American Historical Association and the Organisation of American Historians are all examples of such organisations. Canada and New Zealand have also formed similar associations. The case of Great Britain is more complicated as no similar association exists. There is a Royal Historical Society (RHS), which began as an amateur venture but became an academic one, and an Historical Association (HA), which links up teachers of history from both schools and universities across Britain. Historical societies in this essay will refer to 'para-professional' organisations – the Royal Australian Historical Society (RAHS) and American state-based historical societies such as the New York Historical Society and the Royal Historical Society in its amateur incarnation. Obviously, these two types of historical organisations overlap considerably – the para-professional historical societies have, in many cases, strong relationships with the profession – but they are essentially symbiotic organisations, supporting historical research through the collection of documents and similar activities, rather than acting as representatives for the academic profession.

Women and historical organisations
What role have women played in the historical society? The RHS in Britain was founded in 1868 as a private venture of Dr Charles Rogers (Kenyon 1983: 202). Through the nineteenth century, the RHS was an amateur organisation and was probably closer to a gentleman's club than anything else. Women played little, if any, part in its early work. But from the beginning of the twentieth century, it became an essentially academic and professional organisation. The United States modelled its first historical societies on the British example, but quickly developed a quite different type of organisation. Some of the first historical societies such as the New York Historical Society and the Massachusetts Historical Society were established early in the nineteenth century. As historical writers began to write new histories of the young nation, historical societies began the task of collecting a history through documents and artefacts to complement this task. In the early years of these organisations, few women had a place. Indeed, the New York Historical Society remained largely elitist and restrictive with

only a small percentage of women among the membership. Even the library, often the area which saw the highest employment of women, had only one female librarian, Dorothy Churchill Barck, appointed in 1942 (Richards 1984).

In the newer American states historical societies were established early on as a means of giving some united identity and sense of community (Laugesen 2000). They were mostly amateur organisations, usually founded by local notables, often men involved in state government. But their membership was open and women often were included as members and also as writers for the historical society publications. Women often contributed their **memoirs** and also wrote **local history**. In an amateur environment, women were given more of a voice and chance to participate, although there was still a high level of male leadership.

In the early twentieth century many American state historical societies became more heavily professionalised. The profession recognised these societies as valuable resources for their own research, and the publications a valuable outlet for their writing. The state historical societies generally embraced this new role of supporting the profession and as a consequence the role of members was redefined. Amateur historians were not as likely to be published within the pages of journals; while professionals (including students of history) were much more likely to find their writing privileged. This new structure sometimes took on gendered dimensions because smaller numbers of women were represented within the profession. Some women turned to patriotic organisations as a better forum for expressing their engagement with the past, such as in the historical and patriotic projects of organisations like the Daughters of the American Revolution and the Society of Colonial Dames.

Nevertheless, some women were active in the profession and thus found their work published. The volumes of the *Proceedings of the State Historical Society of Wisconsin*, for example, or the journal of the Oregon Historical Society, the *Oregon Historical Quarterly*, included the work of numerous female graduate students in the early part of the twentieth century. In this sense, historical societies provided an important means for women's historical writing to be put into the public realm. But if the work was by an 'amateur' woman historian, it was likely to be viewed with disdain by many who held out professionally trained historians as the only contributors of serious history. Women's historical writing within the historical society forum, therefore, gained credibility only when written purely to the professional criteria and the publications could at best reflect women's limited participation in the profession.

Historical societies also involved women in other ways, primarily in administrative and librarian roles. This work helped to support the historical endeavour at many levels. Edna W Watkins, for example, was the head cataloguer of the New York Historical Society. Miss M R Curran was assistant secretary and librarian to the British Royal Historical Society for years, and after her death in 1945 *Transactions of the Royal Historical Society* reported that she was sadly missed as 'the principal repository of its traditions'. Few of the stories of these women have been preserved for history and they are now largely forgotten. Their role was largely one of support, rarely fully appreciated, and even within the administration and library, women usually failed to reach higher positions.

The RAHS began publishing its journals and proceedings early in the twentieth century and a survey of its contents provides a useful summary of the relative position of women vis-à-vis the historical society. There were some women contributors to the writings, although they only made up a small percentage. Women generally have made up significant memberships of historical organisations, despite traditional marginalisation within such organisations. Probably one-third of the membership of the RAHS in the sample year of 1929 were women but there were few female Honorary Fellows and few office bearers. Through the 1920s, only two women held office-bearing positions. This is fairly typical of most historical organisations through the first half of the twentieth century. The women of the RAHS formed their own committee within the administration to give themselves a special role in the Society's work. The Women's Auxiliary Committee throughout the 1920s and 1930s largely dedicated itself to fund-raising and other support activities. The Committee, it was noted, also played an important social role, bringing many women together.

As the modern profession established itself, professional associations were established to complement and support the discipline. Typically, such associations held annual meetings, published a journal and organised links between the profession and the general community (for example, supervising archival collection activities). Britain was an exception to this with no single organisation representing the historical profession's interests. Nevertheless, a few important historical associations emerged from the profession. The Economic History Society (EHS) was founded in 1926 and one of the founders was **Eileen Power.** She was the EHS's secretary and a 1927 membership list recorded 100 female members out of 500 (Berg 1996). The HA was a teaching organisation established in 1906, and women played an important role in its foundation. Rachel Reid of the London Day Training College and several local female school teachers helped to establish the HA. While women helped to establish the HA, university men took on the leadership roles. One woman, H M Friend, was secretary and librarian from 1927 to 1956, and in a comment echoing that of Miss Curran, was described as 'the chief guardian of continuity' in its bulletin in 1957. Women thus played an important role in the HA, but probably more because of the Association's links with schools than because of women's involvement in the profession in that period.

A question should be asked as to whether women in the profession have been helped by historical associations. One of the advantages of a professional association is that it allows for issues to be discussed and dealt with at a level beyond the institution. An institution might have an entrenched culture that allows for few women to establish themselves or get promoted, but a professional association can help raise awareness and make it harder for institutions with a poor record to justify their actions. However, the associations can also reflect gender discrimination. In both the United States and Australia, historical associations have played a role in raising the profile of women in the profession, and have provided a forum for women's concerns.

In Australia the establishment of the Women in History Committee within the Australian Historical Association in 1976 was a significant step in raising awareness of the challenges women faced within the profession. The Committee aimed to perform many functions including providing a community for women historians, to ensure continuing and increased employment of women within the profession in Australia and to help promote the subject of women's history. The *AHA Bulletin* in October 1987 presented statistics that illustrated just how few women were establishing careers within the profession. They also conducted research in the 1980s into how many women were publishing in leading journals and revealed the limited number – up to October 1986, only eight articles out of 75 were written *about* women, and only 21 *by* women. The Organisation of American Historians in the United States established their Committee on the Status of Women in the Historical Profession in 1972 with similar aims and similar findings. Such committees have helped to improve women's position within the profession, although it has been a long struggle and questions could still be asked as to whether women have achieved suitable recognition within the profession. The limitations of gender discrimination within the broader culture and society are all too often apparent. Nevertheless, the committees have helped to legitimate women's work in history.

Amanda Laugesen

References

Berg 1996; Historical Association 1957; Jones 1995; Kenyon 1983; Laugesen 2000; Levine 1986; Soffer 1994; Van Tassel 1960.

Related essays

Australia; Canada; Dominions; Memoirs; Local History; United States.

Hrotsvitha of Gandersheim c.932–1002

Saxon playwright, poet, historian. Canoness of the Benedictine monastery of Gandersheim. Hrotsvitha, who called herself the 'strong voice of Gandersheim', was probably related to an earlier abbess of Gandersheim, Hrotsvitha I (919–926), and hence a distant relative of the royal house. Gandersheim, a small independent principality ruled by women, was an important centre of learning. Hrotsvitha was schooled in philosophy, mathematics, astronomy and music, was fluent in Latin and probably Greek and was familiar with classical writers as well as Scripture and the writings of the Church fathers. There is also evidence that she spent time at the Ottonian court and maintained contacts with the court throughout her life.

Like earlier women writers Hrotsvitha was first drawn to **hagiography**, producing eight structurally related verse 'legends' depicting the lives of saints and martyrs. In legends such as 'Pelagius' and 'Gongolf' Hrotsvitha played with the masculinist conventions of martyr history by focusing upon male martyrs who are passive and virginal. Hrotsvitha displayed a concern with the historicity of these 'legends', explaining the authenticity of each tale by giving its provenance. She next produced six dramas in rhymed prose, patterned on the comedies of Roman playwright Terence, but converted into Christian morality plays. These texts are the first plays known to be written by a woman. In the second prose preface to these plays Hrotsvitha self-consciously usurps the masculinist and misogynist nature of the genre, claiming that she followed Terence 'to glorify . . . the laudable chastity of Christian virgins in the self-same form of composition which has been used to describe the shameless acts of licentious women'. Hrotsvitha celebrated the power of 'fragile woman' in these plays, giving women an agency hitherto unrepresented on the stage. Triumphant virginity was also a major theme throughout her writing.

The reputation Hrotsvitha established through her writings led to the request from her friend, the abbess Gerberga, for her to write the *Gesta Ottonis*, an epic poem and panegyric to Otto the Great, uncle of Gerberga and patron of Gandersheim, and his son Otto II. Hrotsvitha's last work, the epic poem *Primordia Coenobii Gandeshemensis*, recounts the foundation of Gandersheim and its history until the death of abbess Christine in 919. Both these texts celebrate the Ottonian dynasty, granting special honours to Otto's female relatives, employing epic conventions to 'describe the establishment of a female community whose right to power surpasses that of any earthly authority'.

It is likely that Hrotsvitha's plays and her later epic poems were read aloud at court. Although they were neglected for many centuries, *Paphnutius* was performed by the Pioneer Players in London in 1914, translated by Christopher St John (Christabel Marshall) and directed by the suffragette Edith Craig, with her mother Ellen Terry taking the lead. The words of Hrotsvitha were also used in St John's suffrage-inspired historyplay, *The Pageant of the Stage*. Hrotsvitha appears in several nineteenth-century collections of **Female Biography** including Jane Williams' *The Literary Women of England* [*sic*] (1861) and Ellen Fries' *Remarkable Foreign Women* (1890). **Lina Eckenstein** also wrote on Hrotsvitha in *Women Under Monasticism* (1896) as did Alice Kemp-Welch in *Of Six Medieval Women* (1913).

Mary Spongberg

Further reading

Cockin 1998; Dronke 1984; Haight 1965; Lerner 1993; Thiébaux 1987; Wilson 1987.

Major works

Anne Lyon Haight (ed.) *Hroswitha of Gandersheim: Her Life, Times and Works* (New York: The Hroswitha Club, 1965).

Hurd-Mead, Kate Campbell 1867–1941

American physician, historian of women in medicine. Born at Danville, Quebec, Canada, the eldest of three children of Sarah Elizabeth Campbell and Edward Payson Hurd, a physician. Educated at the public high school at Newburyport, Massachusetts, graduating in 1883. She studied further with tutors, then in 1885 entered the Women's Medical College of Pennsylvania in Philadelphia, graduating in 1888. She completed a year's internship at the New England Hospital for Women and Children in Boston in 1889 and in the following year undertook postgraduate work in Paris, Stockholm and London. Married William Edward Mead, professor of Early English at Wesleyan University in 1893.

Following her studies Hurd-Mead had a long and distinguished career in the medical profession. In 1890 she was appointed medical director at the newly founded Bryn Mawr School in Baltimore. Following her marriage she moved to Middletown, Connecticut, where she was one of the incorporators and later secretary of Middlesex County Hospital. She completed postgraduate studies in Vienna in 1904. Specialising in the diseases of women and children, she served as consultant gynaecologist to the Middlesex Hospital between 1907 and 1925. She was vice-president of the State Medical Society of Connecticut between 1913 and 1914 and president of the American Medical Women's Association (AMWA) from 1922 to 1924. She provided financial support to the American Women's Hospitals, the AMWA's service committee which supported women physicians in undeveloped countries worldwide. She helped organise the Medical Women's International Association in 1919 and served as corresponding secretary for the United States. Hurd-Mead was also a member of the League of Women Voters and of the Child Welfare Association.

Hurd-Mead began studying the neglected history of women in medicine after attending meetings of the Johns Hopkins Hospital Historical Club in Baltimore in 1890. She studied and wrote history for the rest of her life, especially after she retired from practice in 1925. She spent two years researching in the British Museum Library and travelled for several years in Europe, Asia and Africa, collecting data on women physicians. In 1933 she published *Medical Women of*

America and in 1938 a *History of Women in Medicine*. *Medical Women of America* detailed the contributions to medicine of individual women; the establishment of medical schools for women, women's employment in the medical profession and the admission of women to medical societies. *History of Women from the Earliest Times to the Beginning of the Nineteenth Century* is a similarly broadly based narrative of women's participation in medicine, drawing on literary references, mythology and archaeology, as well as sources in Spanish, French and German. Hurd-Mead planned two more volumes of *History of Women*. Volume two, covering the Eastern hemisphere, from Australia to Ireland, exists in manuscript. Volume three, on the Western hemisphere, was in progress when she died. Hurd-Mead's historiographical approach was openly feminist as she sought to reveal and rehabilitate women as subjects in the history of medicine. This saw her work being criticised by the medical establishment. Her extensive medical history collection was given to the Women's Medical College of Pennsylvania, where she also established a fund to provide an annual lecture on the history of women in medicine.

Sarah Howard

References

Bass 1956; Des Jardins 2003; Lovejoy 1941.

Major work

A History of Women in Medicine from Earliest Times to the Beginning of the Nineteenth Century (Winchester: Longwood Press, 1979).

Hutchinson, Lucy 1620–1681

English poet, translator, historian. Born in Tower of London, daughter of Sir Allen Apsley, Lieutenant of the Tower, and Lucy St John, his third wife, of Tregoze in Wiltshire. She was a precocious child who received an extensive education under the influence of her mother. She recorded in an autobiographical fragment that she could read by the age of four and became a competent linguist, able to work in both Latin and French. She developed an interest in Calvinist theology, a highly unconventional area of scholarship for women. In 1638 she married John Hutchinson who became an officer in the parliamentarian army and the governor of Nottingham. During the civil wars and interregnum they lived at Owthorpe, the Hutchinson family estate in Nottinghamshire. John Hutchinson was one of the Regicides, though he was not incarcerated until accused of plotting an uprising in 1663. He died in prison in 1664 and Lucy Hutchinson was left with debts which she paid off through the sale of family estates. Lucy Hutchinson had nine children, at least two of whom died in infancy.

John Hutchinson's death prompted Lucy Hutchinson to write her main historical work, 'The Life of John Hutchinson', though it was not published until 1806 in an edition by Julius Hutchinson re-titled *Memoirs of the Life of Colonel Hutchinson*. This went through several editions in the nineteenth century and was re-edited with the inclusion of some correspondence of C H Firth in 1906. Hutchinson's account of her husband reveals their shared 'puritan' sympathies. The political narrative and Republican sentiment is interwoven with a providential interpretation of events. For example, 'the hand of God was mightily seen prospering and preserving the parliament till Cromwell's ambition unhappily interrupted them' [1906 edn, 273]. Hutchinson's text is also littered with evidence of her taste for poetry: Captain Charles White is described as 'the devil's exquisite solicitor'. It is very detailed factually drawing on her own notebooks and Thomas May's 'history'. *Memoirs* features

John Hutchinson as Plutarchan hero; his greatness and magnanimity are demonstrated constantly through unflattering portraits of others. Lucy Hutchinson's own role during the civil war is seen in snatches, for example when she describes herself nursing the sick of both sides in Nottingham Castle. However, she diminished her authorial presence by describing her husband as 'a very faithful mirror, reflecting truly, though but dimly, his own glories upon him'. She allowed some oblique personal praise, recording her husband's judgement of her work as 'beyond the customary reach of a she-wit'. *Memoirs of the Life of Colonel Hutchinson* is primarily a scholarly narrative of the English civil wars, commonwealth and restoration and, as such, it ranks with the work of Edward Hyde, Earl of Clarendon.

Hutchinson was a remarkable scholar, a rigorous Calvinist and arguably the finest woman historian of the English Renaissance. Her translation of Lucretius' *De Rerum Natura* was published in a modern edition in 1996. It has also been suggested that she was the author of an anonymous poem 'Order and Disorder' (1679), a meditative exploration of the Fall. She was an admirer of Cromwell's chaplain, John Owen, and wrote two theological treatises – *On the Principles of the Christian Religion* and *On Theology* – published in 1817. However, her historical biography of her husband is usually regarded as her greatest achievement.

Amanda L Capern

References

Hudson 1993; *NDNB* 2004; Norbrook 2001; Todd 1989.

Major works

Lucy Hutchinson, *Memoirs of the Life of Colonel Hutchinson: With a Fragment of Autobiography* (ed.) N H Keeble (London: Dent, 1995).

I

Industrialisation

Recently there has been a great deal of writing about women's experience of industrialisation as part of a range of industrial developments. Gender is now critical to all assessments of the experience of and the impact of industrialisation. It was not always the case; the history of industrialisation tended to focus on factory systems and male workers. Once the Industrial Revolution was thought to have been a discrete historical phase that began in Britain in the last part of the eighteenth century and resulted in improved agricultural efficiency, accelerated population growth and improved transport and distribution infrastructure. The surplus labour thus freed was able to urbanise and work in larger and increasingly mechanised workplaces. Histories of industrialisation elsewhere frequently took this British experience as the touchstone to measure other industrialisations. Most accounts now emphasise slow continuous change with more gradual productivity gains and a range of work practices. Change was uneven. Indeed for many the notion of industrialisation having ended is premature as well as thoroughly British and ethnocentric.

Despite historians in general concentrating upon male factory workers, there are examples of women writing about industrialisation from the early nineteenth century. Britain has the earliest tradition of industrialisation and most developed accompanying writing. While there was no sudden revolution, clearly Britain was the 'first industrial nation' and industrialisation may best be understood discursively (Zlotnick 1998: 1). British women writers' interest in industrialisation partly flows from Britain's comparative advantage, and also from the feminist project itself. **Feminism** starts from the view that women are systematically disadvantaged in modern society. It suggests that men and women should have equal opportunities. The idea of industrialisation has been associated with the most profound economic changes. A highly unequal sexual division of labour is seen as a central characteristic of both industrialisation and **modernity**. Commentators have been drawn then to industrialisation as a defining social as well as economic force, although their research questions have changed over time. A relatively small circle of middle-class novelists in the mid-nineteenth century debated the moral effects of industrialisation in fiction. Political women had fewer common interests and could not agree over what the state should do about industrialisation. It did not help that they were not clear as to the extent of women's involvement in industrialisation. Turn-of-the-century reformers did better research but they were deeply divided over the effects of the state's industrial measures especially over protective labour legislation. Professional women historians exhibit variations in argument and approach over the twentieth century although they all, to some extent, maintain the Industrial Revolution changed gender relations. A survey of British women's writings about industrialisation since the early nineteenth century does not settle the issue of whether women's position improved as a result of the Industrial Revolution but it reveals the extent to which women's work and change has been put in the spotlight and mainstream history.

Fiction and industrialisation

Charlotte Bronte was at the centre of a small and far-flung circle of friends writing about industrialisation. In June 1850 Mary Taylor having emigrated to New Zealand wrote to her Roe Head schoolfriend, Charlotte Brontë back in England, about Brontë's book *Shirley* (1849). The novel was about the introduction of cropping machines and Luddite riots earlier in the century which Brontë had heard about at Roe Head and then subsequently researched in the columns of the *Leeds Mercury* newspaper of 1812–1814 (Gaskell 1857/1966: 378). Taylor complained that Brontë took as her subject the first duty of women to be in paid employment but only for some women, those who eschewed marriage and men. Taylor accused Brontë of being 'a coward and a traitor' for all women ought to earn money: 'A woman who works is by that alone better than one who does not and a woman who does not happen to be rich and who *still* earns no money and does not wish to do so, is guilty of a great fault – almost a crime – a dereliction of duty which leads rapidly and almost certainly to all manner of degradations' (Smith 2002: 392). In 1865 and 1870 she returned to England having earned sufficient in colonial retailing to retire comfortably. Taylor wrote a series of articles in the new feminist journal, *The Victorian Magazine*, that were later republished as *The First Duty of Women* in 1870 on the theme of women's obligation to earn money. This theme, the morality of women's paid employment in a new order, was the backdrop too for her 1893-novel *Miss Miles* (Stevens 1972; Bellamy 1997).

Harriet Martineau, a second literary female friend, had a different criticism of Brontë's work. In her obituary of Brontë in 1855 she noted an undue concern with poor conditions of the middle-class women workers. Martineau wrote a novel too, but at the time she began her friendship with Brontë she had revealed her sense of history in her *Illustrations of Political Economy* (1832),

34 novelettes which covered 'the growing division of labour and the effects of machinery; the relation between wages, prices, and profits; the importance of individual initiative and labor and the negative effects of state support' (Hoecker-Drysdale 1992).

Not all of Brontë's literary friends were so critical. In 1850 Brontë met Elizabeth Gaskell whose *Mary Barton* was published a year before *Shirley*. It was another novel about industrialisation but in this case working people struggling in Manchester including an unsuccessful effort to present the Charter to Parliament. Gaskell had been writing on working-class characters in Manchester since she wrote 'Sketches Among the Poor' with her husband, a Minister, in the *Blackwell's Magazine* in 1837 (Staff 2002). Gaskell concentrated on the gap between rich and poor and the temptation for the working class to respond to social injustice violently. Brontë confided to Gaskell that there were parts of *Mary Barton* which she 'never dare read a second time' (Smith 2002: 476). After her death Gaskell wrote a commemorative biography of Brontë. She explained that Charlotte thought 'she had described reality' albeit fictively (Chapple and Pollard 1966: 308). They were both engaged in 'female novelistic and in so doing offered historical understanding of these events'. Others have noted the documentary nature of these women's fiction: Brontë read newspapers and Charlotte Elizabeth Tonna's *Blue Book*, although this can be taken too far (Koacevic and Kanner 1970; Shelston 1989).

This circle of women writing about industrialisation indicates how widely ideas about industrialisation were circulating in society. These women were widely read and had transatlantic reputations too. Gaskell was quite adamant that 'I am, (above every other consideration) desirous that it should be read . . . my own belief that the tale would bear directly upon present circumstances' (Chapple and Pollard 1966: 345). The famous authors were the tip of a literary phenomena. Many middle-class Victorian women displayed their understanding of the historical process in their diaries, letters to friends and editors, magazine articles, poetry, book and reviews of other people's writings (Kovacevic 1975). As early as 1894 Amy Bulley and Margaret Whitely's *Women's Work* was drawing attention to 'the multitude of scribblers of lesser fame . . . An immense amount of second class fiction is written by women, who seem to have a special gift for producing tales that are readable and brightly written without ever rising above the level of mediocrity' (1894: 4). These sources reveal above all a spirited debate as well as intense conversations about how to construct historical and literary accounts of industrialisation.

An examination of women poets serves a similar purpose. Ellen Johnston wrote her *Autobiography, Poems and Songs of Ellen Johnston, The Factory Girl* in 1867. This text was significant because she was pre-eminent among just a few female muses. Her popularity was not unrelated to the fact that her poetry seems at odds with her description of her life as a factory worker with an illegitimate daughter, for instance, 'Kennedy's Dear Mill' is a paradise: 'The workers are as free As the sunshine of the hill' (Jump 1999). Lesser-known Janet Hamilton, mother of ten, a tambourer (embroiderer), shoemaker's wife, had her narrator in 'Lay of the Tambour Frame' denounce working-class men who opposed better pay for needlewomen: 'Selfish, unfeeling men! Have ye not had your will? High pay, short hours; yet your cry, like the leech Is, Give us, give us still. She who tambours – tambours for fifteen hours a day – Would have shoes on her feet, and dress for church, Had she a third of your pay.' 'Marie', for example (her last name is not known), was a dye-worker from Chorley who published several poems in William and Mary Howitt's *The People's Journal and Howitt's Journal* beginning in 1847, and in assorted journals for a few years thereafter including *Eliza Cook's Journal* (Alves 1996). Eliza Cook, the eleventh child of a tinsmith and brazier, published *Melaia, and Other Poems* (1838) and managed to find the financial and other resources to edit *Eliza Cook's Journal* as a penny-biweekly from 1849 to 1854. In her poems, she commented on the factory conditions, the dignity of labour and working.

Over and above their differing regard for industrialisation and their common theme of moral choices, Brontë, Gaskell and the others have been criticised for their romantic content and the modest change they portray. In the end the woman are married off. Indeed some have argued that later feminists and cultural historians ignored their work because of its non-radical feminism (Shelston 1996: 414–34). More recently Rohan A Maitzen (1998) has catalogued the numerous historical texts written by women and taking women as their subjects, arguing that there was a challenging of conventional beliefs about historical authority and relevance that had long relegated women to the margins. We can rehabilitate the writers further. Together they shared a desire to challenge stereotypes of women in paid employment. Factory women were assumed to possess few moral scruples in the early nineteenth century. The promiscuity of the mill girl was such a common stereotype that one writer in the *Morning Chronicle* flatly declared that there was scarcely a thing as a 'chaste factory girl' (Rule 1986: 1999). And it is here that literary women's engagement with the effects of industrialisation are so potent. Bessie Rayner Parkes in her essay 'The Market for Educated Female Labour' (1859) argued that industrial employment did not unsex women (2002: 141–50). *Mary Barton* challenged the promiscuous characterisation and it was read in large numbers. The contrast is clear with novels written in the twentieth century about eighteenth- and nineteenth-century industrialisation. Tracie Paterson and Judith McCoy Miller's trilogy, *Daughters of the Loom* (2003), *A Fragile Design* (2003) and *These Tangled Threads* (2003) are historical fictions without contemporary engagement.

Until recently analysis of the nineteenth-century fiction has been largely left to literary commentators. Their central question was whether there were contrasting literary treatments of the effects of the industrial revolution by male and female writers. Susan Zlotnick argues in *Women, Writing, and the Industrial Revolution* (1998) that novelists Gaskell, Brontë, Trollope and Tonna were more sympathetic to industrialism than their male counterparts. Valerie Kossew Pichanick made the same observation two decades earlier in relation to Harriet Martineau (1980: 54). Both Pichanick and Zlotnick characterise male writers as viewing industrialisation gloomily and 'critically', writing nostalgically about the past. British women writers were not so pessimistic and some even foresaw the prospect of real improvement for women in modernity. In the absence of much material by industrial workers themselves, on the basis of the middle-class novelists, should we accept that writing about industrialisation above all reveals a gendered experience? A different characterisation would be made if we included the political and professional women who were not optimistic about or favourable to the possibilities offered by industrialisation.

Political women's writings

Political commentators noticed contemporary social and economic changes but were initially slow to suggest that they impacted in any particular way upon women. Their gaze lingered upon the cities and the developing working-class political organisation. Flora Tristan's 'Tour de France' during 1842 took in 19 French industrial centres but she was still struck by the misery of urban English industrial workers. Tristan assured her readers that '[u]nless you have visited the manufacturing towns and seen the workers of Birmingham, Manchester, Glasgow, Sheffield, Staffordshire, etc you cannot appreciate the physical suffering and moral degradation of this class of the population'. Bread was a luxury for English industrial workers who did not sing, talk and laugh like French factory workers. The British worker died young, killed by work, followed quickly by his wife and children who were 'harnessed to the same machines' or else died more quickly because they had 'no work'. Tristan was not against a machine age but rather its social organisation. There had to be a social revolution in order to realise the potential advantages the machinery age offered: 'brute force banished, less time expended on physical labour, more leisure for Man to cultivate his intelligence' (1842/1982: 67).

For a while it seemed that even the 'gloomy' English would revolt at the new economic order. A brief moment of Owenite class and gender radicalism in the protest movements during the 1830s was followed by the working-class Chartist movement. Women did not take positions of active engagement or leadership in the Chartist movement. This did not mean, of course, that they were politically unaware or that they did not write of their experiences. It is certainly true that few women activists penned political pamphlets. The early nineteenth-century Chartist movement's commitment to the rights of woman is questionable but Dorothy Thompson (1971) was not short of material when she began researching women and Chartism in the 1960s. Moreover she was able to draw upon contemporary feminists such as Harriet Taylor Mill who wrote critically about the Chartists.

To some extent the later period is more difficult to trace, for none of the leading women trade unionists or left-wing workers wrote about their industrial experiences. Jill Liddington devotes some space in her biography of Selina Cooper, *The Life and Times of a Respectable Rebel* (1984), to make clear her rarity. Few women organisers like Cooper who helped her fellow women cotton mill workers into cotton trade unionism in 1893 and 1894 had the rich sources, oral histories, continuous occupancy by the family of a home from 1901 to 1983 and family members loyal to the same causes. Even here, Liddington did not manage to find one letter that Cooper wrote (1984: 450–55). Cooper's contemporary, Ada Neid Chew (1982), 'helped to expose tailoresses' appalling wages and conditions in a series of anonymous letters to the local paper, signing herself just "Crewe Factory Girl" '. These women belonged to the second wave of industrialisation and any earlier generation of women writing on industrialisation is difficult to locate.

Thoroughgoing explanations have been offered for this silence of industrial, working-class and left-wing women. They are twofold: prosaic and poststructuralist. Women were less likely than men to write about their experiences, particularly in the form of **memoirs** or autobiography. As Jonathon Rose has shown for Britain, working-class '[w]omen account for only about 5 per cent of the memoirists born before 1870 rising to about 15 per cent for the 1870–89 cohort and about 30 per cent for the 1890–1929 cohort' (2001: 2). This is indicative of the relative paucity of texts that embody female working-class voices. In keeping with such an estimate, Mrs William (Elizabeth) Sharp included just eight poems by working-class women out of 120 in her 1887 anthology *Women's Voices* (Tyler-Bennett 1995). David Vincent suggested that working-class women lacked 'the self-confidence required to undertake the unusual act of writing an autobiography' or, one might add, most publications. Working-class women were relatively literate but they were excluded from working-class organisations, subordinate in families and lacking the authority to be storytellers (1981: 8–9). The nineteenth-century working-class women who committed their thoughts about their experiences to paper were indeed singular. Some like Hannah Cullwick and Ann Yearsley wrote about domestic and rural labour rather than industrialisation but their distinctive relationships to mentors Hannah More and Arthur Munby have also been well-documented. The paucity of working-class women's writings means that it is difficult to trace 'authentic' accounts of the historical experience of industrialisation for women.

Harriet Martineau outshone other contemporary women political authors. However, Martineau's objective was shared by the other women writing about industrialisation: to show that women were critical to the process. Martineau wrote *The History of England During the Thirty Years' Peace 1816–1846* (1849–1850) but it is in her writing in the ephemeral press that she concentrates upon women. In her classic article on 'Female Society' (1858) in the *Edinburgh Review*, she showed that two-thirds of women were likely at some stage to be in paid employment. She began 'contributory women's history' over a century before second-wave feminists insisted that the Industrial Revolution was powered by working-class women's labour. She paints a grim picture of working women's circumstances, but was hopeful that industrialisation would ultimately emancipate women.

Reforming women's writings

In Britain, state intervention began with the Factory Acts from 1802. Although there were few women as part of the first official commissions of inquiry and local reports on industrialisation that focused on the factory, the state figured prominently in women's writing about industrialisation over the course of the nineteenth century. Middle-class women such as Emily Faithful and Barbara Boudichon came to write through reform and philanthropic work. The extent to which there ought to be protective labour legislation became a new axis of debate in women's writings by the end of the nineteenth century. Concern developed in Britain from the 1870s about the consequences of working conditions and the failure of the minimal state interventions to date, both in the form of factory legislation and in its enforcement. It was generally agreed that trade unionism alone would not solve women's employment situation. A more visible debate emerged between a variety of different interest groups about state intervention for women workers against the backdrop of economic depression, male unemployment and national competitiveness. Symbolically the East End of London, with its slums, crime and 'sweated' industries, was metaphorically represented as 'outcast' or 'darkest' England (Harrison 1999: 20–46). A number of strikes and demonstrations in the late 1880s intruded physically into West End terrain contributing to middle-class concerns about the threats to social stability that unemployment, sweated labour and poverty posed. This combination fuelled the fears of physical and social degeneration. As **Beatrice Webb** was to note in *My Apprenticeship*, it was here that the Industrial Revolution had 'thrust hundreds of thousands of families into the physical horrors and moral debasement of chronic destitution and chronic tenements in the midst of mean streets' (1926: 287).

Drawing on their experience of social observation, groups of feminist reformers, philanthropists and social scientists worked together to produce a range of studies of the working life of women such as Clara Collet's special study of women's work (appended to Charles Booth's famous survey of London, *Life and Labour of the People of London* 1889). Beatrice Webb recorded her experiences as a needleworker in her essay 'Pages from a Work-Girl's Diary' which she published in the contemporary journal *Nineteenth Century* (1888). Webb's experiences with Booth's work undoubtedly contributed to her views about the necessity for state intervention. In the United States the connection between Hull House and the University of Chicago allowed women social scientists to gain practice at the Settlement and theory at the School of Civics and Philanthropy and to produce sources of women writing about industrialisation.

At first, reformers' reports were uniformly useful to those lobbying for state intervention. Groups such as the Fabian Society's Women's Executive Committee or the National Federation of Settlements focused on the working conditions of women and children such as work hours and the physical impact of factory labour. Interest culminated in the 1891–1892 Royal Commission of Labour that took an unprecedented step of not only setting up a separate investigation of women's work, but appointing women to undertake it. Some of those eventually appointed to the British Women's Factory Inspectorate had worked for the Royal Commission or in sanitary inspection. Others associated with the Fabian Women's Committee Executive and the Women's Industrial Council argued for reforms. Indeed there was a raft of institutions publishing women's demands for reforms including the Anti-Sweating League, Women's Cooperative Guild, Women's Labour League and the Women's Industrial Council from 1889.

The women's factory inspectors were responsible for many of the new historical sources on industrialisation from the 1890s, generating unique records of women in industry. Inspectors visited up to 7000 factories and 3000 workshops as well as homes and hospitals annually. In addition, they prosecuted cases in the courts, and undertook special inquiries into particular kinds of work. By 1910 the inspectors were receiving 2025 written complaints representing the 'genuine' experience of women's factory work. Such state intervention led to the institution of gender-specific protective legislation that limited the number of hours and the types of work that women could undertake.

Calls for state intervention came to be increasingly challenged by other women worried that gilded cages of protection would prevent women's equality in the long term (Harrison and Nolan 2004). **Josephine Butler** and **Helen Blackburn** and others believed that there should be no 'special' legislation for women in industrial society. In the early years of the twentieth century the demand for protective labour legislation tested women's movements. The International Council of Women deliberately 'ducked from resolutions on controversial questions' such as protective labour legislation 'in an attempt to build a truly broad coalition of women's societies' (Wikkander 1995: 46).

Women historians on industrialisation

When **Ivy Pinchbeck** wrote her classic account *Women Workers and the Industrial Revolution* (1930), she was regarded as a 'remarkable pioneer', conspicuous and 'alone' in her choice of writing about women and work. Commentators suggested that while the second feminist wave promoted women's history, Pinchbeck's work permitted those histories to be written. Pinchbeck's work was considered path-breaking not only because she drew upon a wide range of sources but because she was part of a wider phenomena of women academics writing about industrialisation.

As Maxine Berg has shown, a critical number of women economic historians emerging from the London School of Economics (LSE) turned their gaze on industrialisation (1992: 308–12). The LSE proved to be the crucial institution. Formed by Fabian Socialists, Sidney and Beatrice Webb in 1895, the LSE set out to change social research and it is not surprising that a number of women academics found it congenial. **Lilian Knowles** joined LSE in 1897 and her students included Ivy Pinchbeck and Dorothy Marshall. This nursery influenced their research topics. They focused on women's economic role in the past and changes in women's status generated by the slow development of industrial capitalism. They concentrated upon the pre-industrial economy and the phase of proto-industrialisation. But more importantly their history focused almost entirely on women's labour in this period (Berg 1987: 64–9). The connection between the Fabian Movement and the LSE meant that it became an important centre for the study of women's work and their role in the economy. On the fringe non-academics but Fabian Women's Group members wrote more popular works such as Maud Pember Reeves and Mabel Atkinson's *The Economic Foundation of the Women's Movement* (1914). By the 1920s and 1930s women associated with the LSE shaped some of the most critical debate in economic and social history in the period.

The LSE work attracted a response. Knowles was a committed Tory who maintained that the Industrial Revolution brought positive changes to production and insisted that the factory system was a marked improvement on home-based industry. Her student **Alice Clark** disagreed, arguing in her *Working Life of Women in the Seventeenth Century* (1919) that women's labour had declined in status over time. Clark's account suggested that women in the seventeenth century had been more economically active than those in later centuries and she argued that their standard of living was higher. Barbara Leigh Hutchins' *Women in Modern Industry* (1915) drew on historical examples 'to argue that marriage had been an "industrial partnership" before the rise of the factory system and recognised the importance of reproduction to this partnership'. **Helen Laura Sumner [Woodbury]** drew similar conclusions about the history of women's economic production in America. **Barbara Hammond** and her husband, J L Hammond wrote about the 'apocalyptic decline' for both men and women in *The Town Labourer* (1917) and *The Skilled Labourer* (1919). Thereafter 'decline' has sometimes been in ascendancy in the women's writing about industrialisation and 'improvement' the dominant view at other times. Dorothy M George's *London Life in the Eighteenth Century* (1925) argued for positive changes. Bridget Hill's *Britain's*

Married Women Workers (1965) argued that the decline in employment opportunities for women in an agrarian economy was overtaken by industrial capitalism and that industrialisation was largely to women's paid employment disadvantage.

Since the 1980s there has been an emphasis on examining the way gender has affected economic relations during the industrial revolution in works such as Leonore Davidoff and Catherine Hall's *Family Fortunes* (1987) and Catherine Hall's *White, Male and Middle Class* (1992). Sonya Rose has examined the construction of masculine and feminine identities within the working class in *Limited Livelihoods* (1992). Judy Lown supplied a case study of gender at work in the Courtauld silk mills in mid-Victorian Essex in *With Free and Graceful Step* (1990). Anna Clark's the *Struggle for the Breeches* (1995) goes the farthest in positing a direct relationship between the decline of Chartism and the rise of a domesticated working class. Deborah Valenze's *First Industrial Woman* (1995) demonstrates changes in how women were regarded; they became 'other', weak and in need of protection. This developed out of discussion about the masculinity of the organised labour movement in works such as Sheila Lewenhak's *Women and Trade Unions* (1977) and Barbara Taylor's *Eve and the New Jerusalem* (1983). While a number of lost women leaders have been found most work has been on how skilled working-class men and their unions excluded or at least marginalised women and about the uneasy relationship with organised labour and working-class political institutions. Jane Humpheries in her essay 'Protective Legislation, the Capitalist State and Working Class Men' (1981) has stressed the sexual threat women in workplaces presented. In *Hidden Hands* (2002) Patricia E Johnson has noted that working-class women were seen as both dangerous sexual beings and victims in need of protection. One can explain and compensate for women's exclusion but the fact remains women's unionism was weaker than male unionism. Indeed, Katrina Honeyman's *Women Gender and Industrialisation* (2000) argues that gendered identities in the long run impeded industrialisation and working-class prospects.

Joan Scott and Sonya Rose have also revealed the extent to which gendered identities were institutionalised as the language of class was rendered masculine (Scott 1992; Rose 1993). Industrialisation gave rise to a working-class movement that involved activism and necessitated the creation of language that facilitated the mobilisation of a mass movement. Men came to dominate that language of commentary and take centre political stage in the histories of industrialisation. Catherine Hall in her 'tale of Samuel and Jemima' makes this point (1990: 78–102). Given this semantic and political hegemony, doubt is cast upon the degree to which 'genuine voices of women' remain in the scripts we have. Recent texts such as Pamela Sharpe's edited collection *Women's Work the English Experience* (1998) have focused on the definition of women as dependent particularly in the rise of the male breadwinner wage model. Jane Humpheries stresses the communitarianism of this while others have pointed to a divided working class (1977: 214–58; Seccombe 1993).

Other works such as Sally Alexander's *Becoming a Woman* (1994), Angela V John's *Unequal Opportunities* (1985) and Jane Lewis' *Women in England* (1984) have considered the sexual division of labour more closely. Deborah Valenze and others have emphasised the extent to which economic change for women has been overdrawn: the 'factory girl's liberation from the family economy was probably overestimated by contemporary observers' and her 'much vaunted independence may have been more widely discussed than experienced' (1995: 103–4). Karen Sayer's *Women of the Fields* (1993) has considered the continuing importance of agricultural work and the growth in domestic labour at the same time as industrialisation.

The insertion of women into the narrative of the Industrial Revolution in works such as Berg and Hudson (1992) has led to a revisionist perspective that reimagines the history of industrialisation. This has involved a rethinking of class. It has become commonplace in studies on industrialisation to combine class analysis with gender (Clark 1995; Koditschek 1997). Effectively there has been a collective project to gender British class analysis in regard to industrialisation. Undoubtedly there are fewer voices of women than there are of men experiencing and witnessing industrialisation. However, despite the imbalance of sources, the history has not been hobbled in the long run. Historians of industrialisation have successfully learnt to read across the grain.

Melanie Nolan

References

Alves 1996; Bellamy 1977; Berg 1987, 1992, 1996; Berg & Hudson 1992; Bulley & Whitely 1894; Chapple & Pollard 1966; Clark 1995; Gaskell 1857/1966; Hall 1990; Harrison 1999; Harrison & Nolan 2004; Hoecker-Drysdale 1992; Humpheries 1977; Jump 1999; Kovacevic 1975; Koacevic & Kanner 1970; Koditschek 1997; Parkes 1865; Rose 1993; Rule 1986; Scott 1992; Seccombe 1993; Shelston 1989; Shelston 1996; Smith 2002; Staff 2002; Stevens 1972; Valenze 1995; Vincent 1981; Webb 1926; Wikkander 1995; Zlotnick 1998.

Related essays

Great Britain; Historical Fiction; Feminism; Modernity; Memoirs.

Ireland

Women have been central to the development of patriotic and nationalist history in Ireland, and indeed to the development of Irish nationalism itself. Since the emergence of nationalism in Ireland and the emergence of a strongly nationalist tradition in historical writing are key themes in Irish history, it is therefore unsurprising that women should have engaged with those themes. But perhaps because of the development of a specifically cultural form of nationalism in Ireland, alongside political nationalism, the marginalisation of women in Irish and British political life did not have quite the same affect in Ireland as it did in other emerging **nations**.

Cultural nationalism

Women were active in shaping nationalist discourse at its core. Irish **memoirs, biography** and **historical fiction** during the eighteenth and nineteenth centuries have been seen as part of a British tradition in women's historical writing and many have identified writers like Maria Edgeworth and Sydney Owensen, **Lady Morgan** as major influences on the development of the English gothic novel, and on Sir Walter Scott's historical novels. As was usual for the Irish elite, these women moved between England and Ireland in a fluid way and many nineteenth-century Irish women writers chose London as a base because of the publishing opportunities and wider audience that were available there. Irish women were writing in a context of sharply contested and changing political circumstances that were quite different from those in England at the same time. When writing about Ireland these women frequently engaged in a wider cultural and political debate and were much more explicit about this than was usual for English women writers of the period despite the fictional form that they used. It is helpful to look at a particular example, Maria Edgeworth's *Castle Rackrent*, in order to understand the connection between women's historical writing and their political engagement. Maria Edgeworth wrote within the tradition of Irish patriotism in which her father was a key figure and which had produced a bloodless coup in Ireland in 1782 and a relatively independent Irish parliament. However, this Irish patriotic tradition had to be re-thought and re-invented in the first decades of the nineteenth century after the 1798 Rebellion came close to toppling the Irish government. The rebellion resulted in Ireland's constitutional absorption into the United Kingdom in 1801, in opposition to everything that Irish Patriots had fought for in the 1780s. English readers may have seen Maria Edgeworth's historical novels as merely small-canvas tales set in provincial Ireland. But readers with even the barest grasp of Ireland's political and social turbulence could not have missed the fact that Edgeworth's Irish novels dealt with highly politicised issues. Together with her letters and her unpublished Memoir, the Irish novels *Castle Rackrent, Ennui* (1809), *The Absentee* (1812) and *Ormond* (1817) offered a historically framed critique of the Protestant Ascendancy to which the Edgeworths belonged and an assessment of their relationships with other social groups in Ireland. Her historical fiction was emblematic of Irish society in general rather than accurate in all its historical details. The novel's apparent focus on the period before the establishment of the Irish Parliament, when Ireland was under direct British rule allowed her to draw a parallel with her contemporary period and to explore issues that were re-emerging in the context of the re-absorption of Ireland into Britain through an Act of Union. Historical fiction thus provided her a space in which she could re-think the basis of Irish patriotism in the period of post-Rebellion reconstruction and to wrestle with the issue of how Ireland and its Protestant elite could survive the process of absorption into Britain by an Act of Union which she and her father opposed.

The book was rushed through the publication process so that it could be released in the limbo period between the Act's passage through the two Parliaments in 1800 and its enactment the following year. There were fears that Ireland would descend again into Revolution, especially when King George III refused to agree to the Act of Catholic Emancipation, which had been promised as an accompaniment to the Act of Union and indeed Robert Emmet did lead a second failed Rising just two years later. Historical fiction allowed Edgeworth to explore these political issues in a way that insulated her from the full force of criticism that a political pamphlet would have attracted. By presenting an 'amusing' historical novel she could avoid the accusation that she was encouraging further rebellion. The historical fiction form gave her access to a much wider audience in England than would have been the case for an Irish political pamphlet, and helped her avoid the possibility of alienating that audience. Finally, although the Edgeworths continued to view the Union with considerable unease, by the time *Castle Rackrent* was published they saw it as inevitable. As a result, Maria used her novel as a device with which she could combat English prejudices against the Irish and encourage sympathy with the Irish predicament. She pointed out the social problems which existed in Ireland and which needed resolution if the Union was to be successful. Finally, the novel warned against the social deterioration which was likely to result from the politically corrupt methods that had been used to force the Act through the Irish parliament and it addressed the issue of how the Anglo-Irish elite should reform itself in order to maintain legitimate rule within Ireland (Hollingworth 1997: 75–82). This kind of historical discussion of the Anglo-Irish elite was later taken up by Irish novelists such as Jennifer Johnston in *The Captains and the Kings* (1972) and Elizabeth Bowen in *The Last September* (1929) which examined the declining fortunes of the Anglo-Irish in Irish society. Elizabeth Bowen also wrote a popular history, *Bowen's Court* (1959), which charted her family from the Cromwellian settlement until the mid-twentieth century and a wartime memoir *Seven Winters* (1942) in which she explored the middle-class sensibilities of her Dublin childhood.

Lady Morgan (Sydney Owenson) emerged from a similar Irish patriotic tradition as Maria Edgeworth. Her most famous historical novel *The Wild Irish Girl* (1806) explores Irish society and identity from the perspective of a young Englishman, whose family had been responsible for ruining the Gaelic family he had come to love. Lady Morgan's work was as politicised as Maria Edgeworth's, but she argued a more nationalist case. Historical fiction did not insulate her from trenchant criticism and her publisher initially refused to publish *The Wild Irish Girl* because of its nationalist tendencies. However, it went through seven editions in two years because it was so controversial and was championed by the Catholic and Liberal parties in Ireland. Both authors can be seen as part of a process in which Irish women used historical writing to examine, critique and 'thicken' the early nineteenth-century debate about how best to resolve Ireland's problems (Connolly 1995).

The examples of Edgeworth and Morgan raise a question which has been taken up by women historical writers all over the world, namely, whether women writers were active in shaping nation-based history, or whether they were utilised and absorbed into a nationalist project which was essentially masculine and which increasingly marginalised women (Smith 1998). In the case of Ireland, women historical writers were marginalised in political nationalist movements in the later nineteenth century, but were also key figures in the development of Irish cultural nationalism. Historical writing played a key role in the creation of cultural nationalism. Both Edgeworth's and Morgan's Irish novels were closely connected with the Gaelic revival from its beginnings, which emphasised the scholarly recovery of Gaelic language, history and culture and which formed a base for cultural nationalism in the later nineteenth century. Maria Edgeworth had a detailed knowledge and interest in the antiquarian research being published in the *Transactions of the Royal Irish Academy* and she included a glossary in *Castle Rackrent* which helped to popularise that research and which emphasised the historical tenor of the novel. Similarly, Clare O'Hallaran shows that Lady Morgan's historical novels helped to popularise the scholarship of key figures in the Gaelic revival movement such as Charles O'Conor, Francis Walker and Sylvester O'Hallaran (O'Hallaran 1989: 91–2). This kind of historical fiction became a core part of the cultural nationalist attempt to oppose the anglicisation of nineteenth-century Ireland (Connolly 2001). Edgeworth and Morgan were both concerned with issues of language in Irish culture, but they represented different approaches to its use in their historical writing. While Morgan made Gaelic language one of the key focuses of *The Wild Irish Girl* (1806), as an emblem of Irish national culture, Maria Edgeworth's Irish vernacular was actually a 'Hibernicised' form of English and she avoided any reference to the Gaelic language.

Cultural nationalism sought to recover a Gaelic past that could be used to legitimise and demonstrate the existence of an Irish culture in the present. It focused especially on the recovery of historical and mythical figures that could be used as heroic exemplars of Irish-Gaelic culture. Since Irish culture was a largely oral culture, this frequently involved the recording of folklore and **oral traditions**, as well as the re-telling of Gaelic tales within modern fiction. Irish women were active participants in Ireland's oral tradition, although there is continuing scholarly debate about whether the high bardic tradition and more localised traditions were divided along gender lines. Some of Ireland's most famous storytellers were women, such as Peig Sayers who, in the period after Ireland gained political independence, dictated several volumes of Irish tales as well as her autobiography in Irish. Published originally in 1936 and used as an Irish-language school set text, it was later translated into English and published as *Peig: The Autobiography of Peig Sayers of the Great Blasket Island* (1973).

In the nineteenth century, those women that were prominent in the cultural nationalist movement were also key figures in recovering and popularising Irish oral traditions, especially those that dealt with Gaelic heroic figures. Lady Augusta Gregory was a major figure in the Gaelic League and in the Anglo-Irish literary movement and she published popular and children's editions of myths and legends from the Gaelic past (sometimes collaborating with W B Yeats), as well as the faerie tales that were an important part of Irish popular culture. The most famous example was her re-telling of the heroic Cuchulain Cycle, which gained great symbolic importance in republican nationalist ideology and was used by Patrick Pearse in historical teaching at St Enda's School, afterwards called a 'school for nationalism' in which a generation of Ireland's nationalist leaders were educated. It became an important part of the heroic symbolism that formed the basis and justification of the Easter Rising in 1916 (see Edwards 1977; Gilley 1987). Women were also active in writing historical epic poems in this period, such as Emily Lawless' *With the Wild Geese* (1902), which retold and commemorated the experiences of those Irish soldiers who were exiled to Europe under the terms of the Limerick Treaty in 1691 and which was a key episode in the heroic nationalist tradition.

Women have also been active in writing down Irish oral traditions in which modern historical themes were frequently interwoven. In addition to her re-telling of Gaelic myths and legends, Lady Augusta Gregory published a two-volume collection of Irish folklore, *Visions and Beliefs in the West of Ireland* (1920) and a compilation of the folk history *The Kiltartan History Book* (1909). The latter collection moved seamlessly between narrative figures like Fion ma Cumhail, tales about Oliver Cromwell and tales about nineteenth-century nationalists like Daniel O'Connell and Charles Stewart Parnell. In the process, it presented Irish History as a continuous and unbroken Gaelic tradition which could be explored at the popular level and which did not rely on professional history or on the exploits of elite men. Women's involvement in oral traditions has continued to play an important role in Ireland, and has undergone revival recently in English- and Irish-language poetry and fiction, in such works as Angela Bourke's Irish language *Inion Ri an Oileain Dhorcha* ([1991] The Daughter of the King of Dark Island), written in the tradition of Royal Irish faerie tales.

After the establishment of the Free State, an Irish Folklore Commission was set up to record Irish oral traditions. When this recovery process became professionalised it quickly became masculinised as well, however some recordings were still made by female storytellers. Work within the Commission could be used as one route into professional history; Maureen Wall is a case in point. She joined the Folklore Commission as a typist after completing her History degree, but the experience of archival work that she gained was unusual among Irish historians in the 1940s and 1950s. This put her in a strong position when historical revisionism began to emphasise evidence-based historical writing, which in turn allowed her to move into an academic position at University College, Dublin.

Patriotism and political activism

Many Irish women used short biographies to identify and exemplify a set of key national virtues and characteristics that had a specifically female aspect. Lady Morgan explained that her history of women, *Woman and Her Master* (1840), blended 'the imaginary though improbable incident with the interesting fact' in a womanly way, in order to tell the story of Ireland's past and at the same time identify 'Irish virtue, Irish genius, and Irish heroism'. But some Irish women such as Mary Aikenhead drew upon historical evidence to write within a tradition that explicitly contested the ideals of Irish womanhood. She drew a picture of women's roles in the Gaelic past that formed a direct contrast to nineteenth-century English Protestant views, which represented Irish women as morally depraved and uncivilised. Drawing on the work of Gaelic scholars and antiquarians she used the high status of women in Gaelic society as evidence that Irish Catholic culture was an appropriate and legitimate basis for the virtuous and educated Irishman in the nineteenth century. As she explained, in her *History of the Foundation of the Congregation of the Irish Sisters of Charity* (1879):

> The careful mother, who could not grace her home with the presence of the learned [bards], sent forth her sons to encounter the risks of a perilous voyage and the dangers of foreign travel, so that they might escape the dreaded doom of ignorance; she lent her best efforts to the fostering of that magnanimous loyalty so requisite for the preservation of the ancient faith.

In the process, Aikenhead and others adapted an existing discourse in which Irishness was already infused with notions of femininity and in the process she placed women at the centre of an emerging culturally based nationalist discourse (Warner 1976; Kelleher 1997; Kelleher and Murphy 1997).

Elizabeth Owens Blackburne's two-volume *Illustrious Irishwomen: Being Memoirs of Some of the Most Noted Irishwomen from the Earliest Ages to the Present* (1877) was a work of what she called 'silent patriotism'. Feminist scholars have pointed out that it departed markedly from the masculine heroic tradition of Irish cultural nationalism, because it was an unusually eclectic collection which included many non-heroic figures such as actresses, literary figures and even a 'miscellany' section (Kelleher 2001). This marks her off from her more numerous counterparts who, like Mary Aikenhead, reinforced 'separate spheres' ideology that confined women to the domestic and cultural spheres while men were active in the public or political sphere.

During the 1920s and 1930s, Helena Concannon published more work on Irish women's history within the biographical genre than has been published before or since, using evidence from **private writings** such as diaries, letters and so on. Working outside the formal historical discipline, she popularised the scholarly and antiquarian work that had emerged from the Gaelic revival, as had women historical writers before her. Her 'lives' promoted an ideal of Irish Catholic republican motherhood that fitted very well with the needs of an emerging republican but conservative Catholic State. Her writing also fitted well with the way the Catholic Church saw its role, as the guarantor of that new state and society and with the Church's assumption that Irish womanhood was associated with the ideal of self-sacrificing motherhood. Consequently, she was given substantial financial and practical support by both the new Irish State and the Catholic Church, and in this sense she might be seen as contributing to a masculinist nationalist agenda. However, the fact that women had been, and continue to be, so active in promoting cultural nationalism in their published work does belie the assumption that women were wholly confined within the private sphere.

The notion that women should remain in the private sphere had long been contested by politically active Irish women. Many of these women were engaged in historical writing as well. The Ladies Land League (1879–1884) is a good example. Created as an auxiliary organisation to the National Land League led by Charles Stewart Parnell, the Ladies Land League took over the Land War's leadership when the National Land League's male leaders were in gaol. Their activities sparked a contest over the roles women should play in the public sphere and the nationalist struggle, and why this led to a permanent split between Anna Parnell and her brother Charles (Côté 1991). Debate on the Ladies Land League generally favoured the view that women should remain in the private sphere, a view powerfully backed by the Church, but the Ladies Land League presented a countervailing view in both their actions and their members' historical writing. Anna developed a sharp critique of the activities and aims of the male leadership and in her memoir of the Land League, *The Land League: Tale of a Great Sham* (c.1906), she presented a gendered view of nationalism which diverged markedly from Mary Aikenhead's, making a direct public claim for women's involvement on equal terms with men in the nationalist cause. Even so, while the Gaelic League and Sinn Fein both allowed women prominent roles, most Irish political associations continued to exclude or marginalise women. Some women engaged in gun-running like Mary Spring Rice, or were militarily active like the members of Cumann na mBan, or were prominent nationalist politicians like Constance Markievicz, the first woman MP to win a seat in the Westminster Parliament in 1918 (She did not however take her seat because of the Sinn Fein boycott.) In her *Women, Ideals and the Nation* (1909), Markievicz articulated a vision of the Irish nation which was closely identified with Gaelic Ireland, and which used the Gaelic past to justify the view that men and women should participate in the public sphere on an equal footing with men.

As in the nineteenth century, the use of the Gaelic past to justify particular gender roles in the Irish present was a strong theme in women's writing during the early decades of the twentieth century, and this was brought into even sharper focus by the debate in that period about whether nationalism and feminism were compatible. On one hand, Hannah Sheehy Skeffington argued in the *Bean na hÉireann* in November 1909 that:

> [I]t is barren comfort for us Irishwomen to know that in ancient Ireland women occupied a prouder, freer position than they now hold even in the most advanced modern states, that all professions, including that of arms, were freely open to their ambitions.

However, Skeffington concluded that the 'degradation of the average Irishwoman' was only partly the result of anglicisation; it was also perpetuated in contemporary Irish life and politics, and enforced by the nationalist Sinn Fein party which refused women the vote just as did the British Parliament. Margaret Cousins, who co-founded the Irish Women's Franchise League (IWFL) with Skeffington, explained in her *Memoirs* that:

> We were as keen as men on the freedom of Ireland, but we saw the men clamouring for amendments which suited their own interests, and made no recognition of the existence of women as fellow citizens. We women were convinced that anything which improved the status of women would improve, not hinder, the coming of real national self-government. (Owens 1993: 15–19)

On the other hand, Skeffington's critics argued that IWFL confused Irish with English ideas, but that women's suffrage granted by an English parliament would not free Irish women. The Irish Free State's constitution of 1922 did enfranchise women, but it was the last piece of progressive legislation that affected women for some 50 years (Owens 1986).

Revisionism

The process of masculinisation in historical writing did occur in Ireland and was associated with the development of a much more professionalised History discipline, but the process seems to have occurred later than elsewhere and was closely connected with the emergence of a revisionist historiography. A new generation of Irish women historians emerged as a result of the Irish University Act of 1909, which established a National University of Ireland and provided education for women and men on an equal basis. Irish women established a foothold as lecturers, and the first professors of history at University College, Dublin and University College, Galway were women, Mary Hayden appointed in 1911 and Mary Donovan appointed in 1914. When Constantia Maxwell was appointed to Trinity College, Dublin in 1908 she was the first woman member of staff and she was later appointed professor of economic history in 1936 and then Lecky Chair of History in 1947. Maud Violet Clarke, a medieval historian, held the chair of history at Queen's University, Belfast temporarily between 1916 and 1919 when its permanent incumbent F M Powicke was in the army. These women were prominent in the development of Irish economic and social history, though they chose not to focus specifically on the history of Irish women. They emphasised social and economic history, in part because this allowed them to recover a national past that was associated with the 'true' Irish people rather than with the Protestant elite. Thus, their work was infused with the continuing debates about the nature of Gaelic society.

These academic historians were joined by other women who were prominent as historical writers in the first decades of the twentieth century, including **Alice Stopford Green**, founding member of the Historical Association in England in 1909. She believed that her historical writing for children and for a popular audience was bringing 'about a new study of Irish history' because it focused on the history of the Irish people including women, rather than the history of politicians. Like other schoolbook authors such as Eleanor Knott and Ada K Longfield, Stopford Green presented the view that Irish Gaelic culture had been civilised before the English influence debased it and that the recovery of that culture through school-history and literature was an important basis for the Irish nation. In *The Making of Ireland and Its Undoing 1200–1600* (1908), she used the Gaelic legal and literary sources which Gaelic scholars had discovered, in order to demonstrate that women participated fully in the Gaelic public sphere, and in turn she used this as evidence that Gaelic society was more civilised than English society (MacCurtain 1967: 168–85).

In Ireland, women were most marginalised within the historical profession in the 1950s and 1960s, when a new revisionist school of Irish history emerged. This movement was led by the new professorial appointees Thomas Moody and Owen Dudley Edwards and was represented by the journal *Irish Historical Studies* that they produced. They mounted a damning critique of the older nationalist tradition, which had focused on subaltern Gaelic groups and Gaelic culture and which most of Ireland's women's historical writing reflected. In contrast, the new revisionism involved attacks on the nationalist tradition in which history served the needs of the nation state, on the historical techniques upon which it relied and on popular rather than academic history. Revisionists championed more 'scientific' historical methods which involved a more rigorous approach to evidence and emphasised academic analysis, and which tended to focus much more on elite political history than popular history, despite the fact that this tended to be more masculine in focus. The earlier generation of women historians was therefore roundly criticised for their failure to conform to these 'scientific' historical methods, and the older styles of social history and of biography which most women writers practised were marginalised within academia (O'Dowd 1997: 38–58). Even so, women's historical writing continued to dominate Irish school history textbooks. Alice Stopford Green's texts remained dominant until well into the 1960s, because they were accessible and utilised more traditional but popular writings including moral tales about national heroes.

The marginalisation of women historians was also affected by the growing conservatism of Irish social and political life in the 1950s and 1960s. While the first generation of formally educated women had obtained academic posts in the early decades of the twentieth century, these successes were reversed during the 1950s and 1960s. By 1954 there were no women students at all enrolled for research degrees in Irish History in Irish universities and a very small number of women were appointed in this period (although this small group included some outstanding historians such as Maureen MacGeehin, later Wall and

Margaret MacCurtain at University College, Dublin). Irish academia resembled a men's club in which it was difficult for women to participate and the National University of Ireland operated a marriage ban. Maureen Wall was asked to resign when she married and although she continued to write history under a different job-title she was not recognised as a member of the academic staff until the 1960s when she was re-appointed on the lowest possible grade. Margaret MacCurtain did not marry, but neither was she promoted beyond the lowest grade (college lecturer) in over 30 years of distinguished service. Women are now well represented as undergraduate and research students in History departments in Ireland, but the number of women in full-time permanent academic jobs remains small (around 20 per cent is typical, although University College Galway History Department is exceptional with now around half its staff female). Some of Ireland's most influential women historians are employed outside Ireland, because larger academic communities have provided some limited opportunities for Irish women historians. An obvious example is Marianne Elliott who had to publish two award-winning books on the 1798 Rebellion, *Partners in Revolution: The United Irishmen and France* (1982) and *Wolfe Tone: Prophet of Irish independence* (1989) before she was successful in obtaining a permanent academic post in the early 1990s in England. She quickly became a major force in the development of Irish Studies in Britain, as Professor of Irish History and Director of the first fully funded Centre for Irish Studies in Britain at the University of Liverpool.

This small group of women academic historians have generally engaged with the key issues and political events that feature in 'mainstream' scholarly revisionism, using the kind of archival work and scholarly analysis that was championed by the Irish revisionist school. Maureen Wall's work on the way the Penal Laws were implemented in eighteenth century Ireland has become a core part of the debate about the nature of eighteen-century Irish society. Jacqueline Hill has recently assessed the process by which Irish Protestant Patriots were transformed into Conservative supporters of the Union in the decades after 1798, in her book *From Patriots to Unionists: Dublin Civic Politics and Irish Protestant Patriotism, 1660–1840* (1997). Her work therefore connects with debates about the nature of early nineteenth-century Irish politics and about the development of British political identity in Ireland. Nancy Curtin's *The United Irishmen: Popular Politics in Ulster and Dublin, 1791–1798* (1998) provided an important counterpoint to Marianne Elliott's work on the 1798 Rebellion's leadership, exploring how popular political mobilisation created new liberal traditions which, though short-lived, were different from those republican traditions upon which nationalist historiography had focused. Another key topic in Irish historical debates is the 1840s Famine, where a revisionist interpretation has been put forward by Mary Daly, *The Famine in Ireland* (1986) which contrasts sharply with Christine Kinealy's many books on the Famine including her *This Great Calamity: The Irish Famine, 1845–52* (1994). This group of historical writers have generally chosen not to focus on women as historical subjects and they have had variable success in incorporating women's historical voices, but they have been crucial in the gradual professional acceptance of women historians in what is generally regarded as 'mainstream' Irish history.

Women's history

A second reaction to the marginalisation of women historians and of women as subjects within revisionist history was the emergence of women's history in the 1970s and 1980s. This movement was closely connected with emergence of second-wave feminism in Ireland. Irish women historians have aimed to recover women's stories using the techniques of oral history, and economic and social history. This movement went against the tide in the Irish historical profession, which had focused on the formal political sphere and on elite history and consequently tended to marginalise women's historical voices. The new women's history also provided an answer to the revisionist criticism that the older economic and social history was not sufficiently scholarly.

Irish women's historians have often worked in relative isolation from the broader international developments in women's history, but recently some cross-fertilisation has occurred. In line with women's history elsewhere, feminist historians in Ireland are increasingly questioning separate spheres ideology and are arguing that historians' conceptions of the public sphere need to be broadened to include informal political activity in order to better appreciate women's public and political roles. Maria Luddy has examined the concepts of equality and difference that were expressed in women's political activities in the later nineteenth century. She has identified a flow-on from charitable and other informal organisations into formal political activity, which blurred the boundary between public and private, and between domestic and political (Luddy 1997: 89–108). This emerging work on Irish women's political activities has been matched by the discussion of women's economic roles by such historians as Joanna Bourke, in her book *Husbandry to Housewifery: Women, Economic Change, and Housework in Ireland, 1890–1914* (1993). Working out of English universities, Luddy's and Bourke's work connect with that of historians such as Kathryn Gleadle and Sarah Richardson (eds) *Women in British politics, 1760–1860: The Power of the Petticoat* (New York, 2000) and Clare Midgley *Women Against Slavery: The British Campaigns, 1780–1870* (London, 1992). Such connections have encouraged new explorations of women's roles in the public sphere that were derived from feminist challenges to models of republican citizenship that marginalised women and that are well represented by Mary O'Dowd and Sabine Wichert's edited collection *Chattel, Servant or Citizen? Women's Status in Church, State and Society* (1995). There has been growing interest in women's roles in political Unionism paralleling the re-thinking of republican nationalism. One of the best examples is Diane Urquart and Janice Holmes' edited collection *Coming Into the Light: The Work, Politics and Religion of Women in Ulster, 1840–1940* (1994). The feminist criticism of Irish writing as a mainly male endeavour has led to the publication of two additional volumes in the *Field Day Anthology of Irish Writing* (2002: Vols 4–5), which have made available wide-ranging examples of women's writing since 1500, together with important interpretative essays.

Irish women historians have worked to bring women's stories into the nation's historical narrative and to consider how this might change the overarching narratives. This has involved a robust feminist critique of the masculinisation of Irish professional history. The first major example was Mary Cullen's 'Telling It Our Way: Feminist History' (1985), which was a sustained critique of the leading revisionist historian FSL Lyons' book *Ireland Since the Famine* (1971), the most widely read history of modern Ireland, but which hardly mentioned women. Second, there has been a growing reassessment of the argument that nationalism subordinated feminist concerns, and that nationalism and feminism were historically incompatible. Irish feminist historians have been concerned both to uncover women's political involvement as well as to reassess the perception that nationalism was necessarily played out in the political sphere.

Women historical writers have been active in the debates about historical understanding, rhetoric and re-thinking which have been at the core of the Northern Ireland conflict and the development of the peace process and in the debates about the role played by History in the development and maintenance of cultural traditions. Women politicians have been particularly prominent in autobiographical and historical writing about the development of cross-community women's groups in the 1960s and 1970s in Northern Ireland, from which the Northern Ireland Women's Coalition (NIWC) emerged. This cross-community activity could not be sustained, but there has been recent interest among peace activists in using women's groups as a model for the re-building of civil society as one way forward in the peace process. The NIWC has been particularly associated with the development of new thinking about the importance of civil society in building peace and about the role of civil society in the development of new ideas about citizenship. Many of the NIWC's leaders have become actively involved in autobiographical and historical writing on the Troubles and on women's roles in those events, as a way of explaining their contemporary approaches to politics, and of developing a new way forward, in works such as Eilish Rooney and Margaret Woods' *Women, Community and Politics in Northern Ireland: A Belfast Study* (1995), Bronagh Hinds' *Women Working for Peace in Northern Ireland* (1999), and Kate Fearon's, *Women's Work: The Story of the Northern Ireland Women's Coalition* (1999). In a similar vein, women historical writers like Margaret Ward have played an important role outside academe, in think tanks such as Democratic Dialogue, which have drawn strong links between historical analysis and contemporary political initiatives and which is strongly connected with civil society-based approaches to peace. Similarly, the Republic of Ireland's two women Presidents have been active in re-interpreting Irish History, both since the 1970s and beforehand, in order to contribute to the discussions about community-based peace initiatives in the Northern Ireland peace process and the growing reassessment of women's political and civil society roles in the South. Alongside these explorations of civil society and women's organisations, women have also begun to write in ways that blend autobiography and personalised accounts with reassessments of broader issues in contemporary history and society. These include, for example, Eileen Doherty's book on *Bloody Sunday in Derry: What Really Happened* (1992), Bernadette McAliskey (nee Devlin)'s autobiographical *The Price of My Soul* (1969) which discusses the emergence of the Civil Rights movement, Anne Noble's *The Riot* (1985) on the Ulster Workers' Strike in 1974 which led to the fall of the Legislative Assembly in Northern Ireland, and the work of journalists including Susan McKay who has explored the loyalist tradition in Northern Ireland through a series of oral-history interviews in her *Northern Protestants: An Unsettled People* (2003).

Finally, women historical writers have been prominent in the wider debates about historical memory in nineteenth- and twentieth-century Ireland and in Northern Ireland, which connect with contemporary political debates in Northern Ireland in particular. Again, Marianne Elliott has been prominent in the discussion of historical memory in Irish political and cultural debates since the early nineteenth century, including her book *Robert Emmet: The Making of a Legend* (2003) on the development of Emmet's heroic and 'blood sacrifice' status during the nineteenth and twentieth centuries. Her recent book *The Catholics of Ulster* (2001) has reassessed the historical understandings about Northern Catholics which underlie many of the political stances of modern nationalists and unionists in Northern Ireland, and which has been controversial as a result. Beyond academic history, her membership of the Opsahl Commission in Northern Ireland is an example of the mix between historical writing and contemporary politics that every Irish historian shares. This Commission interviewed representatives from all social, political and cultural groups in Northern Ireland and allowed them to present their views, including their historical understandings. It was a major element in the emergence of the Northern Ireland peace process and in the development of the idea of 'parity of esteem' between the two major cultural and historical traditions in Northern Ireland. Other examples include the historical work of Jane Leonard as a European Union-funded Community Outreach Officer in the Ulster Museum, and of Nuala Johnson's co-edited collection *Ireland, the Great War and the Geography of Remembrance* (2003). Both explore the connections between the history of war commemoration and more recent issues in Ireland and Northern Ireland.

Jennifer Ridden

References

Connolly 1995, 2001; Côté 1991; Cullen 1985; Edwards 1977; Gilley 1987; Hollingworth 1997; Kelleher 1997, 2001; Kelleher & Murphy 1997; Luddy 1997; MacCurtain 1967; O'Dowd 1997; O'Hallaran 1989; Owens 1986, 1993; Smith 1998; Warner 1976.

Related essays

Female Biography; Great Britain; Historical Fiction; Memoir; Nation; Oral Traditions; Peace; Private writings; War.

Italy

Women's production in the field of history in Italy can probably be traced back several centuries, especially if we consider the *Libri di ricordanze,* a genre which appeared in merchants milieus of early modern Italy, family letters and the first biographical writings which developed around hagiography. Recent studies on the monasteries of the **Middle Ages** as well as of the early modern age would suggest the inclusion of nuns as historical writers (see **Convent** essay). Their activity extended almost continuously into the nineteenth century, when we can find several works which could be ascribed to both **hagiography** and history. Yet this somehow secluded world shows little resemblance to the new scholarship and even the works of lay amateurs in the nineteenth century. These are more interesting for us since we could find in the writings of these women the beginning of the new historiography of the 'century of history' as the nineteenth century has been called. Women were extremely active in the production of history during this period. As a recent and extremely broad survey has pointed out, we can identify at least 700 historical texts written by women between 1800 and 1900 (Casalena 2003).

While nuns were still writing hagiography, secular women began to tackle the subject of ancient history. Maria Fulvia Bertocchi, born in Rome around 1760, published a general history of the Greeks, the *Istoria generale dei popoli della Grecia compendiosamente trattata,* in five volumes with maps, geographical descriptions and a well constructed chronology. A few years later Chiara Vicentini's short history of roman antiquity, *Compendio delle antichità romane* (1816) came out. However comprehensive, broad and imposing these studies were, they were not openly presented as works of scholarship but as textbooks devoted to a young public of students with an educational aim. Unfortunately we do not know the degree of recognition that Vincentini was able to receive, nor we know if she was known as an historian or as an educator. Bertocchi on the other hand was also a well-known author of biblical history, but was celebrated explicitly for her volumes on Greek history. In 1805 she was awarded a life long pension from Pope Pius VII. Hopefully new research will help us to better understand the role of these women in a very special age of transition, when women's role in education began to be highly recognized even in the absence of a public system of schooling, but at the same time the 'letterate' started to be seen with increasing suspicion.

Around 1820 several academies of sciences, letters and arts partly devoted to history, which had been suppressed during the Napoleonic era, were reopened. Unlike in France, where at least some women played a certain role in the local *sociétés savante,* in Italy no woman was active in these academies in the field of history: instead, women were present as poets, artists or novelists. Yet some of these women, especially aristocratic women living in Northern and Northern-Eastern Italy, were in fact active in the field of history writing. As amateurs and biographers most of these women had taken advantage of the demand of biographies that increased during the age of Napoleon. In 1807 already Silvia Curtoni Verza from Verona, a cosmopolitan *salonnière* and a friend of important intellectuals such as Scipione Maffei and of the poet Giuseppe Parini wrote biographies of the numerous friends who used to meet in her salon. As recent scholarship has pointed out, history as a precise genre did not appear neatly defined and fully formed. If the boundaries between history and fiction have a history which 'is not continuous and uniform', as Suzanne Gearhart (1984) writes, if history can be permeated by sensibility (Epple 2004) the boundaries between biography and history are even more open and almost osmotic. In Veneto and especially in Verona, a few women continued writing in the old tradition of wise women interested in an antiquarianism. They were certainly not innovative in their approach to the writing of history. Most of them engaged with the genre of **female biography**. Isabella Teotochi Albrizzi, a well-known *salonnière,* called by Lord Byron 'the Venetian **Germaine de Stäel**', wrote about the life of the woman poet Vittoria Colonna. In the same years Bianca Milesi Mojon, known as 'the emancipated Milesi', a Swiss born protestant who played an important role in propagating the new role of mothers in breast feeding and child caring, wrote about the Greek woman poet Sappho and Maria Gaetana Agnesi, an Italian mathematician who lived all through the eighteenth century. Camilla Paltrinieri Triulzi, the daughter of the famous female intellectual, Anna Maria Vettori, and a member of several important academies, wrote the lives of the illustrious Italian Camillas. Following the model of the Plutarch these women chose to write about **women worthies**, celebrating the lives of famous women of the past.

Giustina Renier Michel represents the first shift towards a new way of writing and towards a new form of patriotic if not political engagement. She was also an aristocrat: her grandfather was the last Doge of Venice before the end of the Republic. Like Teotochi Albrizzi she was a salonnière and like Curtoni Verza she shared the friendship of the most important intellectuals of her time. Yet her work is more original. After the end of the Republic and the annexation to the Austrian Lombardo Veneto she abandoned her previous activity of translation and gave up the study of natural sciences in order to concentrate on the history of Venice. In spite of the bitter interventions of Austrian censorship which was suspicious of her patriotic interest in Venetian traditions, her masterpiece in six volumes on the origins of Venetian festivals, *Origine delle feste veneziane,* first published in 1829, enjoyed large success and was republished in shorter versions in 1830 and again in 1852 and 1860. This large study, resulting from anthropological interest in everyday life, rituals and apparently non-political, is in fact typical for a new kind of historical writing produced by women in the nineteenth century (Smith 1998). Such an approach to the history of Italian or regional traditions had in fact a very political scope. In the case of Renier Michel it represented a way of reminding of the original characters of the Republic and of keeping alive 'Italian' anti-Austrian feelings. Writing about traditions as well as about biographies would soon be a way of constructing a historical national consciousness, of writing about the **nation.**

The impact of politics and nation

Some of the first women who were to play an important role in patriotic history writing approached it through the pattern of biography. Yet these biographies were to be very different in scope and aim. Carolina Bonafede born in Piacenza in 1812 as Carolina Pizzigoni, belonged to a new generation, brought up after the Napoleonic era. Bonafede is one of the first examples of women who passionately embraced the political position of their male relatives and who found their way to history starting out from this discovery of politics and patriotism. Her interest in politics began, she says, when her husband was arrested in 1843. Although enrolled in the papal army, he was in fact a patriot, and refused to participate in the political repression of the democrats. Soon also one of her sons was exiled in Turin and entered the Anglo-Italian legion fighting for unification, while the other was arrested and was forced to exile.

We do not know if Bonafede began to write and publish primarily in order to be able to earn her living. It might have helped, since she was a widow with little support. Like some of her forerunners she concentrated on the lives of Italian women both in the form of the dramatic plays (she wrote one play on the Bolognese painter Elisabetta Sirani) and the history of women worthies. But the difference with the previous patterns of biographical works on Italian famous women is evident. Patriotic feelings were now strongly and vividly expressed. Bonafede clearly aimed to tell the story of the family of the Italian nation through the history of her own family. Her books were aimed specifically at a female readership, especially Italian mothers. Writing about her own son was a way of connecting nation and emotions and of keeping alive the memory of the fight against the repression and the battle for liberty and for the nation. The connection between the family and the nation, which was strong in this generation of women patriots, was even more evident in the dedication of her works. *Memorie biografiche di Luigi Sabatini Bonafede* (1863), a book dealing with the experience of her husband, was dedicated to her brothers and sisters, and her second book, published immediately after the accomplishment of unification (1870), was dedicated to her grandchildren.

With Bonafede we enter the first generation of men and women who wrote about the history of the Italian Risorgimento through their memories using as sources the papers which they had kept in the years of the struggle for unity, while their relatives, fathers, brothers, sons and lovers were hiding from Austrian police. The works of these men and women, who had an important role in keeping and hiding letters and papers, attain legitimacy not only through the sources, but through the own experiences of the writers as witnesses.

In the absence of professional historical training for Italian women (and men), women who engaged in historical writing were largely influenced by the reading of the patriotic novels which, during the first half of the 1800s, represented one of the grounds (perhaps the core) of the formation of the national consciousness. Others were influenced by the charisma of heroic characters such as Garibaldi. For the Lombard princess **Cristina Trivulzio di Belgiojoso** and the democrat Jessie White, wife of patriot Alberto Mario, the writing of history represented a way of continuing their conspiratorial work within secret societies or battles fought first-hand in the Milan of the *Cinque Giornate* of 1848 or in the Roman Republic of 1849.

The first element to be underlined is that the first generation of women took a direct part in political (and sometimes even military) action towards the conquest of national independence. They wrote as witnesses. Most of these women were on the side of democrats. Both the concept of *pariah*, according to Bonnie Smith's definition, and of *traumatic history* can be applied to these women and their writings. Studying them implies a link to a whole series of recent studies focusing on women's participation in the 1848 revolutions or the conspiratorial activities of patriotic women in southern Italy (Guidi 2004).

The 'long Italian 1848' (1846–49) was a very important moment for the political struggle for independence and eventually unification. The very fact that political demonstrations had begun under the auspices of the church and had been developed in the form of processions which were so similar to the Catholic ones which used to be attended by the greatest number of women probably helped to facilitate and bridge the presence of women on the scene of political protest. Recent contributions on the history of the European revolutions of 1848 have pointed out the relevance of the presence of women in many countries. Yet Italy was perhaps special in that respect. Here, some women – generally ignored from historiography until very recent years – played a relevant role in both participating in the events and supporting the political movement through historical writings (Porciani 2000).

The best known of them is Cristina Trivulzio di Belgiojoso who devoted most of her life equally to historical writing and fighting for unification. In 1847 she had already written an important and politically engaged essay on the history of Lombardy in the last 30 years, *Studi intorno alla storia della Lombardia degli ultimi trent' anni e delle cagioni del difetto d'energia dei Lombardi.* This study was printed in Paris since the Austrian censorship would have not allowed its publication. In 1848 when the war broke out she intensely supported and personally financed the military campaign against Austria from Milan. One year later during the short and tragic life of the Roman democratic Republic she organized together with **Margaret Fuller** a service of assistance for the wounded entirely relying on lay women. She published influential articles on the very recent history of the 1848 uprising in the *Revue des Deux Mondes, L'Italie et la revolution italienne de 1848,* immediately translated into Italian and widely received in the clandestine democratic milieus. In the 1850s she rejected the democratic ideals and became a strong supporter of the liberal and moderate as well as monarchist Piedmontese leadership in the process of unification. Her work was very important in popularising the image of the Savoia Monarchy. In 1850 she published in her Paris exile *Premières notions d'histoire à l'usage des enfants: Histoire romaine* and confirmed the pedagogical vocation of many of these women historians which was going to be reasserted after unification, when many women entered the teaching profession and wrote textbooks especially for girls, in some cases published by important publishers and even in co-authorship with relevant historians. Finally, she wrote *Etudes sur l'Asie Mineure et les Turcs*, an important essay on Turkey, where she lived for a while and a series of observations on international politics, *Sulla moderna politica internazionale* (1869).

This cosmopolitan aristocrat could be easily compared with another cosmopolitan woman patriot and writer of important historical works: Jessie White. Daughter of a ship builder, whose second wife was engaged in popular education, she was already a cultivated young lady since she had even studied at the Sorbonne. She came to Italy in 1854 as the companion of a rich widow and became acquainted with supporters of democracy. She met Garibaldi, and was fascinated by him. She decided to join his troops as a nurse, ready to take care of the wounded. She married the patriot Alberto Mario, and later devoted herself to the conservation and organisation of the first archives of the patriots, playing a critical role in the preservation of the sources for the recent history of Unification. White's most relevant works were the very successful biographies of Mazzini and Garibaldi.

For many of these women, writing history was also a way of constructing their own identity as women and as members of the nation if not really citizens in a full sense. The limits placed on access of women to the public sphere – the most evident being the exclusion from the right to vote – are obvious. However, on the terrain of the nation, these women negotiated their right to enter the public sphere, sometimes taking their inspiration from traditional women's charitable activities such as the collection of funds through charity sales. But they transformed this ancient practice by acting as protagonists and authors. Instead of selling embroidery or the other products of activities traditionally defined as 'women's', they sold books they had written themselves. An example of this can be seen in the group of women consisting of Gualberta Alaide Beccari, editor of the Veneto magazine *La Donna*, Caterina Croatto Caprin, Adele Butti, Giulia Ballio, Matilde Ferluga Fentler, Ernesta Margarita, Elisa Panizza Scari, Adele Pelliccia, Rosa Piazza, Felicita Bozzoli, Caterina Tetamanzi Boldrin and Annua Verta Gentile. They wrote biographies of Italian patriots for a volume entitled *Martiri italiani. Scritti storici raccolti da alcune donne a favore dei danneggiati poveri dell'inondazione di Roma* (1871). Unfortunately the correspondence leading up to this work cannot be located: therefore it is impossible to understand how the participation of each of these women was obtained. These women considered themselves authors and were recognized as such. This is the case of Anna Vertua Gentile, author of a famous *Galateo* and editor of a volume entitled *L'istruzione in famiglia* containing educational texts for young women with a marked conservative tone. Felicita Pozzoli who made her debut with this text went on in 1874 to write *Le donne nelle lotte italiane* and later *Le vicende più memorabilia d' Italia* (1889) and *Eroi ed eroine del Risorgimento nazionale* (1896).

Out of the institutions

These women, however, are absent from the traditional histories of Italian historiography. Benedetto Croce does not name even one in his standard work on the history of nineteenth-century Italian historiography. Walter Maturi in his *Interpretazioni del Risorgimento* – the standard work on this topic – names Zellide Fattiboni, author of *Memorie storico biografiche al padre suo dedicate* (1885) just once and not for this work, but for a letter that she had given to male historian, Carlo Tivaroni. Belgiojoso and Rosetta Campo, who wrote *Vita politica della famiglia Campo dal 1848 al 1860* (1884) on the uprisings in Palermo, are also absent. Jessie White Mario is mentioned just three times, on the basis of the writings of Tivaroni or to express highly misogynous judgements. Yet at the end of the nineteenth century the intellectual and poet Carducci, one of the first to write on Risorgimento, included at least Fattiboni in his *Letture del Risorgimento italiano*. The erasure seems to have been introduced by academic historians as the theory of the Risorgimento began gradually to take the shape of a well-defined discipline through the foundation of periodicals and later, in the 1930s, of the first university chairs.

Throughout the nineteenth century the place of women historians was totally extra-institutional. Neither State (Deputazione di storia patria in Turin, created in 1832) nor private enterprises for the publication of sources (Archivio Storico Italiano, founded in 1841) offered them any space of scientific cooperation for decades. In these first national historical enterprises, some wealthy and influential women acted as fund-raisers and financial contributors: a role which deserves greater attention as historians come to understand the gendering of intellectual space during this period. There was no place for women in the very few university chairs of history in Italian universities after the Casati law of 1859: small wonder since it was so everywhere. Yet even at the turn of the century the academic situation was less unfavourable to Italian women than, for instance, to German ones (Porciani and O'Dowd 2004). While women were still inhibited from getting university degree in Germany, in Italy women were openly admitted to obtain university degrees. Many women studied history and became teachers of national history in secondary schools for girls long before 1914.

Just before the First World War a few hundreds of arts graduates – 'laureate in Lettere' – had written dissertations on historical subjects. Some of them continued their research for a few years after finishing university. Unlike the witnesses and biographers of the first generation, these women did not concentrate on recent national history: they started to devote themselves to the history of the Middle Ages, often with a **local history** approach characterised by erudition and they frequently wrote about very specific and limited subjects concerning their particular towns and regions. As contributors to regional historical journals, they seldom dared to challenge wide national matters.

Since the 1880s, this dimension of local history helped some women to be admitted to the Deputazioni di storia patria, a series of institutions, established after unification in every region. Due to the increasing interest in local identities, these institutions, prestigious but entirely relying on voluntary work, were also founded in most of urban centres with the aim to publish sources for the local history and promote historical research. Yet the number of female correspondents was extremely restricted and the number of women full members was very rare. It is also interesting to point out that women were more present in smaller, peripherical Deputazioni. The most important ones, as those in Turin, Naples and Florence, had strong connections to history chairs in the universities, but were not open to women until the First World War.

In this context, one exception is worth mentioning, the Princess Ersilia Caetani Lovatelli. Encouraged by her father Michelangelo, one of the leaders of the liberal aristocracy of Rome, to study archaeology and ancient history, she became very early on a member of the Deputazione di Storia Patria of Bologna and was the only woman invited to sit in the national Lincei Academy. More generally, the participation of women in historical societies such as the Deputazioni became important as well as geographically equally widespread in the 1920s and 1930s, where a large number of women had careers as archivists and librarians.

In Italian classical secondary schools history was taught together with philosophy. The minister of education and philosopher Giovanni Gentile theorized explicitly that women were unfit for philosophy. Female students were instead encouraged to study pedagogy. This may be a reason why some women started studying the history of **education**. Emilia Formiggini Santamaria, the wife of a very well-known publisher of Modena, was the first to focus on the history of female education and opened the path to other women dealing with women's schools and education such as Dina Bertoni Jovine.

Yet this did not mean the exclusion of women from studying and doing original research in history. In the same years important intellectual enterprises such as the Italian *Encyclopaedia* as well as scholarly journals gave some room to women's contributions in the field of history. Thirty-three women historians contributed to the Italian *Encyclopaedia* promoted by the fascist regime. Eight more entries of the *Encyclopaedia* were written by women under the direction of the anti-fascist historian Gaetano De Sanctis, after the Second World War.

In spite of the early involvement of women in patriotic historical writing, the institutions devoted to national political history of the Risorgimento such as the *Società Italiana per la Storia del Risorgimento Nazionale* allowed the presence of women only as financial contributors or as widows and daughters of eminent patriots and politicians. Yet many young women continued to write about the nation and devoted themselves to the history of the struggles for unification (*Storia del Risorgimento*) publishing hundreds of contributions and reviews in scientific journals, which would meet the standards of the scholarship of the time. Finally under the fascist regime the history of unification became a university discipline and in 1935 the first chairs were created. No woman was admitted to teach the history of the Risorgimento as a full professor, although there were many experts among Italian women who could have submitted excellent curricula and publications. A few women could attain a 'libera docenza' (a qualification to teach at university level) in Storia del Risorgimento nazionale before 1939. One of them was Angela Valente, who had written about 50 articles along with several books on medieval and modern history. She was allowed to teach Storia del Risorgimento at university level only as a private professor, but had to keep her job as a secondary school teacher, as Maria Avetta did, in spite of publishing several important works especially on 1848. Only later was she able to concentrate on research as the director of the Cavour Archieve in Santena, near Turin. Yet it may be relevant to remark that doing research and working as a secondary school teacher was a usual step since the number of university chairs was extremely restricted.

Ancient history and archaeology

The first women to teach within the Italian university system were ancient historians. Carolina Lanzani, born in 1875, the daughter of an important civil servant, received her degree at the University of Pisa. From 1908 she started to write in the most prestigious journal of classical antiquity *Studi storici per l'antichità classica*. She published a handbook for the schools together with her sister, also a graduate in history working as a secondary school teacher. Co-authorship was important; many women engaged in research activities as a part of a pair, as wives of scholars or as sisters. Maria Cleofe Pellegrini published several schoolbooks together with the prominent historian and university professor Cirrado Barbagallo. Apart from schoolbooks, Lanzani published important works on political history (concentrating on the crisis of the Roman republic) and on the history of religions. She enjoyed a remarkable recognition since she was called to teach in the Milan University as early as 1920. Lanzani was an early supporter of fascism and had a prominent role in the promotion of Roman history and antiquities in a time when it was absolutely crucial for the regime. She was also the director of the popular journal *Historia* (1927–1935) that was edited by the same publisher as the fascist newspaper *Il Popolo d' Italia*. She was one of the stars of the international conferences on Roman History promoted by fascism in the 1930s. After the Second World War she wrote still important books on Greek antiquities such as *Lezioni di antichità greche, Milano* (1949) and a monograph on the myth of Camillus, the *Mito storico di Camillo* (1951).

As the ancient history essay in this volume has suggested it was sometimes easier for women to gain recognition in subsidiary fields such as archaeology rather than in history itself. This is the case of Orsolina Montevecchi, from 1954 director of the school of papyrology of the Catholic university of Milan and full professor of Greek and Roman antiquities as well as honorary president of the International association of papyrology; Momolina Marconi, who graduated in 1936 and immediately became assistant of her professor and in the 1950s taught history of religions at the state university of Milan; Medea Norsa egyptologist, papyrologist and president of the International association of papyrologist from 1947 to her death. Others such as Luisa Banti (Firenze) and Paola Zancan (Padova) were very young when they started working at the Italian Encyclopedia and later became professors of archaeology. To a different generation belongs Lelia Cracco Ruggini, member of the national Lincei Academy, still active today, author of countless contributions in various languages and well known for her innovative work on Italian economy and society: *Economia e società nell' Italia annonaria*.

Fascism and anti-fascism

In the decade 1935–1945 several young women who were to publish relevant contributions in the field of history received their 'libere docenze' in ancient history, archaeology and auxiliary sciences, as well as in literature or art history. This is the case of Barbara Allason who also played an important role in cultural transfers as a translator and published influential works on German romanticism including a study of Caroline Schlegel, *Caroline Schlegel, Studio sul Romanticismo* (1919). She gathered around her private home in Turin many anti-fascist intellectuals from the liberal anti-fascist 'Giustizia e libertà' movement. More than her participation in clandestine anti-fasciast activity, it was her protest against the Patti lateranensi, the State–Church agreement of 1929, which made it impossible for her to teach at university. Thus she was forced to work in a different direction and she ended up writing novels. Nevertheless it is worth mentioning that her **memoirs,** *Memorie di un'antifascista 1919–1940*, published in 1961 are an important historical work for the understanding of the anti-fascist movement.

The fascist regime created a number of university chairs in the history of the Risorgimento in 1935 although as mentioned above no women was able to get one in the first decades. In spite of the large number of women who wrote on the Italian Risorgimento only a few, such as Angela Valente (Naples) and Emilia Morelli (Rome) were able to reach the libera docenza in Storia del Risorgimento before 1940. other younger women now entered university ranks as libere docenti in History of Law and History of Middle Ages. Some of them who graduated in law were quite prominent legal historians. Maybe this happened because women who got a degree in Law were prohibited from becoming lawyers or judges. This was the case of Ginevra Zanetti, born in 1906, who became an expert on legal history and taught first at University of Sassari and then at the State University in Milan. Dina Bizzarri too was the author of a number of important contributions on the Middle Ages – who managed to obtain a chair at the University of Camerino at the age of 46 in 1935. A more singular case is the one of Paola Maria Arcari, daughter of a prominent figure of the Catholic movement and university professor Paolo Arcari, who wrote an influential work on France, which was later to be tailored to the propaganda needs of the Regime.

Gina Fasoli born in Bassano del Grappa in 1905 deserves a particular attention, for she reached a wide recognition, testified by the fact that as early as 1950 she obtained a university chair in the prestigious field of the History of Middle Ages. Fasoli was first employed at the university in the Sicilian town of Catania as the follower of another women historian, Carmelina Naselli. She wrote around 280 contributions, many of them seminal for historians of medieval institutions. She studied the Bolognese statuti; urban history, but also economic and social history of Italy between 535 and the beginning of the tenth century. Her works were also translated into German. Urban aristocracy and urban lower classes, town and feudality, power between medieval and early modern history, local history and sumptuary laws were her most important fields of activity. She also played a critical role in important research organisations such as the Centro Italiano di Studi sull' Alto Medioevo, the Commission internazionale d'histoire des villes and the Istituto per la storia di Bologna.

Only five years after, Emilia Morelli who had started as the vice director of the Central Museum for the unification in Rome (Museo Centrale del Risorgimento) immediately after her degree in 1935, became a full professor in Storia del Risorgimento nazionale. She was the first woman officially recruited as an expert of national history, to teach regularly at University level. Her works followed with no innovation the lines of her professor Carlo Ghisalberti. Her major books were on Mazzini: a subject which proved to be very familiar to women historians.

The innovation of women's and gender history

Since the 1970s there has been a large number of women active in the production of history in Italy, therefore it might be more useful to say a few words about the important innovation of women's and gender history. Paola Di Cori, a feminist and gender historian, has been very active in the field since the 1970s and, as one of the editors of *Memoria*, has published a detailed study of the impact of feminism on Italian history. As she pointed out 'anyone attempting to do historical research on women in Italy in the early 1970s faced with problems unknown to her counterparts in England, the United states, or France' (Di Cori 1991: 443–56). Women's s history and gender history courses were introduced very late in Italy and the first tenured appointment in this field were made in the late 1990s. Given the politicisation of contemporary Italian history, the strong influence of the political parties on the writing on contemporary history and the innovative currents of Gramscian Marxist historiography, gender as a category of history analysis had problems breaking through.

It is interesting to note that while some women had an important role in writing the history of the nation in the first phase after Unification, this did not happen immediately after the Second World War, when virtually no woman took part in the process of discussing the fascism and the birth of the Republic. The mainstream narrative was soon occupied by militant male historians, belonging to different traditions and to the newly-founded political parties. Contemporary history obtained a relatively late recognition in Italy, the first chairs for comtemporary history being founded essentially as a consequence of the student protests of 1968.

Such conditions led to the marginalisation of women as both historians and historical subjects until the mid-1970s, when Franca Pieroni Bortolotti, a real pioneer in women's studies, opened up a new stream of historical investigation focusing on the question of women's emancipation. Pieroni Bortolotti was born in Florence in 1925, in a working-class anti-fascist family. Her experience of anti-fascist politics shaped her historical analysis. As she later recalled in her autobiography her father did not want her to engage in politics directly to become 'one of these horrible suffragettes'. In 1943 she became a member of the Resistance and a clandestine communist organisation. After the war, as her father denied her permission to become a full-time functionary of the communist party she would then turn to the University instead, studying with important historians such as Carlo Morandi and later the anti-fascist exile historian Gaetano Salvemini who had returned from Harvard. Later she would also study under the direction of Delio Cantimori, an extremely original historian who had written very important studies of heretical movements of early modern Europe.

Her first projects to write on women in the Resistance or on women and fascism were never accomplished. Instead she published a quite traditional history of the worker's movement, *Movimento operaio e lotta politica a Livorno 1900–1926* written together with Nicola Badaloni (1977). Next she concentrated on the first emancipationist, Anna Maria Mozzoni, publishing her writings as well as monograph on her work. Franca Pieroni Bortolotti can be regarded as the founder of the women's and gender history in Italy, but she worked in earlier tradition of the history of the workers' movements. In her last work *La donna la pace l' Europa* however there is a real interest in the issues of race, gender and class, while surprising analogies with Natalie Zemon Davis's work have been observed. The place of Pieroni Bortolotti is now widely recognised and the Italian Society for Women Historians together with the Florence Municipality organised a Prize for dissertations on women's history named after her.

Neo-feminist movements and issues produced in Italy as elsewhere both a sudden acceleration and innovation in women's history and women's studies. Much of this innovation took place outside the academy around feminist groups and the first feminist journals. Rome was the most important centre, where both *DWF Donna Woman Femme* and the first journal of women's history, *Memoria* were founded. The journal *DWF Donna Woman Femme*, established in the mid-1970s, was co-founded and edited by Annarita Buttafuoco, who established the Archivi riuniti in Milan, served as president of the Italian Society of Women historians and directed in the first phase its summer school at the University of Siena. She published one of the firsts monographs entirely devoted to Italian women's history, *Le Mariuccine. Storia di un'istituzione laica* (1985), on Milanese women's networks in the nineteenth century devoted to helping lower class women to get access to the little welfare provided by the local government. When she had undertaken her first work on Eleonora Pimentel Fonseca, the heiress of the Neapolitan republic of 1799 already studied by Benedetto Croce, she had already dealt with a critical moment connected to the origins of the awakening for national consciousness and struggle for independence and constitution. Following the steps of Pieroni Bortolotti she later focussed essentially on women's social and political citizenship in liberal Italy, therefore approaching one fundamental issue of the national history: the struggles for the inclusion of women in the nation state, in her *Questioni di cittadinanza. Donne e diritti sociali nell'Italia liberale Siena* (1997).

On modern and contemporary Italy

Although it has been primarily men who have written on the Italian nation, there have been important exceptions, such as Mariuccia Salvati's book on State and enterprise after the Second World War, *Stato e industria nella ricostruzione: alle origini del potere democristiano, Milano, Feltrinelli* (1982) or Elena Aga Rossi's work on the critical moment of the 8th of September 1943. It is also important to note that studies on women's political participation have not been limited to the left-wing women historians such as Pieroni Bortolotti and Buttafuoco. One should not forget the role of the Catholic Paola Gaiotti De Biase who started as early as the 1950s to write women's history in works such as *Le donne oggi* (1957). Later she pointed out the original role of women in the social and political life of the Italian Republic in her *La donna nella vita sociale e politica della repubblica* (1979) and the role of the catholics in women's enfranchisement.

Annamaria Bruzzone and Rachele Farina's *La resistenza taciuta. Dodici vite di partigiane piemontesi* (1976) innovated the history of another starting point of the life of republican Italy focusing on the participation of women in the resistance, which had been silenced if not denied. In the last decade, a series of enquiries, essays and interviews, which is still ongoing, have pointed out the way; after the Second World War women started to engage in local politics in Piedmont as well as in Emilia Romagna and in Tuscany.

Other and deeper innovations were produced by women historians such as Luisa Passerini and Anna Bravo who focused on new methodological issues, such as subjectivity, and practices, such as oral history, and investigated crucial and yet overlooked dimensions of important moments of modern and contemporary Italian history. Anna Rossi Doria translated and edited the first works of Anglo-Saxon feminism, and thus introduced and developed the theme of political citizenship among Italian feminist historians. Her work on women's enfranchisement, *Il voto alle donne in Italia* (1996) and her broad synthesis of women's role on the political scene in republican Italy testify of the importance of a women's approach in recent Italian history.

More recently, Mariuccia Salvati has concentrated on middle classes and fascism, in an original book (*L'inutile salotto*) which evocates in the title the 'unuseful living room' of the middle classes and together with Dianella Gagliani has promoted research on women's citizenship and social and political spaces. The topic of women and war and of women being raped during the Second World War is at the centre of Gabriella Gribaudi's more recent research (published in the journal *Genesis* 2000). Previously, Gribaudi worked with great attention to anthropology and focused on political patronage and family's networking in southern Italy.

Emigration was a central issue for Italian people between the late 1800s and the 1950s. Andreina de Clementi introduced a strong gender approach in this topic in her *Viaggi di donne* (1995). More developed is the large work on the topic of the different aspects of women's work, often bypassing the conventional boundaries between early modern and modern ages, as in Angiolina Arru's enquiries on house servants. Angela Groppi, who edited an important collection of essays on women's work, has pointed out the importance of the work of women within the Italian family and outside of it. *Il lavoro delle donne* (1996) has demolished the common place that women's work is just a complement to one of the breadwinners: often it was and has been an autonomous experience, which has marked the life of the many women living alone, as Maura Palazzi's important book *Donne Sole* (1997) has pointed out. Barbara Curli's *Italiane al lavoro, 1914–1920* (1998) centred on one of the most important turning points, analysing women and labour market and mapping the feminisation of certain areas of work during the First World War. She studied also the parallel phenomenon of the construction of enterprise welfare. Curli and Pescarolo have also considered the problem of women's work in censuses, for instance in the article on gender, work and statistics in Franca Bimbi's edited collection *Differenze e disuguaglianze: Prospettive per gli studi di genere in Italia* (2003).

Gender and the nation

A group of women working in different Italian universities have more recently joined their efforts in a large research on gender and nation building. Some of them have focused on women's direct participation in the political movements which led to constitution and independence pointing out of the Italian specificities already quoted in a previous paragraph. Aware of the necessity to deconstruct the theory of the separate spheres, these historians studied the interconnections between the public and the private, the family and the nation. They have investigated the interrelationship between the public sphere and the private sphere, in order to understand how the private sphere – the nation at first, and later the nation state – pervaded the salons, shaped private writings such as diaries and memoirs and most of all correspondence, and was able to influence family models and strategies in both aristocratic and bourgeois milieus. Ilaria Porciani's book *La festa della nazione* (1997) on the construction of a national festival from 1848 to 1914 devoted a chapter to gender roles within the nation building, while she has also underlined the deep interconnection between family and nation in a broad comparative framework in articles such as 'Famiglia e nazione nel lungo ottocento' (2002).

In a Catholic country where the Church was often set against the state it is important to consider what role religion plays in the gendering of family and educational strategies, models of sanctity and the particular role played by church schools and by other Catholic institutions in relation to the development of Italian national identity. Recent scholarship has also raised the issue of the contribution of Catholicism and women religious orders (active in both charity and education) in offering Italian women new chances of visibility, participation in the public sphere and even emancipation in the framework of old models of discipline. Lucetta Scaraffia and Gabriella Zarri's *Donne e fede: Santità e vita religiosa in Italia* (1993) suggests that we should keep in mind the *longue durée* and the persistence as well as the transformations of Catholic models in the nineteenth century, while Emma Fattorini's *Il Culto Mariano* (2003) points out the importance of the cult of the Virgin Mary.

Women's history in Italy

This contribution had to give account especially about the role women historians played in studying modern and contemporary history of the Italian nation state. Yet it would be impossible not to recall, however briefly, their contributions, often extremely innovative, in other fields, which are particularly important in the case of a country like Italy, and which we have recalled for previous periods. In ancient history Giuliana Lanata's essays on Aristotle and Sappho (1966) were groundbreaking. Giuliana Sfameni Gasparros' contributions to religious history and Eva Cantarella's researches on the border line between cultural and institutional history and history of law and her works on women in the ancient world have enjoyed a broad international acknowledgment. The theme of bisexuality, Eva Cantarella's *Bisexuality in the Ancient World* (1988) and of virginity, Giulia Sissa's *Greek Virginity* (1987) have deeply innovated the picture of the anthropology of the ancient world, as have Elena Giannarelli's works on women's monasticism and on the materfamilias in ancient Rome. In medieval and early modern history many women have focused on women's access to informal power and their role in patronage networks as both clients and patrons. In early modern Italy family was a real agency even on the ground of politics, economy and patronage. Following Christiane Klapisch-Zuber's fundamental works on Renaissance Florence, women historians have brought to light history of the family as history of the kinship and relationships. Comparative studies on family and gender in different cities have focused on patrimonial transmission and dowry, suggesting that women's rights to property and control over children were not so severely limited as previously thought, as Sandra Cavallo, Cesarina Casanova, Daniela Lombardi and Renata Ago have underlined. Giulia Calvi's study on widowed mother's claims for the custody of their children in early modern Tuscany cast light on the sort of 'moral contract' which takes place between women and state officials who entrusted mothers with guardianship of their offspring in spite of the dominant patriarchal culture. Thus women's exclusion from patrimonial transmission was gradually compensated by the state's recognition of their role in the sphere of responsibility and care. Gianna Pomata, who edited and co-edited fundamental works of women's history in the 1980s, is also the author of a number of works on gender history as well as the book *Contracting a Cure: Patients, Healers and the Law in Early Modern Bologna* (1998). Family was also a concern for legal historians such as Giorgia Alessi or social historians such as Margherita Pelaja or Raffaella Sarti, who concentrated on a comparative study of the structuring of the domestic space in different European households. Gabriella Zarri's many books deserve particular mention as she studied female monastic institutions in a very innovative way discovering that counter-reformation monasteries gave women a great opportunity to influential patronage and even political bargaining, while their correspondences proved to be an extraordinary source.

In conclusion, it is worthwhile to point out several new works which can provide a general account on women historians, on the state of the art on women's history in Italy and on the innovations brought by gender in recent historical perspectives: Gianna Pomata's 'Family and Gender' in John A Marino's *Short Oxford History of Italy: Early Modern Italy 1550–1796* (2002); *Storiche di ieri e di oggi* (2004) edited by Maura Palazzi and Ilaria Porciani; *A che punto è la storia delle donne*, edited by Anna Rossi Doria (2003); and *Innesti*, edited by Giulia Calvi (2004) (see also Mantini 2000).

Ilaria Porciani

References

Casalena 2003; Di Cori 1991; Epple 2003; Gearhart 1984; Guidi 2004; Mantini 2004; Porciani 2000; Porciani 2002; Porciani & O'Dowd 2004.

Related essays

Convents; Female biography; Family; Feminism; Nation; Religion; Revolution; War; Women worthies; Women's liberation.

J

Jameson, Anna Brownwell Murphy 1794–1860

Anglo-Irish feminist, art historian, biographer. Born in Dublin, daughter of Dennis Murphy, Irish painter of miniatures. Emigrated to England in 1798. Largely self-educated, she was first employed as a governess in 1812. She worked intermittently in this capacity until her marriage to barrister Robert Jameson in 1825. This marriage broke down almost immediately. The need to support herself and her impecunious extended family led her to become one of the most prolific women writers of the nineteenth century.

Her first major work, *Diary of an Ennuyée*, was published in 1826. Reminiscent of **Germaine de Staël**'s *Corinne*, the fictionalised diary recounts the tragic tour of a young woman in Italy and France. Interspersed with travelogue and commentaries on art and literature, the text signalled many of Jameson's future historical concerns. In the same year she published a series of articles in the *New Monthly Magazine* on the women of the Court of King Charles II, accompanying engravings of miniatures painted by her father. These articles were republished as the *Beauties of the Court of King Charles II* (1833). While not obviously historical these texts recall earlier traditions of women's **Memoirs**, merging fact and fiction, politics and romance. Focusing on the interior world of love, emotion and intrigue not represented in the masculinist historical tradition, such memoirs showed that women's influence in the private sphere shaped the actions of men in the public sphere, anticipating later feminist criticism of masculinist history. Jameson too made this connection in the *Beauties* when she argued that the influence of women in 'our nurseries and boudoirs' shaped 'the principles and opinions of men who are to legislate for the happiness and welfare of nations' (*Beauties* 175–6).

Her later biographical studies, *Loves of the Poets* (1829), *Memoirs of Celebrated Female Sovereigns* (1831) and *Characteristics of Women, Moral, Poetical and Historical* (1832), continued in this vein, reflecting an ambivalence towards the masculinist historical tradition. 'History', Jameson wrote in *Characteristics*, 'informs us that such things have been done or have occurred; but when we come to inquire into motives and characters, it is the most false and partial ... authority we can refer to'. Acknowledging the gendered nature of historical writing, Jameson sought to feminise history by focusing on the domestic and personal lives of her subjects and stressing the importance of the moral truths such lives revealed. This involved the rehabilitation of women traditionally scorned and the creation of her own models of ideal womanhood women who embodied the domestic ideology of the period, while simultaneously being powerful, public and historic figures. These texts were extremely popular: *Characteristics of Women* went through a hundred printings under three different titles, enhancing the trend in female prosopography throughout the Victorian era.

In 1836 Jameson moved to Canada, attempting to reconcile with her husband. While they remained estranged, she travelled widely, writing on North American social and political conditions. In 1838 *Winter Studies and Summer Rambles in Canada* was published, drawing immediate comparisons with **Mary Wollstonecraft**'s *Letters from Norway*. The influence of Wollstonecraft in Jameson's work was tacit but significant and is best evidenced in her desire to rationally educate women. This desire led Jameson to publish her first serious work of art criticism, *A Handbook to the Public Galleries of Art in London* in 1842. She spent the rest of her life writing works of art history, including the *Companion to the Private Galleries of Art in London* (1844) and *Sacred and Legendary Art* (1848–1864).

The *Handbook* was the first British text to make appreciation of fine art accessible to a mass audience, reflecting the new importance placed on art as a means of improving society. Jameson, however, aimed at improving the condition of women. In her art historical writing she focused on the female subject. Her texts functioned as feminine pedagogy on several levels, allowing women readers to acquire both historical knowledge and social skills, while also prescribing a distinct ideal of womanhood. The shift from secular to sacred subject matter in *Legends of the Madonna* (1852) saw Jameson describe the Virgin Mary and other saintly women as role models for Victorian womanhood. The Madonna was depicted as 'the most perfect type of intellectual, tender, simple, heroic woman'. Jameson suggested that the equality or near-equality of the Mary to Christ was evidence that God created man and woman equal. She was also critical of the declining status of women within the Church, prefiguring recent feminist debate about the gendered legacy of the **Reformation**.

Jameson's feminist purpose became more marked in her later works and by the 1840s she engaged in direct social criticism. In her public speaking and published lectures she concentrated on the need for better educational and employment opportunities for women. Not content to simply comment on the wrongs she saw in society, Jameson involved herself in various campaigns to improve society including the abolition of slavery and the reform of the Poor Laws. Through these campaigns she became involved in an international feminist network. Her influence can be seen in the works of **Margaret Fuller** and Sarah Grimke. She was also a mentor to mid-Victorian English feminist Barbara Bodichon and the Langham Place Circle, to whom she suggested the idea of the *English Woman's Journal*.

Following her death Jameson became the subject of both favourable and unfavourable biographical writing. While **Harriet Martineau** and **Sarah Josepha Hale** underestimated Jameson's significance as a woman of letters, later observers were more generous. **Ray Strachey** described her as 'the idol of thousands of young ladies', reflecting her posthumous importance to first-wave feminism. The importance of art to the suffrage campaigns can be attributed to Jameson's influence.

Mary Spongberg

References

Adams 2001; Clarke 2000; Fraser 1998; Holcomb 1983; Johnson 1997.

Major work

Shakespeare's Heroines: Characteristics of women, moral, political and historical (New York: Gramercy Books, 2003).

Japan

We can trace the writing of history by women and of women's history in Japan back more than one hundred years. Japan came into the modern period with a relatively high rate of literacy and one of the first actions of the modernising governments of the 1870s was the creation of a compulsory education system. The seeds were thus sown for a population with a consciousness of the possibilities of documenting their individual experiences in writing. History was also, of course, important to the project of nation-building. The writing of women's history, feminist history and gender history has engaged with the documentation of the gendered experiences of industrialisation and modernisation, coming to terms with Japan's place as a colonising power in the late nineteenth and early twentieth centuries, reflecting on the contemporary legacy of these events, and reflecting on the unresolved history of the Second World War. Debates around these issues have led to debates around the gendering of history, the need to transcend national boundaries in the writing of history, questions of the methodologies of reading the records of the past and the limitations of the historical sources that are passed on to future generations.

Women's life-writing

One important genre connected with women's history is life-writing. In the 1870s Wada Ei kept a diary of her experiences as a worker in one of the textile factories being developed in newly industrialising Japan (Wada 1978). Due to the circumstances of industrialisation, some elite women had been co-opted into the new factories in order to give the factories some legitimacy and make it easier to recruit other women. The employment of *women* as factory operatives is evidence that work in the textile factories was already being seen as a gendered occupation. Industrialisation was inextricable from the development of new class and gender structures to replace the prior feudal status groups, and it was the least privileged rural women who would eventually form a feminised proletariat in the textile factories which were the major industry and the major export product in the early decades of industrialisation in Japan.

Wada Ei's diary was thus a pioneering text. While not usually treated as an example of history-writing, life-writing or even literature, it has nevertheless come to be seen as an important historical document, to be read and re-read according to the concerns of subsequent generations. Due to the fortuitous case of an elite, literate woman being placed in a factory at the earliest stages of industrialisation, we have a rare and valuable account of the factories. Wada's diary demonstrates a transformation of experience into private record, a transformation of private diary into published account, published account then becoming historical document, with the text eventually being placed in the canon of women's life-writing. It would be some decades before we would see similar texts emerging from the masses of women who came to staff the factories.

The genre of **autobiography** in Japan is usually traced to the autobiography of the male liberal intellectual Fukuzawa Yukichi, *Fukuô Jiden* (1899). The first woman's modern autobiography is usually agreed to be Fukuda Hideko's *Warawa no Hanseigai* (*My Life So Far*), published five years later. Although there are some extant women's diaries from the Heian period (794–1152), these did not take the form of the linear exposition of the trajectory of a life, as found in modern autobiographies (Bowring 1987). Fukuda's reference point was the autobiography of Benjamin Franklin rather than the female diarists of the pre-modern period. Fukuda had been an activist in the movement for Liberty and People's Rights in the 1880s, and was the subject of a biography in the heyday of her participation in the liberal movement (Dokuzen 1887). She became involved in an unsuccessful plot to support the cause of Korean Independence by sending explosives. She was imprisoned on a charge of treason, but released in 1890 due to an amnesty on the occasion of the promulgation of the Constitution, and then became involved in the fledgling socialist movement. Her autobiography appeared in 1904, when she was active in the Commoners' Society, an early socialist group (Fukuda 1958).

In subsequent scholarship Fukuda's autobiography has been analysed as a literary text; as an example of women's life-writing; as a primary document of the early liberal, socialist and feminist movements; as an example of the socialist interest in the conditions of women workers under capitalism; as one way of working through the relationship between **feminism**, history and activism; and as a reflection on the choices faced by the subjects of an imperialist state. Fukuda would also edit a pioneering women's magazine, *Sekai Fujin* (*Women of the World* 1907–1909), that provided an early forum for the discussion of socialist views of the 'woman question', another impetus for the documentation of women's lives (Loftus 1991; Mackie 1997).

Other female activists and thinkers in the early twentieth century would also complete autobiographies. Ishimoto Shizue, who became active in the movement for birth control and population control under the influence of Margaret Sanger, published her first autobiography in English in 1935 – a text which has only recently been translated into Japanese (Ishimoto 1935). Others would devote their energies to documenting the lives of other women, through oral history and the gathering of testimonials. The socialist and labour movements provided a particular impetus for the documentation of the lives of working women.

Socialism and the woman question

The debates on the relationship between capitalism and patriarchy, and between socialism and the woman question were advanced in the first decades of the twentieth century. The government also had an interest in documenting the conditions of women workers, due to concerns about the health of women workers as the potential mothers of the next generation of workers and soldiers. The official government report *Shokkô Jijô*, later published in monograph form (*Conditions of Factory Workers* [1903]), the journalistic work *Nihon No Kasô Shakai* (*The Lower Classes in Japan*), Hosoi Wakizô's volume of reportage *Jokô Aishi* (*The Pitiful History of the Factory Women* [1925]) and Maruoka Hideko's *Nihon Nôson Fujin Mondai* (*The Problem of Rural Women in Japan* [1937]) now form part of the documentary corpus for our understanding of the history of early twentieth-century working women. All of these volumes are still accessible, most in cheap paperback editions.

Women workers make an almost perfunctory appearance in what have come to be known as the Japanese capitalism debates (Hoston 1986). These debates, conducted by socialists, hinged on the proper understanding of the events of the mid- to late-nineteenth century, when the military rule of the shogunate was overthrown, the rule of the emperor was restored and imperial rule was justified through a modern constitutional and legal system which gave the vote to propertied males. Although male historians recognised the importance of textiles to Japan's early industrialisation, and made occasional mention of the fact that women formed the majority of factory labour for much of the Imperial period, the situation of women workers was rarely seen in terms of what we would now call 'gender relations' or the 'gender order'. Rather, their situation was seen as a reflection of the conjunction of feudal relations in rural areas and the need of capital for the minimisation of labour costs. Nevertheless, the socialist interest in the 'woman question' gave impetus to the documentation of the lives of working women, providing resources for later generations of historians (Tsurumi 1990; Hunter 2003).

The journals of the unions and the left-wing political parties which were formed after the enactment of universal (manhood) suffrage in 1925 provided a forum for the discussion of strategies for mobilising women workers, for theorising the relationship between capitalism and patriarchy, and for disseminating the writings of European socialist writers. The works of Marx, Engels and Lenin, as well as those of Bebel, Morgan, Bachofen Kollontai and Luxemburg were progressively translated into Japanese. Yamakawa Kikue was a major contributor to the debates on mobilising women and an important translator of the works of such writers as Bebel on socialism and the woman question. Until the 1930s, Yamakawa's major writings were polemical articles and translations. In the wartime and post-war years, however, Yamakawa published several volumes of personal memoirs, including a **memoir** which brought together her own life and that of her mother, and a study of the samurai culture of her forebears. Her own writings moved into the field of history, while her early writings form some of the primary sources for the study of socialism and feminism in the period before the Second

World War (Yamakawa 1943; Yamakawa 1981–1982).

In parallel with Yamakawa's involvement with the socialist movement, a young woman from southwestern Japan – Takamure Itsue – came to Tokyo and became involved with political and literary circles, eventually finding a place in the anarchist wing of the left-wing movement. Male activists were at this time engaged in the above-mentioned debates on the understanding of Japanese capitalism and on the relative merits of anarchist and bolshevist strategies for the transformation of Japanese society. Two journals – *Fujin Sensen* (*The Women's Front* [1930–1931]) and *Nyonin Geijutsu* (*Women's Arts* [1928–1932]) – provided a space for a debate on whether anarchism or bolshevism would provide better prospects for the liberation of women. The debates focused on the role of the state, whether waged work was part of a strategy for women's liberation, and on the socialisation of childcare versus communal or family-based solutions (Tsurumi 1985).

Takamure's early writings were in the genres of poetry, life-writing and polemical articles. Eventually, however, she came to the conclusion that only a proper understanding of the past could provide a basis for developing strategies for the liberation of women. The socialist publications of the first decades of the twentieth century had included reference to the works of Engels, Morgan and Bebel. These writers had engaged in theoretical debates about matriarchy and patriarchy, matriliny and patriliny, and believed in an evolution from hunter-gatherer society to agricultural society then to feudalism, capitalism and socialism. These theoretical debates could be transposed to the Japanese context, but these debates could only be effective if argued from a solid empirical base. For Takamure, the study of history demonstrated that women had not always been subordinated to men, and that it was therefore possible to imagine future societies which would not be based on patriarchal domination.

Writing the history of women in Japan

Takamure retreated to her 'house in the woods' in the suburbs of Tokyo. With the practical and domestic support and research assistance of her partner Hashimoto Kenzô, she devoted her life to the documentation of women's pasts. Her work took her into a re-evaluation of the situation of women in pre-modern Japan. Her genealogical research revealed the existence of female emperors – women who had succeeded to the throne and ruled in their own right. Since the passing of legislation on imperial succession in the late nineteenth century, the throne can only be passed to male heirs through the male line. Although this had already become the accepted custom by this time, the Imperial Household Law of 1889 was the first time this had been codified. This was reaffirmed in the post-1945 laws on imperial succession, leading to a potential crisis in the early twenty-first century where the grandchildren of the current emperor are all female. Takamure's research documented a time when women had not been barred from succession in their own right.

Takamure's examination of the naming practices of pre-modern aristocrats revealed the existence of duolocal, matrilocal and 'wife-visiting' marriage systems and the transmission of names and property through both male and female lines. While not providing evidence of matriarchy – the rule of women – this research did provide a challenge to existing understandings of the past, revealing that the patriarchal systems of recent centuries had not existed from time immemorial. Rather, they were transformations of earlier systems and could be subject to further transformation in the future. The culmination of her work was her four-volume History of Women (*Josei no Rekishi*) which appeared through the 1950s (Takamure 1966–1967). Some of the details of Takamure's conclusions have been challenged on the basis of new research and new evidence. There has also been criticism of her failure to distance herself from the ultranationalism of the Japanese regime of the 1940s (Germer 2003). Nevertheless, she has an important place in any genealogy of feminist history in Japan. Her work also provided an important source for a pioneering English-language work on pre-modern Japan: Joyce Ackroyd's (1959) article 'Women in Feudal Japan'.

People's history

Japan's defeat in the Second World War, the liberation of its former colonies and the institutional changes of the period of Allied Occupation from 1945 to 1952 provided a new framework for gender relations, a new institutional relationship between individual and state and a new discursive context for the writing of history. In the latter half of the twentieth century, there would be tensions between competing narratives of history. There were celebratory narratives of progress from totalitarian militarism and imperialism to liberal democracy. In some circles there was alternation between guilt over and disavowal of the actions of an imperialist and colonialist state supported to a greater or lesser extent by the actions of ordinary people. These views co-existed with narratives of victimhood as the first nation to have suffered nuclear holocaust. Although the scale of destruction caused by the dropping of atomic bombs on Hiroshima and Nagasaki has not been experienced in any other places, it needs to be acknowledged that the effects of radiation were suffered by scientists, soldiers and indigenous communities in the initial testing in the Nevada desert. Since 1945, communities in the Pacific and outback Australia have also suffered the effects of nuclear testing, providing the potential space for the writing of a transnational history of the experiences of nuclear holocaust. So far, the transnational dimension of this history has only been addressed in such places as Oda Makoto's semi-documentary novel, *The Bomb* (Oda 1981, 1990). For many, the response to this history was a commitment to pacifism and an antipathy to the use of nuclear power, expressed most forcefully and in clearly gendered terms in the annual meetings of the 'Mother's Convention' (*Hahaoya Taikai*) which started in 1955.

The socialist and communist parties and labour unions achieved a new legitimacy in the immediate post-war period (notwithstanding the contradictions and reversals of official policy and the purges which were at times directed at communists as well as former militarists). This gave further impetus to the documentation of the experiences of workers and the heroism of labour activists during the imperial period. Several women who had been involved with the labour and socialist movements of the early twentieth century published autobiographies in the early post-war years (Loftus 2004). As early as 1948, Inoue Kiyoshi published his Marxist-influenced *History of Women in Japan (Nihon Joseishi)*, and Kamichika Ichiko produced her *History of Women's Thought (Nihon Josei Shisôshi)* in 1949. Others produced biographies of prominent women, such as Murata Shizuko's (1959) biography of pioneering liberal and socialist activist Fukuda Hideko, or turned to oral history. The post-war years saw the development of grassroots movements for the documentation of individual lives, the experiences of local communities and the experiences of groups which had experienced oppression. This also resulted in the documentation of the lives of women in local areas. These local women's history circles have been responsible for the publication of several volumes of research on the history of women in local areas (Gayle 2004).

In the 1960s, a mass political movement developed to protest against the renewal of the US–Japan Security Treaty whereby Japan continued to host US bases on Japanese soil and was unable to pursue an independent defence policy. This movement led to the largest demonstrations in the post-war era, but the protestors were unable to stop the renewal of the treaty. This led to reflections on the history of progressive and democratic thought in Japan, and led to the naming of the field of '*minshûshi*', or 'people's history', a movement which had much in common with the 'new social history' in English-speaking countries in its focus on documenting the lives of non-elite groups.

Women's liberation and history

In the 1970s, women formed groups to explore issues of sexuality, reproductive control and identity. These groups were known by the Japanese phrase for the women's liberation movement (*josei kaihô undô*) and by the transliteration of 'women's liberation' from English into Japanese. The media soon started to abbreviate this to *uuman ribu* (women's lib). The women's liberation movement provided a further impetus for the documentation of women's experiences (Tanaka 1995). This took several forms: a celebration of the achievements of feminists of earlier times; the production of document collections and facsimile editions of the writings of women of earlier generations; the documentation of the experiences of women in the past in order to better understand women's current situation; consciousness-raising on the power relations behind women's own experiences; reflection on the temporal links between women who had grown up after the Second World War and their mothers' generation which had experienced the war; and reflection on the spatial links between women and men in Japan and women and men in other countries in the region. A consciousness that many of these neighbouring countries were also former colonies of the Japanese empire led to a complex interplay of gender, spatiality and temporality. The first Women's Liberation conferences were held in 1971 and 1972.

A group of women formed a collective to disseminate information about the situation of women in Japan to an international audience. They called their venture 'Femintern Press' (from the phrase 'feminist international'). An important early publication was Tanaka Kazuko's *A Short History of the Women's Movement in Japan*. In just 56 pages, the pamphlet surveys the history of feminism in Japan from the Freedom and Popular Rights movement of the 1880s and the socialist movement of the early 1900s to the most recent developments in Women's Liberation in Japan (Tanaka 1974). Sexuality was a major focus of the women's liberationists of the 1970s, but for many activists, this still focused mainly on heterosexuality. Radical lesbian groups were formed in the 1970s. Publications such as *Subarashii Onnatachi* (*Wonderful Women*) and *Za Daiku* (*The Dyke*) attempted to retrieve a history of lesbians in Japan, a significant gap in accounts of Japanese feminism until recently (Chalmers 2002).

A group of women formed a collective in 1977, calling themselves 'Women Questioning the Present' (*Josei no Ima o Tou Kai*). They established a journal which they called *Notes for a History of the Homefront*

(*Jûgoshi Nôto*). The journal appeared until 1996, with two incarnations. The first series, which appeared from 1977 to 1985, looked at women's experiences in Imperial Japan (1890–1945), from the beginnings of Japan's imperialism to the end of the Second World War. The second series, which appeared from 1986 to 1996, looked at the legacy of Imperial Japan (that is, the period from 1890 to 1945 under the political system of the Meiji constitution) in the post-war period, ending with an examination of their own youth – that is from 1945 to the 1970s. Their group had been born out of the women's liberation movement of the 1970s, itself a reaction against the masculinism of the 'old left' of the established left-wing parties and 'new left' of the counter-culture, the student left and movement against the Vietnam war. In their research on women's experiences of militarism and imperialism, they tried to go beyond narratives of victimhood, and came to see women as complicit in supporting the actions of a militarist and imperialist government, notwithstanding the fact that they had been unable to vote to change that government, as women did not gain suffrage until the revision of the Electoral Law in December 1945 (Mackie 2002).

Other writers also showed an interest in discovering Japan's own feminist tradition, with one journal, *Feminist*, using the subtitle 'the new *Seitô*' ('the new Bluestocking journal', a reference to the pioneering women's journal which appeared from 1911 to 1916). The journal *Feminist* first appeared in 1977 and was able to draw on, and help to construct, a tradition of Japanese feminism. The title of the journal, *Feminist*, was an important intervention. The Japanese transliteration of the English word 'feminist' (*feminisuto*) was a familiar word to most educated people in Japan. Its connotation, however, was rather distinctive. The word had come to be used to describe a man who was kind to women, rather than a campaigner for women's political rights. The use of the word 'feminist' as the title of the journal reclaimed the word itself, and reclaimed the concept of women's militancy as political agents engaged in a project of social transformation. At the same time, the name 'feminist' linked them with similar movements in other countries, and perhaps distanced them from some of the negative connotations apparent in sensational media portrayals of the women's liberationists who had been trivialised by the label *uuman ribu*. The contents included articles about the Japanese situation, translations from overseas, advertisements for the reissued works of feminist pioneers and the facsimile editions of early feminist journals. *Feminist* No. 5 included a series of articles reflecting on Women's Studies, and each edition included academic articles on feminist research into literature, popular culture, history and anthropology (*Feminist* 1977–1980). By the end of the 1970s, several women's studies associations had been established within Japan (Fujieda and Fujimura-Fanselow 1995). There are several academic women's studies journals and journals devoted to women's history, such as *Sôgô Joseishi Kenkyû* (Women's History Research), and several multivolume sets exploring the history of women in Japan. Important document collections include the ten-volume Collection of Documents on Women's Issues in Japan (*Nihon Fujin Mondai Shiryô Shûsei*) (1977–1980), the ten-volume Collection of Documents on Women's Movements in Japan (*Nihon Josei Undô Shiryô Shûsei*) (1996–1998) and the three-volume Documents of the History of Women's Liberation in Japan (*Shiryô Nihon Uuman Ribu Shi*) (1992).

As in many other countries, women's studies courses survive through the dedication of groups of feminist researchers who find solidarity in networks which cross several institutions, and may bring together academics, activists, journalists, women in the law and other professions and freelance writers and researchers. The women's universities, such as Ochanomizu University, Japan Women's University and Tokyo Women's University have provided a rather more hospitable environment for academic women's studies than the 'mainstream' universities. Ochanomizu University has one of the more established gender studies centres. Originally established as an archive in 1975, it became the Centre for the Study of Women's Culture in 1986, changing its name to the Institute for Gender Studies in 1996. The change of name reflected an increasing academic recognition of the usefulness of **gender** as a category of historical analysis although some researchers still preferred to speak of 'women's history' and 'women's studies' (Hayakawa 1991). The Institute for Gender Studies at Ochanomizu University has recently been designated a Centre of Excellence by the Department of Education and Science, and is in receipt of research funding for a major interdisciplinary international collaborative research project on 'The Modern Girl and Colonial Modernity in East Asia' (see http://www.igs.ocha.ac.jp/igs/igs_e.htm). This project is informed by recent developments in gender theory and **postcolonial** theory, and is explicitly transnational in focus.

As we have seen, practitioners of women's history have developed grassroots, community-based ways of writing history, while other community-based research is tied to specific issues such as sexual harassment, domestic violence, the situation of immigrant workers or support for claims for compensation by survivors of forced military prostitution in the Second World War. The Asian Women's Association also contributed to the development of feminist history with an activist emphasis through its journal *Ajia to Josei Kaihô* (*Asian Women's Liberation*) which included articles on military prostitution and women's experiences of colonialism alongside articles on more contemporary issues. Like the journal *Feminist, Asian Women's Liberation* tried to integrate feminist groups in Japan into international channels of communication by producing regular English-language editions.

Gender, history and revisionism

Questions of the writing of history have been the subject of much public controversy in Japanese political circles in recent years. Controversies over the treatment of the Second World War in school history textbooks, the long-running legal cases about textbook censorship waged by Ienaga Saburô (1913–2002) from 1965 to 1997, the renewed public debate about the military prostitution system in the wake of several elderly women 'coming out' in the 1990s with their stories of routinised sexual violence perpetrated by the Japanese military, and the debates about war responsibility which were current in the years either side of the death of Emperor Hirohito (who lived from 1901 to 1989 and reigned from 1926 to 1989) all contributed to a renewed consciousness of the political importance of the writing of history. A distinctive feature of the debates on Japanese history is that they are carried out in a transnational space. Since the 1980s, activists from Korea and other former colonies of the Japanese empire have commented on the debates about the writing of Japanese history, as the colonial past is a history which cannot be contained by the current boundaries of the Japanese nation state.

Several conservative politicians, academics and public figures in the 1990s attempted a revisionist denial of such events as the Nanjing Massacre and the abuse of women from Korea and southeast Asia in the military prostitution system. A group of conservatives embarked on the creation of new social science and history textbooks for schools. Although much controversy has been generated by these textbooks, they have in fact been adopted by very few schools. One conservative commentator's lament about 'masochistic' views of history has led to an extended debate about the ways in which the Second World War is to be remembered, comparable in some ways to the debates about so-called black armband history versus whitewash history in Australia (Hein and Selden 2000; Macintyre 2004).

Feminist historians have entered into debates with the conservative revisionists who have denied atrocities committed during the Second World War including the state's responsibility for the wartime military brothels. Their research into the military prostitution system, and the experiences of women under colonialism and militarism meant that they were well placed to enter into these debates. Leftist, feminist and resident Korean historians had for some time been collecting testimonials of the experiences of 'ordinary' people during wartime, the experiences of colonial subjects, the experiences of colonial subjects resident in the metropolis and the experiences of enforced labour under the military regime (Senda 1973; Kim 1976; Suzuki 1989a,b, 1996a,b; Fujime 1997). It was during such research that the experiences of the survivors of the military prostitution system came to light. The history of the military prostitution system, however, had not really been 'hidden from history', as there was evidence in the soldiers' memoirs which started to appear in the 1950s, in the military war crimes tribunals and in the memories of the soldiers and the women who survived. Nevertheless, a new discursive context was necessary before there could be a public debate about the history of this system. It was not till the early 1990s that some elderly Korean women named themselves in public as survivors of the system, gradually followed by survivors from other countries. Their resolve to bring a suit against the Japanese government for compensation was strengthened when historian Yoshimi Yoshiaki revealed documents that he had found in the archives of the Ministry of Defence. These documents revealed that the government had been directly involved in the running of the military brothels (Yoshimi 1992; Mackie 2000). At the time of writing, their claims for compensation have still not been recognised.

While there were debates between conservative and progressive historians on the interpretation of the events of the Second World War, there were also debates among feminist historians on the interpretation of the military prostitution system. At times this was presented as a debate between those who privileged the gendered dimension of the oppression of the women in military brothels – that they had been oppressed as women – and those who emphasised the nationalist dimension – that they had been oppressed as colonial subjects. Clearly, however, the system can only be explained with a consciousness of the complex interplay of gender, class, ethnicity and colonial power relations, and a sensitivity to the different speaking positions available to the participants (Wöhr 2004).

The debates were carried out by activists supporting the survivors, feminist historians, historians of colonialism, and gender studies scholars seeking explanations for militarised sexual violence. Feminist sociologist Ueno Chizuko engaged in the historical debates and brought her thoughts together in a monograph Nashonarizumu to Jendâ (1998). The book has been translated into English with a new chapter and an epilogue, as *Nationalism and Gender* (2004). In addition to the controversies mentioned above, Ueno argued that bringing the existence of Japanese women in the military brothels into the discussion made it impossible to sustain a simple equation of Japanese = oppressor and non-Japanese = victim. Ueno conducted a detailed discursive analysis of the writings of other feminists, as well as the writings of the conservative revisionists (Ueno 2004).

The importance of history to feminist activism was revealed by the Women's International War Crimes Tribunal on Japan's Military Sexual Slavery, held in Tokyo in December 2000, and attracting over 5000 participants, including 60 survivors from the Second World War, testimonials from survivors from North and South Korea, the People's Republic of China, Taiwan, the Philippines, the Netherlands, Indonesia, East Timor and Japan, lawyers and scholars, and spectators from over 30 countries. The Tribunal was jointly sponsored by organisations from North Korea, South Korea, China, Taiwan, the Philippines, Indonesia, Malaysia, the Netherlands and Japan. The organisers of this tribunal presented their judgments in legalistic terms and justified their action in terms of 'moral responsibility' and participation in 'global civil society', but history was also vital to the tribunal, in the form of testimonies and reference to the sparse documents which remain. The importance of gender – an understanding of both masculinity and femininity – also became apparent in the tribunal. In addition to the testimonies of the women who had suffered under the enforced military prostitution system, there were testimonies from former soldiers.

Feminist history and historiography in Japan has thus moved from the documentation of women's lives, to an analysis of the gendered structures of modern Japanese society, a consciousness of the political importance of history-writing, and a consciousness that modern history cannot be contained by the boundaries of one nation-state.

Vera Mackie

References

Ackroyd 1959; Bowring 1987; Chalmers 2002; Dokuzen 1887; Fujieda & Fujimura–Fanselow 1995; Fujime 1997; Fukuda 1958; Hayakawa 1991; Hein & Selden 2000; Hoston 1986; Hunter 2003; Ishimoto 1935; Gayle 2004; Germer 2003; Kim 1976; Loftus 1991, 2004; Macintyre 2004; Mackie 1997, 2002; Mackie 2000 Murata 1959; Oda 1981; Senda 1973; Suzuki 1989a,b, 1996a,b; Tachi 1994; Takamure 1966–1967; Tanaka 1974, 1995; Tsurumi 1985, 1990; Ueno 2004; Wada 1978; Wöhr 2004; Yamakawa 1943, 1981–1982; Yoshimi 1992.

Related essays

Feminist Auto/biography; Industrialisation; Memoir; Oral Traditions; Peace; Postcolonial; Private writing; War.

K

Kavanagh, Julia 1824–1877

Irish novelist, biographer, historian of women. Born in Thurles, Ireland. Only child of Bridget (Fitzpatrick) and Peter Morgan Kavanagh. Childhood spent in France and England. Abandoned by her father and responsible for the care of her mother, Kavanagh turned to writing. She began writing children's literature, publishing in magazines and several novels. Her first adult novel *Madeleine* (1848) drew on her extensive knowledge of France and was loosely based on the life of Jeanne Jugan, founder of the Little Sisters of the Poor. Kavanagh never married and her novels are subtly critical of the institution and the loss of women's freedom it entailed. Her novels were critically acclaimed and her influence is evident in Charlotte Bronte's *Villette* and the works of George Eliot.

In 1850 Kavanagh produced her first historical work, a collective biography *Women in France during the 18th Century*. Written as a corrective to masculinist histories that denied women's agency, Kavanagh's text documented women's activities at Court, in the salons and during the Revolution. *Women in France* drew upon and echoed sentiments expressed in French women's **memoirs**. Kavanagh argued that 'without that rule of woman . . . many of the pages of their stateman's policy, court intrigue, civil strife, or foreign war, need never have been written'. Of women's influence in these public realms she wrote: 'This power was not always pure and good; it was often corrupt in its source, evil and fatal in its results; but it was power.' In 1852 she published *Women of Christianity, Exemplary for Acts of Piety and Charity*. A collective biography of holy women, *Women of Christianity* merged religious and feminist sentiment arguing that Christianity allowed women equality before God. Kavanagh challenged the notion that female piety required women to be restricted to the domestic sphere. Although a staunch Catholic Kavanagh was ecumenical in her treatment of holy women. This ecumenicalism was later criticised in more sectarian works such as Anna Sadlier's *Women of Catholicity* (1888). Kavanagh did more than merely recover women lost to history; she challenged the boundaries of masculinist history, claiming that such 'History has been written in the old pagan spirit of recording great events and dazzling actions'. In 1862 she produced two volumes of literary biography *French Women of Letters* and *English Women of Letters*, which recovered many women writers lost to male literary traditions. In these works Kavanagh anticipated recent feminist readings of authors such as **Jane Austen** and **Madeline de Scudéry**.

Like earlier romantic writers Kavanagh argued that women transmitted 'ideal history' through novels, history that went 'beyond facts' to show what 'men aspired to be'. She also published travel writing *Summer and Winter in Two Sicilies* (1858). Biographical sketches of Kavanagh appear in Margaret Oliphant's *Women Novelists of Queen Victoria's Reign* (1897) and C J Hamilton's *Notable Irishwomen* (1904). Recently Eileen Fauset (1996) and Michael Forsyth (1999) have produced detailed studies of Kavanagh depicting the proto-feminist nature of her historical writing.

Mary Spongberg

References

DNB; Fauset 1996; Forsyth 1999; Oldfield 2000; Todd 1989.

Kelly, Joan 1928–1982
American historian of women. Born in New York to Ruth (Jacobsen) and George V Kelly. Received her BA (summa cum laude) from Saint John's University College in 1953, an MA from Columbia in 1954 and a PhD in 1963. Began teaching at City University of New York in 1956, becoming full professor in 1972. Her first book *Leon Battista Alberti* (1969), a study of the Renaissance artist, anticipated her later interest in the nature of Renaissance universalism. Approached by Gerda Lerner to consider teaching women's history, Kelly first resisted, suggesting that as a Renaissance historian 'there was nothing much [I] could offer about women'. Encountering Lerner personally Kelly began to rethink everything she 'had known about the Renaissance'. Together they co-directed the first Masters programme in Women's Studies at Sarah Lawrence College between 1972 and 1974.

Kelly's work anticipated the more gendered approach to historical understanding that developed within feminist and poststructuralist scholarship during the 1980s by examining the social relationships of the sexes 'as a fundamental category of historical thought' (see **Gender** entry). Anticipating the work of Joan Wallach Scott, Kelly argued in her essay 'The Social Relations of the Sexes' (1976) that it was necessary to effect 'a new, systematic relation between men and women, and between the particular and universal as fundamental to the analysis of human history as the social relationship of classes'. Kelly's pioneering essay 'Did Women have a **Renaissance**?' (1977) transformed the way in which historians considered concepts of periodisation by underscoring the masculinist notion of progress defining events and eras. Challenging historians to take 'the emancipation of women as our vantage point', Kelly questioned the possibility that women 'had a Renaissance' while simultaneously opening up the field to feminist scholarship. Kelly was also interested in the relationship between feminist history and feminist theory, and in 'The Doubled Vision of Feminist Theory' (1979) she sought to merge Marxism and Radical feminism to generate a more critical understanding of the functioning of patriarchy in its many historical forms and thus 'put an end to it'.

In later work on the *querelle des femmes* (1982) Kelly traced the development of feminist consciousness through an examination of **defences of women** written by women from **Christine de Pizan** to **Mary Wollstonecraft**. In contesting misogynist ideologies such defences Kelly suggested form a deep-seated tradition, underpinning many of the historical critiques of patriarchy generated within both first- and second-wave feminism. Kelly was also involved in **collective** feminist writing projects such as the Sarah Lawrence women's studies programme's *Workbook on Sterilization and Sterilization Abuse* (1978) and a feminist family text *Household Kith and Kin* (1980) co-written with Renate Bridenthal, Amy Swerdlow and Phyllis Vine.

Kelly engaged in feminist activism within the profession, chairing the American Historical Association's Committee on Women Historians from 1975 to 1977. She also co-chaired the New York chapter of the Coordinating Committee for Women in the Historical Profession between 1973 and 1974. Shortly before her death from cancer in 1982 Kelly drew upon the example of **Charlotte Perkins Gilman**, writing:

> I want women to take the lead and I know in the depth of my being and in all my knowledge of history and humanity, I know women will struggle for a social order of peace,

> equality, joy. Women will make the world concern itself with children. Our problem is, how do we 'make' the world do that? Oh, I want to end patriarchy! Passionately!

Following her death Catherine R Stimpson, Blanche W Cook, Alice Kessler Harris, Clare Coss, Rosalind Petchesky and Amy Swerdlow worked together to edit a collection of Kelly's major essays, *Women, History and Theory* (1984).

Mary Spongberg

Reference

Kelly 1984.

Kéralio [Robert], Louise Félicité Guyenement de 1758–1822

French novelist, historian of women. Born in Paris, only child of Marie François Abeille, a translator and author of fiction, and Félix Guyenement de Kéralio, military historian. Educated at home by her father. Married Pierre François Robert in 1790. Early literary works were translations from English and Italian and a novel or pseudo-memoir, published anonymously, *Adélaide ou les mémoires de la marquise de**** (1782). In 1786 she published under her own name the first volumes of her two major historical works, the *Histoire d'Elisabeth* and the *Collection des meilleurs ouvrages français composés par des femmes* (1786–1789). Unlike many **Royal Lives** written by women, Kéralio situated her Elizabeth within the history of male sovereignty, establishing her reign as the linchpin in the history of English constitutional law. The *Collection*, a multi-volume literary history of women in France since Héloïse, was equally innovative. With the *Collection* Kéralio created a feminist literary tradition, documenting the lives of women writers and anthologising their works. Unlike earlier anthologies Kéralio specifically located the lives and works of her subjects historically. In 1787 Kéralio won the title of France's first *Historienne* from French journalist Jacques Mallet du Pan.

During the revolution Kéralio engaged in political journalism, editing the radical newspapers the *Journal de l'Etat et du Citoyen* and the *Mercure National*. Although initially praised by radical men, her efforts were subsequently condemned. In 1791 Kéralio published *Les Crimes des reines de la France* under a male pseudonym. This sanguinary assault on female authority, focusing on much-despised queens such as Catherine de' Medici and Marie Antoinette, was no doubt meant to garner support for the Revolution. Kéralio was, however, accused in the radical press of being both unwomanly and 'dominated by uterine furies'. In 1793 Kéralio published an open letter announcing her retreat from public life. She published nothing until 1808 when a five-volume historical novel set during the English Revolution, *Amélia et Caroline, ou l'amour et l'amité*, appeared. Clearly allegorising the French Revolution, *Amélia et Caroline*, like much historical fiction produced by women, was meticulously researched and quoted directly from primary sources, drawing on historians such as Claredon and Hume.

Mary Spongberg

References

DeJean 1991; Hesse 1993; Hunt 1992.

Knowles, Lilian Charlotte Anne 1870–1926

English economic historian. Born in Truro. Educated at Truro High school and Girton College, Cambridge, where she took the Historical Tripos in 1893 and part one of the Law Tripos in 1894. Studied economic history under William Cunningham and worked as his research assistant. Married C M Knowles, a former student. One son.

Came to the London School of Economics as a Research scholar in 1896, appointed as first full-time lecturer in Economic History in Great Britain in 1904. In 1906 she obtained a D. Litt. from Trinity College, Dublin. Promoted to Reader in 1907, Knowles became the professor of Economic History in 1921, the second person in Britain to hold such a chair. She also served as Dean of Economics and Political Science between 1920 and 1924. Knowles was actively involved in public life, serving as a member of the Royal Commission on Income Tax in 1912 and the Departmental Committee on the Cost of Living of the Working Class in 1918. She was a member of the Royal Economic Society.

Knowles's work explored the impact of the Industrial Revolution on world trade and the relations of states. In *Industrial and Commercial Revolutions in Great Britain during the Nineteenth Century* (1921) Knowles criticised the domestic system of industrial production, arguing that the factory system markedly improved the working conditions of women and children. Basing her opinion on Parliamentary reports written when domestic production was in a debased state Knowles generated a debate that would influence the writing of her students **Alice Clark** and **Ivy Pinchbeck**. Although Knowles noted the declining status of middle-class women she broadly welcomed the changes wrought for women by Industrial Revolution. She published the *Economic Development of the British Empire Overseas* in 1924 while *Economic Development in the Nineteenth Century* was published posthumously in 1932.

Mary Spongberg

References

Berg 1992; Thirsk 1985.

Komnene, Anna 1083–1153

Byzantine Princess, only secular woman historian of the European Middle Ages. Born in Constantinople, daughter of Irene Doukis and Alexios I. Made heir to the Byzantine Empire at birth and betrothed to her maternal cousin Constantine Doukas. Received both a classical and religious education. The birth of her brother John saw Anna disinherited and the death of Constantine further stifled her ambition to rule. In 1118 Anna attempted to seize the throne for herself and her husband following the death of her father. This rebellion was thwarted by her husband and while he remained at court, Anna was exiled to a convent. Between 1143 and 1148 she wrote the *Alexiad*, a history of her father's reign. Anna claimed that she wrote so the deeds of her father would 'not be consigned to Forgetfulness' although the *Alexiad* also demonstrated and justified her own actions and defended the right of women to rule in Byzantium, a right she herself had been denied. The *Alexiad* also demonstrated Anna's knowledge of the classical traditions of historical writing. Recent scholarship has suggested that the authorial voice is more present in the *Alexiad* than in other contemporary Byzantine histories and that more than any other Byzantine historian Komnene was deeply concerned with the social antecedents of the people of whom she wrote. The first major study of Anna Komnene was written by Georgina Buckler in 1929 and she has been the subject of more recent feminist interpretation by Thalia Gouma-Peterson and Barbara Hill, *Anna Komnene and Her Times* (2000).

Mary Spongberg

References

Hill 2000; Laiou 2000.

Major work

The Alexiad of Anna Comnena (trans.) E R A Sewter (Baltimore: Penguin Books, 1969).

L

Lesbian history

In December 1968 Esme Langley, editor of the lesbian magazine *Arena Three*, wrote cogently in that journal about the importance of history to the lesbian community and the research problems this raised:

> The homosexual minorities differ in many respects from those racial and other minorities whose rights a democratic government is pledged to protect. One major difference is our lack of historic past, a treasure house of tradition, of folklore, folk heroes and the origins of a specific and generally accepted culture.
>
> We may suppose, or guess, that one or another woman in history was powerfully drawn to her own sex, but we can rarely be quite certain. Unless her own writing or her own public utterances, carefully preserved up to our own time, have made it plain, supposition and guesswork are all we have to rest our cases on. (*Arena Three* 5 (12) Dec 1968: 11)

The 'lesbian hunger for genealogy' (Doan and Waters 2000: 15) reflects the need to validate the experience of love between women by showing that it has existed in all periods and societies. The longevity of same-sex love gives lesbians a stake in history, and by extension in contemporary society. When prominent individuals can be claimed – in 1906 the sex reformer Edward Carpenter cited Queen Christine of Sweden and Sappho among the great leaders and artists of the 'intermediate sex' – this also challenges the marginal social status of lesbianism (1906: 134). The construction of a lesbian genealogy may help build a contemporary group identity, based on a common philosophy or political framework, strengthened by the supposed continuities between past and present.

Lesbian history, identity and community

Yet the modern idea of the 'lesbian' gained currency only during the course of the twentieth century, and has carried a diverse range of meanings throughout that period. Some elements of lesbian identity were emphasised in sexological writing from the end of the nineteenth century, including the importance of same-sex eroticism and desire, but sexology also confused same-sex love with gender identity. The female 'invert' was figured as having masculine desires and attributes; she was a member of the 'Intermediate Sex' (Bland and Doan 1998: 48–57). The modern lesbian identity of sexual love between women took some time to filter into all areas of culture; arguably popular knowledge of this sexual category was not complete until after the Second World War. At various points over the century, love between women was connected with the feminist struggle and the rejection of patriarchal heterosexuality. While this approach was spelt out by late twentieth-century lesbian-feminism, it can also be found in less concretely expressed forms since the rise of first-wave **feminism**.

Esme Langley pointed out the difficulty of ascribing lesbian identity to historical figures. As with all history-writing, lesbian history will reflect the individuals, groups and periods of time which produce it. 'The process of making and remaking the past is . . . not so much cognitive as creative: less about "finding out", and more about attributing meanings' (Baxendale and Pawling 1996: 6). As lesbian culture, politics and identity change, then so will lesbian interpretations of the past.

This essay will examine the importance of history in the creation of lesbian identity and community through the historical writing in two British periodicals, *Urania* (1916–1940) and *Arena Three* (1964–1971), published in periods when modern lesbian identity was becoming established but before the arrival of the gay and women's liberation movements. Both journals echoed the feminist lament that love between women has been deliberately ignored, denied and suppressed by the mainstream heterosexist view of past societies (see also Lesbian History Group 1989: 1–4). They each used lesbian history to bolster political consciousness and confidence in their particular ideological positions, and to challenge patriarchal discourses about the past and present.

Because sexual love between women has been tabooed and unacknowledged in the past, it is impossible to trace a tradition of lesbian historical writing as one might, for example, follow women's production of family history. The journals *Urania* and *Arena Three* are thus important sites for women's historical writing on lesbian experience. They represented a range of perspectives on women's same-sex love in the interwar years and 1960s respectively, and anticipate many of the debates that have formed lesbian historiography since the 1980s.

This essay will focus on three key figures and models which consistently appeared in both *Urania* and *Arena Three*, though sometimes interpreted very differently. Sappho of Lesbos, the poet of classical Greece, who wrote of her love for women and whose birthplace contributed to the modern term 'lesbian', was a significant figure in both journals and other twentieth-century lesbian writing. The Ladies of Llangollen, the Irish couple who lived the perfect romantic friendship in Wales for 50 years from the late eighteenth century, were important as the archetypal domestic partnership. A third more controversial exemplar in her androgyny and queer notoriety, the cross-dressed women or female husband was also claimed for lesbian heritage by both journals.

Twentieth-century lesbian journals

The journal *Urania* (1916–1940) might be read as a cryptically coded lesbian magazine since it frequently reiterated the joys of love between women, was antagonistic to heterosexuality, and often reported on women's cross-dressing. Yet it also condemned physical sexuality. Valuing boldness in women and sweetness in men, the central philosophical aim of *Urania* was 'the abolition of the "manly" and the "womanly"', in a sense, a 'queer' dissolving of the boundaries of sex and gender altogether.

The small group of women and men who set up the journal had their political roots in suffrage era sexual politics. However while **romantic friendship** was part of suffrage feminist culture, it was rarely explicitly discussed or publicly advocated. Eva Gore-Booth – one of *Urania*'s editorial group – went further than most feminists in her poetry which celebrated love between women (Tyler-Bennett 1998: 124). *Urania*'s worldview was particularly influenced by feminist theosophy, which favoured 'psychic love' and celibacy (Dixon 1997). Their spiritual ideal of same-sex love explains why *Urania* could simultaneously publish a steady stream of material about the delights of love and passion between women, and at the same time condemn physical sexual expression as 'perversion' (Oram 2001a).

Urania's continuing allegiance, over a period of 25 years, to a vision of same-sex spiritual love challenges historians' assumptions that sexology led to a modern lesbian and gay identity in the interwar years (Oram 1998). It is difficult to judge the significance of the community that it served, though it claimed a circulation of 200–250, and did debate with its readers. *Urania* is interesting as a radical late flowering of a suffrage perspective on love between women, and also because it drew on a wide range of cross-cultural histories of same-sex love.

While we can trace lesbian social networks in the 1920s and 1930s among wealthy, bohemian circles, among the modernist literary elite and among more ordinary women, it is difficult to find wider communities organised around lesbian sexual identity until after the Second World War, when limited commercial subcultures began to develop in the larger British cities (see Benstock 1987; Gardiner 2003). The magazine *Arena Three* (1964–1971) was published by the Minorities Research Group (MRG), the first national organisation for lesbians in Britain. Like *Urania*, *Arena Three* created a 'virtual' community among its often isolated readers, though the MRG functioned partly as a social group, with branches across the United Kingdom. It also had a political focus, seeking to change the negative public perception of lesbianism by challenging the attitudes of psychiatrists and the media. In these activities it anticipated gay and women's liberation of the 1970s and 1980s. While both periodicals were radical in their aims, *Arena Three* was much more in the mainstream of its era, promoting a modern lesbian identity and defending its readers' position as a sexual minority. *Arena Three's* circulation was 500–600 but it probably reached considerably more women during its years of publication (Oram 2005).

Its founder and editor Esme Langley had a sophisticated understanding of the importance of the past to lesbian identity. In its early years especially, *Arena Three* published a number of articles which traced a long-standing lesbian literary tradition ranging from Katherine Mansfield to Gertrude Stein. Several long biographical pieces on lesbians in history were published in the mid- to- late 1960s, knitting *Arena Three* readers into a long and varied past. Readers wrote in suggesting figures who could be researched, to recommend books on Sappho, to describe their own responses on first reading *The Well of Loneliness* and occasionally with their reminiscences of prominent lesbians from the recent past such as Radclyffe Hall or Naomi Jacob. There was discussion of lesbian heritage tourism: to Mitylene (Lesbos), the birthplace of Sappho; to Rye, one-time home of Radclyffe Hall, or to the Ladies of Llangollen's Plas Newydd. *Arena Three* served an active community of lesbians discussing, among other issues, their heritage – and also aware that in seeking social and political change, their own organisation was part of lesbian history.

Sappho: Lesbianism and cultural heritage

Very little is known about the poet Sappho – allowing much to be imagined or projected on to her – and only fragments of her poems have been recovered. She was an iconic figure before the twentieth century: late nineteenth-century New Woman feminists lauded her as a figure of female learning, and some among them for her voicing of same-sex passion (Reynolds 2000: 260–2). *Urania's* ideas about spiritual passion between women are illustrated in their reading of Sappho as 'an erotic and pagan mystic' (*Urania* 51 & 52 May–Aug 1925: 4). The journal published several articles celebrating Sappho, but rejected any suggestion of sexual immorality in her life or work. Typically, her 'sublime passion' and 'ardent feelings' were compared to those of the saints; in more than one article to Saint Teresa: 'She followed not the whims of her flesh but the commands of her visions' (*Urania* 51 & 52 May–Aug 1925: 4; *Urania* 121 & 122 Jan–Apr 1937: 5).

In 'Sappho Up-To-Date', published in 1933, *Urania*'s editor noted 'We know next to nothing about Sappho, except that she wrote magnificently, and that she surrounded herself with ladies with whom she was accused of physical intimacy.' She rejected suggestions that Sappho had a husband or child, or was sexually immoral, while describing her as a 'passionate and possessive adorer of beauty and charm in women' (*Urania* 99 & 100 May–Aug 1933: 1–2). Yet the journal also reprinted Bliss Carmen's poem 'Mitylene', based on a Sapphic fragment, which celebrated the love between Sappho and Atthis in sensuous and powerful language. 'The bitter longing and the keen desire, / The sweet companionship through quiet days / In the slow ample beauty of the world, / And the unutterable glad release / Within the temple of the holy night / O Atthis, how I loved thee long ago / In that fair perished summer by the sea!' (*Urania* 51 & 52 May–Aug 1925: 3).

Urania's ambivalent perspective on Sappho straddles the debates about the poet that raged during the early twentieth century. The lesbian circles around Natalie Barney in Paris adopted Sappho as inspiration for their salons, poetry and drama. At the same time, a number of classical scholars sought to defend Sappho's pure idealised vision; a teacher of young women perhaps, but not tainted by homosexuality (Benstock 1987: 277–94; Reynolds 2000: 290–97). Ancient Greece had long been a cultural reference point for educated gay men. The classics offer much less scope for allusion to love between women, though *Urania* tried to develop what there was. Admiration cloaked desire in a 1919 poem to the mythological Artemis: 'Your eyes' bright strength, your lips' soft valour / Your supple shoulders and hands that dare' (*Urania* 14 Mar–Apr 1919: 2–3). *Urania*'s Theosophical background also made the editors aware of **orientalist** ideas about same-sex love outside the European tradi-tion, including, for example, passionate friendship within the harem and myths from Asia (*Urania* 21 May–Jun 1920: 8). 'Amazons in the Ancient East' described legends of kingdoms in Tibet and Manchuria ruled by female princes, whose children were conceived by supernatural means: 'old men said that in the sea there was a Woman State without males' (*Urania* 47 & 48 Sept–Dec 1924: 3). These stories demonstrated that societies where women lived together without men were possible. In modern times the tradition of the Chinese women silk workers who refused to marry and took other women as life companions was similarly inspirational for *Urania* (79 & 80 Jan–Apr 1930: 1–2), and indeed also for 1980s lesbian-feminists such as Adrienne Rich (1980) and Janice Raymond (1986: 123–47). Like *Urania* they decentred the significance of sexual desire, emphasising the political challenge posed to heteropatriarchy by bonding between women.

For *Arena Three*, Sappho was undoubtedly a woman who loved women passionately and sexually, in ways familiar to 1960s lesbians. As a poet she was central to the lesbian cultural tradition they were constructing, inspiring early twentieth-century writers. A discussion of Katherine Mansfield's bisexuality concluded with a Sappho quote Mansfield often used, to cement the argument that she had lesbian relationships and sensibility (*Arena Three* 1 (4) Apr 1964: 6). Sappho's fragments were published from time to time, together with modern variations, including the Bliss Carmen poem favoured by *Urania* (*Arena Three* 3 (1) Jan 1966: 15). Like *Urania, Arena Three* treated Sappho in a serious and scholarly way. Their first major article discussed the speculation about her life, whether she had a daughter and her apocryphal suicide leap and sparked off several months of discussion (*Arena Three* 2 (12) Dec 1965: 17–20). Readers described their searches for material on Sappho and for translations of her poetry, and discussed the feasibility of publishing *Arena Three*'s own collection of Sappho's work, since there was no complete collection then in print (*Arena Three* 3 (2) Feb 1966: 14–16; 3 (3) Mar 1966: 21–3).

Arena Three was anxious at times to defend Sappho's reputation as a poet as more important than her association with lesbianism. They pointed out that in the ancient world she was regarded as the greatest of the Greek lyric poets, admired by her peers and called the Tenth Muse (*Arena Three* 3, 2 Feb 1966: 16; 3, 3 Mar 1966: 21). In 1968 Esme Langley, the editor, wrote: 'unfortunately, far too many have seen her not as the pillar of a culture but as the high priestess of a mere cult'. Seeking to rescue her reputation, however, was also a way of establishing the centrality of lesbian love to culture from the originating moment of Western civilisation. The magazine criticised the distortion of writers who invented 'legends designed to "prove" that she was really heterosexual or, at any rate, an ardent lover of men as well' (*Arena Three* 5 (12) Dec 1968: 11; See also 4 (6) Jun 1967: 7). Sappho's status in literature meant that, like other lesbian and gay worthies from the past, she could be invoked in the present day as a moral authority to counter contemporary denigration and persecution of homosexuality. An editorial in 1968 condemned police witch hunts of gay men despite the recent change in the law: 'Sappho and her contemporaries took love of one's own sex as natural and proper. It is fortunate for them that they do not live today in our "civilised" society' (*Arena Three* 5, 3 Mar 1968: 1).

But *Arena Three* at times took a less reverent and even playful approach to Sappho. One article evoked her as an actively sexual woman with similar emotional and relationship preoccupations to *Arena Three* readers, a bitter rift occurring when Sappho's beloved Atthis was stolen by her friend Andromeda (*Arena Three* 2 (12) Dec 1965: 17–20). Another lighthearted story had Sappho comment on the present day when she and her women friends received a copy of *Arena Three* through a time machine. She adjusted her 'pearl-studded pince-nez' and lamented the 'centuries of ill opinion' visited on the love to which they gave their name, while eyeing up the slave girl and discussing the quality of the wine (*Arena Three* 7 (1) Jan 1970: 4–5).

Arena Three lauded Sappho as perhaps their greatest lesbian heroine. For editor Esme Langley, Sappho was significant because she declared her passion for women in the historical record: 'Our only "folk heroes" are those who did make their position plain for all time to come. Of these rare and excellent women there are very few indeed, and Sappho was the first among them to live on through the pages of history' (*Arena Three* 5 (12) Dec 1968: 11). For both *Urania* and *Arena Three*, Sappho showed that love between women was a cornerstone of western civilisation. *Urania* constructed her as a mystical poet devoted to higher thought without altogether denying the embodied nature of her passion for women. A more modern figure in *Arena Three*, Sappho became both a sexually active woman who shared the pains and delights of lesbian relationships and a heavyweight cultural figure validating contemporary same-sex love. Sappho subsequently inspired lesbians in gay liberation with the establishment in 1972 of *Sappho* magazine and social group by Jackie Forster and other women who had previously worked on *Arena Three*. She continued to be an inspiration to late twentieth-century lesbian poets, and to theorists inventing lesbian utopias and new mythologies such as Monique Wittig in her book *The Lesbian Body* (Wittig 1973; Snyder 1995: 113–23).

The Ladies of Llangollen: Lesbianism and romantic friendship

Sarah Ponsonby and Eleanor Butler eloped from their aristocratic Irish families in 1778 to live together in Wales for over 50 years with their dog named Sappho. Celebrated in literary circles for their romantic life of 'sweet retirement' and self-improvement, they received many visitors at their cottage in Llangollen and became the model of ideal **romantic friendship** between women. The Ladies represent an important paradigm in lesbian history – the devoted female partnership that continues for a lifetime, triumphing over all difficulties. Women of independent means, they achieved the ultimate fantasy of creating a home together while maintaining respectability, a possibility which was out of reach for many subsequent lesbian couples. Like Sappho, they have been appropriated by different generations of lesbian writers to fit their own conceptions of the perfect kind of passionate relationship between women (Oram 2001b).

A pioneer woman doctor, Mary Gordon was the first writer to place the Ladies in a history and tradition of love between women in her biography, *Chase of the Wild Goose* (1936). Her philosophy and identity – and thus her interpretation of the Ladies – was similar in many respects to that of *Urania*'s editors. Like them she was rooted in an early twentieth-century feminist culture which valued intense female friendship and resisted the sexological redefinition of passion between women as homosexuality. Gordon celebrated love between women in a way which suffrage feminism did not or could not, in her semi-fictionalised and very personal interpretation of the ladies' life together. In the book she stresses the depth of their love and the seriousness of their commitment, quoting Sarah Ponsonby as saying 'I will live and die with Miss Butler' (1936: 135). While she suggests that one or two people in their circle believed their relationship was improper in its intensity, she is concerned to defend them against twentieth-century readings of homosexuality: 'And since no terrible scientific names were in existence to describe phenomena of the kind, the escapade remained romantic, to the entire peace of the subjects themselves' (1936: 136–7).

Mary Gordon believed the ladies had appeared to her as ghosts while she was visiting Llangollen and they had carried on a conversation in which she honoured them as spiritual forerunners and role models for later women like herself who loved women.

> Is it nothing to have shown the world a perfect love . . . Had you any idea how many women have been on a pilgrimage to this little old house of yours? Silently, saying nothing to anybody – but they came. . . . You made the way straight for the time that we inherited. You meditated among your books and dreamed us into existence. (1936: 269–70)

Not surprisingly, *Urania* welcomed Gordon's book, printing a review that stated:

> [I]t is history, not poetry. Something it speaks of happened, and went on happening for over fifty years. When history is poetry, it is more poetical than poetry itself. I do not remember to have read a page of print more soul-satisfying than this abstract from The Ladies' journal. . . . The ultimate

charm of the book, of course, is that it is a rhapsody in praise of friendship by one who understands how love endures. (*Urania* 121 & 122 Jan–Apr 1937: 2–3)

Two of the founders of *Urania*, the poet and mystic Eva Gore-Booth and her partner Esther Roper, secretary of the Manchester Suffrage Society, themselves enjoyed a similar romantic friendship. Meeting in Italy in 1896, the two women fell in love, and Eva moved to Manchester to live with Esther, both women actively campaigning for suffrage, women's trades union issues, and later for pacifist causes (Roper 1929). The journal's desire to make love between women visible meant they published a number of passionate extracts from women's **private writings**, such as Sophia Jex-Blake's declaration in her diary: 'I believe I love women too much to love a man . . .' (*Urania* 21 May–Jun 1920: 2). *Urania* also cited Geraldine Jewsbury's letters to Jane Carlyle as evidence of 'an authentic grand passion': 'I feel to love you more and more every day, and you will laugh, but I feel towards you much more like a lover than a female friend!' (*Urania* 115 & 116 Jan–Apr 1936: 8).

This perspective on love between women that stressed idealistic passion rather than sexual feeling was still important between the wars, but it was not the only version. Lesbianism was emerging as a definite sexual identity and lesbian sub-cultures were beginning to develop, at least among metropolitan artists and writers. With this growing awareness, the Ladies of Llangollen could become more sexualised reference points. The novelist Sylvia Townsend Warner and her lover, the young poet Valentine Ackland, joked about the Ladies when in 1931, soon after the start of their relationship, Valentine gave Sylvia a toothpick box with a plait of blonde hair in the lid: 'we decided on no evidence that Sarah Ponsonby gave it to Eleanor Butler' (Pinney 1998: 62). Colette, part of the Paris lesbian set for a while, and sometime lover of Natalie Barney, brought the Ladies right up to date in her novel *Ces Plaisirs* (1932): 'Can we imagine two ladies of Llangollen in this year of 1930? They would own a car, wear dungarees, smoke cigarettes, have short hair, and there would be a bar in their apartment.'

Colette's representation of the Ladies as modern role-playing lesbians was subsequently reprinted by *Arena Three* when the English translation of her book was published in 1968 (*Arena Three* 5 (5) May 1968: 12). On the whole, *Arena Three* treated the story of the Ladies in similar vein to Mary Gordon and *Urania*, as both a thrilling romance and a key part of lesbian heritage. One early article used all the conventions of the romance genre, detailing exciting but inaccurate events, such as how the two women contrived to meet at a dance in Dublin where they kissed for the first time. The couple overcame all obstacles to their love – attempts to marry off Sarah, their first elopement foiled by illness, accusations of being wicked and unnatural – and finally achieved an idyllic life together: 'a mutual devotion and serenity which would wear into legend' (*Arena Three* 4, 9 Sept 1967: 2–9). *Arena Three* also discussed Plas Newydd, the ladies' home in Llangollen, as a site for lesbian tourism – as indeed had Mary Gordon with her earlier pilgrimages of loving women friends. In 1971, *Arena Three* expressed concern about the sad neglect of the property – its furniture riddled with woodworm, and gardens overgrown: 'A great pity that it has not passed into the hands of the National Trust and received the care and attention it deserves. But it is worth a visit all the same.... one may remember, and pay silent homage' (*Arena Three* 8 (2) Feb 1971: 6).

Arena Three published a number of other stories of romantic friendships in history and developed some sophisticated discussion of the boundaries between intense female friendship and lesbian love, much of which would be rehearsed again by lesbian-feminist historians in the 1980s (Vicinus 1985; Lesbian History Group 1989). Clare Barringer's 1965 article on lesbian literature, 'The Fringe Benefits of Marginal Reading' discussed 'the ill-defined borderline between loving friendship and romantic love' and recommended reading against the grain across a range of literature by women. She quoted Virginia Woolf's writing on friendship between women from *A Room of One's Own*: 'those unrecorded gestures, those unsaid or half-said words' as an example of what Judith Bennett would later call 'lesbian-like' behaviour in literature and history (*Arena Three* 2, 1 Jan 1965: 8; Bennett 2000). Esme Langley developed the problem of sexuality in relation to the Ladies, when she argued that evidence of sexual consummation was not demanded by historians of heterosexual relationships and the key issue was same-sex rather than heterosexual choice of partner:

> When two women who are not related prefer to reject the 'heterosexual' way of life entirely in favour of a life together, this is a same-sex choice on both sides. Whether or not they 'did' or 'didn't' with one another is nobody's business, any more than it need concern historians what Samuel Pepys 'did' or 'didn't' do with Mrs Pepys in their two-sex relationship. Platonic or passionate friends, the Ladies are a lasting proof of the value of the Same-Sex Relationship. (*Arena Three* 8 (2) Feb 1971: 6)

Lesbian-feminist reappraisal of nineteenth-century romantic friendship was inspired in the 1970s and 1980s by the work of Carroll Smith-Rosenburg (1975) on the 'female world of love and ritual' and developed by Lillian Faderman into the preferred model of lesbian love. In *Surpassing the Love of Men: Romantic Friendship and Love between Women from the Renaissance to the Present* (1981), Faderman described the loving words written in the Ladies' diary and the references to their sharing a bed, but argued that while this was a committed, loving relationship, it was probably not a sexual one: 'Women dreamed not of erotic escapades but of a blissful life together' (1981: 117; also 84, 123). Similarly she asserted that most lesbians in the 1970s did not see their lesbian identity as primarily sexual but as a powerful emotional bond between women, likely to be cemented by feminist politics and representing resistance to patriarchy (1981: 18, 142; See also Lesbian History Group 1989). In the decentring of sexual desire and emphasis on gender politics, there are echoes here of *Urania*'s position.

The shift back to embracing sexual pleasure in lesbian politics in the late 1980s led to historians searching for evidence of erotic passion between women in the past. In relation to the Ladies of Llangollen, this meant re-engaging with the evidence of press insinuations about their masculine clothes and the private allegation by their friend Mrs Hester Thrale Piozzi that they were 'damned Sapphists'. She claimed that women were reluctant to spend the night in their cottage unless accompanied by men (Stanley 1992: 196–7; Donoghue 1993: 149–50). Romantic friendship, like other archetypes of lesbian love, was open to a variety of interpretations and did not necessarily connote asexual respectability. The erotic charge and complexity of intimate female friendships over the long nineteenth century have been given the most nuanced and contextualised readings by Martha Vicinus (Vicinus 1985, 2004). Focusing on how educated middle-class women used a variety of metaphors in their 'sexual self-fashioning', she has examined the ways in which the Ladies of Llangollen successfully deflected occasional accusations of debauchery and masculinity to create a widely admired vision of marital devotion (Vicinus 2004: xvi, 5–15).

Cross-dressing women: Lesbianism as transgressive desire

Wearing men's clothes, passing as a man or adopting other aspects of female masculinity has been associated with women's same-sex desire for a considerable period of time. In sexological writing lesbian desire was linked with gender inversion and hence with cross-dressing, but these ideas took some time to be disseminated in popular culture. Laura Doan has shown that it was not until after the trial of *The Well of Loneliness* in 1928 that short hair and a masculine cut of clothing became a widely recognised visual image of lesbianism (2001: 164–94). Nevertheless, masculinity in dress was certainly significant among lesbians themselves at an earlier date.

Urania resisted sexological definitions of love between women as gender inversion, but celebrated cross-dressing women as part of their particular sexual politics. From its first publication during the First World War, *Urania*'s pages were full of powerful, athletic, androgynous young women who exhibited physical prowess in sports competitions such as swimming or motorcycling events. The journal also demonstrated the cross-cultural history of the 'girl-soldier', from the Napoleonic Wars to the American Civil War (*Urania* 51 & 52 May–Aug 1925: 4; 69 & 70 May–Aug 1928: 4–9). These androgynous young heroines might become entangled in relationships with other women, if passing as men, and themselves become objects of same-sex desire. The many historical accounts of cross-dressed women who married other women suggested same-sex love and commitment across diverse cultures. *Urania* published the story of the eighteenth-century British couple Mary East and her woman partner, who as Mr and Mrs How ran pubs in east London for over 30 years (*Urania* 69 & 70 May–Aug 1928: 5–6), for example, and an account of a Chinese female husband who worked as a barber and was revealed as a woman only on her death (*Urania* 57 & 58 May–Aug 1926: 10).

Urania loved cross-dressing stories, not only for their connections to same-sex love, but because they demonstrated the fluidity of gender boundaries and the truth of their maxim 'sex is an accident'. While often promoting the attractiveness of the masculine woman, it was the androgynous figure whom *Urania* really valued. They condemned the idea that gendered opposites attract, denouncing the heterosexual extremes of masculinity and femininity. But they also applied this criteria to same-sex relationships and on these grounds criticised *The Well of Loneliness* in 1929:

> the moralist and the novelist, in depicting a case of homogeneous affection are prone to slip into attributing the distinctive shortcomings of the other sex to one of the pair. The 'perverted' girl must be masculine. The 'perverted' youth must be feeble and vain. . . . We have been accustomed to hear a great deal of 'the attraction of opposites'. But it is largely nonsense . . . There is no attraction for anybody in mannishness or effeminacy. (*Urania* 75 & 76 May–Aug 1929: 1–2)

Arena Three had a similarly enthusiastic yet ambivalent relationship with cross-dressing. By the 1960s, female masculinity had become a key signifier of lesbian identity. The very first piece of lesbian history published in *Arena Three* was an extract from *The Gentleman's Magazine* of 1746, about the trial and punishment of Mary/Charles Hamilton for pretending to be a man and marrying 14 wives. This was printed alongside a recent case in south-west England of a 20-year-old girl, Danny Turner, who was said to have dressed as a man since she left school at the age of 15 and to have been living with another girl as 'Mr. And Mrs. Turner'. There was no editorial comment, but the juxtaposition suggested that there was a long tradition of women's cross-dressing which was related to lesbianism (*Arena Three* 1 (2) Feb 1964: 9). Yet the desirability of a masculine or 'butch' appearance caused controversy within the MRG and *Arena Three*, especially in the early years. Since their aim was the public acceptance of lesbians as 'normal women', should members be discouraged from wearing 'full drag' to meetings? The debate also raised issues of how class cut across lesbian identities – did butch and femme represent rough and respectable?

In its transgressive flamboyance, cross-dressing could provide stronger evidence of lesbian sexual expression than romantic friendship. A biographical article on the early nineteenth-century aristocrat Lady Hester Stanhope described her unusual height and masculine beauty. At 30, she fell in love with a younger woman, became the subject of gossip and fled abroad with her servants to the Middle East. 'Lady Hester began to dress as a man, and is described as riding about the countryside dressed as a "seraglio page" '. In male attire she visited aristocrats in Turkey and Egypt and was reportedly taken for a beardless youth by the crowds. Realising it would be impossible to return to England, she made her home in the Lebanon with Elizabeth, her constant companion (*Arena Three* 2 (3) Mar 1965: 5–6).

An article about Margaret Allen, who was hanged for murder in 1949, is interesting both as an attempt to record recent lesbian history and because it empathised with her need to wear men's clothing. While her crime was described as senseless and brutal, the author argued there were extenuating circumstances that meant she should have been reprieved and suggested she was hanged because society could not stomach her flamboyant lesbianism. 'Bill', as she liked to be known, 'whenever possible . . . wore "full drag" ' and signed the hotel register as 'Mr. Allen' during a weekend in Blackpool with her woman friend. The article described 'Bill's' clothes at her trial: 'her fawn overcoat, dark blue slacks, checked shirt and brightly striped tie', how she remarked 'my manhood holds back my tears', and noted that she was obliged to wear a dress for her hanging: 'society applied the final turn of the screw, stripping the condemned woman of the "drag" which was her last solace and dignity' (*Arena Three* 3 (2) Feb 1966: 2–7). Male clothing was a significant part of Allen's identity, which would have been understood by many readers of *Arena Three*.

As discussed above, lesbian-feminist historians of the 1970s and 1980s favoured the romantic friendship paradigm as reflecting their own definition of lesbianism. They did not ignore women's cross-dressing in the past, but tended to view it disapprovingly as false consciousness – lesbians being forced to adopt the negative qualities of masculinity as a consequence of women's limited economic and social choices under patriarchy. The 1980s 'sexual turn' led to studies of the more sexually charged aspects of lesbian history including the butch-femme sub-cultures of the 1950s bar communities. These accounts valued the masculine butch as the heroically visible figure of lesbian desire (Kennedy and Davis 1993; Gardiner 2003: 48–67).

Inspired by the emergence of queer theory in the early 1990s and its far-reaching influence since, there has been continuing interest in cross-dressing and the butch lesbian as prime exemplars of the unstable and performative nature of gender and sexual identities, leading to recent wrangling over whether gender crossing is part of a lesbian tradition or a history of transgender. Projecting contemporary identities back into history, some of those working in queer cultural studies claim the mannish invert, including the masculine heroine of *The Well of Loneliness* (1928), as a female-to-male transsexual rather than a lesbian (Halberstam 1998; Prosser 1998).

The questions with which *Urania* and *Arena Three* were grappling – what we are looking for in the lesbian past and how we interpret it – remain important issues. Careful ways of reading the fragmentary evidence for suggestive gaps, for what is not said as well as for what has been overtly recorded, have revealed the 'eloquent silence' about lesbianism in Victorian England (Vicinus 1997: 72) and the strategies used by women post-sexology to hide but not deny same-sex love (Newman 2002). At the same time the breadth and variety of evidence in official discourses, literary sources and popular culture which can be used to mine lesbian history has increasingly been recognised (Doan 2001; Oram and Turnbull 2001).

Whether their preference was for the spiritual, erotic or political meaning of love between women, lesbian groups in the last century prized visibility in their history-making. They drew attention to same-sex desire in classical and mythological traditions, to its socially challenging expression in gender-crossing, and to its longevity within domestic and romantic partnerships between women. Perhaps because community-building around specific identities is no longer so necessary for lesbians – at least in liberal metropolitan areas – historians have relaxed into more inclusive and plural conceptualisations of the lesbian past. Recent work has questioned the usefulness of identity categories and the periodisation of lesbian history. Analysing the language through which nineteenth-century women expressed their same-sex desires and sense of difference, Martha Vicinus argues that gender inversion was a key indicator of lesbian love long before sexology (Vicinus 2004: 230). She shows that female masculinity was often personally meaningful within women's intimate romantic relationships: in its heterogeneity it could be socially acceptable as well as transgressive in other contexts. The centrality of erotic desire and the diversity of its expression remain essential to lesbian historical writing today.

Alison Oram

Related essays

Body & Sexuality; Feminism; Modernity; Private writings; Queer; Romantic friendships; Women worthies; Women's liberation.

References

Arena three; Baxendale & Pawling 1996; Bennett 2000; Benstock 1987; Bland & Doan 1998; Carpenter 1906; Dixon 1997; Doan 2001; Doan & Waters 2000; Donaghue 1993; Faderman 1981; Gardiner 2003; Gordon 1936; Halberstram 1998; Kennedy & Davis 1993; Lesbian History Group 1989; Newman 2002; Oram 1998, 2001a,b, 2005; Oram & Turnbull 2001; Pinney 1998; Prosser 1998; Purvis 1998; Raymond 1986; Reynolds 2000; Rich 1980; Roper 1929; Smith-Rosenberg 1975;

Stanley 1992; Snyder 1995; Tyler-Bennett 1998; Urania Vicinus 1985, 1997, 2004; Wittig 1973/1975.

Local history

Women generally prefer to paint on a small canvas, for they have a sharp eye for detail, a keen sense of place, and an interest in people as individuals and in personal relationships. As these are best observed in small groups rather than in crowds, it is not surprising that women have warmed to the study of local history and were pioneers of the subject. Writing local history allowed their skill in dissecting the interplay of people in a clearly defined space to be given full play, and from those beginnings they have built up their larger generalisations. While women have been important in the development of local history in many parts of the world, my focus here is on Britain which has its own specific local history traditions.

Local history has taken a long time to win approbation in our masculine academic world, which generally prefers large, bold questions pitched at a national and international level. It is only very recently that local history has begun to receive recognition as a serious scholarly subject, claiming its rightful place among the building blocks on which significant generalisations on national and international history can be erected. With local history so late to receive recognition, the many women who laid its foundations have gone unsung and all accounts of the beginnings of historical writing pass them over in silence. It is time to recall the beginnings of local history when women were prominent pioneers, free spirits who roamed wherever their interests took them, exploring some of its many dimensions. It is not easy to find these women, the early local historians. This essay assembles a miscellany of them, found through those chance references that so often bring together stray facts and people to illuminate themes in a larger jigsaw. It is a preliminary foray only, but it should at least help to identify women's favourite themes, and so sensitise us to uncover more women, even when they disguised their gender as authors by using initials rather than a first name.

When the profession of writing history began to take shape at the end of the eighteenth century, it was a task most readily open to men with an academic training. Since women were excluded from higher education, it was the men who laid down the framework of the new discipline's conventions. Aspects of history which appealed to them most were political, constitutional and ecclesiastical and their research in those fields was furthered by the existence of ancient chronicles, memoirs, annals and other printed records. Only exceptional and lucky women had access to private libraries to exploit and develop historical interests. Nevertheless, a curiosity about local history was not altogether thwarted by such handicaps. Without books, it was certainly hampered, but it could still feed on manuscripts and letters, when they lay in the hands of local people, on visual remains on the ground for all to see and on the memories of living persons. These sources of evidence were available in local communities without ceremony or captious restraint. So they gave women a chance to engage in historical research and to select many fresh themes that were in sympathy with their temperament. Because local history was not recognised as a serious academic subject during most of the nineteenth century, women were at liberty to tackle the subject in whatever way they chose. They were exploring new paths, yet one cannot predict in advance the originality or direction of their work. There were as yet no conventions: they could attempt the general survey of a place, take only a few aspects or define single themes.

Historical fiction and non-fiction

Some of women's interest in local history found expression in historical novels. Nineteenth-century publishers looked with extraordinary benevolence on women authors, encouraged no doubt by their remarkable success, and some gave an historical background to their plots. Maria Edgeworth is given credit for establishing the model for the regional, historical novel in her book, *Castle Rackrent* (1800), and Sir Walter Scott acknowledged his debt to her when he followed her example. This choice of a fictional form for history may reflect women's frustration at their constrained circumstances away from libraries, but it may equally well have released an imaginative energy which they were positively glad to couple with their keen interest in history; it added relish to their writing. One novelist who had superlative success with the public in the middle of the century was Dinah Maria Mulock (later Craik), whose novel *John Halifax Gentleman* (1857) sold 260,000 copies, and whose work runs to nine columns in the British Library catalogue. In other circumstances, she could well be remembered as a local historian, with her sensitive account of distinctive landscapes. Her strong sense of place is most effectively demonstrated in *An Unsentimental Journey through Cornwall* (1884), in which she expressed a keen appreciation of its singular hedges, its unique plants, the influence of the sea on local life and the personality of the Cornish people whom she engaged in conversation whenever she could. She finished her account of Cornwall with thoughtful, diffident remarks about the effort needed to understand a local culture, realising that she had visited 'an old country'. Plainly, she had sharp historical sensibilities. But her success as a writer drew her in other directions, and when Mrs Parr wrote a memoir of Miss Mulock's life and fame in 1898, she entirely failed to mention the book about Cornwall.

The earliest non-fictional work by women on local history also began to appear around 1800. Some of it lies concealed in *The Lady's Magazine* and consists of anonymous articles describing places that might attract curious visitors. Tourism was in its infancy, and readers were anticipated who wanted to leave town for 'the air and exercise of the country'. Landscapes featured prominently in their writing, but some articles, like the one on Weymouth, including the island of Portland, for example, assembled snippets of local history. An early book by Miss S Hatfield, a sympathetic account of a journey from London to Lincolnshire in 1815, is a gem of local and family history. Purporting to be a bundle of letters from a Miss Fielden describing the landscape on her journey and at her destination at Burton Stather in the lower Trent valley, it is laced with historical observations. Hatfield consulted local people, with the result that one of them brought her 'an old musty manuscript for your great pleasure', being the parish register for 1665. Mixing past and present, she offered an unusually slanted, absorbing piece of local history, concluding her letters with praise for its pleasures; in her view they far exceeded those of novels. An interest in local life was plainly stirring, and in sensitive hands it could uncover something of the highly varied personalities of regions.

Landscape and language

A striking characteristic of this early women's work was its concern with the great contrasts in landscape over short distances.

Indeed, some women were so captivated by landscape that their history was consigned to footnotes, as in the case of Eliza Lynn Linton writing on *The Lake Country* (1864). Mary Sterndale in *Vignettes of Derbyshire* (1824) wrote of people's stronger attachment to their native heath in such wild places than in more cultivated regions, where 'refinement polishes manners'. 'The glow of hospitality, the spirit of social happiness' seemed to infuse its countryside, and she expressed her sense of place in some brief but memorable accounts of the local people and dwellings that she encountered. These sites included Cressbrook cotton mill, where two or three hundred orphan children worked under a disciplined but humane regime of training. Her description of the mill offers an instructive insight into factory industry, operating in a kindlier, gentler guise than our present-day perspective can accommodate. All in all, she surveyed the scene serenely, while asking the broad questions of one who thought about the future as well as the past. Bewailing the consequences of enclosure, she described the landscape with care – the trees, the plants, the pattern of settlement and the housing that gave her clues to the classes of people inhabiting the place. Then to get a closer view, she talked to the natives and started to 'people' her local places.

Other women became engrossed by local dialects. Among the earliest was Sarah Sophia Banks, sister of Sir Joseph Banks, who prepared *Glossaries in Lincolnshire Dialect* between 1778 and 1783 but never saw her work published. This text was deposited in the British Library, but was not used by Joseph Wright when he prepared his *English Dialect Dictionary*. Some women working on dialect had scholarly brothers, husbands or friends urging them on; thus Anne Elizabeth Baker worked alongside her brother when he was preparing a topographical history of Northamptonshire. She accompanied him on his travels and listened to local words and phrases on the lips of the inhabitants. From her notes emerged her *Glossary of Northamptonshire Words and Phrases* in two volumes (1854). Another pioneer in this field was Georgina F Jackson, gathering up Shropshire words and publishing them in her *Shropshire Word Book* (1879).

Conversations with local people led other women historians beyond an interest in local words and dialect to the customs, superstitions and traditions of different regions. Their conversation seemed to lay a trail into the distant past before the days of written records. Mrs Bray published in 1838 the three-volume *Traditions, Legends, Superstitions, and Sketches of Devonshire*, which incorporated notes that her clerical husband had assembled in preparation for a never-published history of Tavistock. She had been his supportive companion and together they had examined documents in the offices of the Duchy of Cornwall, and perused land surveys and the records of the Stannary Court. She did not neglect her own special interests, however; and pronouncing her strong intention to write for all classes of readers, she presented portraits of memorable local characters, recounted legends and superstitions and illustrated her book with her own sketches. Georgina Jackson also came to the subject from a first interest in dialect, before collecting folklore. When illness prevented her from publishing anything more, she passed her material to Charlotte Sophia Burne who produced *Shropshire Folklore. A Sheaf of Gleanings* (1883). It is sobering to read Miss Burne keenly studying physical boundaries a century ago in a search of cultural regions. Their origins for her went back to settlers in the Anglo-Saxon period. Today, after a long interval, scholars have come back to the same subject with fresh insights, following a trail yet earlier in time in search of explanations, as the work of Charles Phythian-Adams bears witness. A few years later, Mrs Charlotte G Boger wrote *Myths, Scenes and Worthies of Somerset* (1887). She initially intended to collect only myths and legends, but was drawn into history by realising that myths were built on things that had really happened. King Arthur's burning of the cakes lived before her eyes when the legend of the woman at the hearth scolding Arthur was presented to her in dialect 'such as every housewife in Somersetshire would understand'. Listing her sources at the end of each essay, she cited oral tradition alongside the books.

Moving off in another direction from folklore women started to record singing games and local songs. This research is especially associated with Alice Gomme, whose husband was a folklorist, who became President of the Folklore Society and produced *A Dictionary of British Folklore*. She was bringing up seven sons, and pondered folklore from a different angle. In the end, her work on children's singing games is said to have brought her more fame than her husband, and probably to have inspired Cecil Sharp to make his more systematic search for folksongs. Another trail in search of ballads had already been opened up in the 1860s by F J Furnivall and J W Ebsworth, and this prompted Julia H L de Vaynes to assemble the first-ever collection of Kentish ballads. In *The Kentish Garland* (1881) she focused exclusively on Kent, but opened a wide window on events of national significance.

Craft and industry

The domestic lives of women immersed them in handicrafts of many kinds, and drew another group to study local industries. Here again, they were explorers in new territory with the advantage of a discerning eye, sharpened by their own practical skills. The most memorable volume was on lace by Mrs Bury Palliser, revealing the heavy demands it had placed on her scholarly skills, for lace in England had first to be traced back to its origins across Europe. Mrs Palliser revealed in her Preface extended consultations with librarians, archivists and friends who scoured the foreign archives, and her footnotes make impressive reading in a work published in 1865. Yet she referred to lace in her Preface as 'a trivial matter'! Wisely, when Margaret Jourdain and Alice Dryden revised and enlarged Mrs Palliser's work in 1902, they refrained from any reference to lace as a triviality. It had stood high in the estimation of aristocrats and churchmen throughout Europe, and in European trade much money and many people had been employed on it. It was, indeed, a complex story involving several different kinds of lace, and differentiated regional skills that were communicated between countries by migrants. Another work in this same period by Mrs E Nevill Jackson, *A History of Hand Made Lace* (1900), also examined regional profiles, with a note (though far too cursory) on lacemakers' songs. She also bravely experimented with a further problem, though her solution had no future: inserted in the copy of her book in the British Library are samples of lace mounted on card.

From the middle of the nineteenth century all historians were better equipped to fill their canvases with local detail, through the publication of many reference tools opening up both national and major private archives (these last being calendared by the Historical Manuscripts Commission). Interest can be gauged in the bibliography of Essex history, compiled by W R Powell in 1959, for it brings to light the work done in just one populous county near London, notable for attracting many local historians at an early date, of whom not a few were women. The setting up of public libraries further assisted researchers, while some rules that had hindered women's access to documents were now relaxed. Secondary education for girls gave a privileged few the chance of a grammar school education, and they learned Latin and modern languages. Gradually, the local history written by women relied less on imaginative speculations and **oral traditions** and cited more books.

Women travelled more on the new railways, venturing to write books that carried them far beyond their own locality and proving zealous in exploring archives that had till then hardly been opened at home and abroad. Some absolutely insisted on visiting the places where their histories were enacted, and the scenes of momentous events. Mrs S C Hall, in her *Pilgrimages to English Shrines* (1850), enunciated this principle, starting with 'a visit to the birth place of John Bunyan'. She could not understand how Robert Southey could have written his memoir of Bunyan, so 'full of feeling for Bunyan', without visiting Elstow in Bedfordshire; he had allowed an artist to depict the cottage 'with a poet's eye' rather than as it was. In another book on Chertsey, *Chertsey and Its Neighbourhood* (1853), she conjured up a distinctive picture of this wild, forest country in Surrey where its ancient woodland economy was even now being transformed under a new owner, improving the land and the lot of its inhabitants.

By the end of the nineteenth century historical interest was sufficiently aroused to support an ambitious project for writing the local history of all the English counties, in parish by parish accounts. Thus began in 1899 the series of volumes for a *Victoria County History of England (VCH)*. The Adult Education movement was at the same period establishing a network of teaching centres which recruited women, mostly as students, but also occasionally as tutors, to study general history. The universities were also accepting women on history courses. So a considerable number could now be harnessed to the task of systematically examining documents in the Public Record Office which already possessed indexes and hand-lists. The tables of contents of the earliest published volumes of the *VCH* show the results: a great number of parish accounts were written by women. Volume III of the Hampshire *VCH* (1908) is one topographical volume that was almost entirely written by women. Many of the women historians in the *VCH* series had attended the universities of Oxford, Cambridge, London or St Andrews; only in the case of London were they allowed to claim degrees – in the other cases, only their universities, in brackets, followed their names in print.

Local history in the academy

The expected content of local history underwent significant modification when academic history expanded to embrace new facets of the subject. At the centre of one important new trend stood William Cunningham, who taught at Cambridge and made the economic history of England at the level of national policy his speciality. A colleague at the London School of Economics, **Lilian Knowles**, also adopted this viewpoint, specialising in England's industrial and commercial revolutions, but again pitching her subject on a national rather than local plane. Students moved between London and Cambridge, learning and thereafter becoming teachers or researchers who likewise focused on these economic and social aspects of history.

When scholars showed a special leaning towards the local impact and implications of national trends, they exerted a significant influence on writing in the *VCH* volumes. They decentralised some historical studies, by moving investigations from the capital to the provinces, while also winning some grudging academic respectability for these searches. An exemplary study of this kind, clearly proclaiming its origins in its title, was M F Davies' *Life in an English Village: An Economic and Historical Survey of the Parish of Corsley in Wiltshire* (1909). Sidney and **Beatrice Webb** at the LSE had suggested the subject, which was the parish in which Miss Davies lived. Chronologically systematic and comprehensive, the book started with a clear geographical description of the parish, followed by the major phases in its economic development, a sequence of argument that would become conventional in local history. Its search for documents followed a pattern that would also become a convention in local history: archives in private hands (in this case those of the Marquis of Bath and other lesser owners) were the first source; the records in the parish chest came second; a zestful search then began in other less obvious places. The book was unusual in its Part II, in investigating the condition of the village in the present, uncovering the sources of people's livelihoods and even their family budgets. The economists at LSE were obviously hovering in the background. They did not persuade other local historians to follow that lead; they have preferred to remain historians, and not become sociologists as well.

Another resourceful woman, Florence Bell, not trained in Cambridge or at the LSE, but influenced by the social investigations of Charles Booth, was assisted by a team of women helpers to examine and describe the livelihoods of the inhabitants of Middlesbrough, Yorkshire. Although more strictly a sociological study of contemporary life than a local history, *At the Works: A Study of a Manufacturing Town* (1907) was permeated with a deep understanding of Middlesbrough's development from a hamlet in 1811 into an industrial town of over 75,000 inhabitants by 1891. Its gendered viewpoint was emphatically expressed in the author's determination to gauge the iron trade not in abstract terms as a measure of national prosperity but through its impact on the people engaged in it. She penetrated numerous aspects of their personal lives to give an account that stands now as a remarkable piece of local history, written from a woman's point of view.

Meanwhile other women turned their search for local history in fresh and original directions. They fastened with special sympathy on private correspondence since this built up a picture of rounded personalities, drawn to life; they could not rest, content with the public face of public figures, and many times over said as much. They also combed old newspapers for graphic incidents reported by lively journalists and sought out oral traditions. Miss Sturge Henderson, writing between 1902 and 1934, admirably represents that transitional period when women roamed freely in search of archives, while also receiving some training from academic teachers. Her first book, *Three Centuries in North Oxfordshire* (1902), extolled the oral tradition for the unexpected clues that had unlocked for her hidden but factually correct history. She had been captivated by the past through the imaginative links that her mother always made between past and present and by her own contact with oral history (she had spoken to a Chartist in his old age). These experiences remained her inspiration in *A Corner of the Cotswolds*, written in 1914, when she used the local newspaper, *Jacksons Oxford Journal*, and entered solicitors' offices. Her results brought her the warm appreciation of G M Trevelyan in showing him vividly the personal role of JPs at Quarter Sessions in ordering the transportation of criminals to Australia. Meanwhile, she had become Mrs Gretton and her husband, Richard Henry Gretton, worked on more formal, political and administrative history. His publications included *The Burford Records. A Study in Minor Town Government* (1920) and *Modern Kingship* (1930). So while she shared his interest in Burford, she held to her own distinctive viewpoint and wrote *Burford Past and Present* (1920), a work that laid emphasis on Burford's history on aspects different from her husband's; the absence of a dominant squire in the place counted for much in her estimation, and the consequence that Burford's government lay in the hands of shopkeepers and tradesmen; she also gave prominence to Burford's position on the main road from London to Wales, causing it to absorb a host of influences from its travellers passing through. Nothing could better illustrate the differing approaches of a male and female local historian than this example from two people in one family. But finally Mrs Gretton trod the orthodox academic path in her later years, obtaining a B.Litt. degree from Oxford and editing a volume of documents on Oxfordshire JPs for the Oxfordshire Record Society.

One local historian who gazed on her local scene with a distinctive eye was Miss M S Holgate. She lived in Ardingly in Sussex and traversed its lanes and pondered its place names with the sharp eye of an inhabitant who was also a trained historian. For some twenty years, she contributed articles to the parish magazine of St Peter's, Ardingly, elucidating its topography, the place names and their pronunciation, identifying boundary landmarks and listing its inhabitants from the tax lists. She used archives in London, Oxford and Sussex, and finally prepared for scholars a volume on *Inquisitions Post Mortem, 1541–1616*, for the Sussex Record Society. But already, long before, she had demonstrated this attractive and illuminating way of reading a local landscape that was fresh and original in its time, now made familiar by many more recent examples.

The Women's Institutes have built up a tradition of listening to and remembering the traditions of local communities, and from time to time recording them for posterity. From their beginnings in Britain in 1915, they made efforts to cherish local history in the places where it happened. In 1921 the Women's Institutes launched a competition for the best book on old customs, beliefs, stories and ancient monuments. Cambo in Northumberland enlisted the help of everyone in its large parish, to probe their memories, identify old sites, 'camps' and prehistoric remains, and pass on their knowledge. They wrote their book in 1922, edited by Rosalie Bosanquet, one of the first women to study modern history at Oxford in 1902. It was published in 1929, required reprinting in the same year, and was reissued again in 1989. Memories of life in Cambo went back to the Jacobite risings in the early eighteenth century, and incorporated detail which rarely if ever comes our way in more official documents: in 1822 people still had no ovens in their houses and made bread in a pot; in one house people and cows went in and out through the same door; women went out at 4 a.m. to gather wool off the hedges to get it carded at Otterburn and brought home to spin and knit into stockings – if they went any later, the tramps would have taken it all; and when the railway arrived in 1862 the train used to stop to allow the locals to gather mushrooms.

Popular interest in local history was noticeably fired in Britain during the second half of the twentieth century, precipitating the setting up of many new societies and courses of instruction in the subject. Teaching has introduced a certain formality, if not rules, into its procedures, for when local history is *taught*, a syllabus has to be devised, and conventions start to shape the subject. Now at the beginning of the twenty-first century, local history has become a branch of study that has as many practitioners among men as women, benefiting from a partnership of all comers and both genders in assembling the building blocks of documents and memory. Books and documents are so widely available to all that women's style and viewpoint are less distinctive; indeed, we expect all authors to converge and follow a mainstream. Nevertheless, the rivulets that contribute to that mainstream are always changing; widely travelled people nowadays are constantly passing fresh judgements when evaluating the local scene. So we must continue to read local history with an awareness of the distinctive personalities of our authors. They all bring fresh insights to the subject.

Joan Thirsk

References

Bell 1907/1985; Bosanquet 1989; Davies 1909; Du Cane 2002; Gandy 1989; Goldman 1995; Phythian-Adams 2000; Rudkin 1973; Smith 1984; Stapleton 1895; Thirsk 1996.

Related essays

Australia; Canada; Great Britain; Historical Fiction; Historical Organisations; Oral Traditions; Travel; United States.

Lutz, Alma 1890–1973

American suffrage biographer, historian of women. Born in Jamestown, North Dakota, daughter of Mathilde (Bauer) and George Lutz. Educated at the Emma Willard School and Vassar College. Leaving Vassar in 1912 Lutz moved to Boston, with her Vassar room-mate Marguerite Smith. Lutz and Smith lived together for 41 years. A member of the National Women's Party for much of her life, Lutz was deeply committed to the struggle for the Equal Rights Amendment. She contributed to national magazines on the subject, campaigning in various organisations and spoke on the amendment before the President's Committee on the Status of Women.

Published her first book, a biography, *Emma Willard, Daughter of Democracy*, on the founder of her alma mater in 1929. In the early 1930s Lutz was chosen by Harriet Stanton Blatch to write the biography of her mother. In 1940 she produced the first full-length biography of **Elizabeth Cady Stanton**, *Created Equal.* Blatch was assisted by Lutz in the preparation of her own memoirs, *The Challenging Years* (1940). In these texts Lutz began a revision of suffrage history, celebrating Stanton and presenting Susan B Anthony as 'the secondary attraction'. Lutz also published a biography of Anthony in 1959. She edited a collection of women's letters written during wartime, *With Love, Jane* (1945). Inspired by the civil rights movement, her final work *Crusade for Freedom* (1968) celebrated the work of women in the abolition movement.

In 1953 she began an association with Radcliffe College, where she served as a member of the Advisory Committee for the Schlesinger Library. She also taught a graduate seminar on Women in American History at Radcliffe, as she believed it was important to teach young women about the achievements of their foremothers.

Mary Spongberg

References

Des Jardins 2003; Rupp & Taylor 1987.

Major work

Emma Willard: Daughter of Democracy (Washington: Zenger Publication, 1975).

M

Macaulay, Catharine Sawbridge 1731–1791

English historian and political writer. Born in Kent, youngest daughter of Elizabeth Wanley and John Sawbridge. Largely self-educated, Macaulay immersed herself in Roman history and developed a life-long interest and commitment to Republican politics. In 1760 married George Macaulay, Scottish physician, who was well connected in London's radical and non-conformist circles. One daughter.

With her husband's encouragement Macaulay began work on the first volume of her *History of England from the Accession of James I to the Elevation of the House of Hanover*, which was published in 1763. Her Whig history of seventeenth-century Britain was the first overtly political history to be written by a woman in Great Britain. Dismissing '[t]he invidious censures which may ensue from striking into a path of literature rarely trodden by [her] sex', Macaulay refused to remain 'mute in the cause of liberty and virtue', publishing seven more volumes of her history between 1766 and 1783. Her *History* was a spirited defence of the development and preservation of 'Liberty' in England and was intended to inculcate 'the general principles of the rights of mankind'. Written to counter David Hume's 'partisan Tory history' of the English Revolution, Macaulay's *History* was favourably compared. Certain Tory reviewers, however, characterised it as a 'Romance'. The *Gentleman's Magazine* referred to her only as 'Dr Macaulay's wife' while other reviewers suggested that he had in fact penned the *History*. James Boswell scorned the idea of an English republican, especially a woman. The success of her *History* saw Macaulay become a literary celebrity in London, where Horace Walpole described her as 'one of the sights that all foreigners are carried to see'.

Although not writing a history of women, Macaulay missed no 'anecdote that does honour to the female sex', often dwelling on women whom she believed male historians had traduced or omitted. Her discussion of women such as Rachel Russell and **Lucy Hutchinson** presented important political role models for women and their lives were frequently revisited in the **female biographies** that proliferated in the nineteenth century. Macaulay believed that History told the story of the loss of the rights of man and the progress of man towards realising these rights again in a more perfect state; consequently, she framed her history around the notion that Britons had lost the rights of their ancient Saxon constitution following the invasion of William the Conqueror. This discourse of lost ancient rights would inflect the historical writings of suffragists such as **Helen Blackburn** and **Charlotte Carmichael Stopes** in the nineteenth century.

Macaulay based her history on extensive archival research drawn largely from parliamentary records and histories and political **memoirs**, including those of Lucy Hutchinson, which she tried unsuccessfully to have published. All volumes of her *History* were exhaustively footnoted. When following her death she was accused of destroying materials she had used for her Histories, the Assistant Librarian of the British Museum defended her, writing in the *Gentleman's Magazine*: 'There is another characteristic of Mrs Macaulay's History, still more respectable than her love of Liberty and that is her love of truth' (See **Archives**).

Following the death of her husband in 1766 Macaulay held a radical salon in her London home and began to engage in contemporary political debate producing polemical pamphlets such as *Loose Remarks on Certain Positions to be Found in Mr Hobbes Philosophical Remarks on Government and Society* (1767) in which she critiqued his theory of monarchical government. When the House of Commons refused to validate the election of John Wilkes as representative for Middlesex, Macaulay became involved in the first major parliamentary reform movement of the eighteenth century. In 1770 she attacked Edmund Burke following the publication of his *Thoughts on the Cause of the Present Discontents* and developed her own ideas regarding the basis of a truly popular government in a pamphlet entitled *Observations on a Pamphlet, Entitled, Thoughts on the Cause of the Present Discontents*. Burke dismissed her criticism as 'the patriotick scolding of our republican Virago'. Macaulay's ideas became known in America, where her next pamphlet *Address to the People of England, Ireland and Scotland, on the Present Important Crisis of Affairs* (1775) was more widely circulated than in Britain. In this pamphlet she condemned Britain's treatment of the American colonies, earning herself the reputation in America as a 'Friend of Liberty'.

Plagued with ill health Macaulay took the waters at Bath, moving there in 1774. She lived there in the house of her friend and political ally the Reverend Thomas Wilson, Rector of St Stephen's Parish Walbrook. Macaulay addressed her epistolary *History of England from the Revolution to Present Times* (1778) to Wilson. In December 1778 Macaulay married William Graham a naval officer, 26 years her junior. Scandal ensued and she became an object of scorn and derision. The marriage destroyed her friendship with Wilson and caused embarrassment among her friends. Political enemies produced a barrage of scandal literature in which Macaulay's marriage was celebrated as a victory of male sexual privilege over female intellect.

Macaulay had frequently corresponded with American patriots such as Benjamin Rush, James Otis and John Adams, sometimes sending them complimentary copies of her *History*. In 1784 she spent a year in America and was toasted by political figures including Martha and George Washington. Through these radical circles she became acquainted with **Mercy Otis Warren** who would be called the 'Mrs Macaulay of the American Revolution'. Macaulay had intended to write a history of the American Revolution, a task Warren eventually took up. Macaulay also supported republican politics in France, where she visited in 1777, meeting Madame Roland who was inspired to be 'la Macaulay de son pays'. She was vocal in support of the French Revolution and wrote a vigorous response to Edmund Burke's scathing *Reflections on the Revolution in France*. A translation of her *History* appeared in France in 1791 and greatly influenced the Girondin faction. Macaulay believed that the French Revolution promised 'the highest degree of freedom with the highest degree of order' and did not live to see this illusion shattered. In her last work Macaulay turned to the rights (and wrongs) of women. In her *Letters on Education* (1790), she wrote poignantly, 'Woman has everything against her'. Such sentiment no doubt reflected a sense of the gender conflict she had experienced as a woman writing history. Despite her pessimism Macaulay sought changes to the condition of women, particularly emphasising the importance of education.

Mary Wollstonecraft with whom Macaulay corresponded, would write following her death, that the 'very word respect brings Mrs Macaulay to my remembrance' and claimed that she was 'the woman of the greatest abilities, undoubtedly, that England had ever produced'. **May Hays** wrote the first major study of Macaulay's life in her *Female Biography* (1803). More recently Bridget Hill has produced a critical biography, *The Republican Virago: The Life and Times of Catherine Macaulay, Historian* (1992).

Mary Spongberg

References

Hays 1994; Hill 1992; Kucich 1998; Schnorrenberg 1979; Withey 1976.

Major work

Letters on Education (London: William Pickering, 1996).

Manley, Delarivier 1663–1724

British playwright, political journalist, secret historian. Born Jersey, daughter of Sir Roger Manley, Lieutenant Governor of Jersey and historian. Robbed of her chance to become maid of honour to Mary of Modena, by the Glorious Revolution, Manley was made ward of her cousin John Manley, a Whig lawyer, following the death of her father in 1687. In 1689 John Manley bigamously married his cousin, abandoning her shortly after with a young child. Introduced to Barbara Villiers, Duchess of Cleveland by Ann and Elizabeth, daughters of **Ann, Lady Fanshawe**. Manley came under her patronage around 1694. The pair fell out almost immediately. Manley's time with the Duchess, however, gave her an insider's perspective on courtly scandal that shaped her later writing. Manley travelled through the West Country of England, seeking support from her husband for their infant son.

From 1695 Manley supported herself entirely by the pen. Her first literary works were for the theatre in 1695 she provided a prefatory poem to Catherine Trotter's dramatic version of Aphra Behn's novella *Agnes de Castro*, which shows Manley trying to situate herself within a tradition of English women's writing. *The Lost Lover*, a comedy by Manley, was first performed at Drury Lane in 1696. *The Royal Mischief*, a tragedy performed later that year at Lincoln's Inn Fields, established Manley's literary reputation. Around this time she also produced *Letters Written by Mrs Manley* (1696) (retitled *A Stage Coach Journey to Exeter* in 1725) which documented her travels through the West Country.

Around 1702 Manley began to publish a series of **secret histories**, scandal chronicles modelled after the French courtly *roman à clef*. Manley's secret histories were satires drawn from contemporary history in which she represented abuse of political power as sexually scandalous behaviour. Sarah, Duchess of Malborough, was the butt of Manley's satire in *The Secret History of Queen Zarah and the Zarazians* (1705) and in the more (in)famous *Secret Memoirs and Manners . . . From the New Atalantis* (1709). These texts comment on contemporary political events, while also serving as Tory political propaganda. *The New Atalantis* (1709) has been described as being the single most harmful publication to the Whig ministry in 1709 and was instrumental in the downfall of the Whig government the following year. Manley was arrested and imprisoned for seditious libel in 1709. She was released after claiming in her defence that *The New Atalantis* was a work of fiction, thus allowing her to protect her sources and placing the burden of identification on her prosecutors. In 1710 she produced *Memoirs of Europe* (1710) a panegyric to Tory leaders Robert Harley and Lord Peterborough. Later efforts such as *Court Intrigues* (1711) did not live up to the heady scandal generated by the *New Atalantis*.

Friendship with Jonathan Swift saw her interest shift to political journalism and in 1711 she replaced him as editor of *The Examiner*. In this capacity Manley continued to allegorise recent political history. She also published a series of mock Whig political pamphlets. In 1714 Manley produced her 'autobiography' the *Adventures of Rivella*; however, like her earlier work she mixed biographical detail with rumour and innuendo and consequently the text is regarded as unreliable. Fidelis Morgan's 'Autobiography of Mrs Manley' *A Woman of No Character* (1986) draws together these and other details of Manley's life found throughout her writings. Manley's later works include *Lucius, the First Christian King of Britain*, an historical tragedy first performed in 1717.

Mary Spongberg

References

Ballaster 1992; Gallagher 1992; Zelinsky 1999.

Major works

The New Atalantis (ed.) Rosalind Ballaster (New York: New York University Press, 1992) and *The Adventures of Rivella* (ed.) Katherine Zelinsky (Peterborough: Broadview, 1999).

Martineau, Harriet 1802–1876

English economist, historian. Born in Norwich, the sixth of the eight children of Thomas Martineau, a cloth manufacturer descended from an old Huguenot family, and Elizabeth. Educated at home, attended an excellent school headed by the Rev. Isaac Perry between 1813 and 1815 and for 15 months between 1818 and 1819 she was a boarder in a small school in Bristol run by an aunt. As a child, Harriet Martineau felt unloved and unhappy. To add to her misery, she had limited senses of both taste and smell. Moreover she was increasingly deaf – indeed, her deafness had become virtually total by the time she was 20, adding to her sense of isolation. Although the family was quite wealthy in her childhood, a financial disaster in 1829 meant that Harriet had to support herself. Although she was a talented seamstress, she decided to do so as a writer. She had already published a number of essays in Fox's *Monthly Repository*, so this was an obvious direction. Martineau's health, which had been poor in her childhood, continued to be a problem. She suffered from acute abdominal pains in 1838, which reduced her to semi-invalidism – but from which she was apparently cured some years later by mesmerism. In the 1840s, she was well enough to travel to Egypt and the Near East. In the 1850s, she was again ill and fearing that death was near, she wrote her autobiography, driven to do so, or so she insisted because she had learnt much from the autobiographies of others, and so felt an obligation to record her own story, especially as her life was increasingly a remarkable one. This sense of obligation was increased because, some years earlier, Martineau had demanded the return of all her correspondence.

Martineau's major historical writing was *The History of the Thirty Years' Peace, 1816–1846* (1849–1850). This work was extremely well received and the following year, she wrote an extended introduction to it, entitled *History of England, A.D. 1800–1815* (1851). Martineau's widely acclaimed contemporary history was one of the few nineteenth-century works to include discussion of the condition of women, alongside other questions that were of importance to her, including the anti-slavery movement, education, political economy and free trade, and considerable discussion of ecclesiastical and clerical misdeeds.

In addition to this work, Martineau wrote about the history of women in a number of other ways. Her first essay was a comparison of Anna Laetitia Barbauld and Hannah More as devotional writers published in the *Unitarian Monthly Repository* in 1822. She also discussed the history of women's employment in her essay 'Female Industry' in the *Edinburgh Review* (1859), a work that was very important to the mid-nineteenth-century British women's movement.

Martineau's writing was not confined to Britain, and her visits to America in 1834–1836 and to Egypt and the Near East a decade later both resulted in important works, *Society in America* (1837) and *Eastern Life: Present and Past* (1848), that combined travel with discussions of contemporary society and earlier history. Her autobiography (written in 1855, but published in 1877) continues her analysis of contemporary history, both in her discussion of her immediate and familial life and in the extensive detail she provided of her career, her travels and of the people she had known and the activities in which she had engaged. It is most significant, however, as a study of an individual self and subjectivity across the nineteenth century, and its introspection offers an incomparable insight into the life and mind of an unusual and troubled Victorian woman.

Barbara Caine

References

Hoecker-Drysdale 1992; Webb 1960.

Masculinity

In the past two decades an increasing number of women historians have been drawn to investigate the history of men as a sex. Although men have always been central to historical study, these scholars sought to untangle how men were shaped by gender expectations as they interacted with the world. Male historians who pioneered this field were interested in traditional environments like the military, single-sex schools, fraternal organisations or the boy scouts. Initially spurred by questions which arose from their study of women, female historians were often more interested in integrating men into the study of groups such as the family or into spaces where men exercised power or responsibility. In much the same way that historians of the working class found that they needed to understand elites to clarify the way economic power relationships worked, female historians saw men as shaping and being shaped by the gender imperatives of both sexes. Later works increasingly focused on how definitions of masculinity were employed as a tool by some groups of men to control other men, particularly in an imperial or racial context. One constant thread in their analyses is a sensitivity to the difficulties faced by men and the compromises forced upon them. This enables the reader to recognise that masculinity is not a biological category, but culturally constructed and subject to a variety of subtle pressures over time. This essay focuses on few of the women whose work best illustrates the field, before concluding with a consideration of what makes their work distinctive.

One of the earliest works to try to push analysis in a new direction was co-authored by Leonore Davidoff and Catherine Hall. *Family Fortunes* (1987) investigates the creation of the middle class in Britain during the Industrial Revolution. They focus not on the public sphere, but on the private sphere and the role that domesticity had in defining this new class. Davidoff's earlier work, *The Best Circles* (1973), had explored the role of elite women in forging new alliances through hospitality, but *Family Fortunes* carries the analysis further by revealing that bourgeois men had increasingly embraced the family as part of their sphere of influence. Catherine Hall's subsequent work probes more deeply into the role of gender in shaping men's ideas and actions. Her collection, *White, Male and Middle Class* (1992), offers a nuanced look at controversies such as the mid-Victorian debate over Edward John Eyre, governor of Jamaica, and his brutal quelling of a revolt in 1859. Hall employs this as an opportunity to uncover the way attitudes towards masculinity influenced the British elite in their response to this event. Thomas Carlyle's support for Eyre, for example, was animated by a range of beliefs about the way 'men' should respond to such challenges. Hall's work is also moulded by an awareness of the way masculinity and ideas about race and empire intertwined. These are explored more deeply in her later studies *Civilising Subjects* (2002) and (with Jane Rendall and Keith McClelland) of the 1867 Reform Act (Defining the Victorian Nation, 2000).

The relationship between race and masculinity is also the focus of Mrinalini Sinha, Gail Bederman, Lindsay Clowes, Dana Nelson and Hazel Carby. Sinha's *Colonial Masculinity* (1995) reveals the way British imperialists exploited ideas about manliness to underpin their rule in the nineteenth- and twentieth-century Raj. Here the growing pressures from Indian nationals for self-government were dismissed by defining Bengali men (who were pursuing more education in order to enter the Indian Civil Service) as 'effeminate', and thus by definition unable to govern themselves. Sinha's analysis reveals how ideas about gender were thus employed to reinforce the British empire and to revise the requirements for self-government which had been set out earlier. Ideas about gender were used in other campaigns within India as well to shore up British imperial rule.

Similarly, Gail Bederman's *Manliness and Civilization* (1995) explores the way the construction of masculinities worked to shore up the white elite at a time when their power was being challenged. Through an examination of the way concerns about manliness were recast at the turn of the century in matters like black boxer Jack Johnson's victory in the ring over the white Jim Jeffries, Bederman demonstrates masculinity's centrality in American society as it worried about decline in the face of increasing urbanisation and the closure of the frontier. Her volume also examines Ida B Wells' dissection of the gender anxieties which manifested themselves in a wave of lynchings across the nation, G Stanley Hall's fears about the softening nature of civilisation on white teenaged boys and Theodore Roosevelt's insistence on demonstrating that the fully evolved white man had not lost his masculine edge. Her treatment of the fictional hero, Tarzan, establishes how a cultural construction allows a society to imagine both its greatest fear and a possible solution. Edgar Rice Burroughs' iconic character embodied the possibilities of uniting the eponymous son of the Anglo-Saxon race with the training of a primitive upbringing to create a worthy exemplar in a time of masculine crisis. The turn of the nineteenth to the twentieth century saw worries about masculinity in European as well as American society; Bederman makes it clear how racial thinking was crucial to the construction of masculine examples.

Dana Nelson's *National Manhood* continues this theme by investigating the way white American men have been socialised to perceive independence as a key constituent of masculinity. Working mainly from texts ranging from Jefferson's *Notes on the State of Virginia* to Herman Melville, Nelson explicates what she terms the 'fraternal articulation of white manhood to civic identity' (1998: ix). For her this has two implications. First, white American men have perceived the troubles of society to be rooted in the failures of individuals rather than in systemic problems. Second, this individualism is so centred for them in the person of white men that other groups in society (African-Americans and women, for example) are not perceived as part of the polity as they cannot, almost by definition, embody this independence. Nelson goes on to demonstrate that this idea gives white American men a feeling of fraternity which is exclusive rather than inclusive, so that even when other groups exhibit the characteristics of independence integral to their definition of masculinity, they see it as an aberration. For Nelson, race and gender work together to define political ideas practised in the USA.

Similarly, Hazel Carby's *Race Men* (1998) reveals how masculinity was at the centre of African-American struggles to achieve equality in American society. This series of lectures takes a detailed look at such figures as W E B Du Bois and Paul Robeson to uncover the way they focused on a certain definition of masculinity as appropriate to the struggle for equal rights. Carby demonstrates how Du Bois painted Booker T Washington's achievements as unmanly as they urged African Americans to work hard and fit into the dominant culture. Thus a certain vision of masculinity became one of the litmus tests of African-American culture, marginalising not only men who did not conform to this image, but also women. For Carby, this focus on men and masculinity is a problem that continues to impede the achievement of real equality.

Race and masculinity are also at the heart of Lindsay Clowes' examination of competing masculinities in the post-war South African magazine *Drum*. This magazine, which described itself as a 'magazine of Africa for Africa', sought its readership in the millions of Africans who had moved from rural to urban areas in the 1940s. In order to attract subscribers, it abandoned initial efforts to attract readers with an emphasis on heritage when it realised that readers were eager to leave that behind. Clowes discusses the unease demonstrated by the editors when men entered their competition to find a beautiful Miss Africa. The editors' vision of modern masculinity centred around work, not personal appearance. Clowes argues that this illustrates the competing masculinities emerging in Africa during a shift from a culture which emphasised physical appearance to one which focused on deeds. For many of *Drum*'s readers, however, looking sharp remained a clear indicator of cool masculinity.

In contrast, language is at the heart of Michèle Cohen's *Fashioning Masculinity* (1996), an exploration of the system by which English gentlemen came to be constructed. Cohen argues that for Englishmen learning to speak, acquisition of the French language came to be seen as a feminine accomplishment. Its emphasis on form and politeness was perceived to be detrimental to the construction of the English gentlemen then taking shape. Instead of learning French, therefore, boys were taught Latin which emphasised rigour and was seen to train the male mind for intellectual tasks. French, on the other hand, seemed to be useful for conversation alone, which was best left to the women. Cohen thus demonstrates how taciturnity became a key male virtue which gentlemen had to cultivate.

Kelly Boyd's *Manliness and the Boys' Story Paper, 1855–1940* (2003) explores some of the same issues. Tracing the way masculine exemplars were reshaped over a long period of time in periodicals aimed at the young male market, she reveals that class was the most important factor in defining masculinities in Britain, although issues of race and empire also occasionally intruded. Her analysis suggests that the characteristics of masculinity reflected in these periodicals shifted from an arrogant domineering model of upper-class manliness in the years up to 1890, to a model stressing cooperation, community support and family loyalty between 1890 and 1920, and then to a more violent and individualistic masculinity in the interwar years. At the same time, worries about middle-class masculinity focusing on boys raised in the British Isles led to colonial archetypes being elevated at the turn of the century due to their constant contact with nature in the Australian outback or the untamed regions of Canada. After the Great War, this mattered less and home-grown heroes again took centre stage. Boyd's analysis stresses the way periodical literature picks up the wider anxieties of society while offering a new reading of lowbrow fiction.

What perhaps makes the work of this group of women historians distinctive is that all of their writings situate men and masculinity within interlocking sets of relationships. They demonstrate an attentiveness to the contradictions of masculinity for different groups within a society. Repeatedly these historians demand that we recognise the contingent nature of masculinity as it is inflected by age, class, race, sexuality and a variety of other conditions. If many of these women historians emerged from the study of women's history, it is clear that as gender historians they (along with some of their male peers) have enabled readers to look past the simple biological categories of male and female to see the interactions of a variety of influences which historically define men.

Kelly Boyd

References

Bederman 1995; Boyd 2003; Carby 1998; Clowes 2001; Cohen 1996; Davidoff 1973; Davidoff & Hall 1987/2002; Hall 1992, 2002; Hall *et al.* 2000; Nelson 1998; Sinha 1995.

Related essays

Body and Sexuality; Canada; Dominions; Empire; Great Britain; Modernity; Orientalism; Travel; United States.

Memoir

In the preface to her 2003 memoir *Madame Secretary*, Madeleine Albright stresses the exceptional nature of a text designed to relate the even more extraordinary life of the highest-ranking woman in the history of the United States' government. As the first female Secretary of State, Albright was expected to join the ranks of her predecessors in that powerful position and write her personal account in order to illuminate events of the past from the unique perspective of the eyewitness. But like many women before her, Albright distinguishes her literary and historical effort from those of her male predecessors, stressing that she desires to 'combine the personal with policy and describe not just what happened but also why and how events were influenced by human relationships' (2003: xi). She meticulously weaves together the account of her personal experience with that of the important political events she lived and shaped, feminising this genre that has strong ties to history. The resulting text, while unique given Albright's position, is also a continuation of a long tradition of female memorialists who, like Albright, have sought to alter the fabric of historical narrative and the way we conceive of history itself.

Definitions

The definition of memoir is as vague as the concept from which it is derived, the French term *mémoire* or 'memory'. The *Oxford English Dictionary* gives the standard definition in the singular as 'a historical account or biography written from personal knowledge' and in the plural as 'an account written by a public figure of their life and experiences'. In French the written account founded upon memory is always plural and is traditionally defined, as in the *Robert Dictionary*, as

> an account or narrative that a person gives in writing of things and events in which s/he participated or which s/he witnessed during her/his lifetime. Historical memoirs relating historical facts suitable for use in history; see annals, chronicles, commentaries and also memorialist. Memoirs more or less autobiographical; see autobiography, journal, recollection.

The genre thus occupies an often nebulous critical territory between history and literature. It has obvious ties with other personal narratives such as autobiography, letters and diaries, but statesmen have also used it for centuries to write official history from the perspective of the eyewitness, with little regard to the personal nature of that experience. Many reference works, scholars, and the general public conflate memoirs and autobiography, due in large measure to the fact that the term 'autobiography' did not enter many lexicons, such as French, until the nineteenth century. Prior to that time, all first-person accounts were referred to as memoirs. The vast array of texts that can be labelled memoirs thus adds to the ambiguity of the term. In the present context, memoirs will be used to designate texts in which the emphasis is less on telling one's personal story than in recounting events from one's unique perspective. A distinction will thus be made between purely autobiographical texts corresponding to Philippe Lejeune's (1975) now standard definition, according to which an autobiography traces the evolution of a personality from childhood and is composed by someone the reader can identify as the voice of the narrative, most frequently a well-known figure. In contrast, memoirs focus not on the development of an individual personality but on the interplay between that individual and historical events. The self forcibly comes through these accounts of the past, as the individual's memory processes and shapes experience, but the self is not the overriding preoccupation. Memoirs are frequently composed by a high-ranking, famous person as a chronicle of actions and draw much of their value from the fact the author was an eyewitness to the events.

Clearly the above definition does not describe the situation of the historical experience of the typical woman. The majority of women have not occupied official positions in government, the events of which constitute the backbone of historical narrative, and have been more active in what is referred to as the 'private' sphere. Indeed from the sixteenth century critics have been quick to deny women's memoirs any affiliation with history, labelling them personal, gossipy accounts of court intrigues or unimportant women's lives. Yet when one examines the history of the memoir genre, it becomes apparent that women from all walks of life, from many different countries and across centuries have been drawn to the medium. They have found it a particularly appropriate genre to inscribe themselves and female experience into history. The gender consciousness that is prevalent in the majority of women's memoirs distinguishes them from the texts penned by their male counterparts. As both actors on the stage of history and as writers, women saw themselves and their texts as doubly transgressive. In assuming both these roles, female memorialists have been acutely aware that they are treading upon territory in which they have traditionally been considered interlopers at best and unwelcome, unqualified and unnatural figures at worst. Female memorialists are acutely conscious of these universal gender stereotypes regarding women and the public and literary sphere and their texts attest to the difference they perceive when a woman holds the pen. Contrary to popular belief, many female memorialists viewed themselves as historians, as did some of their contemporaries.

In addition to a heightened gender consciousness, women's perspective in memoirs is often very different from that found in texts authored by men: most female-authored memoirs tend to focus on the less-celebrated and less-commemorated aspects of life and are often valued for their inscription of everyday life. Even when a woman occupied a position of prominence in the public sphere, such as that of princess, respected author, queen or secretary of state, when she composed memoirs, it was frequently in the desire to tell an alternative version of well-known events. This version was often one infused with the personalities and human relationships of the time, as opposed to the more externalised narrative associated with men's memoirs. Given this more personalised form of public history, the publication history of women's memoirs is often problematic. These texts frequently appeared decades or even centuries after the author's death, often due to the stigma associated with being a woman writer, or to the controversy that an alternative, more interiorised version of events might provoke. This was the case in seventeenth-century France where a number of texts were composed by women during the reign of the absolutist monarch, Louis XIV. Texts such as Mlle de Montpensier's *Mémoires* (1718), Mme de Motteville's *Mémoires pour servir à l'histoire d'Anne d'Autriche* (1723), the duchesse de Nemours' *Les Mémoires de M L D D N* (1709) and Mme de Lafayette's *Mémoires de la Cour de France pour les années 1688 et 1689* (1731) appeared in the eighteenth century. However, these memoirs and others like them often circulated unofficially during the author's lifetime and could achieve a certain notoriety for the author. European women frequently chose one form of the genre, the spiritual memoir, as early as the fifteenth century. Memoirs that traced a woman's spiritual itinerary, such as Margery Kempe's *Book* (1436), St Teresa of Avila's *Libro de la vida* (1562) and Jeanne-Marie Guyon's *La Vie de Mme J M B de la Mothe Guyon* (1709), often escaped oblivion because their subject matter conformed more to society's expectations for acceptable occupations for women. Moreover, some of these narratives were composed following the direct order of a priest or other male spiritual adviser.

Memoir and history

The genre's relationship to the venerable narrative of history is complex and the evolution of this relationship reveals the changing nature of gender stereotypes and of historical writing itself. Whereas men's memoirs were usually valued without question as a source for history, women's memoirs have traditionally occupied a less honourable and ambiguous place.

As men were the official actors of history, their accounts were considered welcome additions to the narrative of mainstream events. Women's memoirs were most frequently characterised as private musings of only marginal importance for 'real' history. But with the development of history as a discipline and in particular the genesis of social history, historians began to reconsider these texts and value them as documents for understanding the past. Contrary to previous gender-biased assumptions, historians realised that women have composed memoirs to reflect on more than their personal condition. They have used their texts to reach out to other women with similar experiences, to comment on women's position in society, to provoke change, such as attitudes towards marriage, to inscribe other women into history or to comment upon political situations such as civil wars, among other purposes. These texts are thus of immense value to social historians in particular, who use them to reconstruct the mindset of a given society at a particular historical juncture. Women's memoirs have been re-evaluated following the studies of such historical theorists as Hayden White (1987) and Jacques Le Goff (1988) who stress that all historical narratives contain elements of subjectivity given that they are composed through language that is necessarily affected by the historian and his/her perspective. The further acknowledgement that history is forcibly a construction of the past affected by the preoccupations and perceptions of the present has led to a re-examination of all sources, especially memoirs. In this perspective, women's memoirs can contain historical truth just as a narrative by a supposedly objective, omniscient narrator can.

Social and cultural historians now recognise that women's memoirs are often the only texts that go beneath the surface to tell a story that perhaps was not officially considered worthy of inscription during the period when it was composed, but one that is an invaluable source for understanding the past. Women's memoirs are valued not only for the 'private' narrative they contain, but also for the new light they can shed on the well-known events of official history. For many memorialists, such as Mlle de Montpensier in seventeenth-century France, there is a clear effort to inscribe a female subject into history, to offer an alternative, more detailed, account of official history, as well as to tell the 'private' side of the past. It is interesting to note that while most historians today tend to speak unpejoratively of women's memoirs in terms of 'private' history, most early modern female memorialists would not have labelled their narratives 'private' but rather as 'particular' accounts of the past. Such women considered themselves to be composing a 'particular' version of official history, not a private story running alongside the narrative of the events deemed worthy to be inscribed into history. Many women underscore the fact that when their 'particular' history is taken into account, official history itself changes, for their contributions often provide motives and details that change the way one interprets well-known events.

It is obviously impossible here to pass in review all the texts of the women who have been drawn to the memoir genre. A brief analysis of a few representative traditions and exemplary texts will illustrate how women appropriated and developed the genre for their own ends. More interiorised narrative forms associated with self-writing are usually considered to have begun in the seventeenth century. The case of France illuminates some of the conditions that foster a strong, sustained tradition of female memorialists. Beginning in the early modern period, many women played exceptional roles on the historical stage. Marie de Medici at the end of the sixteenth century and Anne d'Autriche in the 1640s and 1650s served as regents until their sons were of age to assume the throne. This female leadership in government inspired and authorised other primarily aristocratic women to occupy positions of power not normally associated with their gender, such as leaders of armies during the Civil War known as the Fronde. Mme de Longueville and Mlle de Montpensier, both of the royal family, defied their future King, Louis XIV, and fought openly against the regency of his mother. Longueville took over for her husband, the Prince de Condé, when he was imprisoned. Montpensier, frustrated by the indecision of her father, Louis XIV's uncle, decided to take things into her own hands and led rebellions. She battled for and won control over the city of Orleans for the rebels' cause and even fired upon the King's troops from the top of the Bastille in Paris. When the Civil War ended, women such as Montpensier and Longueville were exiled for their seditious behaviour. Desirous that their actions should not be relegated to historical oblivion, some of these rebellious figures, such as Montpensier, took up the pen and wrote memoirs. Marie d'Orléans, the Duchesse de Nemours, wrote a particularly detailed account of the Fronde. Her ambition was to become an official historian of Louis XIV's reign, but as her gender prohibited her from occupying such a position, she opted to compose her memoirs, which are noteworthy for their inclusion of a variety of perspectives. Nemours inscribes not only her first-person aristocratic experience, but also the opinions and perspective of a larger public, including the people. Another aristocratic court figure, Mme de Motteville, Anne d'Autriche's lady-in-waiting, also viewed herself as a particular type of historian when she composed the biography of her female monarch. Her *Mémoires pour servir à l'histoire d'Anne d'Autriche* (1723) contain personal observations of the workings of monarchy during the first half of the seventeenth century and include the royalist perspective on the Fronde.

The case of these women warriors and court insiders underscores the interrelationship between women's decisions to compose memoirs and their positions in society. In this instance, women who played exceptional roles viewed their story essential to complete the historical record and worried that traditional historians would not consider their stories worthy of memory. When Louis XIV assumed power, he in fact sought to erase controversial events such as the Fronde from the historical record. Women such as Montpensier, Motteville and Nemours thus saw themselves as completing history, as well as offering an alternative narrative composed from a particular perspective. Exceptional events can thus encourage women to inscribe their own views into history. A century later Mme de Campan, first lady-in-waiting to Marie Antoinette, also drew upon her exceptional position to compose her *Mémoires sur la vie privée de la Reine Marie Antoinette* (1823) bearing witness to the Revolution from her unique perspective.

But wars and revolutions cannot entirely account for the flourishing of women's memoirs in France. Two other factors in particular provided a foundation for this desire to combine the first-person female voice with history: the more public roles women were assuming in society at large and a burgeoning tradition of women writers. Already in the sixteenth century,

France could boast of a number of women poets, themselves following the lead of **Christine de Pizan** who from the 1380s until 1435 had composed essays, poetry, first-person allegorical memoirs and even a biography of the king. In the following century, Queen Marguerite de Navarre had encouraged female authorship with her own *Heptaméron* (1569) and other works. Queen Margot, Marguerite de Valois, composed her *Les memoires de la reine Marguerite*, which were first published in 1628 and widely circulated during the seventeenth century. Early modern French women were thus aware of their female literary precursors and authorised by them. The association of women with the literary sphere was enhanced by the creation of salons, which flourished from the 1620s. These gatherings were not feminocentric, but in the seventeenth century in particular they were initiated and led by women. There were over 70 salons in Paris alone during the heyday of the movement in the 1650s, organised by aristocratic and bourgeois women alike. The salons attracted academicians, political figures and writers of both genders. Contemporaries often noted the freedom women in France had to associate with men and even attributed the development of certain literary genres such as the novel to this exceptional social interaction. Memoirs evolved out of this milieu. Writers such as Mme de Lafayette, author of France's first modern novel, turned her talents to writing memoirs in order to inscribe women's participation in society into what she considered a genre allied with history and not simply personal outpourings. In her *Histoire de Mme Henriette d'Angleterre* (1664) and her *Mémoires de la Cour de France*, Lafayette uses her personal perspective to construct a detailed history of the court that is consciously different from official history. Other figures such as Hortense and Marie Mancini chose the genre to tell their version of public lives that resembled fiction more than fact. Such narratives enrich our understanding of the social fabric of French society and the lives of women in particular. In addition to recounting the events of the Fronde, Montpensier used her memoir to address the status of women in society, particularly with respect to marriage. As the wealthiest woman in France, Montpensier found herself a pawn for Louis XIV's political ambitions. Marriage was a political tool to create alliances and Montpensier was constantly offered to various rulers by Louis XIV. In her memoir, Montpensier turns philosopher to reflect on the institution of marriage, mirroring a principal preoccupation of all women during her time period.

The relatively highly developed tradition of women's memoirs in France during the early modern period can thus be explained by a confluence of societal traits: active female participation in events considered worthy of historical inscription; a sense of a female literary tradition authorising women's creativity; and public roles in society such as that of the salonnière. Memoirs continued to attract women throughout the eighteenth century, as French women sought to inscribe their position in society on the literary and historical record. Marguerite-Jeanne Cordier de Staal-Delaunay used her *Mémoires* (1775) to recount life as an attendant to the duchesse du Maine at Sceaux. These memoirs offer an insider's perspective on the Bastille, where she was imprisoned for two years, and of the circle she frequented, including her friendship with Mme du Deffand. Having composed two comedies, Staal-Delaunay was known as a writer as well as a learned woman. She did not marry until she was over 50 years old. Her much celebrated *Mémoires sur la fin du règne de Louis XIV* (1775), published five years after her death, attest to her exceptional life as she recounts court life in the seventeenth century and the emergence of the French Enlightenment in the eighteenth. The memoir is permeated with the narrator's personality, thus prefiguring the more interiorised accounts that eventually come to dominate first-person narratives. Occupying an equally exceptional albeit very different position, Elizabeth Vigée-LeBrun chose the memoir genre to inscribe her experience as a renowned artist during the eighteenth century. Stéphanie Félicité de Genlis offered her story and her voice in her ten-volume *Mémoires* (1825), lamenting what she considered to be the deteriorating status of women, especially women writers, as France moved into the nineteenth century. Mme de Rémusat, lady-in-waiting to the Empress Josephine, gives a detailed portrait of aristocratic society in her *Mémoires* (1889). By the nineteenth century, many women opted to compose autobiographies, as opposed to memoirs. Autobiography has in many respects replaced the memoir as the preferred term for first person non-fictional accounts in the modern era. Many French women writers have been attracted to the more introspective genre of autobiography, George Sand and Simone de Beauvoir being only two of a long line of women who focus inward. The effects of such autobiographies are often similar to those of memoirs in that they all attest to women's place in society at a given moment.

The history of women's memoirs in England both contrasts with and was inspired by the tradition in France that largely preceded it. Even though the histories of the two countries were often enmeshed from the **Middle Ages** on, memoirs composed by women were more rare in the early modern period in England than in France, because the conditions for women as well as for women writers were not the same. Women were not prohibited from occupying the throne in England as they were in France, where Salic Law limited them to the role of regent. Yet even as rulers English women did not choose to add to written history through the genre of memoirs in the same numbers as their French counterparts. Elizabeth I composed hundreds of letters but not her memoirs, perhaps because there was no female literary tradition authorising such a narrative. In the fifteenth century Margery Kempe had composed the first autobiography in England, but her account of a personal, spiritual pilgrimage remained an isolated literary event. Memoirs and even a female literary tradition were yet to be established when Elizabeth assumed the throne. Seventeenth-century English women, perhaps inspired by the works of French women they were able to procure, turned to writing theatre, poetry and novels, but were not drawn to the genre of memoirs. The sole exception was **Margaret Cavendish**, Duchess of Newcastle, who in 1667 composed a memoir/biography of her husband that, like the narratives of Montpensier and Motteville, added to history from a 'particular' perspective. It is interesting to note that Cavendish accompanied Queen Henrietta Maria to France during England's Civil War. She would thus have had personal access to the French women who were composing memoirs at precisely this period. This exceptional position, combined with Cavendish's sense of her own importance deriving from such connections, enabled her to follow in the footsteps of the French female memorialists. In the eighteenth and nineteenth centuries, many adventurous English women travelled the globe and then composed narratives of their adventures. These travel narratives can be considered a variation on the memoir genre, but their affiliation with official history is less overt and direct. In the eighteenth century the actor and cross-dresser Charlotte Charke wrote of her exceptional experiences in her memoir, *The Narrative of the Life of Miss Charlotte Charke* (1755) and in the nineteenth century the equally transgressive philosopher **Harriet Martineau** inscribed her life in writing in her *Autobiography* (1877). As autobiography rather than a memoir, this text has a very psychological bent, although it does give a certain portrait of the author's cultural context. Anne Thackeray, a novelist, literary critic and essayist, depicted the literary scene of late nineteenth-century England in her *Chapters from Some Memoirs* (1895).

The emergence of autobiography

Other countries and time periods have shared some of these same conditions that contributed to the development of female memorialists in France and, to a lesser extent, England. One characteristic that unites female memorialists across geographical boundaries and chronological periods is the transgressive nature of their lives. These women challenged the roles ascribed to their gender and do not hesitate to compound these transgressions by inscribing them into writing for posterity. Particularly after the French Revolution, women's first-person non-fictional accounts became more insular and self-reflective as women adopted the ideology of separate spheres into their writing. As autobiography became a more established medium, women were drawn to the genre perhaps because those whose lives were confined primarily to the domestic realm could appropriate it to tell their particular stories. Memoirs, however, have remained the genre of choice for those women who straddled the private and public realms and especially for those public, transgressive figures who challenged the limited roles assigned to women because of their gender. Memoirs of the modern era, like those of the early modern period, place the emphasis on political events as opposed to self-reflection, although it should be noted that most modern critics do not distinguish between memoirs and autobiography and use the terms interchangeably. One of the first Russian women to find her way into print was Nadezhda Durova, a nineteenth-century renegade who disguised herself as a man in order to become a Czarist Calvary Officer. Like Montpensier before her, Durova detailed her exploits in her memoir *The Calvary Maiden* (1836). Unlike Montpensier, however, Durova addressed her text to a specifically female public in the desire to inspire them to go beyond the confines society prescribed for them. Her highly developed sense of the definitive role gender played in her society underscores the differences between nineteenth-century Russia and seventeenth-century France. Whereas Montpensier's experiences reflected those of some of her contemporaries, Durova found herself to be an isolated, totally exceptional case and her memoir attests to this unique status. Catharine Waugh's memoir dating from the 1880s tells the story of one of the first women to practise law in the United States. In her book *Evita* (1953) Eva Peron provides another striking example of a woman in an exceptional historical position who produced a text focused outward on the events of her country, as opposed to creating an interiorised narrative of her thoughts. These exemplary figures felt the need to attest to women's power to transgress society's gender boundaries and found the genre of memoirs the best form to enter society's general discourse and to contribute to and shape the vision of their time period that posterity would inherit.

It is interesting to note that the existence of a female literary tradition or the number of prominent women active in the public sphere in a particular country does not necessarily translate into a prevalent tradition of female memorialists. In medieval Japan, for example, women dominated prose writings, but their texts, while occasionally introspective, were not conscious additions to the historical record as were the memoirs of many early modern European women. There are many examples of Italian women who played prominent roles in society, but very few memoirs. One noteworthy exception is Camilla Faa Gonzaga's memoir, composed in 1622, but only published in the nineteenth century. Gonzaga's *Historia* is considered to be the first female autobiography in Italy. It intersects with the memoir genre when Gonzaga turns to recounting the political situation in her duchy, although much of the text is an effort to justify herself to her contemporaries and to posterity. Other European memorialists include the seventeenth-century Danish princess Eleonora Christina who composed her memoir during her imprisonment of 22 years due to the misdeeds of her husband. That Christina considered her text a memoir as opposed to a more personal autobiography is attested to by the fact that she also composed her autobiography. Interestingly, she opted to compose her autobiography in French, while choosing Danish for her memoir, perhaps because she destined her memoir to be a contribution to her country's national memory.

In addition to bearing witness to the life stories of exceptional women and inscribing women's stories into history, memoirs are often valuable for their ability to shed light on the life scripts in general available to women of a particular culture at a particular juncture in their history. As such these texts provide an additional and essential dimension to social history. Many women's memoirs have political overtones and in fact owe their existence to tumultuous periods of political crisis or upheaval. For example, Fadwa Tugan, a Palestinian Arab, recounts the struggles inherent in her life as a Palestinian and a woman in the twentieth century. In such cases, memoirs overtly use individual experience to represent a much larger social picture that goes beyond the self. In the nineteenth and twentieth centuries, many Indian women were drawn to memoirs and also more autobiographical literary enterprises to bear witness to the varied lives of women across the continent. In the nineteenth century Rassundarai Devi composed the first memoir/autobiography in Bengali. Her *Amar Jiban* (1876) attests to the trapped lives of Bengali women. In her memoir, *India Calling* (1934), Cornela Sorabji describes her experience as the first woman to graduate from Bombay University and her subsequent career as a lawyer. These texts, like those of the general tradition of female-authored memoirs, provide information that history and literary history have censored, often on the grounds of gender.

Historians, social scientists and literary scholars have increasingly recognised the importance and diversity of women's memoirs and their invaluable contribution to the construction of the fabric of human history. Once dismissed as the inconsequential musings of transgressive women and denied relevance to 'real' history, women's memoirs are now often the first step to constructing a complete vision of the past. More of these texts are coming to light, adding forgotten figures and alternative perspectives to the narrative of the past. Women's memoirs add voices to the silences of the past, fill in the voids of official history, allow us to understand the specificity of female experience and lead to a more complete understanding of the workings of human history in general.

Faith E Beasley

References

Albright 2003; Beasley 1990; Brodski & Schenck 1988; Davis 1980; Ferguson 1985; Goldsmith 2001; Kelly 1984; Le Goff 1988; Lejeune 1975; Miller 2000; Otten 1992; Personal Narratives Group 1989; Scott 1988; Smith 1987; Stanton 1987; Tharu & Lalita 1993; White 1987; Wilson & Warnke 1989.

Related essays

Female Biography; Feminist Auto/biography; France; Middle Ages; Private Writings; Reformation; Secret History.

Middle Ages

Women writers of history in the Middle Ages share with modern women medievalists a consciousness of gender difference and of barriers to writing erected by institutional and cultural misogyny. Medieval women historians feminised their material, reflecting the larger cultural differences that structured their lives as women. Like their medieval counterparts, modern women medievalists consequently reflect gender difference in their historiography, in particular in the writing of women's history.

I. Medieval women

The writing of history

As a result of ecclesiastical affiliations, 'history' in the Middle Ages almost always referred to the working out of divine Providence in time, through human agency. Therefore any work purporting to be a history of the world would start with the biblical description of Creation from Genesis, culminating in the Passion and Resurrection of Christ and would end with the Apocalypse and Last Judgment. The boundary between history and literature was porous, as texts dealing with visionary revelation and spiritual experience were regarded as essentially 'true' because dictated by God directly to the individual and, therefore, 'historical'. Legend, myth and the miraculous bled into chronicles and vitae to suggest the interrelationship between the inner and outer lives of the individual, as there were few boundaries between objective observation and subjective experience. Little distinction was made between legendary or mythical history and political or contemporary history. To move from the origins of the world the historian had to trace to the present all that was known about those intervening kings, queens, warriors, learned men and women and saints who had come before.

Through the twelfth century, history was written primarily in Latin, a language relatively few women learned to read and fewer still could write. Until the thirteenth century women who wrote history belonged either to the first or second estates (aristocracy or clergy), because they possessed the requisite wealth, leisure and education. While this class privilege also affected male historians, the latter group enjoyed institutional prerogatives, greater numbers and positions of power that allowed their historical writing a broader canvas. A male monastic or university author did not earn credit for being innovative or original in writing a text but, in fact, was regarded as learned and authoritative if he drew upon the vast storehouse of prior texts by ancient and earlier medieval thinkers. Because the less educated women in convents also generally experienced fewer privileges than monks (Gilchrist 1994, 1999) and university teachers, they also had more limited access to earlier manuscripts. Further, the modern sense of authorship, that is, of one who earns authority through the actual writing down of a particular text, did not necessarily apply in the Middle Ages. This is true especially in the case of these religious women, many of whom were counselled by their confessors in the practice of humility, which might have demanded anonymity.

In the thirteenth century a radical change in gender and culture took place, opening up spaces to record history outside the cloister for women from the third estate (the commons). Mendicant orders (mainly Franciscan and Dominican) with houses of their own permitted tertiaries and lay women to travel to cities and relay their visions or preach their sermons outside churches. Because such lay women were often uneducated, their vernacular discourses took an oral form and were only later written down (translated, expanded or edited) by a (male) scribe, confessor or mentor. Because they lacked access to the libraries of cloistered convents, their visionary works did not necessarily include those references to Church fathers and ancient poets and scholars revered by their educated male counterparts. Generally mendicant women alluded to the Bible (especially the Psalms and the Gospel), the liturgy and other authorities available in what was known as the *Biblia Paupera* – the Bible of the Poor, found inside churches and cathedrals on frescoes, sculpture, stained glass and other forms of iconography.

Gender manifested itself in all the various forms of historical writing, whether in Latin or the vernacular, produced by medieval women. Generally, this writing can be defined as **'family' history**, whether personal, dynastic, institutional (ecclesiastical, legal or courtly) or legendary. It assumed the form of letters that might reveal personal or local or family history; memoirs or biographies (*vitae*) of holy men or women; or finally family or local history, or chronicle. Even the so-called Matilda Roll – a mortuary or obituary roll produced for an abbey headed by Matilda of La Trinité in Caen – shows evidence of feminine authorship in its emphasis on signal life events (Sherrin 2002). Aristocratic women (in or out of the convent) wrote history for dynastic purposes, while other nuns wrote history for their 'sisters' to chronicle familial events within the convent. What is most curious is that this personalisation, or domestication, of history is recognisable not only in the historiography of medieval women, but also in that of modern medievalists.

Letters

Letter-writing constituted one of the earliest genres available to women (Cherewatuk and Wiethaus 1991). The letter served as a convenient genre under whose rubric the other main genres of the Middle Ages, epic, *planctus* (complaint) and memoir, might be subsumed. Through the writing of epic letters and letters of complaint, women constructed details of personal, familial and political history. The early Merovingian St Radegund of Poithier wrote an epistolary epic, 'The Fall of Thuringia,' to accompany her request for a relic from the Holy Cross, which she used to found an abbey of the same name. In this letter Radegund, slave queen of the Frankish king Clothar, compares her native Thuringia, a barbarian city, with Troy. She also addresses her older male cousin, Hamalafred, who had fled to Constantinople after the fall of their family's home and city and laments the death of her brother, slain by Clothar. In another letter, to her nephew Artachis, Radegund records not only the deaths of her father, uncle and brother but also that of the very cousin Hamalafred to whom she had previously written (Thiebaux 1994: 85–124). Evidence of gender appears in both letters when she describes herself as a captive barbarian woman. This deprecation offers a variation on the modesty topos, a rhetorical device often used by medieval women to disarm criticism.

Formal letters, like the Latin letters of the twelfth-century abbess Héloïse of the Paraclete to her former lover and teacher, Abelard, might be used as spiritual admonition and educational correction; they also allowed women to chronicle the founding history of their convents, in Héloïse's case, of the convent of the Paraclete for which Abelard had composed a rule (Wheeler 2000). Letter-writing was favoured by royal and aristocratic women and women gentry, who had difficulty in leaving isolated castles for extended trips to visit their families, or, if living near or within a town, in travelling alone for visits. The fifteenth-century English Paston women and their contemporaries, the Czech Rožmberk sisters, relay aspects of their families and individual histories in letters written in the vernacular (Watt 2004; Klassen 2001). These letters document the cultures of the women's particular regions and the larger historical events then taking place. Instructive letters to daughters, sons and sisters (and other family members) record difficult and tumultuous events in their own personal lives, or their family's, in local regions throughout England and Europe.

Vitae: Lives, spiritual autobiographies and memoirs

Medieval women also wrote biographies, or spiritual lives and, if writing about themselves, spiritual autobiographies that documented the history of their spiritual life. Such texts 'convey what their authors perceive to be a universal spiritual rather than a personal truth' (Greenspan 1996: 219) and record spiritual crises such as conversion, the loss of family, the rejection of marriage and the experience of temptations (Greenspan 1996: 220). Often in form an imitation (*aemulatio*) of the life of Christ, these histories relay the lives of holy men and women, figures mentioned in the Gospel and saints or founders of the early church. Frequently women writers take as their model the Holy Family, in particular the Virgin Mary, the mother of Christ, but even Jesus himself, as mother (Newman 1987; Bynum 1982). Vitae were also written to support the case of individuals considered for canonisation because of their working of miracles, or other commendable spirituality.

One of the earliest examples of vitae written by women is that of St Radegund of Poitiers written by **Baudonivia** of Poitiers, a nun at Radegund's convent. Although other male-authored vitae of Radegund exist, Baudonivia's *Radegund* (c.609–614), attentive to Radegund's political as well as spiritual life, praises the authority of the queen as much as the sanctity of the abbess. Such proximity between woman author and subject helped define other existing vitae. The *Life of Balthild* (c.680) was written by a 'nun of Chelles' about the Frankish queen and founder of the convent of Chelles, just as the *Lives of Willibald and Wynnebald* (c.780), two brothers and Benedictine saints, were written by their sister Huneberc of Heidenheim (St Walburga). In the late eleventh century, Berta of Willich traced the life of the tenth-century German Abbess Adalheid, the first abbess of Willich. In the fourteenth century Katharine Guebeswiller and Elisabeth Kempf of Unterlinden wrote collective biographies of their community.

Less common were vitae of figures unknown to their female authors but important to them for their symbolism such as Hildegard of Bingen's twelfth-century minor vitae, the *Vita Sancti Disibodi* (life of the seventh-century Irish bishop St Disibod, who founded Disibodenberg, the convent where she first lived) and the *Vita Sancti Ruperti* (life of the eighth-century Frankish founder of her second convent, at Rupertsberg) and the vitae of male Gospel figures Lazarus and John the Baptist by Adelheid von Streitberg and Agnes Santpach (or Santpeck).

Vitae such as Clemence of Barking's life of Saint Catherine of Alexandria (c.1153–1175) reflected the learning and eloquence of the female communities that created them. There exists also an Occitan life of Douceline de Digne (c.1215–1274), founder of the Beguines of Marseilles and also Mother of Roubaud, a convent in Provence. Other, similar vitae by women include the *Offenbarungen in Octenbach* by Elspeth von Oye and Elsbeth Stagel's life of her mentor *Henry Suso* (c.1340). Stagel also produced a collective biography of the nuns of Toss. The same kind of spirituality as that of the nuns reappears in vitae of exemplary royal women who often retired to the convent after their public lives as queens were finished, as was the case with Queen Mathilde, by the nuns of Nordhausen (Van Houts 53–68).

Mendicant and lay women's visionary memoirs of their own spiritual lives, 'histories' of interior revelation, blossomed in the late Middle Ages. Among many instances are the *Memoriale* (c.1296) of the Franciscan beguine mystic Angela of Foligno and the *Dialogue* (c.1378) of Dominican preacher and mystic St Catherine of Siena. Other famous examples include the *Revelations* (c.1393) of English anchorite mystic Julian of Norwich and of the mystic St Birgitta of Sweden, who founded the Brigittines with a new Augustinian rule in the fourteenth century. In the case of English mystic Margery Kempe's *Boke* (c.1436), travels and pilgrimages provide interior glimpses of northern England, Jerusalem and Italy and record a medieval environment in rich detail (Arnold and Lewis 2004). Several centuries earlier crusader-pilgrim Margaret of Beverly, born in Jerusalem, had described the events of the Third Crusade at the time of Saladin's siege of the city (20 Sep 1187) and the deeds of Richard the Lionheart in the Middle East. She was repeatedly captured and kept in chains. When she was eventually returned to England, her brother Thomas, a Cistercian monk, wrote down these details on her behalf in the prosimetrum of the *Travels*, switching from the third person in the Latin prose preface to first person in the poetic portion.

Epic biographies, legends and chronicles

For aristocratic women the production of history often served to define their place within a dynasty. For cloistered women the history of an abbey or convent from the time of founding serves to illustrate the importance of the founder in its creation and of the convent leaders as a memorial to the sanctity and spirituality of the order, its members, or God's will in time. The Saxon canoness Hrotsvitha of Gandersheim produced a dynastic Ottonian Latin history, *Carmen de gestis Oddonis imperatoris* (c.970), a Christian epic about the contemporary emperor Otto the Great and the *Primordia coenobii Gandeshemensis* (c.968), in which she chronicles the history of her own convent, the Gandersheim abbey, up to 918, the time of the death of Abbess Christina. Indeed, Hrotsvitha's entire body of work (including eight legends, six plays, two epics and a short poem) can all be considered 'histories' in the sense that they record the events occurring to key religious, political and martial figures at a moment of dramatic change. These works pinpoint changes in the history of the Church and the Holy Roman Empire, ranging from the broadest of institutions – the Church and the state – to the most narrow and personal – Hrotsvitha's own abbey. In almost all cases Hrotsvitha genders these histories by relegating supernal and superior spiritual powers to the religious women and Christian converts of the early Church about whom she writes.

Hrotsvitha's Latin legends, for example, move chronologically but with feminist emphasis from the life of the Virgin Mary (according to an apocryphal *Pseudo-Evangelium* of Mattheus) to one on the 'Ascensio' of Christ (from a Greek source), then to the eighth-century Frankish knight Gondolf (in Pippin the Short's reign) and the tenth-century Spanish knight and martyr Pelagius. She then turns to the Greek saints Basilius and Theophilus and – like her source mistaking Dionysius the Areopagite for the martyr Dionysius, the first bishop of Paris – finally returning to late antiquity with the martyred Roman saint Agnes.

Her most important works, her six Latin plays, centre on early Church history – involving converted Roman generals, desert fathers and transformed prostitutes. They begin with the story of the conversion and martyrdom of Emperor Constantine's pagan royal general in *Gallicanus* through his daughter Constantia; the martyrdom of three Christian virgin sisters during Diocletian's persecution of the Christians in *Dulcitius;* the resurrection of Drusiana, Fortunatus and Callimachus by St John and the conversion of the latter by means of Drusiana, in *Callimachus;* and finally, the conversion of courtesan Thais by the anchorite Paphnutius in *Paphnutius* and of the prostitute Mary of Egypt by her uncle, the anchorite Abraham, in *Abraham*.

Hrotsvitha's epics appear even more directly 'historical' in the modern sense. In the *Carmen de gestis Oddonis imperatoris,* she finds a model for Otto (1081–1118), aided by two queens, Edith and Adelheid, in King David as an ideal ruler. Here she follows (whether knowingly or not) the Byzantine historian **Anna Komnene**. Anna wrote the family history of her father the Emperor into a Latin prose epic biography, the *Alexiad,* a history as well of the First Crusade and a window into the Byzantine Empire. But she injected into her narrative her own autobiography, in particular, her relationship with her mother and her paternal grandmother (Gouma-Peterson 2000).

What Hrotsvitha accomplished in the entire body of her work – the history of the Church from late antiquity to her own day – is also comparable to the chronicle of the world written by abbess Hildegard of Bingen. Hildegard composed two important theological historical works, the *Scivias* [*Know the Ways*] (1151) and the *Liber divinorum operum* [*Book of the Divine Works*] (1173). In the *Scivias,* Hildegard traces the beginning of the world in the Creation through the Redemption to the Apocalypse. At the end of the *Liber divinorum operum,* Hildegard concludes with a Christianised history that focuses on Adam and the biblical fathers and continues to the coming of the Antichrist.

Women also constructed secular histories similar to these founding narratives of Church and state, although not always defined as chronicles. Like the examples of earlier ecclesiastical and institutional histories found in letters, vitae and founding histories, secular histories appear in unexpected genres – for example, visionary allegories – as well as in letters and memoirs. Christine de Pizan wrote secular history in a number of these genres, creating a diverse and innovative historiography that 'not only departed from earlier predominant patterns of medieval French historiography, but . . . followed an Augustinian model of sacred history' (Richards 1994: 14–30).

Christine turned to classical Greek and Roman fables and stories to write a gendered mythologised history of Troy and Greece in her *Epistre d'Othea à Hector*, or *Letter of Othea to Hector* (1399–1400). But Christine then personalised her epistolary fables. In the Middle French *Epistre d'Othea* Christine circumscribes 100 fables – a mythological *prosimetrum*, or a mixture of poetry and prose – within an epistolary frame. In this frame Othea, an invented goddess of wisdom, writes to her nephew, the 15-year-old Trojan prince Hector. The youth serves as a model for the French dauphin. Christine feminises her work by having the goddess send Hector this legendary history of the world as an example of the failure of male leadership – of what not to do and not to be – while she counters with her own moral instruction in the chivalric and Christian virtues in the gloss that follows each poetic fable. Personalising the patriarchal and theological, Christine conceives of Othea and her alter-ego, Minerva/Pallas Athena, as maternal guides for a youth the same age as her son.

Christine de Pizan also composed a long *Livre de la Mutacion de Fortune* (1401–1403) that, as sacred history, describes events involving changes in fortune from the ancient to the contemporary. Borrowing from Augustine's *On the City of God* and the *Histoire ancienne jusqu'à César, Mutacion de Fortune* might also be considered as visionary allegory in which she embeds her own autobiography. In recognition of her gifts as a historian and her connections of patronage with the ruling family in France, she was selected by Philip II to write the royal biography, *Livre des Fais et bonnes meurs de sage Roy Charles V* (1404). She also traces a **world 'history'** of women in her *La Cité des Dames* (1405). Finally, her allegorical, philosophical and spiritual autobiography, *L'Avision-Christine* (1405), describes the history of France personified in the figure Francia. Christine's visionary 'autobiography' might well be described as a secular form of the vita, although it mixes genres. As a form of 'history', or partial chronicle, it merges genres innovatively, like so many of her works, personalising those used more conventionally by male poets and scholars. A similar secularised 'chronicle' or **memoir** (1439–1440) by Helene Kottanner, chambermaid to the Hungarian queen Elizabeth, provides insight into the political and social history of the court and town in the fifteenth century.

By the end of the Middle Ages there is evidence that women had begun to become conscious of their own literary traditions and genres. Queen Anne of France wrote an instructional manual, *Lessons for My Daughter* (c.1497–1498), addressed to her daughter, Suzanne of Bourbon, and modelled it on her predecessor Christine de Pizan's 'syllabus' of instruction, *Le Livre des trois vertus* (1405). In each of these hortatory works, the cultural politics of the times in which the authors lived filters through the idealised portraits of women. Such idealised portraits of behaviour secularised the spiritual vita or life.

II. Women Medievalists

Women Medievalists and the Academy

Since the beginning of the nineteenth century, women historians have contributed to the history of the Middle Ages and especially the history of its women. Women historians have contributed to understanding the social, political, intellectual, artistic, economic and cultural world of the Middle Ages by editing and translating important texts (wills, chronicles, cartularies, memoirs, letters, lyrics, romances, epics and dramas) and by classifying and studying works of art (frescoes, cathedrals, stained glass, statuary, monuments, paintings, misericords). Along the way women historians have invented new fields of study by means of pioneering works of historiography, history, biography and criticism.

As in the Middle Ages, women's participation in the Academy was restricted even into the twentieth century, and thus scholarly women who wrote history of the Middle Ages had to be independently wealthy and usually self-educated, or educated within the home by a male family member or tutor. Often women scholars emerged because of a father who was himself an educator or who encouraged their study. Such was the case with **Mary Bateson**, associated with Newnham College, Cambridge, most of her life and career, although she did not officially teach there. She published 13 edited volumes centring on local social history, including the *Register of Crabhouse Nunnery* (1899). Her biographer Mary Dockray-Miller surmises that edited volumes were in her day perceived as more 'feminine' than monographs (Dockray Miller 2004).

Resourceful women interested in medieval history early in the twentieth century often had to take up entirely different, nonacademic, professions. Women who researched medieval history outside of academia nevertheless published major books (often, as a result, receiving a harsh reception from the men in the Academy). Jessie L Weston published editions of works of Arthurian literature that she had translated from many different languages and research on Grail legends that culminated in the controversial *From Ritual to Romance* (1920) on the influence of fertility rites on the Grail legend. **Lina Eckenstein**, without any formal education, succeeded in publishing a dozen books, the most important of which was *Women under Monasticism: Chapters on Saint-Lore and Convent Life between A.D. 500 and A.D. 1500* (1896), which recovered the lives of medieval women writers but which also included a strange mythical history of the Germanic people. Hope Emily Allen, whose key work advanced identification of the *Ancrene Riwle*, a thirteenth-century anchorite rule, the mystical works of Richard Rolle of Hampole and the annotation and edition of Margery Kempe's fourteenth-century mystical *Boke*, was an independent scholar financially able to pursue her research interests. Even in her independence, she suffered from the intolerance of a male colleague, the young coeditor of her project on Kempe. Helen Waddell, without an academic post, spent her life translating for the public the Latin lyrics of the Goliard (clerical) student-poets, other Latin lyrics of the twelfth century and the lives of the saints and desert fathers. She fictionalised the life of Peter Abelard while she worked part-time at a press. Waddell was attacked for her scholarship by academic G C Coulton, who seems to have prevented her from becoming a member of the British Academy. Unlike her fellow Inklings C S Lewis or J R R Tolkien, who enjoyed university education, university positions and endowed chairs all their lives, Dorothy Sayers wrote detective novels that featured a woman protagonist from Oxford, and translated and commented on Dante for the popular press.

Because of the climate of academic misogyny that prevailed during the early twentieth century, women historians rarely obtained teaching positions at the best universities, or they did so only after several tries. Elise Richter, a Romance philologist also interested in literature, who had been educated at the University of Vienna, published a trailblazing edition of *Chronologische Phonetik des Französischen bis zum Ende des 8. Jahrhunderts (Chronological Phonetics of French up to the End of the Eighth Century)* (1934). For much of her career Richter worked as an unpaid university lecturer at the University of Vienna because of the exclusion of women from the professoriate, even though she was the first woman in Austria to receive her habilitation, in 1907. When women did obtain positions because of family or academic connections, they were not always promoted or given premier positions. Distinguished Anglo-Saxon historian Dorothy Whitelock at St Hilda's College, Oxford, author of two important books, was denied the Rawlinson and Bosworth Professorship of Anglo-Saxon in 1946 by a three to two vote; the chair was given instead to a less distinguished male scholar, C L Wrenn. In 1957 Whitelock was elected as Elrington and Bosworth Professor of Anglo-Saxon at Cambridge; she went on to publish another nine books. At the Dutch Catholic University of Nijmegen, Christine A E M Mohrmann – who specialised in Christian and Medieval Latin and who published ten books on the early Church, the sermons of St Augustine, the letters of St Cyprian, the Latin liturgy, Medieval Latin and Greek grammar – was initially denied by a board of Dutch bishops the chair in Greek and Latin linguistics previously held by her mentor. In 1961, late in her career, Mohrmann finally attained the chair.

Once in university positions, these women scholars were expected to remain unmarried or, if married, childless, in order to serve their disciplines or their institutions more fully. Many women historians of the mid-twentieth century – for example, Marjorie McCallum Chibnall, who specialised in Orderic Vitalus, and Margaret E Reeves, who specialised in Joachim of Fiore – owed their early success at obtaining fellowships or appointments to male mentors with a sense of gender equity. Others married academic husbands who obtained a university position that allowed a wife (no matter how talented in her own right) to teach at least part-time. Laura Hibbard married Roger Sherman Loomis and became known to her students at Wellesley as 'Mrs. Arthur,' in part because of her scholar husband and in part because she was the author of a book on romances, *Medieval Romance in England, A Study of the Sources and Analogues of the Non-Cyclic Metrical Romances* (1924). Nora Kershaw and her much older husband, Hector Munro Chadwick (who had been her professor), both taught at Cambridge University, at Newnham, and together they published the three-volume *The Growth of Literature* (1932, 1936, 1940). She also published editions of *Anglo-Saxon and Norse Poems* (1922) and *An Early Irish Reader* (1927) and popular studies including *The Druids* (1966) and *The Celts* (1971). **Doris M Stenton** married the much older historian Frank M Stenton, her history professor at Reading University where she herself eventually taught. She authored many studies and editions of medieval English legal history, most especially of the Pipe Rolls published by the Selden Society, for which she functioned as secretary. She was finally appointed a fellow of the British Academy, although, reflective of the misogynistic period in which she lived, she was never regarded as the scholar her husband was.

A rare subject for women to pursue without obstacles has been the history of medieval Latin literature and philosophy. However, some women, such as Eleanor Shipley Duckett at Smith College, published on these areas in works such as *Latin Writers of the Fifth Century* (1930) and *Anglo-Saxon Saints and Scholars* (1947). In 1965 she wrote her final work, *Women in Their Letters in the Early Middle Ages*. Also researching tenth-century Latin scholars, Cora E Lutz, a Yale PhD in classical languages, published editions of the commentaries of Martin of

Laon and Remigius of Auxerre for which she received some harsh reviews. Yet Lutz ended her career by describing and cataloguing pre-1600 manuscripts at the Yale Beinecke Library. Specialising in twelfth-century scholasticism and intellectual history, Marie-Thérèse d'Alverny worked at the *Bibliothèque Nationale* in Paris but was never promoted to director of the Department of Manuscripts. Nonetheless, she published important books on the School of Chartres/University of Paris, including the previously unedited works of twelfth-century scholar Alan of Lille (1965), two collections of essays on the manuscripts of the Latin Avicenna (1993, 1994) and a collection of studies on the iconography of Wisdom in the twelfth century (1993). Other scholars also braved the obstacles and published on late medieval philosophical and theological history, including Anneliese Maier, who published at least 12 books on fourteenth-century natural philosophy; Elisabeth Gössman, on medieval theology and women's spirituality; Marcia Colish, on medieval Stoicism and Platonism; Beryl Smalley, on the medieval history of the Bible and late medieval commentators; and Pearl Kibre, on the history of universities and medieval science.

Twentieth-century women historians also pursued formal study of medieval history defined more narrowly as legal, economic and institutional history and they did so within the university, although not without resistance from within or without the halls of Academe. In these fields various women historians excelled, perhaps because of the extension of the 'local and family' custodianship inherited from the Middle Ages. Legal and judicial history offered a subject that attracted a handful of important and stalwart twentieth-century women scholars. **Bertha Haven Putnam** was one of the most important historians of English law. Her specialty was labour history and her study *The Enforcement of the Statutes of Labourers during the First Decade after the Black Death* (1908) was regarded as especially noteworthy because of its concern with the legislation passed during the reign of Edward III to deal with the consequences of the plague. **Nellie Neilson**, medieval constitutional historian and first woman president of the American Historical Association, taught at Mount Holyoke College, specialising in medieval economic history. Despite her stature as a scholar, she was forced to retire early in 1939 and suffered financial hardship as a result. **Helen Maud Cam**, a specialist in medieval institutional history who traced the evolution of various medieval institutions during her career, despite suffering institutional bias against women at Radcliffe, Royal Holloway College and Cambridge, taught at Girton College, Cambridge and also as the Zemurray Professor at Harvard. **Eileen Power**, like other modern women historians, excelled in economic history. Her chosen field, however, was *women's* economic history, especially the economy of the convent, as in *Medieval English Nunneries, c.1275–1535* (1922). The study of individual men and women fascinated her and she is best known for her popular histories, *Medieval People* (1963) and *Medieval Women* (1975).

Because of the background of war and totalitarianism in which women pursued the course of their research during much of the twentieth-century, some women were prevented or blocked from teaching at universities not only because of their gender but also for political reasons. Social reformer and activist Elisabeth Busse-Wilson was prevented for political reasons from teaching at German universities both before and after the Second World War. Avowed Communist Margaret Schlauch, specialist in Old and Middle English and Old Norse philology and literature, fled the United States and New York University in the fifties to take up a post at the University of Warsaw in Poland, where she ended her career. Schlauch authored and translated numerous books, including one on Chaucerian women, *Chaucer's Constance and Accused Queens* (1927). She also distinguished herself in books on broader but related topics: the history of English philology in *Outline History of the English Language: 1400 to the Present* (1952) and the social construction of medieval English literature in *English Medieval Literature and Its Social Foundations* (1956).

As a particularly favoured (appropriately decorous) subject for women, the study of art history enabled the success of several important modern women medievalists. The pioneering research into Spanish Romanesque architecture by Georgiana Goddard King of Bryn Mawr College resulted in nine books, among them *The Way of St James* (1920) and *Pre-Romanesque Churches of Spain*. Margaret Rickert at the University of Chicago studied Chaucer manuscripts with her sister Edith. For the independent scholar Dame Joan Evans the study of French art and jewellery and classical archaeology resulted in books such as *English Jewellery from the Fifth Century to 1800* (1921) and *Pattern, a Study of Ornament in Western Europe from 1180 to 1900*, 2 volumes (1931), as well as broader cultural histories such as *Life in Medieval France* (1925) and *Monastic Life at Cluny, 910–1157* (1931). In Ireland, Helen M Roe created a whole field in medieval Irish art and archaeology through her tireless scholarly efforts to record the material culture of her country, especially its high crosses, grave slabs, medieval fonts and doorways. Although Roe was employed outside the academy, mostly in county library service, she was the first woman to serve as president of the Royal Society of Antiquaries of Ireland. The material culture of the Middle Ages inspired a number of other scholars: stained glass was the subject for pioneering scholar Jane Hayward at the Cloisters and for Meredith Parsons Lillich at Syracuse University; Romanesque and Byzantine architecture, for Ilene Forsyth at the University of Michigan; and misericords (choir-stall carvings), for Elaine C Block of the Hunter College of the City University of New York. Block single-handedly invented the study of misericords by means of indefatigable independent travel to photograph, document and classify the extant evidence. Her lifelong studies are only now being published in multiple volumes.

Writing women's history

Women medievalists have found the study of women's history a most congenial subject, in part because most male scholars have avoided the topic and in part, I speculate, because the very masculinity of the Academy compelled them to seek out female counterparts from the past as subject and model, forming a modern variation on medieval women's vitae intended for instruction and consolation.

In the area of religion, women have been most drawn to and most successful in tracing the history of affective spirituality, especially as it has involved nuns, women mystics, mendicants and tertiaries. Although not affiliated with a university and not formally educated, Evelyn Underhill redefined the history of mysticism in several editions, biographies and the groundbreaking *Mysticism: A Study of the Nature and Development of Man's Spiritual Consciousness* (1911). Other women explored medieval history through biography, letters, autobiography, saints' lives and social life or through the life and writings of a particular historical woman, such as

Elisabeth Busse-Wilson, who recovered the work and life of St Elizabeth of Thuringia; Suzanne Solente and Charity Cannon Willard, who edited and translated the works of Christine de Pizan; and Ruth Dean, who wrote on the English manuscripts of Elizabeth of Schönau. More recently, women scholars have advanced the study of medieval women through more specialised research, with Régine Pernoud publishing on *Héloïse and Abelard* (1973), *Joan of Arc* (1975) and *Christine de Pizan* (1982); Joan Ferrante, on medieval women's history and their depiction in literature by men and women in *Woman as Image in Medieval Literature* (1975) and *To the Glory of Her Sex: Women's Roles in the Composition of Medieval Texts* (1997); Susan Mosher Stuard, on women's social history in *Women in Medieval Society* (1976); Caroline Walker Bynum, on medieval religious women's history in works such as *Jesus as Mother* (1982), *Holy Feast and Holy Fast* (1987) and *The Resurrection of the Body in Western Christianity* (1995); Sister Benedicta Ward, on the religious history of the early Middle Ages, including *Harlots of the Desert: A Study of Repentance in Early Monastic Sources* (1987); and Jo Ann McNamara, on the history of medieval nuns in *Sainted Women of the Dark Ages* (1992) and *Sisters in Arms* (1996).

Like the medieval church before them, the Academy in the twentieth century has attempted to bar access by some of the most significant recent women historians writing on medieval women. Some of the brightest stars have, nevertheless, resisted through perseverance and continuing research and scholarship. Denied her habilitation in theology at the Ludwig-Maximilians-Universität München in Germany because she was a layperson and not a priest or deacon, Elisabeth Gössmann earned her professorship at Seishin Women's University in Japan and travelled back and forth to lecture in Munich, accumulating materials on Alexander Hales until she did receive it. At Columbia University, outspoken Joan Ferrante was never given an endowed chair, despite her many books. Denied tenure at Harvard, Caroline Walker Bynum went on to publish ground-breaking historical studies of medieval women's spirituality. She has retired from Columbia to the Institute for Advanced Study, Princeton. Both Ferrante and Bynum have served as president of the Medieval Academy and Bynum has also served as president of the American Historical Association.

Jane Chance

References

Arnold & Lewis 2004; Bijvoet-Williamson 1998; Brown 2004; Brown, McMillan & Wilson 2004; Bynum 1982; Chance 1996, 2005; Cherewatuk & Wiethaus 1993; Churchill, Brown & Jeffrey 2002; Ferrante 1997; Gilchrist 1994; Gouma-Peterson 2000; Greenspan 1996; Jansen 2004; Klassen 2004; Meale 1996; Newman 1987; Richards 1994; Rosenthal 1990; Sherrin 2002; Stuard 1987; Thiébaux 1994; Van Houts 1992; Watt 2004; Wheeler 2000; Wilson 1984.

Related essays

Convents; Female Biography; Hagiography; Memoirs; Renaissance.

Modernity

Recent historical consensus suggests that we need to see modernity as a period defined by industrialisation, mechanisation, urbanisation, mass media, the rise of science and political movements including nationalism, colonialism and democratisation, as well as an escalating process of global interconnection. Scholars have contended, moreover, that modernity has had spatial, geographic, philosophical and racial, as well as social and cultural dimensions. One of the hallmarks of modernity has been a belief in the possibility of personal transformation, of altering one's individual socio-economic status and subjectivity through education, geographical mobility or capital accumulation, among other possibilities. While hegemonic modern notions of individual development have been gendered masculine, as with political citizenship, economic autonomy and other gendered attributes of modern personhood, women have actively contested their notional and practical exclusion. For at least the last two centuries, women have sought to improve their lives through political and legal rights, travel, education, work and various forms of economic negotiation.

Work on modernity has revealed its complexities and contradictions. There is no strict consensus as to the roots of modernity, although it is usually assumed to have emerged in tandem with Europe's 'discovery' of other parts of the world and the early stages of capitalism and proto-industrialisation from the sixteenth century, as well as interest in science. Scholars have considered the path of modernity's development from the eighteenth to the twentieth centuries; its high period usually thought to be from the late nineteenth to the mid-twentieth century; and the question of whether 'postmodernity' has indeed been as new an epoch as that name suggests, or rather a discernibly distinct but connected phase of modernity itself since perhaps the 1970s. Postcolonial theorists have insisted on the need to see modernity as a global phenomenon, with originary points outside the (over) developed world; while Euro-American imperialism has been one of its central structures, modernity was not invented and imposed by 'the West' but rather evolved globally in interconnected ways.

Most importantly for my purposes, feminist scholars have begun to chart the gendered dimensions of modernity, to interrogate the masculinist assumptions of at least some analyses and to explore the ways in which women have participated in, and been affected by, modernity and modernist cultural movements. We are now aware of ways in which modernity has at once subordinated women (through, for example, a feminised reification of the private and domestic) and supported their struggles for equality (via, for example, discourses of universal human rights that were available to challenge elite Western men's political hegemony). Birth control, expressive and transgressive sexualities, racial hierarchies and challenges to them, women's struggles for social equality and political citizenship, notions of individual autonomy and personal transformation, experimental cultural forms and all kinds of mobility have been elements of the modern.

This essay draws upon a mix of genres, albeit mostly scholarly, to consider the ways in which women have shaped our historical understanding of modernity. The first section addresses the ways in which women as historical subjects since the late eighteenth century have written about the meanings for women of the historical period we now call modernity and its constituent elements. Both women as historical actors and women historians in earlier periods recognised and analysed the significance for women of economic, technological, political and cultural changes. Not just observers, some writers engaged these issues from a feminist perspective, seeking to improve their own and other women's status. The second section assesses the period of so-called high modernity in the early twentieth century and its obsession with the modern and the new. A review of recent scholarly historical writing shows it to have been a mixed era for women, with some changes allowing women more possibilities and social, economic and political freedom, while there were also elements of misogynist backlash. If the 'modern women' of the 1920s and 1930s considered themselves to be distinctly different from an earlier generation, especially in their embrace of sexuality, the third section argues that there was much overlap and slippage among the 'New Woman', the 'modern woman' and the *flaneuse*, even as these categories and their representations varied from country to country. The final section examines works that emphasise the need to see modernity as a global phenomenon in which gender, colonialism and racial hierarchies have been interlinked and considers some historical examples of what this has meant for women.

Women's writing and modernity in the 19th and 20th centuries

If the term 'modernity' has only recently acquired broad currency in history writing, the substance of what can be defined as 'modernity' has been the subject matter of historians and other writers for much longer. In her landmark 1790 manifesto 'Declaration of the Rights of Woman and Citizen', French feminist Olympe de Gouges argued that a revolutionary nation state, freed from old corruption, should extend the rights of man to woman and thus consist of women and men citizens equal in all political, legal and economic rights and duties (Riemer and Fout 1980: 62–7). While political rights remained a concern, a century later some Western feminists became more concerned with the economic conditions of women and with the dependence that they sometimes saw as the product of industrialisation and other aspects of modernity. **Charlotte Perkins Gilman** condemned women's economic and social dependence upon men in her celebrated 1898 treatise *Women and Economics*. In 1911, in her book *Woman and Labour* Olive Schreiner identified the subordination of women as existing in all cultures, including those in an 'untouched primitive condition'. She recorded a conversation with a 'Kafir woman' in her native South Africa, who 'painted the condition of the women of her race; the labour of women, the anguish of woman as she grew older, and the limitations of her life closed in about her, her sufferings under the condition of polygamy and subjection' (1911: 5–6). Paradoxically, Schreiner argued that it was the historical changes that comprised 'modern civilisation' that had resulted in Western women's unhappy and 'parasitic' condition. 'Woman' had been '[robbed] almost wholly, of the more valuable part of her ancient domain of productive and social labour' (1911: 46). Robbed by mechanisation and industrialisation of their traditional occupations such as spinning, hoeing, grinding, brewing, dairy work and sewing, women had lost three-quarters of their 'ancient and traditional labours' (1911: 64). Central to the women's movement, Schreiner contended, was the demand that 'we also shall have our share of honoured and socially useful human toil' (1911: 65).

Disturbed by the suffering of poor women around them, some women historians at this time investigated the effects of the industrial revolution on women in earlier centuries, as recent historiographical studies, particularly *The Gender of History* (Smith 1998: 177) and *Writing Women's History since the Renaissance* (Spongberg 2002: 147, 166–7) have shown. Georgiana Hill argued in her 1896 book *Women in English Life from Mediaeval to Modern Times* that women in the mediaeval period had had more economic possibility and responsibility than women in the nineteenth century. In 1919 **Alice Clark** published her book *The Working Life of Women in the Seventeenth Century*, in which she contended similarly that industrialisation had reduced women's productive competence and skills. Clark's argument was soon challenged by other women historians. **Ivy Pinchbeck**, in *Women Workers and the Industrial Revolution 1750–1850* (1930), saw industrial work for women in a far more positive light. Pinchbeck argued that, despite hardships for women in the early stages of industrialisation, by the mid-nineteenth century English women industrial workers were enjoying a higher standard of living than ever before and an unprecedented degree of economic autonomy. Indeed, she claimed, women industrial workers' improved economic and social position led the way for middle-class women to demand greater independence. As Julie Des Jardins has shown in her study *Women and the Historical Enterprise in America* (2003: 81–3), for historian **Mary Beard**, also writing in the century's early decades, historical enquiry into women's daily lives, their economic and political work, was directly linked to her desire for reform in the present.

The gendering of productive labour that was central to industrialisation was not the only aspect of modernity that preoccupied women historians of the early twentieth century. Caught up in the suffrage movements of various countries, women who wrote historically focused too on the history of women's political status, their exclusion from the political citizenship articulated by modern bourgeois liberal individualism that Olympe de Gouges had protested. Suffragists themselves were imbued with a sense of the movement's historical importance and many documented their struggles with a keen eye towards posterity. Mary Spongberg argues that the major nineteenth-century genre of women's historical writing, biography, was transformed by the suffrage movement into a celebration of radical and proto-feminist women (2002: 138–9), at the same time that suffragists engaged in autobiographical writing created versions of suffrage history and preserved their records. First-wave feminist movements commonly invoked a sense of their own breaking with tradition, resonating with modernity's emphasis on rupture and change. In Australia, two feminist magazines, one in the late nineteenth century and one in the early twentieth, were both titled *The Dawn* to evoke the new order feminists hoped to bring about. The Indian feminist Atiya Begum Fyzee Rahamin used the same image to link modernity and feminism in her speech 'The Citizen Rights of Women within The British Empire' to the British Commonwealth League conference in July 1925: 'The East had slept for two centuries, but the Rising Sun heralded the awakening of the Indian woman once more to contribute her share of knowledge and culture as she had done in the past. Woman was even now playing her part in important movements. The more modern woman adopted up-to-date methods,' including women already working in the law and politics in India. First-wave feminism, as both a political and cultural formation, was tightly interlinked with both the 'New Woman' and the 'modern woman' of the late nineteenth and early twentieth centuries.

Writings by innumerable women from a range of time periods illustrate the connections among the perceived possibilities of modernity, colonialism and imperialism and desires to expand women's options. Feminist and pro-imperialist travel and fiction-writer Mary Gaunt left her native Australia for London at age 40 in 1901.

Gaunt forged a long and successful career from her travel accounts. As a staunch feminist, she advocated women's engagement in the world of work, both for their sake and for the larger public good – specifically, often, the good of the British Empire. Her fantasies about what colonialism could offer in the way of prospects for a modern woman were most excited by a young Jamaican-born woman of English descent whom she met in her post-war travels. Gaunt considered Charlotte Maxwell Hall a 'modern representative' of colonising English women in Jamaica, one who would make her female ancestors 'turn in their graves' (1922: 291). Hall had inherited a cattle pen from her father, which she managed by herself with her workers, at the same time as being 'the Government Meteorologist' and running a small milk business on the side. For Gaunt, Hall exemplified the feminist goal of having 'made a place for herself in the world' and therefore being 'able to hold up her head as a valuable citizen' (1922: 288). She showed how colonial modernity afforded colonising young women possibilities to rewrite the script of feminine lives; in contrast, Gaunt had little interest in the possibilities for colonised women. Gaunt envisioned new femininities facilitated by modernity, but dependent on its racial hierarchies.

Jamaica was the birthplace of another colonial woman writer who illuminates the possibilities and hierarchies of modernity, but one whose life and autobiography reveal a determination to challenge racist exclusion as well as gender circumscriptions. Mary Jane Grant Seacole was Creole, born in Kingston in 1805 to a Scottish army officer father and a free black mother who ran a boarding house that included a well-regarded nursing and medical practice. Seacole apprenticed herself to her mother, learning at her side a blend of traditional African-Caribbean medicine and some elements of European medicine from the naval and army officers who were their clientele. In the 1840s, after her mother's death Seacole took over her hotel and medical practice. In 1850 she helped to deal with the Kingston cholera epidemic. In 1853, the colonial authorities invited her to supervise nursing provision at the local military base. On the basis of this relevant experience she volunteered her services to Florence Nightingale's new nursing organisation as part of the imperial war in Crimea in 1854. Faced in London with a clearly racist rejection, Seacole paid her own way to the Crimea and established a business combining a hotel, canteen and medical practice, catering to all military ranks. Her business thrived during the war but collapsed at the war's end in 1856, and back in England Seacole was faced with bankruptcy charges. Military officials and veterans organised benefits on her behalf and it was in the context of financial need that she wrote her successful autobiography *Wonderful Adventures of Mrs. Seacole in Many Lands* published in 1857. By tying her story to the military challenges of the imperial nation-state and by arguing for her own professional skills and contribution, Seacole invoked aspects of modernity in writing her life (1857/1984: 9–45).

Gaunt and Seacole were both highly mobile women, who exploited the possibilities of travel and publishing to create arguably modern lives and to write their own stories, stories that transgressed dominant feminine subjectivities. While Gaunt was overtly racist and Seacole had to fight racism, both were active supporters of the British Empire, thus showing the complex interconnections between modernity, colonialism, race and gender. Gaunt's travel and fiction-writing and Seacole's autobiography are instances of women's use of writing to contest and to shape modernity in the nineteenth and twentieth centuries.

Periodising modernity

Several historians of women have focused upon the interwar decades as the high period of modernity. Not coincidentally, these were the decades when women of many nations were enfranchised. If modernity was in fact a period comprised of centuries, the early twentieth century was distinctive in its valorisation of 'the modern', the currency of that term and its redolent cultural meanings. The decades either side of the turn of the century are often regarded as the era of accelerated modernity. Technological change (the telephone, the automobile, huge steamships, the camera, movies), rapid urbanisation, high rates of migration, the invention of the assembly line, escalated imperialist competition for colonies and the 'Great War', all combined to produce a sense of dramatic change and the collapsing of space and time often seen as quintessentially modern. What was distinctive about the 1910s and 1920s especially was a cultural embracing of change as inherently good. As literary critic Rita Felski has suggested in *The Gender of Modernity* (1995: 170), this period's modernist impulse included a flaunting of the term 'modern' and an 'assuming of the necessary value of the new.'

For women, embracing the new had quite specific implications. Birgitte Soland has used documentary sources, autobiographies and oral histories to investigate what being 'modern' meant to rural and urban Danish women born between 1895 and 1911 in her book *Becoming Modern: Young Women and the Reconstruction of Womanhood in the 1920s* (2000). Based on this extensive research, Soland concludes that young Danish women in the 1920s were active agents in the production of gendered modernity. With their cropped hair, their short skirts, slender figures, jobs and wages, young Danish women in the 1920s insisted on more leisure and pleasure than their parents had enjoyed. Often better educated than their mothers, this generation of women insisted on trying new jobs, going out at night, playing sports, expressing their greater freedom through bodily movement, pushing at boundaries of sexual expression and enjoying the mobility and speed offered by the bicycle and for some at least, the motor cycle and the car. Soland emphasises that these women conceived of themselves as a new generation, one that explicitly invoked the term 'modern'. In an argument in harmony with Soland's, in her book *Dance Hall and Picture Palace* (2005), Jill Julius Matthews shows that the 'dance craze' in 1910s and 1920s Sydney constituted an important context in which young women embraced joyous bodily movement in a transnational cultural form. Young women constituted their own modernity by pushing at cultural boundaries of respectability, in the careful pursuit of pleasure and desire. Wearing fashionable clothes, using make-up and cigarettes and wearing high heels even if just in certain ways, times and places, Australian women selectively and self-consciously embodied modernity.

The essays in Katharina von Ankum's anthology *Women in the Metropolis: Gender and Modernity in Weimar Culture* present a more troubled picture of German women's encounter with high modernity, suggesting that what seemed the promise of the post-war years already contended with misogyny, which by the latter 1920s was joined by a conservative nationalist backlash. The Weimar Republic gave women the vote and young women flocked into clerical work and hence from the countryside into the city. The relative freedom and cultural modernism of the Weimar city, especially Berlin, encouraged women's sexual expression, cultural experimentation, consumerism and the pursuit of commercial forms of leisure. Yet women's negotiations with urban modernity ran up against nationalist pronatalism, the category and label of prostitute and various forms of misogyny, including recurrent images of the murder and mutilation of women in the work of male artists. A rather more hopeful study of the intersections between femininities and modernity is Laura Doan's analysis of the emergence of an identifiably English lesbian subculture in the 1920s, *Fashioning Sapphism: The Origins of a Modern English Subculture* (2001). This subculture, which she calls 'Sapphic modernity', was recognisably modern in its embrace of women's changed post-war political and cultural status, of new technologies such as the motorcycle and the camera and of the new science of sexology. European culture in the interwar period was characterised by pervasive cross-dressing and gender transgression. As Doan argues, English lesbians took advantage of androgynous fashions such as boyish haircuts and men's clothing worn by women, to develop their own subculture in a way that blended with current styles. Lesbians' expressive appropriation of transgressive fashion was a distinctly modern manoeuvre.

Sexual experimentation and expression was characteristic of interwar modernity, in marked contrast to the pre-war period. Literary critic Elaine Showalter argued a quarter-century ago that American feminists of the 1920s, while themselves espousing a range of political positions, differed from earlier feminists in their insistence on having sexual relationships, marriage and children as well as public careers. In her introduction to her collection of autobiographical essays *These Modern Women* (1978), all first published in *The Nation* in 1926 and 1927, Showalter contends that 'modern' feminists of the 1920s were self-consciously different from what they saw as an older generation of women activists. The essayists discussed the difficulties of balancing marriage, motherhood and a career, but were insistent that they were not prepared to make what they saw as the older generation's sacrifice of a sexual and emotional life – a charge that is undercut to some extent by evidence that some women of the earlier generation chose to live with each other. Despite the younger interwar generation asserting its own distinctive modernness and despite changing patterns of sexual behaviour and expression, there were important connections between the interwar generation and its predecessors.

The 'New Woman' and the 'modern woman'

The 'modern woman' and the 'New Woman' of the 1890s, 1900s and 1910s had a good deal in common. For all of the emblematic espousal of the term 'modern' in the 1910s and 1920s and the interwar generation's insistence on its difference from the turn-of-the-century generation of 'New Women', there was much interconnection between these terms and slippage in their usage. Moreover, the timing of the celebration of these iconic feminine types and their nuances varied somewhat from country to country. While in Britain the 'New Woman' was a figure of the 1890s and 1900s, as Laura Engelstein has shown in her monograph *The Keys to Happiness* (1992), in Russia she gained attention in the 1900s and 1910s as an assertive single woman who earned her own living, was delineated in sensational novels and associated with the arts and in particular transgressed convention through her sexual expression.

In Korea, in contrast, 'New Women' constituted a visible and controversial social movement at its height in the 1920s. Insook Kwon argues in her essay '"The New Women's Movement" in 1920s Korea' (1999) that Korean 'New Women' challenged Confucian patriarchy, advocated free love and free choice in marriage and were relatively well educated. Moreover, some had travelled to Japan and Europe. Linked as they were to Western feminism, opposition to them in Korea stemmed partly from their association with both Western imperialism and the Japanese occupation of Korea.

Even in Western Europe, there was overlap between the 'New Woman' and the 'modern woman'. Indeed, the very term 'modern woman' was used in the late nineteenth century to demarcate women who sought careers, pursued higher education, were active feminists, rode bicycles or espoused dress reform. In her book *Love and Freedom: Professional Women and the Reshaping of Personal Life* (1997), Alison Mackinnon has explored the links between the dramatic drop in fertility rates in Western Anglophone nations in the decades either side of 1900, women's entrance into higher education and their experiments with social autonomy. Education enabled women to have satisfying and challenging careers, which in turn offered them alternatives to marriage and emboldened them to shape new feminine subjectivities. In English feminist Ella Hepworth Dixon's 1894 novel *The Story of a Modern Woman*, the protagonist Mary Erle is a young woman forced by her father's death to find a career to support herself and her younger brother, who, unlike Erle herself, goes to university. Erle first tries to become an artist, then turns to journalism and writing popular romantic fiction. She does not marry (having been betrayed by her callow suitor) but learns from both her best friend and her own observations the importance of solidarity among women: women need to help each other practically, but they also need a united front to resist the moral and emotional depredations of men. Kate Flint points out in her introduction (1894/1990: xiv) to the 1990 reprinting that Hepworth Dixon's novel exemplified W T Stead's dictum that '"The Modern Woman" novel is not merely a novel written by a woman, or a novel written about women, but it is a novel written by a woman about women from the standpoint of Woman.' Both the 'modern woman' and the 'New Woman' were aligned with first-wave feminism (a term, of course, coined in the 1890s), although not all were overt or active suffragists. More than the 'modern woman' of the 1920s and 1930s, the earlier 'modern woman' or 'New Woman' was seen as a freethinker engaged in social criticism and movements for reform. According to an 1894 panegyric poem by 'D N B', 'The New Woman', 'She is listening to the heart-beats / Of the people in its pain; She is pondering social problems / Which appeal to heart and brain. She is daring for the first time / Both to think – and then to act; She is flouting social fictions, Changing social lie – for FACT' (Gardiner 1993: 14).

The late-nineteenth century 'modern woman' or 'New Woman's' alignment with social criticism and reform was directly linked to her being seen as an urban product. Numerous historians have contributed to our understanding of the ways in which the city offered women employment and social and sexual possibilities and thus drew them from rural hinterlands as well as across oceans. Much of the scholarly debate on women and the nineteenth-century city has centred on the issue of respectable women's ability to move around in the city, their cultural permission to negotiate public spaces and perhaps specifically whether or not there was such a woman as the *flaneuse*, or only the *flaneur*, the rambling male observer of urban life. The *flaneur* was a bourgeois man, usually considered bohemian, who was at home in the flux of modern urban traffic and who appreciated and often recorded the aesthetic and cultural possibilities of the city landscape. The definition of the *flaneur* and hence the possibility of the *flaneuse* centred on cultural aspects of urban geography, particularly whether a woman could attain the same status as the autonomous male subject and observer of urban life. Thus the 'New Woman' was not reducible to the *flaneuse*, but the latter's access to the city was directly linked to issues of women's changing economic and cultural status.

Elizabeth Wilson has argued in *The Sphinx in the City: Urban Life, the Control of Disorder and Women* (1992) that since the Industrial Revolution the city has offered women both possibility and constraint: they have been drawn to its amenities and anonymity, but at the price of becoming a sexualised part of the urban spectacle, objects of the male gaze. Other scholars, especially those who have focused on the last decades of the nineteenth century and afterwards, have been more optimistic in their assessments of women's lives in the city. Joanne Meyerowitz's study of *Women Adrift: Independent Wage Earners in Chicago, 1880–1930* (1988) documents the scale of the phenomenon of women leaving home and family to seek work in the turn-of-the-century Midwest. These women included black and white, younger and older, American- and foreign-born. If not as culturally celebrated as more affluent and better educated 'New Women', such women challenged Victorian bourgeois moral codes by achieving measures of economic and social independence, despite the low rates of pay for their work in offices, factories, hospitals and department stores. They lived in rooming houses, enjoyed new urban commercial entertainment, negotiated sexual and economic relationships and formed new urban subcultures. In all of these ways, they contributed to feminine modernity in the city.

Mica Nava has explicitly refuted the notion that were no *flaneuses* in the nineteenth-century city. In her study of London titled 'Modernity's Disavowal: Women, the City and the Department Store' (1996), she argues that, especially in the latter part of the century, women defied their notional restriction to domestic space in a myriad of ways. Women traversed public space on buses, trains, bicycles and on foot. If working-class women were always compelled to negotiate public space, middle-class women did so increasingly as the century wore on, not least in their philanthropic enterprises that took them, ironically enough, into slum neighbourhoods. Women availed themselves of public parks, galleries, exhibitions, libraries, tearooms and department stores. In all of these venues, they too were urban spectators and their presence in the city contributed to the anxieties and instability of this period of modernity. In her monograph *Shopping for Pleasure: Women in the Making of London's West End* (2000) Erika Rappaport demonstrates that gender dynamics were integral to the commercial development of London's West End in the late nineteenth and early twentieth centuries. London's fashionable centre was reshaped in an interdependent economic and cultural relationship with the growth of affluent suburbia. The rise of the department store and the feminised phenomenon of 'shopping for pleasure', were integral to middle- and upper-class women's escalating incursions into London's West End; when women went shopping, they became urban spectators as well as consumers. Rappaport shows that feminist concern with women's access to urban public space (through their demand for and provision of women's clubs, tearooms, restaurants and the essential amenity of toilets for women) was linked to the modern emergence of consumer culture, mass retailing, fashion, commercial leisure pursuits and women's visibility in the marketplace.

The global and colonial dimensions of modernity

Several scholars have pointed towards the global and colonial dimensions of the connections between modernity, the city and women's travel. In my book *To Try Her Fortune in London: Australian Women, Colonialism and Modernity* (2001), I sought to explicate the ways in which the attraction of tens of thousands of Australian women to London between 1870 and 1940 was related to modernity. In this high period of colonialism (which overlapped, not coincidentally, with high modernity), the cultural logic of colonialism naturalised the attraction of the imperial metropolis, at the same time that the technology of the steamship greatly facilitated the 12,000-mile voyage. Colonial women's very ambitions and desires for the educational, cultural and career possibilities of the metropole both shaped and were shaped by a modern belief in changing the self. Similarly, Antoinette Burton has argued in her book *Dwelling in the Archive: Women Writing House, Home and History in Late Colonial India* (2003) that Indian women who travelled between London and India and whose lives and writing challenge traditional assumptions about gender, the public-private dichotomy and historical change, were agents as well as chroniclers of modernity in both India and Britain.

The connections between colonialism and modernity that are significant for women's history, of course, go well beyond travel. Some theorists insist, for example, that we identify the interconnections between racial hierarchies, gender, colonialism and modernity. Paul Gilroy (1993) has argued influentially that modernity has comprised not only racial hierarchy but transnational ethnic identities; not only Western ideologies of dominance and superiority but vibrant countercultures which challenge them. Other scholars, too, have pointed towards the mixed nature of both the Enlightenment and modernity more broadly, their emphasis on science, rationality, control and measurement that coexisted with cross-cultural fantasies and desires. As Edward Said contended a generation ago, European desire to 'know' the exotic 'other' has been at the heart of **Orientalism** and thus of imperial power. And as Ann Stoler has argued in her critique of Foucault, *Race and the Education of Desire*, colonial discourses, regulation and practices of sexuality were central to the construction of European bourgeois codes and thus of racial categories and of modernity (1997: 7–8). Colonialism's racialised dichotomy of 'modernity' and 'tradition' was often produced through definitions of women's sexuality. Small wonder, then, that colonial modernity has been a complex and multivalent affair for women.

Mary Hancock, in an essay titled 'Gendering the Modern' (1999), has explored the gendered meanings of colonial modernity within the specific framework of the growth of the Home Science movement in late colonial India. Home Science, Hancock argues, was a transnational movement that sought to bring the technologies of science to domesticity and thus to create a modernist project from girls' and women's education in home management, maternity, child welfare, nutrition and public health. In India in the

1920s and 1930s, Home Science was sponsored, among others, by the Women's Indian Association, an elite feminist organisation with direct links to both transnational and Western feminisms and Gandhian nationalisms. The meanings of modern domesticity within the discourses of Indian Home Science were fissured over issues of women's political activism and sectarianism. Yet Home Science offered a scientific domain specifically for women, a feminised form of engineering and management that blended with especially Hindu traditions and that turned 'Home' into both a nationalist and modern project. If the modern project of Home Science perhaps helped some colonised women better than others, other gendered aspects of colonial modernity, the interlinked systems of concubinage and prostitution, were both a source of oppression and economic strategies for women. In her essay 'Making Empire Respectable' (1997), Ann Stoler has described the centrality of concubinage to the domestic and sexual arrangements of various colonial regimes; in tension with prostitution and marriage, concubinage was a racially structured and historically contingent system that maintained colonial rule both practically and symbolically.

Prostitution has been tightly linked to colonialism, as Philippa Levine demonstrates in detail in *Prostitution, Race & Politics* (2003) her study of regulated prostitution, racialised definitions of sexuality, venereal disease and colonial medicine in four British colonies (Queensland, the Straits Settlements, Hong Kong and India) from the mid-nineteenth to the early-twentieth century. In the context of British colonialism in Africa, Luise White has shown in *The Comforts of Home* (1990) that the twentieth-century evolution of prostitution in Nairobi was a shifting product of women's and men's negotiations amidst economic change produced by colonial capitalism, migrant labour and urbanisation, all aspects of colonial modernity. From the 1890s, British colonisation disrupted East African marriage systems and an economy based on cattle-owning and agriculture. In the early twentieth century, within the new context of migrant labour, women turned to prostitution as a survival strategy and as a means of capital accumulation that would enable them to buy property; thus they became Nairobi's first year-round residents. Evolving in response to imperial wars, colonial state policies and economic change, prostitution expanded and took on different forms. White argues convincingly that women who engaged in prostitution served to reproduce the labour force by sustaining male workers in ways that the colonial state could not. At the same time, they made money both through prostitution and as landlords, made choices about family and households and established areas of social autonomy beyond the limits of colonial control. Gail Hershatter, too, has made a significant contribution to this subject by demonstrating the centrality of prostitution to debates concerning modernity and the nation in the context of what she calls (borrowing from Mao) the 'semicolonialism' of China. *Dangerous Pleasures: Prostitution and Modernity in Twentieth-Century Shanghai* (1997) is a richly detailed study of the city that was at the centre of the informal colonisation of China by European powers, the United States, and Japan. Hershatter shows how nationalists, reformers and revolutionaries debated forms of gender and sexuality in relation to the Chinese modernity that they sought in order to resist colonisation.

The ubiquity of the term 'modernity' in historical writing is a notably recent phenomenon. Historians' current engagement with the concept of 'modernity' is, arguably, a reaction to the critical vogue of 'postmodernism' and 'postmodernity' in the late 1980s and the 1990s. Since the mid-1990s, historians, it would seem, have been provoked to respond to the implicit question: post- what? If, as David Harvey has suggested in *The Condition of Postmodernity*, the central question addressed by philosophers of postmodernity is whether or not the Enlightenment project should be abandoned, that is an issue still strongly contested (1989: 14). The work of women writers reveals both the possibilities and the historically evolving constraints that not only the Enlightenment but modernity in its entirety, entailed for women and the ways that women responded. The mix of genres discussed in this essay, from scholarly monographs to political treatises, autobiography and fiction, reflects the diversity of ways in which women have contributed to our historical understanding of modernity. If we are still struggling with the question of whether or not we are in a late stage of modernity, the writing of the women surveyed here and many others allows us to explore modernity's complex and historically contingent structures. We can interrogate at once the ways in which it has shaped women's material, technological, political and cultural circumstances and the ways that women have shaped, interpreted and interpellated modernity itself.

Angela Woollacott

References

Burton 2003; Des Jardins 2003; Doan 2001; Engelstein 1992; Felski 1995; Gardiner 1993; Gaunt 1922; Gilroy 1993; Hancock 1999; Harvey 1989; Hepworth Dixon 1894/1990; Hershatter 1997; Kwon 1999; Levine 2003; Mackinnon 1997; Matthews 2005; Meyerowitz 1988; Nava 1996; Rappaport 2000; Riemer & Fout 1980; Said 1979; Schreiner 1911; Seacole 1857/1984; Showalter 1978; Smith 1998; Soland 2000; Spongberg 2002; Stoler 1995, 1997; White 1990.

Related essays

Australia; Canada; Dominions; Industrialisation; Postcolonialism; Travel; United States.

N

Nation

The study of women's writing, even their writing of history, does not usually take as its subject the historiography of nations. If, until recently, women have had only a whisper of a place in the history of nations, that whisper is reduced to an eerie silence when the topic is women as historians of nations or the national idea. This is at least partly because of the curious past of history as a discipline and the legal and social history of the nation. As Bonnie G Smith (1998) has so convincingly shown, in the nineteenth century the hardening of history as a discipline featured the masculinisation of the practice of history-writing. Significantly for the concerns of this essay that past also intersected with the rise of nations. In the same period that the nation became the natural unit of study for modern historians, history helped firm up the ideology of separate spheres, which associated men and masculinity with the public sphere, and women and femininity with the private.

For most of the nineteenth and twentieth centuries certain areas of historical writing, particularly the history of High Politics and diplomacy, all of them nation-bound, were regarded as the domains of male historians and their subject matter was the agency and activities of men. At the same time women's place in both the history profession and in the nation was circumscribed by conventions regarding femininity and the idealised relegation of women to the domestic/private sphere (Scott 1988). It is somewhat ironic then that even before women invaded the professional world of history there was no shortage of women who took up pens to write about the past, although their work was not recognised in the same way as that of their male counterparts. Moreover, women who embraced history-writing in whatever forms they found accessible to them as women – whether non-fiction, fiction or folklore – commonly adopted the nation as an implicit setting (Smith 1998: 37–69).

Many literary theorists now regard the nineteenth-century novel as an important vehicle for nationalism. The English Gothic novel, for example, combined the delineation of individual pasts and selves with historical narratives of national pasts (Schmitt 1997). There is still a question mark, however, over whether women authors merely rehearsed existing views of the nation or, given their marginal political status in the new nineteenth-century nations, challenged them. Indeed Bonnie Smith has argued that female-authored fictional writing did more than just replicate the cultural boundaries of nations; it traversed and transgressed them through the experiences of travel and exile, evoking a cultural rather than merely political or military view of the nation (Smith 1998).

The question of women's contribution to historical writing about the nation becomes even more complicated when one considers the changes that occurred in the latter decades of the nineteenth century in the conceptualisation not only of the nation, but of history. Neither history, nor nation (let alone women) are stable signifiers. While the idea of the nation was increasingly linked to new biological and Social Darwinist understandings of race, the study of the past too assumed an increasingly fixed identity as the scientific discipline of History pursued in specific empirical and narrative forms, and most often in relation to the study of nations. Women also began to contribute to this form of History in a professional manner, locating themselves and their work according to particular national criteria.

Romantic nationalism

The intellectual history of writing about the nation is usually traced back to the late eighteenth century – a period influenced by the Enlightenment and French Revolution's emphasis on the democratic virtues of the 'people' as a unit – and to the philosophical writings of Johann Gottfried von Herder, who is then followed by the German philosopher Johannes Fichte, the Italian Giuseppe Mazzini and French philosopher Ernest Renan. Interrupting this nineteenth-century genealogy of the nation idea, although rarely commented upon, is the work of the imposing Enlightenment figure **Germaine de Staël**. As the author of numerous essays and works of fiction and non-fiction, de Staël is difficult to classify as an historian in any modern sense. She is more obviously an acute observer of her times, almost anthropological and at least sociological in her dissection of the manners and mores of the people with whom she came into contact. But her non-professional status and her lack of specific vocation as an historian mark her most fully as a figure of her time. It was in this capacity that de Staël contributed to an idea of nation and to the increasing importance of the idea of national past. *On Germany* (1810), for example, was one of the first studies to address the notion of a German culture. De Staël, visited the German-speaking Weimar and Berlin, where she met numerous influential political and cultural figures. She studied the idea of Germany 'explicitly in order to interpret German history and culture to non-Germans, drawing clear boundaries between national groups, and commenting as a foreigner in their midst' (Smith 1998: 56).

De Staël also argued the superiority of the novel over conventional history for relating the dimensions of human experience and understanding national pasts. Her most famous novel *Corinne, or Italy* (1807) evoked in great detail the idea of an Italy historically anchored in a classical Roman past. Indeed *Corinne* is a celebration of a past Italian culture embodied in nostalgic images of the culture of ancient Rome. This was at a time when, like the notion of a German state, an Italian state was merely a glimmer in the eye of the beholder. De Staël's novel offered a representation of Italy that helped the idea of an Italian nation capture the imagination of male and female Europeans, at a time when the peninsula was under Napoleon's tutelage. The plot of *Corinne* has the English Lord Nelvil, Oswald, fall in love with Corinne, the great genius and beauty who lives in Rome and embodies the imaginative, if undisciplined and unsocialised, spirit of Italy. Later it emerges that she was born of an English father and Italian mother and raised in Florence. As Oswald and Corinne's fated courtship takes them across the Italian peninsula 'each looks at the Italian past and then tries to persuade the other of the virtues of his or her interpretation' (Smith 1998: 20).

Significantly, both *Corinne* and *On Germany* develop the idea that a proper gender order is a sign of social order. Thus in the politically fragmented German- and Italian-speaking regions, where national association and a national public opinion were lacking, society was less homogenous, and the gender order was less predictable than was the case, for example, in England. While these were hardly novel assumptions, de Staël's fictional and non-fictional writing renewed their relevance for a wide audience. For example, gendered national stereotypes are critical to the plot of *Corinne*. Her Italy is merely an emasculated spirit present in the Italian-speaking regions or principalities in the absence of a centralised national government, army, administrators and soldiers. Male honour can only be restored through duty to the nation, a mode of masculinity evident in England and embodied in the figure of the (Scottish!) Oswald, a man who is consistently selfless, has a determined sense of social responsibility and ultimately puts duty to the nation and filial piety before his love for Corinne (de Staël 1808/1987: 101).

Works such as the non-fictional *On Germany* and the novel *Corinne, or Italy* shaped the nineteenth-century gendered cultural imaginary of both Germany and Italy respectively, and contributed in very specific ways to the idea of the political relevance of the past, particularly the national past. For de Staël, as for other nineteenth-century theorists before and after her, some nations were more masculine than others, with 'masculinity' itself seen as a desirable national quality. This is evident particularly in her descriptions of Italy, which, in some contexts, de Staël regarded as effeminate (Besser 1994: 56). Certainly de Staël's work also perpetrated cliches about national characteristics. In *Corinne* the English love politics, the Italians are too drawn to aesthetics and do not love politics enough and the French love social discourse. In *On Germany*, German women are bland, and Germans sincere, loyal, articulate, slow and inert. Yet the fact that de Staël was attentive to broad cultural notions of history also suggests the ways in which the past for her was not merely national, and national character was not the only element shaping the fate of individuals or, indeed, of states.

De Staël understood national character to be primarily the product of political institutions. National differentiation both reflected and underlay social organisation. Society for her was a form of 'association' ruled by public opinion, which was in turn formed over time by government, laws and customs. Her view of the historical status of nations was mediated to some extent by her understanding of racial difference, which had a more deterministic role to play in the constitution of national characters. In her autobiographical *Ten Years of Exile* (1821), for example, she indicated her contempt for Napoleon by describing him as a fake Frenchman, whose Corsican origins and behaviour rendered him akin to Africans (1821/1966: 138). In *On Germany* too, she articulated the idea of a cohesive German culture in the context of a Europe comprising three great races: Latin, Germanic and Slavic (1813/1968: 45). To be sure, de Staël's notion of race and its political significance differed substantially from the biological version of race introduced in the latter half of the nineteenth century under the influence of evolutionary theory. Instead, race and nation were more ambiguously imbricated in debates about culture and nature. Most importantly de Staël described a European world divided by national differences that were symptomatic of, and relevant to, gender identities and gender relations. In many ways, de Staël's often ambiguous views of the importance of the nation as a form of political as well as cultural association corresponds to her own place in history, at the centre of the cosmopolitan Enlightenment and at the threshold of a Romantic era and its interest in the nation that she helped define. To the extent that she was interested in the influence of the past on the origins of nations, de Staël argued that the age of chivalry was the most important to the delineation of national character. Curiously, the same age of chivalry that, according to de Staël, defined Germany's tendency to civilisation and Russia's salient barbarity had also encouraged a transnational European patriotism (1813/1968: 70).

De Staël, then, had an important role to play in the development of the novel as a vehicle for 'national tales', that is hybrid texts that merged romantic fiction with history and political polemic. But embedded in these texts was a tension between national and transnational identity, which was tied to changing views of the past and of its political and cultural significance. As Todd Kontje has argued, in the early nineteenth century – the period that coincides with de Staël's work – '[n]ascent nationalism confronts the cosmopolitan legacy of the Enlightenment as authors use their novels to explore conflicting models of collective identity, and to rethink gender roles within imagined communities' (1998: 98). Another example of this tension appears in the work of the English author and poet **Helen Maria Williams**, whose eyewitness accounts of the French Revolution, *Letters from France* (1790–1801), evoked the idea of the French patriot without assuming an exclusive view of the world or the constraints of ethnic origin (Keane 2000: 56–7). In this context the literary historian Angela Keane suggests that Williams outlines an ' "extra-national" public sphere; not the Romantic national kind, the part which stands for the whole and which speaks with the logic of imperialism, but an (albeit ideal) democracy of correspondents from a heterogeneous, international public' (2000: 78–9). **Mary Wollstonecraft**'s *Historical and Moral View of the Origins and Progress* *of the French Revolution* (1794) is similarly subversive in that it argues not for a definition of the nation anchored in the idea of its origins and emotional force, but for a view of the nation that illuminates and extends the political underpinnings of society and community (Keane 2000: 112).

Women and national histories

Such readings of women's historical writing on the nation, like Smith's critique of 'amateur' women's history, point to the role that women had in articulating a view of nations as nestled in other forms of association, whether narrower, as in the family, or broader, as in (implicitly European) humanity. Judith Martin has shown that the early nineteenth-century female-authored German novel emulated both possible versions of the themes of national characteristics and gender relations evoked by de Staël. Caroline Paulus' *Wilhelm Dumont* (1805), for example, drew on 'cultural cliches of national character' that focused in particular on growing German national consciousness under Napoleon's occupation. But this view of the world was also undercut by Friederike Helene Unger, who developed an internationalist strand in fictional works such as *Die Franzosen in Berlin* (1809) (Martin 2002: 140).

The tension between nationalism and internationalism evident in women's historical writing on the nation was played out in the context of the contradictions and ambiguities surrounding the status of women in nations in this period more generally. The idea of the nation in the nineteenth century promised women liberty, but, as we have seen, the nation was also associated with a gender order that stifled women's publicity and political agency. Some German-language novelists made the point that women had a role to play in the politics of nationhood, as for example in the work of Caroline de la Motte Fouque, such as *The Magic of Nature: A Story of the Revolution* (1812), *Edmunds Ways and Byways* (1815) and *The Heroic Maiden of the Vendée* (1816). Fanny Lewald's *Prinz Louis Ferdinand* (1849) is an historical novel set around the Franco-Prussian wars of the early nineteenth century and celebrating the promise of gender equality that she associated with the cause of German unification in the mid-nineteenth century. Of course, once Germany was unified, the incorporated German territories were forced to adopt the conservative patriarchal gender code of the Prussian state which bestowed upon fathers the prerogative of nationality. These thematic tensions in the national theme pursued, and predicated, changing perspectives on the idea of nation and its role in bringing about political change.

Throughout the late eighteenth and the nineteenth centuries, the nation remained only erratically a 'safe house' for what we might regard as progressive views of women's issues. In the 1790s the writer Hannah More used her pen to promote a relatively conservative national cause identified with the English gender order de Staël so celebrated. In this version, 'the economy of the household was the analogue of the economy of the nation' (Keane 2000: 30–31ff.). Women's place at home or in the private sphere – as wives, mothers and daughters – became the seat of their symbolic and practical public role as members of a nation. The intention of More's advice books was to indoctrinate young girls into a national identity as English, diluting the influence of foreign languages, mores, religions and foreign authors. There are other examples that could be drawn into this turn of the nineteenth-century history of the idea of nation and the narrativisation of national pasts, particularly the novels of Sydney Owenson, Lady Morgan (such as *The Wild Irish Girl*, 1806 and *Italy*, 1821) and Maria Edgeworth (*Castle Rackrent*, 1800 and *Popular Tales*, 1804), whose fictional writing was enmeshed in the Irish question (Trumpener 1997). Again Smith provides us with a useful summary of their contribution to historical writing about the nation: 'Amateurs were assiduous in writing the histories of other countries, mining these narratives especially for the ingredients of citizenship and sound political rule; but this was an area with ragged contours and not necessarily a closed issue on the subject of women and virtue' (1998: 57).

It was the Italian national cause that featured in the nineteenth-century narratives linking women and the idea of the nation. By the mid-nineteenth century, Italian unification was among the greatest inspirations for all forms of polemical and political writing on the significance of the national past by women, many of them, like their predecessor de Staël, writing from a position as outsider or at least exile. Their work was not as influential as that of de Staël, nevertheless it offers a useful indicator of the extent to which women's writing on the nation mirrored and perpetuated a gendered national agenda. Princess **Cristina Belgiojoso** also wrote on the present and future of an Italian state that she could only imagine rather than visit. *Reflexions sur l'état actuel de l'Italie et sur son avenir* (1869) was written after the unification of Italy as a summary of its claims to national status, as well as testimony to her disillusion. Her first chapters take Italy seriously as a place that needs (since its political unification) to be mapped geographically and historically and thus legitimated.

Belgiojoso did her part for the Italian cause by outlining an historical narrative of the formation of the Italian state. Although she did not single out women, including herself, or the social ambitions for women which were at the time associated with the cause of Italy's 'liberation' from Habsburg rule, her implicit account of the relationship between a national ideal and gender order reinforced de Staël's views. Her assessment of Italian 'character' was that its 'natural' tendencies (which she shared) had to be quashed in order for Italians to develop morally, intellectually and nationally (1869: 143). In other words, Italian men had to emulate English 'activity' in order to more fully realise their masculine and political potential (1869: 155). Englishness was thus characterised as the most vital and masculine, and most politically functional of national characters. In this sense, Belgiojoso, like de Staël, established the importance of an English model in the formation of nations, a model that was by definition fundamentally gendered. She assumed that men embody the characters that inform, shape and develop national destiny. This emphasis on masculinity was linked to her placement of the family at the centre of the image of the nation. Such an association could be used to support quite different conceptions of women's place in the state, but ultimately tied the rights of both men and women to their familial standing.

If women's contribution in the nineteenth century to the writing of national histories has been significant to the history of gender, it has also been relentlessly ungendered in terms of the differences brought by men and women to this idea. Alternatively, it could be argued that female authors not only narrated national pasts, but gendered them in ways that were often contrary to their own needs and experiences. It is as if the idea of nation itself was ineluctably linked with a specific gender order that defined it. Thus the theme of appropriate masculinity was embroidered into nineteenth-century women's literature on the national past. Madame la Comtesse Drohojowska's *History of the French Colonies* (1853) extolled the bravery of French men in the establishment of the colonies – their private virtues were the source, she claimed, of public virtues. This literature also emphasised, much more than de Staël, the public role of women as mothers. Drohojowska celebrated women as the propagators of French children, maintaining the continuity of the French presence in the colonies, raising the moral standard and preventing miscegenation (Gaffarel 1899).

Feminism and the nation

By the latter half of the nineteenth century the themes of colonialism, sexuality and race were definitive of writing about nations and their pasts. As the nation became increasingly important to political life across the European world, whether in the old country or new settler societies, and implicated in the struggle for colonies and the scientific polemics of race, so its presence in women's writing became more and more a given, in tune with the writing of men on these same themes. Susan Sheridan has remarked in the context of Australian history that women novelists such as Katharine Susannah Prichard, Nettie Palmer and Marjorie Barnard identified with the cultivation of a national literary tradition and racially based imperial world-view (1995: 155). In the context of the idea of race particularly, European women often had more in common with their male nationals than with the colonised women who challenged the role of imperial nations by supporting their own national causes (1986: 52).

The twin themes of gender order and national order persisted in women's early twentieth-century 'amateur' and fictional writing about the past, of their own and other societies, albeit in altered forms. In most European societies the nationality of women could not be taken for granted. Men were the assumed citizens of nations, women could have symbolic and even practical roles, but they had no similar natural right to nationality. Indeed, the nationality of married women was a prime cause of the feminist struggle in the first half of the twentieth century. Virginia Woolf's *Three Guineas* (1938) is exemplary of the critique of the gendered basis of nations and nationalism that underlined women's exclusion from national pasts and presents. Woolf argued that women were without countries and should muster that marginalised experience as a basis for challenging the male versions of national politics and of the past. Alternatively, Rebecca West's *Black Lamb and Grey Falcon* (1941), partially a history of 'the Balkans', partly political narrative and partly travelogue, in many ways continued the concerns of de Staël, but with a reversal of symbolism. In West's schema, the English male had been rendered effete and emasculated by modernity and urbanisation. The lessons for a successful gender order were to be gleaned instead from Yugoslavia, a country on the eastern fringes of Italy pieced together at the end of the First World War and on the brink of civil war. West identified Yugoslavia with a primal state of society, where men had gloriously retained their 'natural' and potent masculinity and women were conventionally feminine, and where, as a result, there was no demographic crisis.

The latter half of the twentieth century marks a more critical trend in thinking about the nature of history. The Second World War acted as a watershed in writing about the nation, particularly its relationship to racial thought. The growing self-consciousness about these themes under the spectre of the Holocaust and anti-colonial movements is reflected in the German-American philosopher Hannah Arendt's master work *Origins of Totalitarianism* (1951), one of the most insightful and lasting historical accounts of the nature of nationalism and its relationship to liberalism as well as totalitarianism. In her endeavour to understand the roots of the Holocaust, Arendt traced the origins of nationalism to nineteenth-century Western European liberalism and the nation idea. She argued that in the nineteenth century it was the French and English intellectuals who insisted long before Germans on the *idée fixe* of German superiority. She identified the race-thinking immanent in the idea of 'the rights of Englishmen' that emerged in England in the wake of the universalist claims of the French Revolution. She also claimed that to a significant extent responsibility for the status and legitimacy of racism in the twentieth century had to be borne by the forms of nationalism and race-thinking nurtured at the height of late nineteenth-century Western European imperialism. Arendt concluded that nationalism was not the same as racism, indeed its opposite, and did not conflate race-thinking and racism. She did maintain, however, that the existence of race-thinking 'proved to be a powerful help to racism' (1951/1973: 184). Interestingly Arendt did not focus on the question of gender in this historicisation of the idea of the nation and its relationship to nationalism and racism.

In the decade after Arendt wrote, women, and the idea of women's history, came to the fore in the discipline of History, under the influence of feminism and Marxist theory. Women's history aimed to resuscitate the lost experiences of women, to revive the voices of women in accounts of the past and thus to empower them in the present. Much of this work occurred in the context of national history, and the restoration of women's rightful place in the nation. It did not challenge the nation, rather it bolstered the idea of national history by reinforcing the importance of recovering women's contributions to that history. However, from the 1980s the so-called linguistic turn in historical thinking, taken under the auspices of poststructuralism and then postcolonialism, led to changing perspectives on the place of the nation in history, and the contribution that could be made to this shift by exploring the role of representations of men and women in the construction and consolidation of the nation state. At the forefront of this change was the work of feminists, not all of them historians, who began to question the absence of women in history-writing and the gender assumptions perpetrated in national historiographies. Indeed the contribution of women to the critique of national historiography is as extensive as the previous engagement with nations. The difference, of course, is that increasingly this contribution has been made by women as professionals, whether historians, sociologists, anthropologists, philosophers or literary and political theorists interested in the formative role of historical narratives.

Late twentieth-century feminist critiques of national historiographies both rehearsed the women's history view that the role of women in the national story needed to be recovered, and emphasised the gendering of national forms of identification. Thus in *Creating a Nation, 1788–1990* four Australian women historians attempted a recasting of Australian history that asserted 'the agency and creativity of women in the process of national generation' (1994: 1). Pat Grimshaw, Marilyn Lake, Ann McGrath and Marian Quartly argue that nationalist mythologies are gendered and, more specifically, at the heart of Australian identity is a white masculinity.

Rather than celebrate the role of women in the national tale, they describe the complicity of white women in the 'imperialist civilising project' of the nation. Consequently, their national history focuses on the connections between domestic government and the male head of house on the one hand, and the government of state and institutionalised male political rule on the other. The result is a different kind of national history about patriarchal states, about the correspondence between family and state, about the public/private split and its significance.

Over the last decade the reconceptualisation of national histories around the category of gender and the inclusion of women into the national story have taken place in a number of national contexts. Women historians, particularly historians of imperialism, have been central to the reassessment of 'British' national history, and to the idea of nation in that history. Antoinette Burton's *The Burdens of History* (1994) questions the framework of British history; Maura O'Connor's *The Romance of Italy and the English Political Imagination* (1998) focuses on the influence of Italian nationalism on British women and Mrinalini Sinha's *Colonial Masculinity* (1995) examines the impact of British colonisation on Indian gender and national identity. Linda Colley's *Britons: Forging the Nation 1707–1837* (1992) looks at the development of British identity through the experience of conflict, particularly wars with France. In separate chapters on men and women and the growth of British patriotism and nationalism in the eighteenth century, Colley argues that British identity grew more pronounced during the Napoleonic wars 'as a reaction to the other beyond their shores'. During this time a specific form of femininity – much as idealised by de Staël – was identified as particularly British. It emphasised women's moral responsibility for the family, and their roles as wives and mothers – a negative version of the femininity identified by the English with revolutionary France and the figure of Marie Antoinette.

The important volume *Nation, Empire, Colony: Historicizing Gender and Race* (1998) presents papers delivered at the International Congress of Historical Sciences held in Montreal in 1995 addressing the history of 'Women, Colonialisms, Imperialisms and Nationalisms through the Ages', and sponsored by the newly formed International Federation for Research in Women's History (Pierson *et al.* 1998). Its editors, like those of *Creating a Nation*, claim that their aim is to restore women and the workings of gender to histories of the construction of nation, empire and colony. Many of its contributors want to affirm the place of women and centrality of gender to nationalist ideologies and movements, and focus on the status of feminism in national struggles, and on documenting and understanding, and perhaps learning from, the complicity of white women in the colonising aspects of nationalisms in the past. Kumari Jayawardena's *Feminism and Nationalism in the Third World* (1986) similarly examines the historical reasons for the close association of feminists with nationalist projects. Jayawardena looks at women's participation at the turn of the twentieth century in political struggles against colonisation in Egypt, Iran, Turkey, India, Sri Lanka, China, Japan, Korea, the Philippines, Vietnam and Indonesia.

As feminist historians have begun writing women back into gender histories of the nation, the question of the place of women as historians of nations rehearses the more general problem of women's relationship to the idea of nations and the processes of nation-making or imagining. It also raises questions about the significance of recovering the place of women in the writing of the history of nations. These questions have been most substantially put in feminist writing on British history and its imperial implications. In an essay entitled 'Who Needs the Nation? Interrogating "British" History', Antoinette Burton has taken issue with the popularity of critiques that recast the British nation as an imperialised space but leave intact the sanctity of the nation itself as the proper stuff of history (1997: 146). Burton's work takes a sceptical view of those feminist critiques of national historiographies that want to make women fully part of the nation, as opposed to those that use the historical position of women within nations – as marginal or excluded – to articulate a kind of post-national or, at least, transnational notion of citizenship and subjecthood. Ien Ang has gone further arguing that feminism as well as history 'must stop conceiving itself as a nation, a "natural" political destination for all women, no matter how multicultural' (Burton 2000: 146).

Contemporary feminist critics of writing about the nation focus not only on the complicity in nationalism of women in the past, but of feminist historians in the present. They accentuate the ways in which national imaginaries are discursively constructed and history-writing reproduces and reifies nations and forms of national identification. They also supplement the work of postcolonial theorists engaged in deconstructing the category of nation, and with it the nature of history-writing. These theorists, from a range of disciplines, have shown that 'colonial history also reveals a reverse pattern whereby colonial officials and native men "came to share very similar language and preconceptions about the significance of women and their proper sphere and duties" ' (Loomba 1998: 219). In this context, traditions such as veiling, clitoral excision, polygamy, widow immolation, matriliny or same sex relations are seen as essential aspects of national self-definition (Loomba 1998: 218). Drawing on examples from colonial India, Ania Loomba argues there are some tensions in this postcolonial national narrative, and anticolonialism did open up some avenues for women's agency, so that '[t]he self-fashioning of the nationalist male thus required his fashioning of his wife into a fresh subservience, even though this new role included her education and freedom from some older orthodoxies' (1998: 221). Feminists such as Loomba also criticise existing interest in the place of women in historical debates about national identity on the basis that the women themselves are irrelevant in these debates, they are merely sites rather than subjects of discussion about tradition and modernity. Rather than letting the subaltern 'speak', academic discussions about women have tended to render their experiences and problems as beyond the realm of historical responsibility. This kind of feminist critique of nationalism and of the study of nationalism has led to criticism of the very practice of professional history-writing. At the turn of the twenty-first century, postcolonial historians, among them a number of women, have concentrated on the possibilities for non-national forms of historical writing. As the British sociologist Himani Bannerji writes in her *Nation, Empire, Colony* essay 'Politics and the Writing of History', history itself might be limited in its ability to represent the nation's subaltern, and to challenge the national hierarchies that have infused historiography (Bannerji 1989: 289).

Woman Nation, State

In *Woman Nation-State* (1989), a classic text for students of gender and nationalism,

Nira Yuval-Davis and Flora Anthias list five fundamental ways in which women have been symbolically and actually involved in ethnic and national processes: as biological reproducers of national collectivities; as reproducers of the boundaries of national groups; as transmitters of national cultures; as signifiers of national difference; as participants in national struggles. None of these categories, not even the role of women as transmitters of national cultures, normatively situates women as historians of nations or as national historians. It is hardly surprising then that feminist analysts of ethnicity and nations/nationality/nationalism have complained about the 'failure of theories of nationalism to address either the role of women in national projects or the impact of gender cleavages on our understanding of nations and nationalism' (A Smith 1998: 208). Here I have tried to show that although the views of the past adopted in the national histories and histories of the idea of nation written by women have been varied, in recent years feminist historians and theorists in particular have cast a critical eye on the dominance of the nation theme in historiography and on the consequences of these national characteristics of historiography for our historical understanding of the distinctive social, political, economic, public and private experiences of men and women. Adding women to the historiography of nations may not uncover a predictably 'feminine' response to the narratives of nationhood and national identity. But it does go someway to restoring the place of women in the narratives of history-writing, a position all the more significant for its absence in mainstream accounts of the nation and of history.

Glenda Sluga

References

Arendt 1951/1973; Bannerji 1998; Belgiojoso 1869; Besser 1994; Burton 2000; De Staël 1808/1987, 1813/1968, 1821/1966; Gaffarel 1899; Grimshaw *et al.* 1994; Jayawardena 1986; Keane 2000; Kontje 1998; Loomba 1998; Martin 2002; Pierson 1998; Schmitt 1997; Scott 1988; Sheridan 1995; A Smith 1998; B G Smith 1998; Trumpener 1998; Yuval Davis & Anthias 1989.

Related essays

Australia; Empire; France; Great Britain; Ireland; Postcolonial; Revolution; War.

Neilson, Nellie 1873–1947

American medievalist. Born in Philadelphia, eldest child of Mary Louise Cunningham and William George Neilson, metallurgical engineer. Attended Miss Cooper's School in Philadelphia, then undertook tertiary education at Bryn Mawr. Neilson received her bachelor's degree in 1893, majoring in Greek and English and in 1894 was awarded a master's degree in history. Undertook doctoral study at Bryn Mawr, travelling to England in 1896 where she studied at Cambridge with F W Maitland and at Oxford with Sir Paul Vinogradoff. She received her doctorate in 1899, publishing *Economic Conditions on the Manors of Ramsey Abbey* in the same year. Nelson was appointed in 1902 as an instructor in history at Mount Holyoke College, she was promoted to Professor of European History in 1904 and made Chair of the department in 1905, a position she filled until she retired. Working with fellow medievalist **Bertha Putnam**, Neilson built up the department making Mount Holyoke 'a notable focus of medieval, legal and economic historical studies'.

Neilson was a member of the seminar established by Vinogradoff to research and edit the volumes published as the *Oxford Studies in Social and Legal History* and the *British Academy Records of the Social and Economic*

History of England and Wales. She published *Customary Rents* (1910) in the Oxford series and a *Survey of the Honour of Denbigh* (1914) for the British Academy, also editing *A Terrier of Fleet, Lincolnshire* (1920) and *The Cartulary and Terrier of the Priory of Bilsington Kent* (1928) for that series. She wrote for the *Harvard Law Review* on 'Custom and Common Law in Kent' (1925); published a textbook *Medieval Agrarian Economy* (1936) and contributed to **Eileen Power** and J H Clapham's *Cambridge Economic History of Europe*. She also edited various Year Books for the Selden Society.

In 1926 Neilson was the only woman to be a Charter member of the Medieval Academy of America and she served on the advisory board of its journal *Speculum*. Neilson received two honorary degrees, an L H D from Smith College in 1938 and a LittD from Russell Sage in 1940. In 1940 Neilson was appointed vice-president of the American Historical Association and in 1943 she became its president, the first woman to hold this office. Her presidency was the result of years of lobbying by women historians to attain greater representation in that organisation. Neilson was critical of the discrimination women faced, especially their lack of access to research professorships. In 1944 Neilson was made president of the Medieval Academy, a position she held until her death.

Mary Spongberg

References

Glazer & Slater 1987; Hastings & Kimball 1979; *NAW* 1971.

Nursing and medicine

Issues of gender have been distinctive, enduring and fundamental features of studies about the history of nursing and medicine. They shape the very meanings of those histories, in large part because the human body is so central to all kinds of medical endeavour. Furthermore, the longevity of the belief articulated by Jacqueline Felicie de Almania (c.1313), that 'a man ought to avoid the secrets of women and fly from their intimate associations', illustrates that the practice of medicine also raises vexing questions about morality and its gendered dimensions (Rowland 1981: 9). No historical writing can isolate itself from such pervasive influences. In many different times and cultures, moreover, women's primary role as providers of 'care and cures' – and in some views, their 'natural' or divinely ordained role – was taken to be axiomatic. Yet equally persistent features of this history have been demands for stronger control over the craft of medicine (in whatever form it was practised), and the exclusion of those who were deemed to be 'outsiders'. Women were certainly consistent targets of these pressures. This 'contest' has waxed and waned for almost a thousand years, at least in the Western world, usually accompanied by parades of force by institutions such as universities, churches and states. As a result, theories about medicine and care of the sick have never strayed far from questions of gender, 'sexual difference' and the abilities that were believed to be inherent in each sex.

Perhaps as a product of these twin influences, women's contribution to the history of medicine has been substantial. Yet it is equally apparent that this contribution has been erratic: to identify women historians of medicine who were writing during the Renaissance, for example, is even more difficult than for other fields of historical enquiry. One reason is that the meaning of the terms 'medicine' and 'nursing' profoundly changed since the Middle Ages. What we might understand by 'medicine' in the twenty-first century bears little resemblance to its medieval and early modern usages;

indeed the degree of change even across the nineteenth and twentieth centuries makes direct comparisons risky. 'Nursing' poses equivalent semantic difficulties. Comparing the roles and responsibilities of medieval women in holy orders with those of a woman emerging from the nineteenth-century's Nightingale 'revolution' can illustrate the diversity of forms that this profession has assumed. The pervasive image of women who were called 'nurses' because of their ability to feed the young, whether paid or unpaid, illustrates how closely the term has been associated with 'womanliness'.

Spiritual beginnings

Nonetheless, as many current commentators acknowledge, medical practice in the **Middle Ages** was largely dominated by women. Furthermore, in the vast majority of cases, medieval practitioners performed the dual roles of doctor and nurse. Hildegard of Bingen, the twelfth-century Benedictine abbess of the Rhineland, was one of the best-known medieval practitioners and her writings clearly portray the combined nature of these roles. Historical writing likewise changed a great deal over these centuries, and what we find in the earliest of women's medical writings is an attitude which perceived the past not as something external to be sought out in special repositories of information, but rather as something internal, intrinsic to everyday life and fundamental to the practice of medicine. Hildegard typified this attitude. Like other medical writings of the time, Hildegard's major medical work *Causae et Curae* (c.1158) drew heavily upon historical knowledge. Equally, ancient traditions of practice were the foundation of the work by the renowned woman practitioner and author Trotula from eleventh-century Salerno. The longevity of such notions can further be seen through Elizabeth Grey, Countess of Kent's *A Choice Manuall* (1655) in which her 'rare and select secrets in physick and chirurgery' were valued precisely because of their antiquity. Invention and discovery held no great claims to worth in this world-view; rather it was a practice's historic value that was esteemed by practitioners across many centuries.

Calling upon the authority of the past could fulfil different functions, however. Fifteenth-century Europe gave rise to a variety of legislative mechanisms that attempted to confine the legal practice of 'physick' to men. During the same period we find some rare examples of women celebrating the works and reputations of earlier female practitioners, defending their contemporary practice. While it is commonly accepted that such early proscriptions had little impact on the healing practices of most women, some women were prosecuted and an elite group of medical men began to form, **Christine de Pizan's** father among them. Nonetheless Pizan's **defence of women**, *The Book of the City of Ladies* (1405), set out to remind its readers of the ancient roots of women's many gifts and skills as manifested in the goddesses and women of times past.

Pizan's work highlights a further theme running through women's writings on women's role in the history of healing. Women had abilities in medicine, as Hildegard embodied in an earlier century, because this had been given to women by god – or more accurately, by his mother. Pizan revealed the source of the unparalleled medical skills possessed by Florence of Rome, for instance: on falling asleep Florence encountered an apparition of the Virgin Mary, who directed her to a particular plant in the garden, after which she became famous 'everywhere in the world' for her infallible cures. The influential role that Mary played in the history of Christian Europe is widely recognised. Alongside the increasing ubiquity of images such as the Pietà, the association between Mary and ministering to the ill and inflicted became deep-seated. Her special relationship with women completed the chain that linked women, healing and Christian duty. Thus Florence's visitation was merely one example of the myriad women whose medical skills were attributed to Mary. Nevertheless, Florence's work was not confined to the mere curing of bodies, for through her skill she cured souls and thus ensured the spiritual health of her patients as well.

This connection between women's work in the curing of bodies and souls has an astonishing longevity and remains influential right up to the present. Lives of saints are acknowledged as one of the most influential literary genres in the medieval period, and the healing power of female saints was equally well recognised. In the fifteenth century St Catherine of Genoa, the creator of the 'modern' hospital, following her mystic conversion dedicated her life to God and to healing the sick. St Catherine wrote numerous reflections on her life and work, which were published after her death in the mid-sixteenth century. Perhaps the spiritual status of these women and their medical work made them easier for later historians to identify. Whatever the reason, when there was a general flourishing of women's historical work during the nineteenth century, writers such Catherine Thérèse Woillez returned to the medical powers of medieval female divines in works such as *Les Médecins Moralistes* (1862).

But the connections between women's spiritual lives and their work in caring and curing went beyond the lives and works of the saints – important though they continued to be as models for later women. Even after women religious lost their authority over providing health care, making clinical decisions and running hospitals, we find many women writing about other women whose medical work was informed by their spiritual beliefs. Indeed, the notion of a 'calling' forms a recurrent theme in the way that women have presented their medical and nursing work. This sub-genre of women's medical writings, born of the nineteenth century and prominent throughout the twentieth, spans the works of medical missionaries such as Mabel Pantin's autobiographical *Flashlights on Chinese Life* (1926) and *Sister Dora* (1880), Dorothy Clark Wilson's biography of Ida Scudder, *Dr Ida* (1959), as well as more general medical texts. In all such works the themes of medicine, religion and sacrifice structure the form.

The feminine practice of medicine

Despite the fact that strictures against women's practice of medicine became increasingly common from the seventeenth century, they were slow to enjoy success, largely because of the ubiquity of female practitioners and indeed the widespread lack of alternatives. This was perhaps nowhere so noticeable in women's writings as in the particular form known as the 'receipt' (or recipe) book. Among the earliest extant examples of this genre in the Wellcome Library, London, are those by Anne de Croy (1535) and Elisabethe von Gradnekh (1544). Consisting of compilations of received medical treatments and cures, hundreds of these manuscripts have survived and share much, at least in form and intent, with the medicinal writings of Hildegard. The seventeenth century saw a flowering of this form of women's writing, identifying and detailing the use of various herbs and medications. Jane Jackson, for example, produced her *Very Shorte and Compendious Methode of Phisicke and Chirurgery* in 1642. Katherine, Countess of Chesterfield, produced hers a few years earlier (1635), while Elizabeth Jacob and her fellow compilers continued to add to their

Physicall and Chyrurgicall Receipts for well over 30 years (c.1654–1685). Generally categorised as 'domestic medicine' this sub-genre by women continued to thrive throughout the eighteenth century right across Europe, slowly diminishing to a trickle by the late nineteenth century.

Nonetheless, developing philosophical notions of the seventeenth century promoted the role of 'scientific' observation over 'received wisdom'. Consequently, it might be argued, influential sectors of male medicine turned away from history during this period in favour of experiment and observation, convinced that the past had nothing to offer and that knowledge about the world had to be made anew. In medicine, this created new imperatives to 'view' the patient, simultaneously undermining notions about ancient wisdom which informed the medical world-view of the receipt books. One field of medical practice in which these competing ideas were played out was midwifery. In such a period of ideological conflict, these works produced by women tended towards a more 'public' role than that envisaged for the receipt books, promoting a form of professionalism among midwives while subliminally reinforcing the right of women to this form of medical practice.

Louise Bourgeois' *Observations Diverses sur les Stérilité, Perte de Fruit, Foecondité, Accouchemens, et Maladies des Femmes et Enfants Nouveaux* (1609) on the role and practice of midwives may well be the best-known early example of the genre, not least as a consequence of her own standing as the midwife to Marie de Medici, and thus responsible for birthing Louis XIII. Her marriage to a surgeon gave her access to 'professional' medical knowledge widely denied to women. One impetus for such works, however, was the new interest being shown by male experimentalists during the seventeenth century in the physiology of maternity and the 'diseases of women'. Consequently, other women produced similar works. English midwife Jane Sharp followed Bourgeois' lead in her *Midwives Book* (1671) which interpreted 'midwifery' to encompass a wider notion of responsibilities than the mere delivery of babies. Justine Siegemund's *Die Konigl. Preussische und Chur-Brandenb* (1690) took to task male obstetrical practices. Sarah Stone's *Complete Practice of Midwifery* (1737), on the other hand, inscribed on the frontispiece her unambiguous belief in the value of women's role. The work was, she pointed out,

> interspersed with many necessary cautions and useful instructions, proper to be observed in the most dangerous and critical exigencies, as well when the delivery is difficult in its own nature, as when it becomes so by the rashness or ignorance of unexperienc'd [*sic*] pretenders. Recommended to all female practitioners in an art so important to the lives and well being of the sex.

As the eighteenth century unfolded and the notion of the 'male-midwife' became more firmly entrenched, women's voices on obstetrical matters started to be drowned out by the clamour of enthusiastic men. Nevertheless the eminence attained by Louise Bourgeois a century before could still be had, despite these new pressures on women's practice. Another Frenchwoman, Marie Anne Boivin produced several publications dealing with a variety of uterine pathologies (*Nouveau Traité sur les Hémorragies de l'Utérus* 1818 and *Traité Pratique des Maladies de l'Utérus et de Ses Annexes* 1833). Her *Observations et Expériences sur le Développement Naturel et Artificiel des Maladies Turberculeuses* (1825) on tuberculosis gives an idea of how far from simple 'delivery' Mme Boivin understood the work of midwives to be. On the other side of the Atlantic, Martha Ballard the Maine midwife, so brilliantly introduced to us by Laurel Thatcher Ulrich's sensitive analysis of her diaries *A Midwife's Tale* (1990), illustrated the pivotal role played by such women in the eighteenth and nineteenth centuries, but equally importantly the rich historical value gained from looking into the lives of women healers from the past.

The professionalisation of medicine

The philosophical and intellectual shift of the Enlightenment had profound ramifications for women's work in health and healing beyond midwifery. As recent scholarship has suggested, the Enlightenment solidified notions of a public/private dichotomy in spatial and intellectual conceptions of the world, and then assigned them gender-specific qualities and prerequisites. As one consequence, women's (public) healing roles were usurped and then transformed into systematised (private) knowledge. Women continued to practise in private domestic spaces, but here too their legitimacy was diminished and their skills denigrated as the work of 'empirics' or quacks. Consequently, eighteenth-century examples of women's writing specifically on the history of health and medicine are few. This seems to go against the grain of a general increase in women's writing during this century. More in line with that trend, however, are the allusions that we can find to this theme in fiction. In the midst of the 'Age of Reason', these works tended to recall an earlier ideal of women as the ultimate health-care providers for families and communities. Sarah Scott's **utopian** vision, *Millenium Hall* (1762), shared elements of Pizan's work of four centuries earlier, not least in her fictional depiction of women caring for the ill and infirm, and their 'natural' abilities in these matters. 'Moralising' novels, as this genre is sometimes known, could therefore have a subversive edge: while seemingly depicting moral women doing good works, its usurpation of that ever-increasingly male prerogative of medicine subtly questioned social hierarchies. Fiction remained an important form for women's critique of medical developments. From Sophia Lee's *The Recess; or, A Tale of Other Times* (1785), an historical depiction of insanity as the outcome of woman's subjection, through George Eliot's nineteenth-century man of medicine in *Middlemarch* (1871) as a combination of pride and pathos, to Eleanor Dark's woman doctor tormented by male professional jealousies and physical desire in *Slow Dawning* (1932), novelists have woven together the historically changing but interrelated roles of gender and medicine.

Among those who wrote of the history of medicine during the nineteenth century were the first generation of university-trained and professionally accepted medical women. America's first locally trained and licensed medical women, Elizabeth and Emily Blackwell, turned early to historical writing with *Medicine as a Profession for Women* (1860). For these two women, closely linked with the moral and political reform movements of nineteenth-century America, the history of medicine was an important piece of evidence in their overall argument for opening the profession to women. Looking to history, it was clear to them that male physicians had neglected their responsibilities in educating women about the domestic applications of scientific knowledge, thus it was up to other women to do so.

But for the Blackwells as for many subsequent women, there was another overriding reason for turning to history: medical history was about 'rediscovering' the lost world of medicine of women's making. The 'naturalness' of women's roles in medicine was legitimised by histories of 'traditional' women's medical work. These histories turned common teleological accounts of medical history upside down. The French physician, Mélanie Lipinska took a wide view, looking for evidence of women's medical practice since antiquity in her *Histoire des Femmes Médecins depuis l'Antiquité jusqu'à Nos Jours* (1900). In the same vein US physician **Kate Hurd-Mead**'s *History of Women from the Earliest Times to the Beginning of the Nineteenth Century* (1938) found in the broad sweep of history a political buttress for women's place in medicine.

Similar lessons were also sought closer to home, often in the form of autobiography. The American practitioner Harriet Hunt failed in her attempts to gain admission to a recognised medical college, and was thus compelled to accept an apprenticeship. While she subsequently enjoyed a successful medical career, she nonetheless shaped her autobiography *Glances and Glimpses* (1856) in the form of a political tool, wielded in support for women's rights to a university education. A pioneer medical women in Britain, Sophia Jex-Blake offered her own history in *Medical Women: A Thesis and a History* (1886) as evidence for the 'rightness' of winning the 'women's struggle'. Elizabeth Blackwell too turned to autobiography as a means of addressing and shaping public opinion over the 'woman doctor question' (1895). Elizabeth Garrett Anderson chose to pursue the same objective via a new and different medium: her history appeared in the form of a journal article 'The History of a Movement' in the *Fortnightly Review* (1893). Many women physicians during the twentieth century kept faith with this tradition by penning their autobiographies (Sirridge 1996).

Nursing histories

As part of the 'women's emancipation' movement, the new field of the 'history of nursing' emerged in the late nineteenth century. And for nursing history too, linking current practice into longer 'female traditions' was important. Of the most successful of these early texts were those of Nutting and Dock's *A History of Nursing* (1907–1912), Minnie Goodnow's *Outlines of Nursing History* (1916) and Dock and Stewart's *A Short History of Nursing* (1920). Through their histories of nursing 'from earliest times' to the present, these writers linked into the practitioner-historian tradition. A little later, British writer Lucy R Seymer took an equivalently long view, incorporating the work of women healers from the medieval and early modern period through to the scientific reforms of the nineteenth century in her *A General History of Nursing* (1932). Bonnie and Vern Bullough's *The Emergence of Modern Nursing* (1964) while sharing some of these features (such as locating the origins of nursing in the prehistoric world) might nevertheless also be seen as heralding a new tradition: a critical attitude to the ramifications of nursing philosophies on women's work.

Nineteenth-century women were also active in documenting the work of significant nurses. Among the earliest of this genre was Mary Gardner Holland's celebration of the 'noble women' who had served their nation during the Civil War, *Our Army Nurses* (1895). The early connections between war and nursing may seem obvious, with Florence Nightingale and the Crimean conflict naturally featuring in representations of the profession's *raison d'être*. Late nineteenth-century and early twentieth-century nursing histories also focused on connections with the patriotic, nationalist and imperial politics of the day, in work such as Constance Wakeford's *The Wounded*

Soldiers' Friends (1917) on Nightingale, Barton and others or Elizabeth Sanderson Haldane's *The British Nurse in War and Peace* (1923). General histories of nurses almost inevitably contained a chapter or more on this theme. Nonetheless, this close identification between nursing and that most masculine arena, the battlefield, had overtones beyond that of simply bolstering nurses' professional status. As Margaret Higonnet's *Nurses at the Front* (2001) demonstrated, nurses' accounts of their wartime experiences were not always warmly received. Such a chequered response, particularly in a genre that claimed a 'timeless' appeal, suggests that as a sub-genre, nurses' war histories had a rather different tenor from the more acceptable tales of men's military adventures.

Women's emergence as professional historians during the twentieth century saw medical histories undertaken increasingly by medical/nursing 'outsiders' – particularly since the 1950s. In that time not only have the range and quantity of these writings vastly increased, but their style and content have changed significantly. Yet one constant has been writing that celebrated the lives and work of 'greats' and 'pioneers'. Throughout these tales, the prevailing indignation at perceived gender discrimination found an outlet in narratives about women's valour in the face of adversity. In doing so, these 'compensatory' works helped to shape and re-shape attitudes to these professions. As demands for the political rights and the franchise metamorphosed into campaigns for equal pay, contraception and on into the 'second wave', these forms of history remained popular. **Eileen Power** introduced the medical women of her period to the Royal Society of Medicine in 1921. E Moberley Bell's *Storming the Citadel* (1953) located her medical women as important actors in breaking down barriers to women's full participation in society and the professions. Carole Lopate's *Women in Medicine* (1968) positioned this form of historical research as an important scholarly field while Carlotta Hacker identified Canadian women as a part of this development in *The Indomitable Lady Doctor* (1974). More recently still, Carol Dyhouse's article 'Driving Ambition: Women in Pursuit of a Medical Education' (1998) mapped a convincing explanation for the enduring strength of a sense of 'calling' or 'mission' in women's self-representation of their medical work and ambitions.

The impact of feminism

The 1970s, however, stood as a crucial decade for women's medical and nursing history. One pivotal point around which the nursing history genre has revolved was the mid-nineteenth century development of formal 'nurse training' and the 'rise' of the nursing profession. This has long been used as the measure against which nurses were judged: pre-nurse training was exemplified by Dickens' 'Sairy Gamp' and the legions of unkempt and 'dangerous' women, who 'interfered' in medical work. The rise of nursing was believed to stem from the introduction of nurse training by Nightingale – a rise in public estimation, in the success of medical treatment, and as a professional niche for women. For many nursing insiders who wrote about the history of their profession at this time, an obvious subtext to 'the introduction' of nurse training was 'the emergence of real nursing'.

Beverley Kingston captured the essence of a new 'standard' story being written by women in the history of nursing: a rise from the status of a slattern, the 'ubiquitous Sarah Gamp', to the professional, respectable, ladylike, and above all, deferential health-giver (1975: 81, 83). This perspective made much of the quintessential second-wave concern that Nightingale nursing was 'trapped' within notions of 'lady-like' behaviour and genteel expectations. Such views encapsulated an interpretative dilemma. This created a tension between a need to chart progress within this most female of jobs, by identifying its increasingly scientific basis and its growing professionalism, while also finding it hard to reconcile a progressivist epistemology with awareness of the exploitative effects on these women as workers. This doubled vision of 'good for patients' but 'bad for women' coalesced with the prevailing politics in which women's health featured strongly, leaving many feminist historians uncertain over how to deal with the history of nursing. The conflict between 'woman-as-victim' and 'woman-as-change agent' left little space to manoeuvre.

Yet these theoretical constructions have been re-examined in their turn. Nursing historians in the last years of the twentieth century revisited many of these arguments in order to re-theorise the role of women in history. Eva Gamarnikow in her article 'Nurse or Woman' (1991) argued the need for a closer awareness of the specificities of time and place to understand the revolutionary potential that Nightingale offered to female contemporaries. Kathryn McPherson's *Bedside Matters* (1996) suggested that Canadian nurses of the early twentieth century represented a privileged group in terms of their education levels and professional opportunities. In 1998 Alison Bashford asked new questions about gender, embodiment and power through an analysis of nineteenth-century British nursing in her *Purity and Pollution* (1998).

Women's medical history writing in the 1970s equally reflected the dramatic shift in women's politics. Many medical histories produced in this decade set out to challenge their predecessors' attitudes to medicine's 'progress' and to medical practitioners, which had been, if not positively hagiographic, quite benign. Part of second-wave feminism – with its manifesto for changing normative gender roles – was a new critical vision brought to bear on a profession perceived as 'patriarchal' and necessarily damaging to women. The path-breaking work by Barbara Ehrenreich and Deirdre English, *Witches, Midwives and Nurses* (1973), detailed how women had been forcibly evicted from their historical place in the practice of medicine, and even burned as witches for this offence. Regina Morantz wrote in her article 'The Lady and her Physician' (1974) on the troubled history of women patients and their doctors, and Linda Gordon's work *Women's Bodies, Women's Rights* (1977) focused on the historical interrelationship between birth control and politics.

A significant new character to appear within the history of medicine towards the end of the twentieth century was 'the patient'. As part of the more general 'history from below' movement which shifted the historians' 'gaze' from the 'powerful to the powerless', the doubled impact of seeing the patient as powerless and as woman proved an especially potent mixture for women historians, as Mary Poovey's 'Scenes of an Indelicate Character' (1986) clearly showed. Yet women had themselves written as patients for hundreds of years. Fanny Burney, a 'lettered woman' of considerable reputation, wrote a harrowing account of her pre-anaesthetic mastectomy in her letters of 1811 (Hemlow 1975). Virginia Woolf's *On Being Ill* (1930) poignantly depicted the subjective experience of chronic illness just over a decade before her death. More recently, illness memoirs have developed as a sub-genre in their own right, and contributions such as Rose Kushner's personal history *Breast Cancer* (1975) have challenged and ultimately changed medical policy and practice. In one landmark publication, Susan Sontag's *Illness as Metaphor* (1979) drew together two women's writing traditions, linking the history of her experience of illness to that wider women's literary world to produce an influential work analysing the role of illness metaphors.

Medicine and motherhood

This new focus found particularly fertile ground in the history of women as mothers and the 'medicalisation' of maternity. Ann Oakley's (1984) phrase 'the captured womb' perhaps summed up the spirit of the decade. Historians such as Rima Apple's *Mothers and Medicine* (1987) presented a new vision of women's experience with scientific medicine, questioning its claims of progress, and criticising especially the development of the paternalist male-physician model. These works also challenged the notion of 'timelessness' which had long surrounded the topic of motherhood. For Oakley, motherhood was a 'myth'; rather than being an eternal truth about women and a 'natural' attribute of femininity, it was a construction that was potentially repressive (1984: 187). From there developed the notion that all aspects of femininity were products of an historical context, and that attitudes towards maternity reflected specific times and places, as Judith Walzer Leavitt's *Brought to Bed* (1986) illustrated. Barbara Brookes' *Abortion in England* (1988) gave an historical perspective to a fraught and vicious policy debate, thereby showing how beliefs about abortion were influenced by these same historical forces. Valerie Fildes' *Bottles and Babies* (1985) took another 'fixed' physiological verity, breast feeding, and gave it historical fluidity. Within this new critique, women sought to establish their historical place at the centre of medical practice.

Carroll Smith-Rosenberg's *Disorderly Conduct* (1985) likewise explored the question of abortion from an historical perspective: in this case, the efforts of the American Medical Association (AMA) to criminalise abortion during the nineteenth century. Her work represents an illuminating example of yet another change occurring in women's historical writing during this period. Indeed, the application of psychoanalytic theories to historical interpretation at this time may have represented one of the most potent interweavings of medical and historiographical traditions within women's writing. The new interpretive framework of psychoanalytic approaches offered an opportunity to understand past *motives*: for historians of any bent, this has been a difficult task, and for feminist historians, a challenge of particular import. While the work of Freud and others was founded on ways to define and identify sources of sexual difference, for feminist historians the analytical potential of such approaches was the 'discovery' of those 'embedded' motives that underpinned the social and cultural manifestations of discrimination.

Intersections among motherhood, medicine and history remained important issues for women writing medical history in the 1990s and into the twenty-first century. Pronatalism, scientific hospitals and the increasingly specialised nature of medical practice have all been analysed through the lens of motherhood by women writers during these years. Hilary Marland's *The Art of Midwifery* (1993) turned back to the midwives of early modern Europe to do so, while Ornella Moscucci's *The Science of Woman* (1990) traced intricate threads in the development of gynaecology as a male-dominated profession. Barbara Duden examined how 'the modern fetus and woman have shaped each other' in *Disembodying Women* (1993: 5), while Naomi Pfeffer's *The Stork and the Syringe* (1993) extended the notion of the medicalisation of maternity to the laboratory and the test tube. Helen King's *Hippocrates' Woman* (1998) and Rebecca Flemming's *Medicine and the Making of Roman Women* (2000) were among those to re-imagine and reinterpret the Ancient world as a gendered medical landscape.

One theme often taken to be a distinguishing characteristic of the history of health, and particularly the history of medicine, has been intimately connected with its professional practice. Conceptualised by Gert Brieger as 'bio-history', it involves the historical investigation of disease, epidemiology and the impact of biology on history (1993: 24–44). This historiography was driven by a combination of antiquarianism and the desire to track 'progress', but another impetus was its potential to contribute to medical knowledge, as distinct from historical knowledge. Women's works in this field include the influential studies of pellagra by Daphne Roe, *A Plague of Corn* (1973), and cholera by Margaret Pelling, *Cholera, Fever and English Medicine* (1978). More recently Margaret Humphrey's *Yellow Fever and the South* (1992) and Maryinez Lyons' *The Colonial Disease* (1992) on sleeping sickness have illustrated the intimate connections between imperialism, medicine and policy. Lucinda McCray Beier's *Sufferers and Healers* (1987) and Sheila M Rothman's *Living in the Shadow of Death* (1994) on tuberculosis have helped to shift the focus from the idea of disease as understood by the practitioner to the experiences and perceptions of the patient. As a final refinement, women historians such as Gianna Pomata, *Contracting a Cure* (1998), and Mary Spongberg, *Feminizing Venereal Disease* (1997), have demonstrated how diseases themselves were accorded gendered characteristics, thus making significant changes to the ways in which we imagine and write about health and illness in the past.

Christine de Pizan's *City of Ladies* would look different if it had had a different architect; in the same way others might envision a different city of women who undertook to write medical and nursing histories. I offer this as a foundation perhaps, which others may wish to build on or reconceptualise. However, one distinct pattern that I see in these writings involved a search for the 'forgotten' medical women of the past, and an attempt to re-incorporate them within the institutions of medicine and nursing for the sake of both the past, and the present. This quest linked into works that have challenged the epistemological claims of medicine's status as 'value-free' and 'scientific', and alternatively charted its masculinist preconceptions and the ways these have affected women and medical practice. From such a perspective, we see not least that women's explorations of history have long questioned medicine's methodologies and philosophies of practice. Second-wave feminist critiques of the 1970s were important in setting out new ways for women to write about health and medicine. This essay reminds us, though, that these innovations neither began nor ended then. Cultural historians in the 1990s underlined the importance of gendered bodies, and reminded us that objectifying and thus controlling them has always had political ramifications. Developments within the world of history writing have therefore had profound influences on the ways in which women wrote histories of nursing and medicine. Yet as historians turn their attention from the practitioner to the recipient of treatment, from the objectified body to the body as subject, the practices of medicine and nursing have themselves been affected by these critiques.

Louella McCarthy

References

Anderson 1893; Brieger 1993; Dyhouse 1998; Gamarnikow 1991; Hemlow 1975; Kingston 1975; Morantz 1974; Oakley 1984; Poovey 1986; Rowland 1981; Sirridge 1996.

Related essays

Catalogs; Defences; Body & Sexuality; Middle Ages; Religion; Utopian.

O

Oral traditions

Some scholars of oral traditions might think it a little odd to include an essay on this topic in a companion to women's historical writing. This is because some of the most established scholarship in the field is premised on the belief that oral traditions ought to be defined in contra-distinction to writing. It is often argued that what is most important in the study of oral traditions is to account for oralness on its own terms, with little or no reference to literacy. (For summaries of these types of debates, see Vansina 1965; Ong 1982; Finnegan 1988.) Yet, while scholars differ in their analyses about the nature of the relationship between literacy and oracy, most agree that a distinguishing feature of oral traditions is that, unlike writing, they leave no tangible trace. 'When an oft-told oral story is not actually being told, all that exists of it is the potential in certain human beings to tell it,' observes Walter Ong in his *Orality and Literacy: The Technologizing of the Word* (1982: 11). Yet, History (with a capital H) requires, indeed depends upon, literacy, both in terms of its sources and its form. This does not necessarily mean, however, that oral traditions have had no place in History. Indeed, as Ong argues, literacy and the literary professions like History did not completely eschew oracy, despite the history profession's own claims to the contrary from time to time. 'But in all the wonderful worlds that writing opens,' Ong observes, 'the spoken word still resides and lives' (1982: 8). With this in mind, the aim of this essay is to chart the changing place and function of women's oral traditions within, and in relation to, the literary world of History.

The relationship between women's oral traditions and women's historical production, particularly historical writing, can be approached from (at least) two interrelated perspectives. Firstly, women's oral traditions can themselves be examined as a form of historical production and a means for transmitting historical information among women. Secondly, one needs to examine the ways in which they have been and continue to be used as a source for histories produced by women and as a subject for women historians. But it is also worth noting that the significance of oral traditions to a study of women's historical writing is not simply as an alternative form of history or as a critical source for it. The 'oral' also occupies a prominent place in almost all analyses that seek to explain women's exclusion from the history profession. Most include recourse to the commonplace association between women (or femaleness/femininity) and gossip, implying that women's love of what is often deemed to be frivolous or superficial talk made them supposedly unsuitable for such a literary profession.

Women's oral traditions as a form of women's historical production

Over the last 30 years a large, interdisciplinary scholarship on women's oral culture has been produced, particularly in the fields of history, literary studies and psychoanalysis. Although diverse in a disciplinary sense much of the work is united through having been motivated by the feminist politics of the second half of the twentieth century. In general terms it can be characterised as a reclamation and a celebration of women's particular and peculiar ways of making sense of their world, in which oracy plays a significant role. This scholarship reinforced, and to some degree reified, the notion that women's worlds are constituted more by talk than text.

Within this broad project to reclaim women's past oral culture a type of feminist folklore study emerged, exemplified by the work of writers such as Marina Warner (1994) and Angela Carter (1990). In different ways they each turned to the fairy tale, casting it as the feminine oral genre *par excellence*. Other oral genres associated with women were also examined such as nursery rhymes, tales, riddles and songs. Along with an analysis of specific genres or narrative styles the sites of women's oral culture were critically examined. For instance, spinning rooms were recast as places of cultural as well as economic production. Much was made of the double meaning of phrases such as 'spinning a tale', 'weaving a story', or 'yarning'.

The historical significance of women's oral traditions and specific oral narratives was addressed, sometimes explicitly but mostly obliquely. To take one example, feminist folklorists often suggested that fairy stories contained historical details that offered their modern-day readers significant insights into the lives of women in the past, dealing as they often did with the themes of marriage, work and family. Although it is worth noting that Marina Warner has characterised them as 'rebarbative as historical documents' (1994: xix). Yet, the question about whether they were also a form of historical production that women engaged in is less common in this scholarship. That these women's oral narratives belonging to times past were not interpreted in the late twentieth century as a form of women's historical production is not surprising. At the most basic level the obvious mythical and fabulous qualities of the fairy tale and similar oral genres made it difficult to define them as history, particularly at a time when history prided itself on having banished those qualities from its own practice. Given that other-worldliness was the fairy tale's leitmotif and real-worldliness history's, many if not most of the narratives or genres studied by feminist folklorists were almost automatically disqualified as acceptable historical narratives. This is not to suggest that feminist scholars blindly accepted the traditional (masculine) definition of history in their analysis of women's oral traditions. Rather, it is to underscore the fact that this feminist folklore project gained much of its theoretical and political strength from conceptualising women's oral traditions not as history but rather as a type of 'anti-history'.

It was not only the generic form or the content of women's oral traditions that helped to define them as anti-history. They were also conceptualised in these terms through reference to their own history. The conventional argument proffered by feminist scholars was that oral traditions, especially those of women, had been excluded from history as it became increasingly professionalised, institutionalised and gendered from the eighteenth century onwards. History, as a literary profession that valued text highly both as source and as medium, denigrated the oral, and, as perhaps one might expect of a gendered profession dominated by men, it particularly derided women's talk. The reclamation of women's oral culture and traditions, which gained ground in the 1970s and 1980s, is embedded in a feminist orthodoxy that explained the devaluation of all things female in terms of the concomitant elevation of men. Thus, having explained the fate of women's oral traditions in these broad terms, the typical response was not to seek to have those hitherto excluded traditions re-admitted into the realm of history, but rather to celebrate the very qualities that had kept them outside the limited masculine world that professional history had increasingly become. For this generation of feminist scholars, women's oral traditions were not celebrated as a hitherto unacknowledged form of historical production, but rather as History's other.

Much has changed since then, in both historical and feminist praxis. History is no longer tied to its positivist and scientific moorings, but is rather conceived primarily as a system of meaning about the past, rather than say a method for reconstructing the past in the present. Hence history now often embraces the very qualities – narrative, myth, imagination – that had once made the oral tales women spun unacceptable to it. An emphasis on the social function of telling stories about the past in the present allows one to pursue a type of analysis that conceives of women's oral traditions as a form of history, overcoming some of the hurdles, such as periodicity or change over time, upon which it once would have foundered. Applying this expanded definition of history, the question becomes: Do fairy tales, gossip or various other forms of women's speech that draw upon the past perform the same types of social functions as more conventional historical narratives? To this question, a tentative yes might be proffered. The argument would be that within the storehouse of women's oral traditions can be found many examples of modes of storytelling that performed the function of representing the past in the present in order for tellers and listeners alike to make sense of their lived experience and to imagine the future. Those stories, it might be argued, contributed to giving a group of people a sense of collective identity grounded in shared past experience and in a shared stock of stories about it. To this might be added that they served the function of instructing the young and of transmitting historical information from one generation to the next. From this position, past and present oral traditions belonging to women, once celebrated by twentieth-century feminist scholars as a type of anti-history, might now be feted as an example of women's historical production, and moreover one might argue that they are suggestive of a continuous tradition pre-dating women's entry into more institutionalised forms of history.

While the scholarship on women's past oral traditions in the 'West' has, by and large, paid relatively little attention to the question of whether or not they constitute a distinct form of historical production, this same criticism certainly cannot be levelled at the scholarship on oral traditions in the 'non-West'. Beginning with Jan Vansina's introductory text *Oral Tradition: A Study in Historical Methodology* (1961), the focus in this scholarship on non-Western societies was squarely on the explicitly historical form and function of the oral traditions that came from predominantly oral societies outside Europe. While highly theoretical, preoccupied with questions about what constitutes an oral tradition, this scholarship has significant limitations. The early scholarship especially, although concerned with what an oral tradition is, does not directly engage with the question of what history is, or how historical consciousness might be conceptualised, theorised and historicised. The 'history' element in the formulation of oral traditions-as-history is taken as self-evident and is thus used somewhat imprecisely. Scholars working in this field, particularly in its early phase, tended to think about history as a universal concept. The failure to grapple with history's history is partly a product of this field being dominated by anthropologists and partly because it is concerned with seeking to understand the historical traditions of traditional oral societies outside (indeed prior to coming into contact with) European forms of historical consciousness. But this raises the question, now commonly posed by postcolonial theorists, about whether or not history is fundamentally a European construct and thus not easily applicable to non-European contexts. Another major limitation of the scholarship, particularly for our purposes, is that it does not address gender in any sustained way, often simply noting in passing that men tended to perform the public role of historian in traditional societies more than women; or that particular oral genres belonged to women, although these were invariably less prestigious than those performed publicly by men.

Turning for a moment to the matter about oral traditions as a subject of women's historical production it is worth noting that the collection of oral traditions has long been an acceptable female historical pursuit. This has been the case in the past and in more recent times. As Joan Thirsk points out in her entry on women local and family historians in the *Oxford Companion to Local and Family Historians* (1996), the preservation of local men's and women's folk cultures including oral traditions in Europe and Britain particularly in the seventeenth and eighteenth centuries was an activity in which women often engaged. One example is Sarah Sophia Banks, sister of the acclaimed naturalist Joseph Banks, who, while her brother was at the centre of a vast global collecting enterprise incorporating the newly 'discovered' and colonised lands of the European empire, compiled 'glossaries of the local dialects of their ancestral seat' (Spongberg 2002: 79). This antiquarian activity was in keeping with the typically localised nature of women's historical production. Similarly, women participated in a comparable type of work within professional anthropology, engaged either independently or with their husbands in the collection of (threatened) oral traditions in societies undergoing rapid change due to colonisation in the nineteenth and twentieth centuries.

While the feminist scholarship on oral traditions and the anthropological scholarship on oral traditions both provide useful empirical and theoretical material for understanding oral traditions as a form of women's history, neither provides a model for analysing the relationship between women's oral traditions and women's historical production. Such an analysis would require the historicising and theorising of the three key terms in the equation – 'oral traditions', 'women' and 'history' – but more importantly teasing out the nature of the articulation between any or all of them in specific historical contexts. Of critical significance here would be the question of how to assess the influence of history itself, as practice and as discourse, on the oral traditions under consideration. This issue comes even more sharply into focus when one considers how women historians have used women's oral traditions in the production of histories.

Women's oral traditions as a source for women's history

If feminist scholars of women's oral traditions were engaged in the project of writing a history of women's oral cultures from times past, in part to show some type of continuity between women's pasts and women's presents, then what might be called the feminist oral history project, emerging in roughly the same period in the 1970s and 1980s, was concerned with writing history from women's oral testimony. Dissatisfied with conventional historical sources and methods for writing the history of women, some feminist historians at this time embraced oral history and began to record women talking about their very own past experiences. This was partly a response to the perception that written records were biased in favour of men.

Recorded oral history interviews were rich sources for the new women's history being written in that period. To showcase the types of historical production which oral history methods were making possible in the field of women's history, feminist scholarly journals such as *Frontiers* devoted entire editions to the topic, and in turn specialist journals such as *Oral History* produced special issues that focused on women's history. The women's history issue of *Oral History* in 1977 included articles about work, marriage and family, popular topics for feminist historians generally. When *Frontiers: A Journal of Women Studies* published its second Women's Oral History Special Issue in 1983 the focus had shifted since the first had been published over five years earlier in 1977. The articles in this later issue were not historical analyses based on oral sources, but rather analyses of oral history as an historical method for women's history. Initially simply embraced as providing new sources for the writing of women's history, oral history as a practice used by women historians with women informants had become far more theoretically complex in a relatively short time. Some asked whether or not women's oral testimony was evidence for a universal feminine sensibility or consciousness. (For a review of these debates, see Geiger 1990.) As this suggests, from the outset, quite considerable claims were made for oral history and the potential it had for revolutionising women's history. This was not unique to the field of women's history; similar claims were being made in the burgeoning field of social history in the same period.

The gathering of women's oral testimony for the writing of history was perhaps not as novel as some practitioners initially claimed, although, as will be discussed below, it certainly accrued new significance via the feminist politics with which it was so closely associated in the 1970s and 1980s. Bonnie G Smith in *The Gender of History: Men, Women, and Historical Practice* convincingly shows that women historians, prior to the late twentieth century, had drawn upon women's testimony as a source for the his-tories they wrote. She particularly focuses on the emergence of the 'working woman' as a subject for histories written by mainly middle-class women, a process she argues begins in the late nineteenth century. An interest in the 'poor' was not necessarily pioneered by women (as the work of Henry Mayhew demonstrates), but it is clear that this was an area of research that attracted women historians and social scientists and that in their work they displayed a special interest in the women within working-class .communities. As Smith notes:

> From the late nineteenth century on, researchers entered the home and factory to obtain knowledge and to urge working women to speak and write about their lives in the present and about their families' lives as far back as oral traditions could take them. (1998: 75)

As this quote indicates, the activity was aimed at historical preservation and at historical and social science research. Individual women identified by Smith involved in this general project included Clementina Black, Gabrielle Duchene, Marianne Pollack and Rosa Kempf, among others. That it was working-class women whose oral testimony was most keenly sought is worth noting. This interest in working women re-emerges a hundred or so years later when, as already noted, it was a hallmark of the late twentieth-century feminist oral history project. This common subject could constitute a thread that linked women's historical production, in the late nineteenth century and that belonging to the late twentieth.

But it is important to stress that there were considerable differences too. In particular, the nineteenth-century women researchers who gathered the testimony of working-class women do not appear to have made the same types of claims for and about women's oral testimony that accompanied the feminist oral history project a hundred or so years later. For example, within the more recent women's oral history scholarship it was, for a time at least, claimed by some practitioners that oral history with women was a particularly feminist method. Moreover, it was also commonly claimed that the oral testimony provided to historical researchers by women was itself a form of women's history. These claims do not seem to be made in the late nineteenth century. Indeed, Smith seems to suggest that the very opposite was the case. She describes, somewhat dismissively, the histories produced in this period about working women living in poor neighbourhoods as 'ventriloquist narratives', whereby the voices of the subjects of the study were muted by the historians or social scientists who had collected the oral testimony but who authored the study. In contrast, in the late twentieth century, especially in the heady early days of women's oral history, it was consistently claimed that 'ordinary' women, once denied a place in history, were now, through the recording of their oral testimony, able to speak for themselves. However, it did not take long for these quite bald claims about 'speaking her-story' to become increasingly qualified as the nature of the relationship between the interviewer and the interviewee was interrogated and consequently understood in more complex ways. Indeed, the idea of the unmediated voice gave way to considerable angst about the influence of the oral historian on the testimony recorded.

While the women historians and social science researchers collecting women's oral testimony in the late nineteenth century did not appear to entertain the notion that the accounts they were given, or the stories they were told, were themselves a form of history, one might speculate that the working-class women who agreed to give their testimony saw it as an opportunity to make 'history'. The act of telling one's story to a stranger might have been perceived as an occasion for making public their personal, private, unwritten histories and for giving them a more permanent form by being written down. Perhaps the passing visit of the social scientist might have been akin to other intermittent opportunities to tell histories, however quotidian and domestic, such as in the courtroom dock or at the local police station. This extract from a late nineteenth-century portrait of London's Whitechapel area evokes the figure of the woman given the public stand:

> If there is a sight on earth prone to move a man to wrath, it is an East End woman in the witness box. The female witness has not changed her character since the days of the famous Mrs Cluppins; she still enters into a dissertation on her domestic affairs, and informs the court about the decease of her late beloved, the illness of her last baby, and the wickedness of people in general. It is impossible to make her stick to business . . . (Tebbutt 1995: 39)

The domestic details that the woman witness speaks about in public are here contrasted with 'business' and thus the description reiterates a commonplace view that women talk mainly about personal, intimate, familial details. But it also underscores the reality that women were the keepers of family and community histories, and that their oral traditions were the means they used to preserve and communicate this knowledge. The obvious implication here is that these diminutive histories held in memory by women have only survived as historical trace when they have had occasion to be scripted. This reinforces what is now widely acknowledged among historians: that the revered archival documentary trace often began life as mere babble.

It is sometimes claimed in the women's oral history literature of the late twentieth century that the emergence of oral history as a critical historical method within women's history represented the continuation, or at least the renaissance of, women's oral traditions from times past. This narrative, in which contemporary women's oral history is seamlessly sewn onto a supposedly pre-existing women's oral tradition, while undoubtedly compelling, is probably more imagined than real and, moreover, masks more than it reveals. A more productive mode of analysis is to pose the question about how women's changing role in professional historical practice and its relationship to a broader feminist politics might have provided the conditions of possibility for the creation of completely new oral traditions belonging to, if not to all, then certainly some, women. A genre worth contemplating from this perspective is the originally orally narrated life story translated into text and published for a wide readership. This genre mushroomed in the 1970s and has continued to retain considerable valency both in the field of women's history and as a form of it.

The oral autobiographical narrative is today a genre most closely associated with poor, oppressed, colonised and predominantly non-literate women. Whether or not it had any origin in earlier forms is an open question. In her article 'Women's life histories: Methods and Content' published in *Signs* (Winter, 1986), Susan Geiger catalogues some published women's life stories that began as oral narratives that pre-date the 1970s, focusing mainly on 'slave narratives'. For instance, from East Africa she cites *Baba of Karo: A Woman of Muslim Hausa* 'recorded by Mary Smith during six weeks of interviews in 1949–50' (p. 340). An even earlier tradition she cites are nineteenth-century published narratives, such as Linda Brent's (Harriet Jacob's) *Incidents in the Life of a Slave Girl*, edited by **Lydia Maria Child**, first published in 1861.

Regardless of whether or not the orally narrated life story has precedents, what is clear is that by the late twentieth century some women's oral life stories had been given new meaning and significance, mainly as a result of the political contexts that produced them and the critical analysis that they have received from history scholars and also in literary studies and other specialist areas. For our purposes, what is probably most significant is that the woman telling her life story, usually with the explicit intention of having it turned into text, almost universally and often extremely self-consciously claims to be engaged in the production of history. Take for example one of the most celebrated of this genre, *I Rigoberto Menchu*, the story of an Indian woman in Guatemala, in which Elisabeth Burgo-Debray introduces Menchu as a 'privileged witness' and suggests that her life story is a form of history-making aimed at changing the 'course of history' (1984: xi, xii). According to Burgo-Debray, Menchu's testimony has the potential to change the course of history because by speaking about the oppression of her people she overturns a previous historical silence and challenges the wilful forgetting on the part of the 'colonial oppressors' (1984: xii). These types of claims and this type of framing is also evident in the many life stories of Australian Aboriginal women that began as oral narratives and that have been published since the 1970s. In many, the autobiographical narrator makes clear that she is 'telling history', and that the audience for her history lesson is both her 'own people' and the wider community.

The oral witness to one's own lived experience has in more recent times accrued yet more credence in highly political contexts where the past is being held to account, particularly in former settler societies such as South Africa and Australia. The various tribunals for historical reparation in countries around the world now provide a public and state-sanctioned forum especially for those who suffered dispossession or colonial or other brutality to orally narrate their experiences, not simply because it is seen as valuable in its own right, but because it is an act of witnessing to collective and hitherto suppressed or denied pasts. However, as Fiona Ross, research on the South African Truth and Reconciliation Council clearly shows, these court-like forums often circumscribe the type of narratives that women can tell and implicitly apply quite strict understandings of proper womanliness when eliciting and interpreting the experiences that individual women make public. A subtle shift can often be detected in the final published testimony whereby, for instance, a political activist who happens to be female is by complex discursive processes transformed into mother and martyr and often in ways that serve to ignore her political activism.

Finally, as alluded to above and as others have noted, women's historical practice has walked hand in hand with feminist politics, at least from the nineteenth century onwards. In turn, feminist politics has deployed history in raising consciousness among women about the causes of their oppression and exploitation and when making a case for legislative and social change. Indeed, if one were unwaveringly committed to finding threads of continuity about the role of oral traditions in women's history between the late nineteenth century and the late twentieth century, then it is in the realm of feminist politics that one might find most satisfaction. In both periods, women talking about their shared history as women has featured strongly. This can obviously be conceived in terms of 'consciousness-raising'. Oral history projects with women in the late twentieth century-period were often conceptualised as a means for developing feminist consciousness among women. A hundred years earlier discussion groups functioned in a similar way, although the emphasis on talking about one's own life was perhaps less valorised than it was later to become. Speaking history was also a crucial tool used by feminist activists to reach out to women, to educate them and to rally their support. The public speech is critical here. In this particular example the relationship between talk and text is reversed. Rather than women without literacy talking their own history, in this case it was literate women who adopted the oral mode, translating their historical tracts, books and pamphlets into speech, or more precisely speeches, in order to reach those many women who did not read and write.

Women's oral traditions, however defined, have been present throughout the history of women's historical production since the Renaissance. Their role has been diverse: to make sense of the past in the present in quite diminutive and domestic ways, to pass historical information from one generation to the next, to educate women about their shared historical experiences across time and place, or as a critical source for histories about women. The development of history as a literary profession dominated by men has meant that the oral mode, perhaps more than other forms of communication among women, has fared badly. But to simply argue that oral traditions constitute a type of anti-history or conversely that they are a superior form of women's history is to over-simplify them and particularly their relationship to institutional historical practice more generally, which itself has played a key role in the shape, form and function of women's oral traditions, at least the ones that it is possible to know about. By focusing on this integral relationship between changing forms of historical practice and changing forms of women's oral traditions is not to suggest however that women's talk *always* exists in relationship to historical discourse. There are many oral traditions, genres, narratives and practices that will forever remain hidden from view, either purposefully secreted by women or lost over time due to their essential ephemeralness.

Maria Nugent

References

Burgo-Debray 1984; Carter 1990; Finnegan 1988; Geiger 1986, 1990; Ong 1982; Ross 2002; Smith 1998; Spongberg 2002; Tebbutt 1995; Thirsk 1996; Vansina 1961/1965; Warner 1994.

Related essays

Feminism; Historical Fiction; Local History; Memoir.

Orientalism

Few words have had their meanings so dramatically transformed within such a short period of time as the term 'Orientalism'. Before the publication of Edward Said's *Orientalism: Western Conceptions of the Orient* in 1978, Orientalism referred to a particular genre of painting as well as the academic study of 'the Orient' – a geographically indeterminate place focusing on the Middle East, particularly Turkey and Egypt, but also ranging through South Asia, sometimes extending as far east as Japan. It was a respectable, scholarly term, albeit suffused with notions of the exotic. Orientalists were mostly men but also included among their ranks erudite women such as the travellers and **archaeologists**/historians Amelia Blandford Edwards, Gertrude Bell and Freya Stark.

Said and Orientalist discourse

After Said's book, however, 'Orientalism' was imbued with negative connotations of European imperial fantasy and domination over the Orient, while Western Orientalists were accused of complicity with the colonial project through their study of the East. Orientalism now referred to the discursive (mis)representations of the Orient – academic, political, commercial, religious, psychological, aesthetic and literary – produced and circulated through Western imperial power or cultural hegemony. But Orientalism involved more than false or negative images of the Orient. It was a process by which the West 'Orientalised' the Orient, actively constructing it in such a way that heterogeneous regions, peoples, religions, cultures and histories were subsumed under the Western-created category of 'Orientals', marked by their difference, exoticism and inferiority to the West. Said argued that Western discourses on the Orient confirmed the West's beliefs about its own difference and cultural superiority, thus facilitating or strengthening domination over the Orient, especially during the age of European colonialism. The fantasy of Orientalism was crucial to Western self-definition. In all statements about the Orient, the West was placed in a position of superiority, mastery and control. Thus in his critique of Orientalism Said posited another monolithic geo-fantasy – 'the West' – which constructed ahistorical representations of the Orient as its political, cultural, social and sexual 'Other'.

In Orientalist discourse, the Orient was depicted as a place of violence, cruelty, corruption and despotism. It was a region of political and cultural stagnation or primitivism, outside the progressive march of historical development. Yet European assessments of the Orient were not always negative, nor were they necessarily in agreement with each other. For instance, the French experience of the Orient differed in small but significant ways from that of the British. Nineteenth-century French discourses of Orientalism, for example, were shot through with ambivalence because certain perceived characteristics of the Orient were sometimes nostalgically idealised by travellers disenchanted with their own societies (Behdad 1994: 13–17). The frenetic pace and mercenary values of modern industrial societies could be disparaged in favour of the sensuality, grace, physicality, slowness of time, generosity and careful maintenance of cultural traditions in the Orient; the seeming sterility of Western scientific knowledge disdained for the 'wisdom of the East'; and the sexual repression of Western society contrasted unfavourably with fantasies of the Orient as a sexual paradise for men. Such discourses portrayed the Orient in a more positive light, seemingly elevating it to a position of cultural superiority. Nevertheless these elegiac jeremiads are identifiable as Orientalist discourses because they are unrelentingly Eurocentric in their focus – the East forms the romanticised rod with which to whip the unsatisfactory West – and because they propagate a homogenising Orientalist fantasy which overlooks modernising processes at work, perpetually imprisoning the vast region of the Orient in representational primitivism.

Gender and Orientalism

From the start, Said's conception of Orientalism was a profoundly gendered one because Orientalism was conflated with Western patriarchy. He argued that Orientalism 'encouraged a peculiarly . . . male conception of the world' because the academic discipline of Orientalism 'was an exclusively male province' and the focus of such studies was the Oriental male (Said 1978/1991: 207). As a gendered discourse Orientalism was crucially implicated in the construction of Western masculinity in contradistinction to the mythical Oriental male: a weak, effeminate, brutish, degenerate, childish, deceitful and irresponsible creature, driven by instincts and emotions rather than reason. The Oriental was akin to a beast, ruled by his own concupiscence, cruelly dominating women through sexual slavery that was epitomised in the harem system. By contrast, the Western male was represented as rational and progressive, moral and modern, disciplined, strong, energetic, just, free and politically and culturally mature. Such qualities justified European colonial rule and American neo-colonial intervention after the Second World War.

To Said, Oriental women were of interest insofar as they shed light on Western male fantasies of power and sexual access. In these discourses, Oriental women merely 'express unlimited sensuality, they are more or less stupid and above all they are willing' (Said 1978/1991: 207). Flaubert's relationship with the Egyptian courtesan, Kuchuk Hanem, was emblematic of the West's relationship with the Orient. Said argued that Kuchuk Hanem

> never spoke of herself, she never represented her emotions, presence, or history. He spoke for and represented her. He was foreign, comparatively wealthy, male, and these were historical facts of domination that allowed him not only to possess Kuchuk Hanem physically but to speak for her and tell his readers in what way she was 'typically Oriental'. (1978/1991: 6)

The silenced, passive, over-sexualised Oriental woman was a symbol of the pacified, feminised East embracing Western imperial penetration and domination. This argument was repeated in a number of subsequent works on Europe's relation to the Orient, such as Rana Kabbani's *Imperial Fictions: Europe's Myths of Orient* (1986), Malek Alloula's *The Colonial Harem* (1986), Sarah Graham-Brown's *Images of Women: The Portrayal of Women in Photography of the Middle East* (1988) and Joanna De Groot's essay '"Sex" and "Race": The Construction of Language in Image in the Nineteenth Century' (1989).

Taking visual representations of the Orient as their starting point, Alloula's and Graham-Brown's works critiqued the way Orientalist photographs of women catered to Western men's sexual fantasies by deliberately constructing Oriental women as sexual and cultural 'Others', constituting them as objects to be appropriated and dominated. Purporting to represent an Oriental reality through photography, Orientalist photographers actually *created* the Orient of their fantasies. The inaccessibility of Oriental women and certain desired locations such as the harem meant that photographers could only imagine such scenes, which were then invested with their own fantasies of exotic sensuality. Western painters and photographers constructed supposedly Oriental scenes using models dressed in exotic costumes, surrounded by Oriental props. Alloula showed that the same model would appear in different costumes, standing in for different types of Oriental women, while the same props turned up in different photographs of various cultures (1986: 62–65). The visual images of these women were political representations, for the Oriental woman came to symbolise the state of the nation. This was an idea that continued well into the **postcolonial** period when (male) nationalists used pictorial representations of working women as an indication of national progress and modernity (Graham-Brown 1988: 19). As Schick commented, 'Once again reduced to mere objects, women were, in these images, at the service of a political discourse conducted by and for men' (Schick 1990: 369).

Historians such as De Groot had emphasised that European male art and literature which constructed racially or culturally subordinated non-Western 'Others' were paralleled by discourses creating sexually subordinated 'Others' within the West: women. But the focus remained on male-authored texts and, historically, women seemed as much the victims of European patriarchy as other races. Thus in these critiques, Orientalism was an overwhelmingly male enterprise; an extension of Western patriarchal and imperial politics. Oriental women served as passive sexual objects of desire while Western women were largely invisible. The few European women discussed were treated as 'honorary men' who echoed a primarily masculinist discourse. No attention was paid to how European women's changing political, legal and professional status over the course of the nineteenth and twentieth centuries might affect their representations of the Oriental Other. Kabbani, for instance, argued that Western women were of little relevance to the Orientalist project because they 'were forced by various pressures to articulate the values of patriarchy' (1986/1994: 7). Thus, in Kabbani's *The Passionate Nomad* (1987), the traveller Isabelle Eberhardt

> became a mouthpiece for patriarchy, voicing traditional male views on sex, culture, religion and politics. Perhaps this position gave her a sense of power; after all, many women travellers adopted a similar stance, thereby hoping to win acceptance as token men. (1987: ix)

Kabbani's argument was disturbingly in accord with traditional male imperialist notions that the **empire** was no place for a white woman and that women played a limited role in the whole colonial enterprise.

Western women and Orientalism

This assumption was challenged by feminist scholars who, by the late 1980s, were paying considerable attention to European women's historical role in colonialism, particularly the role of English women who travelled abroad, in works such as Katherine Frank's essay 'Voyages Out: Nineteenth-Century Women Travellers in Africa' (1986), Helen Callaway's *Gender, Culture and Empire* (1987), Nupur Chaudhuri and Margaret Strobel's *Western Women and Imperialism: Complicity and Resistance* (1992), Laura E Donaldson's *Decolonizing* (1992), Moira Ferguson's *Colonialism and Gender Relations* (1993), Antoinette Burton's *Burdens of History* (1994) and Anne McClintock's *Imperial Leather* (1995). The gendered process of travel and writing was examined by authors such as Shirley Foster in *Across New Worlds* (1990) and Sara Mills in *Discourses of Difference* (1991) who argued that women's representations of the non-Western world were not simply palimpsests of men's because women were constrained by the 'discourses of femininity' which circulated in metropolitan Europe, prescribing not only their style of writing and the authority with which they could speak, but also proscribing certain types of subject matter (Mills 1991: 3). Therefore Western women's voices were 'not straightforwardly orientalist in the way Said has described it' (Mills 1991: 62).

But it was Billie Melman's landmark study, *Women's Orients: English Women and the Middle East, 1718–1918* (1992), which posed the most detailed and comprehensive challenge both to ahistorical assumptions of an unchanging Orientalist discourse and to the assumption that Western women were not involved in creating and shaping European ideas of the Orient. Melman's argument was simple: 'Europe's attitude towards the Orient was neither unified nor monolithic' nor historicist in direction. 'Nor did it necessarily derive from a binary vision sharply dividing the world into asymmetrical oppositions: male–female, West–East, white–non-white and Christian–Muslim' (1992/1995: 7). Rather, ever since Lady Mary Wortley Montagu's letters from Turkey were posthumously published in 1763, Western women had developed alternative views of the Orient which often challenged male Orientalist assumptions and representations. Studying the travel writing and harem literature produced by English women in the Middle East, Melman argued that changing metropolitan experiences of gender and class shaped English women's representation of the Orient and, particularly, Oriental women. In the eighteenth century an upper-class, Augustan 'tolerance towards the different – particularly the sexually different' – characterised women's writing (1992/1995: 310). Far from reiterating Oriental inferiority, Lady Mary Wortley Montagu went as far as to assert the superior position of Turkish women in the harem and the freedom they enjoyed *vis-à-vis* English women. But the discourse changed during the nineteenth century. Victorian women travellers were more concerned with domesticating the harem, seeing in harem life a recognisable reflection of middle-class family life (1992/1995: 137–62). To male writers, who could only imagine what they could not access, the fantasy of the sequestered Oriental woman might have been the titillating embodiment of Oriental violence, despotism, sexual excess and female subordination. But English women travellers were able to observe and participate in harem life and the result was a notably different response. To English women, Oriental women were not the apotheosis of 'Otherness' but, rather, the 'feminine West's recognisable image in the mirror' (1992/ 1995: 316). Instead of reproducing a simple and absolute contrast of cultures and morals, English women were comparing similarities in the lives of Oriental women with their own. There were undoubtedly a number of women who insisted on the unameliorated oppression of Oriental women and the unquestionable inferiority of Oriental culture. Nevertheless, many other nineteenth-century English women noted and emphasised

> the sameness of womankind, regardless of culture, class or ethnicity. Innate and indelible female characteristics and aptitudes are emphasised by virtually all writers. The domesticity, the readiness to serve others and the maternal instincts of Muslim women are repeatedly referred to and commended, because these are values which *bourgeois* culture idealised. (Melman 1992/1995: 309–10)

Female subordination to patriarchal authority was recognised in both the West and the East but the conclusions drawn from these comparisons – for instance, that the harem could be 'freer of most forms of exploitations of sex and class which characterised nineteenth-century Britain' (1992/1995: 308) – were sometimes surprising. While practices such as polygamy and the segregation of women were frowned upon, they gave rise, not to fantasies of lust and perversion as in male Orientalist discourse, but rather, to speculation about alternative systems of gender and familial relations. In short, there emerged in women's Orientalist writing a degree of empathy with racial and cultural Others based on the assumption of shared (middle-class) womanhood. Such gender solidarity, Melman argued, 'undercuts the differences of religion or race' (1992/1995: 310).

This was a persuasive argument anticipated by *Critical Terrains* (1991) – Lisa Lowe's reading of French and British female Orientalist writings – and reinforced by Reina Lewis' recuperative work on nineteenth-century European female Orientalist painters in *Gendering Orientalism* (1996). Lewis unearthed and analysed the production and reception of the paintings of such British artists as Margaret Cookesley, Eliza Fox Bridell, Emily Mary Osborne, Sophie Anderson, Barbara Leigh Smith Bodichon, Edith Martineau and Frances E Nesbitt; the French artists Henriette Browne, Jacqueline Commère Paton, Laure Houssaye de Léoménil; and the Polish-Danish painter Elisabeth Jerichau-Baumann. She concluded that Orientalism was a fractured, multivocal discourse considerably influenced by gender politics. Many of the European women artists she studied did not reproduce 'pejorative' male Orientalist fantasies of seductive Oriental women because, first, they chose to portray 'the Oriental domestic as [an] analogy for the Occidental domestic' (1996: 127). Second, their gender meant that their paintings were received differently from men's. Artists such as Henriette Browne had already established artistic reputations on the basis of 'womanly' representations of female spaces in the European middle-class home. As a result, Browne's Oriental paintings were viewed as a continuation of the feminine genre of domestic painting. These women's choices of subject matter – quotidian life in the harem, often featuring mothers and children – and the assumptions of womanhood that guided their public reception meant that although an exotic difference was being established through these paintings, the Orientalist discourse they produced challenged the dominant masculinist representations of Orientalism. Masculine Orientalist authority was subverted because male claims to knowledge about the Orient, which often found a convenient shorthand in the fantasy of the violently sexualised harem as an emblem of the absolute Otherness of Oriental culture, could not be sustained on the basis of women's paintings or writings – and women were the only ones who had actual access to the Oriental harem. That European women were able to produce alternative – and sometimes subversive – visions of the Orient did not mean that they were exempt from complicity in the colonial project that accompanied the production of Orientalist discourse. It simply meant that

> Orientalism functioned through contradiction rather than despite it . . . The myriad ways in which middle- and upper-class European women positioned themselves in relation to the various possible others of Orientalist discourse indicate both the flexibility of imperial power and the contingency of resistance. (Lewis 1996: 239)

Thus the historical writings of Mills, Lowe, Melman and Lewis on Western women and the Orient all argued against the unified, monolithic discourse of Orientalism posited by Said. Women's representations of the Orient not only developed and changed over time, but simultaneously fractured and even undermined the dominant (and domineering) colonial discourse because of their feminine/feminist experiences.

However, this conclusion was disputed by Meyda Yegenoglu's *Colonial Fantasies* which pointed out that just because Western women portrayed favourable aspects of the Orient or disagreed with male Orientalists' representations did not mean that Orientalism as a project was discredited or subverted (1998: 87). Yegenoglu reinvoked Said's distinction between 'latent' Orientalism (the unconsciously held attitudes and assumptions both about the Orient and about the Western individual's authority to comment on the Orient) and 'manifest' Orientalism (how those attitudes were given expression historically through statements which were shaped and differentiated by authorial style and argument) to explain how Western female challenges to Western male Orientalism are nevertheless recognisably 'Orientalist' (1998: 70). First, Yegenoglu argued, Orientalism is not monolithic in the sense of its unchanging internal unity or coherence. Rather, it retains its recognisable form through a process of *citation* of previous Oriental authorities or *contradiction* of the same in order to establish new Western authority over the Orient (1998: 71–2). In other words, an internal struggle for Orientalist authority goes on constantly in the West, but in this process, the Orient continues to be 'Orientalised' through new assertions about the 'truth' of the Orient. Second, the more sympathetic, normalising picture of the harem portrayed by European women travellers such as Sophia Poole or Mary Wortley Montagu did not necessarily act as a challenge to male Orientalist authority, but rather, as a *supplement* to male Orientalist *lack*, reinforcing women's complicity in the male Orientalist project through their deliberate act of 'unveiling' the Oriental woman (1998: 75–6). Ingres's use of Montagu's description of lolling Turkish ladies in the harem as background research for his painting *Le Bain Turc* (1862) is an instance of this (1998: 91).

Ultimately, for Yegenoglu, Orientalism is not a matter of distorted positive or negative images produced respectively by Western women and men. Rather, it is about the power and process which permit this occurrence: 'Orientalism is an economy of signification in which the difference that inscribes the unequal relation between the subject and the object is constituted' (1998: 86). For this reason, even Montagu's 'feminist' statement about the relative freedom and superior status of Turkish women with respect to English women is subordinated to its Orientalising gesture. It should be noted, however, that Montagu's claim is somewhat of an aberration in the history of Western feminist writing. The more usual pattern is to claim parallels between Western and Oriental women and then to denounce Western society – supposedly more enlightened, more just and morally superior – for this state of affairs.

Feminist Orientalism

In an early intervention into feminism and postcolonial studies, Gayatri Spivak, in her essay 'Three Women's Texts and a Critique of Imperialism' (1985), argued that Western liberal feminism was historically founded on the silencing of colonial/colonised women, hence Western feminists have been complicit in the violence of the colonial project. Taking feminist readings of Charlotte Brontë's *Jane Eyre* as a germinal text of Western feminism, Spivak contended that the Western woman – Jane Eyre – is only able to achieve full domestic authority at the expense of the incarceration and pathologisation of the colonial 'Other' woman – Bertha Mason. This reading subsequently became the archetypal topos in debates about Orientalism, feminism and women's history. Joyce Zonana's essay 'The Sultan and the Slave' developed this reading further, examining the ways in which the discourse of Orientalism in *Jane Eyre* was enunciated, not for the purpose of securing 'Western domination over the East, though they certainly assume and enforce that domination', but primarily for the ends of British women's rights (1993: 594). Zonana traced a line of argument, which she labelled 'feminist Orientalism', from the eighteenth through the nineteenth centuries in the writings of Mary Wollstonecraft, Charlotte Brontë, Mary Shelley, Elizabeth Barrett Browning and Florence Nightingale among others. Wollstonecraft's *A Vindication of the Rights of Woman* (1792) – 'the founding text of Western liberal feminism' (Zonana 1993: 599) – presented the most fully explicated argument of feminist Orientalism: a 'rhetorical strategy . . . by which a speaker or writer neutralises the threat inherent in feminist demands and makes them palatable to an audience that wishes to affirm its occidental superiority' (Zonana 1993: 594). By depicting tyranny, despotism and gender inequality as Oriental traits, it was argued that the West could only become more like itself – more enlightened, rational, just and superior by removing Oriental ways from Occidental life.

The inclusion of Western women into liberal political history, the triumphant story of the historical march of Western women towards gender equality, was therefore established through an Orientalist discourse which placed degraded Oriental culture in an unchanging ahistorical time and space. Melman's conclusion that the nineteenth-century liberal feminist reformers – Harriet Martineau, Amelia Blandford Edwards, Frances Power Cobbe or Florence Nightingale, for instance – were among the most unsympathetic in their portrayals of the Orient (1992/1995: 312) should therefore occasion little surprise. In arguing for reform and Western women's rights, they had to distinguish themselves as historical agents and Enlightened beings from the ahistorical, unenlightened Oriental Other woman. As Antoinette Burton argued with respect to British feminist activism on behalf of oppressed Indian women during the age of high imperialism in *Burdens of History*:

> If Indian women, as imagined by British feminists, were used as an argument for white women's social-imperial usefulness, they were believed to constitute additionally a special burden for British women and, more particularly, for British feminist women. . . . This was the essence of the white feminist burden, premised among other things on the expectation that British women's emancipation would relieve Indian women's suffering and 'uplift' their condition. (Burton 1994: 10)

Barbara Ramusack has shown that most British 'maternal feminists' continued to support British imperialism for the improvements they believed colonial government brought to Indian women's lives (1990), while Kumari Jayawardena agreed that British feminists regarded Indian women as their special burdens to be lifted to the high standards of British womanhood (1995: 95–100).

Orientalism and modern Western feminism

Orientalism continued to be a problem for second-wave Western feminism as well as for women's history. A number of post-colonial critics have demonstrated the pervasive racism and Orientalising or 'Third Worlding' practice implicit in key Western feminist writings. Kabbani asserted that 'the imperial torch has been passed to a new group of Orientalists' who assume 'that Western women have it all and Muslim women have nothing' (1986/1994: ix). Chandra Talpade Mohanty argued that feminist histories of non-Western women continue to portray the latter as oppressed victims of their own culture, of Western imperialism, or of their own religious beliefs. Such non-Western women are placed outside history in a category of 'sexually oppressed women', serving to universalise or normalise Western women's experiences of modernity and to reaffirm Western women's difference, subjecthood, liberation and control over their own lives (Mohanty 1993: 214–15).

These attitudes and assumptions have led to significant problems for women's historical writing, particularly in the use some feminist writers make of non-Western women's history. As Joanna Hicks pointed out, prominent feminists such as Kate Millett could not properly contextualise contemporary events such as Iranian women's attitudes towards veiling because she viewed them through a feminist Orientalist lens which regarded 'Mohammedanism' as sexually oppressive for women while modernisation and liberty were measured by the yardstick of Western women's experiences (1982: 20). The Orientalist failings of some Western feminists' histories of non-Western women were also raised by Joanna Liddle and Shirin Rai who singled out for criticism Mary Daly's *Gyn/Ecology: The Metaethics of Radical Feminism* (1978). This was a book which perpetuated the discourse of feminist Orientalism by making unquestioning use of Katherine Mayo's deeply flawed, biologically and culturally racist polemic, *Mother India* (1927), a piece of imperialist propaganda which reduced 'Indian women to the status of victims' and characterised 'Indian culture and people as uniformly uncivilised and barbarous' (Liddle and Rai 1998: 504; Sinha 1994). 'Nowhere in the book is there reference to the Indian women's movement and its campaigns against women's oppression.' (Liddle and Rai 1998: 504) Liddle and Rai argued that because Daly unquestioningly accepted the 'facts' in *Mother India*, she was able to detect agency and resistance in Western women's history, but not in non-Western women's history. Such a piece of feminist historical writing has contemporary political consequences, because

> What is emphasised in this portrayal is the strength of resistance among European and American women and the power of their common history of struggle, compared to the absence of resistance among Indian, Chinese and African women. This image both draws from and feeds into the hierarchical global positioning of these countries, but in a relocated context of radical political opposition, the impact of which is to erase the history of the women's movement in the non-Western world and to elevate American women as the leaders of global feminism. (Liddle and Rai 1998: 512)

This discourse has the added effect, moreover, of reinforcing the Western political story of the modern nation-state (and women's participation therein) as *the* model for all national histories. Thus, as Dipesh Chakrabarty argued, the histories of all post-colonial/Third World/non-Western nations are really European histories (1992: 1), taking as their silent referent the modern European nation-state.

Orientalist women's histories of the so-called Third World female subject have not, of course, gone unchallenged. Works such as Kamaladevi Chattopadhayay's *Indian Women's Battle for Freedom* (1983), Joanna Liddle and Rama Joshi's *Daughters of Independence* (1986), Kumkum Sangari and Sudesh Vaid's *Recasting Women* (1989) and Lata Mani's *Contentious Traditions* (1998) among many others, have dehomogenised and historicised women in India, bringing to the foreground their varied experiences and agency in resisting both imperialism and patriarchal oppression. Works such as Lila Abu-Lughod's *Veiled Sentiments* (1986) and *Remaking Women* (1998), Fatima Mernissi's *Women and Islam* (1991), Leila Ahmed's *Women and Gender in Islam* (1992), Leslie Peirce's *The Imperial Harem* (1993) and Beth Baron's *The Woman's Awakening in Egypt* (1994) have embarked on the same project in Said's original Oriental locus – the Middle East – deconstructing the monolithic 'Orient' of the West in the process of providing historically and culturally specific explanations of phenomena such as the harem or veiling practices. Meanwhile feminist historians such as Antoinette Burton (1994; 1998) and Catherine Hall (2002) have refused the historiographical Orientalising gesture in their efforts to blur the boundaries between the metropolitan imperial Self and the marginalised colonial Other, examining the historical processes by which colonisers and colonised were involved in mutual configurations of identity.

Orientalism and history

The topic of Orientalism in women's history therefore refers to a number of different things. It is the history of how 'the Orient' and, particularly, 'Oriental women' have been 'Orientalised' by both Western men and women. It is also a problematic historiographical practice arising from, and implicated in the maintenance of, Western imperial dominance over the non-Western world – militarily, politically, culturally and academically. What it is *not*, however, is the history of a particular geographical region or a particular group of people. The far-ranging boundaries of the nebulous Orient and, consequently, the usage of the term 'Oriental' to describe non-Western peoples slide into semantic absurdity when, in addition to the abovementioned works on India and the Middle East, critiques of Orientalism now include Hollywood films about Hong Kong, China, Thailand and Vietnam, American Chinatowns and American women travellers in Japan. It should come as no surprise, then, that an argument is even made for the Orientalising of Pacific islands in Hollywood musicals such as *South Pacific* or American novels such as James Michener's *Hawaii*. Among other things, it is the unsatisfactorily monolithic geo-fantasy of an all-encompassing Orient which has led certain critics to doubt the usefulness of the 'totalising gesture' of Orientalism and to call for more empirical, historically specific analyses of the culture and practice of colonialisms in particular times and places. There is much to be said for historical particularity and the recognition of heterogeneity in these vastly disparate regions. Nevertheless latent Orientalism – those historically developed Western ideas of the Orient and Oriental peoples that begs the question: 'what is it that compels us to name these representations Orientalist, despite their differences?' (Yegenoglu 1998: 70) – refuses to disperse, not only from public and popular culture, but also from academic institutions that continue to re-Orientalise the Orient. To use a rather Orientalist metaphor, perhaps Orientalism is something of a mirage whereby the perception of difference is a result of the observer's or critic's distance. From a sufficiently far distance in time and space, from a sufficiently wide perspective, Orientalism seems to be there. Indeed, it seems to be everywhere. Viewed through the lens of historical particularity, however, Orientalism dissolves into difference and heterogeneity. Nevertheless what remains constant is the authority and power of the observer/historian to see and to speak on behalf of Orientalised Others.

Hsu-Ming Teo

References

Alloula 1986; Behdad 1994; Burton 1994, 1998; Frank 1986; Graham-Brown 1988; Hall 2002; Lewis 1996; Liddle and Rai 1998; Millet 1982; Mills 1991; Said 1978/1991; Spivak 1986; Zonana 1993.

Related essays

Archaeology and ancient history; Empire; Postcolonial; Travel.

Owenson, Sydney, Lady Morgan c.1776–1859

Irish poet, novelist, librettist, biographer, historian of women. Daughter of English heiress Jane Hill and Irish actor Robert Owenson. Educated at Madame Terson's Ladies College in Clontarf and finishing school in Dublin. The failure of her father's theatre forced Owenson into employment as a governess to several Anglo-Irish families. In 1809 she joined the household of the Marquis of Abercorn, where she met and married their physician Sir Charles Morgan. The marriage was happy and they formed a literary partnership, with Sir Charles contributing to a number of her publications. Her marriage settlement gave her full control over all money she acquired from her writing.

During her time as a governess Owenson began to write, initially producing a small volume of poetry including an Ode to **Helen Maria Williams** and then *St Clair* (1802), an epistolary novel, 'written in imitation of Werter'[*sic*]. This novel signalled Owenson's interest in the antiquities of Ireland and she corresponded with leading Irish antiquarians such as Charlotte Brook. She travelled to London in 1804 acquiring the radical publisher Sir Richard Phillips who produced her next novel *The Novice of St Dominick* (1805) and introduced her to William Godwin. With the *Wild Irish Girl* (1806) Owenson achieved major literary success creating a hybrid genre, the 'National Tale'. According to Owenson she 'found it difficult and uninteresting to confine [herself] to the cold detail of facts' and thus spun the tale 'from those materials of ancient and modern history' and the manners and habits of Ireland. Ostensibly an epistolary novel, *The Wild Irish Girl* contains a parallel text made up of discursive footnotes drawn from antiquarian sources, folklore, **local history** and **oral traditions**. Richard Edgeworth, father of the novelist Maria, wrote to Owenson assuring her that this work would convince even 'infidels' among the English, the importance of Irish history.

Owenson was forever associated with Glorvina, the eponymous heroine, a figure shaped by her romantic nationalism, embodying Ireland. Although she was sometimes referred to as 'the Irish **de Staël**', *The Wild Irish Girl* predates *Corinne* by a year. Her acquaintance with that novel shifted her interest towards feminism. Her next novel, *Woman, or Ida of Athens*, was concerned with both nationalism and women's rights. Her feminism was, however, tempered by a desire to be considered 'every inch a woman'. Her political commentary in *Patriotic Sketches of Ireland* (1809) is thus romanticised as 'national affection' inseparable from women's love of home and family. She returned to the 'Irish Question' in three later novels, *O'Donnel* (1814), *Florence Macarthy* (1818) and *The O'Briens and the O'Flahertys* (1827), which she described as 'my Irish histories', and in *Dramatic Scenes and Sketches* (1833).

Like de Staël, Lady Morgan believed that fiction constituted 'the best history of nations'. However, de Staël's infuence can also be seen in Morgan's writings on France which are modelled on *l'Allemagne*. Following the surrender of Napoleon, Lady Morgan was among the first Briton to visit France in 1816. She was feted in Paris, meeting **Helen Maria Williams**, General La Fayette and Augustin Thierry. She published her impressions, *France*, a pioneering piece of 'romantic sociology' in 1817. This book was highly successful and won her admiration on both sides of the channel. De Staël was said to have read it on her deathbed. She was, however, also subject to the same misogynistic diatribes addressed to **Mary Wollstonecraft** and Helen Maria Williams from British conservatives and the French translator of the work who added his own vitriolic notes. Undeterred Lady Morgan followed up *France* with a study of Italy, where she travelled the following year. She was kept under surveillance by the Italian police, who noted that she was a 'most determined constitutionalist'. Her book was banned throughout the Austro-Hungarian Empire and she was never allowed to visit Italy again. *Italy* did not sell well. It was, however, much loved by Byron. She would not write on Italy again, but produced a second volume on France in 1830.

Upon return from Europe the Morgans settled in London. Lady Morgan continued writing, producing a biography of the artist Salvator Rosi in 1824 and several novels, *The Book of the Boudoir* (1829) and *The Princess or the Beguine* (1834). In 1837 she received the first literary pension given to a woman of £300 p.a. In 1840 Owenson published the first two volumes of a proposed four-volume history examining the position of women in society from antiquity to the Middle Ages, *Woman and Her Master*. Owenson was critical of the nineteenth century's claims to **modernity**, given the position of women. She wrote: 'she alone [had] been left at the very starting post of civilisation, while all around her progresses and improves.' *Woman and Her Master* drew upon and complicated the rational tropes of linear history and the theories of cultural development posited by Philosophical or conjectural history. Her romanticised representation of 'woman' as 'the foundress of nations and the embellisher of races' generated antihistorical tendencies in the text, anticipating later 'feminised' versions of history by writers such as **Julia Kavanagh** and **Clara Lucas Balfour**. The work represents an important early attempt at showing women's agency in history, anticipating **Mary Ritter Beard**'s *Woman as Force in History*. It was savagely reviewed. Failing eyesight inhibited her writing and the final two volumes never appeared.

Passages from her autobiography appeared posthumously. She figured in a number of literary biographies in the nineteenth century including Julia Kavanagh's *English [sic] Women of Letters* (1863). She was the subject of a major biography *The Wild Irish Girl* by Lionel Stevenson in 1936 and more recently by Mary Campbell in 1988.

Mary Spongberg

References

Atkinson & Atkinson 1986; Burstein 1999; Campbell 1988; Oldfield 1999; Stevenson 1936.

Major works

The Wild Irish Girl (ed.) Claire Connelly and Stephen Copely (London: Pickering & Chatto, 2000).

P

The Pankhurst women: Emmeline 1858–1928, Christabel Harriette 1880–1958, Estelle Sylvia 1882–1960 and Adela Constantia Mary 1885–1961

English suffragettes, historians of women. In 1879, Emmeline Goulden married Dr Richard Pankhurst, a radical barrister. Their children, who spent their early years in Manchester and London, were brought up in a household where their parents supported advanced causes of the day, especially women's suffrage and socialism. From an early age the girls were taken to political meetings and encouraged to believe that they should work for the good of the common people.

The death of Richard Pankhurst in 1898 was a severe blow that left the family in straitened circumstances. Emmeline became increasingly disillusioned with the lukewarm attitude of the Independent Labour Party (ILP) towards women's suffrage. When she heard that the hall built in her husband's name was to be used by a branch of the ILP that would not admit women, she was so indignant that she founded the Women's Social and Political Union (WSPU) in 1903 as a women-only organisation that would campaign for the parliamentary vote for women on the same terms as it is, or shall be, granted to men. Thus was born what has been termed a 'militant' suffrage society that was to dominate the Edwardian political landscape for the next 11 years. With the slogan 'Deeds, not words' the suffragettes engaged not only in constitutional protest but also in activities that involved public disorder, such as setting fire to empty buildings and the large-scale breaking of plate glass windows. Over 1000 suffragettes were imprisoned for their activism. Throughout, the WSPU campaign was led by the charismatic Emmeline Pankhurst and Christabel, the WSPU's Chief Organiser and key strategist. All four of the Pankhurst women wrote accounts of the suffrage movement but Adela's writings were limited to long essays that remain unpublished and have only been used by scholars in recent years. The main focus here will be on the published books of the three elder Pankhurst women.

The first of the histories of the militant movement, Sylvia's *The Suffragette* (1911), was published before the campaign had ended. Using the convention of **feminist biography**, Sylvia writes of the militant suffrage struggle which she ranks as 'amongst the great reform movements of the world, in terms of the great women leaders of the WSPU, namely, Mrs. Pankhurst the founder, with her magnetic personality, and Christabel, the daring political genius and originator of the [militant] tactics'. Sylvia places her mother and her elder sister centre stage in a story that casts them as influential women of courage, determination and strength who are in the process of changing the course of history. Any possible continuities with the nineteenth-century campaigns were, however, ignored. Thus *The Suffragette*, which emphasises the role of heroic individuals in social change and new gendered forms of protest, established a plot that was adopted by future militant writers.

Emmeline Pankhurst's *My Own Story* (1914) follows the same format but is a more personal history of the campaign, told by its leader. The book originally appeared as a series of articles and was dictated as an oral history to an American journalist, Rheta Childe Dorr. Emmeline not only considered herself incompetent with a pen but her life was punctuated by imprisonments, hunger strikes and periods of convalescence at the time of its preparation. Under a three-year penal sentence, she was continually in and out of prison, due to the provisions of the notorious 'Cat and Mouse' Act. *My Own Story* is a moving apologia for militancy, especially the more violent forms that were adopted from 1912. The focus is not on philosophical argument but on the drama of the campaign, especially the injustices against defenceless women, the agonies of imprisonment and the prevarication of a stubborn, insensitive, male Liberal Government. 'Governments have always tried to crush reform movements', she wrote, 'to destroy ideas, to kill the thing that cannot die.' As a body of male politicians, they upheld a double standard, 'a law of leniency for militant men and a law of persecution for militant women'. Throughout *My Own Story* Emmeline Pankhurst presents herself as a powerful feminist leader of a movement in which she passionately believed, a heroic figure following a long, noble tradition of popular protest against injustice.

There were two major splits in the WSPU, in 1907 and in 1912, but Emmeline Pankhurst glosses over them in *My Own Story*, emphasising not division but the bonds of womanhood in a common cause.

Nor does she mention the expulsion of Sylvia from the WSPU in 1914 and the sending of her youngest daughter, Adela, to Australia. *My Own Story* is the statement of a political leader on a public stage in which private life and family tensions have no place. Despite the fact that Emmeline Pankhurst's voice speaks to us clearly in her autobiography, the text has usually been dismissed by historians, unfairly, as an unreliable, ghost-written source.

Part of the reason for this under-valuation of *My Own Story* is due to the influence of Sylvia's second book, *The Suffragette Movement* (1931), which became the dominant narrative of the militant suffrage campaign. Since writing her first book, Sylvia's relationship with her mother and Christabel had deteriorated. The bitterness that Sylvia felt at her expulsion in 1914 was compounded during the First World War which she, a socialist-feminist, opposed and Emmeline and Christabel patriotically supported. The gulf widened further when Christabel converted to Second Adventism and, in the 1920s, moved to America. For Sylvia, an agnostic like her father, such a religious turn was incomprehensible. The final betrayal came in 1927, when she heard that Emmeline was to stand as a Conservative parliamentary candidate. Estranged from her elder sister and mother and politically isolated on the Left since her expulsion from the Communist Party in 1921, the unmarried Sylvia secretly gave birth to a baby later that year. Sylvia made the news public during the spring of 1928 when her mother was campaigning, an action that hastened the ageing Emmeline's death. Shortly after this Sylvia wrote *The Suffragette Movement*.

Her memories as both a rejected daughter and an angry socialist shaped her interpretation of suffrage events in particular ways that differ markedly from the approach of her first book. In the detailed and richly textured *The Suffragette Movement*, Emmeline and Christabel were continually criticised. Emmeline is a weak leader who defers to Christabel as Sylvia wrote: 'From the day of Christabel's imprisonment, Mrs. Pankhurst, to whom her first-born had ever been the dearest of her children, proudly and openly proclaimed her eldest daughter to be her leader.' After the 1907 split Emmeline becomes 'the dictator of the WSPU', a woman so selfish and driven that when, in 1910, her son Harry falls ill with infantile paralysis a few days before her planned lecture tour in the USA, she fails in her motherly duty. Throughout *The Suffragette Movement* Sylvia portrays the charming and influential Christabel as an evil force upon their easily swayed mother. When the WSPU breaks formally with the ILP in 1907, Sylvia reports it as Christabel's doing. And as a feminist who wanted to unite all women, irrespective of party, Christabel is labelled a Tory. When Sylvia is expelled from the WSPU, she presents it as an action she did not want, carried out by her ruthless sister.

In *The Suffragette Movement*, Sylvia brings herself as well as her two socialist heroes, namely her father and her former lover, Keir Hardie, to the fore. For Sylvia, it was her success in persuading Prime Minister Asquith to receive her East London delegation in June 1914 that was the key to winning the vote. In Sylvia's version of events, she is the heroine who keeps the socialist faith of her father. Although Sylvia's *Life of Emmeline Pankhurst* (1935) offers a less hostile picture, Emmeline is still presented as a weak leader, 'a follower in many things' especially of Christabel's policies.

When Christabel read *The Suffragette Movement* she was hurt, but kept a discreet silence. She too, since the death of Emmeline, had been working on a manuscript which was completed in the mid-1930s.

However, as she did not wish to disagree with a member of her family in public, she would not agree to its publication during her lifetime. When she died in 1958, the manuscript was found amongst her papers and prepared for publication, almost unaltered, by Fred Pethick Lawrence. The following year the book was published under the title Lawrence chose, *Unshackled: The Story of How We Won the Vote. Unshackled,* written in a common-sense style, with sparse attention to detail, was no literary match for *The Suffragette Movement.* Nevertheless, it offers a moving celebration of militancy. Christabel's passion and determination to free women from the stigma of inferiority that the denial of the vote embodied shines throughout. Writing from a radical feminist perspective, she emphasises the uniting of all women 'as one independent force' as the key reason why the formal link between the ILP and WSPU was broken. We could not let the votes for women movement become 'a frill on the sleeve of any political party', she observes. Although the help of men was welcome, Christabel wrote, 'a women's movement must be led by women'.

Despite its differing emphasis, *Unshackled* follows the plot of the previous militant histories in that the focus is on the role of heroic individuals in the WSPU, namely Christabel and Emmeline. However, unlike the portrayal in *The Suffragette Movement,* the two WSPU leaders are painted in a positive light. 'Mother and I were not the "born autocrats" we have been reported to be', Christabel stated. 'We had no love of power for the sake of power. The vote was all we wanted.' Further, she points out how there was no compulsion but voluntarism as the heart of the relationship between the leaders and the rank and file. Although there are frequent references throughout the book to 'Mother and I', Christabel understates her own importance and emphasises the valiant role of her mother, to whom she was devoted. No mention is made of the split with Sylvia and Adela. Christabel merely states that the two younger Pankhurst daughters would have preferred to associate the WSPU with the Labour Party, a decision that led to an inevitable 'parting of the ways'. Throughout she writes as political leader for whom the losing of oneself in the 'great impersonal' of the women's cause was the key aim rather than family tensions. Christabel also offers a different account of why Emmeline sailed for America when Harry was ill; it was based on the necessity of having to earn enough money to secure the best of medical care for her sick son.

By the time of Sylvia Pankhurst's death in 1960, it was not *Unshackled* but Sylvia's *The Suffragette Movement* that had become the standard reading of events. Recent scholarship, however, has questioned the story that it tells. Nevertheless, Sylvia has been seen as a much more acceptable feminist figure. She has been the subject of at least six biographical studies of which Patricia Romero's *E. S. Pankhurst: Portrait of a Radical* (1987) and Shirley Harrison's *Sylvia Pankhurst: A Crusading Life* (2003) offer widely differing interpretations. *Emmeline Pankhurst: A Bio-graphy* by June Purvis (2002) is the only full-length study of the leader of the WSPU and offers a much more sympathetic understanding than Sylvia's earlier brief biography of her mother. David Mitchell published a vituperative account of Christabel Pankhurst's life in his *Queen Christabel* (1977) while the Pankhurst family have also been the subject of a recent group biography by Martin Pugh, *The Pankhursts* (2001), which nevertheless draws heavily on Sylvia's *The Suffragette Movement.*

June Purvis

References
Dodd 1993; Holton 2000; Marcus 1987; Pugh 2001; Purvis 2002.

Major works
E Sylvia Pankhurst's *Life of Emmeline Pankhurst* (New York: Kraus Reprints, 1969) and *The Suffragette Movement* (London: Virago, 1977) with introduction by Richard Pankhurst. Emmeline Pankhurst's *My Own Story* (New York: Kraus Reprints, 1971).

Peace

Women's historical writing on peace has a long history, shaped by the experience of **war**, and by several intellectual traditions. While some women's writings on peace have not been about women at all, they mostly are; and in recent times historical writings by women on women and peace and women's peace movements have made a distinct contribution to knowledge. Women have also contributed extensively to the resources now available for the writing of peace history.

The field has not previously been surveyed. There have been a number of anthologies, but so far no comprehensive bibliographies or review essays. Nor is it always easy to identify relevant writers, for gender-blind initials often prevailed until the 1960s. It is clear, however, that a great many women writers have written about peace over time, and the field has thickened in the modern period. In the twentieth century and today, historians and activists, it turns out, are often one and the same people. Perhaps they always have been.

Experiences of war and the emergence of traditions

Women's experience of war has led them to write histories of war and peace from early medieval times. It is often supposed that the earliest western expression of women's commitment to peace dates back even further, to *Lysistrata*. But this play was written by a male, Aristophanes, and is essentially a satire on men, albeit an appealing one. Nearer to the point of much modern writing is Sophocles' *Antigone*. Antigone defied her uncle Creon and enunciated the right of resistance in the name of higher moral laws. That ancient writing on peace was by men is not surprising. In ancient cultures, the pursuit of peace was entirely a male enterprise. Men devised the treatise of antiquity, and in the world of late antiquity, where male envoys and ambassadors were the prototypes of peacemakers, there was little space for women to write about peacemaking.

The oldest intellectual context in which to locate women's historical writings about peace is religious and the earliest evidence of a woman writing on peace appears to be the grieving verses written by Saint Radegund of the Holy Cross in the seventh century. These epic poems written to lament the dead also record details of Radegund's life – the sacking of her father's kingdom Thuringia, her family's slaying and her forced marriage to Clothar, king of Neustria. Not only do they express her desire to live in peace, they also provide a unique feminine perspective on these brutal times (see **Religion** essay).

The combined effect of the brutality of early medieval warfare and the emergence of Christianity occasionally led women to advocate peace in their historical writings. This is evident in the Byzantine princess **Anna Komnene**'s *Alexiad* (1143–1148), a history of her father's reign and her own unsuccessful attempts to gain the throne. During the Hundred Year's War **Christine de Pizan** recorded contemporary history while also calling for peace in her *Lamentations on the Evils that have befallen France* (1412) and her *The Book of Peace* (1412). In an earlier work, *The Book of the Deeds* *and Arms of Chivalry* (1410), Christine had taken the unprecedented step of advising men on just warfare. In the latter **Middle Ages** the invocation of peace was one of the duties of women, especially nuns, but this mostly meant inner peace rather than worldly concerns. The gentle Julian of Norwich may have been an exception in reflecting on 'the likeness of God and the restoration of humanity'. By way of contrast, it has been remarked of the celebrated Hildegard of Bingen that she was 'not one to miss a good fight if there was one to be had' (Beer 1992).

Over two centuries later, radical Protestantism opposed all fighting on religious grounds, and in 1660, that rare spirit Margaret Fell drafted the first Quaker peace testimony (Ross 1949). Ever since, as pacifists Quakers have been vital to the maintenance of a peace tradition (Isichei 1970). A 'pacificist', or political, position – conditional and circumstantial opposition to war – has attracted many more (Ceadel 1980). Catholic teaching had long distinguished between just and unjust wars (Elshtain 1994). In the seventeenth century, 'laws of war' were formulated; and in time peace by arbitration would find many women advocates. Meanwhile, under certain circumstances, women could and did avail themselves of more traditional expressive behaviours, such as the great peace petition of 1643, and during the English Civil War the *Midwives Just Complaint* in 1646 that claimed fighting undermined their trade (Fraser 1984). Intellectual women of the period appear desirous of peace in their diaries and letters. Margaret Cavendish, whose husband fought with King Charles during the English Civil Wars, asserted in her *Sociable Letters* (1664) that disturbance in the country was no cause for a breach in women's friendships (Cambridge Women's Peace Collective 1984: 19–20). Aphra Behn, too, lamented the loss of a peaceable Golden Age in her poetry (Cambridge Women's Peace Collective 1984: 21–3).

In the late eighteenth century, **Mary Wollstonecraft** ought in theory to represent the start of a new tradition in women's historical peace writing; but it is not so, owing to unresolved difficulties both she and her compatriot **Helen Maria Williams** found in addressing violence in the French **Revolution**. The preface of Wollstonecraft's *Historical and Moral View of the French Revolution* (1795) notes the challenge of contemplating 'stupendous events', given the 'calamitous horrors' observed first-hand. While Claire Tomalin points out that Wollstonecraft no longer sought to extenuate violence (1974: 171), her history is now seen to be lacking on this basic issue.

The inauguration of new traditions had to wait a little longer. The first half of the nineteenth century saw a growing interest in the idea of a peaceful alternative to war, in part owing to the widening of wars, also to the rising tide of humanitarianism. Humanitarianism, defined in this context by recent scholarship as 'a secularly based internationalism, derived from humanistic ideals' and dated from the founding of peace societies at the end of the Napoleonic wars (Cooper 1991: 4), is the second great tradition in which women's historical writings on peace is situated. The ideals of international socialism, ultimately constituting a third, troubled tradition, also date from the early nineteenth century, at least notionally. The goal of utopian socialism was universal peace and harmony, although Barbara Taylor has argued with respect to Owenite socialism that its women adherents were more preoccupied with problems of patriarchy than peace. In 1854 Swedish suffragist Frederika Bremer appealed for women to unite to end the Crimean War. Florence Nightingale was no peacenik, but her work there created another dimension, in that army **nurses** were among the first women to see war first-hand and some wrote about it afterwards, as they have continued to do.

Although it is commonly believed that peace 'took a back seat' during the American Civil War despite the link made between peace and the suffrage at Seneca Falls, the pacific impulse was not entirely submerged. **Sarah Josepha Hale**'s mammoth *Woman's Record* states 'the condition of the female sex decides the destiny of the nation' and she campaigned for a peaceful solution to the problem of slavery. Even during the conflict, some American feminists reiterated women's special commitment to peace. The 'little women' of Louisa M Alcott's eponymous novel (1868) certainly knew something of war's horror. Moreover, although little has yet been written about it, the Civil War also brought many women into the public sphere as nurses. Mary Gardner Holland *Our Army Nurses: Stories from Women in the Civil War* (1895) is a pioneering first-hand history.

In the later nineteenth century, especially after the Franco-Prussian War (1871), both men and women responded to the rise of modern militarism with liberal and pacifist ideas, seeking arbitration as an alternative way of resolving conflict. This period saw the emergence of the first generally acknowledged woman peace writer Bertha von Suttner. In 1889 von Suttner, who once worked for Alfred Nobel in Paris and was the first woman to win the Nobel Peace Prize in 1905, published *Lay Down Your Arms: The Autobiography of Martha Von Tilling*, who is said to have lost two husbands to mid-century European wars. This influential work went beyond arbitration to disarmament. There were numerous other influential European pacifist advocates in the late nineteenth century, such as Anita Augspurg and Hubertine Auclert.

By the time of the South African War at the end of the century, European women liberals were well and truly involved with the interlocking issues of war and peace. Outstanding were Emily Hobhouse, whose exposé of the conditions in the concentration camps (Fry 1929) highlighted the plight of women and children, and Olive Schreiner, famous since the publication of *The Story of an African Farm* (1883) and later a great beacon for peace during and after the South African War. In her classic work *Woman and Labour* (1911) Schreiner argued that woman's reproductive capacity gave her 'a controlling right' over the resort to war.

The idea that women have something special to contribute to peace is an old one, but late nineteenth-century evolutionary thought brought new agency, combining scientific and sociological perspectives. If the measure of progress was the position of women and women were more evolved than men, then women should be the standard-bearers of a new, peaceable world order. As Jill Liddington argues (1989), **Charlotte Perkins Gilman** was the other robust thinker here. In *The Man-Made World* (1911) she upheld the doctrine of women's moral superiority and mocked the ultra-masculinism of war ('Maleness means war'). Moreover, to liberal evolutionists like Gilman, war made bad eugenic sense.

The struggle for the suffrage and for peace was in large part sustained by this gender-in-evolution version of progress; but Swedish maternalist Ellen Key struck a discordant note with her oft-reiterated notion of motherhood as race/national service and disdain for the suffrage (albeit somewhat modified in *War, Peace and the Future* [1916]). Key's essentialism retains its purchase to the present day, and serves as springboard in much late twentieth-century historical debate on gender and peace.

The most dramatic demand for peace by women in the First World War came from the International Congress of Women at The Hague. Jane Addams was presiding officer at the International Congress, and second female co-winner Nobel peace laureate (1931). Her own writings on peace are of historical significance, especially *The Newer Ideals of Peace* (1907) and *Peace and Bread in Time of War* (1918). For Addams, peace was not simply the absence of wars but the nurturance of life; and it was a deft touch on the times to stress 'maturing concepts of peace'. Strongly committed to mutuality and mediation, she set a new benchmark for peace-makers.

Among women's responses to the Great War are writings and images of enduring import. **Vera Brittain**'s *Testament of Youth* (1933) captured the trauma of a generation, as did the art of Käthe Kollwitz, whose powerful woodcuts such as 'The Widow' (1922) are iconic. And if Jane Addams saw the way forward, it was **Virginia Woolf** who in *Three Guineas* (1938) pinpointed the obstacles, emphasising that women were still outsiders in many ways: 'The outsider will say "in fact as a woman, I have no country. As a woman I want no country. As a woman my country is the whole world" '. For Australian writer Miles Franklin the despair and disillusion of war were hard to bear, and peace became the basic issue.

In the interwar years, a noble dream died. But the new women citizens of the world could not foresee that. Instead, as recent writings explain, from 1919 they determined on a second crusade, this time to get rid of the world of war. Like some men, activists embarked to an unprecedented extent on work and writings for peace, through prior organisations such as the International Alliance of Women, which channelled a good deal of peace-oriented energy into the League of Nations, the empire-based women's British Commonwealth League; and especially, as noted below, the new organisations for peace founded after the war.

As the focus on peace sharpened in the early twentieth century, so internationalism led to a new 'women's world', revolving around Geneva with women from colonised countries introducing challenges to it there. A new dimension was added to 'the pacific impulse' in the 1930s by Gandhian non-violence, which had its roots in Hinduism but also the teachings of Tolstoy and suffragette 'militancy'. It seems a pity that to date only passing mention of this fourth and alternative tradition is essayed by historians of any stripe, though it is surely the case that as many women as men were attracted to non-violence, as oral histories sometimes reveal. Judith Porter Adams' *Peacework* (1990) includes an interview with Erna Harris (b.1908, Okalahoma) who recalled that 'We had pictures of Gandhi all over the house.' An entirely different angle comes with Elizabeth Abbott's *History of Celibacy* (1999), with its notion of spinster commitment to underlying agendas and the empowering effect for Gandhi.

Women's historical writing on peace skates over the Second World War. This is unsurprising. The few remaining pacifists had a tricky time and it was difficult to maintain the faith with different war aims to counter in different parts of the world, as experienced by Eleanor Moore, stalwart of the Women's International League for Peace and Freedom (WILPF) in far off Australia who wrote *The Quest for Peace as I have Known It in Australia* (c.1948) in the war's aftermath. Thus, while women and the Second World War has been a growth area in women's historical writing, only a few references pertain to peace. Yet Simone Weil starved herself to death in protest at the blockade of German-occupied France; and the young pacifist Sophie Scholl of the German White Rose movement was beheaded for her anti-Nazi activities in 1942. Caroline Moorehead's *Troublesome People* (1987), comparing the fate of conscientious objectors in Britain in both wars, concludes that individual conscience was by then respected (though women COs were new issue) and emphasises the historical importance of moral witness. However, to leave it there would be to overlook the long-run effects of humanitarian war work such as that of Swedish Nobel laureate of 1982 Alva Myrdal and the core message of Margaret Gowing's majestic *Britain and Atomic Energy 1939–1945* (1964). The historian **Mary Ritter Beard** was a life-long pacifist; underpinning her magnum opus *Woman as Force in History* (1946) was the desire to show that women could be a force for peace in world history. She was also one of the few contemporaries to note that women entered the armed services in numbers for the first time in history.

In 1927 Eleanor Roosevelt had urged that the time to prepare for world peace was during the time of peace and not during the time of war. With the formation of the UNO after the Second World War, perhaps the time had come. But the concurrence of war and peace, as in Jane Austen's novels, has often been remarked upon; and from 1946 with the onset of the Cold War, that was again the case. After the dropping of the A-bomb on Japan in 1945, it was no longer relevant to cry 'lay down your arms'. With the liberal defence of individual conscience at default and the effects of an historically backed existentialism still to come, the onset of the Korean war-reinforced old-time feminists' thinking and the need for new energy was apparent, even at the time.

Studies of women's peace movements

Women's experiences of war thus led them to write about it and, increasingly, to advocate peaceable solutions and alternatives. But advocacy is never enough. In modern democratic societies it must be backed by active, organised support, that is by strong peace movements. Hence in recent times women's peace history has predominantly focused on the modern period, especially the twentieth century. Linda Grant De Pauw's important survey *Battle Cries and Lullabies: Women in War from Prehistory to the Present* draws attention to this emphasis (1981: 81).

The International Congress of Women at The Hague, seeking a mediated peace, is the main reference point for many twentieth-century studies. The history of main institutional outcome and enduring women's peace organisation, the WILPF, is presented in Gertrude Bussey and Margaret Timms' *Pioneers for Peace* (1965), updated and extended by Carrie Foster's *Women for All Seasons* (1987); Henry Ford's not-so-quixotic Peace Ship, the year after the Congress, is accounted for in Barbara S Kraft, *Peace Ship* (1978); and the Congress itself is studied by Josephine Eglin in *Campaigns for Peace* (1987), also in Regina Braker's 'Bertha von Suttner's *Spiritual Daughters*' (1995).

Of the four main US organisations in the interwar years, two have been closely studied by women historians. Carrie Foster's *The Women and the Warriors* (1995) is a comprehending critical account of the US section of the WILPF (1915–1946) written from the sources, as is Harriet Hyman Alonso's *The Women's Peace Union and the Outlawry of War 1921–1942* (1989). The WILPF survived through to 1946, just, while the latter, which aimed at a constitutional amendment, did not. Both suffered generational decline and elsewhere Alonso notes the unwillingness of the older generation to relinquish power. Interestingly the new writings study effects of 'burnout'. It is helpful that the US writers take the story through the Second World War.

Writings on post-Second World War peace movements tell not of progress but of reaction. Amy Swerdlow's study of the Left-oriented Congress of American Women 1946–1950 (1995) shows why years immediately post-1945 scarcely make a showing in women's peace writing. The Congress was hounded out of existence by the House Un-American Activities Committee for internationalism and links with the Soviet Union. An interesting comparison is with the campaigns of Communist women in Australia, considered beyond the pale for their efforts (Curthoys and MacDonald 1996). Only recently have women historians begun to consider how rising fear of nuclear war in the 1950s led to new anti-war protest, with the rise of the Campaign for Nuclear Disarmament in Britain from 1957 and the strike for peace in Washington in 1961 (Liddington 1989; Swerdlow 1993).

The Vietnam War and anti-war protest brought not so much a resurgence of women writing histories of peace as a realisation that they would have to recover their own perspectives. The UN Decade of Women 1975–1985 is regarded by Alonso as a significant consolidator and extender of this realisation. But it was the women's protest from 1981 against US cruise missiles at Greenham Common in England which really focused minds. Evidently gender was still a significant variable or weapon in anti-war movements. At the Greenham peace camp, women wrote more songs and poems and pamphlets than ever before; and a new, disconcerting, spirituality was on display. A flood of writings ensued, mostly of record. Something of the early spirit is conveyed in the dedication in *Greenham Common: Women at the Wire* (1984) edited by Barbara Harford and Sarah Hopkins: 'This book is dedicated to all our oppressors. Your time is up!'. Beth Junor's Greenham Common Women's Peace Camp (1995) is a year-by-year history, 1984–1995.

The biographical approach

Biography is of increasing importance to women historians of peace. To date subjects have mostly come from 'the golden age' of women's peace activism in the first half of the twentieth century, with American studies again preponderating. Jane Addams is studied by Sondra Herman in *Eleven Against War* (1969), the only woman, and a new biography of Addams appeared in 2002, with Jean Bethke Elshtain's *Jane Addams and the Dream of American Democracy* and Victoria Bissell Brown's *The Education of Jane Addams* (2004), providing insights into her early years more recently still. In her biography of Emily Greene Balch, entitled *Improper Bostonian* (1964), Mercedes Randall draws attention to an often overlooked figure, including her inner life: Balch was a sacked Wellesley professor, WILPF stalwart, and in 1946 the third woman Nobel peace laureate. The boldest to date, on Mildred Scott Olmsted; Margaret Hope Bacon's *One Woman's Passion for Peace and Freedom* (1993) pays due attention to Olmsted's WASP position and the threesome she maintained throughout her life. Blanche Weisen Cook's immensely impressive study of Eleanor Roosevelt (1992) points out that Eleanor Roosevelt seldom spoke in public in the interwar years without mentioning world peace. Interestingly, Cook herself was a recruit to WILPF in the 1960s. Significant also is the story of Jeannette ('I cannot vote for war') Rankin, told by Hannah Josephson in *Jeannette Rankin, first lady in Congress (1974)*. At 90 Rankin led 'the Jeannie Rankin Brigade' to protest the Vietnam war and later made contact with Ralph Nader.

Fewer British/European peace workers of the period have attracted full-scale biographies as yet. The overshadowing effect of the older Pankhursts' about-face in 1914 has a bearing on British coverage, depicted in Jo Vellacott's 'Anti-war suffragists' (1977). **Memoirs** and other contemporary writings remain the main guide to other outstanding British peace advocates (1914–1918), such as Helena Swanwick, Chrystal McMillan and Vernon Lee. Similarly, Liddington's 'The Women's Peace Crusade' (1983) on north England working-class women (1917–1918), and Sheila Rowbotham's play on framed Midlands activist Alice Wheeldon *Friends of Alice Wheeldon* (1986) are rare instances of researching peace history from below, as urged by Dorothy Thompson (Pierson 1987). European biographical studies such as Elzbieta Ettinger's *Rosa Luxemburg* (1988), murdered in Berlin in 1919, renders her 'flesh and blood'. Barbara Evans Clements published *Bolshevik Feminist: Aleksandra Kollontai* in 1979. Unfortunately the available titles on Hague Congress sponsor Dr Aletta Jacobs have not been translated into English, though her *Memories* (1996) have. And due attention is paid to peace in Sheila Fletcher's *Maude Royden* (1989).

There are also useful biographical collections available to strengthen the field. Sybil Oldfield's *Women Against the Iron Fist: Alternatives to Militarism 1900–1989* (1989) is a sampler from 'a neglected tradition'. Anne Wiltsher's Greenham-inspired *Most Dangerous Women: Feminist Peace Campaigners of the Great War* (1985) is also biographically driven, starting with details of the life of that remarkable Hungarian activist, 1974 Rosika Schwimmer, who died stateless in 1947. A thematic study worth noting due in part to its distinguished author is Vera Brittain's 50th anniversary short history of the pacifist International Fellowship of Reconciliation, *The Rebel Passion* (1964), with its re-assertion of 'the politics of compassion' and non-violence in the nuclear age.

Some recent developments

Jo Vellacott's outstanding study of Bertrand Russell and the Pacifists of the First World War (1980), which also shows the importance of Catherine Marshall to the anti-conscription cause, serves to mark the coming of a new generation of women historians writing on peace movements and women's role in them. By the 1980s, with the growth in both women's history and peace history (though some queried the separation of peace from war studies in the universities), there was a growing market for histories of female pacifism. The need for a broad perspective was met in England by the work of participant-observer, Jill Liddington, *The Long Road to Greenham* (1989). In the US, where the peace/women studies programmes are mainly to be found, a key text was Alonso's *Peace as a Women's Issue*, which also begins at 1820. Both offer fluent narratives spanning two centuries and, in dealing with the troubled interwar years, arrive at comparable conclusions, though differently configured, due to national differences. In both instances, however, 'the long hiatus' revolved around the failure of world disarmament and the rise of fascism.

These surveys share two striking characteristics. First, they seek to demonstrate continuities, however fragile. Second, they necessarily break new ground source wise post-1950. Previously unexamined written sources, oral history, group biography and cameo studies are all utilised. Alonso conducted many interviews, and like Liddington, includes cameo studies (Denver; Golders Green). Notably, both books appeared under sympathetic imprints. *The Long Road* was published by Virago and *Peace as a Women's Issue* appeared in the respected Syracuse Studies on Peace and Conflict Resolution series. Similarly, Foster's *Women for All Seasons* (1987) was a collective effort, supported by the Jane Addams Peace Foundation.

By 1987 several strong collections on war, peace and gender had appeared to address theoretical issues arising. These included: Jean Bethke Elshtain's critique of biological essentialism in her edited collection *Women, Militarism and War*; feminist peace talk, she suggested, too often traffics in 'binary opposites' and 'Manichean' constructions which rely on particular constructions of male and female, the irony being that they finish up endorsing that which they would oppose (1990: 265). Other contributions to this growing field included Canadian Ruth Roach Pierson's *Women and Peace* (1987), with Dorothy Thompson's forceful contribution, previously noted, and Margaret Kamester and Jo Vellacott's *Militarism versus Feminism* (1987). Women historians attracted to the early twentieth century have studied the ways in which new energies were brought to the quest for peace, and looked for the ways in which these energies were experienced in and then transformed by war. Notable British studies in this vein are Jo Vellacott's *From Liberal to Labour: The Story of Catherine Marshall* (1993) and Beryl Haslam's *From Suffrage to Internationalism* (1999). A more theoretical approach to the making of middle-class pacifists in the First World War via sibling analysis is to be found in Miriam Cooke and Angela Woollacott's *Gendering War Talk* (1993); and there is a useful overview by political scientist Jan Jindy Pettman in *Worlding Women* (1996).

The 1980s also brought a rush of source books to teach the new activists their heritage. Two stand out. In 1984, the Cambridge (UK) Peace Collective, echoing Virginia Woolf, produced the anthology *My Country is the Whole World*, chronologically organised. In America, the prize-winning *Women on War: Essential Voices of the Nuclear Age* (Gioseffi 1988) served the same purpose, re-appearing in revised but still polemical format as *Women on War* in 2003. There was even a Gaia Peace Atlas in 1988.

Reference works came later. Like the anthologies they are mostly skewed to the twentieth century, and overlap is inevitable; but they may serve as first port of call for future historical writings, and informative and well-crafted entries by women contributors are often to be found. The multi-volume *World Encyclopedia of Peace* (1986), for example, has articles on women Peace Prize winners by Ruth C Reynolds; and in Helen Rappaport's *Encyclopedia* of Women Social Reformers (2001) there are over 60 entries under 'Peace/Anti-militarism', with brief bibliographies. Similarly there are numerous listings under 'Pacifism and Peace Activists' in the *Routledge International Encyclopedia of Women* (2000), which includes minor essays on peace by Laura Daly and war by Jean Bethke Elshtain. The *Macmillan Dictionary of Women's Biography* (1998) provides diverse shorter entries, including one on Nobel peace laureate, Aung San Suu Kyi.

With so much historical and biographical information now available, it is disconcerting to find that women constitute a mere 5 per cent of the entries in *Peace Mir*, an anthology of historical alternatives to war co-edited by Ruzanna Ilukhina, possibly because most peace organisations have been mixed and male-dominated; and the fact is that after 100 years, only 12 Nobel peace prize winners have been female. Discouraging too is the limited supply of bibliographies after Blanche Wiesen Cook's *Bibliography on Peace Research in History* (1969) and Elise Boulding's *Bibliography on World Conflict and Peace* (1979).

The US-based Peace History Society was founded in 1963 and has its own website; there is also a Peace Resources website to assist future researchers. They will have plenty to write about. In recent times women's writing about peace has often been a matter of ephemera, pamphlets and the like, grist to the historian's mill, and it has never been easier to print it. Autobiographical and other writings of activists such as anti-nuclear campaigner Helen Caldicott's *A Passionate Life* (1996) will be highly significant; and more memory work will surely be productive.

It seems possible that a new phase in women's historical writing about peace/war is beginning. The entry of women into the military and even combat as in the Gulf War, and research into 'women warriors' now appearing is one sign. Another is the course of events post-Cold War, creating new constituencies for peace beyond those served by the North American and European histories which have thus far dominated the field. Pacific Women Speak (c.1987) on anti-nuclear activism in the Pacific is one sign. The names of 1992 Guatemalan Nobel laureate Rigoberta Menchoe Tum and 2003 Sydney Peace Prize winner Hanan Ashrawi are likewise suggestive. Certainly some new directions are evident in other areas, such as international relations and psychology.

The upsurge of the 1980s brought dismay as scholars realised how resistant the world of international relations is to gender, as outlined in Carol Cohn's 'Sex and Death in the Rational World of Defense Intellectuals' (1987), and there were calls to reclaim the discourse in collections such as Diana Russell's *Exposing Nuclear Phallacies* (1989). It was in this context that American political scientist Cynthia Enloe called for a new emphasis, on militarisation as social process (Hess and Ferree 1987), and has since sought to demonstrate in a series of lively works incorporating historical data over the past 20 years, from *Does Khaki Become You?* (1983) to *Maneuvers: The International Politics of Militarizing Women's Lives* (2000). Psychological research rejecting 1960s aggression theory is also telling. *Cultures of Peace: The Hidden Side of History* (2000) by long-time peace writer Elise Boulding is a reminder that alternative traditions may usefully be revisited.

Continuity and complexity are now major preoccupations of women's historical writing on peace, and there is a quest for new approaches. The myriad faces of war ensure that they will be needed to maintain and extend the intellectual traditions which have served women's peace histories well to date and to illuminate the issues and perspectives arising in the era of globalisation.

Jill Roe

References

Alonso 1993; Beer 1992; Braker 1995; Cambridge Women's Peace Collective 1984; Ceadel 1980; Cohn 1987; Cook 1992; Cooper 1991; Curthoys & MacDonald 1996; Elsthain 1990, 1994; Fraser 1984; Fry 1929; Gioseffi 1988; Herman 1969; Hess & Ferree 1987; Isichei 1970; Liddington 1983, 1989; Pierson 1987; Swerdlow 1993, 1995; Vellacott 1980.

Related essays

Feminism; Middle Ages; Memoirs; Nursing & Medicine; Reformation; Religion; Revolution; War.

Pinchbeck, Ivy 1898–1982

English historian of women. Studied at the University College, Nottingham, where she took a BA in 1920. Taught history at Queen Mary's High School, Walsall, between 1921 and 1925. Went to the LSE to study under **Lilian Knowles** and **Eileen**

Power. Awarded an MA in 1927, Pinchbeck went to lecture in the London branch of the Worker's Education Association. A Charlotte Shaw Fellowship allowed her to continue her studies. Pinchbeck was awarded a PhD in 1930, publishing *Women Workers and the Industrial Revolution* in the same year. Took up a job in the Department of Sociology, Social Studies and Economics, Bedford College, University of London in 1929. Retired as Reader from Bedford in 1961.

Like other contemporaries such as **Alice Clark** and M Dorothy George, Pinchbeck's focus was on the impact of **industrialisation** on women's work and draws on extensive records. Less pessimistic than Clark's *Working Life of Women* (1919), *Women Workers and the Industrial Revolution* depicts both the positive and negative effects of industrialisation on the life of women workers in England. Pinchbeck describes how changes in agriculture and industrialisation transformed women's work, but more significantly showed how integral women's labour was to shaping England as the 'first Industrial Nation'. Pinchbeck's work heralded a different perspective on 'industrialisation', creating a paradigm that would be dominant until the 1970s. Developing the social aspects of economic history, Pinchbeck argued that the breakdown of the family economy affected not just the sexual division of labour, but began to diminish the degree of patriarchal power within the family unit. For Pinchbeck the advent of industrial work for women was critical to the possibilities of emancipation. In the 1968 edition of *Women Workers* she was incredulous about the amount of historical interest that had been shown in suffrage and the historical neglect of women's work outside the home.

Although she retired from her position as Reader in Bedford College in 1961 she continued to research, producing a two-volume study *Children in English Society* co-written with her former student Margaret Hewitt in 1969. *Children in English Society* deals with changing social attitudes to children in England and the resulting influences on social policy and legislation. It came about following her preparation of a course of postgraduate lectures on the Child in English Society for students of the University of London who were preparing to enter Child Care Services. When preparing these lectures it became apparent that there existed no adequate systematic study of children in English society, nor any study of the social and economic forces that shaped legislation dealing with children. Like *Women Workers*, this text is meticulously researched, drawing on Parliamentary Papers, an esoteric range of contemporary books and pamphlets, local records and biographical and literary texts. It anticipated more recent work in its focus on child marriage, delinquent and illegitimate children and the education and training of children.

Mary Spongberg

References

Berg 1992; Boyd 1999.

Major work

Women Workers and the Industrial Revolution 1750–1850 (ed.) Kerry Hamilton (London: Virago, 1981).

Pizan, Christine de c.1365–1430

Italian poet, philosopher, historian of women. Born in Venice, daughter of the physician and astrologer Tommaso da Pizzano. Raised in the Court of Charles V of France, Christine described her education as 'crumbs I gathered at my father's table'. Married at 15 to Etienne de Castel, a notary at the Royal Court, she was widowed around 1389 and left with the care of three children, her mother and a niece. Following the death of her husband Christine chose to write to support her family. Attracted first to lyric poetry Christine produced hundreds of love poems between 1392 and 1400, including many written in the voice of a lady and autobiographical poems of widowhood. Around 1400, however, she turned away from 'pretty things' to produce her first non-lyric work the *Epistre d'Othéa*, a 'mirror for princes' or conduct manual, in which she drew lessons from mythology to instruct men in morality.

Christine first expressed interest in the representation of women in the *Epistre au dieu d'amours* (1399). This work playfully challenged the authority of texts such as Ovid's *Art of Love* and Jeun de Meun's *Romance of the Rose*, accusing both authors of maligning women. In this text Christine undercut the arguments made in the *Rose* by drawing on examples of women such as Medea and Dido and revising their history to show their virtue and constancy in the face of male perfidy, a theme she wrote on for the next six years. Having found a political voice Christine created the first vernacular literary quarrel in France when she commented on a treatise by Jean de Montreuil praising *Romance of the Rose* in 1401. Questioning the dubious literary merits of that work Christine defended women against their misogynist representation in the *Rose*, drawing upon Scriptural and French history to provide counter-examples of women as chaste and faithful wives whose virtues greatly benefited their husbands. Christine documented this debate, presenting a dossier of the letters exchanged between herself, Jean de Montreuil and others and the sermons and pamphlets written on this subject to Queen Isabeau de Baviére.

Part of Christine's attack on *Romance of the Rose* ultimately questioned long-standing essentialist arguments that women were unfit for letters. She continued on this theme in *Livre de la mutacion de Fortune* (1403). A universal history depicting the role of fortune in determining human fate, this text also presented an allegorical autobiography tracing Christine's development as a writer. It was in this text that she claimed that fortune had transformed her 'from a woman into a man', alluding to her new familial role as bread-winner and professional role as author. Other texts such as *Le chemin de longue étude* (1402–1403) and *L'Avision Christine* (1405) also present details of her life in allegorical form. Christine's fame as a writer was now established and in 1404 she was commissioned by the Duke of Burgundy to write a life of his brother Charles V. In this work, *Le livre des faits et bonnes moeurs du roi Charles V le Sage*, Christine created an encomiastic account of the king's life, presenting Charles as an outstanding example of noble leadership.

In the following year Christine created another universal history, *Le Livre de la cité des dames*, making women again the subject of her study. Rewriting history from a feminine perspective, this text marked a sharp departure with all previous historical writing as Christine restored speech to women traduced in the masculinist tradition and radically reinvented their lives. Christine also altered the genre of universal history by making women's experience an allegory for all human experience, usurping the tradition of a masculine 'universal' and anticipating later feminist criticism. Shortly after completing the *City of Ladies*, Christine produced the *Le livre des trois vertus* (1405). Akin to her earlier works on conduct, the *Three Virtues* also provided models of political, moral and spiritual leadership for noblewomen. Christine particularly stressed that such women had an important role to play as peacemakers in society. These books were read by women wielding political power at this time. Margaret of Austria, Margaret of Hungary, Louise of Savoy and Queen Leonora of Portugal all held copies of Christine's manuscript in their libraries.

Christine's interest in women's role as peacemakers was articulated further in later works born out of the political unrest that shattered France in the early fifteenth century. *Le Livre du corps de policie* (1407) dedicated to the dauphin, Louis of Guyenne, drew on the political theories of John of Salisbury and Giles of Rome and astutely suggested that just government prevented civil unrest. *Le Livre des faits d'armes et de chevalerie* (1410), an innovative political work commissioned by the Duke of Burgundy, laid out standards for chivalrous warfare. Christine's works on war were read for several centuries, though her name and sex were sometimes suppressed. Christine also wrote on the worsening political situation in France in *La Lamentacion sur les maux de la France* (1412) and in the *Livre de la Paix* (1412). Her *Epistre de la prison de vie humaine* (1418), written after Agincourt, was addressed to Mary of Berry who had lost many members of her family at the battle. Written as a consolation this text reflects Christine's desire to retreat from the worldly realm of politics, which she did when she entered the convent at Poissy. Christine's final work *Ditié de Jehanne d'Arc* (1429) was one of the first literary celebrations of Joan. In this text she synthesised many of the themes most dear to her – patriotism, virtue, female power and the miracle of divine intervention.

Following her death Christine became part of the **catalog** tradition she had used to defend women, with male authors such as Jean de Marconville, Johann Caspar Eberti and Gustave Lanson using her as an example of female excellence. Her writings were 'rediscovered' in the early nineteenth century and she was the subject of several male-authored critical studies. With the onset of first-wave feminism Christine became an iconic figure. Alice Kemp-Welch wrote in *Six Medieval Women* that de Pizan 'may be regarded not merely as a forerunner of true feminism, but also as one of its greatest champions.' Nearly 70 years later **Joan Kelly** connected Christine with modern feminism, claiming that she was the first feminist theorist. The first modern biographical study of Christine de Pizan was written by Marie-Joseph Pinet in 1927. More recently Enid McLeod has produced *The Order of the Rose, The Life and Ideas of Christine de Pizan* (1976) and Charity Cannon Willard, *Christine de Pizan: Her Life and Works* (1984).

Mary Spongberg

References

Blumenfeld-Kosinski 1997; Ferrante 1997; Kelly 1984; McLeod 1991; Richards 1996.

Major works

Livre de la cité des dames [English] translated Earl Jeffrey Richards; foreword by Natalie Zemon Davis (New York: Persea Books, 1998) *Avision-Christine* [English] (ed.) Glenda K McLeod (New York: Garland Publishing, 1993) *Livre du corps de policie* [English] (ed.) Kate Langdon Forhan (Cambridge: Cambridge University Press, 1994) and *Le Livre des faits d'armes et de chevalerie* [English] (ed.) Charity Cannon Willard (University Park, PA: Pennsylvannia State University Press, 1999).

Postcolonial women writers

Postcolonial history

Postcolonial women historical writing is a diffuse category of historical production. It has two distinct streams: a non-academic tradition that is characterised by **autobiographies** and **biographies** written from experience by non-Western women; and an academic tradition distinguished by the confluence of ethnohistory, minority histories, women's history as well as the application of postcolonial and feminist theories. Both streams have challenged the basis of Western knowledges, and induced a shift away from male and Western-centred narratives to a mode of writing aimed at offering alternate, woman-centred and non-Western perspectives of the colonial past.

Postcolonialism as an intellectual concept emerged after the Second World War during the global processes of decolonisation. There has been much discussion about the definition of postcolonialism amongst scholars. Gyan Prakash most clearly outlines what postcolonialism is, along with its intents, when he describes it in 'Subaltern Studies as Postcolonial Criticism' as having 'compelled a radical rethinking of knowledge and social identities authored and authorised by colonialism and Western domination' (1994: 1475). For historians, it is a critique that places colonialism and its accompanying discourses of racial superiority at the epicentre of historical cause and effect.

The majority of postcolonial women's historians examine how colonial and race ideologies operated with the added dimension of gender in historical processes. Working from the premise that colonialism created a state of flux for both colonised and colonising societies, many historians have examined how colonialism's reordering of traditional social structures and economies impacted upon men and women differently. They also consider colonialism's impact on gender relations in non-Western cultures.

Postcolonial women's historical writing is geographically diverse. It encompasses writing on the colonial regions of Africa, South Asia, Asia and SouthEast Asia, the Middle East, South America and the Pacific, and the histories of settler societies and their indigenous peoples in Canada, Australia and New Zealand. In many cases, especially the United States, this history includes studies of slavery as well as relations between indigenous and incoming peoples.

Autobiographical and biographical writing

Writing in the 1830s Mary Prince told of her life as a female slave born on a plantation in Bermuda. Her account, 'related by herself', became a classic articulation of the female slaves' experience and, according to Henry Louis Gates Jr, this narrative 'broke the silence of the black woman slave' (1987: xvi). Prince's account was generated and timed with a specific intent: to draw attention to the plight of slaves and slave women, at the height of debate on the **abolition** of slavery in the British Empire.

A History of Mary Prince: A West Indian Slave, first published in London in 1831, is a chronicle of the multitude of brutalities endemic to slave societies and the particular perils that befell women bound by slavery. Prince revealed the sadistic treatment of herself and other slave women at the hands of malevolent masters: she was sold away from her family 'like sheep or cattle'; subjected to arduous labour; and endured sexualised corporal punishment. This was graphically conveyed when she described her master, Mr D—— stripping her naked and hanging her up by the wrists, beating her with a cowskin or his bare hands 'till my body was raw with gashes'. This treatment was 'nothing very remarkable' as it characterised the power exercised over both male and female slaves. Yet Mr D——'s 'ugly fashion of stripping himself quite naked and ordering me to wash him in a tub of water' was the most despised treatment she experienced, intimating that this practice also entailed sexual violation (Gates 1987: 191, 199, 202).

At the same time that Prince was highlighting injustices in the British Caribbean empire, a parallel tradition of African women's writing was emerging in the United States. The writings of Maria Stewart, *Religion and the Pure Principal of Morality* and *Productions of Mrs Maria W. Stewart* first published in 1829 and 1835 respectively, advocated a special role for black women in moral Christian African-American society that centred upon 'solidarity, self-help and racial pride'. This would be fortified by the establishment of institutions of 'higher learning by and for themselves' (Andrews 2003: viii–x). Stewart's writing which commenced with a sketch of her personal story also contained an overt critique of the United States for sustaining slavery. The worst indictment against America was that 'thou hast caused the daughters of Africa to commit whoredoms and fornications; but upon thee be their curse' (Andrews 2003: 13).

Following Stewart, a number of other African-American women writers authored 'moral essays' that focused upon women's experiences of slavery as well as 'spiritual autobiographies' that charted personal experience and the self-improving Christian path that led them 'to speak out for freedom' (Gates 1987: xxix–xxx; Andrews 2003: xi–xii). Of these, *The Narrative of Sojourner Truth* (1850) was one of the most influential in the years before the Civil War in highlighting the experiences of slave women. Yet, this was not an autobiography but a biography. Although Truth was renowned for her oratory skills she was not literate and so collaborated with Olive Gilbert, a white 'out-spoken opponent of slavery', whose name did not appear in Truth's published book (Andrews 2003: xv). William Andrews, along with other historians of early slave literature, has shown the limits of such literature as the voice of Gilbert is clearly present in the text censoring and revealing colonial condescension (2003: xvi).

The issue of how African-American writers were limited and influenced by white collaborators, editors and publishers was an issue at the time of publication as it is for current analyses of their works. The inclusion of the phrase 'written by herself' on title pages was key to indicating the degree of 'authenticity' of these accounts. Such was the case with Harriet Jacobs' *Incidents in the Life of a Slave Girl*, 'written by herself' and first published in 1861. This account 'brought this category of slave narratives to its summit' although, like Truth, the silent hand of abolitionist **Lydia Maria Child** may have been at work. It not only outlined her own history, it also revealed broader women's experiences – the fracturing of families, the routine sexual violation by masters, the accompanying scorn from the white mistress, the punishments and the degradations of the system that impacted upon white slave-owners, as well as their enslaved families (Gates 1987: xvi).

Like Prince's account it is not a story of unrelenting victimisation. Jacobs portrays herself as a determined young woman who is supported by her respected and monied grandmother who instilled Jacobs with a strong sense of honour and virtue that ran counter to the predominating stereotypes of black women's depraved sexuality (Gates 1987b: 349–51, 362, 383). Jacob's account accentuated the centrality of women to slave families and the manner in which slaves resisted the overwhelming power of slavery. The full impact of Jacobs' account, despite its powerful rendering of the experiences of slave women, was not felt until over

100 years after its publication as it was 'overshadowed' by the Civil War. With the emergence of an academic tradition of African-American women's history, Jacobs' account was rediscovered and has become 'the best-known and most widely read' African-American woman's text from the nineteenth century (Andrews 2003: xxv).

Autobiography and biography continued in the twentieth century to expose the continuing injustices of colonialism upon women and their communities. It remained a very powerful medium for promoting empathy within democratic nations so as to put continuing institutionalised racism on political agendas in those countries, evidenced by Maya Angelou's iconic work *I Know Why the Caged Bird Sings* (1969). Within Australia, for instance, following the nation-wide Aboriginal rights movement that sought the redress of legal, social and economic inequities and land rights in the 1960s, a literature of Aboriginal women's autobiographies emerged. Autobiographies and biographies by Aboriginal women were particularly potent literary forces to bring to light the human impact of eugenic policies of child removal and the accompanying practice of using these children as labourers. These works gave far greater insight into the extent that government policies effected Aboriginal lives and the impact they had upon individuals, thus putting a human face on detached scientific and state procedures.

Political activist Margaret Tucker's autobiography *If Everyone Cared* (1977) echoed a number of themes of nineteenth-century American slave narratives – the break-up of her family, institutionalised violence, drudgery and exploitation, and her conversion to a doctrine that she saw as a salvation for herself and other Aboriginal people. Tucker's autobiography recounts her life in Depression-era New South Wales, her removal from her family by police and her placement in a state-run institution to train Aboriginal girls for domestic service in affluent Sydney homes. Her experience led her to Communism, the doctrine that appealed to her and others in her situation in the years before the Second World War, as they readily identified with the downtrodden workers this political party professed to represent. Long before her autobiography was published, Tucker had gained a public profile as a musical performer and speaker at political rallies.

Other Aboriginal women's autobiographies detailed conditions in different times and places in Australia. Amongst these works those of Ruby Langford Ginibi, *Don't Take Your Love to Town* (1988), Glenyse Ward, *Wandering Girl* (1987) and *Unna You Fullas* (1991), and Sally Morgan, *My Place* (1987), have gained wide popularity. All contributed to the watershed in Australian society in the 1990s when this aspect of its colonial history became more widely recognised and acknowledged. More recently Doris Pinklington Nugi Garimara's *Follow the Rabbit Proof Fence* (2002) that told the story of her mother's escape from a West Australian institution was the basis for the acclaimed 2002 feature film *Rabbit Proof Fence*. This highly successful film alerted the international community to Aboriginal Australia's 'Stolen Generations' and the government policies that underlay the forced removal of children from their families.

Autobiographies and biographies of this nature, written by women who experienced colonialism in its worst excesses in both the nineteenth and the twentieth centuries, became the foundational sources for scholars investigating colonialism from the 1970s. The issues explored in these works – the destruction of the family, the place of women in non-white societies, labour, sexual exploitation, the social and scientific construction of the female black body, the question of victimisation – were all questions that scholars would take up from the 1970s.

Minority histories, national histories and histories of imperial regions

Writing in 1979 in her landmark work, *The Majority Finds Its Past*, Gerda Lerner dwelt upon the 'double neglect' of African-American women in historical writing because they were women and because they were black (1979: 63). Lerner was one of the first historians who acknowledged the shortcomings of feminist historiography that had concentrated exclusively upon white women as historical subjects. Lerner's identification of the absence of black women from American history sparked similar scrutiny of other national historiographies followed by an effort to place minority women into a broader historical framework.

The subsequent field of African-American women's writing grappled with the tensions between the practice of writing history, feminist historical models and the stark differences in historical experience for black women. Whereas 'the patriarchy' had been identified as the source of women's oppression by feminist theorisers, historians of minority women instead concentrated on racism and imperialism as the predominating source of oppression as Ranu Samantrai has argued in *AlterNatives* (2002: 10). This schism between white feminist and black feminist or 'womanist' historical models reflected a wider debate about the limitations of the women's liberation movement that was strongly informing historical writing. Black critics of the feminist movement exposed it as a predominantly white, middle-class movement that had little knowledge of, or empathy for, the plight of black women. In particular, critics of white women's liberation objected to the notion of 'universal sisterhood' that assumed that all women suffered equally in comparative social, economic and political situations. Liberation for black women entailed diametrically opposing objectives from those of the white feminist movement as writers such as bell hooks, *Ain't I A Woman?* (1984) and 'Postmodern Blackness' (1993), Bonnie Dill Thornton, 'Race, Class and Gender: Prospects for an All-inclusive Sisterhood' (1983), and Michelle Wallace, *Invisibility Blues* (1990), pointed out.

Writers and activists from many different contexts echoed this objection to feminism. American Indian Movement activist Mary Dog Crow (Shoemaker 1995: 12) argued in the 1970s that feminism was 'irrelevant' to Native American Indian women; and Australian Aboriginal writers, Pat O'Shane, 'Is There Any Relevance in the Women's Movement for Aboriginal Women?' (1976), and Jackie Huggins, 'A Contemporary View of Aboriginal Women's Relationship to the White Women's Movement' (1994), followed. Yet, as Nancy Shoemaker accents in *Negotiators of Change*, many Native American Indian writers also accepted that Native American women had a distinct historical experience from their menfolk, but this could not be conflated within a universal history of women and their struggle against the patriarchy. Instead liberation for women in their societies involved benefits for the extended family and wider community rather than individual women (1995: 12–13). Such interventions and refinements of feminist arguments impacted upon postcolonial historical writings by women in many national arenas.

This critique of feminist scholarship was also taken up on a theoretical front from 1986 by Chandra Talpade Mohanty's influential critique 'Under Western Eyes: Feminist Scholarship and Colonial Discourses' (1986) and Gayatri Chakravorty

Spivak in 'Can the Subaltern Speak?' (1988). Spivak objected to what she perceived as the depoliticisation of colonial studies, the inference that colonialism was an historical artefact that is implicit in 'postcolonial'. Like Mohanty, Spivak found feminism to be another Western hegemonic discourse that was acting to silence or speak on behalf of non-Western women. Spivak, amongst others, advocated the adoption of the terms 'subaltern' and 'Third World' to differentiate between the work produced by 'ventriloquist' white scholarship and that produced by scholars of non-Western heritage. This position *vis-à-vis* feminism was furthered most notably by Trinh T Minh Ha in *Woman Native Other* (1989) and *The Moon Waxes Red* (1991) and Sara Suleri, 'Woman Skin Deep' (1992). These works compelled feminist scholars who worked in colonial studies, such as Margaret Jolly in 'Colonising Women: The Maternal Body and Empire' (1993), to re-examine their position, politics and intents in light of these far-reaching critiques.

So how did this contemporary debate about feminist historical models, the writing of minority women's history and postcolonialism intersect? One critical development was the rejection of the notion that non-white women were unmitigating victims under the weight of the 'dual burden of racial and gender oppression' (Higginbottom 1989: 52). Rather, women exercised 'agency' in order to gain advantages and better conditions when they could. Evelyn Brooks Higginbottom in her pioneering essay, 'Beyond the Sounds of Silence: Afro-American Women in History', argued that the African matrifocal family structure was 'revitalised in New World slave societies'. She argued that as slavery undermined the role of the male provider, the economic power and autonomy of women within the household were a fundamental feature of black women's history that differed greatly from their white bourgeois counterparts (1989: 54). Deborah G White in 'Female Slaves: Sex Roles and Status in the Antebellum Plantation South' (1983) and Jacqueline Jones in *Labor of Love, Labor of Sorrow: Black Women, Work and the Family from Slavery to the Present* (1986) likewise grappled with linkages between economics and slave women's familial and social status during and after the fall of southern slavery. This remodelling of power made all historical subjects actors. This had extensive ramifications for this field of historical writing. In the writing of frontier histories indigenous women were posited as critical go-betweens between traditional indigenous cultures and colonial societies. This revision of the frontier decentred the overwhelmingly masculine character of the frontier that existed in previous historical constructions of frontiers.

From the 1980s, feminist histories of the frontiers in the United States, South America, Australia, the Pacific and beyond resurrected indigenous women from the confines of victimhood and infused their history with new dynamism. Yet, this new outlook also required refinement as the critique of colonialism became obscured in many instances by an emphasis upon the opportunities that indigenous women were exposed to, and neglected to account for the impact upon the wider indigenous community. Aboriginal historian Jackie Huggins, writing with Heather Goodall in 'Aboriginal Women are Everywhere', also censured writers who adopted this vision of the historic past as it portrayed Aboriginal men in a 'denigratory manner' (Huggins and Goodall 1992: 415). Such histories tended to blame Aboriginal men for violence within indigenous communities rather than incorporating colonial violence into the causes of upheavals within Aboriginal communities or women's decisions to move into frontier societies. Aboriginal writers insisted that their main objective was the cohesion of their communities rather than the politics of individualism advocated by feminism. This point is supported by Cheryl Johnson-Odim and Margaret Strobel who argued in their introduction to the Restoring Women to History series:

> As with any major societal upheaval resulting in challenges to existing authority, colonialism both created opportunities and oppressed women. In the final analysis however, the vast majority of women have opted to work for the independence of their societies. (1999: xli–xlii)

Another very important outcome of this dialogue between postcolonial theory and postcolonial historical writing was a rethinking of the limits of postcolonial approaches to history. As Florencia E Mallon in 'The Promise and Dilemma of Subaltern Studies: Perspectives from Latin American History' outlined there is an 'unfulfilled promise' of even-handedness in postcolonial methodology in which the colonial and colonised would supposedly be given equitable treatment by the historian. Mallon argued, through a review of postcolonial or 'subaltern' histories of Latin America, that despite the best intentions of a number of scholars, the limitations of sources, particularly archival sources, necessarily results in European bias. She also laments that 'like Spivak, I, too, want to touch pictures of the historical subjects I struggle to retrieve' but often these lives are irretrievable given the requirements of the empirical method that remain central to historical practice despite the postmodern critique (1994: 1507). Such critiques drew attention to the limitations of unearthing the past and resulted in an adjustment of the claims of postcolonial writers and a rethinking of the achievable parameters of such studies. The limitations and remoteness of the academic tradition have been countered by many non-western cultural producers by re-telling historical stories through oral traditions, fiction, performances and the new media of film. Toni Morrison's *Tar Baby* (1981), *Beloved* (1987), *Jazz* (1992), Alice Walker's *The Color Purple* (1985), Tracey Moffatt's *Nice Coloured Girls* (1987) and *Nightcries* (1989), Rachel Perkins' *Radiance* (2001) and various writers in Suseila Nasta's *Motherlands: Black Women's Writing from Africa, Caribbean and South Asia* (1992) have chosen to make their statements on colonialism via these mediums.

As postcolonial historians had to rethink what they could retrieve of colonised people's history, so too did they need to rethink the universal categories of 'colonised' and 'coloniser' and the notion that colonisation was experienced in uniform ways. This flaw in early postcolonial theory, clearly outlined by Ella Shohat in 'Notes on the Post-Colonial' (1992) that it collapsed the experience of all colonised peoples into one homogenous experience, overlooked that colonialism varied enormously throughout all colonised zones. Historical writing, as opposed to ahistorical postcolonial critiques, emphasised the specificity of time, place, environment, colonising powers and indigenous social structures as critical factors that differentiated indigenous experience. Through their attention to temporal specificity, historians have shown how divergent colonialism was even within national or larger colonial boundaries. Native American women who lived around Hudson Bay experienced colonialism differently from women from The Plains in many ways as women historians Sylvia Van Kirk in *Many Tender Ties* (1980), Jennifer Brown in *Strangers in Blood* (1980) and Olive Dickason in *The New People* (1985), amongst others, have shown.

An example of this attempt to variate American Indian women's history is the anthology *Negotiators of Change: Historical Perspectives on Native American Women* (1995). It set out to detail the vast differences in Native American women's historical experience across a 400-year period and vastly divergent colonial zones. Yet what bound their various historical quests were three common questions that reflect concerns of broader scholarship on women in native societies. According to editor Nancy Shoemaker, these questions revolved around whether women have had status and power equivalent to that of men and since the answer to that question has often been 'yes', historians have asked why. Secondly, they have tried to identify what the source of women's authority has been and finally how European settlement of the Americas affected the gender balance within native societies. Also, the writers in this volume sought to 'sift through' the stereotype of Indian women generated in Euro-American literature 'in order to appreciate Indian women's viewpoints and motivations' that Shoemaker cites as their 'greatest challenge' (1995: 2). Methodologically, these historians used archaeology, oral traditions and anthropological fieldwork from the late nineteenth and twentieth centuries in addition to traditional source authored by colonisers. The methods adopted by the authors of this volume reflected wider trends in postcolonial women's historical writing in the late 1980s and 1990s characterised by the work of Kumkum Sangari and Sudesh Vaid (1990), in Indian colonial history; Ann McGrath, *Born in the Cattle* (1987) and 'Whiteman Looking Glass' (1990), Kay Saunders, 'Pacific Islander Women in Queensland' (1982), Caroline Ralston, *Grasshuts and Warehouses* (1977) and 'Prostitution, Pollution and Polyandry' (1988), Patricia Grimshaw, *Paths of Duty* (1989), and Patty O'Brien, 'The Gaze of the Ghosts' (1998), in Australian and Pacific history; and Ann Laura Stoler in her works on SouthEast Asian colonial history, *Race and the Education of Desire* (1995) and 'Tensions of Empire' (1997).

The multi-authored volume, *Women in African Colonial Histories*, has likewise challenged colonial conflations of African women. It aimed to undermine any image of African women as 'hapless victims' and instead uncover the complexities of African women's historical experiences (Allman *et al.* 2002: 1). It also attempted to decentre eurocentrism by challenging the periodisation of African history that has been based upon 'formal political markers' and rather structure their histories according to the themes of 'encounters and engagements', 'perceptions and representations' and the reconfiguration and contestation of power. The essays range in focus from Tanya Lyons' study of women's involvement in guerilla warfare and national liberation struggles in Zimbabwe from the 1970s, to Holly Hanson's work on women's loss of political power in nineteenth-century East Africa to interactions of Kwena women with European missionaries in the second half of the nineteenth century, an examination by Wendy Urban-Mead. The essays in this volume built upon a substantial historiography demonstrating how vibrant and extensive postcolonial women's historical writing on Africa has become since the first works were published in the 1970s (Allman *et al.* 2002: 10–15).

Imperial feminism and feminist history

The tensions between feminism and postcolonial women's political objectives of decolonising western knowledges that we have examined in part above are also clearly evident in histories that explore white women's drive to 'uplift' and 'save' their colonised sisters from oppressive cultural practices. Clitoridectomies in Africa, *sati* and dowry murder in South Asia and various other practices are a dilemma for feminist historians. On the one hand these practices contravene western feminist sensibilities about the social empowerment of women and the fundamental need to protect women's bodies from violence and mutilation. Within the traditional feminist social models, men are the agents who exploit women's bodies and enforce cultures of oppression. Yet a number of postcolonial women's historians have shown that it is often women who perpetuate these practices against other women and it was not necessarily older women imposing cultural regimes on their younger counterparts.

Lynn M Thomas in her important study, 'Ngaitana (I will circumcise myself)' (1997), showed that it was a cross-section of women, including adolescent girls, who defied the 1956 ban on female circumcision in Kenya in the 1950s by excising each other. Her findings opposed earlier feminist scholarship that argued this practice, along with infibulation, was the epitome of patriarchal oppression against women. Thomas argued that within the complex colonial circumstances of the Mau Mau rebellion, the proliferation of this practice by adolescent girls was more than an act of resistance against an imposed colonial regime shaped by Christian missionary politics or 'about maintaining a valued practice'. It 'became a test and demonstration of their strength and determination as an age group' (1997: 29). Thomas came to understand their motivations through collecting oral testimonies of the women who were involved as young girls in the defiance of laws created ostensibly to protect them.

Veena Talwar Oldenburg in *Dowry Murder: The Imperial Origins of a Cultural Crime* has also complicated the historical picture by examining dowry murders and female infanticide in India. She has shown that these 'cultural crimes', long blamed by British imperialists upon Hindu culture, were the outcome of the 'masculinisation of the economy' by colonial policies (2002: 4–5). When viewed sociologically, it is mother-in-laws, accompanied by sister-in-laws or husbands, who perpetrate such crimes against brides. When viewed historically, in the colonial microcosm of the Punjab, the causational reasons for the emergence of dowry-related crimes are found in nineteenth-century economic restructuring undertaken by Britain.

Examining the role white women played in colonial history has been a vibrant genre in postcolonial women's historical writing as it continues to be. Since the 1980s, there have been numerous studies that have examined relations between white women and colonised women that have further complicated the sentimentalised vision of a universal sisterhood. The works by Helen Callaway, *Gender, Culture and Empire* (1987), Nupur Chaudari and Margaret Strobel, *Western Women and Imperialism: Complicity and Resistance* (1992), Felicity Nussbaum, *Torrid Zones: Maternity, Sexuality and Empire in Eighteenth Century Narratives* (1995) and Angela Woollacott, *To Try Her Fortune in London: Australian Women, Colonialism and Modernity* (2001) have been prominent in this field. More recently historians such as Victoria Haskins with John Mundine, 'Could you see to the return of my daughter?' (2003), have commenced the examination of the equally complex history of relations between white women and colonised men in the empire. Amongst these works, Antoinette Burton's *Burdens of History* (1994), has shown that the notion of universal sisterhood comes from Victorian-era feminism. Examining the work and lives of British feminists in India, Burton demonstrated how the feminist vision of women like Josephine Butler was structured around improving the lives of Indian women particularly through education and the reformation of imperial culture. Butler was especially concerned with prostitution and repealing the Contagious Diseases Acts, a campaign that Burton characterised as 'the white woman's burden'.

Following close upon Burton's seminal work, Kumari Jayawardena in her book *The White Woman's Other Burden* (1995) has investigated the historical complexity of white women in the empire. Rather than solely being memsahibs or reformers, Jayawardena uncovers the multiple roles that white women played in the empire. She distinguishes between the white women who came to South Asia bringing 'Christianity, Western education and values, social reform, women's rights and some modernising processes to the women of Asia within an acceptance of British rule' from those 'who were rejecting Christianity, negating Western values and rediscovering Oriental religions and culture in a context of Home Rule and nationalism, or even Socialism' (1995: 267). She found that many of the white women she studied dissented from British Rule and acted to undermine it through radical education and lending their support to nationalist movements. It was these women who were 'most appreciated by local women, especially by those who were politically active' (1995: 267).

Deconstructing discourses on race and gender

Whilst numerous postcolonial women's historians seek to understand white women's relationship with empires and colonised peoples, other historians deconstruct stereotypes of black and colonised women. Sarartje Bartman, the South African woman who became known as the Hottentot Venus in the early 1800s when she was displayed in Paris, has been a focal point for a number of scholars, such as Rosemary Wiss (1994) and Anna Fausto-Sterling (1995), delving into the Enlightenment scientific construction of black female sexuality and the black female body. Londa Schiebinger's *Nature's Body: Gender in the Making of Modern Science* (1993) examined Enlightenment scientific discourses and uncovered their dual purpose of circumscribing the social, political and economic role of European women particularly after the French Revolution and entrenching brutal practices towards women of the empire. Schiebinger demonstrated how the configuration of the 'black woman's body' through scientific discourses had ample uses by slave-owners and others who deployed colonised labour. For instance, enlightenment scientists posited that black women did not experience any significant physical trauma during childbirth, therefore their owners and employers could insist upon their return to hard labour soon after parturition with a clear conscience. Schiebinger demonstrates how these constructions had multiple applications in colonial practices.

Reina Lewis, *Gendering Orientalism* (1995), Susan Mendus and Jane Rendall, *Sexuality and Subordination* (1989) and Joanna De Groot 'Sex and Race: The Construction of Language and Image' (1989), amongst others, have examined art and literature as colonial texts and explored the linkages between colonial practice and the colonial imagination. A number of these scholars undertook to further the gendered dimension of Orientalism as set out by Edward Said, either in Said's Middle East or other colonial regions. For instance, the art works of Paul Gauguin in Tahiti and the Marquesas at the turn of the twentieth century have proved a rich subject for scholars such as Griselda Pollock, *Avant-Garde Gambits* (1992), Ann Solomon-Godeau, 'Going Native' (1989), and Margaret Jolly and Teresia Teaiwa in a special edition of *Pacific Studies* (2000), who have explored the politics of cultural production, in this case that of sexualised images of women in a colonial setting. Anthropologists, art historians and cultural studies scholars have also delved into the meanings of these cultural artefacts with differing purposes. Postcolonial historians have utilised the visual heritage of colonialism from art to films as a means to assess historical shifts, altering colonial practices and their intersection with changing attitudes to race, gender and sexuality. The inclusion of visual analysis in postcolonial women's historical writing is becoming increasingly commonplace, an acknowledgment of how important these documents are in reinforcing colonial thought and practice.

Contact histories

As we have seen, the predominant body of work by postcolonial women historians has concentrated upon gendered relations and the status of women in the colonial context. Yet a number of historians have written histories that focus less upon the gendered consequences of colonialism and seek to deconstruct and decentre eurocentric imperial narratives thereby recasting imperial episodes within the context of extant indigenous societies. Inga Clendinnen and Anne Salmond, for instance, are two historians whose work has been important for offering colonised peoples' perspective on imperial history in particular regional contexts. Clendinnen's *Ambivalent Conquest: Mayan and Spaniard in Yucatan 1517–1570* (1987) and Anne Salmond's *Two Worlds: First Meetings between Maori and Europeans 1642–1772* (1991) both contributed to a rethinking of colonial history by highlighting the continuities of indigenous societies after colonisation had ostensibly commenced. Both stressed the diffusion of power in these early contact histories thus dismantling traditional historic models of imperialism that posited the coloniser as dominating the colonised from the outset. By foregrounding non-European evidence, these historians formed a quite different view of what colonisation entailed in these two instances.

Patty O'Brien

References

Allman *et al.* 2002; Andrews 2003; De Groot 1989; Gates 1987; Haskins 2003; hooks 1993; Higginbottom 1989; Huggins 1994; Huggins & Goodall 1992; Johnson-Odim & Strobel M 1999; Jolly 1993; McGrath 1990; Mallon 1994; Mohanty 1986; O'Brien 1998; O'Shane 1976; OdiPrakash 1994; Ralston 1988; Saunders 1982; Shoemaker 1995; Shohat 1992; Spivak 1988; Sterling 1995; Stoler 1997; Suleri 1992; Thomas 1997; Thornton 1983; White 1983; Wiss 1994.

Related essays

Abolition; Australia; Body and Sexuality; Dominion women writers; Empire; Orientalism; Travel; Prostitution; Slavery; United States.

Power, Eileen Edna le Poer 1889–1940

English social and economic historian, historian of women. Born Manchester, eldest daughter of Mabel (Grindley Clegg) and Philip Ernest le Poer Power. Raised by unmarried aunts following her mother's death, Power was educated at the Oxford High School for Girls; obtaining a Clothworker's Scholarship she went up to Girton College, Cambridge in 1907. Power won the Pioneer's Prize for history in 1908, 1909 and 1910 as well as obtaining firsts in Parts 1 and 2 of her historical examinations. Awarded the Gilchrist scholarship in 1910, she travelled to France to study at the Sorbonne and the *École des Chartes* for a year under the supervision of Charles-Victor Langlois.

Returning in 1911 Power took up the Charlotte Shaw scholarship at the London School of Economics (LSE). There she began to study the social and economic position of women in Britain in the later medieval period, eventually narrowing her focus to the history of pre-Reformation English nunneries. Left the LSE in 1913 to take up a lectureship at Girton, where she became the Director of Historical Studies. At Girton she became involved in the National Union of Women's Suffrage Societies. With the outbreak of war, Power campaigned for **peace**, working with the League of Nations Union and lecturing on the Congress of Vienna. In 1917 she was awarded the Gamble Prize for her essay, 'The Enclosure Movement in English Nunneries'.

In 1920 Power became the first (and only) woman to receive an Albert Khan Travelling Fellowship. She spent a year travelling in India, Burma, China, Java and Japan. Power's travels encouraged her to take a less Eurocentric view in her historical understanding. Her innovative perspectives on comparative social and economic history were formed at this time. Returning to England, Power took up a joint appointment in medieval economic history at the LSE and in economic history at King's College, University of London. Although disappointed to leave Girton, Cambridge's failure to allow women full membership of the university strengthened her resolve as she reported: 'I've never felt so bitter in my life.' At the LSE she worked extensively with R H Tawney, with whom she published *Tudor Economic Documents* (1924) and formed the Economic History Society. Power's early commitment to social history was framed by a desire to write history for the newly enfranchised – 'a new kind of history of interest to ordinary people – social and economic and world history'. Her first published work the *Paycockes of Coggeshall* (1920) had rewritten rural history from below, shifting the focus from political study of the manor to the everyday life of ordinary people. This was the framework for her most famous work *Medieval People* (1924) in which she defended social history as a form of history that allowed the past to 'be made alive again'. Her understanding of the power of social history was further expanded by her pacifism and her travel, and she used her position to attack militarism and nationalism. She worked actively to promote **peace** through teaching **World history**, arguing that the success of the League of Nations depended on a community with common historical ideas.

Power's major contribution to women's history *Medieval English Nunneries, c1275 to 1535*, a detailed social and economic history of the convent system, appeared in 1922. While Power maintained that medieval communities were more favourable to women, she did not engage in the speculation about mother-right that characterised the work of **Lina Eckenstein.** Power's interest in women's social and economic position during the Middle Ages was not limited to the convent. Although she never completed her planned study of medieval women, she published numerous articles on their status, on ideas about women and on women as medical practitioners, and in *Medieval People* she produced studies on Chaucer's prioress Madame Eglentyne and the *ménagier's* wife. She also translated the *Goodman of Paris* (1928), a fourteenth-century manual on female deportment, and Johannes Herolt's *Miracles of the Virgin Mary* (1928). Power lectured on the Cult of the Virgin in the Middle ages, medieval women and their work and Joan of Arc. Some of her unpublished writings on women's history appeared as *Medieval Women* in 1975.

At the LSE Power developed a reputation as an innovative teacher. Her seminars on medieval economic history proved highly influential, creating an interdisciplinary environment drawing together economic, social and comparative history, anthropology and sociology. These seminars trained a generation of medieval economic historians including a number of women, such as Eleanora Carus-Wilson and Sylvia Thrupp, who dedicated her book *The Merchant Class of Medieval London* to Power's memory. A number of significant collaborative publications grew out of these seminars: *Studies in English Trade in the Fifteenth Century* (1933) which Power wrote with M M Postan and the Cambridge *Economic History of England* (1941) which she initiated but did not live to see published.

Power did much to popularise the study of history in Britain, publishing works such as *Medieval People* and teaching history at the Workers' Education Association. She made history accessible to children through books such as *The Boys and Girls of History* (1926), which she wrote with her sister Rhonda, and through her history lectures to children on BBC radio. A textbook for children on World history was left unpublished due to her sudden death. She also wrote reviews and essays in the popular press and broadcast her views on international politics on the BBC throughout the 1930s. Power was awarded an honorary doctorate from the University of Manchester in 1933 and another from Mount Holyoke in 1937. She became a member of the editorial board of *Economic History Review* in 1934. She was a fellow and Vice-President of the Royal Historical Society and a corresponding member of the Medieval Academy of America; and a fellow and member of Girton's Council. In 1937 she married her former student and collaborator M M Postan. Power was the first woman to give the Ford Lectures at Oxford in 1939. These lectures were also published posthumously as *The Wool Trade in English Medieval History* (1941).

Mary Spongberg

References

Berg 1992, 1996; Jacob 1995.

Major works

Medieval Women, Foreword by Maxine Berg (Cambridge: Cambridge University Press, 1995) *Medieval People*, Introduction by Emanuel Le Roy Ladurie (London: London Folio Society, 1999) *The Wool Trade in English Medieval History* (New York: Greenwood Press, 1987) *Medieval English Nunneries c1275–1535* (New York: Biblo & Tannen, 1964).

Private writings

In their letters, diaries and fragments of personal papers, women's voices speak compellingly from and of the past. They do not speak *to* us – for 'we' are in most cases not merely an unintended, but an unimaginable audience. But they do speak – evocatively, authoritatively or intimately – to themselves, to their friends, sisters, companions, husbands and mothers, or, more rarely, to kings, governments, seigneurial lords, political representatives or corporations. And in so doing, they also speak for us. Women's private writings present their lives, identities and circumstances in particular lights; and thus shape our present-day understandings of their lived past.

To include 'private writings' as a specific category in a 'Companion' to women's historical writing implies that such writing is, in itself, history. It would be problematic to assume that every act of 'writing the self' entailed the cultural consciousness, the sense of purpose, the imagining of posterity that may seem to be implied by the act of writing 'history'. But it would be equally problematic to assume that diaries and letters simply record the transitory, unreflective moment, and are converted into 'real' history only through the mediation and superior awareness of the historian (Swindell 1989: 25–9). This essay will avoid the pitfalls of these two possible approaches by blending them: attending not only to the debates and practices in the writing of women's history that arise from the use of private writings as sources, but also to the ways those writings themselves at once record and insist upon particular versions of 'history'. History is produced somewhere in the imagined spaces between past writers, recent historians and present readers. This article focuses on the engagements between the first two elements in this equation, although the reader never drops entirely from sight.

The attractions of women's private writings to historians are obvious. When women's history took off in the 1970s it did so on the basis of an intense curiosity about the lives of women who had been 'hidden from history'. If the first impulse in this act of recovery was to read, with a renewed sense of purpose and outrage, centuries of prescriptive literature urging women to 'suffer and be still', the second was to ask how women actually responded to those prescriptions – how their lives were affected by shifts in social mores and gendered ideology; and how they resisted or contributed to such shifts. As Nancy Cott wrote in her pathbreaking work, *The Bonds of Womanhood*, her interest was in women's *lives*, not just in what was written about them. She turned to the personal documents of women in order to 'broaden [her] inquiry into the relation between the change in the material circumstances of women's lives and their outlook on their place as women' (1977: 3). Women's diaries and letters spoke simultaneously of material constraints and of ideological response. Their written words positioned them as historical subjects, produced by and producing the ideas and circumstances in which they were embedded. Their words spoke from, but also of, the past.

It has become something of a truism that early acts of 'recovery' history in the later decades of the twentieth century betrayed a naïve faith in 'experience' as something that lay, inert and readily visible, in the written documents of the past. To re-read some of the key texts of 1970s feminist history offers a valuable corrective to that assumption. Nancy Cott's introduction not only speaks eloquently of the limits of written sources as produced by literate, white, middle-class, Protestant women, but also ponders the varied impact of literacy, leisure and religion on the production of those texts. Religious faith and spiritual introspection, Cott concludes, provided the most important source of energy for these eighteenth and nineteenth-century diaries (1977: 9–18). She writes, too, of the problem of silence – silences which leave present-day readers unaware of what is not said. Even if we become aware of an absence or omission, we cannot interpret its significance. We cannot know what has been accidentally lost, what was left out because it seemed unimportant, and what was kept secret because it carried all-too-weighty significance. 'In an ironic sense', Cott interpolates, 'the writers thus protect their "unknownness" from historians' prying' (1977: 17). We cannot as readers force these texts to yield up information that their writers have omitted: we may speculate on silence, but we cannot conclusively fill the gaps.

Only the text remains; but a text which historians have been increasingly willing to subject to multiple readings, seeking its buried meanings rather than lamenting over its lacks. As Carroll Smith-Rosenberg observed in 1986, in such texts may be traced 'the complexity of our semantic experience'; there an historian may analyze the 'process by which words are formed out of experiences and experiences are shaped by words' (1986: 3). Words, wrote Smith-Rosenberg, 'are cultural constructs, imaginative mediations of social experiences', which 'reflect the social location and relative power of the speakers' (1986: 35). Women's contributions to discourse and language therefore illuminate class, gender, identity and social positioning. She might have added race.

Intimacy and experience

Pursuing this relationship between words, meaning and experience, a number of historians have made diaries, as a specific genre of autobiographical writing, the particular focus of their research. Creating a diary, writes Cynthia Huff, 'is a skill which requires the manipulation of the vastness of experience' (1985: ix). Nineteenth-century women, she suggests, wrote in order to store the flux and nuance of life 'in a place of safe keeping, so that when the time came they could sift and evaluate the past, whether it was measured by the recurrence of birth and death or by the tallying of accounts' (1985: ix).

> By exhibiting the indelible stamp of each woman's existence and the ways in which she wished to present her being, diaries act as a monument to, and a recreation of, the life of their writer. . . . Through their diverse subject matter and a variety of forms and styles, these diaries nonetheless exhibit recurrent patterns which indicate how each writer evaluated her milieu and herself, and chose to construct a record which mitigated against the chaos of death. (1985: xxxiv)

Exploring the agency of self-representation and the patterns of female narrative, Huff and others conclude that women's diaries offer alternative perspectives on historical time. In their daily chronicling of the intimacies and mundanities of life, diaries at once record and produce vivid impressions of time as cyclical or diurnal: driven not by the linearity of conventional historical time, but by the repetitious rhythms of women's domestic labour and reproductive bodies. The idea of what Julia Kristeva (1981) called 'women's time' informs the structure – and titles – of such studies as Harriet Blodgett's *Centuries of Female Days* (1988), Margo Culley's *A Day at a Time* (1985) or Katie Holmes' *Spaces in her Day* (1995). As Holmes writes: 'In writing a diary a woman shaped her day, her week, her life. From the language and meanings available to her, she constructed her world' (1995: xii). Read in this way, diaries are not valued solely for the marginal flashes of insight they supply into the events of 'real' history, but for the way they reconfigure our understanding of historical time, decentring the authority of teleology.

If diaries map the rhythms of time, letters forge the connections of intimacy. In Smith-Rosenberg's analysis of the 'female world of love and ritual', letters are cited again and again not merely for their content, their assurances of affection, interest and concern, but for their frequency and constancy, their bridging of separation and absence, their clear identification of relationships of kin and friendship that mattered and were worth sustaining. For Smith-Rosenberg, letters and diaries, through their existence as much as their content, are eloquent testimony to the 'emotional proximity' to each other in which eighteenth and nineteenth-century women lived (1975: 3).

There is much to be gained from reading diaries and letters for the shape and structures inherent in the texts themselves. But inevitably, historians are also interested in their content. Not surprisingly, such interest has tended to concentrate on their perceptions of, and perspective on, intimacy and domesticity. The 'analysis of women's private letters and diaries which were never intended to be published', writes Smith-Rosenberg, 'permits the historian to explore a very private world of emotional realities central both to women's lives and to the middle-class family' (1975: 3). For Sarah Gristwood (1988), women diarists are 'recording angels', their diaries a compendium of reflections and records of their 'secret world' and intimate preoccupations. Linda Pollock (1983) found in personal writings from 1500 to 1900 a cumulative testimony to the intensity of parent–child feeling, with which to challenge the assumption of historians such as Edward Shorter and Lawrence Stone that family affection was an indulgence only possible in the modern age. Writing subjectively and familiarly, female diarists and correspondents hint at the intimacies of an unknown and ultimately unknowable world. In so doing they stir us, their later readers, to a sense of imaginative empathy, but at the same time draw attention to the limits of empathy as a means of historical understanding. Stella Tillyard reacts to the letters of the Lennox sisters, eighteenth-century English aristocrats, with a 'dual sense of closeness and distance', a 'mixture of sympathy and astonishment' (1984: ix). A powerful sense of intimacy, she writes, imbues the letters and their continued preoccupation with 'things that are as important to us as they are to them.' Their expressive emotions 'create a resonant feeling that seems to erase the centuries between its writing and our recording. . . . But when we look again, sympathy dissolves into strangeness' (1984: ix–x).

The strangeness is mainly of circumstance, but creates subjectivities alien to the experience of the present. The same can be said of Margaret Paston, whose letters have long been seen as offering a unique insight into the fifteenth century and into the domestic and familial consequences of the Wars of the Roses. In a letter to her husband in 1448, Margaret Paston knuckles down to business with the brisk efficiency of a woman beset by pressing domestic concerns:

> Ryt wurchipful hwsbond, I recomawnd me to you, and prey yow to gete som crosse bowis, and wyndacys to bynd them wyth, and quarell; for yowr hwsis here ben so low that there may non man schete owt wyth no long bowe, thow we hadde never so moche

> nede . . . And also I wold ye xuld gete ii or iii schort polle-axis to kepe wyth doris . . . (Davis 1958: 9)

Already ousted from the Pastons' manor, Grantham, by her enemies, 'Lord Moleynys men', Margaret was now hard pressed to maintain her occupancy of the smaller house to which her household had retreated. Yet amidst her preoccupation with cross-bows, poleaxes and the challenges of defence, other matters of domestic moment could not be ignored. Towards the end of her hasty letter she added a few more items to her list of requisitions: a quantity of almonds and sugar, and 'summe frese to maken of your childeris gwnys'. The frieze, she advised her husband, should be purchased from 'Hayis wyf', who would give him 'best chepe and best choyse' (Davis 1958: 10).

Margaret Paston's casual linking of the dual need to guard her house and dress her children defines her, for me, as a woman of agency and immense competence: so much so that this remembered quotation obliterated all surrounding material. When I recently went back to check the reference I was startled, and somewhat abashed, to be reminded of another letter Margaret Paston had written only months later, in which after beseeching her husband not to be displeased that she had 'com from that place that ye left me in', she explained that she had been brought 'seche tydngys' that she felt obliged to flee for her safety. Lord Moleynys' men now said that 'if thei myt gete me they xuld stele me, and kepe me wythinne the kastell' until her husband came to fetch her, to his grave danger and her own. On hearing this 'I kowd no rest have in myn hert tyl I was here' (Davis 1958: 13).

This reminder of female physical and sexual vulnerability shocks and unsettles precisely because Margaret Paston's letters otherwise construe her as a figure of authority, a confident agent of her own destiny. Written, as editors and commentators insist, out of the exigencies of the moment and with no thought to future readers, her letters yet produce a series of vivid and usually controlled images with which to chronicle a life. Through their preservation, Margaret Paston's preoccupations with the pressing concerns of the present and her lifelong efforts to defend the property interests of the Paston family have been woven into history, leading to her prolonged discursive existence as a vital, active and defining figure in the Wars of the Roses. The Lennox sisters' faith in terrifying medical remedies, like Margaret Paston's urgent need for crossbows, remind us that their voices, however direct, speak from a world we have lost and can recover only through a reach of the imagination.

Political correspondence

The fascination of this intimate world, at once so appealing and so mysterious, has formed one of the strongest and most recurring facets of women's history in recent decades. Yet as Mary Favret has more recently argued, feminist historians have been perhaps too willing to accept the 'sentimental fiction of letters' (1993: 10). This fiction, says Favret, 'dresses the letter in feminine roles and scrutinises the private spaces, the physical and emotional vulnerability, that such roles shape and define' (1993: 10). Feminists have accepted that letters provide a 'window into the intimate . . . self', and have celebrated the letter as 'a form which allows unregulated fluctuations of thought and feeling at the same time that it documents the minutiae of domestic life' (Favret 1993: 10). More generally, they have thus contributed to a gendered division of history in which the domestic world belongs to women's history while the world of strife and political action, once thought of as 'universal', is now understood as masculine. Favret reminds us that, in contrast, the boundaries of 'private writing' are as permeable as those of 'domestic', 'public', 'male' or 'female' worlds. Letters have served not only as intimate links, but as 'tools for political agitation or propaganda' (1993: 10). In the years following the French Revolution, she argues in *Romantic Correspondence*, women writers 'used the familiar letter for entry to the world of politics', fusing the world of epistolary romance and domestic tragedy with the 'world of political revolution' (1993: 7). As a political tool, the letter was available 'to anyone with a pen' (1993: 9). Letters might be addressed directly as appeals to authority; pamphlets and propaganda could be packaged as a familiar correspondence. Transgressing the boundaries between public and private, letters could make the intimate at once public and politically powerful. Regarded in this light, letters did not simply chronicle an alternative domestic history, but represented for some women a point of entry onto the historically visible public stage: their active intervention into and representation of historic events of stirring significance.

Conversely, letters might charge the atmosphere of intimacy itself with a politics of dissent, division or resistance. Norma Clarke (1990), like Favret, is sceptical of the 'sentimental fiction' of letters, but for different reasons. For Clarke, the domestic world itself was riven with dispute, with profound significance for the politics of gender. She points to one well-known attempt to package epistolary combat as sentiment: the publication in 1908 of the early letters of Thomas Carlyle and Jane Baillie Welsh, under the unconvincing title of *The Love Letters of Jane and Thomas Carlyle*. These 'love letters' delineate a relationship far more complex than that of courtship. Clarke characterises it in stark terms as something nearer a 'battle to the death' (1990: 6), during which Jane Welsh gradually relinquished her claims to an independent writing life, opting at last to marry the historian who had initially seemed willing to accept the role she had assigned him, that of tutor and mentor. The correspondence can be described as an exchange of love letters, argues Clarke, only within the romantic convention in which a young woman learns to give up all for a young man's genius, finding her reward in love and marriage. 'A high-spirited, highly intelligent, independent-minded, voluble and witty young woman is reduced, in the course of this specific text, to silence and extreme emotional dependency on an exceptionally egotistical and controlling young man, and the process is naturalised as the necessary prelude to marriage' (1990: 6).

In her later life, and still more after her death, Jane Carlyle took her revenge. In defence against the dismal intimacies of her marriage to a cantankerous historian, she developed, in Aileen Christianson's words, 'a finely honed talent for the epistolary art: the art of a miniaturist creating mock-heroic struggles out of her daily life, in contrast to the blocks of monolithic history hewn by Thomas as he sat at the centre of her domestic life, essential to her both as rationale and as material' (1987: 283). Thomas Carlyle himself, as overbearing husband, became 'a fine tragi-comic creation', artful product of Jane Carlyle's genius for letter-writing (Christianson 1987: 283; Amigoni 1996). It was these letters from her later married life, plus the diary that chronicled her particular and acute unhappiness during her husband's brief passion for Lady Ashburton, that helped persuade Thomas Carlyle after Jane's death of his defects as a husband. Overwhelmed with remorse, he poured out grief and anguish into his *Reminiscences*, and handed them over with his wife's private papers to his designated biographer, James

Anthony Froude. Froude, true to his training at Carlyle's hands, deemed it proper to publish the full details after Thomas Carlyle's own death, resulting in a startling revelation of domestic misery that caused Victorian society to reel with horror and speedily drop its former idol from the pantheon of heroes (Gilbert 1991: 295–314; Hamilton 1993: 158–76). It was in response to this public repudiation that Alexander Carlyle attempted to rescue his uncle's good name by packaging his earlier correspondence with Jane as an unexceptionable romance.

As this case demonstrates, the editing and publication of correspondence can impart it with a particular flavour, but letters remain susceptible to multiple interpretations. Just as Clarke found a 'battle to the death' amidst those 'love letters', Antoinette Burton and Meera Kosambi, working within the framework of postcolonial history, have both found alternative stories of conflict and negotiation amidst *The Letters and Correspondence of Pandita Ramabai* (Shah 1977). These letters were originally arranged and edited by the Anglican nun, Sister Geraldine, who had endeavoured to advise and guide Ramabai through her conversion to Christianity in 1883 and the years following. Ramabai, an Indian Brahmin scholar, had gone to England to pursue higher studies, including the study of medicine. Once there, she converted to Christianity, and the efforts of her mentors and the Anglican church hierarchy more generally were focused on making her an appropriate and effective missionary for the Anglican church in India. In assembling the correspondence, Sister Geraldine believed she was making a 'contribution to the history of the conversion of India' (Kosambi 2000: 50) and incidentally displaying the 'childishness, untrustworthiness and vanity' to which she attributed all of Ramabai's rational questioning and religious doubts (Burton 1995: 40). But Kosambi probes aspects of Sister Geraldine's methods 'which she perhaps had not visualized as being the possible subject of scrutiny' (2000: 51), in particular focusing on her use of the ideological language of maternalism as a tool in her disputes with Ramabai; while Burton reads in Ramabai's letters 'her determination to speak in "a voice of my own" ' (1995: 37). For Burton, Ramabai's relationship with Sister Geraldine, and even with her other, more sympathetic mentor Dorothea Beale, was 'a struggle for authority – authority over which version of reform for women would prevail in India' (1995: 42). The context of Church and empire shaped the relationships amongst these women, and their encounters 'signal, if not the impossibility of women's international solidarity, then certainly some of the contradictions inherent in the ideal of international sisterhood' (Burton 1995: 30). Amidst the threads of Sister Geraldine's patronising ordering of Pandita Ramabai's doubts and challenges, the force of Ramabai's claims to intellectual, cultural and spiritual equality rings clear:

> I must tell you that when I find out that you or your friends have no trust in me, and they want directly or indirectly to interfere with my personal liberty, I must say 'goodbye' to you and go my own way, by which my Lord God will guide me. (Burton 1995: 50)

For Ramabai, if not for her self-styled mentors, letters served not as an expression of intimacy but as the site for reasoned discourse and the articulation of disputes: disputes in which she assumed, often on explicitly nationalist terms, an equal right to have and to hold on to her opinion. It is this aspect of private correspondence that Burton, Clarke and Favret all seek to capture: letters which do not chronicle an unchanging domestic world but are themselves crucial currency in an intrinsically dialectical struggle. Such letters map a dynamic world of combat and contest, and in so doing challenge any conventional assumptions of the even flow of female lives.

Cultural production

If the attempt to grapple with the conflicted and conflictual nature of women's private writing has been one key development in women's history, another has been the growing attention to the cultural production of the writing itself. The craft of letters is as important as – and inseparable from – their ideological purpose. The tone of Pandita Ramabai's letters is that of a confident rhetorician. Jane Carlyle's epistles, at once intimate revelations and sharply pointed weapons in a domestic dispute, were also products of wit, artistry and style. Stella Tillyard defines the elements of epistolary style that prevailed amongst the aristocracy of the previous century and to which the Lennox sisters consciously aspired: letter-writing, she says, was 'an art that at once informed, entertained and revealed the self. The most perfect style was both artless and arch, intimate and allusive, with frequent gestures towards a rarified culture of print' (Tillyard 1994: 94). The letters of the Lennox sisters emulated a relaxed style of conversation through an element of 'deliberate sloppiness': letters, they believed, 'were conversations between writer and recipient in which both could construct and (paradoxically) display a private self' (Tillyard 1994: 96). In 'unburdening' their minds they also constructed them for a sympathetic audience.

In her study of women's letters and diaries from nineteenth-century New England, Catherine Kelly (1999) similarly emphasises the evident *craft* of the writing, the self-conscious style and literary conventions that shape the text. Like Smith-Rosenberg before her, Kelly insists that these texts are not, therefore, 'simply unmediated reflections of experiences', the preserve of social historians. Through private writing, women did not only articulate experience and the meanings they attached to experience, but were also able to define themselves as *thinkers*, 'participants in a community of letters'. On this basis Kelly claims the possibility of an intellectual rather than (or as well as) a social history of women's private writing, one that blurs the distinction between 'the history of persons and behaviour on the one hand and intellect and imagination on the other' (1999: 6–7). In offering an intellectual history of women's words, Kelly does not seek to abstract the sources from the 'social contexts and material realities of women's lives', but rather advocates a blending of approaches.

> Indeed, much of the power of these documents lies precisely in their defiance of the fine distinctions between social and intellectual history. Put another way, these documents served multiple purposes in the lives and minds of their creators; they can certainly withstand multiple readings at the hands of historians. (1999: 7)

The idea of an intellectual history of diarists and correspondents implies that the craft of their texts was conscious and self-determined. It is perhaps most easily applied to those writings – the majority in this genre – that were the products of leisure and privilege. But the 'multiple purposes' for which diaries and letters were originally created could lie not only in the minds of their creators, but in their audiences. This is manifestly true of letters, written always to a defined audience and sometimes at least with the desire to please the known sensibilities of the intended recipient. But it can also be true of diaries. If Jane Carlyle's initial purpose in writing her diary about her husband's relationship with Lady Ashburton was to relieve an overcharged heart, her careful packaging of the material into a bundle that Thomas Carlyle would certainly read after her death suggests that she came to imagine a reader for it all other than herself, and thus imbued the writing with a new and still more serious purpose. Thomas Carlyle's own act in placing the diaries into the hands of his biographer, who in turn made their contents available to the public, ensured that the purpose of communication acquired more and more layers and complex twists. For each new audience, the meaning of the writing carried a very different significance.

In a still more celebrated case, a diary was itself created, apparently, entirely for the pleasure of its first reader. Hannah Cullwick's diary has generated more controversy than perhaps any other over the precise problem of how far, if at all, it can be thought to represent the subjectivity of its writer. Many critics have gone so far as to assert that it tells us far more of its first intended reader, Arthur Munby, than it does of Hannah Cullwick herself.

Certainly the circumstances of the production of this diary were unique. Arthur Munby, a classic example of the middle-class fascination with exploring the underworld of Victorian England, had a voyeuristic passion for female labour. In Hannah Cullwick he found a domestic servant whose enthusiasm for her menial labours, strength and skill satisfied his passion and who was, moreover, willing to add to the labours of her domestic drudgery by writing in a diary each evening of the work she had performed. That her diary played a role in their curious relationship is clear: the precise nature of that relationship remains profoundly ambiguous. But historians have been as puzzled by the problem of how, therefore, to read the diary as they have been by the more immediately salacious question of what Hannah Cullwick and Arthur Munby actually got up to. For Liz Stanley, editor of Hannah Cullwick's diaries, Hannah's words are direct testimony to the agency she gained through her own strength and skill: 'the drudgery that was everyday life for the maid-of-all-work also in a sense liberated her' (1984: 4). It made her 'not a woman' and thus freed her from the prescriptive ideology of femininity. To Leonore Davidoff (1983), the diaries are a useful, if ambiguous, testament to the spaces and relationships of power that shaped a domestic servant's life. Julia Swindells more sceptically suggests that ultimately 'the diaries leave us knowing little about Hannah Cullwick' (1989: 36). As Hannah Cullwick first 'experiences' a day of drudgery for the gratification of her 'Massa' and then engages in the further service of writing it all down, 'rendering up that experience to male reconstruction' and male desire, the role of Arthur Munby in the production of the text increasingly seems inescapable. 'If the subject has anything to do with power and the power of defining and prescribing the object, then the subject here is the man and the male fantasy; and the fantasy is primarily of labour as sexual aesthetic' (Swindells 1989: 31–2). Anne McClintock (1995) in turn protests against readings of Hannah Cullwick that present her as Munby's plaything, the 'creature of his fancy'. She seeks to reinstate Cullwick's pride in her labour and her 'lifelong resistance to limitation'. Without suggesting that her relationship to Munby was one of 'libertarian equality and mutual power', McClintock argues that 'Cullwick's life expressed a sustained determination to negotiate power within circumstances of great limitations', and seeks an analysis that acknowledges her 'agency and desires' and her 'lifelong power over Munby' (1995: 139–44). McClintock argues that Cullwick's power lay in her ambiguity and theatricality: but in order to sustain this argument she must read Cullwick's diary as expressive of her own subjectivity and not, as in Swindells' analysis, as a text produced out of and on behalf of Munby's fantasies alone.

Hannah Cullwick's diaries, and their contested use by feminist historians, speak eloquently of the problems and paradoxes of women's private writing in history. To reject her account as merely an act of ventriloquism by Arthur Munby is to perpetuate the erasure of her subjectivity begun during her lifetime: to accept it as a true record of her working life and 'experience' ignores the manifold influences and contexts that produced her text. These dilemmas are present in any historical reading of private writings: to either accept or reject them as authoritative accounts of experience is equally problematic. But the dilemma is most acute when reading texts produced by those, like Hannah Cullwick, whose circumstances have not given them what Carolyn Steedman refers to as the 'privilege' of interiority (1994: 64–7). For many women, including servants like Hannah Cullwick or colonial subjects locked in encounters with the West, diaries and letters were often produced at the behest and to serve the purposes of an intrusive, authoritative audience. Such writings may still testify to a specific subjectivity, but of a subject produced through power relationships that inhere in the text, rather than as an autonomous writing voice.

Once, such diaries and letters might have been read as raw material, biased and subjective but full of information that could be cross-checked, verified and then accepted or discarded. But historians in recent times, feminist historians amongst them, have been less enamoured of the quest for 'objective' truth. Joan Scott has forcibly and repeatedly reminded us of the hazards of seeking 'experience' as the heart of historical research, of assuming pre-existing categories of identity (such as 'women') and then trying to find out what happened to them. Instead, suggests Joan Scott, we should be distrustful of both the identities and the experiences, and read the texts of the past for evidence of *how* identities were produced, culturally and discursively (1991: 773–97). There can be no instant and easy recognition of 'women' between one century, one society and another – only 'imagined repetitions or repetitions of imagined resemblances' (2001: 286). Not only was experience 'mediated' by text, Scott suggests, but the mediations of texts constructed both the experience and the identity behind it.

Feminist historians have never agreed on the value of deconstructive approaches for feminist history. But at the very least Scott reminds us that diaries and letters are as interesting for what they tell us of the constitution of identity as for what they say about women's lives. Female subjectivity itself is a core concern of women's history; and the mysteries of difference are as compelling and important as the 'recognition' or assumption of sameness. Individuals make history through the act of writing as much as they do through social action. Personal writing in this sense constitutes a vital piece of 'history', rather than fragments of 'evidence' capable of being continually sifted, broken and reassembled.

Women's letters and diaries speak of lives embedded in social, historical meaning: they speak of social position shaped by class, race and gender; intimacy and emotion;

political interventions and domestic battlefields; intellectual and cultural interpretations of the world. They offer not 'unmediated experience', but experience clothed in, and produced by, history; texts that served a complex array of motives and purposes for their creators and original audiences. Serious scholarly engagement with women's personal writings, then, demands that historians read them at multiple levels: as at once records of experience and textual constructions of meaning. Historians have traced not only the events recorded in such texts, but the apparent choices of what to record, the relationships that are assumed or created in the text between the writer and her world, the rhythms of time and historical movement, and the presentation and significance of self. They have plunged into worlds of experience, language, feeling and imagination; they have delighted in and dissected narratives; they have striven to catch new glimpses of the outer world recorded on those frail pages, or to understand the internal logic of the words themselves. In short, historians have read women's private writings as the raw material for their own interpretations; but they have also read them as history.

Penny Russell

References

Burton 1995; Christianson 1987; Clarke 1990; Cott 1977; Davidoff 1983; Davis 1958; Favret 1993; Fox 1993; Gilbert 1991; Gristwood 1988; Holmes 1995; Huff 1985; Kelly 1999; Kosambi 2000; Kristeva 1981; Stanley 1984; Steedman 1991; Scott 2001; Swindells 1989; Tillyard 1994.

Related essays

Archives; Australia; Female Biography; Feminist Autobiography Memoir; Great Britain; United States of America.

Prostitution

Although prostitutes have always been considered women with 'a history' the study of prostitution did not begin until the nineteenth century with the monumental work of the Parisian public hygienist Alexandre-Jean-Baptiste Parent-Duchatelet's *De la Prostitution de la ville Paris* (1836). For Duchatelet, prostitution was not a sexual practice or a form of work, but rather a public health problem waiting to be rectified. Parent-Duchatelet imagined prostitutes to be biological specimens to be examined and classified. Recording the histories of prostitutes as he did in this work, he developed theories around the practice of prostitution and its relation to the spread of venereal disease that shaped medical, legal and government intervention in prostitution for the next century. The message medical reformers and government officials took from his work was that prostitutes were like public sewers or cesspits, and should be subject to proper legislation or medical controls.

Underpinning the system of regulation of prostitution embraced by most European governments throughout the nineteenth century (and ensuring its failure) was the assumption that prostitutes were the principal vectors of the disease in society and that only the prostitute, and not her client, needed to be subject to this system of medical inspection. The idea that promiscuous women were the source of sexually transmissible diseases was ancient and reflected long-standing myths about the innate pathology of the female body. Venereal disease, its control and prevention were the principal concerns of most works depicting the history of prostitution in the nineteenth and early twentieth centuries. Often such texts served as defences for the system of regulation established in Europe under the Napoleonic code and in Britain with the enactment of the Contagious Diseases (CD) Acts. Even scholarly works such as William W Sanger's *History of Prostitution* (1858) and Abraham Flexner's *Prostitution in Europe* (1914) were primarily concerned with finding 'remedial measures' to 'stay the march of this devastating plague [prostitution] in its ravages on the health and morals of the public' (Sanger 1858/1896: 627).

The Contagious Diseases Act

The CD Acts were legislation passed by the British government in the 1860s introducing the compulsory medical inspection of prostitutes in garrison towns and naval ports in England and various outposts of Empire, to curtail the spread of syphilis and gonorrhoea. The system of regulation created by such laws allowed police special powers to arrest those suspected of being 'common prostitutes' and order them to undergo an internal examination at a certified hospital. Women were roughly treated in these places. Doctors, who were neither gentle nor particularly hygienic, conducted internal examinations in rooms that were often not properly screened. If women were found diseased they were detained for treatment until they were pronounced cured. Not surprisingly, many groups objected to this abuse of human rights. Britain became the centre of a vast campaign to repeal regulation throughout Europe and her empires. A radical coalition of liberals, medical men and social puritans, led by the charismatic feminist **Josephine Butler** of the National Ladies' Association for the Abolition of Government Regulation of Vice, brought an almost superhuman energy to the opposition towards the Acts.

Butler was the first feminist writer to engage in writing on the subject of prostitution, through her history of the campaign to repeal the CD Acts in her *Personal Reminiscences of a Great Crusade* (1896). *Personal Reminiscences* was an historical account of the 'Women's Revolt' against what Butler referred to as the 'instrumental rape' of women as a direct result of the Acts. Butler recorded her version of the lengthy legal and political struggle to repeal the Acts, frequently interjecting moral outrage at the double standard that characterised Victorian sexual relations. In this respect she was an early feminist theorist, 'advocating sex equality while celebrating the virtues of a distinctive women's culture' (Walkowitz 1980: 117).

Personal Reminiscences also served as a **memoir** and a spiritual autobiography, as Butler fashioned her burgeoning feminism into a narrative of conversion and redemption. In her account, her desire to 'rescue' prostitutes was born out of her immense grief following the accidental death of her only daughter Evangeline. Her engagement in the unladylike spectacle of publicly decrying the double standard of sexual morality inherent both in the practice of regulation specifically, and in Victorian attitudes to prostitution more generally, was thus described as a holy cause, one in which Butler was drawn to by God. Butler's maternal suffering and her desire 'to Save Daughters' has shaped many later histories of the CD Acts and has ensured an hagiographic quality to most of the biographical studies of Butler, as is amply demonstrated in the title of books such as Lionel Williamson's *Josephine Butler, Forgotten Saint* (1977), although recent studies of Butler such as Jane Jordan's biography offers a more nuanced account.

Such hagiographic accounts also depended upon an idea of prostitution that emphasised the victim status of the 'fallen' woman and allowed prostitutes agency only in terms of their rescue and recovery. The representation of prostitutes as 'victims' of male sexual tyranny would influence historical studies of prostitution, such as Kathleen Barry's *Female Sexual Slavery* (1979), Sheila Jeffrey's *The Spinster and her Enemies* (1986) and Margaret Jackson's *The Real Facts of Life* (1995).

The CD Acts would also shape second-wave feminist engagement with the history of prostitution. The first major study of Victorian prostitution, Judith Walkowitz's *Prostitution and Victorian Society* (1980) details the moves towards and the campaigns against the three British Contagious Diseases Acts of 1864, 1866 and 1869. This work demonstrates the ways in which class and gender informed the introduction, the implementation and the repeal of the CD Acts. Echoing Butler, Walkowitz showed how the CD Acts were consistent with a set of attitudes towards women, sexuality and class that permeated Victorian society. They were clear examples of the double standard of Victorian morality whereby it was acceptable for a man to engage in non-marital sex, but highly sinful for a woman. By focusing on women as the carriers of venereal diseases, the CD Acts officially sanctioned this double standard of morality. As Walkowitz argues 'sexual and social ideology became embedded in laws, institutions and social policy' (1980: 5). Thus the CD Acts both shaped and were shaped by social attitudes, creating both a 'technology of power' and a political resistance. Although Walkowitz was not the only historian to have examined the CD Acts (see also Paul McHugh's *Prostitution and Victorian Social Reform* [1980]) her study was unique in its emphasis on both the agency of feminist women involved in the campaigns and in her insistence on demonstrating prostitute's resistance, both to regulation and to their would-be rescuers. In this and her later work, *City of Dreadful Delight* (1992), Walkowitz clearly evoked the experience of women working as prostitutes in Victorian England. *City of Dreadful Delight,* however, also deals with the representation of 'fallen women' and child prostitutes within the cultural context of the Jack-the-Ripper murders in the 1880s. Walkowitz demonstrates how the tabloid exposés of child prostitution, generated by Social Purity and Repeal campaigns, provided a backdrop to this grisly tale of the mass murder. These reports, particularly W T Stead's 'Maiden Tribute of Modern Babylon' which depicted his purchase of young girls for the purposes of prostitution (and for which he was subsequently arrested), invented a new genre of sensationalist newspaper reporting, causing a furore in Victorian England. Most importantly Walkowitz demonstrates the complex dramas of power, politics and sexuality, which characterised late Victorian England, at play in these sensationalised newspaper reports and the manifestation of class anxiety, racial prejudices and gender antagonism that such texts revealed. More recently Lynda Nead has focused on similar territory in *Victorian Babylon: People, Streets and Images in Nineteenth-Century London* (2000). As with her earlier study *Myths of Sexuality* (1988) Nead is primarily concerned with the visual representation of 'fallen women'. Nead argued in *Myths of Sexuality* that the figure of the prostitute, in art and in other discourses, functioned in Victorian society to regulate the behaviour of all women.

The influence of Walkowitz can be seen in other studies of regulation in Europe such as Jill Harsin's *Policing Prostitution in Nineteenth-Century France* (1985) and Mary Gibson's *Prostitution and the State in Italy* (1986). Following Walkowitz, Harsin and Gibson focus on the system of regulation and the double standard of morality it enshrined, the campaigns for repeal and women's resistance to the Acts, both feminist resistance and the individual resistance of prostitutes. For Harsin the French system of regulation provided another lens through which to view the decline of women's social status following the **Revolution.** Like Walkowitz she examines the impact of regulation on the lives of the women of Paris, testing the theories of Parent-Duchatelet and other public hygienists regarding the efficacy of the system. Gibson's focus too is largely on the experience of regulation for Italian women. Drawing on the rich police records of Bologna, Gibson's work follows the life cycle of the Italian prostitute, 'as they "interacted" with the officials who enforced the regulation laws at a local level' (1986: 7).

These studies sought to place the experience of prostitution within the broader framework of working-class culture. Other texts such as Marion S Goldman's study of prostitution on the Comstock Lode, *Gold Diggers and Silver Miners* (1981), and Christine Stansell's *City of Women: Sex and Class in New York 1789–1860* (1982) moved beyond the study of regulation and resisted the image of prostitutes found in reform literature in order to examine the material life and conditions of the working-class women who engaged in prostitution. For Goldman this entailed examining the ideologies that separated 'Good Women and Bad'. Although this separation was virtually impossible given the nature of the sexual economy on the Frontier, Goldman argued that the laws relating to prostitution in Nevada functioned to 'clarify rules about feminine social and sexual behaviour, emphasizing the respectable communities behavioural boundaries, and heightening solidarity among respectable women' (1981: 137). The ideological function of prostitution as a means of defining appropriate female behaviour would become a major theme in feminist histories of prostitution, particularly those examining prostitution in the colonial context.

In *City of Women,* Stansell pushed such ideas further suggesting that the very experience of being a working-class woman 'violated some of the dearest held genteel precepts of "woman's nature" and "woman's place" ' (1982/1987: xi). Viewing prostitution within the context of the emergence of a distinct community of women workers in New York, Stansell argued that prostitution should be seen as one of a number of social and economic choices 'presented by the severities of daily life' (1982/1987: 172). Advocating resistance to 'the Victorian view of prostitution as utter degradation' Stansell urged historians to consider 'the opportunities that commercial sex offered women rather than the victimisation it entailed' (1982/1987: 191). Written over a decade later Marilynn Wood Hill's *Their Sister's Keepers* (1993) also examined the daily life of prostitutes in New York City in the nineteenth century. Clearly influenced by Stansell but also drawing on studies of women's networks in the nineteenth century, Hill's book focused on the more organised brothel-based forms of the profession, presenting an image of prostitutes as women 'better able to cope with their difficult lives because they were given support, protection, and a sense of self-worth by other women in the subculture of urban prostitution' (1993: 5).

Rescue, reformatories and reform

Questions of victimhood and agency, pleasure and danger have become framing arguments for much feminist historical writing on prostitution, especially in works studying the rescue of prostitutes and the movements involved in the reform of prostitution. For many women involved on the campaigns to abolish regulation in Europe and its colonies the desired aim was not merely the end of regulation, but the abolition of the practice of prostitution itself. To this end, moral reformers, social puritans and feminists joined together to establish penitentiaries, asylums and homes to take women off the streets and convert them into decent moral citizens. These institutions were part of a Christian archipelago of reform that stretched all over the colonised world. Research by feminist historians, who have examined reform institutions, suggests that the attitudes of asylum managers towards prostitutes, whether located in Britain, Sweden or America, were informed by a set of similar gender, class and religious assumptions. Although desiring to save 'fallen' women and critical of the sexual double standard, reformers tended to view prostitutes as sexualised women who undermined this principle of female propriety and posed a threat to the institution of marriage, to the sanctity of the family and ultimately to the moral order. While regulationists were concerned at the impact prostitution had on public health, reformers feared that prostitution contaminated the whole of society, eating like a cancer at the heart of the nation's life.

Frances Finnegan's study of prostitution in Victorian York, *Poverty and Prostitution* (1979), was perhaps the first to examine the experience of rescue and reform for prostitutes. Finnegan presented a troubling portrait of the Victorian prostitute, 'brutalised, humiliated and degraded' (1979: 166) and depicted refuges such as the York Penitentiary as an inevitable stage in their life cycle. Although she reports much resistance to the discipline of these institutions (numerous escapes, insolence and recidivism) she viewed such refuges as constituting 'society's major effort to ameliorate the *evils* of prostitution' [our emphasis] (1979: 209). Later studies of reform movements were more inclined to understand the practice of rescue and the processes of reform in terms of the social control they represented. Linda Mahood's *The Magdalenes: Prostitution in the Nineteenth Century* argues that the creation of reformatories for prostitutes served two social control functions directly: sexual control and vocational control. Examining the methods used to reform prostitutes Mahood demonstrates the punitive nature of such rescue arguing that these institutions functioned to create a gendered regime in which working-class women were encouraged to take up (or resume) careers as servants to middle-class women.

Other studies such as Maria Luddy's 'Prostitution and Rescue Work in Nineteenth-Century Ireland' (1990), Peggy Pascoe's *Relations of Rescue* (1993), Susan Mumm's *Stolen Daughters, Virgin Mothers* (1999) and Paula Bartley's *Prostitution Prevention and Reform in England* (2004) detail the daily grind of life within institutions of reform, depicting the punitive nature of such rescue as the penitent prostitute's freedom was completely curtailed. Such studies suggest that reformed prostitutes were treated little better than prisoners, as 'inmates' were denied access to the ordinary pattern of life. They were compelled to wear clothing like prison garb that marked their status. Hair was frequently cropped and inmates were forbidden to go out alone. They were also denied regular contact with friends and family. Isolation was deemed necessary because it was hoped that inmates might internalise the cultural values of the penitentiary more readily if they were not distracted by corrupt influences from outside.

All these studies follow Mahood in stressing the importance of domestic work to the process of reform. As Maria Luddy has reported reformers believed that engagement in domestic industry allowed 'the mind to be tranquilised and made penitents more amenable to religious instruction' (1990: 65). Occupations in these institutions ranged from weaving carpets, making lace, toys, gloves and artificial flowers, but most inmates worked in the laundry. Laundry work reinforced class and gender conformity by preparing inmates for the lowliest type of domestic service and, as Paula Bartley has demonstrated, laundry work was seen as particularly appropriate as cleanliness was the grand metaphor of religious purity (2004: 52). In eliminating physical dirt, she has suggested, order was seen to be established in the spiritual world of the inmates. It was also a metaphor of absolution. In scrubbing sheets white as the purest snow, inmates washed away their sins and regained their shining soul. In addition, laundry work may have been favoured because hard physical labour acted as a penance: in working hard in hot and steamy rooms inmates certainly atoned for their sins.

While feminists like Josephine Butler saw the rescue of prostitutes as a means of attacking male sexual privilege, other people involved in this activity appear more concerned to police the behaviour of working-class women and girls. The motives behind the reform movement have proved a critical focal point for debate among feminists. Ellen DuBois and Linda Gordon's essay, 'Seeking Ecstasy on the Battlefield: Danger and Pleasure in Nineteenth Century Feminist Sexual Thought' (1984), was the first major intervention into this discussion and raised questions about the motivations of first-wave feminists involved in campaigns to 'save' prostitutes. DuBois and Gordon highlighted the repressive nature of such campaigns, suggesting that they involved the establishment of protectionist mechanisms that imposed bourgeois codes of morality upon working-class women. They also suggested that these campaigns reinforced the ideological function of prostitution, separating women in categories of 'good' and 'bad' and consequently limiting the potential for feminist reform. For DuBois and Gordon, the 'negative consequences' of social purity feminism 'overwhelmed its liberatory aspects and began to throw a pall over feminism's approach to sexuality' (1984: 37) that had continued to inflect feminist discussions of prostitution and pornography.

In Britain women historians were less critical of the nexus between first-wave feminism and the social purity movement. Radical feminism inflected works such as Sheila Jeffrey's *The Spinster and Her Enemies* and Margaret Jackson's *The Real Facts of Life*. Such works argued that first-wave feminist campaigns around prostitution should be seen as politicising sexuality and protecting women and children from sexual exploitation at the hands of men. Sheila Jeffreys has been critical of other historians' views of social purity as an evangelical, anti-sex and repressive movement engendered by moral panic. Instead, she placed the feminist contribution to social purity on the moral map by examining the way in which the ideas and personnel of the women's movement shaped its course. Social purists, Jeffreys maintains, believed that men, not women, were responsible for prostitution. Women involved in such campaigns saw that men who were rapists, child abusers, sexual harassers and who indecently exposed themselves were prosecuted. They also campaigned to tighten the law on incest, to raise the age of consent and to make affiliation summonses (whereby men who had fathered 'illegitimate' children were forced to pay for their upkeep) more effective (1985/1997: 6–26). While DuBois and Gordon were critical of first-wave feminism's failure to embrace sexual radicalism, Jeffreys believed that sexual radicalism merely reinforced masculinist and phallocentric ideas about sexuality through 'the new "science" of sexology' (1985/1997: ix).

Tensions between Radical feminist historians and Pro-Sex feminist historians reflected shifts in understanding around the practice of prostitution within the women's movement more generally. The emergence of the Prostitutes' Rights movement brought competing conceptions of prostitution. Committed to an economic analysis of prostitution those involved in the Prostitutes' Rights movement came to see prostitution as 'sex work' and prostitutes as part of a 'sex industry'. Such terms attributed agency to women's engagement in prostitution and sought to challenge the idea that women involved in prostitution were deviant or pathological. Prostitutes were seen as workers who should have trade union rights and other civil rights associated with legitimate work. Radical feminists such as Sheila Jeffreys, however, objected to the idea of prostitution as sex work and questioned the degree of agency experienced by prostitutes in their choice of 'career'. In her book-length study, *The Idea of Prostitution* (1997), Jeffreys would articulate the view that even the term 'prostitute' did not adequately describe the exploitative nature of this exchange. Instead she used the term 'prostituted woman' viewing prostitution as a male form of violence against women, 'somebody must be doing something to the woman for her to be prostituted' (1997: 5).

Clearly influenced by Jeffreys, Margaret Jackson's *The Real Facts of Life* argued that 'male power, was axiomatic in Victorian and Edwardian England and was exhibited in sexuality as much as in high politics, economics, war and diplomacy' (1993: 21–33). This work charts the history of the feminist challenge to this patriarchal model and examines the ways in which women attempted to construct a female-centred sexual identity. Both Jeffreys and Jackson assume a unity of ideas between feminists and social puritans and tend to gloss over the tensions between the two camps. Their single-minded focus on gender has also led to criticism about lack of interest in issues of class. Lucy Bland's *Banishing the Beast: English Feminism and Sexual Morality 1885–1914* (1995), however, recognised the tensions both within the social purity movement and between social puritans and feminists. She acknowledges the middle-class background of social purity workers, the complicated motivations of women like Ellice Hopkins and the contradictions which arose between a radical sexual politics and a repressive political framework. Lucy Bland's meticulously researched book is concerned with the ways in which the state increased its influence over the lives of its citizens but, rather than viewing the state as a monolithic structure, she demonstrates its fragmentary nature. She explores the tensions within social purity by noting that on the one hand it espoused radical sexual politics: it campaigned, for example, against child prostitution. On the other hand, it rested within a middle-class framework of repression: as it helped to close down brothels and police prostitutes. The class and gender contradictions within the social purity movement are not easily reconciled but are ones that still face feminists campaigning against prostitution and pornography today.

This discussion has also influenced the ways in which major figures involved in reform such as Josephine Butler and Jane Ellice Hopkins have come to be represented in more recent histories of prostitution. Particularly the work of Hopkins, an influential social purity campaigner who worked to prevent young women from becoming prostitutes, has been subject to varied analyses. Hopkins through her efforts with the Ladies' Associations for the Care and

Protection of Young Girls worked tirelessly to prevent young women from becoming prostitutes. In male-authored histories of prostitution and reform such as Edward J Bristow's *Vice and Vigilence* (1977) Hopkins and other reforming women had been represented as unfulfilled spinsters who sublimated their sexual passions to become wholly focused on reform. In Sheila Jeffreys *The Spinster and Her Enemies* Hopkins has been characterised as a heroine and as an important precursor of radical feminism's sexual politics. Later works such as Susan Morgan's major biography of Hopkins *A Passion for Purity: Ellice Hopkins and the Politics of Gender in the Late-Victorian Church* present an even more complex picture of the reformer. Morgan rejects these crude polarities in favour of a more nuanced analysis in which Ellice Hopkins is understood in the religious as well as cultural and historical context of her time. Morgan argues that when it became evident that both the reform and the prevention movements had failed to end prostitution Ellice Hopkins and other social purity workers attempted to create a moral climate in which prostitution would inevitably disappear. A number of different organisations were founded with a set of common aims: to enforce the law against prostitutes, to encourage male chastity, to end child prostitution and to censor obscene literature.

White slavery and child prostitution

Morgan's work and other studies have shown how social purity organisations came to view prostitution as an international trade, the 'white slave trade'. The first feminist history of white slavery was Kathleen Barry's pioneering study *Female Sexual Slavery* (1979) which presented the history of 'the traffic in women' as a trajectory from Josephine Butler's campaigns for the repeal of regulation to the modern day pornography industry. Other studies have tended to focus on the moral panics around white slavery in particular national contexts, especially the United States during the Progressive era (1900–1918). The Progressive era was 'the setting for one of society's most zealous campaigns and best-recorded campaigns against prostitution' (Rosen 1982: xi) and the subject of works such as Ruth Rosen's *The Lost Sisterhood* (1982) and Barbara Meil Hobson's *Uneasy Virtue* (1982). Both these works view 'white slavery as a highly charged metaphor of the Progressive era' (Hobson 1982: 142). The idea of an international white slave trade luring young women into a life of vice fired the imagination of the popular press, moral reformers and government agencies during this period. The moral panic generated by the idea of white slavery, however, created something more scandalous, an awareness that most women who engaged in prostitution 'had not been trapped unknowingly in a house of bondage' but chose to work in prostitution. Both Rosen and Hobson conclude that reform campaigns worsened the lives of prostitutes as surveillance and policing of their activities increased. Control of prostitution moved out of women's hands (prostitutes and madams) and into those of pimps and organised crime syndicates.

Such studies have also shown how campaigns around prostitution embraced discourses of **modernity** in the early twentieth century. Rosen writes that 'prostitution became a cultural symbol of the birth of modern industrial culture in which the cold, impersonal values of the market place could invade the most private areas of other people's lives'. More recently Mara L Keire (2001) has argued that Progressive Era reformers eschewed the 'classical language of labyrinths and minotaurs' (that characterised the British campaigns of the 1880s to adopt a language of economics. Keire traces the idea of the white slave back to its origins in the American labour movement of the 1930s, adopting the argument that such campaigns should not be viewed as the 'irrational rantings of a paranoid social group' but rather as part of a broad campaign of economic reform (2001: 7).

Other studies such as Mary E Odem's *Delinquent Daughters: Protecting and Policing Adolescent Female Sexuality in the United States 1880–1920* (1995) and Mary Spongberg's *Feminising Venereal Disease: The Body of the Prostitute in Nineteenth Century British Medical Discourse* (1997) have depicted the campaigns around white slavery and child prostitution as part of a broader programme of social control that allowed middle-class reformers to assert control over the sexual behaviour of female youth. Spongberg's work also deals with the medical treatment of child prostitutes and the failure of regulation and other forms of intervention to prevent the sexual abuse of children. In line with other studies of prostitution and reform, such works trace the evolution of the female delinquent, demonstrating how moral reformers replaced earlier models of female victimisation with a model of 'female delinquency that acknowledged the sexual agency of young women' (Odem 1995: 4).

Discussion of sexual slavery has also been focused on the issue of the enforced prostitution of women in wartime, particularly the experience of the so-called comfort women used by the Japanese military to service soldiers during the Second World War. Works drawing on personal testimony such as that of Jan Ruff O'Hearne's in *Fifty Years of Silence* (1994) and Maria Rosa Henson's *Comfort Women* (1999) present detailed accounts of the brutal sexual exploitation of women and children at the hands of the Japanese Imperial Army. 'Comfort women' were used to help maintain army discipline and to avoid the spread of sexual disease and serve as a reminder that the brutality of war can be found just as easily in the bedroom as on the battlefield.

Prostitution and Empire

The regulation of prostitution was one of the many other aspects of European civilisation that colonial power exported throughout their empires. Prostitution of the indigenous population was deemed by colonial authorities an unfortunate but necessary by-product of the colonial endeavour and as Ronald Hyam has effectively demonstrated many men involved in this process assumed that prostitution was 'an essential part of its [the British Empire's] cosmoplastic [*sic*] activity' (1990: 141). Although feminist historians have criticised Hyam's celebratory narrative, few have disagreed with his premise that sex and empire went hand in hand. Prostitution has served as an important vehicle through which historians have examined the sexualised nature of the imperial endeavour. Works such as Luise White's *The Comforts of Home: Prostitution in Colonial Nairobi* (1990), Donna J Guy's *Sex and Danger in Buenos Aires* (1991), Gail Hershatter's *Dangerous Pleasures: Prostitution and Modernity in Twentieth-Century Shanghai* (1997), Eileen Suarez Findlay's *Imposing Decency: The Politics of Sexuality and Race in Puerto Rico, 1870–1920* (2000), Leslie Ann Jeffreys' *Sex and Borders: Gender, National Identity and Prostitution Policy in Thailand* (2002), Sumanta Banerjee's *Prostitution in Colonial Bengal* (2002) and Katherine Bliss' *Compromising Positions: Prostitution, Public Health, and Gender Politics in Revolutionary Mexico City* (2002) have all explored the nature of prostitution in colonial centres and its relation to the expansion of Empire. In these works prostitution has been the vehicle through which broader questions about concepts of work, family, class, citizenship, race and nation have been explored. Guy's *Sex and Danger* demonstrates how the figure of the prostitute raised questions about the proper role of women in Argentina, allowing men to reaffirm patriarchal dominance within the newly formed nation state. In *Sex and Borders: Gender, National Identity and Prostitution Policy in Thailand,* Leslie Ann Jeffreys illustrates how colonisation was about the control of female sexuality as well as the control of lands, goods and chattels. This control of women's sexuality, she argues, is all too often central to ideas of national identity: women are responsible both biologically and culturally for providing the next generation. If women's purity stands as a metaphor for the purity of the nation then women's immorality stands for its defilement. Thai national identity, she suggests, was threatened by the sexual invasion of foreigners because the idealised perception of the Thai women as either virgin or wife and mother was undermined by the seemingly overwhelming number of prostitutes within the country. Thus the rise in prostitution signalled the 'disintegration of national culture and identity'. Hershatter too demonstrates that the concerns about prostitution in early twentieth-century Shanghai reflected anxieties around the question 'about what kind of sex and gender relationships could help constitute a modern nation in a threatening semicolonial situation' (1997: 7).

It is perhaps Australian women's historical writing, however, that marks out most clearly this relationship between prostitution, colonisation and national identity. The experience of convict society did much to encourage an idea that the earliest female settlers to **Australia** were, to borrow a much-used phrase, 'damned whores'. The notion that white Australia's founding mothers were prostitutes has been immensely significant within Australian women's historical writing. Indeed two of the first second-wave feminist accounts of Australian history, Anne Summer's *Damned Whores and God's Police* (1975) and Miriam Dixson's *The Real Matilda* (1975), explicitly link women's second-class citizenship in the present, to the enforced prostitution of convict women. As Dixson explained 'The central question in this book is why do Australian women have a much lower overall standing than women in other democracies? One important reason lies with our "founding mothers", the convict women' (1975: 115). For Dixson and Summers these 'early mothers' constituted enduring models for female identity formation. Their enforced prostitution and the scandal and shame they evoked in male commentators (and later historians) left deep and disfiguring scars on the national psyche. While few feminist historians followed this polemical analysis the spectre of the 'damned whore' remains firmly entrenched in most accounts of early settlement. While Portia Robinson wholly discounts the work of Summers and Dixson in her *Women of Botany Bay* (1988) her narrative is nonetheless shaped by their analysis.

Kay Daniels' wonderful collection *So Much Hard Work* (1984) was the first history of prostitution to be published in Australia. Daniels and other historians in this collection attempted to shift the history of prostitution beyond its role in the founding mythology of Australia by treating prostitution as a form of labour, albeit one which often entailed sexual exploitation. Deborah Oxley's account of the working life of convict women, *Convict Maids* (1996), adds much nuance to our understanding of the sexual economy of early settlement as she identifies prostitution as a structural part of the capitalist patriarchy that characterised the colonial endeavour. Rae Frances' work on the history of prostitution in Australia has added another dimension to our understanding of the connection between prostitution and empire, in that she argues that prostitution did not occur in Australian Aboriginal societies, societies where neither private property nor private wealth existed. According to Frances' account prostitution only materialised in the seventeenth century when Macassar fishermen visited northern Australia and exchanged their canoes for Aboriginal women (1994: 29). Frances also depicts the often coercive and violent nature of sexual exchange between aboriginal women and white men, suggesting that 'Aboriginal women [were] being conquered and taken in the same way that Aboriginal lands were' (1994: 33).

As in Europe, female prostitutes in the colonies were identified as the principal source of venereal disease and were required to register officially as prostitutes and undergo regular internal examinations designed to detect venereal disease. In her path-breaking book *Prostitution, Race and Politics*, Philippa Levine has examined how and why these Contagious Diseases ordinances were put in place. In her view the colonial authorities used them not only to protect the health of the armed forces but as a conscious instrument of colonial domination. Drawing on an international range of primary sources, Levine reveals the ways in which ideas about race and colonisation were intertwined with ideas about prostitutes and prostitution. Indigenous prostitution was acceptable since non-westerners were assumed to share a permissive sexual morality, believe in strange religions and adhere to bizarre customs and values. (Levine 2003: 232). In contrast, white female prostitutes were thought to undermine the cultural and moral values of the British Empire. Each colonial power enacted laws which re-inforced these sexual multiple standards of the time, both abroad and at home. The law is also the subject of Helen Self's book *Prostitution, Women and Misuse of the Law* (2003). This work provides a detailed exposure of the ways in which an unjust and discriminatory legal system sought to regulate women working as prostitutes in Britain during the 1950s.

Paula Bartley and Mary Spongberg

References

Bartley 2004; Frances 1994; Gibson 1986; Harsin 1985; Hobson 1982; L A Jeffreys 2002; S Jeffreys 1985/1997, 1997; Keire 2001; Levine 2003; Littlewood & Mahood 1991; Mahood 1990; Rosen 1982; Spongberg 1997; Walkowitz 1980.

Putnam, Bertha Haven 1872–1960

American medievalist. Born in New York, daughter of Rebeccca (Kettel Shepard), teacher and social reformer, and Major George Haven Putnam, publisher. Attended Miss Gibbons School and then Bryn Mawr, graduating in the same class as **Nellie Neilson** in 1893. Taught at the Bryn Mawr school in Baltimore, before returning to New York to care for her widowed father. Upon his second marriage to **Emily James Smith [Putnam]**, Putnam returned to study, attaining her doctorate from Columbia University in 1908. Her doctoral work was published as *The Enforcement of Statutes of Laborers 1349–1359* (1908) in *Columbia University's Studies in History, Economics and Public Law*. Through this work Putnam gained an interest in justices of the peace in medieval England and her second major work *Early Treatises on the Practice of the Justices of the Peace in the Fifteenth and Sixteenth Centuries* (1924) focused on this field. In 1940 Putnam was awarded the inaugural Haskins medal by the Medieval Academy of America for her *Proceeding Before the Justices of the Peace in the Fourteenth and Fifteenth Centuries* (1938), the culmination of 30 years of original research.

Putnam was appointed to the Mount Holyoake History Department in 1908, becoming a full professor in 1924. With **Neilson**, Putnam worked to make the history department at Mount Holyoke 'a notable focus of medieval, legal and economic historical studies'. Retiring in 1938 Putnam continued research for her last book, *The Place in Legal History of Sir William Shareshull*, completing this in 1950, inspite of being rendered partially blind by shingles. To undertake research on Shareshull, Putnam had been assisted by a grant from Harvard Law School in 1938, the first ever to be given to a non-lawyer and a woman. In 1945 she was awarded an honorary doctorate from Smith College and was elected a member of the Medieval Academy in 1949.

Mary Spongberg

References

Glazer & Slater 1987; Hastings & Kimball 1979; *NAW* 1971.

Major works

Enforcement of the Statutes of Labourers during the Last Decade after the Black Death (New York: Arno Press, 1970); *Early Treatises on the Practice of Justices of the Peace in the Fifteenth and Sixteenth Centuries* (New York: Octagon Books, 1974) and *Place in legal History of Sir William Shareshull* (Holmes Beach: W W Gaunt, 1986).

Putnam, Emily James Smith 1865–1944

American translator, educator, historian of women. Born in New York. Graduated from Bryn Mawr College with first class in 1889, attended Girton College, Cambridge, between 1891 and 1893. In 1892 she published translations from the Greek sections of Lucian, joining the Classics department at the University of Chicago the following year. In 1894 she was appointed Dean of Barnard College and was instrumental in bringing Barnard into line with Columbia, by opening up Columbia's graduate courses and library to Barnard women and encouraging Columbia faculty to teach at Barnard. Married publisher George H Putnam, father of historian **Bertha Putnam**, in 1899 and resigned as Dean of Barnard the following year when she became pregnant. From 1901 to 1904 she served as president of the League for Political Education and from 1901 to 1905 she was a trustee of Barnard.

In 1910 she published *The Lady: Studies of Certain Significant Phases of Her History*, a major historical study of women in society. Pre-empting **Virginia Woolf**, Putnam's study sought to discover what daily life was like for women of 'the favoured class'. Despite its quaint-sounding title, *The Lady* is decidedly modern in its analysis of the role of women in patriarchal societies, its ambivalence towards maternity and its discussion of the impact of class upon the lives of women. Putnam recognised that '[E]very discussion of the status of woman is complicated by the existence of the lady'. She believed that until women had all the advantages of men, it was impossible to truly grasp women's full potential or the true meaning of femininity. In the early chapters on Greece and Rome, Putnam drew upon her own extensive knowledge of classical literature, while later chapters owe much to **Lina Eckenstein** and **Harriet Martineau**.

Putnam resumed teaching at Barnard in 1914 in the history department and from 1920 taught in the department of Greek.

In 1926 she published *Candaules' Wife and Other Old Stories*, a revisionary study of Herodotus. Through her commitment to adult education, Putnam helped establish the New School for Social Research in 1919 and lectured there until 1932. She retired from Barnard in 1930.

Mary Spongberg

References

NAW 1971.

Major work

The Lady: Studies of Certain Significant Phases of Her History (Chicago: University of Chicago Press, 1970).

Q

Queer history

Queer history is less a formalised enterprise for the historical exploration of particular **lesbian** and gay identities than it is a set of critical practices for interrogating the historical, political and epistemological preconditions of sexual identity in general. Like lesbian and gay history, queer history is influenced by social history, black history, women's history and gender history. It is also centrally informed by recent innovations in critical theory, such as poststructuralism, deconstruction, queer literary studies, postcolonialism and cultural studies. 'Queer history' is distinguished from earlier historiographical paradigms by its deconstructionist bent. Where social constructionist history has been concerned primarily with tracing the emergence of sexually dissident and distinct identities (most notably homosexual identities), queer history is concerned instead with tracing the social and epistemological conditions of possibility for the production and articulation of sexual identities themselves. One of the founding assumptions is the idea that 'sexuality is constituted as a field of meaning by terms that are always and necessarily relational' (Jagose 2002: xv). As an (deconstructive) interrogation, queer history can be viewed as a critical supplement to lesbian and gay history, to feminist history and history-writing in general. Queer history is thus an historiographical impulse that combines simultaneously a rereading of history with the deconstruction and critique of identity.

The single most influential figure in the development of queer history is Michel Foucault. His monumental genealogy, *The History of Sexuality* (1980), demonstrated how central the category of sexuality has been to the historical formation of forms of modern selfhood. For Foucault, the *Scientia Sexualis*, that scientific apparatus for 'telling the truth of sex', has throughout the course of the seventeenth to the nineteenth and twentieth centuries worked to create modern sexual subjects by imposing the illusion of an inner sexual depth and by inventing and cataloguing human beings according to myriad sexual species of sexuality, such as gay, lesbian, bisexual, heterosexual and so on. Drawing on Nietzsche, and in order to contest what he called 'traditional history', a mode of historical interpretation embedded in notions of linearity, teleology, continuity and the self-identical subject as the driving force of history – Foucault developed a form of history writing he called 'effective history'. This was a set of historiographic practices which, rather than reading off sexual categories as descriptions of biological or social reality, aims to analyse the social, political and discursive operations through which certain subjects come to be socially constituted as different to others.

Poststructuralist critiques of the idea that human experience and identity are the building blocks of history furthered this decentring of history writing that has become characteristic of queer history. Noteworthy here is feminist poststructuralist historian Joan Wallach Scott, who in her influential essay, 'The Evidence of Experience' (1991), sees human experience and identity as an effect rather than the generator of history. Queer history has also taken from Foucauldian, feminist, poststructuralist and deconstructive approaches a concern to expose how difference has been discursively and binarily produced in contrast to a privileged heterosexuality. Jennifer Terry in her essay 'Theorizing Deviant Historiography' (1991) offers historians a way to reveal how the social construction of dissident sexual identities is part of a broader process of delimiting the boundaries between the so-called normal and the deviant. So instead of aiming to find lesbians or lesbianism in history, as much gay and lesbian history writing has done, a queer history would compel us, as Donna Penn suggests in 'Queer: Theorising Politics and History', to historicise 'the politics of drawing the line' (1995: 39). This helps the researcher avoid forms of social, political and historical anachronism, by refusing to colonise past peoples and societies with contemporary categories of analysis. It also enables us to broaden the historical field of vision in order to seek out rather than repress differences.

Eve Kosofsky Sedgwick called on scholars, in *Epistemology of the Closet*, to 'incorporate a critical analysis of modern homo/heterosexual definition' in any interrogation of modern sexuality has been particularly influential in demonstrating the ways in which the demarcation of the 'normal' from the 'deviant' has been shown to have been magisterially played out through the hetero/homosexual opposition (1990: 1). Sedgwick has shown how all forms of modern sexuality have been constituted by and assimilated to this dominating opposition.

Annamarie Jagose's *Inconsequence: Lesbian Representation and the Logic of Sexual Sequence* is an example of the emergent queer history that is concerned not with tracing lesbian identities per se but with historicising the epistemological conditions that have 'governed the emergence of lesbian as a meaningful category of identity' (2002: 8). Although the subject of her study is lesbian representability, Jagose's approach is distinctly queer in its broader concern with exposing the ways in which all of our modern categories of sexuality are relationally constituted against the norm of heterosexuality. Combining an historiographical rereading of history with the deconstruction of identity, Jagose's queer history is 'a strategic attempt to recognise the secondariness and derivation that indispensably animate the reification of all sexual identities' (2002: xv).

Queer history, in keeping with the political motivations of both Foucauldian genealogy and queer theory's exposure of the operations of heteronormativity, might best be viewed as a kind of historiographical practice, or even, to use Jennifer Terry's terms, a form of 'historiographic activism' (1991: 57).

Steven Angelides

References

Angelides 2001; Dollimore 1991; Foucault 1980, 1991; Jagose 2002; Penn 1995; Scott 1991; Sedgwick 1990; Terry 1991.

R

Reformation

Soon after Luther's explosive defiance against the Church in Rome in 1517, women began to produce polemical texts in support and against the new Reformation movements. The new technologies of the printing press spread women's works on the subject across the breadth of Europe. If women were widely condemned by authorities for preaching, printed publications served as a means of disseminating their views publicly. These factors brought distinct changes to the ways in which women created historical writings. When women received criticism for speaking publicly, they drew upon their thorough knowledge of classical and religious texts to demonstrate the historical tradition of female public and religious speech that provided precedents for their actions and voices in public religious debate. Argula von Grumbach, a Bavarian noblewoman, reconstituted new visions of the history of the Church in order to propose biblical women as models for her own actions in pamphlets, letters and poems she wrote between 1523 and 1563. Many women wanted to prove that they had a justified place in public debates, particularly in the debates about religion that characterised the period.

Memoirs and eyewitness accounts

The Reformation enabled women to find new means of authority to create historical and religious accounts. Not all women-writing needed access to archival sources as the basis for their historical works. Some produced accounts based on their own experiences. Many women who spoke of religious matters in this era argued their authority to contribute to history on the basis that they were eyewitnesses to religious events. Queens Marguerite de Valois and Jeanne d'Albret wrote **memoirs** of their involvement in political and religious events of the Reformation era. The latter composed *Ample déclaration sur la jonction de ses armes des Reformés en 1568* (1570), as a record of her spirituality and actions over the past decade. She justified her political and military actions as leader of the Huguenot movement in France.

The Reformation also led to a democratisation of memoir writing. Less wealthy or politically involved women witnessed changes to their lives that they felt were also worthy of historical record. Most women were personally affected by the religious and political turmoil that engulfed Europe and they recorded their experiences of religious wars and destruction, historicising them in the broader explanations of religious events of their era. Nuns produced records of their experiences during religious fighting, strict enforcement of enclosure or the disbandment of their **convents**, some in journals as it happened and others as reflective accounts after the events transpired. A number of nuns kept eyewitness accounts of the destruction of their convents and way of life. The *Petite Chronique* (c.1555) by Jeanne de Jussie, abbess of the Poor Clares of Geneva, described how Protestants had forced the convent to move from its original establishment. Jussie's history demonstrated how the sisters retained their Catholic fervour in spite of the community's move to France.

The Counter-Reformation also produced such narratives. In 1695, the Ridler community and, in 1721, the Pütrich community of Munich produced chronicles celebrating how smoothly the changes introduced by the Counter-Reformation Church, including strict enclosure, had been implemented. So too did Beaumont-les-Tours in France, which used an account of convent life during the Wars of Religion as the basis of a later history depicting convent life during the Reformation period. Later histories reveal less of the difficulties faced in convents than contemporary accounts, such as the chronicle written by the 'gatekeeper' of the Pütrich convent, have suggested. Elizabeth Shirley, an Augustinian nun of St Monica's of Louvain, also wrote a history of the founding of her order in 1612. Combining this text with a biography of her mentor, Margaret Clement, she also appended an autobiography detailing the traumas she experienced as a result of these upheavals. The *Chronicle of St Monica's* became a composite historical narrative as other women, such as Catherine Holland, appended their histories to it (Grundy 1992: 128). Holland, an English nun who entered the Augustinian convent in Bruges after the closure of English convents during the sixteenth century, narrated her life experiences around 1664, merging spiritual autobiography with the community's history (Grundy 1992: 132). In recording the history of these events nuns adopted a publicly positive view of the Counter-Reformation transformations as a result of their expectations of male supervision and the prospect of a wider audience (Strasser 2002). Moreover, these accounts differed in perspective to those produced during the Reformation because the purpose of the history was less concerned with historical accuracy, as we might understand it, and more with the moral purpose of edification of the soul of the reader (Woodford 2002: 119).

Other women recounted how and why they had come to leave convents and these accounts were sometimes published as Protestant polemic. In the early days of the reform movement, Marie Dentière, an Augustinian nun from Tournai, left her convent to join Protestants in Geneva. She produced a number of texts supporting the reform, including her *Très Utile Epistre* (1539), which encouraged women to reject papal authority. She also produced an urban religious history of Geneva's conversion, *La Guerre et deslivrance de la ville de Genesve* (1536), using a similar framework to Augustine's *City of God*, but depicting the history of the model Protestant city as a conflict between the earthly and the heavenly. Female converts to Protestantism also made records of their personal experiences of religious turmoil. Martha Elisabeth Zitter's letter to her mother, explaining her reasons for leaving the convent at Erfurt, was published in 1678 by reforming authorities in Jena as part of a triumphant narrative of Protestant history. In such writing Dentière and Zitter were participating in a new understanding of history informed by Protestantism.

Martyrology and family history

As conflict between Catholics and reformers became more violent, the production of martyrologies celebrating the lives and deaths of Protestants became one way in which women could engage in historical writing. These texts inscribed women's participation in contemporary religious history, making women visible as part of the ongoing religious struggles in Europe. English Protestant **Anne Dowriche** produced her own version of contemporary martyrologies in her tragedy *The French History* (1589). Margaret Roper, daughter of Sir Thomas More, almost certainly assisted her husband, William Roper, in writing his biography of Thomas More. This text was critical to establishing Sir Thomas More's reputation as a martyr in English Catholic hagiography. Margaret Roper also translated Erasmus' study of the Lord's Prayer – *A Devout Treatise on the Pater Noster* (1542). Translation of religious texts and partisan histories were another way in which women engaged in both theological debate and historical production. Texts such as **Elizabeth Cary**'s translation of Cardinal Perron's reply to King James (c.1630) proved so controversial that it was confiscated and publicly burned by the Archbishop of Canterbury.

As the organisation of religion in various European countries became increasingly formalised, women were progressively excluded from aspects of the theological and political decision-making. Both Catholic and Protestant theology celebrated the family as a key locus of religious instruction and encouraged women to express their religious fervour through this forum. The domestication of faith encouraged women to develop new forms of historical writing which were located in the household and familial setting. While Protestant men trawled the archives to produce religio-political history, their womenfolk contributed family history from readily available local sources. Luther had argued that the family, as well or even more so than the convent, was a significant site of piety. Family histories written by Protestant women which documented their family's godliness and devotion now became part of the religious historical record. Charlotte Arbaleste, wife of Huguenot statesmen Philippe Duplessis-Mornay, wrote a biography of her husband *Mémoires de messire Philippe de Mornay* around 1595. As well as recording her husband's life she made detailed digressions concerning her own life and spiritual experiences. For French Huguenot women, family history took on particular significance. After the unprecedented St Bartholomew's massacre in 1572, those who escaped celebrated familial survival against the odds, provided evidence of God's mercy and commemorated relatives who died in the conflicts in their family histories. Arbaleste included details of both her and her future husband's separate escape from Paris during the height of the carnage. Family histories in the hands of Huguenot authors were often intended to inspire and maintain Protestant faith in future generations.

Gendering the Reformation

Women historians have been instrumental in shaping the historiography of the Reformation since the nineteenth century. Ann Marsh-Caldwell published a study of the *Protestant Reformation in France* in 1847 and Anna Eliza Bray on the *Revolt of Protestants in Cevennes* in 1870. Writers of **Royal lives** such as **Agnes Strickland, Lucy Aikin** and **Elizabeth Benger** depicted the tumult of the Reformation from a feminine perspective in the collective biographies and courtly memoirs they produced. In the twentieth century, analysis of gender has produced much innovative research, reconfiguring the Reformation by making the status of women an important indicator of the extent of Protestantism's influence. The opinions of the key theologians on women have been explored by Susan Karant-Nunn (1986) for Martin Luther, and Jane Dempsey Douglas (1984) and Mary Potter (1986) for John Calvin. Charmarie Jenkins Blaisdell (1982) has examined Calvin's practical and political interactions with influential women through his correspondence.

Much early debate centred on examining the nature of changes brought by the Protestant Reformation and determining how they might have decreased or improved women's position in books and articles such as Miriam U Chrisman's 'Women and the Reformation in Strasbourg' (1972), Merry E Wiesner's 'Women's Responses to the Reformation' (1988), Sherrin Marshall's 'Women and Religious Choices in the Sixteenth-century Netherlands' (1984), Retha M. Warnicke's 'Women of the English Renaissance and

Reformation' (1983) and Natalie Zemon Davis' 'City Women and Religious Change' (1978). Early studies by Nancy L Roelker (1972) emphasised the potential appeal of Protestantism for French noblewomen. Protestantism brought some women freedom from monastic life without vocation, and new roles as preachers and writers in the early days of the Reformation movements. Furthermore, historians examined the development of Protestant rhetoric of maternity and family life, which might have altered the perceptions of women's roles as wives and mothers. Similarly, Kathryn Norberg's 'Women and the Family and the Counter-Refomation' (1978) and Barbara B Diefendorf's 'Les Divisions Religieuses Dans Les Familles Parisiennes Avant La Saint-Barthelemy' (1988) have examined the diverse impact of new Catholic Reformation ideology on familial practices and relationships. Ellen Macek's 'The emergence of a feminine spirituality in the *Book of Martyrs*' (1988) and Jenifer Umble's 'Women and Choice: an examination of the *Martyr's Mirror*' (1990) have focused on women's opportunities for spiritual expression through martyrdom during this period. Research also emphasised the disadvantages which removal of Catholic rituals and practices brought about for women. Merry E Wiesner's *Convents Confront the Reformation* (1996) and Marilyn Oliva's *Convent and Community in Late Medieval England* (1998) explored the prospects and realities for women who were forced from a much-loved conventual life by the dissolution of monasteries in Protestant areas. Other scholars have pointed out the reduced spiritual expression open to women as veneration of saints and religious confraternal activities were removed from Reformed practices.

Early assessments have become more nuanced as female historians learn more about the wide range of potential possibilities and disadvantages which the Reformation could bring women depending on their social status, location and individual situation. The possible attractions of Protestantism for French women, for example, were later nuanced by Natalie Zemon Davis' aforementioned study of middling women in urban France, where she did not find evidence of the same causes of appeal as Roelker had argued for noblewomen. Moreover, Roelker and Sherrin Marshall's work has examined how, as Protestantism became increasingly institutionalised, women's roles were often restricted. While medieval Catholicism tended to celebrate virginity as the supreme virtue, historians have debated whether women benefited from the new status accorded to wives and mothers by Protestant and then Catholic reformers. In *The Holy Household* (1989) Lyndal Roper has argued that since these roles were subservient to men, women were more controlled and less free to pursue a role outside the familial. Gender relations were a key concern during the Reformation, she has argued. Certainly there were differences in women's roles and expectations between Catholic and Protestant ideologies, but questions of advantages and disadvantages for women have often been negated by the evidence of continuity in women's life experiences across Europe. Susan Karant-Nunn's *Zwickau in Transition* (1982), Patricia Crawford's *Women and Religion in England* (1993) and Susan M Johnson (1992) in her study of Luther's lasting impact on the European family have argued that continuity reflects better the experiences of women's lives both before and after the Reformation. Similar social attitudes towards women were reinforced by changing authoritative bodies so that in many cases expectations of women's roles often remained largely unchanged by the religious transformations.

In areas which experienced the Catholic Reformation, texts such as Merry E Wiesner's

'Ideology Meets the Empire: Reformed Convents and the Reformation' (1991), Gabriella Zarri's *Le sante vive* (1990) and *Donna, disciplina, creanza cristiana dal XV al XVII secolo* (1996), and P Renée Baernstein's *A Convent Tale* (2002) have examined the often detrimental impact of the enforcement of cloister in women's convents, and the ways in which women negotiated their altered position in the Church and community. Both the experiences of women in contemplative orders and the newly emerging active orders of the Catholic Reformation have been explored in such works as Claire Walker's *Gender and Politics in Early Modern Europe* (2003), Ulrike Strasser's *State of Virginity* (2003), Jutta Sperling's *Convents and the Body Politic in Late Renaissance Venice* (1999) and Elizabeth A Lehfeldt's *Religious Women in Golden Age Spain* (2005). Women's involvement in the religious politics of New World colonisation as missionaries and patrons of such movements have been explored in Natalie Zemon Davis' *Women on the Margins: Three Seventeenth-Century Lives* (1995) and Elisa Sampson Vera Tudela's *Colonial Angels* (2000). Examination of many individual convents across Europe has led historians to observe the flexible and varied implementation of such Church-endorsed regulations by local communities.

Of course, historians have not neglected the evidence produced by women themselves about their views of the Protestant and Catholic Reformations. The writings of nuns have been given new recognition as literary and historical sources of significance in works such as Charlotte Woodford's *Nuns as Historians in Early Modern Germany* (2002), Merry E Wiesner's *Convents Confront the Reformation* (1996) and K J P Lowe's *Chronicles and Convent Culture in Renaissance and Counter-Reformation Italy* (2003). The voices of religious women on church politics and spirituality, as well as the opportunities provided for such religious speech, have also been a subject of recent focus. In *Visionary Women* (1992), Phyllis Mack has likewise highlighted the importance of prophetic speech as a means of expression for radical Protestant women in England. In *Oedipus and the Devil* (1994) and *Witchcraze* (2004) Lyndal Roper draws on insights from psychoanalysis to cultural anthropology in order to explore the meanings behind witchcraft accusations and testimony as she seeks to understand how men's and women's self-perceptions may have altered after the Reformation.

While many studies by female historians have focused on the hitherto neglected area of women's experiences during this era, Roper and Wiesner have also argued for a need to integrate these findings into a gendered analysis of the Reformation itself. Complex studies of Reformation gender politics and discourse, as well as the emerging field of masculinity, are increasingly being undertaken by scholars.

Susan Broomhall

References

Blaisdell 1982; Chrisman 1972; Davis 1988; Dempsey Douglas 1984; Diefendorf 1988; Grundy 1992; Johnson 1992; Karant-Nunn 1982, 1986; Macek 1988; Marshall 1984; Norberg 1978; Potter 1986; Roekler 1972; Strasser 2002; Umble 1990; Wiesner 1987, 1988, 1991; Woodford 2002.

Related essays

Memoir; Religion.

Religion

Women have been producing religious histories since at least the **Middle Ages**. It is a particularly strong tradition of women's historical writing because of the comparatively early access which convents gave women to space, time and archival sources. The structure of religious life encouraged monasteries to keep records of their institutions, and nuns could undertake historical writing as a pious Christian endeavour. Histories of religion written by nuns and secular women have usually taken different trajectories to those of men, bringing both alternative perspectives to the historical record of religion and diverse historiographical approaches to their materials.

Christian lives by medieval women

In the medieval period convents gave women access to space, time and archival sources. Consequently, nuns were some of the earliest female historians. Many monasteries became wealthy organisations that provided spiritual focus to surrounding communities, and formed part of the history of medieval Christianity. Nuns frequently produced histories of their orders or houses. Some chronicled internal matters of elections and professions such as Bartolomea Riccoboni whose necrology of the Venetian convent of Corpus Domini created a vision of spiritual continuity through small biographies of its nuns (Bornstein 2000). German sister-books recording the daily life of the convent were a similar phenomenon of the same period (Jaron Lewis 1996). Other histories documented external affairs with the local community or religious bodies. While the abbey of Gandersheim disputed with episcopal authorities, **Hrotsvitha** detailed its early history in ways which significantly renegotiated the role of the bishop. Through convent histories, nuns recognised important female contributions to the local religious and social landscape.

To the medieval mind, the physical world was less significant than the hereafter. History could provide edifying texts to prepare readers for salvation, which female historians contributed as biographies of holy men and women. The *Revelations* (1157) of St Elisabeth of Schönau relate the history of the virgins who accompanied St Ursula to Jerusalem before they were martyred on their return to Cologne. Her account popularised the accepted version of the legend. Hrotsvitha wrote hagiographic works that included poems of the life of Mary and the ascension of Christ, as well as plays about early Christian converts and martyrs. Many of these works were based on extant accounts that Hrotsvitha expanded and developed. Moreover, she also wrote histories of model Christian lives based on eyewitness accounts of the events. She constructed an epic history of Otto the Great in which she depicted Otto as the ideal Christian ruler. Women also chose to write about those who were associated with their particular convent or order. The first known vitae of this kind was written by **Baudonivia**, a nun from Sainte Croix in Poitiers, who wrote the hagiography of the convent's founder, Saint Radegund.

Other women wrote of their life experiences in mystical works, documenting their visions. Gertrud from Helfta analysed how her religious thought had developed in *Legacy of Divine Piety* (c.1290). This text put together by nuns at her convent at Helfta also contains a history of Gertrud's life written by a Helfta nun after her death. *The Flowing Light of the Godhead* (c.1240) by the Beguine Mechtild of Magdebourg contained autobiographical writing about the experience of receiving visions as well as letters of advice, criticism and prayers. In a different vein, a few women wrote about their religious travels, particularly to significant sites of pilgrimage. One of the earliest is Egeria's fourth-century history of her pilgrimage to the Holy Land, which contains descriptions of liturgical practices in Jerusalem. In the eighth century, the nun Huneberc encountered St Willibald, bishop of Eichstätt, staying at the Heidenheim convent. Huneberc's record of his journey, the *Hodoeporicon of St. Willibald* (c.780), was one of the earliest records circulating in Northern Europe of travel to Palestine. Norfolk laywoman Margery Kempe travelled to the Holy Land and her *Boke* (c.1436) contains details of both her revelations and her pilgrimages and is considered among the earliest examples of autobiography in English.

Medieval women did not limit their historical endeavours to the personal or local; some also wrote universal histories founded on the biblical narrative. The abbess Herrad of Hohenbourg compiled a massive encyclopedic work, the *Garden of Delights* (c.1185), which documented contemporary learning and provided an account of world history from creation to the end of the world. As she was writing for the edification of her nuns, Herrad anticipated both advanced and debutant readers, so the text was written in both Latin and German and provided illustration from biblical history. Like much writing by nuns Herrad's text also records contemporary experiences of the nuns at Hohenbourg. Hildegard of Bingen's *Scivias* (1141–1151) and *Book of Divine Works* (1163–1173) were based on a series of visions from which she constructed a complex prophetic history of salvation, from Genesis to the Apocalypse. In this period, scholars were developing rhetorical and rational techniques to understand Christianity, but female historians rarely shared the education that enabled men to participate in scholasticism's theological debates. Even learned women like Hildegard argued that her understanding of Christian history came through divine intervention. As with biographical and hagiographical works, these histories were used as pedagogical texts for readers; most events could be explained by divine causality and the analysis assisted the reader to achieve knowledge of the path to salvation.

Spiritual biography and autobiography

The tumultuous events of the Reformation caused a number of women to write eyewitness accounts of everyday life that could also be considered as religious history. Other women internalised these events, turning to spiritual biography and autobiography as a means of understanding the changes wrought by the Reformation and their place in the world subsequent. Some women sought models of religious female behaviour that could justify their participation in the debates and actions of the new religious movements. Marie Dentière, a former nun in Geneva, produced her *Epistre très utile, faicte et composée par une femme chrestienne de Tornay* (1539), a history of strong religious women from the Old and New Testament who served as examples to the active and theologically inclined women of the sixteenth century. Catholic women, too, did not ignore this form of religious history. Catalogues of exemplary women and men from biblical history were models for contemporary Catholic spiritual behaviour. In France, the Dominican nun Anne de Marquets in her *Sonets Spirituels* (1605) celebrated the continuity of female contributions to religious history in her discussion of exemplary holy women.

Reform measures implemented in the Catholic Church also changed Counter-Reformation women's opportunities for producing history. The Counter-Reformation period saw a return for women to many of the schools of historical writing which had flourished during the Middle Ages. Among them were autobiographical forms. However, whereas the medieval autobiographical texts by women could often focus on exterior accomplishments such as pilgrimages, early modern autobiographies borrowed more heavily from the traditions of mystic and spiritual accounts, even when these experiences involved missionary endeavours in other countries such as Marie Guyart's *Relation autobiographique de 1654*. The Counter-Reformation period was concerned with the spiritual and meditative experiences of the individual, unlike the Reformation autobiographies in which women documented their physical experiences in the everyday world. Tridentine Catholicism's emphasis on individual confession encouraged Catholics to reflect on their lives and sins. Holy women often developed mentor relationships with a particular confessor who directed and monitored their spiritual experiences. In this way, the quest for spiritual enlightenment of women, who were seen as particularly susceptible to the influence of the Devil, could be encouraged to follow appropriate Catholic practices. This phenomenon prompted many women, lay and clerical, to write confessional histories that recorded their struggles and sinful behaviour, as well as their meditations and developing spiritual consciousness in their progress towards union with God. St Teresa of Avila created the model for Catholic women's spiritual autobiographies. Her confessional redaction of her life and sins in the *Book of Her Life* (1562) written for her male superiors and *The Interior Castle* (1577), a presentation of her mystical experiences produced for both confessors and sisters, were widely read and imitated by women across Catholic Europe. As with St Teresa, the events recorded in confessional autobiographies were mediated not only by the reconstruction of moments of sin and redemption, but also by the influence of male advisers who were to control, regulate and ultimately validate women's spiritual experiences.

In other ways too, a concern to establish Catholic orthodoxy pervaded women's historical interpretation of religion. Female historians' orthodox accounts of the lives of saints could transmit Tridentine views to a lay Catholic audience as published texts. In Italy, nuns produced a wealth of historical biographies through spiritual plays. Chiara Matraini's *Life of the Virgin* (1590) studied Mary's spiritual and historical life, drawing on familiar sources of the Scriptures but also less typical sources like the Apocrypha for details of Mary's childhood. Maria Clemete Ruoti created morally instructive spiritual comedies, using music and dance, and a history of the *Birth of Christ* published in 1658. In France, Françoise-Madeleine de Chaugy wrote her *Mémoires sur la vie et les vertus de sainte Jeanne-Françoise de Chantal* (1843), a biography of Jeanne de Chantal the aristocratic founder of the Visitandines order. Chantal had herself composed her *Le petit livret*, a memoir of her spiritual journey under the direction of her confessor, the charismatic archbishop Francis de Sales. Chaugy, once Chantal's secretary, followed a particular hagiographic format and her biography was later used as the main document in Jeanne's 1767 canonisation. Chaugy also composed other studies about Francis de Sales and the early congregation of the Visitandines.

Yet carefully constructed texts could also document the history of heterodox Catholic movements. Gilberte Pascal created a public history for the condemned Jansenist movement through her biographies of her brother, Blaise, *Vie de M. Pascal* (1688), and sister, Jacqueline, *Vie de Jacqueline Pascal* (n.d.). Pascal, a scientist and mystic, had supported Jansenism, a rigorously disciplined movement associated with the French convent of Port-Royal. Jesuits, who held sway at the royal court, feared the political and theological independence of Jansenism and this led to the eventual persecution of its leaders. Blaise Pascal's works were banned. Gilberte Pascal's biographies attempted to recover Jansenist history from obliteration, as she focused on the moral integrity, intellectual and spiritual achievements of her brother and sister.

Composition of godly autobiographical works was a particular female phenomenon among Protestants as well. Over the course of the seventeenth and eighteenth centuries, Protestant women historicised their spiritual and household experiences through reflective journals. However, unlike most Catholic women, there was no formal supervision of these compositions. Documenting domestic tasks in journals of pious self-discovery, some were composed on a daily basis, while others were historical records of God's grace to the family jotted down intermittently over the course of a lifetime (Mendelson 1985). Mary, Countess of Warwick, for example, recorded her intensely pious Puritanism in her diary and occasional memoirs between 1666 and 1677. In contrast to female historians of the **Reformation**, whose observation of extraordinary events made them worthy of record, here women's records of everyday domestic routines were drawn into religious history.

Women's documentation of radical religious movements gave their participants a recognised sacred history. Sects were often attractive to female converts because of their lack of hierarchy and the potential for spiritual equality – qualities that featured in women's histories. Anna Maria von Schurmann's *The Good Choice; or, Choosing the Better Part* (1673) explained her decision to follow Labadism in 1669. A second part of this text was published posthumously in which she described her spiritual contentment and the ongoing development of the Labadist movement. Susanna Parr's *Susanna's Apology against the Elders* (1659) provides detailed information about the contemporary process of becoming a member of such radical religious congregations. The late seventeenth-century German movement of Pietism attracted women by its emphasis on practical evangelical experiences rather than dogma. Its strict puritanical discipline eventually led to self-segregation of Pietist communities by the time Charlotte Zeller composed her large biographical work of her female forebears from the seventeenth to the early nineteenth century (Gleixner 2002). Zeller drew upon a variety of primary sources for her narrative of women in Pietist history, including her subjects' own voices through letters, excerpts from diaries, and reports of their devout last hours. The increasingly tight-knit nature of some sects led later female followers to produce a kind of godly family history of the closed community.

The domestication of religion

By the eighteenth century, the place of religion in everyday life was changing. For the intellectual elite, Enlightenment philosophies pushed religion to the margins, as scientific principles of observation and experimentation, and the quasi-deification of rationality gained dominance. Through observation and increasing experience of other lands and peoples, intellectuals like the Deists argued that there were universal moral laws which could be discerned through reason. Yet popular piety remained significant in Europe, and it was largely to this field that female religious historians contributed during the nineteenth century. Even here, however, the influence of Enlightenment and Deist philosophies could be seen, as the focus of such works shifted away from sin and salvation to instruction on everyday moral behaviour in the physical world. Much of the work produced by women at this time came in the form of conduct manuals that would teach women, adolescents and children how to be good Christians by modelling their behaviour on historical examples. Female historians often asserted the moral superiority of women, and many argued that the domestic sphere was the appropriate place to exert this influence. Exemplary texts would show women how to fulfil their divinely appointed moral guardianship in society. Biographical studies of individuals such as Church figures were a popular topic for women's French historical research. Marie-Geneviève-Charlotte Thiroux d'Arconville focused on both men's and women's roles in the past, examining the lives of François II and Marie de Medici, as well as church leaders like the Cardinal d'Ossat (*Vie du cardinal d'Ossat* 1771). Saints remained the most popular topic for the historical research for lay female historians like Adélaïde Celliez who composed *Les Saintes de France* (1856), a collection of French *vitae*. In contrast to many earlier female authors, these works were intended from their inception for a wide public audience and were published in their authors' lifetime. Clarisse Bader produced both a biography of St Claire *Sainte Claire d'Assise* (1880) as well as a study of women's participation in the dissemination of religious ideas during the biblical era, *La Femme biblique, sa vie morale et sociale, sa participation au développement de l'idée religieuse* (1866).

In the early nineteenth century, the evangelical creator of the Sunday School movement, Hannah More, encouraged religious reading for children with a focus on instilling good moral behaviour amongst the poorer members of English society. These kinds of charitable movements identified children's literature as an appropriate locus of female historians' concern. Louise-Cécile Bouffé, better known by her pen name Arvède Barine, published biographies of reformers *François de la Noüe* (1875) and *William Penn* (1877) in a series for French Sunday Schools. Charlotte Mary Yonge is probably the best-known religious historian writing for children. She published over 250 historical works including *The Chosen People: A Compendium of Sacred & Church History for School-Children* (1862), *Aunt Charlotte's Stories of Bible History for the Little Ones* (1875), *Eighteen Centuries of Beginnings of Church History* (1876), *English Church History, Adapted for Use in Day and Sunday Schools* (1883) and *The Patriots of Palestine, a Story of the Maccabees* (1898). Many of these texts simplified Bible stories for juvenile consumption. The historical value of such works was sometimes questionable. The historical and social context in which the subjects lived was largely irrelevant to the author's purpose of highlighting values suitable to the nineteenth-century female reader.

Nineteenth-century women argued that the more Christian and civilised a nation, the more women would be able to participate as members of that society (Burstein 1999). Protestant evangelical authors such as **Clara Lucas Balfour** in her *The Women of Scripture* (1847) and *Moral Heroism; or, The Trials and Triumphs of the Great and Good* (1848) and Harriet Beecher Stowe in *Women in Sacred History: A Series of Sketches Drawn from Scriptural, Historical and Legendary Sources* (1874) argued that Christianity was a liberating force for women in the past and present. As women enjoying the liberties of their superior Christian societies, they could justify their own participation as virtuous contributors to a public religious history. **Sarah Josepha Hale**'s *Woman's Record* (1853), an enormous world history that included description of the lives and virtues of some 1650 women is an example of such self-congratulation. Hale argued that it was the mission of women encourage the world to embrace Christianity and using a linear narrative framework she demonstrated that Christian nations were the most advanced (Baym 1990).

Such histories also involved national narratives, representing women as the civilisers of nations. Some authors, particularly in Britain and the United States, saw Protestantism as a superior form of Christianity. For example, Hale suggested that Catholicism continued to subjugate women while Anglo-Saxon Protestant cultures demonstrated the most social progress for women. This led her to argue that the United States represented the zenith of human achievement, where women were most able to bring about moral change through their divinely appointed realm of the domestic sphere. Few female historians wrote favourably of Catholic history in English, as did the Irish novelist and author of children's tales, **Julia Kavanagh**, who produced *Women of Christianity Exemplary for Acts of Piety and Charity* (1852). In the mid-nineteenth century, there were fears about the revival of Catholicism in England and some women were criticised for 'papist leanings' if they treated Catholic subjects favourably in their works. Agnes and Elizabeth **Strickland** were accused of 'romanism' for their sympathetic portrayal of Catholic queens and clergy in their popular volumes the *Queens of England* (1840–1848) and the *Lives of Seven Bishops* (1866) (Pope-Hennessy 1940).

The growing voice of the nineteenth-century philanthropic, abolition and suffrage movements also influenced women's religious histories, particularly in the United States. The anti-slavery campaigner **Lydia Maria Child** wrote *The Progress of Religious Ideas* (1855) in which she argued that the abolition of slavery would be the pinnacle of women's moral influence on society. By the end of the nineteenth century, however, suffragists began to espouse a radically different perspective about the progress Christianity had brought to women. In her detailed study of women's rights through Christian history, *Women, Church and State* (1893), **Matilda Joslyn Gage** came to see Christianity as an impediment to women's equality and advancement, by depriving women of their basic rights of freedom.

Comparative religious history

The American historian **Hannah Adams** was one of the first women in the nineteenth century to adopt a comparative approach to Christian history. She compiled a reference work that exercised critical detachment and treated sects and denominations as serious religious movements whose teachings and perspectives were to be carefully considered. The result was her *Alphabetical Compendium of the Various Sects Which Have Appeared from the Beginning of the Christian Era to the Present Day* (1784). Although Adams continued to publish comparative studies such as *History of the Jews* (1812) and the updated version of her first reference work, *A Dictionary of All Religions and Religious Denominations* (1817), her own Christian beliefs were never in doubt, as indicated by the title – *The Truth and Excellence of the Christian Religion Exhibited* (1804).

Later female historians adopted comparative approaches to look beyond Christianity to other world religions. This was aided in large part by increased opportunities for travel during the nineteenth century and growing interest in the 'exotic'. This opened up possibilities to observe new cultures and religions, and to study different types of historical sources. An early example of this phenomenon was Lady Mary Wortley Montagu, the wife of the English ambassador whose travels in Turkey between 1716 and 1718 led to her later writings about her observations of Eastern religions. In letters to England she compared the deist theology of Turkish Islam to the Christian theology she knew from her European experiences. **Harriet Martineau** produced *Eastern Life, Past and Present* (1848) as a result of her travel to Egypt, Palestine and the Sinai. Her travels led her to argue that the four great world religions all came from the same region and a human, rather than divine, source. The archaeologist Margaret Benson used her research on religious objects and representation from digs in Karnak, Egypt, as the basis of her study of the religious ideas of ancient Egypt, *The Temple of Mut in Asher* (1899), published with Janet Gourlay. Benson had been the first woman to obtain permission to excavate in Egypt.

The self-educated and widely travelled Russian historian Zénaïde Alexeïevna Ragozin published a number of studies of religion in ancient civilisations. She studied Hinduism and Vedic literature in *Vedic India as Embodied Principally in the Rig-Veda* (1895), and wrote on Zoroastrianism in Babylon in her *Media Babylon and Persia Including a Study of the Zend-Avesta or Religion of Zoroaster from the Fall of Nineveh to the Persian War* (1889). Moreover, she weighed into the widespread contemporary Russian intellectual debate that Jewish capitalism was the cause of anti-Semitic sentiment in Europe, in her essay on Russian Jews and Gentiles in *Century Magazine* (1882). In the early twentieth century, Alexandra David-Néel studied eastern religions in Paris and later travelled to the forbidden city of Lhasa to research Buddhism. She became the first women to interview the Dalai Lama in 1911 and later published her eyewitness history of early twentieth-century Buddhism in *Tibetan Journey* (1936).

By the late nineteenth and early twentieth century, female historians had entered academic institutions, and were producing rigorous religious histories intended for an academic, rather than popular, audience. Historical writing about religion in the early years of women's entrance into the academy showed a marked interest away from studies of Christianity, towards the less-studied religious history of the ancient or Eastern world. In doing so, women created interest in new areas of religious history. As women were increasingly debating whether Christianity had aided or hindered women's progress to equality, women in the academy were exploring women's contributions to, and place within, other world religions. At Cambridge, **Jane Ellen Harrison** drew upon archaeological and artistic discoveries for her research on Greek mythical and religious ideas. Harrison argued that religion had begun not as a theological theory, but as part of everyday rituals. She saw an older pacifist matriarchal culture of myth and fertility rites pre-dating the more patriarchal Olympian gods, articulating such ideas in her extensive body of work. Margaret Smith, one of the foremost scholars on Sufism, has written on the relationship between Christian and Islamic mysticism, *Studies in Early Mysticism in the Near and Middle East* (1931), as well as producing biographical studies and translations of the life and teachings of individual mystics and women saints, including the first academic biography of the ninth-century Muslim holy woman, Rabi'a al-Adawiyya Al-Qaysiyya, *Rabia the Mystic, A.D. 717–801* (1928). Smith's work provided an innovative perspective on the contribution of women to the history of Islam.

Twentieth-century feminism

In the early twentieth century, female historians increasingly challenged the dominance of male historians' interpretations of Christian history. At a time when women were arguing publicly for recognised rights in the first-wave feminist movements, evidence of sites of female power and control in the Christian past took on contemporary significance. Thus, the history of women's monasticism, where historians could demonstrate the widespread economic, intellectual, social and religious power of abbesses and convent communities over both men and women, was a particular focus. **Lina Eckenstein** analysed female spirituality and writings, documenting numerous and hitherto little known, medieval women writing religious texts in *Women under Monasticism* (1896) and *The Women of Early Christianity* (1935). The medieval economic historian **Eileen Power** also tackled the subject of female monasticism in *Medieval English Nunneries c. 1275 to 1535* (1922), but her approach was very different. She analysed convents as economic institutions and depicted convent life as something akin to a professional career for the medieval woman. In an era where women's abilities to participate in public life were hotly debated, female historians were drawn to study women-centred institutions like the convent, to prove an historical basis to the social disempowerment of women.

The impact of second-wave feminism on female historians' study of religion has been undeniable. Feminist theorisation has opened up new perspectives and areas of research within religious history. Recovery of female voices and experiences within the Christian tradition has continued to be important, but understanding of the social, cultural and historical contexts of women' participation has also come to the fore. This has also involved the recognition of the influence of earlier women historians of religion. Following Gage, texts such as Margaret Ruth Miles' *Carnal Knowing: Female Nakedness and Religious Meaning in the Christian West* (1991), Caroline Walker Bynum's *Fragmentation and Redemption: Essays on Gender and the Human Body in Medieval Religion* (1991) and Roberta Gilchrist's *Gender and Material Culture: The Archaeology of Religious Women* (1994) have examined the history of Christianity with a view to understanding how theological discourses and prescriptive literature have influenced women's lives in practical, social and even spatial terms. Female historians have also turned their attention to women participating in and redefining these theological notions about appropriate behaviour for women with texts such as Rosemary Skinner Keller and Rosemary Radford Ruether's *In Our Own Voices: Four Centuries of American Women's Religious Writings* (1995).

Stemming from the work of Power, the significance of the convent and the importance of nuns and abbesses as managers of large, international institutions has been reassessed in works such as Patricia Ranft's *Women and Religious Life in Premodern Europe* (1996), Penelope D Johnson's *Equal in Monastic Profession* (1991) and Elizabeth Rapley's *A Social History of the Cloister* (2001). Eckenstein's interest in female spirituality has also been renewed by modern historians, who analyse visionary and mystical experiences as key arenas for female expression. Eckenstein's influence is evidenced in works such as Caroline Walker Bynum's *Holy Feast and Holy Fast* (1987) on the religious significance of food; Phyllis Mack's *Visionary Women* (1992) on women's ecstatic prophecy and Elizabeth Rapley's *The Devotes: Women in the Church in Seventeenth-Century France* (1990). Feminist scholars have also questioned the validity of the periodisation of Christian history, examining events from the perspective of women. The Reformation, in particular, has undergone detailed re-examination and the continuities and the changes it brought to the lives of women are now being clearly articulated by historians such as Lyndal

Roper in *The Holy Household* (1989) and Patricia Crawford in *Women and Religion in England* (1993).

The important work of Protestant and Catholic women as nineteenth- and early twentieth-century missionaries, and as missionaries' wives, has been highlighted and incorporated into religious history. This has led historians such as Eliza Kent (1999) and Judith Rowbotham (2000) to examine the gendering of indigenous populations by religious groups and to document the spiritual experiences of women who received missionary teachings. Scholars are just beginning to historicise the experiences and politics of female ordination in Protestant churches in the later twentieth century and evaluate the resulting re-interpretations of Christian theology and practice in works such as Muriel Porter's *Women in the Church* (1989).

The influence of feminist theories can also be seen in women's historical writings on religions other than Christianity. There are now large-scale studies of the historical status of women and gendered history of Islam such as Lois Beck and Nikki Keddie's *Women in the Muslim World* (1978), Margaret Strobel's *Muslim Women in Mombasa* (1979) and more recently Leila Ahmed's *Women and Gender in Islam: Historical Roots of a Modern Debate* (1992) and Margot Badran's *Feminists, Islam and Nation* (1995). There has also been much debate generated about the utility of applying feminist theories of the Western world to other religions and cultures. Feminist theories have, however, created an historical interest in the religious experiences of Buddhist women, rather than conventional study of Buddhist texts as is evidenced in Tessa Bartholomeusz's study of Buddhist nuns in Sri Lanka, *Women under the Bo Tree* (1994). Indrani Iriyagolle has argued that women's status declined after the introduction of Christian religions to Buddhist regions, in her study of women's position from the fourth to the twentieth century (1989–1990). Lata Mani in *Contentious Traditions* (1998) and Catherine A Robinson in *Tradition and Liberation* (1999) have paid close attention to the seemingly misogynistic practice of suttee in Hindu history as well as the impact of Hinduism on feminist movements.

Female historians have been particularly instrumental in arguing the validity and utility of oral sources for understanding religious experiences, especially those of women, which have often not been recorded in official documentation of world religions. By studying different narrative techniques and subjects of Holocaust survivors' accounts, feminist historians have highlighted how Holocaust studies have been dominated by universalised male memories. Collective oral histories include Carol Rittner and John K Roth's *Different Voices: Women and the Holocaust* (1993) and Brana Gurewitsch's *Mothers, Sisters, Resisters: Oral Histories of Women Who Survived the Holocaust* (1998). Feminist theories, that have contextualised women's experiences within a narrative of disadvantages and even persecution by patriarchal forces, have made women historians particularly interested in other forms of persecution and marginalisation in religious history.

Finally, there is growing popular interest being shown in the history of women's pagan beliefs, expressed in the modern 'female religion' of Wicca. Although this has not received significant academic investigation to date, the notion of continuity in female pagan spirituality has been foreshadowed in Harrison's pre-Olympian Greek matriarchal religiosity and Margaret Murray's arguments about pre-modern witchcraft as the survival of a primitive feminine cult in *The*

Witch-Cult in Western Europe (1921), resurfacing more recently in Miranda Green's study of ancient Celtic feminine spirituality *Celtic Goddesses: Warriors, Virgins and Mothers* (1995). It remains to be seen whether academic feminism will historicise Wiccan practices as the latest in a long tradition of women's religious participation.

Susan Broomhall

References

Baym 1990; Bornstein 2000; Burstein 1999; Gleixner 2002; Iriyagolle 1989–1990; Jaron Lewis 1996; Kent 1999; Mendelson 1985; Miles 1991; Pope-Hennessy 1940; Rowbotham 2000; Smith 1998.

Related essays

Convents; Female Biography; Hagiography; Middle Ages; Reformation.

Renaissance

The coining of 'Renaissance' as an historical term is nineteenth century in origin. Drawing upon the earlier concept of 'rinascità', 'Renaissance' was used as a concept first by Jules Michelet in a series of lectures at the Collège de France 1838/1839 and later in his *History of France* (1855). The term is even more firmly associated with Jacob Burckhardt's *The Civilisation of the Renaissance in Italy* of 1860, which argued, like Michelet, for a period of intellectual creativity based upon the revival of the classics and associated with the visual arts of *quattrocento* Italy. In Burckhardt's formulation, modern historical scholarship originated in Renaissance historical method. However, feminist medievalist **Joan Kelly** once famously asked 'Did *women* have a Renaissance?' [Authors italics]. Kelly's interest was women's capacity to benefit from changing intellectual fashions. She concluded that women failed to experience 'Renaissance' in the way that men did because of their limited education and exclusion from public life. This essay tests that general conclusion against the evidence of women's education and female historical subjectivity.

Historians speak of two overlapping 'Renaissances' – an Italian Renaissance (c.1300–1550) and a Northern European Renaissance (c.1450–1700). Renaissance literally means 'rebirth'. By Burkhardt's definition, historical writers during the Renaissance drew upon the secular Greek and Roman histories of wars, states and 'heroes'. Historical writing in the Italian Renaissance was exemplified by the work of Francesco Petrarch, whose 'discovery' of ancient Rome arose out of his fascination with the ruins of the Roman fora that littered Rome's medieval sheep pastures. Petrarch became a collector of Roman antiquities and his *Liber de Viris Illustribus* established the model for other celebratory civic histories such as Leonardo Bruni's *Historiarum Florentini Populi* and Florentine histories from the pens of Poggio Bracciolini, Niccolo Machiavelli and Francesco Guicciardini. Guicciardini's most famous history was his *Storia d'Italia.*

At the heart of all Renaissance scholarship was the *studia humanitatis*, or study of human affairs and nature, through, not only history, but also classical poetry, rhetoric and grammar. Humanism was more than a system of education; it was a process of enculturation that involved the creation of the individual of *virtù*. In theory this individual was genderless, but in practice the classical exemplars of virtuous public life produced the public 'man' of letters. Books of manners, like Baldassare Castiglione's *Il Libro del Cortegiano* (1528), envisaged separate roles for the sexes that privileged a male 'public' sphere. Castiglione's belief that men 'rule[d] cities and armies' was a Renaissance commonplace and was borne out by the evidence of lived lives. Christiane Klapsiche-Zuber's *Women, Family and Ritual in Renaissance Italy* has painted a fairly bleak picture of patriarchal families in which 'men *were* and *made* the houses . . . [t]he determination of a woman's identity thus depended on her movements in the relation to the "houses" of men' (1985: 117–19). Even decisions about wet-nursing were made by men, and women were symbolic of a man's public reputation.

***The* querelle des femmes**

The Renaissance was not an uncomplicated cultural moment, nor was it characterised by the total social and educational subordination of all women. Some European noble families came to regard educated women as socially desirable. The woman who attained a feminised *virtù*, combining female scholarship with chastity, was seen to promote the social status of her family. Learning gave elite women social capital. But it also rendered women's femininity ambiguous and scholarly women were regarded quizzically as a 'third sex' (King 1980: 75). Some female intellects took advantage of the fashion for the 'educated lady' and challenged their exclusion from the *studia humanitatis*. Lisa Jardine (1985) points out that there was a difference between *accomplishment* and *profession*; a humanist education, while designed to give men both, only offered women *accomplishment* and a tense choice between an intellectual celibate life and marriage. The Venetian noblewoman Cassandra Fedele, author of the treatise *The Order of Sciences* (n.d.) and numerous Latin poems, exhorted women 'to seek and embrace these studies'. In 1492 she declared that an educated woman could not have both a profession and marriage (Robin 2000: 6). Although Fedele eventually chose marriage, it appears to have been an unhappy choice and there is little evidence that she pursued research while her husband lived. Humanist women became the 'virgin Muses' of humanist men and living experiments in the philosophical debates of the *querelle des femmes* or 'quarrel about women' that emerged within the literary culture of the Renaissance.

The tension around the 'learned woman' was first expressed in Giovanni Boccaccio's *Concerning Famous Women*, sometimes called the first Renaissance '**defence**' of women and this text was unique in its praise of learned women. Yet feminist historians have noted that Boccaccio's praise of women is often ambiguous. Even in his dedication to Andrea Acciaiuoli, Countess of Altavilla, Boccaccio praises her powers of intellect and generous soul, while also noting that such qualities 'are all the more remarkable for being found in a woman' (McLeod 1991: 66). Such comments produced a dualistic version of femininity within the text that persisted in the *querelle des femmes*, rendering female learning antithetical to the achievement of true femininity, thus unsexing female intellectuals.

In spite of this tension a number of women from elite Italian families pursued a humanist education. They learnt Latin, Greek, poetry and history, often tutored by their male kin. Allesandra Scala, a celebrated Hellenist as well as a Latinist, was educated by her father, Bartolomeo, a humanist scholar and Florentine chancellor. Laura Cereta's father had her rigorously schooled in a convent and at home; her autobiography recorded immersing herself 'night and day . . . in long vigils of study' (Robin 1997: 27). Annibal Guasco's *Discourse* to his daughter Lavinia praised her learning and accomplishment, advising on her conduct as a woman at the court of Turin. In northern Europe too the first generation of female humanist scholars were patronised by fathers and 'kin'. The English humanist, Thomas More, educated all of his daughters in a 'school' in his large household in Chelsea. In his *Utopia* (1516) he envisaged a world in which men and women were equally educated.

Learned women of the Renaissance were also patronised by male humanist scholars who corresponded with them, arranged for them to give orations and praised them in florid terms for their 'chastity' and 'virginity' thus imbuing them with *virtù*. Isotta Nogarola's letters to Guarino Veronese paid tribute to the male influence on her learning which gave her 'virtue and probity' and acknowledged, with necessary modesty, his own comparison of her with the learned women of antiquity (King 2004: 48–51). Cassandra Fedele too established close ties with the leading patrons of humanism and was praised for her mind in extravagant terms (Robin 2000: 6). Aware that in study she put aside women's work to engage in 'manly pursuits', Fedele's letters to her noble patrons are characterised by ambiguity and confusion around her gender (Robin 1995: 197). Her correspondents sometimes positioned her within **catalogs** of women who challenged the gender order with their intellectual pursuits.

The defence of women

Throughout the Renaissance, European humanist intelligentsia linked debates about sexual equality with female education in a nature/nurture debate that became central to the *querelle des femmes*. Following on from Boccaccio's 'praise' of the learned, numerous humanist men engaged in various rhetorical exercises designed to determine the true nature of womanhood. While early male-authored defences of women were rarely concerned with women's capacity for learning or potential for civic virtue, by the beginning of the sixteenth century a discursive shift had occurred that saw men more concerned with the question of 'what constituted a woman in theological and social terms'. With this shift came an increased interest in the educability of women.

Thomas More was influenced by Erasmus' essay 'The Sileni of Alcibiades' and by Juan Luis Vives' two texts on female education, *Instruction of a Christian Woman* and *The Office and Duty of a Husband* (1529). More's employee, Richard Hyrde, was responsible for translating Vives' *Instruction of a Christian Woman* into English in 1529. Thomas Elyot's *The Governour* published in 1531 advocated a gender inclusive Renaissance education that embraced logic, rhetoric, music, dancing and painting and his *Defence of Good Women* (1540) joined the *querelle des femmes* in support of women's education. *The Defence of Good Women* drew on earlier Renaissance defences of women like Boccaccio's to suggest that the classical civic virtues were attainable by women as well as men. His subject was the life of the Lady Zenobia, Queen of Palymyra in Syria and a widow, who was a Latin and Greek scholar and whose education of her children and government of her country was outstanding. Thus, in sixteenth-century Europe some male humanist scholars brought together a philosophy and practice of education that resulted in sexual equality with obvious implications for future scholarship, publication and the creation of historical knowledge and memory.

Humanist women followed the example of their male mentors in deploying historical example in their rhetorical works, particularly in defence of their right to an education. At the same time, however, they also challenged and rewrote the masculinist tradition within which they worked. In so doing they were emulating **Christine de Pizan**, author of the first defence of women, *Cité des Dames* (1405). In *Cité des Dames* Pizan created an alternative civic history; her rhetorical strategy was to use an extended urban allegory as a framework for the insertion into history of the biographies of virtuous women. Pizan is credited with saying 'I betook myself to history' and 'now I am truly a man' and her commissioned history of Charles V and *Corps de Policie* (1406) do indicate her acceptance on these terms. Although it is not known whether Laura Cereta was familiar with Pizan's *Cité des Dames*, like Pizan she ignored Boccaccio's emphasis on Semiramus' incest to concentrate instead on her erudition to defend the liberal education of her female contemporaries. She also inserted women like Almathea to feminise her work.

The extent to which women contributed defences of their sex to the *querelle des femmes* is an important measure of the impact of Renaissance humanist education on women. After 1600 there was a steady stream of such women, the first being Lucrezia Marinella whose *The Nobility and Excellency of Women and the Defects and Vices of Men* was published in 1600. Around this time French and British women scholars also began to engage in their own defence. Marie le Jars de Gournay belonged to the second generation of humanist-trained girls in France, though she claimed to teach herself Latin and to have found her own tutor in Greek. She is principally remembered as the editor of Montaigne's *Essays* (1595), but made her name for her advocacy of female education in her rhetorical essay *The Equality of Men and Women* (1622) and *The Ladies Grievance* which appeared in 1626. *The Ladies Complaint and Apology for the Woman Writing* reworked the material and both appeared in 1641. These rhetorical texts drew upon the historical example of women such as Nicostrata found in Boccaccio and male-authored defences, while also usurping the authority of such texts (Hillman and Quesnel 2002).

Other women used different literary forms to write in defence of women. Louise Labé was the well-educated daughter of a rope manufacturer whose *Debate Between Folly and Love* cast the Roman goddess, Folly (helped by Mercury) against Cupid (aided by Apollo) with a dedication that sought to inspire women to use their education. Labé's preface to a collection of her sonnets exhorted women to become as engaged in cultural activity as men. In sixteenth-century England, Lady Anne Southwell consigned her verses on Julius Caesar to a commonplace book. Jeanne Flore turned to the genre of short stories. Helisenne de Crenne's fictional autobiography of 1538 defended women who wanted to 'occupy themselves with the solace of literary exercises' and recommended 'the learning of the ancients'. In this way too history was deployed by learned women to defend the education of women and education became embedded as a sub-topic of the *querelle des femmes*.

Religious writing

The **Reformation** and Counter-Reformation came partly to shape the historical production of women humanists. Marguerite of Navarre, sister of King Francis I, who established a court that was the centre of humanist learning, became iconic amongst women humanist scholars in sixteenth-century northern Europe for her two works – *Le Miroir de l'ame Pecherese* (1531) and *Heptaméron* – modelled on Boccaccio's *Decameron*. The Seymour sisters – Anne, Margaret and Jane – daughters of Edward Seymour, Duke of Somerset, wrote an extended elegy to her that was published as the *Hecatodistichon* in 1550. The *Heptaméron* was Renaissance history as morality tale and an exploration of gender relations and may be classified as the first of many fictional histories written by French women the historical focus of which was love and its multiplicity of outcomes. However, Marguerite of Navarre was also part of the network of women who developed a religious reformist zeal that informed their work. She patronised Marie Dentiere who dedicated to her a 'letter against false Christians' in 1539. Margaret More, one of the highly educated daughters of Sir Thomas More, received not just a humanist education from her father, but a *Christian* humanist education. Her published output and historical preoccupations reflected this Christian humanism. She translated Erasmus' study of the Lord's Prayer – *A Devout Treatise on the Pater Noster* (1542) – and almost certainly assisted her husband, William Roper, in writing a biography of Thomas More. The altered political and intellectual culture associated with religious reform resulted in religious chronicles and annals, as well as religious biography. Christianised humanism dominated the intellectual climate. Scholars sought the historical 'truth' behind the claims to legitimacy of the Catholic and Protestant churches through scholastic obsession with Biblical accuracy and chronology.

However, scholastic historical writing was accompanied by more modest attempts to lend legitimacy to religious causes through the histories of institutions, saints, martyrs and family members. Women contributed through works of translation and partisan 'histories'. The multilingual Mildred Cooke published a translation of the works of St Chrysostom and her sister, Ann, published a translation of the *Fouretene Sermons of Barnardine Ochyne* (1550), the Italian Calvinist reformer. Catholic women religious wrote the histories of their convents in the tradition of the medieval 'sister histories', but with renewed vigour after the Council of Trent. Elizabeth Shirley, an Augustinian nun, first of St Ursula's and then St Monica's of Louvain, wrote a history of the founding of her order in 1612, combining it with a biography of her mentor, Margaret Clement, in *The Chronicle of St Monica's*.

Arguably the most important humanist woman writer of the Counter-Reformation was Lucrezia Marinella. Marinella was educated within the Venetian patriciate and was described by a male contemporary as 'a woman of wondrous elegance and learning' (Dunhill 1999: 1). She wrote the lives of male and female saints, often in epic and sacred verse punctuated with sections of allegorical prose. She concentrated on some of the female martyrs of the early Church, such as St Justine and St Colomba, publishing a lengthy prose account of St Catherine of Siena in 1624. Her biographical history of the Virgin Mary was published in Venice in 1602 and was her most successful work going through further editions in 1604, 1610 and 1617. Indeed, it was the single most successful work on its subject during her lifetime. Marinella depicted Mary as 'Empress of the Universe', a title that brought her Catholic historical concerns together with a quintessential feminism. It was also a work of Renaissance civic pride, attributing the defeat of the Turks in the battle of Lepanto of 1571 to Mary's intervention on behalf of the Venetian state.

Post-Tridentine Catholicism inspired women like Marinella to deploy their Catholicism and feminism in defence of one another. Marinella's *The Nobility and Excellence of Women* demanded not only women's spiritual equality with men through the Marian model, but cited Petrarch to argue for a female nature with a 'divine beauty' that was at once natural and God-given. It was an answer to Giuseppe Passi's vitriolic and unpleasant diatribe *The Defects of Women* (1599) and she challenged Passi's Aristotelian ideas about 'natural' female inferiority in a philosophical and rhetorical tract that deployed life exempla (drawn from Boccaccio) to prove that women were 'learned', 'temperate', 'strong' and 'prudent'. In Renaissance style, the first half of the work formed the refutation of Passi through a defence of women and the second part reinforced the first through an attack on 'the defects and vices of men'. Here again, history proved useful and Marinella trotted out men who were brutal and violent, like Herod and Achilles, men who killed family members, like Egbert, King of Anglia, and men who were just vile in all respects, like Caligula, who she rather understatedly described as 'excessively fickle'. Marinella's contemporary Arcangela Tarabotti wrote *Convent Life as Paradise, Convent Life as Hell* (1643) and *Paternal Tyranny* (1643) which collectively argued that women were the means of Christian redemption, that the Virgin Mary was 'the strongest and most faithful of God's creatures' and that the disabled and 'ugly' daughters (like herself) dumped in convents by tyrannical fathers were condemned to a life of 'hell' because without 'liberty' and 'vocation' they suffered torment. Her works were deeply bitter and forthright in their attack on men's social power, though they drew on the same language of Mary as 'Empress of the Universe' to defend women. The historical content of her works, such as her argument that Seneca drew advice from Livia and that King Ferdinand of Aragon followed the advice of his wife, Isabella, was also chosen as rhetoric in defence of women.

Protestant women throughout Europe were similarly inspired to write historically in defence of religion. English Quaker women were instrumental in writing the histories of their 'sufferings' especially after the 1672 Quaker policy that all Quaker works be preserved. Women's stories flowed forth in the guise of interpretation of God's wider plan. Alice Curwen's life was narrated in *A Relation of the Labour* (1680). Between 1651 and 1700 Quaker women's 'sufferings' accounted for 177 published works (not counting reprints) or 37.5 percent of the total published output in England of women for those decades. The same reforming impulse resulted in providential and prophetic writing, both of which were inherently historical in their attempts to interpret God's plan and both of which offered a literary space in which women could claim spiritual and even political authority. Providential writings are exemplified by Alice Thornton's *Book of Remembrances* (c.1668) and Katherine Austen's diary (1650s). Both women wrote after being widowed and they reflected back on their lives in an attempt to interpret events according to a divine plan that had Creation as an exactly timed beginning. Austen recorded that God was 'the great governour of the world [who] ordered it by the variety of changes and accidents'. Both she and Thornton wrote what were essentially, to their minds, the 'histories of those "accidents" '. Austen interpreted the death of her husband when she was only 29 as being a sign from God. Thornton recorded in tragic detail the deaths of several of her infant children. Yet for both women, their historical writing was intended to have salvific power and they both stressed what they termed God's 'deliverances' and 'mercies' and made 'thanksgiving' a motivating force in their writing. Thornton spoke of 'perticuler remembrances of His favours', indicating that this form of historical writing looked not to the posterity of a future reading audience but to the salvation of the soul that it might facilitate.

Puritan fervour in England generated other providential diaries, like that of Mary Boyle, Countess of Warwick who recorded her life as 'vain' and 'idle' and filled with reading romances until her conversion at the age of 21 years. She wrote a short autobiography and a 'Diary' that combined family history of the Boyles of Herefordshire and the first Earl of Cork (her father) with an autobiographical account of her illicit courtship with Charles Rich, later earl of Warwick and leading puritan earl during the civil wars. Her writing is frequently punctuated with 'meditations' and she reflected on personal tragedy, such as the death of her only son in 1664, with remorse and repeated devotion to God. Writing, reading and meditations were inseparable activities in the quest of the soul for a favourable place in God's preordained plan. Elizabeth Pindar had printed bookplates made that read 'Elizabeth Pindar. God's Providence is mine inheritance'. Her reading was woven into the Christian historical process.

The denominational boundaries drawn during the sixteenth and seventeenth centuries make it difficult to argue in favour of what Gerda Lerner has called 'affinity clusters' of women. However, Marie le Jars de Gournay, the French (Catholic) scholar, Latinist, novelist and editor of Montaigne's *Essays*, corresponded with and influenced strongly the German Protestant scholar Anna Maria van Schurman, whose sympathies were staunchly and ascetically Calvinist (and later Labardian pietist) and who also wrote a defence of women's education in 1641.

Prophetic writings, spiritual auto/biography, secular biography

By the seventeenth-century Protestant women's Christian humanist *mentalité* had been disrupted by a systematised Calvinism that empowered female subjectivity in the sense that women could write themselves into God's plan, yet at the same time it diminished their agency in the historical narrative. The future and present became conflated with the past and Biblical exegesis became the key to prophesying God's plan for the future. In England alone, 90 prophetic works were written by women during the mid-seventeenth-century 'wars of religion'. Through prophetic writing women could legitimately publish 'history' for a partisan audience. Prophets viewed current events as 'history' already planned by God. Historical writing of this sort harked back to and drew upon the methods of medieval historical universalism. The universalist historical quest enabled women to seek a literary camouflage not available to them in other forms of Renaissance historical writing. In other words, more women 'had' a Renaissance once it included, involved and was intrinsically linked to religion.

The most prolific prophetic writer was Eleanor Davies who co-opted the voice of the male prophets and used the anagram of her name 'Reveale O Daniel' to sign *All the Kings of the Earth* in 1633. She established her prophetic authority in one tract on Revelation 1:8: 'I am Alpha and Omega, the beginning and the ending.' She wrote and published over 60 prophetic works, mostly published during the 1640s when she felt most keenly the sense of history unfolding and her own responsibility as an interpreter of historical process. She translated her family motto – *je le tien* – as a variant of 'Hold fast till I come' from Revelation 2:25, thus conflating the idea of the second-coming of Christ with her central role in its prophecy. However, the legitimacy she claimed came from the 'voices' she co-opted of male prophets.

Davies felt no need, as other women prophets like Anna Trapnel did, to transcend her conscious state when prophesying, regarding herself primarily as a writer. Her instant response to seeing Daniel at the end of her bed was to prepare his message in written form for Archbishop George Abbot. This ultimately turned into a 100-page text on Daniel 7:12 called *Warning to the Dragon* which she re-worked during a period of exile in the 1630s. Her 1640s tracts became a weaving together of opaque Old Testament exegesis and current events viewed as stages of a pre-ordained historical chronology. In *Samsons Legacie* (1643) she combined the anagram of Samson with an apologue to warn 'James Son' about his loss of strength; she equated Delilah with Henrietta Maria. The apogee of her prophetic career came when Archbishop William Laud was executed nineteen-and-a-half years after her original vision. When the execution of Charles I followed in 1649 she felt vindicated in her prophetic capacity to interpret a God who was at once Word and time itself.

The civil wars in England in the 1640s inspired secular, biographical and autobiographical writing by women. Four biographies of note survive: two sets of *Memoirs* by **Ann, Lady Fanshawe** and **Anne, Lady Halkett**, the *Memoirs of the Life of Colonel Hutchinson* by **Lucy Hutchinson** and *Life of the Thrice Noble... Duke*, a biography of her husband, by **Margaret Cavendish**. Only the latter was published in the seventeenth century in 1667 and of these four biographers, Margaret Cavendish demonstrated the greatest knowledge of historical writing as a subject with a professional methodology. Cavendish's views on history are interesting despite her apology that she was 'ignorant of the rules of writing histories.' The ignorance she claimed was only rhetoric, her opening remarks being that she asked her husband for an expert 'assistant' but he claimed that 'truth cannot be defective.' The 'historical truth' she claimed, came from the subject – the duke – himself. Her further bold claims that many histories are applauded 'merely for their elegant style... well-observed method... [and] feigned orations' lead her to dismiss 'pleasant romances' and highlight the historical truth in her own 'plain style.' Her claim to historical method was ironic given her anti-empirical scientific work and earlier forays into whimsy. However, Cavendish did also develop an interesting argument about the three 'chiefest' histories – these being 'general history' or the 'history of the known world,' 'national history' and 'particular history' or biography. Her odd equation of the first and second with democratic and aristocratic polities respectively seems to have been a way of declaring monarchical political sympathies by privileging the worth of 'particular histories' which she associated with monarchy. Her equation of historical styles with different polities found no enduring favour as biographical writing slowly became marginalised as a form of historical writing.

Cavendish called her subject/husband 'prince' in the title of her biography, though it is instructive that her autobiography predates the biography of her husband by 11 years. Cavendish was a writer for whom work was a form of self-projection and even the biography of her husband/prince (as he is referred to in the title) has her own life appended as *A True Relation of My Birth, Breeding and Life*. However, in her *Life of the Thrice Noble... Duke* the style is that of a celebration of character, social pedigree and her husband's actions as royal commander during the civil wars.

In Renaissance style she viewed history as a vehicle for tales of heroism and public virtue. She noted her husband's victory at Adwalton Moor in June 1643 and commented on him committing 7000 men to conduct Henrietta Maria out of Yorkshire 'which in such a conjuncture would have weakened Caesar's army.' More prosaically she presented lists of her husband's estates and their rentals to quantify his losses as a royalist. Cavendish's biography is the most 'typical' of Renaissance biographies. Her husband's life is woven as a tale of heroic virtue and public service propped up by the overblown claim that she has committed no crimes of 'partiality or falsehood'. Her self-legitimisation as a historian is made stronger by the earlier false modesty when she claims to have asked her husband for an assistant because she is 'ignorant of the rules of writing histories'. The claims for her husband's legitimacy as heroic subject are bolstered by his response that she needed no 'elegant and learned historian' to prevent a 'defective' history because 'truth cannot be defective'.

Dramatic works, poetry and romance

Feminine identification with Sappho rather than Clio made women's historical writing in the Renaissance potentially a poetic rather than scientific genre: 'Did not Sappho's poetry flow with wondrous sweetness', Isotta Nogarola asked of Damiano dal Borgo in 1439. The context was defence of women against the charge of loquaciousness, an accusation that de-legitimised the 'female voice' in history. Poetry could be co-opted by this 'voice' and history camouflaged as sonnets and songs in the works of writers such as Louise Labé, Pernette de Guillet, Madeleine Neveu and Gabrielle de Coignard.

It is also the case that the late sixteenth century witnessed the simultaneous growth in the numbers of women whose historical writing was secular in impulse and looked back to the Classical world for inspiration. Mary Sidney, sister of the poet the Arcadian Philip Sidney, was a translator, poet and historian in her own right. Following the death of her brother she prepared his work for publication and in 1592 published her own translation of Robert Garnier's *The Tragedie of Antonie*. Although Sidney diminished her role as author by peddling only translations, her choice of texts reveal her as a humanist-educated woman interested in historical writing. *Antonie* drew upon Plutarch to weave a tale of love and drama, beginning with the 'overthrow of Brutus and Cassius' and the destruction of the liberty of Rome. She followed this work with translations of Petrarch's *A Discourse of Life and Death* and *The Triumph of Death*. In the latter Sidney historicised classical mythology and smuggled Clio into her writing disguised as Sappho: 'A few, for Nature makes true glorie rare, . . . Claym'd whole historians, whole Poete's care' (Clarke 2000: 193). Sidney was part of a second wave of humanist-educated women in England that included also **Elizabeth Cary** (née Tanfield) who was tutored in Latin and Hebrew as well as French and Spanish. Despite having 11 children between 1609 and 1624 and becoming involved in a bitter separation from her husband, Henry Cary, Lord Falkland, she managed to produce *The Tragedy of Mariam* (1613), a Senecan tragedy based on Josephus' *Antiquities of the Jews* and is believed to have written the verse-drama *The History of the Life, Reign and Death of Edward II* (c.1627).

Mary Wroth's *The Countess of Montgomery's Urania* (1621) co-opted the well-established male genre of chivalric romance exemplified by texts like *Guy of Warwick* and, indeed, *Arcadia*, the work of Wroth's uncle, Philip Sidney. Wroth was a court-product, a favourite of Anne of Denmark. *Urania* was written during her affair with William Herbert, Earl of Pembroke and was taken by many courtiers to be a thinly disguised account of several court scandals, particularly that involving the illicit post-marital affair of Honora Denny, daughter of the Baron of Waltham. Wroth wrapped up her contemporary account of the court in a rhetorical tale about Pamphilia's undying love and constancy for Amphilanthus while under continuous pressure from his desertions and philandering. The model was the ever-popular tale of 'patient Griselda' and so this was a gender construct of the most conformist kind while delivering scandal to contemporaries, many of whom were both the readers and the satirised actors in Wroth's drama.

French women historical writers of the seventeenth century used the *topos* of love to frame their histories, sometimes fictionalising historical characters for dramatic tension and at other times developing their historical writing through the *roman à clef.* The development of the romance as a framing device and the self-conscious identification as *précieuse* mark the beginnings of a feminine Enlightenment historiography and the distinction that came to be drawn between masculine, *serious* history and feminine, 'unprofessional' history as is evidenced in texts such as Madeleine de Scudéry's *Clélie* (1654), Marie Catherine Desjardins's [Madame de Villedieu] La Princess de Montpensier (1662) and Mémoires de la vie de Henriette Sylvie de Moliere (1672). Beyond France other women were working in similar idioms. Influenced by French writers the satirical politics dramatised by Aphra Behn included the tripartite *Love Letters between a Noble-Man and His Sister* (1682–1687) which was a serialised *roman á clef* of the elopement of Lady Henrietta Berkeley with her brother- in-law, Lord Grey.

Did women have a Renaissance?

The Renaissance both in Italy and Northern Europe produced many scholarly and educated women though a far smaller number of women wrote Renaissance histories. In this sense, Christine de Pizan's *Book of the City of Ladies,* as an allegorical configuration of the separate 'space' in which women could write was a telling precursor to Virginia Woolf's declaration that women writers needed a 'room of [their] own'. What united Renaissance defences *of* women *by* women was the humanist argument that female education was paramount. Women like Anne-Marie-Louise d'Orléans wrote philosophical treatises against marriage as a constraint on female learning while Lucrezia Marinella included her learned predecessors like Isotta Nogarola and Christine de Pizan in her defence of the female sex to prove her claim that women could achieve 'excellence and virtue'. Writing at the end of the seventeenth century, Mary Astell recommended in her *Serious Proposal to the Ladies* that women be segregated from men in 'academies' to foster female intellect. Women's contributions to the *querelle des femmes* indicate that in the seventeenth century a tension emerged between those writers who argued, like Astell, that the learned woman could only thrive in isolation (secular 'convents') and those who used a new 'enlightened' rhetoric about the learned woman's central role as a 'civilising' influence in society. Once Cartesianism replaced Aristotelianism as the dominant way of understanding the female mind, women at least had the potential (though it was potential only) to move on from the Renaissance position of the learned 'trophy wife'.

If gender is applied as a category of analysis to Michelet and Burkhardt's 'Renaissance', the very concept of Renaissance requires revision. Women's learning did not move from *accomplishment* to *profession* and women's historical writing rarely strayed into masculine-style civic histories, congregating instead in the key areas of auto/biography, defences of the female sex, religious histories, romantic tales and 'secret histories'. Only the last two were an advance upon the female historical writing of the early medieval period, between them forging alternate feminine historical genres. The answer to Joan Kelly's question is that *some* women had a Renaissance in the sense that they gained an education that made them accomplished women, rather than historians. However, asking if women 'had a Renaissance' in the end proves less enlightening than asking what women's historical writing and sense of place in the history of their times tells us about 'the Renaissance' itself.

Amanda L Capern

References

Clarke 2000; Dunhill 1999; Hillman & Quesnel 2002; Jardine 1985; Kelly 1977/1984; King 1980, 2004; Klapische-Zuber 1985; McLeod 1991; Robin 1997a, 1997b, 2000.

Related essays

Catalogs; Defences; Memoir; Middle Ages; Reformation; Religion; World History.

Revolution

Revolution has often meant the irruption of the marginalised and powerless into the public sphere. This has also meant that in the course of the social revolutions which, since the seventeenth-century English Revolution, have shaped **world history**, women have broken out of the private, subordinate spheres into which they have been historically relegated, forcing their way on to the centre stage of the historical process, at least for the duration of the revolution if not beyond. However, the capacity of women to contribute to historical discourse has been limited by their subordination to men of their class. Anti-female prejudices, illiteracy, the exclusion of women from public life and women's own internalisation of their subordination have been major impediments to their being recognised as historians in their own right. In these circumstances, women have generated their own genres of writing about revolutions. Ironically, the bourgeois order engendered by the revolutions of the seventeenth and eighteenth centuries reinforced the separation of the public and private spheres and effectively excluded women from the academy which in the nineteenth century was emerging as a professional, public space. Nevertheless, generations of women – as historians, chroniclers, observers, participants or opponents of revolution – have paved the way for the gendered perspectives on revolution that have become such a force in contemporary Western historiography. This essay examines the evolution of women's historical writing on the revolutions that have shaped the modern Western world.

The English Revolution (1640–1660)

The collapse of censorship on the eve of the English Civil War opened the way to many challenges, including those offered by women, sometimes inspired by Puritanism, to the patriarchal institutions that governed their lives. England became a cauldron of polemical publications about the prerogatives of king and parliament. Women, who hitherto had rarely written for publication, seized their first opportunity to vent their concerns *en masse*. At a time when a mere 11 per cent of women were literate, publications by women suddenly accelerated. Women, particularly members of sects such as the Quakers, became vigorous pamphleteers, petitioners, publicists and rhetoricians. In doing so they put their stamp on political events. Polemics on monarchical and church authority spilled over into questions of patriarchal authority and gender roles. In 1640 'Mary Tattle-well and Jan Hit-him-home, Spinsters' published a pamphlet entitled 'The Women's Sharpe Revenge' which railed against anti-female sentiment.

This was not political feminism, rather it was a call for 'moral improvement' in women's relations with men, not equality between them (Rowbotham 1972: 24–5). Yet there were instances when women demanded an equal voice in public affairs. In 1649 women petitioned parliament in defence of the Leveller John Lilburne, declaring 'that we [women] have an equal share and interest with men in the Commonwealth.'

While some women were adding to contemporary debates, others were contributing to the written historical record in a distinctly female way. Poetry, letters and diaries captured the immediacy of events, coupled with the vagaries of personal life. Whereas traditional, male-authored 'national history' chronicled ruling families and decisive battles, women's letters and diaries, whether royalist or parliamentarist, wove together marriage, family, home, birth, love, death, religion and contemporary politics – in these most political of times.

Seventeenth-century women were reluctant to write for publication, fearing they would be viewed as immodest. But the revolution and increasing literacy encouraged women to publish. In the wake of the Restoration, educated women published letters, memoirs, autobiographies and biographies. In these writings women frequently had recourse to 'the language of revolution as a source of metaphors for private or emotional life', thereby crossing the boundaries between the private and the public (Keeble 2001: 159–60). This traffic between the private and the public was to become a hallmark of women's historical discourse, foreshadowing the social and cultural concerns of much later feminist historiography.

In the main, these women's writings were politically conservative reactions to Civil War disorder and death (overwhelmingly of their menfolk). A rare parliamentarist perspective was provided in the letters of Lady Brilliana Harley. Written mainly in 1638–1643, they revealed the breakdown of established society and how her Puritan beliefs had strengthened her support for parliament against the king.

In keeping with their subservient status to their husbands, female autobiography was often inserted into biographies of husbands who had played an important role in the Civil War. This was the technique of the god-fearing Calvinist republican **Lucy Hutchinson.** As author of the life of her regicide husband, which vindicated him and their divinely ordained marriage in opposition to courtly corruption, she wrote anonymously to avoid restorationist anti-republicanism. Even so, her *Memoirs of Colonel Hutchinson* remained unpublished until 1806. The times were far more propitious for the royalist **Margaret Cavendish** who in 1667 published her *Life of the Duke of Newcastle*, in which she praised her husband while apologising for her ignorance 'of the Rules of Writing Historie.' Cavendish, like the High Church, Tory philosopher Mary Astell, author of the royalist tract *An Impartial Enquiry into the Causes of Rebellion and Civil War in this Kingdom* (1704), also displayed the principal paradox of these conservative women: staunch absolutism coupled with a keen awareness of female subordination to male authority (Smith 1998).

Not until the eighteenth century would a few women venture into serious historical writing on the English Revolution. **Catharine Sawbridge Macaulay**, embarking on her eight-volume *History of England* (1763–1781), anticipated 'the invidious censures which may ensue from striking into a path of literature rarely trodden by my sex.' Macaulay's history was informed not by an incipient feminism but by her radical republicanism. She supported the trial and execution of Charles I. Likewise, she supported the Glorious Revolution, which she saw as an expression of popular will. Not surprisingly she saw the French Revolution as yet another opportunity for popular rule but this time fuelled by an 'enlightened spirit'. Close on the heels of **Mary Wollstonecraft**, with whom she corresponded, Macaulay challenged Edmund Burke's vehemently counter-revolutionary *Reflections on the Revolution in France* (1790), in her own *Observations on the Reflections of the Right Honourable Edmund Burke, on the Revolution in France* (1790). Macaulay believed that writing history was 'the best possible way for a woman to practice public virtue'. She excelled at it. Ahead of her time in using narrative and documentary sources, she wrote possibly the best eighteenth-century account of the New Model Army's revolution of 1647–1649.

The American Revolution

Between the end of the Revolution and the Civil War, history pervaded American women's writing. Rising literacy among late eighteenth-century white, well-to-do women opened the way for them to contribute to historical discourse in a variety of genres: textbooks, poetry, fiction, journalism, drama, **biography** and **travel** stories. Antebellum women's historical works, such as Elizabeth Peabody's *Chronological History of the United States* (1856) offered a biblical perspective on the American Revolution as divine 'destiny' realised. Female-authored, popular, sentimental romance – from Susanna Rowson's *The Fille de Chambre* (1792) to Ellen T H Putnam's *Captain Molly: The Story of a Brave Woman* (1857) – employed familial metaphors. The War of Independence was a 'family quarrel' with Washington as the father of the nation (Baym 1995: 169–70). Thus American women's popular historical writing provided a Protestant patriotic affirmation of patriarchy.

The post-revolution emphasis on 'republican motherhood' impeded women contributing to serious historical scholarship. But there were exceptions. A belief that men were too busy making the revolution to write about it was how **Mercy Otis Warren**, America's first female historian, justified her three-volume *History of the Rise, Progress and Termination of the American Revolution* (1805). Political agitation on behalf of an independent American republic served as the well-connected Warren's apprenticeship for amateur historian. Warren combined a patriotic, radical republicanism with reticence about the role of women in public life. Writing to the revolutionary leader John Adams she begged 'pardon for touching on war, politicks, or anything thereto . . . so far beyond the line of my sex'.

Preserving republican 'civic virtue' also motivated the only antebellum woman historian to write on the role of her own sex in the revolution: **Elizabeth Ellet**, who produced three biographical volumes on *Women in the American Revolution* (1848–1850). Ellet was celebrating exemplary 'matrons', a conventional concern, but by highlighting women her work also gendered the focus of the predominant republican historical paradigm on the role of ordinary people (Baym 1995: 233–7). Ellet subsequently made significant strides towards narrative, social history in her *Domestic History of the American Revolution* (1850). Of course, Ellet's history reflected the limits of the republican historiographical paradigm, driven by Puritan patriotism: there was no place in it for enslaved African Americans. It would take the Enlightenment and the French Revolution to generate a more secular, emancipatory, women's historiography.

The French Revolution

Before the revolution the obstacles to women writing history were immense.

Nevertheless, on the eve of the revolution, France's first publicly acknowledged female '*historienne*', **Louise de Kéralio** published her first historical writings: a biography of Elizabeth I and an anthology of French women's writing. In doing so, Kéralio made a conscious decision to enter the hitherto exclusively male domain of public political history based on documentary sources. Her histories were devoted to women, though not out of any sense of female solidarity. On the contrary, she wrote to warn of the threat posed by women occupying positions of unbridled power. Yet Kéralio's actions belied her anti-female sentiments. With the outbreak of the revolution she took the unprecedented step for a woman of becoming a journalist-printer. Her bloodthirsty *Crimes des reines de France* (1791) implicated every woman associated with the French throne on the grounds that 'a woman who becomes queen changes sex'. Kéralio herself renounced public life in 1793, the year the women's clubs were dissolved and Olympe de Gouges, author of *The Declaration of the Rights of Woman* (1791), was guillotined. Thereafter she returned to prose fiction – a harbinger of a generalised retreat to more traditional forms of female historical writing in the wake of the revolution.

The importance of the salon, of the Romantic enthusiasm for classical republicanism, the penchant for letter-writing and the **memoir**, which particularly characterised women's historical discourse in the late eighteenth and early nineteenth centuries, are all manifest in the creative activities of the Girondist republican, Marie-Jeanne Roland. Born into the artisan classes of Paris, steeped in a classical education, in 1792 Roland became actively involved in 'patriot' politics. The appointment of her husband as minister for the interior 'gave scope to my taste for political argument and for studying men'. But she was a woman of her time: 'I knew the proper role of my sex and never exceeded it.' One of the most belligerent Girondists, she made enemies among the radicals, eventually going to the guillotine in November 1793. During her incarceration she compiled her 'Historical Notes'. A selection of her memoirs was published in 1795 as *An Appeal to an Impartial Posterity*. Mixing memoir with reflection she summed up the despair that she felt for the fate of the revolution: 'Farewell, our sublime illusions, our generous sacrifices, our hopes, our happiness.' Her memoirs have been characterised as 'the prose masterwork of the first revolutionary years' (Shuckburgh 1989).

The romantic reaction

The French Revolution undoubtedly inspired women to new heights in historical writing. Foremost among them was **Germaine de Staël**, daughter of Jacques Necker, banker to Louis XVI, who was reared in the elite *philosophes* salon conducted by her mother. De Staël was the author of a number of outstanding historically based works which for most of the nineteenth century were regarded as models of female 'genius'. Among them was her *Considerations on the Principal Events of the French Revolution* (1818). Published in the shadow of the Bourbon restoration (1814), de Staël's 600-page *Considerations* was an amalgam of memoir, history, political theory, anecdotes, biography and autobiography. In accordance with her 'meritocratic' outlook, for de Staël the pre-Jacobin years of the revolution, when 'political affairs were still in the hands of the first class', was the revolution's defining moment. Despite her republican liberalism, de Staël's depiction of women in the September 1792 blood-letting contributed to their malevolent image as 'furies'. Reflecting her intimate knowledge of high politics, *Considerations* was a 'masculine' work, atypical of female historical writing insofar as it neglected domestic issues. Conceived as an act of 'revenge on Napoleon' (who exiled her), *Considerations* also embodied her dubious historiographical legacy, given the multiplicity of genres within her work and her virtual denial of historical knowledge. Ironically, *Considerations* also reflected the moment when the political presence of women in the revolution was being cut short.

Memoirs

In addition to more formal histories, the 'generation of 1789' spawned an unprecedented volume of **memoirs.** Of the 1000 published during the half century after the revolution, 80 were by women. They bore the stamp of the class polarisation the revolution had entailed. Aristocrats made up two-thirds of women memoirists, reflecting not only educational but also political advantage. The restored Bourbon monarchy promoted hostile accounts of 'that time of horrible memory', as the Comtesse de Bohm put it (1830), while making it politically hazardous to publish memoirs sympathetic to the revolution. Surprisingly, the *Mémoires de Charlotte Robespierre* appeared in 1835, which, in depicting the lives of her famous brothers, took a form then common to female writers of 'ascent to authorship through connection to a famous man' (Yalom 1993: 3).

Few women's memoirs, however, were political. While they told of their observation of and participation in events, they did so from the perspective of the sex traditionally held to be responsible for sustaining family life. Accordingly, they demonstrated a particular sensitivity to death and suffering and the 'connection between victimisation and gender'. Given these factors, aristocratic women in particular wrote with an eye to the conservative 'moral lessons' about the disasters of the revolution to be conveyed to their descendants (Yalom 1993: 1–12). In their writings, at least, there was no sense that the revolution held the promise of emancipation for either women or men.

British writers on the Revolution in France

Burke's anti-revolutionary *Reflections* voiced the British ruling classes' horror of the French Revolution. Given the misogynist logic and rhetoric of his tract, it is not surprising that it generated a backlash from radical British women writers. Among the first published ripostes was Wollstonecraft's *A Vindication of the Rights of Men* in November 1790, followed a month later by Macaulay's *Observations*. Ironically, the 'Revolutionary feminist' Wollstonecraft critiqued Burke in gendered terms, accusing him of indulging in 'effeminate', pretentious 'sensibility' at the expense of 'reason' and 'virtue'. Wollstonecraft herself went to Paris in December 1792, where she associated with the British expatriate **Helen Maria Williams** and the Girondist Roland. While still in France in mid-1794 Wollstonecraft published *An Historical and Moral View of the Origin and Progress of the French Revolution, and the Effect It has Produced on Europe*. Focused chiefly on 1789, the first year of the revolution, her *View* attempted to straddle both female 'sensibility' and 'manly' 'reason', hoping that revolutionary feminism could save the revolution from the masculine excesses of Jacobin radicalism, a perspective that reflected her stance as both radical critic of the 'effeminate' *Ancien regime* and middle-class defender of property rights (Kelly 1993).

The influence of the Enlightenment, dissenting Protestantism, and the importance of the salon and the epistolary genre of historical writing for women is exemplified in the work of one of the few other British women to write on public affairs, the poet

Helen Maria Williams, author of an eight-volume eyewitness account *Letters from France* (1791–1796). Forsaking the feminine pastime of 'literary conversation . . . for the sublimer delights of the French Revolution', she was lured to France in 1790. Mindful that in writing non-fiction prose she was trespassing on a masculine domain, Williams defensively set out to convince her readers that the same feminine, emotional sensibility that had informed her poetry informed her writing on the revolution: 'my political creed is entirely an affair of the heart.' As a result, Williams 'feminised' the revolution, by a 'sentimental', epistolary depiction of events. As the revolution descended into violence Williams blamed the Jacobins for the revolution's masculine degradation. Yet, as a 'friend of liberty', she retained her confidence in the virtues of the revolution. Like most other middle-class British intellectuals, she supported the bourgeois, anti-aristocratic thrust of the revolution but baulked at its uncompromising plebeian violence (Kennedy 2002).

The revolutions of 1848–1849

Women were amongst the most militant participants in the European revolutions of 1848–1849. When these liberal-democratic revolutions were brutally suppressed by an unholy alliance of the liberal intelligentsia and their absolutist foes, fearful of unleashing the socialist-inclined working classes, women militants were punished for challenging the accepted boundaries of gender in action and print. 'When they say the people, women do not count', protested the Saxony *Frauen-Zeitung* (*Women's Journal*) in April 1849, the founder of which, Louise Otto, had even countenanced women taking up arms against foreign troops. The emerging bourgeois order, which defeat of the revolutions helped consolidate, was definitely a 'male project' (Hauch 2000). So too was historical writing about the revolution.

Despite their active participation, women on either side of the barricades produced very little in the way of formal history of the 1848 revolutions. Radical 'women of letters' preferred the written word to political action and the novel as the appropriate medium. 'Novels speak to the heart and the imagination', declared the romantic socialist George Sand, author of *La Petite Fadette* (1848), which expressed her view that female domestic activity rather than male politics was the most efficacious means of achieving social change (Walton 1994: 1017). The singular exception to this tendency to eschew formal history was the Comtesse Marie d'Agoult. Writer, journalist and liberal critic, her *Essai sur la liberté* (1847), published under the nom de plume Daniel Stern, established her as a feminist thinker in the vein of Wollstonecraft and de Staël. Welcoming the revolution she published eyewitness accounts of events 'at the heart of the struggle'. Her three-volume *Histoire de la Revolution de 1848* (1850–1853) has influenced many subsequent treatments of 1848. But d'Agoult's work exemplified the limits of the liberal republicanism of these middle-class, female literati. Aghast at the workers' insurrection of June 1848, she disdained the militant *clubistes* and *Vesuviennes* as women 'of questionable morality'. Her feminism was circumscribed by her acceptance of a male-dominated, bourgeois, political order in which women belonged in the private realm, from whence they might gradually improve their lot through moral persuasion.

The Paris Commune (March–May 1871)

This short-lived experiment in participatory democracy, drowned in blood by the national government at Versailles, saw unprecedented participation in revolution by '*femmes fortes*', later reviled as monstrous '*petroleuses*' (Schulkind 1985: 138). As in 1848, however, few women wrote the history of the revolution. The female Communards were overwhelmingly the urban poor, uneducated and inarticulate. But those that did contribute to historical discourse on the Commune uncompromisingly espoused their revolution. Whereas previously middle-class women historians of revolution, baulking at the most popular and repressive phases of revolution, had qualified their support, the participant-historians of the Commune showed no such reservations.

The socialist-feminist journalist Andre Leo threw herself into writing and speaking on behalf of the Commune during the siege, editing the journal *La sociale* and publishing a defence of the Commune: *La guerre sociale* (1871). However her memoirs, which have been lauded for their 'penetrating analyses of deep-rooted attitudes and political behaviour patterns prevailing among Parisian working people in the late nineteenth century', remained unpublished (Schulkind 1985). In contrast, the published recollections of the notorious anarcho-feminist, Louise Michel, *Les Mémoires* (1886) and *La Commune* (1898), have been derided as anecdotal and lacking in interpretative historical method. No respecter of social or gender norms, she transgressed the conventions of autobiography and historiography, offering a hotchpotch of quotes, texts, perspectives and discourses, reflecting her eclectic historical thinking. On returning to Paris from exile in New Caledonia (1880), she lectured and wrote apocalyptic poetry, novels and plays on revolution, which for her was violent theatre. A semi-educated primary teacher, Michel, lacking the literacy of the female *salonniere* or the training of the male academic, was neither novelist nor historian, but a revolutionary activist, whose vivid, eyewitness accounts of the Commune are regarded as invaluable for the historian seeking to understand this most gendered of revolutions.

The Russian Revolution (1917)

The 1917 revolution inspired women to write about it and its aftermath, as participants, observers and subsequently trained historians – or as émigré memoirists. None could be politically neutral towards the revolution, though most were gender neutral. Class eclipsed gender as the touchstone for the revolution. Further, the onset of Stalinism in the 1930s took a particular toll on Soviet historical writing. Women were not immune from that.

Foreign journalists and sympathisers were among the first to write about the Russian revolution. The American Louise Bryant provided eyewitness reports of events, politics and personalities with a view to winning international sympathy for the revolution: 'Socialism is here . . . just as woman [*sic*] suffrage is here.' Not everybody wrote with sympathy. The American anarchist Emma Goldman, initially supportive, expressed her disillusionment after the Bolshevik suppression of the Kronstadt uprising in 1921. Goldman wrote with a keen sense of the distinction between history and the 'personal reactions of the participants and observers which lend vitality to all history.' She drew parallels between the French and Russian revolutions and the writing of their histories. 'I myself . . . have felt and visualised the Great French Revolution much more vitally from the letters and diaries of contemporaries, such as Mme. Roland . . . than from the so-called objective historians.' In this light, she envisaged her contemporary account of the revolution's demise injecting a necessary 'human element' for future historians.

Of course, the revolution of 1917 and the subsequent civil war between 1918 and 1920 also generated a considerable volume of female émigré literature which recounted the revolution in the bleakest terms. For Princess Sofia Volkonskaya, who in 1919 forsook exile in England to return to Russia to save her imprisoned husband, the 'revolution is primarily about invasion [of their homes] – by neighbours, strangers, policemen and lice'. For women opponents of the revolution, home, family and, especially, husband were paramount and the only alternative to 'nonliving' was 'death through emigration' (Fitzpatrick and Slezkine 2000: 19–20).

In pre-revolutionary Russia only intelligentsia women could write. The establishment of the Soviet state opened up unprecedented opportunities for previously illiterate, ordinary women to record their experiences of the revolution. A number of Soviet practices encouraged them to do so. In the 1920s 'exemplary lives' of revolutionaries, following a tradition in pre-revolution Russia, were popular. In the 1930s Stakhanovite workers and peasants, rewarded for outstanding production, wrote their lives, sometimes aided by journalists, or more often recounted them at celebratory public meetings. After Stalin's death (1953), Khruschev's 'thaw' relaxed censorship somewhat and encouraged less embellished memoirs.

A striking feature of Soviet women's life stories, unlike much Western women's writing, was that they favoured 'testimony' over 'confession', public events over private life. Revolution, war, collectivisation and industrialisation were their markers – not romance, marriage or childbirth. The Soviet woman's proclivity for testimony was reinforced by the imposition of 'socialist realism' in the Stalinist 1930s, which proscribed personal themes as 'backward', 'women's writing'. Women writers were forced to comply with the socialist realist straight-jacket in depicting the revolution and the 'new Soviet women' (Marsh 2001).

Soviet women historians

The 1917 revolution opened the way for the first time for Russian women to become professional historians. But as the revolution faltered under Stalin, historians and historiography were amongst his first victims. Women, no less than men, had to toe the politically determined historical line. Several women did this, with varying degrees of success. Militsa Nechkina, an outstanding student from an intellectual background, went on to become in 1958 one of only two women historians admitted as full academicians. Motivated by the revolution to pursue history, she survived by keeping a distance from the party and researching less controversial topics, notably the nineteenth-century Russian revolutionary movement.

The career of Nechkina's sister academician, Anna Pankratova was more fraught. Born into an impoverished working-class family, she rose to the pinnacle of academic success, courtesy of the revolution. Embracing Marxism, joining the communist party in 1919, and admission to the Institute of Red Professors in 1922 were essential steps on this path. The history of the Russian industrial working class – not women – was the focus of her prodigious research. Subordinating herself to the requirement of 'party-mindedness' in historiography imposed in the 1930s probably saved her from Stalin's purges. But Pankratova was not simply a minion of Stalin. After Stalin's death (1953) she became an academician and editor of the leading journal *Problems of History*. In this capacity she played a key role in the destalinisation of Soviet historiography, even before party secretary Khrushchev famously denounced Stalin at the XXth Communist Party Congress (1956).

The gendered historiography of revolutions

It is no accident that revolutions, particularly the French and Russian, have emerged as the locus of contemporary developments in women's historical writing. Revolutions have been, after all, the great way stations of human progress, although often promising more than they have delivered, particularly for women, as Sheila Rowbotham argued in her important work, *Women, Resistance and Revolution* (1972), written at a time when women's liberation and socialism seemed to go hand in hand. But since Rowbotham's cautious attempt to marry Marxism and feminism, the latter has eclipsed the former in the historiography of revolutions, and recovering the 'invisible' history of women in revolutions has been displaced by gendered analyses of revolutions.

French and North American professional women historians have increasingly set the agenda in relation to the French Revolution. Initially the priority was to recover the neglected role of women in the revolution. A signal achievement in this regard was Dominique Godineau's *The Women of Paris and Their French Revolution* (1988, trans. 1998). Reflecting Godineau's dialogue with her Marxist mentor Albert Soboul, her empirically rich study links the material conditions to the everyday lives, mentalities and political activism of the ordinary women of Paris. Godineau concludes that although women were excluded from formal citizenship after 1793, the revolution cannot be dismissed as simply 'anti-feminist' because the silencing of the popular voice was not gender-specific.

In pursuing this argument, however, voices such as Godineau's have been increasingly isolated. In the wake of the call by the anti-Marxist Francois Furet for historians to 'return to the event' of the revolution, rather than research its societal and political drives, has come an historiographical turn that questions the nature of the revolution itself and interrogates its visual, symbolic and linguistic representations. The 'poetics of power' have been the focus of the work of Lynn Hunt, especially *Politics, Culture and Class in the French Revolution* (1986), Mona Ozouf, *Festivals and the French Revolution* (1976), and Genevieve Fraisse, *Reason's Muse: Sexual Difference and the Birth of Democracy* (1989). Such analyses of female subjectivity and identity, of the relationship between gender and power and of the discursive gendering of revolutions have not only challenged simply equating the revolution with the emancipation of women but in some cases denied it. Dorinda Outram sees the pre-eminence of the male 'sexed body' for the 'purging of the female from the body politic' (1989: 126), while both Joan Landes (1988, 2001) and Joan Scott (1996) argue that, pace Habermas, the revolution excluded women from the resultant bourgeois public sphere – denying them citizenship and hence liberation.

Just when French Revolution revisionist historiography was undermining the dominant Marxist paradigm in the 1980s, North American revisionist historiography of the Russian Revolution was laying siege to the predominant anti-Marxist paradigm: 'Totalitarianism'. Increasingly, a 'social interpretation', influenced by class analysis, displaced the previous focus on high politics, ideology and personality (Suny 1994: 165), particularly in relation to the Stalin period. A leading player in this assault was the historian Sheila Fitzpatrick, who, extending the revolution of 1917 to encompass Stalin's industrialising 'revolution from above' in the 1930s (Fitzpatrick 1994a: 4), exposed the conservative 'cultural revolution' that accompanied the rise of the upwardly mobile former plebeians, the *vydvizhentsy* who would form the Soviet technocratic ruling caste (Fitzpatrick 1992). Fitzpatrick's 'history from below' approach has resulted in major studies of peasant resistance and adaptation to the Stalinist state (Fitzpatrick 1994b) as well as 'Everyday Stalinism' in the cities (Fitzpatrick 1999).

The social interpretation of the course of the Russian Revolution, fuelled by feminist studies of the other great European revolutions, undoubtedly facilitated research into the roles and experiences of women in 1917 and after. Particularly since the opening up of former Soviet archives, there has been a sustained attempt to restore the authentic voices of women long muted by Soviet historiographical silence or idealising of Soviet female emancipation. Studies of women as workers, mothers, wives, writers, Bolsheviks (Wood 1997), flyers and soldiers have revealed the degree to which women were not only 'Midwives of the Revolution' (McDermid and Hillyer 1999), but crucial to its industrialisation (Goldman 2002), survival in the Second World War (Simmons and Perlina 2002) and its subsequent reconstruction. At the same time they have exposed the inherent tension between the promise of women's emancipation and the reality of their subordination, a tension that shaped Soviet female identity (Chatterjee 2002). An increasing engagement with the subjective cultural and discursive universe of Soviet women reflects both the historiographical interaction between the French and Russian revolutions and a destabilising of certainties about social categories such as class in the wake of the demise of the Soviet experiment (Fitzpatrick 2000). Potentially rich as the cultural approach to Soviet women's history undoubtedly is, much of it also reflects uncertainty about whether the Russian revolution, indeed any revolution, has contributed anything to the liberation of women. Analyses in which gender derives from discursively generated difference rather than the raw experience of women's oppression tend to discount the enduring potential unleashed by the French (Hesse 2001) and Russian revolutions for women both to realise their liberation and to write the history of their revolutions.

Roger D Markwick

References

Baym 1995; Chatterjee 2002; Fitzpatrick 1992, 1994a, 1994b, 1999, 2000; Fitzpatrick & Slezkine 2000; Fraisse 1989/1994; Godineau 1988/1998; Goldman 2002; Hauch 2000; Hesse 2001; Hunt 1986; Keeble 2001; Kelly 1993; Kennedy 2002; Landes 1998; Landes 2001; Marsh 2001; McDermid & Hillyar 1999; Mitchell 1998; Outram 1989; Ozouf 1976/1988; Rowbotham, 1972; Scott 1996; Shuckburgh 1989; Schulkind 1985; Simmons 2002; Smith 1998; Suny 1994; Walton 1994; Wilson 1976; Wood 1997; Yalom 1993.

Related essays

France; Great Britain; Memoirs; Romantic Women Writers; War; United States.

Romantic Friendship

Also known as the 'Boston marriage', the 'love of kindred spirits' and 'sentimental friendship', the Romantic Friendship was a loving, intimate attachment formed between same-sex partners. Though appearing from the Renaissance right through to the twentieth century, it is generally associated with Western society in the eighteenth and nineteenth centuries. The idea of the Romantic Friendship was historicised in feminist, lesbian and gay histories in the 1970s and 1980s. Elizabeth Mavor's 1973-study *The Ladies of Llangollen* followed the romance of two Irish women in 1788. In 1975, in an important article on female love and ritual, Carroll Smith-Rosenberg demonstrated that in eighteenth- and nineteenth-century America, relationships between women were not necessarily seen as a challenge to the social order and indeed were a space where intimate relationships were quite acceptable (Smith-Rosenberg 1975: 1).

Lillian Faderman expanded on the idea of the Romantic Friendship in *Surpassing the Love of Men* (1981). According to

Faderman, the Romantic Friendship was a close, loving even passionate relationship, but it was not necessarily erotic or genital. The women were dependent on each other for emotional, spiritual and sometimes economic or sexual support. It was, as Adrienne Rich had earlier suggested, a 'woman-identified experience', the 'sharing of a rich inner life' (Rich 1980). Faderman thus used the concept of the Romantic Friendship to illustrate the historically specific ways that women could experience love, desire, intimacy and sex. Similarly, Martha Vicinus explored a specific form of Romantic Friendship: the late nineteenth-century schoolgirl 'crush' or 'rave'. Like the non-genital romances described by Faderman, the rave was ideally to be in love without sexual contact. Desire was to be disciplined, and 'sacrifice' and 'self-denial' were seen to enhance and intensify the intimacy (Vicinus 1989: 217). Through such work, the historical definition of lesbian was widened to include women who lived a life centred upon women, as well as those who had sex with women.

Romantic Friendships quite explicitly drew on the language of heterosexual love and romance. Evidence of the Romantic Friendship has been drawn from a wide range of literary sources, including letters, diaries, poems and literature. Faderman's own interest was stimulated by her study of Emily Dickinson, who wrote loving, passionate letters to Sue Gilbert, who was later to become her sister-in-law. Other women who were involved in or wrote of Romantic Friendships include **Lady Mary Wortley Montagu, Germaine de Staël, Mary Wollstonecraft, George Eliot** and Louisa May Alcott. Amongst the most famous examples are the nineteenth-century diaries of Anne Lister, which celebrated both emotional and physical love amongst women (Whitbread 1988).

In the early twentieth century, the idea of the socially condoned Romantic Friendship rapidly faded, with the development of sexology and the 'morbidification' of lesbian relations (Faderman 1978). The medicalisation of sexuality ensured close relationships between women were sexualised and made to seem perverse and threatening to hetero-sociability.

The concept of the Romantic Friendship has enabled historians to uncover and explore the meanings of same-sex relationships in the past. It provided contemporary lesbians with a sense of historical continuity, while avoiding the anachronism of present-centred history. Crucially, it allowed an understanding that same-sex relationships had varied considerably over time and space. It also undercut the duality of lesbian/heterosexual, which was not necessarily polarised before the twentieth century.

It is, however, not unproblematic: in minimising the impact of sexual liaisons, aspects of women's erotic lives have been overlooked. Further, recent histories have questioned the extent to which same-sex romantic love was socially acceptable, suggesting that the work of feminist historians in the 1970s and 1980s over-emphasised the 'normality' of close female relationships (Vicinus 1989). Rather than focusing on absence and silence, recent work has begun to explore more visible same-sex eroticism and to consider the ways that lesbian sexuality has a discontinuous and often disrupted history (Binhammer 2003: 472, 492).

Lisa Featherstone

References

Binhammer 2003; Faderman 1978, 1981, 1991; Mavor 1973; Rich 1980; Smith-Rosenberg 1975; Vicinus 1989; Whitebread 1988.

Romantic women writers

'Romanticism' is an elusive concept, describing both an era (which may be loosely represented as the late eighteenth and early nineteenth centuries) as well as an abundantly diffuse set of ideas and aesthetics. While Romanticism eludes neat definition, it may be said that one of this period's central concerns is the creation of ideal worlds, both earthly and imaginary. The question of how to engender a perfect world, whether through a new political order, imaginative freedom or sexual liberation, is one of the great concerns of Romanticism. As part of the response to contemporary political upheavals, Romantic theories of history are richly varied and range from optimistic visions of progress to dystopian narratives of inevitable decline. In Romantic interpretations of history, the hope of a bright future is often shadowed by the potential for decay and decadence.

Frequently excluded from mainstream discourses as both subjects and writers, women bear a unique relationship to Romantic histories. The Romantic historiography that finds expression in women's writings engages not simply with the question of how the past is reconstructed, but more specifically with the gendering and content of historical narratives. The language of private, domestic life and the Romantic emphasis on interiority and individual perception gave women the means of writing alternative histories. One of the effects of the eighteenth-century culture of sensibility, with its fascination with feeling and sensation, was the knowledge that the history of private life was as significant as political history. In their poetry, novels, memoirs and histories, the women writers of the Romantic period reconfigured mainstream historical debate by historicising private life and placing it squarely in the public domain. Enlightenment political discourses were extended with an epistemological emphasis on individual affective ties.

Mary Wollstonecraft wrote her seminal *Vindication of the Rights of Woman* (1792) inspired by a consciousness of her historical moment, as a response to the French legislators' disregard of women's rights in framing the new revolutionary constitution. She hoped to place female education and political rights on the agenda so that women, too, might contribute to 'the progress of knowledge and virtue' (Wollstonecraft 1792/1989: 66). Criticising Jean-Jacques Rousseau for his idealisation of a primitive past, she writes firmly that '[he] exerts himself to prove that all *was* right originally: a crowd of authors that all *is* now right: and I, that all will *be* right' (Wollstonecraft 1792/1989: 84). Her determination to re-cast the political future has much in common with other radical writers of the era who, living in a flawed present, looked to the past for inspiration and to the future for the fulfilment of utopian ideals. The writers considered here share a concern with historical antecedents as well as posterity. They also profess great esteem for eminent female predecessors and, like Wollstonecraft, demonstrate a sense of the connection between personal history and the political. To demonstrate the diversity of Romantic women's writing, this essay will consider how female subjectivity, sensibility and the very political ends of the Romantic novel are used to reconfigure the ways in which history is made and recorded.

Enlightenment antecedents

Catharine Sawbridge Macaulay's historical writings are pre-Romantic, and merit consideration here as they foreshadow the political and philosophical concerns of Romanticism. A significant Enlightenment figure, Macaulay's status as a model of female learning and wisdom ensured her eminence in the late eighteenth century, especially among fellow writers. Wollstonecraft writes glowingly of Macaulay in her *Vindication,* calling her '[t]he woman of the greatest abilities, undoubtedly, that this country has produced' (Wollstonecraft 1792/1989: 174).

Macaulay's central work, the eight-volume *History of England from the Accession of James I to the Elevation of the House of Hanover* (1763–1783), is an important example of national political history, representative of the Enlightenment ideal of continuous progress and improvement. A Whig history of seventeenth-century England, this work affirms the virtues of classical antiquity as well as a localised sense of English political rights. In outlining the purposes of her work, Macaulay makes fleeting reference to her gender, dismissing potential critics who would insist that the writing of history is not the province of women: 'The invidious censures which may ensue from striking into a path of literature rarely trodden by my sex will not permit a selfish consideration to keep me mute in the cause of liberty and virtue' (Macaulay 1769: Vol. 1, x). Macaulay's history serves to contrast eighteenth-century theories of representation and historical practice with Romantic theories of history. This essay will trace the shift from the Enlightenment belief in 'virtuous' historical progress to the Romantic concern with the individual's relationship to history.

In the 'Introduction' to the 1769 edition of the first volume, Macaulay describes history as a moral and didactic science, and by applying the lessons of seventeenth-century English history she hopes to provoke a rational, patriotic response in her readers, rather than an affective or sympathetic one. Macaulay's avowed aim is to recall the actions of England's most illustrious patriots, with the hope of inculcating the virtues of republican antiquity in the young men of England. She is critical of England's public schools and universities, which transform young men into 'slaves to absolute monarchy' and encourage a love of 'every thing foreign' (Macaulay 1769: Vol. 1, xvii, xviii). Coupled with neoclassical notions of virtue and personal sacrifice, Macaulay professes faith in the traditions and institutions of pre-conquest, Saxon England. With its disregard for parliament, the Stuart dynasty imperilled the 'ancient and undoubted rights of every freeman' (Macaulay 1769: Vol. 1, 371) and she writes indignantly of 'the provocations the English had suffered under the government of the Stewart [*sic*] family' (Macaulay 1769: Vol. 3, 316). Macaulay asserts that, in spite of the Stuart tyranny, 'noble principles had taken deep root in the minds of the English people; that the progress of more enlightened reason would bring these to perfection' (Macaulay 1769: Vol. 1, 264). It is through a just restitution of the birthrights of Englishmen that Macaulay seeks to provide an exemplary pattern for future progress.

Metaphors of transparency and opacity inform Macaulay's theories of government and history. Her highest praise is saved for those contemporary historians and writers who 'have endeavoured to direct the judgment of the public to the detection of those masked hypocrites, who . . . have advanced their private interest and ambition' (Macaulay 1783: Vol. 8, 339). She admires 'the protestant succession of the illustrious house of Hanover' but despises the 'ministerial craft' and self-interest of public representatives, which have deprived the English of their constitutional rights (Macaulay 1783: Vol. 8, 337). In her view the subjective fluctuations of 'private interests' are detrimental to the political health of the nation, and politicians and historians who act out of private partialities are bound to 'the false mirror of misrepresentation' (Macaulay 1769: Vol. 1, viii, ix). Macaulay's historiographical practice confronts the Enlightenment distrust of personalised, partial testimony, and invests authority in official, national political records, those 'voluminous collections in which can only be found a faithful representation of the important transactions of past ages' (Macaulay 1769: Vol. 1, ix), by which she means the parliamentary histories, political memoirs and biographies which are her sources. 'It is the business of an historian to digest these, and to give a true and accurate sense of them to the public' (Macaulay 1769: Vol. 1, ix) Macaulay's *History* is a self-conscious memorial to English liberty and to the learning of the author, a reminder to contemporary and future readers to remember the great political lessons of the seventeenth century. It suggests the possibility of 'true and accurate' historical representation and points to the tension between the authority of 'absolute' knowledge and the prerogatives of individual experience, a tension that animates the discourses of history in Romantic women's writing.

Romantic beginnings

Germaine de Staël's *œuvre* marks one of the major theorisations of Romanticism and Romantic history. De Staël's writings situate history in relation to ideas, taste and imaginative literature. Like Macaulay, who looks to England's Saxon heritage for inspiration, de Staël's history is coloured by localised cultures and sharply defined national characteristics. In the Preface to the second edition of *On Literature* (1800), de Staël describes her purpose as the revelation of 'the successive progress of the mind from the beginning of its history'. This ideal of progress is problematic, however, for in her understanding of history the most highly developed societies necessarily contain the potential for decay. For instance, she locates a heightened, decadent sense of 'civilisation' in the culture that existed under the French monarchy, along with a corresponding corruption of taste. Courtly wit, manners and politeness had developed to such a degree, she writes, that life was divorced from nature: 'institutions and social customs had taken the place of natural affections' (de Staël 1800/1987: 189). The ideal of revolutionary improvement falters upon the contemplation of 'the hopes and ruins jumbled together by the French **Revolution**' (de Staël 1800/1987: 173). The Reign of Terror she considers an historical aberration, lying 'completely outside the circle of life's events . . . a monstrous phenomenon nothing ordinary can explain or produce' (de Staël 1800/1987: 186).

Ultimately, de Staël seeks the fulfillment of her revolutionary hopes in the realm of ideas, and contemplates 'how literature and philosophy may be perfectible', even as she questions the purity of civic institutions (de Staël 1800/1987: 186). With *On Germany* (1813) de Staël intended to introduce German literature and philosophy to French readers. She designates 'the poetry of the ancient Greeks and Romans "classical", and the poetry which is somehow related to the traditions of chivalry "Romantic" '. This distinction also separates history into two ages, 'the age before the establishment of Christianity and the era following it' (de Staël 1813/1987: 299). The classical aesthetic is one of simplicity and engagement with 'external objects'; the Romantic, embodied especially in contemporary German and English literature, is characterised by an 'internalized existence' and a devotion to individual feelings and sensations (de Staël 1813/1987: 300–1). If de Staël's history is a dialectical progression, then Romanticism is the condition of modernity itself and the logical culmination of all that has gone before. 'Romantic literature', she asserts, 'is the only literature still capable of being brought to perfection' (de Staël 1813/1987: 302).

De Staël's novel *Corinne; or, Italy* (1807) elaborates her theories of history by representing the eponymous heroine's artistic life as a specifically feminised response to and retreat from the upheavals of history. Corinne is celebrated throughout her native Italy as a brilliant poet and improvisatrice. Her Romantic version of history takes the form of divinely inspired meditations on her homeland and its glorious past. In one extempore performance in the campagna near Naples, Corinne elegises Roman civilisation:

> O memory, noble power, your empire is here in these places! From age to age, strange destiny! Man complains of what he has lost. It is as if times gone by all contain some happiness that is no more; and while the mind grows proud of its progress and looks forward, the soul seems homesick for some former homeland whose past draws near to her once more. (De Staël 1807: 265)

Corinne embodies Italy's cultural inheritance as well as de Staël's hopes for an autonomous, artistic model of femininity. With an emphasis on love for her mother country and mother tongue, Corinne's artistic/historical inheritance is most decidedly a maternal one. *Corinne* contains fruitful tensions between nostalgia for the classical past and hopes for a future modelled on a feminised, Romantic subjectivity.

This same conflict between nostalgia and a modern, feminised artistic consciousness also informs the work of one of Britain's most important Romantic writers, Helen Maria Williams. One of the foremost political commentators of the 1790s, Williams published her annals of the French Revolution from 1790 until the 1820s, which were widely read as books and excerpts in British periodicals. In the eight volumes of her *Letters from France* (1790–1796), Williams portrays the French Revolution as a phenomenon at once affective and political in which personal experience and individual attachment become the very materials of history.

Williams' writing embodies the Romantic fascination with the creative, individual consciousness, exemplified in her exploration of the historical ramifications of affect. At one of the defining historical moments of the Romantic era, she engages with the ways in which partial, personalised testimony shapes the recording of history. Her utopias are founded on familial connections, friendship and sexual love, forming a nexus of affect and political radicalism that typifies Romantic women's historiography. Overriding any distrust of female subjectivity and partial testimony, Williams places herself, the feeling subject, at the centre of the political stage. Her politics are informed by individual feeling and attachment, and sensibility is a means for interpreting history. Williams first travelled to France in July 1790 as the guest of her friends, Monsieur and Madame du Fossé. In the first volume of *Letters from France* she relates their story of marriage across class boundaries as an exemplary triumph of bourgeois affection over patriarchal tyranny. Moreover, her friendship with the du Fosséis is the very source of her admiration for the French Revolution: 'What, indeed, but friendship, could have led my attention from the annals of imagination to the records of politics; from the poetry to the prose of human life?' (Williams 1790/1975: 195). Williams draws attention to her privileged status as an eyewitness and participant in the events she describes, attending sittings of the National Assembly in Paris, visiting her friend Madame Roland in prison, and observing the first festival celebrating the fall of the Bastille.

Williams' first-hand reportage takes the form of letters to an unnamed correspondent. The symbolic language of letters, at once both private and public, bridges the worlds of polite, virtuous society and the politically aspiring middle classes. A potentially transgressive genre, the letter is a particularly apposite form for conveying women's roles in making history, and Williams shows many instances of women as agents of history. 'The women have certainly had a considerable share in the French revolution', she writes, 'for, whatever the imperious lords of creation may fancy, the most important events which take place in this world depend a little on our influence; and we often act in human affairs like those secret springs in mechanism, by which, though invisible, great movements are regulated' (Williams 1790/1975: 37–8). There is a gradual accretion of references to notable women, living and dead, real and symbolic, which inscribes a female tradition and line of inheritance and underscores the iconographic significance of the female form in political culture. She writes admiringly of Madame Roland and Charlotte Corday, both of whom were associated with the Girondin faction, like Williams herself. Meditating on a painting of Jeanne d'Arc, she speculates 'that nature, while she bestowed on the Maid of Orléans the heroic qualities of the other sex, did not deny her the soft attractions of her own' (Williams 1792/1975: 66). Sarah Siddons, the leading tragic actress of the British stage, is referred to repeatedly as an ideal of womanly sensibility and sublime talents: 'There is but one Siddons, one transcendent genius, who has every passion of the human heart at her command' (Williams 1792/1975: 77–8).

At the triumphant close of the first volume of *Letters from France*, Williams relates how she participated in a domestic version of the revolutionary fête with friends. They perform a 'charming little piece . . . called "La Federation, ou La Famille Patriotique" '. She takes the role of a statue, 'the representation of Liberty', and the tricolour 'scarf of national ribband' is draped across her shoulder to symbolise the triumph of the new revolutionary state (Williams 1790/1975: 203–4). Layers of historical precedent lie underneath this iconography, and Williams is highly aware of the Catholic and classical traditions that inform the revolutionary goddesses of Liberty and Justice. The revolutionary interpretation of these traditions is history made flesh, and in a significant act of re-interpretation Williams dispenses with the static passivity of the female statue in favour of the politically engaged, affective female author.

Williams shares Macaulay's belief in the inevitability of historical progress. She celebrates the sheer novelty of events in France when visiting Rouen cathedral, for instance. After several cursory remarks on its age and magnificence she comments enthusiastically that 'in France, it is not what is antient, but what is *modern*, that most powerfully engages the attention' (Williams 1790/1975: 104). In spite of such claims to modernity, however, Williams' history in the *Letters* is overlaid with echoes of the classical and Christian past. 'The history of the French Revolution', she writes, 'abounds with circumstances that would embellish the pages of the Greek or Roman annals.' The awareness of making modern history remains inseparable from antiquity: 'Succeeding generations will perhaps associate the Tennis-court of Versailles, and the Champ de Mars, with the Forum and the Capitol' (Williams 1792/1975: 22–3). 'History' is imagined in terms of past and future, and as the autobiographical subject of the *Letters* Williams emphasises the role of the author in framing history for the benefit of posterity:

> [The Revolution] is that glorious event which will probably in its consequences change the face of this earth, and will be marked in the page of history as that luminous point of human annals, from which a better order of things is seen to arise: and this event has surely been the work of literature, of philosophy, of the enlarging views of mankind. (Williams 1792/1975: 70)

Following the death of many of her friends during the Terror, Williams' support for the French Revolution was never again so unambiguously enthusiastic. However, she retained her belief in the principles of equality and progress, writing confidently in 1801 of her hope that the revolution 'will yet ultimately terminate in the establishment of a perfect government' (Williams 1801/1975, 'Preface'). Following the vicissitudes of the French revolution there is a perceptible shift in radical Romantic writings from the real to the utopian, in which the ideal of continuous amelioration gives way to a less certain conception of progress.

Williams' work renders history in terms of sensibility and draws on the affective authority of the sentimental novel. Frequently characterised as ephemeral and inconsequential, the novel occupied an unstable position in the eighteenth-century hierarchy of literary genres. However, of all Romantic genres, the novel is the most potent vehicle for an historical exploration of class, gender and manners, the codes that are the central concerns of these predominantly female-authored texts. The Romantic novel closely examines the intersection of private life and public, social existence. In the eighteenth-century novel, a character's virtue is rewarded with success and material improvement; like history, personal stories progress according to the laws of perfectibility.

Historical fictions

Dating from the early Romantic period Clara Reeve's literary history *The Progress of Romance Through Times, Countries and Manners* (1785) participates in the debate about the status of the novel. In her Preface, Reeve gives a broad definition of 'romance' to include 'the fictions of the Ægyptians and Arabians, of the Greeks and Romans . . . as well as those of the middle ages' (Reeve 1785/1970: xii). Her literary and cultural history traces 'the progress of this species of composition' from the ancient past to the eighteenth century and, by establishing the historical precedents of the form, imbues the modern novel with credibility and the capacity to instruct. As she delineates the progress of the romance (and its modern offspring) and articulates the achievements of women writers in the contemporary novel, Reeve links this exceptional literary evolution with historical progress and the gradual improvement of the human mind: 'As a country became civilized, their narrations were methodized, and moderated to probability. From the prose recitals sprung History, from the war-songs Romance and Epic poetry' (Reeve 1785/1970: 14). The *Progress* takes the form of a series of conversations between two learned ladies, Euphrasia and Sophronia, and a gentleman, Hortensius, and their convivial discussions hinge on the relationship between history and fiction, the relative truths contained in different genres, and the distinctions between 'probability' and fantasy.

Euphrasia, the learned lady who acts as Reeve's mouthpiece, places romance high in the literary hierarchy and correlates it to history. Euphrasia sees history and fiction as emerging from the same source – oral culture – and fulfilling similar functions. She imagines romances spurring the young men of Elizabeth's court to act for the glory of their country: 'The effects of Romance, and true History are not very different. When the imagination is raised, men do not stand to enquire whether the motive be true or false' (Reeve 1785/1970: 102). However, the marriage of fact and fiction is problematic. Euphrasia cautions against some French romances of the sixteenth and seventeenth centuries, which contain a mixture of 'some obscure parts of true history' and 'fictitious stories', so that 'young people especially imbibed such absurd ideas of historical facts and persons, as were very difficult to be rectified' (Reeve 1785/1970: 64–5).

Reading in the eighteenth century was a matter of social responsibility, morals and education. Especially where girls and young women were concerned, reading was considered both a pleasurable and a potentially dangerous activity requiring considerable surveillance. To imbue the novel with respectability, Reeve's literary history emphasises the form's didactic and moral possibilities. In the Preface she cautions that '[romances] are not to be put into the hands of young persons without distinction and reserve, but under proper restrictions and regulations they will afford much useful instruction, as well as rational and elegant amusement' (Reeve 1785/1970: xvi). The superiority she attributes to the modern novel over chivalric romance lies in her distinction between fables and reality, the latter being preferable as an instructive medium: 'The Romance is an heroic fable, which treats of fabulous persons and things', claims Euphrasia. 'The Novel is a picture of real life and manners, and of the times in which it is written' (Reeve 1785/1970: 111). The novel is an improvement upon its ancestor and indeed exceeds it because of a closer relationship to reality and truth, an aesthetic comparable to that 'faithful representation' advocated by Macaulay in her *History of England*. The concerns of modern fiction, such as domestic and sexual life, the individual's passage into society, and the formation of class, if faithfully represented, become the concerns of true history.

The Gothic novel embodies a particular response to history, combining an antiquarian fascination with the past with a decidedly contemporary critique of outmoded social institutions. This last feature is especially prominent in the female Gothic, in which women could explore gender relations and patrilineal inheritance through the lens of the barbaric, Gothic past. Clara Reeve's most famous work of fiction, *The Old English Baron: A Gothic Story* (1778), examines the Gothic novel's conventions of historical representation by consciously rewriting Horace Walpole's *The Castle of Otranto* (1764). Set in the time of Henry VI, Reeve's novel tempers the supernatural horrors of Walpole's text and replaces his aesthetic of excess with mild Gothic machinery that can be rationally explained. Despite an historical setting it contains little direct reference to historical events, focusing instead on the sentimental tale of Edmund, a gallant young peasant who is discovered to be of noble birth and the rightful owner of the old baron's estate. It is a characteristically Romantic narrative of class conflict and the just restitution of property and the triumph of true virtue over false aristocratic privilege. The novel's historicity lies in the significance it imparts to the details that create domestic life, in the form of the intimate tokens and relics of family history such as family jewels, portraits and costumes. These tokens are the means through which Edmund pieces together his true identity and social role, and they constitute a secret, subversive history that contests the prevailing formulation of political power.

The Gothic enabled female authors to challenge the way power was defined and conferred, chiefly by associating patrilineal inheritance with the dark, unenlightened past. The female Gothic, like the domestic novel, is concerned with familial relationships, inheritance, tradition and property, and the Gothic offered a unique historical consciousness for revising notions of how history is conceived. Sophia Lee's novel *The Recess; or, A Tale of Other Times* (1783–1785) combines elements of historical romance and the Gothic with the sentimental novel. Historical figures mix with invented characters, and historical events are embellished with fictional diversions. Set during the reign of Elizabeth I, *The Recess* concerns twin daughters, Matilda and Ellinor, the offspring of a clandestine marriage between Mary, Queen of Scots, and the Duke of Norfolk. Due to the conflict between their mother and the queen, the girls are raised in a secret recess hidden among some ruins on Lord Scrope's estate. The recess is presided over by the twin's guardian Mrs Marlow, who is herself part of a submerged, banished history (she is the illegitimate daughter of Lord Scrope). Once a hiding place for Catholic clergy in the time of Henry VIII, the recess has symbolic resonance as a subversive, maternal space and the twin protagonists represent an alternative, feminised history. On her deathbed Mrs Marlow bequeaths to the twins a 'casket' containing papers proving the girls' parentage (Lee 1783–1785/2000: 6). The casket is a symbolic repository, representing a secret history and a female line of inheritance that is constituted by talismanic personal objects that contain the potential to contest the dominant political order (see **Great Britain**).

The discursive possibilities of the novel expanded in response to the various reactions to the French Revolution, which cemented the political significance of the gendered concepts of sensibility and sexuality. In 1792 the poet and novelist Charlotte Smith published *Desmond, A Novel,* in which the intimate epistolary form combines lengthy discussions of Enlightenment philosophy and enthusiastic news of contemporary French politics with a romance plot concerning the hero's illicit love for a married woman. As Smith described it to her publisher Thomas Caddell in September 1791, the novel 'is meant to convey in the form of Letters & render the illusion of a Love story, the present state of France'. The knowledge that the novel could portray history in the making also informed her next work, *The Old Manor House* (1793). Set during the American war of independence, the novel concerns the lovers Orlando and Monimia and the familial prejudice against their marriage. In *The Old Manor House* Smith allegorises the French Revolution (and English reactions to it) through an experience of recent American history, so that contemporary political anxieties are displaced onto the new world. This imaginative exchange flows both ways, for the past is, quite literally, another country, which is re-imagined in terms of present debates about political legitimacy and inheritance. The marriage of the virtuous lovers represents the re-ordering of society according to the bourgeois values of virtue and talent, and the utopian possibilities of the new world are mapped back onto the old. The rejuvenated estate is transformed into an ideal domestic space and the model of a regenerated England.

The transformation of public life brought about by the domestic sphere in Smith's novels evinces the political and historical resonance of the domestic novel. **Jane Austen**'s novels enact a similar transformation, whereby the virtue and energy of the middle classes (or the gentry) are joined with the cultural potency and property ownership of the aristocracy. The marriage of Anne Eliot and Captain Wentworth in *Persuasion* (1818), for instance, represents the felicitous union of the landed (though impoverished) upper classes with the enterprising bourgeoisie. Like *The Old Manor House*, Austen's *Mansfield Park* (1814) takes as its central metaphor the improvement of the English (domestic and political) landscape, a metaphoric system in which nature, politics and sexual conduct are inseparable. Framed as a domestic romance, *Mansfield Park* discusses notions of 'the modern', moral improvement and the inevitable historical progress of the middle classes.

Romantic reaction

Cycles of decay and renewal come to characterise late Romantic historiographies, exemplified in the Comte de Volney's *The Ruins; or, A Survey of the Revolutions of Empires* (1791), a visionary work in which a spirit observes the rise and inevitable fall of the world's great imperial nations. Undoubtedly influenced by Volney's work and by the pervasive Romantic fascination with sublime ruins, Anna Letitia Barbauld's poem *Eighteen Hundred and Eleven* (1812) discusses the decline of empires and the state of the British nation. The poem is a radical satire on the current state of Britain that after years of war with France it suffers widespread poverty, disease and famine. In the face of such desolation, Britain cannot remain '[a]n island Queen'; her moment of imperial glory must pass:

> Yes, thou must droop; thy Midas dream is o'er;
> The golden tide of Commerce leaves thy shore . . .

Barbauld imagines the future following the demise of Britain, when the once brilliant capital will be viewed through the eyes of visitors from the new world. The imaginary perspective is that of the 'ingenuous youth . . . / From the Blue Mountains, or Ontario's lake' who, '[w]ith fond adoring steps', will come to admire the remnants of the parent culture. The American tourist is imagined viewing the collections of the British Museum, itself a monument to fallen empires:

> And when, midst fallen London, they survey
> The stone where Alexander's ashes lay,
> Shall own with humbled pride the lesson just
> By Time's slow finger written in the dust.

As a *memento mori* to the British nation, *Eighteen Hundred and Eleven* was not well received by conservative critics, not least because it asserted the ephemerality of British commerce and empire. With the death of Europe, Barbauld's cyclical version of history sees power pass to the new world of the Americas. The poem closes with references to the nascent revolutionary movements of South America, to which Barbauld attributes the true fulfilment of the revolutionary principles of equality and justice: 'Thy world, Columbus, shall be free.'

The Romantic reaction to the disappointments of the French Revolution finds particular expression in apocalyptic literature. Mary Shelley's novel *The Last Man* (1826) is one such work that dramatises Romantic apprehensions about the entrapment of individual consciousness within the processes of history. In the 'Introduction' to the novel Shelley's narrator describes a visit to an ancient grotto near Naples associated with the Cumaen Sybil, the prophetic priestess of Apollo. *The Last Man* is framed as a divine prophecy, pieced together by the author from the fragmented leaves found in 'the Sybil's cave' (Shelley 1826: 5). 'I present the public with my latest discoveries in the slight Sybilline pages. Scattered and unconnected as they were, I have been obliged to add links, and model the work into a consistent form' (Shelley 1826: 8). The novel is set in twenty-first-century Europe, when Britain has become a republic (and with Sybilline prescience, Shelley changes the name of the British royal family to Windsor). The population decimated by plague, the novel centres on a small community of idealistic survivors who, one by one, succumb to the disease; only the narrator, Lionel Verney, survives, sailing the Mediterranean endlessly and vainly searching for signs of human existence.

A partially autobiographical text expressing Shelley's own sense of isolation, this novel approaches questions about the nature of progress with the same combination of subjectivity and historical awareness that I have outlined above in the domestic and historical novels of the late eighteenth century. *The Last Man*, however, offers neither a redemptive belief in the inevitable progress of bourgeois society, nor a vision of the new world. Shelley's prophesied future is a dystopian, solipsistic nightmare rather than a republican utopia. A qualified redemption is offered only in the guise of the protagonists' isolation from humanity and, consequently, their absolute transcendence of the processes of history. *The Last Man* inverts the earlier Romantic ideal of progress and instead presents historical consciousness as a divinely inspired, introspective utterance, of which the ultimate antecedent is the Sybil herself.

The writers considered here interpret history as a record of subjective, private life and as more than a catalogue of political and economic patterns. Women's approaches to history in the Romantic era are characterised by a defiance of conventional eighteenth-century attitudes towards gender and genre, which sought to protect political and historical writing as a male prerogative. The variety of historiographical practices represented here bears witness to the fact that women (and, by extension, the private realm with which they are symbolically associated) do not exist outside of history. This is not to say that history somehow becomes domesticated; rather, history and private life are inseparable.

Donna Robson

References

Armstrong 1987; Barbauld 1812/1994; Chandler 1998; De Staël 1987; Lee 1783–1785/2000; Macaulay 1769, 1783; Phillips 2000; Reeves 1785/1970; Temple 2003; Williams 1975; Wollstonecraft 1792/1989; Zimmerman 1996.

Related essays

Great Britain; France; Historical Fiction; Memoir; Nation; Revolution.

Royal lives

The lives of rulers have always found an appreciative audience, whether out of moral rectitude, political practice or sheer prurience. This essay, however, examines the very modern incarnations of such life-writing: the 'royal lives' of the nineteenth century and their afterlife in more recent decades. More specifically still, it considers royal lives, especially the lives of queens and princesses, as a feminised genre – meaning not that royal lives were never written by men but that they were predominantly written *by* women and, just as importantly, that in the critical imagination they were predominantly associated *with* women. But this gendering process was hardly stable. Anthony Trollope's Lady Carbury, cobbling her 'Criminal Queens' together out of an unlikely hodgepodge of Shakespeare and

Gibbon, represents one end of the critical stick with which these female biographers could be thrashed, but Trollope's satire in *The Way We Live Now* would not necessarily have rung true earlier in the century, when royal lives were a relative novelty.

Royal life as genre

The royal life as a popular genre emerged from and helped shape the transformations of the nineteenth-century monarch's image. In the medieval period, lives of queens were often written specifically for and at the request of aristocratic women. In histories like the *Encomium Emmae Reginae* (eleventh century) or William of Malmesbury's *Gesta Regum Anglorum* (c.1120s), the elite subject was matched to the elite audience as a means of supplying practical political advice, warnings or support (Ferrante 1997). But by the late eighteenth century, George III and Queen Charlotte had effectively 'domesticated' the monarchy: the court was both praised and critiqued on the grounds of its private morality, frugality and general exemplarity (Colley 1992: 195–236). This process came to its triumphal fulfilment after Victoria's ascension to the throne. Biographers and illustrators relentlessly figured Victoria as a queen *mother* – despite her actual antipathy to infants – whose wholly feminine domesticity was both wholesome anecdote to the thoroughly unwholesome reigns of George IV and William IV and a model of national virtue. Moreover, Victoria's image was not just contained within the allegories of state power so beloved by the Tudors and Stuarts: it multiplied on knick-knacks, visiting cards, commemorative cups and plates and, indeed, even advertisements. Biographers loved to dwell pointedly on the differences between Elizabeth I and Victoria, pronouncing that, in the end, 'Elizabeth enjoyed no real and solid happiness, Mary died heartbroken, but Victoria dwells in an atmosphere of purity, of love, and joy' (*Illustrious Women* 1852: 10).

That last quotation also signals the shifting *meanings* of the royal life. In its classical form, the royal life offered models of exemplary morality and spirituality to potential leaders, identifying worthy or dangerous patterns of behaviour. The nineteenth-century royal life was something very different. It grounded the royal life's ultimate meaning in its moral import, but that morality was now something available to anyone; indeed, perhaps the strongest testament to the virtue of any queen was that her life was no different from anyone else's (Burstein 1999). By downplaying the queen's actual political function, writers could sidestep history in favour of charting the growth of the queen's mind. It was possible for the queen as biographical subject to exist almost entirely apart from her historical context; Emma Willsher Atkinson in her *Queens of Prussia* indicated that these women had no 'share in government' nor did they interfere in 'political affairs'. She advised her readers that 'I have thought it more consonant with my subject to give only such outlines of contemporary historical events, as were necessary for the clearer connection of my narrative, or the better development of cause and effect' (1858: v–vi). The author thus universalises the queen, stripping her of her temporal, social and national particularities, the better to make her accessible to a reader of any 'condition'. This semi-democratisation of the royal life received a considerable push from the growth of cheap publishing and the spread of literacy among both women and the lower classes. Thus, the work of **Agnes Strickland**, the most popular of all royal biographers, was available in both deluxe multi-volume editions and economical one-volume abridgments, with some of the lives spun off on their own.

Royal lives appeared singly or in collections, but it was the latter which were associated most closely with women writers. The nineteenth-century biography collection was the generic descendant of two related forms: the Plutarchan biography and the biographical dictionary. Modern Plutarchan biographies used the individual life in order to miniaturise large national movements, making the biographical subject an exemplar in terms of both morality and representation. In such biographical collections, history 'progressed' through the interplay of moral types across time; it was part of the reader's duty to learn how to detect and interpret the signs of moral progress, and apply those lessons to their own lives (cafarell: 1990). While biographical dictionaries abandoned any pretence of constructing a linear narrative in favour of an alphabetical taxonomy, they nevertheless dovetailed with the Plutarchan biography collection in their insistence on judging subjects, especially female subjects, on their intrinsic virtues instead of their accomplishments.

Collective biographies solely devoted to royal lives *and* written by women were not, in reality, all that numerous; their tenacious foothold in the minds of later readers derives from their relative prestige. The royal life was the biographical form closest to history and their attraction for the most ambitious women historians of the period. It was far more common for queens and princesses to find themselves mixed in with other 'illustrious' women as part of the '**women worthies**' genre. Royal lives written within this tradition domesticated the queen's public duties to the fullest possible extent. Thus, whenever Queen Mary II took up the reins of government, '[l]ike the fabled intelligence of some planetary system, she seemed to direct all these movements with order and harmony, and to diffuse an atmosphere of purity and brightness around her' – a description of sufficient vagueness to make running a country sound like running a household, with the rhetoric of women's influence thrown in for good measure (*Select* 1829: 127). In such anthologies, the toll public life took on queens could make them anti-exemplars. One American writer set down Elizabeth I as 'repulsive, mean, and disgusting' – just the first in a long list of equally uncomplimentary adjectives (*Sketches* 1834: 52). Marie Antoinette, in some ways more problematic than Elizabeth, often confused authors who tried to appropriate her for uncontroversial ends. The Catholic biographer **Julia Kavanagh**, more sophisticated than most, mused that 'it seems strange harshness to dwell on indiscretions of temper and conduct, destined to be expiated by years of weeping anguish and death on a scaffold', even though she also thought that the queen bore much of the responsibility for the collapse of the monarchy (1850: Vol. 2, 258–9, 303). Like Mary, Queen of Scots, Marie Antoinette attracted simultaneous vilification for her pettiness and sympathetic pity for her sufferings. Those who desired to reclaim her as some sort of heroine often did so by drawing on the post-Hanoverian rhetoric of the domestic court. It is important to bear in mind, however, that the rhetoric of exemplarity could cover up a multitude of sins. Hence bizarre compilations like Mme. Laure Junot's *Memoirs of Celebrated Women of All Countries* (1834), a hyper-sensationalist collection that somehow included the great Protestant martyr Lady Jane Grey in with transgressive figures like Maria Letizia Bonaparte, Catherine the Great and the transvestite soldier Dona Catalina de Erauso.

Romantic royal lives

While the nineteenth-century royal life would eventually be associated most closely with the collective form, it nevertheless achieved its first generic foothold in the form of **Lucy Aikin**'s informal trilogy, the *Memoirs of the Court of Queen Elizabeth* (1818), of James I (1822) and of Charles I (1833). Unlike her earlier *Epistles on Woman* (1810) which rewrote and versified Enlightenment conjectural history into a feminist critique of woman's subjugation, the *Memoirs of the Court of Queen Elizabeth* offers a detailed account of the relationship between cultural history and personal identity. '[D]ismal scenes of religious persecution and political cruelty' cast an 'indelible' influence on Elizabeth's mind, we are told early on, and one of the narrative's frequently iterated points is that Elizabeth's public and private behaviour is not anomalous when interpreted in historical context (1818: Vol. 1, 15). Aikin's practice exemplifies what would become standard procedure for later writers: she freely interpolates extensive quotations from letters and other primary documents, drawing liberally on chroniclers and historians like Strype and Camden, and augments her biographical narrative with excurses into contemporary fashion, 'manners' and theology. But Aikin quite explicitly distinguishes her project from 'the peculiar province of history' (1818: Vol. 1, vii); she seeks first and foremost to elucidate the personal development and interrelationships of her characters, rather than their political lives. She thus raises the problem of public roles versus private 'character' that dogs royal life-writing to this very day. Early on, in a series of capsule biographies, Aikin imagines her overarching plot in terms of the inevitable doom of many of her key and minor players, enthralled to political machinations whose complications, tragically enough, can be unravelled only belatedly by the biographer. The narrative itself drives towards Protestant Enlightenment, away from the 'reign of terror' (1818: Vol. 1, 183) characterising Mary Tudor's Catholic reign; significantly, under Elizabeth's watch the more charitable Protestant public is outraged by the torture and harassment of Catholics (1818: Vol. 2, 132–3), even as they continue to be rendered uneasy by 'the inveterate hostility of the persecuted papists against the queen' (1818: Vol. 2, 143). Moreover, despite repeated critiques of Elizabeth's own hauteur and other moral foibles, Aikin's final verdict on Elizabeth is nevertheless positive, balancing the splendours of her reign between the political and moral disasters of both her predecessor and her successor. As Greg Kucich points out, Aikin finds Elizabeth at her best when she is at her most reasonable (Kucich 1993: 136) and so it is no surprise that James I's 'contempt' for Elizabeth is a damning sign of his own 'vanity and weakness, and even a want of decorum' – although Aikin grudgingly admits that Elizabeth's treatment of his mother might qualify as something of an excuse (1822: Vol. 1, 135–6).

Aikin's immediate cohort included the Methodist biographer and minor novelist **Elizabeth Benger**. Aikin had applauded Elizabeth's role in steering a proper and rational Protestant course in the wake of Mary's violent religion; Benger's *Memoirs of the Life of Anne Boleyn, Queen of Henry VIII* (1821) goes a step farther by rescuing Elizabeth's mother as herself a key agent in the English Reformation. As a historian, Benger shares Aikin's fascination with what she terms the problem of 'the immeasurable distance' between past and present, the cultural and moral gulf that makes it difficult to identify with or even comprehend what once seemed like rational actions; and like Aikin, she tries to delineate the outlines of 'the age', which inescapably shapes the minds of her actors (1821: 9). In a sense, the narrative constitutes a prequel to Aikin's work. Benger's Anne is youthful and misguided, not evil and designing; even her 'love of power' is 'tempered, if not corrected, by benevolence' (1821: 222). Anne comes to prominence in an age of equal 'despotism' (on the part of the monarch) and 'submission' (on the part of the populace) (1821: 11); her aspirations and struggles thus reflect this dangerous imbalance of power, suggestive of an expressly pre-Reformation state of affairs. In other words, we are to understand Anne as helping, in ever so small a way, to establish modern British freedoms. If Anne quickly becomes disillusioned about her potential role in aiding the English Reformers, she nevertheless saves Hugh Latimer out of pure motives and alters court manners to reflect his views (1821: 316, 322–5). But Anne's real value can be perceived only posthumously; somewhat over-confidently, Benger concludes that the enthusiasm for Elizabeth partly derives from 'tenderness' to Anne's memory (1821: 374). Ultimately, Anne's fate symbolises the dangers posed by absolutist monarchs to individual liberties.

Published in the same year, **Mary Hays'** *Memoirs of Queens Illustrious and Celebrated* (1821) foreshadows the direction that much Victorian royal life-writing would take. Aikin and Benger mixed commercial interest with genuine scholarly ambition; Hays had by this point abandoned scholarship in favour of much-needed cash. The book has received nothing like the attention accorded to her earlier *Female Biography* (1804) – which spent far more time on the scandalous Catherine the Great than on the pious Elizabeth Rowe, to the irritation of contemporary reviewers. Perhaps the most intriguing thing about the *Memoirs* is its frontispiece engraving, which features Queen Caroline's bust surrounded by those of Marie Antoinette, Mary, Queen of Scots, Elizabeth I and Anne Boleyn – a somewhat puzzling grouping that might be intended to suggest that Caroline shares Elizabeth I's greatness but also the tragic fates of the rest. In any event, *Female Biography* celebrates the intellectual and political power of the 'masculine' woman, but the virago (in the older and positive sense) quietly drops out of the *Memoirs*. Additionally, *Female Biography* insists more overtly on the social construction of feminine behaviour. Thus, the earlier work – which devotes 130 pages to Elizabeth I – rebukes readers for 'requir[ing] more softness of manners, greater lenity of temper, and more feminine graces' in Elizabeth's character, reminding them that 'these amiable weaknesses, which arise out of a state of subjection and dependence, are utterly incompatible with the situation of an absolute sovereign, and with the exercise of those qualities by which only such a situation can be maintained' (1804: Vol. 2, 348). Hays' early Elizabeth is manly, largely self-controlled, and unapologetically powerful; nor, given her historical circumstances, is it appropriate for readers to expect otherwise of her. By contrast, the Elizabeth of the *Memoirs* – who gets 16 pages – is still equipped with 'energy and prudence', but in the shorter version the reader cannot but notice the increased prominence of her feminine passion for Essex and her jealousy of Mary, Queen of Scots (1821: 299). Perhaps it is not surprising that, as Greg Kucich points out, Hays' Queen Caroline suffers from a purely domestic predicament rather than a very political one (Kucich 2000: 24).

Victorian royal lives

Hays' *Memoirs* eventually dropped out of the literary-historical consciousness, as did, more oddly, Hannah Lawrance's *Historical Memoirs of the Queens of England*

(1838–1840). Lawrance herself is, as Rosemary Mitchell puts it, 'perhaps the most elusive of mid-nineteenth-century women historians', with little surviving correspondence or other MSS (1998: 115). A contemporary of Lucy Aikin and Elizabeth Benger, she began her professional career in the early 1820s, writing historical tales for the popular annuals. Her long association with the *British Quarterly Review*, which persisted almost until her death, suggests a Dissenting background. While her *History of Women* (1843) was never completed, the *Historical Memoirs* proved a more substantive achievement. Lawrance sees the lives of queens as a route to writing British cultural history. At regular intervals, Lawrance shifts from biography to literary and social history, examining such topics as the development of later medieval poetry or the social significance of the convents; the latter in particular would be developed at greater length in the *History of Women*. Lawrance anticipated **Lina Eckenstein** in identifying the medieval convent as a site for female intellectual and artistic development, thereby joining Thomas Carlyle and John Ruskin in glorifying medieval monasticism for its social rather than spiritual significance. While Lawrance is a moralist, she nevertheless strives for charity: we are to remember that Elinor of Aquitaine's character was formed by 'difficulties and irritating circumstances', that Isabel of France has been condemned on the basis of only one historical source, that Margaret of Anjou's ambitions for her son were purely maternal and so forth (1838–1840: Vol. 1, 267; Vol. 2, 100–2; Vol. 2, 392). Most of Lawrance's queens occupy a culturally separate sphere, often having little to do with politics but performing an equally important national function by patronising the arts and letters; they, as much as their husbands, are responsible for establishing England's eventual supremacy.

If Lawrance was forgotten altogether, **Anna Brownell Jameson** established a tenacious hold on the outskirts of Strickland's territory. Her best-known royal biographical endeavour was the *Memoirs of Celebrated Female Sovereigns* (1831). Like Hays, Jameson offers a comparative study of queenly power; unlike Hays, and perhaps unexpectedly for those familiar with Jameson as an early feminist, her judgement on those queens is negative. In this text Jameson defined female government as 'signally unfortunate' and suggested that women 'called to Empire have been in most cases conspicuously unhappy or criminal' (Vol. 1, xv). Jameson deemed them 'unhappy' because they were forced to sacrifice the tender realm of domestic feeling for the cruel world of masculinised politics, or 'criminal' because their desires, no longer kept pure behind the domestic threshold, become warped into a cruel parody of masculine libertinism. Thus, Maria Theresa of Austria would have been 'an exemplary parent' under normal circumstances, but it was her 'misfortune' that 'she was placed in a situation where the most sacred duties and feelings of her sex became merely secondary' (Vol. 2, 240). Jameson's point is not to disallow women from wielding power per se, but rather that feminising military and monarchical power endangers both women and the state.

It was Agnes Strickland, however, whose work effectively dominated the Victorian market in royal lives and ultimately came to symbolise the genre itself. While Strickland's early life of Queen Victoria (1840) was an error-ridden disaster that drew the ire of Victoria herself, she achieved true literary celebrity with the 12 volumes of *Lives of the Queens of England, from the Norman Conquest*

(1840–1848), silently co-authored with her sister Elizabeth. After the *Lives'* first appearance, it was reprinted nearly every year in England or America between 1849 and 1893. American publishers abridged the book as a school text or excerpted individual lives; other editions emphasised the engraved portraits rather than the text, turning what was supposed to be a work of scholarship into the equivalent of a historical 'Book of Beauty'. The initial critical response was highly favourable, but the favour did not last far beyond the mid-1850s. The eight volumes of *The Lives of the Queens of Scotland and English Princesses Connected with the Regal Succession of Great Britain* (1850–1859), while still far more successful than nearly all other royal lives, was nevertheless met with less enthusiasm and less success: in Britain, it was reprinted only twice in the 1850s and twice in the 1860s. By the time Strickland published her last endeavours, *Lives of the Tudor Princesses, Including Lady Jane Gray and Her Sisters* (1868) and *Lives of the Last Four Princesses of the Royal House of Stuart* (1872), she was out of fashion with both the reading audience and historians and her scholarly methods were no longer in touch with leading developments in the practice of scientific history (Burstein 1998).

Like Lawrance, Strickland advertised her project as cultural history; her goal, she said, was 'to present, in a regular and connected chain, the history of female royalty, to trace the progress of civilisation, learning, and refinement in this country, and to show how greatly these were affected by queenly influence in all ages' – a project made all the more timely by the presence of a queen regnant (1840–1848: Vol. 1, xix). For Strickland, this influence is both cultural and political. Thus, William of Normandy's queen Matilda is a great cultural patroness (1840–1848: Vol. 1, 16), but Matilda of Scotland's 'influence' helped bring about the Magna Charta (1840: Vol. 1, 153). As an interpreter of historical evidence, Strickland lays great stress on her own objectivity – which is not to be confused with a refusal to moralise. Indeed, for Strickland the practice of objective evaluation clears the way for critical moral assessments. Anne Boleyn's character may be swamped by 'the enchantments of poetry and romance', but Strickland refuses to accept Benger's revisionist judgement: her Anne may find temporary solace in Christianity, but is not a true convert (1840–1848: Vol. 4, 149, 237). But Strickland's most revisionist and potentially controversial biography is that of Mary Tudor. She lays the blame for the Marian persecutions on parliament and the privy council (1840–1848: Vol. 5, 413), represents her as a truly feminine figure and in general seeks to rehabilitate her as, at the very least, a figure of honest if misguided virtue. Strickland's representation of Mary is unusual not just because of its High Church revisionism, but also because of its very existence: while Elizabeth I and Lady Jane Grey make regular appearances in Victorian royal lives, Mary is far more likely to be found in texts like the Religious Tract Society's *The Days of Queen Mary* – a compendium of horrors from John Foxe's *Book of Martyrs*. By contrast, the traditional Protestant heroine Elizabeth falls victim to the biographer's 'cold calm light of truth' (1840–1848: Vol. 6, 1), which denounces her for her extravagances, political machinations, the execution of Mary, Queen of Scots and, ultimately, her obsession with the 'semi-barbarous display of pomp and homage' (1840–1848: Vol. 6, 367). Ultimately, political significance pales in the light of perceived moral turpitude.

No later author would replicate Strickland's success. If there was a 'Golden Age' of royal lives, it perhaps ended with the work of Strickland's most reputable emulator, **Mary Anne Everett Green**. In her six volumes of *Lives of the Princesses of England, from the Norman Conquest* (1849–1855) she made no pretence at hiding her debt to Strickland's work. Like Strickland, Everett Green uses the presence of a queen regnant as inspiration for her work and similarly joins professional claims for objectivity with heavily moralising judgments, although she is kinder to masculine women like the Countess Adela (1849–1855: Vol. 1, 35). Green takes particular interest in what she terms 'pure-minded womanliness' (1849–1855: Vol. 5, 64), particularly as it manifests itself in maternal virtues – or not; thus, she condemns Henrietta Anne, Charles I's fifth daughter, for elevating 'the glare of pomp and the homage of courtly adulation' above her two children and the attractions of domesticity (1849–1855: Vol. 6, 475). Far less successful was the evangelical Emily Sarah Holt's *Memoirs of Royal Ladies* (1861). Like Green and Strickland, Holt had genuine scholarly ambitions: her few surviving manuscripts indicate that she was at least marginally competent in six languages, including Greek and Latin, and she was clearly proud of her research at the British Library. Rather precocious, she wrote a number of unpublished verse dramas, devotional poems and poetic sequences including *The Queens of England* (1856) and *The Picture Gallery* (1858) – the latter two indebted to both the royal lives tradition and to Felicia Hemans' *Records of Woman* (1828). As the daughter of a landed family, Holt was able to afford a number of earlier royal lives, including those by Lawrance, Strickland and Green. But unlike her more scholarly predecessors, Holt abandoned the rhetoric of objectivity in favour of blunt moralising; the reader opening to the history of Alicia, Countess of Lancaster, is warned that '[a] sad and sinful history is about to disclose itself before the eyes of the reader' (1861: Vol. 1, 47). Holt moved from history into fiction, ultimately producing a virulently anti-Catholic history of England in over 40 novels – some of which would remain in print until the late 1920s. It was only after her success as a novelist that she returned to non-fiction, writing children's biographies, a life of Wycliffe and a study of medieval social life.

After mid-century, 'queenliness' itself floats free from actual royalty and attaches itself to figures whose power was far more ambiguous. In short order, for example, we find 'Grace and Philip Wharton's' [Katherine and John Cockburn Thomson's] *The Queens of Society* (1860) Ellen Creathorne Clayton's *Queens of Song* (1865), and in America, Elizabeth Ellet's *Queens of American Society* (1867). In these instances, queenliness loses its political possibilities, and instead becomes a function of artistic or cultural supremacy. Such queens enjoy a far more fraught rule than Queen Victoria, holding on to their positions through a combination of ambition, professional acumen, innate talent and, perhaps, domestic connections. Americans further rewrote the royal life in their own image, transforming elite circles into 'courts' and First Ladies into the equivalent of queen consorts; hence the popularity of group biographies like Laura Carter Holloway's *The Ladies of the White House* (1869). Significantly, such American queenliness is 'democratised' by losing its association with a particular bloodline – especially because it is overtly dependent on the will of the electorate that chooses the First Lady's husband.

Royal lives after Victoria

While Strickland and Jameson continued to be reprinted, group lives of queens themselves largely faded out as a serious endeavour. The frothy *Crown Jewels*, with its attack on Elizabeth's 'crimes and cruelties' and patriotic celebration of Victoria as 'the model of every virtue', stands as an example of what happened to the genre when all pretence to original scholarship vanished (1897: 180, 263). But royal lives themselves did not vanish; they regrouped. During the twentieth century, the royal life came to occupy a privileged place in the realm of popular, rather than scholarly, biography. In contemporary scholarly biography, particularly the so-called life and times study, the life at the centre actually functions as a meeting point for the multiple historical narratives that at times seem to constitute it. Rather than telling a story replete with colour and character, the historian foregrounds evidence and its evaluation. At its most extreme, the life and times biography may abandon the purported central figure for surprisingly long periods of time. By contrast, the quality popular biography often eliminates footnotes altogether (replacing them with a general list of works cited) or resorts to endnotes. The biographer refrains as much as possible from overt reflection on the historical process itself. Moreover, nuts-and-bolts issues, such as economic history and the minutiae of administrative work, quietly fall by the wayside, replaced by entertaining anecdotes about people, costume, manners and so forth. In that sense, modern royal lives are very much descended from the work of Aikin, Benger, Strickland and Green – with the proviso that many of these lives offer neither larger reflections on history nor, significantly, any pretence to exemplarity. Like its Victorian ancestor, the modern royal life pays close attention to domestic life and 'manners', aided by the advent of photographic illustrations; unlike its Victorian ancestor, the modern royal life also dwells more explicitly on the seamy side of things, with particular attention (not surprisingly) to sexuality. The authors normally try to create a sense of connection between past and present, often, as we shall see, by invoking feminism – although the novelist Norah Lofts turned her sketchy *Queens of England* into a manifesto for modern royalism, comparing England's social stability to that of ex-monarchical countries and former colonies like the United States ('ended with Nixon and Watergate'), Germany ('got Hitler'), and Russia ('got the Politburo') (1977: 192).

With important exceptions, such as Elizabeth Longford's standard life of Queen *Victoria R. I* (1964), modern royal life-writing relies heavily on synthesis rather than original research and the rhetoric of pleasure instead of the rhetoric of professionalism. It is not surprising that royal lives are regularly marketed through book clubs, which, as Janice Radway and Joan Shelley Rubin have shown, position themselves as arbiters of middlebrow taste – quality books for the serious yet not necessarily scholarly reader (Rubin 1992: 93–147; Radway 1997). Moreover, the royal life has developed its own canon of sorts, with some figures enjoying their own minor industries: among the most popular are Elizabeth I, Henry VIII's various wives as a group (and Anne Boleyn as an individual), Mary Stuart, Victoria and Marie Antoinette. The travails of the Windsors have produced their own crop of biographies devoted to Elizabeth II and, in particular, the late Princess Diana. Lives of the latter, some of them 'insta-lives', exploded in quantity after her unexpected death, and have served a function somewhat akin to the poetry that memorialised Princess Charlotte's death in 1819. Such poetry rewrote the death of a youthful princess as a national, not simply personal, tragedy, while also implicitly (or explicitly) critiquing the rest of the royal family by comparison (Behrendt 1997).

Contemporary royal life-writers sometimes treat Agnes Strickland as a slightly unwanted foremother. Antonia Fraser, in her *Wives of Henry VIII*, describes Strickland as writing '[i]n the full flush of promoting Victorian values'; in contrast is our own 'less moralistic age', when readers and writers 'feel more sympathy for the girl whom the freak wave of the King's desire threw up so cruelly ill-prepared on the exposed shore of history' (1994: 317). Similarly, in *Divorced, Beheaded, Survived: A Feminist Reinterpretation of the Lives of Henry VIII*, Karen Lindsey complains that 'Strickland, trapped in Victorian moral values, denied the affair, as though only as a victim of slander could Kathryn be defended' (1995: 169). The twentieth-century writer, freed from an implicitly conservative and anti-woman standard, can now, in a sense, rescue the queen not only from history's judgement but from Henry's as well. Fraser writes with understated feminist 'sympathy' for her queens, all subjected to a man who grows ominously fatter throughout the book, as though devouring his women alive. The characteristics that rated Victorian censure, like Anne Boleyn's sharp tongue, now reappear as signs of personal strength. More emphatically, Lindsey interprets the behaviour of Henry's queens as situational responses to not just Henry but a patriarchal system more generally: they struggle against a marital economy in which women are the notes of trade in an international power struggle. It is perhaps not surprising that Lindsey is least fond of Henry's favourite queen, Jane Seymour, whom she describes as 'puzzlingly, almost eerily absent': 'Nothing as defined as malice or ambition or compassion or warmth or coldness comes through in the descriptions of Jane' (1995: 118). In other words, what contemporary writers now prize is individuality, rather than uniformity; resistance, rather than religious resignation; sexual fulfilment, rather than maternal urges.

A number of British and American women writers have specialised in individual royal lives, including Carolly Erickson, Alison Plowden and Alison Weir. One of the United States' most successful popular biographers, Erickson's numerous lives range widely across both time and geography. Her work is uniformly brief and highly synthetic, relying heavily on imaginative projection when no concrete evidence exists – a stylistic tic particularly noticeable in *Mistress Anne*: 'She cried, she frowned, no doubt she cursed her fate in rich French curses' (1984: 53). Unlike Fraser and Lindsey, Erickson does not necessarily expect her readers to sympathise with her subjects, nor can her work be described as an act of feminist reclamation. *Mistress Anne* is a harshly negative portrait that emphasises Anne's sexuality, whereas *Her Little Majesty* offers a much more balanced account of both Victoria's vices (like her later gluttony and 'cranky irritability') and her virtues (like her resolute bravery in the face of death) (1997: 188, 251). The somewhat more scholarly British biographers Plowden and Weir do not altogether avoid sensationalism or even moralising. Nevertheless, both writers try to meld a fiction-writer's imaginative sensibility, particularly on issues of romance, with background research in both primary and secondary sources. Plowden, a former television dramatist, began writing both lives and popular history in the early 1970s and specialises in the Tudor and Stuart periods; her books, popular enough to have been recently reprinted in England by Alan

Sutton, include multiple studies of Elizabeth I (*Elizabeth Regina* 2000; *The Life of Elizabeth I* 1998; *Marriage with My Kingdom* 1977 and *Danger to Elizabeth* 1973) and a life of Lady Jane Grey (2002). Like Plowden, Weir specialises primarily in the Tudors and Stuarts, including a best-selling life of Elizabeth, *The Life of Elizabeth I* (1998), *The Six Wives of Henry VIII* (1991), and a study of Mary Stuart's role in the death of her husband, Lord Darnley (2002). Both writers insist on Elizabeth's greatness while also emphasising her performance of power – precisely the issue which had caused her such trouble with nineteenth-century biographers. Thus, Plowden's Elizabeth is simultaneously capable of outwitting men decades her senior and of self-consciously performing the role of modest Christian maiden; indeed, pushing the theatrical imagery, Plowden represents her on the verge of her accession to the throne as standing 'in the wings, waiting composedly for her cue to step out into the dazzle of the spotlight and take her place upon the stage' (1998: 207). It is precisely Elizabeth's actress-like quality, her ability to perform a number of politically invested private roles, that ensures her later success – something to be admired here but which had led to overt criticism from writers like Strickland over a century earlier. Similarly, Weir's Elizabeth carefully represents herself as grief-stricken after the execution of Mary Stuart, well after the grief had subsided (1999: 380–1). Even in works that are not overtly feminist, such performativity has now lost its status as a sign of inauthenticity and come instead to represent a canny awareness of the relationship between image and power.

Although the royal life has really lost none of its commercial appeal, it has lost its original function as a guide to moral and public behaviour, whether for the elite or the masses. The nineteenth-century royal life offered women a potential entrée into the political realm occupied by history, but at the same time the tension between queenly power and domestic tranquillity could become too much for the genre to bear. Moreover, its appeal to intellectual women waned as the genre itself gained in popularity – done in by its own success. In the twentieth century, the popular royal life sits firmly outside of history, while the scholarly life eschews the emphasis on narrative and anecdote that makes lives of Elizabeth I (or II) still so popular with contemporary readers. But as twentieth-century invocations of Agnes Strickland also suggest, the modern royal life is a true descendant of its nineteenth-century ancestor in its emphasis on the pleasures of the past.

Miriam Elizabeth Burstein

References

Crown Jewels 1897; *Illustrious Women 1852; Select Female Biography 1829; Sketches of the Lives of Distinguished Females* 1834; Aikin 1819, 1822; Atkinson 1858; Behrendt 1997; Benger 1822; Booth 1997, 1999/2000; Burstein 1998, 1999; Cafarelli 1990; Colley 1992; Drabble 1982; Erickson 1984; Ezell 1993; Ferrante 1997; Fraser 1994; Green 1849–1855; Hays 1803, 1821; Holt 1861; Howitt 1851; James 1999; Jameson 1840; Kavanagh 1850; Kucich 1993, 2000; Laurence 2000; Lawrance 1838–1840; Lindsey 1995; Lingard 1855; Loeb 1994; Lofts 1997; Maitzen 1995; Mitchell 1998; Perry 1980; Plowden 1998; Radway 1997; Rubin 1992; Strickland 1844; Watson 1997; Weir 1998.

Related essays

Catalogs; Defences; Female Biography; France; Great Britain; Memoir; Secret History.

S

Salmon, Lucy Maynard 1853–1927

Educationalist, political historian, historian of women. Born in New York, daughter of Maria Clara Maynard, school principal, and George Salmon, manufacturer. Following the death of her mother in 1860 Lucy attended the Falley Seminary, Massachusetts, previously known as the Fulton Ladies Seminary, her mother's *alma mater*. In 1870 Salmon moved to Ann Arbor High school for preparatory study before entering the University of Michigan in 1871. Failure of the family fortune initially prevented further study, and upon completion of her degree in 1876 Salmon taught in a high school in McGregor, Iowa, eventually becoming school principal. Returned to graduate school at the University of Michigan in 1882, obtaining a master's degree in history. Salmon was then employed as an instructor at the Indiana State Normal School at Terre Haute, where she became involved in educational associations and published a monograph, *Education in Michigan during the Territorial Period* (1885).

Salmon was awarded a fellowship to Bryn Mawr in 1886, where she studied for her doctorate under Woodrow Wilson, whom she later recalled 'never whole-heartedly believed in college education for women' (Brown 1943: 102). Her thesis on the appointing powers of the President won a prize from the newly established American Historical Association (AHA) and was published in the first edition of its *Papers*, the only article by a woman. Salmon was one of the first female members of the AHA, joining in 1883. Throughout her career she lobbied the AHA for more equitable treatment of its women members, becoming the first woman elected to the Executive Council in 1915. Salmon served as the only woman on the General Committee of the AHA, the Membership Committee and the Committee of Seven, concerned with history in secondary schools. She was also the only woman at the founding meeting of the *American Historical Review*.

In 1887 she took up a position at Vassar, founding the department of history, as the only instructor in economics, political science and history. She was appointed full professor in 1889 and chaired the department until her death. At Vassar Salmon shifted the focus and methodology of her historical research towards the household. Her first major work *Domestic Service* (1897) drew upon the new methods of data collection and survey made popular by social scientists such as Florence Kelly and Jane Addams. Disparaged by historians, this work was praised by reformers. Throughout her career Salmon returned to the household as a site for illuminating class conflict, democracy and citizenship, drawing on feminist scholars such as **Olive Schreiner** and **Emily Putnam** to elucidate her theories.

Salmon's work anticipated the history of everyday life and she believed that the historical study of mundane household items such as laundry lists taught students to read evidence and identify historical problems. Her methods challenged the orthodoxies of historical research, particularly the focus on politics and the use of sources found in public archives. Following her decision in 1901 to create a home with Adelaide Underhill, the Vassar librarian, Salmon wrote extensively on the history of the material culture of the domestic environment, publishing *Progress in the Household* in 1906 and numerous essays. Although such essays represented an innovative object-based epistemology, they were often published in popular texts such as *Good Housekeeping*. That a proposed book critical of imperialism also did not find a publisher left Salmon musing that perhaps it would have had the author been listed as L M Salmon. Later essays defining Salmon's historical methodolology such as 'Main Street' and 'History in a Back Yard' were privately published.

A committed feminist, Salmon headed the suffrage movement at Vassar, as an officer of the National College Equal Suffrage League, eventually serving as vice-president of this organisation. She also served on the Executive Advisory Council of the Congressional Union for Woman Suffrage. In spite of resistance from James Monroe Taylor, President of Vassar, Salmon invited prominent suffragists such as **Charlotte Perkins Gilman** and Harriot Stanton Blatch to Vassar to speak. She also engaged in dress reform and, like **Mary Ritter Beard**, was committed to municipal improvement. Salmon was critical of Taylor's policy to have discussions of 'controversial subjects' banned on campus and following his retirement she worked to implement changes in the governance of the college to allow faculty members a greater role in policy making. Salmon's innovative teaching techniques created conflict between her and the Vassar president, who complained that her teaching involved 'too much looking and not enough memorisation'. Her battles with Taylor saw her publish research on education reform and these writings earned her national recognition as an educator. She served on the committee to prepare standards for college entrance and campaigned to improve the teaching of history in secondary schools.

Salmon encouraged independent thinking and judgement, and was much loved by her students. In 1923 the Vassar board of trustees voted to suspend the mandatory retirement requirement so Salmon could continue teaching. In that year Salmon published *The Newspaper and Authority* (1923) and *The Newspaper and the Historian* (1923). Salmon believed that newspapers served as a record 'of all contemporaneous historical interests, activities, and conditions'. These texts examined issues such as freedom of the press, regulation and taxation of the press, and the law of libel sources and bias in newspaper reporting – anticipating media and cultural studies by some 50 years. When Salmon died suddenly in 1927 former students and friends resolved to finance the publication of two volumes on which she had been working. These texts *Why is History Rewritten* (1929) and *Historical Material* (1933) drew together many of her thoughts on how everyday life revealed the past. In 1943 Louise Fargo Brown published her biography of Salmon, *Apostle of Democracy*.

Mary Spongberg

References

Adams & Smith 2001; Bohan 1999; Brown 1943; *NAW* 1971; Scanlon & Cosner 1996; Scott 1988; Smith 1984, 1998.

Major works

Domestic Service (New York: Arno Press, 1972); *The Newspaper and Authority* (New York: Octogon Books, 1976); *The Newspaper and the Historian* (New York: Octogon Books, 1976) and *History and Texture of Modern Life: Selected Essays by Lucy Maynard Salmon* (ed.) Nicholas Adams & Bonnie G Smith (Philadelphia: University of Philadelphia Press, 2001).

Science

Since we early twenty-first century feminist historians tend to run our fingers forever around the elegant mobius strip of public and private, personal and political, I will begin by being personal. I have recently finished an historical book about women in science. I did not write it with the kind of objective, impersonal attitude that has been *de rigeur* ever since Science became academia's flagship enterprise (in the nineteenth century). I started it in order to show a vague, shadowy army of biological determinists (chiefly embodied by my mother who told me that women had the wrong brains for good mathematics and gave me *BrainSex* by Anne Moir and David Jessell [1991] to prove it) that women *could so* be great scientists. Of course other questions quickly occurred to me once I had embarked on the research, such as: What does it mean to be a 'woman scientist', and how does this affect the science they do? Whilst I found a variety of interesting answers to these questions, to scientists they could appear as trespasses. A few affronted interviewees, reminding me of the harmful absurdities that 'Aryan science', not to mention 'proletarian' or 'communist' science, have produced in the past, told me in no uncertain terms that scientists are scientists, pure and simple. After all, science is methodologically and institutionally designed to eliminate as much of such crass human follies as pride and prejudice as possible (Longino 1990). Can the same be said of history?

To seek some insight into this question it seems logical to apply the questions that scholars have typically directed at women scientists to women historians of science. The first set of questions concerns the factors affecting the structure of the careers of female historians of science. Are there considerably fewer women historians of science than men, and is the history of science more masculinist, more discriminatory, than other kinds of history? What barriers to success do these women confront? The second set of questions is about the nature of their discipline. Is history inherently masculine? Was the birth of History another chapter in the history of patriarchy, as the birth of Science was said to have been (Keller 1995)? The third set of questions concerns whether or not women historians of science practise their craft or arrive at conclusions any differently to their male colleagues. Can there be a 'feminist history of science' just as some optimists have posited the possibility of a 'feminist science' and if so, what would be its characteristics (Harding 1991)? The final set of questions returns us to the personal. What motivated women historians of science and how have their individual identities informed their work? Whilst these questions cannot be adequately answered here, I will offer some preliminary musings about them and the larger questions about historical writing that they touch upon.

The history of science

Women historians of science may in fact have more in common with women scientists than with other women historians since the history of science has been, and to a large extent remains, mentally and institutionally segregated from 'mainstream' history. After all, the history of science is relatively recent. It was born at the very end of the nineteenth century, as the men of the West became awed by the power of this new Thing called Science (the word 'scientist' was not even coined until 1830) and wondered how it came into being. Those first histories, few written by women, were largely either celebratory, teleological histories of ideas that traced 'how we got it right' about vaccination, the atom and other marvels, or were used to prove theories about *how* science managed to produce what was considered to be objective true knowledge. Science history only really flowered and matured in the hothouse of the new critical science studies, kick-started by what is still almost certainly the best-selling work of history of any kind, Thomas Kuhn's *The Structure of Scientific Revolutions* (1962). Whole science-studies departments arose as anti-racist, feminist and environmentalist movements added fuel to the debates between philosophers and sociologists of science as to whether the nature of science was 'rational' or 'social', and these debates invariably turned to history for answers. Whilst soon more than mere fodder for philosophic debate, the history of science is still very much shaped by these questions.

The history of science remains distinct from mainstream history in several ways. First, it has often been built by scientists-turned-historians, rather than by those trained first in history. It is still well populated by such people; many of the brightest female stars in its galaxy were scientists *first*, including Donna Haraway, Evelyn Fox Keller, Lily Kay, Betty Dobbs and Judith Grabiner (to name but a few: see the bibliography for their work). Their awe at discovering that maybe facts are not as stable as they had thought when they were in the lab still rings through all their writing. Secondly, this scientific training means that a high level of technical discussion is normal and often necessary (especially in the older generation, this training also led to a pedantically rigorous attention to detail and accuracy.) Thirdly, because their goal was to understand the nature of science, history was in effect a marvellous databank to use in testing models of theory, growth and change in science. Mary Jo Nye's early work, *From Chemical Philosophy to Theoretical Chemistry: Dynamics of Matter and Dynamics of Disciplines, 1800–1950* (1993), for example, attempted to put the Strong Programme of the sociology of scientific knowledge (SSK) into action, causally explaining how both 'right' and 'wrong' scientific outcomes were produced by the same set of social factors. Finally, the history of ideas was and remains an extremely prominent tradition, even in these days of searching for social context. Donna Haraway's first book, *Crystals, Fabrics, and Fields: Metaphors of Organicism in Twentieth-Century Developmental Biology* (1976), for instance, elegantly traced how metaphors of organicism shaped concepts in twentieth-century biology, while her latest have been philosophical considerations concerning gender and science, rather than historical.

So how have women fared in the distinct world of science history? The *Isis* cumulative bibliographies for the history of science, which tabulate works published since 1913, show a low female-to-male ratio until their 1976–1985 volume, when the increase was gradual but noticeable (it has not yet reached 50 per cent). This increase came as a result of three interrelated late twentieth-century phenomena: 'second wave' feminism, the radical science movement/science studies and University expansion. Most of those women historians who stand out today graduated in the 1960s or 1970s and had to face battles about unequal promotion and pay, the sidelining of women-oriented curricula and the low status of *de facto* women's work in the academy (like teaching). So far as numbers go, then, it seems that women historians of science and women scientists are on a par. They certainly have the barriers and discrimination they have faced in common, both suffering the effects of horizontal and vertical discrimination that Margaret Rossiter, pre-eminent historian of women scientists, has so brilliantly described in *Women Scientists in America* (1995).

The stories of barriers are familiar: Jane Oppenheimer, from the interwar generation and a brilliant embryologist and historian of developmental biology and author of *Essays in the History of Embryology and Biology* (1967), worked her whole life at a women's college, Bryn Mawr. Like her American scientific sisters she found her career only in a highly respected, yes, but carefully separate institutional realm. Betty Dobbs, who revolutionised studies of Newton as much as his work revolutionised physics in *The Foundations of Newton's Alchemy*, or '*The Hunting of the Greene Lyon*' (1975) and *The Janus Faces of Genius: The Role of Alchemy in Newton's Thought* (1991), was a housewife for 20 years before becoming an historian, a transformation not managed by many. Mary Jo Nye (Nye 1993, 1999; Sanders 1999) credits her move into her research to the lucky chance of a great role model for a chemistry teacher when other girls thought scientists were all men. Women who have confronted these and other problems continue to form and support listservs for women historians of science and to act on the women's caucus of the History of Science Society. So barriers, or 'leaky pipelines', the current preferred metaphor for describing how women opt or are pushed out on the way to the top, are important for women historians of science. So is the fact that all three mentioned above were very strongly supported by their male colleagues, something women scientists often found as well: the norm of universalism has served women historians well at times too (Merton 1973). Searingly intelligent, kindly, carrying the gravitas of peer acclamation from around the world, these women continue to be role models for a new generation of female hopefuls.

Concepts and methods

Women historians of science trained with their male counterparts, and so their methods and interests were similar. Indeed, the history of science is perhaps less horizontally segregated than are the sciences themselves. Sciences that have remained fairly steadily masculine, such as physics and mathematics, are reasonably well served by women historians. The history of mathematics contains a subset of prominent women contributors, who between them have tackled virtually the entire sweep from most ancient to modern in the subject. As with their colleagues, the underlying theme is understanding *why* certain mathematical problems were conceptualised, and solved, as it happened they were. Eleanor Robson, for example, in *Mesopotamian Mathematics, 2100–1600 BC: Technical Constants in Bureaucracy and Education* (1999), has examined the evolution of ancient Mesopotamian mathematics, making sense of stone tablets of cuneiform calculations and showing how practical problems in building or economics were understood as mathematical ones. Similarly, Serafina Cuomo in *Pappus of Alexandria and the Mathematics of Late Antiquity* (2000) and *Ancient Mathematics* (2001) has examined the importance of mechanics, counting, measuring and surveying land in the development of mathematics in the Graeco-Roman period, understanding the work of the famous Greek philosophers such as Euclid and Archimedes by and through their political and religious context. Pycior (1997), Stedall (2002, 2003) and Neal (2002) have conducted studies of seventeenth-century number concepts and Judith Grabiner (1981, 1990), the origin of the calculus. Lorraine Daston's *Classical Probability in the Enlightenment* (1988) has suggested that the science of probability, which underlies so much of our late modern world, was shaped by notions of what it meant to be reasonable in the Age of Reason: 'nothing more at bottom than good sense reduced to a calculus'. Women are not so prominent in the history of engineering, although they have produced an abundance of histories of technologies, such as L Hoddeson and M Riordan's *Crystal Fire: The Birth of the Information Age* (1997).

The history of chemistry has likewise garnered considerable attention, especially as the developing concepts of atoms and molecules in the late eighteenth and early nineteenth centuries have always been canonical cannon-fodder for theories of scientific change. Informed by SSK, women historians and their colleagues have complicated these questions of paradigm-shift, asking instead how laboratory scientists in the nineteenth and early twentieth centuries represented the invisible particles about which they theorised and how these practices of representation – signals, processing marks, tables, graphs, diagrams – shaped the differentiation of meaning of scientific concepts, in works such as Ursula Klein's edited collection *Tools and Mode of Representation in the Laboratory Sciences* (2001) and *Experiments, Models, Paper Tools: Cultures of Organic Chemistry in the Nineteenth Century* (2003). Other works such as Nye's *Before Big Science: The Pursuit of Modern Chemistry and Physics, 1800–1940* (1999) and Diana Barkan's *Walther Nernst and the Transition to Modern Physical Science* (1999) have traced how the half-romantic chemistry and natural philosophy of the 1800s, conducted almost wholly in small, private laboratories, turned into the research team-based modern disciplines of physics and chemistry. Geology, too, has had its female chroniclers and queryists, including Naomi Oreskes' discussion of American geology in *The Rejection of Continental Drift: Theory and Method in American Earth Science* (1999) and Rachel Laudan's exploration of the foundations of the science in the seventeenth and eighteenth centuries in *From Mineralogy to Geology: The Foundations of a Science, 1650–1830* (1987). The history of molecular biology, which may be said to have replaced physics as the pre-eminent Science, is not without female practitioner/historians, from Evelyn Fox Keller who argues that genetics represents the ultimate masculine endeavour to control nature in *Secrets of Life, Secrets of Death: Essays on Language, Gender and Science* (1992), to Lily Kay who looks at the social and institutional matrix of Caltech and the Rockefeller in which the 'molecular vision of life' developed, in *The Molecular Vision of Life* (1993).

Gendering science

Yet while their intellectual reach and disciplinary preoccupations have mirrored their male counterparts', it is also true that women historians of science have transformed their field. The radical science and sociological movements that gave such impetus to history of science were shaped by the struggles of 'second wave' **feminism** and the ideas about 'equality' and 'difference' and 'other' and 'duality' in them. An early, important part of this process was the result of women scientists and historians wondering why the history of science contained no women. A reclamatory history came into being, from collections of **biographies** such as Margaret Alic's *Hypatia's Heritage: A History of Women in Science from Antiquity to the Late Nineteenth Century* (1986), Olga Opfell's *The Lady Laureates: Women Who have Won the Nobel Prize* (1986) and Ruth Howes and Caroline Herzenberg's *Their Day in the Sun: The Women of the Manhattan Project* (1989), to outraged rightings of the record about women passed over for Nobel prizes won by their male colleagues, such as Anne Sayre and now Brenda Maddox's studies of Rosalind Franklin and her role in the discovery of DNA (1975, 2002). Others asked why women have been under-represented in science, leading to analyses of the barriers and battles women scientists have faced, pre-eminently explicated in Margaret Rossiter's outstanding history *Women Scientists in America* (1995). As in other disciplines reclamatory biography led to increasingly sophisticated thinking about gender. Recent studies, from Marina Benjamin's *Science and Sensibility* (1992) study of women naturalists, to Mary Terrall's award-winning essay about Emilie du Chatelet (1995) and the small library of works by historians of both sexes about **Margaret Cavendish** and Mary Somerville, analysed how gender shaped these women's choices and self-image. The gendering of science has become the larger inquiry, in studies of the women 'behind' the men of science, the wives and scribes and bottle washers, such as Henrietta Huxley, T H's domestic wife (White 1996). Women historians – and not only them, for many men have turned their attention to gender as well – have traced how some sciences, like botany and physiology came to be gendered feminine in a self-fulfilling circle that led more women to study them, and how these sciences were often deliberately de-feminised by professionalisation processes aimed at 'raising their status'.

Of course, the women in this essay mostly get mentioned because they have published more or won more medals or become Professor at some high status university or otherwise got ticks on the board. Yet this singling out, which excludes many others of equal weight to those mentioned here, replicates exactly the kind of 'linear succession of great men/great ideas' history that women historians of science – usually under a feminist banner – have leapt to critique. Historians of science are especially sensitive about this because of their awareness of how people who happened to get it wrong – wrong according to us – can so easily get lost to history; worse, how such a teleological history obscures the actual development of science. It is therefore important to remark that the history of science is made mostly of the accumulated work of little-known specialists (who reads the history of phycology?), antiquarians, popularisers, graduate students who leave to become moms, scholars with low publication records since as women they do more teaching and so forth. Can *their* history be written and not marginalised? Is it possible to invent a feminine/feminist history of sci-ence that would methodologically avoid creating losers?

Pondering the struggles of women scientists, and asking what kind of beast it was that created unspeakably destructive bombs and corrosive pollutants, mutilated wombs, and 'proved' the inferiority of female and black intelligences led feminist historians to wonder similarly about the nature of science itself. It did not take long to show that, whatever origin one cared to choose for science (the Greeks, where Margaret Wertheim began in her popular study of the gendering of mathematics and physics *Pythagoras' Trousers: God, Physics and the Gender Wars* [1995]?), it was built around strongly gendered dualisms and firmly defined by the masculine side of them: rational, objective, intellectual, mechanical, not emotive, subjective, embodied and organic. The valorising histories of the nineteenth and early twentieth centuries told how the heroes of empiricist rationality – Copernicus, Galileo, Newton, Bacon – sturdily won out in their battles with that superstitious She, the Church, so women historians re-examined that era to ask whether science was born 'a man, bourgeois, and infected too'? The answer seemed to be 'yes': Carolyn Merchant's *The Death of Nature* (1980) and Evelyn Fox Keller's *Reflections on Gender and Science* (1995) have found Bacon's science writing to be full of rape and slavery metaphors. They showed that science was imagined as a project of dominion over Others: nature, women, the 'new' world and its people. These historians wrote in dialogue with the new, energetic discipline of feminist science studies, giving more weight to criticisms that science was an inherently masculine endeavour: its gaze was alienated, distanced, objectifying; its methods made mere machines of organisms, and sorted wholes into collections of diminished parts; it classified and ranked what was multiple and interactive; it cheered the emperor's new cloak of simplicity, and eschewed the accuracy of his complicated nudity; it *knew* only to *exploit*; it killed.

This view of science, in many ways compelling but in point of fact eschewed as overly simplified in most feminist science studies, directed women's historical attention towards the changing relationship between science, gender, nature and culture. Led by Carolyn Merchant, this has given rise to histories of the environment that describe the cultural, economic and intellectual systems (science!) that have validated the colonisation and devastation of so much of the world – histories in which the postmodern luxury of fluid and unstable meaning was often foregone in anger and horror at the abuses of (however you like to call it) white capitalist patriarchy. Others became fascinated with charting different cultural understandings of nature. The late eighteenth and nineteenth centuries have garnered an especially large amount of attention, since this is when science first started to develop social organisations, such as specialised societies, and then to professionalise. The nineteenth century holds particular interest for women historians, who have been delighted to discover that the middle- and upper-class social culture in which science thrived at that time was a highly feminised one, and that an interest in seaweed or fossils was as graceful a feminine adornment as puffed sleeves and ringlets in works such as Patricia Phillips' *The Scientific Lady: A Social History of Women's Scientific Interests, 1520–1918* (1993) and Ann B Shteir's *Cultivating Women, Cultivating Science: Flora's Daughters and Botany in England, 1760–1860* (1996). A number of very sophisticated women's works have now explored this 'culture of natural history' with its women practitioners, illustrators, popularisers, amanuenses and taxidermists. In the twentieth century, Donna Haraway has led studies of the nature/culture/gender nexus in her exceptional history of primatology, *Primate Visions: Gender, Race, and Nature in the World of Modern Science* (1989) – the science where the distinction between human and animal is most blurred.

These kinds of histories revealed as much about the nature of middle-class western society as they did about the nature of science. They are perfect examples of the turn towards situated, culturally embedded studies of science that emerged most recently from the history of science's engagement with both SSK and social and cultural history. Curiosity, like Truth, has been granted a social history (Shapin, 1995). Recent works have brought the whole vividly coloured panoply of belief and practice into connections with science, from witchcraft to navigation. For example, Shelley Costa's look at marketing mathematics in the eighteenth century (2002), Joan Richards' non-traditional look at the interface between logical/mathematical thinking and everyday life in the nineteenth and twentieth centuries and Lorraine Daston's *Classical Probability in the Enlightenment* and Barbara Shapiro's *'Beyond Reasonable Doubt' and 'Probable Cause': Historical Perspectives on the Anglo-American Law of Evidence* (2000) probing into the history of probability and, consequentially, into what exactly it is we mean when we talk about 'facts', all give an apparently impenetrable subject – mathematics – a warm, living cultural context. Similarly, women have returned to the Scientific Revolution, tracing how alchemical writings were not distinct from, but shaped, 'scientific' ideas (Betty Dobbs on Newton [1975, 1991] and Deborah Harkeness' *John Dee's Conversations with Angels: Cabala, Alchemy, and the End of Nature* [1999]), and to show

how contextualising science in its setting of collecting, Carnivale and Machiavelli can shed light on Renaissance Europe in works such as Margaret Jacob's *The Cultural Meaning of the Scientific Revolution* (1988) and Paula Findlen's *Possessing Nature: Museums, Collecting, and Scientific Culture in Early Modern Italy* (1994).

So in sum: is there anything special about women historians of science? Insofar as they trained with and were shaped by the same post-war social and intellectual movements as men, the answer would seem to be no. In terms of output alone, from style of writing to conceptual interest, women vary amongst each other so much that it seems foolish to compare them, as a group, with men. Today women historians write prose as dense and luscious and difficult as poetry (Donna Haraway) and as clear and simple as a novel (Lilian Hoddeson). A lot write popularising works, and biographies, as women have always done; but then so do men, because editors inform them that pop sci of a certain kind sells well. And these days, as men historians take on board the importance of gender in analysis and carefully situate their knowledges, different approaches to history-writing are perhaps less obviously linked to the gender of the writer.

On the other hand, insofar as there was a 30-year period when women increasingly entered the field and wrote from hitherto marginalised positions, uncovering the power relations that structure science through and through, the answer is, they are utterly special! As with women scientists, gender shaped everything from their choice of research topic to their choices about *how* they researched it. For women scientists, the how has often been famously related to their sense of the importance of connecting to life, of having a 'feeling for the organism,' that Evelyn Fox Keller found was central to the research methodology of Nobel prize winner Barbara McClintock (1983). (Later feminist theorists discarded the notion that this 'feeling' might form the basis for a 'feminist' science, but women scientists still discuss it as important in their practice [Mayberry *et al.* 2001; Hooker 2004].) It is hard, and probably foolish, to identify an equivalent for women historians of science that defines their process and overall concerns, but I would suggest one possibility as a subject for future research, and that is that an awful lot of feminist and critical science studies seems to me to bear strong links to the cultural rubric of Romanticism. The tensions between the objective and the emotional, detail and grand theory, nuance and fact, connection and distance, that are particularly noticeable in the longings and disenchantments of current feminist studies of science were forged there. One can trace these concerns backwards to those of 'first wave' feminists and their foremothers throughout the nineteenth century, concerns with what science is and how it might affect the world.

Women scientists and historians of science share an interminable curiosity and passionate pleasure in working out how to understand the subject of their study. Their primary rewards are not those whose unequal distribution with men can cause great anger – not, after all, those of money and status and power. In this sense scholarship can transcend gender: an historian can sometimes be just that, unqualified by social or disciplinary categories. And yet, even given the great diversity of women, and knowing that 'there is not even such a state as "being" female, itself a highly complex category constructed in contested sexual scientific discourses and other social practices,' there are times when it is meaningful to see a scholar as explicitly a *woman* historian of science.

Claire Hooker

References
Costa 2002; Grabiner 1981, 1990; Haraway 1976, 1989, 1997; Harding 1991; Hooker 2004; Keller 1983, 1995, 2002, 2003; Longino 1990; Maddox 2002; Merton 1973; Neal 2002; Pycior 1997; Sanders 1999; Sayre 1975; Shapin 1995; Stedall 2002, 2003; Terrall 1995; White 1996.

Related essays
Female Biographies; Feminism.

Scudéry, Madeleine de 1607–1701

French novelist, historian of women. Daughter of Madeleine de Martel de Goutimesnil. Orphaned at an early age, she was taken to Rouen where she was educated by her uncle. She developed a facility for languages, learning Italian and Spanish as well as how to write and spell in French. Moving to Paris in 1637, she lived with her brother Georges de Scudéry, playwright. A number of her works were published under his name and there seems to have been an element of collaboration. In Paris she became involved in literary society, although it was not until 1653 that she began to hold her own salon. Her salon or *Samedi* [Saturday] was named for the day of the week on which it was held and was frequented by many political and artistic celebrities including Mme de Lafayette and the Duchesses de Longueville and de Montpensier (see **Memoirs**).

Her first novel *Ibrahim; ou, L'illustre Bassa* was published in 1641, as was her *Lettres amoureues de divers auteurs de ce temps*, an epistolary collection modelled on Ovid's *Heroides*. In 1642 she produced *Les femmes illustres; ou Les harangues héroïques*. Derived from and usurping the **women worthies** tradition, this collection of 'autobiographical' speeches by figures such as Sappho, Cleopatra and Agrippina restored the voice of women frequently vilified by male historians and encouraged contemporary women to engage in similarly glorious exploits (see **Catalogs** and **Defences**). Between 1649 and 1653 Scudéry produced *Artamène; ou, Le Grand Cyrus*, in ten volumes. Written in the early days of the Fronde, Scudéry's heroine Mandane represented the Duchess de Longueville, one of the principal instigators of the revolt. Thus Scudéry's most popular novel celebrated contemporary women's political and military subversion. In this novel Scudéry observed that 'the intrigues of war and peace are better many times, laid open and satyriz'd in a Romance, than in a down-right History, which being oblig'd to name the persons is often forc'd for several reasons and motives to be too partial and too sparing' (see **Historical Fiction**). Male critics of Scudéry's work believed that she corrupted 'History' by placing the heroine at its centre. Another novel, *Clélie, Histoire romaine*, appeared in ten volumes between 1654 and 1660. Set in ancient and exotic locations her 'Romances' drew extensively on historical sources and suggest collaboration between Scudéry and classical scholars familiar with Latin and Greek. Their contemporary political commentary, however, contributed to her brother's disgrace and he went into voluntary exile following the Fronde.

In the 1660s Scudéry turned to shorter fiction with three *nouvelles*, *Célinte* (1661), *Mathilde d'Aguilar* (1667) and *La Promenade de Versailles* (1669). In 1671 she published *Discours de la gloire*, a hyperbolic celebration of Louis XIV, for which she was awarded the first *Académie Française* Prize. Scudéry was granted a royal pension in 1683 and dedicated all her works published after this date to Louis XIV. Later works such as *Conversations sur divers sujets* (1680), *Conversations nouvelles sur divers sujets* (1684) and *Entretiens de morale* (1692) instructed women in rhetorical strategies for conversation, wit and letter-writing.

Mary Spongberg

References

Ballaster 1992; Dejean 1991; Donawerth & Strongson 2004; Newman 2003.

Major works

Scudéry's *Histoire de Sapho from Artamène, ou Le grand Cyrus* and Sappho's harangue from *Les femmes illustres* are published in Karen Newman (ed.) *The Story of Sapho* (Chicago: University of Chicago Press, 2003) and extracts from *Lettres amoureues de divers auteurs de ce temps, Les femmes illustres,* and *Conversations sur divers sujets* are published in Jane Donawerth & Julie Strongson (eds) *Madeleine Scudéry's Selected Letters, Orations and Rhetorical Dialogues* (Chicago: University of Chicago Press, 2004).

Secret history

During the last third of the seventeenth century, books and pamphlets carrying the title 'secret history' or *histoire secrète* appeared in the English and French book trades in noticeable numbers. The emergence of this term and the shifting uses made of it through the early eighteenth century indicated social and material conditions integral to the flowering of print culture that were relevant to the development of women's history. Early secret histories exploited the amorously and critically charged ambivalence surrounding the figures of women in narratives of public history. As writers used secret histories to critique the conventions of print culture, however, some women writers appropriated the genre's self-consciousness and its reputation for scandal to engage the public's conceptions of history. The expanding market in printed books opened to women writers the prospect of financial solvency and, more problematically, fame. At this time, a woman selling her work to entertain 'the public' also risked selling her character.

Scandalous beginnings

The title secret history has been used since the seventeenth century to market books by courting readers' appetite for being made privy to scandals, often sexual in nature, among the most important people and institutions in the land. The flurry of secret histories that entered the book trade in England around 1690 provided an indication of more than a fashion, however. The Civil Wars and the ousting of James II in 1688 had demonstrated that English people, mobilised to form collective 'public' opinions by the printing press, possessed the ability to make and unmake kings. Contemporary ideas of secrecy came to include the sense that the nation's leaders concealed their actions from the people, since a reading public could now use the medium of print to exert the pressure of opinion on national policies.

A confluence of circumstances made English 'secret history' available for use by polemical writers warning darkly about the councillors to the king and behind-the-scenes plotting in the government. After the traumatic divisiveness of the Civil Wars, the emerging political parties had strong incentive to produce a series of national histories and collections of documents. The Whigs needed to retell England's story in order to demonstrate the antiquity of the parliament's check on the king's power, and the Tories discounted their evidence with histories illustrating royal prerogative. Furthermore, the Stuart royal court that had been restored to power in 1660 had not shed its aura of scandal. Charles II's personal flamboyance and shifts in policy drew many writers to attribute to him the Machiavellian 'dissimulation' that was said to have characterised the Stuart line since the time of James I, who had drawn suspicion of cover-up when his court favourite was implicated in the poisoning of Overbury (Bellany 2002). James' grandson Charles II embodied and inspired the literature of court scandal and intrigue coming over from France. Charles had publicly taken as his chief mistresses not only Lord Castlemaine's wife and the actress Nell Gwynn, but also a lady in waiting brought directly from the French court, on whom he conferred the title of Duchess of Portsmouth. These liaisons provoked conflicting moral responses among the people and created anxiety over the destabilising of policy and the succession. The Duchess of Portsmouth became emblematic of English fears that France and Spain would lure the Stuarts into making England once again a Catholic nation.

These fears gained confirmation after the end of Charles' reign, when published French documents disclosed that Charles II had in fact signed a secret treaty in 1670 to join forces with Louis XIV against the Protestant Dutch. The best-kept secret out of the extensive negotiations between the two monarchs involved Charles' promise to increase tolerance for English Catholics and to make public his own conversion to Catholicism. In return, Louis freed Charles from relying on Parliament by paying England hundreds of thousands of pounds to refurbish English military and naval capabilities. Charles had signed this treaty, moreover, when his sister Henrietta had handed him the finalised version at Dover. Henrietta, together with Charles' mother and the Duchess of Portsmouth, emblematised France's undue influence on Charles. Pamphleteers who fancied incestuous relations between Charles and his sister used this symbolism to imagine the extent of what the Whigs and many others considered a betrayal of Protestant England's national interests.

The revelation of the Secret Treaty of Dover consequently served Whig efforts to reframe understanding of the monarchy and national government with the claim that citizens had a right to know the *arcana imperii* or 'secrets of state'. When the nation's Protestants welcomed the army of William and Mary in 1688, the flight of their Catholic king James II consolidated the Whig party's power to interpret monarchy as government accountable to the governed, whose scrutiny of their leaders' actions and debates with one another could take place by means of the printing press (Patterson 1997). A flurry of secret histories appeared that included *The Secret History of the Duchess of Portsmouth* (1690) and a series published by Nathaniel Crouch that detailed the scandalous motives and evil councillors corrupting the reigns of the last four Stuart kings. For Whig writers, the theme of *cherchez la femme*, the hint to look for a woman's secret influence to explain mysterious transactions among the powerful, emblematised their quarrel with the old Royalist regime.

Secret history supplies traces of the position of women in relation to emerging concepts of public knowledge. Humanist methods of representing and verifying knowledge carried over into the market in printed works as writers and booksellers on both sides of the English Channel sought means of legitimising the authority of the truths they printed (Mayer 1997; Stone 1997). The intensive efforts that men of letters devoted in the later seventeenth century to codifying rules to govern each genre of writing sought to regulate the reader's perceptions of the status and authority of publications in the burgeoning book trade. 'History', for example, could refer to a wide variety of narratives, including true or fictional 'lives' of individuals. The specialised meanings that scholars had given to the word in order to signify the accurate, impartial and document-based representation of the past had yet to restrict the word's enormous range of meanings in the book trade (Mayer 1997). By the early eighteenth century, distinctions between fact and fiction had consolidated enough to be complicated by secret history (Gallagher 1994). Many of these works sported with generic form in ways that unsettled conventional evaluations of what counted as historical actuality and significance. Secret histories, on the whole, represented women in order to condemn their interventions in history, and yet some women made use of the genre's ambiguities in order to reinterpret what counted as significance, veracity, and historical agency. Invoking the proverbial truth that trivial things can bring down the great, women's writings transmuted the historical glory associated with military conquest and the movement of events on a national scale by inviting sceptical rereading for causes behind the scenes, for which they supplied models. Still, readers would have had little difficulty in observing the equivocation of distinctions between fiction and fact in these works. Secret history suggestively called up the image of seductive women in the minds of readers but, like women themselves, these works took positions in print culture fraught with impropriety and turned into signs of shifts in historical value rather than representing history itself (Bowers 1994).

Derivations

'Secret history' first appeared in a book title as a translation of the word 'anecdotes' (Greek *anekdota*), meaning 'not given out' and therefore 'unpublished'. The sixth-century historian Procopius, commissioned by the Byzantine emperor Justinian to write the official histories of his reign, had kept a secret record of the outrages committed by this emperor and his regime for the benefit of posterity. A Vatican library copy of this manuscript ultimately gained acceptance as Procopius' truth-telling corrections to his multi-volume *History of the Wars of Justinian*. Translated into French as *Histoire secrète* by 1669, it was translated for the bookseller Richard Bentley in 1674 as *The Secret History of the Court of the Emperor Justinian*. Writers in both France and England subsequently seized on the *Secret History* as an exemplar justifying the publication of shocking reports as high-minded history. Procopius had supplemented his official history with hair-raising accounts of the gang warfare and orgies that Justinian brought to Constantinople and showed the heroic general Belisarius as subservient to his wife Antonina, a 'prostitute' capable of having her opponents, including her own son, murdered. Belisarius forfeited imperial territory through fear of marching too far away to stop his wife's amours, while she conspired with the empress Theodora, another 'prostitute', to control the empire. Secret history became associated with the violation of taboos, especially by transgressive women. Fetishising the revelation of such outrageous behind-the-scenes misconduct by the great, the legacy of secret history brought the image of the suppressed manuscript to signify the dangerous power of the act of publishing itself to intervene in contemporary political affairs.

It was English booksellers who turned the marketing value of 'secret history' into a specific category or genre. In France, an assortment of literary works circulated for the amusement of the upper classes, who read their often *à clef*, or encoded, stories with the knowingness of high society's insiders.

Under a welter of genre labels, including *histoire, annales,* **memoirs**, *chroniques, galanteries, intrigues, amours, lettres,* and so forth, which could be *petite, amoreuse, galante, secrète* or *scandaleuse,* these works and their translations drew wider readerships among people seeking to participate in their aura of exclusive community (Beasley 1990). In England, however, the seventeenth-century political context brought writers and readers to fix on 'secret history' as evoking both fascination with an elite French world of amour and intrigue and English anxiety over betrayal of the nation's interests to French cultural power. Some French works were retitled 'secret history' when translated into English. *Le Comte d'Essex* became *The Secret History of Queen Elizabeth and the Earl of Essex* (1680). Charles Vanel's *Royal Mistresses of France* was described as a secret history in its 1695 subtitle and the translator of Madame de La Fayette's *History of Henrietta of England* (1722) added the insinuating prefix '*Secret*'.

This French legacy of secret history served English Tories as well as Whigs. Whigs usually presented their secret histories as correcting the official accounts of events. This lineage of 'secret' political counter-history carried into the early eighteenth century as John Oldmixon, Daniel Defoe and others took part in the adversarial process through which writers struggled to establish authoritative historical narratives and the historical methods for creating them. Royalist Tories emulated the heightened social awareness of the French stylists who wrote of court intrigue and amorous gallantry. Aphra Behn's *Love Letters between a Nobleman and His Sister* (1684), for instance, invited ambivalent readings that were as likely to convey the refinement of aristocratic worldliness as to use sexual scandal to carry out political attacks (Ballaster 1992). Behn inspired a generation of women writers, including **Eliza Haywood** and **Delarivier Manley**, to write amorous narratives supporting the Tory cause. Nevertheless, prominent women remained vulnerable to the stigma of scandal whether Whig or Tory.

The pattern of Procopius' original scandal chronicle had allowed writers to present a wide variety of printed works as purveying at least a truth of principle, if not fact. While voyeuristic illustrations for *The Amours of Messalina* (1689) guided readers to imagine James' queen having an affair with Louis XIV, no boundaries defining fiction made it clear that counter-histories such as Crouch's *Secret History of the Reigns of K. Charles II and K. James II* (1690) should be read differently. All resembled at least some aspects of Procopius' narrative. During the early eighteenth century, however, the differentiation of history from fiction left secret history in a position that called attention to that differentiation.

The lapsing of several Licensing Acts after 1679 had not freed booksellers, writers and printers in England from the threat of prosecution, but latitude of expression and form did increase over subsequent decades. The possibility of engaging in political discourse became especially apparent by contrast with the system of censorship operating in Louis XIV's France. English booksellers' marketing strategies, moreover, encouraged desire for novelty in every aspect of book form, style and subject matter, contributing to a context of constant innovation. Under these circumstances, readerships took readily to the works of women writers, bringing them success so noticeable that they experienced a degree of backlash during the early eighteenth century. Some of the period's most famous satirists, including Alexander Pope and Jonathan Swift, criticised the decline of literary taste that accompanied the expansion of the book trade, of which women's commercial success stood as embarrassing proof.

Writers used secret history opportunistically, typically in order to react to other printed works and their arguments. This generation broke away from the Procopian style of counter-history to create an enormous variety of works, including letters, a periodical, satire, verse, an affidavit, reportage, rogue biography, critical history, apology and history of an object, in addition to the usual *roman à clef*. Particularly suggestive were the overt satires *A Satyr upon King William, Being the Secret History of His Life and Reign* (1703), Daniel Defoe's *Secret History of the Secret History* (1715), and *Terrae-Filius, or, the Secret History of the University of Oxford* (1721), which attributed to the genre a position outside of convention and a viewpoint critical of accepted knowledge. Secret history now called attention to the fabricated nature of printed representation.

Although the conventions of historical prose continued to consolidate and to exclude secret histories, these works complicated the boundaries that historians, whether classically humanist or antiquarian, had set to define their practice. Individual secret histories made it difficult to see histories as distinct from them in form or purpose, since secret histories made their political objectives explicit and demonstrated the adversarial rather than disinterested nature of historical representation. Their example called attention to how historical representations shaped the reading process and controlled the evaluation of significance and methods of legitimising and verifying knowledge. Furthermore, secret histories could be seen as imagining an ideal depth of knowledge about historical circumstance – person to person transactions in private – which challenged the limits of possibility for historical research. Secret history exposed the limits of the historian's ideal of achieving a disinterested, comprehensive survey of material facts from the most significant transactions of the past.

Secret history and women's history

The work of recovering women's history has depended on extending the range of writings to be considered as historical matter. Scholars venture beyond the early modern forms of universal, general or national, and particular history, this last usually the account of a single reign, in order to find women represented through 'lives', memoirs, eulogies, chronicles and portraits (Harth 1983: 132). Adding secret histories to this list makes the problematic position of early modern women in relation to history conspicuous, calling attention to the process by which history formed as an institution.

The least impeachable women's history took the form of lives of **women worthies**, since the women depicted had not put themselves forward by writing memoir and set edifying examples for the reading public. Secret histories often represented the women worthies' scandalous opposites: women who gained illegitimate influence on events of national importance from a position behind the scenes. While many national histories treated the women who gained sway by scandalous means primarily as reflections on the corrupt characters of the kings and leaders, secret history formed a genre that exposed the conventions of publishing truth claims.

Few women risked writing in so unstable a genre, and yet secret history signified women's relation to history much as did the genres of romance and amatory fiction. It is important to remember that during the later seventeenth century even the legitimacy of national histories remained at issue because readers and critics such as René Rapin were aware that powerful interests funded historians. Furthermore, history claimed to record a nation's public knowledge of itself, but the narrative genres competing with one another for the attention of readers made an issue of who counted as 'public' and whether the representation of truth took the same form for all. Seventeenth-century women writers could write for their own circle of acquaintance and their own 'public' apart from the reading public addressed by men of letters, and yet their collective knowledge could be ruled out of history's bounds by the men of letters.

The pervasiveness of anti-romance throughout Europe exemplified this issue, reacting to the power of a mid-century cult of female heroism that a remarkable circle of aristocratic women had developed in France after finding examples of heroic women such as the Amazons handed down by Classical literature. Seizing on the idea that women were physically capable of engaging in battle, a number of noblewomen joined the rebellion known as the Fronde in an attempt to overthrow the regents who ruled during Louis XIV's minority. Some noblewomen even took part in military action. After the rebellion failed, the aristocratic women channelled their energies into literary pursuits and vast heroic romances appeared. Subsequent historians omitted the actions of these women from their accounts of national history. Moreover, men of letters made it a fashion to ridicule the grand romances in order to dismiss the entire movement as absurd (DeJean 1991).

While writers relegated romance to the domain of the literary, secret history remained a genre that reflected on the sharpening cultural divide between history and fiction. Humanist tradition had worked to blur the divide between fact and fiction as much as to set out methods for instituting knowledge. It was the purpose of history to supply examples of past actions that would instruct readers by conveying the principles explanatory of human affairs, in effect providing a political science. Narratives, such as Daniel Defoe's fictions, that provided an experiential understanding of social manoeuvring and its political and economic interests merely extended that humanist objective into additional, private domains of human conduct (Mayer 1997). Some French writers, contemptuous of national history's overt biases, sought fresh truth in romances (DeJean 1991: 178–9). In fact, as the eighteenth century wore on, historical narratives enhanced their attempts to represent more comprehensive, social truth by expanding their accounts of each age's manners (Phillips 2000).

Social perceptions of women writers remained a material condition of women's history that complicated these matters of genre, however. Aristocratic women who published their writings risked compromising their social status (Goldsmith and Goodman 1995: 6). Secret history resembled court memoirs and amatory fiction and so took on some of the associations with impropriety that gathered around the making public of intimate, private conduct. Casting light on the legacy of women's history is one theme common to all these genres: the inexorable power of love. This theme carried ideological significance for French aristocratic society, for whom gallantry mediated political influence. Ambivalence towards female agency registered in contemporary fascination with scandalous works such as those by Marie Catherine Hortense Desjardins, better known by the appropriated name Madame de Villedieu. Already notorious for depicting women who actively sought, even initiated, sexual pleasure for themselves, Villedieu argued the actuality of women's amorous influence on the men most powerfully acting on the course of events (Lalande 2000). Even the 'sundry philosophers' Solon, Socrates and Julius Caesar could not transcend love's sway, according to her fictionalised *Les Amours des grands hommes* (1671).

The period's most influential philosopher of history, René Rapin, found it worthwhile in his *Instructions for History* (1680) to denounce the idea 'that Pericles occasioned the Peloponnesian War, upon the score of his Amours to the Curtezan Aspasia.... That Anthony lost the Empire, only to avoid losing Cleopatra. That Francis the First of France had no motive to bring an Army into *Italy*, but the fair Eyes of a Milanese Lady named Claricia.' At stake in this list of romance exaggerations is authoritative understanding of historical causality. According to Rapin's classical guidelines, historical narratives must represent their material in proportion to its hierarchical significance. The idea that love covertly influenced affairs of national importance opened the prospect of instability in both the order of actual events and the narrative accounts that established their significance.

The model of causality described by romance, amatory fiction and secret history led narrative into intimate spaces where private conversations and subtle erotic influences comprised and explained historical agency. Remarkably, the keeper of the king of France's library, Antoine Varillas, chose secret history as the vehicle for establishing conventions for history that represented precisely such spaces. In the Preface to his *Secret History of the Medicis* (1685), Varillas defended his method of finding truth in idiosyncratic details and person-to-person transactions under the inoffensive label 'anecdotography'. Still, while Varillas gave his historian-interpreter the authority to read intuitively, his account ignored the narratives in the print culture around him that represented women exerting influence in such intimate and seductive spaces. Verisimilitude in descriptions of elite conversation and intrigue among lords and ladies had a long pedigree among *petites histoires*, and at the turn of the century some women came to be called 'secret history' writers for their talents with this style of narrative, notably Charlotte-Rose de Caumont de la Force through her *Histoire secrète de Marie de Bourgogne* (1694), *Histoire secrète des amours d'Henri IV, roy de Castille* (1695), *Ane[c]dote Galante; ou Histoire secrète de Catherine de Bourbon* (1703). Marie Catherine d'Aulnoy in particular exploited the contiguity between narratives of fact and fiction when she presented her spritely writings for an upper-class audience as documentary witnesses to actual events in *Nouvelles ou memoires historiques* (1693) and memoirs of the courts of England, France and Spain. Her marketable reputation earned several false attributions of secret history and memoir to her authorship, including *Secret History of Mack-Beth* (1708). The term 'secret history' raised expectations for both French and English readers of participating in insider's knowledge about an exclusive, elite community.

The Procopian tradition of using secret history in order to injure the reputation of important political figures persisted in England among the rest of the early eighteenth-century innovations in print form. *The Secret History of Queen Zarah and the Zarazians* (1705) struck at Queen Anne's confidante, Sarah, Duchess of Marlborough, wife of the great general. According to this account, Sarah ruled England on behalf of the Whig party through her friendship with the queen. It was evidently not only the Whigs who could lay claim to moral high ground by writing *exposé*. Secret history came naturally enough to Tory writers as well, since their critiques of Whig corruption could continue the cryptographic *à clef* literary fashions shared by the out-of-power Royalist community during the middle seventeenth century (Potter 1989).

In the absence of evidence of authorship, *Queen Zarah* has been attributed to the Tory pamphleteer **Delarivier Manley**, since she produced the more famous roman à clef *Secret Memoirs and Manners ... from the New Atalantis* (1709). This probably false attribution served to consolidate the image of the woman writer wielding amorous narratives in the Tory cause whose choice of printed forms called attention provocatively to women's position in the conventions of public representation. In *The New Atalantis*, Manley has her narrator describe Manley herself in amorous terms. The body of the text and the body of the woman writer are placed in similar positions (Gallagher 1994). Manley transforms the reader's spectator view of public events by revealing the seductive and politically argumentative activity of her own discourse. Along the lines of current satiric tradition, her commentary furthermore implicates the surrounding print culture in its critical suggestion to view all representations as themselves politically interested fabrications. Manley also features herself in the storyline when she participates in an elaborate con game that combines the hoodwinking of members of parliament with an attempt to set up a stooge to claim an inheritance. Reminding readers that an individual like her writerly self could move among and intervene in the affairs of the leadership, Manley calls attention to the active agency of writing, and so creates contiguity across genres of literary works, including history, and across social worlds. A buzz of gossip followed this publication as readers sought the key to its allegory of high society.

At least equal notoriety surrounded **Eliza Haywood** as she sustained her writing career with constant shifts of strategy, including working the vein of secret history during the 1720s. Her *British Recluse* and *City Jilt*, both called secret histories, together with the collection *Secret Histories, Novels, and Poems* established her reputation for amatory fiction. In narratives that emphasised the problematics of female agency, Haywood forcefully represented to vulnerable young women the dangers of the world, often embodied in the desires and power of lords presented as typical. Beyond giving substance to women's interests in the book trade, these works could be seen as extending the humanist purposes for which history was written: history supplied to young readers examples from which principles for evaluating human affairs could be drawn. While national history taught future diplomats how to see the motives of their rivals and opponents in a larger context of events and political motives, Haywood's works suggested that the ability to read motive and to scrutinise conduct in person-to-person encounters was at least as crucial for young women to learn as for men. She did place her themes in more direct connection with national affairs in the longer *Secret History of the Court of Caramania* (1727), a work gossiping that the unpopular and Whig-leaning English king George I had made his choice of a queen in order to gain access to his mistress. At stake in many amatory narratives, including those by Haywood and Manley, remained the value of the young women in the network of social relationships as they were manoeuvred through plots and counterplots among the powerful (Saxton and Bocchicchio 2000).

The meaning of secret history for women writers venturing to publish their work during the early eighteenth century can be supplemented by considering the many anonymous secret histories used to present the characters of women to the reading public. Where Manley and Haywood worked to reinterpret the significance of relations between 'private' domains of women and public political affairs, their accounts of domestic relations often providing political allegory (Saxton and Bocchicchio 2000), the seductive power of scandalous women remained of dubious status as 'historical' material. As icons appearing in printed works, living women who figured in court intrigue or wielding worldly power also underwent the Whig critique of their illegitimate personal influence. The Procopian legacy of secret history was adapted to turn the reputations of individual women into a matter of public record. *The Secret History of an Old Shoe* (1734) pursued secret history's traditional attack on the 'great', relishing Robert Walpole's shady finances and his affair with Molly Skerrett. Complicating the status of these early eighteenth-century secret histories as printed works were their deliberate innovations. *Old Shoe* appeared entirely in verse, while *The Secret History of Betty Ireland* (1741) offered rogue biography. Secret histories even served as public notice of the status of individual women's social reputations. In *The Fair Concubine: or, The Secret History of the Beautiful Vanella* (1732), titillating moral indignation appeared at the expense of a woman moving in high society, whose name, Anne Vane, was barely disguised. The hounding tone with which this anonymous writer recounts her affairs with a series of noblemen, including John Hervey, Baron Hervey and Frederick Louis, Prince of Wales, and her current pregnancy attempts to fix public judgement of this woman and suggests the difficulty of controlling the forces of social ostracism. In an inversion of the scandal of *Vanella*, another writer published a secret history in the following year for the opposite purpose: to champion a woman who had lost her reputation and to glory over the probable discomfiture of the nobleman responsible. *The Secret History of Meadilla* reviewed a case in which a 'Count Onslorio' had despoiled the virtuous 'Meadilla', whose shepherdess name signifies her modest rank. This work reprints letters documenting the facts of the case, including the nobleman's arrangement of a false marriage.

Secret histories – the author of *Meadilla* calls them 'Histories' – left the domain of knowledge to be understood as public history amenable to reader's private habits of distinguishing among published representations claiming to be true. The genre remained a provocative category in part because these works challenged the legitimacy of other works, other knowledge. The knowledge in question included the authoritative category of historical causality, which these works explicitly expanded into the dimension of human interpersonal relations and affective influence. Historical reckoning can consequently consider secret histories as embodying the active agency of writers, including women writers, often deliberately intended as agency moving the 'public' through its sensations. Evidence that early modern observers could view secret history as action in itself comes from the fact that Delarivier Manley had stood trial for libel for writing the *New Atalantis* (Gallagher 1994: 88). Moreover, secret history's relation to public knowledge of history resembled women's position in history: carrying an air of ambiguity, impropriety and scandal in being in public at all. Readers grew accustomed to interpreting the variable category of secret history as signalling slippage in the conventions of printed form as well as arguing a position. In particular, it was the agency of reading itself, the mutual implication of subject with object made obvious by these works' sensational eroticism, that history stood to take into reckoning, requiring historians to be self-conscious about the affective structuring of their own narratives.

Secret history ultimately stands comparison with its Greek namesake, the anecdote. A word that conveys the most basic act of storytelling, an 'anecdote' is commonly told to relate an elementary fragment of experience not necessarily connected to any larger idea. The anecdote serves as a reminder of the small-scale acts of interpretation on which the larger orderings of historical knowledge have been built. Secret history offers a similar reminder that the significance and structure attributed to women's history depend on established practices that guide how fragments of knowledge are set into interpretive contexts and predetermine what those contexts are.

Judith A Dorn

References

Ballaster 1992; Beasley 1990; Bellany 2002; Bowers 1994; DeJean 1991; Gallagher 1994; Harth 1983; Lalande 2000; Mayer 1997; Patterson 1997; Phillips 2000; Potter 1989; Stone 1997.

Related essays

France; Great Britain; Memoir.

Simcox, Edith Jemima 1844–1901

English anthropologist, journalist and political activist. Only daughter of George and Jemima Price Simcox, Edith was born into an educated middle-class family and given a good education that included French, German, Latin and some Greek, Italian and Spanish. She also had a smattering of Dutch and Flemish. From her earliest years, Simcox was interested in social reform, particularly in regard to working conditions and in the improvement of the status of women. In 1875 she was one of the first female delegates admitted to a trade union conference in Glasgow, and subsequently became involved in a small co-operative shirt-and-collar manufacturing enterprise in Soho, which employed women under decent conditions in one of the worst of the sweated trades. A prolific writer of articles in the serious periodicals, Simcox also wrote a number of books. Her first, *Natural Law: An Essay in Ethics* (1877), was an analysis of the ethical underpinning of utilitarian and scientific rationalism. This was followed by her major historical work, *Primitive Civilizations: Outlines of the History of Ownership in Archaic Communities* (1894), a two-volume study that took 15 years to complete and combined an analysis of systems of ownership in ancient Egypt, Mesopotamia and China with a critique of the capitalist system of her own day. She lauded the ways in which earlier civilisations had incorporated notions of community and reciprocity evident in family life into other forms of social organisation – and argued that, contrary to much anthropological and historical discussion and to contemporary ideas of progress, women had enjoyed a higher status in these earlier civilisations than they did in nineteenth-century Britain.

Barbara Caine

Reference

Beer 1995.

Skelton, Isabel 1877–1956

Canadian historian. Born in Ottawa, eldest child of Mary Jane Holliday and Alexander Murphy. Encouraged by her parents Skelton studied first at Arnprior high school, then transferred to Alemonte high school. She proceeded to Queens University in Kingston in 1897, where she studied English and European History. She excelled academically receiving the magisteriate degree in 1901. She graduated with an MA and the medal for history. She married the political-economist Oscar Skelton in 1904 and together they had three children.

Literary criticism was the only viable option available to her during the early years of motherhood. During this time she completed studies of six late nineteenth-century British intellectuals, published by the Toronto Globe under the title, 'Rearguard of the Victorian Age'. She also produced 'Two Women Novelists', a provocative study of American and British novelists Edith Wharton and Mary [Mrs Humphry] Ward, and a portrait of British playwright and novelist John Galsworthy. In 1913 she published an analysis of the women's suffrage movement in Canada, 'Canadian Women and Suffrage'. Skelton's main concern in this article was to ascertain why Canadian women's achievements in this area were so slow to materialise. She highlighted the significance of a limited population, vast geography and, most importantly, the absence of the American tradition of natural rights. She was also critical of some of the contemporary arguments against woman suffrage. She argued that through the vote women could secure legislative 'justice in regard to property rights, marriage and divorce and the guardianship of their children'.

Skelton published three main historical works: *The Backwoodswoman: A Chronicle of Pioneer Home Life in Upper and Lower Canada* (1924); a biography of Thomas D'Arcy McGee, a father of Confederation and literary nationalist, *The Life of Thomas D'Arcy* McGee (1925); and *The Rev William Bell: Man Austere, Parson and Pioneer* (1947), a study of the settlement of eastern Ontario. Skelton was particularly interested in cultural history and *The Backwoodswoman* exemplifies her approach to this kind of history. *The Backwoodswoman* began as a volume on Canadian heroines commissioned by Robert Glasgow for his Chronicles of Canada series. Glasgow wanted Skelton to write a popular history of heroines. Skelton, however, was more interested in writing about ordinary women in the settlement process. In order to make her project manageable Skelton refined her focus to a regional study of central Canada. In writing about New France she anticipated some important historiographic concerns that would not be reconsidered until much later in the twentieth century. Skelton argued that women in New France were better off in terms of their social standing than was previously thought, and portrayed women less as a generalised category, viewing them in their cultural settings as part of social and ethnic groups. She also expressed concerns about other social groups historians had previously ignored.

Skelton did not consider herself a women's historian. She defined herself as 'a historian whose purpose was to reveal the past in a fuller amplitude than her male scholarly counterparts'. Recently Terry Crowley has published a joint-biographical study of Isabel and Oscar Skelton: *Marriage of Minds: Isabel and Oscar Skelton Reinventing Canada* (2003).

Sarah Howard

References

Crowley 1997, 2003.

Skinner, Constance Lindsay 1877–1939

Canadian author and historian. Born in Quesnel, British Columbia. Only child of Annie Lindsay and Robert James Skinner, agent for the Hudson's Bay fur trading company. As a child she lived on the frontier, at a fur trading post in the Peace River area. Skinner was tutored by her parents from their extensive library of British literature until aged 14 when she enrolled in a private school in Vancouver. Skinner began her writing career as a journalist for the Vancouver Evening World. Around the turn of the century she left for the United States where she worked as a journalist in California and Chicago. In 1912 she moved to New York City working as a freelance writer. During her lifetime Skinner published extensively across a wide range of genres: historical monographs, adult and juvenile fiction, poetry, plays, newspapers and magazine features and short stories, two of which were made into films.

Around 1918 Skinner became one of 'The New Historians', a group of 36 who wrote for Yale University Press' 50-volume Chronicles of America series. The goal of the series was to present all of American history in a lively, easily digestible series of short narratives intended for students and the general reader. Skinner was one of just three women who wrote for the series and one of 11 authors who wrote more than one volume: *Pioneers of the Old Southwest: A Chronicle of the Dark and Bloody Ground* (1919) and *Adventurers of Oregon: A Chronicle of the Fur Trade* (1920). Skinner wrote as an experiential historian. Her own upbringing on the Canadian frontier and her parents' experiences served as her most significant qualification and as a major source of historical material for her work. In 1919 she published a defence of experiential history in an essay, 'History as Literature: And the Individual Definition'. In it she argued that the writing of good American history required attention to the drama of human feelings, motives and inspirations, and a telling of the character, habits and customs, domestic and social, of the common people during significant periods.

Skinner's final project with Yale University Press was her co-authored *Adventures in the Wilderness* (1925) which was published as the first volume of a new pictorial history of the United States, *Pageant of America*. In 1933 she published a popular historical account of the fur trade, *Beaver, Kings and Cabins*. This was a sophisticated work that linked fictionalised autobiography with general history. Skinner drew on her memories, interviews with fur-traders and her own reading on the subject. In the mid-1930s Skinner became involved in a major new project that also drew on her reputation as an experiential historian, the Rivers of America series, which combined folklore, literature and history. The series was conceived by Skinner though she commissioned experts on each of the rivers to be featured in the series to write their own particular volumes. The first volume, Robert P Tristram Coffin's story of Maine's Kennebec River, had sold almost 12,000 copies by the time Skinner died. The series was a critical, commercial and popular success. In total more than 40 volumes were published. Much of Skinner's work related to the frontier and she was greatly influenced by Frederick Jackson Turner, particularly identifying with Turner's interest in geography as a key historical factor.

Throughout her writing career Skinner remained on the fringes of an emerging profession. She was the only woman, and one of very few non-academics, among a group of 15 invited to found a new Society of American Historians in 1939. She used insights gained from academic history to further her writing career. She built on her identification with the frontier to write in a style that was essentially international and interdisciplinary. She identified with Canada and the United States and believed that the writing of American history 'served both Canada and all Great and Greater Britain'. In her historical writing Skinner understood the importance of individual accounts and **oral traditions**, as well as the written record.

In all of her writing Skinner sought to recover the everyday experiences of women and men in mainstream society as well as those on the margins. Her historical writing anticipated later academic interest in social history. Although she did not consider women as historical subjects in their own right, the literary nature of her historical writing enabled Skinner to include a broader range of detail about the daily lives of the pioneers than might otherwise have been acceptable in the standard historical fare of the day. Subsequently, her histories include significant information about the roles and experiences of women pioneers. In the same vein, she acknowledges romance in her recording of marriages and refers to loving as well as practical relationships. Skinner's treatment of Aboriginal people and especially people of mixed race is particularly significant. Though she succumbed to romantic stereotypes she also endowed her Aboriginal characters with humanity, and she boldly raised issues of race and hybridity at a time when Canadians, along with most of the Western world, preferred to obscure them. This aspect of Skinner's writing as part of a 'strong, but long-hidden strand in Canadian history' is exemplified in the work of Sylvia Van Kirk and Adele Perry (See **Canada** essay).

In the year after her death the Women's National Book Association (WNBA), of which she had been a member, established the Constance Lindsay Skinner Award, a bronze plaque presented annually to a woman who made 'an outstanding contribution to the world of books'. As well as being an active member of the WNBA Skinner founded *The Bookwoman*, a WNBA publication, and was one of the first women to hold a major editorial post in the field of adult book publishing in the United States. A recent biography of Skinner has been published by Jean Barman: *Constance Lindsay Skinner: Writing on the Frontier (2002)*.

Sarah Howard

References

Barman 1997, 2002; Eastman 1980; *NAW* 1971.

Slavery

'Slavery is terrible for men; but it is far more terrible for women', declared the formerly enslaved woman, Harriet Jacobs/Linda Brent in *Incidents in the Life of a Slave Girl* (1861), her autobiographical narrative. Harriet's searing indictment of the particular burdens exacted by the 'peculiar institution' of slavery on enslaved women has long been, and continues to be, a persistent refrain in anti-slavery literary writings. Yet, until recently, traditional historiographies of slavery paid scant attention to the specific experiences of women, black or white, free or unfree within slave societies. From the 1970s onwards, feminist historians launched a provocative challenge to the masculinist bias of 'mainstream' or traditional history that privileged white and black males as the central historical actors, while marginalising white and black women's diverse historical roles. Feminist historians such as Gerda Lerner and Joan W Scott forcefully argued that the absence of women from historical narratives served to elide women's varied, complex and significant historical, social, economic, political and cultural roles (Lerner 1980; Scott 1988). The invisibility of women within the historiography of slavery cannot simply be explained away by the absence of women's writings on the subject. Since the critically acclaimed publication of Aphra Behn's *Oronokoo; or, The History of the Royal Slave* (1688), generally accepted as the first anti-slavery tract, black and white women have staked out their rights to publicly engage in the discourses of slavery. Behn's willingness to step beyond the conventional private sphere of English womanhood and to speak out against the iniquitous institution of slavery served to give inspiration to other women to utilise the literary canon as a means of inserting their voices into the debates surrounding slavery. Throughout the era of colonial slavery, women utilised diverse media and genres – novels, prose, poetry and personal narra-tives – to add their voices to debates on slavery and to contribute to its history. Yet, the sources on which the historiography of slavery rests are derived primarily from male-authored sources such as plantation journals and the accounts of slave traders.

Feminist historians of slavery and women's histories have plundered women's own writings in their efforts to better understand women's experiences and perspectives. Drawing on women's personal correspondence, journals, **auto/biographies**, prose and poetry, feminist historians have imaginatively reconstructed women's worlds in the slaveholding societies of the American south and the Caribbean. Subsequently, they have significantly enriched and transformed scholarly understanding of women's worlds within slaveholding societies. Less successful, however, has been the integration of black women's multiple experiences into the broader stream of women's history. Black feminist historians on both sides of the Atlantic have drawn attention to the marginalisation of black women's experiences within women's histories, underlining the problematics of privileging the analytical concept of gender over that of race. Published histories of the diverse experiences of free and enslaved black women remain sparse, prompting black feminist historians to insist on closer scholarly attention to the centrality of race in shaping black women's realities under slavery. Notwithstanding the well-known narratives of Harriet Jacobs and Ellen Craft, few enslaved black women left behind them personal testimonies, and in weaving together the fragmented strands of their lives, black feminist historians have of necessity relied heavily on white sources in order to recover enslaved and free black women's histories, an approach that has carried multiple methodological and epistemological problems.

Women and anti-slavery

Through their literary writings, white and black women strove to awaken the public conscience to the inhumanity of slavery. American, British and Caribbean women of all social classes, races, ethnicities and religious convictions offered profound critiques of an economic, political, cultural and social system that rested on the dehumanisation of Africans. From the seventeenth century, religion proved a decisive force in shaping women's anti-slavery discourses. Their religious convictions of a common equality of all humanity before God compelled Quaker women such as Alice Curwen, Elizabeth Hooton and Joan Vokins to publicly denounce the incompatibility of slavery with Christianity. Quaker missionaries such as Ann Austin, Betty Fox and Alice Curwen who visited the Caribbean slave colony of Barbados during the seventeenth century constructed a discourse of anti-slavery that was rooted within a shared sense of religious persecution. Many Quaker women who voiced opposition to the iniquitous system had observed slavery first hand; in the colonies, female Quaker missionaries observed, met with, and talked with the enslaved, and could therefore claim firm grounds on which to construct their critiques of the evils of slavery (Ferguson 1993). Until the eighteenth century, few other British women who entered the slavery debates could claim such authority. The travel accounts of the intrepid Scottish 'Lady of Quality', Janet Schaw throughout the Americas between the years 1774 and 1776 represents one of the few first-person, female-authored accounts of colonial slavery by an eighteenth-century British woman. While many of her contemporaries condemned slavery for its dehumanising effects, Schaw's encounters with enslaved Africans did little to awaken an anti-slavery consciousness. Indeed, Schaw's depictions of enslaved Africans as 'monkeys' reinforced contemporary racist beliefs. Her writings served not only to justify slavery as a civilising imperative, but, by extension, to rationalise and legitimise the violent mastery of slave-owners, for whom she reserved her sympathy. Schaw's acceptance of white racial superiority, her belief in the necessity for colonial rule, and her own privileged positioning within the colonial order prevented her attentiveness to the complex interplay between patriarchal colonial slavery and the subordination of white women and non-white peoples (Andrews 1923).

Women writers commonly deployed the metaphor of slavery to describe women's subordinate status. **Mary Wollstonecraft** drew on the iniquities of colonial slavery to compare the subordinate conditions of white women under patriarchy with that of enslaved peoples. *A Vindication of the Rights of Woman* (1792) highlighted the common dependence of enslaved peoples and white women upon a white male patriarch, and, in so doing, illuminated the conjoining of race and gender relations. It was perhaps this recognition of their shared subordination that inspired thousands of white women to throw their energies into the burgeoning anti-slavery campaigns for the abolition of the British slave trade in the latter decades of the eighteenth century. The anti-slavery campaign was perhaps the first large-scale social movement in which mass numbers of British women were involved, and within which women would become the dominant force. As members of mixed sex and female-only anti-slavery societies, British women organised boycotts of West Indian slave-produced products, circulated petitions, wrote and distributed tracts and pamphlets proselytising against the slave trade. These literary protests began with 'sentimental pleas for improvements in the conditions of the enslaved, and developed over time to more radical demands for freedom' (Ferguson 1992). Women's anti-slavery writings emerged as potent weapons in the campaigns against slavery. Through books, newspapers, pamphlets, poetry, published sermons and other forms of literature, female abolitionists spread their anti-slavery messages to the public. Both historians and literary critics generally concur that anti-slavery protests in prose and poetry were second only to the French Revolution in their impact on the social consciousness of British writers from 1780 to 1830 and the literary contributions of women to the anti-slavery campaigns were undoubtedly of significant import (Mellor 1996).

The poet and writer Hannah More rose to become the most influential female member of the Anti-Slavery Society, and her candid attack on the slave trade in 'Slavery, A Poem' (1788), in which she insisted on the common humanity of Africans with Europeans, came to be recognised as one of the most important anti-slavery verses of the period. More's other tracts, particularly *The Sorrows of Yamba; or, The Negro Woman's Lamentation* (1795), vivified the terrors of slavery through her imaginings of the horrors of the Atlantic passage, the forced sale and painful separation of families and the callous brutality of slave-owners (Hole 1996). More's protégé Ann Yearsley, also took up her pen on behalf of the enslaved, writing a much-celebrated 'Poem on the Inhumanity of the Slave

Trade' (1788). Yearsley, one of the few successful working-class writers in this period, also portrayed the suffering and inhumane treatment of enslaved Africans, and bitterly castigated those who used Christianity to defend the trade.

The 1773 publication of Poems on Various Subjects, Religious and Moral, by Phillis Wheatley, a young enslaved woman of Boston, brought its author international acclaim. Wheatley, recognised as the first African-American poet to be published, represented a restrained, though powerful racial consciousness in her subtle condemnations of slavery that foregrounded a tradition of black women's anti-slavery literary productions. Slavery, Wheatley insisted, was inimical to Christianity, and whites could not 'hope to find/Divine acceptance with th' Almighty mind' when 'they disgrace/And hold in bondage Afric's blameless race'. Wheatley's accomplishments – her demonstrable ability to master English and Latin and Greek languages in an age when enslaved peoples were forbidden to read and write – must be read as her own personal mode of resistance to the strictures of slavery. Though Wheatley died in poverty, abolitionists would reclaim her poetry in the struggle for emancipation.

From the 1830s onwards, the movement for the emancipation of enslaved African-Americans took on a decidedly more urgent, militant and political character. Black and white women launched sustained attacks on the 'peculiar institution', denouncing slavery as a moral and political evil, and successfully forced the issue onto national political agendas. *In An Appeal in Favor of That Class of Americans Called Africans* (1833) **Lydia Maria Child** made an impassioned plea for an end to slavery, using history to refute racist myths. Freeborn Maria W Stewart, believed to be the first American woman to lecture in public, articulated a nascent black feminist and abolitionist consciousness in her writings published in the *Liberator*, the organ of the abolitionist movement. In public lectures, Stewart urged black women to take on responsibility for the building of strong black families as the building block of a free black community. 'How long,' Stewart railed, 'shall the fair daughters of Africa be compelled to bury their talents beneath a load of iron pots and kettles?' Stewart's vision was far-reaching: abolitionist pressure would inevitably emancipate African-Americans, but they had to be prepared to take their rightful places as citizens in the new society. Stewart's writings and speeches combined a commitment to the liberation of blacks and women as a group.

Though they condemned slavery, many white female anti-slavery activists were less prescient in recognising the complex relationships between racism and sexism, a point reiterated forcefully by the ex-enslaved woman Sojourner Truth. Disturbed by the racism of many white female abolitionists at the 1851 women's rights convention in Akron, Ohio, Truth vociferously challenged them in her speech, 'Ain't I A Woman?'. Truth demanded that hostile white women recognise her personhood as a woman and in doing so, forced the realisation that discourses of slavery and racial equality also implicated gender. Truth foregrounded the still intractable problem of women's difference from each other, disrupting white feminists oft-claimed assertions of common sisterhood between women.

Shirley J Yee (1992) has documented the secondary status of black women and men within the abolitionist movement and, in particular, highlighted the problems endured by black women activists as they confronted the racial prejudices of white feminists who sought to distance the abolitionist cause from the women's rights movement. When in Fall River, Massachusetts, two white sisters

Elizabeth Chace and Lucy Lovell invited a few respectable black women to join the women's rights group, some white members threatened to quit in indignation, rather than allow black women membership of the society. Few white feminists-abolitionists made the connections between racial slavery and white female subordination as perceptively as did Sarah and Angelina Grimke. The efforts of these white abolitionist sisters, daughters of a South Carolina slaveholding family, to synthesise the nexus of gender and race were unprecedented among white women abolitionists. In 1836, Angelina wrote *An Appeal to the Christian Women of the South* in which she encouraged southern white women to join the abolitionist movement. She argued that slavery was equally destructive of white womanhood, for the widespread sexual exploitation of black women undermined the strength of the white family. In *Letters to Catharine Beecher in Reply to an Essay on Slavery and Abolitionism Addressed to A. E. Grimke* (1837), Angelina equated woman's subordination to slavery, and staunchly defended both abolitionism and their right to publicly speak out on behalf of that cause. In 1838, Sarah published *Letters on the Equality of the Sexes and the Condition of Women*, the first woman's rights pamphlet in the United States, in which she too linked the rights of enslaved peoples to the rights of women. Deploying liberal rhetoric of natural rights, the Grimke sisters argued that the fight for women's rights and the fight for abolition both supported human rights (Lerner 1967). Following their lead, Ernestine Rose, a Jewish women's rights advocate of the 1850s pointed out similarities between slaves and white wives: a white wife who attempted to leave an abusive husband was in exactly the same legal position as a fugitive slave. Like the slave, she had no rights over her children, could not testify against her husband, serve on juries, vote or hold public office (Suhl 1990). Many white feminists, however, considered the women's question unrelated to abolitionism, insisting that the struggle for women's rights would be weakened by any connection between the two groups. As Rosalyn Terborg-Penn (1981) has argued, discrimination against Afro-American women reformers was the rule rather than the exception within the women's rights movement from the 1830s to the 1920s. Black feminist abolitionists therefore found themselves caught between the sexism of the anti-slavery movement on one hand and the racism of the white women's movement on the other. The 1852 publication of Harriet Beecher Stowe's *Uncle Tom's Cabin*, a fictionalised account of enslaved experiences, has often been described as the most influential of American anti-slavery texts. Angered by the passage of the 1850 Fugitive Slave Law which punished runaway slaves and those who aided them, Stowe sought to portray the immorality and iniquity of 'the institution of slavery just as it existed'. Deploying the conventions of popular nineteenth-century sentimental novels, *Uncle Tom's Cabin* told the story of an enslaved family's suffering and tribulations under the peculiar institution. While evoking Northern sympathy for the enslaved, the novel inflamed southern pro-slavery ideologues and provoked angry debate and partisan acrimony across the Mason-Dixon line, prompting Abraham Lincoln's description of Stowe as 'the little woman who made this great war'.

Narratives of enslaved peoples

Historians of slavery acknowledge the significant influence of *Uncle Tom's Cabin* to American abolitionism, yet they have also drawn attention to its damaging stereotypical representations of black peoples. It was these stereotypes of blacks as 'childlike' and 'immoral' that the narratives of formerly enslaved peoples sought to counter as a response to pro-slavery advocates who represented plantation slavery as a pastoral idyll.

The eloquent, articulate and impassioned voices of former slaves relating their experiences powerfully contradicted such claims. In the very act of writing, ex-slave narrators sent a powerful message to slave-owners that though legislation might prohibit enslaved people's right to learn to read and write, they were willing to risk punishment and even death to acquire skills that could bring them to eventual freedom. The acquisition of literacy skills then represented a powerful mode of enslaved resistance and the act of publication of a narrative of a literate slave such as Harriet Jacobs made evident to the world the enslaved individual's will to resist. Whether self-penned or dictated to an amanuensis, slave narratives rudely dispelled the pro-slavery paternalistic representations of plantation life, skilfully depicting instead both the abject misery that slavery inflicted on enslaved peoples and the inhumanity and depravity of slave-owners as they struggled to impose their mastery. In taking up the pen to write their own stories, slave narrators undermined the myth of blacks as ignorant and unintelligent beings, revealing instead their mastery of language. Unlike the fictionalised characters of *Uncle Tom's Cabin*, these were real people, speaking with authoritative experience of the horrors from which they had escaped. Such narratives constituted an alternative history of slavery written from the perspective of the enslaved.

An essential element of the transatlantic anti-slavery and abolitionist movements, the narratives of ex-slaves such as Harriet Jacobs, Frederick Douglass, Ellen and William Craft and Mary Prince forced the British and American public to confront the full extent of the brutalities of slavery while simultaneously countering pro-slavery propaganda. Often drawing on biblical imagery, the rhetoric of abolitionism, the traditions of the captivity narrative and the spiritual autobiography, these narratives vividly painted for northern white middle-class readers the abjection under which millions of enslaved peoples were forced to exist on both sides of the Atlantic. Nearly a hundred slave narratives were published as books or pamphlets between 1760 and 1865, most of these written by formerly enslaved people in the United States.

Few among the enslaved of the Caribbean left behind personal testimonies of their experiences of slavery. *The History of Mary Prince* (1834) remains still the sole known surviving slave testimony to have emerged from the Caribbean. Bermuda-born Mary Prince is remembered not only as the first black British woman to escape bondage, but also as the first formerly enslaved woman of the English-speaking Caribbean to publish a first-person account of the enslaved experience. Born into slavery, Prince's life was spent with a succession of indifferent or cruel owners. While still a young girl, Prince was sold at auction, a commercial transaction that resulted in the separation of her family. In a heart-rending passage describing her sale, Mary revealed the abject powerlessness of the enslaved and in particular, the absolute denial of enslaved women's rights to motherhood. Her distraught mother was forced to collude in her children's sale and Mary recalled her mother's desperate attempts to arrange her daughters' clothing and bodies in such a manner as to distract attention away from their burgeoning sexuality. On the auction block, Mary and her sisters were subjected to the fondling of strange men who examined them as though they were cattle. Prince would later identify her sale as the moment of coming to consciousness of herself as an enslaved person, and as a commodity that could be bought, sold, mortgaged, leased or hired out. Following the sale, Prince came to experience the systematic exploitation and degradation shared by enslaved Africans. She was forced to labour for long hours without remuneration or gratitude. Daily she bore witness to the unrestrained brutality of owners as they tortured and murdered enslaved men, women and children, without fear of legal retribution. Yet, Prince retained a passionate belief in her rights to the very same freedom enjoyed by her owners and set about pursuing strategies that would eventually secure her own survival and autonomy. She carefully secreted away income from the sale of ground provisions towards her manumission fund, forged allegiances with sympathetic whites and in an outright assertion of her own sexual agency, married Daniel James, a free black man, without first obtaining the necessary approbation of her owners. In slave societies, legal matrimony remained the prerogative of whites and Prince's marriage represented the assertion of her autonomous self, her right to choose a partner of her own liking, the right to enjoy her own sexuality. Mary Prince's efforts to secure freedom finally came in 1828, when she accompanied her owners Mr and Mrs Woods on a visit to England. In London, after suffering further abuse, Mary left their dwelling and made her way to the offices of the Anti-Slavery Society. Moved by her story, the Society provided her with accommodation and domestic work and with the assistance of an amanuensis, helped Prince to publish her autobiography.

Mary's **memoirs** represent a direct assault on the institution of slavery, but above all, the *History* bears testimony to how the powerless may, with tenacity, courage and strength, become the instruments of their own freedom. Prince used her *History* to reveal to the British public the brutal and dehumanising conditions under which millions of enslaved Africans forcibly laboured on Caribbean plantations. In the act of writing her History, Mary Prince literally wrote her way to the freedom she regarded as her natural right. But the *History* is not simply Mary's individual story; it is a polemic against slavery, and a history of all voiceless enslaved peoples, bearing testimony to their resilience, their desire for freedom and their persistent will to survive in the face of great inhumanity and brutality.

Fictionalised voices

Autobiographical narratives represented the most common genre of formerly enslaved people's literary writings. Many enslaved women and men also found expression through poetry, while speaking circuits gave voice to many African-American women such as Maria Stewart and Sojourner Truth. Despite the increasing popularity of the novel as literary form during the nineteenth century, African-Americans were slower to adopt the novel as a source of protest and a site to record their history. Indeed, until the recent discovery of a hand-written manuscript dating from the 1850s, and purporting to be the autobiographical novel of Hannah Crafts, it was widely believed that only one African-American woman had published a novel before the 1890s. *The Bondswoman's Narrative*, allegedly written by Hannah Crafts, represents the only novel known to have been penned by a fugitive slave woman, and, if authentic, would also be the first novel known to have been written by an African-American woman. In *The Bondswoman's Narrative*, Crafts relates the tale of a young, enslaved self-taught mulatto woman, whose quest for freedom eventually leads her to 'pass' for white and thus instigating a literary tradition addressing racial ambiguity among black writers. Drawing on diverse literary genres of the nineteenth century, Crafts scripted a compelling history of slavery from the perspective of the enslaved. Going against the conventions of the slave narratives, Crafts represented the enslaved community as heterogeneous, stratified by occupation and skin colour, thus giving to enslaved peoples multi-layered and complex identities. Moreover, unlike the discrete veil drawn over the sexual lives of the enslaved by other slave narrators, Crafts gave to the enslaved a sense of sexual agency. Going against the grain of abolitionists who promoted legal marriage among the enslaved, Crafts argued against such unions on the grounds that children born to enslaved parents would inherit their parents' unfree status. Crafts also drew attention to the peculiarly ambiguously racialised position and status of the mulatto, a theme further explored by Harriet Wilson in *Our Nig* (1859), an autobiographical novel, which, until the discovery of Craft's manuscript, was believed to be the first novel penned by an African-American female. In *Our Nig,* Wilson related the trials and mistreatment of a young African-American mulatto woman, Frado, an indentured servant in the household of a white Massachusetts family. Though legally 'free', Frado is treated by her employers as inhumanely as are enslaved peoples in the south and the tale narrates her quest for economic security for herself and her son.

Fusing two dominant literary modes of the nineteenth century – the sentimental novel and the slave narrative – Wilson created the novelised autobiography in order to confront complacent Northerners with the harsh realities of life facing free African-Americans in their midst. In exposing the structural racism of the North, Wilson highlighted the continuing inequalities endured by free blacks who were denied full political and legal equality.

Gender and race in women's slave histories

The historiography of slavery has benefited immeasurably from the integration of gender as an analytical category, for it has deepened understanding both of the centrality of gender in shaping slave societies and the importance of slavery in shaping gender relations. As historians now acknowledge, slavery was not a gender-neutral process and beliefs about gender underpinned the nature of social relations between individuals in slave societies. Gender impacted on the lives of every individual, whether free or unfree, white or black, male or female, elite or poor, in profoundly different ways. Ann Firor Scott's *The Southern Lady* (1970) raised the veil on the distinctive experiences of slaveholding white women in the American south, arguing that the prevailing image of passive and submissive, pampered and leisured was a myth derived from the slave-holding patriarch's desire to establish and maintain control over all his subjects. White women, along with slaves, were expected to know their subordinated place and defer to the head of the household. As Scott argued, any tendency on the part of any of the members of the system to assert themselves against the master threatened the whole and therefore slavery itself. Thus, Scott argued that the patriarchal imperative to maintain the institution of slavery rested on the subordination of white women. Catherine Clinton's *Plantation Mistress* (1982) also gave analytical privilege to elite southern white women, arguing that their identity and material reality was indelibly shaped by slavery and patriarchy. Clinton insisted that slavery be understood not merely as an economic mode of organisation underpinned by the forced extraction of the unfree labour of enslaved Africans, but as an overarching system of sexual and social control in which patriarchal planters asserted dominance and control over the social and sexual freedoms of white women and enslaved peoples alike. Clinton highlighted the resultant damage wrought on enslaved women and their families, as planters exercised their masterly prerogatives expressed through their sexual abuse and exploitation of enslaved women.

Feminist investigations of slave societies through the lens of gender have helped to explicate more clearly the complex social positioning of white women, but white women's gendered identity cannot be understood in isolation from their racialised identities. White women were always first and foremost white women. Their place in the social hierarchies of the plantation society was determined, not solely or even primarily by their gender, but by their identity as white people, in societies that promulgated white supremacist ideologies. In *Within the Plantation Household* (1988) Elizabeth Fox-Genovese highlights the intersection of gender, race and class as structural factors in the shaping of women's lives. Fox-Genovese argues that white '[w]omen contributed to the hegemony of the slave-holding class, even though [white] men normally figured as its primary spokesmen . . . Slave-holding women, who never figured as merely passive victims of male dominance, benefited from their membership in a ruling class' (1988: 44). Racial ideologies and practices always intervened to complicate relations between women. Slave-owning women owed allegiance not to their slaves – however much they might empathise with their conditions, but to their race and class. Moreover, Fox-Genovese diluted the authority of the master, offering instead a narrative that revealed white slave-owning women not as mere passive bystanders or victims of slavery, but as active slave-owning agents, exercising power and control over their slaves. Masters might wield ultimate authority over the plantation, but on a daily level, the domestic arrangements of the plantation Big House were more likely to bring female slaves into greater contact with their mistresses, and often with violent results.

Contemporary feminists have argued that the fact of women's shared gender identity and their common subordination to patriarchal authority should provide a common ground for understanding and solidarity between women. A nuanced reading of narratives by formerly enslaved women such as Mary Prince and Harriet Jacobs, however, abruptly disrupts and problematises the universalist category of woman, instead highlighting the cruciality of race in structuring women's multiple experiences and the relations between different groups of women, especially in racially ordered societies, where white women's shared racial identity with white males places them in privileged positions over black 'others'. In describing the tense relationships that flowed between mistress and slave, Mary Prince's narrative revealed the complicity of white women within the institution of colonial slavery. Mary did not experience white women as passive bystanders or victims of slavery, but as active participants in a system that denied her humanity. Prince revealed the equal capacity of mistresses to inflict cruel and sadistic punishments on their slaves. Yet Prince was not ignorant of the iniquitous patriarchal gender order that deprived white women of meaningful social and political power. Prince understood, however, that ownership and management of slaves conferred on white women the ability to exercise a perverse power over the bodies of black men and women. Some among her mistresses were 'kindly', but Mary was in no doubt that their economic, social and racialised privileges were derived from her own racialised subordination.

Lucille Mathurin Mair (1974) not only challenged the prevailing androcentrism of traditional Caribbean historiography, but also highlighted the implicit racism of white women and their implications within racialised hierarchies. In her pioneering and reconstructive study of enslaved women's experiences of slavery in the Caribbean colonial world, Mair highlighted the historical marginalisation of enslaved women while also bringing to the fore the multiple experiences of black, coloured and white women in

Jamaican colonial society, clarifying the significance of race and colour as well as gender in shaping women's experiences of slavery. In slave society, Mair argued, 'black women produced, coloured women served and white women consumed'. In asserting the primacy of racial difference in shaping the contours of women's lives, Mair's typology disrupted universalist and essentialist categorisation of a singular 'woman', revealing the gendered and racialised fragmentation of Caribbean womanhood. Barbara Bush (1981), however, sought to identify the common ground on which white and black Caribbean women stood. Turning her attention to the social positioning of white Caribbean women, Bush insisted that despite the racially derived privileges of white woman, all women, irrespective of race or status, were in the final analysis subordinated to white male patriarchy. However, Bush conceded that as members of the dominant white social group, white women held and wielded power over all black people. Black feminist historians have insisted that gender represents only one category of historical analysis, for as **Anna Julia Cooper** in *A Voice from the South* (1892) noted, black women confront both a 'woman question and a race question'. Under slavery black women were doubly oppressed: as economic producers, but also endured widespread sexual abuse and exploitation (Giddings 1984). Sexual abuse of black women was central to southern and Caribbean slave societies, where in a peculiar inversion of British inheritance principles, individual legal status derived from the mother's status. Enslaved black women were thus the literal reproducers of unfreedom, since their children inherited their status. Freedom resided solely in the body of the white women, and hence, controlling the sexuality of free white and unfree black women became a patriarchal imperative. Scholars of Caribbean women's histories have similarly revealed the plantocracy's damaging interference in the family lives of the enslaved, as planters sought to manipulate the sexuality of black and white women. On both sides of the Atlantic, negative constructions of black women as lascivious 'hot constitution'd ladies' served to justify their sexual abuse, but conversely, it was this gender-specific form of exploitation that shaped enslaved women's specific modes of resistance to enslavement. Paula Giddings (1984) has documented efforts by enslaved women to resist the imposition of racially informed stereotypes of black women as sexually licentious beings and who refused to perform their most essential role – the reproduction of the enslaved population by natural increase (Hine 1986; Higginbotham 1989).

The disruption of the familial lives of enslaved peoples forms a substantial and recurrent theme within American and Caribbean slave historiographies. Earlier scholarship had argued that slavery destroyed the ability of enslaved Africans to sustain stable family life, and created family households that were characteristically fragile and matrifocal. Recent reappraisals of enslaved family life in the slave societies of the Americas has severely undermined this paradigm, arguing instead that in the face of adversity, enslaved peoples managed to sustain strong family units. Marietta Morrisey (1991) argued that women's integration into Caribbean plantation agricultural production did not preclude the formation of strong nuclear families in some plantation societies. Barbara Bush (1990) similarly highlighted the tenacity of enslaved peoples in maintaining durable familial and kinship structures in the face of the plantocracy's disrespect for the sanctity of enslaved marital and familial relationships. Bush argued that the extended family, rather than the western nuclear model, characterised enslaved Caribbean people's family formations, and further argued that though matrifocal in nature, this did not presuppose women's familial dominance. Deborah Gray White's groundbreaking *Ain't I a Woman: Female Slaves in the Plantation South* (1985) vigorously refuted some enduring myths surrounding black womanhood under slavery and freedom. White's study offered a sterling challenge to the traditional historiography of slavery that privileged enslaved male experience and status while peripheralising complex roles of enslaved women in sustaining their community. White examined multiple aspects of enslaved women's realities – their daily lives, occupations, familial roles and female networks, and, in so doing, eroded stereotypes of black womanhood as sexualised Jezebels and of the mammy who identified more with 'her' white family than with the enslaved community. Further, White drew attention to the articulations of gender and race and illuminated the significance of women's role to the survival of the black family. Though constrained by the double burdens of racism and sexism, enslaved women assumed pivotal roles within their families and communities that were often at variance with accepted gendered roles for white women. Their capacity to forge networks of supportive female friendships enabled enslaved women to foster a strong sense of individual and group identity that ultimately enabled them to withstand and survive the adversities of slavery. Jacqueline Jones (1985) similarly argued that throughout slavery and into freedom, African-American women shouldered the double burdens of racism and sexism as they struggled to ensure their families' survival. Jones, however, suggested that black women's strong sense of gender identity derived not primarily from their networks of female friends, but from their relationships with black males. By reappraising the impact of slavery on enslaved family life through the lens of gender and race, black feminist historians have disrupted previous analyses of enslaved family life. The character of enslaved families was shaped as they adapted to their conditions, and to some extent, by the influence of white cultural and religious values. Most enslaved peoples retained and shared some elements of their African heritage, which laid great stress on the importance of kinship relations.

Through postcolonial eyes: Toni Morrison's Beloved

Slavery continues to exert a powerful hold on the literary and theoretical imaginations of contemporary writers. Slavery's abiding impact on the psychic consciousness of formerly enslaved peoples and their status in the post-slavery world forms a dominant thread within **postcolonial** literature. Mindful of Edward Said's dictum that enslaved peoples 'speak through and by virtue of the European' postcolonial writers have sought to uncover the authentic submerged voices of the formerly enslaved (see **Orientalism** essay).

Continually defined by debilitating colonising and oppressive discourses that objectified blacks as commodities, formerly enslaved peoples remain unable to develop a self-empowered subjectivity, even though no longer physically confined by the iron shackles of enslavement. It is this search for self-actualisation that is at the heart of Toni Morrison's novel *Beloved* (1994) which narrates Sethe's struggles to escape first slavery and in post-Civil War America, to escape her slave past. Morrison, however, insists that slavery cannot be relegated to 'past history' for the past remains alive in the present. Sethe's struggles to disremember the horrors of slavery cannot be realised, for years after her legal emancipation, Sethe is haunted by the angry ghost of Beloved, her infant daughter, murdered by Sethe herself, rather than countenance her child's enslavement. Beloved's presence forces Sethe to construct her 'rememory' of the past, to face up to her deeds, and only when she has done so, is Sethe finally freed from the psychological traumas of the past.

Beloved, then, insists that we attend not only to the physical abuse perpetrated against the enslaved, but that we recognise the terrible psychological trauma inflicted on the enslaved, and the continuing repercussions on African-Americans who in post-slavery/postcolonial society continue to carry with them the internalised discourses of their subjective inferiorities. Slavery represents 'unfinished business', for its powerful discourses remain potent in shaping not only African-American realities, but white America's attitudes and relationships with and towards black Americans. Self-actualisation, the development of subjectivity, can be realised for Sethe only outside the limits of a colonial discourse and within a collectively defined alternate discourse, found within the black community to which she flees. In this new adopted community, Sethe, her daughter Denver and the community damaged by the colonising terrors of slavery must recognise their acceptance of internalised ideologies of oppression before they may acquire the subjectivity that will set both individual and community free (Elliot 2000). Hence, Morrison's novel calls for both a collective decolonisation and a collective 'rememory' before America – and by extension all former colonising societies and colonised people's societies – can truly be set free from the legacies of their slave pasts.

Cecily Jones

References

Andrews 1923; Beckles 1989, 1998; Bush 1981, 1990; Clinton 1982; Elliot 2000; Ferguson 1992, 1993, 1997; Fox-Genovese 1988; Gates 1990; Giddings 1984; Gray White 1985; Higginbotham 1989; Hine 1986; Hole 1996; Jones 1985; Lerner 1967, 1980; Mair 1974; Mellor 1996; Midgley 1995; Morrisey 1990, 1991; Morton 1996; Scott 1970, 1988; Suhl 1990; Terborg-Penn 1981; Yee 1992; Yellin 1987.

Related essays

Great Britain; Historical Fiction; Orientalism; Postcolonial women's writings; Romantic women's writings; USA.

Spruill, Julia Cherry 1899–1986

American historian of women. Born in Rocky Mount, North Carolina. Married economist Croydon Spruill in 1922. Throughout her life Spruill's academic writing was secondary to her family duties. She defined herself as a 'housewife who does a little writing and research in history'. Although primarily occupied with the social responsibilities associated with her husband's position as Dean at the University of North Carolina, her interest in the history of women remained strong even when she had no time for research and writing. She was vice president of two historical societies and president of the University Women's Club as well as of the local chapter of the American Association of University Women.

Spruill published only one book, *Women's Life and Work in the Southern Colonies* (1938), a study of the daily lives and status of women in the English colonies of the South, funded by a grant from the Institute for Research in the Social Sciences. Although Spruill's original plan had been to make a study of the changing attitudes towards women in the South, she changed the focus of her work 'to find out as much as possible about the everyday life of women'. Spruill's work proved ground-breaking because it focused on the lives of ordinary women, rather than **women worthies**, although she did concentrate almost exclusively on the upper classes and did not attempt to include the African-American experience on its own terms. The book is considered a classic in early American social history. It was unique not only for its focus on women and their families, but also for the sources consulted. She drew almost entirely on primary sources, including colonial newspapers, court records and other legal documents, housekeeping manuals, diaries, letters and other manuscript materials to reconstruct colonial society. It took her a decade to complete the research for the book. Her method of writing was new. She used the words of individuals to tell the story of the past and this methodology enabled her to demonstrate the impact of otherwise elusive and unquantifiable social attitudes on colonial society. She gained most of her insight into social attitudes about women's roles in colonial southern society through the writings of women themselves. Such documents provided Spruill with a deeper layer of historical understanding, as women's **private writing** revealed that the stigma placed on women's sexual transgressions often overrode any legal sanctions against them. This fact was not borne out in court decrees but was confirmed in the 'ladies' morality books' that enabled Spruill to read between the lines of legal records.

Women's Life and Work in the Southern Colonies received much critical acclaim, although, Spruill would never have earned a reputation outside the South without the sponsorship of Harvard professor Arthur Schlesinger, and even with his commendation, her research was virtually ignored by academics until social historians reinvigorated interest in it in the early 1970s.

Sarah Howard

References

Des Jardins 2003; Hall & Scott 1987; Scott 1993.

Major work

Spruill, Julia Cherry, *Women's Life and Work in the Southern Colonies* (New York: W W Norton & Company, 1972).

Staël, Germaine de 1766–1817

French novelist, salonnière, historian. The daughter of Jacques Necker, one-time finance minister of Louis XVI, and Suzanne, salonnière, Anne Louise Germaine Necker was born in Paris. Educated at home, she absorbed early the intellectual and political atmosphere of her mother's salon. In 1786 she married Baron Stael-Holstein, a Swedish diplomat, in what was accepted by both as a marriage of convenience: it enabled him to pay his gambling debts and assisted his political career, while she acquired a title and, later, some measure of protection as the wife of a foreign diplomat. They had one daughter, who survived only 18 months, and separated in the early 1790s. Staël had felt some initial enthusiasm for the French revolution in 1789, but it soon waned and her efforts to establish a constitutional monarchy, as well as her title as baroness, made it impossible for her to remain in France after 1792. She returned to Paris under the Directory, and established a salon that became an influential political and intellectual centre. In 1794, she met Benjamin Constant, with whom she worked politically as they both attempted to keep alive the liberal ideals of 1789. Initially, both Staël and Constant welcomed Napoleon when he returned from Italy in 1797, regarding him as the saviour of the republic. When he became First Consul in 1800, however, Staël began to oppose him, speaking out so strongly that in 1803, Bonaparte exiled her from Paris. Mme de Staël retired to her estate at Coppet, on the Lake of Geneva, where she wrote and entertained a brilliant circle (see **Revolution** essay).

Madame de Staël's historical concerns are evident in her novels, her discussions of contemporary literature and society, and in her essays. Her most important novel in this regard is *Corinne* (1807), an immensely popular and influential work in its time. Corinne was the first fictional heroine depicted as a woman of genius, and one who was unapologetic about living for her art. The novel's direct influence can be traced through the works of George Sand, George Eliot, Elizabeth Barrett Browning, Charlotte Bronte, Harriet Beecher Stowe and Willa Cather. Titled *Corinne or Italy*, it encompassed the history of the Italian peninsula, a region with a glorious past that, in de Staël's view, also promised future greatness as a nation. Access to this past, which was necessary if the great future was to be possible, however, came only through imagination. Staël depicts the character of Corinne as having the kind of historical sensibility that allowed her to feel and connect with this past. Staël herself felt she had a particular genius for History, *albeit* a kind of history that depended on inspiration and emotion, rather than facts and critical analysis.

Of greater and longer lasting importance was Staël's comparative approach to the history of literature and to the understanding of German romanticism. Her pioneering study *De la littérature considérée dans ses rapports avec les institutions sociales* (*On Literature Considered in Its Relationship to Social Institutions*, 1800) relates the literatures of France, Italy and Germany to their particular religions, customs, governments, and was very important in establishing new ways of thinking both about the national foundations of literature, and more broadly about national differences (see **Nation** essay). Drawing on Montesquieu's ideas about the significance of climate for emotion and outlook, Staël sought to differentiate between southern and northern temperaments, literatures and cultures. This approach was extended in *De l'Allemagne* (*Germany*, 1810), which explored German Romanticism, comparing it favourably with contemporary French literature and culture and making it much more widely understood throughout Europe and the United States.

For many years, Staël's attention was dominated by Napoleon. His opposition and decision to exile her from Paris in 1803 both increased her hostility towards him and focussed her attention on a form of European liberalism that was absent from France. Some critics argue that all her books written after 1800 bear the mark, implicitly or explicitly, of her defiance of Napoleon. Her most direct accounts of this clash appear in her posthumously published, *Considerations on the French Revolution* (1818), and in her unfinished memoirs *Ten Years of Exile* (1918). The first of these presents the post-Revolutionary excesses, the Terror and Napoleon's despotism as necessary evils in the fulfilment of the Revolution's underlying ideals, a novel historical view at that time. The latter is an account of her years in exile at her family estate Coppet outside Geneva and of her desperate attempt to reach the safety of England via Vienna, Kiev, Moscow, St Petersburg and Sweden, skirting Napoleon's empire, always just a few weeks ahead of the Grande Armée.

Barbara Caine

References

Gutwirth *et al.* 1991; Smith 1998.

Stanton, Elizabeth Cady 1815–1902

United States women's rights leader, writer, historian. Born in Johnstown, New York, daughter of Margaret Livingston and lawyer, state assemblyman and congressman, Daniel Cady. Educated at the Johnstown Academy and Emma Willard's

Troy Female Seminary, and informally by her father and her abolitionist cousin Gerrit Smith. Married anti-slavery agent Henry Stanton in 1840 and attended the World's Anti-Slavery Convention, London, where she met Lucretia Mott. Seven children between 1842 and 1859. From 1841 to 1862 lived in Johnstown, Albany, Boston and Seneca Falls, New York, till 1869 in Brooklyn and New York City, and from 1870 in Tenafly, New Jersey, with long periods of residence in England and Paris between 1882 and 1891.

As a young housewife, Stanton initiated the call for a woman's rights convention held in July 1848 at Seneca Falls, where she was then living. Attended largely by dissident anti-slavery Quakers, the convention issued a Declaration of Sentiments and resolutions attacking the English common law principle that a woman lost her identity and rights when she married, and arguing that the principles of the American Revolution required an end to government without women's consent. In articles and public letters published in the antebellum anti-slavery and women's press Stanton used her considerable intellectual skills to advocate women's autonomy in dress and occupation, their right to vote, married women's right to a separate legal identity, their right to control sexual access and child bearing and their right to divorce.

In 1852 Stanton formed the Woman's New York State Temperance Society with her lifelong partner in reform, **Susan B Anthony**, whom she met in 1850. In their first campaign to change laws regarding women in 1854 they established their *modus vivendi*, with Anthony circulating petitions and tracts, organising meetings and lobbying the legislature, and Stanton crafting the arguments on her kitchen table surrounded by a growing family. In 1863, with the establishment of the Women's Loyal National League to lobby for a constitutional amendment to end slavery, she and Anthony turned their attention to national politics. In 1869 they established the National Woman Suffrage Association (NWSA), which lobbied for a national amendment for woman suffrage, while Lucy Stone's American Woman Suffrage Association (AWSA) focused on state amendments. Stanton was president of the NWSA and its successor, the National American Woman Suffrage Association, which merged the two.

Lucretia Mott had frequently urged Stanton to write a history of the woman's movement. The events of the Centennial convinced her that someone must document their campaign. In the fall of 1876 she signed partnership papers with Anthony and their colleague **Matilda Joslyn Gage** 'for the purpose of preparing and editing a history of the woman suffrage movement'. Stanton and Gage would 'write, collect, select and arrange material' and Anthony would 'secure publication'. In the fall of 1880 they gathered to assemble the documents, personal reminiscences, biographical sketches, photographs, state reports, speeches and resolutions, excerpts from the Congressional Record, newspaper clippings they had solicited from individuals and state organisations and dredged from their own files. Stanton enjoyed the work immensely, writing much of the material. Although they initially envisaged a one-volume illustrated general history of 600–800 pages, the first volume alone of the *History of Woman Suffrage*, which took them only to 1860, was 878 pages. Volume Two, covering 1861–1876, was published in May 1882. By the time they published Volume Three (1886), covering 1877–1885, Gage had dropped out and they were ready to consign the work to younger hands. Volume Four (1902), covering 1883–1900, was begun half-heartedly by Anthony and Stanton in 1891 and finally completed by Anthony's young housemate Ida Husted Harper. After Anthony's death in 1906 Harper completed the *History* up to ratification with Volumes Five and Six (1922). These final three volumes are essentially the reports on legislation gathered at the end of each congressional term suggested by Stanton and Anthony in their 1886 preface. But the first three volumes contain, amongst much other useful material, 'Reminiscences' by Stanton of her early partnership with Anthony that provide important accounts of female friendship and child rearing along with a history of the movement. Aware of possible problems in being 'historians of a reform in which we have been among the chief actors', Stanton points out for the authors that 'history written from a subjective point of view' gets 'nearer the soul of the subject'.

Stanton was a prodigious thinker and writer. Between 1881 and her death she published five books and hundreds of articles as well as delivering several major speeches a year. In the 1890s she published her two-volume *Woman's Bible* (1895, 1896), and the *Woman's Tribune* serialised her reminiscences, which she published as *Eighty Years and More* in 1898. Both were histories of women's struggle against religious superstitions that perpetuate women's bondage. The *History of Woman Suffrage* symbolised for Stanton everything she and her fellow activists had achieved. Her 1887 portrait by Anna Klumpke has a volume of the *History* on the table to her left; and when she died, the *History* was displayed at the head of her coffin on the table on which the Declaration of Sentiments had been written.

Desley Deacon

Reference

NAW 1971.

Major works

Elizabeth Cady Stanton, Susan B Anthony & Matilda Joselyn Gage's *History of Woman Suffrage* (Salem: Ayer Co: 1985) and Stanton's papers are microfilmed and indexed as the *Papers of Elizabeth Cady Stanton and Susan B. Anthony* (eds) Patricia G Holland and Ann D Gordon (1991).

Stenton, Doris Mary 1894–1971

English Medievalist, historian of women. Only child of Amelia (Wadhams) and Joseph Parson. Educated at the Abbey School and the University College at Reading. Began work on the Lincoln records in 1916 supervised by Sir Frank Merry Stenton, the first chair of history at Reading whom she married in 1919. She was appointed an assistant lecturer in the history department at Reading in 1917, became a senior lecturer in 1952 and a reader in 1955. Awarded the degree of Doctor of Letters from Reading in 1948, she was elected to the British Academy in 1958. In 1968 she was awarded an honorary LLD from Glasgow and was made an honorary fellow of St Hilda's College, Oxford.

Her primary interest was in legal history and she edited numerous volumes of legal documents including *The Earliest Lincolnshire Assize Rolls AD 1202–1209* (1926), *Rolls of the Justices in Eyre for Lincolnshire 1218–19 and Worcestershire 1229* (1934) for the Selden Society and the four volumes of *Pleas Before the King or his Justices 1198–1202* (1952–1968). She was instrumental in re-establishing the Pipe Roll Society, overseeing numerous editions of the pipe rolls of Richard I and John. As well as editing and compiling legal documents, Stenton wrote *English Society in the Middle Ages* for the Penguin History of England series in 1951.

Stenton's interest in social and legal history came together in *The English Woman in History* which she completed in 1957. In this work she attempted to show the ways in which women had influenced English society since ancient times. Like earlier historians of British women Stenton presented the Anglo-Saxon period as a golden age for women and charted the decline of women's autonomy following the Norman invasions. Drawing largely on legal records and the auto/biographical writings of women, the book contains brief sketches of **Anne Clifford, Elizabeth Cary, Margaret Cavendish** and **Lucy Hutchinson.**

Mary Spongberg

Stopes, Charlotte Carmichael 1841–1929

English suffragist, legal and literary historian. Born in Edinburgh, youngest child of Christina (Brown Graham) and James Ferrier Carmichael, landscape artist. Educated in Edinburgh where she attended university classes open to women and became the first woman to take out a university certificate in Scotland in lieu of a degree. She married Henry Stopes, architect, civil engineer and anthropologist, in 1879. Two daughters, one of whom was Marie Stopes, author of *Married Love* (1918). After marriage, she travelled in Europe and Africa. Returning to England she settled in Upper Norward and founded a discussion society for ladies and a Shakespeare reading society. She was a founding member of the New Shakespeare Society (1874) and authored a number of literary histories pertaining to Shakespeare and his world. She received the Rose Mary Crawshay prize from the British Academy for her article 'Shakespeare's Industry' in 1916.

A member of the Rational Dress Society and active in the campaigns for womanhood suffrage, Stopes wrote a number of works pertaining to the history of women's political and legal rights in Great Britain, the most important of these, *British Freewomen, Their Historical Privileges,* was published in 1894. *British Freewomen* documented many examples of women's ancient rights as citizens through an analysis of state papers, parliamentary writs, journals of the House of Commons, works of law, history and archaeology. The whole first edition of this work was bought by **Helen Blackburn** and numerous copies were sent to Members of Parliament. She also wrote a number of articles for the feminist journal *Shafts: A Magazine for Progressive Thought.*

Mary Spongberg

References

Boas 1931; Purvis 1995; Smith 1998.

Stopford Green, Alice 1848–1929

Irish nationalist historian. Seventh child of Anne Catherine (Duke) and Reverend Edward Adderley Stopford, archdeacon of Meath. Largely self-educated. Had mastered German, Greek and metaphysics by the age of 16. Following the death of her father Alice moved with her mother to England. Married John Richard Green, Anglican cleric, social historian and author of the *Short History of the English People* (1874) in 1877. Stopford Green began her career as an historian working as her husband's collaborator. The couple produced *A Short Geography of the British Islands* (1879) and were working on the *Conquest of England* when he died of consumption. In 1883, Stopford Green completed this text and revised earlier editions of his work. Using the skills she had acquired working with her husband, Stopford Green began her own career. Her first book *Henry II* (1888) was published by John Morley as part of his English Statesman series and in

1894 *Town Life in the Fifteenth Century* appeared in two volumes.

Moving to London, Stopford Green made her Kensington home a literary centre, with friends including Florence Nightingale, Mary Kingsley, Louisa Creighton and Mrs Humphrey Ward. Encouraged by Mrs Ward, Stopford Green was one of the signatories of the 1889 'Appeal against Women's Suffrage', although she later changed her mind. Acquaintance with Irish journalist John Francis Taylor caused Stopford Green to become involved in Irish politics, taking on an anti-English and anti-Imperialist stance. She visited Boer prisoners on St Helena and founded the Africa Society in 1901.

Stopford Green identified herself with the movement for Irish cultural revival and began to write on Irish history, producing *The Making of Ireland and Its Undoing* (1908), *Irish Nationality* (1911) and *The Old Irish World* (1912). She had learnt from Green to study the landscape to examine the remains of material culture and of ritual and celebration and she brought these ideas to her studies of Ireland. Her histories demonstrated the longevity of the national culture, contributing to the Gaelic revival and sustaining the nationalist movement. While English critics viciously reviewed her works and her *Making of Ireland* was banned by the Royal Dublin Society, Stopford Green became a nationalist heroine said to have brought 'a new spirit' into the writing of Irish history. She moved to Dublin in 1916 and became further embroiled in nationalist politics. In 1918 she published an incisive pamphlet 'Ourselves alone in Ulster' pleading the nationalist cause.

Stopford Green supported the Treaty of December 1921 and was among the first Irish senators appointed in 1922. She was concerned with the educational role of history and engaged in debate about the school history curriculum, writing a series of booklets for use in Irish schools. She advocated the introduction of rigorous scholarly standards to the study of early Irish history and helped to establish the school of Irish studies in Dublin. Her final work *A History of the Irish State to 1014* was published in 1925.

Mary Spongberg

References

DNB; Holton 2000.

Strachey, Ray 1887–1940

Suffragist, feminist activist, biographer and historian of the women's movement. One of the two daughters of Mary (Pearsall Smith) and Frank Costelloe, who separated in 1891, leaving Ray to be brought up by her grandmother, the American feminist and religious writer, Hannah Whitall Smith. She attended the Kensington Girls School before going to Newnham College where she read mathematics. Although her aunt, Alys Pearsall Russell, and her grandmother were both strongly committed to women's suffrage, it was through the Strachey family whom she met in 1906, in the course of her student days at Newnham, that Ray became actively engaged in suffrage campaigns. She became formally connected to the Stracheys when she married Oliver Strachey in 1911. From the time she left Newnham, Ray devoted herself to feminist campaigns, beginning with the moderate suffrage movement, as an organiser and sometime parliamentary secretary for the NUWSS, and moving on during and after the First World War to women's employment. Whenever possible, she worked alongside her beloved sister-in-law, Philippa (Pippa) Strachey.

Writing came easily to Ray Strachey and her first work, a semi-autobiographical novel, *The World at Eighteen* (1907), chronicling an episode in her own life, was published when she was just 20. After that, she turned her hand to biography. Her chosen biographical subjects were prominent feminist activists and she sought to make clear their historical role and significance, while offering also an informal view of them as private individuals. Her biographies were also a way of paying homage to women who had been important to her personally. The first of these dealt with Frances Willard, the American suffragist and temperance advocate. Willard had been a close friend of Hannah Whitall Smith, and Ray Strachey's book, *Frances Willard: Her Life and Work* (1912), written shortly after the death of Whitall Smith in 1911, was intended to pay homage to her too. Ray Strachey did this in a more personal way a couple of years later in *A Quaker Grandmother: Hannah Whitall Smith* (1914).

Only once did Ray Strachey stray from her predominant interest in feminist biographies and histories of women's activities, in a slim volume, *Keigwin's Rebellion (1683–4): An Episode in the History of Bombay* (1916), written on her honeymoon – in part as an attempt to find in the history of British India a possible career for her husband, Oliver, who showed little inclination to seek any form of work himself. In the 1920s, Ray turned her attention briefly to the history of religious movements, and women's involvement in them, in the United States, producing both a book of documents and a novel on these questions. Her major historical work, *The Cause: A Short History of the Women's Movement in Great Britain* (1927), was produced after this, not apparently through her own desire to write on the women's movement, but rather because she was asked to do so by a publisher. Initially reluctant, she eventually agreed to write this book because she felt it would help to lay the foundation for the biography of Millicent Garrett Fawcett, the suffrage leader to whom she was devoted, which she was planning to write. Her veneration of Fawcett can be seen clearly in the whole framework and the broad interpretation of the women's movement provided by *The Cause*, with its emphasis on the importance of women's earlier role in philanthropy in anticipating the demand for women's rights – and on the role of Fawcett and the constitutional NUWSS in the development and ultimate success of the suffrage movement. The militants are depicted always as extremists, lacking in any political sense or indeed in any appropriate understanding of procedure. Although the book was a product of the late 1920s, a period when the meaning, the programme and the concerns of feminism were the subject of extensive and intense debate in which Strachey herself participated, it remains very much 'the product of the mainstream feminism of the turn of the century', setting out a view of feminism and the women's movement which took into account little of the questioning of earlier feminism which was so central to the 1920s.

The Cause was followed by *Millicent Garrett Fawcett* (1931) in which Strachey extolled at greater length the virtues and the contributions Fawcett had made to the emancipation of women.

Barbara Caine

References

Caine 1999; Strachey 1982.

Major work

The Cause: A Short History of the Women's Movement in Great Britain (London: Virago, 1978).

Strickland Sisters: Elizabeth 1794–1875, Agnes 1796–1874, Jane Margaret 1800–1888, Catherine Parr 1802–1899 and Susanna 1803–1885

English poets, children's writers, novelists, travel writers, biographers, naturalists, historians. Daughters of Elizabeth (Homer) and Thomas Strickland. Educated in Latin and mathematics all six sisters, Eliza(beth), Agnes, Sarah, Jane Margaret, Catherine Parr, and Susanna, were encouraged by their father to 'publish books' – an ambition five fulfilled. Their early life was spent in Suffolk, but the family also resided in Norwich, where Elizabeth and Agnes joined the literary circle around their friend **Sarah Taylor Austin.**

The death of Thomas Strickland in 1818 left the family in straitened circumstances. Their poverty brought forth 'talents that might have remained buried had circumstances been less adverse'. Between 1818 and 1823 the sisters published moral tales for children. Elizabeth moved to London becoming editor of the *Court Magazine,* published by Henry Colburn, who later published Elizabeth and Agnes' historical writing. Agnes moved between Suffolk and London, trying to establish her reputation as a poet. Both sisters immersed themselves in London literary circles, becoming acquainted with **Sydney Owenson, Lady Morgan** and **Anna Jameson.**

Susanna began her literary career as a poet and, with Catherine Parr, produced children's fiction. Through connections with, the Anti-Slavery League Susanna became involved in **Abolition** campaigns, writing several anti-slavery pamphlets and transcriptions of the sufferings of Mary Prince and Ashton Warner. In 1831 she met the author of *Ten Years in South Africa,* Lieutenant John Moodie, and the pair married. Catherine Parr met Lieutenant Thomas Traill and married in 1832. Both couples migrated to Canada in 1832. They suffered much hardship on arrival. Catherine Parr recorded their terrible journey as *The Backwoods of Canada* (1836), a guide to the 'domestic economy of British America'. Susanna too wrote out of adversity, confessing in *Roughing It in the Bush* (1839) that she hoped it might deter families from 'sinking their property and ship-wrecking all their hopes . . . in the backwoods of Canada'. In spite of the hostile environment both women became established literary figures in North America. They wrote exclusively on their new homeland: travelogues, hints for new emigrants, children's stories and natural histories. Neither returned to England.

In England Agnes published a number of epic poems, some on historical themes, such as 'The Escape of Mary of Modena' (1827), a tale she revisited in *Lives of Queens;* others depicting contemporary events such as *Demetrius: A Tale of Modern Greece* (1827) but with references to historical texts, such as Blaquière's *Greek Revolution.* She published an historical romance, *The Pilgrims of Walsingham* (1835) that rehearsed themes more fully developed in her **Royal Lives.** Neither her poetry nor the *Pilgrims* gave her literary success, so she decided to 'abandon light literature for that higher walk for which her education fitted her'.

The idea to write a series on the history of the queens of England had originally been Eliza's, but it was Agnes' suggestion to move beyond journalism and into the realms of history. The sisters agreed to work together on the series, with Agnes named as the sole author. Queen Victoria's ascension to the throne was the occasion for many such collections of Royal Lives, however, the Stricklands' *Lives of the Queens of England from the Norman Conquest* (1840–1848) and associated Royal Lives were the most popular and critically acclaimed. In these works the Stricklands promised to 'portray equally the grandeur of the Queen, the attachments of the wife and the affection of the mother . . .', rendering their subjects emblematic of the bourgeois values of the age. Victorian domestic ideology infused their work, as they presented a thoroughly domesticated version of British history. The sisters imagined their books would be read in the private sphere and would be 'associated with the sacred joys of home'. The Stricklands brought to history women's particular sensibilities, claiming women's biographical writing as their unique quarter. The facts and artefacts they analysed required feminine understanding. Male historians who they described as the 'lords of creation', they believed, should 'direct their intellectual powers to more masculine objects of inquiry'. Such criticisms earned Agnes scorn in some quarters and she was accused of introducing into '[our] households ... the reduced pretensions of the historic muse'.

The Stricklands were conscious of avoiding the fictitious nature of women's **Memoirs**, announcing their credo 'facts, not opinions' and basing their work on detailed archival research. Their use of **Archives** was sometimes impeded because they were women. Their analysis of 'facts' gleaned from women's private papers, however, allowed them to revise a number of women reviled in the masculinist historical tradition such as Mary Tudor and Mary Stuart. This revision was inevitably read in sectarian rather than feminist terms. Indeed both sisters avoided connection with any of the campaigns of first-wave feminism.

Agnes believed that her kinship with 'eight of the early queens' and her 'ancestral connection to Katherine Parr' gave the sisters particular historical authority. Such connections likened their biographical writing to family history, the accepted province of women. The sisters happily used their kinship networks to access documents and artefacts that might otherwise have remained private. This familial connection would be continued in the biographical writing produced about Agnes Strickland following her death in 1884. Her sister Jane Margaret, who had written a domestic history of Ancient Rome, *Rome, Regal and Republican* (1853), produced a biography of Agnes in 1887. Jane Margaret's *Life of Agnes Strickland* also contains a fragment of Elizabeth's life. Another biographical study of Agnes was produced in 1940, by Una Pope-Hennesy, the daughter of Agnes' godson.

While Agnes' posthumous fame declined, that of her younger sisters Catherine Traill and Susanna Moodie has definitely increased. Susanna Moodie has been the subject of much interest, with major Canadian literary figures Carol Shields and Margaret Atwood producing works on her life. The sisters have also been the subject of a recent joint biography by Charlotte Gray.

Mary Spongberg

Further reading

Atwood 1970; Gray 1999; Pope-Hennessy 1940; Sheilds 1977; Strickland 1887.

Sumner [Woodbury], Helen Laura 1876–1933

American child rights advocate, historian of women and labour. Born in Sheboygan, Wisconsin, only daughter of Katherine Eudora (Marsh) and George True Sumner, a judge. Educated at East Denver High School, she undertook undergraduate study at Wellesley, receiving a BA in 1898. While at Wellesley she became involved in the College Settlement Association, beginning a lifetime's commitment to political activism. A committed socialist and member of the Intercollegiate Socialist Society, she also served on the National Council of the League for Industrial Democracy.

Her first book, a novella *The White Slave, or 'The Cross of Gold'* (1896), demonstrated an early interest in issues of social justice and feminism. Her experience of the strikes by Western Federation miners in Colorado turned her attention to labour history and she undertook graduate work at the University of Wisconsin, with the radical political economist Richard Ely. Working first as Ely's secretary, Sumner attained a fellowship in 1904 and began collaboration with labour historian John R Commons of the American Bureau of Industrial Research. She contributed a chapter to Commons' *Trade Unionism and Labor Problems* (1905). Her doctoral thesis 'The Labor Movement in America, 1827–1837' (1908) constituted a segment of Commons' pioneering *History of Labor in the United States*. She also worked with Commons as assistant editor on *A Documentary History of American Industrial Society* (11 vols, 1910–1911).

In September 1906 she took leave from graduate work to undertake a 15-month investigation of woman suffrage in Colorado for the Collegiate Equal Suffrage League of New York State. This resulted in her book *Equal Suffrage* (1909) which included a short history of the granting of suffrage in the United States and provided an important account of the immediate impact of womanhood suffrage. Her acquaintance with feminism may have changed her position in regard to women in labour. In her collaborative work she maintained a trade-unionist position, defending the male wage. In later work, such as the study of the history of women in industry as part of the Bureau of Labor Statistics, a multi-volume *Report on the Condition of Women and Child Wage-Earners in the United States*, Woodbury adopted a stance more supportive of women in industry.

Sumner left the University of Wisconsin in 1909 when she was told that she would not find a permanent position in the history faculty. Unsatisfied with the 'drudgery and obscurity' of collaborating with more prominent male colleagues, she undertook various forms of contractual studies for government agencies. In 1910 she travelled abroad to study the industrial courts in Germany, France and Switzerland and attended the Copenhagen Congress of the Socialist International. In 1913 she joined the Children's Bureau conducting policy research on industry and was then appointed Assistant Chief of the Children's Bureau in 1915. In 1918 she became director of investigations, a position held until her marriage when she resigned from full-time work. She claimed her research for the Children's Bureau had allowed her to establish herself 'as a scholar with a deeper social purpose'. In her later years Sumner Woodbury contributed to the *Dictionary of American Biography and the Encyclopedia of the Social Sciences*.

Mary Spongberg

References

Des Jardins 2003; Folbre 1997.

Major works

Equal Suffrage (New York: Arno Press, 1972) and *History of Women in Industry in the United States* (New York: Arno Press, 1974).

T

Taylor, Lily Ross 1886–1969

American ancient historian. She was born in Auburn, Alabama, the eldest of three children of Mary (Ross) and William Dana Taylor, railway engineer. Her mother died during her childhood, leaving her father to remarry. In 1901, when he was appointed as professor of railway engineering at the University of Wisconsin, Taylor attended Madison High School. She obtained her AB degree at Wisconsin in 1906, having changed her major from Mathematics to Classics. She entered the Graduate School at Bryn Mawr in 1906, later graduating with a PhD on 'The Cults of Ostia' (1912). Much of her early research was focused on the study of Roman religion. The publication of her PhD dissertation was followed by her second book *Local Cults in Etruria* (1923). From 1912 until 1927 she taught at Vassar College and in 1917 she became the first woman Fellow of the American Academy in Rome. In 1927 she was appointed Professor of Latin and Chair of the department at Bryn Mawr. She served as President of the American Philological Association in 1942. After retirement from Bryn Mawr in 1952 she was professor in charge of the Classical School of the American Academy in Rome and held visiting posts at a number of universities in the United States and at the American Academy in Rome.

Her publications include six books, over 70 articles and more than 60 reviews. Her work in Roman religion, history and institutions was influenced primarily by Italian and German scholarship, most notably Theodor Mommsen's analyses of Roman political and constitutional forms. Taylor's research was characterised by an emphasis on the functioning of institutions and how people operated within these institutions. She wrote: 'I am a student of Roman civilization. I want to understand how the Romans thought and felt and acted, what their religion, their institutions, their economic system, their laws, their poetry, their histories meant to them.' Her monograph *The Divinity of the Roman Emperor* (1931) was the first comprehensive investigation of the Roman ruler cult. She went on to a series of studies on Caesar, culminating in her next major work, *Party Politics in the Age of Caesar* (1949), a study which has been characterised as the first application on a large scale in English of the methodology of Gelzer's *Die Nobilität der römischen Republik* (1912), a work which changed the shape of Roman historiography. Study of party politics led to a major study of the territorial tribe in Roman political assemblies, *The Voting Districts of the Roman Republic: The Thirty-five Urban and Rural Tribes* (1960), still a major work of reference. The following *Roman Voting Assemblies from the Hannibalic War to the Dictatorship of Caesar* (1966) was a ground-breaking description of the procedures in the various assemblies as they performed their electoral, legislative and judicial functions.

Taylor had strong views on the philosophy of teaching. As Dean of the Graduate School at Bryn Mawr from 1942 until 1952 she was a critic of graduate exploitation. In an article in the *Journal of Higher Education in 1952* she suggested: 'The subjects of the dissertations are assigned topics suggested not by the student's interest but by the professor's desire to have someone do a laborious job which he requires for his own investigations. The professor may have some light but the poor student is a slave laborer groping in darkness.' Taylor herself was an outstanding teacher, amongst other accolades, being listed in *Life* magazine as one of America's great teachers.

Taylor was killed by a hit-and-run driver near her home in Bryn Mawr at the age of 83, still an active and productive scholar. She was working on a major study of the Roman senate at the time of her death.

J Lea Beness
T W Hillard

References

Broughton 1990; *NAW* 1980.

Major works

Party politics in the Age of Caesar (Berkeley: University of California Press, 1949). *The Divinity of the Roman Emperor* (New York: Garland, 1979).

Travel

Although histories of western women travellers have proliferated since the 1970s, the debate about the gendered subject matter and style of women's travel writing has largely taken place in literary studies. This debate has important implications for the historiographical content and quality of women's travel writing. Arising from the question of whether women's travel writing was as 'imperialistic' or 'racist' as men's travel writing, certain scholars claimed that women's travel writing was generically shaped by nineteenth-century notions of femininity which precluded 'masculine' topics such as politics, science, racial or imperialistic generalisations and judgements. Shirley Foster, for example, in her study of nineteenth-century women travellers *Across New Worlds* maintained that these women did not adopt the language of 'colonial discourse' because their writing was subject to a 'feminine' set of literary conventions that focused on 'topics of romance and home and family life, . . . feeling and sentiment and delicacy and emotionalism of expression' (1990: 18). Women's travel writing was concerned with the 'appearance, costume and manners of women; details of domestic life such as household management and culinary habits; behaviour towards children; marriage customs and female status' (Foster 1990: 24). This is a list that noticeably excludes historical writing. Sara Mills in *Discourses of Differences* makes a similar argument, suggesting that nineteenth-century 'discourses of femininity' shaped the writing and reception of women's travel texts so that they were unlikely to produce 'the type of "factual" writing which requires "authorising", for example, history and scientific writing' (1991: 80–1). This view has, however, been challenged by others such as Maria Frawley who observed that there was no homogeneous 'Victorian woman traveller' and argued that travel writing by women encompassed the areas of art, sociology and history (1994: 205). Nevertheless, women's travel writing is not usually studied for its historiographical component. Melman's careful consideration of the Middle Eastern historiography of **Harriet Martineau,** Amelia Blandford Edwards and Lady Anne Blunt remains the exemplary exception (Melman 1992/1995: 235–305). This essay takes a chronological look at the role of history in women's travel writing: the pilgrim's historical consciousness and desire to authenticate a particular world view; the notion of history as the doings of great men and women, particularly monarchs and political leaders; the Grand Tour as a confirmation of national and cultural histories; the 'customs and manners' social histories of New Worlds; the Orientalist and imperialist histories arising from travel to European colonies; and women travellers' own consciousness of themselves as historically significant agents.

Spiritual journeys

The earliest form of travel women undertook was pilgrimage, and pilgrimages of all sorts – sacred and secular – involve an obligatory genuflection at the altar of history. In the fourth century CE, the Spanish nun Egeria arranged her travel itinerary according to the 'historical' sites of Biblical tradition. As Glenn Bowman (1999) has suggested, Egeria's *Diary of a Pilgrimage* (1970) was 'Mapping History's Redemption' in the diary of her travels. It was a project of enduring popularity, with Margery Kempe following in her footsteps in the fifteenth century and Georgiana Damer doing the same in the mid-nineteenth century in her *Diary of a Tour in Greece, Turkey, Egypt and the Holy Land* (1841). By the twentieth century, European spiritual pilgrimages could serve as quests for alternative cultures, spiritualities and histories. Alexandra David-Néel's *My*

Journey to Lhasa (1927) or Lady Evelyn Cobbold's *Pilgrimage to Mecca* (1934) detailing her conversion to Islam and the hajj she subsequently undertook are cases in point.

But pilgrimages tend to confirm existing world-views, particularly of linear, progressive, teleological histories culminating in the status quo of religious, national, imperial or cultural power and privilege. The eighteenth-century Grand Tour was a pilgrimage of sorts, albeit a secular one. European men and women traversed the Continent to mark the cultural history of 'Western Civilisation' and to marvel at the shrines of Roman and Renaissance sculpture, painting and architecture. Such pilgrimages generally served to reinforce a conviction of European cultural supremacy which had resulted in (western) European dominance in trade and exploration. Pilgrimages could also justify histories of colonisation. After 1857 British women travelled to Lucknow, Kanpur and the Kashmiri Gate in Delhi to remember the female victims of the 'Mutiny' which brought India under British governance (Ramusack 1995: 72). In the nineteenth and twentieth centuries, travellers from the colonised margins also visited the imperial metropole to reconnect themselves with imperial history and to authenticate that history. This was true of Australians such as Margery Tripp in 1872 or Anne Donnell in 1917 (Hassam 2000: 119–20). As Woollacott observed, 'For most white Australians, London – the rest of the British Isles – was the locus of inherited cultural memory, the site of ancestral connections and the setting of major historical episodes' (2001: 4–5). Britain was where history happened. But by the late twentieth-century, in the postcolonial era, British travellers themselves would make nostalgic pilgrimages to sites of former imperial glory to commemorate and mourn the passing of the empire (Teo 2001). Pilgrimages serve to authenticate histories for pilgrims; they rarely challenge them or produce new historical writing.

The Grand Tour

If the medieval pilgrimage provided the sacred topography for historical travel, it was the Grand Tour which gave women travellers the opportunity to produce secular history. Until the late 1990s, discussions of the Grand Tour tended to focus on upper-class European men, with the exception of women such as Lady Mary Wortley Montagu, Lady Bessborough, Lady Holland, **Mary Wollstonecraft**, Marianna Starke and Mary Shelley. These women seemed the exceptions proving the rule that the Grand Tour was primarily about the socialisation of men into a particular type of ruling-class masculinity and the cultivation of knowledge and aesthetic appreciation as social power. In more recent times, however, attention has shifted to the gendered experience of the Grand Tour: how women negotiated masculine notions of Romantic travel, landscape and aesthetics. While works such as Elizabeth Bohls' *Women Travel Writers, Landscape and the Language of Aesthetics, 1716–1818* (1995) have emphasised the liberating aspects of the Grand Tour which gave women the opportunity to escape rigid family and gender roles, to compare the restrictions placed on English womanhood with their Continental counterparts, to develop their intellectual or artistic talents, as well as to intervene in and renegotiate the Romantic principles of masculine aesthetics, others such as Chloe Chard's *Pleasure and Guilt on the Grand Tour* (1999) have explored the relationship of women to the gendered representation of the past. For women travellers to produce historical writing was not easy since, in the dominant masculine tradition of Grand Tour literature, they were elided with antiquity (Chard 1999: 126–44) – spectacles rather than spectators; the objects rather than the authors of history.

Women travellers' first forays into historical writing tended to be chronicles of kings, queens and courts scattered through their letters, diaries and memoirs. From the seventeenth to nineteenth centuries their travels within Europe followed the well-worn route of the Grand Tour. As Mills observed, these itineraries 'were fairly fixed; there were only certain towns and cities in Europe which were considered worth visiting and describing. Texts decreed which sights should be seen and how these sights should be viewed' (Mills 1991: 83–4). As a result of the sheer familiarity with and common knowledge about sites visited, historical descriptions were few and far between, especially since most of the travel literature from this era was in the form of letters and women were hesitant to bore their correspondents with excessive historical detail. Lady Mary Wortley Montagu, for instance, apologised to her sister, Lady Mar, for the 'tedious account' of her Hungarian travels in 1717. 'It was not an affectation of showing my reading that has made me tell you some little scraps of the history of the towns I have passed through,' Montagu hastened to add. 'I have always avoided anything of that kind, when I spoke of places that I believe you knew the story of as well as myself' (Montagu 1725/1993: 50).

Madame Marie-Catherine d'Aulnoy, travelling in the late seventeenth century, was among the first women travellers to fill her letters with the chronicles, intrigues and scandals of various European courts. Aulnoy's *Memoirs of the Court of England in 1675* (1930), recounts the intrigues and lovers of the kings and nobles of England, while her *Travels into Spain* (Aulnoy 1930, 1691) contains anecdotes and genealogical information about the Catalonian king and his family as well as an account of the hostility between Aragon and Castile and a short explanation on the invasion of the Moors. But these were diverting stories to while away the tedium of travel between towns, thus Aulnoy's explanation of the origins of the Spanish Inquisition was incomplete because, she wrote, she arrived at Toledo halfway through the narrative. Like Aulnoy, most other women travellers in the seventeenth and eighteenth centuries were from the aristocracy and their historical interest remained with royalty and their own class. Lady Elizabeth Craven's *Memoirs* (1914) chiefly related details of royalty and military figures, particularly Frederick the Great of Prussia. Countess Marguerite Blessington 'idled' her way through Italy (1839) and France (1841), writing desultorily of various monuments and Roman towns but also recounting the events and political repercussions of the French Revolution.

Travel often served to reinforce national myths. Majorie Morgan has pointed out that while English, Scottish, Welsh and even Irish travellers willingly identified themselves as 'British' in Europe, national differences came to the fore when they were travelling within Britain. Nationalism manifested itself through historical interest. English travellers to Scotland, for example, were primarily interested in Highland landscape and revealed 'not only an ignorance of but also an indifference and even an hostility to Scotland's past' whereas Scottish travellers made a point of visiting and writing about Scottish monarchical, political and literary history (Morgan 2001: 192–3). When these women went to Europe, however, they emphasised the pre-eminence of England's position and tended to confirm a particular narrative of England's unique strength and liberty – consequences, so they believed, of the historical development of its political culture, parliamentary institutions and the effects of Protestantism (Morgan 2001: 159–60). Fanny Kemble and Elizabeth Carne exulted in England's freedom after their Grand Tours, while Mary Shelley 'assumed that the English had already been active in exporting the love of freedom' to the American colonies even though she had never set foot there (Morgan 2001: 161, 166–7).

The 'New World'

Travel writing in the New World generally contained little historical content. To be sure, late eighteenth-century European women were acutely aware of the historical times through which they travelled, conscientiously bearing witness to the events of the American revolutionary wars in their letters and journals in texts such as Janet Schaw's *Journal of Lady of Quality* (1923) or the Baroness von Riedesel's (Frederica Massow) *Letters and Journals* (1867). But women's travel writing in the United States and Canada during the nineteenth century was overwhelmingly sociological in focus, perhaps because it was accepted that women should write about 'customs and manners', or perhaps because of the short time span of white settlement and the fascination with the US as an experiment in modernity. Hence we have Frances Trollope's highly critical *Domestic Manners of the Americans* (1832), or Harriet Martineau's *Retrospect of Western Travel* (1838) and *Society in America* (1837) which purported to measure American society against 'the principles on which it is founded'. Contemplation of slavery in antebellum America such as Fanny Kemble's *Journals* (1835, 1839) focused on the harshness of contemporary conditions, but brief mentions were sometimes made of its historical roots, as when Isabella Bird reminded readers in her *The Englishwoman in America*, 'that England bequeathed this system to her colonies, though she has nobly blotted it out from those which still own her sway' (1856: 132).

Central and South America tended to be of greater historical interest to travellers. Lady Winefred Howard recorded her journey 'across the pond' to New York, then travelled down to Mexico to view Aztec antiquities (1897) in her *Journal of a Tour in the United States, Canada and Mexico*. Of the women who travelled in the western hemisphere, Lady Callcott (Maria Graham) was singular in her passion for politics and historical detail. Her *Journal of a Voyage to Brazil* (1824) contains vivid descriptions of the insurrections of the northern states against the Portuguese in the south of the country. She travelled widely through the Sandwich Islands and stayed in India, including snippets of Hindu religious beliefs in her *Journal of a Residence in India* (1812). Callcott later became famous for a popular children's history book, *Little Arthur's History of England*, which was reprinted and revised with updates about 20 times between its first publication in 1835 and 1975. It is a perfect example of the kind of Whig potted histories of England no doubt familiar to many of these women.

But for other women, new worlds and colonies did not elicit great historical interest. Eighteenth-century texts such as Anna Maria Falconbridge's *Two Voyages to Sierra Leone* (1794) or Mary Ann Parker's *A Voyage Round the World* (1795) were undoubtedly governed by a notion of history which focused on the doings of white monarchs and military men (Coleman 1999). African or Australian Aboriginal societies were regarded as timeless and unchanging, arrested in primitivism and outside the course of history because, as Mignolo has pointed out, from the Renaissance onwards Europeans believed that 'people without writing were people without history and that people without history were inferior human beings' (Mignolo 1995: 127). The entry of non-literate peoples into history was marked by contact with Europeans, especially through colonisation. By the mid-nineteenth century, however, sufficient time had passed for certain European colonies to be considered historically. Of the many British women who travelled to Australia in the nineteenth century, Rosamond Hill and Florence Davenport were probably the most conscientious in recording historical details in their prosaically-titled travel book, *What We Saw in Australia* (1875). Hill and Davenport's work is interesting from an historiographical perspective because they not only recounted the usual history of colonisation and convicts, they also described political and institutional histories: the formation of South Australia as a state; the expansion of Melbourne as a city; the telegraph service in South Australia; and the historical background of 'destitute asylums' and reformatories for girls.

Orientalism

These women dipped into historical detail to pad out their travel narratives. It remained for late nineteenth-century women travellers to the Middle East to produce substantial historical works. The Middle East had, of course, elicited significant historical interest since the early Christian pilgrimages mentioned above. Women travelled there to authenticate the historical accuracy of the Scriptures. In doing so, they reinforced a tradition of historiography that ignored and effaced the histories of contemporary Muslim inhabitants or Ottoman imperial influence in the region in favour of pre-Islamic pasts (Melman 1992/1995: 241). Lady Mary Wortley Montagu was the first to write at length about contemporary Turkey in her *Turkish Embassy Letters* (1725), followed in the nineteenth century by Julia Pardoe's *The City of the Sultan and Domestic Manners of the Turks in 1836* (1837) which has been described as 'probably the most detailed, most sympathetic description of the Turkish élite before the *Tanzimat*, or reform era' (Melman 1992/1995: 50). Pardoe was also an historical novelist, producing, among many other works, two Turkish books – *Romance of the Harem* (1839) and *Beauties of the Bosphorus* (1839) – before turning to European historical fiction: *Louis XIV and the Court of France in the Seventeenth Century* (1847), *The Court and Reign of Francis I* (1849) and *The Life of Marie de Medici, Queen of France* (1852).

In many ways the late nineteenth and early twentieth centuries were the golden years of women travellers' historical writing, when educated British women who journeyed through the Middle East produced weighty tomes of Orientalist works. These writings were 'Orientalist' in that they arose from the European academic and aesthetic tradition specialising in studies of 'the Orient' – a geographically indeterminate region ranging from Turkey eastwards to South Asia. Travellers such as Harriet Martineau, Amelia Blandford Edwards, Lady Anne Blunt, Gertrude Bell and Freya Stark were Orientalist historians in the modern academic understanding of 'history'. They were conversant with contemporary historiography and methodology and, in the case of Bell and Stark, had actually taken university degrees in history. Despite common clichés about the 'timelessness of the East', educated European travellers understood the Orient to be rich in its heritage of art, archaeology and literature, therefore the Orient had a history worth documenting and studying. Indeed, it was often felt that the past was all that was worthwhile; that contemporary Oriental society had long since degenerated from its cultural zenith. In this way, the works they produced were also 'Orientalist' in Edward Said's (1978) usage of the term: European travellers actively constructed the Orient as Europe's 'Other' – marked by its difference, exoticism, backwardness and inferiority in comparison to the modern imperial, colonising West.

Harriet Martineau's *Eastern Life, Present and Past* (1848) is a ponderous, Whiggish exploration of the evolution of religious ideas beginning with 'primitive' tribal animism, polytheism and 'immature' monotheistic beliefs like Judaism, progressing upwards through Christianity and Islam and ending with a more enlightened European deism. Amelia Blandford Edwards, on the other hand, was more intrigued by the archaeological remains of ancient Egypt – the subject of *A Thousand Miles Up the Nile* (1877) and *Pharaohs, Fellahs and Explorers* (1891). Edwards was a notable scholar who, together with Reginald Poole, was largely responsible for founding the Egypt Exploration Fund in 1882 and she later founded the chair of Egyptology at University College, London. She was skilled at reading Egyptian hieroglyphics and her historical work was meticulously researched with extensively detailed evidence. She was particularly interested in the position of women in ancient Egypt, lecturing on the subject and arguing that 'throughout the Pharaonic era, women enjoyed equality with, sometimes superiority over, men' (Melman 1992/1995: 265). Indeed, she used her historical work on Pharaonic women to critique the position of women in contemporary Britain. Edwards is an interesting historian because she was ahead of her time in many ways, not just in her focus on women's history, but also in the wide variety of sources she used – hieroglyphic inscriptions, illustrations, legal documents such as mortgages, deeds of sale, inventories, receipts, marriage contracts, material remains, literary sources, works of art, handicrafts and utensils – to construct a picture of the ordinary private lives of common people. And this in an age when academic historians were focusing on political states and social elites (Melman 1992/1995: 265).

Martineau and Edwards were both uninterested in the history of the contemporary Muslim inhabitants of the Middle East. It remained for Lady Anne Blunt to document this history in her magisterial and empathetic *Bedouin Tribes of the Euphrates* (1879). Blunt's work is remarkable because she wrote the political and military history of the Shammar and Anazeh tribes with a confidence and authority more typical of nineteenth-century male academic historians, but at the same time she was unafraid to let Bedouin tribal leaders and informants speak for themselves in her text. As Melman pointed out, this was not 'a one-sided process, in which an articulate West represents a speechless, expressionless Middle East' (Melman 1992/1995: 298). Rather, the process was a reciprocal dialogue. Equally remarkable is the fact that Blunt rejected the sort of Eurocentric history critiqued by Mignolo. Not only was Europe marginalised and Bedouin culture made the centre of her historical narrative, but she also demolished the Eurocentric historical hierarchy between literate and non-literate societies. She engaged extensively in early oral history, interviewing many different Bedouin men in order to piece together cultural norms and tribal lores from ancient Arabic poetry, writing about the history of desert politics and conflicts and the effect of Ottoman rule on the region.

Anne Blunt and her husband, Wilfrid Scawen Blunt, were deeply anti-imperialist, championing the Bedouins' political cause as ethnic minorities in their historical writings. But twentieth-century Orientalists such as Gertrude Bell would use their travel writings on the Middle East to push the cause of British imperialism in the region. Bell was a learned scholar and the first woman to achieve a first-class degree in modern history at Oxford in 1888. She studied Farsi and Arabic and travelled widely throughout the Middle East, producing several dry, archaeological tomes such as *Amurath to Amurath* (1911) and *The Palace and Mosque of Ukhaidir: A Study in Early Mohammadan Architecture* (1914), as well as more conventional travel writings of which *The Desert and the Sown* (1907) is perhaps the most well known. *The Desert and the Sown* recounts Bell's journey through Syria and she followed the Blunts' lead in relating historical details about the Bedouins among whom she travelled as well as 'the actual political conditions of unimportant persons' (1907: xi). Like the Blunts, she was highly critical of Turkish rule, but she differed from them in her ardent advocacy of the historical benefits of British imperial rule. '[A]ll over Syria and even in the desert,' she wrote, 'whenever a man is ground down by injustice or mastered by his own incompetence, he wishes that he were under the rule that has given wealth to Egypt and our occupation of that country . . . has proved the finest advertisement of English methods of government' (1907: 58). Her scholarly achievements in the field of Orientalism were recognised by the British government when she became the only female political officer appointed to the Arab Intelligence Bureau in Cairo during the First World War. Her interest in the region's history continued in the aftermath of war and she eventually became the first director of the National Museum of Iraq which she founded in 1923.

Africa

Orientalist history may have facilitated European imperialism, yet on the whole the imperial agenda was rarely overt in a way that women travellers' writings about sub-Saharan Africa tended to be. Apart from Mary Kingsley, whose *Travels in West Africa* (1897) and *West African Studies* (1899) included short histories of early European contact with West Africa and who was staunchly critical of the extension of British imperial rule in favour of European traders' rights, Africa brought out the rampant imperialist in women as well as men. Charlotte Mansfield's *Via Rhodesia* (1911) included a hagiographic account of Rhodes and was written to encourage white settlement after she had travelled through the country. Flora Shaw (Lady Lugard), who travelled through the continent while she was South African correspondent and later colonial editor for *The Times*, was perhaps the most blatant. In 1883 J R Seeley's *Expansion of England* had set out a paradigm for the imperialist history of 'Greater Britain'. Shaw's *A Tropical Dependency* (1906) was in many ways an answer and a challenge to Seeley's work. 'It has become the habit of the British mind to think of the British Empire as a white empire,' she wrote – a habit that Seeley had of course fostered. 'But as a matter of fact, we all know that ours is not a white empire.' The British now stood at 'an interesting moment in our history' when questions of self-government in the white colonies had been settled (1906: 1). It was time, she declared, to deal with Britain's non-white colonies and to harness the energies of 'coloured labour' for the good of the empire. The far-ranging history of the African continent she put together in *A Tropical Dependency* – from ancient Egyptian and Phoenician history, to Roman occupation, Islamic African conquest of southern Spain, to European contact, colonisation and administration in the present time – was designed to reinforce the rightness of

British imperial rule through an account of its ameliorative history:

> A territory which we found in chaos has been brought to order. The slave trade has been abolished . . . Its subject races have been secured in the possession of their lives and property. Its rulers have been converted with their own consent into officials of the British Crown . . . [and] into the veins of a decadent civilisation new blood has been introduced, which has brought with it the promise of a new era of life. (Lugard 1906: 500)

Women travelling through Africa in the early twentieth century also had a sense of the historicity of their own journeys, simply because they were the first European women to travel somewhere or accomplish something. This sense of achieving a history-making trip comes through in Mary Hall's *A Woman's Trek from the Cape to Cairo* (1907) and Stella Court Treatt's *Cape to Cairo: The Record of a Historic Motor Journey* (1927). In 1920–1921, Rosita Forbes masqueraded as a Muslim woman to travel to the Islamic holy city of Kufara in the Libyan desert – a city where no other European had ventured. She wrote of this dramatic journey in equally dramatic purple prose in *The Secret of the Sahara: Kufara* (1921). Forbes was a flamboyant socialite and hardy traveller who relished the prospect of travelling in revolutionary, history-making times, writing of these journeys in *Conflict: Angora to Afghanistan* (1931) and *Eight Republics in Search of a Future: Evolution and Revolution in South America* (1933). The heady sense of excitement at 'being there' during historical upheavals was perhaps typical of the interwar years, for in much the same way, Charlotte Cameron was a witness to 'Mexico in Revolution' (1925). But the Soviet Union was the biggest draw card for British women travellers who wished to see history unfolding before their eyes. The USSR exerted the same kind of fascination in the interwar years that the USA had in the nineteenth century as a modern social experiment for which there was no historical precedent. Women flocked there and produced largely admiring accounts of what they saw, such as Ada Chesterton's *My Russian Adventure* (1931) and *Salute the Soviet* (1942), Eileen Bigland's *The Key to the Russian Door* (1942), Ella Maillart's *Turkestan Solo* (1934) and, of course, Rosita Forbes' *Conflict: Angora to Afghanistan* (1931) and *Forbidden Road – Kabul to Samarkand* (1937).

Histories of women travellers

If, by the late nineteenth and early twentieth centuries, women had an awareness of themselves and their own journeys as historically remarkable, it is a feeling that has been shared by many writers ever since W H Davenport Adams published *Celebrated Women Travellers of the Nineteenth Century* in 1883. A decade later, Ménie Muriel Dowie produced *Women Adventurers* (1893) – a history of women who liked to cross-dress and travel, as she herself did during her travels through the Carpathians (1891). It was in the 1970s and 1980s, however, during the florescence of women's history at the height of second-wave **feminism,** that the list of celebratory, monumental histories of exceptional women travellers burgeoned. Thus we have Dorothy Middleton's *Victorian Lady Travellers* (1965, 1982), Alexandra Allen's *Travelling Ladies: Victorian Lady Adventuresses* (1980), Luri Miller's *On Top of the World: Five Women Explorers in Tibet* (1980), Leo Hamalian's *Ladies on the Loose: Women Travellers of the Eighteenth and Nineteenth Centuries* (1981), Catherine Barnes Stevenson's *Victorian Women Writers in Africa* (1982), Mary

Russell's *The Blessings of a Good Thick Skirt* (1986), Maria Aitken's *A Girdle Round the Earth* (1987), Dea Birkett's *Spinsters Abroad: Victorian Lady Explorers* (1989), Jane Robinson's fascinating bibliography, *Wayward Women: A Guide to Women Travellers* (1990), Marion Tinling's *With Women's Eyes: Visitors to the New World 1775–1918* (1993), Susan Morgan's *Place Matters: Gendered Geography in Victorian Women's Travel Books about Southeast Asia* (1996), Brian Dolan's *Ladies of the Grand Tour* (2001) and Barbara Hodgson's *No Place for a Lady: Tales of Adventurous Women Travellers* (2002).

It is notable that these are overwhelmingly concerned with pre-twentieth-century travellers. Collectively, these works reinforce the perception that whatever the difficulties of pre-modern travel, the voyage abroad was liberating for Western women. Travel provided middle- and upper-class women with opportunities and power denied to them at home. These women escaped the constraints of gender identity and the domestic sphere that was their lot in life, pursuing careers as artists, writers, journalists, scientists and historians in the course of expanding their cultural and geographical horizons. Moreover, the white woman traveller enjoyed all the prestige and authority of the European male in the age of empire (Birkett 1989: 117). If women's travel writing has, on the whole, been rather patchy where historical content and methodology is concerned, nevertheless eighteenth- and nineteenth-century women travellers continue to be popular subjects of history simply because they, as women, actually went somewhere and lived to tell the tale. Thus by the twentieth century, women travel writers occupied a unique position with regard to history: they were both the authors and the subjects of history. Whatever the quality of their historical writing, they themselves had developed a sense of the historical importance of their own journeys and of their exceptional lives as women.

Hsu-Ming Teo

References

Blessington 1839; Blessington 1841; Bowman 1999; Chard 1991; Coleman 1999; Egeria 385CE/1970; Frawley 1994; Hassam 2000; Kempe 1436/1985; Melman 1992/1995; Mills 1991; Mignolo 1995; Montagu 1725/1993; Morgan 2001; Ramusack 1995; Said 1978; Woollacott 2001.

Related essays

Empire; Great Britain; Local History; Memoir; Middle Ages; Orientalism; Postcolonial; Religion; United States.

U

United States of America

The range of women's historical writing on the United States has been incredibly diverse and substantial. From the American Revolution onwards, women writers have engaged prolifically with writing the history of their nation. They have done this in many ways – through working within the historical profession and by operating outside the sometimes constraining bounds of professionalism; from writing the perspective of the white middle class, to writing into the historical record the experiences of the marginalised and oppressed groups of American society. American women historians operated within the context of *American* historiography and their work must be interpreted as part of this tradition. But, at the same time, many women have contributed to reshaping the very nature of that historiography by bringing their own perspectives and agendas to the writing of the history of the United States.

Republican mothers and 'maternal' history

The Revolution and its aftermath encouraged a wave of historical writing that both sought to chronicle the Revolution and to provide a historical narrative for a newly formed, still divided and disparate nation. Women engaged through history with the events of the Revolution and its aftermath as a way to engage with the young nation's political life. **Mercy Otis Warren** was perhaps the most important of these early writers of the United States. During the revolutionary years, she published satirical plays and pamphlets criticising British rule and promoting the Patriot cause. She wrote a history of the American Revolution, *History of the Rise, Progress, and Termination of the American Revolution* (1805), one of three contemporaneous histories of the Revolution. Although in many ways a standard comprehensive account of the period, Warren's intervention into the narrative of revolutionary history differed from other accounts in its depiction of highly dramatic descriptions of abuse, rape and murder of patriot women. (Baym 1991). Warren was inundated with letters containing horrendous reports of bloodshed and devastation, and in recording these events she was reflecting the personal, domestic experience of the revolution seen as unimportant by male historians (Smith 1998: 39). Aside from her obvious involvement in political and intellectual life, Warren set an important precedent for women writers of history to be published and, indeed, many women would write for publication in the years leading up to the Civil War.

The role of women in the new Republic was seen as especially important. The concept of 'Republican Motherhood' assigned women the task of educating the new citizens of the nation and instilling into them virtue and patriotism – this task was conceived within the constraints of gender, but it did ensure that certain women could gain access to education. Many women in the first half of the nineteenth century engaged in historical writing with the aim of instructing the young women of the nation. Elizabeth Peabody wrote a guide, *First Steps to the Study of History*, in 1832; other similar works were produced, such as those Emma Willard's *History of the United States* (1828) and Augusta Berard's *School History of the United States* (1855). Such works emphasised the importance of education to women and the nation (Baym 1995: 26, 35). Reading history was seen to be essential to good citizenship, especially for women, who were entrusted to the critical role of raising a generation of loyal and good citizens.

It was important for this work to be presented within the clearly defined women's sphere, even if these women engaged with public intellectual and political debate. Writing history was viewed as an extension of women's work, because it could be done usually from the home, and complementing their domestic work. But the work itself also reflected the private and domestic nature of the vocation of a woman writer of history. Nina Baym (1995) labels many of these women of the new Republic as 'maternal historians', and it is an apt description. Women brought to their work the distinctive contributions of their gender, and of their role as mothers of the Republic. Many of their works were aimed at young people, the future mothers or citizens of the Republic. They often adopted intimate, conversational tones in their work. The relationship between a mother and her children were critical to works of women such as **Lydia Maria Child** and **Sarah Josepha Hale.** These sentiments are also found in the work of **Elizabeth Ellet**, who sought to preserve the contributions of women to the making of the new Republic: she published a multi-volume chronicle of the history of *Women of the American Revolution* (1848). She also authored *Domestic History of the American Revolution* (1850), adding a distinctively gendered view of the history of the event. Women thus played a central role in shaping the way history was written and presented in the first decades of the United States' existence, doing a great deal for codifying and promoting its values. In the later nineteenth century, such work would be perpetuated in the work of many women's organisations which used history as a vehicle for patriotic instruction.

Women's historical writing was strongly focused on the use of history for the present. Women historians of the new Republic infused their work with the ideals and values of the new Republic, and of the role of women therein. Lydia Maria Child's body of work conveyed her strong religious, patriotic and moral beliefs. Child argued against the poor treatment of Native Americans, championed **abolition** and sought to improve the lot of women, using history as a means of furthering her social and political goals. **Margaret Fuller** presented an ideal of American nationhood that was also linked to the emancipation of women in *Woman in the Nineteenth Century* (1845) and in her dispatches from Europe. Her historical perspective on women's subjection proved critical to the development of a nascent suffrage movement in America.

Historical novels were an immensely popular genre in the first half of the nineteenth century. In the wake of the Revolution, the fate of Native Americans formed the dominant subject in such works, most famously in texts such as Catherine Maria Sedgewick's *Hope Leslie* (1827). Some historical fiction such as Lydia Maria Child's *Hobomok* (1824) and Anna Cumming Johnson's *The Iroquois* (1855) depicted a sympathetic view of Native Americans that was radical for its time. More often, works such as Ann Stephens' *Mary Derwent* (1858) reflected the prejudices of American society in the early nineteenth century. Religious purpose was often explicit in women's historical writing, and tolerance for religious difference was rarely apparent. This intolerance also extended to race. As the United States expanded westward through the early nineteenth century, national histories romanticised this process within the grand concept of 'Manifest Destiny'. Native Americans were reduced to either the 'wild' or 'noble' savage. Women's work sometimes fell within this framework of understanding. Emma Willard's *History of the United States* highlighted and sensationalised alleged atrocities perpetrated by indigenous Americans on the settlers. In ethnographic works such as Mary Henderson Eastman's *Dacotah* (1849), the historical representation of Native Americans was subsumed within a discourse of extinction (Baym 1995: 110).

Slavery was also a critical issue for women writers during this period and some reformist writers like Lydia Maria Child and Angelina Grimke drew upon history to demand abolition. Other women defended slavery or treated it favourably in their historical works. Sarah Josepha Hale argued for the preservation of the Union above all else in her work, even if it meant retaining slavery. In her historical novel ***Liberia*** (1853) and in editorials for *The Lady's Book* she championed the idea that slavery was a necessary step towards a Christian Africa. Other texts written by Southern authors such as Mary Howard Schoolcraft's historical novel *The Black Gauntlet* were viciously pro-slavery (Baym 1995: 55) Slaves themselves also began to write narratives relating their experience of slavery, such as Harriet Jacob's *Incidents in the Life of a Slave Girl* (1861). Jacob's text revealed both her own history and her historical insight into slavery from the perspective of the slave.

As American women settled across the country they claimed attachment to their new homes by recording history as an extension of their domestic interests. Memoirs, eyewitness accounts and local histories found willing readers throughout the nineteenth century, providing an important source of insight into life on the frontier. As early as 1799 Hannah Adams produced a *Summary History of New England* as well as numerous works of religious history. Women often produced local history as religious calling, following the divine command to 'remember the days of old and consider the years of many generations' (Sklar 1976: 174). Frances Manwaring Caulkins *History of Norwich* (1845) and *New London* (1866); Emma Willard's history of California, the *Last Leaves of American History* (1849) and Harriet E Bishop's history of Minnesota, *Floral Home* (1857) presented the history of the USA as Providential history, connecting the settlement of the country to a familiar narrative of historical progress (Baym 1995: 114). Captivity narratives and historical accounts of massacres and other tumultuous events were also popular with nineteenth-century readers. Juliette Magill Kinzie described her life on the Great Lakes frontier in her eyewitness history *Wau-bun* (1856), depicting both the Fort Dearborn massacre and the Black Hawk War.

Preserving the national memory

In the wake of the Civil War, the United States of America began to undergo a process of modernisation and industrialisation. Millions of people entered the United States in this period, ensuring the nation's continuing ethnic and racial diversity. The nation now stretched the width of the continent and it became essential to find new means for bringing (and keeping) such a nation together. History became a primary means of doing this, as programmes of patriotic instruction became essential in schools. Local expressions of history became more common than before, through a variety of societies and organisations in which women actively participated. Women's involvement in the creation of historical culture allowed them to compile archives, collect artefacts, create or restore historical monuments and sites, and promote the study of local and state history as a means of patriotic instruction in schools. They sometimes produced historical writing out of these activities.

An interest in preserving the history of the private sphere inspired writers such as **Alice Morse Earle** who wrote histories of the colonial period such as *Colonial Dames and Good Wives* (1895) and *Child Life in Colonial Days* (1899) as well as antiquarian studies such as *Collecting in America* (1892), *Costume of Colonial Times* (1894) and *Old Time Gardens* (1901). Earle's work on everyday colonial life presented American history from a feminine perspective, allocating much importance to the domestic environment and the work of women. Earle's interest in women's cultural life anticipated major themes in American women's history.

Women were also interested in the preservation of the history of the public sphere and women's clubs were particularly active in this endeavour. The Daughters of the American Revolution and the Society for Colonial Dames were among the most active of such organisations and counted Earle among their members. While women in the Eastern states were more likely to write of their engagement with the history of material culture, in the West, women historians took a more pragmatic approach. The Kansas Daughters of the American Revolution, for instance, organised for the preservation and marking of the Santa Fe Trail through their state. In 1915 Almira Cordry, one of the Daughters, published *The Story of the Marking of the Santa Fe Trail by the Daughters of the American Revolution in Kansas and the State of Kansas*. The book included historical narrative on the Trail itself, as well as chronicling the story of the efforts to preserve it. That particular historical project also involved the Kansas State Historical Society, which collected the tales of many pioneers, including women (Laugesen 2000a). Public historical projects thus came to produce women's historical accounts in many different ways.

In Western states, there was little opportunity, or desire, for a literary culture such as that in the East. However, many people still sought to write a history for their communities, not least to commemorate their achievements in settling the country. **Historical organisations** and pioneer societies blossomed across the United States from the middle of the nineteenth century. While founded by men, many women became members of these organisations. Women engaged with historical writing through writing diaries and memoirs, not necessarily intended for publication. Occasionally such texts found their way into a public forum. One of their primary activities at annual meetings would be for pioneers to get up and address assemblies with tales of their pioneering adventures – many women wrote and told their stories at these forums. Some of the more established pioneer and historical associations organised for annual publications in which these memoirs were preserved (Laugesen 2000b). Women's clubs also involved themselves in this work – the Woman's Kansas Day Club, for example, dedicated themselves to collecting personal stories that they printed as pamphlets.

Women participating in public historical projects through organisations such as the Daughters of the American Revolution or involving themselves in pioneer and historical associations contributed an important type of historical writing. This writing was often personal – notably in memoirs – and rarely was it informed by any deep understanding of historical events. These writings are preserved in the many proceedings and collections of historical societies, state and local, produced through the late nineteenth and twentieth centuries. This work, while perhaps seen as marginal contributions to history, nevertheless reflected the nature of the past for these women – their historical understanding was personal, it was also about patriotism and belonging to the nation. Further, it was often historical understanding produced within a social, rather than individual, context. These women pursued history in a social setting and their understandings were formed within that context. Their work has added importance in being the work of 'ordinary' rather than 'extraordinary' women.

Women historians and the academy

As higher education expanded in the late nineteenth and early twentieth century, history became a subject studied and codified within the academy. The emergence of an idea of 'scientific' history gendered the nature of historical writing and consequently women were frequently marginalised in the new profession and their work was trivialised or ignored. In spite of such discrimination women within the new profession managed to establish a place for themselves and to generate new ways of thinking about the nation's history. The story of Louise Phelps Kellogg is instructive. Kellogg received her doctorate from the University of Wisconsin in 1901, having worked with Frederick Jackson Turner. She went on to write several important studies of Midwestern history, including *Frontier Advance on the Upper Ohio* (1916), *The French Regime in Wisconsin and the Northwest* (1925) and *The British Regime in Wisconsin and the Northwest* (1935). Yet she spent most of her working life outside the academy, working in support areas such as within the State Historical Society of Wisconsin. In 1904, Kellogg had only recently published her doctoral thesis and received the Justin Winsor prize for it, yet Reuben Gold Thwaites, with whom she worked, and director of the State Historical Society, wrote in a letter to a colleague that he sometimes caught her 'jumping at conclusions from insufficient evidence' and that she needed to be watched 'not through desire of hers to do anything but good, honest work; but because of some lack in mental make-up'.

Despite, or maybe because of, such challenges, women historians pursued areas and employed sources deemed to be less conventional by the standards of male professional history. Ellen Churchill Semple used the environment and geography to frame her interpretation of the American past in her 1903 volume *American History and Its Geographic Conditions* (Fitzpatrick 2002: 77). Originally an expert in the appointing powers of the President, **Lucy Maynard Salmon** came to bring the scientific study of history to the mundane arena of the domestic sphere. Like Alice Morse Earle, Salmon drew on the material culture of the home and the conditions of buildings and urban spaces to identify historical problems and to create the potential for a 'more useful civic-mindedness' in works such as *Domestic Service* (1897) and *Progress in the Household* (1906) (Smith 1998: 207, 211). Salmon believed that her innovative historical methodology allowed for a unique perspective on the workings of American democracy, yet many of her essays were published privately, as scholarly journals such as *Yale Review* claimed they lacked 'gravity' (Adams and Smith 2001: 21).

Underpinning Salmon's work was a Progressivist commitment to history as a means of achieving social and economic reforms. Salmon and her contemporaries such as **Katherine Coman**, Professor of Economics at Wellesley, were Progressive historians 'well before men like Beard, Becker or Robinson gave the term any import' (Des Jardins 2003: 60). Coman was a founder of the College Settlements Association, an organisation which set up communal housing for single, mostly university-educated women in poor, urban areas that aimed to uplift their poor neighbours by exemplifying virtue and to cultivate in the working-class homes the value of 'pure, true and simple living'. In essays such as 'The Supreme Court Decision on the Oregon Ten Hour Law' (1908), and 'A Sweated Industry' (1911), Coman wrote of the exploitation of women workers and defended their right to strike. Her commitment to social reform and activism inspired a generation of women who like her engaged in history as a means of achieving social progress and reform. Women such as Edith Abbott, Director of Social Research at University of Chicago's School of Civics and Philanthropy, and **Helen Laura Sumner [Woodbury]**, both students of Coman's at Wellesley, merged social reform interests with their historical production and made significant contributions to American labour history. Abbott's *Women in Industry* (1910) was groundbreaking in bringing women and unskilled workers into focus. Salmon's influence too can be seen in the work of her student Caroline Ware, whose *The Early New England Cotton Manufacture* (1931) drew on a rich and diverse range of source material that threw much light on the employment and exploitation of women workers. Ware too had a history of social activism, participating in the first Bryn Mawr Summer School for Women Workers in Industry in 1922. While her critical views of capitalism were not always received favourably, her work contributed to the establishment of labour history as an important area of historical study.

On the frontier

While it is possible to speculate that women's marginalisation within the profession allowed them greater insight into the history of marginalised groups in the United States, in very real ways, women's exclusion from academic postings frequently led them to innovative approaches to studying American history. This is particularly true of women who engaged in writing the history of relations between colonisers and colonised on the Frontier. The historiography of the American West for a good part of the twentieth century was dominated by the 'Frontier thesis' of Frederick Jackson Turner. Turner first posited his thesis in 1893 and changed American national historiography into a narrative of progress and expansion across the continent. The frontier thesis, in many ways, ignored the complex nature of Western settlement – not least in its dismissal of Native Americans. It was also highly masculinist in its vision of the stalwart male frontier pioneer. Women historians did much to challenge this prevailing interpretation well before the rise of the 'New Western History'.

One of the first women to write on the history of the West was **Frances Fuller Victor**. She was employed by the historian and entrepreneur Hubert Howe Bancroft to research his multi-volume subscription history of the American West. Victor wrote all of the two volumes on *Oregon* (1886–1888), the volumes on *Washington, Idaho and Montana* (1890) and *Nevada, Colorado and Wyoming* (1890), and considerable portions of the volumes on *California* (1884–1890), the *Northwest Coast* (1884) and *British Columbia* (1887); yet Bancroft claimed authorship of this monumental endeavour. Her reputation as an historian, however, was greatly increased by her own claims to the authorship of the Bancroft volumes, which she presented in newspaper articles. When these books were exhibited at the Chicago World Fair in 1893 Victor placed her name alongside Bancroft's on the title page and spine of each volume, with a special preface in each to explain her actions. In spite of this she died in straitened circumstances, her writing career having been an ongoing struggle for survival.

The plight of Native Americans had long been a popular subject for women historians. In the late nineteenth century, historical fiction remained a significant way in which women related their perspective on settlement and conquest. Helen Hunt Jackson is most famous for her historical novel *Ramona* (1884) which challenged prejudice towards Native Americans and Spanish Americans, while her major historical work *A Century of Dishonor* (1881) laid bare the terrible treatment inflicted on indigenous Americans by white settlers. Jackson campaigned passionately on behalf of Native Americans and her work was informed by these views. Eva Emery Dye, an active woman's suffrage campaigner, wrote numerous historical works, usually fictional elaborations of true historical events, including *The Conquest: The True Story of Lewis and Clark* (1902) and *McLoughlin and Old Oregon* (1902). In a later work *Sacajawea* (1934), the story of Sacajawea, a Shoshone woman who helped to lead explorers Lewis and Clark to the Pacific Coast, Dye drew upon three decades of research to show the significance of Native

American women to the settlement of the frontier (Des Jardins 2003: 112).

By the early twentieth century, the dispossession of Native Americans became a field in which professionally trained women historians made significant and innovative contributions. Annie Heloise Abel employed ethnography in her work on Native American history, producing pioneering work including her Yale dissertation on the 'Indian Consolidation of the West Mississippi' (1905), her article for the *American Historical Review* 'The American Indian in the Civil War' (1910) and the multi-volume *The Slaveholding Indians* (1915–1925). Unlike other historians Abel attempted to present American history from a Native American perspective (Fitzpatrick 2002: 85). Her scholarship was widely respected and Abel was appointed to a full professorship at Smith College in 1916. Few other women working in this field attained the same level of professional achievement as Abel. The career of Angie Debo marks an interesting contrast to that of Abel. After graduating from the University of Chicago with a master's degree, Debo found no universities were prepared to hire a woman when they could get a man. She went on to gain a PhD from the University of Oklahoma. Debo's dissertation on the history of the Choctaw nation was published as *The Rise and Fall of the Choctaw Nation* in 1934 which won the Dunning Prize, bestowed annually by the American History Association (AHA) for the best book in American history. Debo's thesis was unusual in its effort to grant historical agency to native peoples and in its depiction of the coercive and dehumanising impact of colonisation on the Choctaw (Fitzpatrick 2002: 129). Debo went onto become one of the most prolific historians of Native American life, publishing *And Still the Waters Run* (1940) and *The Road to Disappearance* (1941) as well as a biography of Geronimo (1976), yet she never attained employment within the academy. Through extensive work in the archives of Oklahoma's Indian Commission, Debo exposed much corruption in relation to land dealings with Native Americans. The University of Oklahoma so feared the repercussions of Debo's findings that their press was unable to publish them (Fitzpatrick 2002: 138). Debo's marginal position as independent scholar may have allowed her the freedom to present an analysis of the frontier less dependent on Turner's thesis and hence more attuned to the relationships of power that shaped contact between settlers and Native Americans (Des Jardin 2003: 106).

Debo was not alone in uncovering the darker side of the frontier. Mari Sandoz, another independent scholar, published Western history in the form of biography, including the life of her father, *Old Jules* (1935), and that of Oglala leader Crazy Horse (1942). Writing from her own experience, Sandoz depicted the frontier in starkly unromantic terms and, like Debo, found herself marginalised from the profession (Des Jardin 2003: 116). Mormon historian Juanita Brooks fought to chronicle the history of the Utah in its entirety, exposing the fact that the Mormon community had covered up the killing of West-bound emigrants by Mormon militia in 1857. Brooks told the story in her *The Mountains Meadow Massacre* (1950) and, in doing so, challenged the conformity of thinking in the Mormon community of the time (Peterson 1988). She would be declared a 'dissenter' by the Mormon Church and she chose to ostracise herself from that institution rather than face disfavour (Des Jardins 2003: 117).

Finding their voice

While historians such as Abel and Debo could draw upon extensive archives when writing of relations between colonised and coloniser, other women recognised that such sources did not lend themselves to finding the voices of those groups marginalised within the national historiography. For women in the African-American community facing the dual barrier of race and gender when developing their perspective on the history of the United States, the need to record and preserve the historical record was most pressing. **Anna Julia Cooper** articulated this sentiment poignantly in her autobiography, *A Voice from the South* (1892), when she described African-American women as 'the mute and voiceless of the race', with 'no language but a cry'. As her title suggested, Cooper did not want African-American women to remain mute, rather she implored them to remember their collective past and generate a history of the United States that reflected their unique perspective.

The recording of oral testimony and life stories was an important way for women to create history and to challenge historical orthodoxies. The exigencies of slavery, particularly the restriction of literacy by the slave-owning classes, meant that oral traditions were critical to an understanding of African-American history, and that other non-discursive modes such as quilting and folktales were also used to preserve and record the past. The Harlem Renaissance and the emergence of a distinctive emphasis on the 'African' part of the 'African-American' identity saw many women become involved by themselves in collecting such narratives. Ophelia Settle Egypt, a graduate student at the Social Science Institute at Fisk University, recorded oral histories of over 100 former slaves in West Tennessee. Egypt's interviews tellingly entitled *The Unwritten History of Slavery* (1945) took the form of verbal autobiographies. Egypt wanted to see slavery through the eyes of the slave and thus provided a unique insight into the cultural world of slavery. Zora Neale Hurston while working in the anthropology department at Barnard College began to collect African-American folklore, compiling many of the narratives she uncovered researching the South, the Bahamas, Haiti and Jamaica in *Mules and Men* (1935) and *Tell My Horse* (1938). Hurston's work on folk culture recognised the importance of such non-discursive sources to an understanding of race history in America, particularly from the perspective of African-American women, who were the bearers and preservers of this culture (Des Jardins 2003: 141).

African-American women's organisations became one vehicle through which women could investigate their history. These club-women produced some valuable work such as *A History of the Woman's Club Movement in America* (1898) and collective biographies such as *Heroines of African Methodism* (1891), thus increasing the number of accounts of African-American women's lives. African-American women also used organisations such as the American Negro Historical Society and the Association for the Study of Negro Life and History as vehicles for the preservation of source materials such as songs, folktales, memoirs and oral testimonies and helped to organise and order the collections of these materials, thus creating an alternate archive in American history. Other women recognised the importance of collecting documents, books and the personal papers of significant African-Americans. Ella Elbert, the second African-American woman to graduate from Wellesley College, built up a collection of nearly 800 volumes of personal narratives, autobiographies, tracts and pamphlets, novels, folklore, poetry, novels and folklore which she donated to her alma mater. Elbert believed that the maintenance and preservation of such materials was critical for African-American women to develop a sense of historical identity (Des Jardins 2003: 133).

By the 1930s a small number of African-American women found themselves within the walls of the academy. Historians such as Margaret Nelson Powley and Elsie Lewis found a venue for their work within the pages of Carter Woodson's *Journal of Negro History*. Woodson, who advocated the 'New Negro History', saw the work of women, with their focus on social and cultural history, as vital to the project (Des Jardins 2003: 154). Mary McLeod Bethune also promoted the work of the New Negro History, initiating the *Negro History Bulletin* through the Association for the Study of Negro Life and History in 1937. Within five years of its establishment, the *Bulletin*'s editorial board and writing staff were made up almost entirely of women (Des Jardins 2003: 159).

Women as force in history

Until **Mary Ritter Beard** presented her unique perspective on women's historical role, mainstream American historiography in twentieth century found little scope for the discussion of women's social, cultural and political achievements. While there was a burgeoning literature devoted to narrating the lives and works of women involved in nineteenth-century reform campaigns such as abolition and suffrage, these texts were usually written by participants such as **Elizabeth Cady Stanton, Susan B Anthony** and **Matilda Joslyn Gage's** multi-volumed *History of Woman Suffrage* (1881–1922) and Carrie Chapman Catt's *Woman Suffrage and Politics* (1881–1923) or biographies written by hand-chosen acolytes such as **Alma Lutz**, who wrote the biography of Elizabeth Cady Stanton, *Created Equal* (1940). Mary Beard's reconceptualisation of American history from a woman's perspective was formed in response to these feminist histories. Reacting particularly to the Stanton collection, Beard argued in *On Understanding Women* (1931) that feminists had unwittingly contributed to the tradition that 'history had been made by man alone'. Beard rejected such a position, making an emphatic argument for women's historical agency, most famously in her *Woman as Force in History* (1946). Such ideas had always inflected her work and in the books on American history she co-wrote with her husband Charles Beard, *The Rise of American Civilisation: America in Midpassage* (1939) and *The American Spirit* (1942), she particularly stressed the importance of American women to the development of American culture. Beard also founded the World Center for Women's Archives in 1935. She saw this project as essential to fighting discrimination in American society as she believed that the material collected would form an invaluable basis for writing more inclusive history. Beard also worked to widely disseminate such historical work on women, participating in numerous public historical projects, including writing popular radio series, such as *Gallant American Women* (aired in 1939).

Woman as Force in History (1946) anticipated the emergence of second-wave feminism, as did **Eleanor Flexner**'s *Century of Struggle* which appeared in 1959. Flexner sought to revise American feminist history and, like Beard, shared a desire to write more inclusive history. *Century of Struggle* documents the history of suffrage in America, but is unusual in its focus on the intersections between class, sex and race that shaped first-wave feminism. This book was a notable achievement in a period that was largely conservative and paranoid about the Left. Both Beard and Flexner wrote history as independent scholars, reflecting the marginal position of women historians within the profession in the interwar years. The 1960s, however, saw a revitalisation of women's position within the academy. The impetus of second-wave feminism saw women fight to gain positions of influence within the university system and challenge discrimination within the historical profession. This shift in women historians' position in the academy was coupled with a general opening up in terms of approaches to historical study, which reflected the turbulent political atmosphere – the foundations of social and economic history were already there, but they gained in influence as areas of significance. Attention was now being paid to the 'ordinary' people of history and their lives. Women's historical writing benefited from these developments, and from second-wave feminism, and forums for publication of work explicitly addressing women's history increased through numerous new journals and publishing houses. Associations for women historians also flourished, such as the Berkshire Conference of Women Historians.

Gerda Lerner is perhaps the historian most pivotal to the development of American women's history and she is the only woman in the recent compilation *Clio's Favorites: Leading Historians of the United States 1945–2000* (2000). Lerner's work placed woman at the centre of historical inquiry, while also paying attention to the nexus between sex, class and race. Like the works of Mary Beard who Lerner viewed as a mentor, Lerner's works such as *The Woman in American History* (1971), *Hidden from History* (1973), *The Female Experience: An American Documentary* (1976) and *The Majority Finds Its Past: Placing Women in History* (1979) can be defined as recuperative history, history that recovers the female experience in American history and demonstrates women's historical agency. Indeed many of the themes Beard espoused in her writings particularly those relating to the importance of women in the development of American cultural life can be evidenced in historical works that emerged in the wake of second-wave feminism such as Lois Banner and Mary Hartman's (eds) *Clio's Consciousness Raised* (1976), Berenice Carroll's (ed.) *Liberating Women's History* (1976), Nancy F Cott's *The Bonds of Womanhood* (1977), Ellen DuBois' *Feminism and Suffrage* (1978), Linda Kerber's *Women of the Republic* (1980), Alice Kessler-Harris' *Out to Work* (1982), Mary Beth Norton's *Liberty's Daughters* (1980), Mary P Ryan's *Womanhood in America* (1975) and *The Cradle of the Middle Class* (1981), and Carroll Smith-Rosenberg's ground-breaking essay 'The Female World of Love and Ritual' (1975).

Dealing with difference

Women's history as informed by second-wave feminism was, in its first decades, all too clearly, the project of white middle-class women. The first feminist-influenced histories tended to tell the story of white middle-class women, making little concession for the differences in the experience of women generated by class and race. The works of African-American women historians such as bell hooks, *Ain't I a Woman* (1981), Paula Giddings, *When and Where I Enter* (1981) and Gloria T Hull *et al.*, *All the Women are White* challenged white feminist understandings of women's place in American history and the universalising tendencies that sprang from this. Echoing the writings of women such as Anna Julia Cooper and Sojourner Truth, hooks, Giddings and Hull presented American history from the perspective of the African-American woman, consequently revising familiar narratives in American history through the nexus of sex and race.

As debates about difference were generated within feminism, more women came to present American history shaped by their particular experience of race and class. In 1986 Paula Gunn Allen published *The Sacred Hoop*, a history of the experience of

Native American women that both recovered the feminine experience in Native American history and challenged dominant narratives of American history more generally. Vicki Ruiz has contributed important histories of the lives of Chicanas/Latinas, including *Cannery Women, Cannery Lives: Mexican Women, Unionization and the California Food Processing Industry, 1930–1950* (1987) and *Out of the Shadows: Mexican Women in Twentieth-Century America* (1998). Iris Chang too made contributions to recent American popular historiography both as a woman and as a Chinese-American, notably in her history of the Chinese-American community *The Chinese in America: A Narrative History* (2003). While her work is more preoccupied with questions of race and identity, it is also perceptive to issues involving women.

Women have continued to explore historical issues through fictional and non-academic forms of writing. Interestingly, many of the most notable achievements have been by women outside the white, middle-class norm, perhaps because until recently they have been the most marginalised from the institutions of power and the academy. Pauli Murray and Maya Angelou used their work and their experiences as African-American women to inform their autobiographical writing, providing a personal and intimate perspective on the history of the United States. Historical novels such as Toni Morrison's *Beloved* (1987) and Alice Walker's *The Color Purple* (1982) have addressed the impact of slavery on African-American women, and the historical experiences of Native American women and Chinese women have been addressed in the work of writers like Louise Erdrich and Amy Tan. These writers might produce fiction, but they have done much to address major historical issues in important ways and have reached a wide audience in doing so.

Gendering history

However, women's history only focused on restoring the history of women. Radical feminism impacted on women's historical writing in an even deeper way, as the very nature of womanhood as a historical construct was investigated. What many of the women mentioned above brought to their work was a distinctive consciousness of, and engagement with, the issue of gender. Gender began to be analysed as a central dynamic of historical understanding. Gender was now, in the words of Joan Wallach Scott, 'a useful category of analysis' (1988: 28). This new perspective had radical implications for the study of history, because it destabilised the very categories of 'man' and 'woman', and, by implication, other previously viewed as essentialist categories, such as racial and class identities.

Gender history has allowed historians new interpretations of the American past. Using gender as a category of historical analysis, works such as Gail Bederman's *Manliness and Civilization: A Cultural History of Gender and Race in the United States, 1880–1917* (1995), Joanne Meyerowitz's *Not June Cleaver: American Women and Gender in Postwar America, 1945–1960* (1994) and Susan Jefford's *Remasculinization of America: Gender and Vietnam* (1989) have revised the familiar narratives within American history, radically reassessing dominant perceptions on period, class and race. These histories have been complemented by studies such as those of Estelle Freedman into the history of American sexuality, notably (with John D'Emilio) *Intimate Matters: A History of Sexuality in America* (1997) and the contributions made towards lesbian history such as Lillian Faderman's *Surpassing the Love of Men* (1981) and *Odd Girls and Twilight Lovers: A History of Lesbian Life in Twentieth Century America* (1991) and Elizabeth Lapovsky Kennedy and Madeline

D Davis' *Boots of Leather, Slippers of Gold: The History of a Lesbian Community* (1993).

Amanda Laugesen

References

Baym 1991, 1995; Clinton 2000; Des Jardins 2003; Fitzpatrick 2002; Laugeson 2000a,b; Peterson 1988; Sklar 1976; Smith 1998; Scott 1988.

Related essays

Canada; Great Britain; Historical Organisations; Local History.

Utopian writings

Until recently, most secondary literature on women's utopian writing viewed the genre as a space for women to imagine an alternative society in which equality between men and women was the paramount concern. This was partly the result of a second-wave feminist desire to historicise a feminist consciousness and thus plot the emergence of woman as a self-conscious subject of history and political philosophy.

While there is a good deal of scholarship on gender in utopian literature, there are fewer studies of utopias written by women, particularly those that place the works in their historical contexts. Indeed much of the interest in this subject is an extension of the feminist tradition of literary criticism, in which the major work to give a comprehensive account of women's utopias is *The Feminist Companion to Literature in English, Women Writers from the Middle Ages to the Present* (1990). In addition, Jean Pfaelzer has conceptualised women's utopian writing in the context of the changing historical objectives of the women's movement. Finally, thematic studies of women's utopias of the nineteenth and twentieth centuries have been of particular interest to scholars, notably to Nan Bowman Albinski in *Women's Utopias in British and American Fiction* (1988) and Carol Farley Kessler's edited collection *Daring to Dream, Utopian Stories by United States Women 1836–1919* (1984).

A central issue when conceptualising women's utopian literature is at what historical moment this form of writing should be understood as a 'genre'. We should be cautioned against locating a feminist voice in pre-modern utopias. Such an approach would anachronistically read into the past a unified subject of 'woman', and thus overlook the complexity of early modern women's writing by assuming that female authors were necessarily addressing issues of gender.

Often, what is utopian about an early modern text is not a self-conscious engagement with a canon of literature, but rather an ideal immersed in a wide range of genres. Women's utopian literature before the eighteenth century, therefore, is better classified as having a utopian *dimension*, because such works experiment with a variety of forms. **Margaret Cavendish**'s 'The Inventory of Judgements Commonwealth, the Author Cares Not in What World It is Established', for example, echoes the renaissance genre of advice to princes and is part of her larger work, *The World's Olio* (1655). Analogously, the millennial setting of Mary Cary's *The Little Horns Doom and Downfall* (1681) places it in a tradition of seventeenth-century apocalyptic literature.

In much of women's pre-modern writing, part of the utopian element consists in an idealised ethos of female friendship and education. In Cavendish's *The Description of a New World, Called The Blazing World*, which was appended to the treatise *Observations Upon Experimental Philosophy* (1666), the character Margaret Cavendish is taught natural philosophy by the Empress of the Blazing World. Cavendish's utopia was nothing if not adventurous. It inverted gender roles by depicting Cavendish herself as the princely commander of her own empire, in which her power relied upon her knowledge of the natural world. Eleven years earlier, Cavendish articulated an ideal of educated and reasoned debate among women in the 'Female Academy', part of *The World's Olio* (1655). Similarly, in Mary Astell's *A Serious Proposal to the Ladies; for the Advancement of Their True and Greatest Interest*, published anonymously in 1694, wealthy, single women were encouraged to establish residential, protestant colleges for their younger counterparts. In part two of the work Astell proposes a series of rules of rational thought for women. The importance of women's education continues in the earliest engagement of utopian writing with a consciously feminist political programme, most prominently in **Mary Wollstonecraft**'s *Vindication of the Rights of Woman* (1792) and Sarah Scott's *Millenium Hall* (1778). Together with Lady Barbara Montagu, Sarah Scott established a community for women at Batheaston, upon which *Millenium Hall* was based.

The late eighteenth to the late twentieth centuries are characterised by an intersection between utopian writing, and political and social movements. In America, first-wave feminism was a major influence upon women's utopian writing during the fruitful period of the last two decades of the nineteenth century and the first two of the twentieth. In America, Mary Ford's 'A Feminine Iconoclast' (1889) and Lois Waisbrooker's *A Sex Revolution* (1894) envisioned women's control of their own bodies. The feminist social critic **Charlotte Perkins Gilman** wrote three utopian novels including *Herland* (1915), a separatist utopia populated by women and governed on a parthenogenic basis through which women were freed from sexual relations with men.

A new theme emerges during the nineteenth and early twentieth centuries. This is the role of racial equality and inequality. In *Account of an Expedition to the Interior of New Holland* (1837) Lady Mary Fox describes a journey into the inland desert in Australia and the discovery of a utopian civilisation comprised of people who fled the European reformation, and who had since interbred with the Aborigines. The utopia is a rational and liberal society of racial equality, as well as a satire of the Australian convict system. In some works, utopian racial equality is imagined in a specifically historical setting, in a way reminiscent of the 'noble savage' topos. In 1947, the Australian authors Marjorie Barnard and Florence Eldershaw, collectively published a censored version of their work, *Tomorrow and Tomorrow*, under the pseudonym 'M Barnard Eldershaw'. Their socialist utopia is partly constructed as a historical narrative in which Aboriginal people lived in harmony with the land, only to be supplanted by the Australians and ultimately usurped by a tyrannous foreign elite. Influenced by the post-war fear of totalitarianism, *Tomorrow and Tomorrow* oscillates between the twenty-fourth and the twentieth century. Not all women's utopias of this period, however, were feminist or promoted racial equality. Central to the American author Mary Griffith's 'Three Hundred Years Hence' (1836), for example, was the return of slaves to Africa as a prerequisite for her racialised utopian vision.

The importance of a historical narrative to *Tomorrow and Tomorrow* raises an important issue. How is women's utopian literature a form of *historical* writing? In structuralist theories of history, utopia is the state of telos in which the Hegelian struggles that define historical change are resolved in a final act of synthesis. Yet many women's utopias take the idea of history as a central theme, constructing the ideal society as a state with its own past. Cavendish's *Description of a New World, Called the Blazing World*, for example, begins with a story to explain how the young Cavendish becomes Empress of the 'New

World'. There are also references to the contemporaneous Civil Wars in England.

In the case of modern women's utopias, from the eighteenth century onwards, the idea of history has a peculiar significance. As the consciousness of woman as a political subject developed, so the idea of history became prominent in women's utopian literature. This is arguably because historical writing is a metaphysical act of bringing an historical subject into being. When women authors told the story of the origins of their utopias, women took centre stage. Women became central to the founding stories of utopias just as, conversely, men's stories constituted the foundation myths of the modern nation state. This emphasis upon origins is the first feature of the increasing prominence of history. In utopias, women become part of the historical, public realm. The American Civil War doctor, journalist and author, Dr Mary Edwards Walker, for example, appropriated and subverted the Biblical historical trope of the Edenic paradise, in her separatist utopia, *An Adamless Eden* (1897).

A second feature of the historical consciousness of modern utopias is the sense of the contingency of the relationships of power that define women's oppression. In twentieth-century utopias, the female body becomes a representation of the problems and possibilities of the way that corporeality is constructed through operations of power. Consequently, the utopia is created through *deconstructing* these relationships. This theme arguably accompanies the broader turn toward poststructuralism and a postmodern aesthetic in intellectual life since the mid-1970s. In Margaret Atwood's *The Handmaid's Tale*, the metaphysical boundaries between humanity and technology are blurred; a fusion which is laden with both utopian and dystopian possibilities. Also significant in this context is the work of Ursula le Guin, particularly *The Eye of the Heron* (1978) and *The Dispossessed: An Ambiguous Utopia* (1974). This fragmentation of categories is accompanied by the abandonment of a linear narrative, a technique also employed by Joanna Russ in *The Female Man* (1974).

Another characteristic of postmodern utopian literature is a critique of the unity of the female subject and authorial voice. In Octavia Butler's *Xenogenesis* science fiction trilogy, racial boundaries are subverted through the exploration of oppressive and dystopian relationships. A similar collapse of categorical distinctions and technological boundaries is found in Marge Piercy's *He, She and It* (1991) and Donna Haraway's essay *A Manifesto for Cyborgs* (1985). Haraway raises the possibility of constructing and reconstructing one's gender and sexuality, a form of postmodern self-fashioning. It should be noted that while postmodern utopias explicitly and playfully undermine their normative force, there has historically been a good deal of slippage between utopia and dystopia. It is an oversimplification, therefore, to see the history of utopian literature as a genre for women's confident emancipatory visions.

Sarah Irving

Related essays
Australia; Dominions; Religion; Renaissance; Science; USA.

Victor, Frances 1826–1902

American poet, journalist, novelist, historian and social critic. Born in New York, the eldest child of Lucy A Williams and Adonijah Fuller. Educated at a female seminary with her sister Metta Victoria. In their teens the sisters published stories and poems in the *New York Home Journal*. In 1848 Frances published a romantic novella *Anzietta the Guajira; or the Creole of Cuba*. A collection entitled *Poems of Sentiment and Imagination, with Dramatic and Descriptive Pieces*, written by both sisters, appeared in 1851. After the death of their father the sisters returned to Ohio to care for their mother. In 1853 Frances married Jackson Barritt. After a period of home-steading they separated. Frances rejoined Metta in New York, where both pursued literary careers, publishing historical romances for *Beadle's Home Monthly*. Obtaining a divorce in 1862 Frances married her brother-in-law, Henry Clay Victor.

In 1863 Victor moved to San Francisco, finding work as a journalist. Writing as Florence Fane, she contributed regularly to the *Golden Era* and the *San Francisco Bulletin*. She reported on political and social events, news and issues that concerned women. She was offered a position as editor of the *New Era* in 1864, but she turned it down to follow her husband to Oregon, where she began to write **local history**. Victor published her first work of history in 1870. *The River of the West* has been described as 'folk literature', but was mostly factual, although it was criticised for embellishing the achievements of its protagonist Joe Meeks. Women appear in several specific contexts in this work, particularly as victims of violence and injustice on the frontier, and in relation to divorce, a subject of personal interest to Victor. Separated from her second husband, Victor wrote numerous articles for the burgeoning suffrage movement, advocating economic independence for women and educational reform, urging women to study history to learn why men became the dominant sex.

Widowed in 1875 Victor had to support herself. She published the historical fiction *The New Penelope* in 1877. Drawn from her writings for the *Overland Monthly*, the novel focuses on a woman establishing herself in the West in the face of much prejudice and adversity and drew upon the writings of John Stuart Mill on the condition and status of women and Victor's knowledge of the history of women during the gold rushes. The novel was commercially successful and received impressive reviews. She also published historical articles in journals such as *West Shore* and *Resources of Oregon and Washington*. In 1878 she drew the attention of Hubert Howe Bancroft, the historical entrepreneur. He employed Victor to help prepare his monumental *History of the Pacific States*. She worked on the 28-volume project until its completion in 1890, writing *Oregon* (1886–1888), *Washington, Idaho and Montana* (1890), *Nevada, Colorado and Wyoming* (1890) and considerable portions of the volumes of *California* (1884–1890), the *Northwest Coast* (1884) and *British Columbia* (1887). Her authorship was not acknowledged by Bancroft. In these works women feature mostly in footnotes and statistics, although Victor demonstrated a particular interest in the lives of women, in the way in which she portrayed their stories, albeit parenthetical to the main text. Returning to Oregon in 1890 she continued writing to survive. In spite of failing health, she published *The Early Indian Wars* (1891) (commissioned by the legislature of Oregon); a biography of *Hall J Kelley* (1901); a history of *The First Oregon Cavalry* (1902); and a collection of poetry and numerous articles in the *Oregon Historical Society Quarterly*.

Sarah Howard

References

Bube 1997; Elgi 1998; Martin 1992.

Major work

Women of the Gold Rush: 'The New Penelope' and other stories (ed.) Ida Rae Egli (Berkeley: Heydey Books, 1998).

W

War

In the *Illiad* Homer wrote, 'The men must see to the fighting', and since then war has been seen as a male domain. Women's role has been to stay at home and suffer as civilians, or to support armies as 'camp followers', and until very recently there has been virtually no space for women to act as combatants on the battlefield. Of course, there have always been exceptions to this rule: from the Amazons to Joan of Arc and Boadicea, mythical female warriors have acted as icons for belligerent nations and have been a recurring source of fascination for authors, artists and academics. Individual women have participated in battle as combatants. Phoebe Hessel of England disguised herself as a man to follow her sweetheart to the Napoleonic wars. Flora Sandes led Serbian soldiers into battle in the First World War and the Russian Women's Battalion of Death was formed to inspire the Russian soldiers suffering in the trenches of the same war. In very few cases, women have been armed and have acted as combatants alongside men. The Dahomey Kingdom of nineteenth-century West Africa was famed for its 'Amazon corps' whilst in the Soviet Union during the Second World War women performed in a wide range of combat tasks, including anti-aircraft units, infantry and aerial bombardment. Women served with the Yugoslav partisans during the same war, in the French and Italian Resistance, and in later wars of liberation such as those in Algeria, Vietnam and Zimbabwe. However, these are exceptions and, historically, women's writing on war has been marginalised in the same way that women participating in warfare have been.

The gender of war

When considering the impact of war on gender roles, wartime can most usefully be seen as a period in which gender divides are highlighted and reinforced, rather than negated. Although war, particularly the total wars of the twentieth century, has often provided a widening of opportunities for women, opening up new areas of employment and new roles within the home, women have always remained subordinate to the fighting man, the key symbolic figure of wartime. Indeed, fighting is often naturalised as an innate feature of masculinity, and the warrior portrayed as a masculine ideal in texts ranging from the chivalric novels of the nineteenth century to the 'Rambo' films of late twentieth-century Hollywood. As Martin Shaw has commented: '[W]arfare has been defined in most societies as a male prerogative, and warlikeness as an attribute of masculinity' (Shaw 1991: 188). This gendered division has often been mirrored in a marginalisation of women's writing on war. Anthologies of war-writing are still predominantly anthologies recording this male experience, and representation, of war. Paul Fussell's *The Bloody Game: An Anthology of Modern War* includes only six women authors amongst its collection of 97 first-hand observations of war. Similarly, the edited collection *The War Decade: An Anthology of the 1940s* has 17 pieces of poetry and prose written by women amongst its 309 pieces. It appears that narrative authority in wartime is primarily acquired through an author's proximity to the battlefield – a physical and ideological terrain closely associated with masculinity. When women's writing, and the female experience of war which it represents, is given equal status with men's it is in work which specifically focuses on gender as a category of analysis, and which seeks to examine the extent to which experiences and representations of war are shaped by gender.

For a long time, this pattern was replicated in historical writing on war. The dominance of military history as a means of approaching and understanding warfare meant that histories of war tended to be dominated by studies of battlefield tactics and political strategies. Martin Gilbert's authoritative histories of both the First and Second World Wars, for example, combine political and military history in their descriptions of the conflicts, and pay only passing attention to the social and cultural impact of the conflicts (Gilbert 1989, 1994). As battles are generally fought by, and high politics overwhelmingly determined by, men, any female perspective on war is largely absent from these histories. The focus upon the battlefield in most military histories has led to this particular branch of history being principally written by men. Joanna Bourke's *An Intimate History of Killing*, which avoids the narrow focus of most military histories by focusing on the largely male experience of killing in combat, and addressing the role of the warrior myth in the creation of male combatants, is a rare exception (Bourke 1999). Bourke's research not only focuses on the battlefield experience, but also examines the wider implications of warfare for the combatants, paying particular attention to the psychological, social and cultural impact of battle upon its participants. *An Intimate History of Killing* sets out to challenge the inclination to see combatants as victims of warfare, as sacrificial figures, instead emphasising that 'the characteristic act of men at war is not dying, it is killing' (1999: 1). Bourke's book is less a military history, characterised by a cataloguing of the minutiae of battlefield planning and action, than a social and cultural history which engages with the impact of conflict upon both combatants and civilians.

The growth of social and cultural history in the 1960s and 1970s did widen the historical perspective on war as historians began to consider the impact of war on civil society, focusing particularly on the concept of war as a force for social change and modernisation. However, it was not until the emergence of feminist history in the 1970s that academics began to fully explore the impact of war on gender roles. Literary historians such as Susan Gilbert interrogated literary and visual texts of the First World War to argue that the conflict effectively emasculated men, whilst women became 'ever more powerful' (Gilbert 1989: 263). Gilbert's contribution to the debate on gender in wartime, with its emphasis on 'high' cultural representations of war, while addressing the disjuncture between symbolic and lived gender roles, has been roundly criticised for focusing on too narrow a range of established sources (Tylee 1988; Braybon 2003). Social historians too began to re-examine the relationship of war to gender roles, and the wider range of sources used here often led researchers to conclusions which opposed Gilbert. While early evaluations of the impact of war on women tended to focus on the opportunities offered by widening access to the workplace, work such as Gail Braybon and Penny Summerfield's *Out of the Cage* (1987) has argued that war, far from liberating women, as exponents of the modernisation thesis had argued, actually reinforced existing gender roles. Similar arguments were made by Leila Rupp in *Mobilizing Women for War* (1978) and Kate Darian-Smith's *On the Home Front: Melbourne in Wartime* (1990). Such texts demonstrated the ways in which new opportunities for women were framed within a discourse which encouraged them to 'help out in the workforce because of their love for male friends and relatives in the forces'. Although total war had meant that women's roles expanded the movement of women out of the traditional fields of women's work into a variety of occupations that had previously been the preserve of men, these historians have argued that freedom was short-lived and circumscribed by existing ideas concerning masculinity and femininity. However, more recent work such as Penny Summerfield's *Reconstructing Women's Wartime Lives* (1998) has suggested that, despite the rapid return to established gender relations and gendered occupational patterns following both wars, many women have expressed the view that their wartime experiences *were* liberating. This sense of liberation through wartime experiences is not something that is quantifiable via an examination of employment patterns or government policy. It only becomes available to the historian through a study of women's personal experiences, recorded through writing and reminiscence work.

The experience of combat

Nonetheless, as Margaret Higonnet has argued, much writing on war continues to privilege the experience of the combatant, reflecting his special status in society as one who will fight, kill and perhaps die for his nation's interests and beliefs (Higonnet 1993). Combatants are seen here as having undergone an experience which 'isolates them from other men – cuts off the men who fought from older and younger men who did not share that shaping experience' (Hynes 1997: 5). The experience of combat, both actual and as a potential, acts to divide men from women. Wars that are fought away from the home, with relatively little immediate danger for civilians, such as the First World War, intensify this divide, as women are intimately linked with ideas of the home in wartime. Although many men will never experience combat first-hand, there is a ready supply of representations of war, both popular and academic, which focus on combat as a peculiarly *male* experience, a male rite of passage which functions as a means by which boys become men. As combat is something that the majority of people will never experience, there is an especial fascination for many in texts that attempt to communicate the realities of battle. This focus on the experience of combat in war-writing has acted to marginalise women's attempts to record their own experiences of wartime.

The sense of wishing to record one's experiences of wartime in some form is widespread, and although women may be much less likely than men to write about combat, there is a large body of historical writing by women on the experience of war. Women writers addressed the impact of the First World War in their fiction: Rebecca West's *The Return of the Soldier* (1918) focused on the impact of shell shock on a relationship whilst more populist literature quickly moved to incorporate the war into the traditional romance narrative. Novels such as Olivia Manning's *The Balkan Trilogy* (1987) and Elizabeth Bowen's *The Heat of the Day* (1948) drew on autobiographical material in these 'fictional' studies of the Second World War. Female war correspondents have reported on both the battle- front and civilian life in wartime from the American Civil War onwards. Feminist historians have examined the impact of war on both women's lives and on society more widely. Women have recorded wartime life in diaries, letters, photographs, family histories and biographies. While the majority of women writing about war may not have experienced combat first-hand, many of them have seen battle at close quarters, or had loved ones participating in conflict. The two 'total wars' of the twentieth century touched, to some extent, the lives of all the citizens of the belligerent nations, and these wars were widely recognised as 'historical events'; extraordinary times to live through and record.

One of the best-known writers on the experience of war is the British feminist author **Vera Brittain**. Brittain captured the mood of August 1914 in her diaries. The entry for 3 August 1914, the day before war was declared in Britain, read:

> Today has been far too exciting to enable me to feel at all like sleep – in fact it is one of the most thrilling I have ever lived through . . . That which has been so long anticipated by some and scoffed at by others has come to pass at last – Armageddon in Europe! (1981: 84)

Brittain's diaries express an ambivalent early relationship with the war which is absent from her later autobiographical writing which sits more consciously within a body of literature which both eulogised the 'lost generation' of the war and attempted graphically to convey the horrors of the conflict. Brittain's transition as a writer from the ambivalence of her wartime diaries to the pacifism of *Testament of Youth* (1933) can also be traced through her fictional writing between the wars: *Not Without Honour* (1924) describes the reaction of two women to the war, one a pacifist and one a romantic idealist, whilst *Honourable Estate* (1936) is more clearly inflected with Brittain's pacifist ideals. Brittain's autobiographical account of the war in *Testament of Youth* remains her most popular and best-known work, perhaps because it sits most easily within an established body of writing which attempted to communicate the war experiences of a particular generation and a particular class to a wider audience.

Many other women have also been driven to record their own particular and unusual activities in wartime. Marguerite Duras' *La Douleur* (1985), Lucie Aubrac's *Outwitting the Gestapo* (1984) and Madeleine Baudoin's *Histoire des Groupes Francs* (1962) draw on autobiography to describe the role of women in the French Resistance. Violette Rougier Lecoq, imprisoned in Ravensbruck concentration camp for her Resistance work, drew the atrocities that she saw there: these drawings went on to become vital evidence in the 1946 war-crimes trials at Hamburg, in which she represented France (Collins-Weitz 1995: 15). The drive to document the unique experiences of wartime was felt as much by women as by men. The civilian perspective on war has been recorded far more often by women than by men, perhaps because male non-combatants are 'silenced' by their uncomfortable position in a time when the dominant model of masculinity is a militarised one.

Wartime diaries, letters and reminiscence work by women are more likely to describe the civilian experience of warfare than the combatant. Indeed, a focus on women's wartime writing can illustrate many of the domestic, private aspects of wartime life. One woman's account of French Resistance to German occupation during the Second World War demonstrates the hidden, yet vital, role of women in the home, remembering that:

> In my parent's house, my father was an official Communist Resistance worker, so he used to have many men and women visiting him. But it cannot be said that my mother was not involved in Resistance activities. . . . Who used to darn socks and do the washing for the Resistance worker who was sleeping? Who used to prepare the food that he would take away with him? And who would be at home when the police called during an alert? I think that in my family my mother was as involved in Resistance activities as my father. (Diamond 1999: 98)

As much of this writing vividly demonstrates, it would be a mistake to assume that non-combatants necessarily suffer less than combatants in modern warfare. Indeed, the use of aerial bombardment against civilians as a feature of modern warfare has sometimes led to higher casualty rates amongst civilians than combatants. The female experience of warfare is often shaped by the need to care for and protect dependents in extremely difficult circumstances. Many responses to the British Mass-Observation Directives during the 1982 Falklands/Malvinas War and the 1991 Gulf War demonstrate the ways in which women used their personal memories of warfare. Such responses show how women's experience of war allows them to identify with the victims of contemporary wars. One woman described 'sitting under the stairs of the house in Liverpool alone with a nine month old baby in my arms while bombs rained down' as a means of supporting and explaining her opposition to war (Mass-Observation Directive No. 5, 1982: Correspondent W563). In the same way, a woman writing for Mass-Observation during the 1991 Gulf War drew on her memories of 'a mentally and physically handicapped boy left in his wheelchair with his mother dying on the ground beside him' to conclude 'that's war. War in the Gulf. NEVER.NEVER. NEVER' (Mass-Observation Directive No. 33, 1990: Correspondent D666). The discourse used in these examples, which draws upon memories of civilian victims of war, was rarely used by male correspondents, suggesting that the valorisation of the male soldier makes it difficult for men to describe wartime experiences which do not fit easily within this identity. Studies of wartime writing by women thus illustrate both the gendered nature of warfare and the variety of ways in which war shapes the lives of non-combatants.

Nella Last, a housewife from the shipbuilding town of Barrow-in-Furness in the North of England, was one of the most prolific diarists for the Mass-Observation project. Nella, who kept diaries for Mass-Observation for almost 30 years, used her writing as a means of expressing her often forceful views on the war, yet they also demonstrate the ways in which the Second World War served to expand Nella's horizons and increase her self-confidence. Although Nella's activities during the war sit comfortably within traditional tropes of femininity, her writings nonetheless display a sense of liberation through wartime work and responsibilities. During the war Nella worked outside the home as a member of the Women's Voluntary Service, nursed a premature baby and saw her youngest son join the army. Her sense of identity was shaped by these wartime experiences and she began to see herself as a citizen with a useful public role, as well as a privately situated wife and mother. Nella's reactions to the aerial bombardment of Barrow demonstrate the linkage between these public and private roles: when her son suggested evacuating into the country to sleep, as many others had done, Nella replied, 'No, not while I've a roof and my nerves can possibly stand it. Do you think I'd feel shame before the women of London and Bristol who have stood it for so long?' (Last 1981: 144). These diaries show the extent to which Nella felt that the war, famously described in Britain as the 'people's war', was her war, as much as any fighting man's.

Feminising war

Women writing about war have used a variety of strategies to record their views and document their experiences. One of these is to claim a particular feminine perspective on war. This can be used politically, both to support a pacifist position that states that war is largely enacted by men, and to endorse a more bellicose and jingoistic view, in which women often use their special status as mothers or wives of combatants to argue in support of military action. In both cases, motherhood is taken as a position from which to argue a uniquely female perspective. In a parallel with the male role of soldier, the female role of mother is seen as providing a particular, gendered standpoint. Indeed, the image of woman as mother has been used time and time again in wartime propaganda, perhaps most grotesquely in Alonzo Earl Forinza's reworking of the Pieta in an American Red Cross poster of 1918 'The Greatest Mother in the World'. Several popular French novels of the First World War reflected legal and moral debate about the nationality of the children of French women raped by German soldiers, emphasising that 'for women motherhood was synonymous with patriotism' (Grayzel 1999: 63). The notorious letter from 'A Little Mother', republished in Robert Graves' wartime **memoir** *Goodbye to All That*, first published in the *Morning Post* in 1916 embodies what Claire Tylee calls the 'motherhood for militarism' campaign of the First World War (Tylee 1990: 70). Purporting to be written by a British soldier's mother, the letter described 'women's sacred trust of motherhood . . . we women pass on the human ammunition of "only sons" to fill up the gaps since women were created for the purpose of making life as men were created to take it' (Tylee 1990: 70). Mrs Alec Tweedie, an upper-class Englishwoman, took a similar view in 1918 when writing of her wish to take an active part in combat:

> The writer is ready to form a women's battalion the moment it becomes necessary for women to fill that fighting breach. Women have done more for their country than handle a rifle and thousands of us are ready to do that too. (1919: 26)

However, Tweedie's wish to fight was framed within a very traditional notion of femininity: she claimed it as her right as a mother, her youngest son having died in battle earlier in the war. Tweedie argued that women should take up arms as a last resort, and that mothers had a special role in defending the home and nation:

> We mothers of England, mothers of Empire, will never see the land of our forebears trampled underfoot. We will fight if necessary. Shed our blood if necessary. (1919: 184)

This image of women acting to defend the home in wartime is common in both inter-state wars and guerrilla warfare, and has been widely used in propaganda intended to inspire male soldiers, reflecting the ideological linkage between women, home and family and a belief that women's willingness to defend the home symbolises a nation or a movement's determination and unity.

Opposing this jingoistic use of motherhood in pro-war propaganda were the feminist pacifists, who have long argued that women's maternal, nurturing capabilities instinctively oppose them to war. Olive Schreiner, the South African feminist and socialist, argued in *Women and Labour* that:

> We have in all ages produced, at an enormous cost, the primal munition of war, without which no other would exist. There is no battlefield on earth, nor has there ever been, howsoever covered with slain, which it has not cost the women of the race more in actual bloodshed and anguish to supply, than it has the men who lie there. *We pay the first cost on all human life*. (Original emphasis; 1911: 169)

Similar arguments have been used by female peace activists throughout the twentieth century. Both the nationalistic and xenophobic Tweedie and her ilk, and the feminist-pacifist campaigners effectively argue their case from a similar essentialist position. Although coming to very different conclusions, both groups of women use the image of a nurturing, maternalistic femininity to claim a particular perspective on wartime.

Writing in another language

Another strategy used by women writing about war has been to try and claim some of the authority attributed to men writing on the same subject by using a 'male language' to describe their war experiences, or by allying themselves with the combatant men. This often backfired, as any female attempt to claim parity with combatant men was seen as demeaning the special status of the male combatant, rather than elevating the position of women. The Women's Volunteer Reserve (WVR), a uniformed, paramilitary organisation which was formed in Britain during the First World War, was often subject to these criticisms, particularly when its female members paraded in khaki uniforms. Formed in reaction to German raids on east coast towns, in which 78 women and children had been killed, the WVR illustrated the changing patterns of war for British people, in which 'non-combatants may suffer very severely'. The feminist campaigner Eleanor Rathbone was one of those to suggest the organisation of a women's reserve army in response to these raids, arguing in the *Common Cause* in 1915 that 'if there are any functions that can usefully be performed by women, they have a right to claim those functions . . . if once the idea could be got rid of that they must not be exposed to danger'. However, the WVR was widely seen as a female encroachment on the masculine, military sphere, providing a space for women to dress as men, act as men and, according to the *Morning Post* in 1915, to 'assume mannish attitudes'. Members of the WVR argued in response that their members were simply fulfilling their patriotic duty as women, not only by learning how to defend their homes and community in times of crisis such as invasion and bombardment, but also as part of the ongoing eugenicist campaign to strengthen the British 'race' by improving the health of its mothers and children through exercise. A poem published in the *Women's Volunteer Reserve Magazine* (1916) used explicitly religious imagery which evoked the 'sacrifice' of dead soldiers to link the women's voluntary work with the combatant men:

> When we are gone
> You will remember then
> We wore the sacred khaki soberly
> As did the men

Thus, women of the WVR attempted to contest claims that their work was 'worse than useless' by endeavouring to align themselves with the spirit of sacrifice popularly associated with the men of the armed forces.

Similar attempts to align the female experience of the war with that of the fighting man were made in fiction. The anonymously authored *WAAC: The Women's Story of the War* (1930) attempts to establish a unity between the men and women serving overseas, both of whom undergo warfare as both a formative and an isolating experience. In a manner similar to Siegfied Sassoon's famous wish to see tanks in the stalls of London theatres as a response to the inability of the civilian public to comprehend the realities of trench warfare, the anonymous author comments of home that:

> The smugness and the apathy and the lack of imagination of many of

> our people at home had made me feel uncharitable. They seemed unable to realise what was actually happening in France. (1930: 44)

However, unlike Sassoon's poem, which expresses the division between combatant and non-combatant in terms of gender, this novel tries to demonstrate the ways in which being close to the front line unified men and women. The sense of 'being there', bearing witness to the horrors of modern, mechanical warfare, normally seen as a male prerogative, is here extended to female non-combatants who served close to the front line. A similar appeal is made in *Not So Quiet . . . Stepdaughters of War*, written by the journalist Evadne Price under the pseudonym Helen Zenna Smith in 1930. A feminine counterpart to the avalanche of male war memoirs published in 1929, Price uses a similar linguistic style in her attempts to describe a wartime experience. Price's novel draws on the diaries of Winifred Young, a British ambulance driver in France, and delights in recounting the hardships of life near the front lines, describing the 'bloody war and wounds and foul smells and smutty stories and smoke and bombs and filth and noise, noise, noise . . . a world of cold sick fear, a dirty world of darkness and despair'. According to her account, women and men suffered these privations in the same way (Zenna Smith 1988: 30). In this novel, women's bodies are destroyed by war alongside men's. After Tosh, the aristocratic heroine, is killed by a bomb, the novel ends with the narrator sheltering from an air raid with members of the Women's Army Auxiliary Corps (WAAC) in which ten of them are killed:

> The trench is like a slaughterhouse. All around me girls are lying dead or dying. Some are wounded. The wounded are trying to staunch one another's blood. A few are shell shocked. One scales the sides of the shelter frantically, scrabbling and digging her toes into the earth like a maddened animal. (Zenna Smith 1988: 237–8)

In these descriptions of the horrors of war, Price attempts to parallel the graphic description of trench warfare found in the work of male authors such as Graves, Sassoon and Remarquez. It is both a satire upon wartime propaganda 'praising the indomitable pluck and high spirits of the female volunteers' and a somewhat overwrought plea for women to be recognised as members of the war generation on the same terms as men (Zenna Smith 1988: 134).

In spite of these attempts to align a female war experience with the male, the key theme which emerges from women's literary responses to war is that wartime is a period in which gender roles can be seen extremely clearly. Indeed, in many ways, this gender divide is just as visible in jingoistic and militaristic writing by women – writing which attempts to take on a male voice, or a male perspective – as it is in more pacific writing. Maria Botchkareva, commander of the Russian Women's Battalion of Death in 1917, argued that the battalion existed in order to 'shame the men . . . in the trenches by having the women go over the top first' (Botchkareva 1919: 157). Despite endorsing women's right to take part in the robustly male world of combat, Botchkareva could be seen as in fact supporting a very traditional ideology of gender. Whilst she did take up arms, the primary purpose of Botchkareva's battalion was propagandist and sacrificial, and after one-third of the women had been killed or injured in one offensive of 1917, they were sent home and told to 'put on female attire' by the new Bolshevik government (Bryant 1919: 212–13). This follows the pattern of demobilisation experienced by women in combatant nations at the end of both world wars identified by feminist historians. When these wars ended, large numbers of conscripted, combatant men returned to civilian life, often displacing the women who had been employed in their place during the conflict. Whilst an examination of national demobilisation, welfare and employment policies demonstrates the extent to which women's wartime work was widely seen as being just 'for the duration', only a focus upon the ways in which women experienced and managed these changes illustrates the impact of these policies.

Reconstructing women's wartime lives

Penny Summerfield's oral history of British women's memories of the Second World War, *Reconstructing Women's Wartime Lives* (1998), reveals the ways in which a gendered policy of demobilisation shaped women's lives. The women interviewed by Summerfield recall a variety of responses to demobilisation, ranging from a sense of marginality, resentment and dismay at having to give up not only their paid work but their sense of themselves as useful citizens, actively contributing to the war effort, to the belief that the end of the war marked a welcome return to the private, female sphere of home and family, one woman describing how 'I was looking forward to married life and having a home of my own' (1998: 216). Women who crossed gender boundaries in their wartime work, perhaps by working in what had previously been seen as male spheres of employment, were possibly the most likely to experience resentment in post-war societies which wanted to return to 'normal'. A focus on processes of demobilisation, and the attempts by societies to re-assert 'normality' in the face of often devastating wartime experiences, has been a recurring feature of feminist analysis of warfare, concerned as it often is with questions of change in both discourses and lived experience of gender. Jane Jenson's examination of women's lives in post-war France demonstrated how conservative social forces worked to assert a linkage between women, motherhood and the state, whilst Denise Riley found similar policies enacted in the post-war British welfare state. The British feminist commentator Irene Clapham, writing in 1935, described post-war Britain as a place in which women in paid employment went from being 'saviours of the nation' to 'ruthless self-seekers, depriving men and their dependents of a livelihood' (1935: 210). Women who had joined the military, either as auxiliary workers or, as in the Soviet Union, as combatants, rarely maintained their position when wars ended; as the most visible examples of gender transgression in wartime, their return to a feminine role was highly symbolic of a society's return to peace. These women had threatened to destabilise gender roles by their appearance and their activities, being widely seen as both 'unfeminine' and as challenging the masculine model of the military. Towards the end of the Second World War in the Soviet Union for example, gender distinctions were reinforced by a new pronatalist family code, which made divorce more difficult to obtain, and, in an echo of the family policies of Nazi Germany, awarded motherhood medals to women with five or more children. In this environment women who had served with the military found themselves the subject of disparaging public opinion, in which they were widely seen as sexualised 'camp followers'. Vera Malakhova, a physician decorated for her service with the Red Army, described in an oral history how 'I didn't like to show myself (with my medals) because many people thought I was some kind of front-line "W" (whore)' (Alpern-Engel 1999: 150). Stories such as Malakhova's reveal the extent to which the post-war reconstruction of gender roles acted to eradicate or misrepresent memories of women's active participation in warfare. This gendered discourse of war, which associates masculinity with militarism, can also work to stigmatise women who have undertaken military roles in wartime.

Although combat has historically been largely seen as the preserve of men, women have always participated in, and suffered in, wars. Wartime is often perceived by those who live through it as a significant life event; a period in which individuals feel a sense of living through important public events which will be recorded for posterity. As such, it is not surprising that so many men and women have attempted to record their own experiences of wartime in a multitude of different written and visual forms. Whilst women do not use one voice when writing about war, this body of representation is undoubtedly shaped by gender. It may not be feasible to identify one female perspective on war, but it is apparent that women's war-writing is produced through a gendered framework. The majority of the authors discussed in this essay recognise and describe the ways in which their experience of war was framed by gender. Gender not only shapes the experience of war, it also moulds the ways in which these experiences are historically recorded, and the audience for these representations. There has long been an avid readership for male accounts of combat, whether these be the bitter, disillusioned poems of First World War combatants such as Sassoon and Owen, or the macho, celebratory narrative of Andy McNab's popular Gulf war fiction *Bravo Two Zero*. Women's writing on war, being less likely to describe the experience of combat, has often found it harder to reach these large audiences. Conversely, when women have been close to combat, the post-war reconstruction of gender roles has acted to marginalise their memories. We need to pay attention to women's writing on war, not only because this body of work can help us to understand the wide-ranging impact and the diverse experiences of wartime, but also because the dominant narratives of war exclude and marginalise women. Vera Malakhova expressed this sense of exclusion in the conclusion of her interview:

> I wish you and I had more time. I could tell you so much, so many good stories. But no one is interested . . . No one is interested now, absolutely no one, and we are dying out, most of us are gone, and we are the last. And that's it. (Alpern-Engel 1999: 154)

Our understanding of wartime is incomplete without the inclusion of these stories.

Lucy Noakes

References

Alpern-Engel 1999; Anon 1930; Aubrac 1984; Baudoin 1962; Botchkareva 1919; Bourke 1999; Braybon 1981, 2003; Braybon & Summerfield 1987; Bryant 1918; Clapham 1935; Collins-Weitz 1995; Darian Smith 1990; Diamond 1999; Duras 1985; Gilbert 1989, 1994; Grayzel 1999; Higonnet *et al.* 1987; Higonnet 1993; Hynes 1997; Jenson 1987; Last 1981; Mass-Observation Directive 1982–1990; Riley 1987; Rupp 1978; Shaw 1991; Summerfield 1984, 1998; Tweedie 1919; Tylee 1988; Wiltsher 1985; Zenna Smith 1931.

Related essays

Great Britain; France; Peace; Revolution; Memoir.

Warren, Mercy Otis 1728–1814
American poet, playwright, patriot and historian. Born in Barnstable, Massachusetts, the third child of Mary (Allyne), a descendent of Edward Dotey who arrived on the Mayflower, and James Otis, a judge and colonel in the militia. Warren was from an early age exposed to political debate. Not formally schooled, she gained her education sitting in on her brothers' lessons. In 1754 Mercy Otis married James Warren, a merchant farmer of Plymouth. They had five sons, three of whom perished in the revolutionary wars.

Warren was 'by nature, friendship, and every social tie', connected to 'many of the first patriots', counting among her friends Abigail Adams, wife of the first President. She corresponded with Republican historian **Catharine Sawbridge Macaulay**, who visited America in 1784. John Adams called Warren 'Mrs Macaulay of the American Revolution'. Warren's early literary endeavours were politically satirical plays in support of the revolutionary cause such as *The Adulateur* (1772), which appeared anonymously in two instalments in the *Massachusetts Spy; The Defeat* (1773), *The Group* (1775), *The Blockheads* (1776) and *The Motley Assembly* (1779). These texts functioned as popular pamphlets, as their enactment would have been illegal at the time and the stage directions were often impossible to carry out. In 1790 she published *Poems, Dramatic and Miscellaneous* which contained two blank verse historical tragedies the 'Ladies of Castile' and 'The Sack of Rome'. Written in the classical style, these texts portray republics undermined by a loss of civic virtue, and present examples of women who fulfil the traditional roles of wife and mother while also taking active part in the political and military turmoil that surrounds them, thus anticipating later discussion of Republican motherhood.

In 1788 she published anonymously a pamphlet, 'Observations on the New Constitution', based on letters she had written to Catharine Sawbridge Macaulay, depicting the contemporary political situation. She also wrote a long commentary on the published letters of Lord Chesterfield to his son, which had severely criticised the nature of women. Abigail Adams arranged for Warren's commentary, originally a letter to her son, to be published in 1781. In it Warren pronounced Chesterfield to be 'beneath the resentment of a woman of education and reflection' and charged him with making 'trite, vulgar, hackneyed observations'. She further criticised Chesterfield's focus on women's faults, arguing that women and men actually had the same natural characteristics, and that 'the foibles, the passions, the vices and the virtues, appear to spring from the same source', rising to the 'same degree of perfection', or falling to 'the same stages of depravity'. Warren's defence of women, however, and of women's intellectual capacities and their right to think and speak out about political issues was framed within the ideology of feminine domesticity, and particularly in terms of Republican motherhood. Warren believed that because of their role in nurturing and educating future generations, women had a vested interest in politics, in the government of their nation and therefore that it was in keeping with this role that they speak publicly about their opinions.

Warren began writing her *History of the Rise, Progress, and Termination of the American Revolution* during the Revolution, but withheld publication until 1805, when she believed the controversies associated with the formation of the new nation and its government had been settled. Hers was one of the earliest accounts of the Revolution, and the only contemporary account written by a woman. Warren drew on a variety of sources including her own recollections of the events she recorded. She was both a participant and observer, and acknowledged her privileged position as such. In many respects Warren's *History* was a standard, comprehensive account of the period including detailed discussion of British policies and American responses to them. As with other contemporary accounts by American historians, Warren's *History* was strongly patriotic, celebrating revolutionary events as major steps towards fulfilling God's plan for mankind and the new nation.

Warren did not write directly on the subject of women, as she considered the conduct of war and diplomacy to be the primary subject of history. Stories of women's experiences during the war, however, do appear in the *History*, indeed the Revolution itself is constituted as a gendered event. Repetitive, highly dramatic descriptions of abuse, rape and murder of patriot women by the British and Loyalist forces, and conversely depictions of the compassionate treatment of women by patriot commanders and soldiers drive Warren's narrative. While representations of female tenderness and helplessness obtain an explanatory force in her text, victimisation tends to define women's revolutionary role. The public reception to Warren's *History* at the time of its publication was disappointing. The only contemporary review criticised Warren for having drawn the characters too freely, as 'a gentleman would not, perhaps, have thought prudent', and that it was 'the product of a mind that had not yet yielded to the assertion that all political attentions lay outside of the road of female life'. John Adams, who had initially encouraged her work, decided after its publication that 'History is not the Province of the Ladies.' They pursued a heated correspondence over her representation of the Revolution. Although she regained the friendship of John Adams, Warren's family's political influence declined following the Revolution and she retired from public life.

Sarah Howard

References

Baym 1991; Hutcheson 1953; Norton 1980; Smith 1998; Zagarri 1998.

Webb, Beatrice 1858–1943

English diarist, social reformer, historian. The eighth daughter of Richard Potter, a successful businessman, and Laurencina, a woman constantly torn between her desire for solitary study and the demands of a large family. Beatrice received little education either at home or in the few months that she spent as a boarder at Stirling House. Nonetheless, although her mother thought little of her intellectual ability, family friends like Herbert Spencer encouraged her intellectual ambition. When she suffered a crisis in religious faith in late adolescence, she read extensively in the social sciences, especially the writings of Comte and Spencer, seeking to reconcile her need for a faith with scientific method. Seeking a meaningful alternative to the social life that preoccupied the women of her class, she began to work for the Charity Organisation Society in 1883, but soon came to the belief that it had little understanding of poverty. Nor did she wish to continue engaging in the social work that she saw essentially as ladies' work. Wanting both to move into an area that was not entirely feminised and to undertake what she thought of as 'social diagnosis', rather than philanthropy, she began to work with her cousin Charles Booth in his survey of the lives of London workers. She was assigned to investigate a number of groups in the East End of London, including dock workers, women in the sweated trades and Jewish migrants.

In the late 1880s, after visiting distant relatives in Lancashire, she became interested in the cooperative movement, and while working in it met Sidney Webb whom, despite his different class background and his lack of physical appeal, she married in 1892. Sidney Webb was a leading figure in the Fabian Society, and through him Beatrice became involved in Fabian research, labour politics and in establishing the London School of Economics. In some ways the gradualism of the Fabians appealed to Beatrice Webb because it was inherent in the developmental framework which she had derived from Spencer and Comte. While engaged in her work for Booth, she noted in her diary, in Comtean terms, that 'all things are in the process of becoming, and yesterday vies with today as a foreteller of tomorrow'. The Webbs undertook a number of major historical projects together and were significant figures in the emergence of labour history and in the history of social administration.

Her book *The Cooperative Movement in Great Britain* (1891) explored the rise and the ongoing development of cooperative societies across Britain, emphasising the importance of consumers rather than producer's cooperatives. This was followed by a number of major historical works that she produced with Sidney Webb. The first of these was *History of Trade Unionism* (1894) with a companion volume describing the philosophy and contemporary. This work set up the pattern for the Webbs' collaborative work, with Beatrice touring the country to unearth 'minute-books, in which generations of diligent, if unlettered, secretaries, the true historians of a great movement, have struggled to record the doings of their committees', while Sidney wrote the final text. Beatrice Webb's careful archival work enabled them to trace the origins of trade unionism to a period – the late seventeenth century – far earlier than contemporaries would have expected, and to carry the development forward to the late Victorian era. This was followed by the Webb's monumental historical study of *English Local Government* which appeared over a period of more than 20 years, from 1903 until 1929, incorporating volumes on the Poor law, liquor licensing, the manor and the borough, roads and highways, the administration of prisons under local government.

In addition to this formal historical investigation, Beatrice Webb's *Diaries*, and the autobiographies, *My Apprenticeship* (1926) and *Our Partnership* (1948), which she based on them, constitute a most important historical contribution. Her interest in combining an analysis of her own intellectual and emotional life with that of her family, on the one hand, and the wider social and political world in which she lived, on the other, make these works of central importance in understanding British social and political history, and particularly the lives of women, in the period from the mid-nineteenth to the mid-twentieth centuries. Beatrice Webb was interested also in the naturalist novel, and some of her diaries are consciously written in ways that serve to anatomise social developments.

Barbara Caine

References

Nord 1985; Seymour-Jones 1992.

Major works

The Diaries of Beatrice Webb (ed.) N MacKenzie and J Mackenzie (Boston: Northeastern University Press, 2001) and *My Apprenticeship* (Cambridge: Cambridge University Press, 1979).

Williams, Helen Maria 1761–1827

British poet, novelist, translator, historian of the French Revolution. Born in London, daughter of Helen Hay and Charles Williams, an army officer. Educated at home. Her first poem 'Edwin and Eltruda: A Legendary Tale' was published in 1782. Its success allowed her to move to London, where she frequented meetings of radicals and Bluestockings. Her collected *Poems* (1786) drew upon numerous radical themes and were enormously popular, with some 1500 subscriptions. A major influence on young **Romantics**, especially Wordsworth, she was the 'foremost poet of sensibility' at this time. In 1790 she published *Julia*, a novel that revised Rousseau's *La Nouvelle Heloïse*.

The French **Revolution** proved the perfect vehicle for Williams' radical sensibility. In 1790 she visited Paris on the invitation of her friend Augustin du Fossé, a nobleman who had been imprisoned by his father for marrying his love. Freed with the fall of the Bastille, du Fossé was for Williams a symbol of both the oppressive nature of the *ancien régime* and the Revolution's liberatory potential. His story formed the basis for her first volume of *Letters from France*, gently rebuking the romanticised feudalism of Burke's scathing *Reflections on the Revolution in France*. The first of 13 volumes she wrote on France, the *Letters* merged the epistolary form with travelogue and poetry to present a feminised history of the Revolution. One of the first observers to praise the participation of women in the revolution, Williams believed the Revolution originated in 'feminine sympathy and humanity'. Later editions covered the heroism of Madame Roland and Charlotte Corday and the resistance French women offered Napoleon following his escape from Elba. Taking up permanent residence in Paris in 1791, Williams's salon became a centre for expatriate radicalism. It was visited by **Mary Wollstonecraft** in 1792 and **Sydney Owenson Morgan** in 1816.

Her support for the Revolution saw her vilified in Britain and later writings were published under the threat of the Traitorous Correspondence Bill. In 1793 she was arrested in Paris as a supporter of the Girondist faction. While imprisoned she translated the work of her friend Bernardin de Saint-Pierre's *Paul et Virginie* (1795). When released she escaped to France, recording her travels in *A Tour of Switzerland* (1798). During the Napoleonic period she was Britain's principal interpreter of events in France. Her writings have all the immediacy and limitations of eyewitness accounts and have been criticised for their subjectivity. Williams was, however, a critic of the 'faction of the impartial'. Moreover she avoided discussing anything that contested her feminised Revolution by having others, such as her lover John Hurford Stone, write on these subjects. News that she was living with Stone generated further misogynistic accusations against her in Britain. Later editions of her *Letters* suggest some disillusionment with the Revolution, although no diminution of her radicalism. The last edition of the *Letters* (1819) welcomed the restoration of the monarchy.

Mary Spongberg

Reference

Kelly 1993.

Major works

Poems (with new introduction by Caroline Franklin) (London: Routledge, 1996) and *Letters Written in France 1790* (Oxford: Woodstock, 1989) Janet Todd (ed.) *Helen Maria Williams: Letters from France 1790–94* (Delmar, New York: Scholars' Facsimiles and Reprints, 1975) 2 vols.

Willoughby, Cassandra Duchess of Chandos 1670–1735

Born in Middleton Hall, Warwickshire, the daughter of Francis Willoughby, a naturalist, and Emma Barnard. Her father died when she was two and she moved to Wanstead, Essex, after her mother's remarriage to Josiah Child, later Baron Middleton. In 1687 she returned with her eldest brother, Francis, to the family property of Wollaton Hall, Nottinghamshire, to act as his housekeeper. On his death in 1688, she continued in this role for her younger brother, Thomas, until he married in 1690. She then embarked on a number of journeys, keeping records of her **travels** in the same fashion as Celia Fiennes. In 1713 she married James Brydges, the son of her maternal aunt, a widower with two young sons. They had no children of their own. The marriage was a happy one and Willoughby became very involved in family financial affairs. James Brydges (later first Duke of Chandos) held the lucrative office of paymaster to the forces of the Duke of Marlborough during the wars of 1705–1713 which enabled him to build Canons, a Palladian mansion to the north-west of London. Their fortunes changed in the 1720s after catastrophic investment in South Sea stock and the failure of Cassandra Willoughby's health.

Cassandra Willoughby's *oevre* was family history. She catalogued her father's natural history collections and constructed a Willoughby family tree using medieval title deeds and other fifteenth- and sixteenth-century documents at Wollaton Hall. The outcome was a two-volume history of the Willoughby family of Wollaton, Nottinghamshire and Middleton, Warwickshire. It was written between 1702 and about 1721, extracts were published in 1911. The history is a family chronicle with antiquarian touches, incorporating copies of letters and transcripts of accounts. A further volume retraced the history of the Willoughbys of Willoughby and Eresby, Lincolnshire. This was published as *The Continuation of the History of the Willoughby Family* in 1958. According to this edition, Willoughby, 'with a woman's instinct for the particular, seized on small homely facts, to give us a true and evocative glimpse of seventeenth century life as it was lived'. Willoughby synthesised family correspondence and papers with information from printed sources like Dugdale's *History of Warwickshire* to produce an ambitious chronological narrative and accurate pedigrees. Her travel writing was also filled with antiquarian, sociological, anthropological and topographical detail. Without any formal training Cassandra Willoughby was one of the first woman writers to use historical evidence and archival sources.

Amanda L Capern

References

Baker 1949; Johnson 1981; Thorold 1999; Willoughby 1958.

Major work

Cassandra Willoughby, *The Continuation of the History of the Willoughby Family*, (ed.) A C Wood (Eton: Shakespeare Head Press, 1958)

Wollstonecraft, Mary 1759–1796

English novelist, essayist, critic, historian, letter-writer. The second child, and first daughter of a silk weaver, Edward Wollstonecraft and Elizabeth, Mary grew up in a troubled family as her father's business ventures failed, and he became increasingly violent and despotic. Her own unhappiness was increased by her sense of being little loved or appreciated by her mother. She picked up what education she could at home, by reading and by attending occasional lectures in the local community. With the help of a small legacy she left home in 1777, attempting to support herself first by becoming a lady's companion, then setting up a small school with her sisters and finally as a governess, before establishing herself as a writer with the help of the radical editor and publisher Joseph Johnson. Her radical sympathies made her welcome the French Revolution, in 1789, and she travelled to France to see it at close quarters in 1792. Once there, however, she was horrified by the Terror and by the execution of the King. She entered into a relationship with an American adventurer, Gilbert Imlay, and gave birth to a child, Fanny in 1794. The relationship did not last and she returned to London in a very depressed, indeed in a suicidal, state, from which she emerged in the course of a trip to Sweden, undertaken at Imlay's behest to investigate some of his business problems. On her return to London in 1794, she met and became involved with William Godwin, whom she married when she discovered she was pregnant in 1795. Although unusual in form, as Wollstonecraft and Godwin maintained separate dwellings, this final relationship was the first in which Wollstonecraft was really fulfilled – but it came to a tragic end with her death in childbirth in 1796.

Most of Wollstonecraft's major work reflects her passionate interest and engagement with contemporary history. Her enthusiasm for the French Revolution and her hostility to Edmund Burke's criticism of it led her to write two books in 1789, first *The Rights of Men* and then her best-known work, the *Vindication of the Rights of Woman* (1792). Neither of these works are histories, but both contain historical reflections and discussions of the relationship between past developments and the current political and social situation. Wollstonecraft felt that reading earlier history did not offer much that was hopeful for women disclosing, rather 'marks of inferiority and how few women have emancipated themselves from sovereign man'. She nonetheless saw the greatest hope for women as coming with the intellectual and political changes associated first with the **Enlightenment** and then with the French Revolution. Her sense of the importance of history is evident throughout the *Vindication* in her constant discussions of the ways in which external social assumptions and institutions affect the morality and the conduct of both men and women. The book itself demonstrates her sense of the need for them to be considered and included as actors and citizens in what she saw as the new world being ushered in by the French Revolution.

Although very closely involved with the radical circle that surrounded Joseph Johnson, Wollstonecraft also took note of contemporary women writers. The one she most admired was **Catharine Sawbridge Macaulay**, whose historical writing she praised and whose *Letters on Education* was very influential for her own thought. She saw herself in some ways as following Macaulay in a consciously created intellectual tradition. The journey that Wollstonecraft made alone to France further demonstrates her wish to be both an eyewitness and a participant in the great historical event of her time and the visit was momentous, although not quite in the way she had anticipated. Shortly after arriving in France, Wollstonecraft wrote her 'Letter on the Present Character of the French Nation' (1793). The letter, written to Johnson and intended as the first in a series which did not in fact appear, expressed both her own unhappiness and her extreme disillusionment with France.

She was confronted there in a dramatic form with developments in the Revolution that she found distressing, and a realisation that her ideal of progress was more problematic than she had seen. She was struck particularly by the conflict between wealth and virtue and the sense that the pursuit of the former, which continued in France, was incompatible with the latter. She had cherished the idea that Liberty and Virtue would have arisen out of the chaos of France, but found to her great distress that human nature had not been reformed by the Revolution, and indeed felt with despair that French character might be inimical to moral progress. A year later, she published her major historical work, *The Historical and Moral View of the Revolution in France* (1794). This work needs to be seen in the context of the other works of philosophical history written in eighteenth-century Britain, by which Wollstonecraft had been influenced and with which her own work was in a constant dialogue. The philosophical histories of Adam Smith, William Robertson, John Millar and Lord Kames were all concerned with the evolution of society through a series of fixed stages, beginning in primitive savagery and concluding with the 'civilisation' of their own day. To the 'philosophic eye', Wollstonecraft insisted, the French Revolution was not produced by a few individuals or the result of a sudden enthusiasm. It was rather 'the natural consequence of intellectual improvement, gradually proceeding to perfection in the advancement of communities from a state of barbarism to that of polished society'. This work has occasioned considerable comment because of the dramatic shift away from her earlier enthusiasm for the Revolution, its lack of apparent interest in or sympathy with either the plight or the political aspirations of women in France and its assumption of a masculine authorial voice. The detached and philosophical tone of their work, and its concern with general principles immediately gendered it masculine, in contrast with the more immediate and personal writing that women undertook. Wollstonecraft accepted absolutely this gendering in declaring her intention to contemplate the revolution through the 'enlightened sentiments of masculine and improved philosophy'. This project was a fraught and difficult one and one in which there was considerable tension between her general belief in the idea that European society and institutions were progressing towards a higher, even a perfect, state and her opposition to developments in France which questioned the very possibility of progress. Her comments on the march of women to Versailles in this work closely resemble those of Edmund Burke, whose comments on the market women she had castigated so strongly in the *Vindication*. This work was well received, on the whole, as Wollstonecraft's opposition to developments in France struck a chord with many of her contemporares.

After Wollstonecraft's tragic and premature death in 1796, her reputation suffered a sudden and dramatic decline. The *Memoir* of her written by her grieving husband, William Godwin, brought to light the irregularities of her relationship with Imlay, whom she had never married, and Godwin himself. This caused such outrage that her writing was for the most part neglected for at least a century until the advent of the 'new woman' in the 1890s provided a framework for her rehabilitation.

Barbara Caine

References

Caine 1997; Rendall 1997; Taylor 2003; Todd 2000.

Major works
An Historical and Moral View of the Origin and Progress of the French Revolution (ed.) Janet Todd (Delmar, New York: Scholars Facsimiles and Reprints, 1975) and *A Vindication of the Rights of Man/A Vindication of the Rights of Woman* (eds) D L McDonald & Kathleen Scherf (Peterborough: Broadview Press, 1997).

Wolstenholme, Elizabeth 1834–1913

English teacher, feminist activist, historian of feminism. Born in Manchester, the daughter of Joseph Wolstenholme, a Methodist minister, and his first wife Elizabeth Clarke, the daughter of a cotton spinner. Both parents died before she was fourteen and she had only a couple of years of schooling at the Moravian School, Fulneck, near Leeds. For the rest, Wolstenholme was self-taught – which did not prevent her from becoming headmistress of a private girls' school at Boothstown. In 1874, she married Ben Elmy three months before the birth of their son.

Wolstenholme Elmy was primarily an activist, with a strong interest in suffrage, and in reform of marriage laws. In the course of the 1890s, however, she became increasingly interested in exploring the nature of feminism and in extending knowledge of earlier women writers and feminist theorists. In a series of articles in the journal *Shafts: A Magazine for Progressive Thought* (1892–1899), she explored the earlier history of the women's movement, republishing key documents, such as the first protest against the Contagious Diseases Acts issued by the Ladies National Association in 1869. Using the pseudonym 'Ignota', she also published a number of articles in the *Westminster Review* looking at the suffrage movement and its development until that time. Writing with her husband under the pseudonym 'Ellis Ethelmer', she published the first article in England to address the term 'feminism', including a history of it as an idea and approach in the *Westminster Review* in 1898.

Barbara Caine

Reference
Holton 1994.

Women worthies

A woman worthy is not just any good woman. She might be a woman whose social origin and virtues transcend those of normal women, and thus fit her for action on the public stage. Or she might be a woman who exhibits the truly feminine virtues in their purest form – a woman to be emulated within the household instead of the world at large. Or her very virtues might be a warning to other women. Worthiness existed at the junction of multiple imperatives, ranging from political considerations to theological disputes to gender ideologies. What constituted worthiness in the twelfth century did not necessarily pass muster in the seventeenth, while the exemplary virtues of the seventeenth century in turn horrified the Victorians.

The lives of the women worthies remained a primarily masculine purview until the early nineteenth century, but with some rare exceptions, the genre has never been about scholarly innovation or primary research. Instead, it draws on received knowledge to emphasise the tutelary potential of each woman's life. In whatever century, the worthy woman's life must always exemplify universal qualities to be either emulated or avoided, whether those qualities are spirituality or sexuality. As a result, the worthy woman is less historical than transhistorical, a figure who speaks to the moral priorities of the present day. Not surprisingly, worthiness often resists historical relativism: if morality (or malice) is the foremost criterion for inclusion in the pantheon, then the woman worthy's example must be applicable in a wide variety of situations. Hence the sameness of many lives; at times, the reader may have a hard time distinguishing between worthy queens and worthy missionaries.

These characteristics of the genre themselves derive from other forms devoted to enumerating the extremes of good and evil, most notably the **catalog** and the saint's life. Whether in prose or verse, at a minimum the catalog listed the core female virtues and vices; the most elaborate catalogs used historical examples to embody those characteristics. Although many of the earliest Greek catalogs have not survived, one of the most famous still extant is Semonides of Amorgos' *On Women* (c.630 BCE), a satire that identifies female behaviours with different animals. The catalog that became the most important model for later writing, however, is Plutarch's *Virtues of Women (Mulierum virtutes)* [c.100 CE], which consists of 27 anecdotes about female heroism. Plutarch begins with anecdotes of women acting virtuously as a group before moving on to women who act as individuals. The overwhelming majority of these anecdotes deal with civic action: resistance to tyrants, struggles against invaders, diplomatic negotiations, governing in the absence of a suitable male leader. If Plutarch's definition of worthiness as political and martial virtue would not survive long past the seventeenth century, his emphasis on women being *called* to action in exigent circumstances remained central.

By contrast, if the qualifications for sainthood were not the same as those necessary for worthiness, saints' lives themselves did exert an obvious influence on the lives of the worthies. Most importantly, saints' lives downplayed the saint's *individuality* in favour of his or her *exemplarity*: the saint's life offered ideal models of lived virtue for the reader's edification and, perhaps, imitation. As students of **hagiography** have often noted, miraculous deeds and cruel martyrdoms often migrate from saint to saint, foregrounding God's work in the world at the expense of the saint's particular experience. In a different register, this interchangeability would become particularly important to nineteenth-century writers, who regularly insisted that what made a woman worthy was not her historical uniqueness but rather her embodiment of peculiarly domestic virtues.

The most famous of the early women worthies texts offer notoriously unstable judgements on the worthiness of the women they represent. Thus, Giovanni Boccaccio's pioneering *De claris mulieribus* (1361–1362), which pays especial homage to the classical virtues of Greek and Roman women while also castigating their vices, assumes that women are by nature man's physical and mental inferiors. Although Boccaccio would not have known Plutarch – he identifies Petrarch as his inspiration – his brief narratives nevertheless share some of Plutarch's suppositions about feminine virtue. In particular, Boccaccio insists that women rightly act in history only when *called* to do so, unlike, say, the ambitious Athaliah, Queen of Jerusalem. Moreover, exemplary women in history transcend their sex in order to become 'manly'. More positive is Geoffrey Chaucer's unfinished *The Legend of Good Women* (c.1380s), in which the poet is set the task of celebrating women constant in love as a penance for his earlier poetry. In the nine legends that follow, Chaucer deals solely with women of classical antiquity, both historical and legendary. Despite praising women normally considered problematic or even evil, like Cleopatra or Medea, Chaucer solely emphasises emotional fidelity; he is uninterested in leadership or civic heroism.

The first woman to undertake a catalog of women worthies was the French poet **Christine de Pizan,** whose *Le Livre de la Cité des Dames* (1405) is today one of the most famous shots fired in the *querelle des femmes.* The book circulated only in manuscript within France itself; it was first printed in Brian Anslay's English translation as *The Boke of the Cyte of Ladyes* (1521), although the English may have had access to manuscript copies before that. Unlike Boccaccio and Chaucer, de Pizan presents her catalog as a critique of male misogyny, arguing that masculine representations of women in history are intended to artificially inflate male authority at the expense of truth and justice. To offer a corrective, de Pizan 'constructs' her city in conversation with the allegorical female figures of Reason, Rectitude and Justice, each figure leading her higher through the scale of feminine virtues until she reaches those embodied by the Virgin Mary and the saints. The bulk of the text consists of brief lives (including saints' lives) drawn from both history and mythology, exemplifying women's work in every sphere from politics to culture to war. Along the way, the allegorical figures critique misogynist generalisations about female morality, trustworthiness, intellect and the like, arguing that men have twisted even the words of Christ Himself in order to justify their perverse views of women. Ultimately, the book sees women as man's equals but not as independent *of* man. While the reader is occasionally cautioned against using the figures at the 'lower levels', like Semiramis, as models, nevertheless de Pizan's worthies are overwhelmingly positive examples.

Sixteenth- and seventeenth-century writing in the women worthies tradition remained overwhelmingly male-dominated, ranging from figures such as John Foxe, who included many women in his martyrology *Acts and Monuments of the Christian Church* (1563), to the playwright Thomas Heywood, author of two collections celebrating the virago, *The Gynaikeion* (1624) and *The Exemplary Lives and Memorable Acts of Nine of the Most Worthy Women in the World* (1640). A number of women writers, however, incorporated women worthies catalogs into polemical or prescriptive texts, where they functioned as shorthand *exemplaria* authorising larger arguments about women's abilities. Thus, in France, Jacquette Guillaume argued for women's intellectual and moral superiority with *Les Dames illustres, où par bonnes et fortes raisons il se prouve que le sexe feminine surpasse en toutes sortes de genres le sexe masculine* (1665), while the novelist **Madeleine de Scudéry** contributed fictional biographies of famous and virtuous women, both historical and legendary, in *Les femmes illustres ou les Harangues Héroique* (1642). Similarly, in Italy, Moderata Fonte had one of the participants in her dialogue *Dei meriti delle donne* (1600) list a number of world-historical female figures; Lucrezia Marinella took a similar approach in her *La nobilit e la eccelenza delle donne, con difetti e mancamenti degli uomini* (1600). In England, Esther Sowernam's *Esther hath hang'd Haman* (1617) responds to Joseph Swetnam's misogynist *Arraignment of Lewd, Idle, Forward, and Unconstant Woman* (1615) by, among other things, listing the contributions of Biblical, mythical and medieval women to the cause of moral, cultural and spiritual advancement. Along the same lines, Bathsua Makin's *An Essay to Revive the Antient Education of Gentlewomen* (1673) incorporates an extensive list of learned female figures from multiple countries and periods to demonstrate that scholarly achievement is hardly incompatible with female virtue. More pragmatically, Hannah Woolley's *The Gentlewoman's Companion; or, A Guide to the Female Sex* (1675) includes among its chapters on marriage, cooking and deportment a discussion of famous classical and Biblical figures, who model the best virtues of feminine heroism, intellectual achievement and, above all, religious devotion.

It is in the late eighteenth and nineteenth centuries, however, that writing in the women worthies tradition becomes feminised. While 'feminised' does not necessarily translate into 'feminist', it is true that writing exemplary lives became a commercial outlet for many women; at the same time, it is also true that women who wrote such lives were *expected* to make them exemplary. That is, if women gained more influence in writing female morality for their readers, they also remained subject to strictures – from both men and women – about what was appropriate material for such biographical accounts. Thus, reviewers praised the poet Matilda Betham's delicate moral sensibilities in assembling *A Biographical Dictionary of the Celebrated Women of Every Age and Country* (1804), but attacked the feminist **Mary Hays**' equally opinionated and far more substantial *Female Biography; or, Memoirs of Illustrious and Celebrated Women, of All Ages and Countries, Alphabetically Arranged* (1803). In France, **Louise de Kéralio** strategically allied exemplary biography with literary history in her massive *Collection des meilleurs ouvrages français composés par des femmes* (1787). While Betham, Hays and de Kéralio aimed to write general reference works, many of the female-authored women worthies texts, like Mary Pilkington's *A Mirror for the Female Sex* (1798), were overtly aimed at children. Such collections were intended to shape budding female virtues, and as such often incorporated explicit directions for both interpreting famous exemplars and applying their lessons to everyday life. At the same time, the range of women adduced as 'worthies' began to stretch. While civic action could still be grounds for worthiness, as in Elizabeth Starling's *Noble Deeds of Woman; or, Examples of Female Courage and Virtue* (1835) and its American imitation, Jesse Clement's *Noble Deeds of American Women: With Biographical Sketches of Some of the More Prominent* (1851), more and more worthiness was associated with domestic culture. The noted evangelical Sarah Stickney Ellis' *The Mothers of Great Men* (1859), for example, certainly pointed to a number of women famous in their own right – St Monica, for example – but also celebrated women whose only claim to fame was their sons.

By the later nineteenth century, the woman worthies tradition ran headlong into feminism. Sarah Bolton, a prolific author of exemplary biographies, celebrated *Successful Women* (1888) whose success was emphatically public, ranging from novelists like Mrs G R Alden (who wrote under the pseudonym 'Pansy') to the famed nurse Clara Barton. In Britain, the well-known feminist Millicent Garrett Fawcett reprinted a series of articles as *Some Eminent Women of Our Time* (1889), which interpreted a number of famous figures as participants in the project of female emancipation, including the scientists Caroline Herschel and Mary Somerville, the novelists Jane Austen and Maria Edgeworth, the prison reformer Mary Fry and indeed Queen Victoria herself. American feminists and non-feminists alike developed vast reference works, including **Sarah Josepha Hale**'s *Woman's Record* (1852), arranged according to a theory of historical progress in which America represented the apex of woman's development, and Frances E Willard and Mary Livermore's *A Woman of the Century* (1893), featuring over 1400 entries. But feminism also generated anti-exemplary texts like 'Sutherland Menzies' [pseudo Elizabeth Stone] in *Political Women* (1873), which adduced famous politicking women like the Duchess of Malborough as examples of the dangers of female involvement in the public sphere.

In the late twentieth century, the term 'women worthies' has come to mean the practice of rescuing 'lost' female figures in order to identify a proto-feminist tradition. This newer model could be said to return to the genre's Plutarchan origins in at least one sense: the feminist woman worthy is above all devoted to civic action. Outside the academy, the women worthies tradition has persisted in the work of such popular biographers and historians as Antonia Fraser and Elizabeth Longford, as well as in Vicki Leon's agreeably pugnacious Uppity Women series. It has also been appropriated by religious, racial and ethnic minorities, who have found the tradition a useful tool for inspiring civil rights activism or simply countering mainstream historical narratives. Inside the academy, the tradition has fallen on hard times as of late: it is associated with the much-derided 'add women and stir' model of feminist history, and has by and large fallen out of favour as a scholarly enterprise. Nevertheless, in *The Creation of Feminist Consciousness* (1993), Gerda Lerner claimed that women worthies were essential to any feminist revision of Western Civilisation's historical plot; significantly, her sweeping account – which stretched from medieval nuns to Victorian novelists – ended with a brief history of the women worthies genre and its place in women's history, making it a way station in the journey towards modern feminist inquiry. New electronic media have offered an additional twist on the tradition, in the form of such websites as 'Brave Women' (http://www.angellpro.com.au/women.htm), celebrating the work of Australian military women, or Danuta Bois's 'Distinguished Women of Past and Present' (http://www.distinguishedwomen.com/), an ongoing collection of eminent figures. If such biographies no longer play a significant moral role, they nevertheless continue to exert a strong inspirational pull.

Miriam Elizabeth Burstein

References

Benson 1992; Brown-Grant 1999; Burstein 1999; Dolnikowski 1998; Ferrante 1997; Jordan 1990; McLeod 1991; Malcolmson 2002; Teague & de Haas 2002; Winstead 1997; Wright 1943.

Related essays

Catalogs; Defences of Women; Female Biography; Royal Lives; World History.

Women's liberation

The term 'women's historians' has been coined in recent years to denote a field of historical study as distinct from 'women historians', which described the sex of the historian. The Women's Liberation Movement, or more generally the feminist movement of the 1970s and 1980s, had an enormous effect on both the field and the historians, in interrelated ways. This essay focuses on the issues feminism raised for women historians for the two decades since 1970. Women historians were both an important part of this movement and deeply affected by it. The new **feminism** had as its basic proposition that the subjection of women (it would have said the oppression of women) was not inevitable, not ordained by biological difference. In this denial, it raised the question, 'why, if sexual inequality is not necessary to social life, is not inevitable, does it in fact exist?' Feminists sought answers in a wide range of disciplines, from anthropology to sociology to philosophy and especially history. If feminists could show how the relationships between men and women developed over time in particular circumstances in particular ways, they could, they hoped, show the mutability of these particular arrangements and the lack of necessity of the current social inequalities based on sex.

Two of the key texts of the new movement – Kate Millett's *Sexual Politics* (1970) and Shulamith Firestone's *The Dialectic of Sex* (1970) – provided an argument about women's history as the groundwork for their radical analysis of women's position in modern society. On the basis of recent scholarship by historians such as **Eleanor Flexner** and Aileen Kraditor, they were able to construct a history of women's earlier struggles for the vote and other legal and political rights. They plundered many other works as well, in literature, anthropology and biological sciences. Millett's *Sexual Politics* argued for the force of patriarchy throughout history, but also emphasised the importance of feminism in the nineteenth and early twentieth centuries. She evoked a 'Sexual Revolution' from 1830 to 1930, with political, rhetorical and literary dimensions. After describing the gains made in the early twentieth century, she then argued there had been a counter-revolution from 1930 to 1960 that in the West had been assisted by the influence of Freud. Firestone's *The Dialectic of Sex* borrowed the idea of the dialectic, used by Marxists to explain the dynamics of the class struggle in history, and applied it instead to sex. She, too, described the earlier American women's rights movement and posited a backlash in the decades since American women gained the vote. Women had lost their earlier political consciousness, diverted by an obsession with glamour in the twenties, other people's causes in the thirties, war in the forties, the ideal of domesticity in the fifties and radical politics in the sixties (1970: 27–33). By contrast, the two key English women's movement texts – Germaine Greer *The Female Eunuch* (1970) and Juliet Mitchell *Woman's Estate* (1971) – were not historical in their approach at all. Greer's book was a meditation on women's need for psychic and cultural liberation, while Juliet Mitchell understood women's subordination in terms of structures (she argued for four – production, reproduction, sex and the socialisation of children) rather than history. Mitchell's book, furthermore, saw Freud and psychoanalysis as valuable for rather than hostile to feminist understandings of women.

Clio's consciousness raised?

The history students and historians who were part of the movement wanted to apply their historical knowledge to the movement's concerns and to use their feminism to rethink their approach to history. They pored over whatever earlier histories of women they could find, usually those dealing with women's work or the suffrage movement. These were not works they had encountered in their historical education, but books they ferreted out in their search for information about women in the past. As Linda Gordon later wrote in 'What's New in Women's History?', 'When I became a feminist and began with a group of historians turned feminist, to find out something about women's situation in the past, I discovered these books, dusty, in the Widener library stacks, untouched for decades' (1986: 20). Some of the favourite earlier histories on women and work included **Ivy Pinchbeck**, *Women Workers and the Industrial Revolution* (1930) and **Alice Clark**, *Working Life of Women in the Seventeenth Century* (1919), while more recent texts on the suffrage movement included Eleanor Flexner, *Century of Struggle* (1959) and Aileen Kraditor, *The Idea of the Woman Suffrage Movement 1890–1920* (1965). It was not long, however, before the historians began writing a flood of programmatic articles advocating a new attention to women's history, one that simply did not add women to existing political and military histories but sought to ask new questions and to develop new methods to answer them.

Most of these contributions were very much within the framework of national history, and within a few years manifestos appeared for American, British, Australian, Canadian and other histories (See essays on **United States, Great Britain, Canada, Australia**). Some of the American essays were influenced by the new Women's Liberation movement but also cautioning against some of its more naïve approaches to history. One of the earliest was Gerda Lerner's essay 'New Approaches to the Study of Women in American History' (1969). She criticised existing scholarship on American women's history for being either absent or 'topically narrow, predominantly descriptive, and generally devoid of interpretation'. The one exception she thought was **Mary Ritter Beard**'s argument against feminist histories for being too often based on an assumption of women's subjection and for an approach that explored women's 'continuous and impressive contribution to society throughout all of history'. Lerner also warned against various current approaches to women's history emerging in the context of the new feminism: seeing women as a unified group; using inappropriate analogies with 'other distinctive groups', such as slaves or ethnic minorities or the economically deprived; presupposing that women's exclusion from formal political rights meant they had no power at all; and assuming that ideas about women's place at any one time accurately reflected their actual status. She recommended breaking down 'women's history' into more specific categories and developing new woman-specific ways of measuring women's achievements. Her essay ended with a ringing call for 'a painstaking search of known sources for unknown meanings'.

The critiques by feminist historians of the new women's movement's approach to history continued. In 'On Writing Women's History' (1971), Lois Banner criticised Kate Millett's *Sexual Politics* as superb polemic but 'flawed history'. While Banner welcomed Millet's emphasis on women's sexual oppression in the mid-twentieth century, she criticised her reliance on individual authors rather than collective data and advocated a social history approach that investigated how women's roles had changed over time, both in theory and in practice. Ann Gordon, Mari Jo Buhle and Nancy Schrom Dye in 'The Problem of Women's History' (1971) also favoured a social history approach, criticising works that focused on the suffrage movement, or individuals, or histories of ideas about women as too limited in various ways. They advocated attention to women's social history, especially through probing connections between women's role in the home and in the workforce. Like Lerner and Banner before them, these authors emphasised just how little we know about women in history and like them argued for attention to the diversity of women's experience at any one time and over time. They were wary of an approach to women's history grounded on the notion of oppression, for it 'freezes and levels their enormously diverse experience' (1971: 86). The situation of the slave woman and the plantation mistress should not be conflated. 'We must know', they wrote, 'as much about what kept women apart as we know about what situation they shared' (1971: 87).

Largely independently, though influenced by the same women's movement activism, programmatic articles appeared at the same time in other countries. Unaware of Lerner's article, I wrote a rather similar essay myself in the Australian neo-Marxist journal *Arena* in 1970 (see **Australia** essay). Here, as a doctoral student, I argued that the ideas of the new Women's Liberation movement could be used to ask new questions about

Australian history, namely women's history. We should, I wrote, attempt a 'far-reaching study of why sex differentiation in all its aspects has occurred, how it has affected the lives of both men and women and how it is related to the maintenance of, or change in, entrenched social and power structures' (1970: 36). It would also, I thought, be important to critique and explain History's emphasis on 'public life and politics'; 'the concepts usually operating in historiography, defining what is important, must be questioned' (1970: 37). As we develop a history of Australian women, 'we should be careful that we do not confine our analyses to "the position of women" but are able to integrate analyses concerning women with the mainstream of historical enquiry'.

Similar discussions were occurring in Britain. There the links between feminist activism and the women historians were especially strong, with most of the young women historians also feminist activists, very often socialist feminist activists. So close was the association between historians and activists that in March 1970, when the women historians at Oxford's Ruskin College set out to organise a small study workshop on women's liberation, it became a very large conference establishing the Women's Liberation Movement itself. The labour, social, socialist and now feminist historians in Britain were very often concentrated in adult education colleges, including Ruskin which in 1967 had developed the radical History Workshop movement, combining labour and social history. One of these young historians teaching in adult education was Sheila Rowbotham, who was still in her twenties when she wrote *Women, Resistance and Revolution* (1972), a history of British women's political struggles. In the preface, she noted women's invisibility in history and wrote, 'The language which makes us invisible to "history" is not coincidence, but part of our real situation in a society . . . which we do not control.' Understanding women's history was essential for women's political activism and historians had been inspired by the new Women's Liberation Movement: 'Women's liberation brings to all of us a strength and audacity we have never before known.' Anna Davin, in 'Women and History' (1972), provided a particularly stirring call to arms, announcing that we know virtually nothing of women's history. 'We now', she wrote, 'have to reject what has passed for history, to redefine the word, to discover the history which is relevant to us now' (1972: 216). It was important to look at the history of women's struggles, as suffragettes for instance, but 'it is still more important to discover first what was the ordinary condition of women' (1972: 217). To understand resistance, she argued, one first had to understand oppression. Davin, too, was wary of taking ideas about women as indicating their actual status, taking the position of Victorian women in England as her example. She emphasised the high levels of women's employment in working-class communities and the hard work undertaken in the home by the working-class married woman. For Davin, knowledge of women's history was important in the present: 'We need to know our past. . . . By showing that the role and "nature" of women changes with each society we are hoping to defeat the argument "that's how it's always been". Since oppressive ideology is justified by reference to a false past, it is important for us to show what the past really was.'

Inspired by such ideas, the new scholarship proceeded apace. In the US, regular conferences on women's history began with the first Berkshire Conference on the History of Women at Douglass College (of Rutgers

University) in 1973, which drew around 300 participants. The following year there was another conference, at Radcliffe, with over 1000 participants. This was followed by conferences at Bryn Mawr in 1976 and Mount Holyoke in 1978. From then on the conferences were held every three years, by the mid-1990s drawing several thousand participants from all over the world. Britain also saw a series of large women's history conferences, such as the Feminist History Conference in London in 1973 and the Women's History/Oral History Conference in Colchester in 1977. Also important were the conferences organised by the History Workshop collective, which though not exclusively on women's history, included a great deal of feminist historical scholarship. In Australia very large Women and Labour conferences, focusing both on history and current issues, were held every two years from 1978 to 1986, after which the practice developed of a separate women's history day held before each bi-annual Australian Historical Association conference. By the later 1980s, the national orientation of women's history was becoming more internationalist in approach. The International Federation for Research in Women's History was founded in April 1987, with the first meeting of national committee representatives held, with the assistance of the Rockefeller Foundation, in 1989 in Bellagio, Italy. The new organisation's inaugural officers were Ida Blom of the University of Bergen, Norway, as President; Ruth Roach Pierson of the University of Toronto, Canada, as Vice-President and Karen Offen of Stanford University, USA, as Secretary-Treasurer. The new organisation had its own newsletter and organised international conferences, either on its own or in association with the International Committee for the Historical Sciences.

New academic journals also sprang up to carry the scholarship in women's and gender history. The American journals included *Signs*, *Feminist Studies*, *The Women's Studies Quarterly* and a little later, from 1988, *The Journal of Women's History*, while in Britain, feminist histories were published in *History Workshop Journal* and *Feminist Review*. Canada had *RFR/DRF* (*Resources for Feminist Research/Documentation sur la Recherche Feministe*), while Australian journals carrying the new feminist history included *Refractory Girl*, *Hecate and Australian Feminist Studies*. These journals published not only substantive essays but also works of debate about questions of interpretation and methodology. A sign of growing international co-operation came with the launch in 1988 of *Gender and History* as a joint UK/US journal.

Liberating women's history

This is, however, to run a little ahead of our story. In 1975, the stream of articles about women's history and how it might be written had by now become a flood, with notable contributions by Carroll Smith Rosenberg, Gerda Lerner, Joan Scott and Louise Tilly, and Natalie Zemon Davis. So many discussions of the new women's history were there in the United States that Berenice Carroll collected them together into a book in *Liberating Women's History* (1976). Many of these essays reiterated the points already made, about the invisibility of women in history and the need to develop new categories, or new criteria for inclusion, in the writing of history. In addition, new methodological and conceptual concerns were discussed. In 'The New Woman and the New History' (1975a), Rosenberg stressed the importance of the New Social History, for it provided a methodological sophistication, for example in detailed family studies, that feminist historians badly needed. Gerda Lerner was one of the first to raise an issue that was to be important for feminist historians over the next decade or so. Many were beginning to feel that the new scholarship tended to portray women as victims of social, cultural and economic institutions, rather than as historical actors. Echoing **Mary Beard** 40 years earlier, they wanted to look not at what women had suffered, or been excluded from, but what they had actually done. Gerda Lerner referred to Beard when she raised this issue in an article, 'Placing Women in History' (1975), pointing out that emphasis on women's 'oppressive restraints' 'makes it appear either that women were largely passive or that at the most, they reacted to male pressures or the restraints of patriarchal society. Such inquiry fails to elicit the positive and essential way in which women have functioned in history' (1975: 358). Too great a focus on oppression returns the historian to the study of the actions of men, or more precisely to a 'male-defined conceptual framework'.

It was probably this feeling that led so many to respond so positively to Carroll Smith Rosenberg's 'Female World of Love and Ritual: Relations between Women in Nineteenth-Century America' (1975b). Here was an essay that focused on female experience, on relationships between women which built 'a sense of inner security and self-esteem' and in which men and male power were either absent or clearly in the background (1975: 14). It was also an essay that embodied the popular notion of 'separate spheres' but recreated it as something more positive, as a form of women's culture that sustained itself without the help of men. Also generally regarded as a landmark was Joan Scott and Louise Tilly's 'Women's Work and the Family in Nineteenth-Century Europe', published in the same year. It addressed one of the key issues for feminist historians of the time, the relationship between family and work, and disrupted the conventional assumption of women's gradual move from home to work. Rather, the essay showed just how prevalent was work outside the home for European peasant and working-class women in the nineteenth century and emphasised the ways older family ties persisted in an industrialised context. This was a thoroughly researched article that indicated that the new enthusiasm for women's history was bearing fruit in detailed historical studies.

The tasks for feminist history were spelt out even more clearly in Natalie Zemon Davis' '"Women's History" in Transition: The European Case' (1976). Davis reminded women's historians that they were not working in quite the vacuum they sometimes proclaimed: there had been writings about women's history since Plutarch. In particular, Alice Clark, for England, and Leon Abensour, for France, had written two excellent histories of women half a century earlier. What the newer scholarship could add, however, was an attention to demography, quantitative history more generally, and sexual and erotic activity. Davis stressed that women's history challenged the discipline generally, in its understanding of power, social structure, property, symbols and especially periodisation. Full attention to women might mean entirely new divisions in European history, marked, perhaps, by demographic changes or changes in sexual practice. The issue of periodisation was to interest feminist historiography over the next decade. Joan Kelly's essays, 'The Social Relation of the Sexes' (1976) and 'Did Women Have a Renaissance?' (1977), pointed out that the meaning of a given historical period for women might be quite different from that for men. Indeed, she wrote in the former: 'What emerges is a fairly regular pattern of relative loss of status for women precisely in those periods of so-called progressive change' (1977: 2). She opposed, however, suggestions that women's history might require entirely new periodisation, based on major turning points affecting human reproduction, as this would detach the history of reproduction from changes in the general social order. Rather, the task of feminist historians would be to insist that the traditional or existing historical periods were understood equally in terms of their meaning for women as for men.

In Britain, most attention was focused on the study of the relationship between women's work and the family. In the new *History Workshop Journal* (1976), a further development of the History Workshop movement that had started at Ruskin, Sally Alexander and Anna Davin drew attention to the failings of both labour history and social history, since both took for granted social institutions, such as the sexual division of labour, which ought to be explained. They reiterated what was by now a common theme, that 'the purpose is not simply to slot women in wherever they have been left out', but rather to explain relationships, between 'the sexual division of labour and class struggle, home and work, or the private and the public' (1976: 5). They also emphasised their political perspective: 'it is only by seeking and recognizing political relevance in history that we can bring it more directly into the battle of ideas – history is too important to be left just to the professional historians' (1976: 6). Sally Alexander followed this with a long essay, 'Women's Work in Nineteenth-Century London' (1976), which emphasised the extent of working-class women's wage-earning and the persistence and tenacity of a sexual division of labour throughout the transformations wrought by industrialisation. Even longer was Anna Davin's essay, 'Imperialism and Motherhood' (1978), which explored the ways in which anxieties about the population's health and growth in a context of national fears and imperial desires in the late nineteenth and early twentieth centuries resulted in a growing attention to women's role as mothers, as distinct from wives. Population was power, making a higher birth rate and lower infant death rate, a matter of national importance in Britain; as a result, to entice women to have more children and to care for them properly, motherhood was accorded a new dignity.

By the 1980s, new issues were emerging, especially around the terms **gender** and difference. Jane Lewis' essay, 'Women Lost and Found: The Impact of Feminism on History' (1981), uses the category 'gender' in an easy way not found in the earlier essays, with their rather clumsy formulations like 'sex role differentiation', or 'relations between men and women'. She notes the considerable increase in the number of histories paying attention to women's experience, but is critical of many of them as descriptive or methodologically narrow. She is more interested in the extent to which attention to women changes the way history is understood generally. Issues of concern include whether a focus on women requires different historical periodisation or simply understanding existing categories in a new way. She is also interested in the question Lerner addressed, of how to balance an interest in the constraints on women with an emphasis on their agency and active choices. Lewis draws attention to feminist interest in the distinction between public and private and the ways the distinction was often dissolved in practice. She was particularly approving of Ellen DuBois' work on the American suffrage movement, which showed how suffragists used the ideology of domesticity to demand a public role for women. In the case of work and family, the former sometimes seen as public and the latter as private, historians were showing how the experience in each sphere structured the other.

A more comprehensively argued challenge to the notion of male public versus female private spheres came with Linda Kerber's 'Separate Spheres, Female Worlds, Woman's Place: The Rhetoric of Women's History' (1988). She outlined the ways in which within American historiography the scholarship of the 1970s, which had so emphasised the separate worlds of men and women, gave way by the 1980s to a greater recognition that the notion of separate spheres was a long-standing idea, or ideology, more than it was an accurate account of actual gender relationships. We are, she wrote, now 'treating the language of separate spheres itself as a rhetorical construction that responded to changing social and economic reality' (1988: 21) and increasingly stressing the connections between, and mutual construction of, the public and private realms. The phrase 'separate spheres' becomes a 'metaphor for complex power relations in social and economic contexts' (1988: 28). In short, Kerber argued for an end to dualistic approaches and recognition of the complexity of gender relationships.

The gender of history

By the early 1980s, feminist historians were wondering about the meaning of their labours for the discipline generally. Elizabeth Fox-Genovese, in 'Placing Women's History in History', probed the question at length. Adding women to history, she pointed out, was not the same as adding *women's history* to history (1982: 6). The implications of women's history for history she saw as multiple; some of her key points were that historians would need henceforth to 'adopt gender system as a fundamental category of historical analysis' and to recognise the variability of male dominance, making the term 'patriarchy' too limited in its application. She emphasised 'the mutability of gender systems', warning that it is 'fruitless to look for a uniform oppression of women, or a universal form of male dominance' (1982: 15). Fox-Genovese was unusual also for the time amongst women historians in emphasising that women had not always been on the side of the oppressed: 'The world we have inherited could not have been built without them, neither the bad in that world nor the good. They worked for all contending parties – for the Klan as well as against lynching' (1982: 28).

Fox-Genovese's approach was still strongly Marxist with its emphasis on structures and systems and forms of exploitation. Joan Scott made some somewhat similar points a year later, but without the Marxist inflection. In effect, she removed the word 'system' from Fox-Genovese's 'gender system' to produce a more open and flexible concept of gender. Scott summarised both the achievements and the difficulties of the field in her essay, 'Women's History', in 1983. Her work was extremely important, not least because she crossed the US/UK divide much more freely than anyone else. Her summary of the state of play bears repeating:

> More than in many other areas of historical inquiry, women's history is characterized by extraordinary tensions: between practical politics and academic scholarship; between received disciplinary standards and interdisciplinary influences; between history's atheoretical stance and feminism's need for theory. (1983: 16–17)

While these tensions were productive, it was time, she argued, to attempt to examine and redefine some of the key terms of analysis, namely 'woman as subject, gender and politics'. Recognition of women as historical actors, she argued, necessitated abandoning earlier frameworks that took men's experience as general and women's as particular, or specific, and instead see all human subjects as particular and specific. How, then, she continued, could all these particularities be conceptualised? How do we relate to one another the multiple differences marking individuals – by race, gender, class, sexual preference? For 'women' to be understood properly, 'gender' was a most important analytical tool.

The question of **gender** became the focus of Scott's most famous essay three years later, 'Gender: A Useful Category of Historical Analysis' (1986), one of the most famous products of the intersection of feminism and history. While the category had been around since the late 1960s and had been used occasionally by feminist historians, it had not been used, as Scott pointed out, very systematically. Scott's contribution was to define the concept much more clearly specifically for historians. Her approach derived partly from the huge body of work women's historians had built up in the previous 15 years and partly from the influence of poststructuralist theory, which led her to pose questions about power, identity and subjectivity rather differently. She argued for the need to distinguish 'between our analytic vocabulary and the material we want to analyze' (1986: 1065) and her achievement was to help effect just that distinction. Women's history from the early 1970s had been based on a binary opposition between male and female expressed in various ways (patriarchy, separate spheres, sexual division of labour, etc.). Scott opposed the binary opposition as a permanent feature of history and sought a more open notion of gender, where the distinctions between male and female could be any kind whatsoever. She also opposed those versions of women's history that tended to equate women's history with social history and more specifically with the relationship between the family and the working life and argued that gender history could be anywhere. Political history, for example, need not be seen as somehow conventional male history, for it, too, was gendered, even when (or especially when) women were formally absent. Scott argued for analyses that explored the connections between hierarchical structures and understandings of gender.

Linda Gordon, in 'What's New in Women's History' (1986), also opposed the tendency to equate women's history and social history. Where Scott wanted to make political history gendered, Gordon wanted women's history to become more political in the conventional sense, attentive to women's political action and also their political oppression. The growing fashion for speaking of 'difference' rather than domination was also a concern, for it tended to imply a 'neutral asymmetry' rather than domination (1986: 26). Gordon also addressed the question of passivity versus action, or domination and resistance, which had first arisen in Lerner's 'Placing Women in History' (1975). She saw the progenitors of the two approaches as **Simone de Beauvoir** (passive) and Mary Beard (active). Using terms that were to be heard very frequently in subsequent years, she likened this dichotomy to the agency versus structure debate within Marxism and argued that in both cases – in feminist history and in Marxist history – structure and agency needed both to be recognised. She thought this was more easily said than done, however, with histories tending to emphasise either one or the other.

That same year, in an essay entitled 'Evidence and Silence: Feminism and the Limits of History' (1986), Australian feminist historian Judith Allen asked whether history could ever be made important and illuminating for feminism. There were limits to history's value, she argued, not because of the particular sexist assumptions of its male practitioners; the problem lay deeper, in history's basic epistemology and methodology. 'Feminism', she wrote, 'seeks a knowledge and understanding of the past; the discipline of history is a poor servant in this quest' (1986: 188). Historians were too ready to read the evidence literally as if facts spoke for themselves and too inclined to say no evidence exists for aspects of social life of major importance for women (for example, unreported crimes by or against women). She urged feminist historians to 'read' for evidentiary silences more carefully, to use both inference and deduction to account for both presences and absences in extant sources (1986: 184).

Dealing with difference

Within the growing field of women's history, one of the main issues had always been how to recognise the differences between women while still maintaining an interest in and focus on women as an historical category. Class differences had long been recognised, especially by those with a Marxist background; race, too, had sometimes been noted as a source of differentiation. But in the early to mid-1980s the question of race became vastly more important. Bell hooks published in 1981 *Ain't I a Woman?*, a reference to a speech by Sojourner Truth to Women's Convention in 1851, which suggested that black women's experience was quite different from that of white woman: Bell hooks picked up Truth's cry to argue that sexism and racism combined to assign black women low status during slavery and that stereotypes created then persisted into the present (see **Slavery** essay). Black women faced a patriarchal black nationalist movement and a white middle-class feminist movement that had no understanding of black women's experience. The critique by black women of white fem-inism continued apace. Bonnie Thornton Dill, in 'Race, Class and Gender: Prospects for an All-Inclusive Sisterhood' (1983), pointed out just how foreign to black women was the women's movement's emphasis on paid work as liberation and domesticity as a constraint; for them, it often seemed the other way around. More importantly, perhaps, she pointed out that white feminists had forgotten their own history, where the women's rights movement had itself been racially discriminatory. Too often, in both past and present, white women sought changes that benefited them alone. Black women also resented white feminists' calling on them to place their allegiance to their womanhood over and above that of race. The structures of race, class and gender had to be separated analytically, in order to work out how they interconnected in complex ways (1983: 37–8).

Paralleling the demands of African-American women for a form of scholarship that fully understood the salience of race as an historical experience were demands from minority and indigenous groups everywhere. As early as 1976, Australian Aboriginal feminist Pat O'Shane had queried feminist expectations that Aboriginal women would foreground their gender rather than their experience as a dispossessed, exploited and discriminated-against racial group. Other Aboriginal women stressed how their suspicion of white feminists had its origin in the role white women had played in the exploitation of Aboriginal women historically and modern feminists' inability to acknowledge that history. It took some time for historians to incorporate these issues into their work, but by the mid-1980s historians such as Ann McGrath were beginning to write histories of colonisation and Aboriginal experience which were attentive to the gendered nature of that experience and the ways gender and race combined in frontier and post-frontier colonial situations. Similar **postcolonial** scholarship burgeoned in Canada, New Zealand and the United States.

The questions of race, class and gender were becoming increasingly difficult for feminist historians. In her essay, 'Eccentric Subjects: Feminist Theory and Historical Consciousness' (1990), Teresa de Lauretis, though a cultural critic rather than a historian helped many historians out of the increasingly conceptual minefield in which they now found themselves. In trying to take account of all the complexities of race, class and gender, they had, she argued, retained their initial gender dualism and then tried to add to it concerns of class and race. Rather than add, Lauretis argued, feminist scholars needed to grasp 'their constant intersection and mutual implication', to understand how gender affects racial oppression, or the ways in which the experience of gender is itself shaped by race relations. Rather than structures, de Lauretis spoke of identities. The new feminist consciousness must see itself as 'multiply organized across positions on several axes of difference and across discourses and practices that may be and often are, mutually contradictory'.

The liberation of gender from 'system' and now 'structure' had long-term consequences. Not only did feminist historians turn their attention increasingly to **masculinity**, but also shifted their focus from women, or men, or gender per se to a whole range of human activities that had a gendered aspect. Feminist historians in the 1990s and 2000s came to the forefront of a range of historiographical movements, from environmental, to colonial and postcolonial, to 'new imperial' to transnational history. They continued to insist on the salience of gender and the importance of women, but now these concerns were embedded in a range of others. They had moved a long way from the enthusiasms of the early 1970s, of rescuing women from invisibility, investigating those aspects of existence where women actually lived, of asking why women were oppressed, exploited and devalued through history and how change to a more equal or liberated future might occur. These changes had not been as internal to women's history as might be implied here. They had been linked to changes in the fortunes of the activist feminism which had initially kickstarted the enterprise, from rapid growth in the 1970s, significant gains at a legislative and social level in the 1980s and faltering in western societies but increasingly influential elsewhere in the 1990s and beyond. Despite these changes, a re-reading of these debates reminds us of some of the continuities as well, of the enormous energising force of second-wave feminism for women's history, a force which still impacts on women's his-torical writing today.

Ann Curthoys

References

Alexander 1976; Alexander & Davin 1976; Allen 1986; Banner 1971; Carroll 1976; Curthoys 1970; Davin 1972, 1978; Davis 1976; De Lauretis 1990; Dill 1983; Firestone 1970; Fox-Genovese 1982; Gordon 1986; Gordon *et al.* 1971; Greer 1970; Hooks 1981; Kelly 1976, 1977; Kerber 1988; Kraditor 1965; Lerner 1969, 1975; Lewis 1981; Millet 1970; Mitchell 1971; O'Shane 1976; Rowbotham 1972; Scott 1983, 1986/1988; Scott & Tilly 1975; Smith-Rosenberg 1975a,b.

Related essays

Australia; Canada; Feminism; France; Gender; Great Britain; Masculinity; Postcolonial; Slavery; USA.

Women's magazines

The genre of women's magazines, which may be defined as magazines that explicitly position their readers as women, has its own history that goes back to the advent of print periodicals at the turn of the eighteenth century. The first English-language periodical to address itself to 'the Fair Sex' was the *Ladies' Mercury* (1693), where London bookseller John Dunton invited questions and promised replies on matters of 'Love, Marriage, Behaviour, Dress and Humour of the Female Sex'. Other male pioneers of women's magazines included Richard Steele (*The Tatler*) and Ambrose Phillips (*The Free Thinker*), who were keen to inform as well as to entertain ladies. Most early periodicals were written and published by individuals and by the middle of the eighteenth century some female editors had appeared, like Charlotte Lennox, who offered their readers a more literary journal. Adburgham and Shevelow stress that such publications should be seen in the context of the emergence of various kinds of texts, including almanacks and novels, addressed principally to the women readers, and increasingly supplied by female writers.

The nineteenth century saw the significant expansion of a literate middle class and the elaboration of an ideal of domestic femininity. Women's magazines were the site of major debates about 'the girl of the period' and other female types, while at the same time they recorded and assessed the rapidly changing fashions in dress and etiquette by which status was measured. While there was little support for women's rights evidenced in such popular titles as *The Englishwoman's Domestic Magazine* and *Queen*, by the late 1850s several smaller-circulation titles like the *Englishwoman's Review* specifically addressed those issues. During the last quarter of the century the 'New Journalism' brought an unprecedented expansion in cheap mass-circulation papers. Newer magazines addressed 'women' rather than 'ladies', as the woman in the home assumed new importance as the target of advertising.

This trend intensified throughout the twentieth century with the rise of consumerism, reaching its apogee with post-war affluence and the vast expansion of consumer spending. From about 1960 in Britain and the USA the women's magazine market diversified into glossies addressed to young women and more specialist fashion and decorating titles, although the older home-and-family titles continue to lead the market. The strongly class-differentiated range of titles which could be identified at the turn of the twentieth century was eventually replaced by a range of titles reflecting differences in age and spending capacity. But other differences among women were ignored: by definition, such magazines must appeal to an average or an ideal of 'woman'. It was not until 1970, for instance, that a popular magazine addressed to Afro-American women (*Essence*) appeared. Women's magazines in the developing world follow Western models closely, reflecting no doubt the global nature of the industries that advertise in them.

Women's magazines have long served as invaluable sources for social historians seeking visual and verbal illustrations of changing fashions, etiquette and household hints. With the recent development of feminist cultural and historical studies, these magazines have been used more analytically to examine changing constructions of femininity and gender relations in texts such as Kathryn Shevlow's *Women and Print Culture: The Construction of Femininity in the Early Periodical* (1989). They have also been used as case studies in histories of **modernity** – of print culture in Alison Adburgham's *Women in Print: Writing Women and Women's Magazines from the Restoration to the Accession of Victoria* (1972), or of consumer culture in

Jennifer Scanlon's *Inarticulate Longings: The Ladies' Home Journal, Gender and the Promises of Consumer Culture* (1995).

There has been a shift in the focus as well as purpose of historical studies using women's magazines, with the magazines themselves becoming objects of analysis, both as texts and as aspects of the media industry. Various disciplinary approaches have fed into this emerging field of study. Most of the available histories focus on developments in England until well into the twentieth century. A pioneering sociological study by Cynthia White, *Women's Magazines 1693–1968* (1970), was presented as a contribution to policy-making in the women's magazine industry, which was perceived at the time to be in crisis due to the increased power of advertisers to determine content. While there has been an intensification of this trend, studies of women's magazines have turned their attention to constructions of femininity, as shaped by both ideological and economic forces, and to women as readers. The impact of feminist textual and cultural studies such as Janice Winship's *Inside Women's Magazines* (1987) and Joke Hermes' *Reading Women's Magazines* (1995) ensured that historians of this genre saw the interaction of readers with their magazines as a crucial question to be addressed. Margaret Beetham's title, *A Magazine of Her Own? Domesticity and Desire in the Woman's Magazine 1800–1914*, indicates this more complex theoretical framework that brings together 'the history of a particular publishing tradition and an analysis of the way "woman" has been defined in and through tradition' (1996: ix).

There is a need for studies of emerging magazine industries, as well as surveys that can compare earlier developments between American, British and European magazines. Relationships between women's magazines and women's modernity would be a key question in such inquiries. As a source for women's history, magazines have the particular advantage of being addressed specifically to women readers (and thus inviting interpretations that emphasise the uses such readers might make of the materials) and of constituting an important component of the media as a social institution that is tied directly to both the economics and the ideologies of global capitalism. Margaret Beetham captures the uniqueness of women's magazines with her remark that, 'It would be impossible to write a comparable history of magazines which defined men in terms of their masculinity' (1996: 3).

Susan Sheridan

Reference

Beetham 1996.

Related

Editors and journalists; Modernity.

Woolf, Adeline Virginia (Stephen) 1882–1941

English novelist, essayist, short-story writer, critic, biographer, diarist, letter-writer. The daughter of Leslie Stephen, man of letters and first editor of the *Dictionary of National Biography*, and Julia Duckworth. Although education was prized for the men of her family, Virginia Woolf was educated at home with occasional private lessons in Greek and Latin. She felt bitterly her lack of the formal education given to her brothers. Woolf benefited greatly, however, from her father's excellent library and the resources this offered her particularly in Elizabethan history and literature and that of the eighteenth century. In 1912, she married Leonard Woolf, another original member of the Bloomsbury group, who had recently returned from Ceylon and with whom she subsequently set up the Hogarth Press.

Both the interest in history, and the critical approach that Woolf took to the existing historical literature reflect the central place that history had occupied in her own early life-education. Leslie Stephen was a very distinguished intellectual and literary historian and critic. He read all his children major contemporary historical works, like Carlyle's *History of the French Revolution,* in their childhood. He took a special interest in Virginia and hoped that she would follow in his footsteps and take up literary history herself. Under his firm guidance, she read all the major nineteenth-century historians, but after his death and in her adult years, she became increasingly critical of their ideas and approach and sought to develop new ones for herself. In place of their concern with politics and formal social and religious institutions, she sought to use literature, diaries and letters to find out how, in earlier periods, people had lived their daily life and talked about ordinary things. Moreover, as she made clear, she sought to know about more than the masculine world and to find out both about significant individuals and more generally about how women in the past had lived. In her many essays on 'Dorothy Osborne's *Letters*', or on 'Dorothy Wordsworth', 'Mary Wollstonecraft', 'Jane Austen', and on 'Geraldine and Jane', dealing with Geraldine Jewsbury and Jane Carlyle, Woolf sought not only to discuss the writing of these women, but to read it in ways that offered insights into their emotional make-up and personalities and daily life – and often also to see whether, and in what ways, these particular women offered insights beyond their own lives and into the wider world of women beyond.

Woolf's historical discussions of women's lives illustrated also her interest in biography. Here too, there was a familial basis to her interest: her father was the founding editor of the *Dictionary of National Biography,* and here too one can see in her work a constant critical commentary on his approach. Like her close friend, Lytton Strachey, Woolf was very critical of the standard monumental Victorian Life and Letters. But she was far more concerned than Strachey with the difficulties biography posed in its combining of historical research with its literary form. The biographer, she argued, lacked the freedom of the writer of fiction and was thus always constrained in ways that limited their freedom both to explore the life of their subject and to deal with it in new forms. Woolf explored these possibilities in her essays and in her own biographical works. These included an excellent biography of *Roger Fry* (1940), in which she dealt with the necessary restraint imposed by the fact that she had been asked to write this by his family, and thus needed to be silent about many aspects of his personal and sexual life, by framing his life in terms of the conflict between his Victorian roots and his desire for modernity. She also wrote two imaginative works: *Flush* (1933), dealing with the life of Elizabeth Barrett Browning's spaniel, and a novel *Orlando* (1929). This work, dedicated to and offering a kind of homage to Vita Sackville West, traces the life of a character who lives for several centuries, changing sex on several occasions and romping through the world of high art and literature from the Elizabethan period till the nineteenth century. Both books are subtitled 'a biography' and both carry in new directions her sense of how biography might move beyond its conventional form so that it could explore and interrogate lives in new and different ways.

Historical questions were the subject of several of Woolf's novels. In some cases this is evident in the treatment of particular issues: the satirising of Victorian courtship and convention and the treatment of women's rights and women's suffrage in *Night and Day,* for example, or the impressionistic and elegaic treatment of the unknowable young men who died in the First World War, in *Jacob's Room* (1922). In others, it involves an extended historical discussion of changes in institutions, values, behaviours and dress over time. *The Years* (1931), in particular, traces the evolution of a family from the 1880s to the present, exploring as it does changes in customs and social values, in expectations of women and marriage, and in London itself across this period.

Woolf's capacity to range across an extended period of British history, encapsulating with both elegance and humour changes in intellectual outlook, literary approach and social mores is evident also in her most significant feminist work, *A Room of One's Own*. Influenced by **Jane Ellen Harrison**, and written as a series of lectures delivered at Newnham College, this work played an important part in the development both of women's studies in general and of women's history in particular. Although literature, or more precisely the question of women and fiction, was her starting point in *A Room of One's Own* (1929) in establishing the ways in which women had written fiction, Woolf provided an imaginative history of women across several centuries in Britain. In the process, she also laid out the framework for a woman-centred literary history in which the relationship between women writers and the existence of a female literary tradition was stressed, almost for the first time.

Woolf's discussions of the lives of women in Britain especially across the late eighteenth and nineteenth centuries was informed by an unparalleled knowledge of the history of feminism that encompassed both earlier feminist ideas and the development of the nineteenth-century women's movement. In her essays, in *A Room of One's Own* and in her later feminist work, *Three Guineas* (1938), it was through her knowledge of the particular lives, and experiences of discrimination that Woolf made clear her own sense of the need to extend the battle of nineteenth-century feminists beyond that of political rights and towards economic independence.

Woolf believed strongly in the need for new research into women's history. In *A Room of One's Own*, she suggested a number of the specific kinds of historical questions that needed to be asked in order to establish the distinctive nature of women's experience in the past. It was impossible at present, she argued, to find out anything about the normal experiences of Elizabethan women, for example, because existing historical work supplied none of the necessary information. Using Trevelyan's *History of England* as a particular case, Woolf showed how his questions and categories, while occasionally allowing for some reference to a particularly prominent woman, allowed no space for the lives of ordinary middle-class women. In place of his concern with major political events and institutions, she argued, when it came to women, one wanted a mass of particular information: 'at what age did she marry; how many children had she as a rule; what was her house like; had she a room to herself; did she do the cooking; would she be likely to have a servant? All these facts must lie some where in parish registers and account books; the life of the average Elizabethan woman must be scattered about somewhere.' This life could be written and, in an exhortation that was certainly taken up some decades later, Woolf suggested the research and writing of it as appropriate tasks for the women students she was addressing.

Barbara Caine

References

Hill 1981; Robinson 2002; Rosenberg 2000.

Major work
A Room of One's Own (London: Hogarth Press, 1991) Introduction by Hermoine Lee.

World history

Historians commonly assume that world history and women's history have only intersected with one another quite recently, despite abundant evidence to the contrary (Bentley 1996: 25; Zinsser 1996: 11; Manning 2003: 209; Dunn 2004: 41–2). At least two assumptions have shaped this perception. First, and most importantly, world historians generally presuppose that they write above gender, documenting the unsexed activities of humanity over time (Zinsser 2005: 209–10). This gender blindness, combined with gendered periodisations, categories of analysis and rhetorical strategies has at its worst fostered the unquestioned use of women as an historiographical device to signal the preservation or destabilisation of world order. Furthermore, it has served to minimise and even disguise the activities of women in the past, including women world historians. Second, 'world history' is a broad field and many of its sub-fields – like universal history, ecumenical history, comparative history, eschatological history, world-system history, macrohistory, big history and the new world and global histories – are not considered in relation to one another. Consequently, surveys of the historiography of world history tend to be limited to the period following global exploration or even to the twentieth century (Bentley 1996; Pomper, Elphick and Vann 1998; Manning 2003; Stuchtey and Fuchs 2003). The cumulative result of these assumptions is that pre-twentieth-century women world historians are routinely overlooked.

This essay seeks to rectify such oversights by treating the genre broadly, focusing on women's historical writing that attempts to comprehend a meaningful 'world', understood as an entire meaningful system of existence. World histories written by women vary widely in narrative structure and emphases and range in time and space. They are united, however, by the purpose of offering a construction of and a guide towards a meaningful 'world' or 'realm or domain *taken for* an entire meaningful system of existence or activity by historians or historical agents' (Hughes-Warrington 2005: 4, 8). Recognising the kinship of 'world history' with 'universal history', for instance, extends the historiography of the field back to Herodotus' *Histories* (c.430–424 BCE). Considerations of women and gender were there at the beginning. The *Histories* comment freely on gender relations; women and men function as symbols of the health of the *polis* and as agents of social order. While few of the male historians that followed Herodotus held to his flexible assignment of typologies, they shared his understanding of history as a source of orientation towards the world and as a guide to action. They persistently used women as an historiographical device to signal the maintenance of – or more commonly threats to – world order.

Ancient and medieval 'universal histories'

Most ancient world historical writing on women belongs to the biographical **catalog** genre, which list and describe particular groups of people, a genre that has lasted ever since. There were, for instance, ancient catalogs of priestesses, queens, women responsible or causing wars and ruining or joining family houses and prostitutes. Ancient catalogs of women are characterised by the apparently random order of their entries (i.e. non-chronological or non-alphabetical), the use of male relatives to place or identify female figures, and the judgement of women according to their physical appearance and sexual passion. Some of these works range far over known space and time, and deserve recognition as universal histories because their authors were evidently interested in drawing together historical events to lay bare universal moral truths. These biographical catalogs expressed a continuum of opinion on women, ranging from sympathetic treatments to misogynistic accounts brimming with vitriol. A notable example of the former is the anonymous *Women Intelligent and Courageous in Warfare* (c.200 BCE), which celebrates the achievements of Greek and barbarian queens without passing comment on their physical appearance or sexuality. The non-standard treatment of women in this work has led commentators to wonder whether the author might have been a woman (Gera 1997). Many catalogs, by contrast, warned of the potential sexual impropriety, idleness and disobedience of women; Juvenal, for instance, connected the idleness, moral and sexual depravity of women with the decline of the Roman state.

In the medieval period, a common fear of the social and intellectual impact of female actions upon world order, along with the New Testament prohibition against women teaching (for example, I Timothy 2:9), made it difficult for women to position themselves as pedagogical writers or authorities. They therefore sought covert opportunities for expression, particularly via the frameworks of **hagiography**, mystical writing and florilegium: compilations or collections of literary and biographical texts. For instance, although Herrad of Hohenbourg positions herself in the florilegium *Garden of Delights* (c.1176–1191) (Green *et al.* 1979) as a little bee of God who simply makes honey out of the different flowers of scriptural, philosophical, scientific and cosmological writings, the resulting fusion is a cleverly crafted contribution to medieval universal historical writing. Hildegard of Bingen, too, though not opting for the Augustinian method of using texts, also documents the epochs and future of mankind in the mystical work *Book of Divine Works* (1163–1173) (Fox 1987).

Over a century later, **Christine de Pizan**'s *The Book of the City of Ladies* (1405) appeared, the earliest extant work in which we see the content and structure of history explicitly modified to empower female readers. In the narrative frame of a dream vision, de Pizan inserts herself as a protagonist. In doing so, she presents herself not as the dispenser but as the receiver of information and as a result generates the impression that she is a model for her readers who can encourage them to 'write' themselves into the city of womanly virtue (Brown-Grant 1999: 74–128). Further, to de Pizan, the examples of female warriors, good wives and saintly women demonstrate their common humanity with men and – as their natural and worthy companions – their contribution to the progressive development of civilisation. Through the use of the word 'city' in her title – an echo of Augustine's *City of God* – de Pizan signals that her account of civilisation is a 'universal history'. When discussing the role of men in the history of civilisation, she looks to contemporary events and echoes the late medieval view of society's decline and decadence. When discussing the contributions of women, however, she looks to events over the long term and observes progress. Women are credited with the invention of the letters of the alphabet, arms and agriculture and the development of cities and education. They are also expected to make valuable contributions to society in future – mostly through their companionship with men. Men, on the other hand, are portrayed as increasingly willing to slander women and as connected with the decadent institutions of the Church and State. De Pizan's work is thus characterised by two gendered narratives of differing timescales and modes of emplotment: male as tragedy and female as romance (Hughes-Warrington 2005: 124).

The defence of women

De Pizan clearly anticipated some of the key developments in renaissance and reformation historiography. Topical issues also continued to be important, particularly those in politics and religion. Both came together in the *querelle des femmes* or literary debate about women from the fifteenth to the seventeenth centuries. Generally, *querelle des femmes* works are characterised by theological, philosophical and legal arguments, but many also included biographical catalogs. Women participated in this debate, with **defences** of women being provided by Moderata Fonte's (Modesta Pozzo) *The Worth of Woman*, Lucrezia Marinelli's *The Excellence of Women Together with the Defects and Deficiencies of Men* (1600), the pseudonymous Ester Sowernam's *Ester Hath Hang'd Haman* (1617), Rachel Speght's *A Mouzell for Melastomus* (1617), Mary Fage's *Fames Roule* (1637) and Bathsua Makin's *An Essay to Revive the Antient Education of Gentlewomen* (1673). Of particular interest to these writers was whether women were morally, socially and intellectually complementary to men, rather than subordinate to them, and capable of being citizens and even sovereigns. For instance, while John Knox presented many historical examples in *The First Blast of the Trumpet Against the Monstrous Regimen of Women* (1558) to show that the rule of any woman is 'repugnant to nature, contumelious to God, a thing most contrary to his revealed will and approved ordinance, and . . . the subversion of good order, or all equity and justice', Diana Primrose in her *Chaine of Pearle* (1630) fragmented Elizabeth I into a pseudo-biographical catalog of allegorical virtues. Defences outnumbered attacks by a ratio of four to one and the number of works by women or purportedly by women increased steadily up to the nineteenth century.

Women, civilisation and universal histories

By the seventeenth century, history writing moved away from theology and towards science and philosophy. Through that century and the next, male historians continued in universal fashion, however, to search for the fundamental principles that shaped the behaviour of individuals and societies. They often sought confirmation of the leading role of Western Europe in progress towards intellectual, moral, aesthetic, technological and social perfection. Very often, the treatment of women was a barometer for degrees of civilisation. With some exceptions, these universal historians thought 'civilisation' saw the transformation of Western women from 'slaves' and 'sexual idols' into 'friends and companions' in the private sphere of the home.

Women's historical writing proliferated in the nineteenth century, and this included world histories. Indeed, right at the beginning of the century, Hester Piozzi (also known as Mrs Henry Thrale) published her ambitious world history, entitled *Retrospection; or, A Review of the Most Striking and Important Events, Characters, Situations and Their Consequences, Which the Last Eighteen Hundred Years Have Presented to the View of Mankind* (1801). Her book was in 24 chapters, starting with 'Containing the First Century; from Tiberius to Trajan' and ending with 'Last four years of the century from 1796 to 1800'. Piozzi is notable for presenting annotated copies to her friends, the annotations often emphasising her views as to the fitness of rulers. Especially popular was the biographical catalog featuring women through the ages. **Mary Hay**'s *Female Biography, or Memoirs of Illustrious and Celebrated Women, of all Ages and Countries* (1803), **Lucy Aikin's** *Epistles on Women, Exemplifying Their Character and Condition in Various Ages and Nations with Miscellaneous Poems* (1810), **Anna Jameson**'s *Memoirs of Celebrated Female Sovereigns* (1832), *Characteristics of Women* (1833) and *The Romance of Biography* (1837), Laure Junot's *Memoirs of Celebrated Women* (1834) and Mary Elizabeth Hewitt's *Heroines of History* (1852) are just some of the many nineteenth-century world histories of women that took the form of biographical surveys.

Burstein has argued that in the period from 1830 to 1870 reader, reviewer and publisher demand for morally edifying works quashed methodological innovation, leading authors to produce didactic and encyclopedic texts 'characterised by instances of dèjá vu, plagiarism and mutual raiding of sources' (Burstein 1999: 48). The biographical catalog genre could, indeed, be imbued with deep moral purpose. Women's lives were thought to be particularly edifying, for as **Sarah Josepha Hale** argued in her biographical catalog *Woman's Record; or, Sketches of All Distinguished Women, from 'The Beginning' until AD 1850*, 'woman is God's appointed agent of morality' and the mainspring of human progress towards 'millennial peace' because she was created last in an ascending scale from matter to man (1853: vii, xxxv, xxxvi). As Sarah Strickley Ellis, the author of *The Mothers of Great Men* realised, the moral needs of readers dictated that historical order be subordinated to moral order (1859: 70). 'World-noted women', as Mary Cowden Clarke called them in her book, *World-Noted Women; or, Types of Womanly Attributes of All Lands and Ages*, were accordingly not so much individuals as a historical exemplars or 'types of particular womanly attributes' (1858: 3). Yet a closer inspection of at least some of the women's world histories from this time reveals the use of narrative arrangement, contradictory statements and asides to deliver oblique and sometimes even quite pointed moral, social and political comments. Sarah Josepha Hale's principles of selection clearly indicate her use of history to support a progressive, womanist political programme; Mary Cowden Clarke notes how quickly men are apt to read feminine intelligence as a vice (*World-Noted Women; or, Types of Womenly Attributes of all Lands and Ages* 1858); and a little later **Clara Lucas Balfour** in *Women Worth Emulating* (1877) complains of the deleterious effects of depriving girls of education.

Not all women's world histories took the form of a biographical catalog. **Lydia Maria Child**, a radical abolitionist with a fascination with world religions, wrote five volumes of the *Ladies Family Library*, the first three of which contained biographies of exemplary women. The last two volumes, however, published as *The History of the Condition of Women, in Various Ages and Nations* (1835), were organised spatially. In the same year, Emma Willard, an American innovator and pioneer in girls' education, wrote a school text book *A System of Universal History, In Perspective: Accompanied by an Atlas, Exhibiting Chronology in a Picture of Nations, and Progressive Geography in a Series of Maps* (1835). Reflecting contemporary stereotypes, however, Child's and Willard's works relate European history diachronically and activities in non-European locations synchronically. Yet Child and Willard were deeply affected by the ideals of the new professional history. Unlike many of her peers, Child consistently refused to deduce overt philosophical or universal explanations from the many and varied facts she assembled.

The 1835 edition lacks even an introduction or preface, and the preface Child added to the 1845 edition confirmed that she did not want her work to be read as a philosophical or universal text: 'This volume is not an essay upon women's rights, or a philosophical investigation of what is or what ought to be the relation of the sexes . . . I have simply endeavored to give an accurate history of the condition of women . . .'

It is ironic that female authors of nineteenth-century world histories argued for the domesticity of women at the same time that they enlarged their own sphere of influence by becoming publicly known figures with opinions on the experiences of women in far flung parts of the globe. Perhaps, like Lucretia, as Mary Cowden Clarke argued in *World-Noted Women*, they would have kept 'peaceful silence' had 'destiny so permitted' and would return to privacy once their moral duty had been performed (Clarke 1858: 37). Furthermore, women's world histories, as Hobbs has argued, were double-edged because while on the one hand they provided reading material designed to reinforce prevailing norms regarding girl and womanhood, they also contributed to and thus promoted the literacy and education of women (Hobbs 1995: 10). Many nineteenth-century women's world histories were conduits for womanist thought, demonstrating that women were not lesser instantiations of humanity than men, but their complementary companions, using the gifts of their separate spheres to enhance the abilities of their partners and to turn them away from iniquity.

Few nineteenth-century world histories are mentioned in historiographical surveys today, but the neglect of women contributors to the field is particularly apparent. As some commentators have noted, this is likely due to their exclusion from academic discussions and privileges and even library facilities: few women could hope to produce the archival research that was increasingly valued (Karcher 1998). It is also worth noting, however, that their biographical, ethnographic and narrative methods meant their easy assimilation into the genres of 'travel writing' and 'biography' and movement out of an increasingly professionalised 'history'. Stigmatised as well intentioned but amateurish, compilations of **women worthies** remain today on the margins of professional world-historical writing, with production limited almost exclusively to the growing market of eight-to twelve-year-old girls or 'tweens'. Girls may have 'rocked the world' as one series of texts declares, but their collective biographers have not shaken the foundations of world-historical writing.

Gender and world history

Mid-way through the twentieth century, Arnold J Toynbee in 'A Woman's Life in Other Ages' asked 'When was the best time in history for women to live?' His conclusion, that 'it was a black day for woman when man . . . [wrenched] the hoe out of women's hands and [transformed] it into a plough', was an early contribution to the debate about whether there was a particular point in world history that ushered in gender inequalities (Corfield and Ferrari 2001: 1–16). Yet the debate over the origins of sexual inequality took on a new life with the advent of second-wave **feminism. Simone de Beauvoir** in *The Second Sex* (1949) and later Gerda Lerner in *The Creation of Patriarchy* (1986) argued that gender inequality began much earlier than Toynbee's suggestion of the onset of agriculture, and was extremely common spatially and temporally. A number of works by women historians have continued this debate, notably Marija Gimbutas' *Civilization of the Goddess* (1991), Margaret Ehrenberg's *Women in Prehistory* (1989) and Rosalind Miles' *The Women's History of the World* (1989).

In the mid-twentieth century, modernisation analysis dominated world-history research and writing. Of interest to modernisation theorists were the paths of development in the West that might be used to study and foster development in the 'developing' world. Works such as Ester Boserup's *Woman's Role in Economic Development* (1970) considered development to lead to female empowerment. A disparate group of neo-Marxist theorists such as A G Frank (1978) and Immanuel Wallerstein (1974) disagreed, noting the inadequacy of modernisation theory for an explanation of Latin American development alongside the marginalisation and exploitation of women, and suggesting an alternative in the form of world-system and dependency theory, which focused on inequalities in the distribution of power worldwide.

World histories based on world-systems and dependency theory, however, have rarely been gendered; though writers like Baron have noted it theoretically could be (Baron 1998). This lack is probably due in part to these approaches' affinity with Marxism, and the generally perceived disjunction between feminism and Marxism. It is also due, though, to the growing preference amongst many women historians for identification under the rubric of 'postcolonial studies'. **Postcolonial** histories emphasise the specificities of race, class, gender, nationality and religion and as such can work against the search for universal patterns of change. First brought to the attention of world historians with the publication of Edward Said's *Orientalism* (1978), postcolonial theorists enhance political and economic criticisms of colonialism with cultural analyses. For example, representation and language are crucial for the construction of an 'Other', as works by Joanna De Groot have demonstrated (1989: 89–128; 1999: 107–35). Postcolonial scholars have been tugged by opposing aims: to establish the alignment of the experiences of women and colonised subjects and to recognise the specificities of race, class, nationality, religion, sexuality, epistemic, social, political and economic hierarchies and gender relations. Some have managed to strike a balance, as with Nupur Chaudhuri and Margaret Strobel's study of the varying impacts of European womens' activities on men and women in colonial societies and Louise Tilly's recognition that industrialisation did not lead to the marginalisation of all women (Chaudhuri and Strobel 1992; Strobel 1993; Tilly 1993). However, as Judith Tucker has argued, the desire to recognise and respect cultural particularity can result in a loss of confidence in one's ability to write about those whose lives are shaped by presuppositions very different from our own. Writing world history can thus appear difficult or even unethical (Tucker 1993; Prazniak 2000). Many historians would agree, and, like Von Laue, argue that history is best written on small scales, or from what he calls 'the ground floor of life' (Von Laue 1998: 233).

Dependency, world-system and postcolonial world histories were part of a wider shift in the twentieth century towards the study of relations between peoples across the globe. With the exception of sociological macrohistories, new global histories and neo-universal 'big' histories, 'new' world histories are smaller in scale and more cross-cultural and comparative in approach than earlier works. This shift is mirrored in new world historical writing on women: for example, recent women's world histories such as Bonnie Anderson and Judith Zinsser's *Women in Early Modern and Modern Europe* (2000), Bonnie G Smith's *Changing Lives: Women in European History Since 1700* (1989) and Pauline Pantel's

A History of Women in the West (1992) are restricted to Europe or the West. Other indications of this trend to smaller-scale approaches include Sarah and Brady Hughes' *Women in World History* (1995) and the American Historical Association's 'Women's and Gender History in Global Perspective' series, both of which derive their large-scale perspectives from the combination of specialist sources and pamphlets.

Mary Ritter Beard in *Woman as a Force in History* worked to shift the emphasis of world history discourse away from finding the origins of 'subjection' and towards an appreciation that 'women have been a force in making all the history that has been made' (1946: vi). This idea has inspired much recent scholarship by women about women, but little of it has been in the field of world history. Unfortunately, Beard's comments have had little impact on the field of world history, as women are still routinely confined to sidebars or paragraphs on inequality and agriculture, and on family and marriage. It is as if, as Zinsser notes, women single-handedly created families and had no part to play in technological change. There have, however, been some attempts recently to argue for the value of a gendered approach to world history. Ida Blom (2000) in 'World History as Gender History: The Case of the National-State' has analysed the ways in which different gender systems shape different understandings of the nation state. Sarah Hughes in 'Gender at the Base of World History' has argued for gender to be brought to the forefront of world history scholarship and education. Marilyn Morris (1998) in 'Sexing the Survey: The Issue of Sexuality in World History Since 1500' surveyed world-history textbooks, finding unconscious biases against homosexuality and its conflation with the East. How much the construction of world histories might change when gender is brought to the forefront is clear when one compares the periodisation, categories and narrative structure of Merry Wiesner-Hanks' innovative global survey, *Gender in History* (2001) with the more traditional approach of Peter Stearns in *Gender in World History* (2000) which are contemporaneous. While Stearns fits women to a chronological survey punctuated by phenomena routinely included in world-history surveys – the invention of agriculture and the industrial revolution, to name just two – Weisner-Hanks questions the dominant techno-centred narratives of world historians, and offers instead a thematic treatment of the various points of intersection between gender and politics in family life, warfare, government and popular social movements.

It is time for studies of gender *in* world history to be joined by those of the gender *of* world history. Until world historians understand that they do not write above gender, they will continue to offer limited and limiting visions of our world.

Marnie Hughes-Warrington

References

Baron 1998; Bentley 1996; Blom 2000; Brown-Grant 1999; Burstein 1999; Chaudhuri & Strobel 1992; Clarke 1858; Corfield & Ferrari 2001; De Groot 1989; De Groot 1999; Dunn 2000; Ellis 1859; Fox 1987; Frank 1978; Gera 1997; Green *et al.*, 1979; Hale 1853; Hobbs 1995; Hughes-Warrington, 2005; Karcher, 1998; Manning 2003; Morris 1998; Pomper, Elphick & Vann 1998; Prazniak, 2000; Stuchtey and Fuchs 2003; Strobel, 1993; Tilly, 1993; Tucker, 1993; Von Laue, 1998; Wallerstein 1974; Zinsser 1996; Zinsser 2005.

Related essays

Female Biography; Nation; Orientalism; Postcolonial; Travel; Women Worthies.

General bibliography

Works of reference

Anonymous, 'The Lady Falkland', in Barry Willer and Margaret W Ferguson (eds) *The Tragedy of Mariam Queen of Jewry* (Berkeley: University of California Press, 1994).

Blain, Virginia, Isobel, Grundy and Patricia, Clements (eds), *The Feminist Companion to Literature in English* (New Haven and London: Yale University Press, 1990).

Boyd, Kelly, *Encyclopaedia of Historians and Historical Writing* (London: Fitzroy Dearborn, 1999).

Briggs, Ward W and William M Calder III (eds), *Classical Scholarship: A Biographical Encyclopedia* (New York and London: Garland Publishing, Inc., 1990).

Diamond, Robert, Mary Ann Dimand and Evelyn Forget, *A Biographical Dictionary of Women Economists* (Aldershot: Elgar, 2000).

James, Edward T, Janet Wilson James and Paul S Boyer (eds), *Notable American Women 1607–1950* (Cambridge, Mass.: The Belknap Press, 1971).

Matthew, H G C and Brian Harrison (eds), *The Oxford Dictionary of National Biography* (Oxford: Oxford University Press, 2004).

Oldfield, Sybil, *Collective Biographies of Women in Britain 1500–1900* (London: Mansell, 1999).

Sage, Lorna (ed.), *The Cambridge Guide to Women's Writing in English* (Cambridge: Cambridge University Press, 1999).

Scanlon, Jennifer and Sharon Cosner, *American Women Historians, 1700s–1990s: A Biographical Dictionary* (Westport: Greenwood, 1996).

Schlueter, P and J Schlueter (eds), *An Encyclopedia of British Women Writers* (New York: Garland Publishing Inc., 1988).

Smith, Jessie Carney (ed.), *Notable Black American Women* (Detroit: Gale Research, 1996).

Spender, Dale and Janet Todd (eds), *British Women Writers: An Anthology from the Fourteenth Century to the Present* (New York: Peter Bedrick Books, 1989).

Books

Ackermann, Jessie, *The World through a Woman's Eyes* (Chicago: Cassell, 1896).

——, *Australia from a Woman's Point of View* (London: Cassell and Company, 1913).

Adams, Kimberley Van Esveld, *Our Lady of Victorian Feminism: The Madonna in the Works of Anna Jameson, Margaret Fuller and George Eliot* (Athens: Ohio University Press, 2001).

Aikin, Lucy, *Memoirs of the Court of Queen Elizabeth*, 2 vols (London: Longman, Hurst, Rees, Orme and Brown, 1819).

——, *Memoirs of the Court of King James the First*, 2 vols (London: Longman, Hurst, Rees, Orme and Brown, 1822).

Albright, Madelyn, *Madame Secretary: A Memoir* (New York: Miramax Books, 2003).

Alexander, W, *The History of Women, from the Earliest Antiquity, to the Present Time, Giving Some Account of Almost Everything Every Interesting Particular Concerning that Sex Among All Nations* [1779] (Bath: Thoemmes, 1994).

Allen, Judith, *Sex and Secrets: Crimes Involving Australian Women since 1880* (Oxford: Oxford University Press, 1990).

Allesbrook, Mary, *Born to Rebel. The Life of Harriet Boyd Hawes* (Oxford: Oxbow Books, 1992).

Allman, J, Susan Geiger and Nakanyike Musisi (eds), *Women in African Colonial*

Histories (Bloomington: Indiana University Press, 2002).

Alloula, Malek, *The Colonial Harem* (Minneapolis: University of Minnesota Press, 1996).

Alonso, Harriet Hyman, *Peace as Women's Issue* (Syracuse: Syracuse University Press, 1993).

Anderson, Bonnie S, *A History of Their Own: Women in Europe from Pre-history to the Present* (New York: Harper & Row, 2000).

Andrews, Evangeline W (ed.), *Janet Schaw, Journal of a Lady of Quality: Being the Narrative of a Journey from Scotland to the West Indies, North Carolina and Portugal in the Years 1774–1776* (New Haven: Yale University Press, 1923).

Andrews, W L (ed.), *Classic African American Women's* Narratives (New York: Oxford University Press, 2003).

Angelides, Steven, *A History of Bisexuality* (Chicago: University of Chicago Press, 2001).

Armstrong, Nancy, *Desire and Domestic Fiction: A Political History of the Novel* (New York: Oxford University Press, 1987).

Arnold, John H and Katherine J Lewis, *A Companion to the Book of Margery Kempe* (Woodbridge, Suffolk: Boydell & Brewer Ltd, 2004).

Astell, Mary, *A Serious Proposal to the Ladies*, ed. Patricia Springborg (London: Brookfield, 1997).

Atkinson, Emma Willsher, *Memoirs of the Queens of Prussia* (London: W. Kent and Co., 1858).

Atwood, Margaret, *The Journals of Susanna Moodie* (Toronto: Oxford University Press, 1977).

Aubrac, L, *Outwitting the Gestapo* (Lincoln: University of Nebraska Press, 1993).

Auerbach, Nina, *Woman and the Demon: The Life of a Victorian Myth* (Cambridge, Mass.: Harvard University Press, 1982).

Backscheider, Paula, *Revising Women: Eighteenth Century 'Women's Fiction' and Social Engagement* (Baltimore: Johns Hopkins Press, 2000).

Bacon, Margaret Hope, *One Woman's Passion for Peace and Freedom* (Syracuse: Syracuse University Press, 1993).

Bair, Deirdre, *Simone de Beauvoir: A Biography* (London: Jonathan Cape, 1990).

Baker, C H C, *The Life and Circumstances of James Brydges, First Duke of Chandos* (Oxford: Oxford University Press, 1949).

Ballard, George, *Memoirs of Several Ladies of Great Britain*, ed. Ruth Perry (Detroit: Wayne State University Press, 1985).

Ballaster, Ros, *Seductive Forms: Women's Amatory Fiction from 1684 to 1740* (Oxford: Clarendon Press, 1992).

Barman, Jean, *Constance Lindsay Skinner: Writing on the Frontier* (Toronto: University of Toronto Press, 2002).

Barnard, Majorie and Flora Eldershaw, *My Australia* (London: Janolds, 1939).

Bartley, Paula, *Prostitution: Prevention and Reform in England 1860–1914* (London: Routledge, 2000).

Barwick, G F, *The Reading Room of the British Museum* (London: Ernest Benn Ltd, 1929).

Baudoin, M, *Histoire des Groupes Francs (MUR): Bouches-du-Rhone de Septembre 1943 a la Liberation* (Paris: PUF, 1962).

Baym, Nina, *American Women Writers and the Work of History, 1790–1860* (New Brunswick: Rutgers University Press, 1995).

Beard, Mary, *The Invention of Jane Harrison* (Cambridge, Mass.: Harvard University Press, 2000).

Beasley, Faith E, *Revising Memory: Women's Fiction and Memoirs in Seventeenth-Century France* (New Brunswick: Rutgers University Press, 1990).

Beckles, Hilary, *Natural Rebels: A Social History of Enslaved Black Women in Barbados* (London: Zed Books, 1989).

——, *Centering Woman: Gender Discourses in Caribbean Slave Society* (Oxford: James Curry, 1998).

Bederman, Gail, *Manliness and Civilization: A Cultural History of Gender and Race in the United States* (Chicago: University of Chicago Press, 1995).

Beer, Frances, *Women and the Mystical Experience in the Middle Ages* (Rochester: Boydell Press, 1992).

Beer, Gillian, *George Eliot* (Brighton: Harvester, 1986).

——, *Darwin's Plots: Evolutionary Narrative in Darwin, George Eliot and Nineteenth-Century Fiction* (Cambridge: Cambridge University Press, 2000).

Behdad, Ali, *Belated Travellers: Orientalism in the Age of Colonial Dissolution* (Durham: Duke University Press, 1994).

Behn, Aphra, *The Complete Works*. Vol. II, *Love Letters Between a Nobleman and His Sister*, ed. Janet Todd (Columbus: Ohio State University Press, 1993).

Behrendt, Stephen, *Royal Mourning and Regency Culture: Elegies and Memorials of Princess Charlotte* (London: Palgrave Macmillan, 1997).

Beilin, Elaine, *Redeeming Eve: Women Writers of the English Renaissance* (Princeton: Princeton University Press, 1987).

Belgiojoso, C T de, *Reflexions sur l'etat actuel de l'Italie et sur son avenir* (Paris: Librairie International, 1869).

Bell, Lady Florence, *At the Works. A Study of a Manufacturing Town* [1907] (London: Virago Press, 1985).

Bellamy, Joan, *Mary Taylor – Strong-minded Woman and Friend of Charlotte Brontë* (Kirklees: M C Cultural Services, 1997).

Bellamy, Joan, Anne Laurence and Gill Perry (eds), *Women, Scholarship, and Criticism: Gender and Knowledge c.1790–1900* (Manchester: Manchester University Press, 2000).

Bellany, Alastair, *The Politics of Court Scandal in Early Modern England: News, Culture and the Overbury Affair, 1603–1660* (Cambridge: Cambridge University Press, 2002).

Benger, Elizabeth, *Memoirs of the Late Elizabeth Hamilton* (London: Longman, 1818).

——, *Memoirs of the Life of Anne Boleyn, Queen of Henry VIII* (Philadelphia: Abraham Small, 1822).

Benson, Pamela, *The Invention of the Renaissance Woman* (Pennsylvania: The Pennsylvania State University Press, 1992).

Bentley, J, *Shapes of World History in Twentieth-Century Scholarship* (Washington, DC: American Historical Association, 1996).

Berg, Maxine, *A Woman in History: Eileen Power, 1889–1940* (Cambridge: Cambridge University Press, 1996).

Berkman, Joyce Avrech, *The Healing Imagination of Olive Schreiner: Beyond South African Colonialism* (Amherst: University of Massachusetts Press, 1989).

Besser, Gretchen Rous, *Germaine de Staël Revisited* (New York: Twayne, 1994).

Blake, Audrey, *A Proletarian Life* (Malmesbury: Kibble Books, 1984).

Bland, Lucy, *Banishing the Beast: English Feminism and Sexual Morality, 1885–1914* (London: Penguin, 1995).

Blessington, Marguerite, *An Idler in Italy* (London: Henry Colburn Publisher, 1839).

——, *An Idler in France* (Philadelphia: Carey and Hart, 1841).

Blodgett, H, *Centuries of Female Days* (New Brunswick: Rutgers University Press, 1988).

Bohls, Elizabeth, *Women Travel Writers, Landscape and the Language of Aesthetics, 1716–1818* (Cambridge: Cambridge University Press, 1995).

Booth, Alison, *How to Make it as a Woman: Collective Biography from Victoria to the Present* (Chicago: University of Chicago Press, 2004).

Bornstein, Daniel, *Life and Death in a Venetian Convent: The Chronicle and Necrology of Corpus Domini 1395–1436* (Chicago: University of Chicago Press, 2000).

Bosanquet, Rosalie E, *In the Troublesome Times. Memories of Old Northumberland Collected by the Cambo Women's Institute* (Stocksfield: Spredden Press, 1989).

Botchkareva, Y, Yashka, *My Life as a Peasant, Officer and Exile* (New York: Frederick A Stokes, 1919).

Boutilier, Beverley and Alison Prentice (eds), *Creating Historical Memory: English-Canadian Women and the Work of History* (Vancouver: UBC Press, 1997).

Boyd, Kelly, *Manliness and the Boy's Papers in Britain: A Cultural History* (London: Palgrave, 2003).

Branson, Susan, *These Fiery Frenchified Dames: Women and Political Culture in Early National Philadelphia* (Philadelphia: University of Pennsylvania, 2001).

Breton, Philipe le (ed.) *Memoirs, Miscellanies and Letters of the Late Lucy Aikin* (London: Longman, 1864).

Brodsky, Bella and Celeste Schenck (eds) *Life/Lines Theorising Women's Autobiography* (Ithaca: Cornell University Press, 1998).

Brombert, Beth Archer, *Cristina: Portraits of a Princess* (New York: Alfred A Knopf, 1977).

Brosman, Catherine Savage, *Simone de Beauvoir Revisited* (Boston: Twayne, 1991).

Brown, Louise, Beatrix Ch de Crespigny, Mary P Harris, Kathleen Kyffin Thomas and Phebe N Watson, *A Book of South Australia: Women in the First Hundred Years* (Adelaide: Rigby, 1936).

Brown, Lucy Fargo, *Apostle of Democracy: The Life of Lucy Maynard Salmon* (New York: Harper & Brothers, 1943).

Brown, Peter, *The Cult of the Saints* (Chicago: University of Chicago, 1981).

Brown-Grant, Rosalind, *Christine de Pizan and the Moral Defence of Women: Reading Beyond Gender* (Cambridge: Cambridge University Press, 1999).

Buchanan-Gould, Vera, *Not without Honour: The Life and Writings of Olive Schreiner* (London: Hutchinson & Co., 1948).

Bulley, A Amy and Margaret Whitely, *Women's Work* (London: Methuen, 1894).

Bumpus, John S, *The Organists and Composers of St. Paul's Cathedral* (London: Bowden, Hudson & Co., 1891).

Burgos-Debray, Elisabeth (ed.) *I, Rigoberta Menchu: An Indian Women in Guatemala*, trans. Ann Wright (London: Verso, 1984).

Burton, Antoinette, *Burdens of History: British Feminists, Indian Women, and Imperial Culture, 1865–1915* (Chapel Hill: University of North Carolina Press, 1994).

——, *At the Heart of the Empire: Indians and the Colonial Encounter in Late-Victorian Britain* (Berkeley: University of California Press, 1998).

——, *Dwelling in the Archive: Women Writing House, Home, and History in Late Colonial India* (Oxford: Oxford University Press, 2003).

Bush, Barbara, *Slave Women in Caribbean Societies* (Oxford: James Curry, 1990).

Buss, Helen M, 'The Different Voice of Canadian Feminist Autobiographers', *Biography*, 13:2 (1990) 154–167.

Buss, Helen M and Marlene Kadar (eds) *Working in Women's Archives: Researching Women's Private Literature and Archival Documents* (Waterloo, Ontario: Wilfrid Laurier University Press, 2001).

Butler, Judith, *Gender Trouble: Feminism and the Subversion of Identity* (New York: Routledge, 1990).

——, *Bodies that Matter: On the Discursive Limits of 'Sex'* (New York: Routledge, 1993).

Butler, Marilyn, *Maria Edgeworth: A Literary Biography* (Oxford: Oxford University Press, 1972).

——, *Jane Austen and the War of Ideas* (Oxford: Oxford University Press, 1989).

Bynum, Caroline Walker, *Jesus as Mother: Studies in the Spirituality of the High Middle Ages* (Berkeley: University of California Press, 1982).

——, *Fragmentation and Redemption: Essays on Gender and the Human Body in Medieval Religion* (New York: Zone Books, 1991).

——, *Resurrection of the Body in Western Christianity 200–1336* (New York: Columbia University Press, 1996).

Caffarelli, Annette Wheeler, *Prose in the Age of Poets: Romanticism and Biographical Narrative from Johnson to De Quincey* (Philadelphia: University of Pennsylvania Press, 1990).

Caine, Barbara, *Victorian Feminists* (Oxford: Oxford University Press, 1992).

Callon, A, *The Spectacular Body: Science, Method and Meaning in the Work of Degas* (London and New Haven: Yale University Press, 1995).

Cambridge Women's Peace Collective, *My Country is the Whole World* (London: Pandora Press, 1984).

Campbell, Mary, *Lady Morgan: The Life and Times of Sydney Owenson* (London: Pandora, 1988).

Carby, Hazel, *Race Men* (Cambridge, Mass.: Harvard University Press, 1998).

Carroll, Berenice (ed.), *Liberating Women's History: Theoretical and Critical Essays* (Urbana: University of Illinois Press, 1976)

Carter, Angela (ed.), *The Old Wives' Fairy Tale Book* (New York: Pantheon Books, 1990).

Cartwright, Julia, *Isabella d'Este, Marchioness of Mantua 1474–1539: A Study of the Renaissance* (London: John Murray, 1903).

——, *Beatrice d'Este, Duchess of Milan 1475–1497: A Study of the Renaissance* (London: J M Dent & Sons; New York: E P Dutton & Co., 1926).

Cary, Elizabeth, *The Tragedy of Mariam Queen of Jewry*, Barry Willer and Margaret W Ferguson (eds) (Berkeley: University of California Press, 1994).

Casalena, Maria Pia, *Scritti storici di donne italiane, Bibliografia 1800–1945* (Firenze: Olschki, 2003).

Caton-Thompson, Gertrude, *Mixed Memoirs* (Gateshead: Tyne & Wear, Paradigm Press, 1983).

Ceadel, Martin, *Pacifism in Britain, 1914–1944* (Oxford: Clarendon Press, 1980).

Chalmers, S, *Emerging Lesbian Voices from Japan* (London: Routledge Curzon, 2002).

Chambers, Sarah C, *From Subjects to Citizens: Honor, Gender and Politics in Arequipa, Peru, 1780–1854* (University Park: Pennsylvania State University Press, 1999).

Chance, Jane (ed.), *Gender and Text in the Later Middle Ages* [1996] (Gainesville: University Press of Florida, 2003).

—— (ed.), *Women Medievalists and the Academy* (Madison: University of Wisconsin Press, 2004).

Chandler, James, *England in 1819: The Politics of Literary Culture and the Case of Romantic Historicism* (Chicago: University of Chicago Press, 1998).

Chapple, J A V and Arthur Pollard (eds), *The Life of Mrs Gaskell* (Manchester: Manchester University Press, 1996).

Chard, Chloe, *Pleasure and Guilt on the Grand Tour: Travel Writing and Imaginative Topography 1600–1830* (Manchester: Manchester University Press, 1999).

Chatterjee, C, *Celebrating Women. Gender, Festival Culture, and Bolshevik Ideology, 1910–1939* (Pittsburgh: University of Pittsburgh Press, 2002).

Chaudhuri, N and Strobel, M (eds), *Western Women and Imperialism: Complicity and Resistance* (Bloomington, IN: Indiana University Press, 1992).

Cherewatuk, Karen and Ulrike Wiethaus (eds), *Dear Sister: Medieval Women and the Epistolary Genre* (Philadelphia: University of Pennsylvania Press, 1993).

Cherry, Deborah, *Painting Women: Victorian Women Artists* (London: Routledge, 1993).

Churchill, Laurie J, Phyllis R Brown and Jane E Jeffrey (eds), *Women Writing Latin*, 3 vols (New York: Routledge, 2002).

Clancy-Smith, Julia and Frances Gouda (eds) *Domesticating the Empire. Race, Gender, and Family Life in French and Dutch Colonialism* (Charlottesville: University Press of Virginia, 1998).

Clark, Alice, *The Working Life of Women in the Seventeenth Century*, ed. Miranda Chaytor and Jane Lewis (London: Routledge, 1982).

Clark, Anna, *The Struggle for the Breeches: Gender and the Making of the British Working Class* (London: Rivers Oram Press, 1995).

Clarke, M C, *World-Noted Women; or, Types of Womanly Attributes of all Lands and Ages* (New York: D Appleton and Company, 1858).

Clarke, Norma, *Ambitious Heights: Writing, Friendship, Love: The Jewsbury Sisters, Felicia Hemans, and Jane Welsh Carlyle* (London: Routledge, 1990).

Clarke, Patricia, *Rosa! Rosa! A Life of Rosa Praed, Novelist and Spiritualist* (Melbourne: Melbourne University Press, 1999).

Clayton, Cherry, *Olive Schreiner* (New York: Twayne Publishers, 1997).

Clery, E J, *The Feminisation Debate in Eighteenth Century England* (New York: Palgrave, 2004).

Clinton, Catherine, *The Plantation Mistress: Women's World in the Old South* (New York: Pantheon Books, 1982).

Clowes, E M, *On the Wallaby: Through Victoria* (London: Heinemann, 1911).

Cockin, Katharine, *Edith Craig 1869–1947 Dramatic Lives* (London: Cassell, 1998).

Cohen, Michéle, *Fashioning Masculinity: National Identity and Language in the Eighteenth Century* (New York: Routledge, 1996).

Coleman, Deirdre (ed.) *Maiden Voyages and Infant Colonies: Two Women's Travel Narratives of the 1790s* (London: Leicester University Press, 1999).

Colley, Linda, *Britons: Forging the Nation 1707–1837* (New Haven: Yale University Press, 1992).

Collier, Frances, *Family Economy of the Working Classes in the Cotton Industry, 1784–1833* ed, R S Fitton and Memoir by T S Ashton (Manchester: Manchester University Press, 1964).

Conrad, Margaret, Toni Laidlaw and Donna Smyth, *No Place Like Home: Diaries and Letters of Nova Scotia Women, 1771–1938* (Halifax: Formac Publishing Company, 1988).

Conrad, Susan Phinney, *Perish the Thought: Intellectual Women in Romantic America* (New York: Oxford University Press, 1976).

Cook, Blanche Wiesen, *Eleanor Roosevelt* (New York: Viking Press, 1992).

Coon, Lynda, *Sacred Fictions: Holy Women and Hagiography in Late Antiquity* (Philadelphia: University of Pennsylvania Press, 1997).

Cooper, Anna Julia, *A Voice from the South: By a Black Woman of the South* [1892] (Ohio: Aldine Printing Press, 1988).

Cooper, Sandi E, *Patriotic Patriotism: Waging War on War in Europe 1815–1914* (New York: Oxford University Press, 1991).

Cope, Esther, *Handmaid of the Holy Spirit: Dame Eleanor Davies, Never Soe Mad a Ladie* (Ann Arbor: University of Michigan Press, 1992).

Côté, Jane McL, *Fanny and Anna Parnell: Ireland's Patriotic Sisters* (London: Macmillan, 1991).

Cott, Nancy J, *The Bonds of Womanhood: 'Woman's Sphere' in New England, 1780–1835* (New Haven and London: Yale University Press, 1977).

—— (ed.), *A Woman Making History: Mary Ritter Beard through her Letters* (New Haven, London: Yale University Press, 1991).

Covert, James, *A Victorian Marriage: Mandell and Louise Creighton* (London: Hambledon, 2000).

Craft, William and Ellen Craft, *Running a Thousand Miles to Freedom: The Escape of Willam and Ellen Craft*, ed. Barbara McCaskill (Athens: University of Georgia Press, 1999).

Crawford, P S and Sara Mendelson, *Women in Early Modern England 1550–1720* (Oxford: Clarendon Press, 1998).

Crowley, Terry, *Marriage of Minds: Isabel and Oscar Skelton Re-inventing Canada* (Toronto: University of Toronto Press, 2003).

Crown Jewels: A Brief Record of the Wives of English Sovereigns from 1066 to 1897 A.D. (London: Elliot Stock, 1897).

Cruikshank, Julie, *Life Lived Like a Story: Life Stories of Three Yukon Elders* (Vancouver: UBC Press, 1991).

Culley, M, *A Day at a Time: The Diary Literature of American Women from 1764 to the Present* (New York: Feminist Press, 1985).

Currie, Emma, *The Story of Laura Secord and Canadian Reminiscences* (Toronto: William Briggs, 1900).

Curthoys, Barbara and Audrey McDonald, *More than a Hat and Glove Brigade: The Story of the Union of Australian Women* (Sydney: Bookpress, 1996).

Damico, Helen and Joseph B Zavadil (eds) *Medieval Scholarship: Biographical Studies on the Formation of a Discipline*, 3 vols (New York: Garland, 1995, 1998, 2000).

Davidoff, Leonore, *The Best Circles: Society, Etiquette and the Season* (London: Hutchinson, 1973).

——, 'Class and Gender in Victorian England', in Judith L Newton, Mary P Ryan and Judith R Walkowitz (eds) *Sex and Class in Women's History* (London: Routledge & Kegan Paul, 1983).

Davidoff, Leonore and Catherine Hall, *Family Fortunes: Men and Women of the English Middle Class, 1750–1850* (London: Hutchinson, 1987).

Davies, Maude F, *Life in an English Village: An Economic and Historical Survey of the Parish of Corsley in Wiltshire* (London: Fisher Unwin, 1909).

Davis, Norman (ed.) *Paston Letters* (Oxford: Clarendon Press, 1958).

DeJean, Joan, *Fictions of Sappho 1546–1937* (Chicago: Chicago University Press, 1989).

——, *Tender Geographies: Women and the Origins of the Novel* (New York: Columbia University Press, 1991).

—— (ed. and trans.), *Against Marriage: The Correspondence of La Grande Mademoiselle* [Orléans, Anne-Marie-Louise d'] (Chicago: University of Chicago Press, 2002).

Dentiere, Marie, *Epistle to Marguerite de Navarre and a Preface to a Sermond by John Calvin*, ed. and trans. Mary B McKinley (Chicago: University of Chicago Press, 2004).

Des Jardins, Julie, *Women and the Historical Enterprise in America: Gender, Race, and the Politics of Memory, 1880–1945* (Chapel Hill: University of North Carolina Press, 2003).

Di Cori, Paola, 'Women's History in Italy', in Karen Offen, Ruth Roach Pierson and Jane Randall (eds) *Writings Women's History. International Perspectives* (London: Macmillan, 1991) pp. 443–456.

Dilke, Emelia, *French Painters of the Eighteenth Century* (London: George Bell & Sons, 1899).

Dixon, Kathleen, *An Appeal to the Women of Empire Concerning the Present Moral Conditions in Our Contonments in India* (London: Association for Moral and Social Hygiene, 1916).

Dollimore, Jonathan, *Sexual Dissidence: Augustine to Wilde, Freud to Foucault* (Oxford: Clarendon, 1991).

Donawerth, Jane and Julie Strongson (trans. and eds), *Madeleine Scudery's Selected Letters, Orations and Rhetorical Dialogues* (Chicago: University of Chicago Press, 2004).

Dronke, Peter, *Women Writers of the Middle Ages: A Critical Study of Texts from Perpetua to Marguerite Porete* (Cambridge: Cambridge University Press, 1984).

Drower, Margaret S, *Flinders Petrie: A Life in Archaeology* (London: Victor Gollancz, 1985; Madison: University of Wisconsin Press, 1996).

Du Cane, Rosamund, *Sicklesmiths and Spear Carriers* (Newbury, Berks: The Village and Family History Project, 2002).

Duden, Barbara, *Woman Beneath the Skin: A Doctor's Patients in 18th century Germany*, *trans*. Thomas Dunlap. (Cambridge Mass.: Harvard University Press, 1991).

Dyhouse, Carol, *Feminism and the Family in England, 1880–1939* (Oxford: Basil Blackwell, 1989).

Eastman, Ann Heidbreder, *Constance Lindsay Skinner, Author and Editor, Sketches of Her Life and Character with a Checklist of Her Writings and the "Rivers of America" Series* (Montclair: Women's International Book Association, Inc., 1980).

Edgeworth, Maria, *Castle Rackrent* [1800] (Oxford: Oxford University Press, 1999).

Edwards, Ruth Dudley, *Patrick Pearse: The Triumph of Failure* (London: Victor Gollancz, 1977).

Egli, Ida Rae (ed.), 'Introduction', *Women of the Gold Rush: "The New Penelope" and Other Stories, by Frances Fuller Victor* (Berkeley, California: Heydey Books, 1998).

Ehrenreich, Barbara and Deirdre English, *Complaints and Disorders: The Sexual Politics of Sickness* (New York: Feminist Press, 1973).

Eldershaw, Flora (ed.), *The Peaceful Army* [1938], ed. Dale Spender (Ringwood: Penguin, 1988).

Ellis, Sarah Stickney, *The Mothers of Great Men* (London: Chatto & Windus, 1874).

Elshtain, Jean Bethke, *Women, Militarism and War* (Totowa: Rowman & Littlefield, 1990).

——, *Just War Theory* (New York: New York University Press, 1994).

Emanuel, Angela (ed.), *Bright Remembrance: The Diaries of Julia Cartwright, 1851–1924* (London: Weidenfeld & Nicolson, 1989).

Engelstein, Laura, *The Keys to Happiness: Sex and the Search for Modernity in Fin-de-Siecle Russia* (Ithaca, New York: Cornell University Press, 1992).

Epple, Angelika, *Empfindsame Geschichtschreibung. Eine Geschlechtergeschichte der Historiographie zwischen Aufklärung und Historismus* (Köln, Weimar Wien: Böhlau Verlag, 2003).

Epstein, Julia and Kristina Straub (eds), *Body Guards: The Cultural Politics of Gender Ambiguity* (London: Routledge, 1991).

Erickson, Carolly, *Mistress Anne* (New York: Summit Books, 1984).

——, *Her Little Majesty: The Life of Queen Victoria* (New York: Simon & Schuster, 1997).

Esdaile, Arundell, *The British Museum Library: A Short History and Survey* (London: George Allen & Unwin, 1948).

Ezell, Margaret J M, *Writing Women's Literary History* (Baltimore: Johns Hopkins University Press, 1993).

Faderman, Lilian, *Surpassing the Love of Men: Romantic Friendship and Love between Women from the Renaissance to the Present* (New York: William Morrow, 1981).

——, *Odd Girls and Twilight Lovers: A History of Lesbian Life in Twentieth-Century America* (New York: Columbia University Press, 1991).

Fallaize, Elizabeth (ed.), *Simone de Beauvoir: A Critical Reader* (London: Routledge, 1998).

Farnham, Fern, *Madame Dacier. Scholar and Humanist* (Monterey, California: Angel Press, 1976).

Favret, M A, *Romantic Correspondence: Women, Politics and the Fiction of Letters* (Cambridge: Cambridge University Press, 1993).

Fedele, Cassandra, *Letters and Orations*, ed. and trans. Diane Robin (Chicago: University of Chicago Press, 2000).

Fenwick, Gillian, *Women and the Dictionary of National Biography* (Aldershot: Scolar, 1994).

Ferguson, Moira, *First Feminists: British Women Writers 1578–1799* (Bloomington: University of Indiana Press, 1985).

——, *Subject to Others: British Women Writers and Colonial Slavery, 1670–1834* (London: Routledge, 1992).

——, *Colonialism and Gender Relations from Mary Wollstonecraft to Jamaica Kincaid: Eastern Caribbean Connections* (New York: Columbia University Press, 1993).

—— (ed.), *The History of Mary Prince, A West Indian Slave Related by Herself* [1831] (Ann Arbor: University of Michigan Press, 1997).

Ferrante, Joan M, *To the Glory of Her Sex: Women's Roles in the Composition of Medieval Texts* (Bloomington: Indiana University Press, 1997).

Ferris, Ina, *The Romantic National Tale* (Cambridge: Cambridge University Press, 2002).

Finnegan, Ruth, *Literacy and Orality: Studies in the Technology of Communication* (London: Blackwell, 1988).

Firestone, Shulamith, *The Dialectic of Sex* (New York: William Morrow and Co., 1970).

Firmager, Gabrielle M (ed.), *The Female Spectator: Being Selections from Mrs Eliza Haywoods Periodical 1744–46* (London: Bristol Classical Press, 1993).

Fitzpatrick, Ellen, *History's Memory: Writing America's Past, 1880–1980* (Cambridge, Mass.: Harvard University Press, 2002).

Fitzpatrick, Sheila, *The Cultural Front: Power and Culture in Revolutionary Russia* (Ithaca: Cornell University Press, 1992).

——, *Stalin's Peasants. Resistance and Survival in the Russian Village after Collectivization* (New York: Oxford University Press, 1994).

——, *The Russian Revolution* (New York: Oxford University Press, 1994).

——, *Everyday Stalinism: Ordinary Life in Extraordinary Times* (New York: Oxford University Press, 1999).

Fitzpatrick, S and Slezkine, Y (eds), *In the Shadow of Revolution. Life Stories of Russian Women from 1917 to the Second World War* (Princeton: Princeton University Press, 2000).

Fletcher, Brian, *Australian History in New South Wales 1888–1938* (Kensington: New South Wales University Press, 1993).

Fletcher, Anthony, *Gender, Sex and Subordination in England 1500–1800* (New Haven: Yale University Press, 1995).

Flexner, Eleanor, *Century of Struggle*, ed. Ellen Fitzpatrick (Cambridge, Mass.: Belknap Press, 1996).

Folkenflik, Vivian (ed.), *An Extraordinary Woman: Selected Writings of Germaine de Staël* (New York: Columbia University Press, 1987).

Fonte, Moderata, *The Worth of Women*, ed. Virginia Cox (Chicago: University of Chicago Press, 1997).

Forster, Penny and Imogen Sutton (eds), *Daughters of de Beauvoir* (London: The Women's Press, 1989).

Foster, Shirley, *Across New Worlds: Nineteenth-Century Women Travellers and Their Writings* (London: Harvester Wheatsheaf, 1990).

Foucault, Michel, *Discipline and Punish: The Birth of the Prison* (London: Allen Lane, 1977).

——, *The History of Sexuality: An Introduction* (New York: Vintage Books, 1980).

Fox, M (ed.), *Hildegard of Bingen's Book of Divine Works with Letters and Songs* (Sante Fe: Bear, 1987).

Fox-Genovese, Elizabeth, *Within the Plantation Household: Black and White Women of the Old South* (Chapel Hill: University of North Carolina Press, 1988).

Fraisse, Genevieve, *Reason's Muse: Sexual Difference and the Birth of Democracy* [1989] (Chicago: University of Chicago Press, 1994).

Frank, A G, *World Accumulation 1492–1789* (London: Macmillan, 1978).

Fraser, Antonia, *The Weaker Vessel. Woman's Lot in Seventeenth Century England* (London: Methuen, 1984).

——, *The Wives of Henry VIII* (New York: Vintage Books, 1994).

Frawley, Maria, *A Wider Range: Travel Writing by Women in Victorian England* (London: Associated University Presses, 1994).

Fry, Anna Ruth, *Emily Hobhouse: A Memoir* (London: Jonathon Cape, 1929).

Fujime, Y, *Sei no Rekishigaku* (Tokyo: Fuji Shuppan, 1997).

Fukuda, H, *Warawa no Hanseigai* [1904] (Tokyo: Iwanami Shoten, 1958).

Gaffarel, Paul, *Les colonies francaises* (Paris: Felix Alcan, 1899).

Gallagher, Catherine, *Nobody's Story: The Vanishing Acts of Women Writers in the Marketplace* (Berkeley and Los Angeles: University of California Press, 1994).

Gallagher, Catherine and Thomas Laqueur (eds) *The Making of the Modern Body: Sexuality and Society in the Nineteenth Century* (California: University of California Press, 1987).

Gandy, Ida, *Round about the Little Steeple* (Gloucester: Alan Sutton, 1989).

Garay, Kathleen and Madeleine Jeay (trans.) *The Life of Saint Douceline, a Beguine of Provence* (Woodbridge, Suffolk and Rochester, New York: D S Brewer, 2001).

Gardiner, Dorothy, *English Girlhood at School* (Oxford: Oxford University Press, 1929).

Gardiner, Juliet (ed.), *The New Woman: Women's Voices 1880–1918* (London: Collins & Brown, 1993).

Garside, Peter, 'The English Novel in the Romantic Era', in Peter Garside, James Raven and Rainer Schowerling (eds) *The English Novel, 1770–1829*, 2 vols (Oxford: Oxford University Press, 2000).

Gaskell, Elizabeth, *The Life of Charlotte Brontë* (New York: D Appleton, 1857).

Gatens, Moira, *Imaginary Bodies: Ethics, Power and Corporeality* (London: Routledge, 1996).

Gates, Henry Jr, *The Classic Slave Narratives* (New York: Mentor Books, 1987).

——, *Collected Black Women's Narratives* (New York: Oxford University Press, 1990).

Gattey, Charles Neilson, *A Bird of Curious Plumage: Princess Cristina di Belgiojoso* (London: Constable, 1971).

Gaunt, Mary, *Where the Twain Meet* (London: John Murray, 1922).

Gearhart, Suzanne, *The Open Boundary of History and Fiction: A Critical Approach to the French Enlightenment* (Princeton: Princeton University Press, 1984).

Gera, D, *Warrior Women: The Anonymous Tractatus de Mulieribus* (Leiden: E J Brill, 1997).

Gibson, Mary, *Prostitution and the State in Italy 1860–1915* (New Brunswick: Rutgers University Press, 1986).

Giddings, Paula, *When and Where I Enter: The Impact of Black Women on Race and Sex in America* (New York: William Morrow and Company, Inc., 1984).

Gilchrist, Roberta, *Gender and Material Culture: The Archaeology of Religious Women* (New York: Routledge, 1994).

——, *Gender and Archaeology: Contesting the Past* (London and New York: Routledge, 1999).

Gimbutas, Marija, *The Living Goddesses* (Berkeley: University of California Press, 1999).

Gioseffi, Daniela, *Women on War: Essential Voices of the Nuclear Age* (New York: Simon & Schuster, 1988).

Glatz, Karl Juliana Ernst (ed.), *Chronik des Bickenklosters zu Villingen 1238–1614* (Tübingen 1881).

Glazer, Penina Migdal and Miriam Slater, *Unequal Colleagues: The Entrance of Women into the Professions 1890–1940* (New Brunswick: Rutgers University Press, 1987).

Godineau, Dominique, *The Women of Paris and Their French Revolution* [1988] (Berkeley: University of California Press, 1998).

Goldberg, Rita, *Sex and the Enlightenment: Women in Richardson and Diderot* (Cambridge: Cambridge University Press, 1984).

Golden, Mark and Peter Toohey (eds), *Sex and Difference in Ancient Greece and Rome.* (Edinburgh: Edinburgh University Press, 2003).

Goldman, Lawrence, *Dons and Workers: Oxford Adult Education and the Working Class since 1850* (Oxford: Oxford University Press, 1995).

Goldman, Wendy Z, *Women at the Gates: Gender and Industry in Stalin's Russia*

(Cambridge: Cambridge University Press, 2002).

Goldsmith, Elizabeth, *Publishing Women's Life Stories* (London: Ashgate Press, 2001).

Goldsmith, Elizabeth and Dena Goodman (eds), *Going Public: Women and Publishing in Early Modern France* (Ithaca: Cornell University Press, 1995).

Goodman, Dena, *The Republic of Letters: A Cultural History of the French Enlightenment* (Ithaca: Cornell University Press, 1994).

Gordon, Linda, *Woman's Body, Woman's Right: A Social History of Birth Control in America* (New York: Grossman, 1976).

Gouma-Peterson, Thalia (ed.), *Anna Komnene and Her Times* (New York: Garland, 2000).

Gournay, Marie le Jars de, *Apology for the Woman Writing* (ed.) Richard Hillman and Collette Quesnel (Chicago: University of Chicago Press, 2002).

Grabiner, J, *The Origins of Cauchy's Rigorous Calculus* (Cambridge, Mass.: MIT Press, 1981).

——, *The Calculus as Algebra: J.-L. Lagrange, 1736–1813* (New York: Garland Publishing, Inc., 1990).

Graham-Brown, Sarah, *Images of Women: The Portrayal of Women in Photography of the Middle East, 1860–1950* (New York: Columbia University Press, 1988).

Gray, Charlotte, *Sisters in the Wilderness: The Lives of Susanna Moodie and Catherine Parr Traill* (Viking: Toronto, 1999).

Gray-White, Deborah, *Arn't I a Woman? Female Slaves in the Plantation South* (New York: Norton & Co., 1985).

Green, Mary Ann Everett, *Lives of the Princesses of England, from the Norman Conquest*, 6 vols (London: Henry Colburn, 1849–55).

Greer, Germaine, *The Female Eunuch* (London: Penguin, 1970).

——, *The Obstacle Race: The Fortunes of Women Painters and Their Work* (London: Weidenfeld & Nicolson, 1979).

Griffin, Penny, *St Hugh's: One Hundred Years of Women's Education in Oxford* (London: Macmillan, 1986).

Griffiths, Tom, *Hunters and Collectors: The Antiquarian Imagination in Australia* (Cambridge: Cambridge University Press, 1996).

Grimshaw, Patricia and Lynne, Strahan (eds), *The Half-open Door: Sixteen Modern Australian Women Look at Professional Life and Achievement* (Sydney: Hale & Iremonger, 1982).

Grimshaw, Patricia, Marilyn Lake, Ann McGrath and Marion Quartly, *Creating a Nation* (Ringwood: McPhee Gribble, 1994).

Gristwood, Sarah, *Recording Angels: The Secret World of Women's Diaries* (London: Harrap, 1988).

Grosz, Elizabeth, *Volatile Bodies: Toward a Corporeal Feminism* (Bloomington: Indiana University Press, 1994).

Guidi, Laura, *Relazioni epistolari di Enrichetta Di Lorenzo, in Scritture femminili e storia* (Napoli: Cliopress, 2004).

Gunn, Peter, *Vernon Lee: Violet Paget, 1865–1935* (Oxford: Oxford University Press, 1964).

Haight, Anne Lyon, *Hroswitha of Gandersheim: Her Life, Times and Works* (New York: The Hroswitha Club, 1965).

Hale, Sarah Josepha, *Woman's Record; Or Sketches of All Distinguished Women, from the Beginning until AD 1850* (London: Sampson Low & Son, 1853).

Hall, Catherine, *White, Male and Middle Class: Explorations in Feminism and History* (Cambridge: Polity Press, 1992).

——, *Civilising Subjects: Metropole and Colony in the English Imagination, 1830–1867* (Cambridge: Polity, 2002).

Hall, Catherine, Keith McClelland and Jane Rendall, *Defining the Victorian Nation* (Cambridge: Cambridge University Press, 2000).

Hall, Lesley, *Sex, Gender and Social Change in Britain since 1880* (London: Macmillan Press, 2000).

Hall, Lesley and Roy Porter, *The Facts of Life: The Creation of Sexual Knowledge in Britain, 1650–1950* (London: Yale University Press, 1995).

Hamilton, Elizabeth, *Memoirs of Agrippina* (London: John Walker, 1811).

Haraway, Donna, *Crystals, Fabrics, and Fields: Metaphors of Organicism in Twentieth-Century Developmental Biology* (New Haven: Yale University Press, 1976).

——, *Primate Visions: Gender, Race, and Nature in the World of Modern Science* (New York: Routledge, 1989).

——, *Modest.Witness@ Second.Millennium: FemaleMan Meets OncoMouse: Feminism and Technoscience* (New York: Routledge, 1997).

Harding, Sandra, *Whose Science: Whose Knowledge: Thinking from Women's Lives* (Ithaca: Cornell University Press, 1990).

Hardy, Barbara (ed.), *Critical Essays on George Eliot* (London: Routledge & Kegan Paul, 1970).

Harris, Sharon M, *Women's Early American Historical Narratives* (New York: Penguin, 2003).

Harrison, Jane Ellen, *Alpha and Omega* (London: Sidgwick & Jackson Ltd, 1915).

——, *Themis: A Study of the Social Origins of Greek Religion* [1927] (Cleveland: The World Publishing Company, 1962).

Harrison, Jane Ellen, Reminiscences of Student Life (London: Hogarth Press, 1926).

Harsin, Jill, *Policing Prostitution in 19th Century Paris* (Princeton University Press, 1985).

Hart, Margaret, *Janet Fisher Archibald* (Victoria, BC.: Colonist Printing and Publishing, 1934).

Harth, Erica, *Ideology and Culture in Seventeenth-Century France* (Ithaca: Cornell University Press, 1983).

Hartman, M and Banner, L, *Clio's Consciousness Raised: New Perspectives on the History of Women* (New York: Harper & Row, 1974).

Haselkorn, Anne M and Betty S Travisky (eds), *The Renaissance Englishwoman in Print: Counterbalancing the Canon* (Amherst: University of Massachusetts Press, 1990).

Hassam, Andrew, *Through Australian Eyes: Colonial Perceptions of Imperial Britain* (Carlton: Melbourne University Press, 2000).

Hawkes, Jean (ed.), *The London Journal of Flora Tristan 1842 or The Aristocracy and the Working Class of England* [1842] (London: Virago, 1982).

Hayden, Michael, *So Much to Do, So Little Time: The Writings of Hilda Neatby* (Vancouver: UBC Press, 1983).

Hays, Mary, *Female Biography; Or, Memoirs of Illustrious and Celebrated Women, of All Ages and Countries. (Alphabetically Arranged)* [1803], 3 vols (Philadelphia: Birch and Small, 1807).

——, *Memoirs of Queens, Illustrious and Celebrated* (London: T and J Allman, 1821).

——, *Memoirs of Emma Courtney* [1796], ed. Eleanor Ty (Oxford: Oxford University Press, 1996).

Heilbrun, Carolyn, *Writing a Woman's Life* (New York: Norton, 1988).

Hein, L and Selden, M (eds), *Censoring History: Citizenship and Memory in Japan, Germany and the United States* (Armonk: M E Sharpe, 2000).

Hemlow, Joyce (ed.), *The Journals and Letters of Fanny Burney (Madame d'Arblay)*, vol. VI, *France 1803–1812* (London: Clarendon Press, 1975).

Hepworth Dixon, Ella, *The Story of a Modern Woman* (London: Merlin Press, 1990) with introduction by Kate Flint.

Herman, Sondra, *Eleven Against War* (Stanford: Hoover Institution Press, 1969).

Herold, E, *Die Tat: Rundbrief des Freundeskreises Oberschönenfeld*, 35-(Quotations from the manuscript: Oberschönenfeld, Klosterarchiv, 'Die Chronik der Elisabeth Herold' (237 fol.) (December 1995–).

Herrad of Hohenbourg, *Hortus deliciarum*, ed. R Green, M Evans, C Bischoff and M Curschmann (London: Warbourg Institute, 1979).

Hershatter, Gail, *Dangerous Pleasures: Prostitution and Modernity in Twentieth-Century Shanghai* (Berkeley: University of California Press, 1997).

Hess Beth and Myra Marx Ferree, *Analyzing Gender* (Newbury Park: Sage, 1987).

Hesse, Carla, *The Other Enlightenment: How French Women Became Modern* (Princeton: Princeton University Press, 2001).

Hildonbrand, Suzanne (ed.), *Women's Collections: Libraries, Archives, and Consciousness* (New York: Haworth, 1986).

Hill, Bridget, *The Republican Virago: The Life and Times of Catherine Macaulay, Historian* (Oxford: Clarendon Press, 1992).

Hill, Georgiana, *Women in English Life from Mediaeval to Modern Times* (London: Richard Bentley & Sons, 1896).

Hill, Mary A, *Charlotte Perkins Gilman: The Making of a Radical Feminist, 1860–1896* (Philadelphia: Temple University Press, 1980).

Hobby, Elaine, *Virtue of Necessity: English Women's Writing 1649–1688* (London: Virago, 1989).

Hobson, Barbara Meil, *Uneasy Virtue: The Politics of Prostitution and the American Reform Tradition* (New York: Basic Books, 1987).

Hoecker-Drysdale, Susan, *Harriet Martineau. First Woman Sociologist* (Oxford: Berg, 1992).

Hollingworth, Brian, *Maria Edgeworth's Irish Writing: Language, History, Politics* (London: Macmillan, 1997).

Holmes, Katie, *Spaces in her Day* (Sydney: Allen & Unwin, 1995).

Holt, Emily Sarah, *Memoirs of Royal Ladies*, 2 vols (London: Hurst and Blackett, 1861).

Holton, Sandra Stanley, *Suffrage Days: Stories from the Women's Suffrage Movement* (London: Routledge, 1996).

Hooker, Claire, *Irresistible Forces: Women in Australian Science* (Melbourne: Melbourne University Press, 2004).

Hooks, bell, *Ain't I a Woman? Black Women and Feminism* (Boston: South End Press, 1981).

Hopkins, J Ellice, The Power of Womanhood; or Mothers and Sons: A Book for Parents and those in Locus Parentis (London: Wells & Gardner, 1899) reprinted in Stormbell (April 1900).

Hosoi, W, *Jokô Aishi* [1925] (Tokyo: Iwanami Shoten, 1954).

Hoston, G A, *Marxism and the Crisis of Development in Prewar Japan* (Princeton: Princeton University Press, 1986).

Howitt, Mary (ed.) *Biographical Sketches of the Queens of Great Britain. From the Norman Conquest to the Reign of Victoria. Or, Royal Book of Beauty* (London: Henry G Bohn, 1851).

Hudson, Roger (ed.), *The Grand Quarrel: English Women's Memoirs of the English Civil War 1649–88* (Stroud: Sutton, 1993).

Huff, Cynthia, *British Women's Diaries: A Descriptive Bibliography of Selected Nineteenth-Century Women's Manuscript Diaries* (New York: AMS Press, 1985).

Hull, Isobel, *Sexuality, State and Civil Society in Germany 1700–1815* (Ithaca, New York: Cornell University Press, 1996).

Hunt, Lynn, *Politics, Culture and Class in the French Revolution* (Berkeley: University of California Press, 1986).

——, *The Family Romance of the French Revolution* (Berkeley: University of California Press, 1992).

Hunt, Margaret R, *The Middling Sort: Commerce, Gender, and the Family in England, 1680–1780* (Los Angeles: University of California Press, 1996).

Hunter, J, *Women and the Labour Market in Japan's Industrialising Economy: The Textile Industry before the Pacific War* (London: Routledge Curzon, 2003).

Hurley, Kelly, *The Gothic Body: Sexuality, Materialism, and Degeneration at the fin-de-siecle* (Cambridge: Cambridge University Press, 1996).

Hutchinson, Lucy, *Order and Disorder*, ed. David Norbrook (Oxford: Blackwell, 2001).

——, *Memoirs of the Life of Colonel Hutchinson: With a Fragment of Autobiography*, ed. N H Keeble (London: Dent, 1995).

Hutton, Ronald, *The Triumph of the Moon. A History of Modern Pagan Witchcraft* (Oxford: Oxford University Press, 1999).

Illustrious Women Who Have Distinguished Themselves for Virtue, Piety, and Benevolence (London: James Blackwood, 1852).

Irvine, E Marie, *Certain Worthy Women* (London: New Century Press, 1939).

Ishimoto, S, *Facing Two Ways: The Story of My Life* [1935] (Stanford: Stanford University Press, 1986).

Isichei, Elizabeth, *Victorian Quakers* (London: Oxford University Press, 1970).

Israel, Jonathon, *Radical Enlightenment: Philosophy and the Making of Modernity 1650–1750* (Oxford: Oxford University Press, 2001).

Jackson, Margaret, *The Real Facts of Life: Feminism and the Politics of Sexuality c.1850–1940* (London: Taylor and Francis, 1994).

Jacobs, Harriet, *Incidents in the Life of a Slave Girl, Written by Herself* [1861] ed. Jean Fagan Yellin (Cambridge, Mass.: Harvard University Press, 1987).

Jacobus, M, Evelyn Fox Keller and Sally Shuttleworth (eds), *Body/Politics: Women and the Discourses of Science* (New York: Routledge, 1990).

Jagose, Annamarie, *Inconsequence: Lesbian Representation and the Logic of Sexual Sequence* (Ithaca: Cornell University Press, 2002).

James, Susan E, *Kateryn Parr: The Making of a Queen* (Aldershot: Ashgate, 1999).

Jameson, Anna B M, *Memoirs of Celebrated Female Sovereigns* (New York: H Colburn & R Bentley, 1832).

——, *Characteristics of Women, Moral, Poetical and Historical* (Annapolis: Jeremiah Hughes, 1833).

——, *Visits and Sketches at Home and Abroad* (London: Saunders & Otley, 1835).

——, *The Romance of Biography, or Memoirs of Women Loved and Celebrated by Poets* (London: Saunders and Otley, 1837).

Jansen, Sharon (trans. and ed.), *Anne of France: Lessons for My Daughter* (Woodbridge, Suffolk: Boydell and Brewer, 2004).

Jayawardena, K, *Feminism and Nationalism in the Third World* (London: Zed Books, 1986).

Jean, Joan de, *Tender Geographies: Women and the Origins of the Novel in France* (New York: Columbia University Press, 1991).

Jeffrey, Julie Roy, *The Great Silent Army of Abolitionism: Ordinary Women in the Anti-slavery Movement* (Chapel Hill: University of North Carolina Press, 1998).

Jeffreys, Lesley Ann, *Sex and Borders, Gender, National Identity and Prostitution Policy in Thailand* (Hawaii: University of Hawaii Press, 2002).

Jeffreys, Sheila, *The Spinster and Her Enemies: Feminism and Sexuality 1880–1930* (London: Pandora, 1986).

——, *The Idea of Prostitution* (Melbourne: Spinafex, 1997).

Johnson, Joan, *Excellent Cassandra: The Life and Times of the Duchess of Chandos* (Gloucester: Alan Sutton, 1981).

Johnson, Judith, *Anna Jameson: Victorian, Feminist, Woman of Letters* (Aldershot: Scolar, 1997).

Jones, Ann H, *Ideas and Innovations: Best Sellers of Jane Austen's Age* (New York: AMS Press, 1986).

Jones, H G, *Historical Consciousness in the Early Republic: The Origins of State Historical Societies, Museums and Collections, 1791– 1861* (Chapel Hill: North Carolinian Society, 1995).

Jones, Jacqueline, *Labor of Love, Labor of Sorrow: Black Women, Work and the*

Family, from Slavery to the Present (New York: Basic Books, 1985).

Jordan, Constance, *Renaissance Feminism: Literary Texts and Political Models* (Ithaca: Cornell University Press, 1990).

Jordanova, L, *Sexual Visions: Images of Gender in Science and Medicine between the Eighteenth and Twentieth Centuries* (Madison: University of Wisconsin Press, 1989).

Jump, Harriet Devine (ed.), *Women's Writing of the Victorian Period 1837–1901: An Anthology* (New York: St Martin's Press, 1999).

Kabbani, Rana, *Imperial Fictions: Europe's Myths of Orient* [1986] (London: HarperCollins, 1994).

Kammen, Michael, *Mystic Chords of Memory: The Transformation of Tradition in American Culture* (New York: Alfred A. Knopf, 1991).

Karcher, Carolyn L, *The First Woman of the Republic: A Cultural Biography of Lydia Maria Child* (Durham: Duke University Press, 1994).

Kavanagh, Julia, *Woman in France during the Eighteenth Century* (Philadelphia: Lea and Blanchard, 1850).

Keane, Angela, *Women Writers and the English Nation in the 1790s* (Cambridge: Cambridge University Press, 2000).

Keeble, N H (ed.), *The Cambridge Companion to Writing of the English Revolution* (Cambridge: Cambridge University Press, 2001).

Kelleher, Margaret, *Feminisation of the Famine, Expression of the Inexpressible? Representations of Women in Famine Narratives* (Cork: Cork University Press, 1997).

Kelleher, Margaret and James H Murphy (eds), *Gender Perspectives in Nineteenth-Century Ireland: Public and Private Spheres* (Dublin: Irish Academic Press, 1997).

Keller, Evelyn, *A Feeling for the Organism: The Life and Work of Barbara McClintock* (San Francisco: W H Freeman, 1983).

——, *Secrets of Life, Secrets of Death: Essays on Language, Gender and Science* (New York: Routledge, 1992).

——, *Reflections on Gender and Science* (New Haven: Yale University Press, 1995).

——, *Making Sense of Life: Explaining Biological Development with Models, Metaphors, and Machines* (Boston: Harvard University Press, 2002).

Kelly, C E, *In the New England Fashion: Reshaping Women's Lives in the Nineteenth Century* (Ithaca and London: Cornell University Press, 1999).

Kelly, Gary, *Women, Writing and Revolution 1790–1827* (Oxford: Clarendon, 1993).

—— (ed.) *Bluestocking Feminism: Writings of the Bluestocking Circle 1738–1785*, 6 vols (London: Brookfield, 1999).

Kelly, Joan, *Women History and Theory* (Chicago: University of Chicago Press, 1984).

Kelso, Ruth, *Doctrine for the Lady of the Renaissance* (Urbana: University of Illinois Press, 1956).

Kennedy, D, *Helen Maria Williams and the Age of Revolution* (Lewisburg: Bucknell University Press, 2002).

Kent-Kingsley, Susan, *Sex and Suffrage in Britain 1860–1941* (Princeton: Princeton University Press, 1987).

Kenyon, John, *The History Men* (London: George Weidenfeld & Nicolson, 1983).

Kerber, Linda, *Women of the Republic: Intellect and Ideology in Revolutionary America* (Chapel Hill: University of North Carolina Press, 1981).

——, *Toward an Intellectual History of Women Essays* (Chapel Hill: University of North Carolina Press, 1997).

Kessler, Carol Farley, *Charlotte Perkins Gilman: Her Progress Toward Utopia with Selected Writings* (Syracuse: Syracuse University Press, 1995).

Kim, I, *Tennô no Guntai to Chôsenjin Ianfu* (Tokyo: San'ichi Shobô, 1976).

King, Helen, *Hippocrates' Woman: Reading the Female Body in Ancient Greece* (New York: Routledge, 1998).

King, Margaret, *Her Immaculate Hand: Selected Works by and about the Women Humanists of*

Quattrocento Italy (Binghampton: Pegasus Books, 1992).
Kingston, Beverley, *My Wife, My Daughter and Poor Mary Ann: Women and Work in Australia* (Melbourne: Thomas Nelson, 1975).
Kitchen, John, *Saints Lives and the Rhetoric of Gender* (New York: Oxford University Press, 1998).
Klapische-Zuber, Christiane, *Women, Family and Ritual in Renaissance Itali* (Chicago: University of Chicago Press, 1985).
Klassen, John M (trans.), *The Letters of the Rożmberk Sisters: Noblewomen in Fifteenth-Century Bohemia* (Woodbridge, Suffolk: Boydell and Brewer, Ltd, 2001).
Kovacevic, Ivanka, *Fact into Fiction. English Literature and the Industrial Scene, 1750–1850* (Leicester: Leicester University Press, 1975).
Kraditor, Aileen, *The Ideas of the Woman Suffrage Movement 1890–1920* (Garden City: Anchor Books, 1965).
Krige, Uys (ed.), *Olive Schreiner: A Selection. Cape Town* (Oxford: Oxford University Press, 1968).
Kuhn, D, *From Midwives to Medicine: The Birth of American Gynaecology* (London: Rutgers University Press, 1998).
Lalande, Roxane Decker, *A Labor of Love: Critical Reflections on the Writings of Marie-Catherine Desjardins* (London: Associated University Presses, 2000).
Landes, Joan B, *Women and the Public Sphere in the Age of the French Revolution* (Ithaca: Cornell University Press, 1988).
——, *Visualizing the Nation: Gender, Representation, and Revolution in Eighteenth-Century France* (Ithaca: Cornell University Press, 2001).
Lane, Ann J, *To Herland and Beyond: The Life and Work of Charlotte Perkins Gilman* (New York: Pantheon, 1990).
Lawrance, Hannah, *London in the Olden Time; Or, Tales Intended to Illustrate the Manners and Superstitions of Its Inhabitants, from the Twelfth to the Sixteenth Century* (London: Longman, Hurst, Rees, Orme, Brown and Green, 1825).
——, *Historical Memoirs of the Queens of England*, 2 vols (London: Edward Moxon, 1838–40).
Leach, W, *True Love and Perfect Union: The Feminist Reform of Sex and Society* (London: Routledge, 1980).
Ledger, Sally, *The New Woman: Fiction and Feminism at the Fin de Siècle* (Manchester: Manchester University Press, 1997).
Lee, Sophia, *The Recess; Or, A Tale of Other Times* [1783–85], ed. April Alliston (Kentucky: The University Press of Kentucky, 2000).
Lee, Vernon, *Euphorion: Studies of the Antique and the Mediaeval in the Renaissance* (London: T Fisher Unwin, 1884).
Lefkowitz, Mary, *Not Out of Africa. How Afrocentrism Became an Excuse to Teach Myth as History* (New York: Basic Books, 1996).
Le Goff, Jacques, *Histoire et mémoire* (Paris: Gallimard, 1988).
Lejeune, Philippe, *Le Pacte autobiographique* (Paris: Seuil, 1975).
Lerner, Gerda, *The Grimke Sisters from South Carolina: Rebels Against Slavery* (Boston: Houghton Mifflin Co., 1967).
——, *The Majority Finds Its Past: Placing Women in History* (New York: Oxford University Press, 1980).
——, *The Creation of Feminist Consciousness from the Middle Ages to 1870* (New York: Oxford University Press, 1993).
Levin, Carole and Jeanie Watson (eds), *Ambiguous Realities: Women in the Middle Ages and Renaissance* (Detroit: Wayne State University Press, 1987).
Levine, Phillippa, *The Amateur and the Professional: Antiquarians, Historians and Archaeologists in Victorian England, 1838–1886* (Cambridge: Cambridge University Press, 1986).
——, *Prostitution, Race & Politics: Policing Venereal Disease in the British Empire* (New York: Routledge, 2003).
Lewis, Gertrud Jaron, *By Women, For Women, About Women: The Sister Books of*

Fourteenth-Century Germany (Michigan and Toronto: Pontifical Institute of Medieval Studies, 1996).

Lewis, Thomas Taylor, *Letters of Lady Brilliana Harley of Brampton* (London: Camden Society, 1968).

Liddington, Jill, *The Life and Times of a Respectable Rebel, Selina Cooper 1864–1946* (London: Virago, 1984).

——, *The Long Road to Greenham* (London: Virago Press, 1989).

Lindsey, Karen, *Divorced, Beheaded, Survived: A Feminist Reinterpretation of the Wives of Henry VIII* (Reading, Mass.: Addison-Wesley Publishing Company, 1995).

Locher-Scholten, Elspeth, *Women and the Colonial State. Essays on Gender and Modernity in the Netherlands Indies, 1900–1942* (Amsterdam: Amsterdam University Press, 2000).

Loeb, Lori Anne, *Consuming Angels: Advertising and Victorian Women* (New York: Oxford University Press, 1994).

Loftis, John (ed.), *Memoirs of Anne, Lady Halkett and Ann, Lady Fanshawe* (Oxford: Clarendon, 1979).

Lofts, Norah, *Queens of England* (Garden City, New York: Doubleday & Company, Inc., 1977).

Loftus, R P, *Telling Lives: Women's Self-Writing in Modern Japan* (Honolulu: University of Hawaii, 2004).

London Feminist History Group, *The Sexual Dynamics of History* (London: Women's Press, 1983).

Longino, H, *Science as Social Knowledge: Values and Objectivity in Scientific Enquiry* (Princeton: Princeton University Press, 1990).

Loomba, A, *Colonialism/Postcolonialism* (New York: Routledge, 1998).

Looser, Devoney, *British Women Writers and the Writing of History, 1670–1820* (Baltimore: Johns Hopkins University Press, 2000).

Lowe, K J P, *Nuns' Chronicles and Convent Culture in Renaissance and Counter-Reformation Italy* (Cambridge: Cambridge University Press, 2003).

Lowe, Lisa, *Critical Terrains: French and British Orientalisms* (Ithaca: Cornell University Press, 1991).

Lowenthal, David, *The Past is a Foreign Country* (Cambridge: Cambridge University Press, 1983).

Lukács, Georg, *The Historical Novel* (1937) (Lincoln and London: University of Nebraska Press, 1983).

Lugrin, N de Bertrand, *The Pioneer Women of Vancouver Island 1843–1866*, ed. John Hosie (Vancouver Island: The Women's Canadian Club of Victoria, 1928).

Macaulay, Catharine Sawbridge, *The History of England from the Accession of James I to the Elevation of the House of Hanover*, vols 1–2 (London: Edward and Charles Dilly, 1769).

——, *The History of England from the Accession of James I to the Revolution*, vol. VIII (London: A. Hamilton, 1783).

——, *Letters on Education* (1791), ed. Gina Luria (New York: Garland Publishing, 1974).

McCarthy, William and Elizabeth Kraft (eds), *The Poems of Anna Letitia Barbauld* (Athens: University of Georgia Press, 1994).

McClintock, *Imperial Leather: Race, Gender and Sexuality in the Colonial Contest* (New York and London: Routledge, 1995).

McClung, Nellie, *Clearing in the West* (Toronto: Thomas Allen Ltd, 1935).

——, *The Stream Runs Fast: My Own Story* (Toronto: Thomas Allen and Son, 1965).

——, *In Times Like These* [1915] (Toronto: University of Toronto Press, 1972).

McCracken, Ellen, *Decoding Women's Magazines: From Madomoiselle to Ms* (London: Macmillan, 1993).

McDermid, J and A Hillyar (eds), *Midwives of the Revolution: Female Bolsheviks and*

Women Workers in 1917 (Athens: Ohio University Press, 1999).

Macintyre, S, *The History Wars* (Melbourne: Melbourne University Press, 2004).

Mackie, Vera, *Creating Socialist Women in Japan: Gender, Labour and Activism, 1900–1937* (Cambridge: Cambridge University Press, 1997).

McKillop, A B, *The Spinster and the Prophet: Florence Deeks, H.G. Wells, and the Mystery of the Purloined Past* (Toronto: Macfarlane, Walter & Ross, 2000).

Mackinnon, Alison, *Love and Freedom: Professional Women and the Reshaping of Personal Life* (Cambridge: Cambridge University Press, 1997).

Maclean, Ian, *Woman Triumphant (1610–1652)* (Oxford: Oxford University Press, 1977).

McLeod, Glenda (ed.), *The Reception of Christine de Pizan from the Fifteenth through the Nineteenth Centuries: Visitors to the City* (Lewiston Queenston Lampeter: Edward Mellen Press, 1991).

——, *Virtue and Venom: Catalogs of Women from Antiquity to the Renaissance* (Ann Arbor: University of Michigan Press, 1991).

McNamara JoAnn, and John E Halborg with 11E Gordon Whatley, *Sainted Women of the Dark Ages* (Durham: University of North Carolina Press, 1992).

Maddox, B, *Rosalind Franklin: The Dark Lady of DNA* (New York: HarperCollins, 2002).

Mahood, Linda, *The Magdalenes: Prostitution in the Nineteenth Century* (London: Routledge, 1990).

Maitzen, Rohan Amanda, *Gender, Genre, and Victorian Historical Writing* (New York: Garland, 1998).

Malcovati, Henrica, *Madame Dacier: Una Gentildonna filologa del gran secolo* (Firenze: Sansoni, 1953).

Manley, Delariviere, *The New Atalantis*, ed. Rosalind Ballaster (New York: New York University Press, 1992).

——, *The Adventures of Rivella*, ed. Katherine Zelinsky (Peterborough: Broadview, 1999).

Manning, P, *Navigating World History: Historians Create a Global Past* (New York: Palgrave Macmillan, 2003).

Marinella, Lucrezia, *The Nobility and Excellency of Women and the Defects and Vices of Men* [1600], ed. and trans. Anne Dunhill (Chicago: University of Chicago Press, 1999).

Marrone, Claire, *Female Journeys: Autobiographical Expressions by French and Italian Women* (London: Greenwood, 2000).

Martin, Catherine, *The Incredible Journey* [1923] (London: Pandora, 1987).

Martin, Jim, *A Bit of a Blue: The Life and Work of Frances Fuller Victor* (Salem, Oregon: Deep Well Publishing Co., 1992).

Matus, Jill, *Unstable Bodies: Victorian Representations of Sexuality and Maternity* (Manchester: Manchester University Press, 1995).

Mavor, Elizabeth, *The Ladies of Llangollen* (Harmondsworth: Penguin, 1973).

Mayer, Robert, *History and the Early English Novel: Matters of Fact from Bacon to Defoe* (Cambridge: Cambridge University Press, 1997).

Meale, Carol M (ed.), *Women and Literature in Britain 1150–1500* (Cambridge: Cambridge University Press, 1996).

Melman, Billie, *Women's Orients: English Women and the Middle East, 1718–1918. Sexuality, Religion and World* [1992] (Ann Arbor: University of Michigan Press, 1995).

Merchant, C, *The Death of Nature: Women, Ecology and the Scientific Revolution* (San Francisco: Harper & Row, 1982).

Meyerowitz, Joanne, *Women Adrift: Independent Wage Earners in Chicago, 1880–1930* (Chicago: University of Chicago Press, 1988).

Midgley, Clare, *Women Against Slavery: The British Campaigns, 1780–1870* (London: Routledge, 1995).

Midgley, Clare, *Gender & Imperialism* (Manchester: Manchester University Press, 1998).

Miles, Margaret Ruth, *Carnal Knowing: Female Nakedness and Religious Meaning in the Christian West* (New York: Vintage, 1991).

Millett, Kate, *Sexual Politics* (London: Abacus, 1971).

——, *Going to Iran* (New York: Coward, McCann & Geoghegan, 1982).

Mills, Sara, *Discourses of Difference: An Analysis of Women's Travel Writing and Colonialism* (London: Routledge, 1991).

Mitchell, Juliet, *Woman's Estate* (Harmondsworth: Penguin, 1971).

Mitchell, Rosemary Ann, *Picturing the Past: English History in Text and Image, 1830–1870* (Oxford: Oxford University Press, 2000).

Moi, Toril, *Simone de Beauvoir: The Making of an Intellectual Woman* (Oxford: Blackwell, 1994).

Montagu, Lady Mary Wortley, *The Complete Letters* [1838] (Oxford: Clarendon, 1965).

——, *Letters from the Levant during the Embassy to Constantinople, 1716–18* [1838] (New York: The Arno Press, 1971).

Montgomery, L, *Courageous Women* (Toronto: McLelland and Stewart, 1934).

Morantz-Sanchez, Regina, *Conduct Unbecoming a Woman: Medicine on Trial in Turn-of-the-Century Brooklyn* (Oxford: Oxford University Press, 1999).

Morgan, Sue, *A Passion for Purity: Ellice Hopkins and the Politics of Gender in the Late-Victorian Church* (Bristol: CCSRG Monograph, 1999).

Morgan, Susan, *Place Matters: Gendered Geography in Victorian Women's Travel Books about Southeast Asia* (New Brunswick: Rutgers University Press, 1996).

Morrisey, Marietta, *Slave Women in the New World* (Kansas: University Press of Kansas, 1990).

Morton, Patricia, *Discovering the Women in Slavery* (Athens: University of Georgia Press, 1996).

Moscucci, Ornella, *The Science of Woman: Gynaecology and Gender in England, 1800–1929* (Cambridge: Cambridge University Press, 1990).

Munich, Adrienne, *Queen Victoria's Secrets* (New York: Columbia University Press, 1996).

Murata, S, *Fukuda Hideko* (Tokyo: Iwanami Shoten, 1959).

Murray, Margaret, *My First Hundred Years* (London: William Kimber, 1963).

Myers, Sylvia Harcstock, *The Bluestocking Circle: Women, Friendship and the Life of the Mind in Eighteenth Century England* (Oxford: Clarendon, 1990).

Neal, K, *From Discrete to Continuous: The Broadening of Number Concepts in Early Modern England* (Boston: Kluwer Academic Publishers, 2002).

Needler, G H (ed.), *Letters of Anna Jameson to Ottilie von Goethe* (London: Oxford University Press, 1939).

Nelson, Dana, *National Manhood: Capitalist Citizenship and the Imagined Fraternity of Men* (Durham: Duke University Press, 1998).

Nestor, Pauline, *George Eliot: Critical Issues* (Basingstoke: Palgrave, 2002).

Newman, Barbara, *Sister of Wisdom: St. Hildegard's Theology of the Feminine* (Berkeley and Los Angeles: University of California Press, 1987).

Nogarola, Isotta, *Complete Writings*, ed. and trans. Margaret L King and Diane Robin (Chicago: University of Chicago Press, 2004).

Nord, Deborah, *The Apprenticeship of Beatrice Webb* (Amherst: University of Massachusetts Press, 1985).

Norton, Mary Beth, *Liberty's Daughters: The Revolutionary Experience of American Women 1750–1800* (Boston: Little Brown & Company, 1980).

Novick, Peter, *That Noble Dream: The 'Objectivity Question' and the American Historical Profession* (Cambridge: Cambridge University Press, 1988).

Nyberg, T (ed.), *Dokumente und Untersuchungen zur inneren Geschichte der drei Birgittenklöster Bayerns 1420–1570* (Munich: C H Beck'sche Verlagsbuchhandlung, 1972).

Oakley, Ann, *The Captured Womb: A History of Medical Care of Pregnant Women* (Oxford: Basil Blackwell, 1984).

O Bróin, Léon, *Protestant Nationalists in Revolutionary Ireland: The Stopford Connection* (Dublin: Gill & Macmillan, 1985).

Oda, M, *Hiroshima* (Tokyo: Kôdansha, 1980).

Offen, Karen, *European Feminisms 1700–1950* (Stanford: Stanford University Press, 2000).

Offen, Karen, Ruth Roach Pearson and Jane Rendall (eds), *Writing Women's History: International Perspectives* (Bloomington: Indiana University Press, 1991).

Okker, Patricia, *Our Sister Editors: Sarah J Hale and the Tradition of Nineteenth-Century American Women Editors* (Athens and London: University of Georgia Press, 1995).

Ong, Walter, *Orality and Literacy: The Technologizing of the Word* (London and New York: Methuen, 1982).

Otten, Charlotte F (ed.), *English Women's Voices, 1540–1700* (Miami: Florida International University Press, 1992).

Oudshoorn, N, *Beyond the Natural Body: An Archaeology of Sex Hormones* (London: Routledge, 1994).

Outram, Dorinda, *The Body and the French Revolution: Sex, Class and Political Culture* (New Haven: Yale University Press, 1989).

Owenson, Sydney, *The Wild Irish Girl* [1806] (London: Pickering & Chatto, 2000).

——, *Patriotic Sketches of Ireland, Written in Connaught* (London: R Phillips, 1807).

——, *Woman and Her Master* (London: Henry Colburn, 1840).

Ozouf, Mona, *Festivals and the French Revolution* [1976] (Cambridge: Harvard University Press, 1988).

Palmer, Helen G and J Macleod, *The First Hundred Years* (Melbourne: Longman, 1954).

Palmer, Vance, *National Portraits* (Melbourne: Melbourne University Press, 1940).

Pardoe, Julia, *The City of the Sultan, and Domestic Manners of the Turks in 1836* (London: Henry Colburn, 1837).

Parker, R and G Pollock, *Old Mistresses: Women, Art and Ideology* (London: Routledge & Kegan Paul, 1981).

Parkes, Bessie Raynor, '*The Market for Educated Female Labour*' [1858], *Essays on Woman's Work* (London: A Strahan, 1865).

Pateman, Carole, The Sexual Contract (Cambridge: Polity, 1988).

Patterson, Annabel, *Early Modern Liberalism* (Cambridge: Cambridge University Press, 1997).

Pedersen, Diana, *Changing Women, Changing History: A Bibliography of the History of Women in Canada* (Ottawa: Carleton University Press, 1996).

Pepper, Mary Sifton, *Maids and Matrons of New France* (Boston: Little, Brown & Company, 1901).

Perham, Margery, *The Colonical Reckoning: The Reith Lectures* (London: Collins, 1961).

Perham, Margery, *African Apprenticeship: An Autobiographical Journey to Southern Africa* (New York: Africana Publishing, 1974).

Perham, Margery, *Pacific Prelude: A Journey to Samoa and Australasia [1929]* (London: Peter Owen, 1988).

Perry, Adele, *On the Edge of Empire Gender, Race and the Making of British Columbia 1849–1871* (Toronto: University of Toronto Press, 2001).

Personal Narratives Group (eds), *Interpreting Women's Lives: Feminist Theory and Personal Narratives* (Bloomington: Indiana University Press, 1989).

Peterson, Levi S, *Juanita Brooks: Mormon Woman Historian* (Salt Lake City: University of Utah Press, 1988).

Petroff, Elizabeth Alvilda, *Medieval Women's Visionary Literature* (New York and Oxford: Oxford University Press, 1986).

Pfanner, Josef (ed.), *Die Denkwürdigkeiten der Caritas Pirckheimer (aus den Jahren 1524–1528)* (Landshut: Solanus-Druck, 1962).

Phillips, Mark Salber, *Society and Sentiment: Genres of Historical Writing in Britain, 1740–1820* (Princeton: Princeton University Press, 2000).

Pichanick, Valerie Kossew, *Harriet Martineau, the Woman and Her Work, 1802–76* (Ann Arbor: University of Michigan Press, 1980).

Pinchbeck, Ivy, *Women Workers and the Industrial Revolution 1750–1850* (London: Virago, 1981).

Pierson, Ruth Roach, *Women and Peace* (London: Croom Helm, c.1987).

Pierson, Ruth Roach and N Chaudhuri (eds), *Nation, Empire, Colony: Historicizing Gender and Race* (Bloomington: Indiana University Press, 1998).

Pilardi, Jo-Ann, *Simone de Beauvoir Writing the Self: Philosophy Becomes Autobiography* (Westport, Connecticut, Praeger, 1999).

Pizan, Christine de, *The Book of the City of Ladies*, ed. Earl Jeffrey Richards (London: Pan, 1982).

——, *The Treasure of the City of Ladies, or The Book of the Three Virtues*, trans. Sarah Lawson (Harmondsworth: Penguin, 1985).

Plant, I M, *Women Writers of Ancient Greece and Rome: An Anthology* (London: Norman, 2004).

Plowden, Alison, *The Young Elizabeth: The First Twenty-Five Years of Elizabeth I* [1971] (Phoenix Mill: Sutton Publishing Ltd, 1999).

Pollock, Griselda, *Differencing the Canon: Feminist Desires and the Writing of Art's Histories* (London: Routledge, 1999).

Pollock, L A, *Forgotten Children: Parent–Child Relations from 1500 to 1900* (Cambridge: Cambridge University Press, 1983).

Poovey, M, *Uneven Developments: The Ideological Work of Gender in Mid-Victorian England* (Chicago: University of Chicago Press, 1988).

Pope-Hennessy, Una, *Agnes Strickland: Biographer of the Queens of England, 1796–1874* (London: Chatto & Windus, 1940).

Porter, Jane, *Thaddeus of Warsaw* [1803] (Montana: Kessinger Publishing, 2004).

——, *The Scottish Chiefs* [1810] (Montana: Kessinger Publishing, 2004).

Potter, Lois, *Secret Rites and Secret Writings: Royalist Literature, 1641–1660* (Cambridge: Cambridge University Press, 1989).

Power, Eileen, *Medieval People* (London: Folio Society, 1999).

Pratt, Mary Louise, *Imperial Eyes: Travel writing and Transculturation* (London: Routledge, 1992).

Purvis, June, *Women's History in Britain 1850–1945* (Bristol: UCL Press, 1995).

Pycior, H, *Symbols, Impossible Numbers, and Geometric Entanglements: British Algebra through the Commentaries on Newton's Universal Arithmetick* (Cambridge: Cambridge University Press, 1997).

Rabil, Albert Jr, *Laura Cereta: Quattrocento Humanist* (New York: Centre for Medieval and Renaissance Studies, 1981).

Rabinowitz, Nancy Sorkin and Amy Richlin (eds), *Feminist Theory and the Classics* (London and New York: Routledge, 1993).

Radice, Betty (trans.), *The Letters of Abelard and Heloise* (London: Penguin, 1974).

Radway, Janice, *A Feeling for Books: The Book-of-the-Month Club, Literary Taste, and Middle-Class Desire* (Chapel Hill: University of North Carolina Press, 1997).

Rafroidi, Patric, *Irish Literature in English: The Romantic Period* (Atlantic Highlands: Humanity Press, 1980).

Reeve, Clara, *The Progress of Romance through Times, Countries and Manners* [1785] (New York: Garland Publishing, Inc., 1970).

——, *The Old English Baron: A Gothic Story* [1778], ed. James Trainer (Oxford: Oxford University Press, 1977).

Rendall, Jane, *The Origins of the Scottish Enlightenment* (London: Macmillan, 1978).

——, *The Origins of Modern Feminism: Women in Britain, France and the United States 1780–1860* (London: Macmillan, 1985).

Richlin, Amy (ed.), *Pornography and Representation in Greece and Rome* (New York: Oxford University Press, 1992).

Rigg, Julie (ed.), *In Her Own Right: Women of Australia* (Melbourne: Thomas Nelson, 1969).

Robin, Diane (ed.), *Collected Letters of a Renaissance Feminist* [Laura Cereta] (Chicago: University of Chicago Press, 1997a).

Robinson, Annabel, *The Life and Work of Jane Ellen Harrison* (Oxford: Oxford University Press, 2002).

Rocheleau, Corinne, *Françaises D'amérique Esquisse Historique. Quelque Traits Vécus De La Vie Des Principales Héroïnes De La Nouvelle-France* (Montreal: Librairie Beauchemin, 1924).

Roper, Lyndall, *Oedipus and the Devil: Witchcraft, Sexuality and Religion in Early Modern Europe* (London: Routledge, 1994).

Rose, Jonathon, *The Intellectual Life of the British Working Classes* (New Haven: Yale University Press, 2001).

Rosen, Ruth, *The Lost Sisterhood: Prostitution in America* (Baltimore: Johns Hopkins University Press, 1982).

Rosenthal, Joel T (ed.), *Medieval Women and the Sources of Medieval History* (Athens: University of Georgia Press, 1990).

Ross, Ellen, *Love and Toil: Motherhood in Outcast London 1870–1918* (New York: Oxford University Press, 1994).

Ross, Fiona, *Bearing Witness: Women and the Truth and Reconciliation Commission in South Africa* (London: Pluto Press, 2002).

Rowbotham, Sheila, *Women, Resistance and Revolution* (Harmondsworth: Penguin, 1972).

Rowland, Beryl (ed. and trans.), *Medieval Woman's Guide to Health. The First English Gynaecological Handbook: Middle English Text* (Kent, OH: Kent State University Press, 1981).

Rubin, Joan Shelley, *The Making of Middle-Brow Culture* (Chapel Hill: University of North Carolina Press, 1992).

Rudkin, Ethel H, *Lincolnshire Folklore* (Wakefield: E P Publishing, 1973).

Rule, John, *The Labouring Classes in Early Industrial England, 1750–1850* (London: Longman, 1986).

Rumbold, Valerie, 'The Jacobite Vision of Mary Caesar', in Isobel Grundy and Susan Wiseman (eds) *Women, Writing, History 1640–1740* (London: Batsford, 1992) pp. 178–199.

Rupp, Leila J and Verta Taylor, *Survival in the Doldrums: The American Women's Rights Movement 1945–1960* (Oxford University Press, New York: 1987).

Said, Edward W, *Orientalism* (New York: Vintage Books, 1979).

Salmon, Lucy Maynard, *History and the Texture of Modern Life*, Nicholas Adams and Bonnie G Smith (eds) (Philadelphia: University of Pennsylvania Press, 2001).

Sama, Catherine M, *Selected Writings of an Eighteenth Century Venetian Woman of Letters* [Elisabetta Caminer Turra] (Chicago: University of Chicago Press, 2003).

Sandford, Mrs John [Elizabeth] *Lives of English Female Worthies* (London: Longman, 1833).

Sarkar, Tanika, *Hindu Wife, Hindu Nation: Community, Religion and Cultural Nationalism* (Bloomington: Indiana University Press, 2001).

Savage, Candace, *Our Nell: A Scrapbook Biography of Nellie L. McClung* (Saskatoon: Western Producer Prairie Books, 1979).

Saxton, Kirsten P and Rebecca P Bocchicchio (eds), *The Passionate Fictions of Eliza Haywood* (Lexington: The University Press of Kentucky, 2000).

Sayre, A, *Rosalind Franklin and DNA: A Vivid View of What It is Like to be a Gifted Woman in an Especially Male Profession* (New York: Norton, 1975).

Schiebinger, Londa, *The Mind Has No Sex? Women in the Origins of Modern Science* (Harvard: Harvard University Press, 1989).

——, *Natures Body: Gender in the Making of Modern Science* (Boston: Beacon Press, 1993).
Schmitt, C, *Alien Nation: Nineteenth-Century Gothic Fictions and English Nationality* (Philadelphia: University of Pennsylvania Press, 1997).
Schreiner, Olive, *An English-South African's View of the Situation: Words in Season* (London: Hodder & Stoughton, 1899).
——, *Woman and Labor* (New York: Frederick A Stokes Co., 1911).
Schurman, Anna Maria van, *Whether a Christian Woman Should be Educated and Other Writings*, ed. Joyce L Irwin (Chicago: University of Chicago Press, 1998).
Scott, Ann Firor, *The Southern Lady: From Pedestal to Politics, 1830–1930* (Chicago: University of Chicago Press, 1970).
—— (ed.), *Unheard Voices: The First Historians of Southern Women* (Charlottesville: University Press of Virginia, 1993).
Scott, Joan Wallach, *Gender and the Politics of History* (New York: Columbia University Press, 1988).
——, *Only Paradoxes to Offer: French Feminists and the Rights of Man* (Cambridge, Mass.: Harvard University Press, 1996).
Scudéry, Madeleine de, *The Story of Sapho*, ed. Karen Newman (Chicago: University of Chicago Press, 2003).
Seacole, Mary, *Wonderful Adventures of Mrs. Seacole in Many Lands* [1857] (New York: Oxford University Press, 1988).
Seccombe, Wally, *Weathering the Storm. Working Class Families from the Industrial Revolution to the Fertility Decline* (London: Verso, 1993).
Sedgwick, Eve Kosofsky, *Epistemology of the Closet* (Berkeley: University of California Press, 1990).
Select Female Biography; Comprising Memoirs of Eminent British Ladies. Derived from Original and Other Authentic Sources (London: Harvey and Denton, 1829).
Senda, K, *Jûgun Ianfu* (Tokyo: Futabasha, 1973).
Seymour-Jones, Carole, *Beatrice Webb: Woman of Conflict* (London: Allison & Busby, 1992).
Shah, A B (ed.), *The Letters and Correspondence of Pandita Ramabai* (Bombay: Maharashtra State Board for Literature and Culture, 1977).
Shapin, Steven, A. *Social History of Truth, Civility and Science in Seventeenth-Century England* (Chicago: University of Chicago Press, 1995).
Shaughnessy Bowers, Toni, *Sex, Lies, and Invisibility: Amatory Fiction from the Restoration to Mid-Century* (New York: Columbia University Press, 1994).
Sheilds, Carol, *Susanna Moodie: Voice and Vision* (Ottawa: Borealis Press, 1977).
Shelley, Mary, '*The Last Man*', in Jane Blumberg and Nora Crook (eds), *The Novels and Selected Works of Mary Shelley*, vol. 4 [1826] (London: William Pickering, 1996).
Sheridan, Susan, *Who was that Woman? The Australian Women's Weekly in the Postwar Years* (Sydney: UNSW Press, 2002).
Sherman, C R with Holcomb, A M (eds), *Women as Interpreters of the Visual Arts, 1820–1979* (Westport, Connecticut and London: Greenwood, 1981).
Shoemaker, N (ed.), *Negotiators of Change: Historical Perspectives on Native American Women* (New York: Routledge, 1995).
Showalter, Elaine (ed.), *These Modern Women: Autobiographical Essays from the Twenties* (New York: The Feminist Press, 1978).
——, *The Female Malady: Women, Madness and English Culture, 1830–1980* (New York: Pantheon, 1985).
Shuckburgh, E (ed. and trans.), *The Memoirs of Madame Roland* (London: Barrie & Jenkins, 1989).
Shuttleworth, Sally, *George Eliot and Nineteenth-Century Science: The Make-Believe of a Beginning* (Cambridge: Cambridge University Press, 1984).
Simmons, C and Perlina, N, *Writing the Siege of Leningrad. Women's Diaries, Memoirs,*

and Documentary Prose (Pittsburgh: University of Pittsburgh Press, 2002).

Simpson, Helen S, *The Women of New Zealand* [1940] (Auckland: Paul's Book Arcade, 1962).

Sinha, Mrinalini, *Colonial Masculinity. The 'Manly Englishman' and the 'Effeminate Bengali' in the Late Nineteenth Century* (Manchester: Manchester University Press, 1995).

Skelton, Isabel, *The Backwoodswoman: A Chronicle of Pioneer Home Life in Upper Canada* (Toronto: Ryerson, 1924).

Skemp, Sheila L (ed.), *Sex, Race and the Role of Women in the South: Essays* (Jackson: University Press of Mississippi, 1983).

Sketches of the Lives of Distinguished Females, Written for Girls, With a View to Their Mental and Moral Improvement. By an American Lady (London: O. Rich, 1834).

Smith, A, *Nationalism and Modernism* (London: Routledge, 1998).

Smith, Bonnie G, *The Gender of History: Men, Women, and Historical Practice* (Cambridge, Mass.: Harvard University Press, 1998).

Smith, Charlotte, *The Old Manor House* [1793], ed. Anne Henry Ehrenpreis (Oxford: Oxford University Press, 1969).

——, *Desmond; a novel* [1792], ed. Gina Luria (New York: Garland Publishing, Inc., 1974).

Smith, Hilda L, *Women Writers and the Early Modern British Political Tradition* (Cambridge: Cambridge University Press, 1998).

——, *All Men and Both Sexes: Gender, Politics and the False Universal in England 1640–1832* (University Park, Penn.: Pennsylvania State Press, 2000).

Smith, Margaret (ed.), *The Letters of Charlotte Brontë 1848–1851* (Oxford: Clarendon Press, 2002).

Smith, Sidonie, *A Poetics of Women's Autobiography: Marginality and the Fictions of Self-Representation* (Bloomington: Indiana University Press, 1987).

——, *Subjectivity, Identity and the Body: Women's Autobiographical Practices in the Twentieth Century* (Bloomington: Indiana University Press, 1993).

Snyder, J, *The Woman and the Lyre: Women Writers in Classical Greece and Rome* (Carbondale: South Illinois University Press, 1989).

Socolow, Susan M, *The Women of Colonial Latin America* (New York: Cambridge University Press, 2000).

Soffer, Reba N, *Discipline and Power: The University, History and the Making of an English Elite, 1870–1930* (Stanford: Stanford University Press, 1994).

Soland, Birgitte, *Becoming Modern: Young Women and the Reconstruction of Womanhood in the 1920s* (Princeton, NJ: Princeton University Press, 2000).

Solomon, Bertha, *Time Remembered: The Story of a Fight* (Cape Town: Howard Timmins, 1968).

Sondergard, Sydney L, *Sharpening Her Pen: Strategies of Rhetorical Violence by Early Modern English Women Writers* (Selinsgrove: Susquehanna University Press, 2002).

Spencer, J, *The Rise of the Woman Novelist: From Aphra Behn to Jane Austen* (Oxford: Basil Blackwell, 1986).

Spender, Dale and Janet Todd (eds) *British Women Writers: An Anthology from the Fourteenth Century to the Present* (New York: Peter Bedrick Books, 1989).

Spongberg, Mary, *Feminising Venereal Disease: The Body of the Prostitute in Nineteenth Century Medical Discourse* (New York: New York University Press, 1997).

——, *Writing Women's History Since the Renaissance* (London: Palgrave, 2002).

Spruill, Julia Cherry, *Women's Life and Work in the Southern Colonies* (New York: W W Norton & Company, 1972).

Staël, Germaine de, *Dix Années d'Exil* (Paris: Bibliotheque 10/18, Union General d'Edition, 1966).

——, *De L'Allemagne* [1813] (Paris: Garnier-Flammarion, 1968).

——, *Corinne, Or Italy* [1808], trans. Avriel H Goldberger (New Brunswick: Rutgers University Press, 1987).

Staiger, c Klara Staigers Tagebuch (ed.) *O Fina* (Regensburg: Pustet, 1981).

Stanley, Liz (ed.), *The Diaries of Hannah Cullwick, Victorian Maidservant* (London: Virago, 1984).

Stanton, Domna (ed.), *The Female Autograph* (Chicago: University of Chicago Press, 1987).

Stedall, J, *A Discourse Concerning Algebra: English Algebra to 1685* (Oxford: Oxford University Press, 2002).

——, *The Greate Invention of Algebra: Thomas Harriot's Treatise on Equations* (Oxford: Oxford University Press, 2003).

Stevens, Joan (ed.), *Mary Taylor Friend of Charlotte Brontë* (Oxford: Oxford University Press, 1972).

Stevenson, Lionel, *The Wild Irish Girl: The Life of Sydney Owenson, Lady Morgan* (London: Chapman & Hall, 1936).

Stodart, M A, *Female Writers Thoughts on Their Proper Sphere, and on Their Powers of Usefulness* (London: Thames, 1842).

Stoler, Ann Laura, *Race and the Education of Desire: Foucault's History of Sexuality and the Colonial Order of Things* (Durham, NC: Duke University Press, 1995).

——, *Carnal Knowledge and Imperial Power: Race and the Intimate in Colonial Rule* (Berkeley: University of California Press, 2002).

Stone, Harriet, *The Classical Model: Literature and Knowledge in Seventeenth-Century France* (Ithaca: Cornell University Press, 1997).

Strachey, Barbara, *Remarkable Relations: The Pearsall Smith Women* (New York: Universe Books, 1982).

Strickland, Agnes (ed.), *Letters of Mary, Queen of Scots* (London: Henry Colburn, 1844).

——, *Lives of the Queens of England, from the Norman Conquest; With Anecdotes of Their Courts, Now First Published from Official Records and Other Authentic Documents, Private as Well as Public*, 9 vols (London: Henry Colburn, 1844).

Strickland, Jane Margaret, *Life of Agnes Stickland* (Edinburgh and London: William Blackwood and Sons, 1887).

Strobel, Margaret, *Gender, Sex, and Empire* (Washington, DC: American Historical Association, 1993).

Stuard, Susan Mosher (ed.), *Women in Medieval History and Historiography* (Philadelphia: University of Pennsylvania Press, 1987).

Stuchtey, B and E Fuchs (eds), *Writing World History 1800–2000* (Oxford: Oxford University Press, 2003).

Suhl, Yuri, *Ernestine L. Rose: Women's Rights Pioneer* (New York: Biblio Press, 1990).

Suzuki, Y, *Joseishi o Hiraku 1: Haha to Onna* (Tokyo: Miraisha, 1989a).

——, *Joseishi o Hiraku 2: Yokusan to Teikô* (Tokyo: Miraisha, 1989b).

——, *Joseishi o Hiraku 3: Onna to Sengo 50nen* (Tokyo: Miraisha, 1996a).

——, *Joseishi o Hiraku 4: 'Ianfu' Mondai to Sensô Sekinin* (Tokyo: Miraisha, 1996b).

—— (ed.), *Nihon Josei Undô Shiryô Shûsei*, 10 vols (Tokyo: Fuji Shuppan, 1996–1998).

Swerdlow, Amy, *Women Strike for Peace* (Chicago: University of Chicago Press, 1993).

Takamure, I, *Takamure Itsue Zenshû*, ed. Hashimoto Kenzô, 10 vols (Tokyo: Rironsha, 1966–1967).

——,'The New Feminist Movement in Japan, 1970–1990', in K Fujimura-Fanselow and A Kameda (eds) *Japanese Women: New Feminist Perspectives on the Past, Present and Future* (New York: The Feminist Press, 1995).

Tarabotti, Arcangela, *Paternal Tyranny*, ed. and trans. Letitia Panizza (Chicago: University of Chicago Press, 2004).

Taylor, Barbara, *Mary Wollstonecraft and the Feminist Imagination* (Cambridge: Cambridge University Press, 2003).

Teague, Frances N, *Bathsua Makin: Woman of Learning* (Louisberg: Bucknell University Press, 1998).

Tebbutt, Melanie, *Women's Talk? A Social History of 'Gossip' in Working-Class Neighbourhoods, 1880–1960* (Aldershot: Scolar Press, 1995).

Temple, K, *Scandal Nation: Law and Authorship in Britain, 1750–1832* (Ithaca: Cornell University Press, 2003).

Tharu, Susie and K Lalita (eds), *Women Writing in India* (New York: The Feminist Press, 1993).

Thiébaux, Marcelle, *The Writings of Medieval Women* (New York: Garland, 1987).

Thompson, Dorothy (ed.), *The Early Chartists* (London: Macmillan, 1971).

Thompson, Homer A, *A Symposium in Memory of Hetty Goldman 1881–1972* (Princeton: Princeton University Press, 1974).

Thomson, Gladys, *Mrs Arthur Strong: A Memoir* (London: Cohen & West Ltd, 1949).

Thorold, Peter, *The London Rich: The Creation of a Great City from 1666 to the Present* (London: Viking, 1999).

Tillyard, Stella, *Aristocrats: Caroline, Emily, Louisa and Sarah Lennox, 1740–1832* (London: Chatto & Windus, 1994).

Todd, Janet, *Mary Wollstonecraft: A Revolutionary Life* (London: Weidenfeld & Nicolson, 2000).

Tristan, Flora, *The London Journal of Flora Tristan 1842 or The Aristocracy and the Working Class of England*, ed. and trans. Jean Hawkes (London: Virago, 1982).

Trumpener, Katie, *Bardic Nationalism: The Romantic Novel and the British Empire* (Chicago: Chicago University Press, 1997).

Tsurumi, E P, *Factory Girls: Women in the Thread Mills of Meiji Japan* (Princeton: Princeton University Press, 1990).

Tuite, Clara, *Romantic Austen: Sexual Politics and the Literary Canon* (Cambridge: Cambridge University Press, 2002).

Ueno, C, *Nationalism and Gender* [1998] trans. Beverley Yamamoto (Melbourne: Transpacific Press, 2004).

Valenze, Deborah, *The First Industrial Woman* (Oxford: Oxford University Press, 1995).

Vansina, Jan *Oral Tradition: A Study in Historical Methodology*, trans. by H M Wright (London: Routledge & Kegan Paul, 1965).

Van Tassel, David D, *Recording America's Past: An Interpretation of the Development of Historical Studies in America, 16-7-1884* (Chicago: University of Chicago Press, 1960).

Vellacott, Jo, *Bertrand Russell and the Pacifists of the First World War* (Brighton: Harvester, 1980).

Vincent, David Bread, *Knowledge and Freedom. A Study of Nineteenth-Century Working Class Autobiography* (London: Methuen, 1981).

Vintges, Karen, *Philosophy as Passion: The Thinking of Simone de Beauvoir* (Bloomington: Indiana University Press, 1996).

Wada, Ei, *Tomioka Nikki* (Tokyo: Chûô Kôronsha, 1978).

Walker, Cherryl, *Women and Resistance in South Africa* (London: Onyx Press, 1982).

Walker, Claire, *Gender and Politics in Seventeenth-Century English Convents* (London: Palgrave, 2003).

Walker, Kim, *Women Writers of the English Renaissance* (New York: Twayne, 1996).

Walker, Nancy, *Shaping Our Mother's World: American Women's magazines* (Jackson: University Press of Mississippi, 2000).

Walkowitz, Judith, *Prostitution and Victorian Society: Women, Class and the State* (Cambridge: Cambridge University Press, 1980).

Wallach, Janet, *Desert Queen* (London: Weidenfeld & Nicolson, 1996).

Wallerstein, Immanuel, *The Modern World System: Capitalist Agriculture and the Origins of European World-Economy in the*

Sixteenth Century (New York: Academic Press, 1974).

Ware, Vron, *Beyond the Pale: White Women, Racism & History* (London: Verso, 1992).

Warner, Marina, *Alone of All Her Sex: The Myth and the Cult of the Virgin Mary* (New York: Alfred A Knopf, Inc., 1976).

——, *From the Beast to the Blonde: On Fairy Tales and Their Tellers* (London: Vintage, 1995).

Warren, Mercy Otis, *History of the Rise, Progress, and Termination of the American Revolution* [1805] (New York: AMS Press, 1970).

Waterfield, Gordon, *Lucie Duff Gordon* (New York: Dutton, 1937).

Watt, Diane (ed.), *The Paston Women: Selected Letters* (Woodbridge, Suffolk: Boydell & Brewer, 2004).

Weaver, F E, *The Evolution of the Reform of Port-Royal: From the Rule of Cîteaux to Jansenism* (Paris: Beauchesne, 1978).

Weaver, S A, *The Hammonds: A Marriage in History* (Stanford: Stanford University Press, 1997).

Webb, Beatrice, *My Apprenticeship* (London: Longman, 1926).

Webb, Sidney and Beatrice Webb, *Indian Diary*, ed. Niraja Gopal Jayal (Oxford: Oxford University Press, 1990).

Weir, Alison, *The Life of Elizabeth I* [1998] (New York: Ballantine Books, 2003).

Wemple, Suzanne Fonay, *Women in Frankish Society: Marriage and the Cloister* (Philadelphia: University of Pennsylvania Press, 1981).

Wheeler, Bonnie (ed.) *Listening to Heloise: The Voice of a Twelfth-Century Woman* (New York: St Martin's Press, 2000).

Whitbread, Anne (ed.) *I Know My Own Heart: The Diaries of Anne Lister, 1791–1840* (London: Virago, 1988).

White, Hayden, *Tropics of Discourse: Essays in Cultural Criticism* (Baltimore: Johns Hopkins University Press, 1978).

——, *The Content of the Form: Narrative Discourse and Historical Representation* (Baltimore: Johns Hopkins University Press, 1987).

White, Luise, *The Comforts of Home: Prostitution in Colonial Nairobi* (Chicago: University of Chicago Press, 1990).

Wildenthal, Lora, *German Women for Empire, 1884–1945* (Durham: Duke University Press, 2001).

Willard, Frances and Mary A Livermore (eds), *A Woman of the Century* (Buffalo: C W Molton, 1893).

Williams, Helen Maria, *Letters Written in France, in the Summer of 1790, to a Friend in England, Containing Various Anecdotes Relative to the French Revolution; and Memoirs of Mons. and Madame du F——* [1790], ed. Janet M Todd (New York: Scholars' Facsimiles & Reprints, 1975).

——, *Letters from France: Containing Many New Anecdotes Relative to the French Revolution, and the Present State of French Manners*, vol. II, Second Edition, ed. Janet M Todd (New York: Scholars' Facsimiles & Reprints, 1975).

——, *Sketches of the State of Manners and Opinions in the French Republic, Towards the Close of the Eighteenth Century. In a Series of Letters. In Two Volumes* (London: G G and J Robinson, 1801).

Williams, Raymond, *The Country and the City* (London: Chatto & Windus, 1973).

Williamson, Maya Bijvoet (trans.), *The Memoirs of Helene Kottanner (1439–1440)* (Woodbridge, Suffolk and Rochester, New York: D S Brewer, 1998).

Willoughby, Cassandra, *The Continuation of the History of the Willoughby Family* (ed.) A C Wood (Eton: Head Press, 1958).

Wilson, Kathleen, *Island Race: Englishness, Empire and Gender in the Eighteenth Century* (London: Routledge, 2002).

Wilson, Katharina M (ed.), *Medieval Women Writers* (Athens: University of Georgia Press, 1984).

——, (ed.), *Hrotsvit of Gandersheim: Rara Avis in Saxona* (Ann Arbor: Marc Publishing, 1987).

Wilson, Katharina M and Frank J Warnke (eds), *Women Writers of the Seventeenth Century* (Athens, Georgia: The University of Georgia Press, 1989).

Winstead, Karen A, *Virgin Martyrs: Legends of Sainthood in Late Medieval England* (Ithaca: Cornell UP, 1997).

Wiseman, T P, *A Short History of the British School at Rome* (London: British School at Rome, 1990).

Wollstonecraft, Mary, *Vindication of the Rights of Woman* [1792], ed. Mariam Brody (London: Penguin Books, 1992).

Women's Division of the New Zealand Farmers' Union, *Brave Days: Pioneer Women of New Zealand* (Dunedin and Wellington: A H and A W Reed, 1939).

Wood, E A, *The Baba and the Comrade. Gender and Politics in Revolutionary Russia* (Bloomington: Indiana University Press, 1997).

Woodford, Charlotte, *Nuns as Historians in Early Modern Germany* (Oxford: Clarendon, 2002).

Woollacott, Angela, *To Try Her Fortune in London: Australian Women, Colonialism, and Modernity* (New York: Oxford University Press, 2001).

Yalom, Marilyn, *Blood Sisters: The French Revolution in Women's Memory* (New York: Basic Books, 1993).

Yamakawa, K, *Yamakawa Kikue Shû*, ed. Tanaka Sumiko, 10 vols (Tokyo: Iwanami Shoten, 1981–1982).

——, *Buke no Josei* (Tokyo: Mikuni Shobô, 1943).

Yee, Shirley J, *Black Women Abolitionists: A Study in Activism, 1828–1860* (Knoxsville: University of Tennessee Press, 1992).

Yegenoglu, Meyda, *Colonial Fantasies: Towards a Feminist Reading of Orientalism* (Cambridge: Cambridge University Press, 1998).

Yoshimi, Y (ed.) *Jûgun Ianfu Shiryôshû* (Tokyo: Ôtsuki Shoten, 1992).

Yuval-Davis, Natalie and Flora Anthias, 'Introduction', *Women-Nation-State* (Basingstoke: Macmillan, 1989).

Zagarri, Rosemary, *A Woman's Dilemma: Mercy Otis Warren and the American Revolution* (Illinois: Harlan Davidson, 1995).

Zimmerman, E, *The Boundaries of Fiction: History and the Eighteenth-Century British Novel* (Ithaca: Cornell University Press, 1996).

Zlotnick, Susan, *Women, Writing and the Industrial Revolution* (Baltimore: The John Hopkins University Press, 1998).

Zuckerman, Mary Ellen, *Sources on the History of Women's Magazines 1792–1960* (Westport, Connecticut: Greenwood Press, 1991).

Articles

Ackerman, Robert, *Introduction to Jane Harrison's Prolegomena to the Study of Greek Religion* (Princeton: Princeton University Press, 1991) pp. xiii–xxx.

Ackroyd, J, 'Women in Feudal Japan', *Transactions of the Asiatic Society of Japan*, Third Series, 7:3 (1959) 31–68.

Adshead, K, 'The Secret History of Procopius and Its Genesis', *Byzantion*, 63 (1993) 5–28.

Alexander, Elizabeth, '"We Must Be About Our Father's Business": Anna Julia Cooper and the In-Corporation of the Nineteenth-Century African American Woman Intellectual', *Signs*, 20:2 (1995) 336–356.

Alexander, Sally, 'Women's Work in Nineteenth Century London', in Juliet Mitchell and Ann Oakley (eds) *The Rights and Wrongs of Women* (Harmondsworth: Penguin, 1976) pp. 59–111.

Alexander, Sally and Anna, Davin, 'Editorial', *History Workshop Journal*, 1 (1976) 4–6.

Allen, Ann Taylor, 'Feminism, Social Science and the Meanings of Modernity: The Debate on the Origin of the Family in Europe and the United States, 1860– 1914', *American Historical Review*, 104:4 (1999) 1085–1113.

Allen, Judith, 'Evidence and Silence: Feminism and the Limits of History', in Carole Pateman and Elizabeth Gross (eds) *Feminist Challenges: Social and Political Theory* (Sydney: Allen & Unwin, 1986) pp. 173–189.

Ambrose, Linda M, 'Ontario's Women's Institutes and the Work of Local History', in Beverly Boutilier and Alison Prentice (eds) *Creating Historical Memory: English-Canadian Women and the Work of History* (Vancouver: UBC Press, 1997) pp. 75–100.

Anderson, Elizabeth Garrett, 'The History of a Movement', *Fortnightly Review*, 59 (March 1893) 404–17.

Applegate, Celia, 'The "Creative Possibilities of Science" in Civil Society and Public Life: A Commentary', *Osiris Annual* (2002) 351.

Atkinson, Colin B and Jo Atkinson, 'Sydney Owenson, Lady Morgan: Irish Patriot and First Professional Woman Writer', *Eire-Ireland*, 15:2 (1986) 60–91.

Atwood, Barbara, P, 'Connecticut's Lady Historians', *New England Galaxy*, 12:3 (1971) 32–41.

Ballanger, Margaret, 'Native Life in South African Towns', *Journal of Royal African Society*, 37:148 (1938) 326–338.

Banner, Lois, 'On Writing Women's History', *Journal of Interdisciplinary History*, 2:2 (1971) 347–358.

Bannerji, H, 'Politics and the Writing of History', in R Roach Pierson and N Chaudhuri (eds), *Nation, Empire, Colony: Historicizing Gender and Race* (Bloomington: Indiana University Press, 1998) pp. 287–302.

Barker, P S D, 'Charitas Pirckheimer: A Female Humanist Confronts the Reformation', *Sixteenth-Century Journal*, 24 (1995) 259–272.

Barman, Jean, 'I walk my own track in life & no mere male can bump me off it': Constance Lindsay Skinner and the Work of History', in Beverly Boutilier and Alison Prentice (eds) *Creating Historical Memory: English-Canadian Women and the Work of History* (Vancouver: University of British Columbia Press, 1997) pp. 129–163.

Baron, E, 'Romancing the Field: The Marriage of Feminism and Historical Sociology', *Social Politics*, 5 (1998) 17–37.

Bass, Elizabeth, 'Kate Campbell Hurd-Mead M D', *Journal of the American Medical Women's Association*, 11 (1956) 155.

Baym, Nina, 'Onward Christian Women: Sarah J. Hale's History of the World', *The New England Quarterly*, 63:2 (1990) 249–270.

——, 'Mercy Otis Warren's Gendered Melodrama of Revolution', *The South Atlantic Quarterly*, 90:3 (1991) 531–554.

Beard, Mary, 'Women on the Dig', *Times Literary Supplement* (October 1994) 7–8.

Beck, F A G, 'The Schooling of Girls in Ancient Greece', *Classicum*, 9 (1978) 1–8.

Beer, Gillian, 'Passion, Politics, Philosophy: The Work of Edith Simcox', *Women: A Cultural Review*, 6:2 (1995) 166–179.

Berg, Maxine, 'Women's Work, Mech-anization and the Early Phase of Indus-trialization in England', in Patrick Joyce (ed.) *The Historical Meanings of Work* (Cambridge: Cambridge University Press, 1987) pp. 64–98.

——, 'The First Women Economic Historians', *Economic History Review*, 45 (1992) 308–329.

Berg, Maxine and Pat Hudson, 'Rehabilitating the Industrial Revolution', *Economic History Review*, 45 (1992) 24–50.

Beveridge, W H, 'Professor Lilian Knowles 1870–1926', *Economica*, 6 (1926) 119–120.

Binhammer, Katherine, 'The "Singular Propensity" of Sensibility's Extremities: Female Same-Sex Desire and the Eroticization of Pain in Late-Eighteenth-Century British Culture', *Gay and Lesbian Quarterly*, 9:4 (2003) 471–498.

Bivar, A D H and J R Hinnells, 'Professor Mary Boyce', *Papers in Honour of Professor Mary Boyce* (Acta Iranica. Hommages et Opera Minora 10 Leiden, E J Brill, 1985) pp. xi–xx.

Blok, Josine, 'Sexual Asymmetry. A Historiographical Essay', in Josine Blok and Peter Mason (eds) *Sexual Asymmetry. Studies in Ancient Society* (Amsterdam: J C Gieben, 1987) pp. 1–57.

Blom, I, 'World History as Gender History: The Case of the Nation-State', *Between National Histories and Global History* (eds) S Tønnesson, J Koponen, N Steensgard and T Svensson (Helsinki: Finnish Historical Society, 1997) pp. 71–91.

Boas, F S, 'Charlotte Carmichael Stopes: Some Aspects of Her Life and Work' *Transactions of the Royal Society of Literature*, Series 3, vol. 10 (1931) 77–94.

Bohan, Clara Hauessler, 'Lucy Maynard Salmon: Progressive Historian, Teacher, and Democrat', in Margaret Smith Crocco and O L Davis, Jr (eds) *'Bending the Future to Their Will': Civic Women, Social Education, and Democracy* (Lanham: Rowman & Littlefield, 1999) pp. 47–72.

Bonfante, Larissa, 'Margarete Bieber', *Gnomon*, 51 (1979) 621–623.

Booth, Alison, 'Illustrious Company: Victoria Among Other Women in Anglo-American Role Model Anthologies', in Margaret Homans and Adrienne Munich (eds) *Remaking Queen Victoria* (Cambridge: Cambridge University Press, 1997) pp. 59–78.

——, 'The Lessons of the Medusa: Anna Jameson and Collective Biographies of Women', *Victorian Studies*, 42 (1999/2000) 257–288.

Bowman, Glenn, '"Mapping History's Redemption": Eschatology and Topography in the *Itinerarium Burdigalense*', in Lee I Levine (ed.) *Jerusalem: Its Sanctity and Centrality to Judaism, Christianity, and Islam* (New York: Continuum, 1999).

Bowring, R, 'The Female Hand in Japan: A First Reading', in Domna Stanton (ed.) *The Female Autograph: Theory and Practice of Autobiography from the Tenth to the Twentieth Century* (Chicago: University of Chicago, 1987) pp. 49–56.

Braker, Regina, 'Bertha von Suttner's Spiritual Daughters', *Women's Studies International Forum*, 18:2 (1995) 103–111.

Braunschneider, T, 'The Macroclitoride, the Tribade, and the Woman: Configuring Gender and Sexuality in English Anatomical Discourse', *Textual Practice*, 13:3 (1999) 513–536.

Breay, Claire, 'Women and the Classical Tripos 1869–1914', in Christopher Stray (ed.), *Classics in 19th and 20th Century Cambridge. Curriculum, Culture and Community* (Cambridge: Cambridge Philological Society, 1999) pp. 49–70.

Brieger, Gert H, 'The Historiography of Medicine', in W F Bynum and Roy Porter (eds), *Companion Encyclopedia of the History of Medicine* (London: Routledge, 1993) pp. 24–44.

Brink, Elsabe, 'Man-Made Women: Gender, Class and the Ideology of the Volksmoeder', in Cherryl Walker (ed.) *Women and Gender in Southern Africa to 1945* (Cape Town: David Philip, 1990) pp. 273–292.

Brooten, Bernadette, 'Early Christian Women and Their Cultural Context: Issues of Method in Historical Reconstruction', in A Y Collins (ed.), *Feminist Perspectives on Biblical Scholarship* (Chico, California: Scholars Press, 1985), pp. 65–91.

Broughton, T R S, 'Obituary of Lily Ross Taylor', *Gnomon*, 42 (1970) 734–735.

Brown, Shelby, 'Feminist Research in Archaeology: What does It Mean? Why is It Taking So Long?', in Nancy Sorkin Rabinowitz and Amy Richlin (eds) *Feminist Theory and the Classics* (New York: Routledge, 1993) pp. 238–271.

Bube, June Johnson, 'Prefiguring the New Woman: Frances Fuller Victor's Refashioning of Women and Marriage in *"The New Penelope"*', *Frontiers*, 18:3 (1997) 40–66.

Burstein, Miriam Elizabeth, '"The Reduced Pretensions of the Historic Muse": Agnes Strickland and the Commerce of Women's History', *Journal of Narrative Technique*, 28:3 (1998) 219–242.

——, '"From Good Looks to Good Thoughts": Popular Women's History and the Invention of Modernity, c.1830–c.1870', *Modern Philology*, 97 (1999) 46–75.

Burton, Antoinette, 'Colonial Encounters in Late-Victorian England: Pandita Ramabai at Cheltenham and Wantage 1883–6', *Feminist Review*, 49 (1995) 29–49.

——, 'Who Needs the Nation?', in Catherine Hall (ed.) *Cultures of Empire* (Manchester: Manchester University Press, 2000) pp. 137–156.

Bush, Barbara, '"White Ladies", Coloured "Favourites" and "Black Wenches": Some considerations on sex, race and class factors in social relations in white Creole society in the British Caribbean', *Slavery and Abolition*, 2:3 (1981) 245–262.

Buss, Helen M, 'The Different Voice of Canadian Feminist Autobiographers', *Biography*, 13:2 (1990).

Bynum, Caroline Walker, 'Why All the Fuss about the Body? A Medievalist's Perspective', in *Critical Inquiry*, 22:1 (Fall 1995).

Caine, Barbara, 'Victorian Feminism and the Ghost of Mary Wollstonecraft', *Women's Writing*, 4:2 (1997) 261–275.

——, 'Mothering Feminism/Mothering Feminists: Ray Strachey and The Cause', *Women's History Review*, 8:2 (1999) 295–309.

Calder III, William M and Judith P Hallett, 'Introduction: Six North American Women Classicists', *Classical World*, 90 (1996–1997) 83–96.

Callen, A, 'The Body and Difference: Anatomy Teaching at the Ecole des Beaux-Arts in Later Nineteenth-Century Paris', *Art History*, 20:1 (1997) 23–60.

——, 'Technique and Gender: Landscape, Ideology and the Art of Monet's Series Paintings', in A G Robins and S Adams (eds) *Gendering Landscape Art* (Manchester: Manchester University Press, 2000) pp. 26–44.

Careless, J M S, 'Limited Identities in Canada', *Canadian Historical Review*, 50:1 (1969).

Caspar, E Scott, 'An Uneasy Marriage of Sentiment and Scholarship: Elizabeth F Ellet and the Domestic Origins of American Women's History', *Journal of Women's History*, 4:2 (1992) 10–35.

Chapman, John, 'The Impact of Modern Invasions and Migrations on Archaeological Explanation: A Biographical Sketch of Marija Gimbutas', in Margarita Díaz-Andreu and Marie Louise Stig Sørensen (eds), *Excavating Women: A History of Women in European Archaeology* (London and New York: Routledge, 1998) pp. 295–314.

Chrisman, Miriam, 'Women and the Reformation in Strasbourg, 1490–1530', *Archiv für Reformationsgeschichte lxiv* (1972) 143–168.

Christianson, Aileen, 'Jane Welsh Carlyle and Her Friendships with Women in the 1840s', *Prose Studies*, 10:3 (1987) 283–295.

Clarke, Norma, 'Anna Jameson: The Idol of Thousands of Young Ladies', in Mary Hilton and Pam Hirsch (eds) *Practical Visionaries: Women, Education and Social Progress 1790–1930* (London: Longman, 2000).

Clinton, Catherine, 'Gerda Lerner', in R A Rutland (ed.), *Clio's Favourites: Leading Historians of the United States 1945–2000* (Columbia: University of Missouri, 2000).

Clowes, Lindsay, 'Are You Going to be Miss or (Mr) Africa: Contesting Masculinity in

Drum Magazine 1951–1953', *Gender and History*, 13:1 (2001).

Cohn, Carol, 'Sex and Death in the Rational World of Defense Intellectuals', *Signs: Journal of Women in Culture & Society*, 12:4 (1987) 687–718.

Conkey, Margaret W and Janet D Spector, 'Archaeology and the Study of Gender', in M Schiffer (ed.), *Advances in Archaeological Method and Theory*, vol. 7 (New York: Academic Press, 1984) pp. 1–38.

Conkey, Margaret W and Joan M Gero, 'Tensions, Pluralities, and Engendering Archaeology: An Introduction to Women and Prehistory', in Gero and Conkey (eds), *Engendering Archaeology. Women and Prehistory* (Oxford: Basil Blackwell, 1991) pp. 3–30.

Connolly, Clare, 'Writing the Union', in Dáire Keogh and Kevin Whelan (eds), *Acts of Union: The Causes, Contexts and Consequences of the Act of Union* (Dublin: Four Court Press, 2001) pp. 171–186.

Costa, S, 'Marketing Mathematics in Early Eighteenth Century England: Henry Beighton, Certainty and the Public Sphere', *History of Science*, 40:2 (2002) 211–232.

Cott, Nancy F, *A Woman Making History: Mary Ritter Beard through Her Letters* (New Haven: Yale University Press, 1991).

Coudart, Anick, 'Archaeology of French Women and French Women in Archaeology', in Margarita Díaz-Andreu and Marie Louise Stig Sørensen (eds), *Excavating Women. A History of Women in European Archaeology* (London: Routledge, 1998) pp. 61–85.

Crawford, Patricia, 'Women's Published Writings 1600–1700', in Mary Prior (ed.), *Women in English Society 1500–1800* (London: Methuen, 1985).

Crowley, Terry, 'Isabel Skelton: Precursor to Canadian Cultural History', in Boutilier Beverly and Alison Prentice (eds) *Creating Historical Memory: English-Canadian Women and the Work of History* (Vancouver: UBC Press, 1997) pp. 165–193.

Culham, Phyllis, 'Ten Years after Pomeroy: Studies of the Image and Reality of Women in Antiquity', in M Skinner (ed.) *Rescuing Creusa: New Methodological Approaches to Women in Antiquity* (A Special Issue of *Helios*, NS, 13:2, (1987), 9–30.

Cullen, Mary, 'Telling It Our Way: Feminist History', in Liz Steiner-Scott (ed.) *Personally Speaking: Women's Thoughts on Women's Issues* (Dublin: Attic Press, 1985).

Cunliffe-Jones, Janet, 'A Rare Phenomenon: A Woman's Contribution to 19th Century Adult Education', *Journal of Educational Administration and History*, 24:1 (1992) 1–17.

Curli, Barbara and Alessandra Pescarolo, 'Genere, lavori, etichette statistiche. I censimenti in una prospettiva storica', in Franca Bimbi (ed.) *Differenze e disuguaglianze. Prospettive per gli studi di genere in Italia* (Bologna: Il Mulino, 2003) pp. 65–100.

Curthoys, Ann, 'Historiography and Women's Liberation', *Arena*, 21 (1970) 35–40.

——, 'Towards a Feminist Labour History', in Ann Curthoys, Susan Eade [Magarey] and Peter Spearitt (eds) *Women at Work* (A special issue of *Labour History*) 29 (1975) 88–95.

——, 'Cultural History and the Nation', in Hsu-Ming Teo and Richard White (eds) *Cultural History in Australia* (Sydney: University of NSW Press, 2003) pp. 22–37.

Daniels, Kay, 'Women's History', in G Osborne and W F Mandle (eds) *New History: Studying Australia Today* (Sydney: Allen & Unwin, 1982) pp. 32–50.

——, 'Feminism and Social History', *Australian Feminist Studies*, 1:1 (1985).

——, '"The Flash Mob": Rebellion, Rough Culture and Sexuality in the Female Factories of Van Dieman's Land', *Australian Feminist Studies*, 18 (1993).

Davidoff, Leonore, 'Class and Gender in Victorian England: The Diaries of

Arthur J Munby and Hannah Cullwick', in J L Newton, M P Ryan and J R Walkowitz (eds) *Sex and Class in Women's History* (London and Boston: Routledge & Kegan Paul 1983) pp. 17–71.

Davin, Anna, 'Imperialism and Motherhood', *History Workshop Journal*, 5 (1978) 9–65.

Davis, Natalie Zemon, '"Women's History" in Transition: The European Case', *Feminist Studies*, 3:3–4 (1976) 83–103.

——, 'City Women and Religious Change' *Society and Culture in Early Modern France* (Stanford: Stanford University Press, 1978) pp. 65–96.

——, 'Gender and Genre: Women as Historical Writers, 1400–1820', in P H Labalme (ed.), *Beyond Their Sex: Learned Women of the European Past* (New York: NYU Press, 1980) pp. 153–182.

Degler, Carl N, 'Charlotte Perkins Gilman on the Theory and Practice of Feminism', *American Quarterly*, 8:1 (1956) 21–39.

De Groot, J, '"Sex" and "Race": The Construction of Language and Image in the Nineteenth Century', *Sexuality and Subordination: Interdisciplinary Studies of Gender in the Nineteenth Century* (London: Routledge, 1989) pp. 89–128.

De Lauretis, Teresa, 'Eccentric Subjects: Feminist Theory and Historical Consciousness', *Feminist Studies*, 16 (1990) 115–150.

Derbyshire, Lynne, 'Paulina Kellogg Wright Davis', in Campbell, Karlyn Kohrs (ed.) *Women Public Speakers in the United States, 1800–1925* (Westport, Connecticut and London: Greenwood Press, 1993).

Díaz-Andreu Margarita and Marie Louise Stig Sørensen (eds), 'Excavating Women: Towards an Engendered History of Archaeology', *Excavating Women: A History of Women in European Archaeology* (London: Routledge, 1998) pp. 1–60.

Diefendorf, B 'Les Divisions religievses dans les familles parisiennes avant La saint-Barthélemy', *Histoire Économic et sociétié* 7:1 (1988) 55–77.

Digby, Anne, 'Women's Biological Straightjacket', in S Mendus and J Rendall (eds) *Sexuality and Subordination: Interdisciplinary Studies of Gender in the Nineteenth Century* (London: Routledge, 1989) pp. 192–220.

Dill, Bonnie Thornton, 'Race, Class, and Gender: Prospects for an All-Inclusive Sisterhood', *Feminist Studies*, 9:1 (1983) 131–150.

Dockray-Miller, Mary, 'Mary Bateson 1865–1906: Scholar and Suffragist', in Jane Chance (ed.) *Women Medievalists and the Academy* (Madison and London: University of Wisconsin Press, 2004).

Doern, Kristin, 'Clara Lucas Balfour: A Woman Campaigner against Drink', *Women's History Notebooks*, 4:2 (1997) 14–20.

Dokuzen, K, *Kageyama Hidejo no Den* [1887] (Tokyo: Eisendô).

Dolnikowski, Edith Wilks, 'Feminine Exemplars for Reform: Women's Voices in John Foxe's *Acts and Monuments*', in Beverly Mayne Kienzle and Pamela J Walker (eds) *Women Preachers and Prophets through Two Millennia of Christianity* (Berkeley: University of California Press, 1998) pp. 199–211.

Douglass, Jane Dempsey, 'Christian Freedom: What Calvin Learned at the School of Women', *Church History*, 53:2 (1984) 155–173.

Drabble, John E, 'Mary's Protestant Martyrs and Elizabeth's Catholic Traitors in the Age of Catholic Emancipation', *Church History*, 51 (1982) 172–185.

Dubois, Ellen C, 'Women's Rights and Abolition: The Nature of the Connection', in Lewis Perry and Michael Fellman (eds) *Antislavery Reconsidered: New Perspectives on the Abolitionists* (Baton Rouge: Louisiana State University Press, 1979).

——, 'Eleanor Flexner and the History of American Feminism', *Gender & History* 3:1 (1991) 81–90.

DuBois, Ellen C and Gordon, Linda, 'Seeking Ecstasy on the Battlefield: Danger and Pleasure in Nineteenth Century Feminist Sexual Thought', in Carole Vance (ed.) *Pleasure and Danger: Exploring Female Sexuality* (Boston: Routledge, 1984) pp. 31–49.

Duff, Wendy, 'Bibliography of the Writings of Phyllis Ruth Blakeley', *The Nova Scotia Historical Review*, 7:2 (1987).

Dunn, R, 'Gender in World History', *The New World History: A Teacher's Companion* (Boston: St. Martin's, 2000) pp. 441–442.

Dyhouse, Carol, 'Working-Class Mothers and Infant Mortality in England, 1895–1914', *Journal of Social History*, 12:2 (1978) 248–267.

——, 'Driving Ambition: Women in Pursuit of a Medical Education, 1890–1939', *Women's History Review*, 7:3 (1998) 321–341.

Dyson, S L, 'From New to New Age Archaeology: Archaeological Theory and Classical Archaeology – A 1990s Perspective', *American Journal of Archaeology*, 97 (1993) 195–206.

Elfenbein, Andrew, 'Lesbian Aestheticism on the Eighteenth Century Stage', *Eighteenth Century Life*, 25:1 (2001) 1–16.

Ellinghaus, Katherine, 'Absorbing the "Aboriginal problem": Controlling Interracial Marriage in Australia in the Late 19th and Early 20th Centuries', *Aboriginal History*, 27 (2003) 183–207.

Elliot, Mary Jane Suero, 'Postcolonial Experience in a Domestic Context: Commodified Subjectivity in Toni Morrison's *Beloved*', *Melus* (2000) 181–204.

Evangelisti, S, 'Angelica Baitelli [1588–1650], la Storica', in G Calvi (ed.) *Barocco al femminile* (Rome: Laterza, 1992) pp. 71–95.

Faderman, Lilian, 'The Morbidification of Love Between Women by 19th-Century Sexologists', *Journal of Homosexuality*, 4:1 (1978) 73–90.

Fauset, Eileen, 'The Politics of Writing: Julia Kavanagh 1824–1877', *Irish Journal of Feminist Studies*, 2 (1996) 58–68.

Fausto-Sterling, A, 'Gender, Race and Nation: The Comparative Anatomy of "Hottentot" Women in Europe', in Jennifer Terry and Jaqueline Urla (eds) *Deviant Bodies* (Bloomington: Indiana University Press, 1995) pp. 19–48.

Fee, Elizabeth, 'Science and the Woman Problem: Historical Perspectives', in Michael Teitelbaum (ed.) *Sex Differences: Social and Biological Perspectives* (New York: Anchor Press, 1976) pp. 175–223.

Fiamengo, Janice, 'A Legacy of Ambivalence: Responses to Nellie McClung', *Journal of Canadian Studies*, 34:4 (1999/2000) 70–87.

Fitzpatrick, Sheila, 'Ascribing Class: The Construction of Social Identity in Soviet Russia', *Stalinism. New Directions* (New York: Routledge, 2000) pp. 20–46.

Folbre, Nancy, 'The "Sphere of Women" in Early-Twentieth Century Economics', in Helene Silverberg (ed.) *Gender and American Social Science: The Formative Years* (Princeton: Princeton University Press, 1997) pp. 35–60.

Foster, A M C, 'The Chronicles of the English Poor Clares of Rouen', *Recusant History*, 18: 1 & 2 (1986) 71–76, 154–158.

Foucault, Michel, 'The Life of Infamous Men', in Meaghan Morris and Paul Patton (eds) *Michel Foucault: Power, Truth Strategy* (Sydney: Feral Publications, 1979) pp. 76–91.

——, 'Nietzsche, Genealogy, History', in Paul Rabinow (ed.) *The Foucault Reader* (New York: Penguin, 1991) pp. 75–100.

Fouquet, C, 'The Unavoidable Detour: Must a History of Women Begin with the History of Their Bodies?', in Michelle Perrot (ed.) *Writing Women's History* (Oxford: Blackwell, 1984) pp. 51–60.

Fox-Genovese, Elizabeth, 'Placing Women's History in History', *New Left Review*, 33 (1982) 5–29.

Frances, Rae, 'The History of Female Prostitution in Australia', in Roberta Perkins, Garrett Prestage, Rachel Sharp and Frances Lovejoy (eds), *Sex Work and Sex Workers in Australia* (Sydney: University of New South Wales Press, 1994) pp. 27–52.

Frank, Katherine, 'Voyages Out: Nineteenth-Century Women Travellers in Africa', in Janet Sharistanian (ed.) *Gender, Ideology and Action: Historical Perspectives on Women's Public Lives* (New York: Greenwood Press, 1986) pp. 67–94.

Fraser, Hilary, 'Women and the Ends of Art History: Vision and Corporeality in Nineteenth-Century Critical Discourse', *Victorian Studies*, 42:1 (1998/1999) 77–101.

Friesen, Gerard, 'Irene M. Spry: A Biographical Note', in Duncan Cameron (ed.) *Explorations in Canadian Economic History: Essays in Honour of Irene M. Spry* (Ottawa: University of Ottawa Press, 1985).

Fujieda, M and K Fujimura-Fanselow, 'Women's Studies: An Overview', in K Fujimura-Fanselow and A Kameda (eds) *Japanese Women: New Feminist Perspectives on the Past, Present and Future* (New York: The Feminist Press, 1995) pp. 155–180.

Gamarnikow, Eva, 'Nurse or Woman: Gender and Professionalism in Reformed Nursing, 1860–1923', in Pat Holden and Jenny Littlewood (eds) *Anthropology and Nursing* (London: Routledge, 1991), pp. 110–129.

Gayle, C A, 'Marxist Appoaches and Women's History in Early Post-War Japan', *Copenhagen Journal of Asian Studies*, 19 (2004).

Geiger, Susan, 'Women's Life Histories: Method and Content', *Signs: Journal of Women in Culture and Society*, 11:2 (1986) 334–351.

——, 'What's So Feminist About Women's Oral History?', *Journal of Women's History*, 1:2 (1990) 169–182.

Gero, Joan M, 'Socio-Politics and the Woman-at-Home Ideology', *American Antiquity* 59 (1985), 342–350.

Gerson, Carole, 'Locating Female Subjects in the Archives', in Helen M Buss and Marlene Kadar (eds) *Working in Women's Archives: Researching Women's Private Literature and Archival Documents* (Waterloo, Ontario: Wilfrid Laurier University Press, 2001) pp. 7–22.

Gibson, Margaret, 'Clitoral Corruption: Body Metaphors and American Doctors' Constructions of Female Homosexuality, 1870–1900', in Vernon A Rosario (ed.) *Science and Homosexualities* (New York: Routledge, 1997) pp. 108–132.

Gill, David W J, 'Winifred Lamb and the Fitzwilliam Museum', in Christopher Stray (ed.) *Classics in 19th and 20th Century Cambridge. Curriculum, Culture and Community* (Cambridge: Cambridge Philological Society, 1999) pp. 135–156.

Gilley, Sheridan, 'Pearse's Sacrifice: Christ and Cuculain Crucified and Risen in the Easter Rising 1916', in James Obelkevich, Lyndal Roper and Raphael Samuel (eds), *Disciplines of Faith: Studies in Religion, Politics, and Patriarchy* (London: Routledge & Kegan Ltd, 1987) pp. 479–497.

Gleadle, Kathryn, ' "Our Several Spheres": Middle-Class Women and the Feminisms of Early Victorian Radical Politics', in Kathryn Gleadle & Sarah Richardson (eds) *Women in British Politics 1760–1860* (New York: St Martin's Press, 2000).

Goggin, Jacqueline, 'Challenging Discrimi-nation in the Historical Profession: Women Historians and the American Historical Association, 1890–1940', *The American Historical Review*, 97:3 (1992) pp. 769–802.

Gollan, Daphe, 'The Memoirs of "Cleopatra Sweatfigure" ', in Elizabeth Windscuttle (ed.) *Women, Class and History: Feminist Perspectives on Australia 1788–1978* (Sydney: Fontana/Collins, 1980).

Gordon, Ann, Buhle, Mari Jo and Dye, Nancy Schrom, 'The Problem of Women's History' [1971] reprinted in Berenice Carroll (ed.) *Liberating Women's History* (Urbana: University of Illinois Press, 1976) pp. 75–92.

Gordon, Linda, 'What's New in Women's History', in Teresa de Lauretis (ed.) *Feminist Studies/Critical Studies* (Madison: University of Wisconsin Press, 1986) pp. 55–66.

Gouma-Peterson, Thalia, 'Gender and Power: Passages to the Maternal in Anna Komnene's *Alexiad*', *Anna Komnene and Her Times* (New York: Garland, 2000) pp. 107–24.

Green, Monica, '"From 'Diseases of Women" to "Secrets of Women": The Gynaecological Literature in the Later Middle Ages', *Journal of Medieval and Early Modern Studies*, 30:1 (2000) 5–39.

Greenspan, Kate, 'Autohagiography and Medieval Women's Spiritual Autobiography', in Jane Chance (ed.) *Gender and Text in the Later Middle Ages* (Gainesville: University Press of Florida, 1996) pp. 216–236.

Grimshaw, Patricia, 'Women in History: Reconstructing the Past', in Jacqueline Goodnow and Carole Pateman (eds) *Women, Social Science and Public Policy* (Sydney: Allen & Unwin, 1985) pp. 32–55.

——, 'Writing the History of Australian Women', in K Offen, Ruth Roach, Pearson and Jane Rendall (eds) *Writing Women's History: International Perspectives* (London: Macmillan, 1991) pp. 151–171.

——, 'Colonising Motherhood: Evangelical Social Reformers and Koorie Women in Victoria, Australia', *Women's History Review*, 8:2 (1999) 329–346.

Grimshaw, Patricia and Jane Carey, 'Kathleen Fitzpatrick [1905–1990] Margaret Kiddle [1914–1958] and Australian History after the Second World War', *Gender & History*, 13:2 (2001) 349–374.

Gutch, Mrs, Peacock, Mabel and Rudkin, Ethel H, 'Articles on Lincolnshire folklore', *Folklore* (Journal of the Folklore Society), LXIII (1908); LXVI (1955).

Haley, Shelley P, 'Black Feminist Thought and Classics: Re-membering, Re-claiming, Re-empowering', in Nancy Sorkin Rabinowitz and Amy Richlin (eds) *Feminist Theory and the Classics* (London and New York: Routledge, 1993) pp. 23–43.

Hall, Jacquelyn Dowd and Anne Firor Scott, 'Women in the South', in John B Boyles and Evelyn Tomas Nolan (eds) *Interpreting Southern History: Historiographical Essays in Honor of Sanford W. Higginbotham* (Baton Rouge: Louisiana State University Press, 1987).

Hallett, Nicky, 'Anne Clifford as Orlando: Virginia Woolf's Feminist Historiology and Women's Biography', *Women's History Review*, 4:4 (1995) 505–524.

Hallman, Dianne M, 'Cultivating a Love of Canada through History: Agnes Maule Machar, 1837–1927', in Beverley Boutilier and Alison Prentice (eds) *Creating Historical Memory: English-Canadian Women and the Work of History* (Vancouver: UBC Press, 1997).

Hancock, Mary, 'Gendering the Modern: Women and Home Science in British India,' in Antoinette Burton (ed.) *Gender, Sexuality and Colonial Modernities* (London: Routledge, 1999) pp. 148–160.

Harrison, Barbara, 'Harsh Lives in Hard Times: Women's Work and Health in the East End 1880–1914', *Rising East*, 2:3 (1999) 20–24.

Harrison, Barbara and Melanie Nolan, 'Reflections in Colonial Glass? Women's Factory Inspectors in Britain and New Zealand 1893–1921', *Women's History Review*, 13:2 (2004) 263–288.

Harrison, Evelyn B, 'Necrology: Margarete Bieber (1879–1978)', *AJA*, 82 (1978) 573–575.

Haskins, V and Mundine, J, '"Could You See to the Return of My Daughter": Fathers and Daughters under the New South Wales Aborigines Protection Board Child Removal Policy', *Australian Historical Studies*, 34:121 (2003) 106–121.

Hastings, Margaret and Elizabeth G Kimball, 'Two Distinguished Medievalists – Nellie Neilson and Bertha Putnam', *Journal of British Studies*, 18:2 (1979) 142–159.

Hauch, G, 'Did Women Have a Revolution? Gender Battles in the European Revolution of 1848/49', in A Koerner (ed.) *1848 – A European revolution? Inter-national Ideas and National Memories of 1848* (New York: Palgrave Macmillan, 2000) pp. 64–84.

Hay, Carla H, 'Catherine Macaulay and the American Revolution', *The Historian*, 56:2 (1994) 301–317.

Hayakawa, N, 'The Development of Women's History in Japan', in Karen Offen, Ruth Roach Pearson and Jane Rendall (eds) *Writing Women's History: International Perspectives* (Bloomington: Indiana University Press, 1991) pp. 171–179.

Hesse, Carla, 'Revolutionary Histories: The Literary Politics of Louise de Kéralio (1758–1822)', in Barbara B Diefendorf and Carla Hesse (eds) *Culture and Identity in Early Modern Europe 1500–1800* (Ann Arbor: University of Michigan Press, 1993) pp. 237–260.

Hewitt, Nancy A, 'On Their Own Terms: A Historiographical Essay', in Jean Fagan Yellin and John C Van Horne (eds) *The Abolitionist Sisterhood: Women's Political Culture in Antebellum America* (Ithaca: Cornell University Press, 1994) pp. 23–30.

Hicks, P, 'Catherine Macaulay's Civil War: Gender, History and Republicanism in Georgian Britain', *Journal of British Studies*, 42 (2002) 170–198.

Higginbotham, Evelyn Brooks, 'Beyond the Sound of Silence: Afro-American Women in History', *Gender and History*, 1:1 (1989) 50–67.

Hill, Barbara, 'Actions Speak Louder than Words: Anna Komnene's Attempted Usurpation', in Thalia Gouma-Peterson (ed.) *Anna Komnene and Her Times* (New York: Garland, 2000).

Hilliard, Chris, 'A Prehistory of Public History: Monuments, Explanations and Promotions, 1900–1970', in Bronwyn Dalley and Jock Phillips (eds) *Going Public: The Changing Face of New Zealand History* (Auckland: Auckland University Press, 2001) pp. 16–30.

Hine, Darlene Clark, 'Lifting the Veil, Shattering Silence: Black Women's History and Freedom', *The State of Afro-American History* (Baton Rouge: Louisiana State University Press, 1986) pp. 224–249.

Hobbs, C (ed.), *Nineteenth-Century Women Learn to Write* (Charlottesville, Virginia: University Press of Virginia, 1995).

Holcomb, Adela, 'Anna Jameson: The First Professional English Art Historian', *Art History*, 6 (1983) 171–187.

Hollis, Karen, 'Eliza Haywood and the Gender of Print', *Eighteenth Century Theory and Interpretation*, 38 (1997) 43–62.

Holt, Lilian, 'One Aboriginal Woman's Identity: Wailing in Both Worlds', *Australian Feminist Studies*, 18 (1993) 175–179.

Holton, Sandra Stanley, 'British Freewomen: National Identity, Constitutionalism and Languages of Race in Early Suffrage Histories', in Eileen Yeo (ed.) *Radical Femininity: Women's Self-Representation in the Public Sphere* (Manchester: Manchester University Press, 1998) pp. 149–171.

——, 'The Making of Suffrage History', in June Purvis and Sandra Stanley Holton (eds) *Votes for Women* (London: Routledge, 2000).

——, 'Gender Difference, National Identity and Professing History: The Case of Alice Stopford Green', *History Workshop Journal*, 53 (2002) 119–127. hooks, bell, 'Postmodern Blackness', in P Williams and L Chrisman (eds) *Colonial Discourse and Post-Colonial Theory: A Reader* (New York: Harvester Wheatsheaf, 1993).

Houts, Elisabeth Van, 'Women and the Writing of History in the Early Middle

Ages: The Case of Abbess Matilda of Essen and Æthelweard', *Early Medieval Europe*, 1 (1992) 53–68.

Hufton, Olwen, 'Women and the Family Economy in the Eighteenth Century France', *French Historical Studies*, 9 (1975) 38–53.

Huggins, Jackie, '"Firing on in the Mind": Aboriginal Women Domestic Servants in the Inter-War Years', *Hecate*, 13:2 (1987/1989) 5–23.

——, 'A Contemporary View of Aboriginal Women's Relationship to the White Women's Movement', in Norma Grieves and Ailsa Burns (eds) *Australian Women: Contemporary Feminist Thought* (Melbourne: Oxford University Press, 1994) pp. 70–79.

Hughes-Warrington, (ed.) M, 'Shapes', *Palgrave Advances in World Histories* (Basingstoke: Palgrave, 2005) pp. 112–134.

—— (ed.), 'World Histories', *Palgrave Advances in World Histories* (Basingstoke: Palgrave, 2004) pp. 1–17.

Hult, David F, 'The *Roman de la Rose*, Christine de Pizan and the *querelle des femmes*', in Carolyn Dinshaw and David Wallace (eds) *Cambridge Companion to Medieval Women's Writing* (Cambridge: Cambridge University Press, 2003) pp. 184–194.

Humpheries, Jane, 'Class Struggle and the Persistence of the Working Class Family', *Cambridge Journal of Economics*, 1 (1977) 214–258.

Hutcheson, Maud Macdonald, 'Mercy Warren, 1728–1814', *William & Mary Quarterly*, 10 (1953) 378–400.

Iriyagolle, Indrani, 'The Unique Position of Sinhala Women: A Historical Perspective', *Journal of the Royal Asiatic Society of Sri Lanka*, 34 (1989–1990) 78–101.

Jacobs, Ellen, 'Eileen Power (1889–1940)', in Helen Damico and Joseph B Zavadil (eds) *Medieval Scholarship: Biographical Studies on the Formation of a Discipline*, Vol. 1, *History* (New York and London: Garland Publishing, 1995) pp. 219–231.

——, 'Eileen Power's Asian Journey, 1920–21: History, Narrative, and Subjectivity', *Women's History Review*, 17:3 (1998) 295–319.

Jardine, Lisa, '"*O Decus Italiae Virgo*": Or, The Myth of the Learned Lady in the Renaissance', *The Historical Journal*, 28:4 (1985) 799–819.

Jeffrey, Julie Roy, 'Permeable Boundaries: Abolitionist Women and Separate Spheres', *Journal of the Early Republic*, 21:1 (2001) 79–93.

Johnson, Penelope D, 'Two Women Scholars Look at Medieval Nuns: Lina Eckenstein and JoAnn McNamara', *Magistra*, 3 (1997) 30–47.

Johnson, Susan M, 'Luther's Reformation and (Un)Holy Matrimony', *Journal of Family History*, 17:3 (1992) 271–288.

Jolly, Margaret, 'Colonizing Women: The Maternal Body and Empire', in S Gunew and Anna Yeatman (eds) *Feminism and the Politics of Difference* (Sydney: Allen & Unwin, 1993) pp. 103–127.

Jordon, Constance, 'Boccaccio's In-famous Women: Gender and Civic Virtue in *De claris mulieribus*', in Carole Levin and Jeanie Watson (eds) *Ambiguous Realities: Women in the Middle Ages and Renaissance* (Detroit: Wayne State University Press, 1987) pp. 25–47.

Karant-Nunn, Susan C, 'The Transmission of Luther's Teachings on Women and Matrimony: The Case of Zwickau', *Archiv fur Reformationsgeschichte*, 77 (1986) 31–46.

Keire, Mara L, 'Vice Trust: A Reinterpretation of the White Slavery Scare in the United States 1917', *Journal of Social History*, 35:1 (2001) 5–41.

Kelleher, Margaret, 'Writing Irish Women's Literary History', *Irish Studies Review*, 9:1 (2001) 5–14.

Keller, Frances Richardson, 'The Perspective of a Black American on Slavery and the French Revolution: Anna Julia Cooper', *Proceedings of the Annual Meeting of the Western Society for French History*, 3 (1975) 165–176.

Kelly, Joan, 'The Social Relation of the Sexes: Methodological Implications of Women's History', *Signs*, 1:4 (1976) 809–823.

——, 'Did Women Have a Renaissance?', in Renate Bridenthal and Claudia Koonz (eds) *Becoming Visible: Women in European History* (New York: Houghton Mifflin Co., 1977).

Kent, Eliza F, 'Tamil Bible Women and the Zenana Missions of Colonial South India', *History of Religions*, 39:2 (1999) 117–149.

Kerber, Linda, 'Separate Spheres, Female Worlds, Woman's Place: The Rhetoric of Women's History', *Journal of American History*, 75:1 (1988) 9–39.

Klein, Lawrence E, 'Gender, Conversation and the Public Sphere in Eighteenth Century England', in J Still and M Worton (eds) *Textuality and Sexuality: Reading Theories and Practice* (Manchester: Manchester University Press, 1993).

Koditschek, Theodore, 'The Gendering of the British Working Class', *Gender and History*, 9 (1997) 331–363.

Koecevic, Ivanka and S Barbara Kanner, 'Blue Book into Novel: The Forgotten Industrial Fiction of Charlotte Elizabeth Tonna', *Nineteenth Century Fiction* 25:2 (1970) 152–173.

Kostroun, D, 'A Formula for Disobedience: Jansenism, Gender and the Feminist Paradox', *Journal of Modern History*, 75:3 (2003) 483–522.

Kovacevic, I and B Kanner, '*Blue Book* into Novel: The Forgotten Fiction of Charlotte Elizabeth Tonna', *Nineteenth Century Fiction*, 25 (1970) 152–173.

Krebs, Paula, 'Olive Schreiner's Racialization of South Africa', *Victorian Studies*, 40:3 (1997) 427–444.

Kristeva, Julia, 'Women's Time', *Signs*, 7:1 (1981) 13–35.

Kronitiris, Tina, 'Style and Gender in Elizabeth Cary's Edward II', in Anne M Haselkorn and Betty S Travisky (eds) *The Renaissance Englishwoman in Print: Counterbalancing the Canon* (Amherst: University of Massachusetts Press, 1990) pp. 137–153.

Krueger, C L, 'Why She Lived in the PRO: Mary Anne Everett Green and the Profession of History', *Journal of British Studies*, 42 (2003) 65–90.

Kucich, Greg, 'Romanticism and Feminist Historiography', *The Wordsworth Circle*, 24 (1993) 133–140.

——, 'This Horrid Theatre of Human Suffering', in Thomas Pfau and Robert F Gleckner (eds) *Lessons of Romanticism* (Durham: Duke University Press, 1998) pp. 448–465.

——, 'Romanticism and the Re-engendering of Historical Memory', in Matthew Campbell, Jacqueline M Labbe and Sally Shuttleworth (eds) *Memory and Memorials, 1789–1914: Literary and Cultural Perspectives* (London and New York: Routledge, 2000) pp. 15–29.

——, 'Women's Historiography and the (Dis)embodiment of the Law: Ann Yearsley, Mary Hays, Elizabeth Benger', *Wordsworth Circle*, 33:1 (2002) 3–5.

Kwon, Insook, '"The New Women's Movement" in 1920s Korea: Rethinking the Relationship Between Imperialism and Women', in Mrinalini Sinha, Donna Guy and Angela Woollacott (eds), *Feminisms and Internationalism* (Oxford: Blackwell Publishers, 1999) pp. 37–61.

Laiou, Angeliki, 'Why Anna Komnene?', in Thalia Gouma-Peterson (ed.) *Anna Komnene and Her Times* (New York: Garland, 2000) pp. 1–14.

Lasser, Carol, 'Beyond Separate Spheres: The Power of Public Opinion', *Journal of the Early Republic*, 21:1 (2001) 115–123.

Lateiner, Donald, 'Elizabeth Hazelton Haight', *Classical World*, 90 (1996/1997) 153–166.

Laugesen, Amanda, 'Making a Unique Heritage: Historical Celebrations in Kansas, 1900–1920', *Kansas History: A Journal of the Central Plains*, 23:3 (2000) 172–185.

Laurence, Anne, 'Women Historians and Documentary Research: Lucy Aikin, Agnes Strickland, Mary Anne Everett Green, and Lucy Toulmin Smith', in Joan Bellamy, Anne Laurence and Gill Perry (eds) *Women, Scholarship, and Criticism: Gender and Knowledge c.1790–1900* (Manchester: Manchester University Press, 2000) pp. 125–141.

Lees, Jay T, 'Hrotsvit of Gandersheim and the Problem of Royal Succession in the East Frankish Kingdom', in Phyllis R Brown, Linda A McMillin and Katharina M Wilson (eds) *Hrotsvit of Gandersheim: Contexts, Identities, Affinities, and Perfor-mances* (Toronto, Buffalo and London: University of Toronto Press, 2004) pp. 13–28.

Lerner, Gerda, 'New Approaches to the Study of Women in American History', reprinted in Berenice Carroll (ed.) *Liberating Women's History* (Urbana: University of Illinois Press, 1976) pp. 26–41.

——, 'Placing Women in History' (1975), reprinted in Berenice Carroll (ed.) *Liberating Women's History* (Urbana: University of Illinois Press, 1976) pp. 357–367.

Lewis, Jane, 'Women Lost and Found: The Impact of Feminism on History', in Dale Spender (ed.) *Men's Studies Modified: The Impact of Feminism on the Academic Disciplines* (London: Pergamon Press, 1981) pp. 55–72.

Liddington, Jill, 'The Women's Peace Crusade', in Dorothy Thompson (ed.) *Over Our Dead Bodies* (London: Virago Press, 1983).

Liddle, Joanna and Shirin Rai, 'Feminism, Imperialism and Orientalism: The Challenge of the "Indian woman"', *Women's History Review*, 4 (1998) 495–520.

Loftus, R, 'Is There a Woman in the Text? Fukuda Hideko's Warawa no hanseigai', in J A Carson and J Rehn (eds) *In the Pacific Interest: Democracy, Women and the Environment*, Willamette Journal of the Arts Supplemental Series 4 (1991) 73–86.

Lovejoy, Esther P, 'Kate Campbell Hurd-Mead 1867–1941', *Bulletin of the History of Medicine*, 10 (1941) 314–317.

Lowe, K J P, 'History Writing from Within the Convent in Cinquecento Italy: the Nuns' Version', in L Panizza (ed.) *Women in Italian Renaissance Culture and Society* (Oxford: European Humanities Research Centre, 2000) pp. 105–121.

Luddy, Maria, 'Women and Politics in Nineteenth-Century Ireland', in Maryann Gialanella Valiulis and Mary O'Dowd (eds) *Women and Irish History: Essays in Honour of Margaret MacCurtain* (Dublin: Wolfhound Press, 1997) pp. 89–108.

MacCurtain, Margaret, 'The Teaching of History in Irish Schools', *Administration*, 15 (1967) 168–285.

Macek, Ellen, *The Emergency of a Feminine Spirituality in the Book of Martyrs Sixteenth Century Journal*, 19:1 (1988) 63–80.

McGrath, Ann, 'White Man's Looking Glass: Aboriginal-Colonial Gender Relations at Port Jackson', *Australian Historical Studies*, 24:9 (1990) 189–206.

Mackie, Vera, 'Sexual Violence, Silence, and Human Rights Discourse: The Emergence of the Military Prostitution Issue', in Anne Marie Hilsdon, Martha McIntyre, Vera Mackie and Maila Stivens (eds) *Human Rights and Gender Politics* (London: Routledge, 2000).

——, 'Women Questioning the Present: The Jûgoshi Nôto Collective', in Janice Brown and Sonja Arntzen (eds) *Across Time and Genre: Women's Writing in Japan* (Edmonton: University of Alberta, 2002).

Maidment, Brian, 'Popular Exemplary Biography in the Nineteenth Century: Edwin Paxton Hood and His Books', *Prose Studies*, 7 (1984) 148–167.

Maitzen, Rohan A, '"This Feminine Preserve?": Historical Biographies by Victorian Women', *Victorian Studies*, 38 (1995) 371–393.

Malcolmson, Cristina, 'Christine de Pizan's City of Ladies in Early Modern England', in Cristina Malcolmson and Mihoko Suzuki (eds) *Debating Gender in Early Modern England, 1500–1700* (London: Palgrave Macmillan, 2002) pp. 15–35.

Mantini, S., 'Women's History in Italy: Cultural Itineraries and New Proposals in Current Historiographical Trends', *Journal of Women's History*, 12:82 (2000) 170–198.

Marsh, R., 'Women Writers in the 1930s: Conformity or Subversion', in M Ilic (ed.) *Women in the Stalin Era* (London: Palgrave, 2001).

Marshall, Sherrin, 'Women and Religious Choices in the Sixteenth-Century Netherlands', *Archiv für Reformationsgeschichte*, 75 (1984) 276–289.

Martin, Judith E, 'Nineteenth Century German Literary Women's Reception of Madame de Stael', *Women in German Yearbook 2002* (Lincoln Nebraska: University of Nebraska Press, 2002).

Mellor, Ann, '"Am I not a Woman, and a Sister?": Slavery, Romaniticism, and Gender', in Alan Richardson and Sonia Hofkosh (eds) *Romanticism, Race, and Imperial Culture, 1780–1834'*, (Bloomington: Indiana Univer-sity Press, 1996).

Melman, Billie, 'Gender, History and Memory: The Invention of Women's Past in the Nineteenth and Early Twentieth Centuries', *History and Memory*, 5:5 (1993) 5–41.

Merton, R, 'The Normative Structure of Science', *The Sociology of Science* (Chicago: Chicago University Press, 1973) pp. 267–278.

Meskell, Lynn, 'Goddesses, Gimbutas, and "New Age" Archaeology', *Antiquity*, 69 (1995) 74–86.

——, 'Engendering Egypt', in Maria Wyke (ed.) *Gender and the Body in the Ancient Mediterranean* (Oxford: Blackwell Publishers, 1998) pp. 173–178.

Miller, Nancy K, 'But Enough About Me, What Do You Think of My Memoir?' *The Yale Journal of Criticism*, 13:2 (2000) 421–436.

Mitchell, Rosemary Ann, '"The Busy Daughters of Clio": Women Writers of History form 1820–1880', *Women's History Review*, 7:1 (1998) 107–134.

Mohanty, Chandra T, 'Under Western Eyes: Feminist Scholarship and Colonial Discourses', *Boundary*, 2:12 (1986) 333–358.

Moody Barry M, 'A View from the Front Steps. Esther Clark Wright and the Making of a Maritime Historian', in Beverley Boutilier and Alison Prentice (eds), *Creating Historical Memory: English-Canadian Women and the Work of History* (Vancouver: UBC Press, 1997) pp. 233–253.

Morantz, Regina, 'The Lady and Her Physician', in M S Hartman and L Banner (eds) *Clio's Consciousness Raised: New Perspectives on the History of Women* (New York: Harper Colophon, 1974) pp. 38–51.

Morris, M, 'Sexing the Survey: The Issue of Sexuality in World History since 1500', *World History Bulletin*, 14 (1998) 11–20.

Morrissey, Marietta, 'Women's Work, Family Formation and Reproduction among Caribbean Slaves', in Hilary Beckles and Verene Shepherd (eds) *Caribbean Slave Society and Economy* (London: James Currey, 1990) pp. 670–682.

Mulvey, Laura, 'Visual Pleasure and Narrative Cinema', *Screen*, 16:3 (1975) 6–18.

Nead, Linda, 'Feminism, Art History and Cultural Politics', in A L Rees and F Borzello (eds) *The New Art History* (London: Camden Press, 1986) pp. 120–124.

Newman, Sally, 'Silent Witness? Aileen Palmer and the Problem of Evidence in Lesbian History?' *Women's History Review*, 11:3 (2002) 505–530.

Nochlin, Linda, 'Why Have There been No Great Women Artists?' *Artnews*, January, 20–39 (1971) 67–71.

Norberg, Kathryn, 'Women, the Family, and the Counter-Reformation: Women's Confraternities in the Seventeenth Century', *Proceedings of the Annual Meeting of the Western Society for French History*, 6 (1978) 55–63.

Norris, John, 'Margaret Ormsby', in John Norris and Margaret Prang (eds) 'Personality and History in British Columbia: Essays in Honour of Margaret Ormsby', *BC Studies*, 32 (1976–1977) 11–27.

O'Brien, P, 'The Gaze of the Ghosts: Images of Aboriginal Women in New South Wales and Port Phillip 1800–1850', in Jan Kociumbas (ed.) *Maps, Dreams, History* (Sydney: Braxus, 1998) 313–400.

O'Halloran, Clare, 'Irish Re-creations of the Gaelic Past: The Challenge of MacPherson's Ossian', *Past and Present*, 124 (1989) 69–95.

Olsen, U S, 'The Late Medieval Chronicle of Marie van Oss', in E Kooper (ed.) *The Medieval Chronicle* (Amsterdam: Rodopi, 1999) pp. 240–250.

Ortner, S, 'Is Female to Male as Nature is to Culture?', in Michelle Zimbalist Rosaldo and Louise Lamphere (eds) *Woman, Culture, and Society* (Stanford: Stanford University Press, 1974) pp. 67–88.

O'Shane, Pat, 'Is There Any Relevance in the Women's Movement for Aboriginal Women?', *Refractory Girl*, 12 (1976) 31–34.

Owens, Rosemary Cullen, 'Votes for Women', *Labour History News*, 9 (1993) 15–19.

Paisley, Fiona, 'Introduction' in 'New Comparisons/International Worlds', special issue of *Australian Feminist Studies*, 16:36 (2001) 271–277.

Palmieri, Patricia A, 'Here was Fellowship: A Social Portrait of Academic Women at Wellesley College, 1895–1920', *History of Education Quarterly*, 23:2 (1983) 195–214.

Park, Katherine, 'The Rediscovery of the Clitoris: French Medicine and the Tribade 1570–1620', in C Mazzio (ed.) *The Body in Parts: Fantasies of Corporeality in Early Modern Europe* (London: Routledge, 1997) pp. 171–194.

Passman, Tina, 'Out of the Closet and into the Field: Matriculture, the Lesbian Perspective, and Feminist Classics', in Nancy Sorkin Rabinowitz and Amy Richlin (eds) *Feminist Theory and the Classics* (New York: Routledge, 1993) pp. 181–208.

Penn, Donna, 'Queer: Theorizing Politics and History', *Radical History Review*, 62 (1995) 24–42.

Perry, A, 'Writing Women into British Columbia History', *BC Studies*, 122 (1999) 85–88.

Perry, Ruth, 'George Ballard's Biographies of Learned Ladies', in J D Browning (ed.) *Biography in the 18th Century* (New York and London: Garland Publishing, 1980) pp. 85–111.

——, 'Colonising the Breast: Sexuality and Maternity in Eighteenth Century England', in J C Fout (ed.) *Forbidden History: The State, Society and the Regulation of Sexuality in Modern Europe* (Chicago: University of Chicago Press, 1992) pp. 107–138.

Phythian-Adams, Charles, 'Frontier Valleys', in Joan Thirsk (ed.) *Rural England: An Illustrated History of the Landscape* (Oxford: Oxford University Press, 2000)

Pieri, Stefania *et al.*, 'Italian Migrant Women, Participation and the Women's Movement', in Margaret Bevege, Margaret James and Carmel Shute (eds) *Worth Her Salt: Women at Work in Australia* (Sydney: Hale & Iremonger, 1982) pp. 389–399.

Pocock, J G A, 'Catherine Macauley: Patriot Historian', in Hilda Smith (ed.), *Women Writers and the Early Modern British Political Tradition* (Cambridge: Cambridge University Press, 2002) pp. 243–258.

Pomper, P, R H Elphick and R T Vann (eds), *World History: Ideologies, Structures, and Identities* (Oxford: Blackwell, 1998).

Poovey, Mary, '"Scenes of an Indelicate Character": The Medical "Treatment" of Victorian Women', *Representations*, 14 (1986) pp. 137–168.

Porciani, Ilaria, *Les historiennes et le Risorgimento*, «Mélanges de l'Ecole Française de Rome. Italie et Méditerranée», tome 112 – 1 –2000, 317–357.

——, *Famiglia e nazione nel lungo Ottocento*, in Famiglia Stato Società civile, special issue of 'Passato e Presente', ed. Paul Ginsborg and Ilaria Porciani, 57 (2002) 9–39.

Porciani, Ilaria and Mary O'Dowd (eds), *History Women*, special issue of Storia della storiografia, 46 (2004).

Potter, Mary, 'Gender Equality and Gender Hierarchy in Calvin's Theology', *Signs*, 11:4 (1986) 725–739.

Prakash, G, 'Subaltern Studies as Postcolonial Criticism', *American Historical Review*, 99:5 (1994) 1475–1490.

Prazniak, R, 'Is World History Possible?', in A Dirlik, V Bahl and P Gran (eds), *History after the Three Worlds: Post-Eurocentric Historiography* (Lanham, MD: Rowman and Littlefield, 2000).

Prentice, Alison, 'Laying Siege to the History Professoriate', in Beverley Boutilier and Alison Prentice (eds) *Creating Historical Memory: English-Canadian Women and the Work of History* (Vancouver: UBC Press, 1997) pp. 197–232.

Pritchard, Sarah, 'Library of Congress Resources for the Study of Women', in Suzanne Hildenbrand (ed.) *Women's Collections: Libraries, Archives, and Consciousness* (New York: Haworth, 1986) pp. 13–36.

Rabinowitz, Nancy Sorkin, 'Excavating Women's Homoeroticism in Ancient Greece: The Evidence from Attic Vase Painting', in Nancy Sorkin Rabinowitz and Lisa Auanger (eds) *Among Women. From the Homosocial to the Homoerotic in the Ancient World* (Austin: University of Texas Press, 2002) pp. 106–166.

Ralston, C, '"Prostitution", "pollution" and "polyandry": The problems of Eurocentrism and Androcentrism in Polynesian Studies', in Barbara Caine, E A Grosz and Marie de Lepervanche (eds) *Crossing Boundaries: Feminism and the Critique of Knowledges* (Sydney: Allen & Unwin, 1988) pp. 71–80.

Ramusack, Barbara, 'The Indian Princes as Fantasy: Palace Hotels, Palace Museums, and Palace on Wheels', in Carol A Breckenridge (ed.) *Consuming Modernity: Public Culture in a South Asian World* (Minneapolis: University of Minnesota Press, 1995).

Randall Martin, 'Anne Dowriche's *The French History*, Christopher Marlow, and Machiavellian Agency', *Studies in English Literature*, 39:1 (1999) 68–87.

Rang, Brita, 'A "Learned Wave": Women of Letters and Science from, the Renaissance to the Enlightenment', in Tjitske Akkerman and Siep Stuurman (eds) *Perspectives on Feminist Political Thought in European History: From the Middle Ages to the Present* (London: Routledge, 1998) pp. 50–67.

Rendall, Jane, 'Writing History for British Women: Elizabeth Hamilton and the Memoirs of Agrippina', in Clarissa Campell Orr (ed.) *Wollstonecraft's Daughters* (Manchester: Manchester University Press, 1996) pp. 79–93.

——, '"The Grand Causes Which Combine to Carry Mankind Forward": Wollstonecraft, History and Revolution', *Women's Writing*, 4:2 (1997) 155–172.

Rich, Adrienne, 'Compulsory Heterosexuality and Lesbian Existence', *Signs*, 5 (1980) 631–660.

Richards, Earl Jeffrey, 'Christine de Pizan and Sacred History', in Margarete

Zimmermann and Dina De Rentiis (eds) *The City of Scholars: New Approaches to Christine de Pizan* (Berlin and New York: Walter de Gruyter, 1994) pp. 14–30.

——, 'Rejecting Essentialism and Gendered Writing: The Case of Christine de Pizan', in Jane Chance (ed.) *Gender and Text: In the Later Middle Ages*, (Gainesville: University Press of Florida, 1996) pp. 96–131.

Richlin, Amy, 'Zeus and Metis: Foucault, Feminism, Classics', *Helios*, 18 (1991) 160–180.

——, 'Hijacking the Palladion: Feminists in Classics', *Gender and History*, 4 (1992) 70–83.

——, 'The Ethnographer's Dilemma and the Dream of a Lost Golden Age', in Nancy Sorkin Rabinowitz and Amy Richlin (eds) *Feminist Theory and the Classics* (New York: Routledge, 1993) pp. 272–303.

Robin, Diane, 'Women, Space and Renaissance Discourse', in Barbara K Gold, Paul Allen Miller and Charles Platter (eds) *Sex and Gender in Medieval and Renaissance Texts* (Albany: State University of New York Press, 1997b) pp. 165–188.

Robinson, Annabel, 'Something Odd at Work: The Presence of Jane Harrison in *A Room of One's Own*', in Eleanor McNees (ed.) *Virginia Woolf. Critical Assessments II Critical Responses to the Short Stories, Sketches and Essays, Feminist Treatises and Biographies* (Mountfield near Robertsbridge: Helm Information Ltd, 1994) pp. 215–220.

Roekler, Nancy, 'The Role of Noblewomen in the French Reformation', *Archiv für Reformationsgeschichte*, 63 (1972).

——, 'The Appeal of Calvinism to French Noblewomen in the Sixteenth Century', *Journal of Interdisciplinary History*, 2 (1972) 391–418.

Rose, Sonya O, 'Respectable Men, Disorderly Others: The Language of Gen-der and the Lancashire Weavers' Strike of 1878 in Britain', *Gender and History*, 5 (1993) 382–397.

Rowbotham, Judith, '"Soldiers of Christ"? Images of Female Missionaries in Late Nineteenth-Century Britain: Issues of Heroism and Martyrdom', *Gender & History*, 12:1 (2000) 82–106.

Rubin, Gayle, 'The Traffic in Women: Notes on the Political Economy of Sex', in Rayna Reiter (ed.) *Toward an Anthropology of Women* (New York: Monthly Review Press, 1975) pp. 157–210.

Saunders, Kay, 'Pacific Islander Women in Queensland: 1863–1907', in Margaret Bevege, Margaret James and Carmel Shute (eds) *Worth Her Salt: Women and Work* (Sydney: Hale & Iremonger, 1982) pp. 16–32.

Schick, Irvin Cemil, 'Representing Middle Eastern Women: Feminism and Colonial Discourse', *Feminist Studies*, 16:2 (1990) 345–380.

Schlesier, Renate, 'Jane Ellen Harrison', in W W Briggs and W M Calder III (eds) *Classical Scholarship. A Biographical Encyclopedia* (New York and London: Garland Publishing, Inc., 1990) pp. 127–141.

——, 'Prolegomena to Jane Harrison's Interpretation of Ancient Greek Religion', in W M Calder III (ed.) *The Cambridge Ritualists Reconsidered*, Illinois Classical Studies Suppl. 2 (Atlanta, Georgia: Scholars Press, 1991) pp. 185–226.

Schnorrenberg, Barbara Brandon, 'The Brood Hen of Faction: Mrs Macaulay and Radical Politics 1765–1775', *Albion*, 11:1 (1979) 33–45.

Schulkind, E, 'Socialist Women during the 1871 Paris Commune', *Past and Present*, 106 (1985) 124–163.

Scott, Joan and Tilly, Louise, 'Women's Work and the Family in Nineteenth Century Europe', *Comparative Studies in Society and History*, 17:1 (1975) 36–54.

Scott, Joan Wallach, 'Women's History', *Past and Present: A Journal of Historical Studies,* 101 (1983) 141–157.

——, 'Gender and Useful Category of Analysis', *American Historical Review,* 91 (1986) 1053–1075.

——, 'On Language, Gender and Working Class History', *International Labour and Working Class History,* 31 (1987) 1–36.

——, 'The Evidence of Experience', *Critical Inquiry,* 17 (1991) 773–797.

——, 'Fantasy Echo: History and the Construction of Identity', *Critical Inquiry,* 27 (2001) 284–304.

Sheerin, Daniel, 'Elizabeth Gaskell's Manchester', *The Gaskell Society Journal,* 3 (1989).

——, 'Sisters in the Literary Agon: Texts from Communities of Women on the Mortuary Roll of the Abbess Matilda of La Trinité, Caen', in Laurie J Churchill, Phyllis R Brown and Jane E Jeffrey (eds) *Women Writing Latin,* Vol. 2, *From Early Roman Antiquity to Early Modern Europe* (New York and London: Routledge, 2002) pp. 93–131.

Shelston, Alan, 'Elizabeth Gaskell's Manchester', *The Gaskell Society Journal,* 3 (1989) 46–67.

——, 'Elizabeth Gaskell and Her Critics', *Elizabeth Gaskell, Mary Barton* (London: Everyman, 1996) pp. 414–434.

Shohat, Ella, 'Notes on the 'Post-Colonial', *Social Text,* 31/32 (1992) 99–113.

Simons, Margaret A, 'In Memoriam', *Yale French Studies,* 72 (1986) 203–206.

Sinha, Mrinalini, 'Reading Mother India: Empire, Nation and the Female Voice', *Journal of Women's History,* 6 (1994) 6–44.

Sirridge, Marjorie S and R Brenda, Pfannenstiel, 'Daughters of Aesculpius: A Selected Bibliography of Autobiographies of Women Medical School Graduates, 1849–1920', *Literature and Medicine,* 15:2 (1996) pp. 200–216.

Skinner, Marilyn B, 'Classical Studies vs. Women's Studies: *duo moi ta noemmata*', *Helios,* 12 (1985) 3–16.

——, 'Rescuing Creusa: New Methodological Approaches to Women in Antiquity', in M Skinner (ed.) *Rescuing Creusa: New Methodological Approaches to Women in Antiquity* (A Special Issue of *Helios,* NS, 13:2 (1987) 1–8).

——, 'Expecting the Barbarians: Feminism, Nostalgia, and the "Epistemic Shift" in Classical Studies', in P Culham and L Edmunds (eds) *Classics: A Discipline and Profession in Crisis?* (Lanham: University Press of America, 1989) pp. 199–210.

Smith, Bonnie G, 'The Contribution of Women to Modern Historiography in Great Britain, France, and the United States 1750–1940', *American Historical Review,* 89 (1984) 709–732.

Smith-Rosenberg, Carroll, 'The Female Animal: Medical and Biological Views of Woman and Her Role in Nineteenth Century America', *Journal of American History,* 60 (1973) 332–356.

——, 'The New Woman and the New History', *Feminist Studies,* 3:1–2 (1975) 171–198.

——, 'Female World of Love and Ritual: Relations between Women in Nineteenth-Century America', *Signs,* 1:1 (1975) 1–30.

——, 'Writing History: Language, Class and Gender', in T de Lauretis (ed.) *Feminist Studies/Critical Studies* (Bloomington: Indiana University Press, 1986) pp. 31–54.

Smyth, Elizabeth, '"Writing Teaches Us Our Mysteries": Women Religious Recording and Writing History', in Beverley Boutilier and Alison Prentice (eds) *Creating Historical Memory: English-Canadian Women and the Work of History* (Vancouver: UBC Press, 1997) pp. 101–128.

Sondheimer, J, 'Helen Cam, 1885–1968', in E Shils and C Blacker (eds) *Cambridge*

Women: Twelve Portraits (Cambridge: Cambridge University Press, 1996) pp. 93–112.

Spivak, Gayatri Chakravorty, 'Three Women's Texts and a Critique of Imperialism', *Critical Inquiry*, 12:1 (1985) 43–61.

——, 'Can the Subaltern Speak?', in C Nelson and L Grossberg (eds) *Marxism and the Interpretation of Culture* (Urbana: University of Illinois Press, 1988).

Staff, Elizabeth, 'A Great Engine for Good: The Industry of Fiction in Elizabeth Gaskell's *Mary Barton* and *North and South*', *Studies in the Novel*, 34:1 (2002) 400–421.

Stanley, Liz, 'Is There a Feminist Auto/Biography?', *The Auto/Biographical I: The Theory and Practice of Feminist Auto/Biography* (Manchester: Manchester University Press, 1992) pp. 240–256.

——, 'Shadows Lying across Her Pages: Epistolary Aspects of Reading "The Eventful I" in Olive Schreiner's Letters', *Journal of European Studies*, 32:125/126 (2002) 251–266.

Stapleton, Mrs Bryan, 'Three Oxfordshire Parishes: Kidlington, Yarnton and Begbroke', *Oxfordshire Historical Society*, 24 (1895).

Starr, Elizabeth, 'A Great Engine for Good: The Industry of Fiction in Elizabeth Gaskell's *Mary Barton* and *North and South*', *Studies in the Novel*, 34:1 (2002) 385–400.

Steedman, Carolyn, 'Bimbos from Hell', *Social History*, 19:1 (1994) 57–67.

Stoler, Ann Laura, 'Carnal Knowledge and Imperial Power: Gender, Race and Morality in Colonial Asia', in Micaela di Leonardo (ed.) *Gender at the Crossroads of Knowledge: Feminist Anthropology in the Postmodern Era* (Berkeley: University of California Press, 1991) pp. 51–101.

——, 'Sexual Affronts and Racial Frontiers: European Identities and the Cultural Politics of Exclusion in Colonial South East Asia', *Comparative Studies in Society and History*, 34:3 (1992) 514–551.

——, 'Making Empire Respectable: The Politics of Race and Sexual Morality in Twentieth-Century Colonial Cultures', in Anne McClintock, Aamir Mufti and Ella Shohat (eds) *Dangerous Liaisons: Gender, Nation, & Postcolonial Perspectives* (Minneapolis: Uni-versity of Minnesota Press, 1997) pp. 344–373.

Strasser, Ulrike, 'Cloistering Women's Past: Conflicting Accounts of Enclosure in a Seventeenth-Century Munich Nunnery', in Ulrike Rublack (ed.) *Gender in Early Modern German History* (Cambridge: Cambridge University Press, 2002) pp. 221–246.

Suleri, S, 'Woman Skin Deep: Feminism and the Postcolonial Condition', *Critical Inquiry*, 18 (1992) 756–769.

Suny, R G, 'Revision and Retreat in the Historiography of 1917: Social History and Its Critics', *The Russian Review*, 53 (1994) 165–182.

——, 'History', in A Motyl (ed.) *Encyclopedia of Nationalism* (San Diego: Academic, 2000) pp. 337–358.

Suzuki, Mihoko, 'Anne Clifford and the Gendering of History', *Clio*, 30:2 (2001) 195–217.

Swerdlow, Amy, 'Abolition's Conservative Sisters: The Ladies' New York City Anti-Slavery Societies', in Jean Fagan Yellin and John C Van Horne (eds) *The Abolitionist Sisterhood: Women's Political Culture in Antebellum America* (Ithaca: Cornell University Press, 1994) pp. 31–44.

——, 'The Congress of American Women', in Linda Kerber, Alice Kessler-Harris and Kathryn Kish Sklar (eds) *US History as Women's History* (Chapel Hill: University of North Carolina Press, 1995) pp. 292–312.

Swindells, Julia, 'Liberating the Subject? Autobiography and "Women's History": A Reading of *The Diaries of Hannah Cullwick*', in The Personal Narratives

Group (eds) *Interpreting Women's Lives: Feminist Theory and Personal Narratives* (Bloomington: Indiana University Press, 1989) pp. 24–38.

Tanaka, K, 'The New Feminist Movement in Japan, 1970–1990', in K Fujimura-Fanselow and A Kameda (eds) *Japanese Women: New Feminist Perspectives on the Past, Present and Future* (New York: The Feminist Press, 1995).

Teague, Frances and Rebecca de Haas, 'Defences of Women', in Anita Pacheco (ed.) *A Companion to Early Modern Women's Writing* (Oxford: Blackwell, 2002) pp. 248–263.

Terborg-Penn, R, 'Discrimination Against Afro-American Women in the Women's Movement 1830–1920', in Filomina Chioma Steady (ed.) *The Black Woman Cross Culturally* (Vermont: Schenkman Books, 1981).

Terrall, M, 'Emilie Du Chatelet and the Gendering of Science', *History of Science*, 33 (1995) 283–310.

Terry, Jennifer, 'Theorizing Deviant Historiography', *Differences: A Journal of Feminist Cultural Studies*, 3:2 (1991) 55–74.

Thirsk, Joan, 'The History Women', in Mary O'Dowd and S Wichert (eds) *Chattel, Servant or Citizen: Women's Status in Church, State and Society* (Belfast: Institute of Irish Studies, 1995) pp. 1–11.

——, 'Women Local and Family Historians', in David Hey (ed.) *Oxford Companion to Local and Family History* (Oxford: Oxford University Press, 1996) pp. 498–504.

Thomas, L M, '"Ngaitana" (I will circumcise myself)': The Gender and Generational Politics of the 1956 Ban on Clitoridectomy in Meru, Kenya', in N R Hunt (ed.) *Gendered Colonialism in African History* (Oxford: Blackwell, 1997) pp. 16–41.

Thornton, B D, 'Race, Class and Gender: Prospects for an all-inclusive Sisterhood' *Feminist Studies*, 9:1 (1983) 131–148.

Tickner, Linda, 'Feminism, Art History and Sexual Difference', *Genders*, 3 (1998) 92–128.

Tilly, L A, 'Industrialisation and Gender Inequality', in M Adas (ed.) *Islamic and European Expansion: The Forging of a Global Order* (Philadelphia: Temple University Press, 1993) pp. 243–310.

Tomaselli, Sylvana, 'The Enlightenment Debate on Women', *History Workshop Journal*, 20 (1985) 101–124.

Toynbee, A J, 'A Woman's Life in Other Ages', in P J Corfield and P Ferrari (eds) *Historical Research*, 74:183 (2001) 1–16.

Traub, Valerie, 'The Psychomorphology of the Clitoris', *Gay and Lesbian Quarterly*, 2 (1995) 81–113.

Travisky, Betty, 'The Feme Covert in Elizabeth Cary's Mariam', in Carole Levin and Jeanie Watson (eds) *Ambiguous Realities: Women in the Middle Ages and Renaissance* (Detroit: Wayne State University Press, 1987) pp. 184–196.

Tsurumi, E P, 'Feminism and Anarchism in Japan: Takamure Itsue, 1894–1964', *Bulletin of Concerned Asian Scholars*, 17:2 (1985) 2–19.

Tucker, J, 'Gender and Islamic History', in M Adas (ed.) *Islamic and European Expansion: The Forging of a Global Order* (Philadelphia: Temple University Press, 1993) pp. 37–74.

Tweed, Thomas, 'An American Pioneer in the Study of Religion: Hannah Adams and her *Dictionary of All Religions*', *Journal of the American Academy of Religion*, 60:5 (1992) 437–464.

Tyler-Bennet, Deborah, 'Women's Voices Speak for Themselves: Gender, Subversion and the Women's Voices Anthology of 1887', *Women's History Review*, 4:2 (1995) 165–175.

Umble, Jennifer, 'Women and Choice: An Examination of the *Martyr's Mirror*', *Mennonite Quarterly Review*, 64 (1990) 135–145.

Vella, Michael W, 'Theology, Genre and Gender: The Precarious Place of Hannah

Adams in American Literary History', *Early American Literature*, 28 (1993) 21–41.

Vicinus, Martha, 'Sexuality and Power: A Review of Current Work in the History of Sexuality', *Feminist Studies*, 8:1 (1982) 133–156.

——, 'Distance and Desire: English Boarding School Friendships, 1870–1920', in Martin Bauml Duberman, Martha Vicinus and George Chauncey, Jr (eds) *Hidden from History: Reclaiming the Gay and Lesbian Past* (New York: New American Library, 1989) pp. 212–232.

Von Laue, T H, 'World History, Cultural Relativism, and the Global Future', in P Pomper, R E Elphick and R T Vann (eds) *World History: Ideologies, Structures, and Identities* (Oxford: Blackwell, 1998) pp. 217–234.

Walton, Whitney, 'Writing the 1848 Revolution: Politics, Gender, and Feminism in the Works of French Women of Letters', *French Historical Studies*, 18:4 (1994) 1001–1024.

Watson, Nicola J, 'Gloriana Victoriana: Victoria and the Cultural Memory of Elizabeth I', in Margaret Homans and Adrienne Munich (eds) *Remaking Queen Victoria* (Cambridge: Cambridge University Press, 1997) pp. 79–104.

Weaver, F E, 'Angelique de Saint-Jean de Port-Royal: The "Third Superior" as "Mythographer" in the Dynamics of Reform Caught in a Controversy', *Cistercians in the Late Middle Ages* (Kalamazoo, Mich: Cistercian Publications, 1981) pp. 90–101.

White, D G, 'Female Slaves: Sex Roles and Status in the Antebellum Plantation South', *Journal of Family History*, 8 (1983) 248–251.

White, P, 'Science at Home: The Space between Thomas Huxley and Henrietta Heathorn', *History of Science*, 34 (1996) 33–56.

Wiesner Merry E, 'Beyond Women and the Family: Towards a Gender Analysis of the Reformation', *Sixteenth Century Journal*, 18:3 (1987) 311–321.

——, 'Women's Responses to the Reformation', in R Po-Chia Hsia (ed.) *The German People and the Reformation* (Ithaca: Cornell University Press, 1988) pp. 148–172.

——, 'Ideology Meets the Empire: Reformed Convents and the Reformation', in S Karant-Nunn and Andrew Fix (eds) *Germania Illustrata: Essays Presented to Gerald Strauss* (Kirksville, MO: Sixteenth Century Journal Publishers, 1991) pp. 181–196.

Wikander, Ulla, 'Some "Kept the Flag of Feminist Demands Waving": Debates at the International Congress on Protecting Women Worker's in Ulla Wikander, Alice Kessler-Harris and Jane Lewis (eds) *Protecting Women: Labor Legislation in Europe, the United States and Australia* (Urbana: University of Illinois Press, 1995) pp. 29–62.

Williams, S, *Rand Women Pioneers:* They did their level best (Johannesburg, 1992).

Wilson, J H, 'The Illusion of Change: Women and the American Revolution', in A F Young (ed.) *The American Revolution Explorations in the History of American Radicalism* (DeKalb: Northern Illinois University Press, 1976) pp. 311–330.

Wiss, R, 'Lipreading: Remembering Saartje Baartman', *The Australian Journal of Anthropology*, 5:1–2 (1994) 11–40.

Withey, Lynne E, 'Catherine Macaulay and the Uses of History: Ancient Rights, Perfectionism and Propaganda', *Journal of British Studies* (1976) 59–83.

Wöhr, U, 'A Touchstone for Transnational Feminism: Discourses on the Comfort Women in 1990s Japan', *Japanstudien* (2004).

Wood, Ann Douglas, 'The Fashionable Diseases: Women's Complaints and Their Treatment in Nineteenth Century America', *Journal of Interdisciplinary History*, 4:1 (1973) 25–52.

Wood, Elizabeth, 'Lesbian Fugue: Ethel Smyth's Contrapuntal Arts', in Ruth Solie (ed.) *Musicology and Difference: Gender and Sexuality in Music Scholarship* (Berkeley: University of California Press, 1993).

Wood, Susan, 'God's Doormats: Women in Canadian Prairie Fiction', *Journal of Popular Culture*, 14:2 (1980) 350–359.

Woolf, Daniel R, 'A Feminine Past? Gender, Genre, and Historical Knowledge in England, 1500–1800', *American Historical Review*, 102:3 (1997) 645–679.

Worth, Rita, 'Introduction: Gendered Ways of Knowing in Archaeology', in R Worth (ed.), *Gender and Archaeology* (Philadelphia: University of Pennsylvania Press, 1996) pp. 1–19.

Wright, Celeste Turner, 'The Elizabethan Female Worthies', *Studies in Philology*, 43 (1946) 628–643.

Wunder, H, ' "Gewirkte Geschichte": Gedenken und "Handarbeit" ', in H Wunder (ed.) *Der andere Blick auf die frühe Neuzeit: Forschungen 1974–1995* (Königstein, 1999) pp. 289–311.

Wylie, Alison, 'Gender, Theory and the Archaeological Record: Why is There No Archaeology of Gender', in Joan M Gero and Margaret W Conkey (eds) *Engendering Archaeology: Women and Prehistory* (Oxford: Basil Blackwell, 1991) pp. 3–30.

Zinsser, J P, 'And Now for Something Completely Different: Gendering the World History Survey', *Perspectives* (American Historical Association) 34 (1996) 11.

——, 'Gender', in M Hughes-Warrington (ed.) *Palgrave Advances in World Histo-ries* (Basingstoke: Palgrave, 2005) pp. 189–214.

Zonana, Joyce, 'The Sultan and the Slave: Feminist Orientalism and the Structure of Jane Eyre', *Signs* (1993) 592–617.

Theses

Alves Susan, '*A Thousand Times I'd Rather Be a Factory Girl': The Politics of Reading American and British Female Factory Workers' Poetry 1840–1915*', PhD Thesis, Northeastern University, 1996.

Connolly, Claire, *Gender, Nation and Ireland in the Early Novels of Maria Edgeworth and Lady Morgan*, PhD Thesis, University of Wales, Cardiff, 1995.

Forsyth, Michael, *Julia Kavanagh in Her Times: Novelist and Biographer 1824–1877*, PhD Thesis, Open University, 1999.

Laugesen, Amanda, *Making Western Pasts: Historical Societies of Kansas, Wisconsin and Oregon, 1870–1920*, PhD Thesis, Australian National University, 2000.

Mair, Lucille Mathurin, *An Historical Study of Women in Jamaica from 1654–1844*, PhD Thesis, University of the West Indies, Jamaica, 1974.

Unpublished manuscripts and papers

Holt, Emily S, *Library Catalogue. Norman F. Colbeck Collection*, vol. 6. University of North Carolina, Chapel Hill.

——, *Poems. Norman F. Colbeck Collection*, vol. 7. University of North Carolina, Chapel Hill, 1864.

Jammal, Nadine, 'La contribution des Quebecoises francophones a l'emergence de la discipline historique au Quebec (1900–1960)', unpublished research report (1999).

Websites

Germer, Andrea, 'Feminist History in Japan: National and International Perspectives'. *Intersections*, 9(2003). wwwsshe.murdoch.edu.au/intersections/issue9/germer.html.

Judy Norsigian, Vilunya Diskin, Paula Doress-Worters, Jane Pincus, Wendy Sanford and Norma Swenson, 'The Boston Women's Health Book Collective and *Our Bodies, Ourselves*: A Brief History and Reflection', *Journal of the American Medical Women's Association* (1999), www.ourbodiesourselves.org/jamwa.htm.

Laura Cottingham, 'Notes on "lesbian." – historical narrative of lesbianism – We're Here: Gay and Lesbian Presence in Art and Art History', *Art Journal* (1996), www.findarticles.com/p/articles/mi_m0425/is_n4_v55/ai_19101787/pg_2.

Index

Abbott, Edith, 564
Abbott, Elizabeth, 407
  History of Celibacy, 407
Abel, Annie Heloise, 566
  The Slaveholding Indians, 566
Abolition, 1–3, 20, 146, 416, 547, 561
Aboriginal women's writing, 50, 388, 418–19, 605–6
Abu-Lughod, Lila, 397
  Remaking Women, 397
  Veiled Sentiments, 397
Ackermann, Jessie, 119
  Australia from a Woman's Point of View, 119, 125
  The World through a Woman's Eye, 119
Ackland, Valentine, 310
Adams, Hannah, 3, 58, 461, 562
  An Alphabetical Compendium of the Various Sects, 3, 461
  History of the Jews, 3, 461
  memoir, 3, religious history, 3, 461
  A Summary History of New England, 3, 562
Adburgham, Alison, 607
  Women in Print, 607
Addams, Jane, 407, 409, 506
  Peace and Bread in Time of War, 407
  The Newer Ideals of Peace, 407
Adler, Ada, 6
Ady, Cecilia Mary, 3–4
  Bentivolgio of Bologna, 4
  daughter of Julia Cartwright, 3–4
  History of Milan under the Sforza, 4
  Lorenzo di Medici and Renaissance Italy, 4
  Pius II: The Humanist Pope, 4
  Renaissance art and culture, 4
  The Role of Women in the Church, 2–3, 4
African-American women writers, 2, 28, 415–29, 560–70, 605–6
Ago, Renata, 288
Agoult, Marie d', 211, 480
  Essai de la Liberté, 211, 480
  Histoire de la Révolution de 1848, 211, 480
Agrippina, Julia, [the elder], 17
  Elizabeth Hamilton's *Memoirs of Agrippina*, 234
Agrippina, Julia, [the younger], 17, 161, 179, 515
  Commentarii, 17, 161, 515
Ahmed, Leila, 397, 464
  Women and Gender in Islam, 397, 464
Aikenhead, Mary, 268, 269
  History of . . . the Irish Sisters of Charity, 268
Aikin, Lucy, 4–5, 25, 453, 498–9, 500, 503, 614
  Epistles on Women, 4, 498, 614
  memoirs of Anna Laetitia Barbauld, 5
  Memoirs of the Court of Charles I, 4
  Memoirs of the Court of James I, 4
  Memoirs of the Court of Queen Elizabeth, 4, 498
  niece of Anna Laetitia Barbauld, 5
  poetry, 4
  relationship with Elizabeth Benger, 5
  relationship with Elizabeth Hamilton, 5
  relationship with Sarah Taylor Austin, 5
Aitken, Maria, 559
  A Girdle Round the Earth, 559
Albert, Jeanne d', 206, 451
  Ample déclaration sur la jonction des ses armes des Reformés en, 206, 451
Albinski, Nan Bowman, 571
  Women's Utopia's, 571
Albright, Madelenie, 330–1
  Madame Secretary, 330–1
Albrizzi, Isabella Teotochi, 276
Alcott, Louisa May, 406, 485
  Little Women, 406
Alessi, Giorgia, 288
Alexander, Sally, 263, 602
  Becoming A Woman, 263
Alexander, William, 153
  History of Women . . ., 153
Alic, Margaret, 511
  Hypatia's Heritage, 511
Allason-Jones, Lindsay, 229
  Roman Women . . ., 229
Allason, Barbara, 283

Allen, Alexandra, 558
Travelling Ladies . . ., 558
Allen, Ann Taylor, 162
Allen, Hope Emily, 345
Ancrene Riwle, 345
Allen, Judith, 50, 70, 605
Rose Scott, 50
Sex and Secrets . . ., 70
Allen, Margaret, 48, 51
Fresh Evidence, New Witnesses, 48
Allen, Paula Gunn, 569
The Sacred Hoop, 569
Allies, Mary Helen, 224
Alloula, Malek, 391
The Colonial Harem, 391
Alonso, Harriet Hyman, 408, 409, 410
Peace as Women's Issue, 410
The Women's Peace Union and the Outlawry of War, 408
Alverny, Marie-Thérèse, 347
Ancient history, 5–15
Ancient world, xvii, 5–15
Anderson, Bonnie, 192, 616
Joyous Greetings, 192
Women in Early Modern and Modern Europe [with Judith Zinsser], 616
Anderson, Carol, 95
Eyes off the Prize . . ., 95
Anderson, Elizabeth Garrett, 376
Ang, Ien, 369
Angela of Foligno, 342
Memoriale, 342
Angelou, Maya, 418, 570
I Know Why the Caged Bird Sings, 418, 570
Ankum, Katharina, von, 354
Women in the Metropolis, 354
Anne of France, 344
Lessons for My Daughter, 344
Anonymous
Women Intelligent and Courageous in Warfare, 612
Anthias, Flora, 370
Woman-Nation-State [with Nira Yuval-Davis], 369–70
Anthony, Susan B., 1, 19, 94, 101, 114, 115, 184, 195, 216, 568
abolition, 1, 20
autobiography,195
friendship with Gage, 21, 217
friendship with Stanton, *History of Woman Suffrage* [with Matilda Joslyn Gage and Elizabeth Cady Stanton], 1, 94, 101, 114, 115, 184, 542–3
Woman's Declaration of Rights [with Susan B Anthony and Elizabeth Cady Stanton], 217
Antler, Joyce, 139
The Educated Woman . . ., 139
Apple, Rima, 379
Mothers and Medicine, 379
Arbaleste, Charlotte, 453
Mémoires . . ., 453
Arcari, Paola Maria, 283
Archaeology, 5–15, 389
Archives, 21–9, 103, 323, 548
Arconville, Marie-Geneviève-Charlotte-Darlus d', 209, 460
Vie de Marie de Médici, 209
Arena Three, 304–314
Arendt, Hannah, 367
Origins of Totalitarianism, 367
Arnauld, Angélique de Saint-Jean, 106, 107
Arria, 18
Arrow, Michelle, 1–3, 94–8
Arru, Angiolina, 286
Art history, 29–38
Artemesia, 93
Ashurst Women, 38
Aspasia, 61, 93, 113
Astell, Mary, 118, 154, 156, 158, 173, 474, 476, 572
The Christian Religion Profess'd . . ., 118, 173
An Impartial Enquiry into the Causes of Rebellion and Civil War . . ., 476
A Serious Proposal to the Ladies, 154, 474, 572
Atkinson, Emma Willsher, 496
Queens of Prussia, 496
Atkinson, Mabel, 99, 262
Economic Foundations of the Women's Movement [with Maude Pember Reeves], 262
Atwood, Margaret, 247, 548, 573
Oryx and Crake, 247
The Handmaid's Tale, 573
Aubrac, Lucie, 578
Outwitting the Gestapo, 578
Audoux, Marguerite [Marguerite Donquichotte], 212
Marie-Claire, 212
L'Atelier de Marie-Claire, 212

Auerbach, Nina, 196
Aulnoy, Marie Catherine, 522, 553
Memoirs of the Court of England in 1675, 553
Nouvelles ou memoires historiques, 522
Travels into Spain, 553
Austen, Jane, xiv, 40–2, 161, 247, 300, 408, 493, 609
Emma, 41
family history, 161
History of England, 40, 222
influence on Walter Scott, 41
Letters, 41
Mansfield Park, 41, 494
Northanger Abbey, xiv, 222
Persuasion, xiv, 42, 493–4
Pride and Prejudice, 41, 247
Austen, Katherine, 470
Austin, Ann, 529
Austin, Sarah Taylor, 5, 42–3
Germany from 1760–1814, 43
Grandmother of Janet Ross, 43
Mother of Lucie Duff-Gordon, 43
Relationship with Anna Laetitia Barbauld, 42
Relationship with Elizabeth and Agnes Strickland, 42, 547
Relationship with Jane Carlyle, 43
Relationship with Lucy Aikin, 5
Three Generations of Englishwomen, 43
translations 43
Australia, xvii, 43–54, 124–6
Autobiographies and autobiographical writing, 17, 21, 59, 158, 182, 192, 291, 337–9, 416–19, 529
Aveling, Marion[Quartly], 48, 49, 101
Creating a Nation [with Patricia Grimshaw, Marilyn Lake, Ann McGrath], 48, 49, 101, 367, 368
Freedom Bound I [with Patricia Grimshaw and Susan Janson], 48
Stepping out of History [with Joy Damousi], 48
Avetta, Maria, 281

Bacon, Margaret Hope, 409
One Woman's Passion for Peace and Freedom, 409
Badaloni, Nicola, 284
Movimento operaio e lotta politica a Livorno [with Pieroni Bortolotti, Franca], 284
Bader, Clarisse, *Sainte Claire d'Assise*, 460
La Femme biblique . . ., 460
Badran, Margot, 464
Feminists, Islam and Nation, 464
Baernstein, P Renée, 455
A Convent Tale, 455
Baillie, Joanna, 5
Baker, Anne Elizabeth, 317
Glossary of Northamptonshire Words and phrases, 317
Balch, Emily Greene, 409
Improper Bostonian, 409
Balfour, Clara Lucas, 54–5, 182, 400, 460, 614
Women Worth Emulating, 614
Women and the Temperance Reformation, 55
Women of Scripture, 55
worker's education, 55
Working Women of the Last Half-Century, 55
Ballard, George, 118, 158, 221
Memoirs of British Ladies, 118, 158, 221
Ballard, Martha, 375
Ballio, Guilia, 279
Marti italiani . . ., 279
Banerjee, Sumanta, 445
Prostitution in Colonial Bengal, 445
Banks, Sarah Sophia, 317, 384
Glossaries in Lincolnshire, 317, 384
Banner, Lois, 66, 569, 598
Clio's Consciousness Raised [with Mary Hartman], 66, 569
Bannerji, Himani, 369
Nation, Empire, Colony . . ., 369
Banti, Luisa, 282
Barbauld, Anna Laetitia, 5, 248, 327, 494
Aunt of Lucy Aikin, 5
Eighteen Hundred and Eleven, 494
memoir by Lucy Aikin, 5
Relationship with Sarah Taylor Austin, 42
Bardounau-Narcy, Eliza Ashurst, 38–40
Barine, Arvède, 460
[Louise-Cécile Bouffé], 460
Barkan, Diana, 511
Walther Nernst . . ., 511
Barman, Jean, 85
Constance Lindsay Skinner, 528
Sojourning Sisters, 85
Barnard, Majorie, 44, 124, 125, 140–1, 366, 572
A House is Built, 44, 141
As M Barnard Eldershaw, 44, 140–1
A History of Australia, 141
My Australia [with Flora Eldershaw], 124, 141

Barnard, Majorie – *continued*
  Sydney, 141
  Tomorrow and Tomorrow, 141
  writing with Flora Eldershaw, 44, 124, 125
Barnes, Catherine A., 95
  Journey from Jim Crow, 95
Barney, Natalie, 307
Baron, Beth, 397
  The Woman's Awakening in Egypt, 397
Barringer, Clare, 311
Barry, Kathleen, 439, 444
  Female Sexual Slavery, 439, 444
Bartholomeusz, Tessa
  Women under the Bo Tree, 464
Bartley, Paula, 438–47
  Prostitution, Prevention and Reform in England, 441–2
Bashford, Alison, 378
  Purity and Pollution, 378
Bassett, Marnie, 45
  The Governor's Wife, 45
Bassi, Laura Maria Caterina, 155
Bates, Daisy T., 97
Bateson, Mary, 55, 225, 345
  Borough Customs, 55
  Cambridge Guild Records, 55
  Charters of the Boroughs of Cambridge, 55
  editor of *Cambridge Medieval History*, 55
  influence of Lina Eckenstein, 55
  Medieval History, 55
  'Origins and Early History of Double Monastries', 55
  Records of the Boroughs of Leicester, 55
  The Register of Crabhouse Convent, 55, 225, 345
  suffrage activities, 55
Baudoin, Madeleine, 578
  Histoire des Groupes Francs, 578
Baudonivia, xv, xvii, 23–32, 56, 174–5, 341, 456
  Life of Radegund, xv, 56, 174–5, 232, 456
Baym, Nina, 27, 560
  American Women Writers and the Work of History, 27
Beale, Dorethea, 133, 433
Beard, Charles Austin, 26, 56, 564
  collaboration with Mary Ritter Beard, 27, 57
  husband of Mary Ritter Beard, 26, 56
Beard, Mary Ritter, 26, 56–9, 186, 221, 352, 400, 408, 568, 569, 598, 601, 604
  America through Women's Eyes, 58
  American Citizenship [with Charles Austin Beard], 57
  The American Spirit [with Charles Austin Beard], 57, 568
  A History of the United States [with Charles Austin Beard], 57, 568
  influence of Charlotte Perkins Gilman, 57
  On Understanding Women, 57, 568
  Relationship with the Pankhursts, 56
  The Rise of American Civilisation [with Charles Austin Beard], 57, 568
  Suffragist, 26, 56–7
  Woman as Force in History, 58, 400, 408, 568
  World Centre for Women's Archives, 27, 58, 568
Beasley, Faith E., 330–9
Beauvoir, Simone de, 59–60, 193, 212–13, 221, 336, 604, 615
  autobiographies, 59, 193, 336
  Force of Circumstance, 59
  The Mandarins, 59
  Memoirs of a Dutiful Daughter, 59
  Prime of Life, 59
  The Second Sex, 59, 193, 212, 615
  She Came to Stay, 59
Beck, Lois *Women in the Muslim World* [with Nikki Keddie], 464
Becker, Lydia, 62, 196
Beddoe, Deirdre, 229
Bederman, Gail, 328, 570
  Manliness and Civilization, 328, 570
Bedford, Jessie, 227
  Home Life under the Stuarts, 227
  Social Life under the Stuarts, 227
Beecher, Catherine, 133
  grand-aunt of Charlotte Perkins Gilman, 219
Beetham, Margaret, 608
  A Magazine of Her Own . . ., 608
Behn, Aphra, 325, 405, 474, 519
  Love Letters between a Noble-Man and His Sister, 474, 519
  Oronokoo, 528
Beier, Lucinda McCray, 380
  Sufferers and Healers, 380

Beifuss, Joan T., 95
At the River I Stand, 95
Belgiojoso, Cristina di, 60, 216, 279, 280, 365
Etudes sur l'Asie Mineure et les Turcs, 279
L'Italie et la revolution italienne de 1848, 60, 278
nursing with Margaret Fuller during Roman Revolution, 216, 277
Premières notions d'histoire à l'usage des enfants, 279
Reflections sur l'etat de Italie, 365
Studia intorno alla storia della Lombardia . . ., 277
Sulla moderna politica internazionale, 279
translation of Vico, 60
Bell, E Moberley, 377
Storming the Citadel, 377
Bell, Flora, 320
At the Works . . ., 320
Bell, Gertrude, 7, 389, 555, 556–7
The Desert and the Sown, 7, 557
The Palace and Mosque at Ukhaidir, 7, 557
Beness, J Lea, 5–15, 235–7, 549–50
Benger, Elizabeth, 5, 60, 453, 498–9, 500, 501, 503,
Biography by Lucy Aikin, 61
Memoir of Life of Anne Boleyn, 61, 498–9, 501
relationship with Elizabeth Hamilton, 60
The Female Geniad, 60
Memoir of Elizabeth Hamilton, 61
Elizabeth of Bohemia, 61
Mary Queen of Scots, 61
Relationship with Lucy Aikin, 5, 60, 61
Benjamin, Marina, 511
Science and Sensibility, 511
Bennett, Judith, 311
Benson, Margaret, 8, 461
The Temple of Mut, 462
Berard, Augusta, 560
School History of the United States, 560
Berg, Maxine, 262, 264
Berkshire conferences, 599–600
Bernier, Isabelle, 37
Berry, Mary, 61
A Comparative View of Social Life in England and France, 61,
Letters of Rachel, Lady Russell, 61
relationship with Anne Seymour Damer, 61
Berta of Willich, 232, 341
Bertocchi, Maria Fulvia, 276
Istoria generale dei popoli della Grecia . . ., 276
Bethune, Mary Mcleod, 568
Bézard, Yvonne, 212
Biase De, Gaiotti, Paola, 285
Le donne oggi, 285
La donne nella vita sociale e politica dell repubblica, 285
Bieber, Margarete, 12, 13
Ancient Copies, 12
History of the Greek and Roman Theater, 12
Sculpture of the Hellenistic Age, 12
Biggs, Caroline Ashurst, 38–40, 119
'British' chapter in Stanton's *History of womem Suffrage*, 39
Editor of *The Englishwoman's Review*, 39
Waiting for Tidings, 40
White and Black: A Story of the Southern States, 40
Biggs, Matilda Ashurst, 39
Bigland, Eileen, 558
The Key to the Russian Door, 558
Bimbi, Franca, 286
Differenze e disuguaglianze, 286
Biographies and biographical writing, xvii, 17, 21, 172–82, 416–19, 511, 529
Biondi, Martha, 95
To Stand and Fight, 95
Bird, Isabella, 554
The Englishwoman in America, 554
Birgitta, Saint, 342
Birkett, Dea, 559
Spinsters Abroad . . ., 559
Birkett, Winifred, 44
Bishop, Harriet E., 562
Floral Home, 562
Black, Clementina, 235, 385
Black, Naomi, 84
Canadian Women: A History [with Alison Prentice, Paula Bourne, Gail Cuthbert Brandt, Beth Light and Wendy Mitchinson], 84
Blackburn, Helen, 61–2, 119, 184, 261, 544
editor of *Englishwoman's Review*, 62
Women's Suffrage, 62, 100, 184, 228
Blackburne, Elizabeth Owen, 268
Illustrious Irishwomen, 268

Blackwell, Elizabeth, 375
autobiography, 376
Medicine as a Profession for Women [with Emily Blackwell], 375
Blackwell, Emily, 375
Medicine as a Profession for Women [with Elizabeth Blackwell], 375
Blaisdell, Charmarie Jenkins, 453
Blakeley, Phyllis, 81
Bland, Lucy, 70, 443
Banishing the Beast, 70, 443
Blessington, Marguerite Countess, 553
Bliss, Katherine, 445
Compromising Positions . . ., 445
Block, Elaine C., 348
Blodgett, Harriet, 429
Centuries of Female Days, 429
Blok, Josine, 14
Blom, Ida, 600, 617
Blumberg, Rhonda Lois, 95, 96
Blunt, Anne, 551, 555, 556, 557
Bedouin Tribes of the Euphrates, 556
Boccaccio, Giovanni, 115–16, 117, 176, 177, 466–8, 470, 593
Concerning Famous Women, 115–16, 176, 177, 466–8, 593
Bocchicchio, Rebecca, 239
The Passionate Fictions of Eliza Haywood [with Kirsten P Saxton], 239
Bodichon, Barbara, 260, 290
Body, 62–74
Boger, Charlotte G., 318
Myths, Scenes and Worthies of Somerset, 318
Bohl, Elizabeth, 552
Women Travel Writers, Landscape and the Language of Aesthetics, 552
Bohm, Comtesse de, 479
Boivin, Marie Anne, 374–5
Nouveau Traité sur les Hémoragies de l'Utérus, 374
Observations et Expériences sur le Développement Naturel et Artificiel des Maladies Turberculeuses, 374
Traité Pratique des Maladies de l'Utérus . . ., 374
Boldrin, Caterina Tetamanzi, 279
Marti Italiani . . ., 279
Bolton, Sarah, 182
Famous Types of Womanhood, 182
Leaders among Women, 182
Successful Women, 182
Bonafede, Carolina [Pizzigoni], 277–8
Memorie biografiche di Luigi Sabatini Bonafede, 277–8
Booth, Alison, xvi, 173
Bosanquet, Rosalie, 321
Boserup, Ester, 616
Women's Role in Economic Development, 616
Botchkareva, Maria, 582
Boulding, Elise, 412
Cultures of Peace, 412
Bourgeois, Louise, 207
Observations Diverses sur les Stérilité . . ., 374
Récit véritable de la naissance, 207
Bourke, Angela, 268
Inion Rian Uileáin Dhorcha, 268
Bourke, Joanna, 273, 576
An Intimate History of Killing, 575
Husbandry to Housewifery, 273
Bourne, Paula, 84
Canadian Women: A History [with Alison Prentice, Gail Cuthbert Brandt, Beth Light, Wendy Mitchinson and Naomi Black]
Bowen, Elizabeth, 266, 577
Bowen's Court, 266
The Last September, 266
Seven Winters, 266
The Heat of the Day, 577
Bowman, Glenn, 551
Diary of a Pilgrimage, 551
Boxer, Marilyn, 188
Boyce, Mary, 6
Boyd, Harriet [Hawes], 7–8, 12
Gournia, Vasiliki and Other Prehistoric Sites . . ., 7
Boyd, Kelly, 327–30
Manliness and the Boy's Story Paper, 329–30
Boyle, Mary, Countess of Warwick, 471
diary, 471
Bozzoli, Felicita, 279
Martiri Italiani . . ., 279
Braker, Regina, 408
Bertha von Suttner's *Spiritual Daughters*, 408
Branca, Patricia, 165
Silent Sisterhood, 165

Brand, Dionne, 84
We're Rooted Here and They Can't Pull Us Up [with Peggy Bristow, Linda Carty, Afua P Cooper, Sylvia Hamilton and Adrienne Shadd], 84
Brandt, Gail Cuthbert, 84
Bourne, Beth Light, Wendy Mitchinson and Naomi Black, 84
Canadian Women: A History [with Alison Prentice, Paula], 84
Braunschneider, Theresa, 71
Bravo, Anna, 286
Bray, Anna Eliza, 317, 453
Revolt of Protestants in Cevennes, 453
Traditions, Legends, Superstitions . . ., 317
Braybon, Gail, 576
Out of the Cage [with Penny Summerfield] 576
Bremer, Fredericka, 405
Bridenthal, Renate, 102, 165
Household Kith and Kin [with Joan Kelly, Amy Swerdlow and Phyllis Vine], 102
Brieger, Gert, 380
Brink, Elsabe, 123
Briquet, Fortunée, 211
Dictionnaire historique . . ., 211
Bristow, Peggy, 85
We're Rooted Here and They Can't Pull Us Up [with Dionne Brand, Linda Carty, Afua P Cooper, Sylvia Hamilton and Adrienne Shadd], 84
British Library, Admittance of women, 22–3
Brittain, Vera, 72–4, 199, 407, 410, 578
Friendship with Winifred Holtby, 73, 199
Honourable Estate, 74, 578
Lady into Woman . . ., 73
Not Without Honour, 578
Pethick-Lawrence: A Portrait, 74
Testament of Experience, 73
Testament of Youth, 73, 578
Testament to Friendship, 73, 199
The Rebel Passion, 74, 410
Women at Oxford, 74
Bronte, Charlotte, 256, 257, 258, 395
influence of Julia Kavanagh, 300
relationship with Elizabeth Gaskell, 257
relationship with Mary Taylor, 256
Shirley, 256, 257
Brooke, Charlotte, 158
Brookes, Barbara, 379
Abortion in England, 379
Brooks, Juanita, 566
The Mountains Meadow Massacre, 566
Broomhall, Susan, 205–15, 451, 455–65
Brooten, Bernadette, 6, 13
Brown, Cynthia Stokes, 97
Brown, Jennifer, 422
Strangers in Blood, 422
Brown, Louise, 125
A Book of South Australia . . ., 125
Brown, Louise Fargo, 507
Apostle of Democracy, 507
biographer of Lucy Maynard Salmon, 507
Brown, Vera, 76
Brown, Victoria Bissell, 409
The Education of Jane Addams, 409
Browne, Stella, 70
Browning, Elizabeth Barrett, 395
Browning, Joan C., 94
Brownmiller, Susan
In Our Times, 203
Bruce, Mary Grant, 126
Bruzzone, Annamaria, 285
La resistenza taciuta [with Rachele Farina], 285
Bryant, Louise, 481
Bryant, Margaret, 136
The Unexpected Revolution . . ., 136
Bryn Mawr, 8, 13, 76, 133, 348, 370, 447, 448, 509, 550, 565, 600
Buci-Glucksmann, Christine, 68
Buckler, Georgina, 303
Buffet, Marguerite, 209
Eloges des illustres savantes anciennes et modernes, 209
Buhle, Mari Jo, 598
'The Problem of Women's History' [with Ann Gordon and Nancy Schrom Dye], 598
Bulley, Amy, 257
Women's Work [with Margaret Whitely], 257
Bullough, Bonnie, 376
Emergence of Modern Nursing [with Vern Bullough]
Burgmann, Verity, 49, 52
A People's History of Australia since 1788 [with Jenny Lee], 49
Power and Protest, 52
Burgo-Debray, Elisabeth, 387
I Rigoberto Menchu, 387

Burne, Charlotte Sophia, 225, 317
Shropshire Folklore, 217, 225
Burney, Fanny, 378
Burstall, Sarah, 133
Education of Girls in the United States, 133
English High Schools for Girls, 133
Burstein, Miriam Elizabeth, 495–505
Burstein, Miriam Elizabeth, xvi, 26, 173, 495–505, 592–6
Burstyn, Joan, 136, 139
Burton, Antoinette, 21, 55, 144, 147, 230, 368, 369, 396, 397, 424, 433
The Burdens of History, 230, 368, 392, 396, 424
Dwelling in the Archive, 21, 358
At the Heart of Empire, 147
'Who Needs the Nation', 144, 369
Burton, Catherine, 111
Bush, Barbara, 537
Bush, Julia, 147
Buss, Frances Mary, 133
Busse-Wilson, Elisabeth, 347, 349
Bussey, Gertrude, 408
Pioneers for Peace [with Margaret Timms], 408
Butler, Eleanor, 309
Butler, Josephine, 39, 74–5, 99, 148, 184, 189, 190, 197, 261, 424, 438, 442–3
An Autobiographical Memoir, 75
Catherine of Sienna, 74
Contagious Diseases Acts, 74, 75, 197, 424, 438
Memoir of John Grey of Dilston, 74, 197
In Memoriam Harriet Meuricofffre, 74, 197
Native Races and the War, 75
Personal Reminiscences of a Great Crusade, 74, 184, 197
Recollections of George Butler, 74, 197, 438
Relationship with Emilie Ashurst Venturi, 39
Women's Work and Women's Culture, 74
Butler, Judith, 219
Gender Trouble, 219
Butler, Marilyn, 242
Butler, Octavia, 573
Buttafuoco, Annarita, 285
Le Mariuccine, 285
Questioni di cittadiananza, 285
Butti, Adele, 279
Marti Italiani, 279
Byles, Rebecca, 78–9
Bynum, Caroline Walker, 64, 463
Fragmentation and Redemption, 463
Holy Feast, Holy Fast, 64, 463
Jesus as Mother, 64
Resurrection of the Body in Western Christianity, 64

Cadden, Joan, 68
Meanings of Sex Differences in the Middle Ages, 68
Caine, Barbara, 72, 74–5, 160–71, 182, 192–203, 525, 540–1, 586–7, 589–92, 608–11
Caird, Mona, 162, 163
Caldicott, Helen, 412
A Passionate Life, 412
Califronia, Rosa, 160
Callaway, Helen, 392, 423
Gender, Culture and Empire, 392, 423
Callcott, Lady, [Maria Graham], 226, 554
Journal of a Residence in India, 554
Journal of a Voyage to Brazil, 554
Little Arthur's History of England, 226, 554
Callen, Anthea, 36
Angel in the Studio, 36
The Spectacular Body, 36
Calvi, Giulia, 288
Innesti, 288
Cam, Helen Maud, 75–6, 228, 347
England before Elizabeth, 76
First woman professor at Harvard, 75
Historical Novels, 76
Liberties and Communities in Medieval England, 76
The Hundred and the Hundred Rolls, 76
Cambridge, Ada, 44
The Three Miss Kings, 44
Cameron, Avril, 14
Agathias, 14
Christianity and the Rhetoric of Empire, 14
Continuity and Change in Sixth-Century Byzantium, 14
History as Text, 14
Procopius and the Sixth Century, 14
The Later Roman Empire, 14
The Mediterranean World in Late Antiquity, 14
Campan, Jeanne-Louise-Henriette Genest, 210, 334
Mémoires . . ., 210, 334

Campbell, Mary, 400
The Wild Irish Girl, 400
Campo, Rosetta, 280
Vita Politica della famiglia Campodal, 280
Canada, xvii, 76–87, 120–3
Cantarella, Eva, 287
Bisexuality in the Ancient World, 287
Capern, Amanda L., 71–2, 152–60, 233–4, 254–5, 465–75, 589
Caprin, Caterina Croatto, 279
Marti Italiani, 279
Carby, Hazel, 329
Race Men, 329
Carlyle, Jane, 43, 216, 310, 432–5, 609
diaries, 432–5
letters to Geraldine Jewsbury, 310, 609
letters to Thomas Carlyle, 432–5
Relationship with Sarah Taylor Austin, 43
Carmen, Bliss, 307
Carr, Lady Mary, 23
Carroll, Berenice, 569, 600
Liberating Women's History, 569
Carter, Angela, 382
Carter, Elizabeth, 6
Cartwright, Julia, 29, 86
Beatrice d'Este, 87
influence of Anna Jameson, 86
Isabelle d'Este, 32, 87
Jean-Francois Millet, 31, 87
Madame, 86
Mantegna and Francia, 31, 32
mother of Cecilia Mary Ady, 87
Raphael, 31, 32
Carty, Linda, 84
We're Rooted Here and They Can't Pull Us Up [with Peggy Bristow, Dionne Brand, Afua P Cooper, Sylvia Hamiliton and Adrienne Shadd], 84
Carus, Eleanora, 228
Cary, Elizabeth, Lady Falkland, 87–8, 453, 473, 544
Authorship of *History and Reign and Death of Edward II*, 88, 473
Catholicism, 87–8
daughter's biography, 88
The Tragedy of Mariam, 87, 473
translations, 87, 453
Cary, Mary, 571
The Little Horns Doom and Downfall, 571
Casanova, Cesarina, 288
Casteras, Susan, 36
A Struggle for Fame, 36
Catalogs of women, 88, 156, 160, 172, 173, 176, 177, 415, 457, 515, 593, 611–12, 614
Catherine of Genoa, 373
Catherine of Siena, 342
Caton-Thompson, Gertrude, 9, 10
Badarian Civilisation, 9
Desert Fayum, 9
Kharga Oasis in Prehistory, 9
work with Elinor Gardner, 9
Caulkins, Frances Manwaring, 90–1, 562
Eve and Her Daughters or Women of the Bible, 91, 562
History of New London, 91
History of Norwich, connection, 91, 562
Cavallo, Sandra, 288
Cavendish, Margaret, 22, 61, 91–2, 336, 405, 472–3, 476, 512, 544, 571–3
The Blazing World, 91, 571
Observations upon Experimental Philosophy, 91, 571
The Life of William Cavendish, 92, 472–3
Sociable Relations, 405
A True Relation of My Birth, Breeding and Life, 92, 336
The World's Olio, 91, 571
utopian writings, 91, 571–2
Caylus, Marquise de [Marthe-Marguerite de Villete de Murcay], 208
Souvenirs, 208
Celliez, Adélaïde, 211, 460
Les Impératrices. France, Russie, Autriche, Brésil 211
Les Reines d'Angleterre, 211
Les Reines de France, 211
Les Reines d'Espagne, 211
Les Saintes de France, 460
Cereta, Laura, 90, 116, 117, 177, 466
Chance, Jane, 339–49
Chang, Iris, 570
The Chinese in America, 570
Chapone, Hester, 155
Chard, Charlotte, 552
Pleasure and Guilt on the Grand Tour, 552

Charke, Charlotte, 337
Narrative of the Life of Miss Charlotte Charke, 337
Chattopadhayay, Kamaladevi, 397
Indian Women's Battle for Freedom, 397
Chaudhuri, Nupur, 392, 423, 616
Western Women and Imperialism . . . [with Margaret Strobel], 392, 423, 616
Cherry, Deborah, 29, 32
Painting Women, 36
Chesterton, Ada, 558
My Russian Adventure, 558
Chevigny, Gale Bell, 217
The Woman and the Myth, 217
Chew, Ada Neild, 259
Chibnall, Majorie McCallum, 346
Child, Lydia Maria, 1, 2, 92–4, 180, 387, 461, 531, 561, 614–15
Abolition activities, 92, 531
An Appeal in Favour of that Class of Americans called Africans, 1, 93, 181, 531
Biographies of Lady Russell and Madame Guyon, 93, 180
Biographies of Madame de Staël and Madame Roland, 93, 180
Condition of Women in Various Ages and Nations, 93, 614,
editor of *Juvenile Miscellany*, 92
Good Wives, 180, 181
Hobomok, 92, 561
Incidents in the Life of a Slave Girl, 387, 417
The Mother's Book, 93
Progress of Religious Ideas, 93, 461
The Rebels, or Boston before the Revolution, 93
relationship with Margaret Fuller, 93, 215–16
A Romance of the Republic, 94
Choo, Christine, 51
Mission Girls, 51
Chrisman, Miriam U., 453
Christianson, Aileen, 432
Chudleigh, Mary Lady, 117
The Ladies' Defence 117
Circé-Côte, Eve, 80
Papineau . . ., 80
Civil Rights, 2, 94–8
Clapham, Irene, 583
Clark, Alice, 98–9, 163, 227, 262, 352, 411, 597, 601
connections to Elizabeth Cady Stanton, 99
influence of Olive Schreiner, 99
supervised by Lilian Knowles, 99, 303
Working Life of Women in the Seventeenth-Century, 99, 163, 262, 352, 597
Clark, Anna, 69, 263
The Struggle for the Breeches, 263
Clarke, Mary Cowden, 614, 615
World-noted Women, 614, 615
Clarke, Maud Violet, 270
Clarke, Norma, 432–3
Clayton, Ellen, 30
English Female Artists, 30
Clemence of Barking, 342
Clement-Hémery, Albertine, 212
Histoire des fêtes civiles et religieuses . . ., 212
Clement, Clara, 30
Women in the Fine Arts from the 7th Century BC to the 20th Century, 30
Clement, Margaret, 451, 468
Chronicle of St Monica's, 451, 468
Clementi, Andrieina, 286
Viaggi di donne, 286
Clements, Barbara Evans, 410
Bolshevik Feminist . . ., 410
Clendinnen, Inga, 51, 425
Ambivalent Conquest, 425
Dancing with Strangers, 51
Clifford, Anne, 62, 99–100, 544
ancestor of Vita Sackville West, 100
Great Books of the Records of Skipton Castle, 100
as Virginia Woolf's 'Orlando', 100
Knole Diary, 100
Clifford, Deborah Pickman, 2
Crusader for Freedom: A Life of Lydia Maria Child, 2
Clifford, Geraldine Joncich, 134, 138
Clinton, Catherine, 535
Plantation Mistress, 535
Clowes, E M [Elinor Mary Mordant], 124
On the Wallaby, 124
Clowes, Lindsay, 329
Cobbe, Frances Power, 194, 396
autobiography [*Life*], 196–7
Cobbold, Evelyn Lady, 552
Pilgrimage to Mecca, 552

Codell, Julie, 36
Orientalism Transposed, 36
Cohn, Carol, 412
Coicy, Madame de, 209
Les Femmes comme il convient de les voir, 209
Coignard, de Gabrielle, 473
Colette, 310
Ces Plaisirs, 310
Colish, Marcia, 347
Collective and Collaborative Writing, 100–3
Collet, Clara, 261
Colley, Linda, 229, 368
Britons, 229, 368
Collier-Thomas, Bettye, 95
Sisters in the Struggle . . . [with V P Franklin], 95
Coman, Katharine, 103–4, 564
Economics Beginnings of the Far West, 104
Industrial History of the United States, 104
Comnena, Anna, 161, 303, 343, 404
Alexiad, 161, 303, 343, 404(2)
Conkey, Margaret, 14
Conlon, Anne, 46
Gentle Invaders [with Edna Ryan], 46
Conrad, Margaret, 84
George Nowlan . . . , 84
Contagious Diseases Acts, 39, 62, 74, 99, 148, 184, 185, 194, 424, 592
Convents, 104–12, 275
Conway, Jill Ker, 137
Cook, Blanche Weisen, 302, 409, 411
Bibliography on Peace Research in History, 411
Cook, Eliza, 258
Melaia, 258
Cooke, Ann, sister of Mildred, 469
Fouretene Sermons of Barnardine Ochyne, 469
Cooke, Mildred, 469
sister of Ann, 469
translations, 469
Cooke, Miriam, 411
Gendering War Talk [with Angela Woollacott], 411
Cooper, Afua P., 84
We're Rooted Here and They Can't Pull Us Up [with Peggy Bristow, Dionne Brand, Linda Carty, Sylvia Hamiliton and Adrienne Shadd], 84
Cooper, Anna Julia, 112–13, 537, 567, 569
A Voice from the South, 112, 537, 567
Cooper, Selina, 259
Cordy, Almira, 563
The Story of the Marking of the Santa Fe Trail . . . , 563
Cornaro, Elena, 155
Cornelia, 17, 18, 19, 117
Corner, Julia, 226
Costa, Shelley, 513
Costello, Louisa S., 100
Falls, Lakes and Mountains, 225
Memoirs of Eminent English Women, 100, 225
Cott, Nancy, 183, 190, 428–9, 569
Grounding of Modern Feminism, 183
The Bonds of Womanhood, 190, 428–9, 569
Cousins, Margaret, 270
Craft, Ellen, 146, 529, 533
Crafts, Hannah, 534
The Bondswoman's Narrative, 534
Craven, Elizabeth Lady, 553
Memoirs, 553
Crawford, Patricia, 68, 229, 454, 464
Women and Religion in England, 454, 464
Women in Early Modern England [with Sara Mendelson], 68, 229
Crawford, Vicki, 95
Women in the Civil Rights Movement, 95
Creighton, Louise, 26
Creighton, Mandell, 26, 55
Crenne, Helisenne de, 468
Critchett, Jan, 50
Untold Stories, 50
Cronin, Kathryn, *Race Relations in Colonial Queensland* . . . [with Raymond Evans and Kay Saunders], 50
Cross-dressing, 311–14
Cross, Suzanne, 83
Crow, Mary Dog, 419
Crowley, Terry, 526
Marriage of Minds . . . , 526
Croy, Anne de, 373
Cruttwell, Maud, 30
Culley, Margo, 429
A Day at a Time, 429
Cullwick, Hannah, 69–70, 260, 435–6
Cummings, Barbara, 51
Take this Child, 51
Cuomo, Serafina, 510
Ancient Mathematics, 510
Pappus of Alexandria, 510

Curli, Barbara, 286
Italiane al Lavoro, 286
Currie, Emma, 121
The Story of Laura Secord, 121
Curry, Constance, 97
Deep in Our Hearts, 97
Curthoys, Ann, 46, 49, 54, 55, 58–9, 140–1, 193, 203–4, 218–19, 596–606
Freedom Ride, 52
'Historiography and Women's Liberation', 46, 598–9
Women at Work [with Susan Eade [Magarey] and Peter Spearritt], 46–7
Curtin, Nancy,
The United Irishmen, 272
Curwen, Alice, 470, 529
A Relation of Labour, 470
Curzon, Sarah, 79, 85
Laura Secord: The Heroine of 1812, 79
Cusack, Dymphna, 44, 125, 132

Dacier, Anne Le Fèvre, 6
Dall, Caroline Wells Healey, 113–14, 182
Abolition activities, 113
The College, the Market and the Court, 114
'conversations' with Margaret Fuller, 114, 215
Historical Pictures Retouched, 182
Lecture on Transcendentalism, 114
Women's Right to Labour, 113
Women's Rights under the Law, 114
work with Paulina Wright Davis, 113
Daly, Laura, 411
Daly, Mary, 272
The Famine in Ireland, 272
Daly, Mary, 397
Gyn/Ecology, 397
Damer, Georgiana, 551
Diary of a Tour in Greece, 551
Damousi, Joy, 48, 53
Depraved and Disorderly, 53
Freud in the Antipodes, 53
Labour of Loss, 53
Living with the Aftermath, 53
Stepping out of History [with Marian Aveling [Quartley]], 48
Daniels, Kay, 47, 48, 50, 446
Convict Women, 51
So Much Hard Work, 50, 446
Uphill All the Way [with Mary Murnane], 48
D'Aprano, Zelda, 47, 201–2
Zelda, 47, 201–2
Darian-Smith, Kate, 576
On the Home Front, 576
Dark, Eleanor, 44, 125, 375
Slow Dawning, 375
The Timeless Land, 44, 51
Dash, Julie, 98
The Rosa Parks Story, 98
Daston, Lorraine, 510, 513
Classical Probability in the Enlightenment, 510, 513
Daveluy, Marie-Clair, 80
L'Orphelinat catholique de Montréal, 80
Davenport, Florence, 555
What We Saw in Australia [with Rosamund Hill], 555
David-Néel, Alexandra, 462, 551–2
My Journey to Lhasa, 552
Tibetan Journey, 462
Davidoff, Leonore, 69, 166, 170, 171, 327, 435
Best Circles, 327
Family Fortunes [with Catherine Hall], 166, 262, 327–8
The Family Story . . ., 170
Davies, Eleanor, 471–2
All the Kings of the Earth, 471
Samsons Legacie, 472
Davies, Emily, 130, 131, 132, 136, 137, 139, 190
Higher Education of Women, 131
Davies, Maud Frances, 320
Life in an English Village, 320
Davies, Stevie, 229
A Century of Troubles, 229
Unbridled Spirits, 229
Davin, Anna, 169, 170, 599, 602
'Imperialism and Motherhood', 169, 602
'Women and History', 599
Davis, Madelaine D., 103, 570
Boots of Leather, Slippers of Gold [with Elizabeth Lapovsky Kennedy], 103, 570–1
Davis, Natalie Zemon, xvi, 105, 285, 454, 455, 600
Women on the Margins, 455
'Women's History in Transition', 218, 601
Davis, Paulina Wright, 114–15
History of the National Woman's Rights Movement, 115
work with Caroline Dall, 114

De Groot, Joanna, 391, 424, 616
De Pauw, Linda Grant, 408
Battle Cries and Lullabies, 408
Deacon, Desley, 19–21, 217–18, 541–3
Managing Gender, 49
Dean, Ruth, 349
Debo, Angie, 566
And Still the Waters Run, 566
The Rise and Fall of the Choctaw Nation, 566
The Road to Disappearance, 566
Dechêne, Louise, 82–3, 85
Habitants et marchands de Montrèal au XVIIe siecle, 83
Le partage des subsistances, 84
Deeks, Florence, 79, 80
Defences of women, 115–19, 172, 173, 174, 176–8, 301, 372, 467–8, 515, 613
Deman, Esther Van, 10
Ancient Roman Construction in Italy, 10
The Atrium Vestae, 10
The Building of Roman Aqueducts, 10
Dentière, Marie, 452, 457, 468
La Guerre et desivrance de la ville de Genesve, 452
Très Utile Epistre, 452, 457, 468
Des Jardins, Julie, 28
Women and the Historical Enterprise in America, 352
Desjardins, Marie Catherine [Villedieu, Madame, de], 474, 521
La princesse de Montpnsier, 474
Memoirs of the life of Henriette-Sylvie de Moliere, 474
Devanny, Jean, 50
Devi, Rassundarai, 338
Amar Jiban, 338
Di Cori, Paola, 284
Diaries, 21, 53, 78, 146, 428–37, 470, 485
Dickason, Olive Patricia, 84
Canada's First Nations, 84
The New People, 422
Dickenson, Donna, 217
Margaret Fuller: Writing a Woman's Life, 217
Dickinson, Emily, 485
Dictionary of National Biography, 9, 225, 609
Diefendorf, Barbara B., 454
Dieulafoy, Jane, 9
Digby, Anne, 66
'Women's Biological Straightjacket', 66
Dilke, Emilia, 29, 33–4, 35
Claude Lorrain: Sa Vie et Ses Oeuvres, 30
French Painters of the Eighteenth Century, 33
Dixon, Ella Hepworth, 356
The Story of a Modern Woman, 356
Dixon, Katherine, 151
An Appeal to the Women of the Empire, 151
Dixson, Miriam, 47, 51, 446
The Real Matilda, 47, 446
Djebar, Assia [Fatima-Zohra Imalayène], 214
L'amour, la fantasia, 214
Loin de Medine, 214
Ombre sultane, 214
Doan, Laura, 312, 355
Fashioning Sapphism, 355
Dobbs, Betty, 509–10, 513
The Foundations of Newton's Alchemy, 510
'The Hunting of the Greene Lyon', 510
The Janus Face of Genius . . ., 510
Dock, Lavinia, 376
A History of Nursing [with Mary Adelaide Nutting], 376
A Short History of Nursing [with Isabel M Stewart], 376
Doherty, Eileen, 274
Bloody Sunday in Derry, 274
Domestic history, xiv
Dominion women writers, 44, 103, 119–28, 146
Donoghue, Emma, 311
Donovan, Mary, 270
Doria, Anna Rossi, 286
A che punto è la storia delle donne, 288
Il voto alle donne in Italia, 286
Dorn, Judith A., 516–25
Douglas, Jane Dempsey, 453
Dowie, Ménie Muriel, 558
Women Adventurers, 558
Dowriche, Anne, 128, 207, 452
The French History, 128, 207, 452
Drake, Judith, 156
Drohojowska, Madame la Comtesse, 366
History of the French Colonies, 366
Droz, Eugénie, 212
Dryden, Alice, 318
DuBois, Ellen Carole, 1, 69, 182, 188, 189, 569, 603
Feminism and Suffrage, 188, 569
'Seeking Ecstasy on the Battlefield' [with Linda Gordon], 69
Duchene, Gabrielle, 385

Duckett, Eleanor Shipley, 346
Anglo-Saxon Scholars, 346
Latin Writers of the Fifth Century, 346
Women in their Letters, 346
Duden, Barbara, 63, 379
Disembodying Women, 379
The Woman Beneath the Skin, 63
Dudziack, Mary L., 95
Cold War Civil Rights, 95
Duff Gordon, Lucie, 42
Daughter of Sarah Taylor Austin, 43
Mother of Janet Ross, 43
in *Three Generations of Englishwomen*, 43
Dufrenoy, Adélaïde-Gillette Billet, 211
Biographies des jeunes demoiselles . . ., 211
Françaises, 211
Dumont, Micheline, 83
Maîtresses de maison, maitresses d'école [with Nadia FahmyEid], 83
Durack, Mary, 46
Keep Him My Country, 46
Duras, Marguerite [Marguerite Donnadieu], 214
La Douleur, 578
L'Amant, 214
L'Amant da la Chine du nord, 214
Durova, Nadezhda, 337
The Cavalry Maiden, 337
Durr, Virginia Foster, 97
Dye, Eva Emery, 565
McLoughlin and the Old Oregon, 565
Sacajawea, 565
The Conquest, 565
Dye, Nancy Schrom, 598
'The Problem of Women's History' [with Ann Gordon and Mari Jo Buhle], 598
Dyhouse, Carole, 16, 138, 163
Girls Growing up in Late Victorian England, 138
No Distinction of Sex?, 138

Earle, Alice Morse, 58, 128–9, 562
Child Life in Colonial Days, 129, 562
Colonial Dames and Good Wives, 129, 562
Eastman, Mary Henderson, 561
Dacotah, 561
Eckenstein, Lina, 4, 9, 55, 129–30, 227, 253, 345, 426, 448, 463, 500
Importance of monasticism to women's history, 4, 55, 129–30
influence on Cecilia Mary Ady, 4
influence on Mary Bateson, 55
Woman Under Monasticism, 129, 227, 253, 345, 463
The Women of Early Christianity, 130, 463
Economic History, 99, 227–8
Edgeworth, Maria, 158, 160, 242–4, 264, 265, 266–7, 316
The Absentee, 242, 243
Castle Rackrent, 160, 242–3, 265, 316
Ennui, 242, 265
Ormond, 242, 265
Education, 130–40, 281
Edwards, Amelia Blandford, 7, 389, 396, 551, 556
A Thousand Miles up the Nile, 7, 556
Pharaohs, Fellahs and Explorers, 7, 556
Egeria, 18, 551
Diary of a Pilgrimage, 551
Itinerarium, 18
Egerton, Sarah Fyge ['Eugenia'], 117
'The Female Advocate', 117
Eglin, Josephine, 408
Campaigns for Peace, 408
Egypt, Ophelia Settle, 567
The Unwritten History of Slavery, 567
Ehrenberg, Margaret, 615
Women in Prehistory, 615
Ehrenreich, Barbara, 66
Complaints and Disorders [with Deirdre English], 66
For Her Own Good [with Deirdre English], 66
Witches, Midwives and Nurses [with Deirdre English], 378
Eick, Gretchen Cassel, 95
Dissent in Wichita, 95
Eisenmann, Linda, 138
Elbert, Ella, 567
Eldershaw, Flora, 44, 124, 140–1, 572
A House is Built, 44, 140, As Barnard Eldershaw, 44, 140–1
My Australia [with Marjorie Barnard], 124, 140
The Peaceful Army, 44, 125
Tomorrow and Tomorrow, 141, 572
writing with Marjorie Barnard, 44, 124, 125
Eldershaw, M Barnard, 140–1, 572
see also Barnard, Majorie; Eldershaw, Flora
Eleonora Christina, 338
Elias, Amy J., 248
Sublime Desire, 248

Eliot, George [Mary Anne Evans], 141–2, 161, 195, 485
Felix Holt, 142
Middlemarch, 375
Mill on the Floss, 195
Romola, 142, 246
Scenes of a Clerical Life, 142
Elisabeth of Schönau, 456
Revelations, 456
Ellet, Elizabeth, 30, 58, 129, 142–3, 180, 477, 502, 561
Domestic History of the Revolution, 143, 477, 561
Queens of American Society, 502
Women Artists in All Ages and Countries, 30
Women of the American Revolution, 142, 180, 477, 561
Ellinghaus, Katharine, 168
Elliott, Marianne, 272
Catholics of Ulster, 275
Partners in Revolution, 272
Robert Emmet, 275
Wolfe Tone, 272
Ellis, Sarah Stickney, 614
The Mothers of Great Men, 614
Ells, Margaret, 81
Elmy, Elizabeth Wolstenholme, 193
Elshtain, Jean Bethke, 411
Women, War and Militarism, 411
Elstob, Elizabeth, 22, 158, 221
Rudiments of Grammar, 158
Source of George Ballard's *Memoirs*, 118, 221
Empire, xvii, 143–51, 230, 422–4, 445
Engelstein, Laura, 68, 355
The Keys to Happiness, 355
English, Deirdre, 66
Complaints and Disorders [with Barbara Ehrenreich], 66
For Her Own Good [with Barbara Ehrenreich], 66
Witches, Midwives and Nurses [with Barbara Ehrenreich], 378
Enlightenment, xvii, 152–60, 208–9
Enloe, Cynthia, 412
Does Khaki Become You?, 412
Maneuvers . . . , 412
Epstein, Julia, 67
Body Guards [with Kristina Straub], 67
Erdch, Louise, 570
Erickson, Carrolly, 504
Her Little Majesty, 504
Mistress Anne, 504
Ernst, Julia, 106, 108–9
Ettinger, Elzbieta, 410
Rosa Luxemburg, 410
Eudocia, 19
Evans, Joan, Dame, 348
Evans, Sara, 96
Personal Politics, 96

Fabian Women's Group, 99, 188, 261
Faderman, Lillian, 311, 484–5, 570
Odd Girls and Twilight Lovers . . ., 570
Surpassing the Love of Men . . ., 311, 484–5
Fage, Mary, 613
Fames Roule, 613
Fahmy-Eid, Nadia, 83
Maîtresses de maison, maitresses d'école [with Micheline Dumont], 83
Faithful, Emily, 260
Falconbridge, Anna Maria, 554
Two Voyages to Sierra Leone, 554
Family history, 17, 158, 160–71, 225–6, 340
Fannia, 18
Fanshawe, Ann, 171, 325, 472
Memoirs of Ann, 171, 472
Farina, Rachele, 285
La resistenza taciuta [with Annamaria Bruzzone], 285
Farnham, Fern, 6
Fasoli, Gina, 283
Fattiboni, Zellide, 280
Memorie storico biografiche al padre suo, 280
Fattorini, Emma, 287
Il Culto Mariano, 287
Faure, Christine, 213
Democratie sans les femmes, 213
Fauset, Eileen, 300
Fausto-Sterling, Anne, 71, 424
Favret, Mary, 431–3
Romantic Correspondence, 432
Fawcett Library, 28, 229
Fawcett, Millicent Garrett, 184, 185, 190, 194, 197, 546
autobiography [*What I Remember*] 194, 197–8
Strachey's biography, 546,
Women's Suffrage, 184, 185
Fearon, Kate, 274
Women's Work, 274

Featherstone, Lisa, 484–5
Febvre, Suzanne, 212
Fedele, Cassandra, 466, 467
Fee, Elizabeth, 66
'Science and the Woman Problem', 66
Fell, Christina, 229
Fell, Margaret, 405
Felski, Rita, 354
The Gender of Modernity, 354
Female Biography, 93, 114, 172–82, 223, 233, 238, 253, 264, 276, 323
Feminism, 596–606
first-wave, 30, 33,58, 182–92, 217, 304, 352, 442, 548
histories of, 182–92
impact on academy, 14, 596–606
second-wave, 14, 216–17, 615
Feminist autobiography and biography, 192–203
Feminist biographies, 192–200
Fentler, Matilde Furluga, 279
Marti Italiani, 279
Ferguson, Moira, 392
Colonialism and Gender Relations, 392
Ferrante, Joan, 176, 349
Woman as Image in Medieval Literature, 349
To the Glory of Her Sex, 349
Ferrier, Carole, 50
Jean Devanny, 50
Radical Brisbane [with Raymond Evans], 52
Ferrier, Suzanne, 161
Marriage, 161
Ferris, Ina, 241
The Romantic National Tale, 241
Fiennes, Celia, 158, 589
Fildes, Valerie, 379
Bottles and Babies, 379
Findlen, Paula, 514
Possessing Nature, 514
Firestone, Shulamith, 59, 597
Dialectic of Sex, 59, 597
First Nations women's writing, 80, 84–6
Fissel, Mary, 68
Fitzgerald, Shirley, 52
Rising Damp, 52
Fitzpatrick, Kathleen, 45, 47, 203–5
Solid Bluestone Foundations, 204
Fitzpatrick, Sheila, 483
Fleming, Cynthia Griggs, 97
Flemming, Rebecca, 379
Medicine and the Making of Roman Women, 379
Fletcher, Sheila, 410
Maude Royden, 410
Flexner, Eleanor, 187, 568, 597
Biography of Mary Wollstonecraft, 205
Century of Struggle, 187, 204–5, 568, 597
influence on Betty Freidan, 205
Flint, Kate, 356
Flora, 18, 19
Flore, Jeanne, 468
Fonte, Moderate [Modesta Pozzo], 116, 594, 613
The Worth of Women, 116, 594, 613
Forbes, Rosita, 558
Conflict: Angora to Afghanistan, 558
Forbidden Road, 558
The Secret of the Sahara, 558
Force, Charlotte-Rose Camount de la, 208, 522
Histoire Secréte de Henry IV, 208
Histoire de Marguerite de Valois . . ., 208
Histoire Secréte de Marie de Bourgogne, 522
Ford, Mary, 572
Formicini, Orsola, 106
Forster, Jackie, 308
Forsyth, Ilene, 348
Forsyth, Michael, 300
Fosl, Catherine, 97
Subversive Southerner, 97
Foster, Carrie, 408, 411
Women for all Seasons, 408, 411
Foster, Shirley, 392
Across New Worlds, 392
Foster, Shirley, 551
Across New Worlds, 551
Foucault, Michel, 67, 139, 248
Fouque, Caroline de la Motte, 364
Edmunds Ways and Byways, 364
The Heroic Maiden of the Vendee, 364
The Magic of Nature, 364
Fouquet, Catherine, 62
'The Unavoidable Detour', 62
Fox-Genovese, Elizabeth, 218, 536, 603
'Placing Women's History in History', 218–19, 603–4
Within the Plantation Household, 536
Fox, Betty, 529
Fox, Mary, 572
Fraisse, Geneviève, 213, 483
La raison des femmes, 213
Muse de la raison, 213, 483

France, 36, 205–14, 363
Frances, Raelene, 53, 446–7
Frank, Katherine, 392
Franklin, Miles, 44, 50, 125, 407
Some Everyday Folk and Dawn, 44
Franklin, V P, 95
Sisters in the Struggle [with Bettye Collier-Thomas], 95
Fraser, Antonia, 224, 504, 596
The Weaker Vessel, 224
Wives of Henry VIII, 504
Fraser, Frances, 125
Centenary Gift Book [with Nettie Palmer] 125–6
Fraser, Hilary, 29–38
Frawley, Maria, 551
Freedman, Estelle, 570
Intimate Matters [with John D'Emilio], 570
Freeman, Kathleen, 5
Work and Life of Solon, 5
Freidan, Betty, 59, 202, 205
Autobiography [*Life So Far*], 202
influence of Eleanor Flexner, 205
The Feminine Mystique, 205
Fries, Ellen, 253
Remarkable Foreign Women, 253
Fukuzawa, Yukichi, 291
Fukuô Jiden, 291
Fuller, Margaret, 93, 113, 114, 215–17, 561
'conversations', 114, 215
despatches for *New York Tribune*, 216
influence of Anna Jameson, 290
nursing with Cristina de Belgiojoso, 216, 277
relationship with Lydia Maria Child, 93, 215
Woman in the Nineteenth Century, 215–16, 651

Gage, Matilda Joslyn, 1, 20, 94, 101, 114, 115, 162, 184, 217–18, 461, 462
abolition, 1
friendship with Anthony, 21, 217
friendship with Stanton, 217, 542
History of Woman Suffrage [with Susan B Anthony and Elizabeth Cady Stanton], 1, 20, 94, 101, 114, 115, 184, 217, 542–3, 568
on matriarchy, 162
Woman, Church and State, 162, 217
Woman's Declaration of Rights [with Susan B Anthony and Elizabeth Cady Stanton], 217
Gagliani, Dianella, 286
Gallagher, Catherine, 68
The Making of the Modern Body [with Thomas Laqueur], 68
Gamarnikow, Eva, 378
Ganter, Regina, 51
Pearl-Shellers of Torres Strait, 51
Gardner, Elinor, 9
The Desert Fayum, 9
Kharga Oasis in Prehistory, 9
work with Getrude Caton-Thompson, 9
Garimara, Doris Pilkington Nugi, 418
Follow the Rabbit Proof Fence, 418
Garrard, Mary, 35
Artimesia Gentileschi, 35
Artimesia Gentileschi Around 1622, 35
Garrod, Dorothy, 10
Environment, Tools and Man, 10
The Upper Palaeolithic Age in Britain, 10
Gaskell, Elizabeth, 161, 256–7, 258
Mary Barton, 257, 258
relationship with Charlotte Bronte, 257
Gaunt, Mary, 352–4
Gearhart, Suzanne, 276
Geiger, Susan, 387
Gender, 218–19, 570, 602, 603–5
Genius, 22, 61, 478
Genlis, Stéphanie Félicité de, 336
Mémoires, 336
Genre, xvi
Gentile, Annua Verta, 279
L'instruzione in famiglia, 279
Martiri Italiani, 279
George, M Dorothy, 99, 228, 262
London Life in the Eighteenth Century, 262
Gero, Joan, 14
Gerson, Carole, 28, 85
Gertrude of Helfta, 456
Legacy of Divine Piety, 456
Giannarelli, Elena, 287
Gibbon, William, 41
Decline and Fall, 41
Influence on Austen's *Pride and Prejudice*, 40
Gibson, Margaret, 71
'Clitoral Corruption', 71
Gibson, Mary, 439
Prostitution and the State in Italy, 439
Giddings, Paula, 96, 112, 168, 537, 569
When and Where I Enter, 96, 537, 569

Giese, Diana, 51
Astronauts, 51
Beyond Chinatown, 51
Lost Souls & Dragons: Voices of Today's Chinese Australians, 51
Gilbert, Olive, 417
The Narrative of Sojourner Truth, 417
Gilbert, Susan, 576
Gilchrist, Roberta, 463
Gender and Material Culture, 463
Gille, Elisabeth, 214
Le Mirador, 214
Gilman, Charlotte Perkins, 58, 163, 190, 219–21, 300, 351, 406, 572
autobiography [*The Living of CPG*], 200, 221
grand-niece of Catherine Beecher, 219
Herland, 220, 572
Man-Made World, 220, 406
The Yellow Wallpaper, 220
utopian writings, 220
Women and Economics, 220, 351
Gimbutas, Marija, 14, 615
Civilisation of the Goddess, 615
Gibini, Ruby Langford, 418
Don't Take Your Love to Town, 418
Girton College, 12, 62, 75, 133, 302, 347, 448
Gleadle, Kathryn, 273
Women in British Politics [with Sarah Richardson], 273
Goddard, Georgiana, 348
The Way of St James, 348
Pre-Romanesque Churches of Spain, 348
Godineau, Dominique, 483
The Women of Paris, 483
Goldman, Emma, 481
Goldman, Hetty, 10
Excavations at Eutresis in Boeotia, 10
Excavations at Gözlü, 10
Excavations at Kule, 10
Excavations at Tarsus, 10
Goldman, Marion S., 440
Gold Diggers and Silver Miners, 440
Goldsmith, Oliver, 40
Gollan, Daphne, 48
Gomme, Alice, 318
Dictionary of British Folklore, 318
Gonzaga, Camilla Faa, 338
Historia, 338
Goodall, Heather, 420
Goodnow, Minnie, 376
Outlines of Nursing History, 376
Gordon, Ann, 598
'The Problem of Women's History' [with Mari Jo Buhle and Nancy Schrom Dye], 598
Gordon, Linda, 69, 169, 442, 597, 604
Heroes of Their Own Lives, 169
Pitied but not Entitled, 169
'Seeking Ecstasy on the Battlefield' [with Ellen Dubois] 69, 442
Woman's Bodies, Woman's Rights, 89, 378
Gordon, Mary, 309, 310
Chase of the Wild Goose, 309
Gore-Booth, Eva, 305, 310
Gorham, Deborah, 83
Gössman, Elisabeth, 347, 349
Gouma-Peterson, Thalia, 303
Anna Komnene and Her Times, 303
Gourlay, Janet, 8
Gournay, Marie de, 117, 468, 471
Equality of Men and Women, 117, 468
The Ladies Complaint, 468
The Ladies Grievance, 468
Gowing, Margaret, 408
Britain and Atomic Energy, 408
Grabiner, Judith, 509, 510
Gradnekh, Elizabethe von, 373
Graham-Brown, Sarah, 391
Images of Women, 391
Graham, Patricia, 134
Grand, Sarah, 162
Gray, Charlotte, 548
biography of Susanna Moodie and Catherine Parr Traill, 548
Grazia, Victoria de, 65
How Fascism Ruled Women, 65
Great Britain, xvii, 221–30, 493
Green, John Richard, 544
collaboration with Alice Stopford Green, 544
husband of Alice Stopford Green, 544
Green, Mary Anne Everett, 25, 223, 225, 230–1, 502, 503
editor of the *Calenders of State Papers*, 231
Letters of the Royal Ladies of Britain, 230
Lives of the Princesses of England, 223, 230, 502
Green, Miranda, 465
Celtic Goddesses, 465
Green, Monica, 66

Greenberg, Cheryl Lynn, 97
A Circle of Trust, 97
Greene, Maxine, 134
Greer, Germaine, 35
The Obstacle Race, 35
Gregory, Lady Augusta, 267
The Kiltartan History Book, 267
Visions and Beliefs in the West of Ireland, 267
Grey, Elizabeth, 372
Gribaudi, Gabriella, 286
Griffiths, Naomi, 84
Grimke, Angelina, 1, 532, 561
'An Appeal to the Christian Women of the South', 532
sister of Sarah, 532
Grimke, Sarah, 1, 532
Letters on the Equality of the Sexes, 532
sister of Angelina, 532
Grimshaw, Patricia, 48, 53, 119–28, 422
Creating a Nation [with Marilyn Lake, Ann McGrath and Marion Quartly [Aveling]], 49, 101, 367, 368
Freedom Bound I [with Susan Janson and Marion Quartly [Aveling]], 48
Paths of Duty, 422
Women's Rights and Human Rights [with Katie Holmes and Marilyn Lake], 53
Gristwood, Sarah, 430
Groppi, Angela, 286
Grote, Harriet, 43
Relationship with Sarah Taylor Austin, 43
Grumbach, von Argula, 451
Guasco, Annibal, 466
Discourse, 466
Guebeswiller, Katharine, 341
Guillet, de Pernette, 473
Guin, Ursula Le, 247
The Dispossessed, 247
The Eye of the Heron, 573
Guizot, François, 25, 43
Translated by Sarah Taylor Austin, 43
Gurewitsch, Brana, 464
Mothers, Sisters, Resisters, 464
Guy, Donna J., 445–6
Sex and Danger, 445–6
Guyart, François, 206
Guyart, Marie, 458
Autobiography, 458
Guyon, Jeanne-Marie, 332
La Vie de Mme JMB de la Mothe Guyon, 332
Habermas, Jürgen, 155, 156, 483
Hack, Maria, 226
English Stories, 226
Grecian Stories 226
Hacker, Carlotta, 377
The Indomitable Lady Doctor, 377
Hackett, Maria, 23, 24
Hagiography, 173, 174, 231–2, 252, 612
Haight, Elizabeth, 13
Haldane, Elizabeth Sanderson, 377
The British Nurse in War and Peace, 377
Hale, Sarah Josepha, 93, 142, 180, 181, 232, 239, 290, 405, 460, 561, 614
Contributor to *Juvenile Miscellany*, 93
editor *Godey's Lady's Book*, 93, 233, 561, 614–15
Liberia, 233, 561
Northwood, 233
Woman's Record, 181, 233–4, 406, 460
Haley, Shelley, 14
Halkett, Anne, 233–4, 472
Memoirs, 233, 472
Hall, Catherine, 54, 144, 230, 328, 397
Civilizing Subjects, 144, 328
Defining the Victorian Nation, 328
Family Fortunes [with Leonore Davidoff] 166, 263, 327
White, Male and Middle Class, 263, 328
Hall, Charlotte Maxwell, 353
Hall, Edith [Dohan], 8
Tomb Groups in the University Museum, 8
Hall, Lesley, 70–1
Sex, Gender and Social Change, 70
Hall, Mary, 558
A Woman's Trek from the Cape to Cairo, 558
Hall, Radclyffe, 306
The Well of Loneliness, 311, 312, 314
Hall, S. C., 319
Chertsey and its Neighbourhood, 319
Pilgrimages to English Shrines, 319
Halstead, Caroline, 224
Life of Richard III, 224
Hamilton, Cicely, 200
autobiography [*Life Errant*], 200
Hamilton, Elizabeth, 234, 244
Benger's *Memoirs*, 60, 234
feud with Mary Hays, 234
Letters of a Hindoo Rajah, 234
Letters of Elementary Principles of Education, 234,

Hamilton, Elizabeth – *continued*
Memoirs of Agrippina, 234, 244
Memoirs of Modern Philosophers, 234
relationship with Elizabeth Benger, 60, 234
relationship with Lucy Aikin, 5, 234
Hamilton, Janet, 257
Hamilton, Sylvia, 84
We're Rooted Here and They Can't Pull Us Up [with Peggy Bristow, Dionne Brand, Linda Carty, Afua P Cooper, and Adrienne Shadd], 84
Hammond, Barbara, 99, 227, 235, 262
collaboration with John Lawrence Hammond, 235, 235
The Skilled Labourer [with John Lawrence Hammond], 235, 262
The Town Labourer [with John Lawrence Hammond], 235, 262
The Village Labourer [with John Lawrence Hammond], 235, 262
Hammond, John Lawrence, 235
collaboration with Barbara Hammond, 235
husband of Barbara Hammond, 235
Hancock, Mary, 358
Hanem, Kuchuk, 391
Hannam, June, 191
Hanson, Holly, 422
Haraway, Donna, 509, 513, 514, 573
Crystals, Fabrics and Fields, 509
'Manifesto for Cyborgs', 573
Primate Visions, 513
Hareven, Tamara, 164
Family Time and Industrial Time, 164
Transitions, 164
Harford, Barbara, 409
Greenham Common [with Sarah Hopkins], 409
Harkeness, Deborah, 513
John Dee's Conversations with Angels . . ., 513
Harley, Brilliana, 476
Harper, Ida Husted, 20
Harris, Alice Kessler, 302
Harris, Mary Dormer, 225
The Story of Coventry, 225
Harrison, Jane Ellen, 6, 11, 12, 15, 162, 235–7, 462
Alpha and Omega, 237
lesbianism, 237
matriarchy, 162
memoir, 237
myth and history, 11, 236
Myths of the Odyssey, 236
The Mythology and Monuments of Ancient Athens, 236
Prolegomena to the Study of Greek Religion, 11
Themis, 11, 236
Harsin, Jill, 439
Policing Prostitution in Ninteenth-Century France, 439
Hart, Margaret, 121
Janet Fisher Archibald, 121
Hartman, Mary, 66, 569
Clios Consciousness Raised [with Lois Banner], 66, 569
Haskin, Victoria, 423
Haslam, Beryl, 411
From Suffrage to Internationalism, 411
Hasluck, Alexandra, 45
Portrait with Background, 45
Hatfield, S., 316
Hayden, Mary, 270
Hays, Mary, 160, 179–80, 237–8, 499, 614
A Victim of Prejudice, 179, 237
Appeal to the Men of Great Britain, 237
Biographer of Catherine Sawbridge Macaulay, 160, 325
Female Biography, 160, 179–81, 238, 325, 499, 614
feud with Elizabeth Hamilton, 234, 238
Letters and Essays, 237
Memoirs of Emma Courtney, 178, 237
Memoirs of Queens, 180, 238, 499
obituaries of Mary Wollstonecraft, 237
relationship with Mary Wollstonecraft, 160, 179, 237
Haywood, Eliza, 157, 238–9, 519, 523–4
Adventures of Eovaai, 157, 238–9
editor of *The Female Spectator*, 157, 238
influence of Delariviere Manley, 238
Memoirs of A Certain Island, 157
Secret History of Mary Queen of Scots, 239
The Secret History of . . . Court of Caramania, 238, 523–4
Heilbrun, Carolyn, 172
Héloïse, 118, 205, 302, 341
Hemans, Felicia, 502
Records of Woman, 502
Henderson, Mary Sturge [Gretton], 320–1
A Corner of the Cotswolds, 320

Burford Past and Present, 321
Three Centuries in North Oxfordshire, 320
Henriette, Sister [Darie Lemyre-Marsolais], 80
Histoire de la Congrégation de notre-Dame de Montréal, 80
Henry, Alice, 44, 50
Herman, Sondra, 409
'Eleven against War', 409
Hermes, Joke, 608
Reading Women's Magazines, 608
Herold, Elisabeth, 105, 106, 108, 109, 110
Herrad of Hohenbourg, 457, 612
Garden of Delights, 457, 612
Hersh, Blanche Glassman, 1
The Slavery of Sex: Feminist-Abolitionists in America, 1
Hershatter, Gail, 359, 445–6
Dangerous Pleasures, 359, 445–6
Herzenberg, Caroline, 511
Their Day in the Sun [with Ruth Howes], 511
Hewitt, Margaret, 170
Children in English Society [with Ivy Pinchbeck], 170, 413
Hewitt, Mary Elizabeth, 614
Heroines of History, 614
Hewitt, Nancy, 1
Heyer, Georgette, 226, 246
Bath Tangle, 246
knowledge of Jane Austen, 247
Regency Buck, 247
These Old Shades, 246
The Black Moth, 246
Hibbaerd, Laura, 345
Medieval Romance in England, 345
Hicks, Joanna, 396
Higginbottom, Evelyn Brooks, 420
'Beyond the Sounds of Silence', 420
Higonnet, Margaret, 377, 577
Nurses at the Front, 377
Hildegard of Bingen, 341, 343, 372, 405, 457, 612
Causae et Curae, 372
Liber divinorum operum, 343, 457, 612
Scivias, 343, 457
Vita Sancti Disibodi, 341–2
Vita Sancti Ruperti, 342
Hill, Barbara, 303
Anna Komnene and Her Times, 303
Hill, Bridget, 229, 262–3
Britain's Married Women Workers, 262–3
Servants, 229
The Republican Virago, 325
Women, Work and Sexual Politics in Eighteenth-Century England, 229
Hill, Georgiana, 227
Women in English Life, 227, 351
Hill, Jacqueline, 272
From Patriots to Unionists, 272
Hill, Marilynn Wood, 440
Their Sister's Keepers, 440
Hill, Mary A., 221
Charlotte Perkins Gilman: The Makings of a Radical Feminist, 221
Hill, Rosamond, 555
What We Saw in Australia [with Florence Davenport], 555
Hill, Ruth Edmond, 96
Black Women Oral History Project, 96
Hillard, T. W., 5–15, 235–7, 549–50
Hinds, Bronagh
Women Working for Peace, 274
Hine, Darlene Clarke, 95, 103
Black Victory, 95
Black Women in America, 103
'Hispana', 18, 19
Histiaea, 17
Historical Dictionary of Women's Education, 138
historical fiction, xiv, 41–2, 160, 161, 226, 240–9, 264, 316–18, 488–95, 515
Historical films, 98
historical organizations, 79, 249–52, 563
Hobhouse, Emily, 406
Hobson, Barbara Meil, 444
Uneasy Virtue, 444
Hoddeson, Lilian, 511, 514
Crystal Fire [with Michael Riordan], 510
Hodgson, Barbara, 559
No Place for a Lady, 559
Holgate, Mary S., 321
Inquisitions Post Mortem, 321
Holland, Catherine, 111, 451
Holland, Mary Gardner, 376, 406
Our Army Nurses, 376, 406
Holloway, Laura Carter, 502
The Ladies of the White House, 502

Holmes, Janice, 273
Coming Into the Light [with Diana Urquart], 273
Holmes, Katie, 48, 53, 429
Freedom Bound II [with Marilyn Lake], 48
Spaces in Her Day, 53, 429
Women's Rights and Human Rights [with Patricia Grimshaw and Marilyn Lake], 53
Holt, Emily Sarah, 502
Memoirs of Royal Ladies, 502
The Queens of England, 502
Holtby, Winifred, 73
Friendship with Vera Brittain, 73, 199
Testament Friendship, 73, 199
Holton, Sandra Stanley, 185, 188, 191
Feminism and Democracy, 188
Honeyman, Katrina, 263
Women Gender and Industrialisation, 263
Hooker, Claire, 507–15
Hooks, bell, 112, 419, 569, 605
Ain't I A Woman?, 419, 569, 605
Hooton, Elizabeth, 529
Hope, Anne, 224
Hopkins, Jane Ellice, 148, 443–4
The Power of Womanhood, 148
Hopkins, Sarah
Greenham Common [with Barbara Hopkins], 409
Houston, Susan, 83, 138
Schooling and Scholars in Ninteenth-Century Ontario [with Alison Prentice], 83, 138
Howard, Sarah, 3, 90–1, 114–15, 219–21, 253–4, 525, 526–8, 539–40, 573–4, 586
Howard, Winefred Lady, 554
Journal of a Tour in the United States, 554
Howe, Julia Ward, 216
Margaret Fuller, Marchesa Ossoli, 216
Howes, Ruth, 511
Their Day in the Sun [with Caroline Herzenberg], 511
Howitt, Mary, 258
Hrotsvitha, 55, 252–3, 342, 456
Gesta Ottonis, 252, 342–3
Primordia Coenobii Gandeshemensis, 252, 342–3
Hudson, Pat, 264
Huff, Cynthia, 429
Hufton, Olwen, 164, 213
'Women and the Family Economy in Eighteenth Century France', 164–5
Women and the Limits of Citizenship, 213
Huggins, Jackie, 50, 419, 420
Auntie Rita [with Rita Huggins], 50
Huggins, Rita, 50
Auntie Rita [with Jackie Huggins], 50
Hughes-Warrington, Marnie, 611–17
Hughes, Sarah, 617
Women in World History [with Brady Hughes], 617
Hull, Gloria T., 569
All the Women are White, 569
Hull, Isabel, 65
Sexuality, State and Civil Society in Germany, 65
Hume, David, 22, 40, 153, 154, 156, 222, 323
Humpheries, Jane, 263
Humphrey, Margaret, 380
Yellow Fever and the South, 380
Huneberc of Heidenheim, 341, 457
Lives of Willibald and Wynnebald, 341, 457
Hunt, Harriet, 376
Glances and Glimpses, 376
Hunt, Lynn, 65, 166–7, 483
The Family Romance of the French Revolution, 65, 166–7
Politics, Culture and Class in the French Revolution, 483
Hunt, Susan Jane, 51
Spinifex and Hessian, 51
Hurd-Mead, Kate Campbell, 253–4, 376
History of Women in Medicine, 254, 376
Medical Women of America, 253–4, 376
Hurley, Kelly, 66
The Gothic Body . . ., 66
Hurston, Zora Neale, 567
Mules and Men, 567
Tell My Horse, 567
Hutcheon, Linda, 247
A Poetics of Postmodernism, 247
Hutchins, Barbara Leigh, 262
Women in Modern Industry, 262
Hutchinson, Lucy, 22, 23, 61, 161, 255–6, 472, 544
Catherine Macaulay's interest in the *Memoirs*, 23

Memoirs of the Life of Colonel Hutchinson, 22, 23, 161, 255–6, 472
Hypatia, 113, 117

I'Incarnation, Marie, Guyart de, 77, 78
Industrialization, xvii, 228, 255–64
Innis, Mary Quayle, 82, 85
Unfold the Years, 82
Ireland, xvii, 241–3, 264–74
Iriyagolle, Indrani, 464
Irvine, E Marie, 126
Irving, Sarah, 91–2, 571–3
Italy, xvii, 275–88, 362–4, 365

Jackson, F Nevill, 318
A History of Hand Made Lace, 318
Jackson, Georgina F., 317
Shropshire Word Book, 317
Jackson, Helen Hunt, 565
A Century of Dishonor, 565
Ramona, 565
Jackson, Jane, 373
Very Shorte and Compendious Methode of Phisicke and Chirurgery, 373
Jackson, Margaret, 70, 439, 442–3
The Real Facts of Life, 70, 439, 442
Jacob, Elizabeth, 373
Jacob, Naomi, 306
Physicall and Chyrurgicall Receipts, 374
Jacobs, Ellen, 149
Jacobs, Fredrika, 36
Defining the Renaissance Virtuosa, 36
Jacobs, Harriet [Linda Brent], 387, 417, 528, 529, 533, 536, 562
Incidents in the Life of a Slave Girl, 387, 417, 528, 529, 562
Jacobs, Margaret, 168, 514
The Cultural Meaning of the Scientific Revolution, 514(3)
Jacoway, Elizabeth, 95
Understanding the Little Rock Crisis, 95
Jagose, Annamarie, 450
Inconsequence: Lesbian Representation and the Logic of Sexual Sequence, 450
James, Barbara, 50, 51
No Man's Land, 50, 51
James, Elinor, 157
Jameson, Anna Brownell Murphy, 29, 31–2, 37, 86, 113, 131–2, 216, 233, 288–90, 500, 502, 547
Characteristics of Women, 289
influence on Margaret Fuller, 290
Legends of the Madonna, 32, 289
Marian iconography, 32, 289–90
Memoirs of Celebrated Female Sovereigns, 289, 500
Janson, Susan, 48
Freedom Bound I [with Patricia Grimshaw and Marion Quartly [Aveling]]
Japan, xvii, 290–9
Jardine, Lisa, 466
Jayawardena, Kumari, 368, 396, 424
The White Woman's Other Burden, 424
Jefford, Susan, 570
Remasculinization of America, 570
Jeffrey, Julie Roy, 2
Jeffreys, Leslie Ann, 445–6
Sex and Borders, 445–6
Jeffreys, Sheila, 69, 70, 189, 439, 442–4
The Idea of Prostitution, 443
The Spinster and Her Enemies, 70, 189, 439, 442–4
Jenson, Jane, 583
Jewsbury, Geraldine, 310, 609,
letters to Jane Carlyle, 310, 609
Jex-Blake, Katharine, 12
Jex-Blake, Sophia, 310, 376
Medical Women, 376
John, Angela V., 229
Unequal Opportunities, 263
Johnson-Odim, Cheryl, 421
Johnson, Anna Cumming, 561
The Iroquois, 561
Johnson, Berenice, 98
Johnson, E Pauline, 85
Paddling Her Own Canoe, 85
Johnson, Nuala, 275
Ireland, the Great War and the Geography of Remembrance, 275
Johnson, Patricia E., 263
Hidden Hands, 263
Johnson, Penelope D., 463
Equal in Monastic Profession, 463
Johnson, Susan M., 454
Johnston, Ellen, 257
Autobiography, Poems and Songs, 257

Johnston, Jennifer, 266
The Captains and the Kings, 266
Jolly, Margaret, 420, 425
Jones, Cecily, 528–39
Jones, Helen, 52, 137
In Her Own Name, 52
Jones, Jacqueline, 168, 420, 538
Labor of Love, Labor of Sorrow, 168, 420
Jones, Kathleen, 92
A Glorious Fame: The Life of Margaret Cavendish, 92
Jones, Lesley Dean, 66
Women's Bodies in Classical Greek Science, 66
Jordanova, Ludmilla, 64
Sexual Visions, 64
Joshi, Rama, 397,
Daughters of Independence [with Joanna Liddle], 397
Jourdain, Margaret, 318
Julian of Norwich, 342, 405
Revelations, 342
Junius, Maria Anna, 111
Junot, Madame Laure, 497, 614
Memoirs of Celebrated Women, 614
Jussie, Jeanne (de), 206, 451
Le commencement de l'hérésie de Genéve, 206
Petite Chronique, 451

Kabbani, Rana, 391, 396
Imperial Fictions, 391
Passionate Nomad, 392
Kamester, Margaret, 411
Militarism versus Feminism [with Jo Vellacott], 411
Kamichika, Ichiko, 294
Nihon Josei Shisôshi, 294
Kamm, Josephine, 133, 134, 137
Hope Deferred, 133
How Different from Us, 133
Indicative Past, 133
Karant-Nunn, Susan, 453, 454
Karcher, Carolyn L., 2
The First Woman of the Republic, 2
Kavanagh, Julia, 181, 233, 300, 400, 461, 497
English Women of Letters, 300, 400
French Women of Letters, 300
influence on Charlotte Bronte, 300
Women in France, 300
Women of Christianity, 181, 300, 461

Kay, Lily, 509
The Molecular Vision, 511
Keane, Angela, 363
Keddie, Nikki, 464
Women in the Muslim World, 464
Keire, Mara L., 444
Keller, Evelyn Fox, 509, 511, 512, 514
Reflections on Gender and Science, 512
Secrets of Life, Secrets of Death, 511
Keller, Rosemary Skinner, 463
In Our Own Voices [with Rosemary Radford Ruether], 463
Kellogg, Louise Phelps, 563–4
Frontier Advance on the Upper Ohio, 564
The French Regime in Wisconsin, 564
The British Regime in Wisconsin, 564
Kelly, Catherine, 434
Kelly, Farley, 52
Double Time [with Marilyn Lake], 52
Kelly, Joan, xvii, 101–2, 119, 136, 301–2, 415, 465, 475, 601
Collaborative writing, 101–2
'Did women have a Renaissance?', 465, 475, 601–2
Household Kith and Kin [with Renate Bridenthal, Amy Swerdlow and Phyllis Vine], 102, 300
'The Doubled Vision of Feminist Theory', 301, 601–2
'The Social Relation of the Sexes', 218, 300
Women History and Theory, 102, 302
Workbook on Sterilization and Sterilization Abuse, 101–2, 300
Kelso, Ruth, 119
Doctrine for the Lady of the Renaissance, 119
Kemble, Fanny, 554
Journals, 554
Kemp-Welch, Alice, 253, 415
Of Six Medieval Women, 253, 415
Kempe, Margery, 336, 342, 457, 551
Boke, 342, 345
Kempf, Elisabeth, 341
Kempf, Rosa, 385
Kennedy, Elizabeth Lapovsky, 103, 570–1
Boots of Leather, Slippers of Gold [with Madelaine D Davis], 103, 570–1
Kent, Eliza, 464
Kent, Susan Kingsley, 70, 189
Sex and Suffrage, 70, 189

Kenyon, Kathleen, 10
Archaeology in the Holy Land, 10
Digging Up Jericho, 10
Kéralio, Louise-Felicite-Guynement de [Robert], 118, 178, 209, 302, 478
Collection des meilleurs ourages français composés par des femmes, 118, 178, 209, 302
Histoire d'Elisabeth, 302
Les Crimes des reines de la France, 210, 302, 477
Kerber, Linda, 569, 603
Women of the Republic, 569
Kershaw, Nora, 346
Anglo-Saxon and Norse Poems, 346
The Growth of Literature, 346
Kessler-Harris, Alice, 569
Out to Work, 569
Kessler, Carol Farley, 571
Daring to Dream, 571
Key, Ellen, 406
War, Peace and the Future, 406
Kibre, Pearl, 347
Kiddle, Margaret, 45, 47
Men of Yesterday, 45
Kinealy, Christine, 272
This Great Calamity, 272
King, Helen, 379
Hippocrates' Woman, 379
King, Mary, 97
Kingsley, Mary, 557
Travels in West Africa, 557
West African Studies, 557
Kingston, Beverley, 47, 377, 378
My Wife, My Daughter and Poor Mary Ann, 47
The World Moves Slowly, 48
Kinnear, Mary, 84
In Subordination, 138
Kinzie, Juliette Magill, 562
Wau-bun, 562
Kirk, Sylvia Van, 83, 422, 528
'Many Tender Ties', 83, 422
Kirkby, Diane, 50, 52, 53
Alice Henry, 50
Klapische-Zuber, Kristiane, 166, 287, 466
Women, Family and Ritual in Renaissance Italy, 166, 466
Klein, Ursula, 511
Experiments, Models, Paper Tools, 511
Tools and Mode of Representation, 511
Knowles, Lilian, 99, 227, 262, 302–3, 319
Economic Development in the Nineteenth Century, 303
Economic Development of the British Empire, 303
The Industrial and Commercial Revolutions in England, 227, 303
Supervision of Alice Clark, 99, 303
Supervision of Ivy Pinchbeck, 303
Kosambi, Meera, 147, 433
At the Intersection of Gender Reform and Religious Belief [1995]
The Letters and Correspondence of Pandita Ramabai, 433–4
Kraditor, Aileen S., 1, 597
Means and Ends in American Abolitionism, 1
The Idea of the Woman Suffrage Movement, 597
Kraft, Barbara S., 408
Peace Ship, 408
Kristeva, Julia, 429
'Woman's Time', 429
Kucich, Greg, xvi, 498, 499
Kuhn, Deborah, 66
From Midwives to Medicine, 66
Kushner, Rose, 378
Breast Cancer, 378
Kwon, Insook, 356
Kyle, Noeline, 138
Her Natural Destiny, 138

Labé, Louise, 468, 473
Debate Between Folly and Love, 468
Ladies of Llangollen [Sarah Ponsonby and Eleanor Butler], 224, 305, 306, 309–12, 484
Elizabeth Mavor's book, 224, 484
Ladner, Joyce, 96
Lafayette, Comtesse de [Marie-Madeleine Pioche de la Vergne], 156, 208, 332, 515, 519
Histoire de Mme Henriette d'Angleterre, 335
La Princess de Clèves, 156, 208
Mémoires, 332, 335
Lake, Marilyn, 48, 49, 50, 52, 101, 169, 191
Australians at Work [with Charles Fox], 48
Creating a Nation [with Patricia Grimshaw, Ann McGrath and Marion Quartly [Aveling]], 48, 49, 101, 367, 368
Double Time, 52
Faith [with Farley Kelly], 50
Freedom Bound II [with Katie Holmes], 48
Getting Equal, 52

Lake, Marilyn, – *continued*
The Limits of Hope, 49
Women's Rights and Human Rights [with Patricia Grimshaw and Katie Holmes], 53
Lamb, Winifred, 10
Excavations at Thermi in Lesbos, 10
Greek and Roman Bronzes, 10
Lanata, Guiliana, 287
Landes, Joan, 64, 190, 483
Women and the Public Sphere in the Age of the French Revolution, 64, 190
Lane, Ann J., 200, 221
To Herland and Beyond, 221
Langley, Esme, 304, 308
Lanzani, Carolina, 282
Lezioni di antichità greche, Milano, 282
Mito storico di Camillo, 282
Last, Nella, 579
Lauden, Rachel, 511
From Mineralogy to Geology, 511
Laugesen, Amanda, 249–52, 559–71
Laurence, Anne, 26, 229
Women in England, 229
Laurens, de Jeanne, 207
La Généalogie des Messieurs du Laurens, 207
Lauretis, Teresa de, 606
'Eccentric Subjects', 606
Laut, Agnes, 81
The Cariboo Trail, 81
Lavigne, Marie, 83
Lawless, Emily, 267
With the Wild Geese, 267
Lawrance, Hannah, 499–500, 501, 502
Historical Memoirs of the Queens of England, 499–500
History of Women, 500
Lawson, Sylvia, 52
The Archibald Paradox, 52
Leach, Abby, 12
Leavitt, Judith Walzer, 379
Brought to Bed, 379
Lecoq, Violette Rougier, 578
Lee, Jenny, 49
A People's History of Australia since 1788 [with Verity Burgmann], 49
Lee, Sophia, 222, 375, 493
The Recess, 222, 375, 493
Lee, Vernon, 29, 32, 34–5, 87, 410
Euphorion, 34
Renaissance Fancies and Studies, 34
Lefkowitz, Mary, 14, 15
Lehfeldt, Elizabeth, 455
Religious Women in Golden Age Spain, 455
Leneman, Leah, 229
Lennox, Charlotte, 607
Leo, Andre, 481
Leon, Vicki, 596
Lerner, Gerda, xvi, 1, 136, 471, 528, 569, 596, 599, 600, 601, 615
Creation of Feminist Consciousness, 596
Creation of Patriarchy, 615
Grimké Sisters from South Carolina, 1
Hidden from History, 569
'Placing Women in History', 601, 604
The Majority Finds Its Past, 419
The Woman in American History, 569
Lesbian history, 224, 304–14
Lesbian History Group, 102
Not a Passing Phase, 102
Letters and letter writing, 17, 18, 78, 146, 340, 427–37
Levine, Philippa, 143–51, 359, 447
Feminist Lives, 190
Prostitution, Race and Politics, 144, 359, 447
Lewald, Fanny, 364
Prinz Louis Ferdinand, 364
Lewenhak, Sheila, 263
Women and Trade Unions, 263
Lewis, Elsie, 568
Lewis, Jane, 170, 602
Lewis, Reina, 36, 393, 394, 424
Gendering Orientalism, 36, 393, 424
Leyser, Henrietta, 229
Christina of Markyate, 229
Medieval Women, 229
Lézardière, Charlotte Pauline Robert de, 159, 209
Théorie des loix politiques de la monarchie français, 159, 209
Library of Congress, 24
Admittance of women, 24
Liddington, Jill, 188, 189, 259, 406, 410
The Life and Times of a Respectable Rebel, 259
One Hand Tied Behind Us [with Jill Norris], 188, 189
The Long Road to Greenham, 410–11

Liddle, Joanna, 397
Daughters of Independence [with Rama Joshi], 397
Light, Beth, 84
Canadian Women: A History [with Alison Prentice, Paula Bourne, Gail Cuthbert Brandt, Wendy Mitchinson and Naomi Black], 84
Linsey, Karen, 504
Divorced, Beheaded, Survives, 504
Linton, Eliza Lynn, 317
The Lake Country, 317
Lipinska, Mélanie, 376
Histoire des Femmes Médecins, 376
Lister, Anne, 485
diaries, 485
Local history, 90, 103, 158, 225–6, 315–22, 399, 574
Lodge, Eleanor, 227
Lofts, Norah, 503
The Queens of England, 503
London Feminist History Group, 69, 102
Sexual Dynamics of History, 69, 102
London School of Economics, 227, 262, 303, 319
Longfield, Ada K., 271
Longford, Elizabeth, 503, 594
Longueville, Duchesse de, 61, 515
Mémoires, 334
Loomba, Ania, 369
Looser, Devoney, xvi, 21–9
Lopate, Carole, 377
Lovatelli, Ersilia Caetani, 281
Lowe, K. J. P., 455
Chronicles and Convent Culture, 455
Lowe, Lisa, 393, 394
Critical Terrains, 393
Lown, Judy, 263
With Free and Graceful Step, 263
Luddy, Maria, 273, 441
Lugrin, Nellie de Bertrand, 121–2
The Pioneer Women of Vancouver Island, 121–2
Lutz, Alma, 1, 322, 568
Created Equal, 322
Crusade for Freedom, 1, 322
Lutz, Cora E., 346–7
Lyon, Mary, 133
Lyons, Maryinez, 380
Lyons, Tanya, 422
Macadam, Elizabeth, 200
McAliskey, Bernadette [Devlin], 274
Macaulay, Catharine Sawbridge, 22, 23, 27, 61, 159, 178, 179, 180, 222–3, 224, 323–5, 474, 486–8, 490, 492
Accused of defacing archival materials, 23, 323
correspondence with Mary Wollstonecraft, 323, 486–7
History of England from the Accession of James I [8 vols], 23, 159, 222, 323, 476–7, 486–8, 492
History of England from the Revolution, 159
interest in Lucy Hutchinson's *Memoirs*, 23, 323
Letters on Education, 159, 178, 323,
relationship with Mercy Otis Warren, 324
use of British Library, 23, 159
McCarthy, Louella, 370–80
McCarthy, Wendy, 52
Don't Fence Me In, 52, 203
McClee, Helen, 5
Study of Women in Attic Inscriptions, 5
McClintock, Anne, 65, 144, 392, 435–6
Imperial Leather, 65, 144
McClintock, Barbara, 514
McClung, Nellie, 122–3
In Times Like These, 122–3
The Stream Runs Fast, 121
McCoy, Judith
Daughters of the Loom [with Tracie Paterson], 258
A Fragile Design [with Tracie Patterson], 258
These Tangled Threads [with Tracie Paterson],258
McCrone, Kathleen, 83
MacCurtain, Margaret, 272
Macek, Ellen, 454
MacGeehin, Maureen, 271
McGrath, Ann, 49, 50, 101, 422, 606
Creating a Nation [with Patricia Grimshaw and Marilyn Lake, Marion Quartly [Aveling]], 49, 101, 367, 368
Machar, Agnes Maule, 79
Mack, Phyllis, 455
Visionary Women, 455, 463
McKay, Susan, 274
Northern Protestants, 274
Mackie, Vera, 290–9
MacKinnon, Alison, 130–40, 137, 138, 355
Love and Freedom, 139, 355
The New Women, 138

McKisack, May, 228
Oxford History of Britain: The Fourteenth Century, 228
McLeod, Enid, 415
The Order of the Rose, 415
MacLeod, Jessie, 124
The First Hundred Years [with Helen G Palmer], 124
Mcmillan, Chrystal, 410
Macmillan, Margaret, 84
Paris 1919, 84
McNamara, Jo Ann, 349
Sainted Women of the Dark Ages, 349
Sisters in Arms, 349
MacNaughton, Katherine, 82
The Development of the Theory and Practice of Education in New Brunswick, 82
McPhee, Hilary, 52
McPhee-Gribble, 52
Other People's Words, 52
McPherson, Kathryn, 378
Bedside Matters, 378
Macurdy, Grace H., 5, 12
Hellenistic Queens, 5
Maddox, Brenda, 511
Magarey, Susan, 43–54, 49, 53
Debutante Nations [with Sue Rowley and Susan Sheridan], 53
Unbridling the Tongues of Women, 50
Women at Work [with Ann Curthoys and Peter Spearritt], 46–7
Magill, [White] Helen, 12
Magnall, Richmal, 226
Historical and Miscellaneous Questions, 226
Mahood, Linda, 441
The Magdalenes, 441
Maier, Annaliese, 347
Maillart, Ella, 558
Turkestan Solo, 558
Mair, Lucille Mathurin, 536–7
Maitland, F. W., 55, 370
Maitzen, Rohan Amanda, xvi, 173, 258
Makin, Bathsua Reginald, 117, 154, 594, 613
An Essay to Revive the Antient Education of Gentlewomen, 118, 154, 594, 613
Malakhova, Vera, 583–4
Malcovati, Henrica, 6
Mancini, Hortense, 335
Mancini, Marie, 335
Mani, Lata, 464
Contentious Traditions, 464
Manley, Delariviere, 222, 240, 325–6, 519, 522–4
influence on Eliza Haywood, 238
plays, 325
Secret Memoirs of the New Atalantis, 240, 325, 522–4
The Secret History of Queen Zarah, 222, 325, 522–3
Manning, Olivia, 577
The Balkan Trilogy, 577
Mansfield, Charlotte, 557
Via Rhodesia, 557
Mansfield, Katherine, 306, 307
Margaret of Beverley, 342
Margarita, Ernesta, 279
Martiri italiani . . ., 279
Marie-Antoinette, Mère, 80
L'Institute de la Providence, 80
Marinella, Lucrezia, 90, 117, 177, 468–70, 474, 613
The Nobility and Excellences of Women, 90, 117, 468–70, 613
Markievicz, Constance, 269
Women, Ideals and the Nation, 269
Markwick, Roger D., 475–84
Marland, Hilary, 379
The Art of Midwifery, 379
Marquets, Anne de, 457
Sonets Spirituels, 457
Mars, Florence, 97
Witness in Philadelphia, 97
Marsden, Susan, 100–3
Travels, 342
Marsh-Caldwell, Ann, 453
Protestant Reformation in France, 453
Marsh, Jan, 36
Pre-Raphaelite Sisterhood, 36
Marshall, Dorothy, 262
Marshall, Henrietta, 226
Our Island, 226
Our Empire Story, 226
Scotland's Story, 226
Marshall, Sherrin, 453, 454
Martin, Catherine, 44, 50
An Australian Girl, 44
The Incredible Journey, 44
Martin, Judith, 364

Martineau, Harriet, 61, 113, 194–5, 216, 256, 258, 260, 290, 327, 396, 448, 462, 551, 554, 555, 556
Autobiography, 194, 327, 337
Eastern Life, 327, 462, 551, 556
History of England During the Thirty Years' Peace, 260
Illustrations of Political Economy, 256
Retrospect of Wastern Travel, 554
Society in America, 327, 554
Maruoka, Hideko, 292
Nihon Nôson Fujin Mondai, 292
Masculinity, 219, 327–30, 606
Mass Observation Archive, 579
Massow, Frederica [Baroness von Reidesel], 554
Letters and Journals, 554
Matraini, Chiara, 458
Life of the Virgin, 458
Matthews, Jill, 48–9
Dance Hall and Picture Palace, 354
Good and Mad Women, 48–9
Matus, Jill, 66
Unstable Bodies, 66
Mavor, Elizabeth, 224, 484
The Ladies of Llangollen, 244, 484
Maxwell, Constantia, 270
Mayo, Katherine, 397
Mother India, 397
Maza, Sara, 214
Private Lives and Public Affairs, 214
Mechtild of Magdebourg, 456
Flowing Light of the Godhead, 456
Melman, Billie, xvi, 143, 392
Women's Orients, 143, 392, 394
Memoir, 17, 161, 171, 207–9, 233, 259, 283, 292, 323, 410, 438, 479, 534, 548, 580
Australian, 48,
Courtly memoirs, 4, 61, 331–9
definitions of, 331–2
and History, 332–7
Irish, 264
Julia Agrippina's *commentarii* as memoirs, 17
religious memoirs, 332, 342
wartime, 580
Mendelson, Sara, 68, 229
Women in early modern England [with Patricia Crawford], 229
Mendus, Susan, 424
Sexuality and Subordination [with Jane Rendall], 424
Merchant, Carolyn, 63, 512
The Death of Nature, 63, 512
Mernissi, Fatima, 397
Women and Islam, 397
Meskell, Lynn, 14
Meyerwitz, Joanne, 570
Not June Cleaver, 570
'Michael Field' [Katherine Bradley and Edith Cooper], 35
'Sight and Song', 35
Michel, Giustina Renier, 276–7
Origine delle feste veneziane, 277
Michel, Louise, 481
Mémoires, 481
Mid-dleton, Dorothy, 558
Victorian Lady Travellers, 558
Middle Ages, 64, 275, 339–49, 372, 404–5, 455, 457
Middleton, Sue, 138
Telling Women's Lives [with Kathleen Weiler], 138
Midgley, Clare, 144, 273
Women Against Slavery, 273
Miles, Margaret Ruth, 463
Carnal Knowing, 463
Miles, Rosalind, 616
The Women's History of the World, 616
Mill, Harriet Taylor, 259
Miller, Luri, 558
On Top of the World, 558
Miller, Pavla, 138
Millett, Kate, 59, 65, 201–2, 396, 597, 598
Autobiographical writing, 201–2
Sexual Politics, 59, 65–6, 201, 597, 598
Mills, Sara, 392, 394, 551
Discourses of Difference, 392, 551
Mitchell, Hannah, 198
The Hard Way Up, 198
Mitchell, Juliet, 187
Mitchell, Margaret, 247
Gone with the Wind, 247
Mitchell, Rosemary Ann, xvi, 221–30
Mitchinson, Wendy, 83
Canadian Women: A History [with Alison Prentice, Paula Bourne, Gail Cuthbert Brandt, Beth Light and Naomi Black], 84

Mitchison, Rosalind, 229
Modernity, 160, 256, 349–60, 444, 607
Moffatt, Tracey, 421
  Nice Coloured Girls, 421
  Nightcries, 421
Mohanty, Chandra, 151, 396, 419
  'Under Western Eyes', 151, 419
Mohrmann, Christiane A. E. M., 346
Moir, Anne, 508
  BrainSex [with David Jessell], 508
Mojon, Bianca Milesi, 276
Mommsen, Theodor, 6
Mongellaz, Fanny de, 211
  De l'influence des femmes, 211
Montagu, Mary Wortley, 145, 158, 392–3, 395, 461, 485, 552, 553, 555
  Letters from the Levant, 145, 158
  Turkish Embassy Letters, 158, 555
Montevecchi, Orsolino, 282
Montgomery, L., 121
  Courageous Women, 121
Montpensier, Mlle de, 332, 333, 515
  Mémoires, 332, 335, 336
Moodie, Susanna, 78, 79, 80, 546–8
  Roughing It in the Bush, 547
  Sister of Agnes and Elizabeth Strickland, 78, 546–8
Moody, Anne, 97
Moore, Eleanor, 407
  The Quest for Peace, 407
Moorehead, Caroline, 408
  Troublesome People, 408
Morantz-Sanchez, Regina, 66
  Conduct Unbecoming, 66
  'The Lady and the Physician', 378
More, Hannah, 42, 55, 185, 327, 364, 460, 530
Morelli, Emilia, 283
Moreton-Robinson, Aileen, 51, 55
  Talkin' up to the White Woman, 51
Morgan, Lady
  see Owenson, Sydney
Morgan, Sally, 50, 418
  My Place, 50, 418
Morgan, Susan, 444
  A Passion for Purity, 444
Morgan, Susan, 553, 559
  Place Matters, 559
Morris, Marilyn, 617
Morrisey, Marietta, 537
Morrison, Toni, 247, 538–9, 570
  Beloved, 247, 421, 538–9, 570
  Jazz, 421
  Tar Baby, 421
Moscucci, Ornella, 66, 379
  The Science of Woman, 66, 379
Moses, Claire, 187, 188
  French Feminism in the Nineteenth Century, 187
Motteville, Madame de, [Françoise Bertaut], 61
  Memoires, 207, 332, 334, 336
Mount Holyoake College, 8, 347, 370, 448, 600
Mulock, Dinah Maria, 316
  John Halifax Gentleman, 316
  An Unsentimental Journey through Cornwall, 316
Mulvey, Laura, 37
  'Visual Pleasure and Narrative Cinema', 37
Mumm, Susan, 441
Munson, Lady Ann, 23
Murata, Shizuko, 294
Murnane, Mary, 48
  Uphill All the Way [with Kay Daniels], 48
Murphy, Caroline, 36
  Lavinia Fontana, 36
Murphy, Sara, 97
Murray, Margaret, 5, 8, 464
  suffragette, 8
  Saqqara Mastabas, 9
  The God of Witches, 9
  The Witch-Cult in Western Europe, 9, 464
  The Osireion at Abydos, 9
Murray, Pauli, 97, 570

Naselli, Carmelina, 283
Nasstrom, Kathryn L., 96, 97
Nasta, Suseila, 421
  Motherlands, 421
Nation, xvi, 241, 277–80, 286–7, 360–70, 541
National tales, 160, 241, 244
Nationalism, 360–70
  and Romanticism, 361–4
Nava, Mica, 357
Navarre, Marguerite de, 335, 468–9
  Heptaméron, 335, 468–9
  Le Miroir de l'ame Pecherese, 468
Nead, Lynda, 36, 37
  Myths of Sexuality, 36, 439
  The Female Nude, 36
  Victorian Babylon, 37, 439

Neatby, Hilda, 77, 83, 85
Nechkina, Militsa, 482
Neilson, Nellie, 347, 370–1, 447, 448
The Cartulary and Terrier of the Priory of Bilsington Kent, 371
Customary Rents, 371
Economic Conditions on the Manors of Ramsey Abbey, 370
Medieval Agrarian Economy, 371
Survey of the Honour of Denbigh, 371
A Terrier Fleet, 371
Nelson, Dana, 328
National Manhood, 328
Nemours, Duchesse de [Marie d'Orléans], 61, 332
Nestor, Pauline, 141–2
Neveu, Madeleine, 473
New Zealand, 126–8
Newcomer, Mabel, 133–4
A Century of Higher Education for American Women, 133–4
Newnham College, 11, 55, 545
Nicobule, 16
Nicolai, Margareta, 107
Nidiffer, Jana, 138
Pioneering Deans of Women, 138
Nightingale, Florence, 185, 194, 372, 376, 377, 395, 405
Noakes, Lucy, 575–85
Noble, Anne,
The Riot, 274
Nochlin, Linda, 35
Women, Art, and Power, 36
Nogorola, Isotta, 117, 177, 467, 473
Nolan, Melanie, 255–64
Norberg, Kathryn, 454
Norris, Jill 188, 189
One Hand Tied behind Us [with Jill Liddington], 188, 189
Norton, Caroline, 185
Norton, Mary Beth, 569
Liberty's Daughters, 569
Nugent, Maria, 381–9
Nun of Chelles, 175, 341
Life of Bathild, 175, 341
Nunn, Pamela Gerrish, 36
Victorian Women Artists, 36
Nuns, writings of, 21, 77–8, 79, 104–11, 206, 275–6, 451
Nursing and Medicine, 371
Nussbaum, Felicity, 423
Torrid Zones, 423
Nutting, Mary Adelaide, 376
A History of Nursing [with Lavinia Dock], 376
Nye, Mary Jo, 509, 510
Before Big Science, 511
From Chemical Philosophy to Theoretical Chemistry, 509

Oakley, Ann, 379
Oberlin College, 112, 133
O'Brien, Patty, 415–26, 422
O'Connor, Maura, 368
The Romance of Italy, 368
Oda, Makoto, 294
The Bomb, 294
Odem, Mary E., 445
Delinquent Daughters, 445
O'Dowd, Mary, 273
Chattle, Servant or Citizen? [with Sabine Wichert], 273
Offen, Karen, 191, 600
Ogbourne, Elizabeth, 225
A History of Essex, 225
Oldenburg, Veena Talwar, 423
Dowry Murder, 423
Oldfield, Sybil, 410
Women Against the Iron Fist, 410
Oliphant, Margaret, 29, 300
Oliva, Marilyn, 454
Convent and Community in Late Medieval England, 454
Olsen, Lynne, 98
Opfell, Olga, 511
The Lady Laureates, 511
Oppenheimer, Jane, 509
Essays in the History of Embryology and Biology, 509
Oral history, 385, 388
Buffalo Lesbian, 103
Civil Rights, 96–7
War, 583–4
Oral traditions, 19, 267, 381–9, 399, 528
Oram, Alison, 304–14
Oresekes, Naomi, 511
The Rejection of Continental Drift, 511
Orientalism, 14, 36, 60, 143–5, 358, 389–98, 538, 555–7

Orléans, Anne-Marie-Louise-Henriette, 207, 474
Memoires, 207
Ormsby, Margaret, 77–6, 81, 85
O'Shane, Pat, 419, 605
Oss, Marie van, 107
Otto, Louise, 480
Oudshoorn, Nelly, 64
Beyond the Natural Body, 64
Outram, Dorinda, 64–5, 483
The Body and the French Revolution, 64, 483
Owenson, Sydney [Lady Morgan], 158, 160, 180, 222, 233, 244, 264, 266–7, 268, 364, 398–400, 547, 588
France, 399
Italy, 365
The Wild Irish Girl, 160, 222, 244, 266, 364–5, 399
Woman and her Master, 180, 268, 400
Oxley, Deborah, 51, 446
Convict Maids, 51, 446
Oye, von, Elspeth, 342
Offenbarungen in Octenbach, 342
Ozouf, Mona, 213–14
La fête révolutionnaire, 213–14

Paisley, Fiona, 54
Palazzi, Maura, 286, 288
Donne Sole, 286
Storiche di ieri e di oggi [with Ilaria Porciani], 288
Palliser, Fanny Bury, 318
History of Lace, 318
Palmer, Helen G., 124
The First Hundred Years [with Jessie MacLeod], 124
Palmer, Nettie, 125–6
Centenary Gift Book [with Frances Fraser], 125–6, 366
Palmieri, Patricia Ann, 138
In Adamless Eden, 138
Pamphila, 16
Historical Commentaries, 16
Pankhurst, Adela, 400–4
daughter of Emmeline, 400
sister of Christabel and Sylvia, 400
Pankhurst, Christabel, 185, 186, 197–8, 400–4
daughter of Emmeline, 400–4
sister of Sylvia and Adela, 400–4
Unshakled, 197–8, 403–4
Pankhurst, Emmeline, 185, 186, 189, 197–8, 400–4
My Own Story, 401–2
Relationship with Ethel Smyth, 199
Pankhurst, Estelle Sylvia, 185, 186, 197, 400–4
daughter of Emmeline, *Life of Emmeline Pankhurst*, 402
Sister of Adela and Christabel, 400–4
The Suffragette, 401
The Suffragette Movement, 185, 186, 401–4
Pankhursts, 56, 182, 185, 400–4
Pankratova, Anna, 482
Pantel, Pauline, 616–17
A History of Women in the West, 616–17
Pantin, Mabel, 373
Flashlights on Chinese Life, 373
Sister Dora, 373
Papaspyridi-Karouzou, Semni, 10
Pardoe, Julia, 555
Life of Marie de Medici, 555
Louis XIV, 555
Romance of the Harem, 555
The City of the Sultan, 555
The Court and Reign of Francis I, 555
Park, Katherine, 71
Parker, Kathleen Langloh, 46, 126
Parker, Mary Ann, 554
A Voyage around the World, 554
Parker, Rozsika, 30, 31, 37
Old Mistresses: Women, Art and Ideology [with Griselda Pollack], 30
The Subversive Stitch, 37
Parks, Rosa, 98
Parnell, Anna, 269
The Land League: Tale of a Great Sham, 269
Parr, Joy, 83–4
The Gender of Breadwinners, 84
Parr, Susanna, 459
Susanna's apology against the Elders, 459
Pascal, Gilberte, 458
Pascal, Jacqueline, 458
Vie de Jacqueline Pascal, 458
Pascoe, Peggy, 441
Relations of Rescue, 441
Passerini, Luisa, 286
Paston, Margaret, 341, 429–31
Pateman, Carole, 153
Paterson, Tracie, 258
A Fragile Design [with Judith McCoy], 258

Daughters of the Loom [with Judith McCoy], 258
These Tangled Threads [with Judith McCoy], 258
Paulus, Caroline, 364
Wilhelm Dumont, 364
Peabody, Elizabeth, 477, 560
Chronological History of the United States, 477
Peace, 404–12
Peace, xvii
Pedersen, Susan, 200
Eleanor Rathbone and the Politics of Conscience, 200
Peirce, Leslie, 397
The Imperial Harem, 397
Pelliccia, Adele, 279
Marti Italiani, 279
Pelling, Margaret, 380
Cholera, Fever and English Medicine, 380
Penn, Donna, 450
Penrose, Elizabeth [Mrs Markham], 226
History of England, 226
Pepper, Mary Sifton, 121
Maids and Matrons of New France, 121
Perham, Margery, 148–50
African Apprenticeship, 150
Pacific Prelude, 149
The Colonial Reckoning, 149
Periodisation, xvii
Perkins, Rachel, 421
Radiance, 421
Pernoud, Régine, 349
Héloïse and Abelard, 349
Joan of Arc, 349
Pernon, Eva, 337
Evita, 337
Perpetua, 18
Perrot, Michelle, 213
Perry, Adele, 144, 528
Pesman, Ros, 38–40, 145
Duty Free, 145
Petchesky, Rosalind, 302
Pethick-Lawrence, Emmeline, 198
My Part in A Changing World, 198
Petrie, Flinders, 7, 8, 9, 130
Petrie, Hilda, 8, 9, 10, 130
Pettman, Jindy, 411
Worlding Women, 411
Pfaelzer, Jean, 571
Pffefer, Naomi, 379
The Stork and the Syringe, 379
Phillips, Patricia, 513
The Scientific Lady, 513
Piazza, Rosa, 279
Marti Italiani, 279
Pichanick, Valerie Kossew, 258
Piercy, Marge, 247, 573
He, She, It, 573
Woman on the Edge of Time, 247
Pieroni Bortolotti, Franca, 284
La donna la pace l'Europa, 285
Movimento operaio e lotta politica a Livorno [with Nicola Badoloni], 284
Pierson, Ruth Roach, 83, 411, 600
'They're Still Women After All', 83
Pilkington, Mary, 178
A Mirror for the Female Sex, 178
Pinchbeck, Ivy, 99, 163, 170, 227, 262, 352, 412–13, 597
Children in English Society [with Margaret Hewitt], 170, 413
Women Workers and the Industrial Revolution, 163, 227, 262, 352, 413, 597
Pindar, Elizabeth, 471
Pindar, Elizabeth, 471
Pinet, Marie-Joseph, 415
Piozzi, Hester Thrale, 311, 613
Retrospection, 613
Pirckheimer, Caritas, 106, 108
Denkwürdigkeiten, 108
Pizan, Christine de, xv, 30, 89, 116, 119, 176–7, 301, 335, 343, 349, 372, 375, 380, 404, 413–15, 467, 474, 594, 612–13
The Book of the Deeds and Arms of Chivalary, 404
The Book of Peace, 404, 415
Corps de Policie, 414, 468
God of Love's Letter, xv, 89, 176, 414
Lamentations on the Evils that have Befallen France, 404, 415
Lavision Christine, 205, 344, 414
Letter of Othea to Hector, 344, 414
Livre de la Mutacion de Fortune, 344, 414
Livre . . . Roy Charles, 344, 414, 468
Plaidy, Jean, 226
Plant, I. M., 15–19
Plowden, Alison, 504
Danger to Elizabeth, 505
Elizabeth Regina, 505

Plowden, Alison – *continued*
  Marriage with My Kingdom, 505
  The Life of Elizabeth I, 505
Plummer, Brenda Gayle, 95
  Window on Freedom, 95
Plutarch, 89, 179, 238, 473, 497, 593
Poetry, 19, 35
Poitiers, Eleanor de, 206
  Les Etats de France, 206
Pollack, Marianne, 385
Pollock, Griselda, 29, 30, 31, 34, 36, 37, 425
  Avant-Garde Gambits, 36, 425
  Differencing the Canon: Feminist Desire and the Writing of Art's Histories, 29–30
  [With Rozsika Parker] *Old Mistresses: Women, Art and Ideology*, 30
Pollock, Linda, 430
Pomata, Gianna, 288, 380
  Contracting A Cure, 288, 380
Pomeroy, Sarah B., 13
  Goddesses, Whores, Wives and Slaves: Women in Classical Antiquity, 13
Ponsonby, Sarah, 309
Poovey, Mary, 66, 68, 378
  Uneven Developments, 66
Pope-Hennesy, Una, 548
  biography of Agnes Strickland, 548
Porciani, Ilaria, 275–88
  La feste della nazione, 287
  Storiche di ieri e di oggi [with Maura Palazzi], 288
Porter, Jane, 222, 244–5
  Owen: Prince of Powys, 222
  Thaddeus of Warsaw, 222, 244–5
  The Scottish Chiefs, 222, 244–5
Porter, Muriel, 464
  Women in the Church, 464
Postcolonial women writers, 214, 415–26, 538, 606, 616
Potter, Mary, 453
Power, Eileen, 81, 85, 99, 149, 163, 227–8, 347, 371, 377, 426–7, 463
  Medieval English Nunneries, 347, 426, 463
  Medieval People, 227, 347, 426
  Medieval Women, 227, 347
Powley, Margaret Nelson, 568
Pownall, Eve, 45, 46
  Mary of Maranoa, 45
Pozzoli, Felicita, 280
  Eroi ed eroine del Risorgimento nazionale, 280
  Le donne nelle lotte italiane, 280
  Le vicende più memorabilia d'Italia, 280
Pradel, Paule, 212
Praed, Rosa, 43
  Lady Bridget in the Never Never Land, 43–4
  Policy and Passion, 43
Prang, Margaret, 82, 85
Pratt, Mary Louise, 150–1
  Imperial Eyes, 150
Prentice, Alison, 75–86, 84, 138
  Canadian Women: A History [with Paula Bourne, Gail Cuthbert Brandt, Beth Light, Wendy Mitchinson and Naomi Black], 84
  Schooling and Scholars in Ninteenth-Century Ontario [with Susan Houston], 83, 138
  Women Who Taught [with Marjorie Theobald], 138
Preston, Margaret, 125
Prichard, Katherine Susannah, 44, 46, 366
  Coonardo, 44, 46
Primrose, Diana, 613
  Chaine of Pearl, 613
Prince, Mary, 416–17, 533–4, 536, 547
  A History of Mary Prince, 416–17, 533–4, 536
Prior, Thelma, 48
Private writing, 269, 310, 427–37
Proba, 19
Prostitution, 53, 70, 148, 359, 437–47
Public Record Office, 25
  Admittance of women, 25
Purvis, June, 138, 197, 400–4
  Hard Lessons, 138
  Women in Nineteenth-Century England, 138
Putnam, Bertha Haven, 347, 447–8
  Early Treatises on the Practice of the Justices of the Peace, 447
  Proceedings Before the Justices of the Peace, 448
  The Enforcement of Statutes of Laborers, 447
Putnam, Ellen T. H., 477
  Captain Molly, 477
Putnam, Emily, 119, 447, 448–9, 506
  The Lady, 119

Quataert, Jean, 188
Queer history, 314, 449–50
querrelle des femmes, xv, 115, 154, 160, 301, 466–8, 474, 594, 613

Rabby, Glenda Alice, 95
The Pain and the Promise, 95
Radcliffe College, 10, 27, 58, 322, 347
Schlesinger Collection, 27, 204, 322
Radegund, xv, 55, 174–5, 340, 404
Baudonivia's vitae, xv, 56, 174–5, 341
epic poetry, 161, 340, 404
Radi, Heather, 52, 200
Australian Women, 52
Radway, Janice, 503
Ragozin, Zénaïde Alexeïevna, 462
Media Babylon, 462
Vedic India, 462
Rahamin, Atiya Begum Fyzee, 352
Rai, Shirin, 397
Ramabai, Pandita, 147, 433
Letters, 433–4
Ramelson, Miriam, 187
Ramusack, Barbara, 396
Ranke, Leopold Von, 26, 43
Scientific history, 26
translation Sarah Taylor Austin, 43
Ransby, Barbara, 8, 97
Rapley, Elizabeth, 463
A Social History of the Cloister, 463
The Devotes, 463
Rapp, Rayna, 165
Rappaport, Erika, 357
Shopping for Pleasure, 357
Rathbone, Eleanor, 200, 581
Rawson, [Wilkinson] Beryl, 13
Raymond, Janice, 307
Reekie, Gail, 52
Reeves, Clara, 222, 240, 491–2
The Champion of Virtue [*The Old English Baron*], 222, 492
The Progress of Romance, 240, 491–2
Reeves, Margaret E., 345
Reeves, Maude Pember, 262
The economic Foundation of the Women's Movement [with Mabel Atkinson], 262
Reformation, 105, 161, 166, 206–7, 227, 231, 290, 451–5, 459, 468–73
Reiger, Kerreen, 48–9
The Disenchantment of the Home, 48–9
Religious writing, 3, 55, 77–8, 79, 93, 104–12, 206, 231–2, 339–40, 404–5, 451, 455–65, 466–73
Reluctant Feminists in German Social Democracy, 188
Rémusat, Mme de, 336
Mémoires, 336
Renaissance, 3, 4, 32, 87, 91, 152, 161, 166, 178, 231, 465–75
Rendall, Jane, 424
Reuben, Julie, 138
The Making of the Modern University, 138
Revolution, 160, 166, 178, 209–11, 213, 224, 240, 337, 405, 475–84, 488–91, 494, 540–1, 588, 590
Reynolds, Myra, 119,
The Learned Lady in England, 119
Rich, Adrienne, 71, 151, 307, 485
'Compulsory Heterosexuality and Lesbian Existence', 71, 485
Richardson, Henry Handel, 44, 45
The Getting of Wisdom, 44
Richardson, Lula McDowell, 119
The Forerunners of Feminism, 119
Richardson, Sarah, 273
Women in British Politics [With Kathryn Gleadle], 273
Richter, Elise, 345
Richter, Gisela, 12
Handbook of Greek Art, 12
Sculpture and Sculptors of the Greeks, 12
Rickert, Margaret, 348
Ridden, Jennifer, 264–74
Rigg, Julie, 46
In Her Own Right, 46
Riley, Denise, 63, 583
Am I That Name?, 63
Rittner, Carol, 464
Different Voices [with John K Roth], 464
Ro_mberk sisters, 341
Roberts, Barbara, 83
Whence they Came, 83
Roberts, Elizabeth, 228
A Woman's Place, 228
Robertson, Mavis, 48
Robertson, William, 22

Robespierre, Charlotte, 479
Memoires, 479
Robin, Libby, 52
Defending the Little Desert, 52
Robinson, Catherine A., 464
Tradition and Liberation, 464
Robinson, Hilary, 38
Robinson, Jane, 559
Wayward Women, 559
Robinson, Portia, 51
The Hatch and Brood of Time, 51
Robnett, Belinda, 96
How Long? How Long?, 96
Robson, Donna, 485–95
Robson, Eleanor, 510
Mesopotamian Mathematics, 510
Rocheleau, Corinne, 121
Roe, Daphne, 380
A Plague of Corn, 380
Roe, Helen M., 348
Roe, Jill, 50, 404–12
Roelker, Nancy L., 454
Roger, Kim, 95
Righteous Lives, 95
Roland, Marie-Jeanne, 478, 479, 480, 489–90, 588
An Appeal to an Impartial Posterity, 478,
"Historical Notes', 478
Rollins, Judith, 97,
All is Never Said, 97
Roma-Bari, Laterza, 286,
Il lavoro delle donne, 286
Romantic friendship, 129, 305, 484–5
Romantic women writers, 485–95, 588
Romanticism, 215, 224, 283, 361–4
Rooney, Eilish, 274
Women, Community and Politics [with Margaret Woods], 274
Roper, Esther, 310
Roper, Lyndal, 166, 454, 463–4
Holy Household, 166, 454, 463–4
Oedipus and the Devil, 455
Witchcraze, 455
Roper, Margaret [More], 452, 469
A Devout Treatise, 452, 469
Rose, Ernestine, 532
Rose, Jacqueline, 37
Sexuality in the Field of Vision, 37
Rose, Sonya, 263
Rosen, Ruth, 444
The Lost Sisterhood, 444
Ross, Ellen, 165, 169
Ross, Janet, 43
Daughter of Lucie Duff-Gordon, 43
Grand-daughter of Sarah Taylor Austin, 43
Story of Pisa, 225
Three Generations of Englishwomen, 43
Rossi, Elena Aga, 285
Rossiter, Margaret, 509, 511
Women Scientists in America, 509, 511
Rothmans, Sheila M., 380
Living in the Shadow of Death, 380
Rothschild, Mary Aickin, 95
A Case of Black and White, 95
Rouillard, Germaine, 212
Rousseau, Jean-Jacques, 155, 179, 200, 238, 486
Rover, Constance, 187, 189
Love, Morals and the Feminists, 187
Women's Suffrage and Party Politics in Britain, 187
Rowbotham, Judith, 464
Rowbotham, Sheila, 187, 228, 483, 599
Friends of Alice Wheedon, 410
Remembering the Sixties, 203
Women, Resistance and Revolution, 228, 483, 599
Women's Consciousness, Man's World, 228
Rowley, Sue, 53
Debutante Nation [with Susan Magarey and Susan Sheridan], 53
Rowson, Susanna, 477
The Fille de Chambre, 477
Roy, Beth, 98
Royal Lives, 180, 223, 453, 495–505, 547
Rubin, Gayle, 218
'sex/gender system', 218
Rubin, Joan Shelley, 503
Ruether, Rosemary Radford, 463
In Our Own Voices, 463
[with Rosemary Skinner Keller], 463
Ruggini, Leila Cracco, 282
Ruiz, Vicki, 570
Cannery Women, Cannery Lives, 570
Out of the Shadows, 570
Ruoti, Maria Clemete, 458
Mémoires, 458
Rupp, Leila, 576
Mobilizing Women, 576

Ruskin College, 228
Ruskin, John, 35
Russ, Joanna, 573
The Female Man, 573
Russell, Diana, 412
Exposing Nuclear Phallacies, 412
Russell, Mary, 558–9
The Blessings of a Good Thick Skirt, 558–9
Russell, Penny, 50, 53
A Wish of Distinction, 53, 427–37
Ryan, Edna, 46–7
Gentle Invaders [with Anne Conlon], 46
Mother of Lyndall Ryan, 50
Two Thirds of a Man, 47
Ryan, Jan, 51
Ancestors, 51
Ryan, Lyndall, 50
Aboriginal Tasmanians, 50
Biography of Edna, 50
Daughter of Edna Ryan, 50
Ryan, Mary P., 166, 569
Cradle of the Middle Class, 166
Womanhood in America, 569
Ryan, Susan, 52
Catching the Waves, 52

Sackville-West, Vita, 100
Said, Edward, 41, 358, 389–90, 397, 425, 538, 616
Salmon, Lucy Maynard, 506–7, 564,
biography, 507
Domestic Service, 506, 564
Historical Material, 507
Progress in the Household, 506, 564
The Newspaper and Authority, 507
The Newspaper and the Historian, 507
Why is History Rewritten, 507
Salmond, Anne, 425
Two Worlds, 425
Salons and salonniéres, 155–6, 276, 277, 481, 515, 588
Salvati, Mariuccia, 285, 286
L'inutile salotto, 286
Stato e industria nella ricostruzione, 285
Samantrai, Ranu, 419
AlterNatives, 419
Sanchez-Eppler, Karen, 2
Touching Liberty: Abolition, Feminism and the Politics of the Body, 2
Sand, George, 39, 213, 216, 336, 480
La Petite Fadette, 480
Sandford, Elizabeth, 173, 224
Female Improvement, 173,
The Lives of English Female Worthies, 173, 224
Woman in her Social and Domestic Character, 224
Sandoz, Mari, 566
Old Jules, 566
Sangari, Kumkum, 397, 422
Recasting Women [with Sudesh Vaid], 397, 422
Sanger, Kerran L., 98
"When the spirits says sing!", 98
Sanger, Margaret, 291
Santamaria, Emilia Formiggini, 281
Sappho, 6, 61, 177, 276, 304, 305, 306–9
Sarkar, Tanika, 144
Saunders, Kay, 50, 422
Race Relations in Colonial Queensland [with Raymond Evans and Kathryn Cronin], 50
Saxby, Jessie M. E., 225
Foys and Fanteens, 225
Saxton, Kirsten P, 239
The Passionate Fictions of Eliza Haywood [with Rebecca P Bocchicchio], 239
Sayer, Karen, 264
Women of the Fields, 264
Sayers, Dorothy, 345
Sayers, Peig, 267
autobiography, 267
Sayre, Anne, 511
Scala, Allesandra, 466
Scanlon, Jennifer, 608
Inarticulate Longings, 608
Scaraffia, Lucetta, 287
Donne e fede [with Gabriella Zarri], 287
Scari, Elisa Panizza, 279
Marti Italiani, 279
Schaw, Janet, 55, 530
Journal of Lady of Quality, 554
Schbeinger, Londa, 64, 68
Nature's Body, 64, 424
The Mind Has No Sex, 64
Schlauch, Margaret, 347–8
Chaucer's Constance and Accused Queens, 347
English Medieval Literature, 348
Outline of the History of the English Language, 348

Schlegel, Caroline, 283
Schoolcraft, Mary Howard, 561
  The Black Gauntlet, 561
Schopenhauer, Johanna, 43
Schreiner, Olive, 73, 123–4, 163, 190, 193, 350, 406, 506, 580
  The Story of an African Farm, 123, 406
  Woman and Labour, 352, 406, 580
Schultz, Debra, 97
  Going South, 97
Schurman, Anna Maria van, 117, 118, 459, 471
  The Good Choice, 459
  Whether the Study of Letters is Fitting for a Christian Woman, 117
Science, 507–15
Sclafert, Thérèse, 212
Scott, Ann Firor, 535
  The Southern Lady, 535
Scott, Joan Wallach, xvi, 136, 139, 263, 436, 450, 483, 528, 570, 600, 601
  'Gender: A Useful Category of Historical Analysis,' 219, 570
  Women, Work, and Family [with Louise A Tilly], 165
Scott, Rose, 44, 50, 190
Scott, Sarah, 375, 572
  Millenium Hall, 375, 572
Scott, Walter, 41, 241–2, 243, 316
Scrine, Clair, 62–72
Scudéry, Madeleine, de, 90, 118, 156, 158, 177, 208, 240, 300, 474, 515–16, 594
  Artaméne ou Le Grand Cyrus, 208, 240, 515
  Clélie, 208, 474, 515
  'Conversations', 156, 515–16
  Ibrahim, 515
  Les femmes illustres, 90, 118, 156, 594
  Story of Sapho, 158
Seacole, Mary Jane Grant, 353–4
  Wonderful Adventures of Mrs Seacole, 353–4
Secret histories, 4, 157, 516–25
Sedgewick, Catherine Maria, 561
  Hope Leslie, 561
Sedgwick, Eve Kosofsky, 450
  Epistemology of the Closet, 450
Semiramis, 177, 217, 468
Semple, Ellen Churchill, 564
  American History and Its Geographic Condtions, 564
Seneca Falls, 19, 216
Seton-Williams, Veronica, 5, 9
  Blue Guide to the Egypt, 5
  El-Amarna, 9
  Ptolemaic Temples, 9
  Short History of Egypt, 9
Sexuality, 62–72
  Sexuality and Subordination [with Susan Mendus], 424
Seymer, Lucy R., 376
  A General History of Nursing, 376
Seymour, Anne
  Hecatodistichon [with Jane and Margaret Seymour], 468
Seymour, Jane
  Hecatodistichon [with Anne and Margaret Seymour], 468
Seymour, Margaret
  Hecatodistichon [with Jane and Anne Seymour], 468
Shadd, Adrienne, 84
  We're Rooted Here and They Can't Pull Us Up [with Peggy Bristow, Dionne Brand, Afua P Cooper, Linda Carty and Sylvia Hamiliton], 84
Shapiro, Barbara, 513
  'Beyond Reasonable Doubt', 513
Sharp, Jane, 374
  Midwives Book, 374
Sharpe, Pamela, 263
  Women's Work the English Experience, 263
Shaw, Flora [Lady Lugard], 557–8
  A Tropical Dependency, 557–8
Sheilds, Carol, 548
Shelley, Mary, 245, 247, 395, 494–95, 552, 554
  Frankenstein, 247
  The Last Man, 245, 494–5
Sheridan, Susan, 53, 366, 607–8
  Debutante Nation [with Susan Magarey and Sue Rowley], 53
Sherman, Cindy, 37
Sherman, Claire Richter, 31
  Women as Interpreters of the Visual Arts, 31
Shevlow, Kathryn, 607
  Women and Print Culture, 607
Shirley, Elizabeth, 452, 469
  The Chronicle of St Monica's, 452, 469
Shoemaker, Nancy, 419
  Negotiators of Change, 419, 422
Shohat, Ella, 421

Showalter, Elaine, 67, 355
The Female Malady, 67
These Modern Women, 355
Shteir, Ann B., 513
Cultivating Women, Cultivating Science, 513
Sidney, Mary, 473
transalations, 473
Siegemund, Justine, 374
Die Konigl, 374
Simcox, Edith, 525
Natural Law, 525
Primitive Civilizations, 525
Simon, Joan, 135
Simpson, Helen, 127
Sinha, Mrinalini, 55, 328, 368
Colonial Masculinity, 144, 328, 368
Sissa, Giulia, 287
Greek Virginity, 287
Sizer, Lyde Cullin, 2
The Political Work of Northern Women Writers and the Civil War, 2
Skeffington, Hannah Sheehy, 270
Skelton, Isabel, 80, 85, 121, 525–6
Backwoodswoman, 80, 121, 526
biography, 526
Skinner, Constance Lindsay, 80–1, 526–8
Adventures of Oregon, 81, 527
biography, 528
Chronicles of Canada, 80
Pioneers of the Old Southwest, 81, 527
Slavery, 1–3, 41, 113, 146, 168, 216, 247, 290, 416–19, 528–39, 605
Sluga, Glenda, 360–70
Smalley, Beryl, 347
Smith College, 27
Sophia Smith Collection, 27, 58, 204
Smith-Rosenberg, Carroll, 67, 190, 311, 379, 428–30, 434, 484, 569, 600, 601
Disorderly Conduct, 379
'The Female Animal', 67
'The Female World of Love and Ritual', 311, 484, 569, 601
Smith, Bonnie G., xvi, 130, 132, 139, 172–3, 360, 365, 616
Changing Lives, 616
'Contribution of Women to Modern Historiography', 172
Gender of History, 219, 351, 385, 386
Smith, Charlotte, 238, 493
Desmond, 493
History of England, 238
The Old Manor House, 493–4
Smith, Charlotte Fell, 225
Smith, Gertrude, 5
Administration of Justice from Hesiod to Solon, 5
Smith, Helen Zenna [Evadne Price], 582
Not so Quite . . . Stepdaughters of War, 582
Smith, Hilda, 136, 153
Smith, Margaret, 462
Studies in Early Mysticism, 463
Smith, Sidonie, 193, 195
Smyth, Elizabeth, 77
Smyth, Ethel, 199–200
autobiographical writings, 199
relationship with Emmeline Pankhurst, 199
relationship with Virginia Woolf, 199–200
Snitow, Ann, 70
Female Desire [with Christine Stansell], 70
Social History, 99, 227–8
Soland, Birgitte, 354
Becoming Modern, 354
Solomon-Godeau, Abigail, 425
Solomon, Barbara Miller, 133, 138–9
In the Company of Educated Women, 133, 138–9
Solomon, Bertha, 124
Somerville College, 73, 76, 203, 204
Somerville, Mary, 23, 512
Sontag, Susan, 247
Illness as Metaphor, 378
The Volcano Lover, 247
Sorajib, Cornela, 338
India Calling, 338
South Africa, 123–4
Southwell, Anne Lady, 468
Souvenirs, 201
Sowernan, Ester [pseud], 90, 594, 613
Ester hath hang'd Haman, 90, 594, 613
Spector, Janet, 14
Speght, Rachel, 90, 117, 613
A Mouzell for Melastomus, 90, 117, 613
Spence, Catherine Helen, 43, 44, 50
Clara Morison, 43
Spender, Dale, 190
Feminist Theorists, 190
Sperling, Jutta, 455
Convents and the Body Politic, 455
Spivak, Gayatri Chakravorty, 395, 419–20
'Can the Subaltern Speak', 420

Spongberg, Mary, 3, 4–5, 42–3, 56–9, 60–2, 66, 86, 87, 88–90, 92–4, 115–19, 172–182, 204–5, 215–17, 230–1, 232–3, 234, 235, 288–90, 300, 301, 302, 303, 322, 399–401, 437–47, 506–7, 543, 544, 545, 546, 548–9,
Feminising Venereal Disease, 66, 378, 445
Writing Women's History, 351
Spruill, Julia Cherry, 539–40
Women's Life and Work in the Southern Colonies, 539–40
Spry, Irene Biss, 81–2, 85
The Palliser Expedition, 82
Staal-Delaunay, Baronne de [Marguerite-Jeanne Cordier], 207–8, 335
Mémoires, 208, 335
Staël, Germaine de, 22, 61, 93, 113, 156, 160, 210–11, 276, 288, 361–3, 365, 366, 399, 478–9, 480, 485, 488–9, 540–1
Considerations on the Principal Events of the French Revolution, 21–2, 478–9, 541
Corinne, 160, 288, 362, 399, 489, 541
On Germany, 22, 93, 160, 210, 361–3, 399, 488
influence on Lydia Maria Child and Margaret Fuller, 93, 215, 216
On Literature, 488, 541
salon, 156, 540
Ten Years of Exile, 362
Stafford, Pauline, 229
Queen Emma and Queen Edith, 229
Queens, Concubines and Dowagers, 229
Stagel, Elsbeth, 342
Henry Suso, 342
Staiger, Clara, 111
Standley, Ann, 94, 96
Stanley, Liz, 435
Stansell, Christine, 70, 440
City of Women, 440
Female Desire [with Ann Snitow], 70
Stanton, Elizabeth Cady, 1, 20, 39, 58, 93, 94, 99, 101, 114, 115, 162, 184, 186, 188, 189, 190, 193, 194, 195–7, 215, 216, 322, 541–3, 569
abolition, 1, 20, 542
autobiography [*Eighty Years*], 193, 195–7, 543
friendship with Maltilda Joslyn Gage, 21, 217, 542–3
friendship with Susan B Anthony, 21, 217, 542,
History of Woman Suffrage [with Matilda Joslyn Gage and Elizabeth Cady Stanton], 1, 94, 101, 114, 115, 184, 541, 569
on matriarchy, 161
Woman's Bible, 195, 543
Woman's Declaration of Rights [with Susan B Anthony and Elizabeth Cady Stanton], 217
Stapleton, Mary, 225
Three Oxfordshire Parishes, 225
Stark, Freya, 389, 555
Stead, Christina, 132
Steedman, Carolyn, 436
Stein, Gertrude, 306
Stenton, Doris Mary, 119, 228, 543–4
The English Woman in History, 119, 228, 346, 544
Stephen, Ann, 53
'Selling Soap', 53
Stephen, Barbara, 133
Emily Davies and Girton College, 133
Stephens, Ann, 561
Mary Derwent, 561
Sterling, Dorothy, 2
Ahead of Her Time: Abby Kelly and the Politics of Antislavery, 2
Sterndale, Mary, 317
Vignettes of Derbyshire, 317
Stevens, Joyce, 48
Taking the Revolution Home, 48
Stevenson, Catherine Barnes, 558,
Victorian Writers in Africa, 558
Stewart, Iabel M., 376
A Short History of Nursing [with Lavinia Dock], 376
Stewart, Maria W., 417, 531, 533
Religion and the Pure Principal of Moraliy, 417
Stewart, Mary, 226
Stimpson, Catherine R., 302
Stocks, Mary, 200
Eleanor Rathbone, 200
Stoddart, Jennifer, 83
Stoler, Ann Laura, 65, 358, 359, 422
Carnal Knowledge and Imperial Power, 65, 167
Race and the Education of Desire, 358, 422
Stone, Jean Mary, 224

Stone, Lucy, 184
Stone, Sarah, 374
Complete Practice of Midwifery, 374
Stopes, Charlotte Carmichael, 62, 119, 228, 323, 544
British Freewomen, 228, 544
Stopes, Marie, 70, 544
daughter of Charlotte, 544
Married Love, 544
Stopford Green, Alice, 229, 544–5
collaboration with John Richard Green, 544
The Making of Ireland and its Undoing, 229, 271
Story-telling, 18–19
Stowe, Harriet Beecher, 460, 532, 533
Uncle Tom's Cabin, 532, 533
Women in Sacred History, 460
Strachey, Ray, 132, 182–3, 290, 545–6
Millicent Garrett Fawcett, 546
The Cause, 182, 185, 546
Strasser, Ulrike, 107, 455
State of Virginity, 455
Straub, Kristina, 67
Body Guards [with Julia Epstein], 67
Strickland Sisters, 546–8
Strickland, Agnes, 24, 25–6, 27, 28, 78, 160, 180, 223, 224, 230, 233, 453, 461, 496, 500–1, 502, 503, 504, 505, 546–8
Archival research, 24, 548
Lives of the Last Four Princesses of the House of Stuart, 25, 501
Lives of the Queens of England, 24, 180, 230, 500, 547–8
Lives of the Queens of Scotland, 24, 224, 501
Lives of the Tudor Princesses, 501
Sister of Catherine Parr Traill and Susanna Moodie, 78, 546–8
Strickland, Elizabeth, 24, 25, 160, 224, 461, 546–8
Co-authorship with Agnes, 547
Sister of Catherine Parr Traill and Susanna Moodie, 78
sympathetic reappraisal of Mary Tudor, 224
Strickland, Jane, 25, 546–8
Biographer of Agnes Strickland, 25, 548
Strobel, Margaret, 421, 464, 616
Muslim Women in Mombasa, 464
Western Women and Imperialism [with Nupur Chaudhuri], 392, 616
Strong-Boag, Veronica, 83, 85
Strong, Eugénie Sellars, 11–12, 13
Apotheosis and After Life, 11, 13
The Elder Pliny's Chapters on the History of Art, 12
Roman Sculpture from Augustus to Constantine, 11
Stuard, Susan Mosher, 349
Women in Medieval Society, 349
Suffrage, 4, 20, 26, 27, 39, 44, 55, 61–2, 70, 74, 124, 183–92, 352
Suleri, Sara, 420
Sullerot, Evelyne, 213
Histoire et sociologie du travail féminin, 213
Sullivan, Patricia, 95, 97
Days of Hope, 95
Freedom Writer, 97
Summerfield, Penny, 576, 583
Out of the Cage [with Gail Braybon], 576
Reconstructing Women's Wartime Lives, 577, 583
Summers, Anne, 47, 51, 52, 446
Damned Whores and God's Police, 47, 52, 446
Ducks on the Pond, 52, 201
Sumner, Helen Laura [Woodbury], 262, 548–9, 564
Condition of Women and Child Wage Earners, 549
Equal Suffrage, 549
Suttner, Bertha von, 406
Lay Down Your Arms, 406
Swain, Shurlee, 118–29
Swanwick, Helena, 410
Swerdlow, Amy, 2, 102, 302, 409
Household Kith and Kin [with Renate Bridenthal, Joan Kelly and Phyllis Vine], 102
Swindler, Mary, 13
Ancient Painting, 13
Swiney, Frances, 163
Symonds, John Addington, 34, 87

Tacitus, 17, 234
Takamure, Itsue, 293–4
Josei no Rekishi, 294
Tan, Amy, 570
Tanaka, Kazuko, 295
A Short History of the Women's Movement in Japan, 295

Tarabotti, Arcangela, 470
  Convent Life as Paradise, 470
Taylor, Barbara, 159, 193, 228, 263, 405
  Eve and the New Jerusalem, 188, 228, 263
Taylor, Lily Ross, 5, 6, 12, 13, 549–50
  Divinity of the Roman Emperor, 5, 13, 550
  Party Politics in the Age of Caesar, 5, 550
  Roman Voting Assemblies, 5, 550
  The Voting Districts of the Roman Republic, 5, 550
Taylor, Mary, 256
  Miss Miles, 256
  relationship with Charlotte Bronte, 256
  The First Duty of Women, 256
Taylor, Rebe, 51
  Unearthed: The Aboriginal Tasmanians of Kangaroo Island, 51
Teaiwa, Teresia, 425
Tennant, Kylie, 124, 125
  Australia: Her Story, 124
Teo, Hsu-Ming, 389–98, 551–9
Terborg-Penn, Rosalyn, 532
Teresa, of Avila, 332, 458
  Interior Castle, 458
  Libro de la vida, 332, 458
Terrall, Mary, 512
Terry, Jennifer, 71, 450
Tey, Josephine, 226
  The Daughter of Time, 226
Thackeray, Anne, 337
  Chapters from Some Memoirs, 337
  The Petticoat Rebellion, 187
Theobald, Marjorie, 137, 138
  Knowing Women, 138
  Women Who Taught [with Alison Prentice], 138
Theoharis, Jeanne, 95
  Freedom North [with Komozi Woodard], 95
Thickness, Ann, 118, 178
  Sketches of the Lives and Writings of the Ladies of France, 118, 178
Thirsk, Joan, xvi, 384
Thomas, Edith, 213
  Jeanne d'Arc, 213
  Les Femmes de 1848, 213
Thomas, Lynn M., 423
  'Ngaitana [I will circumcise myself],' 423
Thomas, M Carey, 133
Thompson, Dorothy, 259, 410, 411
Thornton, Bonnie Dill, 419
  'Race, Class and Gender,' 419
Thornton, Merle, 47
  'Women's Labour,' 47
Thorton, Katherine, 470
  diary, 470–1
Thrupp, Sylvia, 76–7, 81
Thucydides, 15, 16
  daughter's contribution to *Peloponnesian War*, 16
Tickner, Lisa, 36, 37
  The Spectacle of Women, 36
  suffrage art, 36
Tilly, Louise A., 165, 600, 616
  Women, Work, and Family [with Joan Wallach Scott], 165
Tillyard, Stella, 430, 434
Tinling, Marion, 559
  With Women's Eyes, 559
Tomaselli, Sylvana, 154
Toulmin, Lucy Smith, 225
  York Plays, 225
Traill, Catharine Parr, 78–9, 80, 546–8
  Sister of Agnes and Elizabeth Strickland, 78, 546–8
  The Backwoods of Canada, 547
Trapnel, Anna, 471
Traub, Valerie, 71
Travel and travel writing, 18, 60, 144–6, 158, 551–9, 589
Treatt, Stella Court, 558
  Cape to Cairo, 558
Trinh, T Minh Ha, 420
  The Moon Waxes Red, 420
  Woman Native Other, 420
Tristan, Flora, 259
  'Tour de France,' 259
Triulzi, Camilla Paltrinieri, 276
Trollope, Frances, 554
  Domestic Manner of the Americans, 554
Trotula, 372
Trumpener, Katie, 241
Truth, Sojourner, 531, 533, 569, 605
Tucker, Margaret, 50, 418
  If Anyone Cared, 50, 418
Tudela, Elisa Sampson Vera, 455
  Colonial Angels, 455
Tugan, Fadwa, 338
Tuite, Clara, 40–2, 240–9
Turra, Elisabetta Carminer, 157

Ueno, Chizuko, 299
Ulrich, Laurel Thatcher, 375
A Midwife's Tale, 375
Umble, Jennifer, 454
Underhill, Evelyn, 348
Mysticism: A Study of the Nature and Development of Man's Spiritual Consciousness, 348
Unger, Friederike Helene, 364
Die Franzosen in Berlin, 364
United States, xvii, 1–3, 94–8, 559–71
Urania, 305–314
Urban-Mead, Wendy, 422
Urquart, Diane, 273
Coming into the Light [with Janice Holmes], 273
Utopian writings, 91, 247, 375

Vaid, Sudesh, 397, 422
Recasting Women [with Kumkum Sangari], 397, 422
Valente, Angela, 281, 283
Valenze, Deborah, 263
First Industrial Woman, 263
Valois, Marguerite de, 206, 451
Memoires, 206, 335, 451
Vance, Carol, 69
Pleasure and Danger, 69
Vansina, Jan, 383
Oral Traditions, 383
Varga, Louise, 212
Vassar College, 12
Vayne, Julia H L de, 318
The Kentish Garland, 318
Vellacott, Jo, 410
From Liberal to Labor, 411
Militarism versus Feminism [with Margaret Kammester], 411
Venturi, Emilie Ashurst, 38–40
editing *The Shield*, 39
Joseph Mazzini, 39
The Duties of Man, 39
relationship with Josephine Butler, 39
The Life and Writing of Joseph Mazzini, 39
Mazzini's Foreshadowings of the Coming Faith, 39
The Owl's Nest, 39
Verza, Silvia Curtoni, 276, 277
Vicinus, Martha, 312, 314, 485
Vickery, Amanda, 229
The Gentleman's Daughter, 229
Women, Privilege and Power, 229
Victor, Frances Fuller, 565, 573–4
contribution to Hubert Howe Bancroft's *History of American West*, 565, 574
The New Penelope, 574
The River of the West, 574
Vigée-Le Brun, Elizabeth, 336
Mémoires, 336
Vine, Phyllis, 102
Household Kith and Kin [with Renate Bridenthal, Joan Kelly and Amy Swerdlow], 102
Virgin Mary, 32
Vitae, 174–6, 232–3, 341, 596
Vokins, Joan, 529
Volkonskaya, Sofia, 481
Volude, Béatrix-Etiennette Renart de Fuchsamberg d'Omblimont de Lage de, 210

Wada, Ei, 290–1
Waddell, Helen, 345
Waisbrooker, Lois, 572
A Sex Revolution, 572
Wake, Joan, 225–6
The Brudenells of Deene, 226
How to Compile a History, 226
Wakeford, Constance, 376–7
The Wounded Soldiers Friends, 377
Wakizô, Hosoi, 292
Jokô Aishi, 292
Walker, Alice, 421
The Color Purple, 421
Walker, Claire, 108, 455
Gender and Politics in Early Modern Europe, 455
Walker, Mary Edwards, 573
An Adamless Eden, 573
Walker, Melissa, 98
Down from the Mountaintop, 98
Walkowitz, Judith, 70, 190, 439
City of Dreadful Delight, 439
Prostitution and Victorian Society, 70, 190, 439
Wall, Maureen, 271–2
Wallace, Michelle, 419
Invisibility Blues, 419
War, 575–85

Ward, Glenyse, 418
Unna You Fullas, 418
Wandering Girl, 418
Ward, Jennifer, 229
Women of the English Nobility and Gentry, 229
Ward, Sister Benedicta, 349
Harlots of the Desert, 349
Ware, Caroline, 564
The Early New England Cotton Manufacture, 564
Ware, Vron, 144,
Beyond the Pale, 144, 230
Warner, Marina, 382
Warner, Sylvia Townsend, 310
Warnicke, Retha M., 453
Warren, Mercy Otis, 27–8, 560, 585–6
Archival research, 28
History of the Rise, Progress, and Termination of the American Revolution, 27–8, 560, 585–6
relationship with Catherine Sawbridge Macaulay, 324, 585
Waugh, Catherine, 337
Webb, Beatrice, 99, 150, 227, 235, 261, 262, 320, 586–7
The Cooperative Movement in Great Britain, 587
Diaries, 587
Indian Diary, 150
London School of Economics, 262
My Apprenticeship, 261, 587
Webb, Jessie, 5
Weiler, Kathleen, 138
Telling Women's Lives [with Sue Middleton], 138
Women Teaching for Change, 138
Weir, Alison, 224, 504–5
Life of Elizabeth I, 505
Six Wives of Henry VIII, 505
Wertheim, Margaret, 512
Pythagora's Trousers, 512
West, Rebecca, 366, 577
Black Lamb and Grey Falcon, 366
The Return of the Soldier, 577
Weston, Jessie L., 345
From Ritual to Romance, 345
Wheatley, Phillis, 531
Wheeler, Tessa, 5
Whitaker, Kate, 92
Mad Madge: Margaret Cavendish, Duchess of Newcastle, 92
Whitbread, Nanette, 135–6
White, Cynthia, 608
Women's Magazines, 608
White, Deborah Gray, 420, 538
White, Jessie [Mario], 278, 279, 280
White, Luise, 144, 359, 445
The Comforts of Home, 144, 359, 445
Whitehead, Kay, 138
The New Women Teachers Come Along, 138
Whitelock, Dorothy, 346
Whitely, Margaret, 257
Women's Work [with Amy Bulley], 257
Wiesner [Hanks], Merry E., 453, 454–5
Convents Confront the Reformation, 454, 455
Willard, Charity Cannon, 349, 415
Christine de Pizan, 415
Willard, Emma, 133, 560, 561, 562, 614
A System of Universal History, 614
History of the United States, 560, 561
Leaves of American History, 562
Willard, Myra, 44
History of the White Australia Policy, 44
Williams, Helen Maria, 61, 210, 245, 399, 405, 479–8, 489–91, 588
Letters from France, 210, 245, 363, 489–91, 588
Williams, Jane, 253
The Literary Women of England, 253
Williams, Justina, 48
Anger and Love, 48
Willoughby, Cassandra, 158
Continuation of the History of the Willoughby Family, 589
Willoughby, Cassandra [Duchess of Chandos], 589
Wilson, Dorothy Clark, 373
Dr Ida, 373
Wilson, Harriet, 535
Our Nig, 535
Wilson, Kathleen, 65, 144
The Island Race, 65
Wiltsher, Anne, 410
Most Dangerous Women, 410
Windschuttle, Elizabeth, 50
Women, Class and History, 50

Winship, Janice, 608
Inside Women's Magaiznes, 608
Winterson, Jeanette, 247
Sexing the Cherry, 247
Wiss, Rosemary, 424
Witches and witchcraft, 9
Witt, Henriette Guizot de, 211
Les Femmes dans l'histoire, 211
Wittig, Monique, 309,
The Lesbian Body, 309
Woillez, Catherine Thérèse
Les Médecins Moralistes, 373
Wollstonecraft, Mary, 42, 119, 131, 152, 159, 160, 173, 179, 181, 182, 184–5, 188, 190, 193, 210, 215, 217, 234, 247, 289, 363–4, 395, 399, 405, 479–80, 485, 486–7, 530, 552, 572, 588, 589–91, 609
correspondence with Catherine Sawbridge Macaulay, 324, 486–7, 590
Enlightenment feminism, 42, 159, 590
Historical and Moral View of the French Revolution, 159, 210, 363, 479, 591
Memoir, 193, 591
Thoughts on the Education of Daughters, 159
The Rights of Man, 590
Vindication of the Rights of Woman, 131, 152, 159, 173, 182, 185, 395, 486, 530, 572
Wolstoneholme, Elizabeth, 592
Women Worthies, 90, 93, 156, 160, 172, 173, 223, 276, 497, 515, 520, 592–6, 615
Women's Liberation, 596–606
Women's Magazines, 607–8
Wood, Ann Douglas, 67
'The Fashionable Diseases', 67
Woodard, Komozi 95
Freedom North [with Jeanne Theoharis], 95
Woodford, Charlotte, 21, 104–12, 455
Nuns as Historians in Early Modern Germany, 21, 455
Woodham-Smith, Cecil, 224
Florence Nightingale, 224
Woolf, Daniel R., xvi, 158
Woolf, Virginia, 100, 102, 199, 311, 366, 407, 448, 608–11
Anne Clifford as Orlando, 100, 609
On Being Ill, 378
Jacob's Room, 610
'Journal of Mistress Martin', 100
My Country is the Whole World, 411
Night and Day, 609
Orlando, 609
relationship with Ethel Smyth, 199–200
A Room of One's Own, 311, 610
Three Guineas, 366, 407, 610
The Years, 610
Woollacott, Angela, 145–6, 350–60, 423, 552
Gendering War Talk [with Miriam Cooke], 411
To Try Her Fortune in London, 146, 358, 423
Woolley, Hannah, 594
The Gentlewoman's Companion, 594
World Centre for Women's Archives, 27
World History, 79, 181, 426, 475, 611–17
Worth, Rita, 14
Wright, Esther Clark, 81–2
The St John River, 81
Wroth, Mary, 473–4
Guy of Warwick, 473–4
The Countess of Montgomery's Urania, 473–4
Wykes, Olive, 134

Yamakawa, Kikue, 292–3
Yearsley, Ann, 260, 530
Yee, Shirley, 2, 531
Black Women Abolitionists, 2
Yegenoglu, Meyda, 394–5
Colonial Fantasies, 394–5
Yellin, Jean Fagin, 2
An Untrodden Path: Antislavery and Women's Political Culture, 2
Yonge, Charlotte Mary, 226
religious writing, 460
Yourcenar, Marguerite, 246
Memoirs of Hadrian, 246
Yuval-Davis, Nira, 370
Woman-Nation-State [with Flora Anthias], 369–70

Zainu'ddin, Ailsa, 134, 136, 137
Zancan, Paola [Padova], 282

Zarri, Gabriella, 287, 455
Donna, disciplina, creanza cristiana, 455
Donne e fede [with Lucetta Scaraffia],287
Le sante vive, 455
Zeller, Charlotte, 459
Zenobia, 17–18, 467
Zimmern, Helen, 29
Zinsser, Judith, 617, 618
Women in Early Modern and Modern Europe [with Bonnie Anderson], 617
Zitter, Martha Elisabeth, 452
Zlotnick, Susan, 258
Women, Writing, and the Industrial Revolution, 258
Zonana, Joyce, 395